Lecture Notes in Artificial Intelligence 10423

Subseries of Lecture Notes in Computer Science

More information about this series at http://www.springer.com/series/1244

Eugénio Oliveira · João Gama
Zita Vale · Henrique Lopes Cardoso (Eds.)

Progress in Artificial Intelligence

18th EPIA Conference
on Artificial Intelligence, EPIA 2017
Porto, Portugal, September 5–8, 2017
Proceedings

 Springer

Editors
Eugénio Oliveira 🆔
Universidade do Porto
Porto
Portugal

João Gama 🆔
Universidade do Porto
Porto
Portugal

Zita Vale 🆔
Polytechnic Institute of Porto
Porto
Portugal

Henrique Lopes Cardoso 🆔
Universidade do Porto
Porto
Portugal

ISSN 0302-9743 ISSN 1611-3349 (electronic)
Lecture Notes in Artificial Intelligence
ISBN 978-3-319-65339-6 ISBN 978-3-319-65340-2 (eBook)
DOI 10.1007/978-3-319-65340-2

Library of Congress Control Number: 2017948190

LNCS Sublibrary: SL7 – Artificial Intelligence

This Springer imprint is published by the registered company Springer Nature Switzerland AG
The registered company address is: Gewerbestrasse 11, 6330 Cham, Switzerland

Preface

The EPIA Conference on Artificial Intelligence came back to Porto. EPIA's first edition, in 1985, followed by the 1993 and 2001 editions, already took place in this unique city.

Today, AI is experiencing a new age of social recognition as well as increasing ethical responsibility, which makes this event, in 2017, even more attractive and challenging.

The main goal of the EPIA conferences has always been to foster research, scientific knowledge exchange, and new insights in the AI scientific area. This is achieved through judicious presentations and critical discussions on selected topics by, among others, researchers, practitioners, scientists, and engineers.

The 18th EPIA Conference on Artificial Intelligence (EPIA 2017) took place at the Faculty of Engineering of the University of Porto during September 5–8 (www.fe.up.pt/epia2017/).

This edition included several novelties. First, it was mandatory to include international AI community researchers, from different countries, in each track's Organizing Committee.

The international flavor of this EPIA edition was confirmed by the origin of the Program Committee (PC) members, coming from 42 different countries, and accepted paper authors, who belong to 17 different countries (Argentina, Austria, Brazil, Finland, France, Germany, Italy, The Netherlands, New Zealand, Poland, Portugal, Russia, South Africa, Spain, Turkey, USA, Ukraine).

Secondly, we promoted a journal special issue for papers specifically submitted to the journal (*New Generation Computing*, Special Issue on "Computational Models for Social and Technical Interactions"). The accepted papers were also presented orally during the conference.

EPIA 2017 encompassed a record of 16 tracks devoted to different topics, plus a doctoral symposium and a panel session on "Beneficial AI." The selected tracks are: ABM4Crime – Agent-Based Modelling for Criminological Research, AICPDES – Artificial Intelligence in Cyber-Physical and Distributed Embedded Systems, AIG – Artificial Intelligence in Games, AIM – Artificial Intelligence in Medicine, AIPES – Artificial Intelligence in Power and Energy Systems, AITS – Artificial Intelligence in Transportation Systems, ALEA – Artificial Life and Evolutionary Algorithms, AmIA – Ambient Intelligence and Affective Environments, BAAI – Business Applications of Artificial Intelligence, IROBOT – Intelligent Robotics, KDBI – Knowledge Discovery and Business Intelligence, KRR – Knowledge Representation and Reasoning, MASTA – Multi-Agent Systems: Theory and Applications, SE4AIS – Software Engineering for Autonomous and Intelligent Systems, SSM – Social Simulation and Modelling, TeMA – Text Mining and Applications.

The invited speakers at EPIA 2017 were Francesco Bonchi, Research Leader at the ISI Foundation, Turin, Italy, with a talk on "Data Science"; Simon M. Lucas, from the

School of Computer Science and Electronic Engineering, University of Essex, with a talk on "AI and Games"; and Philipp Slusallek, from the German Research Center for Artificial Intelligence (DFKI), Germany, with a talk on "Agents and Simulated Reality".

There were 177 paper submissions to the thematic tracks, plus another 20 to the special session on "Business Applications of Artificial Intelligence" open to students and industry and to the doctoral symposium. The 18th EPIA also accommodated two AI-related competitions (Geometric Friends Game AI Competition and Discovery Challenge).

The papers acceptance rate was circa 38% which means that 71 (almost all full papers) out of 177 papers are published in these proceedings, plus six out of 26 in the journal special issue.

All the papers were carefully revised and the track organizing chairs, together with their respective Program Committee members, have to be praised for their hard work on scientific reviewing.

Thanks are also due to the supporting organizations (University of Porto, Faculty of Engineering of the University of Porto and Informatics Engineering Department) and, finally, the conference sponsors, starting with SISCOG, our main sponsor to whom we sincerely address our thanks, but also ShelfAI, MASDIMA, LTP, and DevScope. Our colleagues of the Organizing Committee, Ana Paula Rocha and Goreti Marreiros, were also crucial for the successful realization of EPIA 2017.

Thank you all.

June 2017

Eugénio Oliveira
Henrique Lopes Cardoso
João Gama
Zita Vale

Panel Session on Beneficial AI @EPIA2017
Porto, September 5, 2017

Members of the panel:

- Cristiano Castelfranchi (Italian National Research Council and University of Siena, Italy)
- Ernesto Costa (Universidade de Coimbra, Portugal)
- Luís Sarmento (TonicApp, Portugal, former applied Scientist at Amazon)
- Philipp Slusallek (DFKI, Germany)
- Simon M. Lucas (University of Essex, UK)
- Eugénio Oliveira (Universidade do Porto, Portugal) (Moderator)

Moderator: What do I mean by beneficial AI?
Besides the obvious, pointing to the production of new technology at the service of new businesses, corporations, armies, or governments, I am more in favor that beneficial AI should be measured by how much it complies with human rights and harmonious progress of humanity as a whole.

It is an accepted fact that the most relevant outcomes of civilization derive from the fair use of intelligence. How can we improve and enlarge those benefits, through AI-based systems?

Q1: Can AI continue to provide a new revolutionary conceptual and formal instrument for understanding and modeling (human) mind, intelligence, intentional behavior, emotions, communication, social structures and their dynamics? Can AI develop a theory of cognitive and social phenomena of its own, not imported from social sciences?

Q2: About the possibility of the so-called strong AI. Is consciousness a possible state for an AI-based system to achieve?

Q3: Considering purposeful systems that truly integrate humans and machines, would it be possible to formulate general rules for humans to retain control?

Organization

The 18th EPIA Conference on Artificial Intelligence (EPIA 2017) was co-organized by the Artificial Intelligence and Computer Science Laboratory (LIACC) of the University of Porto (UP), the Laboratory of Artificial Intelligence and Decision Support (LIAAD) of INESC-TEC, and the Intelligent Engineering and Computing for Advanced Innovation and Development Research Group (GECAD) of the Institute of Engineering, Polytechnic of Porto (ISEP/IPP).

Conference and Program Chairs

Eugénio Oliveira	LIACC, Universidade do Porto, Portugal
João Gama	LIAAD/INESC-TEC, Universidade do Porto, Portugal
Zita Vale	GECAD, Instituto Superior de Engenharia do Porto, Portugal
Henrique Lopes Cardoso	LIACC, Universidade do Porto, Portugal

Organizing Chairs

Ana Paula Rocha	Universidade do Porto, Portugal
Goreti Marreiros	Instituto Superior de Engenharia do Porto, Portugal

Steering Committee

Ana Bazzan	Universidade Federal do Rio Grande do Sul, Brazil
Ana Paiva	UL/Instituto Superior Técnico, Portugal
Ernesto Costa	Universidade de Coimbra, Portugal
François Pachet	Sony Computer Science Laboratory, France
Helder Coelho	Universidade de Lisboa, Portugal
José Júlio Alferes	Universidade Nova de Lisboa, Portugal
José Maia Neves	Universidade do Minho, Portugal
Juan Pavón	Universidad Complutense Madrid, Spain
Luís Paulo Reis	APPIA/Universidade do Minho, Portugal
Manuela Veloso	Carnegie Mellon University, USA
Marco Dorigo	Université Libre de Bruxelles, Belgium
Paulo Novais	APPIA/Universidade do Minho, Portugal
Pavel Brazdil	Universidade do Porto, Portugal
Peter McBurney	Kings College London, UK
Ulrich Furbach	University of Koblenz, Germany

ABM4Crime Track Chairs

Charlotte Gerritsen   NSCR, Amsterdam, The Netherlands
Tibor Bosse   Vrije Universiteit Amsterdam, The Netherlands
Corinna Elsenbroich   University of Surrey, UK

AmIA Track Chairs

Paulo Novais   University of Minho, Portugal
Ana Almeida   ISEP, Porto, Portugal
Sara Rodríguez González   University of Salamanca, Spain
Goreti Marreiros   ISEP, Porto, Portugal

AICPDES Track Chairs

Jean-Paul Jamont   University of Grenoble Alpes, France
Stamatis Karnouskos   SAP, Germany
Thiago RPM Rúbio   FEUP/LIACC, Porto, Portugal
Henrique Lopes Cardoso   FEUP/LIACC, Porto, Portugal

AIG Track Chairs

Rui Prada   INESC-ID/IST, Lisbon, Portugal
João Dias   INESC-ID/IST, Lisbon, Portugal
Frank Dignum   Utrecht University, The Netherlands
Pedro Nogueira   FEUP/LIACC, Porto, Portugal
Alberto Simões   IPCA, Barcelos, Portugal

AIM Track Chairs

Manuel Filipe Santos   Universidade do Minho, Portugal
Carlos Filipe Portela   Universidade do Minho, Portugal
Allan Tucker   Brunel University London, UK

AIPES Track Chairs

Zita Vale   ISEP/GECAD, Porto, Portugal
Pedro Faria   ISEP/GECAD, Porto, Portugal
Juan Manuel Corchado   University of Salamanca, Spain
Tiago Pinto   University of Salamanca, Spain

AITS Track Chairs

Alberto Fernandez   CETINIA, Universidad Rey Juan Carlos,
                               Madrid, Spain
Luis Moreira-Matias   NEC Labs Europe, Germany
Rosaldo Rossetti   FEUP/LIACC, Porto, Portugal

ALEA Track Chairs

Sara Silva	University of Lisbon, Portugal
Mauro Castelli	NOVA IMS, Portugal
Leonardo Trujillo	Instituto Tecnológico de Tijuana, Mexico
Leonardo Vanneschi	NOVA IMS, Portugal

BAAI Track Chairs

Célia Talma Gonçalves	P.Porto/LIACC, Portugal
Ana Paula Appel	IBM Research, São Paulo, Brazil
François Pachet	Sony CSL, Paris, France
Carlos Soares	FEUP/INESC TEC, Porto, Portugal

IROBOT Track Chairs

Luís Paulo Reis	Universidade do Minho/LIACC, Portugal
Nuno Lau	Universidade de Aveiro, Portugal
João Alberto Fabro	UTFPR, Curitiba, Brazil

KDBI Track Chairs

Paulo Cortez	University of Minho, Portugal
Albert Bifet	Université Paris-Saclay, France
Luís Cavique	Universidade Aberta, Portugal
Nuno Marques	New University of Lisbon, Portugal
Manuel Filipe Santos	University of Minho, Portugal

KRR Track Chairs

Ricardo Gonçalves	NOVA LINCS, Universidade Nova de Lisboa, Portugal
Minh Dao-Tran	KBS, Vienna University of Technology, Austria
Matthias Knorr	NOVA LINCS, Universidade Nova de Lisboa, Portugal
Jörg Pührer	ISG-CSI, Leipzig University, Germany

MASTA Track Chairs

Alberto Fernandez-Gil	CETINIA, Universidad Rey Juan Carlos, Spain
Daniel Castro Silva	LIACC, University of Porto, Portugal
Jomi Fred Hübner	Federal University of Santa Catarina, Brazil
José Machado	ALGORITMI, University of Minho, Portugal

SSM Track Chairs

Luis Antunes	FCUL, Lisbon, Portugal
Pedro Campos	LIAAD-INESC TEC, FEP, Porto, Portugal
Luiz Izquierdo	University of Burgos, Spain

SE4AIS Track Chairs

Ana Paula Rocha	LIACC, Universidade do Porto, Portugal
António J. M. Castro	LIACC, Universidade do Porto, Portugal
Pavlos Moraitis	LIPADE, Paris Descartes University, France
Jorge Jesus Gomez-Sanz	Universidad Complutense de Madrid, Spain

TeMA Track Chairs

Joaquim Francisco Ferreira da Silva	FC-UNL, Lisbon, Portugal
José Gabriel Pereira Lopes	FC-UNL, Lisbon, Portugal
Hugo Gonçalo Oliveira	CISUC, DEI, Universidade de Coimbra, Portugal
Bruno Martins	INESC-ID, IST, Lisbon, Portugal
Pável Calado	INESC-ID, IST, Lisbon, Portugal
Altigran Soares da Silva	Federal University of Amazonas, Manaus, Brazil

ABM4Crime Program Committee

Daniel Birks	Griffith University Brisbane, Australia
Tibor Bosse	Vrije Universiteit Amsterdam, The Netherlands
Henk Elffers	Netherlands Institute for the Study of Crime and Law Enforcement, The Netherlands
Corinna Elsenbroich	University of Surrey, Uk
Vasco Furtado	University of Fortaleza, Brazil
Charlotte Gerritsen	NSCR, Amsterdam, The Netherlands
Elizabeth Groff	Temple University, USA
Nicola Lettieri	INAPP, Italian National Institute for the Analysis of Public Policies, Italy
Lin Liu	University of Cincinnati, USA
Nicholas Malleson	University of Leeds, UK
Klaus Troitzsch	University of Koblenz-Landau, Germany

AmIA Program Committee

Amal Seghrouchni	Pierre et Marie Curie University, France
Amilcar Cardoso	University of Coimbra, Portugal
Ana Almeida	Polytechnic of Porto, Portugal
Ana Paiva	IST, Portugal
Andrew Ortony	Northwestern University, USA
Ângelo Costa	Universidade do Minho, Portugal
Antonio Caballero	University of Castilla-La Mancha, Spain
Antonio Camurri	University of Genoa, Italy
Boon Kiat-Quek	National University of Singapore, Singapore
Carlos Bento	University of Coimbra, Portugal
Carlos Ramos	Polytechnic of Porto, Portugal

Carlos Iglesias   Universidad Politécnica de Madrid, Spain
Cesar Analide   University of Minho, Portugal
Dante Tapia   University of Salamanca, Spain
Davide Carneiro   Polytechnic of Porto, Portugal
Davy Preuveneers   K.U. Leuven, Belgium
Diego Gachet   European University of Madrid, Portugal
Eva Hudlicka   Psychometrix Associates Blacksburg, USA
Fábio Silva   Universidade do Minho, Portugal
Florentino Fdez-Riverola   University of Vigo, Spain
Gordon Hunter   Kingston University, UK
Goreti Marreiros   Polytechnic of Porto, Portugal
Grzegorz Nalepa   AGH University of Science and Technology, Poland
Hoon Ko   Sungkyunkwan University, Republic of Korea
Ichiro Satoh   National Institute of Informatics, Japan
Javier Bajo   Pontifical University of Salamanca, Spain
Javier Jaen   Polytechnic University of Valencia, Spain
Jean Ilié   LIP6, Pierre et Marie Curie University, France
José Machado   University of Minho, Portugal
José Molina   University Carlos III of Madrid, Spain
José Neves   University of Minho, Portugal
Juan Corchado   University of Salamanca, Spain
Laurence Devillers   LIMS-CNRS, France
Lino Figueiredo   Polytechnic of Porto, Portugal
Luís Macedo   University of Coimbra, Portugal
Paulo Novais   University of Minho, Portugal
Ricardo Costa   Polytechnic of Porto, Portugal
Ricardo Santos   Polytechnic of Porto, Portugal
Rui José   University of Minho, Portugal
Rui Costa   Ubiwhere, Portugal
Sara González   University of Salamanca, Spain
Shin'Ichi Konomi   University of Tokyo, Japan
Vic Callaghan   Essex University, UK
Vicente Julián   Polytechnic University of Valencia, Spain

AICPDES Program Committee

Olivier Boissier   ENS Mines Saint-Etienne, France
Luis M. Camarinha-Matos   New University of Lisbon, Portugal
Jose Francisco Cervantes   ITESO, Mexico
  Alvarez
Yacine Challal   Ecole Nationale Supérieure dInformatique, Algeria
Vincent Chevrier   Université de Lorraine, France
Armando Colombo   University of Applied Sciences Emden/Leer, Germany
Natalia Criado   Kings College London, UK
Christopher Frantz   University of Otago, New Zealand

Benjamin Gateau	Luxembourg Institute of Science and Technology, Luxembourg
Marie-Pierre Gleizes	IRIT, Université de Toulouse, France
Mouloud Koudil	Ecole nationale Supérieure d'Informatique, Algeria
Claude Le Pape	Schneider Electric, France
Laurent Lefevre	G.INP, France
Paulo Leitão	Polythecnic Institute of Braganca, Portugal
Marin Lujak	Ecole des Mines de Douai, France
Simon Mayer	SIEMENS, USA
Marco Mendes	Schneider Electric Automation GmbH, Germany
Michael Mrissa	Université de Pau et des Pays de lAdour, France
Thanh Binh Nguyen	Danang University of Technology, Vietnam
Michel Occello	University of Grenoble Alpes, France
Gauthier Picard	ENS Mines Saint-Etienne, France
Clément Raievski	LCIS Grenoble-Alpes University, France
Juan Antonio Rodriguez-Aguilar	IIIA-CSIC, Spain
Tiberiu Seceleanu	ABB Corporate Research, Sweden
Vlasios Tsiatsis	Ericsson Research Ericsson AB, Sweden
Laurent Vercouter	LITIS lab, INSA de Rouen, France
Alois Zoitl	Fortiss Gmbh, Germany

AIG Program Committee

Alexander Zook	Georgia Institute of Technology, USA
Antonios Liapis	University of Malta, Malta
Carlos Martinho	IST, Universidade de Lisboa, Portugal
David Carneiro	Universidade do Minho, Portugal
Diego Perez	University of Essex, UK
Duarte Duque	Instituto Politécnico do Cávado e do Ave, Portugal
Ian Horswill	Northwestern University, USA
Joost Broekens	TU Delft, The Netherlands
José Valente de Oliveira	Universidade do Algarve, Portugal
Mike Preuss	University of Dortmund, Germany
Penousal Machado	Universidade de Coimbra, Portugal
Sandy Louchart	Glasgow University, UK
Stavros Vassos	Sapienza University of Rome, Italy
Stefanos Kollias	National Technical University of Athens, Greece
Matthew Bedder	University of York, UK

AIM Program Committee

Álvaro Silva	Abel Salazar Biomedical Sciences Institute, Portugal
Andreas Holzinger	Medical University Graz, Austria
Antonio Manuel de Jesus Pereira	Polytechnic Institute of Leiria, Portugal

Barna Iantovics	Petru Maior University of Trgu-Mure, Romania
Beatriz de la Iglesia	University of East Anglia, UK
Cinzia Pizzi	Università degli Studi di Padova, Italy
Danielle Mowery	University of Utah, USA
Do Kyoon Kim	Pennsylvania State University, USA
Giorgio Leonardi	University of Piemonte Orientale, Italy
Göran Falkman	Universitet of Skövde, Sweden
Helder Coelho	University of Lisbon, Portugal
Helena Lindgren	Ume University, Sweden
Inna Skarga-Bandurova	East Ukrainian National University, Ukraine
José Maia Neves	University of Minho, Portugal
Luca Anselma	University of Turin, Italy
Michael Ignaz Schumacher	University of Applied Sciences Western, Switzerland
Miguel Angel Mayer	Pompeu Fabra University, Spain
Mohd Khanapi Abd Ghani	Technical University of Malaysia, Malaysia
Panagiotis Bamidis	Aristotelian University of Thessaloniki, Greece
Pedro Gago	Polytechnic Institute of Leiria, Portugal
Pedro Pereira Rodrigues	University of Porto, Portugal
Rainer Schmidt	Institute for Biometrics and Medical Informatics, Germany
Ricardo Martinho	Polytechnic Institute of Leiria, Portugal
Rui Camacho	University of Porto, Portugal
Salva Tortajada	Polytechnic University of Valencia, Spain
Shabbir Syed-Abdul	Taipei Medical University, Taiwan
Shelly Sachdeva	Jaypee Institute of Information Technology, India
Szymon Wilk	Poznan University of Technology, Poland
Ulf Blanke	Swiss Federal Institute of Technology in Zurich, Switzerland
Werner Ceusters	University at Buffalo, USA

AIPES Program Committee

Alexandre Alves da Silva	General Electric Global Research, Brazil
Ana Estanqueiro	LNEG National Research Institute, Portugal
António Gomes Martins	University of Coimbra, Portugal
Bo Norregaard Jorgensen	University of Southern Denmark, Denmark
Carlos Ramos	Polytechnic of Porto, Portugal
Chen-Ching Liu	Washington State University, Pullman, USA
Dagmar Niebur	Drexel University, USA
Fernando Lopes	LNEG National Research Institute, Portugal
Gerhard Krost	University of Duisburg-Essen, Germany
Germano Lambert-Torres	Dinkart Systems, Brazil
Goreti Marreiros	Polytechnic of Porto, Portugal
Gustavo Figueroa	Instituto de Investigaciones Eléctricas, Mexico
Hélder Coelho	University of Lisbon, Portugal
Isabel Praça	Polytechnic of Porto, Portugal

Jan Segerstam	Empower IM Oy, Finland
João P.S. Catalão	University of Porto, Portugal
João Peças Lopes	University of Porto, Portugal
João Tomé Saraiva	University of Porto, Portugal
José Rueda	Delft University of Technology, The Netherlands
Juan F. De Paz	University of Salamanca, Spain
Kevin Tomsovic	University of Tennessee, USA
Kwang Y. Lee	Baylor University, USA
Maxime Lefrancois	École Nationale Supérieure des Mines de Saint-Étienne, France
Nikos Hatziargyriou	National Technical University of Athens, Greece
Nouredine Hadj-Said	Institut National Polytechnique de Grenoble, France
Nuno Fidalgo	University of Porto, Portugal
Olivier Boissier	École Nationale Supérieure des Mines de Saint-Étienne, France
Pablo Ibarguengoytia	Instituto de Investigaciones Eléctricas, Mexico
Peter Kadar	Budapest University of Technology and Economics, Hungary
Rui Castro	Instituto Superior Técnico, Portugal
Seung-Jae Lee (Paul)	Myongji University, Korea
Vladimiro Miranda	University of Porto, Portugal
Zbigniew Antoni Styczynski	Otto von Guericke University Magdeburg, Germany

AITS Program Committee

Ana Bazzan	UFRGS, Brazil
Carlos Lisboa Bento	University of Coimbra, Portugal
Constantinos Antoniou	MIT, USA
Eduardo Camponogara	UFSC, Brazil
Eugénio Oliveira	University of Porto, Portugal
Franziska Klügl	Örebo University, Sweden
Giuseppe Vizzari	University of Milan-Bicocca, Italy
Gonçalo Homem De Almeida Correia	TU Delft, The Netherlands
Harry Timmermans	Eindhoven University of Technology, The Netherlands
Hussein Dia	Connell Wagner, Australia
Javier Sanchez Medina	Universidad de Las Palmas de Gran Canaria, Spain
Jihed Khiari	NEC Laboratories Europe, Germany
João Mendes-Moreira	University of Porto, Portugal
José Telhada	University of Minho, Portugal
Josep Salanova	CERTH-HIT, Greece
Kai Nagel	Technical University of Berlin, Germany
Luís Nunes	ISCTE, Portugal
Marcela Munizaga	University of Santiago, Chile
Oded Cats	TU Delft, The Netherlands

Sascha Ossowski	Rey Juan Carlos University, Spain
Soora Rasouli	Eindhoven University of Technology, The Netherlands
Thahn Lam Hoang	IBM Research Dublin

ALEA Program Committee

Khulood Alyahya	University of Birmingham, UK
Wolfgang Banzhaf	Memorial University of Newfoundland, Canada
Tiago Baptista	CISUC, University of Coimbra, Portugal
Stefano Cagnoni	University of Parma, Italy
Mauro Castelli	NOVA IMS, Portugal
Luís Correia	University of Lisbon, Portugal
A.E. Eiben	VU Amsterdam, The Netherlands
Gianluigi Folino	CNR-ICAR, Italy
James Foster	University of Idaho, USA
Mario Giacobini	University of Turin, Italy
Jin-Kao Hao	University of Angers, France
Ben Kovitz	Indiana University, USA
William B. Langdon	University College London, UK
Antonios Liapis	Institute of Digital Games, University of Malta, Malta
Penousal Machado	CISUC, University of Coimbra, Portugal
Luca Manzoni	Università degli Studi di Milano-Bicocca, Italy
James McDermott	University College Dublin, Ireland
Rui Mendes	Universidade do Minho, Portugal
Pablo Mesejo Santiago	Inria, France
Julian Miller	University of York, UK
Jason Moore	University of Pennsylvania, USA
Luis Muñoz	Instituto Tecnológico de Tijuana, Mexico
Enrique Naredo Garcia	CentroGeo, Mexico
Gabriela Ochoa	University of Stirling, UK
Francisco B. Pereira	Instituto Superior de Engenharia de Coimbra, Portugal
Riccardo Poli	University of Essex, UK
Sebastian Risi	IT University of Copenhagen, Denmark
Juan Romero	University of A Coruña, Spain
Marc Schoenauer	Inria, France
Lukas Sekanina	Brno University of Technology, Czech Republic
Sara Silva	University of Lisbon, Portugal
Leonardo Trujillo	Instituto Tecnológico de Tijuana, Mexico
Leonardo Vanneschi	NOVA IMS, Portugal

BAAI Program Committee

Adam Woznica	Expedia, Switzerland
Albert Patrick	ILOG, France
António Castro	FEUP/LIACC-NIADR, University of Porto, Portugal
Carlos Rodrigues	Marionete, UK

Efi Papatheocharous	Swedish Institute of Computer Science, Sweden
Elaine Ribeiro de Faria	Universidade Federal Uberlândia, Brazil
Eunika Mercier-Laurent	Innovation3D, France
Hanen Borchani	SimCorp Technology Labs, Denmark
Jean-Charles Régin	ILOG, France
Jean-Pierre Briot	Laboratoire dInformatique de Paris 6 (Paris6-CNRS) and PUC-Rio, Brazil
Kaustubh Patil	MIT, USA
Marisa Affonso Vasconcelos	IBM Research, Brazil
Maritza Correa	Universidad Autónoma de Occidente, Colombia
Paulo Cavalin	IBM Research, Brazil
Pedro Henriques Abreu	FCTUC-DEI/CISUC, Portugal
Peter Van der Putten	Pegasystems/University of Leiden, Netherlands
Ricardo Sousa	Farfetch, Portugal
Rodrigo Mello	Universidade de São Paulo, Brazil
Victor Cavalcante	Motorola Mobility R&D, Brazil
YongHong Peng	University of Sunderland, UK

IROBOT Program Committee

André Marcato	Universidade Federal de Juíz de Fora, Brazil
André Scolari Conceição	Federal University of Bahia, Brazil
Anibal Ollero	University of Seville, Spain
Anna Helena Costa	EPUSP, São Paulo, Brazil
António Paulo Moreira	Universidade do Porto, Portugal
Armando J. Pinho	Universidade de Aveiro, Portugal
Armando Sousa	Universidade do Porto, Portugal
Augusto Loureiro da Costa	UFBA, Salvador, Brazil
Axel Hessler	TU Berlin, Germany
Brígida Mónica Faria	Instituto Politécnico do Porto, Portugal
Carlos Cardeira	Instituto Superior Técnico, Portugal
Carlos Carreto	Instituto Politécnico da Guarda, Portugal
César Analide	Universidade do Minho, Portugal
Fernando Osório	Universidade São Paulo/SC, Brazil
Flavio Tonidandel	FEI University, S. Bernardo Campo, Brazil
Guy Theraulaz	CRCA, University of Toulouse III, P. Sabatier, France
Josemar Rodrigues de Souza	Universidade Estadual da Bahia, Brazil
Luís Correia	Universidade de Lisboa, Portugal
Luis Moreno Lorente	Universidad Carlos III Madrid, Spain
Luis Mota	ISCTE-IUL, Portugal
Luis Seabra Lopes	Universidade de Aveiro, Portugal
Marco Dorigo	Université Libre de Bruxelles, Belgium
Mikhail Prokopenko	CSIRO ICT Centre, Australia
Nicolas Jouandeau	Université Paris 8, France

Paulo Urbano   Universidade de Lisboa, Portugal
Reinaldo Bianchi   IIIA-CSIC, Barcelona, Spain
Saeed Shiry Ghidary   Amirkabir University, Iran
Sanem Sariel Talay   Istanbul Technical University, Turkey
Urbano Nunes   Universidade de Coimbra, Portugal

KDBI Program Committee

Fernando Bacao   NOVA-IMS, Universidade Nova de Lisboa, Portugal
Orlando Belo   University of Minho, Portugal
Agnès Braud   University of Strasbourg, France
Alberto Bugarín   University of Santiago de Compostela, Spain
Margarida Cardoso   ISCTE, Portugal
Andre Carvalho   University of Sao Paulo, Brazil
Ning Chen   GECAD, Instituto Superior de Engenharia do Porto,
                                    Portugal
Jose Alfredo Ferreira Costa   Federal University, UFRN, Brazil
Marcos Aurélio Domingues   State University of Maringá, Brazil
Mark Embrechts   RPI, USA
Elaine Faria   Federal University of Uberlandia, Brazil
Manuel Fernandez Delgado   University of Santiago de Compostela, Spain
Carlos Ferreira   LIAAD INESC Porto LA, Portugal
Mohamed Gaber   Birmingham City University, UK
Stéphane Lallich   University of Lyon 2, France
Philippe Lenca   Telecom Bretagne, France
Sérgio Moro   ISCTE, Portugal
Filipe Pinto   Polytechnic Institute of Leiria, Portugal
Rita P. Ribeiro   FCUP/LIAAD INESC TEC, University of Porto,
                                    Portugal
Fátima Rodrigues   Institute of Engineering of Porto, Portugal
Murat Caner Testik   Hacettepe University, Turkey

KRR Program Committee

Slim Abdennadher   German University in Cairo, Egypt
Salvador Abreu   University of Evora, Portugal
José Júlio Alferes   Universidade Nova de Lisboa, Portugal
Mario Alviano   University of Calabria, Italy
Gerhard Brewka   Leipzig University, Germany
Pedro Cabalar   Corunna University, Spain
Esra Erdem   Sabanci University, Turkey
Cristina Feier   University of Bremen, Germany
Johannes Klaus Fichte   Vienna University of Technology, Austria
Sarah Alice Gaggl   Technische Universität Dresden, Germany
Amelia Harrison   University of Texas, Austin, USA
Martin Homola   Comenius University, Slovakia

Daniela Inclezan	Miami University, USA
Adila A. Krisnadhi	Wright State University and Universitas Indonesia, USA/Indonesia
Joao Leite	Universidade Nova de Lisboa, Portugal
Francesca Alessandra Lisi	Università degli Studi di Bari Aldo Moro, Italy
Ines Lynce	University of Lisbon, Portugal
Joao Marques-Silva	University of Lisbon, Portugal
Loizos Michael	Open University of Cyprus, Cyprus
Özgür Lütfü Özcep	University of Lübeck, Germany
David Rajaratnam	University of New South Wales, Australia
Orkunt Sabuncu	TED University Ankara, Turkey
Peter Schüller	Marmara University, Turkey
Mantas Simkus	Vienna University of Technology, Austria
Edjard de Souza Mota	Federal University of Amazonas, Brazil
Daria Stepanova	Max Planck Institute for Informatics, Germany
Hannes Strass	Leipzig University, Germany
Matthias Thimm	Universität Koblenz-Landau, Germany
Ivan Varzinczak	Université dArtois, France
Carlos Viegas Damásio	Universidade Nova de Lisboa, Portugal
Antonius Weinzierl	Vienna University of Technology, Austria
Stefan Woltran	Vienna University of Technology, Austria
Guohui Xiao	Free University of Bozen-Bolzano, Italy

MASTA Program Committee

Alejandro Guerra-Hernández	Universidad Veracruzana, Mexico
Ana Bazzan	Universidade Federal do Rio Grande do Sul, Brazil
Ana Paula Rocha	LIACC, University of Porto, Portugal
Andrea Omicini	Università di Bologna, Italy
António Castro	TAP Air Portugal, LIACC, Portugal
António Rocha Costa	Universidade Federal do Rio Grande do Sul, Brazil
Brigida Mónica Faria	Polytechnic Institute of Porto, Portugal
Carlos Martinho	INESC-ID, Technical University of Lisbon, Portugal
César Analide	University of Minho, Portugal
F. Amílcar Cardoso	University of Coimbra, Portugal
F. Jordan Srour	Lebanese American University, Lebanon
Diana Adamatti	Universidade Federal do Rio Grande, Brazil
Felipe Meneguzzi	Pontifical Catholic University of Rio Grande do Sul, Brazil
Filipe Portela	ALGORITMI, University of Minho, Portugal
Francisco Grimaldo	Universitat de València, Spain
Frank Dignum	Utrecht University, The Netherlands
Graçaliz Dimuro	Universidade Federal do Rio Grande, Brazil
Gauthier Picard	Ecole Nationale Supérieure des Mines de Saint-Etienne, France

Henrique Lopes Cardoso	LIACC, University of Porto, Portugal
Ingrid Nunes	Universidade Federal do Rio Grande do Sul, Brazil
Javier Carbó	Carlos III University of Madrid, Spain
Jerusa Marchi	Federal University of Santa Catarina, Brazil
Joana Urbano	LIACC, University of Porto, Portugal
João Leite	Universidade Nova de Lisboa, Portugal
John-Jules Meyer	Utrecht University, The Netherlands
Jordi Sabater-Mir	IIIA-CSIC, Spain
Juan Antonio Rodriguez-Aguilar	IIIA-CSIC, Spain
Juan Burguillo	University of Vigo, Spain
Juan Corchado	University of Salamanca, Spain
Laurent Vercouter	École Nationale Supérieure des Mines de Saint-Étienne, France
Luís Botelho	ISCTE-IUL, Portugal
Luís Correia	University of Lisbon, Portugal
Luís Macedo	University of Coimbra, Portugal
Luís Moniz	University of Lisbon, Portugal
Matt Webster	University of Liverpool, UK
Michael Schumacher	University of Applied Sciences Western Switzerland, Switzerland
Neil Yorke-Smith	American University of Beirut, Lebanon
Nuno Lau	University of Aveiro, Portugal
Olivier Boissier	École Nationale Supérieure des Mines de Saint-Étienne, France
Paolo Torroni	Università di Bologna, Italy
Paulo Novais	University of Minho, Portugal
Paulo Trigo	Superior Institute of Engineering of Lisbon, Portugal
Paulo Urbano	University of Lisbon, Portugal
Pedro Mariano	University of Lisbon, Portugal
Penousal Machado	University of Coimbra, Portugal
Rafael Bordini	Pontífica Universidade Católica do Rio Grande do Sul, Brazil
Ramón Hermoso	University of Zaragoza, Spain
Reyhan Aydogan	Özyegin University, Turkey
Rosa Vicari	Universidade Federal do Rio Grande do Sul, Brazil
Rosaldo Rossetti	University of Porto, Portugal
Virginia Dignum	Delft University of Technology, The Netherlands
Viviane Torres Da Silva	Universidade Federal Fluminense, Brazil
Wamberto Vasconcelos	University of Aberdeen, UK
Yves Demazeau	Laboratoire d'Informatique de Grenoble, France

SSM Program Committee

| Frederic Amblard | University of Toulouse 1, France |
| Klaus Troitzsch | University of Koblenz, Germany |

SE4AIS Program Committee

Daniel Silva	University of Porto, Portugal
Francisco Garijo	Universidad Complutense de Madrid, Spain
Franco Zambonelli	University of Modena and Reggio Emilia, Italy
Frédéric Migeon	IRIT, University of Toulouse III, France
Juan Botia	Kings College London, UK
Juan Garcia-Ojeda	Universidad Santo Tomás, Colombia
Holder Giese	University of Potsdam, Germany
Laszlo Gulyas	AITIA International Inc, Hungary
Massimo Conssentino	ICAR-CNR, Italy
Medhi Dastani	Universiteit Utrecht, The Netherlands
Michael Winikoff	University of Otago, New Zealand
Nikolaos Spanoudakis	Technical University of Crete, Greece
Ruben Fuentes	Universidad Complutense de Madrid, Spain
Rui Maranhão	University of Porto, Portugal
Tom Holvoet	KU Leuven, Belgium
Vincent Hilaire	Belfort-Montbeliard Technology University, France

TeMA Program Committee

Alberto Diaz	Universidade Complutense de Madrid, Spain
Alberto Simões	Algoritmi Center, University of Minho, Portugal
Alexandre Rademaker	IBM/FGV, Brazil
Aline Villavicencio	Universidade Federal do Rio Grande do Sul, Brazil
Altigran Silva	Universidade Federal do Amazonas, Brazil
Antoine Doucet	University of Caen, France
António Branco	Universidade de Lisboa, Portugal
Béatrice Daille	University of Nantes, France
Belinda Maia	Universidade do Porto, Portugal
Brigitte Grau	LIMSI, France
Bruno Martins	Instituto Superior Técnico, Universidade de Lisboa, Portugal
Christel Vrain	Université dOrléans, France
Denilson Barbosa	University of Alberta, Canada
Eric de La Clergerie	Inria, France
Fernando Batista	Instituto Universitário de Lisboa, Portugal
Francisco Couto	Universidade de Lisboa, Portugal
Gabriel Pereira Lopes	Universidade Nova de Lisboa, Portugal
Gaël Dias	University of Caen Basse-Normandie, France
Hugo Gonçalo Oliveira	Universidade de Coimbra, Portugal
Ioannis Korkontzelos	Edge Hill University, UK
Irene Rodrigues	Universidade de Évora, Portugal
Isabelle Tellier	University of Orléans, France
Jannik Strötgen	Max Planck Institute for Informatics, Germany
Jesús Vilares	University of A Coruña, Spain

João Magalhães	Universidade Nova de Lisboa, Portugal
Joaquim Ferreira da Silva	Universidade Nova de Lisboa, Portugal
Luísa Coheur	Instituto Superior Técnico, Universidade de Lisboa, Portugal
Manuel Vilares Ferro	University of Vigo, Spain
Marcelo Finger	Universidade de São Paulo, Brazil
Maria das Graças Volpe Nunes	Universidade de São Paulo, Brazil
Mário Silva	Instituto Superior Técnico, Universidade de Lisboa, Portugal
Mark Lee	University of Birmingham, UK
Nuno Mamede	Universidade Técnica de Lisboa, Portugal
Nuno Marques	Universidade Nova de Lisboa, Portugal
Pablo Gamallo	University of Santiago de Compostela, Spain
Paolo Rosso	Universitat Politècnica de València, Spain
Paula Carvalho	Universidade Europeia, Portugal
Paulo Quaresma	Universidade de Évora, Portugal
Pavel Brazdil	Universidade do Porto, Portugal
Pável Calado	Instituto Superior Técnico, Universidade de Lisboa, Portugal
Pierre Zweigenbaum	CNRS-LIMSI, France
Sérgio Nunes	Universidade do Porto, Portugal
Vitor Jorge Rocio	Universidade Aberta, Portugal

Additional Reviewers

Alexandre Lemos	Johannes Oetsch	Markus Hecher
Diana Haidar	Khaled Fawagreh	Nada Sharaf
Diana Haidar	Leandro Pasa	Natalia Boldyrev
Elem Güzel	Magdalena Ortiz	Reda Yaich
Fábio Pinto	Marcial Guerra	Sorin Moga
Ioannis Hatzilygeroudis	de Medeiros	Thanh-Nghi Do
Jianmin Ji	Mariam Adedoyin-Olowe	Victor H. Barella
Jim Prentzas	Marie Schmidt	Vladimir Lifschitz

Contents

Artificial Intelligence in Games

Artificial Intelligence in Medicine

Artificial Intelligence in Power and Energy Systems

Artificial Intelligence in Transportation Systems

Artificial Life and Evolutionary Algorithms

Business Applications of Artificial Intelligence

Intelligent Robotics

Agent-Based Modelling for Criminological Research

An Agent-Based Aggression De-escalation Training Application for Football Referees

Tibor Bosse[✉], Ward van Breda, Nousha van Dijk,
and Jelmer Scholte

Department of Computer Science, Vrije Universiteit Amsterdam,
De Boelelaan 1081a, 1081 HV Amsterdam, The Netherlands
t.bosse@vu.nl

Abstract. An ongoing problem associated with sports such as football is the regular occurrence of aggressive behavior against referees. Campaigns and meetings for players and football clubs that are organized by the Dutch football federation must reduce aggression on the pitch. To support referees, this paper introduces a mobile application that simulates a football related environment for referees to train with aggression de-escalation. It replicates an aggressive scenario between football player (agent) and referee (user), in which the referee must approach appropriately to decrease the aggression level of the agent. A preliminary evaluation pointed out that the application has potential to be used as a training instrument for football referees.

Keywords: Conversational agents · Aggression de-escalation · Football

1 Introduction

Service and aid workers in occupations of the public sector are regularly exposed to verbal and physical violence. This concerns employees in governmental services that provide safety, health care, education, social security, social services and rail services. Almost 60% of these employees frequently encounter aggressive behavior [1]. To better prepare employees for aggressive incidents, resilience training is offered in which they learn how to communicate with aggressive clients.

Similarly, aggressive behavior regularly occurs to (voluntary) employment in public activity, such as in the sports domain in which much threatening and physical intimidation appears. This is striking, since sports are typically seen by governments and sports organizations as an important means to prevent aggression. For instance, exercising decreases aggressive behavior, especially for young unprivileged people. Additionally, sports have been shown to be beneficial in terms of improved health, meaningful leisure activities, team building, social control, ethics and integration of minorities [6].

Nevertheless, aggressive occurrences are not uncommon in the domain of football and similar sports. An extreme example of this took place in the Netherlands in December 2012, when a 41-year-old male serving as a voluntary linesman of a Dutch football club was fatally attacked by a few aggressive players on the pitch [14]. After an argument in which the players accused him of having made biased decisions, the

© Springer International Publishing AG 2017
E. Oliveira et al. (Eds.): EPIA 2017, LNAI 10423, pp. 3–14, 2017.
DOI: 10.1007/978-3-319-65340-2_1

man was knocked down by six teenage players and a 50-year-old father. The next day the afflicted man died as a result of head injury. The widespread shock of this fatal incident caused many debates about violence associated with football in the Netherlands. Moreover, the KNVB, the governing body of football in Netherlands, started with new advertising campaigns in a public response to the death of the voluntary linesman.

According to the KNVB [12] the overall type of aggressive behavior that occurs most often on a football pitch is physical violence against referees, followed by fights between players or spectators. To reduce the number of incidents, the KNVB organizes various training programs, including aggression de-escalation programs for (upcoming) referees. However, the arbitration training that is offered, which is similar to the resilience training of employees in the public sector, is financially expensive and time-consuming [2].

Hence, as a complementary approach, the aim of this paper is to introduce a simulation-based training application for referees in order to practice with aggression de-escalation. This is in line with various recent initiatives to use virtual agents in simulated environments to train people's social skills (e.g., [2, 4, 7]). The proposed training application has the form of a mobile app that can be used to practice scenarios involving a conversation between the user (referee) and an aggressive player (simulated by the system). Based on this, the communication skills of the referee will be trained as the application will constantly adapt the scenario in such a way that the situation will de-escalate if the referee uses an appropriate communication style towards the aggressive player. However, the player will show more aggression when he is treated inappropriately by the referee. To define what is an 'appropriate' communication style, the theory of Leary on interpersonal communication will be used.

The remainder of this paper is structured as follows. Section 2 provides some scientific background of the research, both in terms of existing tools and underlying theory. The functioning of the application is described in the next two sections, both from a technical perspective (Sect. 3) and from a user perspective (Sect. 4). Next, Sect. 5 describes a preliminary evaluation of the application, and Sect. 6 concludes the paper with a discussion.

2 Background

The application presented in this paper builds upon several earlier studies, which are described in this section. Section 2.1 addresses existing tools for simulation-based training of aggression de-escalation. Section 2.2 describes the theory on interpersonal stance (called Leary's Rose) that is used as a theoretical basis for our application.

2.1 Existing Tools

Simulation based training is an area that has been researched before, for example in a project enabling police students to train the skills required for successfully conducting negotiations with virtual suspects [4]. Another project delivered a role-playing session with a virtual human to help officers learn and practice interpersonal and counseling skills [7]. Likewise, virtual humans are used in a project aimed to improve the aggression de-escalation skills of public transport employees [2]. In this project, which was taken as the main source of inspiration for the current research, employees are able to practice their social and communication skills by engaging in an aggressive conversation with a virtual traveler. The purpose of this virtual agent is to provide personalized training support which can assess and respond accordingly to aggressive behavior. To enable users to engage in a conversation with a training agent, a dialogue system based on conversation trees and cognitive models is used [3]. At the start of the dialogue the virtual agent passenger shows behavior involving a certain level of aggression. The trainee must respond by selecting the most appropriate response from a multiple-choice menu. In addition, the project described in [2] distinguishes two types of aggression; emotional and instrumental aggression [5]. Emotional aggression implies an angry reaction to a negative event, whereas instrumental aggression does not contain the presence of anger and is used to achieve a certain predetermined goal [9]. The user should be able to recognize the emotional state in order to choose the communication style that suits this emotional state. Regarding the style of communication, the aggression level of the agent decreases when it is being approached correctly, but increased if it is being treated incorrectly. Experimental results show positive evaluation of the system presented in [2] regarding both the content and interaction of the virtual scenarios and the potential of the system as an effective learning tool.

2.2   Leary's Rose

In order to determine the most appropriate approach to de-escalate aggressive behavior, the communication model Rose of Leary is used in this paper. This is a general theory about interpersonal communication [8]. The main idea is that a person's 'interpersonal stance' during a 1:1 conversation can be represented as a point in a two-dimensional space. Here, the vertical y-axis determines the level of *dominance* and focuses on the relationship with others, whereas the horizontal x-axis determines the degree of *affiliation* and focuses on the attitude to others (see Fig. 1). For instance, a person that behaves high on dominance and low on affiliation towards the interlocutor can be labelled as 'disagreeable', as represented in the upper-left part of the circle.

In addition, the theory predicts how the interpersonal stance of one person influences the stance of the other person. Here, two propositions are put forward. First, people typically tend to mimic the level of affiliation of the conversation partner (e.g., if A behaves positively, B will also act more positively). Second, with respect to dominance, people mostly tend to take a stance that is opposed to the stance of the conversation partner (e.g., if A behaves dominantly, B will take a more submissive stance).

When it comes to de-escalating aggressive behavior on the football pitch, it is advisable that the referee takes a communication style that is very high on affiliation (since positive behavior triggers positive responses [8]) and moderately (but not too) high on dominance (since too dominant behavior is known for triggering more aggression [13]). This optimal behavior that is expected from the referee is denoted by the yellow circle in Fig. 1.

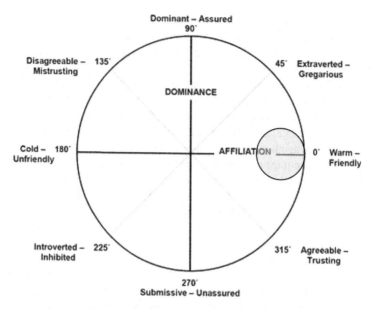

Fig. 1. Leary's rose. (Color figure online)

3   Application Design

In this section, the technical design of the application will be explained. This includes the description of the dialogue system to simulate the interaction between user and agent as well as the underlying computational model to generate the agent's behavior.

3.1   Dialogue System

The basis of the application consists of a dialogue system that can be used to simulate a conversation between a referee (the user of the system) and a football player that shows aggressive behavior (the simulated agent). The behavior of the agent is represented in textual format on the screen, and the user can respond to this by speaking to the application. A turn-based protocol is used, initiated with a sentence by the agent. After this, the user can respond, which in turn triggers a new sentence by the agent, continuing until the dialogue ends. It is important to state that, each turn, the agent selects one of a number of predefined sentences. The sentence that is selected depends on the agent's level of aggression at that moment. This level of aggression is dynamic, and depends on the agent's initial state as well as an ongoing evaluation of the sentiment of the user's spoken inputs. The exact dynamics of the agent's aggression level are determined by a computational model described in the next sub-section. The current system does not aim to interpret the semantics of the spoken inputs in detail), but it does interpret the 'stance' of the input in terms of the dominance and affiliation of the words that are used.

Aggressive behavior mostly occurs when the player disagrees with the decision of the referee. Four scenarios were created that address these kinds of situations, e.g., cases in which the referee gives a red or yellow card, or when the linesman (unfairly) flags offside.

In each scenario, the aggressive agent starts the conversation. Three start levels of the agent's behavior are distinguished; aggressive, not calm and calm. The user of the application decides which type of behavior to practice, after which the agent proceeds by selecting the first sentence that corresponds with the chosen start level. Then, the trainee responds by free speech, and so on (see Fig. 2).

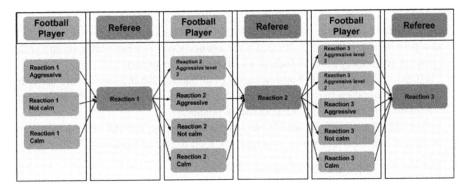

Fig. 2. Dialogue system.

The contents of the speech are processed automatically based on sentiment analysis, using an approach described in [11]. This approach makes use of a commercial tool[1] that takes free text as input and automatically computes to what extent the text contains certain characteristics (such as affiliation, dominance, and various more subtle emotions). This is done by identifying relevant keywords, matching them with domain-specific vocabularies, and applying some linguistic analysis. For the current application, the main idea is that the sentiment analysis assigns two numerical values to each spoken sentence in the $[-1, 1]$ domain: one for affiliation and one for dominance. For instance, a sentence like 'I am very sorry, but I would kindly like to ask you to stay calm' may have an affiliation value of 0.7 (due to keywords like 'kindly' and 'calm') and a dominance value of -0.7 (due to keywords like 'ask' and 'would like'). Hence, in terms as illustrated in Fig. 1, this sentence would be positioned in the 'agreeable' segment.

Next, based on the value of the spoken sentence, the system will automatically calculate the effect on the state of the virtual agent. When the referee responds 'correctly', the player will show less aggressive behavior and respond more kindly. However, when the user does not give an appropriate reply, the player's aggression level will increase. This might provoke an even higher aggression level than the start level. Therefore, at this point two levels are distinguished in the aggressive reaction of the

---

[1] http://www.sentimentics.com/.

agent; Aggression level 1 (cursing) and Aggression level 2 (threatening), as shown in the third column of Fig. 2. In the last iteration, a third Aggression level (beating) is added to allow for the possibility of reaching a state where the situation escalates into physical violence. The dialogue finishes when the trainee has spoken three times. The final value of the player's aggression level determines whether the referee has passed the test.

3.2   Computational Model

This section introduces the computational model that is used to calculate the aggression level of the virtual agent (player). The system assumes the following parameters:

- Od (Optimal Dominance): the optimal level of dominance that the user should apply in a particular situation to calm down the agent, which is a real value on the scale from −1 (extremely submissive) to +1 (extremely dominant)
- Oa (Optimal Affiliation: the optimal level of affiliation that the user should apply in a particular situation to calm down the agent, which is a real value on the scale from −1 (extremely negative) to +1 (extremely positive)
- w (Weight Factor): weight factor determining the relative importance of dominance, compared to affiliation, which is a real value on the scale from 0 to 1

In addition, the following numerical variables are used:

- A (Aggression Level): the virtual agent's level of aggression, which is a real value on the scale from −1 (extremely calm) to +1 (extremely aggressive)
- Ld (Level of Dominance): the level of dominance in the user's text, which is a real value on the scale from −1 (extremely submissive) to +1 (extremely dominant)
- La (Level of Affiliation): the level of affiliation in the user's text, which is a real value on the scale from −1 (extremely negative) to +1 (extremely positive)
- Id (Impact of Dominance): the impact of the user's level of dominance on the virtual agent's aggression level, which is a real value on the scale from −1 (extremely negative impact) to +1 (extremely positive impact)
- Ia (Impact of Affiliation): the impact of the user's level of affiliation on the virtual agent's aggression level, which is a real value on the scale from −1 (extremely negative impact) to +1 (extremely positive impact)
- Ic (Combined Impact): combined impact of the user's dominance and affiliation on the virtual agent's aggression level, which is a real value on the scale from −1 (extremely negative impact) to +1 (extremely positive impact)

Based on these variables, the following rules have been defined:

Rule 1 - Determine Optimal Values
    Od = 0 and Oa = 1   //see yellow circle in Fig. 1[2]

---

[2] Although we assume one fixed set of optimal values in this paper, the model can also deal with other values. For instance, to deal with certain cases of more instrumental aggression, the optimal dominance is 1 and the optimal affiliation is 0. This makes the approach also applicable to other domains, such as aggression in public transport [2].

Rule 2 - Calculate Impact

Basically, if the distance between real and optimal value is 0, the impact is +1, but if the distance gets larger, the impact moves towards -1 (where a *positive* impact is assumed to *calm down* the agent, and vice versa):

IF $Ox = 1$ THEN $Ix = 1 - |Ox - Lx|$ //case where the optimal value is 1

IF $Ox = 0$ THEN $Ix = 1 - 2 * |Ox - Lx|$ //case where the optimal value is 0

$Ic = w * Id + (1 - w) * Ia$ //combined impact is the weighted sum
//of the impact of
//dominance and affiliation

$Ic = -1 * Ic$ //now, a *positive* impact is assumed to
//make the agent
//*more aggressive* (and vice versa)

Rule 3 - Calculate New Aggression Level

Take the old aggression level and add (or subtract) a value from that, which is proportional to the impact (* speed factor δ):

IF $A * Ic > 0$ THEN $Anew = A + Ic * (1 - |A|) * \delta$ //positive impact on positive
//aggression level OR
//negative impact on negative
//aggression level

ELSE $Anew = A + Ic * (1 + |A|) * \delta$ //positive impact on negative
//aggression level OR
//negative impact on positive
//aggression level

4 Using the Application

In this section, design choices of the application that is in line with the intended user group will be explained and illustrated with reference to a few screenshots of the application in action.

4.1 Intended Users

The design choices are based on the intended users of the application, which are football referees. The application can also be used by referees in different sports, but the scenarios would need to be slightly adapted. The intended user group is described in research from 2009 made by "Masterplan Arbitrage" which shows that 99% of the referees are men with the average age of 44.5 years old. The minimum age of a referee is 16 years old, whereas the limit of the maximum age does not exist anymore since 2005 [12].

4.2   Application Behavior

The application is built with Android Studio, a platform that facilitates building applications for all types of Android devices. The style of the application is based on ARAG Group, a multinational insurance corporation in Germany and partner of the KNVB professional football referees, that is mostly represented by the colors yellow and black. This is done in an attempt to make the application feel coherent for referees and the KNVB. Other design components needed for the application's functionality are explained below, with reference to a few screenshots.

The main screen (Fig. 3a) is built to enable the user to select both a scenario and the emotional state of the player using radio groups including radio buttons. The start settings are shown by the yellow-filled radio button (i.e., the left most one), which indicates that the user is talking to an aggressive player that just received a red card. When the user wants to modify the settings, (s)he simply needs to touch the corresponding radio button. Then, the yellow underlined words will transform in the chosen setting. Afterwards, the user can touch the yellow "Oefen deze situatie" ("Practice this situation") button in order to start practicing. The size and the contrast of the button and radio groups are built significantly greater as those are most important on the main screen. The white colored text views including the yellow underlined varying texts are also greater than other text boxes.

Fig. 3. Screenshots showing (a) main screen and (b) conversation screen 1. (Color figure online)

When the referee has entered the ideal settings, the conversation starts with a sentence of the agent represented in a white message box (Fig. 3b). The reaction of the player is in line with the chosen settings. As now it is the referee's turn to speak, a loading message box is shown. Also, a button with a microphone icon pops up to make it obvious for the referee to use the button to talk. This speaker button is bigger because it has a great importance. When the user hits the yellow speaker button, a Google Speech-to-Text interface pops up that allows the user to speak. After the user has spoken, the sentence will be shown in the conversation screen in the same form as the message box from the player.

The spoken sentence of the referee is now shown in a yellow message box (Fig. 4a). The sentence will be analyzed and the dominance and affiliation values will be determined due the sentiment analysis. This results into a modified aggression level that leads to a new response of the player. For example, when the player is treated inappropriately by the referee, the response will be more aggressive. In contrast, when the referee approaches the player in a friendlier way, the player will most likely be calmer and respond in a kind manner. Again, the reaction of the player is shown in a white message box. The loading message box will also be displayed again as the referee should speak. After that, both player and referee have the opportunity to speak once more in order to finish the conversation.

Fig. 4. Screenshots showing (a) conversation screen 2 and (b) results screen. (Color figure online)

When the conversation is finished, and both agent and user have been able to speak three times, results will be shown depending on whether the referee was able to calm down the agent. When the referee treated the player appropriately, a green thumb up appears on the screen. The user is also able to read a short advice message. Then, two options are given; a button that allows the user to read more about the scenario and a button that leads back to the main screen in order to practice another scenario. The re-practice button and the thumbs up/down have been given a central position on the screen as they have a high importance. For the same reason, the objects that give more information about the conversation have been made less salient.

5   Preliminary Evaluation

After extensive testing and tuning of the parameters of the computational model to make the application representative, a small pilot experiment has been done to investigate the usability of the application. Five participants who satisfy the target group were asked to practice with the application for a small number of trials. After that, they were asked to fill in a short survey, where they had to rate various aspects of the application on a 5-point Likert scale. The average results are displayed in Fig. 5.

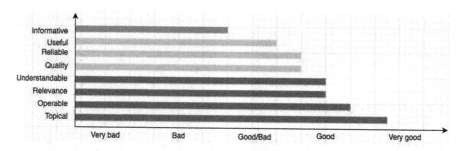

Fig. 5. Results of the pilot experiment.

As shown in the figure, overall the users were rather positive about the tool and its potential to help reduce aggression, although it should be mentioned that the sample was too small to draw crisp conclusions. Aspects of the application such as whether it is topical, operable, relevance and understandable were ranked high by the participants. On the contrary, the informative section of the application needs more improvement and therefore scored low. The feedback of a few participants stated that the application lacks particular desired information; for example, they longed for hints or a progression bar throughout the conversation as they were unaware of the progression. Also, two participants mentioned that the homepage should be clearer for the user. They were uncertain what to do after they had started the application. This will be further examined in the discussion section. Finally, the participants were asked to rate the overall quality of the tool on a 10-point scale, and the average rating they gave was 7.5 (not shown in Fig. 5).

6 Discussion

The current paper introduced a prototype of an agent-based training application that enables football referees to practice their aggression de-escalation skills during simulated conversations with aggressive football players. The prototype combines three elements, namely a dialogue system, a computational model of Leary's Rose, and a module for sentiment analysis. All this is implemented within an application that runs on Android devices.

The prototype was evaluated using a pilot experiment involving 5 users, who were moderately positive about it. All in all, these results are encouraging, in the sense that participants from a possible group of end users sees the potential of human-agent interactions as an instrument for aggression de-escalation training.

Nevertheless, there is room for improvement on several aspects. First of all, the dialogue system could be expanded in various ways. The current application simulates a conversation in which both user and agent are allowed to speak three times. A straightforward way to make the system more flexible would be to increase the number of interactions. Also, the current application users three possible emotional states to initialize the agent: aggressive, not calm and calm. These states could be extended to allow for mode sophisticated differences in agent behavior. In addition, to enhance realism of the scenarios, virtual bystanders could be added. After all, in a real-life scenario on the football pitch, the player will easily get influenced by the surrounding players. This extension could be realized by using existing methods to generate realistic interactions in small groups [10].

In terms of the design of the application, usability research showed that the application does not provide all the information the user needs. The participants of the survey stated they were unaware of their progress during the conversation. Therefore, small notifications can be added to the conversation screen, in such a way that it either shows the result after every individual spoken sentence or a hint that implies what the user should say next. Also, the design of the main screen was not clear enough, as the users were uncertain of what to do after starting up the application. Therefore, an improved main screen can be implemented that contains an expandable list including buttons, so that it is clearer to the user to choose between scenarios.

In addition, an interesting extension would be to graphically visualize the conversation partner, e.g. in terms of an avatar (e.g., as in [2]) or a short video. Such an approach could possibly enhance the user's engagement in the scenario, potentially leading to a more effective training instrument.

On the long term, further testing of the tool is required, with a larger number of participants and a more sophisticated experimental design. Ultimately, it would be interesting to investigate to what extend the tool really prepares referees for incidents of aggressive behavior in the football pitch.

References

1. Abraham, M., Flight, S., Roorda, W.: Agressie en geweld tegen werknemers met een publieke taak. In: Research for the Program 'Veilige Publieke Taak 2007–2009–2011'. DSP, Amsterdam (2011)
2. Bosse, T., Gerritsen, C., de Man, J.: Evaluation of a virtual training environment for aggression de-escalation. In: Proceedings of Game-On 2015. Eurosis (2015)
3. Bosse, T., Provoost, S.: Integrating conversation trees and cognitive models within an ECA for aggression de-escalation training. In: Chen, Q., Torroni, P., Villata, S., Hsu, J., Omicini, A. (eds.) PRIMA 2015. LNCS, vol. 9387, pp. 650–659. Springer, Cham (2015). doi:10. 1007/978-3-319-25524-8_48
4. Bruijnes, M., Linssen, J., op den Akker, R., Theune, M., Wapperom, S., Broekema, C., Heylen, D.: Social behaviour in police interviews: relating data to theories. In: D'Errico, F., Poggi, I., Vinciarelli, A., Vincze, L. (eds.) Conflict and Multimodal Communication. CSS, pp. 317–347. Springer, Cham (2015). doi:10.1007/978-3-319-14081-0_16
5. Dodge, K.A.: The structure and function of reactive and proactive aggression. In: Pepler, D., Rubin, H. (eds.) The Development and Treatment of Childhood Aggression, pp. 201–218. Erlbaum, Hillsdale (1990)
6. Gabler, H.: Lexicon der Ethik im Sport, pp. 22–30 (Ed. by Gruppe, O., Mieth, D.). Verlag Schorndorf, Karl Hoffman (1998)
7. Hays, M., Campbell, J., Trimmer, M., Poore, J., Webb, A., Stark, C., King, T.: Can role-play with virtual humans teach interpersonal skills? In: Interservice/Industry Training, Simulation and Education Conference, I/ITSEC (2012)
8. Leary, T.: Interpersonal Diagnosis of Personality. Ronald Press, New York (1957)
9. Miller, J.D., Lyna, D.R.: Reactive and proactive aggression: similarities and differences. Pers. Individ. Differ. 41(8), 1469–1480 (2006)
10. Ravenet, B., Cafaro, A., Biancardi, B., Ochs, M., Pelachaud, C.: Conversational behavior reflecting interpersonal attitudes in small group interactions. In: Brinkman, W.-P., Broekens, J., Heylen, D. (eds.) IVA 2015. LNCS, vol. 9238, pp. 375–388. Springer, Cham (2015). doi:10.1007/978-3-319-21996-7_41
11. Scholte, J.: Towards realistic virtual communication training - integrating semantics into human-agent conversations. Technical report, VU University Amsterdam (2016)
12. Veldboer, L., Boonstra, N., Duyvendak, J.W.: Agressie in de sport; Fysieke en verbale agressie in de Rotterdamse amateursport: ervaringen en verklaringen. Verwey-Jonker Instituut, Erasmus Universiteit Rotterdam, Utrecht (2003)
13. Wierema, T.: Scheids, what the fuck doe je nou? Technical report, University of Amsterdam (2014)
14. Zantingh, P.: Wat gebeurde er bij Buitenboys - Nieuw Sloten? Vandaag begint de rechtszaak. NRC (2013)

Agents Shaping Networks Shaping Agents: Integrating Social Network Analysis and Agent-Based Modeling in Computational Crime Research

Nicola Lettieri[1]([✉]), Antonio Altamura[2], Delfina Malandrino[2], and Valentina Punzo[1]

[1] INAPP, Rome, Italy
{n.lettieri,v.punzo}@inapp.org
[2] Department of Computer Science, University of Salerno, Fisciano, Italy
antonioaltamura7@gmail.com, dmalandrino@unisa.it

Abstract. The paper presents a recent development of an interdisciplinary research exploring innovative computational approaches to the scientific study of criminal behavior. The attention is focused on an attempt to combine social network analysis and agent-based modelling into *CrimeMiner*, an experimental framework that seamlessly integrates document-enhancement, visualization and network analysis techniques to support the study of criminal organizations. Our goal is both methodological and scientific. We are exploring how the synergy between ABM and SNA can support a deeper and more empirically grounded understanding of the complex dynamics taking place within criminal organizations between the individual/behavioral and social/structural level.

Keywords: Agent-based modeling · Social network analysis · Computational crime analysis

1 Introduction

Over the years, the theoretical debate about the foundational issues of social science has been marked by a move towards the integration of different research approaches to the investigation of social phenomena. The idea of overcoming what has been called the "war of paradigms" [19], has gradually led to the emergence, in discipline after discipline, of a pluralist perspective [18] according to which social research is ever more understood as the integration of different scientific traditions. Faced with the impossibility to identify common epistemic foundations for all the social sciences, researchers are adopting an "eclectic" [35] stance, geared towards discovering the complementarities across concept and

---

The authorship of this work can be attributed as follows: N. Lettieri (Sects. 1, 2.1, 2.2, 4, 4.2, 4.3 and 5); D. Malandrino and A. Altamura (Sects. 3.2, 4.1 and 4.2); V. Punzo (Sects. 2.3, 3.1 and 4.3).

© Springer International Publishing AG 2017
E. Oliveira et al. (Eds.): EPIA 2017, LNAI 10423, pp. 15–27, 2017.
DOI: 10.1007/978-3-319-65340-2_2

visions belonging to different research communities. Far from being limited to the epistemic dimension, the choice of an eclectic research approach involves also the methodological dimension as the sharing of different methods [38] is proving to be crucial in enhancing the scientific investigation of social phenomena. This is true not only in the more traditional areas of social science research, but also in the emerging field of the computational social science [12] where the integration of heterogeneous research perspectives and methods is essential to gain a deeper understanding of foundational issues of social science spanning from the emergence of collective phenomena to the dynamics of social learning. In this scenario, following substantially the same line of thought, researchers are increasingly often exploring the combination of different computational techniques to better deal with the problems arising from the empirical investigation of crime.

This paper presents a development of a research in the direction of exploring innovative and cross-methodological computational approaches to the academic and investigative study of crime. Our objective is a first attempt to combine social network analysis (hereinafter SNA) and agent-based modeling (hereinafter ABM) into *CrimeMiner*, an experimental framework that seamlessly integrates document-enhancement, visualization and network analysis techniques to support the study of criminal organizations starting from real data. Our goal is to explore how the synergy between ABM and SNA can support a deeper and more empirically grounded understanding of the complex dynamics taking place within criminal organizations both at individual and structural level.

2   Theoretical Background: Three Premises

From a theoretical point of view, our research is rooted into three main premises that can be summarized as follows.

2.1   From Instrument-Enabled Science to Science-Enabled Instruments

A first theoretical premise behind the work presented in this paper originates from the relationship that links the scientific investigation and the development of new methodologies and research tools. The scientific endeavor has been over the centuries mediated by increasingly complex artifacts offering new and more insightful representations of the world. Research can be conceived an "instrument-enabled" activity, the result of an iterative process in which technological development is at the same time an enabling factor and an outcome of scientific progress. On this process depended the birth of entire research areas: the nano-sciences, to give just a recent example, would not have come into being without the invention of the electronic microscope.

In the same way, the computational investigation of social phenomena has been marked since its origins by a strong relation between the technological-instrumental and the scientific dimension. As underlined in [11], even in social sciences, doing research also means designing new methods, new tools, new ways of processing data. Instruments enable science but, at the same time, the adoption of new scientific perspectives leads to the creation of new tools that will in turn bring about new knowledge. Against this backdrop, our analysis tries to explore how the creation of new tools and the combination of different scientific perspectives can result into a deeper understanding social phenomena.

2.2   Strange Loops: Agents Shaping Networks Shaping Agents

The second premise of our work is connected with the longstanding clash between individualism and structuralism, the two opposed metatheoretical positions that have marked so far a large part of the contemporary history of social science. As is well known, while individualists assume that only individuals exist and that sociological objects and properties are nothing but combinations of the individual participants and their properties, in the structuralist perspective, society is somehow the sum of interrelations in which individuals stand with respect to one another [32].

The debate has remained substantially unresolved despite a long history also because of the lack of research methodologies [4] allowing to bridge the gap between two research perspectives looking at phenomena belonging to different ontological levels: the individual and the social structure. What has been missing so far is the possibility to explore how individual behaviours turn into social networks and networks shape individual behaviors. Agents and networks are locked into a perpetual coevolution, a dynamic that can be well depicted through the illuminating metaphor of *"strange loops"* [28], a paradigmatic concept developed by Douglas Hofstadter to describe *"the phenomenon that occurs whenever, by moving upwards or downwards through the levels of some hierarchical system, we unexpectedly find ourselves right where we started"*. The struggle to shed new light on this loop is a worthy effort: social influence is crucial in all social phenomena. In this scenario, while useful to explore the causal path connecting individual/micro and social/macro emergent phenomena, ABM alone may be insufficient to account for the role played by the structure and the features of social networks in shaping human behavior. Agents change under different types and degrees of social influence as entities at the macroscopic level network affect them and their behavior: we therefore *"must understand how this can happen if we want to drive, enforce, or prevent such an influence"* [14]. It is no coincidence at all, in this scenario, the attention paid by the simulation study of norms to the topology of social networks, growingly considered as a *"key factor of all phases of norm development"* [2].

2.3   Networks in Criminological Research

The third theoretical premise is related to one of the main goal of criminological research: understand the relationship between social networks and criminal behavior. As a matter of fact, social influence processes taking place in social networks are traditionally considered as one of the main factors responsible of different aspects of criminal behavior ranging from the development of an individual's own deviant behavior to the micro criminality as well as the spreading of some forms of criminal patterns [34].

Sutherlands Differential association theory [37] states that criminal behavior patterns (motives, attitudes and techniques of committing a crime) are learned in interaction with others. Differential association theory can be seen as a specific instance of the more general network theory of social learning. The role of the social environment is crucial within the explanatory framework of situational models of crime. Both the Routine activity theory [13] and the Situational Action Theory [39], for example, suggest that some social environmental conditions are more criminogenic than others. According to these approaches, acts of crime are an outcome of the convergence between people and setting and social networks are considered a natural way to explain the emergence of criminal offending [9, 33]. In addition to providing a highly visual and detailed way to describe a set of relations and actors, social network analysis facilitates the testing of structural hypotheses about criminal patterns emerging from patterns of relations.

3   Methodological Background

3.1   Agent-Based Modeling and Crime

The use of Agent-Based Social Simulation (ABSS) in the social sciences has grown over the past 15 years [25] proving to be successful also for the study of the social dimension of crime [31]. Early applications of simulative approach to crime analysis appeared in the field of Environmental Criminology [8].

There are many reasons to investigate the relationship between Agent-Based Simulations and crime analysis. The principal argument in criminology is the need for complementarities between the experimental or quasi-experimental approach and the simulation one [31]. An important argument is the possibility to advance, test or refine theory [27], to anticipate consequences coming from one type of intervention over another [3] as well as to provide new policy evaluation tools. ABM allows researchers to create artificial societies [20] and to explore how individual-level criminal action might translate into observable macrolevel crime patterns. As already highlighted, social scientists can grasp within a formalized model those relevant features of the complexity of social systems: autonomy and heterogeneity of agents, adaptive rationality, spacial and local interactions, non-equilibrium dynamics [36]. In the field of crime research, for example, the spatial nature of crime and interaction between agents (criminal, police, victim, etc.) often requires the agent-based models to include space and time [26]. An important challenge is in fact to investigate the spatio-temporal dynamics of crime [7,31]. Within this area, the key object is the study of crime, criminality, and victimization as they relate to particular places and how offenders, targets (victims), and guardians (control agents) shape their activities spatially. In this field, a relevant question is which factors influence the emergence of hot spots [6,24]. Computer simulations of criminal patterns are implemented to identify potential hotspots and flashpoints. As a consequence they can supply support to police forces in order to allocate resources to areas where particular crimes are most likely to occur. After this brief overview, it emerges how agent-based simulations have becoming increasingly important in crime research since they allow us to overcome some of the limitations which characterize the traditional research methods in criminology bounded both temporally and spatially.

3.2   From Social to Criminal Network Analysis

Recent years have witnessed a growing interest towards the use of SNA techniques in the study of criminal organizations both for scientific and investigation goals. SNA made a key contributions to criminological issues in several areas such as, the role of peer selection and influence in delinquency, gang boundaries and collaboration among gang members, the structure of criminal and terrorist organizations. Criminal Network Analysis (CNA) is today a well-established interdisciplinary research area in which network analysis techniques are employed to analyze large volume of relational data and gain deeper insights about the criminal network under investigation. There are many examples of application of the principles of SNA in the analysis of criminal organizations [5,17,22,34,40]. As an example, in [5] authors found out that drug trafficking networks tend to spread from a relatively dense core in short chain-like structures. Their studies also show that these structures are apparent across the drug distribution system. Disruption strategies targeting individuals with high centrality and human capital are likely to include the leaders and other visible members of the drug distribution network, and this should, lead to a more successful crime control.

4   Integrating ABM and SNA

The scenario described makes easier to understand the reasons that led us to explore the intersections between social simulation, network analysis and criminal research. ABM and SNA can be mutually beneficial and their integration can result into a significant contribution to the explanatory and predictive power of social research. SNA allows to better investigate the evolution of social phenomena in all the situations in which topological properties of the network become a key factor affecting social outcomes - think about the spread of epidemics [41] or opinion dynamics [10]. This is even truer when the structural knowledge provided by SNA is based on the analysis of real data, a circumstance that makes more empirically rooted the investigation. ABM, on its own, allows to account for the individual attributes and the internal, cognitive dynamics of the agents involved in the target social phenomenon, a possibility that becomes crucial whenever we deal with events for which individual behavior is relevant and we want not only to predict and understand but also to somehow affect the process e.g. by shortening, delaying or preventing it [14]. The project here presented has to be seen in this perspective: the experiment described in the following sections is based on *CrimeMiner*, an experimental computational crime analysis environment dealing with data coming from real investigations.

4.1   The CrimeMiner Project

CrimeMiner [29, 30] is an ongoing research project aiming to explore innovative computational methods to support the study of the societal dimension of crime for both scientific and investigative purposes. In more details, the goal of the research is to see how the combination of data mining, SNA, and data visualization techniques can contribute to a deeper understanding of structural and functional features of criminal organizations starting from the analysis of even simple relational and investigative data. The considerations developed during the project led to a holistic approach deployed into a computational framework intended to be used in investigative and research settings to gather, markup, visualize and analyze all the information needed to apply SNA techniques to criminal organizations. The environment has been validated during a case study based on data coming from real criminal investigations (telephone and environmental tapping used to map the social structure of a criminal organization belonging to the Italian Camorra). System requirements were discussed with domain experts involved in the project and then translated into several functionalities that can be summarized as follows.

- *Document-enhancement.* Its goal is to structure the content of documents (in our case study, a set of procedural documents belonging to a criminal trial) providing all the metadata needed to implement SNA and visualization features [40]. We implemented a structured Text Editor combining the traditional word-processor facilities with the background creation of structured data containing relevant information for CNA (e.g., police records, etc.).
- *Graph visualization, interactive charts, tabular visualization.* Data currently handled by *CrimeMiner* consist in people records and telephone/environmental tapping: people are transformed into vertices (or nodes) of a graph; telephone and environmental tapping depicting a relationship between two or more people are represented as edges to be analyzed using SNA metrics. To make the graph visualization easy to read, drawing inspiration from experiences already made [15], we have implemented some algorithms for force-directed graph drawing allowing users to filter nodes by a minimum threshold degree. *CrimeMiner* generates also line charts showing the trends of the communications between given nodes (see Fig. 1). The whole list of the persons and tapping can be also browsed in the form of interactive tabular data with an advanced filtering feature.
- *SNA, statistical analysis, GIS features.* *CrimeMiner* offers a set of SNA metrics to allow the study of the distinctive features of the criminal organization and the identification of the role of single individuals within it. The current implementation supports the most popular features such as the dominance, subordination, influence or prestige of social actors [23]. Among the implemented measures we can mention: degree centrality, betweenness centrality, Page Rank and Modularity. The network can be plotted into a geographical map to better understanding the relations in popular place and known location (see Fig. 1).

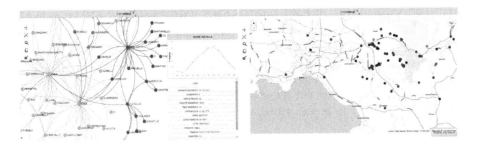

Fig. 1. *CrimeMiner:* screenshots of the SNA and GIS user interfaces

4.2 Widening the Scope of the Research

Starting from the work above described, we decided to widen the scope of the research complementing former *CrimeMiner* functionalities (mainly devoted to data collection, visualization and network analysis, see Fig. 2) with a simulation component. The goal was twofold: (i) Enhancing ABM theory making: a first goal of our experiment is to support and enhance the ABM exploration of criminological theories by adding to the simulation both empirical evidences and topological properties of criminal networks derived from the analysis of real data; (ii) Making SNA more "generative": a second goal is to add a generative dimension to the analyses underway within our project, by making it possible to complement the structural analysis with the study of the interactions taking place between agents and the environment. The overall outcome of our effort is sketched in Fig. 2 where research goals (level 1) are wrapped in four macro-sections (Data

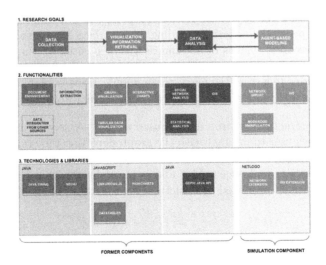

Fig. 2. An overview of *CrimeMiner* project: research goals, functionalities and technologies. Dotted boxes at level 2 represent functionalities under development.

collection, Visualization/Information retrieval, Data Analysis, ABM), each of which is mapped into a group of system functionalities (level 2). Level 3 finally lists the technologies used for each research goal.

We have implemented an extension of *CrimeMiner* (the "Simulation component") enabling a two-way, circular communication between the original system and an ABM environment (in this case NetLogo). The attempt resulted into a set of features that can be described as follows.

Data Exchange Between CrimeMiner and ABM Environment. A first group of functionalities allows to export from *CrimeMiner* and import into an ABM environment the whole set of real world and network data stored and produced within *CrimeMiner* in the SNA stages of the research:

- Real data about individuals and their criminal profile: personal data of individuals brought into the investigation (name, age, residence, criminal records etc.); criminal records.
- Real data about social interaction and criminal activities: date and time of telephone tappings; date time and location of in person meetings harvested by means of environmental tapping
- Network data: topological features of the network identified by *CrimeMiner*. These data include nodes/individuals measures (Degree, Betweeness, Page Rank etc.), edges/social interactions (orientation and weight) and overall network (e.g. density, sub-communities, etc.)

Depending on the research goals, users can select and export, in standard structured format (csv and XML), only the information considered to be relevant for the design and the implementation of the simulation experiment. Even in this preliminary stage of the project, it's easy to imagine different experiments based on the fusion of real/network data and ABM models. It is for instance possible to recreate the real world network topology into a simulation assigning to the agents specific behaviors depending on real data like personal attributes (e.g. criminal records); values of SNA measures or position of the agent in real space. In the same way, it's possible to model in the simulation the nature of social interactions (e.g. the frequency of communications between agents) so as to reflect the actual properties of the interaction in real world.

User-Graph Interaction Within ABM Environment. A second group of functionalities allows user to interact with the graph depicting the criminal network within the NetLogo environment. Users can add, remove or modify the properties of both nodes and edges. This allows to explore, within the simulation, the effect potentially produced by structural modifications of the network under investigation.

4.3 Experimenting with ABM Criminological Models

We are working, both at a theoretical and application level, on a first set of experiments aiming to understand how the workflow and the tools so far developed can support both the analysis of the implications of criminological theories and the study of real criminal organizations. To move in this direction, we have decided to merge SNA and ABM using, on the one hand, the data coming from the *CrimeMiner* project (network data, attributes and properties of individuals involved into the investigation) and, on the other, an agent-based model of criminal dynamics [34]. We have chosen a model investigating the mechanisms of social influence and their effects both on individual criminal choices and on the spread of crime on social networks. The study started from the hypothesis that of different criminal outcomes generated by different mechanisms of imitation at the micro level of social interaction. In particular, the model introduces a distinction between *rational imitation* (based on the performance observed) and *social imitation* (based on the degree of connectivity observed) on the basis of the motivations that are behind the imitative behavior. To test this hypothesis, the model simulates individual agents interacting in their social networks. Individual decisions to be engaged in crime and their consequent behavior towards crime, are influenced by both personal and social learning factors. The model formalizes the structure of different social network topologies (random, scale-free and small-world) on which agents are connected. The main substantive implications emerging from the study concern the different effects of rational and social imitation mechanisms on crime. Summarizing some of the main results, the network topology seems to have more influence on crime when individuals influence each other through social imitation. In such cases, as already said, agents imitate other actors connected on their network, on the basis of their degree of connectivity. Secondly, results suggest that a small world network structure allows to better account for the spreading of crime through social imitation.

Starting from the model just sketched and exploiting the functionalities described in Sect. 4.2 we imported *CrimeMiner* data into a *NetLogo* implementation of the model so to start a series of simulation experiments that can be traced back to the two research directions above listed:

(i) *Enhancing ABM theory making:* a first set of experiments is and will be devoted to place the conceptual insights and hypotheses of the theoretical model taken as reference into a more realistic environment. The goal is to explore the outcomes produced by the imitation mechanisms presented in [34] in different experimental conditions variously connected with topical issues in criminological research. Here below a list of both started and forthcoming experiments grouped by topic.

– *Network structure:* network topologies (random, scale-free, small-world) already tested have been replaced with the topology derived by real data in the *CrimeMiner* project. The attention is focused on monitoring of how different and more realistic topologies affect specific features of the simulated phenomenon (first of all the emergence and spread of criminal behaviors, the speed and the diffusion of crime at the end of the simulation). Other experiments will be done adding/deleting specific nodes/edges so to explore the effect produced on the evolution of the network (emergence or disappearance of sub-communities) and give an answer to questions like the following. How does criminal models/leaders and participation relate to behavioral patterns? Which types of ties predict social status, power, or influence within the group, and how do these translate into collective action?

- *Nodes attributes:* behavioral profiles (e.g. the propensity to commit a crime) and individual attributes (e.g. the criminal prestige) will be assigned to simulated agents according to the attributes (e.g. type of criminal records) of the corresponding real individuals/nodes as defined in *CrimeMiner*. This will allow to give a "realistic flavour" to the ABM exploration of fundamental theories of crime like, just for instance "social learning theory" [1].

- *Environment:* agent behavior will be varied not only depending on the imitation mechanism taken into account, but also according to the spatial information (of the agents, of the criminal activities) derived from *CrimeMiner* GIS data. We will imagine new *in silico* explorations of the role played by the environmental/spatial dimension in the genesis/evolution of crime [21].

(ii) *Making generative SNA:* another set of experiments will be devoted to explore the potential evolutions of the criminal network under investigation exploiting the expressiveness and the simplicity of ABM. This will allow to complement more complex and less "semantic" (at least for social scientists and investigators) approaches like probabilistic approaches to link prediction [41].

5 Conclusion

Even if in its early stages, the work presented in this paper has already produced interesting preliminary results depicting the integration of ABM and SNA as a promising way to support the study of criminal organizations both for scientific and investigative purpose. The merging of these methodologies seems capable to enhance criminological research offering new ways to investigate how the evolution of crime relates to the structural features of criminal organization and to the dynamics of agency (autonomy, learning etc.). In that direction, evolutionary techniques, that we applied in other research areas [16], could be used to gain more and different insights about the phenomenon under investigation. Advances in this field could not only shed a new light on the core dynamics of crime, but could also result in the creation of more effective tools to be gradually introduced into the daily activity of crime researches and public agencies involved in the fight against organized crime. In more general terms, the integration of heterogeneous research methods like ABM and SNA appeared to be helpful also in other ways: providing more chances for communication between otherwise bounded communities, teasing out complementarities across problems sliced in different ways in separate scientific and application areas. The experience made provided us with a meaningful example of how scientific perspectives, methods and tools evolve together in a continuous and circular process. So far we have focused our attention on extending the functionalities of *CrimeMiner* devoting a still limited time to the experiments. The network data and the simulation model have been correctly merged in *NetLogo* and the first simulations performed so far have produced results that, in addition to being different from the ones presented in [34], have given us food for thought bringing about new challenges for research areas spanning from criminology to computational social science, from legal informatics to computer science. It should not come as no surprise. According to the scenario above sketched speculating about epistemological issues, the future of social science is not only computational, but also eclectic.

References

1. Akers, R.L.: Deviant behavior: a social learning approach (Wadsworth, Belmont, 1977). An upper level text written from a cultural transmission perspective. Evaluates major theories of deviance and examines a wide variety of deviant activities (1973)
2. Balke, T., Cranefield, S., Di Tosto, G., Mahmoud, S., Paolucci, M., Savarimuthu, B.T.R., Verhagen, H.: Simulation and NorMAS. In: Dagstuhl Follow-Ups, vol. 4. Schloss Dagstuhl-Leibniz-Zentrum fuer Informatik (2013)
3. Berkes, F., Colding, J., Folke, C.: Rediscovery of traditional ecological knowledge as adaptive management. Ecol. Appl. **10**(5), 1251–1262 (2000)
4. Bhargava, R.: Individualism in Social Science: Forms and Limits of a Methodology. Clarendon Press, Oxford (1992)
5. Bichler, G., Malm, A., Cooper, T.: Drug supply networks: a systematic review of the organizational structure of illicit drug trade. Crime Sci. **6**(1), 2 (2017)
6. Bosse, T., Elffers, H., Gerritsen, C., et al.: Simulating the dynamical interaction of offenders, targets and guardians. Crime Patterns Anal. **3**(1), 51–66 (2010)
7. Bosse, T., Gerritsen, C., Klein, M.C.: Agent-based simulation of social learning in criminology. In: ICAART, pp. 5–13 (2009)
8. Brantingham, P., Groff, E.: The future of agent-based simulation in environmental criminology. American Society of Criminology, Nashville (2004)
9. Calvó-Armengol, A., Zenou, Y.: Social networks and crime decisions: the role of social structure in facilitating delinquent behavior. Int. Econ. Rev. **45**(3), 939–958 (2004)
10. Castellano, C., Fortunato, S., Loreto, V.: Statistical physics of social dynamics. Rev. Modern Phys. **81**(2), 591 (2009)
11. Cioffi-Revilla, C.: Computational social science. Wiley Interdiscip. Rev.: Comput. Stat. **2**(3), 259–271 (2010)
12. Cioffi-Revilla, C.: Introduction to Computational Social Science: Principles and Applications. Springer Science & Business Media, London (2013). doi:10.1007/978-1-4471-5661-1
13. Cohen, L.E., Felson, M.: Social change and crime rate trends: a routine activity approach. Am. Sociol. Rev. **44**, 588–608 (1979)
14. Conte, R., Paolucci, M.: On agent based modelling and computational social science. Front. Psychol. **5**, 668 (2014)
15. De Prisco, R., Esposito, A., Lettieri, N., Malandrino, D., Pirozzi, D., Zaccagnino, G., Zaccagnino, R.: Music plagiarism at a glance: metrics of similarity and visualizations. In: 21th International Conference Information Visualisation, IV 2017. London South Bank University, London (2017)

16. De Prisco, R., Zaccagnino, G., Zaccagnino, R.: A multi-objective differential evolution algorithm for 4-voice compositions. In: 2011 IEEE Symposium on Differential Evolution, SDE 2011, Paris, France, 11–15 April 2011, pp. 65–72 (2011); De Prisco, R., Zaccagnino, G., Zaccagnino, R.: A genetic algorithm for dodecaphonic compositions. In: Di Chio, C., et al. (eds.) EvoApplications 2011, Part II. LNCS, vol. 6625, pp. 244–253. Springer, Heidelberg (2011)

17. Décary-Hétu, D., Dupont, B.: The social network of hackers. Global Crime **13**(3), 160–175 (2012)

18. Della Porta, D., Keating, M.: Approaches and Methodologies in the Social Sciences: A Pluralist Perspective. Cambridge University Press, Cambridge (2008)

19. Eckstein, H.: Unfinished business reflections on the scope of comparative politics. Comp. Polit. Stud. **31**(4), 505–534 (1998)

20. Epstein, J.M., Axtell, R.: Growing Artificial Societies: Social Science From the Bottom Up. Brookings Institution Press, Washington, DC (1996)

21. Felson, M., Clarke, R.V.: Opportunity makes the thief (1998)

22. Ferrara, E., De Meo, P., Catanese, S., Fiumara, G.: Detecting criminal organizations in mobile phone networks. Expert Syst. Appl. **41**(13), 5733–5750 (2014)

23. Freeman, L.C.: Centrality in social networks conceptual clarification. Soc. Netw. **1**(3), 215–239 (1978)

24. Furtado, V., Melo, A., Coelho, A.L., Menezes, R., Belchior, M.: Simulating crime against properties using swarm intelligence and social networks. In: Artificial Crime Analysis Systems, pp. 300–318 (2008)

25. Gilbert, N., Troitzsch, K.: Simulation for the Social Scientist. McGraw-Hill Education, New York (2005)

26. Groff, E., Mazerolle, L.: Simulated experiments and their potential role in criminology and criminal justice. Exp. Criminol. **4**(3), 187–193 (2008)

27. Groff, E.R.: Simulation for theory testing and experimentation: an example using routine activity theory and street robbery. J. Quant. Criminol. **23**(2), 75–103 (2007)

28. Hofstadter, D.R.: Gödel, escher, bach. Un eterno y grácil bucle (1980)

29. Lettieri, N., Malandrino, D., Vicidomini, L.: By investigation, I mean computation. Trends Organ. Crime **20**, 31–54 (2017)

30. Lettieri, N., et al.: Text and (social) network analysis as investigative tools: a case study. Inform. Diritt. **22**(1), 263–280 (2013)

31. Liu, L.: Artificial crime analysis systems: using computer simulations and geographic information systems: using computer simulations and geographic information systems. IGI Global (2008)

32. Mayhew, B.H.: Structuralism versus individualism: Part II, ideological and other obfuscations. Soc. Forces **59**, 627–648 (1981)

33. Ormerod, P., Wiltshire, G.: 'Binge' drinking in the UK: a social network phenomenon. Mind Soc. **8**(2), 135 (2009)

34. Punzo, V.: How crime spreads through imitation in social networks: a simulation model. In: Cecconi, F. (ed.) New Frontiers in the Study of Social Phenomena, pp. 169–190. Springer, Cham (2016). doi:10.1007/978-3-319-23938-5_10

35. Sil, R.: The foundations of eclecticism the epistemological status of agency, culture, and structure in social theory. J. Theor. Polit. **12**(3), 353–387 (2000)

36. Squazzoni, F.: The micro-macro link in social simulation. Sociologica **2**(1), 1–26 (2008)

37. Sutherland, E.H., Cressey, D.R.: Principles of Criminology. Lippincott, Philadelphia (1947)

38. Teddlie, C., Tashakkori, A.: Foundations of Mixed Methods Research: Integrating Quantitative and Qualitative Approaches in the Social and Behavioral Sciences. Sage, Thousand Oaks (2009)
39. Wikström, P.O.H.: Individuals, settings, and acts of crime: situational mechanisms and the explanation of crime. The explanation of crime: context, mechanisms and development, pp. 61–107 (2006)
40. Xu, J., Chen, H.: Criminal network analysis and visualization. Commun. ACM **48**(6), 100–107 (2005)
41. Zhou, T., Lü, L.: Link prediction in complex networks: a survey. Phys. A: Stat. Mech. Appl. **390**(6), 1150–1170 (2011)

An Agent-Based Model Predicting Group Emotion and Misbehaviours in Stranded Passengers

Lenin Medeiros[(✉)] and C. Natalie van der Wal

Behavioural Informatics Group, Vrije Universiteit Amsterdam,
De Boelelaan 1081, 1081 HV Amsterdam, Netherlands
{l.medeiros,c.n.vander.wal}@vu.nl

Abstract. Airline passengers can get stranded in an airport due to a number of reasons. As a consequence, they might get frustrated. Frustration leads to misbehaving if a given individual is frustrated enough, according to the literature. In this work, an agent-based model of stranded passengers in an airport departure area is presented. Structured simulations show how personal and environmental characteristics such as age, gender and emotional contagion, among others, influence the frustration dynamics, number and type of misbehaviours in such a scenario. We also present simulation results with two implemented support models (a chatbot and multilingual staff) aiming to reduce the overall frustration level of passengers facing this type of situation. Important findings are that: men are more likely to use force than women, the crowd composition plays an important role in terms of misbehaviours, the effect of emotional contagion leads to more misbehaviours and a chatbot might be considered as an alternative for supporting stranded passengers.

Keywords: Computational modelling · Multi-agent based modelling · Emotional contagion · Misbehaviour prediction · Crime prevention · Chatbots

1 Introduction

On February 2017, as storm Doris battered European regions as UK and The Netherlands, hundreds of passengers, including holidaymakers and commuters, faced flight delays.[1,2] In such a situation in which passengers are stranded in a delimited area as a boarding gate lounge, it is always a challenge for the air companies as well as security professionals to deal with the fact that people may start to get frustrated and angry. Having people intimidating or yelling at others is a risk in such a scenario.

---

[1] Available on: https://goo.gl/ZrVeHT. Accessed 12 April 2017.

[2] Available on: https://goo.gl/8Me4ve. Accessed 12 April 2017.

© Springer International Publishing AG 2017
E. Oliveira et al. (Eds.): EPIA 2017, LNAI 10423, pp. 28–40, 2017.
DOI: 10.1007/978-3-319-65340-2_3

In previous work, a similar situation to the one stated above - stranded passengers in a train - was addressed by van der Wal et al. [21] In the current research it is described how this approach was adapted to deal with stranded passengers (in a boarding gate area) of a delayed flight.

The aim of this work is to propose a realistic domain model that: (1) can predict misbehaviours in stranded passengers at an airport boarding gate area and (2) that can be used by emergency management and prevention professionals as a preparation for or managing crowds during emergency scenarios. The word 'domain' refers to modelling the process as it is in reality. Besides that, we also implemented different 'support' models, added to the 'domain' model, to simulate the effects of a chatbot offering support or multi-lingual staff members on the group frustration level and number and types of misbehaviours.

Via the developed domain model we can predict how likely a given set of stranded passengers is to misbehave. This is calculated based on personal and environmental characteristics as gender, boarding time information, etc.

The rest of this paper is organized as follows. Section 2 provides concepts and lessons from the literature that were used to develop the models. Section 3 presents the developed formal domain and support models. Section 4 presents the structured simulation results to investigate the correctness of our models and to extract insights regarding the stranded passengers situation. Finally, Sect. 5 provides a discussion and our final conclusions.

2   Related Work

2.1   Computational Models of (Group) Emotions

Affective Computing is the field of developing and studying systems and devices that can interpret, simulate, process and recognize human emotion [16]. Marsella et al. [12] give an overview of the research on computational models of human emotions and emotional processes. They describe how the field of computational models of emotion is not mature yet, as there are very competing and complementary computational models. Often, such models do not seem to state their goals clearly or assumptions and design decisions are not articulated. They make a distinction between appraisal models, dimensional models and other approaches.

In appraisal theory, emotion is argued to arise from patterns of individual judgements concerning the relationship between events and an individual's beliefs, desires and intentions. This stems from the beliefs-desires-intention model for simulating agent behaviour and thoughts [9]. These judgements are formalised in variables representing aspects of the personal significance of events and can also trigger cognitive responses, or so called coping strategies. These models are mainly applied in human computer interaction applications, such as real-time interactive characters exhibiting emotions.

Dimensional theories argue that emotions should not be conceptualized as discrete entities, but as points in a continuous dimensional space. Dimensional computational models of emotions are applied in systems attempting to recognize human emotions and in animated character generation, as virtual avatars, in computer games or online therapies, that recognise the user's emotions to adjust the content of the game or therapy upon.

Among the other approaches are (1) anatomical approaches (models based on neural links and processes underlying emotional reactions), (2) rational approaches (that view emotions as a cognitive function with its own architectural constraints on how it operates) and (3) communicative theories of emotion (incorporating the dissociation between internal emotional processes and social emotion displays).

These computational models of emotion are mainly meant for individual emotions. Bosse et al. [2,3] have created a computational model for group emotions in which mental and emotional states can be socially distributed representing people being able to affect each other's states: the ASCRIBE model. The approach of Bosse et al. is a mix of computational social science and affective computing. The social contagion mechanisms are modelled and simulated, based on neurological findings as well (the anatomical perspective on computational models of emotions). Tsai et al. [20] evaluated computational emotional contagion models beforehand. The ASCRIBE model outperformed the other two models on reproducing real crowd panic scenes.

Concluding, in this paper a combination of the ASCRIBE model (social contagion of emotion) with an appraisal model (individual emotion) suits the goal of modelling frustration dynamics in stranded passengers best.

2.2   Chatbots and Multi-lingual Professionals Supporting People

Concerning the developed support models, we based ourselves on the literature to come up with the ideas of a chatbot and multi-cultural staff to regulate the overall frustration level of stranded passengers.

First, the concept of peer support, defined by Kim et al. [11] as people supporting each other within a social network context, has been addressed by researchers from Artificial Intelligence field. As examples for that we can point out the works conducted by: van der Zaan et al. [22], that provided a virtual buddy for helping victims of cyberbullying, and DeVault et al. [7], that developed virtual agents as depression therapists. In addition, Medeiros and Bosse [13] started to develop research about chatbots for messaging apps providing social support to users in order to help them to deal with everyday stressful situations. Hence, our paper addresses the role played by a chatbot in a network of people getting frustrated over time due to a flight delay and whose goal is to reduce the overall network frustration level. More precisely, a chatbot is a software that simulates human conversation through voice commands, text chats or both. Thus, during critical as well as emergency situations, an interaction with users and a chatbot would be useful to help people to receive instant instructions on how to handle the situation via providing social and/or practical support.

Second, we were also interested in investigating the role played by multi-lingual staff in our support model. A multicultural or at least bilingual staff may be helpful to effectively interact and respond to passengers' requests and claims

[23]. Indeed, verbal announcements and written information should be provided in English as well as the local language to increase clarity of communication, given the popularity of this language (according to Crystal [5], for example, it might be the case that approximately 2 billion people speak English).

3   Modelling a Flight Delay Situation

In this section, the formal domain and support models that were developed, are presented. Due to lack of space, only part of the formal definitions and code (written in NetLogo[3]) is presented. Nevertheless, for purposes of checking and replicating our simulations, the code is available on a GitHub repository[4].

3.1   Domain Model

Based on one of Fiumicino Airport's boarding areas[5], we designed an airport departure lounge in NetLogo with seats, restaurants, toilets, help desks and boarding gates. Then, we constructed a computational agent-based model in accordance with requirements provided by stakeholders from the H2020 IMPACT project[6]. In general terms, the model acts as follows: (1) as soon as there is no information regarding the boarding time, the passengers' frustration levels keep increasing over time; (2) when a given passenger reaches a frustration level equal or higher than 0.8, he or she will start to misbehave (it was decided it would be simpler to model the phenomena of becoming aggressive by implementing a standard frustration threshold for each passenger that triggers potential misbehavior rather than having different frustration thresholds for different groups); (3) a given passenger's frustration level growth rate depends on his or her personal characteristics (e.g. age, whether he or she is a commuter or a holidaymaker, etc.); (4) the intentions of a given passenger depend on his or her frustration level as well as respective personal characteristics; (5) the actions performed by a given passenger depend on his or her frustration level, personal characteristics and intention. A pseudocode for this model is given in Algorithm 1. As a basic setting (adjustable), the domain model runs for 2 h.

The agent's age and gender affect the selection of actions. According to literature, young men are more prone to exert aggressive behaviour compared to any other age group or gender [15]. Based on the frustration level in combination with the characteristics of the passenger, an intention and an action is chosen. The higher the frustration level, the more aggressive the behaviour and men are more likely than women to express aggression [1,4]. This is modelled with different chances to misbehave, for each passenger type. The chance a passenger will yell, intimidate or use force, depends on both gender and age. The chances of misbehaviours were based on the statistics of disruptive behaviour on board

---

[3] Available on: https://ccl.northwestern.edu/netlogo/. Accessed 30 April 2017.

[4] Available on: https://git.io/vH5ma. Accessed 14 June 2017.

[5] Available on: https://goo.gl/HS95SI. Accessed 30 April 2017.

[6] Available on: http://www.impact-csa.eu/. Accessed 14 June 2017.

Algorithm 1 Pseudo code for the domain model.

---

procedure MAINLOOP(void)
    time ← 0:00 *a.m.*
  repeat
    UPDATEFRUSTRATION()
    ▷ Updating the passenger's frustration level according to the pre-defined rules, taking into account: the individual's personal characteristics, boarding time and availability of toilets and restaurants.

    UPDATEINTENTION()
    ▷ Updating the individual's intention according to his characteristics and frustration. The possible values are: "to enjoy the trip", "to seek for information" and "to become aggressive".

    ACTIONSELECTION()
    ▷ Selecting the individual's action according to his characteristics and intention. The possible values are: "to go to a restaurant", "to go to the toilet", "to walk", "to sit", "to ask questions", "to yell", "to intimidate", and "to use force". This procedure is called every 2 minutes.

    EMOTIONALCONTAGION()
    ▷ Spreading the effect of emotional contagion among passengers in a radius of 5 meters.

    time ← time + 1*s*
  until *time* = 2:00 *a.m.*

---

of UK airlines[7]. Therefore, we assumed that male passengers are more likely to misbehave than female passengers for each type of misbehaviour.

In agent-based modelling, agent behaviour might be modelled with some randomness in order to make it more realistic [24]. To accomplish this, an internal random constant assuming values between −0.04 and 0.04 called INT_THRESHOLD was created in every stranded passenger. It is aimed to simulate internal personal characteristics that differentiate the passengers from each other as individuals.

In the model, the passengers are divided into different clusters of culturally similar nationalities based on previous research [18]. Data concerning the percentage of English speakers for each country in each cluster were then obtained, where available, from multiple verified and official sources compiled by Wikipedia[8]. We then calculated a weighted average percentage of English speakers in each cluster – using the population sizes of each cluster's constituent countries – and these were the values used in the simulation model to determine the percentage of passengers from each cluster who could understand an English instruction by a staff member or public announcement.

Social contagion of frustration, according to the concept of social identity [8,10,17], also plays a role in our model. Passengers compare themselves to others and the more similar (based on age, gender and traveller type) they are, the more they can infect others' frustration levels. This influence is causing a strengthening or diminishing of the frustration experienced. This mechanism is based on social identification theory [19] and emotional contagion [3]. The formula in the current model works as follows for passengers in a radius of 5 meters: if 2 passengers are travelling together, one will fully affect the other's frustration level; if 2 passengers are not travelling together, the influence one exerts on the other's frustration level is proportional to the similarity between them considering 4 personal characteristics (age, gender, nationality cluster and traveller type); therefore, if 2 passengers that are not travelling together have the same age, gender, nationality cluster and if both are commuters, one will

---

[7] Available on: https://goo.gl/lBUK5H. Accessed 30 April 2017.

[8] Available on: https://goo.gl/vrEQip. Accessed 30 April 2017.

fully affect other's frustration level, i.e., 4 times more than if they had only the same gender, for instance.

The following is an example of a formal rule we used in our domain model. Consider: P as a set containing all the passengers, $p \in P$ as a given passenger, the functions $g : P \rightarrow G = \{$"male", "female"$\}$, $ag : P \rightarrow AG = \{$"young", "adolescent", "adult", "elder"$\}$ and $i : P \rightarrow I = \{$"to enjoy the trip", "to seek for information", "to misbehave"$\}$ as gender, age group and intention of the passenger p, respectively. Besides, consider the function $yell : P \rightarrow \mathbb{R}$ as the chance p has to yell when he or she is intending to become aggressive (i.e., $i(p) = $"to misbehave"). Hence, the chance a given male passenger has to yell when intending to misbehave (30%) is defined as follows: $\forall p \in P \wedge g(p) = $"male"$\wedge ag(p) = $"adult"$\wedge i(p) = $"to misbehave"$\Rightarrow yell(p) = 0.3$. Figure 1 shows how this rule is implemented in NetLogo. A conceptual representation of the domain model is presented in Fig. 2.

```
ask passengers with [intention = "to become aggressive" and gender = "M" and age_group = "adult"] [
  set chance random 100
  ; ...
  if chance >= 16 and chance <= 45 [ ; 30%
    set action "to yell"
  ; ...
  ]
]
```

Fig. 1. Excerpt of NetLogo code regarding the chance a given adult male passenger will yell when he is intending to misbehave (i.e., to become aggressive).

3.2   Support Models

In previous research, a model of how people are collectively coping with stressful situations within social networks was developed [14]. The authors realized that, by providing support to peers, a given individual might also get stressed as a consequence of such an emotional effort. As an attempt to deal with this implication, the idea of a chatbot emerged from a study about strategies used by social network users when helping their friends to cope with stress online [13]. Based on these previous works, we came up with the concept of a supportive chatbot for stranded passengers in the current model. It is assumed a reasonable idea that some passengers might get even more stressed by receiving such a type of support, since its efficacy needs more concrete results. Therefore, when a given stranded passenger receives support from the chatbot, in 80% of cases his or her frustration level will become lower than before. On the other hand, in 20% of cases, it will become higher than before.

Finally, we also implemented the concept of multi-lingual staff as a support strategy. In our model, when a given staff member is able to speak more than one language, the chance a given passenger will get less frustrated by talking to him or her is 3 times higher than if he or she had no such a multi-cultural background.

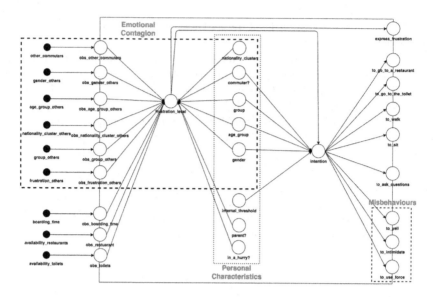

Fig. 2. Representation of the stranded passengers' domain model at a departure gate at Fiumicino Airport. A given passenger's internal states are located within the big (non-dashed) rectangle.

4   Experimental Analysis

In order to answer our research questions and check our hypotheses, we performed structured simulations with our model, adjusting parameters in a structured way (10 runs per configuration as there was not enough variance to need more repetitions).

All environmental and personal factors were kept constant among simulations and they are as follows: 2 h of simulation time (delay), unknown boarding time throughout the hour delay, cultural clusters evenly distributed, 50% chance of misbehaving towards staff or other passenger, age distribution according to De Wulf [6], presence of children 'on', effect of emotional contagion 'on', 50% men and 50% women, 50% commuters and 50% holidaymakers, toilets and restaurants 'available', effect of chatbot 'off', non-multilingual staff, 50% of passengers in a hurry, 50% travelling alone, 50%, 30% and 20% travelling in groups of 2, 3 and 4, respectively and, finally, the total amount of passengers equal to 250. Only the factors and levels stated in each subsequent experimental setup were systematically varied.

Concerning the effect of gender, we had the following research question: what is the effect of gender on number and types of misbehaviour? We checked 2 hypotheses to answer this question: (1) Men will show more misbehaviours in total than women; (2) There will be differences in types of misbehaviour for men and women. We simulated changing gender, crowdedness (number of passengers) and boarding time. All factors and levels were reproduced, only the most important findings are presented here, namely the difference between 100% males and 100% females.

The results show us that: men and women misbehaved equally much (see Fig. 3) and, when the passengers are misbehaving: (1) men are more likely to use force and to yell than women and (2) women are more likely to intimidate than men (see Fig. 4). Interestingly, men and women misbehaved equally. This could be explained by the fact that, in our model, the growth rate of the frustration level function for a given passenger depends on other personal characteristics different than gender as age, traveller type, etc. and, besides that, all the passengers have the same frustration threshold that determines if they will start to misbehave. Also interesting is the difference in types of misbehaviours between men and women. A difference was expected, but it was unknown which types of misbehaviours would be dominant for men and women. These results can give an insight to how men and women can differ in their types of misbehaviours, to better estimate the risks for certain crowd compositions.

Fig. 3. Effect of gender on misbehaviours.

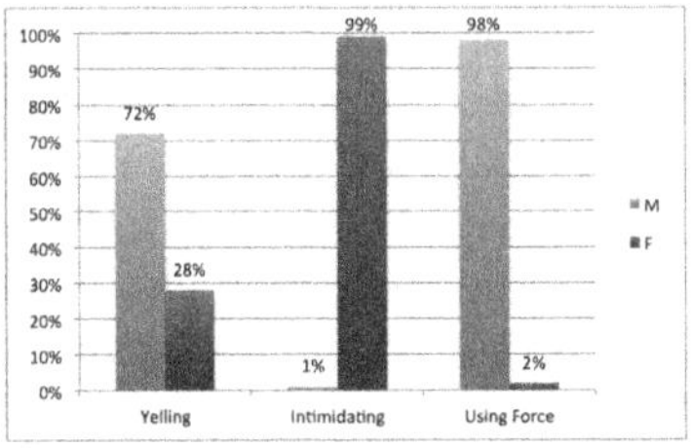

Fig. 4. Effect of gender on types of misbehaviours.

For crowd composition and the definitions of conditions 1 (emotional contagion 'on', more groups with 4 people than 2 and 3 and most of the passengers having the same nationality cluster) and 2 (emotional contagion 'off', number of groups of people travelling together and nationality clusters evenly divided), we had this research question: what is the effect of crowd composition on number and types of misbehaviour? We checked this hypothesis: It is expected that passengers will misbehave more in condition 1 than in 2. We simulated changing crowdedness, groups of passengers, cultural clusters and emotional contagion effect. Even though we reproduced all the combinations for the parameters, we only checked the results regarding the stated conditions since we were aiming to check the differences between populations of passengers with very strong and very weak social ties (conditions 1 and 2, respectively).

Indeed, people misbehaved more in condition 1 than condition 2 (in general as well as for every type of misbehaviour). See Figs. 5 and 6. We verified, therefore, that group frustration level reaches higher values faster in condition 1 than condition 2 and, as a consequence, passengers tend to misbehave more in condition 1 than in condition 2. This conclusion can be explained by emotional contagion. The model was developed taking into account that the effect of emotional contagion influences the passengers' frustration levels more if they have similar personal characteristics such as nationality clusters and they are travelling together within the same group of passengers.

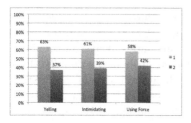

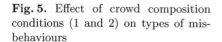

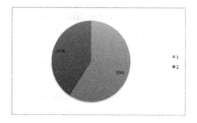

Fig. 5. Effect of crowd composition conditions (1 and 2) on types of misbehaviours

Fig. 6. Effect of crowd composition conditions (1 and 2) on misbehaviours

For the effect of emotional contagion, we had the following research question: what is the effect of emotional contagion on passengers' misbehaviours? We checked the following hypothesis: it is expected that passengers will start to misbehave faster when the effect of emotional contagion is 'on' than when it is 'off'. Here we used all the default values for the parameters and we only changed the effect of emotional contagion ('on' and 'off'). On average, passengers misbehaved 8.95 times when the emotional contagion was 'on' versus 0 times when it was 'off'. Besides that, they always started to misbehave sooner with the emotional contagion 'on' than when it was 'off' (Fig. 9 shows an execution of this simulation to illustrate what was stated). These are interesting findings, as they indicate that through emotional contagion there appear more misbehaviours. This is something emergency managers and prevention professionals should take into account. Perhaps in some cases certain passengers should be separated from each other, to avoid emotional contagion between them and consequently misbehaviours that follow out of that.

For the effects of a chatbot and multi-lingual staff, we had the following research questions: (1) What is the effect of a chatbot on overall frustration level and misbehaviours? (2) What is the effect of a multi-lingual staff on frustration levels and misbehaviours? To answer these questions we checked the following hypotheses: (1) More misbehaviours are expected when the chatbot is 'off' than when it is 'on'; (2) Less misbehaviours are expected 'with' multi-lingual staff than 'without'. We simulated changing crowdedness and (1) chatbot or (2) staff and cultural clusters of the passengers – depending on the research question.

Indeed, passengers misbehaved more when the chatbot was 'off' than when it was 'on' (see Fig. 7). Interestingly, we found no statistical difference in terms of misbehaviours when we compared multi-lingual versus non-multi-lingual staff (see Fig. 8). We were not expecting this result and an explanation could be that in the period of asking questions, the multi-lingual staff couldn't lower the frustration levels enough to avoid the passengers from reaching higher levels and misbehaving. In reality, this seems similar to the situation where after a certain level of frustration, talking to the staff makes no difference on the passengers' frustration levels. We presume it is reasonable to think that passengers would like practical information about what to do rather than simple supportive messages or generic instructions when they are already frustrated. Finally, the overall frustration level of the passengers always tended to be lower when the chatbot was 'on' than when it was 'off' (Fig. 10 shows an execution of this simulation to illustrate what was stated). Such a chatbot is always available for the users that have access to it. Additionally, as we mentioned in Sect. 2, there are some insights on the literature about chatbots being useful for helping people to cope with stress. Therefore, that is why we believe that having better results for a chatbot than for a multi-lingual staff might be reasonable and we developed our model taking this into account. Nevertheless, this should be investigated further using real data and being simulated in different scenarios.

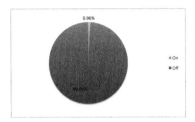

Fig. 7. Effect of a chatbot (on/off) on misbehaviours

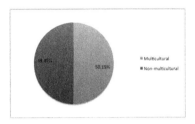

Fig. 8. Effect of a multicultural staff on misbehaviours

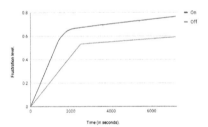

Fig. 9. Passengers' overall frustration level over time. 2 scenarios: with (on) and without (off) emotional contagion.

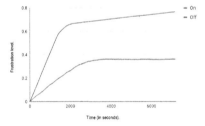

Fig. 10. Passengers' overall frustration level over time. 2 scenarios: with (on) and without (off) support from a chatbot.

5   Discussion

The aim of this work was to provide a computational agent-based domain model of stranded passengers at an airport to help stakeholders in dealing with these passengers. Besides that, we also investigated the effects of 2 support models (a supportive chatbot and multi-lingual staff) aiming to decrease the overall frustration level of the passengers in such a situation. We tried to do so by constructing these models according to the concepts found in the literature as well as requirements provided by stakeholders. Via the domain model we developed we can predict how likely a given set of stranded passengers is to misbehave. This can be calculated based on passengers and environments characteristics such as age, gender, nationality and amount of information.

Strengths of this work are: the inclusion of the socio-cultural aspects in the crowd modelling, the specific communication solution under analysis, both domain and support models being based on input (concepts) from specialist stakeholders and empirical findings from the literature, the facts that we carefully designed the simulation experiments and we have showed that it is useful to implement new emergency communication strategies and to estimate their effectiveness. The main weakness of this work is the fact that there are many cultural aspects that may play a role in this scenario, so we could not model all of them since it would become too complex to analyze. Although, it is an advantage to have a well defined parameters setting and they were most relevant to the stakeholders. Furthermore, the results coming out of the simulations cannot be taken for granted. Therefore, they will remain estimations. However, because they are based on a set of concepts taken from the literature, research and interaction with stakeholders, we believe they are representative enough as estimations.

As future work, we suggest (among others): to investigate the effect of a different layout, to investigate the effect of the number of staff members, to address multiple delayed flights and to come up with more cultural aspects and to investigate them in such a context.

We believe the implications of this work to be as follows. Transport operators, emergency managers and prevention professionals can use this kind of agent-based models to see what happens and choose the best solution at design time, to support periodic safety and security risk assessments and mandatory risk assessment when something changes in the environment, procedures and/or when new communication measures/technologies are put in place. Also, policy makers could use these models to support the identification of mandatory regulations and standards with respect to communication for emergency prevention and management.

Acknowledgements. This research was undertaken as part of the EU HORIZON 2020 Project IMPACT (GA 653383) and Science without Borders – CNPq (scholarship reference: 235134/2014-7). We would like to thank our Consortium Partners and stakeholders for their input as well as the Brazilian Government.

References

1. Berkowitz, L.: Frustration-aggression hypothesis: examination and reformulation. Psychol. Bull. **106**(1), 59 (1989)
2. Bosse, T., Duell, R., Memon, Z.A., Treur, J., van der Wal, C.N.: Agent-based modeling of emotion contagion in groups. Cogn. Comput. **7**(1), 111–136 (2015)

3. Bosse, T., Hoogendoorn, M., Klein, M.C.A., Treur, J., van der Wal, C.N., Van Wissen, A.: Modelling collective decision making in groups and crowds: integrating social contagion and interacting emotions, beliefs and intentions. Auton. Agents Multi-Agent Syst. **27**, 1–33 (2013)
4. Challenger, R., Clegg, C.W., Robinson, M.A.: Understanding Crowd Behaviours. Supporting Theory and Evidence, vol. 2. The Stationery Office (TSO), London (2010)
5. Crystal, D.: Two thousand million? Engl. Today **24**(01), 3–6 (2008)
6. De Wulf, M.: Population pyramids of the world from 1950 to 2100 (2016)
7. DeVault, D., Artstein, R., Benn, G., Dey, T., Fast, E., Gainer, A., Georgila, K., Gratch, J., Hartholt, A., Lhommet, M., et al.: SimSensei Kiosk: a virtual human interviewer for healthcare decision support. In: Proceedings of the 2014 International Conference on Autonomous Agents and Multi-agent Systems, pp. 1061–1068. IFAAMAS (2014)
8. Drury, J., Cocking, C., Reicher, S.: Everyone for themselves? A comparative study of crowd solidarity among emergency survivors. Br. J. Soc. Psychol. **48**(3), 487–506 (2009)
9. Georgeff, M., Pell, B., Pollack, M., Tambe, M., Wooldridge, M.: The belief-desire-intention model of agency. In: Müller, J.P., Rao, A.S., Singh, M.P. (eds.) ATAL 1998. LNCS, vol. 1555, pp. 1–10. Springer, Heidelberg (1999). doi:10.1007/3-540-49057-4_1
10. Jackson II, R.L., Hogg, M.A.: Encyclopedia of Identity, vol. 1. Sage, Thousand Oaks (2010)
11. Kim, H.S., Sherman, D.K., Taylor, S.E.: Culture and social support. Am. Psychol. **63**(6), 518 (2008)
12. Marsella, S., Gratch, J., Petta, P., et al.: Computational models of emotion. Bluepr. Affect. Comput. Sourceb. Man. **11**(1), 21–46 (2010)
13. Medeiros, L., Bosse, T.: Empirical analysis of social support provided via social media. In: Spiro, E., Ahn, Y.-Y. (eds.) SocInfo 2016. LNCS, vol. 10047, pp. 439–453. Springer, Cham (2016). doi:10.1007/978-3-319-47874-6_30
14. Medeiros, L., Sikkes, R., Treur, J.: Modelling a mutual support network for coping with stress. In: Nguyen, N.-T., Manolopoulos, Y., Iliadis, L., Trawiński, B. (eds.) ICCCI 2016. LNCS, vol. 9875, pp. 64–77. Springer, Cham (2016). doi:10.1007/978-3-319-45243-2_6
15. Mileti, D.S.: Factors related to flood warning response. In: US-Italy Research Workshop on the Hydrometeorology, Impacts, and Management of Extreme Floods, pp. 1–17. Citeseer (1995)
16. Picard, R.W.: Affective Computing. MIT Press, Cambridge (1995)
17. Reicher, S., Drury, J.: Social identity and social change: rethinking the context of social psychology (1996)
18. Ronen, S., Shenkar, O.: Mapping world cultures: cluster formation, sources and implications. J. Int. Bus. Stud. **44**(9), 867–897 (2013)
19. Tajfel, H.: Social Identity and Intergroup Relations. Cambridge University Press, Cambridge (2010)
20. Tsai, J., Bowring, E., Marsella, S., Tambe, M.: Empirical evaluation of computational emotional contagion models. In: Vilhjálmsson, H.H., Kopp, S., Marsella, S., Thórisson, K.R. (eds.) IVA 2011. LNCS, vol. 6895, pp. 384–397. Springer, Heidelberg (2011). doi:10.1007/978-3-642-23974-8_42

21. van der Wal, C.N., Couwenberg, M., Bosse, T.: Getting frustrated: modelling emotional contagion in stranded passengers. In: Benferhat, S., Tabia, K., Ali, M. (eds.) IEA/AIE 2017. LNCS, vol. 10350, pp. 611–619. Springer, Cham (2017). doi:10.1007/978-3-319-60042-0_67

22. van der Zwaan, J.M., Dignum, V., Jonker, C.M.: A conversation model enabling intelligent agents to give emotional support. In: Ding, W., Jiang, H., Ali, M., Li, M. (eds.) Modern Advances in Intelligent Systems and Tools. Studies in Computational Intelligence, vol. 431, pp. 47–52. Springer, Heidelberg (2012). doi:10.1007/978-3-642-30732-4_6

23. Veenema, T.G.: Disaster Nursing and Emergency Preparedness: for Chemical, Biological, and Radiological Terrorism and Other Hazards. Springer Publishing Company, New York (2012)

24. Wilensky, U., Rand, W.: An Introduction to Agent-Based Modeling: Modeling Natural, Social, and Engineered Complex Systems with NetLogo. MIT Press, Cambridge (2015)

Towards Understanding the Impact of Crime on the Choice of Route by a Bus Passenger

Daniel Sullivan[1](✉), Carlos Caminha[1], Hygor P.M. Melo[2],
and Vasco Furtado[1]

[1] UNIFOR – Universidade de Fortaleza, Av. Washington Soares 1321,
Fortaleza, CE, Brazil
daniel.sullivan@edu.unifor.br,
{caminha,vasco}@unifor.br
[2] IFCE – Instituto Federal de Educação, Ciência e Tecnologia do Ceará,
Av. Des. Armando de Sales Louzada, Acaraú, CE, Brazil
hygor@fisica.ufc.br

Abstract. In this paper we describe a simulation platform that supports studies on the impact of crime on urban mobility. We present an example of how this can be achieved by seeking to understand the effect, on the transport system, if users of this system decide to choose optimal routes of time between origins and destinations that they normally follow. Based on real data from a large Brazilian metropolis, we found that the percentage of users who follow this policy is small. Most prefer to follow less efficient routes by making bus exchanges at terminals. This can be understood as an indication that the users of the transport system favor the security factor.

Keywords: Crime behavior · Human mobility

1 Introduction

The academic community has reported the correlation between human mobility and crime from different perspectives. Examples of this are the works by Felson [11] that found a relationship between the occurrence of crimes and the convergence of routines between offenders and unprotected victims, Brantingham and Brantingham's [35] works on environmental criminology and, most recently, Caminha et al. [17], found that the relationship between clusters of floating population and crimes against property within a large metropolis follows a power law.

Despite the fact that the correlation between mobility and crime is widely recognized and studied, few quantitative studies have been developed to understand the impact of crime on the mobility of people in large cities. However, digitized data on the movement of people are increasingly abundant, opening up the possibility of elaborating more complete social models that can be used in validation.

Our research in this context focuses on data on the movement of people in buses in a large Brazilian metropolis, the city of Fortaleza. These are data concerning one million people who daily use buses on their journeys, which characterizes this mode of

© Springer International Publishing AG 2017
E. Oliveira et al. (Eds.): EPIA 2017, LNAI 10423, pp. 41–50, 2017.
DOI: 10.1007/978-3-319-65340-2_4

transportation as the most important form of city displacement (the total population of the city is 2.4 million people).

In previous studies, we have studied the impact of the movement of people on the occurrence of crime [17] as well as on police allocation strategies [36]. In this article we will follow a different strategy, as we will investigate the impact that crime distribution in the city can have on the choice of bus routes made by people. We have developed a software platform that enables us to use data of movement and crime in the city to simulate the impact on the public transportation system. In particular, we simulate the negative effects that this can have on the behavior of bus users leading them to choose clearly less efficient routes in terms of travel time, comfort and/or distance traveled. In addition, it was possible to estimate the impact on the public bus transportation system in general by evaluating indicators such as the passenger's waiting time at bus stops and bus overcrowding.

The methodology that we followed was to compare two models of bus routes. Firstly, based on the real world data provided on the paths of the users, we evaluated the system of when the users make their actual routes. Then we investigated how the Public Transport System (PTS) would behave if users chose to take more efficient routes in terms of time. In order to achieve this goal, users are likely to seek to make bus line changes in order to minimize route time since many origin-destination routes are impossible to complete from a single direct route. This strategy, favoring the time of the journey, is not necessarily the most efficient in terms of security, since bus stop connections can be criminal hot spots. In fact, It has been found that, in Fortaleza, the bus stops that are more suitable for commuters are significantly more insecure than the places that the users actually use. This result raises the possibility that users of the Fortaleza bus system may be taking more inefficient routes to escape crime.

2   Related Work

Agent-based modeling provides a simplified simulation of the reality, but it is also a powerful technique to replicate social phenomena. The agent-based model uses a bottom up approach simulating the individual behavior of multiple agents in order to predict complex phenomena. These general characteristics allow for a large number of applications in a diverse range of areas, such as: archaeology [1, 2]; biological models of infectious diseases [3]; growth of bacterial colonies [4]; alliance formation of nations during the Second World War [5]; modeling economic processes as dynamic systems of interacting agents [6]; and size-frequency distributions for traffic jams [7]. In this work our main interest is in simulations of crime and urban mobility dynamics. In criminology, the role of urban space and its social relations have been previously emphasized to explain the origin of crime [8, 9]. In particular, the routine activity theory, proposed by Cohen and Felson [8], states that crimes, and more specifically property crimes such as robbery and theft, occur through the convergence of the routines of an offender, motivated to commit a crime, and an unprotected victim. The dynamics of crime and the impact of social relations on the increase of violence has been the object of study in several areas such as Social Sciences [10], Criminology [8, 9, 11], Computing [12–17], Economics [18] and Physics [19–25]. There are also a number of papers that use simulations in Criminology in order to test theories [26]; to study burglary including transportation networks and statistically based human mobility patterns along the network [27]; and to analyze police patrol routes [28].

There is a vast literature on human mobility [29–33], however, less attention is given to its possible connection with crime. Some new researches have shown that human mobility is a key factor in understanding the spatial distribution of crime in the urban landscape [17, 34] yet, works on how crime can affect human mobility are scarce.

3 Data Sets

We used user routes and a bus travel time network produced in a Data Mining project executed on mobility data in the city of Fortaleza [17, 31, 37]. A user's route on a bus network is defined by bus stops visited in sequence by that user within one or more buses. This is defined as: a user route R_u, is a set containing n ($\{p_1, p_2, p_3, ..., p_n\}$) bus stops visited in sequence by a set of bus lines, $L_u = \{l_1, l_2, l_3, ..., l_m\}$, used by u in its course. Furtado et al. [37] estimated these routes from the actual origin of each user to the actual destination, see [31] for details. For each origin and destination, two routes were estimated; one that the authors consider to be the actual route of the user and the other is an optimal route in time. In total, 294870 origins and destinations (representing an average behavior for business days in Fortaleza) were estimated, starting from these origins to their respective destinations, the same number of real and optimal routes was estimated.

Access was obtained to the scheduled route of the city buses, if there is a certain quantity of vehicles available on a weekday for each bus line, capacity of each vehicle, departure time for each trip of each vehicle and the expected arrival time.

Also from [37], a network of time was obtained, where the nodes represent bus stops and the links are the average time between these two bus stops. Each link was assigned a probability function that is based on the mean time (μ) and standard deviation (σ) calculated from the actual GPS data of the buses. Thus the time of an edge at time x is obtained by the function:

$$f(x, \mu, \sigma) = \frac{1}{\sqrt{2\pi\sigma^2}} e^{\left(\frac{-(x-\mu)^2}{2\sigma^2}\right)}, \quad -\infty < x < \infty, \sigma > 0 \tag{1}$$

Crime data refers to crime against property (theft, robbery and burglary) occurring between 9/23/2014 and 10/4/2016 in the city of Fortaleza and metropolitan region. In total, this dataset has 98431 crimes. Figure 1 shows the density map of these crimes in Fortaleza.

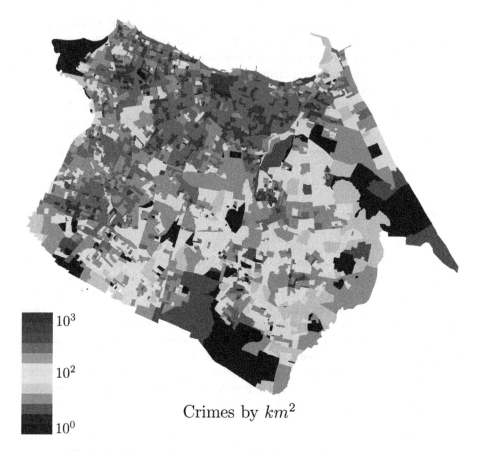

10^3

10^2

10^0

Crimes by km^2

Fig. 1. Density map for property crime in Fortaleza from 2014 to 2016.

4   Simulation

The simulator was developed using Repast, a java multi-agent simulation framework. This simulator handles events whose management and execution of actions is done by a clock, which has a tick as a measure of time. The tick is incremented when all scheduled actions are performed.

The main elements of this tool are: Bus; Line; Route; Passenger; Stops; and Crimes. Buses behave like agents in the simulation, their behavior is stopped by the stops and making trip connections. They have as main attributes the current stop (corresponds to the stop it is at or the last stop it has visited), the next stop to be visited, the time needed to reach the next stop, the list of passengers in the vehicle, the current line and a hash that commits the trips that the bus will make in one day. Passengers, in turn, have information regarding the route they will take, i.e. they have a list with the lines that they will use and another one regarding the stops where they will board and disembark. Passengers are agents who board and disembark from buses when vehicles pass through their initial and destination stops. The lines have a list with all the stops on their route. The crimes include the information of where they occurred (latitude and longitude) and their type.

It was defined that the simulation start time would be two o'clock in the morning, because it is the time when there are fewer buses in circulation and fewer passengers using the system. This minimizes the effect of the simulation starting with empty buses. The simulation closes at two o'clock in the afternoon because of technical limitations, so it is possible to evaluate the system in its peak hours, from 5:00 am to 8:00 am, as well as at low usage times, for example in the early morning. Each minute is called a bus dispatch event, in this event it is checked if the time of departure of each bus has already been reached, if positive, the bus enters the simulation, at the end of this event one minute is increased in the time of the simulator.

Each bus has an event called move, it consists of the logic that makes the buses follow the network. This event is triggered after the dispatch event. After all buses run their event, the process will be finalized and will only start again at the next tick. As already mentioned a bus has a current stop and the next stop, the time in which the bus will take to reach the next stop will be calculated using the average time in which the buses of this line take to pass through this stretch and the standard deviation of those times. These are the input data to apply to the normal or Gaussian distribution so as to get the time in which the bus will take to go along an edge.

Each tick represents one minute in the time of the simulator, if the time for the bus to cross the edge is greater than sixty seconds, the bus will not be able to complete this stretch still within this tick, so the time for it to arrive at the next stop will only be decreased from sixty seconds. If the time is exactly equal to sixty seconds, it will travel this edge still in this movement and will arrive at the next stop. The last case that can occur is the time being less than sixty seconds, that is, one bus will arrive at the next stop and will continue towards another.

Whenever a bus arrives at a stop, it is checked to see if there are passengers intending to disembark or board the vehicle. A bus in Fortaleza has 80 passengers, so if its capacity is reached and some passenger wants to embark, it will have to wait for the next vehicle of that line to pass.

When the bus of a certain line reaches the end of its route, it is checked to so see if there are still trips for that vehicle to carry out, if there is a check that the line is maintained or if there is a line change, the trip changes are made and the bus starts a new trip. When there are no more trips for that bus to perform, it will be removed from the simulation. The simulator closes at 2 o'clock in the morning the next day or when all the buses finish all their trips.

5   Methodology and Empirical Evaluation

In this article, the bus system will be evaluated for waiting time for shipment, stocking of vehicles and safety at the point of transfer. The average waiting time for boarding is calculated by subtracting the time of boarding from the time that the passenger appeared at the stop, and the vehicle stocking distribution, which shows the quantities of vehicles with low occupancy (between 0 and 20 passengers), intermediate occupation (between 21 and 60 passengers) and high occupancy (between 61 and 80).

Security was measured by the ratio of the number of crimes occurring in the vicinity of the transfer point divided by the number of users who are on-site, we call this Rate of Crime.

The behavior of the network with its natural operation was observed, i.e. when all users take their actual route. The behavior of the network was also evaluated in a hypothetical scenario, simulating a situation where all users take optimal routes of time. The contrasts between the values of the individual indicators adopted in this research can be observed in the panel of Fig. 2.

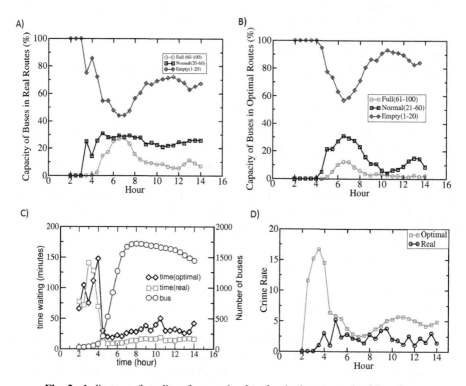

Fig. 2. Indicators of quality of use and safety for the bus network of Fortaleza.

Figure 2(A) shows the stocking of vehicles when all users take actual routes, while in Fig. 2(B) the vehicles are stocked for the optimal routes. It may be noted that when passengers take optimal routes there are less crowded buses. This is because Fortaleza's transit network is not prepared for its users to take optimal routes in time, thus, many passengers are waiting for vacancies to appear on the few crowded buses. In Fig. 2(C) it can be seen that at the beginning of the day, where there are few buses running, the waiting time for the passengers is similar, regardless of the route (real or optimal). However, from the peak time onwards, the number of vehicles in circulation increases and the waiting time for those who take the optimal routes becomes longer than the waiting time for actual routes. This is because when everyone does the correct thing, there are not enough vehicles to meet the demand. In Fig. 2(D) it is possible to visualize the crime rate per stop at optimal and real p. It can be observed that the risk at optimal points of transfer is greater than at the points where users actually pay, especially outside the peak hours (from 5 am to 8 am), possibly the higher number of people on the street discourages criminals from committing crimes at that time. This result raises the possibility that people choose slower routes to escape the crime, essentially because the slower route has its point of transfer in a bus terminal, a place that offers, among other things, greater safety for users.

In Fig. 3 we show the relationship between crimes and the urban public transportation network. Recently, an extensive analysis conducted with real crime data related to a large Brazilian metropolis [38] demonstrated that the spatial distribution of crimes such as robberies, theft, and burglaries follows a power law, more specifically, a Zipfian distribution [39]. We see in Fig. 3A that the distribution of crimes occurring close to bus stops visually follows a power law, with an exponent close to −2.0 as shown by the red guideline. The power law distribution indicates that we can find bus stops with a much larger number of crimes when we compare with an exponential distribution. In order to see the effect of crimes on the usage of the urban transportation system, we computed the number of crimes that occurred close to a bus stop which is used for a connection transfer in the optimal routes. As we already mentioned, a large part of the users do not use the optimal connection transfer, instead of this, they seem to choose a safe route. In Fig. 3B we show that a large percentage of connection transfers on the optimal route (98%) have more than 10 crimes close. This is an indication that the users prefer to go by a safe but longer trajectory.

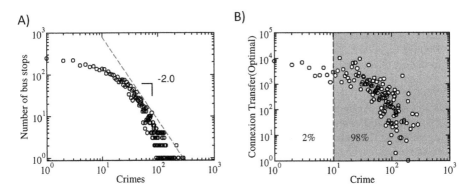

Fig. 3. Histograms of crimes. (Color figure online)

6 Conclusion

In this paper we describe a simulation platform that supports studies on the impact of crime on urban mobility. We present an example of how this can be achieved by seeking to understand the effect on the public transport system, if travelers decide to choose optimal routes of time between origins and destinations. Based on real data from a large Brazilian metropolis, we found that when a bus transfer is necessary, the percentage of users who follow this policy is small. Most prefer to follow less efficient routes by making bus transfers at terminals. This can be understood as an indication that the users of the transport system favor the security factor. This indication is corroborated by the fact that 98% of the optimal routes pass through unsafe bus stops (more than 10 crimes).

Our research is ongoing and new tests are necessary to detail the features that passengers consider the most important. The simulation environment must also be improved to help this process, however, this first work has already shown to us that it is an important to tool to help understand the impact of crime on urban mobility. Based on real data describing the geographical space, we intend to further investigate particular, new and different policies based on features like comfort and overcrowding in order to improve the simulation.

References

1. Axtell, R., Epstein, J.M., Dean, J.S., Gumerman, G.J., Swedlund, A.C., Harburger, J., et al.: Population growth and collapse in a multiagent model of the Kayenta Anasazi in long house valley. Proc. Natl. Acad. Sci. U.S.A. (PNAS) **99**(3), 7275–7279 (2002)
2. Kohler, T.A., Kresl, J., Van Wes, Q., Carr, E., Wilshusen, R.H.: Be there then: a modeling approach to settlement determinants and spatial efficiency among late ancestral Pueblo populations of the Mesa Verde Region, U.S. Southwest. In: Kohler, T.A., Gumerman, G.J. (eds.) Dynamics in Human and Primate Societies: Agent-Based Modeling of Social and Spatial Processes, pp. 145–178. Oxford University Press, Oxford (2000)
3. Yang, Y., Atkinson, P.M.: An integrated ABM and GIS model of infectious disease transmission. In: Batty, S. (ed.) Computers in Urban Planning and Urban Management (CUPUM), London (2005)
4. Kreft, J.U., Booth, G., Wimpenny, W.T.: BacSim, a simulator for individual based modelling of bacterial colony growth. Microbiology **144**(12), 3275–3287 (1998)
5. Axelrod, R., Bennett, S.D.: A landscape theory of aggregation. Br. J. Polit. Sci. **23**(2), 211–233 (1993)
6. Tesfatsion, L.: Agent-based computational economics: a constructive approach to economic theory. In: Tesfatsion, L., Judd, K.L. (eds.) Handbook of Computational Economics: Agent-Based Computational Economics, vol. 2, pp. 831–880. North-Holland, Amsterdam (2006)
7. Nagel, K., Rasmussen, S.: Traffic at the edge of chaos. In: Brooks, R. (ed.) Artificial Life IV, pp. 222–236. MIT Press, Cambridge (1994)
8. Cohen, L.E., Felson, M.: Social change and crime rate trends: a routine activity approach. Am. Sociol. Rev. **44**(4), 588–608 (1979). doi:10.2307/2094589
9. Clarke, R.V.G., Felson, M.: Routine Activity and Rational Choice. Advances in Criminological Theory. Transaction Publishers, New Brunswick (1993)
10. Michael, J., Adler, M.J.: Crime, Law and Social Science. International Library of Psychology, Philosophy, and Scientific Method. K. Paul, Trench, Trubner and Co., Ltd. (1933)
11. Felson, M.: Crime and Everyday Life. SAGE Publications, Thousand Oaks (2002)

12. Guedes, R., Furtado, V., Pequeno, T.: Multiagent models for police resource allocation and dispatch. In: 2014 IEEE Joint Intelligence and Security Informatics Conference (JISIC), pp. 288–291. IEEE (2014)
13. Wang, T., Rudin, C., Wagner, D., Sevieri, R.: Learning to detect patterns of crime. In: Blockeel, H., Kersting, K., Nijssen, S., Železný, F. (eds.) ECML PKDD 2013. LNCS, vol. 8190, pp. 515–530. Springer, Heidelberg (2013). doi:10.1007/978-3-642-40994-3_33
14. Kiani, R., Mahdavi, S., Keshavarzi, A.: Analysis and prediction of crimes by clustering and classification 4(8) (2015)
15. Caminha, C., Furtado, V.: Modeling user reports in crowdmaps as a complex network. In: Proceedings of 21st International World Wide Web Conference. Citeseer (2012)
16. Furtado, V., Caminha, C., Ayres, L., Santos, H.: Open government and citizen participation in law enforcement via crowd mapping. IEEE Intell. Syst. 27(4), 63–69 (2012). doi:10.1109/MIS.2012.80
17. Caminha, C., Furtado, V., Pequeno, T.H., Ponte, C., Melo, H.P., Oliveira, E.A., Andrade, J.S.: Human mobility in large cities as a proxy for crime. PLoS ONE 2(12), e0171609 (2017)
18. Wang, F.: Geographic Information Systems and Crime Analysis. IGI Global, Hershey (2005)
19. Melo, H.P.M., Moreira, A.A., Batista, E., Makse, H.A., Andrade, J.S.: Statistical signs of social influence on suicides. Sci. Rep. 4 (2014). doi:10.1038/srep06239 PMID: 25174706
20. Alves, L.G., Ribeiro, H.V., Lenzi, E.K., Mendes, R.S.: Distance to the scaling law: a useful approach for unveiling relationships between crime and urban metrics. PLoS ONE 8(8), e69580 (2013). doi:10.1371/journal.pone.0069580. PMID: 23940525
21. Alves, L.G., Ribeiro, H.V., Mendes, R.S.: Scaling laws in the dynamics of crime growth rate. Phys. A: Stat. Mech. Appl. 392(11), 2672–2679 (2013). doi:10.1016/j.physa.2013.02.002
22. D'Orsogna, M.R., Perc, M.: Statistical physics of crime: a review. Phys. Life Rev. 12, 1–21 (2015). doi:10.1016/j.plrev.2014.11.001. PMID: 25468514
23. Alves, L., Lenzi, E., Mendes, R., Ribeiro, H.: Spatial correlations, clustering and percolation-like transitions in homicide crimes. EPL (Europhys. Lett.) 111(1), 18002 (2015). doi:10.1209/0295-5075/111/18002
24. Short, M.B., D'Orsogna, M.R., Pasour, V.B., Tita, G.E., Brantingham, P.J., Bertozzi, A.L., et al.: A statistical model of criminal behavior. Math. Models Methods Appl. Sci. 18 (Supp. 1), 1249–1267 (2008). doi:10.1142/S0218202508003029
25. Short, M.B., Brantingham, P.J., Bertozzi, A.L., Tita, G.E.: Dissipation and displacement of hotspots in reaction diffusion models of crime. Proc. Natl. Acad. Sci. 107(9), 3961–3965 (2010). doi:10.1073/pnas.0910921107
26. Birks, D., Townsley, M., Stewart, A.: Generative explanations of crime: using simulation to test criminological theory. Criminology 50(1), 221–254 (2012)
27. Peng, C., Kurland, J.: The agent-based spatial simulation to the Burglary in Beijing. In: Murgante, B., et al. (eds.) ICCSA 2014. LNCS, vol. 8582, pp. 31–43. Springer, Cham (2014). doi:10.1007/978-3-319-09147-1_3
28. Melo, A., Belchior, M., Furtado, V.: Analyzing police patrol routes by simulating the physical reorganization of agents. In: Sichman, J.S., Antunes, L. (eds.) MABS 2005. LNCS, vol. 3891, pp. 99–114. Springer, Heidelberg (2006). doi:10.1007/11734680_8
29. Gonzalez, M.C., Hidalgo, C.A., Barabasi, A.-L.: Understanding individual human mobility patterns. Nature 453(7196), 779–782 (2008)
30. Wang, D., Pedreschi, D., Song, C., Giannotti, F., Barabasi, A.-L.: Human mobility, social ties, and link prediction. In: Proceedings of the 17th ACM SIGKDD International Conference on Knowledge Discovery and Data Mining, pp. 1100–1108. ACM (2011)

31. Caminha, C., Furtado, V., Pinheiro, V., Silva, C.: Micro-interventions in urban transportation from pattern discovery on the flow of passengers and on the bus network. In: 2016 IEEE International Smart Cities Conference (ISC2), pp. 1–6. IEEE (2016)

32. Andrade, J.S., Oliveira, E., Moreira, A., Herrmann, H.: Fracturing the optimal paths. Phys. Rev. Lett. **103**(22), 225503 (2009)

33. Ponte, C., Caminha, C., Furtado, V.: Busca de melhor caminho entre dois pontos quando múltiplas origens e múltiplos destinos são possíveis. In: ENIAC (2016)

34. Frith, M., Johnson, S., Fry, H.: The role of the street network in offender spatial decision making. Criminology **55**, 344–376 (2017)

35. Brantingham, P.L., Brantingham, P.J.: Notes on the geometry of crime. In: Environmental Criminology, pp. 27–54 (1981)

36. Caminha, C., Furtado, V.: Towards understanding the impact of human mobility on police allocation (2017). arXiv:1704.07823v1

37. Furtado, V., Caminha, C., Furtado, E., Lopes, A., Dantas, V., Ponte, C., Cavalcante, S.: Increasing the likelihood of finding public transport riders that face problems through a data-driven approach (2017). arXiv:1704.07823v1

38. Cançado, T.M.L.: Alocação e despacho de recursos para combate à criminalidade. Master dissertation, UFMG, Belo Horizonte (2005). (in Portuguese)

39. Zipf, G.K.: Human Behaviour and the Principle of Least-Effort. Addison-Wesley, Cambridge (1949)

Exploring Anti-poaching Strategies
for Wildlife Crime with a Simple and General
Agent-Based Model

Nick van Doormaal$^{(\boxtimes)}$

Netherlands Institute for the Study of Crime and Law Enforcement,
Amsterdam, The Netherlands
nvandoormaal@nscr.nl

Abstract. Understanding and preventing wildlife crime is challenging because of the complex interdependencies between animals, poachers, and rangers. To tackle this complexity, this study introduces a simple, general agent-based model of wildlife crime. The model is abstract and can be used to derive general conclusions about the emergence and prevention of wildlife crime. It can also be tailored to create scenarios which allows researchers and practitioners to better understand the dynamics in specific cases. This was illustrated by applying the model to the context of rhino poaching in South Africa. A virtual park populated by rhinos, poachers and rangers was created to study how an increase in patrol effort for two different anti-poaching strategies affect the number of poached rhinos. The results show that fence patrols are more effective in preventing wildlife crime than standard patrols. Strikingly, even increasing the number of ranger teams does not increase the effectiveness of standard patrols compared to fence patrols.

Keywords: Agent-based modeling · Wildlife crime · Anti-poaching strategies

1 Introduction

The most common threats to plant and animal species worldwide are the destruction of their habitat and the over-exploitation of natural resources due to human activities like wildlife poaching and the illegal trade in wildlife products [1]. Recently, criminologists have also started to study wildlife crime. Understanding the processes behind crime often leads to practical implications for crime prevention strategies to improve its effectiveness. These strategies are based upon opportunity theories, seeking to create interventions that reduce victimization by removing or disrupting opportunities for crime. This includes increasing offender perceptions of risk and effort while minimizing perceptions of reward [2].

A commonly used strategy to prevent wildlife crime inside a protected area is aimed at increasing the poacher's perception of risk. This is a data-driven approach that includes the analysis and mapping of poaching incidents [3]. Rangers are then deployed at poaching "hotspots" to either prevent or detect illegal activities. The downside of a data-driven approach is that it is heavily biased towards the spatial

© Springer International Publishing AG 2017
E. Oliveira et al. (Eds.): EPIA 2017, LNAI 10423, pp. 51–62, 2017.
DOI: 10.1007/978-3-319-65340-2_5

aspects of how the observation data was collected [4]. Ranger patrols are often not able to cover the whole protected area on a regular basis, leading to an incomplete knowledge of where and when poaching activities occur [5]. This is also referred to as the dark figure of crime [6]. Furthermore, when a new anti-poaching strategy has been put in place, rarely has it been evaluated in a standardized and systematic way.

As an alternative, wildlife crime can be studied as a complex and dynamic system. Its complexity does not only arise from the strategic interdependencies between animals and poachers. Poachers are also being tracked by rangers and seek to avoid interaction. This creates a second layer of strategic interdependence. To tackle the complexity of these systems, formal models allow researchers to study the implications of model assumptions. They help to understand why and under what conditions the models generate unexpected predictions [7]. Formal models allow researchers to explore the effectiveness of anti-poaching strategies even before they are implemented. They also allow to derive testable predictions about the conditions under which they are effective or not. For example, a successful strategy can turn ineffective at one moment, not because rangers failed to implement it, but simply because animals responded to changes in their environment. Subsequently, this motivates different poacher behavior which makes the adopted anti-poaching strategy ineffective.

Agent-based modeling (ABM) is a prominent formal modeling technique and particularly suited to study wildlife crime. In an agent-based model, each individual agent makes autonomous decisions, reacting to its environment and the behavior of other agents. AMB is a rigorous method, but hardly restricts the modeler in the choice of assumptions [8]. ABM allows researchers to tailor models to specific settings, for example by applying their model to a specific protected area, endangered species, or anti-poaching strategy. Such information is not only relevant for practitioners, but also expands the application of ABM into new areas of wildlife crime.

2   Objective

This study is aimed at exploring the dynamic interactions between the agents involved in wildlife crime using agent-based modeling. The objective was to develop a simple and general model that captures these dynamics under different anti-poaching scenarios. As an illustration, the model is demonstrated by applying it to the context of rhino poaching in South Africa.

3   The General Model: Animals, Poachers, and Rangers

For most cases of wildlife crime, there are three types of agents: animals, poachers, and rangers. The interactions between these agents can be described as a triple foraging process [9]: "animals search for food, poachers search for animals, and rangers search for poachers". The model simulates a "world" with a population of animals where poachers go in and out to hunt for this species. The rangers try to disrupt and catch the poachers.

The world is a simplified representation of a protected area, like a national park. This virtual park is divided into grid cells that contain information about the environment, like the amount of resources available to the animal, how long it takes to move through this cell and any signs of animal, poacher, or ranger presence. The advantage of using a simplified model of a park is that dynamics cannot be driven by idiosyncratic characteristics of a specific setting, allowing the modeler to derive general conclusions about the implications of model assumptions. Nevertheless, the model is formulated in such a way that many idiosyncrasies of real parks can be implemented, which allows the study of dynamics also in specific settings.

In this model, animals are distributed over the virtual park and individually make decisions on where to move next based on the characteristics of the surrounding grid cells, choosing cells that are most attractive. At the same time, animals also change their environment by consuming resources. The resources recover over time. While the animals move over the landscape, they leave signs that can be detected by poachers, influencing their movement as they search for a target. Poachers can also detect signs of ranger activity and try to avoid those areas. Hence, poachers make decisions based on, among others, signs of recent animal activity and ranger activity. Poachers always start and end their hunt at the border of the virtual park. If a poacher encounters an animal within his observation radius, he kills it and the poached animal is removed from the park. The poacher then returns to the park's border. When the poacher reaches the border, he successfully escaped and cannot be caught by rangers. Poachers remember the areas where they were successful, areas with high ranger activity and use that information to plan their subsequent incursions.

Rangers carry out patrols and search for signs of poaching. Just as poachers tend to go to areas with the highest animal activity, rangers tend to go to areas with the highest poaching activity. If a ranger detects a poacher within his observation radius, the ranger catches the poacher, removing him from the park. Rangers remember where they found poaching signs and tend to patrol those areas more frequently. Rangers can start either at a base camp inside the virtual park or at one of its borders.

Dynamics are broken down to a sequence of discrete events. At each event, first all animals decide in a random order where to move, followed by the moving decisions of poachers, and rangers. Finally, the simulation program updates the resources available at each cell, taking into account the consumption by animals and resource recovery. The decision-making of all three agents is similar and can be easily adjusted by adding relevant variables for a particular problem. This can also be used to create specific scenarios or conditions.

4   Example: Rhino Poaching in South Africa

Rhino poaching in South Africa has surged since 2008, in response to significant increases in black market prices for rhino horn [10]. This has led to discussion among conservationists, law enforcement and governmental organizations about effective anti-poaching strategies. Protected areas often have limited resources available, and this forces ranger commanders to implement patrol strategies that are as efficient as possible. A standard anti-poaching strategy is to deploy ground based patrol teams around rhino locations and searching for poaching activity. Almost all protected areas in South Africa are fenced or partially fenced, and fence patrols play an important role in the early detection of illegal fence crossings.

The model was applied to study the interactions and dynamics of rhino poaching and two different patrol strategies in a virtual fenced park. The free software 'NetLogo' [11] was used to program the virtual park and agents. The model, its code, and the used parameters are available online at the following website: http://modelingcommons.org/browse/one_model/5016.

4.1   Virtual Park

The virtual park consists of 100 by 100 grid cells. Time in the park is represented by discrete simulation events. In this example, the grid size and events are arbitrary measurements and do not map directly to real world size or time. During one event, all agents make decisions based on the surroundings and move to one of their neighboring cells. The virtual park borders are considered to be outside of the park. The other cells represent areas inside the park and contain information about the environment with the most important ones being resource abundance, terrain roughness, rhino signs, poacher signs, and ranger signs. Resources are randomly distributed over the landscape, and a small number of cells do not contain any resources at all. Clusters of high resources were created around the cells with high resources. Cells increase their resources by 1% when there are no rhino visits within 100 events. The reserve also contains 'rough' grid cells; cells that take more time to pass through. Roughness is represented as values ranging from 1 to 5, with 1 being easily accessible areas and 5 the most difficult areas to move through. The agents "skip several turns", depending on the roughness value of the cell they are in.

4.2   Rhino Agents

Two rhino species still exist today in South Africa: the white rhinoceros and black rhinoceros. While both species suffer from poaching, here the white rhino was chosen to model the rhino agents after. This decision was based upon fact that black rhino populations are low compared to the white rhino population and hence white rhinos are poached more often. This virtual park is inhabited by 70 white rhinos which are randomly distributed over the landscape. Rhinos are territorial animals, so if two rhinos end up within a 10 cell radius of each other, one of them moves to another random spot. The rhinos move by checking which of its surrounding cells is the most attractive. The rhinos do this by checking each of those cells for several variables like, how many resources there are, the roughness, and the distance to other rhinos. Each variable is scaled from 0 to 1 with 1 representing the highest preference. Each variable has a weight assigned to it to prioritize certain variables over the other. Next, the variables are summed and divided by the sum of weights. This information is stored as 'attractiveness' and describes the likelihood that the rhino moves to that cell. Once the rhino has moved to a neighboring cell, it consumes 1% of the resources and it includes that cell in its territory. To reduce the likelihood that a rhino enters another rhino's territory, the cell attractiveness that belong to other rhinos is divided by 10. Finally, the rhino leaves signs at its current location. This probability was set at 0.5 and the signs remain visible for a certain number of events. This is a random number between 500 and 1000 events. At the start of each simulation run only the rhinos move around to establish their territory and to distribute rhino signs over the park. This setup duration is set to 1000 events.

4.3   Poacher Agents

Poachers start with no recollection of hunting grounds or areas to avoid; this is an updated procedure based on what the poacher encounters during his hunts. Poachers start at a random grid cell along the border. While they at the border, they cannot be detected or caught by rangers. Before the poacher decides where to move to, he checks the neighboring grid cells for the ranger presence. If so, the poacher abandons his current hunt, remembers this location as a 'failure site', and moves towards the nearest grid cell that is outside the park. While poachers are hunting, they have a similar decision-making rule as described for the rhinos. The variables that the poacher takes into account are the distance to the nearest ranger agent or camp, rhino activity signs, terrain roughness, and resources. Just as the rhino decision-making, each variable is scaled from 0 to 1, summed and then divided by the sum of weights. This information is stored as 'attractiveness' and describes the likelihood that the poacher moves to that cell. Poachers also leave signs with a probability of 0.5 and remain visible for a random number between 100 and 200 events. A poacher kills a rhino when it is on a neigh-boring grid cell of the poacher's location. A poached carcass is an important poaching sign and remains visible throughout the simulation run. Poachers remember the number of events he has spent inside the park. When it exceeds a specified threshold, the poacher moves to the nearest grid cell that is outside the park. Once the poacher is outside the park, he waits a certain number of events before his next attempt. The waiting time is set at twice the specified threshold plus a random number between 1 and 100. When the waiting time is over, the poacher chooses a new start location based on his recollection of any ranger encounters and signs, poached rhino locations, and rhino activity signs. If the poacher does not remember any good sites, he picks a random grid cell along the border of the virtual park.

4.4   Ranger Agents

Ranger agents have a similar setup as the poacher agents. Rangers start at either a ranger camp or along the border of the virtual park. The camps are randomly dis-tributed. All cells within a 10 cells radius around the camps do not contain any resources to avoid lingering rhinos around the camps. Rangers either perform standard patrols or fence patrols. Rangers on a standard patrol have a similar decision-making rule as poachers. While on patrol, rangers make decisions based on the distance to nearest camp or other ranger teams, rhino signs, terrain roughness, and poaching signs.

Just like the poacher decision-making, each variable is scaled from 0 to 1, summed and then divided by the sum of weights. This information is stored as 'attractiveness' and describes the likelihood that the ranger moves to that cell. Ranger agents carrying out fence patrols do not make decisions; they always move along the border for a certain number of events. When a fence patrol encounters poaching signs, they carry out the so-called "follow up". The number of events that the ranger has been on patrol is then reset to 0. This represents that a 'response team' takes over to follow the poacher's track. The ranger agent checks the neighboring grid cells for other poacher signs and moves to the cell with the highest poacher activity. For the following actions, the decision-making is the same as the standard patrol until the agent reaches the patrol duration threshold. If a poacher is on a neighboring cell of the ranger's location, he catches the poacher. The caught poacher is removed from the virtual park and the ranger ends his patrol. Rangers remember areas where they caught poachers and found poaching signs as risky sites, and tend to patrol those areas more. Rangers also leave signs with the same setup as for the poacher agents. Rangers remember the number of events they have been on patrol. When this exceeds the specified threshold, the ranger moves to the nearest grid cell outside the park or to the nearest camp, depending on which of the two is closest. Just like the poacher, ranger agents wait a certain number of events before going out on their next patrol. The ranger's waiting rule is the same as the poacher's waiting rule. Rangers choose a new start location for their patrols based on the memory of any poacher encounters and signs, poached rhino locations, and rhino activity signs. If the ranger does not remember any good sites, he picks a random border cell or a random camp.

5   Scenarios with Different Anti-poaching Strategies

Having the agents in place, several scenarios or strategies can be simulated and compared in terms of how man rhinos have survived at the end of each simulation run. The different anti-poaching strategies were compared with a 'worst-case scenario': a virtual park without any ranger teams. For each patrol strategy, the number of ranger teams and the duration of their patrols were varied, in combination with different numbers of poachers. Ranger and poacher numbers were considered a categorical variable with three levels: 1, 2, and 4 poachers or rangers. Patrol duration was also considered as a categorical variable with three levels: 50, 100, and 200 events. The number of camps was set at 1 for all scenarios with rangers. Each simulation run lasts no longer than 10,000 events, but ends earlier if either all rhinos are killed, or all poachers are caught. The outcome variable was the number of surviving rhinos at the end of each run. Each combination of settings was ran 100 times.

The Shapiro-Wilk test was used to test for normality. Further analyses were performed with the Kruskal-Wallis test. A post hoc comparison using Dunn's test with the Bonferroni adjustment was performed if the Kruskal-Wallis showed significant differences between the groups [12]. These conservative non-parametric methods were applied to reduce the possibility of type I error.

5.1 Standard Patrols

The effect of adding more ranger teams carrying out standard patrols was studied in a virtual park with 1 poacher, 2 poachers, and 4 poachers. The amount of time that the poachers and ranger teams are allowed to spend inside the park was fixed at 50 events. The number of surviving rhinos was significantly different between the number of poachers and number of ranger teams (Kruskal-Wallis test; H = 567.99; d.f. = 8; P < 0.001). The number of surviving rhinos increased with increasing ranger team numbers (Fig. 1a). There was no significant difference between one ranger or two ranger teams on the surviving rhino numbers when the poacher numbers were kept constant. The same applied for two rangers and four ranger teams for the same number of poachers.

The effect of patrol duration was studied in a virtual park with 1 poacher, 2 poachers, and 4 poachers. The duration of a poacher's hunt was fixed to 50 events.

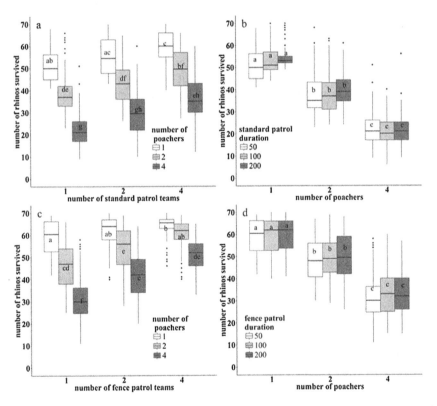

Fig. 1. Scenario simulation results presented in boxplots. The upper row (a, b) shows the results for rangers using a standard patrol strategy. The lower row (c, d) shows the results of fence patrol teams. The left column (a, c) shows the effect of adding more ranger teams. The right column (b, d) shows the effect of increasing patrol duration. The number of surviving rhinos is on the y-axis for all four plots. For statistical comparisons a Kruskall-Wallis was conducted followed by a Dunn's post-hoc test. The bars bearing the same letters are not significantly different at the 5% level

The number of rangers was set to one. The number of surviving rhinos was significantly different between the number of poachers and patrol duration (Kruskal-Wallis test; H = 680.58; d.f. = 8; P < 0.001). While the surviving rhino numbers decreases with increasing number of poachers, the results show no significant difference between the different patrol durations (Fig. 1b).

5.2   Fence Patrols

The effect of adding more fence patrol teams was studied in a virtual park with 1 poacher, 2 poachers, and 4 poachers. The amount of time that the poachers and ranger teams are allowed to spend inside the park was fixed at 50 events. The number of surviving rhinos was significantly different between the number of poachers and number of fence patrol teams (Kruskal-Wallis test; H = 515.58; d.f. = 8; P < 0.001). The number of surviving rhinos increases with an increase in number of fence patrol teams (Fig. 1c). This effect was similar to the increase in rangers for the standard patrols.

The effect of fence patrol duration was studied in a virtual park with 1 poacher, 2 poachers, and 4 poachers. The duration of a poacher's hunt was fixed to 50 events. The number of rangers was set to one. The number of surviving rhinos was significantly different between the number of poachers and fence patrol duration (Kruskal-Wallis test; H = 527.37; d.f. = 8; P < 0.001). While the number of surviving rhinos decreases with increasing number of poachers, the results show no significant difference between the different fence patrol duration (Fig. 1d).

5.3   Comparison of Anti-poaching Strategies

The two anti-poaching strategies were compared with a 'worst-case scenario': a virtual park without any ranger teams. Two parks were created, one with one poacher, and one with four poachers. The duration of a poacher's hunt was fixed to 50 events. The comparison provides insight in how effective each patrol strategy is compared to a park without any patrols. The number of surviving rhinos was significantly different between the different patrol types and number of rangers in the park with one poacher (Kruskal-Wallis test; H = 271.56; d.f. = 6; P < 0.001; Fig. 2a) and in the park with four poachers (Kruskal-Wallis test; H = 451.35; d.f. = 6; P < 0.001; Fig. 2b). As one might expect, the numbers of surviving rhinos was the lowest when four poachers were present. Still, when one poacher was present approximately half of the initial 70 rhinos survived. The average number of rhinos surviving was significantly higher when rangers were present and patrolling. In the virtual park with one poacher the difference between the two types of patrols decreases slightly with increasing rangers. Interestingly, the number of surviving rhinos was not significantly different between one fence patrol team and the two and four standard patrol teams in the one-poacher park. In the park with four poachers the differences between the patrol types are increasing with increasing ranger teams. The number of surviving rhinos was not significantly different between one fence patrol team and two and four standard patrol teams.

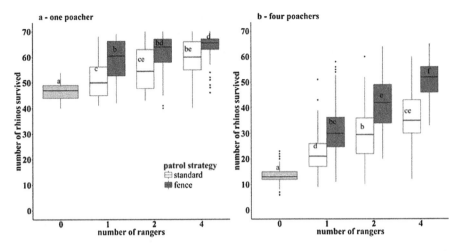

Fig. 2. Results of the patrol strategy comparison presented in boxplots. The left plot shows the result of a virtual park with one poacher and the right plot shows the result of a park with four poachers. The poacher-only scenarios are represented by the boxplot when no rangers where present. The number of surviving rhinos is on the y-axis for all four plots. For statistical comparisons a Kruskall-Wallis was conducted followed by a Dunn's post-hoc test. The bars bearing the same letters are not significantly different at the 5% level.

6 Discussion and Model Improvements

This study introduces an agent-based model to study the dynamic interactions between animals, poachers, and rangers. The model provides a general framework that can easily be applied to a specific setting or context. In this study the model was applied to an abstract, virtually fenced park to explore the effect of an increase in ranger teams and an increase in patrol duration for standard patrols and fence patrols on the numbers of surviving rhinos.

The results show that the more rangers are being deployed, the less rhinos were poached. From a situational crime prevention perspective [2], providing more 'boots on the ground' is a way to increase the risks for poachers. The increase in formal surveillance leads to a higher chance of getting detected and reduces the chances of success. The increase in ranger teams also means that a greater area can be covered or more frequently covered. This improves the knowledge on the spatial and temporal distribution of illegal activities, and hence uncovering the dark figure of crime [6].

The general approach in building this model leads to the assumption that all ranger teams are equal: there are no differences in detection rate and in performance among the ranger agents, regardless of where or when it was deployed in the protected area. However, the effectiveness of one team and their ability to respond to a poaching event is heavily influenced by the amount of training they have received, and the equipment they carry on their patrol [13]. The effect and efficiency of having more patrol teams is only possible when all rangers went through proper training and have adequate supplies of good anti-poaching equipment. The strength of a general model is that it can be easily adjusted. For example, one can introduce variation in the ranger's ability to detect poacher signs, or different levels of experiences. This can then lead into an analysis of the costs and returns for investing more in ranger teams, equipment, or perhaps in technology, like drones or GPS-transmitters for tracking animals. It also allows to test the proposed rule-of-thumb of 1 ranger per 20 km^2 by Bell and Clarke [14]. This was not possible in the current study because the applied context was still a general approach with units that do not map directly to real world measurements.

When resources in protected areas are limited, a different strategy is to go on longer patrols to increase patrol area coverage. However, the results of this study showed that longer patrols were not more effective in protecting rhinos than shorter patrols. Rangers need special training to be able to survive under harsh conditions and in rough environments for an extended period of time. Hence, law enforcement commanders might prefer to send out their teams on shorter patrols, rather than longer ones if indeed they are not more effective. Another study by Nyirenda and Chomba [15] found that shorter patrols of 2 to 8 days were more suitable for the Kafue National Park in Zambia, but stressed that this finding might not be applicable to other protected areas with different environments or in a different social-cultural context. Their statement also applies to the current model. In this study, only three levels of patrol duration were used in a virtual park where poachers only hunt for rhinos. Furthermore, the model also assumed that there are no changes in the ranger's ability to detect signs throughout their patrol. In other words, the model ignores the possible effect of fatigue on the ranger's ability. The longer waiting times between long patrols tries to take that into account, but also results in a lower frequency of patrols. This would also explain why no significant differences between patrol durations were found. The model can be further improved by creating a new variable that represents energy or fatigue of the ranger team and how it influences their detection rate.

The results showed that fence patrols were more effective in protecting rhinos than the standard patrols. More specifically, one fence patrol team was equally effective as two or four standard patrol teams. Fence patrols have a higher likelihood of picking up poacher signs, because poachers always start and end at the borders. In addition to that, while patrolling, the ranger agents also leave signs that influence the poacher's decision-making and likely deflects them. As stated by Eck and Weisburd [16] "offenders avoid targets with evidence of high guardianship". Hence, offenders seek out new areas or time periods with low guardianship. This is referred to as crime displacement [16]. In the case of wildlife crime, poachers might be spatially displaced to other areas with low security, or temporally displaced by operating at different hours. Especially temporal displacement can be of concern when deploying fence patrols as those are much more linear and predictable compared to standard patrols. While spatial displacement can be observed from the current model, it does not explicitly measure it. Hence, it is still unknown if the observed spatial displacement in the model is a good representation of actual displacement. The model can be easily adjusted to study spatial and temporal displacement. For example, evidence suggests that poachers are more active around a full moon period [17], probably because the light allows them to move through the bush more easily or faster. If more teams are being deployed around these times, poachers eventually are displaced to other moon phases or perhaps even to times during the day. It would be interesting to use the model to study how ranger patrols displace poachers in time and space.

The suggestions mentioned above are just some possibilities to further improve the current model. However, before any of these suggestions are worked into the model, it is important to stress a few limitations. First, no sensitivity analysis was performed to see how each parameter influences the model outcomes. This is especially important when one is interested in studying the conditions under which systems can become critical. ten Broeke et al. [18] suggested the 'one-factor-at-a-time' as a good starting point for a sensitivity analysis of an ABM. Furthermore, the current model was not calibrated to a specific protected area, but built around the general context of rhino poaching in South Africa. A true representation of the actual system requires more data on the agent's behavior. In most cases, data on animal behavior is widely available, however data on ranger and especially poacher behavior is more difficult to collect. Such data usually comes from various sources, each with its own standards. This makes it challenging to create accurate rules for the ranger and poacher agents. However, the model can also be used to test different potential poacher strategies to see which one best reflects the observed behavior. Once these limitations are accounted for, a next step can involve applying the model to a specific context or problem.

7   Conclusion

This study presented a general model to study the dynamic interactions between the three agents that are involved in wildlife crime. The general, abstract approach was done intentionally to keep the model from getting too complex, yet with rules that result in realistic behavior of the animals, poachers, and rangers. The general framework of the model can easily be expanded to include more levels of complexity. When applied to rhino poaching under different anti-poaching strategies, the model provides some general insight in how the different strategies influence the behavior of rhino poachers. The results show that fence patrols are more effective in preventing wildlife crime than standard patrols. Strikingly, even deploying more ranger teams does not increase the effectiveness of standard patrols compared to fence patrols. The model presented here should be regarded as a first step to understand the complexity of wildlife crime and only benefits from further improvements and extensions.

Acknowledgments. The author would like to thank Jacob van der Ploeg and Michael Mäs (University of Groningen, the Netherlands) for their help in developing and creating the model. Furthermore, AM Lemieux (Netherlands Institute for the Study of Crime and Law Enforcement) and Craig Spencer (Balule Nature Reserve, South Africa) for their helpful comments and suggestions on the model.

References

1. Banks, D., Davies, C., Gosling, J., Newman, J., Rice, M., Wadley, J., Walravens, F.: Environmental crime: a threat to our future, p. 25 (2008)
2. Clarke, R.V.: "Situational" crime prevention: theory and practice. Br. J. Criminol. **20**, 136–147 (1980)
3. Maingi, J.K., Mukeka, J.M., Kyale, D.M., Muasya, R.M.: Spatiotemporal patterns of elephant poaching in South-Eastern Kenya. Wildl. Res. **39**, 234 (2012). doi:10.1071/WR11017
4. Critchlow, R., Plumptre, A.J., Driciru, M., Rwetsiba, A., Stokes, E.J., Tumwesigye, C., Wanyama, F., Beale, C.M.: Spatiotemporal trends of illegal activities from ranger-collected data in a Ugandan National Park: trends in illegal activities. Conserv. Biol. **29**, 1458–1470 (2015). doi:10.1111/cobi.12538
5. Gavin, M.C., Solomon, J.N., Blank, S.G.: Measuring and monitoring illegal use of natural resources. Conserv. Biol. **24**, 89–100 (2010). doi:10.1111/j.1523-1739.2009.01387.x
6. Biderman, A.D., Reiss, A.J.: On exploring the "dark figure" of crime. Ann. Am. Acad. Polit. Soc. Sci. **374**, 1–15 (1967). doi:10.1177/000271626737400102
7. Epstein, J.M., Axtell, R.: Growing artificial societies: social science from the bottom up. Brookings Institution Press, MIT Press, Cambridge (1996)
8. Birks, D.J., Donkin, S., Wellsmith, M.: Synthesis over analysis: towards an ontology for volume crime simulation. In: Artificial Crime Analysis Systems: Using Computer Simulations and Geographic Information Systems, pp. 160–192. IGI Global (2008)
9. Lemieux, A.M.: Introduction. In: Situational Prevention of Poaching (2014)
10. Milliken, T., Shaw, J.: The South Africa-Vietnam Rhino Horn Trade Nexus: A Deadly Combination of Institutional Lapses, Corrupt Wildlife Industry Professionals and Asian Crime Syndicates. TRAFFIC, Johannesburg (2012)
11. Wilensky, U.: NetLogo (1999). http://ccl.northwestern.edu/netlogo/
12. McKight, P.E., Najab, J.: Kruskal-Wallis Test. Corsini Encyclopedia of Psychology (2010). doi:10.1002/9780470479216.corpsy0491
13. Moreto, W.: To conserve and protect: examining law enforcement ranger culture and operations in Queen Elizabeth National Park, Uganda. Thesis, Rutgers University (2013)
14. Bell, R.H.V., Clarke, J.E.: Funding and financial control. In: Conservation and Wildlife Management in Africa, pp. 543–546. US Peace Corps, Washington, DC (1986)
15. Nyirenda, V.R., Chomba, C.: Field foot patrol effectiveness in the giant Kafue National Park. Zambia. J. Ecol. Nat. Environ. **4**, 163–172 (2012). doi:10.5897/JENE12.010
16. Eck, J.E., Weisburd, D.L.: Crime places in crime theory. Crime Place Crime Prev. Stud. **4**, 1–33 (2015)
17. Eloff, C., Lemieux, A.M.: Rhino poaching in Kruger National Park, South Africa. In: Situational Prevention of Poaching (2014)
18. ten Broeke, G., van Voorn, G., Ligtenberg, A.: Which sensitivity analysis method should I use for my agent-based model? J. Artif. Soc. Soc. Simul. (2016). doi:10.18564/jasss.285

Ambient Intelligence and Affective Environments

A SOA Web-Based Group Decision Support System Considering Affective Aspects

Luís Conceição[1(✉)], João Carneiro[1,2], Goreti Marreiros[1],
and Paulo Novais[2]

[1] GECAD - Research Group on Intelligent Engineering and Computing for
Advanced Innovation and Development, Institute of Engineering,
Polytechnic of Porto, Porto, Portugal
{lmdsc,jomrc,mgt}@isep.ipp.pt
[2] ALGORITMI Centre, University of Minho, Braga, Portugal
pjon@di.uminho.pt

Abstract. The topic of Group Decision Support Systems (GDSS) has been studied over the last decades. Supporting decision-makers that participate in group decision-making processes is a complex task, especially when decision-makers have no opportunity to gather at the same place and at the same time. In this work, we propose a Web based Group Decision Support System (WebGDSS) which intends to support decision-makers anywhere, anytime and through almost any kind of devices. Our system was developed under a SOA architecture and we used a multi-criteria algorithm that features decision-makers' cognitive aspects, as well as a component of generation of intelligent reports to provide feedback of decision-making processes to the decision-makers.

Keywords: Group Decision Support Systems · Group decision-making · Intelligent reports · Cognitive decision-making

1 Introduction

Nowadays, group decision-making is the most preferred way of making decisions in companies around the world. It's known that when decisions are made in group, better results are achieved [1]. Group Decision Support Systems (GDSS) have been studied throughout the last decades with the objective of supporting decision-makers in group decision-making processes. The number of participants in a group decision-making process is variable and each participant may be at the same place at the same time or may be in different countries and with different time zones. Due to this facts, the support to the decision-makers involved in a group decision-making process is a challenge quite difficult to tackle [2].

GDSSs have seen quite an evolution since their introduction [3]. This is mainly attributable to the evolution of general technology, as well as to the need of enhancing the efficiency of the group decision-making processes.

There are many relevant GDSSs in literature [4–9]. However, the success of these systems hasn't been positive because the organizations' acceptance of these systems

© Springer International Publishing AG 2017
E. Oliveira et al. (Eds.): EPIA 2017, LNAI 10423, pp. 65–74, 2017.
DOI: 10.1007/978-3-319-65340-2_6

has been low due to numerous factors. On the one hand, several of the existing systems feature interfaces too complex that won't be filled in by the busy decision-maker, which is what enables the decision-maker to reflect the respective preferences regarding the available alternatives. On the other hand, some of the systems do not allow decision-makers to properly express their preferences [10] or do not fully transmit the decision-maker's opinion to the system, resulting in a loss of relevant information for the decision-making process.

In this paper, we propose a Web Based Group Decision Support System capable of aiding groups of decision-makers in decision-making processes, namely in multi criteria problems. The proposed system has been developed using a Services-oriented Architecture (SOA) to help mainstream the integration of the application in several platforms (e.g.: PCs, tablets, smartphones) which, not only does it feature decision-makers' cognitive aspects, it has a problem configuration interface that simplifies the whole process and allows decision-makers to express their preferences, based on the work of [10, 11]. Moreover, the present GDSS features a component of generation of intelligent reports that presents to decision-makers information about the decision-making process. This feature aims to meet the decision-maker's interests in that same process, while trying to maximize his/her approval of the final decision.

The rest of the paper is organized as follows: in Sect. 2 we describe some existing works in literature. Section 3 describes our proposed GDSS, namely its functionalities and architecture, and in Sect. 4 we present some conclusions and some guidelines regarding future work that we aim to carry on.

2   State of the Art

We did an analysis of some existing GDSSs in the literature in order to analyze the software architectures, their functionalities and applications.

In [7], authors presented a scientific paper where they developed a scenario of simulated medical practice for intelligent support for decision-making on the stages of cancer. Decisions were made in the context of a group meeting to facilitate collaborative work. The authors used agents to represent real participants and to exchange and store information. The developed system emulated the phases of cancer, allowing to increase the performance of the medical team and eliminate the circulation of paper.

In [9] authors have developed a web based GDSS that allows support groups of decision-makers in group decision-making processes. The developed GDSS allows a facilitator to create a decision problem, its alternatives and add the experts who will participate in the decision process. In this system experts only introduce their preferences to alternatives. These preferences are indicated in the form of comparison of the alternatives with each other. Later, at each iteration of the decision process, the computation module evaluates the preferences introduced by the experts and makes suggestions if there are inconsistencies between the preferences.

Another interesting work is the one's presented in [6]. In this work authors have developed a model of a GDSS that uses agents to represent the participants of a meeting. In this approach, the agents were not meant to replace the members of the meeting, but rather the intention to support them in the group decision-making process. In this work, the agents are endowed with an emotional component due to the importance that the emotions have in the negotiation process. The architecture of the participating agents is composed of three layers: Knowledge, Reasoning and Interaction.

In [8], authors bring to us a very relevant and practical work where they proposed a GDSS for the evaluation of alternative pipelines routes to transport oil and natural gas from Caspian Sea to others distant regions. They decompose the route selection process into manageable steps. They combine Strength, Weakness, Opportunity and Threat (SWOT) analysis with the Delphi method to capture the decision-makers' beliefs. They also developed a model called Preference Ranking Organization Method for Enrichment Evaluation (PROMETHEE) to integrate the decision-makers' beliefs with subjective judgments and identify the most attractive pipeline route. They claim that their system encourages decision-makers to think systematically and carefully consider environmental complexities and uncertainties. They see as future challenges the incorporation of simulating and optimization methods in the GDSS.

A more recent work published by [5] where they presented an experimental study of a new web-based called Group Remote Asynchronous Screening Support (GRASS). They used interactive decision maps/reasonable goals method in remote asynchronous group decision-making. They used reasonable goals method where an individual can select a small number of alternatives for subsequent ranking. They claim that the GRASS produces better results when used by someone familiar with the procedure. However, the non-experienced people failed to use GRASS without the help of an instructor.

In [12] addressed a very interested work about how GDSS can facilitate and help the organizations. They performed a good literature review about this thematic and did an experiment to test whether the use of a GDSS increases the quality of a brainstorm sessions. Besides they consider that GDSS promises very potential, they did not find any evidences to say that GDSS increased the quality of brainstorm results.

The systems analyzed are quite different from each other, but they allow us to identify some gaps and it is these gaps that the system proposed in this work intends to satisfy. In the system proposed in [7], although screenshots of their interfaces are not available, according to the authors these are made available as web front-ends, but they do not show usability results nor the level of complexity required for the problem configuration. In relation to the system proposed in [9], in this system each decision-maker has to introduce their preferences in the form of comparison of alternatives, which means that the number of comparisons that each decision-maker has to make is determined by $n \cdot (n - 1)$. If we are in a situation where a problem has 10 possible alternatives, it means that each decision-maker has to introduce his/her preferences on 90 comparisons of alternatives, which makes the process slow and complex. The work described in [6], proposes a GDSS that uses a multi-agent system where each agent represents a decision-maker. In this paper, authors prove that in a GDSS, when emotions are contemplated, it is easier to reach a consensus for a solution. In the system proposed in [8], decision makers also indicate their preferences on the set of alternatives through comparisons of alternative pairs. In [5], preferences of each decision maker are indicated in the form of selection of a subset of alternatives from the initial set. In this way, it is not possible to truly understand the intentions of decision-makers in the problem.

Our system was developed in order to fulfill the interaction failures identified in the analyzed systems, as well as failures in the representation of the actual preferences of each decision maker in relation to the problem.

3 Proposed GDSS

The system recommended in this paper has the objective of being the most ubiquitous system so that it supports decision-makers anytime, anywhere and from any device or equipment, as long as it has an Internet connection.

The developed GDSS aims to aid groups of decision-makers in multi-criteria decision-making processes. In this system, each participant configures his/her preferences regarding the problem and, after every participant has introduced the respective preferences, the system runs the decision algorithm and presents the results in intelligent reports.

3.1 System Architecture

The system architecture (Fig. 1) was designed in such a way that it allows for the usage of the system in any device (e.g. PCs, tablets, smartphones) due to the implementation of the Service-oriented Architecture (SOA) methodology. This way, it is possible to easily develop applications for different devices with different technologies, enabling decision-makers to use the GDSS in any type of device, anytime and from anywhere, as long as they have an Internet connection. The system uses a database to store all the configurations about each problem. These configurations include problem's data, personal configurations of decision-makers preferences for each problem, as well as all the results about each iteration of each problem.

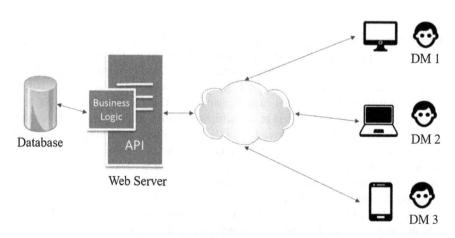

Fig. 1. System architecture

The system offers an Application Programming Interface (API) that implements business logic, responsible for modulating the actions allowed by the application, so that the client applications only need to implement interfaces with the end user (the decision-maker).

The API implements all the system's business layers, as well as the control of the access to the database, implementing all functions of Create, Read, Update and Delete (CRUD), where all GDSS information is stored. Besides this, it implements the multi-criteria decision-making algorithm. In this specific case, the chosen algorithm is the Cognitive Analytic Process (CAP) [13].

CAP is an algorithm for the sorting of alternatives within multi criteria problems that features decision-makers' cognitive aspects. This algorithm evaluates alternatives using criteria preferences indicated by each decision-maker, but it goes beyond that: it takes into account the intentions of the decision-makers. The CAP considers the behaviour style and the expertise level of the decision-maker and it also makes use of the information of which decision-makers are considered credible among the group. All this information is processed by the CAP, presenting a solution that combines the rational component with the irrational one [13].

The developed API implements authentication services in order to ensure data integrity and security, as well as every service of manipulation of the decision-making problems, alternatives, criteria, etc. It is possible to access all system functionalities through the API (e.g. creating problems, criteria, alternatives, and selecting which decision-makers will participate in a given problem, etc.).

3.2   Web Application

The Web Application implements user interfaces between the GDSS and the decision-maker. This application allows the user to configure the multi-criteria problem, namely their alternatives and the criteria that evaluate each of the alternatives. In addition to the alternatives and criteria, the user who creates the problem must also add the users who will participate in that decision-making process. The preferences configuration interface was defined according to the work proposed by [10, 11], Where it presents a multi-criteria system configuration template for a multi-agent system. The results of the system are presented through an intelligent report generation feature [14, 15] which reports to each decision-maker only the information considered relevant according to their profile in the decision-making process.

3.3   System Functionalities

The primary objective of a GDSS is to support a group of decision-makers in a group decision-making process.

The user intending to start a decision-making process (the organizer) has to set up the problem and for that he has to:

1. Define the problem for discussion;
2. Define the criteria to consider;

3. Define the available alternatives;
4. Select the participating decision-makers.

The organizer needs to have all this information previously defined so that he/she is able to input them into the system. This information is usually gathered during brainstorming meetings, or by other methods, depending on the problem for which a decision is being made. In GDSS, the creation of a new problem prompts the user for a problem title and brief description.

The next step is the creation of criteria, which can be Boolean, Numeric or Classificatory. In case they are of the Classificatory type, the organizer has to define a numerical value for each of the classifications. Besides the type of data that measure the criterion, it is necessary to indicate if the criterion is of minimization or maximization type (e.g. if a given criterion is the buying price of a given product, and considering that the intention is to minimize the cost of that purchase, the criterion Price will be a minimization criterion).

Once the problem criteria are set up, the next task is to define the alternatives that may be the solutions for the problem. Each alternative has a name, a field for a brief description, and its evaluation based on the criteria defined in the previous stage. Therefore, for each alternative, the organizer has to specify the value of that alternative in each of the defined criteria.

After inserting the alternatives and the criteria, the organizer is left with the task of adding the decision-makers that will participate in the decision-making process, as well as setting a deadline for the process and finalizing the problem creation.

Upon completion of these actions, decision-makers selected to participate in the process will be alerted via email that a new problem has been created and that their intervention is needed to indicate their preferences regarding the alternatives and criteria to be considered.

The decision-makers who will participate in the process have access to the interface of configuring their preferences through the link received via email. Each decision-maker has now the possibility to configure the preferences of the system on the problem to be discussed. First, begin by setting personal preferences for the problem as shown in the Fig. 2. In this case, each decision-maker can indicate his/her Expertise Level in relation to the issue, the behavior style that he/she wants, and which decision-makers he or she considers to be credible (within the group of participants).

The Expertise Level intends to represent the level of expertise of the decision-maker in relation to the problem being discussed (to read more about this see [13]).

Credibility is related to the decision maker's perception of the credibility of the other participants in the process in relation to their expertise regarding the problem being discussed (to read more about this see [13]).

Behavior style can be seen as the desired behavior or behavior of the system in the "defense" of the interests/preferences of the decision-maker during the decision-making process (to read more about this see [16]). Available styles (presented in Table 1) are: Dominating, Integrating, Compromising, Obliging and Avoiding. These styles differentiate each other through 4 dimensions:

- Concern for Self – This dimension is related to the individual's concern for his own opinion above the others since he is likely to adapt a more one-sided attitude during

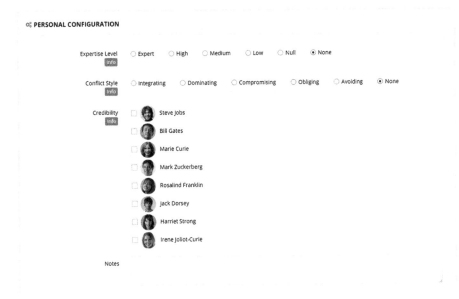

Fig. 2. Personal configuration

Table 1. Behaviour styles and corresponding dimensions, adapted from [16]

Conflict style	Concern for self	Concern for others	Activity	Resistance to change
Dominating	High	Low	High	High
Integrating	High	High	High	High
Compromising	Moderate	Moderate	Moderate	Moderate
Obliging	Low	High	Low	Low
Avoiding	Low	Low	Low	Low

the decision-making process by making statements, questions and requests that detail that opinion;

- Concern for others – This dimension relates to the individual's concern for other individuals' opinion. He adapts a more altruist attitude during the decision-making process, trying to understand other opinions and making an effort to reach a decision that benefits or pleases most of the participants;
- Activity – This dimension relates to the effort put into the decision-making process by the individual, meaning that the more active an individual is, the more questions and statements and requests he is likely to make;
- Resistance to change – This dimension relates to how hard or easy it is for an individual to accept other opinions.

After configuring personal information, each decision-maker has to indicate their preferences regarding the attributes of the problem: the criteria and the alternatives. Preferences are indicated on a scale of 0 to 100 as shown in Fig. 3.

When all the decision-makers involved in the process configure their preferences, the system executes the algorithm and concludes the process. This process is iterative until all members of the group agree on the final decision, or until the organizer completes the process. In the event that a decision-maker does not accept the decision, it can readjust its preferences and then the process returns to the beginning.

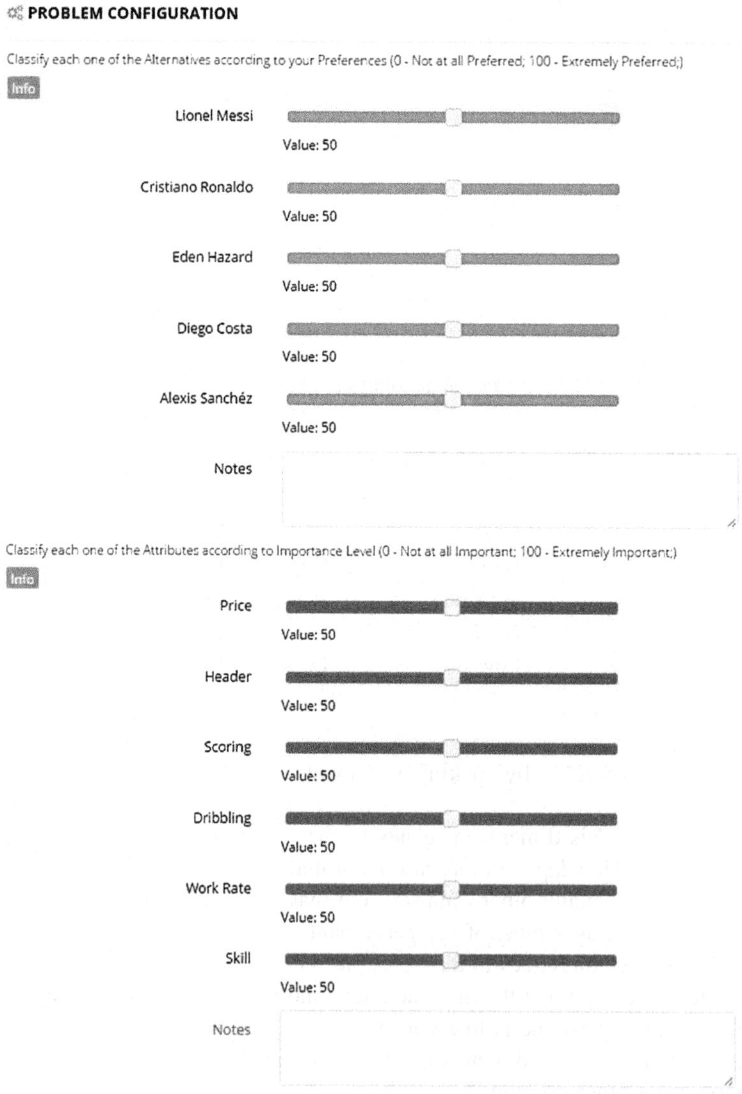

Fig. 3. Problem configuration

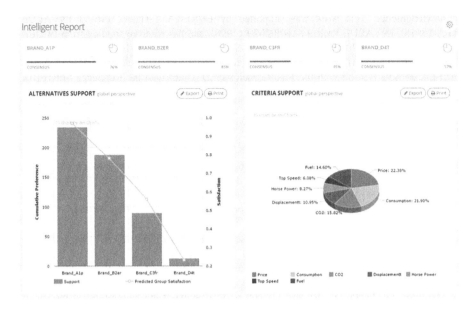

Fig. 4. Intelligent report

The information is reported in the form of intelligent reports as presented in Fig. 4. Intelligent reports have the objective of reporting to each decision-maker only the information that is considered relevant according to their position (their interests) in each group decision-making process. With this functionality, we intend to report to the decision-makers brief and relevant information so that each decision-maker can analyze the results of each iteration of the process by spending as little time as possible (to read more about this see [14, 15]).

4   Conclusions and Future Work

GDSS have become an important topic of study in recent decades. Its benefits and its advantages are recognized by all, especially when it comes to supporting decision-makers who are not in the same place. Despite this, we know that these systems have not been well accepted by organizations. As we mentioned in our previous works [10, 11, 14, 15], the interaction between decision-makers and the system is an essential point regarding the acceptance of systems by users and the organizations themselves.

The development of this system is the result of extensive research related to group decision-making. Our proposal aims to fill some of the flaws identified in the literature, especially in relation to usability factors. In this work, we developed a web-based GDSS where the results of previous works are applied, with the aim of presenting a system that allows the groups of decision-makers to make decisions remotely without the relevant aspects such as the personality and the influence of the relations between the elements of the group being lost.

As future work, we intend to develop a case study with a real group of decision-makers in a real-life context in order to validate the system.

Acknowledgments. This work was supported by EUREKA - ITEA2 Project INVALUE (ITEA-13015), INVALUE Project (ANI|P2020 17990), and has received funding from FEDER Funds through NORTE2020 program and from National Funds through FCT - Fundação para a Ciência e a Tecnologia (Portuguese Foundation for Science and Technology) under the project UID/EEA/00760/2013 and with the João Carneiro Ph.D. Grant with the Reference SFRH/BD/89697/2012.

References

1. Luthans, F.: Organizational Behavior, vol. 46. McGraw-Hill/Irwin, New York (2011). 594 p.
2. Huber, G.P.: Issues in the design of group decision support systems. MIS Q.: Manag. Inf. Syst. **8**, 195–204 (1984)
3. DeSanctis, G., Gallupe, B.: Group decision support systems: a new frontier. SIGMIS Database **16**, 3–10 (1985)
4. Choi, D.-Y.: Aggregation of preferences based on FSAM in GDSS. IEEE Trans. Syst. Man Cybern. Part A: Syst. Hum. **38**, 2–8 (2008)
5. Efremov, R.V., Lotov, A.V.: Multi-criteria remote asynchronous group decision screening: an experimental study. Group Decis. Negot. **23**, 31–48 (2014)
6. Marreiros, G., Santos, R., Ramos, C., Neves, J.: Context-aware emotion-based model for group decision making. Intell. Syst. IEEE **25**, 31–39 (2010)
7. Miranda, M., Abelha, A., Santos, M., Machado, J., Neves, J.: A group decision support system for staging of cancer. In: Weerasinghe, D. (ed.) eHealth 2008. LNICSSITE, vol. 0001, pp. 114–121. Springer, Heidelberg (2009). doi:10.1007/978-3-642-00413-1_14
8. Tavana, M., Behzadian, M., Pirdashti, M., Pirdashti, H.: A PROMETHEE-GDSS for oil and gas pipeline planning in the Caspian Sea basin. Energy Econ. **36**, 716–728 (2013)
9. Alonso, S., Herrera-Viedma, E., Chiclana, F., Herrera, F.: A web based consensus support system for group decision making problems and incomplete preferences. Inf. Sci. **180**, 4477–4495 (2010)
10. Carneiro, J., Santos, R., Marreiros, G., Novais, P.: Overcoming the lack of human-interaction in ubiquitous group decision support systems. Adv. Sci. Technol. Lett. **49**, 116–124 (2014)
11. Carneiro, J., Martinho, D., Marreiros, G., Novais, P.: A general template to configure multi-criteria problems in ubiquitous GDSS. Int. J. Softw. Eng. Appl. **9**, 193–206 (2015)
12. Monteban, J.: Using group decision support systems to facilitate organizational change. In: 21st Twente Student Conference on IT, 23 June 2014, Enschede, The Netherlands (2014). http://referaat.cs.utwente.nl/conference/21/paper
13. Carneiro, J., Conceição, L., Martinho, D., Marreiros, G., Novais, P.: Including cognitive aspects in multiple criteria decision analysis. Ann. Oper. Res. 1–23 (2016). https://link.springer.com/article/10.1007/s10479-016-2391-1
14. Carneiro, J., Conceição, L., Martinho, D., Marreiros, G., Novais, P.: Intelligent reports for group decision support systems. In: Intelligent Environments 2016: Workshop Proceedings of the 12th International Conference on Intelligent Environments, p. 4. IOS Press (2016)
15. Conceição, L., Carneiro, J., Martinho, D., Marreiros, G., Novais, P.: Generation of intelligent reports for ubiquitous group decision support systems. In: Global Information Infrastructure and Networking Symposium (GIIS), 2016, pp. 1–6. IEEE (2016)
16. Martinho, D., Carneiro, J., Marreiros, G., Novais, P.: Dealing with agents' behaviour in the decision-making process. In: Workshop Proceedings of the 11th International Conference on Intelligent Environments, vol. 19, p. 4 (2015)

Monitoring the Progress of Programming Students Supported by a Digital Teaching Assistant

Nuno Gil Fonseca[1,2(✉)], Luís Macedo[1], and António José Mendes[1]

[1] Department of Informatics Engineering,
Center for Informatics and Systems of the University of Coimbra,
University of Coimbra, Coimbra, Portugal
{nunogil,macedo,toze}@dei.uc.pt
[2] Instituto Politécnico de Coimbra - Escola Superior de Tecnologia e Gestão de
Oliveira do Hospital, Oliveira do Hospital, Portugal

Abstract. Several studies have shown that there is an important link between continual monitoring by the teachers and the students' performance. Unfortunately, the teachers cannot be continuously looking for what the students are doing. To overcome this situation, we propose the use of *CodeInsights*, a tool capable of capturing, in an autonomous, transparent and unobtrusive manner, information about the students' performance and then, based on teacher's expectations, notify them about possible deviations in the specific context of programming courses. The decision on whether the system should or should not notify the teacher is supported by an artificial cognitive selective attention mechanism. Although *CodeInsights,* provided with the described mechanism, hasn't been fully tested in a real case scenario, we present some specific examples of how it can be used to assist teachers.

Keywords: Intelligent systems in education · Digital teaching assistant · Programming · Selective attention

1 Introduction

Now more than ever, programming is becoming more and more part of the student's life, even on early stages of their lives [1]. However, programming is not a trivial task, and the students experience a series of difficulties along the way [2]. Due to factors like inhibition, the students may be facing difficulties, and the teacher might be totally unaware of them. As those difficulties can be relevant to their progress, their non-clarification may lead to drastic consequences in terms of the learning process. Furthermore, when the students are capable of expressing their problems to the teachers, it is always difficult trying to understand what the student already knows and has done to solve the problem in hand. This lack of information sometimes leads the teachers to solve the problem themselves without explaining its origin to the students.

Finding ways to overcome these barriers between teachers and students, which includes the problems faced by the teachers in becoming aware whether or not the students are facing difficulties, as well as their nature, has given rise to research on

© Springer International Publishing AG 2017
E. Oliveira et al. (Eds.): EPIA 2017, LNAI 10423, pp. 75–86, 2017.
DOI: 10.1007/978-3-319-65340-2_7

teaching methodologies. As stated by Bloom [3], the most efficient teaching-learning method is individualized tutoring, since the teacher is more aware of the students' difficulties and capabilities, and can more easily adapt the teaching pace, as well as the materials and assignments, proposed to the students. Also, Raabe and Silva [4] claim that students' performance is highly coupled with the capacity that the teachers have to detect their difficulties and react within a useful time. In the specific context of face-to-face learning with a large number of students, this proximity relationship between teachers and students may be hard to achieve.

Finding strategies that increase this proximity relationship has driven researchers to make use of technology. In fact, strategies that include technology in education have provided a promising solution to overcome this problem. One of those strategies includes using agent-based technology. For instance, according to Jafari [5], there are three groups of intelligent agents for teaching and learning applications: digital classmate, digital teaching assistant, and digital secretary. Among these groups, especially related to our interests is the group of digital teaching assistants. In this category, we find those systems whose main purpose is to autonomously collect and analyze data about the student's work, and display it to the teacher in the most suitable way. Eventually, the systems may also generate notifications to the teacher whenever a deviation from the usual path is found. As examples of this type of systems, we may find the *Logic-ITA* system [6], the *AVA* system proposed by Raabe and Silva [4], the teaching assistant agent proposed by Choy et al. [7] or the *AmI-RIA*: Real-Time Teacher Assistant proposed by Mathioudakis et al. [8]. Particularly related to the context of programming, we may find the *ELJT* (E-Learning Java Trainer) [9], the *Retina* system proposed by Murphy et al. [10], the *TestMyCode* system [11] or *ClockIt* [12].

A significant limitation of some of these systems is that they may be highly coupled to a specific set of assignments, or the students may need to use a specific development methodology (e.g. the Test Driven Methodology must be utilized with the TestMyCode tool). Also relevant is the fact that some tools were designed to analyze the code snapshots[1] *a posteriori*, and not in real time, which in our opinion is a significant drawback.

In most cases, these systems are only used to collect and process data coming from the students and make the resulting information available to the teacher. The teacher should then browse through the data available and try to make sense of it, which obviously is very time-consuming. For this purpose, systems should include some notification system that will alert the teachers about specific aspects of the student's performance (e.g. unfinished assignments, plagiarism of code). However, if not carefully designed, systems could rapidly start to notify the teachers about everything, which will lead to a scenario where the overload of information will make the system impossible to use. To avoid this information overload scenario, systems may include selective attention mechanisms, capable of identifying the most relevant information to display to the users.

Although there has been much research in this field, there is not a general theory/model of selective attention. In spite of this, a number of models of selective

---

[1] A code snapshot is a copy of the source code written by the student to solve a designted assignment at a given moment in time.

attention have been proposed in Cognitive Science (e.g., [13–15]). Particularly related to these models is the issue of measuring the value of information. A considerable amount of literature has been published on these measures, especially from the fields of active learning and experimental design. Most of those measures rely on assessing the utility or the "informativeness" of information (see [16] for more details).

A number of models of selective attention have been proposed in Cognitive Science (e.g., [17]). Particularly related to these models is the issue of measuring the value of information. A considerable amount of literature has been published on these measures, especially from the fields of active learning and experimental design. Most of those measures rely on assessing the utility or the informativeness of information (e.g., [18–21]).

In this paper, we adopt the model of selective attention proposed by Macedo [16]. We integrate it into one digital teaching assistant tool to decide if a certain notification should or nor be generated. This tool should be capable of autonomously capturing information about the students' performance and, based on the teacher's beliefs, notify them about possible deviations whenever needed. This way, the teacher can be more aware of the students' performance and be capable of making more educated decisions and at the same time avoid an overabundance of information.

The next section presents Macedo's model of selective attention while Sect. 3 describes how this model is incorporated in our system, called *CodeInsights* [22]. Finally, we discuss our approach and present conclusions.

2   Background Macedo's Model of Selective Attention

The artificial selective attention mechanism that we are using is an implementation of the model proposed by Macedo [16] which has already been used and validated in several different scenarios. This artificial selective attention mechanism is comprised of three distinct components: (i) Surprise Value of Information, (ii) Uncertainty-based Value of Information and (iii) Motive Congruence/Incongruence-based Value of Information.

According to the "Principle of Selective Attention" stated by Macedo, "*A resource-bounded rational agent should focus its attention only on the relevant and interesting information*". Macedo has defined three different real numbers α, β, and γ as levels above which the absolute values of motive congruency (MC), surprise (S) or information gain (IG), respectively, should be such that the information can be considered valuable or interesting according to the following algorithm.

```
IF (MC > α AND (S > β OR IG > γ)) :
    generate notification
ELSE:
    discard notification
```

The initial values for the thresholds are automatically defined based on previous experiments, but the teachers can change them at any time according to their needs.

The Uncertainty-based Value of Information component consists basically of determining the gain of information, *IG*, about the acquisition of new information in an experiment. It does not matter what event in fact happened. The value for *IG* can be determined as described in (1), where *m* stands for the number of mutually exclusive events of experiment *E*, and H_{prior} and H_{post} are, respectively, the entropies before and after the acquisition of new data that might change the probability distribution of the event(s) of interest.

$$IG(E) = \frac{H_{prior}(E) - H_{post}(E)}{\log(m)}$$
$$IG(E) = \frac{-\sum_{i=}^{m} P_{prior}(E_i) \times \left(\log P_{prior}(E_i)\right) - \left(-\sum_{i=}^{m} P_{post}(E_i) \times \left(\log\left(P_{post}(E_i)\right)\right)\right)}{\log(m)}$$

(1)

In our particular case, H_{post} is equal to zero, because we are assuming that the experiment has ended (i.e. no more attempts will be received after the deadline has passed) and therefore all the $P_{post}(E_i)$ but one are zero, this one having the value unity. Thus, only when we are confident of the outcome does H_{post} vanish. Otherwise, it is positive. So the value for *IG* in these cases is obtained by (2):

$$IG(E) = \frac{-\sum_{i=}^{m} P_{prior}(E_i) \times \left(\log\left(P_{prior}(E_i)\right)\right)}{\log(m)}$$

(2)

Next, we will use the Surprise Value of Information component, which is used to determine the extent of the surprise felt by the agent (representing the teachers) when a certain event occurs. According to Macedo et al., the intensity of surprise about an event E_g, from a set of mutually exclusive events $E_1, E_2, ..., E_m$, is a nonlinear function of the difference, or contrast, between its probability and the probability of the most expected event E_h in the set of mutually exclusive events $E_1, E_2, ..., E_m$. So, the value of surprise *S* of some event E_g, $S(E_g)$, is given by (3);

$$S(E_g) = log\left(1 + P(E_h) - P(E_g)\right)$$

(3)

For this purpose, we assume that the set of mutually exclusive events has at least one event whose occurrence is unsurprising (has a higher probability to occur), namely, E_h.

Finally, the Congruence/Incongruence-based Value of Information component is used to assign different degrees of desirability (satisfaction) for receiving notifications about the occurrence of each event (i.e. the teacher may have more satisfaction with the occurrence of some events than with the occurrence of others). Instead of probabilities or expectations, this component takes as input "desires" that can be satisfied or frustrated independently of the probability of occurrence for that event. The "desires" are expressed as a value between −1 and 1. It is important to notice that the negative value for *D* is used to represent "unhappy desires" (i.e. the teacher is not "happy" with that, but still wants to be notified). In the end, the motive congruence value for the outcome of an event – *MC* – is equal to |*D*|.

As mentioned previously, the system will only generate notifications about the occurrence of those events for which $MC > \alpha$ AND $(S > \beta$ OR $IG > \gamma)$. The "OR" between surprise and information gain can easily be explained by looking at Fig. 1. This figure depicts the evolution of the values of S and IG (YY axis) using different values for the probability of the occurrence of a certain event (XX axis), assuming that there are only two possibilities.

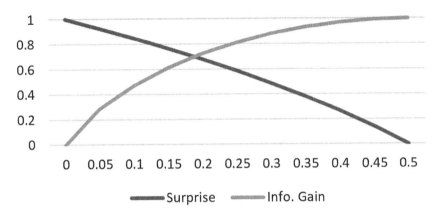

Fig. 1. The distribution of the values of surprise and information gain using different values for the probability of the occurrence of a certain event

As can be seen in Fig. 1, the value for the gain of information increases as the probability of the occurrence of a certain event increases up to 0.5, which means that the occurrence of an event in a very homogenous scenario is more likely to reduce uncertainty than otherwise. In contrast, the value of surprise decreases as the difference between the probability of occurrence of the two events also decreases. Because of this contrast, the OR is used to accommodate those scenarios where the occurrence of an event may not represent a huge gain of information, but will definitively be surprising, and the reverse scenario as well.

3   Using the Selective Attention Mechanism in *CodeInsights*

Our main goal is to develop a tool capable of automatically collecting and analyzing data coming from the students in the form of code snapshots (a copy of their code) and provide the teachers information about how their students are performing.

The code snapshots are automatically sent to a central server each time the students run the developed code, regardless of where they are (at the classes, at home, etc.). When received, the snapshots are automatically processed, and various pieces of information about the students' performance is extracted and immediately made available to the teachers in the form of aggregated statistical data and data visualizations, as well as more individualized information about each student.

In Fig. 2 is shown a partial view of the main dashboard of *CodeInsights* from which the teacher has access to data and visualizations about a series of aspects related to the student's performance such as the more/less popular assignments, daily/hourly distribution of the attempts performed by the students, the most common compilation errors, the amount of attempts made during the classes period (and outside that period), and several other.

Fig. 2. Partial view of the main dashboard of *CodeInsights* which contains a series of data visualizations about the students' performance and behavior

Based on this information, the teacher could "manually" identify some deviations from the normal learning path and provide feedback or take the appropriate measure, via the most suitable means: verbally, directly in *CodeInsights,* via email, Moodle or any other existing platform. However, the teachers most likely don't have time to be constantly looking at the charts or browsing through the data and snapshots within *CodeInsights*. So, for this purpose, we have developed an automatic notification system, which will notify the teacher about a series of aspects concerning each student's performance such as unusual number of lines of code, compilation errors, attempts per assignment, assignments not even attempted, or a number of "unfinished" assignments. In reality, *CodeInsights* is capable of generating notifications about virtually any aspect that can be observed from the data.

Since there are plenty of situations where the system may automatically generate notifications to the teachers about different aspects of a student's performance, it is possible that the system may generate such an overload of information that the teacher may be unable to process it all in useful time. Because of this potential overload, we have decided to incorporate into our system the cognitive mechanism of selective attention previously presented.

Let's, for instance, assume that the teacher is interested in being notified when the percentage of students that have attempted to solve a given assignment is unusual. Additionally, let's consider that we have two assignments A1 and A2 with the probability distribution according to the teachers beliefs/expectations of student completions depicted in Tables 1 and 2.

Table 1. Example of teacher's beliefs for assignment A1

A1		
% of students		Probability
A	<= 20%	0.10
B	]21–79]%	0.75
C	>= 80%	0.15

Table 2. Example of teachers's beliefs for assignment A2

A2		
% of students		Probability
A	<= 20%	0.60
B	]21–79]%	0.25
C	>= 80%	0.15

Estimates for these probabilities can be calculated using aggregated data from previous editions of the courses, or simply using subjective probabilities defined by the teachers based on their personal experience.

Applying the Equation n°2 to the two examples presented above, we obtain for A1 an information gain of 0.665 and 0.853 for assignment A2.

As mentioned previously, the teachers can change the value for the γ threshold (see Sect. 2). High value for γ mean that the teacher is only interested in receiving notifications about situations that represent a high gain of information (i.e. that will contribute to decreasing the uncertainty). The exact opposite happens otherwise – a very low value for γ will mean that even if that event does not help to reduce the uncertainty, the teacher still wants to be informed about its occurrence. This latter scenario should be avoided, because it may result in receiving huge number of notifications.

Assuming that the system is initiated with 0.65 as the value for γ, for the particular scenarios described above, this would mean that any of the possible outcomes for the assignments A_1 and A_2 would be considered valuable. If the value for γ is defined to be 0.8, since only $IG(A_2) > 0.8$, only the occurrence of events related with the assignment A2 would be considered valuable.

Now, let's assume that after the deadline, the percentage of students that had tried to solve this assignment A_1 is 13% (A occurred), using the Equation n°3 we would have a surprise value of 0.72. If the percentage of students attempting A_1 was, for instance, 87% (occurrence of C), the value of the surprise would be 0.67.

An event is considered surprising if the value of surprise is higher than the threshold β previously mentioned (see Sect. 2). Assuming that the value for β is 0.65, the surprise value for the occurrence of these events is greater than β, so we can consider that these events are surprising enough that the teacher should be notified of their occurrence.

If, for the same assignment, the percentage of students that attempted to solve it was, for example, 55% (occurrence of B), the surprise value would be equal to zero - the occurrence of the most probable (expected) event generates no surprise at all.

As happens with the other thresholds, the value for β is defined by default to a certain value, but the teacher can increase or decrease this value at any time. Higher values of β indicate that only very unexpected events (with high surprise values) are considered interesting. If a lower value for β is used, the system will consider more events as being surprising enough. However, that could easily lead to the information overload situation that we are trying to avoid.

Finally, let's focus on the motive congruence component. In our particular scenario, let's suppose that the teacher has defined a certain desirability value, *D*, for each event as shown in Table 3.

Table 3. Example of a table of desirabilities

A1	
% of students	D
<= 20%	−0.85
]20–79]%	0.40
>= 80%	+0.75

These desirabilities indicate that the teacher would feel very satisfied if there is a large portion of students submitting this assignment A1, and very unsatisfied if there is a low percentage of students submitting this assignment, and would feel almost indifferent if the percentage of students submitting is moderate (21-79%).

Assuming the principle that people want to know about situations that are either consistent or inconsistent with their goals, this might also mean in this particular case of the teacher, that it doesn't make sense to notify her/him when the percentage of students that attempted solving A1 is between 21 and 79%. On the other side, it makes great sense to be notified about the fact that the number of attempts for this assignment exceeds 80% or is lower than 20%.

Assuming that the teacher has defined 0.1 as the value for α, in our scenario regardless of the event that occurs, s/he will always be notified, since *MC* is always greater than α. In this case, the teacher could well face a situation of the overflow of undesired notifications, because the value for the threshold is set to a very low value. If the value for α is much higher, 0.8 for instance, it means that the teacher only wants to be notified about the events that really (un)satisfy him/her. In this example, the teacher will only be notified when the percentage of students is lower than 20.

It is important to reinforce that these tables of desirabilities are defined by the teachers and can be considerably different for each assignment. For instance, there may be some assignments for which the teacher may want to be notified, even if the percentage of students that attempt to solve it is entirely "normal".

To conclude, let's have a look on how the system behaves in some of the scenarios presented previously. In Tables 4, 5 and 6 are shown some examples of how the system

Table 4. Using high values for all the thresholds

Assignment	Occurred	Prob.	IG	S	D	γ	β	α	
A1	a(<20 %)	0.10	0.665	0.72	0.85	0.85	0.85	0.85	NO
A1	b(<20 %)	0.75	0.665	0	0.40	0.85	0.85	0.85	NO
A1	c(>80 %)	0.15	0.665	0.67	0.75	0.85	0.85	0.85	NO

Table 5. Using low values for all the thresholds

Assignment	Occurred	Prob.	IG	S	D	γ	β	α	
A1	a(< 20 %)	0.10	0.665	0.72	0.85	0.35	0.35	0.35	OK
A1	b(<20 %)	0.75	0.665	0	0.40	0.35	0.35	0.35	OK
A1	c (>80 %)	0.15	0.665	0.67	0.75	0.35	0.35	0.35	OK

Table 6. Using moderate values for all the thresholds

Assignment	Occurred	Prob.	IG	S	D	γ	β	α	
A1	a(<20 %)	0.10	0.665	0.72	0.85	0.70	0.65	0.80	OK
A1	b(<20 %)	0.75	0.665	0	0.10	0.70	0.65	0.80	NO
A1	c(>80 %)	0.15	0.665	0.67	0.75	0.70	0.65	0.80	NO

would behave in different scenarios. The heighted values for IG, S and D correspond to values below the thresholds. In the last column, the "OK/NO" indicate whether or not a notification on the occurrence of that event should be generated.

As expected, the specific values used for the thresholds are essential for the success of this artificial selective attention mechanism. Because of that, special attention should be taken when defining those values.

Specifying the expectations about a certain event in *CodeInsights* is very easy, the teacher just needs to decide if s/he wants to define expectations about an event related to a particular assignment, a particular class or a global event. The teacher can also define expectations about the occurrence of a certain event concerning a particular student. In any case, the teacher must specify the date and time when the system will check if the expectations are met or not; the type of verification to be performed; and for each possible event, the expectations interval (inferior - superior), the probability of the occurrence of that event and finally, the value of the desirability - D.

For instance, let's suppose that the teacher wants to introduce into *CodeInsights* the expectations and desirabilities shown in Table 4. To accomplish this, the teacher just needs to fill a form similar to the one depicted in Fig. 3.

On the specified date and time, *CodeInsights* will automatically perform the necessary operations to check if the expectations about a certain event are met or not, and

inferior	superior	probability	D
0	20	0.10	0.85
21	79	0.75	0.40
80	100	0.15	0.75

Fig. 3. The form used to insert the expectations and desires chosen by the teacher

according to these expectations and desirabilities defined by the teacher, determine if a new notification should be generated or not. If so, the new notification is generated and presented immediately to the teacher if s/he is using *CodeInsights* at that moment. Otherwise, when the teacher logs in the system, a list of all the new notifications will be available, as shown in Fig. 4.

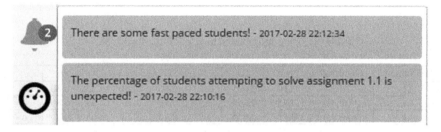

Fig. 4. Example of the notifications list

The teacher can then explore those notifications and take the remedial measures considered necessary to overcome the problems that some students may be facing.

4 Discussion and Conclusions

In this paper, we have presented *CodeInsights*, a monitoring tool capable of collecting data from students in the form of code snapshots and, with the information that results from processing these snapshots, notify the teachers about the situations where their intervention may be crucial.

To avoid exposing the teacher to an overload of notifications, we have decided to integrate into the system a cognitive artificial selective attention mechanism capable of presenting to the teachers only the most relevant notifications, according to the teacher's expectations/beliefs.

It is important to notice that the use of the proposed system *per se* will not have any direct impact on the students' performance. The system provides data, visualizations, and notifications to the teachers, but if they do not check the system regularly and, if based on the information provided, they do not take the most appropriate measures, then the impact of using the system will be null.

Due to academic schedule constraints, we have not yet been able to perform a full evaluation of *CodeInsights* with the cognitive artificial selective attention mechanism integrated. However, preliminary tests that we have performed so far have shown us that the system is, in fact, working as supposed. The system is selecting only the most relevant notifications to present to the teacher, according to the criteria defined by the principle of selective attention.

In the current version of the system, the teacher has to set the values for the expectations, desirabilities and thresholds manually. Although it can be done in a very easy way, we plan to develop a "baseline" student model based on data from previous editions of the course. This way, the teacher would only need to specify the expectations and desirabilities for new assignments or if s/he wants to overwrite certain values (since the students are not the same, some values may not make sense for the new group of students).

CodeInsights was planned to be used in the context of face-to-face classes. Nevertheless, it will also be of great (if not greater) importance in the context of distance learning, where in most cases there is a considerable geographical and even temporal distance between teachers and students.

References

1. Fessakis, G., Gouli, E., Mavroudi, E.: Problem solving by 5–6 years old kindergarten children in a computer programming environment: a case study. Comput. Educ. **63**, 87–97 (2013)
2. Gomes, A., Mendes, A.J.: Learning to program - difficulties and solutions. Presented at the International Conference on Engineering Education September (2007)
3. Bloom, B.S.: The 2 sigma problem: the search for methods of group instruction as effective as one-to-one tutoring. Educ. Res. **13**, 4–16 (1984)
4. Raabe, A., Silva, J.: Um Ambiente para Atendimento as Dificuldades de Aprendizagem de Algoritmos. Presented at the Anais do XXV Congresso da Sociedade Brasileira de Computação (2004)
5. Jafari, A.: Conceptualizing intelligent agents for teaching and learning. Educause Q. **25**, 28–34 (2002)
6. Yacef, K., University of Sydney. School of Information Technologies: Experiment and Evaluation Results of the Logic-ITA. School of Information Technologies, University of Sydney, Sydney (2003)
7. Choy, S.-O., Ng, S.-C., Tsang, Y.-C.: Building software agents to assist teaching in distance learning environments. In: Fifth IEEE International Conference on Advanced Learning Technologies (ICALT 2005), pp. 230–232 (2005)
8. Mathioudakis, G., Leonidis, A., Korozi, M., Stephanidis, C.: Real-time teacher assistance in technologically-augmented smart classrooms. Int. J. Adv. Life Sci. **6**, 62–73 (2014)
9. Mendes, A.J., Ivanov, V., Marcelino, M.J.: A web-based system to support Java programming learning. Presented at the CompSysTech 2005 - International Conference on Computer Systems and Technologies, June 2005
10. Murphy, C., Kaiser, G., Loveland, K., Hasan, S.: Retina: helping students and instructors based on observed programming activities. In: Proceedings of the 40th ACM Technical Symposium on Computer Science Education, pp. 178–182. ACM, New York (2009)

11. Vihavainen, A., Vikberg, T., Luukkainen, M., Pärtel, M.: Scaffolding students' learning using test my code. In: Proceedings of the 18th ACM Conference on Innovation and Technology in Computer Science Education, pp. 117–122. ACM, New York (2013)
12. Norris, C., Barry, F., Fenwick Jr., J.B., Reid, K., Rountree, J.: ClockIt: collecting quantitative data on how beginning software developers really work. In: Proceedings of the 13th Annual Conference on Innovation and Technology in Computer Science Education, pp. 37–41. ACM, New York (2008)
13. Kahneman, D.: Attention and Effort. Prentice-Hall, Upper Saddle River (1973)
14. Wright, R.D., Ward, L.M.: Orienting of Attention. Oxford University Press, Oxford (2008)
15. Feldman, H., Friston, K.: Attention, Uncertainty, and Free-Energy. Front. Hum. Neurosci. **4** (2010)
16. Macedo, L.: Arguments for a computational model for forms of selective attention based on cognitive and affective feelings. In: 2013 Humaine Association Conference on Affective Computing and Intelligent Interaction, pp. 103–108 (2013)
17. Horvitz, E., Jacobs, A., Hovel, D.: Attention-sensitive alerting. In: Proceedings of the Fifteenth Conference on Uncertainty in Artificial Intelligence, pp. 305–313. Morgan Kaufmann Publishers Inc., San Francisco (1999)
18. Horvitz, E., Barry, M.: Display of information for time-critical decision making. In: Proceedings of the Eleventh Conference on Uncertainty in Artificial Intelligence, pp. 296–305. Morgan Kaufmann Publishers Inc., San Francisco (1995)
19. MacKay, D.J.C.: Information-based objective functions for active data selection. Neural Comput. **4**, 590–604 (1992)
20. Lindley, D.V.: On a measure of the information provided by an experiment. Ann. Math. Stat. **27**, 986–1005 (1956)
21. Settles, B.: Curious Machines: Active Learning with Structured Instances (2008)
22. Fonseca, N.G., Macedo, L., Mendes, A.J.: CodeInsights: monitoring programming students' progress. In: Proceedings of the 17th International Conference on Computer Systems and Technologies 2016, pp. 375–382. ACM, New York (2016)

Image Matching Algorithm Based on Hashes Extraction

Alberto Rivas[1], Pablo Chamoso[1], Javier J. Martín-Limorti[1],
Sara Rodríguez[1(✉)], Fernando de la Prieta[1], and Javier Bajo[2]

[1] BISITE Research Group, Edificio I+D+i, University of Salamanca,
Calle Espejo 2, 37007 Salamanca, Spain
{rivis,chamoso,limorti,srg,fer}@usal.es
[2] Departamento de Inteligencia Artificial, Universidad Politécnica de Madrid,
Campus Montegancedo, 28660 Boadilla del Monte, Madrid, Spain
jbajo@fi.upm.es

Abstract. Nowadays, the rise of social networks and the continuous storage of large of information are topical issue. But the main problem is not the storage itself, is the ability to process most of this information, so that it is not stored in vain. In this way, using the shared images within the scope of social networks, possible relationships between users could be identified. From this idea arises the present work, which focuses on identifying similar images even if they have been modified (applying color filters, rotations or even watermarks). The solution involves preprocessing to eliminate possible filters and then apply hashing techniques, just to obtain hashes that are unique for each image and allow the comparison of an abstract but effective way for the user.

Keywords: Image matching · Visual analysis · Social networks

1 Introduction

This article is focused on the analysis of images published in social networks. It has been developed to be integrated in a social network focused on work environments and job searches. The intention of this social network is to connect users with the same interests based on the contents they share. These contents can be published in different ways, for example images (which may or may not be accompanied by a descriptive text, so that text will not be taken into account).

Therefore, the problem that this article faces is the identification of images which are the same from a human point of view, but not from a computational point of view for one or more reasons: (a) the quality has been reduced or the image format has been changed; (b) a watermark has been included; (c) some changes in tonality have been applied; (d) a border has been added or removed; (e) the image has been rotated.

The solution presented in this article tries to solve this problem with an algorithm based on obtaining hashes from the images, so that the system is able

© Springer International Publishing AG 2017
E. Oliveira et al. (Eds.): EPIA 2017, LNAI 10423, pp. 87–94, 2017.
DOI: 10.1007/978-3-319-65340-2_8

to quickly compare the existing images and the new image at the moment it is sent by the user.

The rest of the article describes existing methodologies used in image matching and the mechanisms involved in processing large amounts of information in real time. Next, the proposed algorithm for image processing and matching is described, as well as the platform that supports real-time processing. This system is evaluated in the results section with a set of images. Finally, the article present the conclusions drawn and the lines of future work.

2   Background

As stated, the main focus of this article is to identify images that are the same from a human point of view but differ computationally, in order to put people who publish similar images in contact, as they may share common interests.

When identifying whether two images are the same, it is necessary to perform a series of checks because two apparently identical images may be computationally different due to problems of compression, different quality of the image, number of colors, size, slight modification of the image with filters or watermarks, changes in the tonality, insertion of borders, or rotations.

In the computer vision and the image processing fields, different methodologies have been presented to extract relevant information with an image as input. These techniques are catalogued under the concept of feature detection.

There are different types of image features including edges, corners or interest points, and blobs or region of interest. In this regard, there are multiple algorithms used to process images in search of features, the most common of which are:

- **Edges**: Canny, Sobel, Harris & Stephens, SUSAN [12].
- **Corners**: Harris & Stephens, SUSAN, Shi & Tomasi, Level curve curvature, FAST, Laplacian of Gaussian, Difference of Gaussians, Determinant of Hessian.
- **Blobs**: FAST, Laplacian of Gaussian, Difference of Gaussians, Determinant of Hessian, Maximally stable extremal regions (MSER) [8], Principal curvature-based region detector (PCBR) [3], Gray-level blobs and others algorithms [2,5].

The concept of perceptual hashing is similar to that of the classical paradigm of cryptographic hashes, where the tiniest changes quickly evolve into an entirely different hash. In perceptual hashing the image content is used to try to fingerprint the image, so that even if hashes are not identical they can be used to determine how "close" the images are to one and other.

Another important concept that has been applied when comparing different images is the Hamming distance [9]. It can be used on most of the resulting hashes to determine the perceived difference between two images, so that a perceptually similar image would have a short hamming distance, 0, for the same image. A quick definition for hamming distance, $d(x, y)$, is the number of ways in which x and y differ. In other words, the hamming distance is simply the number of positions in which they are different.

There are different proposed algorithms based on the hash value generation technique: pHash (also called "Perceptive Hash", with different variations) [6], aHash (also called Average Hash or Mean Hash) and dHash Also called Difference Hash) [7]. The typical hash-based algorithms flow diagram is shown in Fig. 1.

Fig. 1. Typical hash-based algorithms flow diagram.

However, all variations of this methodology present different problems when dealing with an image to which a border has been added, or one which has been rotated.

For the latter problem, a modification of these steps is proposed in [1,4] by introducing a rotational system whereby it is possible to differentiate images rotated 22.5°; however, this implies a loss of precision in the corners when the original images are rectangular or square, the most common situations with images uploaded to social networks, so its solution is not applicable to the present problem.

There are online platforms dedicated to the search of images that exist on the Internet and are similar to those provided by a user, without taking into account the meta-data or associated text. Their applicability is oriented to the search of image plagiarism. This is the case of TinEye [13], whose algorithm is not public, but is based on the analysis of hashes.

3   Proposed System

The proposed methodology is based on the application of techniques of image matching based on hash value generation, with certain transformations and pre-processing that are able to discriminate the possible transformations that a social network user may have applied to the image prior to uploading it.

One of the main characteristics of the proposed system, which makes it possible to improve the result of similar systems, is the preprocessing stage. This stage is focused on applying a series of transformations to the images that are received as input by the user. This is followed by a scheme similar to hash-based algorithms.

3.1   Preprocessing

The strategy followed in this first stage ensures that images which have been slightly transformed are stored in the system in the same way. This allows the system to start comparing the same or most similar image.

The present study considered the following possible transformations that a user could perform on an image, after which the image would still be considered the same: (i) insertion of an outer uniform border; (ii) rotation of the image; and (iii) insertion of a watermark. It should be noted that all hash-based algorithms are really robust if a uniform change is applied to the tonality. Therefore, such modifications were not considered for the comparison.

When a watermark is inserted, a hash-based algorithm application can be sufficient to determine if it is the same image or not despite the modification. Therefore, in this first stage of preprocessing, the proposed system focuses only on any modifications based on the insertion of an outer uniform border, and the rotation of the image.

– **Solid border addition:** The proposed system applies the Algorithm 1, allowing the following steps of the methodology to be performed without considering the uniform outer border. The first step is to transform the original image provided by the social network user I to a grayscale image gI, which will also be used in the following steps.

Algorithm 1. Solid border removal algorithm

1: **function** BORDERREMOVAL(I)
2:     gI = grayscale(I)
3:     **if** hasBorder(gI) **then**   ▷ Check border
4:         $value$ = getBorderTonality(gI)   ▷ Get border tonality value
5:         bI = toBinary(gI, $value$)   ▷ Border tonality as threshold
6:         cnt = findContour(bI)   ▷ Get contour
7:         ⟨ x,y,width,height ⟩ = boundingRect(cnt)   ▷ Find bounding rectangle
8:         gI = $gI[x : x + width, y : y + height]$ ▷ Crop grayscale image
9:     **end if**
10:     **return** gI
11: **end function**

– **Image rotation:** The most common rotations that a user applies to an image are based on 90° modifications. This part of the preprocessing is centered on precisely this type of rotation. The objective is for the images to follow a rotation pattern so that they always have the same orientation in the system. Different solutions are possible, depending on whether the shape of the image is rectangular or square.

If the image is rectangular, the system will always work with the image in landscape mode (the two longest sides are in the x-axis) The system must then determine which side is placed on the top and which is placed on the bottom. If the image is square, the previous logic cannot be applied, since the four sides are the same length. In both cases, the key of the final orientation will be the tonality of the image, as described by the Algorithm 2. Although this step appears in the preprocessing section, it is applied in an intermediate step of the Algorithm 3, which will be detailed below, to avoid possible changes in the tonality resulting from the insertion of a watermark.

Algorithm 2. Image rotation algorithm

```
 1: function IMAGEROTATION(gI,sI)
 2:     width = getWidth(gI)
 3:     height = getHeight(gI)
 4:     if width == height then                              ▷ Square image
 5:         nsI = sI[0 : width, 0 : height/2]                ▷ Get North middle
 6:         ssI = sI[0 : width, height/2 : height]           ▷ Get South middle
 7:         wsI = sI[0 : width/2, 0 : height]                ▷ Get West middle
 8:         esI = sI[width/2 : width, height/2 : height]     ▷ Get East middle
 9:         highestMean = getHighestValue(nsI, ssI, wsI, esI)
10:         if highestMean == nsI then                       ▷ Highest tonality on top
11:             rI = rotate(sI,180)
12:         else if highestMean == wgI then
13:             rI = rotate(sI,270)
14:         else if highestMean == egI then
15:             rI = rotate(sI,90)
16:         else
17:             rI = sI
18:         end if
19:     else                                                 ▷ Rectangular image
20:         if width < height then
21:             gI = rotate(sI,90)      ▷ Longest image side over x-axis (landscape)
22:         end if
23:         nsI = sI[0 : width, 0 : height/2]                ▷ Get North middle
24:         ssI = sI[0 : width, height/2 : height]           ▷ Get South middle
25:         if ngI < sgI then                                ▷ Highest tonality on top
26:             rI = rotate(sI,180)
27:         else
28:             rI = sI
29:         end if
30:     end if
31:     return rI
32: end function
```

3.2 Hash-Based Transformations

Hash-based algorithms are the most suited for the problem of image matching because they are very fast. The pHash algorithm extends the aHash approach by using discrete cosine transform (DCT) [11] to reduce the frequencies. We have followed a similar schema; we defined the Algorithm as 3 and used it to obtain the hash associated with the image I, which is provided by a user of a social network. The input of this algorithm is the grayscale image gI, obtained in the preprocessing step.

Top-left 12×12 values are obtained because they represent the lowest frequency range. In contrast, the bottom right is the highest frequency range. The human eye is not very sensitive to high frequencies.

Algorithm 3. pHash-based algorithm

1: **function** GETIMAGEHASH(gI)
2:     sI = reduceSize(gI, 32, 32)   ▷ Reduce size to 32x32 pixels
3:     rI = imageRotation(gI,sI)   ▷ Rotate as defined in Algorithm 2
4:     DCT = computeDCT(rI, 32, 32)   ▷ Get a collection of frequencies and scalars
5:     $sDCT$ = reduceDCT(DCT, 12, 12)   ▷ Get the lowest freq. (top-left 12x12)
6:     **for each** $px \in sDCT$ **do**
7:         **if** $px > \overline{sDCT}$ **then**   ▷ Compare every pixel with sDCT mean
8:             $hash = hash + 1$
9:         **else**
10:            $hash = hash + 0$
11:        **end if**
12:    **end for**
13:    **return** $hash$
14: **end function**

As a result, we have the value of the hash composed of 144 values (12×12) 1 or 0 in order to evaluate the distance by using the Hamming distance algorithm, which simply compares each bit position and counts the number of differences.

4   Results

To perform the tests of the proposed system, a set of 200,000 images available in the public repository of Pixbay [10] was used as image dataset.

Figure 2 presents an example of the processing of two images obtained from the original. On the left side, there is an image with a yellowish hue, rotated 90°, with an outer border, and a watermark in the lower left corner. On the right, the processing of an image obtained directly from the original is shown. The result in both cases is a 144-digit value composed of 1 and 0, as detailed in the Algorithm 3. After calculating the Hamming distance, the system determines that both images are 99.3% equal.

To evaluate the performance of the algorithm, it was compared with the different implementations of hash-based algorithms. 1,000 images were obtained from the total set of the images to which different transformations were applied. The success rate was evaluated by considering the result a success for those cases in which the system associates the modified image with the original image of the dataset as the most similar, having a similarity value greater than 99%. The applied transformations and the images used are shown in Table 1.

All of these images were provided as input using the implementations of the pHash, aHas, and dHash algorithms, the proposed algorithm. Regarding to Tineye, whose algorithm is not public (although it has been published that it is based on hash), images have been processed by using its public API [13].

Following these indications, the results obtained are reflected in Table 2, where all images that have been catalogued as equal, and indeed were, are considered a success.

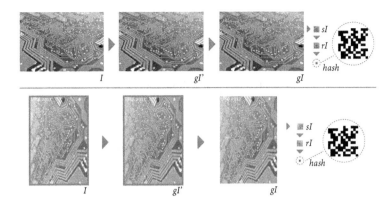

Fig. 2. Example of the system process. (Color figure online)

Table 1. Test dataset

	n	b	w	r	b + w	b + r	w + r	b + w + r	Total
Images	**125**	125	125	125	125	125	125	125	1000

Legend: n = none; b = border; w = watermark; r = rotation

Table 2. Hit rate for hash based algorithms

	n	b	w	r	b + w	b + r	w + r	b + w + r	Avg
pHash	**100%**	0%	75%	0%	0%	0%	0%	0%	22%
aHash	**100%**	0%	74%	0%	0%	0%	0%	0%	21%
dHash	**100%**	0%	75%	0%	0%	0%	0%	0%	22%
Tineye	**100%**	0%	**80%**	0%	0%	0%	0%	0%	22%
Proposed	**100%**	**90%**	75%	**100%**	**74%**	**90%**	**74%**	**74%**	**84%**

Legend: n = none; b = border; w = watermark; r = rotation; avg = average

It can be observed that the proposed system shows a better result in all transformations except when a watermark is included. In that case, Tineye and pHash show a higher success rate. In the case of Tineye, the details of its algorithm are not known. With respect to pHash, the improvement in the success rate is mainly due to the number of frequencies obtained when the DST is reduced (8×8), lower than for the proposed system (12×12).

5 Conclusion and Future Work

The proposed system improves current state of the art of image matching, by including images which have been slightly modified by the inclusion of a watermark, outer borders, or rotations of 90°, 180°, and 270°.

The results are robust in terms of the insertion of edges and rotations. However, with the insertion of watermarks which have considerably altered the image, none of the algorithms was able to associate the images with precision. In fact, in order not to introduce false positives (identify images as equal images when they are in fact not), it is necessary to compromise the detail with which one wants to perform the analysis.

As a future line of work, this solution will be incorporated into an existing job search social network in order to suggest contacts to users who have published or shared equal images. Regarding the image matching system, different solutions capable of associating images whose proportions have been modified by the user, either by trimming and removing part of the exterior of the image or by having deformed the image, are being evaluated. This evolution could make it possible to check rotations in each of the possible 360°.

Acknowledgments. This work was carried out under the frame of the project with ID RTC-2016-5642-6. The research of Pablo Chamoso has been financed by the Regional Ministry of Education in Castilla y León and the European Social Fund.

References

1. Aghav, S., Kumar, A., Gadakar, G., Mehta, A., Mhaisane, A.: Mitigation of rotational constraints in image based plagiarism detection using perceptual hash. Int. J. Comput. Sci. Trends Technol. **2**, 28–32 (2014)
2. De Paz, J.F., Rodríguez, S., Bajo, J., Corchado, J.M.: Mathematical model for dynamic case-based planning. Int. J. Comput. Math. **86**(10–11), 1719–1730 (2009)
3. Deng, H., Zhang, W., Mortensen, E., Dietterich, T., Shapiro, L.: Principal curvature-based region detector for object recognition. In: 2007 IEEE Conference on Computer Vision and Pattern Recognition, pp. 1–8. IEEE, June 2007
4. Hernandez, R.A.P., Miyatake, M.N., Kurkoski, B.M.: Robust image hashing using image normalization and SVD decomposition. In: 2011 IEEE 54th International Midwest Symposium on Circuits and Systems (MWSCAS), pp. 1–4. IEEE, August 2011
5. Kamaruddin, S., Ghanib, N., Liong, C., Jemain, A.: Firearm classification using neural networks on ring of firing pin impression images. ADCAIJ: Adv. Distrib. Comput. Artif. Intell. J. **1**(3), 27–34 (2013). doi:10.14201/ADCAIJ20121312734
6. Krawetz, N.: Looks Like It (2011). http://www.hackerfactor.com/blog/index.php?/archives/432-Looks-LikeIt.html. Accessed 12 Jan 2017
7. Krawetz, N.: Kind of Like That (2013). http://www.hackerfactor.com/blog/?/archives/529-Kind-of-Like-That.html. Accessed 12 Jan 2017
8. Matas, J., Chum, O., Urban, M., Pajdla, T.: Robust wide-baseline stereo from maximally stable extremal regions. Image Vis. Comput. **22**(10), 761–767 (2004)
9. Norouzi, M., Fleet, D.J., Salakhutdinov, R.R.: Hamming distance metric learning. In: Advances in Neural Information Processing Systems, pp. 1061–1069 (2012)
10. Pixabay.com. Free Images - Pixabay (2017). https://pixabay.com/. Accessed 17 Jan 2017
11. Rao, K.R., Yip, P.: Discrete Cosine Transform: Algorithms, Advantages, Applications. Academic Press, San Diego (2014)
12. Smith, S.M., Brady, J.M.: SUSAN—a new approach to low level image processing. Int. J. Comput. Vis. **23**(1), 45–78 (1997)
13. Tineye.com. TinEye Reverse Image Search (2017). https://www.tineye.com/. Accessed 12 Jan 2017

Unsupervised Stress Detection Algorithm and Experiments with Real Life Data

Elena Vildjiounaite[1]([⊠]), Johanna Kallio[1], Jani Mäntyjärvi[1],
Vesa Kyllönen[1], Mikko Lindholm[1], and Georgy Gimel'farb[2]

[1] VTT Technical Research Centre of Finland, 02044 VTT Espoo, Finland
{elena.vildjiounaite,johanna.kallio,jani.mantyjarvi,
vesa.kyllonen,mikko.lindholm}@vtt.fi
[2] University of Auckland, Private Bag 92019, Auckland 1149, New Zealand
g.gimelfarb@auckland.ac.nz

Abstract. Stress is the major problem in the modern society and a reason for at least half of lost working days in European enterprises, but existing stress detectors are not sufficiently convenient for everyday use. One reason is that stress perception and stress manifestation vary a lot between individuals; hence, "one-fits-all-persons" stress detectors usually achieve notably lower accuracies than person-specific methods. The majority of existing approaches to person-specific stress recognition, however, employ fully supervised training, requiring to collect fairly large sets of labelled data from each end user. These sets should contain examples of stresses and normal conditions, and such data collection effort may be tiring for end users. Therefore this work proposes an algorithm to train person-specific stress detectors using only unlabelled data, not necessarily containing examples of stresses. The proposed method, based on Hidden Markov Models with maximum posterior marginal decision rule, was tested using real life data of 28 persons and achieved average stress detection accuracy of 75%, which is similar to the accuracies of state-of-the-art supervised algorithms for real life data.

Keywords: Stress detection · Unsupervised learning · Hidden Markov Models

1 Introduction

Stress is a state of mental tension and worry caused by problems in life, work, etc.; something that causes strong feelings of worry or anxiety [1]. As stress is one of the major problems in modern society [2], intelligent environments should be able to recognise human stresses. According to a recent review [3], however, the majority of studies into stress detection by environmental sensors were performed in a lab and hence are not yet ready for real life conditions, that is, when subjects do not face video, depth or hyperspectral cameras or do not sit in pressure-sensitive chairs. Studies with environmental audio sensors [4] and keyboard/mouse dynamics [5, 6] use real life data, but these modalities do not work when the subjects stay silent or do not use computers.

Wearable sensors allow to monitor humans in greater range of situations than environmental sensors, tested to date, but again, not all wearable sensors suit to real life

© Springer International Publishing AG 2017
E. Oliveira et al. (Eds.): EPIA 2017, LNAI 10423, pp. 95–107, 2017.
DOI: 10.1007/978-3-319-65340-2_9

use. Most of physiological monitoring devices provoke too much discomfort [3] for everyday use, and their improper attachment may cause notable data losses [7]. To date, only wrist bracelets and mobile phones were found sufficiently convenient in real life use [8, 9], but system convenience depends also on algorithm choice. Unfortunately, existing stress detectors typically employ fully supervised algorithms, such as SVM (Support Vector Machines) [2, 4, 9–11] and decision trees [12, 13]. Training of these methods requires fairly large sets of labelled data, and stress labels (i.e., information about stress times and (possibly) severity levels) are usually obtained by asking test subjects to provide self-reports upon periodical system prompts. The reason why it is beneficial to obtain stress labels from each end user is strong person-dependency of stress perception and stress manifestation (stress influence on physiological parameters and behaviour). Hence stress detection models, which training utilised labelled data of the target individual, usually achieve significantly higher accuracies than any other models. Such results were reported by both lab tests [11, 14] and field studies [4, 10, 12], and in the latter training person-specific models on the data of each subject increased stress recognition accuracy by 20% on average compare with general models. This accuracy gain, however, was achieved at the cost of notable data labelling efforts: training data in [10, 12] contained about 100 labelled instances per person; dataset in [4] - even more. Although dataset size of 100 samples is not large for machine learning methods, it seems to be too large for humans: in [8] not every subject provided even 100 labels, and on average the test subjects answered only 28% of system prompts to provide self-reports.

Therefore several alternatives to fully supervised training were proposed to date. One of them is to train a general model using data of many subjects and to adapt it to each target person in a certain way, e.g., by using person-specific input features (such as deviations of sensor values from the average values of the target individual in neutral state [11]) or by modifying class priors according to individual tendency to report more or less stressful events [4]. Another alternative is to exploit similarity between human beings, e.g., by clustering test subjects and training a separate model for each cluster. Then the target individual is assigned to one of these clusters using either his/her labelled [12] or unlabelled [4, 11, 14] data, and the corresponding model is used for detecting his/her stresses. Other proposed methods include combining outputs of models of similar subjects and training a model using a mixture of the target person data with data of similar individuals [13]. Success of similarity-based methods, however, was found to depend on the chosen numbers of similar persons. Another similarity-based reasoning method is k Nearest Neighbours classifier, but this approach was tested only in a limited range of real-life settings: users working on their computers [6]. In addition, although the above-listed approaches reduce the need in labelled data of each target individual, they nevertheless require collecting labelled data of many persons. To the best of our knowledge, only the work [15] proposed an unsupervised stress detection method: to recognise stresses by calculating so-called "additional heart rate" (a deviation between current and recent physiological data) and comparing it with dynamically calculated threshold, taking into account current physical activity. This method required two additional sensors, however: accelerometers on the chest and the right thigh, which is not a realistic setup for long-term real life application.

This work proposes stress detection system for a fairly broad range of real life settings, convenient both sensor-wise and algorithm-wise: it uses mobile phones and wrist bracelets and requires no data labelling. As unsupervised learning typically results in lower accuracies than supervised one, this work aims at recognising only the most dangerous stresses: high level stresses. The main contribution of this work is the following: first, we propose a novel unsupervised method to recognise stress-related data patterns. Then, using real life data, we demonstrate that for training of this method fairly small datasets (two days) suffice and that these datasets should not necessarily contain examples of stresses. In addition, we discuss how the stress recognition results correlate with personality traits of the test subjects.

2   Unsupervised Stress Detection Algorithm

We assume that high stresses occur in human lives less frequently than normal conditions; hence, we detect high stresses by learning a model of normal human condition and evaluating current deviations from this model. As normal behavioural and physiological data may notably vary between different individuals, we learn normal models for each person separately. Although stress may be caused by a short event and may reflect itself in physiological data as a short-term deviation, realising what happened and coping with stress takes some time. Furthermore, due to great varieties of short-term human behaviours, it is difficult to reliably distinguish between normal and unusual data patterns in a short term. Thus we detect stresses by evaluating data sequences within time windows of certain duration, and we employ overlapping time windows instead of consecutive ones to obtain stress detection results as frequently as desirable.

We suggest to classify each time window into two classes, "normal" vs. "unusual", at least when training datasets are small. After the system collects sufficient amount of training data, it may switch to finer classification. For unsupervised classification we propose to employ HMM (Hidden Markov Model) with two hidden states ("normal" and "unusual") and discrete observations because training of such models does not require large datasets. We propose to train HMM in fully unsupervised way, namely:

- use no pre-defined thresholds for classifying data samples;
- use no labels in training, i.e., use all collected data samples in exactly same way.

2.1   Unsupervised Hidden Markov Model Training

First, we use all training data to create a reference model, i.e., a vector of reference samples of physiological, acceleration and mobile phone usage data features. As we don't use any labels in training, we don't know which data samples denote normal condition and which ones denote stress; hence, we calculate feature-wise average over all samples according to formula (1), where $V_{M;i}$ is a reference sample of feature i, $V_{T;i}$ is a data sample of this feature at time T, and m is total number of training data samples.

$$V_{M:i} = \frac{1}{m} \sum_{T=1}^{m} V_{T:i} \qquad (1)$$

Then for each data sample we calculate its deviation from the reference model. A deviation D of the time moment T with n features from the reference model M is:

$$D = \frac{1}{n} \sum_{i=1}^{n} (V_{T:i} - V_{M:i}) \qquad (2)$$

This deviation could be straightforwardly used as degree of normality of the current time moment, but in our tests it did not work well. Instead, we discretise this deviation by dividing an interval $[-1, 1]$ into K appropriate sub-intervals and use the sub-interval's number as an observation in the HMM. The experiments below employed the following $K = 6$ sub-intervals: $[-1.0, -0.6]$; $[-0.6, -0.3]$; $[-0.3, 0]$; $[0, 0.3]$; $[0.3, 0.6]$; $[0.6, 1.0]$. A sequence of the discretised deviations of data samples inside selected time window from the reference model is a sequence of the HMM observations for this time window.

The HMM of a time window has finite sets of states $S = \{1, \ldots, N\}$ (output classes, i.e., "normal" and "unusual") and observations $X = \{1, \ldots, K\}$. An example configuration of the proposed HMM is illustrated in Fig. 1.

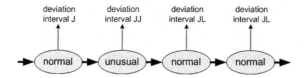

Fig. 1. HMM model of a time window

Let $S_T = \{s_t : t = 1, \ldots, T\}$ be a sequence of the hidden states and $X_T = \{x_t : t = 1, \ldots, T\}$ be a corresponding sequence of obtained observations at T time moments. The HMM assumes that every observation x_t at time t depends, in a probabilistic sense, only on a hidden state s_t and the latter (excluding s_1) depends in turn only on the previous state s_{t-1}. Let $\alpha = [\alpha(s|v) : s, v \in S]$; $\beta = [\beta(x|s) : x \in X, s \in S]$, and $\pi = [\pi(s) : s \in S]$ denote conditional probabilities of transitions between the discrete states; conditional probabilities of observations, given the state, and unconditional probabilities of the initial state, respectively. Then the HMM is characterised by the joint probability of the sequences of evolving states and observations [17]:

$$p(S_T, X_T) = \pi(s_1)\beta(s_1|x_1) \prod_{t=2}^{T} \alpha(s_t|s_{t-1}) \beta(x_t|s_t) \qquad (3)$$

Given a sequence of unlabelled observations X_T, HMM is trained, i.e., its parameters (α, β, π) are learned in a fully unsupervised mode by applying Baum-Welch forward-backward algorithm [16]. In other words, mapping of deviations from a normal model into output classes is learned from the training data and does not require defining any thresholds. This method can be used for training HMM on data of each target individual separately (so-called "***personal model***") as well as on data of all individuals ("**general model**") or of similar individuals ("**similarity-based model**"). Reference models can be built using data of each individual in all cases because stress labels are not required.

2.2   Inference with Hidden Markov Models

To classify the current time window as "normal" or "unusual", a sequence of observations within this window (i.e., a sequence of discretised deviations of data samples from the reference model) is created first. Then a sequence of the hidden states can be obtained by the Bayesian maximum *a posteriori* (MAP) decision rule using the well-known Viterbi dynamic programming algorithm [16]. The MAP rule minimising the error probability assumes that the cost of errors for a given sequence of observations is just the same, irrespectively of their number (i.e., a single erroneous state or all T such errors are equally bad). An alternative way is to account for all the individual errors and minimise their expected number. In this case the hidden states are to be recovered with the Bayesian MPM (maximum posterior marginal) rule that selects for each time moment the hidden state with the maximum posterior marginal probability. The posterior marginals $\{p_t(s|X_T) : s \in \mathbf{S}; t = 1, \ldots, T\}$ are calculated for each hidden state s of time t by the forward and backward message propagation [16]:

$$p_t(s|X_T) = \frac{\mu_t(s|x_1, \ldots, x_t)m_t(s|x_T, \ldots, x_t)}{\sum_{v \in \mathbf{S}} \mu_t(v|x_1, \ldots, x_t)m_t(v|x_T, \ldots, x_t)} \tag{4}$$

where $\mu_t(s|x_1, \ldots, x_t)$ and $m_t(s|x_T, \ldots, x_t)$ denote the forward and backward message, respectively, for the state s at each instant t. These messages are computed successively from the beginning and the end of the observed sequence X_T : $\mu_1(s, x_1) = \pi(s)\beta(x_1|s)$;

$$\mu(s; x_1, \ldots x_t) = \sum_{v=1}^{N} \mu_{t-1}(v; x_1, \ldots x_{t=1}) \, \alpha(s|v) \, \beta(x_t|s)$$

$$\text{and } m_T(s|x_T) = 1; m_t(s|x_T, \ldots, x_t) = \sum_{v=1}^{N} m_{t+1}(v|x_T, \ldots, x_{t+1})\alpha(v|s)\beta(x_{t+1}) \tag{5}$$

Both the conventional MAP and less conventional MPM decisions produce a recovered sequence of hidden states classifying each time moment, for example, "normal, unusual, normal, normal, ...". Due to the HMM based reasoning, the classification of each time moment depends on all the observations and hidden states.

A stress score of the whole window can be then calculated as a conventional likelihood of generating a given sequence of observations by the learned HMM (the lower the likelihood, the less normal the sequence), but this estimation takes into account the order of recovered states. In our experience, learning to recognise truly unusual order of states requires fairly large training datasets. As we had fairly small datasets per subject in this study, we calculated a stress score of each window in a different way, by assigning numerical scores A_S to the recovered hidden states:

$$A_S = \begin{cases} 1, & \text{if state } s \text{ is classified as normal} \\ -1, & \text{if state } s \text{ is classified as unusual} \end{cases} \tag{6}$$

and using an average quantified state as a window stress score:

$$A = \frac{1}{T}\sum_{S=1}^{T} A_S \tag{7}$$

For example, the stress score of a sequence "normal, unusual, normal, normal" is $A = \frac{1-1+1+1}{4} = 0.75$, indicating a normal time window.

In the proposed method all HMM model parameters are learned from the data, just time window length has to be specified. Choice of window length should depend on human behaviour patterns and number of data samples in a window. Short time windows are likely to result in high false stress detection rate because of diversity of short-term human behaviours. HMM does not work well with short sequences of observations either. The proposed HMM inference may additionally benefit from longer sequences: due to crisp digitalisation of deviations between data samples and reference models, HMM observations are sensitive to small changes in sensor values lying on the boundaries between K sub-intervals. This problem is softened by the probabilistic nature of HMM inference and dependency of each hidden state classification on the neighbouring states (HMM may assign exactly same observation to "normal" or "unusual" state depending on its estimations of other states), but this "smoothing" effect is more notable in longer time windows. On the other hand, long time windows are more likely to include a mixture of "stressed" and "normal" (e.g., "not yet stressed") human conditions.

For time window classification it is needed to specify also decision threshold TS: if window score A falls below TS, it denotes stress; otherwise human condition is normal. For classifying each day into "stress" and "normal" classes we also need to specify, how many windows in a day should be classified as "stress" to classify the whole day as stressful. The experiments below compared several lengths of time windows and decision thresholds for the following two inference schemes:

(a) *HMM-Viterbi*: sequence of hidden states is obtained via the MAP decision rule by the Viterbi algorithm and the window score is calculated using Eqs. (6) and (7).
(b) *HMM-MPM*: Each sequence of hidden states is obtained via the MPM decision rule and the window score is formed in accord with Eqs. (6) and (7).

3   Experiments with Field Data

3.1   Data Collection

In this study we used data, collected by the Institute of Behavioural Sciences at the University of Helsinki (Finland). Participants were recruited from the university; they had to satisfy the following criteria: good health, non-smoking, interest in technology, willingness to use mobile applications and possession of an Android smart phone. The subjects were monitored during normal course of their lives during four days, although monitoring of a few subjects lasted for three or five days. Before data collection the subjects answered a questionnaire to identify their Big Five personality traits.

Physiological data were collected once per minute by wrist-worn Basis device [17] that included an optical heart rate sensor and 3-axis accelerometer. Mobile phone data included two parts: (1) an Android service collecting digital behaviour data and (2) self-reporting. Digital behaviour data consisted of logs of usage of six different application types: social (Skype, social networks etc.), entertainment (games, music etc.), infotainment (news, books etc.), business (calendar, editing etc.), wellbeing (weight watching, exercise monitoring etc.) and any other interaction with a phone. These logs only contained information whether a user interacted with an application of certain type or not during each minute; contents of the web pages or keystrokes were not logged.

Self-reporting was prompted by Android notification every 45 min during daytime from 9 am to 9 pm. The subjects had to answer whether stress had occurred during the current reporting period and if so, evaluate it on 7-level Likert scale. The subjects also provided free-from comments on their activities. 28 subjects answered questionnaires fairly regularly. These persons aged from 20 to 47 years old (mean 25.5 years, standard deviation 6); among them were 4 males and 24 females. High stress levels (6–7 on Likert scale) were reported on 12% of days, by the female subjects only.

3.2   Experimental Protocol

In the tests we first evaluated accuracy of classifying each self-reporting period as "stress" (i.e., high stress) vs. "normal" (other conditions). Although Android phone prompted the test subjects to provide self-reports every 45 min, in practice intervals between reports were not so regular because the subjects did not always answer immediately. Thus it was not possible to use HMM time window of 45 min in the evaluation and to compare HMM results with the self-reports directly. Instead, we compared several HMM window sizes in the following protocol: first, HMM labelled each time window as either "stress" or "normal". These HMM results were stored along with the window timestamps. Then for each time interval between self-reports we retrieved HMM results for time windows falling inside this interval.

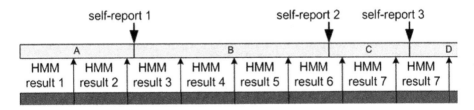

Fig. 2. Evaluation of time intervals between self-reports

If a self-report stated that high stress has occurred and at least one HMM result within this interval was "stress", we considered this interval as real stress, otherwise - as missed stress. Similarly, if self-report stated that high stress has not occurred, we considered this interval as "true normal" if HMM had not labelled any window within this interval as "stress"; otherwise we considered this interval as false stress. For example, in Fig. 2 time interval A includes HMM results 1 and 2. If one of these results is "stress", it means that HMM evaluated interval A as "stress", and this result is compared with the self-report 1. Then we calculated the following criteria:

- stress detection rate, i.e., a ratio between correctly classified "high stress" intervals and the total number of "high stress" intervals;
- non-stress detection rate, i.e., a ratio between correctly classified intervals, not labelled as "high stress", and the total number of these intervals.

These criteria were used to compare the following stress modelling approaches:

- *Personal*: model of each target subject was trained using data of this person only; we used first half of his/her data for training and another half for testing, then swapped training and test sets and averaged the results over these runs;
- *Similarity-based*: first the subjects were clustered via k-means clustering; then for each target subject a model was trained using all data of other subjects in the same cluster and tested on all data of the target subject;
- *General*: for each target person, a model was trained on all data of all other subjects and tested on all his/her data (i.e., leave-one-person-out protocol).

In addition, as timing of self-reports may be imprecise, we evaluated ability of *personal* models to evaluate days, i.e., to detect whether stress occurred during a day or not. For this we needed one more hyper-parameter, TW: if number of HMM results for some day exceeded TW, this day was classified as "stress"; otherwise as "normal".

In all cases neither training of HMM-based stress classification models nor clustering utilised self-reports; hence all above-listed approaches were fully unsupervised.

3.3   Experimental Results

Figure 3 presents accuracies of recognising "stress" vs. "normal" human conditions by personal models for different window sizes and decision thresholds TS.

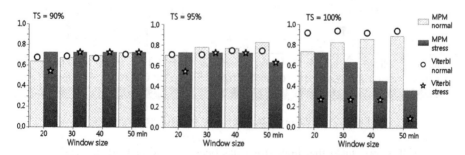

Fig. 3. Classification of time intervals between self-reports by personal HMM models

A window is classified as "stress" if number of its hidden states, classified as "unusual", is greater than TS. For example, window size 50 min and TS = 95% mean that at least 48 min in a window should be classified as "unusual" to classify this window as "stress". As Fig. 3 shows, HMM-MPM behaviour is consistent with respect to hyper-parameter changes: increase in window size and TS leads to increase in true negative rate and decrease in high stress recognition rate. HMM-Viterbi behaves less consistently: its recognition rate of high stress for window size 20 min and TS = 90–95% is lower than that for window sizes 30 and 40 min for the same values of TS. HMM-MPM also achieved higher accuracy for TS = 100% than HMM-Viterbi.

Figure 4 compares accuracies of personal, general and similarity-based models. For the latter we used the following numbers of clusters: two, three, four, five and six. Best result was achieved in case of four clusters; with other numbers of clusters accuracy of recognising stress was slightly lower, whereas accuracies of recognising normal conditions were fairly similar to that with four clusters. Figure 4 shows that general models tend to classify nearly all intervals as normal. Similarity-based modelling resulted in higher false detection rate and lower stress detection rate than that of personal models.

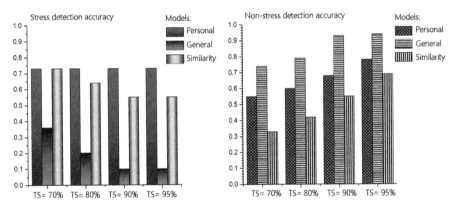

Fig. 4. Accuracies of personal, general and similarity-based HMM-MPM models for window size 30 min and different TS values; similarity-based results are presented for 4 clusters

Figure 4 shows that personal models achieved higher accuracies than other models: 73% accuracy of recognising stress and 75–80% accuracy of recognising normal conditions. Unfortunately, in real life these accuracies would mean large number of false detections if number of normal time intervals is large. On the other hand, in real life it may be sufficient to evaluate stresses on daily basis: to detect whether stress occurred today. Figure 5 presents accuracies of evaluating days by personal models for different values of threshold TW: the best results were achieved for TW equal to 4 or 5, i.e., for our test subjects it was fairly normal to have 4–5 periods of low activity per day, but not more. Figure 5 shows that HMM-MPM again outperformed HMM-Viterbi.

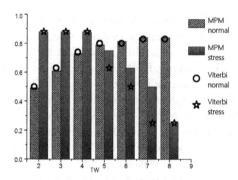

Fig. 5. Accuracies of detecting stresses by personal HMM models on daily basis for window size 30 min and TS = 95% for different values of threshold TW.

4 Discussion

During data collection the test subjects were asked to provide free-form comments regarding their activities in addition to stress labels. Although not all self-reports included free-from comments, from available comments we deduced that the proposed method best of all recognised high stresses which caused subjects' distraction from the current activity and contemplation: e.g., one subject stated that stress caused her to sit and wonder about received message. We also observed that HMM did not recognise stresses when the subjects dealt with them actively, e.g., one stress was not detected because the subject had a long phone call with her husband; another one - because the person went shopping. After checking trained HMM models we found that indeed HMM classified time windows as "unusual" if test subjects were notably inactive during this time: used their phones and moved less than normally. This finding corresponds to findings of the work [2], which reported that high stress significantly correlated with shorter "phone screen on" times, and to observations that stresses decrease physical activity level [13]. Hence HMM detected stress-induced decrease in values of physiological and behavioural features, unlike more common way to treat activity-induced changes in physiological data as non-indicative of stresses [15, 18].

As the subjects' "Big Five" personality data were acquired, we calculated Pearson correlation for our results and the subjects' factors. We found two statistically significant correlations: accuracy of recognising high stress negatively correlated with conscientiousness ($R = -0.91$, $p = 0.01$) and positively correlated with openness ($R = 0.82$, $p = 0.04$). Higher conscientiousness value means that the person is more efficient/organised and less easy-going/careless; higher openness value means that the person is more inventive/curious and less consistent/cautious. Hence the observed correlations suggest that organised and consistent persons were more inclined to keep doing what they were doing when stress occurred, whereas careless and inventive subjects were more inclined to stop and contemplate stresses, which sounds reasonable.

Classification of periods of inactivity as stresses, unfortunately, resulted in errors in cases when test subjects were notably inactive because they focused on studying or slept during daytime. For such cases it appeared important to have accelerometer in a wrist bracelet: normally human beings move their hands fairly often even if other parts of the body are still. In addition, classifying daytime sleeping as unusual behaviour may be correct if it happens only occasionally, because then daytime sleeping is a sign of tiredness and hence is related to stress. Learning whether daytime sleeping is usual or unusual behaviour for each person is fairly straightforward, but it requires longer observation histories than that available for this study. Number of misclassifications of cases when the subjects are highly concentrated on studying can be decreased by analysing user activities in greater detail, e.g., by classifying computer applications. An alternative approach is to learn models of normal behaviour depending on time, location and other available context data: for example, to learn what is normal for each user in the afternoon at home vs. what is normal for the same user in the morning in other places. As the proposed approach does not require any self-reports from the end users, it allows to learn large numbers of context-dependent models effortlessly for the users. Hence in future we plan to evaluate accuracy of context-dependent stress detection.

To the best of our knowledge, this work is the first study into unsupervised learning of person-specific stress detection models on the basis of wrist sensors and mobile phone data. Hence we only aimed at recognising most dangerous stresses (high stresses), moreover that training data, available for this study, were not abundant. Nevertheless the proposed unsupervised HMM-MPM stress detection algorithm achieved accuracies, comparable with the state-of-the-art results of fully supervised methods. For example, two works that trained general models to recognise stresses on the basis of data from wrist sensors (either alone [9] or in combination with mobile phone usage data [2]), achieved 75% accuracies for two-class context-independent stress detection problem in the tests with real life data. Context-dependent stress recognition in [9] was notably more accurate than context-independent one; hence, we also plan to train context-dependent models in future, but unlike [9], in our case learning will not require data labelling. Person-specific models, trained to recognise stresses on the basis of mobile phone usage data, achieved 70–71% accuracy in three-class classification problem in [10, 13], but such training requires significant labelling efforts from end users. We also plan to study capability of unsupervised HMM to recognise several stress levels in future, after collecting larger datasets.

Fully supervised training not only requires fairly large sets of labelled data; it requires these sets to contain examples of all classes. High stresses typically occur less often that normal conditions; furthermore, highly stressed users may feel too badly to report all such cases. Therefore collecting suitable databases for training fully supervised methods may require long time. The proposed unsupervised HMM-based stress detection approach does not suffer from this drawback: in our tests high stresses of several users occurred during one day only and hence recognition of these stresses was performed by HMM models, trained only on the normal data. Nevertheless these stresses were recognised correctly when the users reacted by decrease in activities.

5 Conclusion

This work proposed unsupervised stress detection algorithm, based on discrete HMM with MPM decision rule. The proposed algorithm first learns person-specific models of normal behaviour and then classifies notable deviations from normal behaviour as stresses. In the experiments with real life data of 28 subjects the proposed HMM-MPM approach outperformed more conventional HMM-Viterbi inference method, based on the MAP decision rule.

The main advantage of the employed devices (a wrist bracelet and a mobile phone) is ease of wearing in a broad range of real life settings. The main advantage of the proposed reasoning algorithm is its unobtrusiveness: algorithm training requires no data labelling from the end users. Hence the proposed method allows to provide for person-dependency of stress perception and stress influence on physiological parameters and behaviour of human beings in more realistic way than existing approaches, either employing supervised training (and thus requiring end users to collect fairly large sets of labelled data), or employing data collection devices that suit only to a limited range of conditions (e.g., only to cases of computer work [6], or only to cases of constant monitoring of sensor attachment quality [7]). The main limitation of the proposed approach is that it best of all recognises stresses which cause subjects' contemplation, but may easily fail to detect cases of active coping with stresses (e.g., when the subjects discuss the problems with trusted persons or comfort themselves by shopping). On the other hand, some studies reported that active coping with stresses, such as positive orientation, seeking advice and assistance etc., is correlated with overall wellness [19] and hence is less dangerous than rumination. The main limitation of this study is a fairly small dataset and gender bias: high stresses were reported by females only. The latter may be not so important, however, as emotion-focused coping with stresses, such as rumination, was found to be gender-independent [20].

In future we plan to increase accuracy of HMM-MPM by learning context-dependent person-specific models, i.e., to learn what kind of behaviour is normal in different contexts, and then to evaluate deviations from the normal model in context-dependent way. We also plan to exploit relations between Big Five personality factors and stress detection results in more detail. The initial experiments, presented in this work, seem to be encouraging for further algorithm development and evaluations because in this study the proposed unobtrusive system achieved accuracy, similar to that of the state-of-the-art fully supervised methods, reported by other studies.

References

1. Merriam-Webster dictionary. http://www.learnersdictionary.com/definition/stress. Accessed 23 Mar 2017
2. Sano, A., Picard, R.W.: Stress recognition using wearable sensors and mobile phones. In: ACII 2013, pp. 671–676 (2013)

3. Alberdi, A., Aztiria, A., Basarab, A.: Towards an automatic early stress recognition system for office environments based on multimodal measurements: a review. J. Biomed. Inform. **59**, 49–75 (2016)
4. Hernandez, J., Morris, R.R., Picard, R.W.: Call center stress recognition with person-specific models. In: ACII 2011, pp. 125–134 (2011)
5. Carneiro, D., Novais, P., Pêgo, J.M., Sousa, N., Neves, J.: Using mouse dynamics to assess stress during online exams. In: Onieva, E., Santos, I., Osaba, E., Quintián, H., Corchado, E. (eds.) HAIS 2015. LNCS, vol. 9121, pp. 345–356. Springer, Cham (2015). doi:10.1007/978-3-319-19644-2_29
6. Pimenta, A., Carneiro, D., Novais, P., Neves, J.: Detection of distraction and fatigue in groups through the analysis of interaction patterns with computers. In: Camacho, D., Braubach, L., Venticinque, S., Badica, C. (eds.) Intelligent Distributed Computing VIII. SCI, vol. 570, pp. 29–39. Springer, Cham (2015). doi:10.1007/978-3-319-10422-5_5
7. Rahman, M.M., et al.: Are we there yet?: feasibility of continuous stress assessment via wireless physiological sensors. In: ACM-BCB 2014, pp. 479–488 (2014)
8. Adams, P., Rabbi, M., Rahman, T., Matthews, M., Voida, A., Gay, G., Choudhury, T., Voida, S.: Towards personal stress informatics: comparing minimally invasive techniques for measuring daily stress in the wild. In: PervasiveHealth 2014, pp. 72–79 (2014)
9. Gjoreski, M., Gjoreski, H., Lutrek, M., Gams, M.: Continuous stress detection using a wrist device: in laboratory and real life. In: Ubicomp 2016 Adjunct, pp. 1185–1193 (2016)
10. Ferdous, R., Osmani, V., Mayora, O.: Smartphone app usage as a predictor of perceived stress levels at workplace. In: PervasiveHealth 2015, pp. 225–228 (2015)
11. Shi, Y., et al.: Personalized stress detection from physiological measurements. In: International Symposium on Quality of Life Technology (2010)
12. Garcia-Ceja, E., Osmani, V., Mayora, O.: Automatic stress detection in working environments from smartphones' accelerometer data: a first step. IEEE J. Biomed. Health Inform. **20**(4), 1053–1060 (2016)
13. Maxhuni, A., Hernandez-Leal, P., Sucar, L.E., Osmani, V., Morales, E.F., Mayora, O.: Stress modelling and prediction in presence of scarce data. J. Biomed. Inform. **63**, 344–356 (2016)
14. Xu, Q., Nwe, T.L., Guan, C.: Cluster-based analysis for personalized stress evaluation using physiological signals. IEEE J. Biomed. Health Inform. **19**(1), 275–281 (2015)
15. Kusserow, M., Amft, O., Troster, G.: Modeling arousal phases in daily living using wearable sensors. IEEE Trans. Affect. Comput. **4**(1), 93–105 (2013)
16. Rabiner, L.R.: A tutorial on hidden Markov models and selected applications in speech recognition. Proc. IEEE **77**(2), 257–286 (1986)
17. https://www.mybasis.com/. Accessed 12 Jan 2016
18. Hovsepian, K., al'Absi, M., Ertin, E., Kamarck, T., Nakajima, M., Kumar, S.: cStress: towards a gold standard for continuous stress assessment in the mobile environment. In: ACM International Joint Conference on Pervasive and Ubiquitous Computing (2015)
19. Aalto, J.K., Brotheridge, C.M.: Resources, coping strategies and emotional exhaustion: a conservation of resources perspective. J. Vocat. Behav. **63**(3), 490–509 (2003)
20. Folkman, S., Lazarus, R.S.: An analysis of coping in a middleaged community sample. J. Health Soc. Behav. **21**, 219–239 (1980)

Artificial Intelligence in Games

Artificial Intelligence in Games

Iterative Parallel Sampling RRT for Racing Car Simulation

Samuel Gomes$^{(\boxtimes)}$, João Dias, and Carlos Martinho

INESC-ID and Instituto Superior Técnico, Universidade de Lisboa, Lisbon, Portugal
samuel.gomes@tecnico.ulisboa.pt

Abstract. Graphics Processing Units have evolved at a large pace, maintaining a processing power orders of magnitude higher than Central Processing Units. As a result, the interest of using the General-Purpose computing on Graphics Processing Units paradigm has grown. Nowadays, big effort is put to study probabilistic search algorithms like the Randomized Search Algorithms family, which have good time complexity, and thus can be adapted to massive search spaces. One of those algorithms is Rapidly Exploring Random Tree (RRT) which reveals good results when applied to high dimensional dynamical search spaces. This paper proposes a new variant of the RRT algorithm called Iterative Parallel Sampling RRT which explores the use of parallel computation in GPU to generate faster solutions. The algorithm was used to construct a CUDA accelerated bot for the TORCS open source racing game and tested against the plain RRT. Preliminary tests show lap time reductions of around 17% and the potential for reducing search times.

Keywords: General-Purpose Computing on Graphics Processing Units · Randomized Search Algorithms · Rapidly-Exploring Random Trees · The Open Racing Car Simulator · Planning

1 Introduction

The need to search big continuous state spaces led to the creation of stochastic search algorithms (algorithms that have a probabilistic approach on search) like the Randomized Search Algorithms (RSA) family. Most known RSA include Rapidly-Exploring Random Tree (RRT) [13], R* [7] (based on A*) or Monte-Carlo Tree Search (MCTS) [4]. In particular, RRT can adapt to rapidly changing worlds and/or high dimensional state spaces, dynamically generating the representation of those spaces. Besides that, it has a good behaviour for non holonomic[1] and kynodynamic[2] problems.

To speedup the exploration of massive state spaces, major effort has recently been put to use the (GPGPU) programming paradigm to create parallel versions

---

[1] Problems with non holonomic constraints. These are characterized by implying variables that change with time (not time itself), like gravity or angular velocity.

[2] Problems which are defined by manipulating force attributes like velocities or accelerations.

© Springer International Publishing AG 2017
E. Oliveira et al. (Eds.): EPIA 2017, LNAI 10423, pp. 111–122, 2017.
DOI: 10.1007/978-3-319-65340-2_10

of RSA, namely MCTS [2,11], R* [6] and even the RRT itself [1,5]. However, those parallelizations have not been much explored in real time applications such as videogames, where the processing time assigned to the search algorithm needs to be balanced with the execution of high graphical requirements. In order to achieve good results on time constrained applications such as those, a parallel version of RRT using the GPGPU paradigm is proposed, the Iterative Parallel Sampling RRT (IPS-RRT).

To analyse and test the properties of IPS-RRT we implemented it in CUDA and applied it to a car racing videogame extensively used for academic research, (TORCS)[3], which is a multi-platform open source game that serves as a base for the construction of AI controllers. Racing games can benefit from the use of RRT versions like IPS-RRT, as directional speed and steering generate a big continuous state space.

2   Related Work

Several techniques have been applied to improve the performance of RRT. RRT*, referred in [1], is an optimization of the RRT algorithm to asymptotically converge to a better solution. It achieves this through multiple neighbour selection and node rearrangement. A big drawback of RRT* is that it implies a big number of dependencies as the additional phases use previously calculated information. This makes it much less prune to parallelization than the plain RRT. Constraint parallelization [1] also helped to improve RRT's performance by parallelizing the process that checks constraints and culls invalid points. When searching potential object collisions in the motion planning problem, parallel threads checked the collision with each obstacle concurrently. This approach has the drawback of only parallelizing one part of RRT's execution. If only one obstacle is considered there is no gain because the only thread is going to process the collision of all RRT states. Also, a parallelization method called (SRT) [10] parallelizes RRT by creating several independent trees in parallel, joining them to produce a global tree. That tree can then be searched to find a solution. Another approach for parallelizing RRT is presented in [5], Bulk Synchronous Distributed RRT. In that algorithm, processes create several RRT samples and synchronize them to a global tree through message broadcasting. Approaches such as the ones in [5] revealed to be applied in distributed computation contexts.

Although, to our knowledge, no work applied RRT to TORCS, other approaches have been explored. An Inverse Reinforcement Learning bot [3] was developed with the objective of testing a framework for autonomous road driving. This approach involved two sub controllers: a speed and pose sub controllers. An MCTS racing bot [4] was also developed, that uses a state space based on physical aspects like positions and velocities. The bot uses that spatial representation to predict future states through a physics based forward model.

---

[3] http://torcs.sourceforge.net/ (as consulted on June 15, 2017).

3   Iterative Parallel Sampling RRT

Instead of applying constraint parallelization (like in [1]) or creating parallel trees (like in SRT [10]), IPS-RRT focuses on executing several iterations of parallel tree samples. At each iteration, a number of samples are concurrently generated and checked for constraints (using a thread for each sample). The valid samples are added to local trees which are then synchronized to the global tree at the end of each iteration. IPS-RRT's pseudocode is presented in Algorithm 1.

Algorithm 1. IPS-RRT

1: **procedure** GENERATERRT(numIterations,numParallelSamples,T)
2:    **loop** *from 0 to numIterations*:
3:       *launch numParallelSamples threads computing this*:
4:          $T' \leftarrow T$
5:          $x_{rand} \leftarrow randomState()$
6:          $x_{near} \leftarrow nearestNeighbor(x_{rand}, T')$
7:          $x_{new} \leftarrow applyDelta(x_{rand}, x_{near})$
8:          **if not** $validPoint(x_{new})$ **then**
9:             $endThread()$
10:          add vertex x_{new} to T'
11:          add edge (x_{near}, x_{new}) to T'
12:       $syncronizeThreads()$, $T \leftarrow$ all T's
13:    **return** T

IPS-RRT receives three parameters: (1) the number of iterations, (2) the number of concurrent samples to be generated in each of those iterations and (3) an empty search tree T that corresponds to the global tree. Partial trees (represented by T') are used inside each thread. They consist in snapshots of the contents of T at the start of the iteration (line 4).

A state x_{rand} is randomly generated (line 5). Then, the algorithm searches for the closest state x_{near} to x_{rand} in the tree T' (line 6). However, x_{near} is not added directly to the tree. In order to expand the tree in a controlled way, a new state x_{new} is generated by moving x_{near} a small distance *delta* in the direction of x_{rand} (line 7). If the new state is not valid (does not verify the problem constraints), it is not added to T' (nor to T) and the thread stops its execution (lines 8 and 9). Otherwise, the new state x_{new} is added to T' (line 10) along with a new edge between x_{near} and x_{new} (line 11) to represent a parent/child connection between the two states. At the end of each iteration, threads are synchronized[4] and the samples generated in each thread are copied over to T (line 12). Lastly, the algorithm returns the global tree T (line 13).

It is important to compare our proposed algorithm with Bulk Synchronous Distributed RRT (BSD) [5] because it also parallelizes the build of a single RRT

---

[4] By thread synchronization it is meant that the threads wait for the slowest one before the execution continues, just like a barrier.

tree. However, the process of creating the trees is different, because of the way IPS-RRT's schedule works. IPS-RRT iteratively builds partial trees by thread synchronization instead of incrementally broadcasting them in a distributed process context. IPS-RRT process is more adequate for a GPGPU implementation, as message passing would not efficiently work in such contexts. Another difference is that in BSD broadcast is done only after a number of new valid states are added, while in IPS-RRT synchronization occurs after each thread processes a sample independently of being added to the tree or not. The reason for this change is that since the synchronization must wait for the slowest thread, it would not be appropriate to wait for an unlucky thread processing several invalid samples.

3.1   IPS-RRT Characteristics

By selecting different number of iterations and number of parallel samples, IPS-RRT presents different characteristics. Figure 1 illustrates how IPS-RRT trees can significantly differ from the classic RRT trees.

If one tries to maximize the parallelization by having just one iteration and performing all samples in parallel, then all resulting new states will connect to the initial state (given that each partial tree only has the initial state). This is illustrated in the second leftmost picture from Fig. 1. By increasing the number of iterations, the algorithm will increase the span of the search tree, and will be able to reach more distant states. When the number of iterations is equal to the number of RRT generated samples and only one sample is created for each iteration, then the IPS-RRT becomes equivalent to the traditional RRT, as illustrated in the rightmost picture from Fig. 1.

Sequential 800 Samples	1 Iteration of 800 Parallel Samples	2 Iterations of 400 Parallel Samples	4 Iterations of 200 Parallel Samples	8 Iterations of 100 Parallel Samples	800 Iterations of 1 Parallel Sample

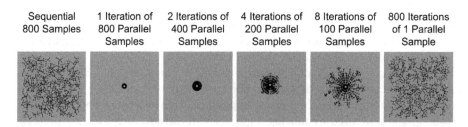

Fig. 1. Schematic comparison between an 800 state search tree generated by the sequential RRT version and trees generated by IPS-RRT. The state space is projected to a 2D plane. Black points represent 2D states, black connections represent parent-child relations and the bigger red point is the initial state. (Color figure online)

4   TORCS Bot Implementation

This section presents the implementation of our developed CUDA accelerated TORCS bot using IPS-RRT. The solution architecture is presented and its components analysed. The state representation and restrictions are detailed and depicted for better reader comprehension.

4.1   Bot Architecture

Our TORCS bot consists of several modules, similar to the approach in [12]. A schematic representation of the solution can be found in Fig. 2. It includes:

- **A planning module** which is composed by IPS-RRT as well as the plain RRT (for comparison purposes);
- **A control module** which receives the plan from the planning module and coordinates the actions needed to drive the car by calling TORCS back-end;
- **The TORCS back-end** which provides the necessary game core procedures to describe and control the car and query track information.

The planning module is called when the control module checks that either the car passed the last point of the current intermediate plan or a time limit is reached. When the planning module returns, the control module follows the new intermediate plan. This procedure is repeated until the end of the race.

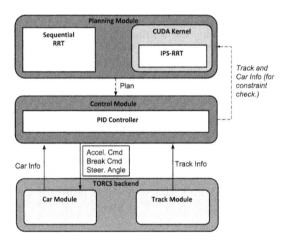

Fig. 2. Diagram of the TORCS bot's architecture and modules.

Planning Module. The planning module consists of an abstraction for the execution of both the plain RRT and IPS-RRT. The output of this layer is the best plan found without the initial point (the initial point represents the current state which is redundant to seek).

Control Module. The module that controls the car is divided in two components: the pedals component and the steering component (similarly to the speed and pose controllers described in [9]). It drives the car using the TORCS control parameters depicted in Fig. 4.

The pedals are controlled by a PID controller[5] as the relation between their position and the car's acceleration varies from car to car and cannot be directly acquired. The objective of using PID is to minimize the errors incurred by the search, getting practical action results close to the theoretical predictions. The use of this type of controller revealed to be a good compromise. There was no need for a steering PID controller given that the steering angle can be directly determined as described in Fig. 3.

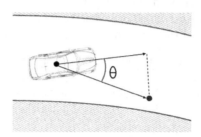

Fig. 3. Used method to determine the steering angle. The target search point is represented in blue. The position of the car is displayed in black along with the car direction vector. The angle between the car's direction and the current state position, displayed as θ, is obtained by the arc-tangent of the legs of the triangle. (Color figure online)

4.2   TORCS Search State Representation

The objective of each state is to represent a predicted car situation. Thus, the representation that seemed more adequate was including attributes like position and velocity. While the position of the car is represented in the cartesian space defined by the TORCS back-end, the velocity is represented in a polar space aligned to the same cartesian space. The function of each state attribute is clarified by the scheme provided in Fig. 4.

4.3   IPS-RRT Applied to TORCS

This subsection details the implementation of the IPS-RRT methods presented on page 3. First, a velocity is randomly sampled and used to generate a new state x_{rand} (line 5 of IPS-RRT's pseudocode). A forward simulation method considers a simple physical model to generate the position of x_{rand} based on its velocity. The position is obtained by multiplying the velocity by a fixed search action time. The nearest neighbour x_{near} (line 6) is determined by choosing the state which has the lowest velocity angle variation to x_{rand}[6]. To calculate x_{new} (line 7), a set of intermediate states are generated between x_{near} and x_{rand}. Such states are computed by interpolating their velocities. Figure 5 illustrates the procedure.

---

[5] The article [8] introduces PID and refers how to generally implement and tweak a PID controller so that it can adapt to a racing environment.

[6] The angle variation between two velocity vectors is the minimal angle between them.

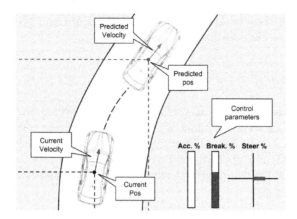

Fig. 4. Visual identification of the attributes in each state. The darker car represents its current position and the red vector the car's current velocity (lower in the figure); The blue line represents the theoretical trajectory; The lighter car represents the predicted position and the lighter red vector, the predicted velocity (upper in the figure); Finally a visual telemetry represents the control parameters (pedals position and steering axis). (Color figure online)

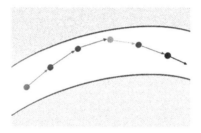

Fig. 5. Intermediate states and delta representation. x_{rand} is represented in dark blue and x_{near} in light blue. The states' velocities are also depicted accordingly. Intermediate states are represented in grey. x_{new}, represented in orange, is determined by choosing one of the intermediate states. In this case, the third furthest state from x_{near} was chosen. However, the chosen intermediate state is defined initially, just like a *delta* variation in RRT. (Color figure online)

Finally, x_{new}'s validity (lines 8 and 9) is checked by verifying if all intermediate states are positioned inside the track. After the search tree is built and returned (line 13), the best tree state is picked as the one estimated to maximize the covered track distance[7] in the minimum amount of time. This is calculated by the ratio between the track distance and the depth of the state in the tree[8].

---

[7] The track distance for a state s is determined by projecting the line segment between the initial state and s along the centre of the track, and calculating the length of the projection.

[8] Since a connection in the tree represents a fixed time span, the depth of the state in the tree can be used as an estimation of the time required to reach that state.

The best state is then backtracked to the initial state and the corresponding path is returned as the solution.

5   Evaluation

In this section, the hardware and software used to develop and test this work are presented, along with the analysis of several preliminary tests results. These tests were performed using preliminary versions of the algorithms which were not yet optimized. The goal was to determine if there is a potential advantage when using the explored approach. A screenshot of the bot running the test cases can be seen in Fig. 6.

Fig. 6. This work's bot in action.

5.1   Tools

The work was developed in the C++ programming language, using Microsoft Visual Studio[9] 2013 and CUDA development toolkit 7.5[10]. This combination was chosen because despite more recent ones being available, it was the most stable and well documented when the development started.

The used graphical card was a Nvidia GTX 960M (laptop) GPU with 4 GB of VRam (which is a middle range laptop gaming GPU). It has a 5.0 compute capability and a 1.176 Ghz clock rate. The used CPU was an Intel(R) Core(TM) i7-4720HQ (laptop) CPU with a 2.6 GHz clock.

5.2   Performance of One Search Procedure

The mean of search times (around 3 laps) for both implementations on the representative road track "Speedway-1" can be consulted in the chart of Fig. 7.

---

[9] https://www.visualstudio.com/ (as consulted on June 15, 2017).

[10] https://developer.nvidia.com/cuda-toolkit (as consulted on June 15, 2017).

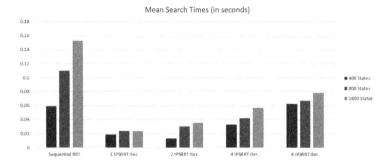

Fig. 7. Chart displaying the mean search times.

IPS-RRT appears to be more time consistent along lap searches than the sequential version, because of the way the parallel schedule works. The overall search time seems to be reduced in practically all cases, supporting the idea that the parallel implementation can improve the efficiency. There are however situations where the GPU IPS-RRT implementation is actually slower than the sequential RRT search, so more tests are required in order to properly understand in which situations is preferable to use the GPU implementation of IPS-RRT.

By using the Visual Studio Performance Wizard with CPU sampling[11] on each sequential method call in the whole TORCS execution, it was confirmed that the time is spent mostly on constraint checking (13.63% of the samples). The random state generation and nearest neighbour checking procedures are much faster (they both took only a sum of 0.21% of the samples). It can then be concluded that constraint checking is the procedure that mostly affected the duration of each IPS-RRT iteration.

5.3 Bot Racing Performance

This metric is tested by examining the lap times produced by the bot. As the lap time decreases, it is assumed that the bot performs better. A mean of three lap times on the test track "Speedway-1" regarding various searches can be consulted in the chart of Fig. 8. The acronym "NC" (Not Consistent) means that the search executed some recoverable mistakes (the data was measured on three non-consecutive clean laps). A recoverable mistake means that the car gets out of track but can return by itself. The acronym "DNF" (Did Not Finish) means that the search failed to finish a lap, committing an unrecoverable mistake (like when the car gets out of track and the search span is not big enough to bring it back).

---

[11] The reader can check https://msdn.microsoft.com/en-us/library/ms182372.aspx (as consulted on June 15, 2017) and https://blogs.msdn.microsoft.com/visualstudioalm/2016/04/28/how-cpu-sampling-works/ (as consulted on June 15, 2017) for more information about Visual Studio Profiling features and CPU sampling.

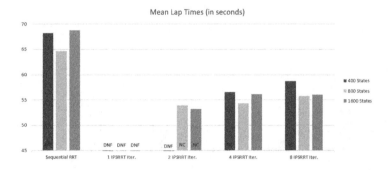

Fig. 8. Chart displaying the mean lap times.

As can be seen in the chart presented in Fig. 8, there is a considerable lap time reduction (around 17% across all tests) when IPS-RRT is applied, as the generated paths are faster. However, the bot gets more inconsistent as less iterations are applied (the extreme being only one). This happens because the search span gets so small that the algorithm is not able to look ahead and detect an incoming curve. Nevertheless, with enough iterations and parallel threads, consistency can be achieved. Although non consistent, less iteration searches produced slightly better results (whenever they could) because the smaller search time decreased the prediction model error. All in all, the most successful parametrization for this scenario was using 800 states search with four IPS-RRT iterations (of 200 parallel samples).

6   Discussion

Based on the experience gained with the work described in this paper, some conclusions can be taken about IPS-RRT's characteristics. First of all, IPS-RRT is a simple and straightforward way of dividing the work done in the sequential RRT. Secondly, when the number of iterations is low, IPS-RRT is not applicable to problems where a distant solution needs to be calculated in the first search, because in that case, the generated trees are small and compact (as presented on Subsect. 3.1). However, in problems where the solution can be obtained by determining smaller intermediate plans and executing them (as in the case of TORCS), the previous IPS-RRT limitation is not as problematic and IPS-RRT becomes a good choice as a global solution can be obtained by a composition of solutions of smaller span plans.

Some aspects about the particular application of IPS-RRT to TORCS (using the hardware presented in Subsect. 5.1) were discovered. When parallelizing IPS-RRT, a low number of threads is not useful, as thread overhead overwhelmed the gains obtained by parallelization. When using a low number of IPS-RRT iterations, the algorithm was not able to search far enough to detect incoming corners (left picture of Fig. 9). Another problem arose when using a big number of tree samples. Given that TORCS simulation is frame independent, the search took so long that the returned solution was no longer consistent with the car's current position (right picture of Fig. 9).

It is important to understand that in frame independent applications like TORCS, IPS-RRT's benefits are tightly coupled to the used hardware. If more resources are available, best search and lap time reductions can possibly be achieved, because the problems presented in Fig. 9 emanate directly from the number of IPS-RRT samples that can be processed in a given amount of time.

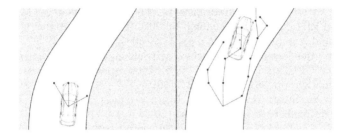

Fig. 9. Occurrences that can increase lap times.

7   Conclusion and Future Work

In this paper, we presented a new GPU parallelization technique for RRT and described how we created an effective bot for the game TORCS. Our proposal, Iterative Parallel Sampling RRT, seems to create faster solutions by running the main RRT loop in parallel, and performing parallel sampling. Our preliminary results indicate that the GPU implementation of IPS-RRT can achieve an increase on racing performance (reduction of around 17% in lap times), but also shows potential for improving RRT search times. However, a longer and more detailed evaluation of the system is required to further corroborate these findings.

Additional possible improvements to this work include optimizations to the algorithm implementations, such as improving the constraint checking and nearest neighbour processes or the development of a mechanism to use previously computed trees instead of starting from an empty tree. Another interesting idea would be to create and test a version of the algorithm that automatically adjusts the number of iterations to the available system resources.

Acknowledgments. This work was supported by national funds through Fundação para a Ciência e a Tecnologia (FCT) with reference UID/CEC/50021/2013.

References

1. Bialkowski, J., Karaman, S., Frazzoli, E.: Massively parallelizing the RRT and the RRT*. In: IEEE International Conference on Intelligent Robots and Systems, pp. 3513–3518. IEEE (2011)

2. Chaslot, G.M.J.-B., Winands, M.H.M., Herik, H.J.: Parallel Monte-Carlo tree search. In: Herik, H.J., Xu, X., Ma, Z., Winands, M.H.M. (eds.) CG 2008. LNCS, vol. 5131, pp. 60–71. Springer, Heidelberg (2008). doi:10.1007/978-3-540-87608-3_6
3. Dizan, V., Yufeng, Y., Suryansh, K., Christian, L.: An open framework for human-like autonomous driving using inverse reinforcement learning. In: 2014 IEEE Vehicle Power and Propulsion Conference (VPPC), pp. 1–4. IEEE (2014)
4. Fischer, J., Falsted, N., Vielwerth, M., Togelius, J., Risi, S.: Monte Carlo tree search for simulated car racing. In: Proceedings of the Foundations of Digital Games Conference. ACM (2015)
5. Jacobs, S.A., Stradford, N., Rodriguez, C., Thomas, S., Amato, N.M.: A scalable distributed RRT for motion planning. In: 2013 IEEE International Conference on Robotics and Automation (ICRA), pp. 5088–5095. IEEE (2013)
6. Kider, J.T., Henderson, M., Likhachev, M., Safonova, A.: High-dimensional planning on the GPU. In: Proceedings - IEEE International Conference on Robotics and Automation, pp. 2515–2522. IEEE (2010)
7. Likhachev, M., Stentz, A.: R* search. In: Proceedings of the National Conference on Artificial Intelligence (AAAI). ACM (2008)
8. Melder, N., Tomlinson, S.: Racing vehicle control systems using PID controllers (Chap. 40). In: Rabin, S. (ed.) Game AI Pro: Collected Wisdom of Game AI Professionals, p. 10. CRC Press, Boca Raton (2013)
9. Perez, A., Quigley, P., Yu, H.: Driving in TORCs with a Reinforcement Learning Agent. Stanford University, Technical report (2014)
10. Plaku, E., Bekris, K.E., Chen, B.Y., Ladd, A.M., Kavraki, L.E.: Sampling-based roadmap of trees for parallel motion planning. IEEE Trans. Rob. **21**(4), 597–608 (2005)
11. Rocki, K., Suda, R.: Parallel Monte Carlo tree search on GPU. In: Eleventh Scandinavian Conference on Artificial Intelligence, pp. 80–89. IOS Press (2011)
12. Soares, R., Leal, F., Prada, R., Melo, F.: Rapidly-exploring random tree approach for geometry friends. In: Proceedings of 1st International Joint Conference of DiGRA and FDG. DIGRA (2016)
13. LaVelle, S.M.: Rapidly-Exploring Random Trees: A New Tool for Path Planning. Iowa State University, USA, Technical report (1998)

Multi-agent Double Deep Q-Networks

David Simões[1,2,3(✉)], Nuno Lau[1,3], and Luís Paulo Reis[1,2,4]

[1] IEETA - Institute of Electronics and Informatics Engineering of Aveiro,
University of Aveiro, Aveiro, Portugal
[2] LIACC - Artificial Intelligence and Computer Science Lab, Porto, Portugal
[3] DETI/UA - Electronics, Telecommunications and Informatics Department,
University of Aveiro, Aveiro, Portugal
david.simoes@ua.pt
[4] DSI/EEUM - Information Systems Department - School of Engineering,
University of Minho, Braga, Portugal

Abstract. There are many open issues and challenges in the multi-agent reward-based learning field. Theoretical convergence guarantees are lost, and the complexity of the action-space is also exponential to the amount of agents calculating their optimal joint-action. Function approximators, such as deep neural networks, have successfully been used in single-agent environments with high dimensional state-spaces. We propose the Multi-agent Double Deep Q-Networks algorithm, an extension of Deep Q-Networks to the multi-agent paradigm. Two common techniques of multi-agent Q-learning are used to formally describe our proposal, and are tested in a Foraging Task and a Pursuit Game. We also demonstrate how they can generalize to similar tasks and to larger teams, due to the strength of deep-learning techniques, and their viability for transfer learning approaches. With only a small fraction of the initial task's training, we adapt to longer tasks, and we accelerate the task completion by increasing the team size, thus empirically demonstrating a solution to the complexity issues of the multi-agent field.

1 Introduction

In recent years, there have been many successes using deep representations in reinforcement learning. One such example is Deep Q-Networks (DQN) [12], a reinforcement learning algorithm that allowed a single agent to achieve human-level performance across many Atari games. However, in most situations, agents interact with other agents in order to solve a given problem. Multi-agent Systems research focuses on building a system with multiple independent agents, and how to coordinate them [16]. We propose to extend the DQN algorithm to the multi-agent scenario and describe two variants for cooperative scenarios. We show how these variants behave in different tasks and how they can generalize to similar tasks, with more agents or more goals to accomplish.

The remainder of this article is structured as follows: Sect. 2 introduces Markov Decision Processes, Q-learning, Double Deep Q-Networks, and the multi-agent reward-based learning paradigm. Section 3 describes similar work in the

© Springer International Publishing AG 2017
E. Oliveira et al. (Eds.): EPIA 2017, LNAI 10423, pp. 123–134, 2017.
DOI: 10.1007/978-3-319-65340-2_11

field, and Sect. 4 describes our proposed algorithms. Section 5 shows the results obtained, and Sect. 6 draws our conclusions and lists future research options.

2   Background

In single-agent reinforcement learning, the environment of an agent is commonly modeled by a Markov Decision Process (MDP). A Decentralized Partially-Observable Markov Decision Process (Dec-POMDP) is a multi-agent generalization of a MDP. It is defined by the tuple $\mathcal{E} = (\mathcal{S}, \{\mathcal{A}_i^n\}, F, \{\mathcal{O}_i^n\}, O, R)$, where n is the number of agents, $\mathcal{S} \in \mathbb{N}^d$ is a finite set of possible d-dimensional states of the environment $\mathcal{E}$, $\mathcal{A}_i, i = 1, \ldots, n$ is a set of possible actions for agent i, $\mathcal{A}$ is the joint-action set $\mathcal{A} = \mathcal{A}_1 \times \ldots \times \mathcal{A}_n$, $F : \mathcal{S} * \mathcal{A} * \mathcal{S} \to [0,1]$ is a state transition probability function $F(s'|s,a)$ for transitioning to state s' after taking joint-action a in state s, $\mathcal{O}_i, i = 1, \ldots, n$ is the set of observations for agent i, $\mathcal{O}$ is the joint-observation set $\mathcal{O} = \mathcal{O}_1 \times \ldots \times \mathcal{O}_n$, $O : \mathcal{S} * \mathcal{A} * \mathcal{O} \to [0,1]$ is a state observation probability function $O(o|s,a)$ for observing o after taking joint-action a in state s, and $R : \mathcal{S} * \mathcal{A} * \mathcal{S} \to \mathbb{R}$ is the associated reward function of all agents. The state transitions and observations are the result of the joint-action $a_k \in \mathcal{A}$. The joint policy π is gathered from the policies $\pi_i : \mathcal{S} * \mathcal{A}_i \to [0,1], i = 1, \ldots, n$. At time-step t, agent i observes observation $o_{t,i} \in \mathcal{O}_i$ from the environment and the reward r_t. In Dec-MDP, the state can be computed from the set of agent observations $\{\mathcal{O}_0, \ldots, \mathcal{O}_n\}$, i.e., $O(o|s,a) = \{0,1\}$.

Q-learning [19] is a model-free MDP-based algorithm, from which many multi-agent reinforcement learning algorithms are derived [2]. The action-value function, also known as Q-function, $Q_\pi : \mathcal{S} * \mathcal{A} \to \mathbb{R}$, is the expected return of policy π based on the current state and action performed. A discount factor $\gamma \in [0,1[$ represents the importance of future rewards. Discount factors closer to 1 increase the amount of fore-planning the agent takes into account. The optimal Q-function is defined as $Q^*(s,a) = \max_\pi Q^\pi(s,a)$. The agent determines Q^* and then uses a greedy policy to choose its actions, which is optimal when applied to Q^*. Q-learning is an iterative approximation procedure, where the current estimate of Q^* is updated using samples collected as rewards from actual experiences with the task, i.e.,

$$Q_{t+1}(s_t, a_t) = (1 - \eta_t)\{Q_t(s_t, a_t)\} + \eta_t\{r_{t+1} + \gamma \max_{a'} Q_t(s_{t+1}, a')\}, \qquad (1)$$

where $\eta_t \in [0,1]$ represents a learning rate. In single-agent systems, the Q-function provably converges to Q^* as long as the agent tries all actions in all states with non-zero probability (usually by using an ϵ-greedy exploration method). In multi-agent systems which are not fully cooperative, due to the non-stationarity of the environment and the conflict of interests between agents, such theoretical guarantees are lost.

2.1   Double Deep Q-Networks

In single-agent systems, this basic approach is also impractical in high dimensional tasks, because the action-value function is estimated separately for each state, without any generalization. The Deep Q-Networks (DQN) algorithm [12] uses a deep neural network with weights θ as a function approximator, where $Q(s, a; \theta) \approx Q^*(s, a)$. Agents compute a processed state $\phi_t = \Phi(o_t)$ (dependent on the problem; Mnih et al. [12] used a stack of the last 4 frames to compensate for partial observability) and, under the policy $\pi(\phi, a)$, the sequence of loss functions in iteration i with target y_i, denoted by

$$L_i(\theta_i) = \mathbb{E}_{\phi, a \sim \pi(.)}[(y_i - Q(\phi, a; \theta_i))^2], \tag{2}$$

is minimized, in order to train the Q-network. A target network is kept, whose parameters θ_{i-1}^- for iteration i are fixed, and only updated (copied from the on-line network) every τ time-steps. The target of the Double DQN [7] extension is

$$y_i = \mathbb{E}_{\phi' \sim \varepsilon}[r + \gamma \max_{a'} Q(\phi', \arg\max_{a'} Q(\phi, a'; \theta_{i-1}); \theta_{i-1}^-)|\phi, a], \tag{3}$$

which decouples action selection and evaluation over the on-line and target networks. This successfully reduces overoptimism, and results in a more stable and reliable learning process. The gradient of the loss function with respect to the weights can be optimized by stochastic gradient descent. The agent's experience at each time-step $e_t = (\phi_t, a_t, r_t, \phi_{t+1})$ is stored in a data-set $\mathcal{D} = e_1, \ldots, e_N$, known as a replay memory. Updates are performed with mini-batches (k samples of experience $e \sim \mathcal{D}$) drawn uniformly from the replay memory.

2.2   Multi-agent Reinforcement Learning

Reinforcement Learning in the multi-agent paradigm (MARL) has several advantages over the single-agent counterpart. Parallel computation leads to speedups in the learning phase when agents exploit the decentralized structure of the task [2]. MARL also benefits from the multi-agent systems' advantages, such as robustness and scalability.

Q-learning has been widely adopted by the scientific community as a viable option to find good strategies in cooperative multi-agent environments. Claus and Boutilier [3] describe multi-agent Q-learning with Independent Learners (IL) and Joint-Action Learners (JAL). In IL, each learner's Q-values are based solely on its own actions. In JAL, on the other hand, the learner's Q-values are based on the joint-action of all the agents. In practice, this implies that JAL agents require knowledge about the other agent's actions during the learning phase to form their Q-tables, while IL agents do not.

3   Related Work

There are many approaches to multi-agent coordination, both with hand-made policies and with multi-agent learning techniques. Hand-made policies usually rely on domain-knowledge, and use both situation- and role-based mechanisms [10,14,15] to achieve flexibility among cooperative agents. Multi-agent learning techniques, like multi-agent Q-learning [3] have shown good results in fully

cooperative or fully competitive scenarios. However, since state-action representations are stored in tables, without any generalization to unseen states, these
algorithms suffer from the curse of dimensionality, and require specific techniques
to decrease the state- and action-spaces. Other techniques [8,11] worsen these
problems by relying on state-based or agent-based lists and counters to improve
upon the agents' coordination. Other algorithms focus on Decentralized MDPs
and POMDPs, but assume unrealistic assumptions, such as complete independence from other agents [1] or the ability to observe other agents' actions [13].
Most of these have also only been evaluated in the context of single-stage games.

Multi-agent adaptations of deep-learning algorithms, on the other hand, have
recently emerged as a solution to multi-agent learning. Tampuu et al. [17] use the
Pong video-game and adjust the rewarding schemes of the game to range from
cooperative to competitive behaviors. The authors use the Independent Learners
approach (which would be necessary in non-cooperative scenarios), and report
great results, such as cooperative agents learning to hit the ball parallel to the
x-axis. Egorov [4] has also adopted the original DQN algorithm to a multi-agent
scenario using the Pursuit environment and the Independent Learners technique.
The author demonstrates how the algorithm can generalize to similar tasks, with
a different number of agents, or different obstacles. Finally, the author uses a
Transfer Learning technique, by transferring the network weights between similar
scenarios, to speed-up learning. Foerster et al. [5] propose a set of techniques for
multi-agent DQN, such as inter-agent weight sharing, where the same network
is used by all agents, instead of several separate ones. The authors also suggest
feeding each agent's last action to its input and disabling the experience replay
feature of DQN, and demonstrate how multi-agent riddles can be solved by
learning communication protocols.

4   Multi-agent Double Deep Q-Networks

Our proposal, which we call Multi-agent Double Deep Q-Networks (MaDDQN)
is a multi-agent version of Double DQN, using the Joint-Action Learners (JAL)
and Independent Learners (IL) strategies for fully cooperative scenarios. JAL is
a technique where agents learn the value of joint-actions, instead of just their
own, where Q-values represent the expected return of the joint-action $\mathcal{A}$. In
fully cooperative scenarios, the optimal action for each agent is their respective
component of the joint-action with the largest Q-value. IL is a technique where
agents learn the value of their own actions, and thus do not require knowledge
about the actions performed by other agents. When the number of agents $n = 1$,
the algorithm is the original Double DQN.

The full JAL algorithm is described in Algorithm 1. Each agent interacts with
the environment and executes a random action with probability ϵ. Agents observe
the new state and the obtained reward, and store the joint-action transition in a
replay memory. For JAL, a global processed state ϕ_t must always be computable
by any agent, a requirement satisfied in all POMDP and fully observable Dec-
MDP, but not in all Dec-POMDP. In the simplest case, the processed state is

Input: Learning rate η, mini-batch size k, discount factor γ, network update period τ, replay memory $\mathcal{D}$ with capacity N, action-value function Q with random weights θ

1: **for** iteration $= 1, M$ **do**
2:     **for** agent $p = 1, P$ **do**
3:         Sample state $s_{1,p}$
4:     **end for**
5:     Compute ϕ_1
6:     **for** step $t = 1, T$ **do**
7:         **for** agent $p = 1, P$ **do**
8:             Select random action $a_{t,p}$ with probability ϵ, otherwise best action $a_{t,p} = \max_a Q^*(\phi(s_t), a; \theta)$
9:             Execute $a_{t,p}$
10:            Sample state $s_{t+1,p}$ and reward r_t
11:        **end for**
12:        Compute ϕ_{t+1}
13:        Store transition $(\phi_t, a_{t,1}, ..., a_{t,p}, r_t, \phi_{t+1})$ in $\mathcal{D}$
14:        Sample random mini-batch of k transitions $(\phi_j, a_{j,1}, ..., a_{j,b}, r_t, \phi_{j+1})$ from $\mathcal{D}$
15:        **for** transition $i = 1, k$ **do**
16:            Update $\theta \leftarrow \theta + \eta \nabla_{\theta_i} L_i(\theta_i)$
17:        **end for**
18:        Update network weights $\theta_{target} \leftarrow \theta$ every τ time-steps
19:    **end for**
20: **end for**

Algorithm 1. Joint-Action Multi-agent Double DQN

simply the latest observed state stripped of any agent-specific information (such as agent perspective). The full IL algorithm is described in Algorithm 2. In this case, the processed state ϕ_t can be different for any agent, thus relaxing the requirements of JAL. Transitions are stored by each agent and no longer contain the joint-action, but simply the action of their corresponding agent. Unlike Tampuu et al. [17], who focus on the diversity of coordinated behaviors between two agents through different rewarding schemes, we assume fully cooperative agents and instead focus on their adaptability to similar tasks and to larger team sizes. We also train all our agents at the same time, as opposed to Egorov [4], who fixes the network weights of all-but-one agents during training and periodically distributes the learned weights to the remaining agents.

The input of the network is the processed state ϕ_t (which is usually dependent on the observation o_t), implying that larger observations (like larger maps) will require a change in network architecture. The output of each network is the optimal action for IL, and optimal joint-action for JAL. Since the joint-action is dependent on the number of agents, the JAL variant of MaDDQN cannot generalize for different numbers of agents, as opposed to the IL variant.

5   Results

Our proposal was tested in two multi-agent environments: a foraging task and a predator-prey game. The foraging task is a task where agents are tasked with foraging items and bringing them back to specific places. Our implementation of the Foraging Task provides homogeneous agents with complete vision, but no communication. An exemplary map is shown in Fig. 1(a). The starting positions of agents and berries are randomized across the lower and upper parts of the

Input: Learning rate η, mini-batch size k, discount factor γ, network update period τ, replay
   memory $\mathcal{D}$ with capacity N, action-value function Q with random weights θ

1: **for** iteration $= 1, M$ **do**
2:    **for** agent $p = 1, P$ **do**
3:       Sample state $s_{1,p}$ and compute $\phi_{1,p}$
4:    **end for**
5:    **for** step $t = 1, T$ **do**
6:       **for** agent $p = 1, P$ **do**
7:          Select random action $a_{t,p}$ with probability ϵ, otherwise best action
             $a_{t,p} = \max_a Q^*(\phi(s_t), a; \theta)$
8:          Execute $a_{t,p}$
9:          Sample state $s_{t+1,p}$ and reward r_t
10:          Compute $\phi_{t+1,p}$
11:          Store transition $(\phi_{t,p}, a_{t,p}, r_t, \phi_{t+1,p})$ in $\mathcal{D}$
12:       **end for**
13:       Sample random mini-batch of k transitions $(\phi_{j,b}, a_{j,b}, r_t, \phi_{j+1,b})$ from $\mathcal{D}$
14:       **for** transition $i = 1, k$ **do**
15:          Update $\theta \leftarrow \theta + \eta \nabla_{\theta_i} L_i(\theta_i)$
16:       **end for**
17:       Update network weights $\theta_{target} \leftarrow \theta$ every τ time-steps
18:    **end for**
19: **end for**

Algorithm 2. Independent Multi-agent Double DQN

map, respectively. Each agent can only carry one berry at a time, and can only release it in the base. Agents move simultaneously and, if they would collide, no movement occurs. All state transitions and rewards are deterministic, and agents observe the map from a global perspective. A time limit of 200 steps was set for each simulation. The Predator-Prey game is also known as the Pursuit task, where a team of homogeneous predators must capture the elements of the team of semi-randomly moving prey in a toroidal grid. Communication was disabled and predators must on top of a prey to capture it. An exemplary map is shown in Fig. 1(b). The starting positions of predators and prey are randomized across the map. Movements occur alternatively for predators and prey, but are simultaneous for members of the same team. Predators are penalized if they collide, and set randomly on the map. The prey are intelligent and move randomly away from the closest predator. We use unreliable communication channels, and the prey move semi-randomly, so state transitions and rewards are stochastic. Agents observe a local perspective of the relative positions of other elements in the map, and there is no time limit. For a single agent, catching the prey is impossible, as both move at the same speed.

Based on the DQN algorithm, an average network value V was used to determine the learning performance for our tests, which corresponds to the average Q-value of the best action in all steps of a fixed simulation. Tests were performed on a 7 by 7 grid, whose size is small enough for a policy with Q-tables to be learned, and on a 15 by 15 grid, too large for table-based methods. For the small maps, a fully connected neural network with 2 hidden layers of 50 neurons was deployed. The hidden layer units are activated with a rectified linear function $f(x) = \max(0, x)$, and the output layer units with the identity function $f(x) = x$. In our tests, the Replay Memory had a capacity $N = 5000$ transitions, and the discount factor, network update period, mini-batch size, and learning rate took

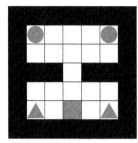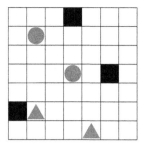

Fig. 1. The initial state of a Foraging map (left) and of a random toroidal Pursuit map (right). The berries and prey are represented in circles, the agents and predators in triangles, the base in squares, and obstacles in black.

values $\gamma = 0.9$, $\tau = 500$, $k = 32$, $\eta = 0.001$, respectively. The exploration rate ϵ was annealed from 1 to 0.1 during the first 75% steps. We use the Adam Optimizer [9] for optimization and Xavier initialization [6] for the weights' initial values. In order to compare our proposal with table-based Q-learning, we also learned standard Q-learning policies with a discount factor and learning rate of $\gamma = 0.9$ and $\eta = 0.5$, respectively. For tests on 15 by 15 environments, 2 hidden layers of 250 neurons were used. Training took five times as long, and a trainer was used to guide the initial exploration phase, by guiding the agents or handicapping the prey with some probability.

5.1 Joint-Action Learners and Independent Learners

The Foraging Task and the Pursuit game were used to compare the learning performance of the JAL and IL approaches. Both environments provide agents with a categorical grid of the observed world, which is converted to a 1-hot grid. The input layer consists of $w * h * m$ neurons, where w is the map width, h the map height, and m the number of map cell categories (empty, obstacle, base, berry or prey, agent). The output layer, for JAL, contains a^n neurons, where a is the number of possible actions, and n is the number of agents in the team. In the Forager Task, $a = 7$ (move in any of four directions, pick up, drop, do nothing), while in the Pursuit Game, $a = 5$ (move in any of four directions, do nothing). For IL, the output layer contains simply a neurons. Foerster et al.'s inter-agent weight sharing [5] was used for a faster and more consistent learning, by providing each agent with its own network, but using the same weights across all networks, which takes advantage of the fact that our agents are homogeneous. In a 7×7 map, with only a narrow gap between both halves of the map, we expected the IL approach to be harder to learn than its JAL counterpart. The results in Fig. 2(a) show, however, that both approaches have very similar learning curves. We conclude that this is due to the homogeneity of the agents and the inter-agent weight sharing technique, which allows the independent agents to quickly learn a homogeneous cooperative policy. In the Pursuit game, agents observe a local perspective of the map, and their perspectives were concatenated in the

JAL approach. Figure 2(b) shows how the learning process evolved, for a team of 2 agents attempting to catch a team of 2 prey. We see that JAL is now easier to learn, due to the strong coordination requirements of the environment. The agents learn to converge and surround each prey, until they eliminate it, before moving on to the next. We also trained our networks in large 15 by 15 maps, with up to 6 agents and up to 10 berries or prey. In the Pursuit environment, we added some random obstacles for increased complexity. Using regular Q-learning, the amount of states was intractable for the learning process and no policy was learned. However, MaDDQN managed to learn highly successful policies for the both environments (over 80% perfect score in less than 200 time steps).

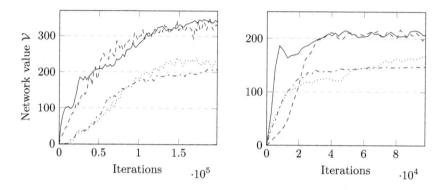

Fig. 2. The average and standard deviation of $\mathcal{V}$ in fixed Foraging (left) and Pursuit (right) simulations during the learning process. IL (solid) and JAL (dashed) strategies with MaDDQN, and IL (dotted) and JAL (dash dotted) strategies with Q-tables, are averaged over 3 trials.

5.2 Generalization

We also evaluated the generality of our proposal, by directly measuring the task performance when the task conditions were changed. Transfer learning approaches [18] allow learning in one task to improve the learning performance in a related, but different, task. We used 7 by 7 maps with 2 agents for the Foraging task, to demonstrate how MaDDQN behaves in narrow complex global-perspective environments, and 15 by 15 maps with 4 agents for the Pursuit games, to contrastingly demonstrate MaDDQN's behavior in large toroidal local-perspective environments. After training both MaDDQN and standard Q-learning (using Q-tables in 7 by 7 maps), the policies were then progressively re-trained for a fraction of the original training for different numbers of berries or prey and their performance was re-evaluated. The fractions of the original training for these tests, which we call Generalization Fractions (GF), ranged from 10% to 2.5%. The results of DQN generalization for the Foraging environment are shown in Fig. 3, where the ratio of successful simulations represents simulations where the agents captured all the berries within the time limit. The average

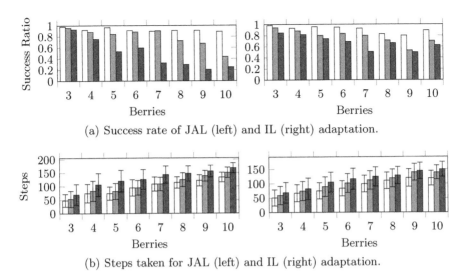

(a) Success rate of JAL (left) and IL (right) adaptation.

(b) Steps taken for JAL (left) and IL (right) adaptation.

Fig. 3. Adapting to Foraging scenarios with progressively more berries, over 1000 test simulations, using the JAL and IL approaches, with a GF of 10% (white), 5% (gray), and 2.5% (dark gray). (a) The ratio of successful attempts. (b) The average and standard deviation of the steps taken in successful attempts.

amount of steps per successful simulation is also shown, with the simulation time limit being kept at 200 steps. Both figures show how DQN-based algorithms are generalizable to more complex scenarios with only a limited amount of training of the network's weights, by achieving a success rate of over 80%, with at least 10% training. Using Q-tables, however, despite achieving a near perfect success rate on the original scenario, generalization achieved only a 12% and a 5% success rate with a GF of 10% for 3 berries in JAL and IL, respectively, and could not generalize any further. In some of our tests, we saw that policies actually improved, despite the increased complexity of the tasks. One of the initial policies consisted on only one of the agents picking up berries, while the other simply tried to avoid collisions. With 10% training, however, the agents learned a better policy, where both alternate behaviors and both carry berries. The same approach was tried in the Pursuit domain as well, as shown in Fig. 4, where a simulation is considered successful when all the prey were caught within 200 time-steps and without any agent collisions. Despite the increased map size, great results can be observed, with a success rate of over 60% with a GF of only 2.5% on the IL approach. The JAL approach, however, on large or complex maps, has issues generalizing. In fact, we used only 2 predators (for a simpler network output) and prey who only escaped with a 50% probability, and still the results show that after an increase of only 2 prey, predators already have an unsatisfactory behavior. In the Pursuit game, even with the small 7 by 7 map, Q-tables also failed to generalize with positive results. Generalization with a GF

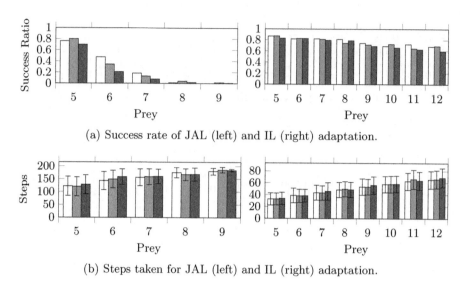

(a) Success rate of JAL (left) and IL (right) adaptation.

(b) Steps taken for JAL (left) and IL (right) adaptation.

Fig. 4. Adapting to Pursuit scenarios with progressively more prey, over 1000 simulations, using the JAL and IL approaches, with a GF of 10% (white), 5% (gray), and 2.5% (dark gray). (a) The ratio of successful attempts. (b) The average and standard deviation of the steps taken in successful attempts.

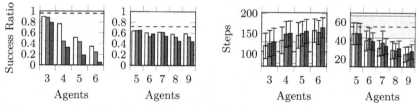

(a) Success rate of Foraging (left) and Pursuit (right) adaptation.

(b) Steps taken for Foraging (left) and Pursuit (right) adaptation.

Fig. 5. Adapting to Foraging and Pursuit scenarios with progressively more agents, over 1000 simulations, using the IL approach, with a GF of 10% (white), 5% (gray), and 2.5% (dark gray). The dashed line represents the original training's baseline, with 200000 training steps for Foraging and 400000 for Pursuit. (a) The ratio of successful attempts. (b) The average and standard deviation of the steps taken in successful attempts.

of 10% achieved only a 17% and a 4% success rate for 3 prey in JAL and IL, respectively, and could not generalize further than 4 prey.

Unlike the JAL counterpart, the IL approach also allows the generalization of the number of agents performing the task. The scenarios were trained with 6 berries and only 2 agents, and 4 predators and 10 prey. The network was then re-trained, as before, with up to 6 agents and up to 9 predators, and re-evaluated. The results for the Foraging and Pursuit tasks are shown in Fig. 5. In the Foraging narrow map, a larger amount of agents are not expected to help parallelize the task performance. Indeed, the results show that agents disturb each other and conflict in an attempt to cross the narrow bridge. On the other hand, we expect the same generalization to improve the performance of tasks where a broad map allows more agents to speed up the task completion. In the Pursuit environment, given a toroidal map, increasing the amount of agents with a small fraction of training speeds up the completion of the task, while decreasing its success rate (due to a larger amount of predator collisions).

6 Conclusion

We formally extend the Double DQN algorithm to the multi-agent paradigm. The Independent Learners and Joint-Action Learners techniques are described, and their viability for learning complex policies in multi-agent scenarios is shown, in comparison with regular Q-learning. The algorithm code, experiments, and demonstrations have been published on-line at https://github.com/bluemoon93/Multi-agent-Double-Deep-Q-Networks.git.

We demonstrate how MaDDQN can generalize and corroborate previous results, where transfer learning is shown to speed up convergence. With only a small fraction of the original training, IL can generalize not only on more complex tasks, with a higher success rate, but also with a larger number of agents. On the other hand, JAL has issues adapting its policy to more complex environments, due to the increased complexity of the network. We conclude that the independent approach with implicit coordination is not only more generalizable, but also a more realistic solution than a centralized approach, on highly complex environments. Transfer learning techniques allow for gradually harder tasks to be learned, whose complexity might be prohibitively high without any previous knowledge, as well as an increase in the speed of a parallel task's completion, by increasing the team's size. We believe that these are stepping stones to solving the complexity problems commonly associated with multi-agent systems.

In the future, we plan on extending MaDDQN to make use of other multi-agent adaptations of Q-learning, apart from IL and JAL, which allow for non-deterministic policies and non-cooperative scenarios. Finally, other deep reinforcement learning techniques, aside from DQN, must also be extended to the multi-agent paradigm and compared against MaDDQN.

Acknowledgements. The first author is supported by FCT (Portuguese Foundation for Science and Technology) under grant PD/BD/113963/2015. This research was partially supported by IEETA and LIACC. The work was also funded by project EuRoC, reference 608849 from call FP7-2013-NMP-ICT-FOF.

References

1. Becker, R., Zilberstein, S., Lesser, V., Goldman, C.V.: Transition-independent decentralized markov decision processes. In: Proceedings of the Second International Joint Conference on Autonomous Agents and Multiagent Systems, AAMAS 2003, pp. 41–48. ACM, New York (2003)

2. Busoniu, L., Babuska, R., De Schutter, B.: A comprehensive survey of multiagent reinforcement learning. Trans. Syst. Man Cybern. Part C **38**(2), 156–172 (2008)
3. Claus, C., Boutilier, C.: The dynamics of reinforcement learning in cooperative multiagent systems. In: Innovative Applications of Artificial Intelligence, IAAI 1998, pp. 746–752. American Association for Artificial Intelligence (1998)
4. Egorov, M.: Multi-agent deep reinforcement learning. University of Stanford, Department of Computer Science, Technical report (2016)
5. Foerster, J.N., Assael, Y.M., de Freitas, N., Whiteson, S.: Learning to communicate to solve riddles with deep distributed recurrent q-networks. CoRR abs/1602.02672 (2016)
6. Glorot, X., Bengio, Y.: Understanding the difficulty of training deep feedforward neural networks. In: AISTATS, vol. 9, pp. 249–256 (2010)
7. van Hasselt, H., Guez, A., Silver, D.: Deep reinforcement learning with double q-learning. CoRR abs/1509.06461 (2015)
8. Kapetanakis, S., Kudenko, D.: Reinforcement learning of coordination in cooperative multi-agent systems. In: Eighteenth National Conference on Artificial Intelligence, Menlo Park, CA, USA, pp. 326–331. American Association for Artificial Intelligence (2002)
9. Kingma, D.P., Ba, J.: Adam: a method for stochastic optimization. CoRR abs/1412.6980 (2014)
10. Lau, N., Reis, L.P.: FC Portugal - high-level coordination methodologies in soccer robotics. InTech Education and Publishing, Vienna, December 2007
11. Lauer, M., Riedmiller, M.: An algorithm for distributed reinforcement learning in cooperative multi-agent systems. In: Proceedings of the Seventeenth International Conference on Machine Learning, pp. 535–542. Morgan Kaufmann (2000)
12. Mnih, V., Kavukcuoglu, K., Silver, D., Graves, A., Antonoglou, I., Wierstra, D., Riedmiller, M.: Playing atari with deep reinforcement learning. CoRR abs/1312.5602 (2013)
13. Nair, R., Tambe, M., Yokoo, M., Pynadath, D., Marsella, S., Nair, R., Tambe, M.: Taming decentralized pomdps: towards efficient policy computation for multiagent settings. In: IJCAI, pp. 705–711 (2003)
14. Reis, L.P., Lau, N., Oliveira, E.C.: Situation based strategic positioning for coordinating a team of homogeneous agents. BRSDMAS 2000. LNCS, vol. 2103, pp. 175–197. Springer, Heidelberg (2001). doi:10.1007/3-540-44568-4_11
15. Stone, P.: Layered Learning in Multiagent Systems: A Winning Approach to Robotic Soccer. MIT Press, Cambridge (2000)
16. Stone, P., Veloso, M.: Multiagent systems: a survey from a machine learning perspective. Auton. Robot. **8**(3), 345–383 (2000)
17. Tampuu, A., Matiisen, T., Kodelja, D., Kuzovkin, I., Korjus, K., Aru, J., Aru, J., Vicente, R.: Multiagent cooperation and competition with deep reinforcement learning. CoRR abs/1511.08779 (2015)
18. Taylor, M.E., Stone, P.: Transfer learning for reinforcement learning domains: a survey. J. Mach. Learn. Res. **10**(1), 1633–1685 (2009)
19. Watkins, C.J., Dayan, P.: Q-learning. Mach. Learn. **8**(3–4), 279–292 (1992)

Artificial Intelligence in Medicine

A Deep Learning Method for ICD-10 Coding of Free-Text Death Certificates

Francisco Duarte[1]([✉]), Bruno Martins[1], Cátia Sousa Pinto[2], and Mário J. Silva[1]

[1] INESC-ID, Instituto Superior Técnico, Universidade de Lisboa, Lisbon, Portugal
{francisco.ribeiro.duarte,bruno.g.martins,
mario.gaspar.silva}@tecnico.ulisboa.pt
[2] Direção-Geral da Saúde, Lisbon, Portugal
catiasousapinto@dgs.min-saude.pt

Abstract. The assignment of disease codes to clinical texts has a wide range of applications, including epidemiological studies or disease surveillance. We address the task of automatically assigning the ICD-10 codes for the underlying cause of death, from the free-text descriptions included in death certificates obtained from the Portuguese Ministry of Health. We specifically propose to leverage a deep neural network based on a two-level hierarchy of recurrent nodes together with attention mechanisms. The first level uses recurrent nodes for modeling the sequences of words given in individual fields of the death certificates, together with attention to weight the contribution of each word, producing intermediate representations for the contents of each field. The second level uses recurrent nodes to model a sequence of fields, using the representations produced by the first level and also leveraging attention in order to weight the contributions of the different fields. The paper reports on experiments with a dataset of 115,406 death certificates, presenting the results of an evaluation of the predictive accuracy of the proposed method, for different ICD-10 levels (i.e., chapter, block, or full code) and for particular causes of death. We also discuss how the neural attention mechanisms can help in interpreting the classification results.

Keywords: Classification of death certificates · Clinical text mining · Deep learning · Natural language processing · Artificial intelligence in medicine

1 Introduction

The systematic collection of high-quality mortality data is essential in the context of monitoring a population's health, also serving as a basis for mortality and epidemiologic studies. For this and other legal purposes, doctors write death certificates, i.e. reports including the deceased personal data and textual descriptions for the cause of death, as well as any contributing conditions or injuries. In Portugal, doctors are now submitting death certificates in electronic format, using a national Death Certificate Information System (SICO [1]) for data collection and registry purposes. The analysis and classification of causes of death are

© Springer International Publishing AG 2017
E. Oliveira et al. (Eds.): EPIA 2017, LNAI 10423, pp. 137–149, 2017.
DOI: 10.1007/978-3-319-65340-2_12

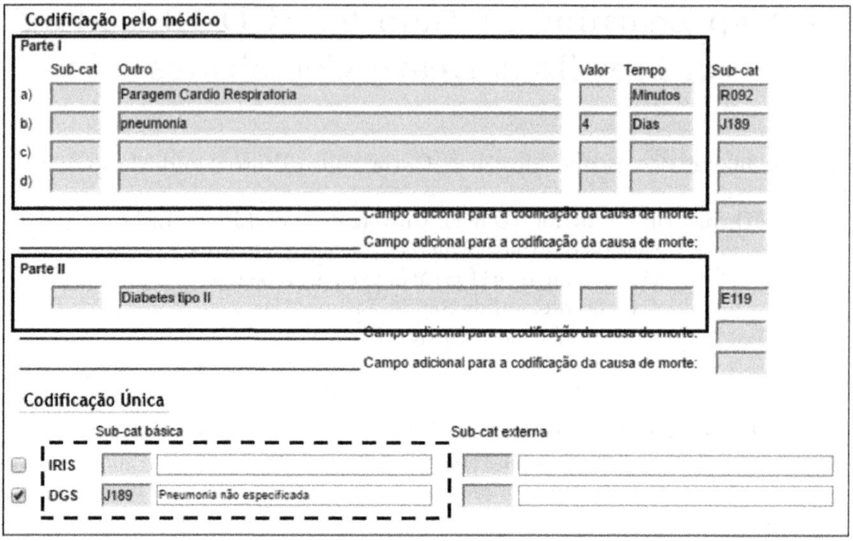

Fig. 1. The form in the SICO platform that is used for coding the death certificates.

based on Revision 10 of the International Classification of Diseases, ICD-10, the standard medical classification list developed and reviewed by the World Health Organization. However, the assignment of ICD codes to the death certificates provided by doctors is is still made manually by mortality coders with specific expertise, based on the free-text descriptions included in the death certificates.

Figure 1 presents a screenshot of the SICO form used by mortality coders in Portugal to assign ICD-10 codes to death certificates. The form has two parts (delimited by the solid lines). Part I has four rows of text, labelled *(a)*, *(b)*, *(c)* and *(d)*, for reporting a chain of events leading directly to death. The underlying causes of death should be provided in the lowest line(s) and the immediate cause of death in the first one. Part II is filled-in only if necessary for reporting other significant diseases, conditions or injuries that contributed to death, but are not part of the main causal sequence leading to it. After the manual review of the data, the mortality coder should assign the corresponding ICD-10 code, in the box shown under the dashed line of Fig. 1.

The manual coding of the free-text contents in death certificates is a challenging, expensive, and time consuming task [2], which slows down the dissemination of mortality statistics and prevents real time surveillance. However, we believe that the large number of certificates that have been manually coded in the past can be used to support supervised machine learning of models for automatically assigning codes to the certificates. Automated approaches can be used to speed-up the process of publishing mortality statistics by quickly producing results that can latter be revised through manual coding. When integrated into existing platforms, automated approaches can also provide suggestions to assist the manual coders. If sufficiently accurate, automatic coding also has the potential to significantly reduce the costs with human experts, and to increase coding consistency.

Several previous studies have already addressed the ICD coding of free-text death certificates [3–6]. Recently, increasing attention has been given to this problem due to the organization of CLEF eHealth clinical information extraction tasks in 2016 and 2017, which involved large-scale datasets prepared from French and English death certificates [7,8]. However, previously published methods are still relatively simple in comparison to the current state-of-the-art in other text classification problems, either leveraging dictionary projection methods or supervised machine learning with linear models and manual feature engineering.

In this paper, we propose to leverage a neural network based on a two-level hierarchy of recurrent nodes together with attention mechanisms, inspired on previous work by Yang et al. [9]. The first level of the model uses Gated Recurrent Units (GRUs) [10] for modeling the sequences of words given in individual fields of the death certificates, together with attention to weight the contribution of each word, producing intermediate representations for the contents of each field. The second level uses GRUs to model a sequence of fields, using the representations produced by the first level and also leveraging attention in order to weight the contributions of the different fields. The representations produced by the second level are passed to feed-forward nodes, which leverage a softmax activation to predict the most likely ICD-10 codes. The entire model can be trained end-to-end from a set of coded death certificates, leveraging the back-propagation algorithm in conjunction with the Adam optimization method [11,12].

The paper reports on experiments with a dataset of 115,406 death certificates from the years of 2013 up to 2015, through which we evaluated the predictive accuracy of the proposed method. The available data was randomly split into two subsets (i.e., 75% for model training and 25% for testing), and we measured results in terms of classification accuracy, as well as macro-averaged precision, recall, and F1-scores. Given the hierarchical organization of ICD-10 (i.e., the codes are organized hierarchically into chapters, blocks and full codes), we also measured results according to different levels of specialization.

Our best model achieved an accuracy of 86%, 78%, and 75%, respectively when considering ICD-10 chapters (i.e., a total of 22 different classes appearing in our dataset), blocks (i.e., 697 different classes) and full codes (i.e., 1,674 different classes). Our full model also achieved F1-scores of 96% and 90%, respectively in terms of correctly identifying causes of mortality related to ICD-10 Chapters II (i.e., neoplasms) and IX (i.e., diseases of the circulatory system), that together represent 58.7% of the death causes in the dataset. We argue that the obtained results indicate that automatic approaches leveraging supervised machine learning can indeed contribute to a faster processing of death certificates, given the relatively low classification error. Moreover, although our experiments failed to show that neural attention mechanisms lead to an increased performance, these methods can offer much needed model interpretability, by allowing us to see which parts of the input are attended to when making predictions.

2   Related Work

Various previous studies have addressed automatic ICD-10 coding. For instance Koopman et al. described the use of Support Vector Machines (SVMs) for identifying cancer related causes of death in natural language death certificates [5]. The textual contents were encoded as binary feature vectors (i.e., vectors encoding the presence of terms, term n-grams, and SNOMED CT concepts recognized by a clinical natural language processing system named Medtex), and these representations were used as features to train a two-level hierarchy of SVM models: the first level was a binary classifier for identifying the presence of cancer, and the second level consisted of a set of classifiers (i.e., one for each cancer type) for identifying the type of cancer according to the ICD-10 classification system (i.e., according to 85 different ICD-10 blocks, of which 20 instances corresponded to 85% of all cases). The system was highly effective at identifying cancer as the underlying cause of death (i.e., a macro-averaged F1-score of 0.94 for the first level classifier). It was also effective at determining the type of common cancers (i.e., a macro-averaged F1-score of 0.7), although rare cancers, for which there was little training data, were difficult to classify accurately (i.e., a macro-averaged F1-score of 0.12). The principal factors influencing performance were the amount of training data and certain ambiguous cases (e.g., cancers in the stomach region).

In a separate study, Koopman et al. described machine learning and rule-based methods to automatically classify death certificates according to four high impact diseases of interest, namely diabetes, influenza, pneumonia and HIV [6]. The rule-based method leveraged sets of keyword-matching rules, while the machine learning method was again based on SVM classifiers, using binary feature vectors (i.e., presence of terms, term n-grams, and SNOMED CT concepts recognized by Medtex) for encoding the texts. In the case of the machine learning approach, a separate model was trained for each of the four diseases of interest, and the authors also experimented with more fine-grained classifiers trained for each of the relevant ICD-10 blocks. An empirical evaluation was conducted using 340,142 certificates (i.e., 80% for model training and 20% for testing) covering deaths from 2000–2007 in New South Wales, Australia. The results showed that the classification of diabetes, influenza, pneumonia and HIV was highly accurate (i.e., a macro-averaged F1-score of 0.95 for the rule-based method, and 0.94 when using machine learning). More fine-grained ICD-10 classification had nonetheless a more variable effectiveness, with less accurate classifications for blocks with little training data available, although results were still high (i.e., a macro-averaged F1-score of 0.80, when discriminating over 9 different ICD-10 blocks). The error analysis revealed that word variations (e.g., *pneumonitis* or *pneumonic* as variants for *pneumonia*) as well as certain word combinations adversely affected classification. In addition, anomalies in the ground truth likely led to an underestimation of the effectiveness (i.e., the authors observed some class confusions, e.g. in ICD blocks E10 versus E11).

Mujtaba et al. tested different text classification methods in the task of coding death certificates with nine possible ICD-10 codes [4], aiming to assist pathologists in determining causes of death based on autopsy findings. The dataset used in these experiments was composed of 2200 autopsy reports obtained from one of the largest hospitals in Kuala Lumpur, and the methods under study involved different feature selection schemes, and also five different learning algorithms. Random forests and J48 decision models, parametrized using expert-driven feature selection and leveraging a feature subset size of 30, yielded the best results (e.g., approximately 90% in terms of the macro-averaged F1-score).

Lavergne et al. described a large-scale dataset prepared from French death certificates, suitable to the application of machine learning methods for ICD-10 coding [8]. The dataset comprised a total of 93,694 death certificates referring to 3,457 unique ICD-10 codes, and it was made available for international shared tasks organized in the context of CLEF. The 2016 edition of the CLEF eHealth shared task on ICD-10 coding attracted five participating teams, which presented systems relying either on dictionary linking or statistical machine learning [7]. The shared task was defined at the level of each statement (i.e., lines varying from 1 to 30 words, with outliers at 120 words and with the most frequent length at 2 tokens) in a death certificate, and statements could be associated with zero, one or more ICD-10 codes. The best-performing system achieved a micro-averaged F1-score (i.e., harmonic mean of precision and recall weighted by the class size) of 0.848, leveraging dictionaries built from the shared task data.

Leveraging the CLEF eHealth dataset, Zweigenbaum and Lavergne. presented hybrid methods for ICD-10 coding of death certificates [3], combining dictionary linking with supervised machine learning (i.e., an SVM classifier leveraging tokens, character tri-grams, and the year of the certificate as features). The best hybrid model corresponded to the union of the results produced by the dictionary- and learning-based methods, outperforming the best system at the 2016 edition of the CLEF eHealth shared task with a micro-averaged F1-score of 0.8586.

3   The Proposed Approach

We propose a neural network model for assigning ICD-10 codes to free-text death certificates, taking inspiration on previous work by Yang et al. [9]. Considering the SICO platform from the Portuguese Ministry of Health's Directorate-General of Health (DGS), illustrated on Fig. 1, we modeled the coding task as follows: given different textual strings encoding events leading to death, an automated system should output the ICD-10 code corresponding to the underlying cause of death. Figure 2 presents the neural network architecture, which is briefly explained next. For an in-depth introduction to deep neural networks for natural language processing, the reader can refer to the tutorial by Goldberg [13].

Noting that the certificates can be seen as having a hierarchical structure (i.e., words form different fields, and the fields from Parts I and II, as shown in Fig. 1, form the certificate), our model first builds representations of individual fields, and then aggregates those into a representation for the certificate. Both hierarchical levels are illustrated in Fig. 2, with the word-level part of the model

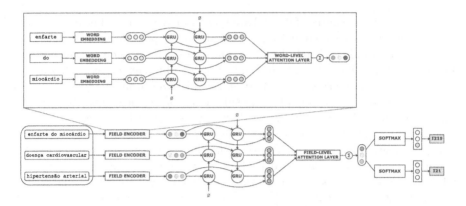

Fig. 2. The proposed neural architecture (with 3 fields instead of 6, for illustration).

shown in the box at the top. A recurrent neural network node known as a Gated Recurrent Unit (GRU) is used at both levels to build the representations, and we specifically considered bi-directional GRUs [10]. Notice that the GRUs in the first level of the model leverage word embeddings as input, whereas the second level uses as input the field representations generated at the first level.

GRUs model sequential data by having a recurrent hidden state whose activation at each time is dependent on that of the previous time. A GRU computes the next hidden state h_t given a previous hidden state h_{t-1} and the current input x_t using two gates (i.e., a reset gate r_t and an update gate z_t), that control how the information is updated, as shown in Eq. 1. The update gate (Eq. 2) determines how much past information is kept and how much new information is added, while the reset gate (Eq. 4) is responsible for how much the past state contributes to the candidate state. In Eqs. 1 to 4, $\tilde{h}_t$ stands for the current new state, W is the parameter matrix for the actual state, U is the parameter matrix for the previous state, and b is a bias vector.

$$h_t = (1 - z_t) \odot h_{t-1} + z_t \odot \tilde{h}_t \tag{1}$$

$$z_t = \sigma\left(W_z x_t + U_z h_{t-1} + b_z\right) \tag{2}$$

$$\tilde{h}_t = \tanh\left(W_h x_t + r_t \odot (U_h h_{t-1} + b_h)\right) \tag{3}$$

$$r_t = \sigma\left(W_r x_t + U_r h_{t-1} + b_r\right) \tag{4}$$

Bi-directional GRUs perceive the context of each input in a sequence by outlining the information from both directions. Concatenating the output of processing a sequence forward $\overrightarrow{h}_{it}$ and backwards $\overleftarrow{h}_{it}$ grants a summary of the information around each position, $h_{it} = [\overrightarrow{h}_{it}, \overleftarrow{h}_{it}]$.

Since the different words and fields can be differently informative in specific contexts, the model also includes two levels of attention mechanisms (i.e., one at the word level and one at the field level), that let the model pay more or less attention to individual words/fields when constructing representations.

For instance, in the case of the word-level part of the network, the outputs h_{it} of the bi-directional GRU encoder are provided to a feed-forward node (Eq. 5), resulting in vectors u_{it} representing words in the input. A normalized importance α_{it} (i.e., the attention weights) is calculated as shown in Eq. 6, using a context vector u_w that is randomly initialized. The importance weights in α_{it} are then summed over the whole sequence, as shown in Eq. 7.

$$u_{it} = \tanh\left(W_w h_{it} + b_w\right) \tag{5}$$

$$\alpha_{it} = \frac{\exp(u_{it}^T u_w)}{\sum_t \exp(u_{it}^T u_w)} \tag{6}$$

$$s_i = \sum_t \alpha_{it} h_{it} \tag{7}$$

The vector s_i from Eq. 7 is finally taken as the representation of the input. The part of the network that processes the sequence of fields similarly makes use of bi-directional GRUs with an attention mechanism, taking as input the representations produced for each field, as shown in Fig. 2.

The representation resulting from the different fields is finally passed to two feed-forward nodes with softmax activations, which respectively attempt to predict the corresponding ICD-10 block and the ICD-10 full-code. The entire model is trained end-to-end from a set of coded death certificates, leveraging the back-propagation algorithm [11] in conjunction with the Adam method [12] for optimizing loss functions corresponding to the categorical cross-entropy (i.e., we combine loss functions computed from ICD-10 blocks and full-codes, respectively with weights 0.5 and 1.0). The idea of leveraging two separate outputs relates to the large number of ICD-10 full-codes that are sparsely used. We expect that information on ICD-10 blocks can be used to better inform model training.

4   Experimental Evaluation

This section describes the experimental evaluation of the proposed method. We first present a statistical characterization of the dataset that supported our tests, together with the considered experimental methodology. Then, Subsect. 4.2 presents and discusses the obtained results, also giving illustrative examples.

4.1   Dataset and Experimental Methodology

The dataset used in our experiments consisted of death certificates emitted from the years of 2013 to 2015, collected from the SICO platform. We excluded all instances involving a supplemental autopsy report, mostly corresponding to accidents, suicides, or homicides. Table 1 presents characterization statistics.

Figure 1 already presented the general layout of the SICO online platform that is currently being used for manually coding the death certificates. For each certificate, we use the textual contents of fields labeled from *(a)* to *(d)* in Part

Table 1. Statistical characterization of the dataset used in our experiments.

Number of distinct ICD-10 codes	1,674
Number of distinct ICD-10 blocks	697
Number of distinct ICD-10 chapters	22
Number of certificates	115,406
Average number of fields with textual data	2.3
Average number of words per field	7.5
Maximum number of words per field	71
Vocabulary size	16,778

I, as well as the contents from Part II, in each case concatenating the strings labeled as *Outro*, *Valor* and *Tempo* (i.e., the fields named *Valor* and *Tempo* can be used to encode the approximated interval between the onset of the respective condition and the date of death, which can be relevant in cases like a stroke that occurred much before the time of death). Thus, each instance in the dataset consists of 6 different strings (i.e., we noticed that the field from Part II often contained two sentences), some of them possibly empty, padded with special symbols to encode the beginning/termination of the textual contents, together with the ICD-10 code corresponding to the main cause of death.

The available data was split into two subsets, with 75% (86,554 death certificates) for model training and 25% (28,852 certificates) for testing. Table 3 presents the distribution of the number of instances associated to each ICD-10 chapter (i.e., the column named *percentage* gives the fraction of instances, in the training plus the testing splits, corresponding to each chapter). Notice that some ICD-10 chapters have no instances in our dataset, given that the corresponding health problems are seldom related to death (i.e., Chapter VII, corresponding to diseases of the eye and adnexa), or are instead related to external causes that require an autopsy report (e.g., Chapter XIX, corresponding to injury, poisoning and certain other consequences of external causes).

All experiments relied on the keras[1] deep learning library. The word embedding layer in the first level considered a dimensionality of 50, and the output of the GRU layers had a dimensionality of 25. Model training was made in batches of 32 instances, using the Adam optimization algorithm [12] with default parameters. Model training considered a stopping criteria based on the training loss, finishing when the difference between epochs was less than 10^{-6}.

For accessing prediction quality, we measured the classification accuracy over the test split, as well the macro-averaged precision, recall and F1-scores (i.e., macro-averages assign an equal importance to each class, thus providing useful information in the case of datasets with a highly unbalanced class distribution).

---

[1] http://keras.io.

Given the hierarchical organization of ICD-10, we also measured results according to different levels of specialization (i.e., ICD-10 chapters, blocks, and full codes).

4.2   Experimental Results

Our experiments compared three different neural architectures: (i) a hierarchical model with two levels of GRUs but without the attention mechanisms, thus using the hidden states produced at the edges of the sequences in order to build the representations, an also considering only a single output node for the full ICD-10 code; (ii) a hierarchical attention model that also considers only a single output; (iii) the full model with two output nodes, as described in Sect. 3. Models (i) and (ii) correspond to variations were some of the components were removed.

Table 2 presents the results, and Table 3 further details the results obtained with Model (iii), by showing evaluation scores for each individual ICD-10 chapter. The best values is terms of accuracy were actually obtained with the simpler model, corresponding to 86%, 78%, and 75%, respectively when considering ICD-10 chapters, blocks and full-codes. To further access the overall performance of our method, we also computed the Mean Reciprocal Rank (MRR) of the correct class, when sorting classes according to the probability assigned prior to performing the softmax operation. Model (iii) has a MRR of 0.795 when assigning full codes, 0.830 for blocks, and 0.899 for chapters.

ICD Chapters II (i.e., neoplasms) and IV (i.e., diseases of the circulatory system) correspond to the most common causes of death in our dataset and, together, they represent approximately 58.1% of the instances. Table 4 further details the results obtained by Model (iii) in these two important chapters. We can also see that deaths with underlying cause in Chapter XVIII (i.e., symptoms, signs and abnormal clinical and laboratory findings, not elsewhere classified) were predicted with high effectiveness (i.e., an F1-score of 93.925%).

Table 2. Performance metrics for different variants of the neural model.

	ICD-10 level	Accuracy	Macro-averages		
			Precision	Recall	F1-score
Hierarchical model	Chapter	**86.417**	60.200	57.893	58.781
	Block	**78.459**	**35.786**	**32.824**	**32.892**
	Full code	**74.567**	**25.550**	**24.727**	**23.920**
+ attention mechanisms	Chapter	85.297	59.133	55.069	56.319
	Block	76.314	30.473	28.642	28.579
	Full code	72.480	20.760	20.417	19.471
+ two outputs	Chapter	86.372	**73.498**	**69.614**	**71.031**
	Block	78.171	33.919	31.614	31.658
	Full code	73.981	23.360	23.048	22.057

Table 3. Number of instances and obtained results for each of the ICD-10 chapters.

Chapter	Occurences		Percentage	Precision	Recall	F1-score
	Train	Test				
I	1,952	642	2.248	65.994	66.199	66.096
II	23,971	7,921	27.634	95.608	95.922	95.765
III	418	126	0.471	36.947	32.540	34.599
IV	4,836	1,567	5.453	75.925	66.816	71.079
V	2,386	849	2.803	76.162	75.265	75.711
VI	3,033	1,053	3.540	84.747	76.828	80.139
VII	0	0	0.000	—	—	—
VIII	8	1	0.008	100.000	100.000	100.000
IX	26,773	9,036	31.028	89.982	89.464	89.722
X	11,109	3,675	12.810	80.273	86.259	83.158
XI	3,970	1,334	4.596	78.012	80.585	79.277
XII	112	36	0.128	25.000	11.111	15.385
XIII	390	112	0.435	50.980	46.429	48.598
XIV	2,695	905	3.119	64.870	69.171	66.952
XV	0	0	0.000	—	—	—
XVI	10	1	0.003	100.000	100.000	100.000
XVII	105	34	0.120	68.421	38.235	49.057
XVIII	3,725	1,166	4.238	90.778	97.084	93.925
XIX	0	0	0.000	—	—	—
XX	1,171	394	1.356	66.776	51.523	58.166
XXI	0	0	0.000	—	—	—
XXII	0	0	0.000	—	—	—
Total:	86,554	28,852	Average:	73.498	69.614	71.031

Some of the previous research on coding death certificates has focused on deaths related to cancer [5]. When considering the 20 most common ICD cancer blocks in our test split, Model (iii) achieves a macro-averaged F1-score of 90.090%.

Although the results on Table 2 fail to show that neural attention mechanisms lead to an increased performance, these methods can offer model interpretability, by allowing us to see which parts of the input (i.e., which fields and which words) are attended to when making predictions. In Fig. 3, we illustrate the attention weights calculated as shown in Eq. 6, for the contents of two death certificates. The certificate in Fig. 3a was correctly assigned to code C719 (i.e., malignant neoplasm of brain, unspecified) with a confidence of 95.21%, and the figure shows the words *glioblastoma multiforme* having a significant impact. The certificate in Fig. 3b was assigned to code J40 (i.e., bronchitis, not specified as acute or chronic) with a confidence of 92.39%. In this example, the words *insuficiência*

Table 4. Results for blocks and full codes within ICD Chapters II and IX.

	ICD-10 level	Accuracy	Macro-averages		
			Precision	Recall	F1-score
Chapter II	Block	89.673	31.692	27.226	28.619
	Full code	85.216	26.133	23.877	23.960
Chapter IX	Block	76.859	13.596	11.118	11.900
	Full code	73.683	13.162	10.786	11.221

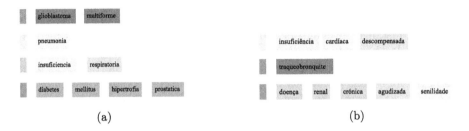

(a)   (b)

Fig. 3. Examples of the attention weights given at the field and word levels.

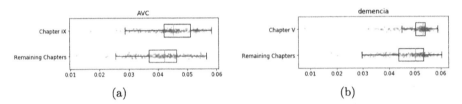

(a)   (b)

Fig. 4. Distribution of attention weights given to tokens *AVC* and *demencia*.

cardíaca descompensada in the first field have much less impact than the word *traqueobronquite* on the second field. Figure 4 instead shows the distribution of the attention weights for two particular word tokens, contrasting 250 death certificates from an ICD chapter related to the tokens, against 250 certificates from the remaining chapters. The token *AVC* (i.e., abbreviation of *acidente vascular cerebral*) is often used to denote a stroke, and the attention weights in Chapter IX (i.e., diseases of the circulatory system) are generally higher, as shown in Fig. 4a. Figure 4b shows a similar example, with the token *demencia* and considering Chapter V (i.e., mental and behavioural disorders).

5   Conclusions and Future Work

In this paper, we proposed a deep learning method for coding the free-text descriptions of the cause(s) of death, included in death certificates obtained from the Portuguese Ministry of Health's Directorate-General of Health, according to ICD-10. Results show that although IDC coding is a difficult task, due to the large number of classes that are sparsely used, we can still obtain a high accuracy, particularly in the cases of the more common causes of death. We argue that our approach can indeed contribute to a faster processing of death certificates, or it can help in the task of manual coding. The attention mechanisms used in our complete model also offer the opportunity to interpret and visualize the classification results, as we can check for each input where the model places more attention and how that impacts the prediction. This last aspect is particularly important for applications involving a human in-the-loop (i.e., a health technician with experience in ICD-10 coding), validating the results of the classifier.

Despite the interesting results, there are still many opportunities for future work. For instance, although previous studies have advanced methods for ICD coding of death certificates, their results are not directly comparable to ours, given the different languages and different formulations of the task – in some cases, the input was a single text, and the prediction tasks also differed in the number of classes or in the fact that multiple labels could be given as output. For future work, we would like to experiment with an adapted version of our neural architecture, over the French dataset from the CLEF eHealth task [8].

Noting that the inclusion two different model outputs (i.e., the ICD-10 full code and the ICD-10 block, for the main cause of death) helped to increase accuracy, for future work we would like to further pursue related ideas by considering multiple outputs corresponding to auxiliary causes of death (i.e., in Fig. 1, one can see that in SICO the input strings *(a)* to *(d)* are individually assigned to ICD-10 codes), also leveraging techniques for exploring class co-occurrences [14]. Given the highly skewed class distribution, we also plan to explore batch training procedures that, taking inspiration on the SMOTE method [15], oversample the minority classes and introduce minor perturbations on these training instances.

Finally, we have that the current model is only exploring six small strings as input, although in some circumstances (e.g., accidents, suicide, or homicide) we could also use the supplemental autopsy report. Currently ongoing efforts, also taking inspiration on previous work on text classification [16], are exploring the extension of the deep neural network introduced in Sect. 3 with different parts for encoding the full-text contents of autopsy reports, or the full-text contents of supplemental clinical information bulletins, when these are available.

Acknowledgements. This work had support from Fundação para a Ciência e Tecnologia (FCT), through the INESC-ID multi-annual funding from the PIDDAC program (UID/CEC/50021/2013).

References

1. Marques, C., Maia, C., Martins, H., Pinto, C.S., Anderson, R.N., Borralho, M.D.C.: Improving the mortality information system in portugal. Eurohealth **22**(2), 48–51 (2016)

2. Dalianis, H.: Clinical text retrieval - an overview of basic building blocks and applications. In: Paltoglou, G., Loizides, F., Hansen, P. (eds.) Professional Search in the Modern World. LNCS, vol. 8830, pp. 147–165. Springer, Cham (2014). doi:10. 1007/978-3-319-12511-4_8

3. Zweigenbaum, P., Lavergne, T.: Hybrid methods for ICD-10 coding of death certificates. In: Proceedings of International Workshop on Health Text Mining and Information Analysis (2016)

4. Mujtaba, G., Shuib, L., Raj, R.G., Rajandram, R., Shaikh, K., Al-Garadi, M.A.: Automatic ICD-10 multi-class classification of cause of death from plaintext autopsy reports through expert-driven feature selection. PLoS ONE **12**(2), e0170242 (2017)

5. Koopman, B., Zuccon, G., Nguyen, A., Bergheim, A., Grayson, N.: Automatic ICD-10 classification of cancers from free-text death certificates. Int. J. Med. Inform. **84**(11), 956–965 (2015)

6. Koopman, B., Karimi, S., Nguyen, A., McGuire, R., Muscatello, D., Kemp, M., Truran, D., Zhang, M., Thackway, S.: Automatic classification of diseases from free-text death certificates for real-time surveillance. BMC Med. Inform. Decis. Making **15**(1), 53 (2015)

7. Kelly, L., Goeuriot, L., Suominen, H., Névéol, A., Palotti, J., Zuccon, G.: Overview of the CLEF eHealth evaluation lab 2016. In: Fuhr, N., Quaresma, P., Gonçalves, T., Larsen, B., Balog, K., Macdonald, C., Cappellato, L., Ferro, N. (eds.) CLEF 2016. LNCS, vol. 9822, pp. 255–266. Springer, Cham (2016). doi:10. 1007/978-3-319-44564-9_24

8. Lavergne, T., Névéol, A., Robert, A., Grouin, C., Rey, G., Zweigenbaum, P.: A dataset for ICD-10 coding of death certificates: creation and usage. In: Proceedings of the Workshop on Building and Evaluating Resources for Biomedical Text Mining (2016)

9. Yang, Z., Yang, D., Dyer, C., He, X., Smola, A., Hovy, E.: Hierarchical attention networks for document classification. In: Proceedings of the Conference of the North American Chapter of the Association for Computational Linguistics (2016)

10. Cho, K., van Merrienboer, B., Bahdanau, D., Bengio, Y.: On the properties of neural machine translation: encoder-decoder approaches (2014). arXiv preprint arXiv:1409.1259

11. Rumelhart, D.E., Hinton, G.E., Williams, R.J.: Learning representations by back-propagating errors. Cogn. model. **5**(3), 1 (1988)

12. Kingma, D., Adam, J.B.: A method for stochastic optimization. In: Proceedings of the International Conference for Learning Representations (2015)

13. Goldberg, Y.: A primer on neural network models for natural language processing. J. Artif. Intell. Res. **57**, 345–420 (2016)

14. Kurata, G., Xiang, B., Zhou, B.: Improved neural network-based multi-label classification with better initialization leveraging label co-occurrence. In: Proceedings of the Annual Conference of the North American Chapter of the Association for Computational Linguistics (2016)

15. Chawla, N.V., Bowyer, K.W., Hall, L.O., Philip, W., Kegelmeyer, S.: Synthetic minority over-sampling technique. J. Artif. Intell. Res. **16**, 321–357 (2002)

16. Joulin, A., Grave, E., Bojanowski, P., Mikolov, T.: Bag of tricks for efficient text classification (2016). arXiv preprint arXiv:1607.01759

Robot Programming Through Whole-Body Interaction

Marta Ferraz[✉]

Biosymtic Robotics, Almada, Portugal
biosymrobots@gmail.com

Abstract. Programmable and non-programmable educational robots are, in most cases, associated with sedentary behavior in children. Children interact with educational robots mostly in indoor environments. Whole-body interaction and natural environments seem to potentiate children's physical and mental health. In order to potentiate children's physical and mental health we have developed a new set of robotic devices - Biosymtic Robotic devices. We describe the main computational models of Biosymtic Robotic devices: a computational model demonstrating how to increase children's physical activity levels and contact with natural environments through automatic feedback control mechanisms; a theoretical cognitive model on how to program robotic devices through whole-body interaction in natural environments.

Keywords: Child-robot interaction · Whole-body interaction · Physical and mental health · Robot programming

1 Introduction

Researchers have been developing robots to interact with children, e.g., for educational and health purposes. Programmable and non-programmable educational robots have been used to support child learning. These robots have been encouraging children to interact with screen-based computer devices involving mostly visual and auditory information-gathering scenarios (e.g., desktop/portable computers) and user interfaces based on hand-eye coordination skills (e.g., keyboard, mouse, multi-touch interfaces). These interfaces are used, e.g., to program physical actions/behaviors performed by the robots - programming autonomous control through source code [16]. Programmable and non-programmable educational robots may also communicate with children through speech and gestures [12].

For the aforementioned reasons, programmable and non-programmable educational robots are linked to sedentary behavior in children - in most cases encouraging sedentary interaction formats based on manipulative actions.

Sedentary behavior is characterized by diminished or complete lack of physical activity and is one of the main factors negatively influencing children's health. It correlates with obesity, type 2 diabetes, ADHD, anxiety, depression, mobility and postural problems, breathing difficulties, sleep and digestive disorders. This type of behavior has also been linked to increased cancer risk and premature death [18]. Nowadays, levels of energy expenditure are still insufficient in order to benefit

E. Oliveira et al. (Eds.): EPIA 2017, LNAI 10423, pp. 150–161, 2017.
DOI: 10.1007/978-3-319-65340-2_13

children's health [4]. Health robots to promote children's physical and mental health - increases in physical activity - are still scarce [7, 10]. Physical activity has a variety of benefits for children's physical and mental health [18].

In addition, children interact with educational and health robots predominantly in indoor environments. It has also been referenced that natural environments may optimize children's physical and mental health [11].

We propose a new format of robotic devices to increase children's physical activity levels, encourage learning and contact with natural environments: Biosymtic (Biosymbiotic Robotic) devices (BSDs).

In the present work we describe the main computational models included in BSDs that aim to potentiate children's physical and mental health. The next section introduces the literature associated with this work. We then describe a computational model demonstrating how to increase physical activity levels, in children, through automatic feedback control mechanisms - describing an experimental study. Followingly, we demonstrate a theoretical cognitive model on how to program robotic devices through whole-body interaction in natural environments, and why this model may represent a benefit for both children's development and Artificial Intelligence.

2 Related Work

2.1 Health Robots and Children

The ALIZ-E project employs a robotic humanoid system - NAO; semi-autonomous robot - to help children with diabetes in hospital environments. NAO helps children learn about and manage their metabolic condition. It is a teleoperated robot: the operator communicates verbally with the child as if he were the robot. NAO incites children to be physically active by suggesting they imitate its dance moves. In a study, it was demonstrated that five diabetic children (aged 8 to 12) increased their knowledge about diabetes by playing diabetes-quiz based games with the robot [7].

A non-mobile robot - "Keepon robot" - was developed to promote healthy physical activity and dietary behaviors in adolescents. The user wears a wristband device measuring physical activity levels throughout the day - number of steps. The obtained data is processed by the robot system, which persuades the adolescent to increase his/her daily physical activity levels - by modeling the user's motivational state. The user communicates with the robot directly or via a phone application (speech or text input). In turn, the robot produces speech as output [10].

2.2 Physical Activity and Natural Environments Benefit Children's Physical and Mental Health

Physical activity benefits human development in multiple ways. It benefits the development of the sensorimotor system; promotes physical fitness; reduces anxiety and depression; boosts self-esteem; and it is associated with the reduction of ADHD symptoms [18].

Moderate vigorous physical activity (MVPA) benefits children's physical and mental health, optimizing the development of the cardiovascular system and contributing to a healthy body weight. The World Health Organization recommends at least 60 min of daily MVPA for children aged 5 to 17 years [18].

In addition, MVPA seems to be the gold standard to optimize cognitive function (including academic achievement) and boost cognitive structure in children [6].

Although scarce, recent studies have demonstrated that the development of gross motor skills (demanding use of large muscular groups) improves the development of cognitive function and optimizes academic achievement [17]. The previous experiences go beyond the manipulative actions (demanding small muscular groups) used to interact with computing devices in most educational robotic systems.

Other recent studies have also demonstrated that whole-body motion computing devices tend to benefit children's cognitive function (e.g., attention and memory) compared to sedentary computing devices [9].

It has been referenced that natural environments optimize children's physical and mental health, e.g., optimizing cognitive function by increasing alertness levels; synthesis of vitamin D for prevention of autoimmune diseases [11].

For the aforementioned reasons, it is urgent to include physical activity, in natural environments, in children's daily lives so as to promote healthy lifestyles.

The central goal of a BSD is to potentiate children's physical and mental health (including cognitive development/performance), while connecting them with challenging natural environments offering multiple possibilities for sensory stimulation and increasing physical and mental stress to the organism.

3 Computational Models Associated with Biosymtic Devices

A BSD is characterized as an artificial system displaying automatic control functions and autonomous behaviors.

A BSD displays automatic control functions while (two modes):

(1) Directly connected to a human organism (human-integrated automatic control);
(2) Disconnected from a human organism (working as an autonomous robot).

A BSD is able to sense and act in the environment, demonstrating adaptive functions in both modes 1 and 2.

3.1 Mode 1 - Automatic Control Functions in a Biosymtic Device While Directly Connected to a Human Organism

Computational models allow robots to control a variety of sensors and actuators in real-time in order to act in the environment.

In mode 1, a BSD encourages a child to be physically active, in natural environments, through computational models - robot software systems - based on automatic feedback control mechanisms. These mechanisms encourage the child to achieve a specific physiological state - e.g., MVPA - associated with physical and mental health. The child's physiological data is always used to persuade a covert response: physical action.

We developed a wheeled mobile BSD, named "Cratus", to test our proposals. "Cratus" mimics a Roman inventor. The physical structure of this device consists of a head connected to a torso, with a three-wheel mechanism on its base. The system includes a touch-based computer, on the back of the torso, displaying visual (virtual) information. Auditory output (e.g., music and verbal speech) is produced by a sound speaker integrated in the apparatus' head (resembling an eye).

System inputs to control visual and audio information (e.g., put a game avatar into motion; robot's speech) are made via whole-body physical action, e.g., the child may push, pull, rotate the apparatus while running on the physical terrain. The child may also skate while using this system - feet on top of the three-wheel mechanism. "Cratus" includes wireless motion sensors to capture motion data (e.g., accelerometer, gyroscope and a tilt sensor on the device's torso and a rotational speed sensor in one of its wheels). Moving "Cratus" on the terrain is translated as virtual locomotion, e.g., of a game avatar. The system also captures the child's physiological data - e.g., communicating wirelessly with a heart rate (HR) biosensor on the child's chest. The device also includes environmental sensors (light, humidity and temperature) and servomotors connected to encoders (actuators integrated in its wheels) (see Fig. 1).

Fig. 1. Biosymtic device "Cratus".

"Cratus" may include a variety of robot software systems, e.g., aiming to improve children's cardiorespiratory performance and/or cognitive performance. These software systems include automatic feedback control mechanisms.

For example, we developed a software - game "Cratus. The Space Traveller" - whose goal is to optimize children's cardiorespiratory performance. In this game narrative, "Cratus" is an old Roman inventor who reinvented his body in order to become a time traveller. The "wheeled teleportation system" is one of his great inventions. This system allows "Cratus" to travel the Universe at the speed of light. "Cratus" begins a journey throughout the Universe to discover the ancient architectural epochs of planet Earth (e.g., Roman coliseum - IV century, Eiffel Tower - XIX century). The game's main goal is to help "Cratus" control his "wheeled teleportation system" while exploring a variety of 3D game scenarios - displayed on the touch-based display. The child is encouraged to move, as fast as possible, in each game scenario in order to score - completing racetracks in the shortest time possible.

In this program, "Cratus", encourages a child to perform MVPA - the automatic feedback control mechanism incites the child to achieve 50% and 85% of maximum HR values (recommended by the American Heart Association) [1].

The inertial wheel mechanism actuator of the apparatus - on two of the wheels - maintains the desired interval of HR values. The inertial mechanism consists of an electromechanical brake system - encoders placed on servomotors - that controls the rotational speed of the apparatus. For instance, if the child presents an average HR value <134.5 beats per minute (<50%, sedentary physical activity levels), while interacting with the device (e.g., while pushing the apparatus during running), the system increases the inertial forces applied to the inertial mechanism (brake system locks the wheels up to a certain degree, e.g., 45%) - the child then needs to move faster to reach the desired interval. If the child exhibits an average HR value >175 beats per minute (>85%, very vigorous physical activity levels), the system decreases the inertial forces applied to the inertial mechanism (brake system unlocks the wheels up to a certain degree, e.g., 36%).

The system also includes a verbal actuator that produces audio output. This actuator follows the principles established for the "inertial wheel mechanism actuator". If, for instance, the child presents an average HR value <134.5 beats per minute (<50%), the verbal actuator emits specific verbal feedback, e.g., "Run faster!" or "Give me more power!". If the child presents an average HR value >175 beats per minute (>85%), the verbal actuator emits specific verbal feedback, e.g., "Slow down!" or "Move slower!". The reference interval of HR values is calculated and adjusted every minute - according to average HR values per minute.

"Cratus" demonstrates adaptive behavior by adapting to the performance of each child. For instance, for a similar task, child "A" may need to be exposed to increased inertial forces to achieve the desired HR values when compared to child "B".

Additionally, real-time HR/motion data can be visualized on the software: a bar graph that changes color according to the child's HR values; a slider (disk) displaying the angles and the rotation velocity in three-dimensional space. The system displays angles and rotation velocity to facilitate the child's performance during the game. This information is also accompanied by verbal instructions - e.g., "Straight ahead!"; "Turn right!"; "Rotate 45 degrees to the right!".

We conducted a study [8] to evaluate the effects of the BSD "Cratus" (cardiorespiratory performance program) on physical activity levels of a group of 20 healthy children aged 6 to 8 years - evaluation via the SenseWear® Arm Band. In the experimental session, children were evaluated once - two children interacting with the "Cratus" device (one device each) in a natural forested landscape - performing a single 12-min session. Children were told to interact freely with "Cratus" in the natural forested landscape - playing the game "Cratus. The Space Traveller". Children's expectations regarding the device - motivation to play - were also collected using the Smileyometer questionnaire - individual evaluation in a classroom context.

Results showed that interacting with "Cratus", in a natural environment, instilled vigorous physical activity levels in children - 8.1 ± 1.4 METs (metabolic intensity). In addition, children achieved the reference (desired) interval of HR values (moderate-intense physical activity) - between 50% and 85% of maximum HR values (recommended by the American Heart Association), instilled by the automatic feedback control mechanism. Furthermore, children were highly motivated to interact with the device in the natural environment.

The latter results demonstrate that the automatic feedback control mechanism included in "Cratus" served the purpose of maintaining children's HR values at adequate exercise intensities. Hence, robotic systems endowed with automatic feedback control mechanisms - establishing a connection with the child's physiological state in real-time (HR) - may be advantageous in promoting adequate exercise intensities and thus favoring health in children.

3.2   Mode 2 - Autonomous Functions in a Biosymtic Device - Bio-Kinesthetic Programming

In mode 2, a BSD builds autonomous functions by interacting with a human. We termed this process Bio-Kinesthetic Programming (BKP). BKP is an approach to Robot Programming by Demonstration, aiming to help a robot build autonomous functions via human guidance techniques, such as whole-body direct physical control and physiological states transfer, while physically and mentally benefiting the human organism. Hence, a BSD and a human form a symbiotic connection.

The child controls the BSD, in the environment, through whole-body physical action, programming autonomous functions - e.g., the child's locomotion works as an example to be replicated by the device during autonomous navigation. The child's physiological states, while controlling the robot, are also used to program autonomous functions - e.g., the robot learns to manage its energy sources according to the child's energy metabolism.

Kinesthetic teaching has been used to help robots learn motor skills associated with a certain goal, e.g., guiding the motion of a robot's arms through direct manual control in order to teach it how to manipulate objects [5]. However, and to our knowledge, there are no references to guidance techniques making use of physiological states transfer between a human - while playing in the natural world - and a robotic system.

Let's take our wheeled mobile BSD "Cratus" as a way of example.

After activating the "learning program" (robot software system to build autonomous functions in the BSD) the child is encouraged to control "Cratus", in the physical environment, through whole-body physical action. For example, the child may push, pull, rotate and throw the apparatus while she walks or runs on the physical terrain. In the "learning program" the child interacts freely with the BSD, e.g., may select a variety of avatars/scenarios included in the software (or even previously build her own avatars/scenarios) to freely explore the physical world.

The child may also define the inertial forces applied to her avatar by controlling software actuators - e.g., "inertial wheel mechanism" changing effort intensity. At the same time, the child establishes physical interaction with the BSD, she may also teach it physical actions/behaviors to be autonomously executed later.

The device includes motion sensors to capture motion data, e.g., accelerometer, gyroscope and a tilt sensor on the apparatus' torso; a rotational speed sensor in one of its wheels. The system captures the child's physiological data - e.g., communicating wirelessly with a HR biosensor on the child's chest. "Cratus" also includes environmental sensors - light, humidity and temperature; four infrared sensors (IR) on its base to detect objects in close proximity; a microphone in its head to record sound; and servomotors in its wheels, which allow for autonomous motion (motion in a straight line and rotation).

The child may visualize motion, physiological and environmental data on the touch-based display: motion intensity scale; angles/velocity of rotations; a virtual heart that changes color according to the child's HR values; light, humidity and temperature scales. The child is encouraged to explore her own biological processes on the software, together with environmental information during the teaching experience.

The "learning program" on BSDs involves a memory-based learning approach grounded on perceptual, motor and physiological states and verbal commands. This approach is inspired by the multimodal simulation system developed by Barsalou (Embodied Cognition) to explain the origins of mental representations in different animal species [3]. Accordingly, mental representations are generated through simulation processes in the brain (brain computations) - reactivation of neural circuits that were active during previous perceptual, motor and introspective experiences. Multimodal representations regarding perceptual, motor and introspective states - perceptual symbols - are stored in the brain's memory system and later recalled during conceptual knowledge - supporting memory recall and other higher-order cognitive abilities such as higher-order perception and conceptual knowledge.

A BSD may learn a variety of tasks via multimodal simulation processes: collecting (recording) motor, physiological and environmental data, while interacting with the child, to be later recalled/used during autonomous functions - gathering information about events in the environment through human guidance. Motor and physiological data - captured via rotational speed sensors, gyroscopes, tilt, IR and HR sensors - represent the sensory state of the BSD. Environmental data - light, humidity and temperature - represents information external to the system.

The child also ascribes verbal labels to the learning experiences - e.g., "stop", "move fast", "move slow", "avoid obstacles", "touch-object", "search-light", "rotate", "dance" - to activate multimodal simulation processes on the device.

For example, after activating the "learning program", on the software, the BSD immediately starts recording sensory data. The child interacts with the device freely in the physical environment - deciding what physical action/behavior to teach the device. When the child determines that the learning activity has ended, she activates a "verbal learning" function on the software - ascribing a verbal label to the previous experience via verbal input to the system - microphone recorded. The software associates this verbal label to the metrics obtained during the interaction (motion, physiological, environmental data) - creating a memory representation of the experience. Later, after a few learning experiences, the child may reactivate this memory via a speech recognition system, included in the software - activating the function "autonomous behavior" in the software and voicing the verbal label to the system. At this moment, the system should be able to reactivate the memory associated with the verbal label (accessing motion, physiological, environmental data associated with the learning experience - multimodal simulation) and autonomously replicate the behavior - also demonstrating adaptive behavior in different environmental settings.

Let's imagine that the child decides to teach the concept of "move fast" to "Cratus".

The child activates the "learning program" and starts pushing the device as fast as possible in the physical world. To end the learning process the child activates the "verbal learning" function in the software. At this moment the software stops recording data and verbal inputs may be given (a verbal label) - "move fast". This behavior may be later reactivated, in the "autonomous behavior" mode, by voicing the same verbal command - "move fast".

During the learning experience, the sensory states of the BSD and information external to it are continuously recorded. The child may enable or disable inputs made to the system by activating or deactivating communication between the sensors and the software.

Data acquired during the learning experience - demonstration phase - represents perceptual symbols to be stored by the software. These perceptual symbols are reactivated during the "autonomous behavior" function, according to specific verbal labels determined by the child. This learning approach allows the BSD not only to create a multimodal memory of a verbal concept - associated with motor and physiological states and environmental information - but also to act, in the environment, according to the earlier experiences. For instance, in the previous example, the verbal label "move fast" is associated with an increase in the rotational speed of the wheels of the apparatus. The "learning program" records the rotational speed of the wheels, from the start of the activity until the "verbal learning" function is activated. In this case, the device records motion data to later manage its locomotion functions, in the environment, autonomously.

The BSD also makes use of the child's physiological data – e.g., HR data – to perform autonomous behavior in the environment. In the previous example, the verbal label "move fast" is associated with an increase in the child's HR. Again, the "learning program" records the child's HR values from the start of the activity until the "verbal learning" function is activated. In addition, the device captures the physical terrain's gradient through the tilt sensor.

The child's physiological data is recorded by the device to later manage its energy sources autonomously while in the environment. The computational model makes an analogy between the human energy metabolism and the energy functions in the BSD. For instance, the verbal label "move fast" is associated with an increase in HR. As the child moves across different terrain gradients, she will show variations in HR - e.g., a slope will increase HR while she tries to push the device as fast as possible. The BSD records and associates data from the child's HR and terrain gradient, obtained during the learning experiences, to manage its energy functions - e.g., providing more power to the servo motors when on a slope in order to maintain speed.

The BSD learns new skills (or builds skill models) by computing the average and variance of continuous motion, physiological and environmental data from multiple learning experiences - in order to apply them to new contexts. To that end, the software makes use of a Gaussian Mixture Model, extracting the statistical regularities and the variability across multiple interactions. For instance, if after a few demonstrations, in different environmental conditions, the average rotational speed of the wheels of the apparatus is "X revolutions/time" then - when the child activates the "move fast" behavior in the "autonomous behavior" function - the apparatus tries to replicate this same speed ("X revolutions/time") in different environmental conditions. Variations regarding environmental conditions - e.g., terrain gradient - and on the child's HR (for different terrain gradients) are taken into account when trying to replicate the behavior "X revolutions/time" to new contexts. If the Biosymtic device is not able to perform the learned behavior in different environmental conditions, then the child needs to provide the system more learning experiences.

While the child guides the BSD through the learning activity, environmental data may also be recorded - light, humidity and temperature. Since the learning process on a BSD results from multiple learning experiences, we may expect the BSD to create associations between not only motor and physiological data, but also environmental data and verbal concepts. In some cases, environmental data may be more important for the BSD to learn how to act in an environment than other types of data. For instance, the "move fast" behavior may be more dependent on motor and physiological data, compared to environmental data, because the learning process results from finding statistical regularities and the variability across multiple interactions. On the other hand, if the child tries to teach behaviors such as "search light" or "search shadow", light data becomes essential for the device. For example, starting the "learning program" with the light sensor and the motion sensors activated and driving the device multiple times to a shaded area and vice-versa (Fig. 2).

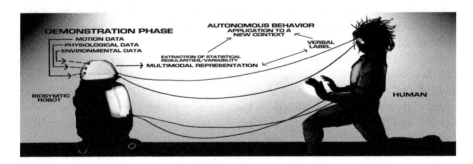

Fig. 2. Bio-Kinesthetic Programming Cognitive Model. The Biosymtic device captures continuous motion, physiological and environmental data during the learning experience (demonstrations phase). Data is used to create a multimodal representation of the learning experience (recorded in the robot software system) - associated with a verbal label.

Bio-Kinesthetic Programming: Benefits for Children's Development and Artificial Intelligence

While programming autonomous behaviors in a BSD, the child is encouraged to be physically active in natural environments that offer a variety of benefits for physical and mental health (including cognitive development and performance). Moreover, while giving commands to a BSD she may engage in social skills practice, e.g., through collaborative play. For example, she may decide to challenge another child to a race/football contest between BSDs - verbally controlling the devices.

One of the goals of the Bio-Kinesthetic teaching approach to robot learning is to make robots acquire autonomous functional features in close proximity to biological organisms; however, autonomy is always subject to previously given commands - according to human will.

Our learning model allows BSDs to develop adaptive functions based on memory processes - multimodal simulation. The device is able to identify human verbal commands - concepts - to perform actions in the physical world. Concepts in a BSD become associated with motor and physiological states - transferred from the human organism to the device - in combination with sensory information from the physical environment (e.g., light, temperature). In fact, BSDs learn how to manage their energy resources by mirroring human energy functions in order to optimize their actions in the physical world. Hence, we may say that BSDs are endowed with cognitive skills, however, under human control.

The central goal of the Artificial Intelligence (AI) field has been to assign biological functions to artificial machines [2, 13–15]. Roboticists have been working on artificial machines aiming to emulate the physical and cognitive features of a variety of biological organisms (e.g., humans, insects, reptiles) [2, 13]. However, electromechanical systems differ from biological organisms in their physical properties. A biological organism is characterized as a contiguous living system consisting of a single or multiple cells: made of organic matter. Life involves chemical reactions to sustain it, e.g., energy production. An electromechanical system integrates mechanical moving parts to carry out electrical operations: made of silicon and metals [15].

According to von Neumann [15:70], *"the natural materials have some sort of mechanical stability and are well balanced with respect to mechanical properties, electrical properties, and reliability requirements. Our artificial systems are patchworks in which we achieve desirable electrical traits at the price of mechanically unsound things"*.

Meyer and Guillot [13:1415] emphasize that billions of years of evolution have made biological functional mechanisms more efficient (*"sensing, actuating and control mechanisms"*) and that it has been difficult for artificial devices to cope with that evolutionary background.

Embodied Cognition researchers claim that cognition, in biological organisms, emerges according to their structural features and associated action possibilities - e.g., a human will perceive a chair differently from a crocodile because these species have different body structures (a chair suggests "seating" for most humans, a crocodile will probably not notice it) [3]. It has also been emphasized that different kinds of biological organisms present particular physiological features that determine, e.g., how those organisms sense and create knowledge about the physical world.

The previous arguments led us to the idea that structural, as well as physiological features, determine how cognition emerges in biological organisms. Taking into account that electromechanical systems differ from biological organisms in their physical and functional properties and that, e.g., biological organisms present more efficient "sensing, actuating and control mechanisms" than current artificial devices, it may be the case that artificial machines come to benefit from a learning approach involving, not only motor, but also physiological learning models. This learning approach may allow artificial machines to demonstrate functional features in close proximity to biological organisms.

The BSD "Cratus" has a different "body structure", and energy mechanism, to that of a human. Hence, it is expected that the perception of the physical world will emerge differently. While operating the device in the physical environment, through physical action, the child teaches the device to generate percepts from the physical world according to the latter's "body structure" - i.e., a torso with no arms connected to a wheeled mechanism. The child also teaches the device to manage its own energy functions more efficiently in the environment - emulating the human energy metabolism to manage its own energy functions.

The BSD may also learn from other types of human physiological response so as to learn how to manage its own functional mechanisms, e.g., emotional response. Hence, the BSD learns to interpret the functional processes of the human body in order to manage its functional processes autonomously. Because the learning process results from several learning experiences it may be characterized as a developmental process.

Researchers in Developmental Robotics and AI have suggested that in order for artificial machines to demonstrate cognitive abilities they must be subject to several learning experiences [14].

We are currently evaluating/testing a computational model allowing children to program Biosymtic devices through Bio-Kinesthetic teaching techniques. This research study will be presented in future work.

4   Conclusions

Whole-body motion robotic systems endowed with automatic feedback control mechanisms - establishing a connection with the child's heart rate in real-time - seem to be advantageous in promoting adequate exercise intensities - moderate-intense physical activity. Researchers showed that moderate-intense physical activity benefits children's physical and mental health - including cognitive development/performance.

Programmable robots are linked to sedentary behavior in children - encouraging sedentary interaction formats to program autonomous control through source code. Biosymtic Robotic devices are an alternative to programmable robots - encouraging whole-body motion interaction formats, in natural environments, to program autonomous control. Research showed that whole-body motion and natural environments benefit children's physical and mental health.

The present work aims to draw the attention of the Child-Robot Interaction community to the fact that children's development may benefit from whole-body interaction in natural environments, and that robot learning - artificial intelligence - may profit from a symbiotic approach with the human organism.

References

1. American Heart Association 2015. Target Heart Rates. http://www.heart.org/HEARTORG/
GettingHealthy/PhysicalActivity/FitnessBasics/Target-Heart-Rates_UCM_434341_Article.
jsp

2. Bar-Cohen, Y., Breazeal, C.: Biologically inspired intelligent robotics. In: Proceedings of the SPIE Smart Structures Conference, San Diego, CA, pp. 1–7 (2003)
3. Barsalou, L.W.: Perceptual symbol systems. Behav. Brain Sci. **22**(4), 577–660 (1999)
4. Boreham, C., Riddoch, C.: The physical activity, fitness and health of children. J. Sports Sci. **19**(12), 915–929 (2001)
5. Calinon, S., Billard, A.: What is the teacher's role in robot programming by demonstration? Toward benchmarks for improved learning. Interact. Stud. **8**(3), 441–464 (2007). Special Issue on Psychological Benchmarks in Human-Robot Interaction
6. Chaddock, L., Erickson, K.I., Prakash, R.S., Kim, J.S., Voss, M.W., Vanpatter, M., Kramer, A.F.: A neuroimaging investigation of the association between aerobic fitness, hippocampal volume and memory performance in preadolescent children. Brain Res. **1358**, 172–183 (2010)
7. Espinoza, R.R., Nalin, M., Wood, R., Baxter, P., Looije, R., Demiris, Y.: Child-robot interaction in the wild: advice to the aspiring experimenter. In: Proceedings of the 13th International Conference on Multimodal Interfaces, ICMI 2011, pp. 335–342. ACM (2011)
8. Removed for blind review 2016
9. Removed for blind review 2017
10. Grigore, E.C., Scassellati, B.: Maintaining engagement in shared goals with a personal robot companion through motivational state modeling. In: 10th ACM/IEEE International Conference on Human-Robot Interaction (HRI), Portland, OR (2015)
11. Jensen, E.: Learning with the Body in the Mind: The Scientific Basis for Energizers, Movement, Play, Games, and Physical Education. The Brain Store, Inc., Chicago (2000)
12. Kirstein, F., Risager, R.V.: Social robots in educational institutions. They came to stay: introducing, evaluating, and securing social robots in daily education. In: The Eleventh ACM/IEEE International Conference on Human-Robot Interaction, HRI 2016, pp. 453–454. IEEE Press, Piscataway (2016)
13. Meyer, J.-A., Guillot, A.: Biologically inspired robots. In: Siciliano, B., Khatib, O. (eds.) Springer Handbook of Robotics, pp. 1395–1422. Springer, Heidelberg (2008)
14. Minsky, M.L.: Robotics. Omni Press Book, New York (1985)
15. von Neumann, J.: Theory of Self-Reproducing Automata. Burks, A.W. (ed.) University of Illinois Press, Urbana and London (1966)
16. Papert, S.: Mindstorms, Children, Computers and Powerful Ideas, 2nd edn. Basic Books, New York (1980)
17. Piek, J.P., Dawson, L., Smith, L.M., Gasson, N.: The role of early fine and gross motor development on later motor and cognitive ability. Hum. Mov. Sci. **27**(5), 668–681 (2008)
18. World Health Organization 2013. Physical Activity and Young People. http://www.who.int/dietphysicalactivity/factsheet_young_people/en/

Wheeze Detection Using Convolutional Neural Networks

Kirill Kochetov[1]([✉]), Evgeny Putin[1], Svyatoslav Azizov[1], Ilya Skorobogatov[2], and Andrey Filchenkov[1]

[1] Computer Technologies Lab, ITMO University, 49 Kronverksky Pr,
197101 St. Petersburg, Russia
{kskochetov,eoputin,szazizov,afilchenkov}@corp.ifmo.ru
[2] Center for Billing Technologies and Printing Services,
17 Bolshaya Raznochinaya St, 197110 St. Petersburg, Russia

Abstract. In this paper, we propose to use convolutional neural networks for automatic wheeze detection in lung sounds. We present convolutional neural network based approach that has several advantages compared to the previous approaches described in the literature. Our method surpasses the standard machine learning models on this task. It is robust to lung sound shifting and requires minimal feature preprocessing steps. Our approach achieves 99% accuracy and 0.96 AUC on our datasets.

Keywords: Wheeze detection · Convolutional neural networks · Machine learning · Deep learning

1 Introduction

According to the World Health Organization (WHO), lung diseases are the third most common cause of the death right after the coronary heart disease and stroke. Prevalence statistics of the pulmonary diseases are impressive. For example, in many countries, approximately 5% of the population suffers from asthma, which is appearing as coughing, dyspnea, and the main factor is wheezes.

Wheezes are adventitious sounds present in the lung that is clinically defined as abnormal. Wheezes can be determined as an undesigned and uninterrupted sounds [1]. Lung sound records generated during breathing can be a good source of information for lung treatment. For example, the presence of wheezes in lung sound records of children have been widely used as a parameter to evaluate the inclination to asthma. From an acoustic point of view, wheezes are characterized by periodic waveforms with a dominant frequency usually over 100 Hz [2].

Traditionally, a stethoscope is used to diagnose and monitor wheezes. Stethoscope is a fast, reliable, non-invasive instrument for diagnosing respiration functions of patients. But due to the fact of the increasing number of patients with asthma and other lung diseases, there is a permanent demand for automatic wheeze detection systems. Among other reasons that complicate lung treatment,

© Springer International Publishing AG 2017
E. Oliveira et al. (Eds.): EPIA 2017, LNAI 10423, pp. 162–173, 2017.
DOI: 10.1007/978-3-319-65340-2_14

maybe, the most important one is the late diagnosis. In many countries with low quality of life, there are simply not enough qualified medical workers to diagnose every patient on time. Thus, for patients with lung diseases uninterrupted and automatic monitoring is very important as the day-to-day state monitoring of lung health can provide key information to the medical diagnosis. The automated wheeze recognition system will also allow any member of medical staff to understand if something is wrong with the respiratory cycle of patient, so it would speed up further treatment. Such systems could help to minimize or eliminate human factor mistakes serving as intellectual decision support systems for medical workers.

The scientific advances in signal processing, speech recognition, time series analysis has been very significant lately, so there are a lot of complex and powerful methods to analyze respiratory cycle sounds nowadays. However, the necessary quality level has not been achieved yet preventing widespread of such systems in real clinics. One of the main problems of most previous studies in wheeze detection is that almost all the methods used there require a lot of complex preprocessing steps of lung sound records to achieve suitable performance. These preprocessing steps are not robust and are sensitive to internal/external noise and quality of records. For example, conventional machine learning (ML) models such as support vector machine (SVM) or k-nearest neighbors (kNN), if being trained on mel-frequency cepstral coefficients (MFCC) features, will work poorly on shifted lung sounds, because MFCC features by nature are not robust to shifting. But in real clinical applications, it is hard to adjust records so they start and end exactly when they are required to. Also, ML models trained on preprocessed data in such ways may not generalize their performance on different versions of stethoscopes.

Deep learning models [3] have recently showed very promising performance on a range of tasks. It has turned out to be a very efficient tool for image recognition [4–6], nature language processing [7–9] and speech recognition [10–13]. In 2012, a convolutional neural network (CNN) was trained to classify 1.3 million high-resolution images into the 1000 different classes [14]. It achieved top-1 and top-5 error rates of 39.7% and 18.9% on the test data. In the area of sound event recognition [15], CNNs beats other feature extraction algorithms and showed great performance in terms of robustness compared with MFCC.

The goal of this study is suggesting an efficient approach for the wheeze detection problem. We propose approach wheeze detection using convolutional neural network (WDCNN) that solves this problem using more flexible architecture. The proposed approach reaches state-of-the-art performance in wheeze detection task and is robust for shifting records and external noise. The contribution of this paper includes:

- To the best of our knowledge, we are the first who presents CNN-based automatic wheeze detection approach.
- Our CNN-based approach on non-processing normalized data like spectrograms are better in terms of evaluation metrics than other approaches that involved a lot of complex preprocessing steps like applying different filters

(FIR, Hamming window, etc.), noise reduction techniques, normalization by frequencies, different feature extraction techniques (MFCC, SBC, Entropy features), etc.
- Our CNN-based solution achieves 99% accuracy and 0.96 AUC measure.

The rest of the paper is organized as follows. In Sect. 2, the previous studies related to the topic are summarized. We describe our deep learning approach, data that we used and methods for preprocessing in Sect. 3. Experiments details are presented in Sect. 4. Results and performance measures are presented in Sect. 5. Finally, conclusions are made in Sect. 6.

2   Related Work

In [16], authors proposed an approach to automatic wheeze detection called Entropy-Based Wheeze Detection (EBWD). On the first stage, digital signal was transformed to domain frequency by commonly used STFT (Short Time Fourier Transform) method. STFT procedure produced the Fourier spectrum for each shorter segment of digital signal. On the second stage, peak detection by masking was applied to identify peaks in the signal. After that the authors empirically estimated that vacancy areas beside the peaks for wheezy breath were much larger than for normal breath. They characterized these discrepancies in signals in terms of informational entropy. On the third stage, several features were extracted with respect to entropy. The authors proposed to use features like the difference between maximum and minimum entropy or their ratio and to perform thus wheeze detection using some threshold on this features. As a result, EBWD was able to identify 85% of wheeze samples based on Microphones (Panasonic WM-64 ON) data.

The authors of another paper [17] have demonstrated how Gaussian Mixture Models (GMM) can be applied to classify respiratory diseases. RALE database and 4 classes (normal, wheeze, crackles and asthma) of lung sounds were used in this research. As the preprocessing steps for digital signals from a stethoscope, the authors applied FIR (Finite Impulse Response) filter followed by FFT (Fast Fourier Transform) algorithm. After that, MFCC (Mel-frequency cepstral coefficients) features were extracted from preprocessed signals. The authors conducted several experiments to evaluate the best number of GMMs in the model and also evaluated the accuracy of their models with and without cross-validation. As a result, their approach obtained average (across all classes) 98.7% accuracy without cross-validation and 52.5% accuracy with cross-validation.

In [18], the authors have used a lot of machine learning methods such as feed-forward multilayer neural network (MLP), random forest (RF), logistic regression (LR), naïve Bayes (NB), support vector machine (SVM) and k-nearest neighbors (kNN) for automated wheeze detection using phonopneumograms from the Internet (called INT dataset) and Dubrovnik General Hospital (DGH) datasets. Their preprocessing stages consisted of applying Yule-Walker filter to reduce the influence of cardiovascular and muscular noise followed by STFT procedure. After that, the commonly used MFCC features were extracted from the preprocessed signals. Also, the authors experimented with some statistical features using FFT (Renyi entropy, Kurtosis, Spectral Flatness (SF), Skewness, etc.) without using MFCC features. As a result, their approach on statistical features achieved 93.62%, 91.77% accuracies for INT and DGH datasets, respectively, by the best model (NN with 2 hidden layers). On MFFC features, their approach with SVM and kNN models obtained 99% on both datasets. The authors claimed that by properly filtering and preprocessing the entry data, and using MFCC features, the signals recorded in suboptimal conditions can be efficiently processed.

Table 1. The comparison table

Author	Year	Processing and feature extraction methods	Classifier	Result
Zhang et al.	2009	Entropy, STFT	Entropy-Based Wheeze Detection (EBWD)	Able to identify 85% wheezes samples and systems have been implemented into wearable sound-based respiration monitoring system
Mayorga et al.	2010	Finite Impuse Response (FIR) filter, Hamming window, Fast Fourier Transform (FFT), Mel Frequency Cepstral Coefficients (MFCC)	Gaussian Mixture Models (GMM)	Accuracy of 98.7% obtained
Milicevic et al.	2016	Yule-Walker filter, STFT, FFT, MFCC	MLP, RF, LR, NB, SVM, kNN	93.62%, 91.77% accuracies for INT and DGH datasets, respectively
Bahoura et al.	2004	MFCC, Subband Based Cepstral (SBC)	Gaussian Mixture Models (GMM), MLP, Vector Quantization (VQ)	GMM on MFCC successfully classify sounds into two category (wheeze and normal sounds)
Palaniappan et al.	2014	MFCC	SVM, kNN	92.19% and 98.26% accuracies obtained for SVM and kNN, respectively

GMM method was used for binary classification of normal and wheezing respiratory sounds in [19] as well as in [18]. At the preprocessing stage, the sound data were divided into overlapped frames from which a reduced dimension feature vectors were extracted using MFCC procedure and Subband based Cepstral parameters (SBC). The GMM-MFCC combination was compared with Vector

Quantization (VQ) and Multi-Layer Perceptron (MLP) neural networks and the best result was obtained by GMM-MFCC. At the postprocessing stage, smoothing of the score function was applied to include the wheezes duration into the model. This led to the significant performance improvement.

In [20], two common classifiers were applied to the data of three categories: normal, airway obstruction pathology, and parenchymal pathology. The MFCC features were extracted from the data and analyzed by one-way ANOVA (analysis of variance). After that, the features were fed separately into the SVM and kNN classifiers. The obtained accuracies of the classification with the SVM and kNN classifiers were found to be 92.19% and 98.26%, respectively.

The most successful recent papers related to wheeze detection are listed in Table 1. These works presented effective techniques that achieved high accuracy values of the exploited classification methods. The Table reflects differences between the techniques, specifically, it shows which processing, feature extraction methods, and classifiers were applied in each work and to what results it has led.

3   Proposed Approach

3.1   Data

Most authors use lung sound data from different internet databases (e.g. [21]) for their research purposes. Such databases were created foremost for educational aims. Each database usually contains a small amount of samples. Unfortunately, most of these databases consist almost only of sick lung sounds.

We collected several datasets from all over the Internet (e.g. soundtracks from YouTube videos and a other sources, e.g. [21]). Some of founded lung sound samples were too long or too short. The number of such samples was 43. These samples were considered as outliers and were dropped. Resulting dataset consisted of 817 samples with 232 healthy and 585 sick lung respiratory cycles. A 2D spectrograms of several samples are shown in Fig. 1.

3.2   Methods

There are many preprocessing techniques and feature extraction methods that can be used for lung sound data. Some of these methods were used as a part of the methodology in the previous studies, which were described in Sect. 2. Most of the observed methodologies included many complex preprocessing steps [22] followed by feature extraction methods like MFCC. There is a good explanation of how MFCC works in [23] A lot of the proposed preprocessing techniques were explained by the fact that there were many data sources with different distributions of frequencies, noises, contents and other characteristics of lung sound data. A methodology has to be insensitive to data changing, data shifting or to some anomalies in the lung sounds. But most of the previously proposed methods were just data cleansing and normalization techniques required to apply

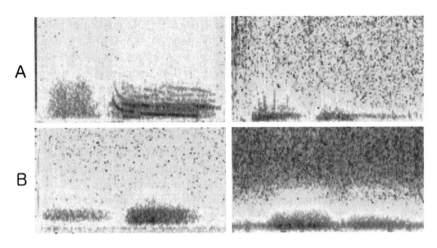

Fig. 1. Examples of respiratory cycle spectrograms. (A) With anomalies. (B) Without anomalies

machine learning models. For example, finite impulse response (FIR) filter [17] and Yule-Walker filter [18] were used for reducing the impact of noise and for the same frequency range in generated spectrograms by STFT. A classifier required clean normalized data to achieve the better performance score on validation data and to give more stable predictions on the future lung sounds (preprocessed in the same way). In this section, we describe some techniques used in our deep learning approach or used in approaches that we implemented for comparison purposes.

Our deep learning approach for wheeze detection is short and clear. We use a minimum of preprocessing steps and give to CNN almost raw lung sound data. Study design of our approach and CNN scheme is presented in Fig. 2.

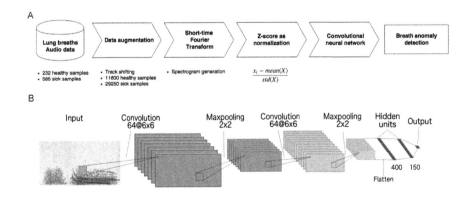

Fig. 2. Deep learning approach. (A) Study design. (B) CNN architecture

Data Augmentation is a technique for artificially enlargement of the original data. Deep learning models (such as CNN) require as much data as possible, thus data augmentation is very helpful here to generate new samples and it is also applied to prevent overfitting. Also, due to data augmentation, we can show CNN robustness in terms of respiratory cycle shifting (it is presented in Sects. 4 and 5 of this paper). Here we consider shifting operation as the biasing of the original lung sound sample by several frames in time.

Data augmentation is the first step of our approach and it is applied to the original data. The soundtracks containing respiratory cycles are shifted several times and are marked by id of the original soundtrack. Marking is required to avoid intersection of train and test sets during model training.

The soundtrack shifting technique helps to simulate real-world conditions and to generate many possible variations of specific respiratory cycle. If a classifier can precisely detect anomalies regardless of location of content in the lung sound sample, it is robust enough. For example, a patient can make a mistake and turn on the electronic stethoscope in the middle of the inspiration or turn it off before the end of the cycle.

STFT. Short-time Fourier transform (STFT) is a general-purpose tool for audio signal processing. It is a time-dependent Fourier transform for a sequence, and it is computed using a sliding window. The STFT is a Fourier-related transform that is used to determine the sinusoidal frequency and the phase content of the local sections of a signal as it changes over time.

$$\text{STFT}\{x[n]\}(m,\omega) \equiv X(m,\omega) = \sum_{n=-\infty}^{\infty} x[n] \times w[n-m] \times e^{-j\omega n} \qquad (1)$$

where $w[n]$ is the window (frame) and $x[n]$ is the signal to be transformed. The magnitude squared of the STFT yields the spectrogram of the function:

$$\text{spectrogram}(t,\omega) = |\text{STFT}(t,\omega)|^2 \qquad (2)$$

which is represented like plots as shown in Fig. 1. We use STFT in our approach for obtaining a raw spectrogram of lung sound.

Z-Score. It is a normalization technique using formula presented on Fig. 3. This type of normalization applies scale on each feature (pixel) of the sample. If we do not scale the input vectors, the ranges of the features (pixels) would likely be different, and this may cause problems related to the specific of gradient based algorithms.

CNN. Convolutional neural network is a type of feed-forward artificial neural network most commonly used for image processing. There is a good explanation of how CNN and it layers works in [24]. Briefly, CNN consist of convolution, pooling and fully connected layers. Convolution layer is a feature extraction part of CNN. It learns filters that are activated when they detect some specific feature (shape) on some position in the input. Max pooling layer is a form of down-sampling. It converts the input image into a set of non-overlapping rectangles and, for each such sub-region, outputs the maximum. Fully connected layers followed by convolutional and pooling layers processes high-level abstract features received by learnable convolutions. Also fully connected layer is a main building block of regular feed-forward neural network, in which all neurons have full connections to all activations in the previous layer. The output of CNN depends on the task. In our wheeze detection task it is binary classification problem and there is one neuron in the output of CNN.

4 Experiments

4.1 Experiments Design

In this study, we conducted three types of experiments, the only difference in which is the data augmentation application.

A. A common experiment was conducted on non-augmented data for comparison. Original dataset without data augmentation was used for this experiment. The purpose of this experiment is to compare CNN and other ML models in terms of classification performance.
B. Each soundtrack was augmented 50 times and then the data were splitted into the train and test sets. There are no augmented copies of any soundtracks from the train set in the test set. The purpose of this experiment is to test CNN and other models for robustness in terms of soundtrack shifting.
C. This experiment is similar to "B". The only difference is that there are no augmented samples in the train set. The purpose of this experiment is to test whenever or not our CNN-based model holds its generalization ability on shifted samples trained on the original ones.

All experiments were conducted on a computer with Intel Core i7-6900 CPU with 32 GB of RAM and NVIDIA 1080 GPU.

4.2 Result Evaluation

Due to the unbalanced dataset, we used Area Under Curve (AUC) and Matthews correlation coefficient (MCC) as the performance measures.

AUC score is an area under ROC (receiver operating characteristic) curve. ROC is a graphical plot that illustrates the performance of a binary classifier system as its discrimination threshold is varied. The curve is created by plotting the true positive rate (TPR) against the false positive rate (FPR) at various threshold settings.

MCC is a robust measure for the binary classification task in the case of very different sizes of classes. It returns a value between -1 and $+1$. A coefficient of $+1$ represents an ideal prediction, 0 corresponds to no better than a random prediction and -1 indicates the total disagreement between prediction and observation. MCC is calculated using Eq. 3. In this equation, TP is the number of true positives, TN the number of true negatives, FP the number of false positives and FN the number of false negatives.

$$\text{MCC} = \frac{TP \times TN - FP \times FN}{\sqrt{(TP + FP)(TP + FN)(TN + FP)(TN + FN)}} \tag{3}$$

Cross-validation was used to evaluate the results. The idea behind cross-validation is to divide the data set into disjoint training and validation subsets K in different but regular ways, after that a performance measure is evaluated as the mean value on all folds. Thus, results from cross-validation experiments are robust. We used 5-fold cross-validation.

5   Results

5.1   Results of the Experiments

The classification performance of different models trained on MFCC features is presented in Table 2. The best result on non-augmented data (MCC 0.88) was achieved by CNN, but MLP, RF and GBM scored just a bit worse (MCC 0.824). In the second (B) and third (C) experiments, CNN completely beat other ML methods in terms of performance and robustness. CNN completely outperformed other models on augmented data, especially when tested on augmented data (0.897 versus 0.32 MCC). CNN robustness in this task is explained by the specificity of model structure. Convolutional layers consist of many learnable filters (feature masks). Filters are independent of content (respiratory cycle) location. Because of this, filters can detect anomalies regardless of soundtrack shifting.

Additionally, Fig. 3 shows the performance of classifiers in the form of ROC curves for experiment "B". By analyzing the shown curves, as well as the corresponding AUC score, it can be seen that the best results are achieved by CNN.

Also, we provide results of CNN trained on almost raw features (spectrograms). The results are presented in Table 3. As expected, CNN showed a good feature extraction ability. Our model showed better performance in experiment "B" because of ability of deep learning models to process and memorize big amount of data. Also, we provide loss curve of the best trained CNN for experiment "B". It is shown on Fig. 3.

Comparison with State-of-the-Art Models. Almost all the approaches overviewed in Sect. 2 contained MFCC as the feature extraction step. Performance of our approach is 96% of accuracy on MFCC features and 99% on spectrograms. The best accuracy scores were achieved in [17] (98.7%) and in [20] (98.26%). But almost all of the experiments conducted in observed papers used a small data set and were not tested for algorithm robustness.

Table 2. Classification performance received with MFCC features. (A) Original train and test. (B_1) Augmented train and test. (B_2) Augmented train and original test. (C) Original train and augmented test

Model	A		B_1		B_2		C	
	AUC	MCC	AUC	MCC	AUC	MCC	AUC	MCC
SVM	0.787	0.523	0.557	0.095	0.731	0.418	0.5	0
KNN	0.631	0.356	0.531	0.158	0.625	0.331	0.509	0.026
LR	0.79	0.546	0.599	0.134	0.784	0.515	0.505	0.01
GBM	0.874	0.824	0.808	0.279	0.823	0.769	0.507	0.053
RF	0.874	0.824	0.744	0.207	0.77	0.729	0.506	0.091
MLP	0.874	0.824	0.729	0.32	0.866	0.819	0.507	0.061
CNN	**0.939**	**0.88**	**0.939**	**0.897**	**0.931**	**0.83**	**0.723**	**0.519**

Table 3. Classification performances of CNN on spectrogram and MFCC features. (MFCC) Augmented train and test. MFCC features were used. (A) Original train and test. Here and below spectrogram features were used. (B_1) Augmented train and test. (B_2) Augmented train and original test. (C) Original train and augmented test

Experiment	Accuracy	F1	AUC	MCC
MFCC	0.961	0.956	0.939	0.897
A	0.989	0.981	0.958	0.916
B_1	0.984	0.977	0.95	0.915
B_2	**0.99**	**0.982**	**0.96**	**0.922**
C	0.904	0.856	0.772	0.546

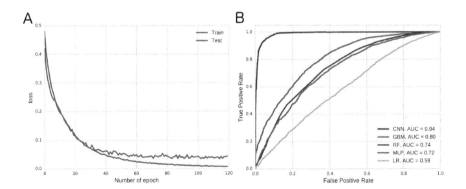

Fig. 3. Performance of best models. (A) Learning curve of the best CNN trained on spectrogramm features for "B" experiment. (B) ROC curves for classifiers trained on MFCC features for "B" experiment.

6 Conclusion

In this paper, we proposed CNN-based approach called WDCNN to detect wheezes in lung sound data. The results showed by the approach on sound signals presented as spectrograms and MFCC features were compared with conventional machine learning models, and WDCNN reaches state-of-the-art performance. Our method outperformed other approaches in the scope in terms of performance measure demonstrating stable 0.96 AUC score on the Internet dataset. Also, several experiments were conducted to prove that WDCNN is the robust method, insensitive to the lung sound shifting and external noise. Our method showed better performance in comparison with the baseline methods.

Our findings showed that the generalization capability and reliability of the proposed CNN-based method is high enough to use it in real-world conditions. Thus, WDCNN is a well-suited and reliable method to use both in clinics and by any people at home.

References

1. Reichert, S., Raymond, G., Christian, B., Andrès, E.: Analysis of respiratory sounds: state of the art. Clin. Med. Circ. Respirat. Pulm. Med. **2**, 45–58 (2008)
2. Bahoura, M., Lu, X.: Separation of crackles from vesicular sounds using wavelet packet transform. In: 2006 IEEE International Conference on Acoustics Speed and Signal Processing Proceedings (2006)
3. Yann, L., Bengio, Y., Hinton, G.: Deep learning. Nature **521**(7553), 436–444 (2015)
4. Farabet, C., Couprie, C., Najman, L., LeCun, Y.: Learning hierarchical features for scene labeling. IEEE Trans. Pattern Anal. Mach. Intell. **35**(8), 1915–1929 (2013)
5. Tompson, J.J., Jain, A., LeCun, Y., Bregler, C.: Joint training of a convolutional network and a graphical model for human pose estimation. In: Advances in Neural Information Processing Systems, pp. 1799–1807 (2014)
6. Szegedy, C., Liu, W., Jia, Y., Sermanet, P., Reed, S., Anguelov, D., Rabinovich, A.: Going deeper with convolutions. In: Proceedings of the IEEE Conference on Computer Vision and Pattern Recognition, pp. 1–9 (2015)
7. Collobert, R., Weston, J., Bottou, L., Karlen, M., Kavukcuoglu, K., Kuksa, P.: Natural language processing (almost) from scratch. J. Mach. Learn. Res. **12**(Aug), 2493–2537 (2011)
8. Hu, B., Lu, Z., Li, H., Chen, Q.: Convolutional neural network architectures for matching natural language sentences. In: Advances in Neural Information Processing Systems, pp. 2042–2050 (2014)
9. Bordes, A., Chopra, S., Weston, J.: Question answering with subgraph embeddings. arXiv preprint arXiv:1406.3676 (2014)
10. Palaz, D., Magimai-Doss, M., Collobert, R.: Analysis of CNN-based speech recognition system using raw speech as input. In: Proceedings of the 16th Annual Conference of International Speech Communication Association (Interspeech), pp. 11–15 (2015)
11. Mikolov, T., Deoras, A., Povey, D., Burget, L., Černocký, J.: Strategies for training large scale neural network language models. In: 2011 IEEE Workshop on Automatic Speech Recognition and Understanding (ASRU), pp. 196–201 (2011)

12. Hinton, G., Deng, L., Yu, D., Dahl, G.E., Mohamed, A.R., Jaitly, N., Kingsbury, B.: Deep neural networks for acoustic modeling in speech recognition: the shared views of four research groups. IEEE Sig. Process. Mag. **29**(6), 82–97 (2012)

13. Sainath, T.N., Mohamed, A.R., Kingsbury, B., Ramabhadran, B.: Deep convolutional neural networks for LVCSR. In: 2013 IEEE International Conference on Acoustics, Speech and Signal Processing (ICASSP), pp. 8614–8618 (2013)

14. Krizhevsky, A., Sutskever, I., Hinton, G.E.: Imagenet classification with deep convolutional neural networks. In: Advances in Neural Information Processing Systems (2012)

15. Zhang, H., McLoughlin, I., Song, Y.: Robust sound event recognition using convolutional neural networks. In: 2015 IEEE International Conference on Acoustics, Speech and Signal Processing (ICASSP), pp. 559–563 (2015)

16. Zhang, J., Ser, W., Yu, J., Zhang, T.: A novel wheeze detection method for wearable monitoring systems. In: 2009 International Symposium on Intelligent Ubiquitous Computing and Education (2009)

17. Mayorga, P., Druzgalski, C., Morelos, R., Gonzalez, O., Vidales, J.: Acoustics based assessment of respiratory diseases using GMM classification. In: 2010 Annual International Conference of the IEEE Engineering in Medicine and Biology (2010)

18. Milicevic, M., Mazic, I., Bonkovic, M.: Classification accuracy comparison of asthmatic wheezing sounds recorded under ideal and real-world conditions. In: 15th International Conference on Artificial Intelligence, Knowledge Engineering and Databases (AIKED 2016), Venice (2016)

19. Bahoura, M., Pelletier, C.: Respiratory sounds classification using cepstral analysis and Gaussian mixture models. In: The 26th Annual International Conference of the IEEE Engineering in Medicine and Biology Society (2004)

20. Palaniappan, R., Sundaraj, K., Sundaraj, S.: A comparative study of the SVM and K-nn machine learning algorithms for the diagnosis of respiratory pathologies using pulmonary acoustic signals. BMC Bioinform. **15**, 223 (2014)

21. Wrigley, D.: Heart and Lung Sounds Reference Library. PESI HealthCare, Eau Claire (2011)

22. Shaharum, S., Sundaraj, K., Palaniappan, R.: A survey on automated wheeze detection systems for asthmatic patients. Bosnian J. Basic Med. Sci. **12**, 249 (2012)

23. Wei, H., Chan, C., Choy, C., Pun, P.: An efficient MFCC extraction method in speech recognition. In: Circuits and Systems (2006)

24. Ciresan, D.C., Meier, U., Masci, J., Gambardella, L.M., Schmidhuber, J.: High-performance neural networks for visual object classification. arXiv preprint arXiv:1102.0183 (2011)

25. Liaw, A., Wiener, M.: Classification and regression by randomForest. R News **2**(3), 18–22 (2002)

26. Friedman, J.H.: Greedy function approximation: a gradient boosting machine. In: Annals of Statistics, pp. 1189–1232 (2001)

Multiclassifier System Using Class and Interclass Competence of Base Classifiers Applied to the Recognition of Grasping Movements in the Control of Bioprosthetic Hand

Marek Kurzynski[✉], Pawel Trajdos, and Andrzej Wolczowski

Department of Systems and Computer Networks,
Wroclaw University of Science and Technology, Wroclaw, Poland
marek.kurzynski@pwr.edu.pl

Abstract. In this paper the problem of recognition of patient's intent to move hand prosthesis is addressed. The proposed method is based on recognition of electromyographic (EMG) and mechanomyographic (MMG) biosignals using a multiclassifier (MC) system working with dynamic ensemble selection scheme and original concept of competence measure. The concept focuses on developing competence and interclass cross-competence measures which can be applied as a method for classifiers combination. The cross-competence measure allows an ensemble to harness information obtained from incompetent classifiers instead of removing them from the ensemble. The performance of MC system with proposed competence measure was experimentally compared against six state-of-the-art classification methods using real data concerning the recognition of six types of grasping movements. The system developed achieved the highest classification accuracies demonstrating the potential of MC system for the control of bioprosthetic hand.

Keywords: Bioprosthesis · EMG signal · MMG signal · Multiclassifier system · Competence measure

1 Introduction

Hands in a human life play a role not only of a skillful manipulator which allows grasping and manipulating a variety of objects, but also of the sensor in order to determine the type of object being touched. The loss of even a single hand significantly reduces the human activity. The people who have lost their hands are doomed to permanent care. Restoring to these people even a hand substitute makes their life less onerous. The hand transplantations are still in a medical experiment, mainly due to the necessity of immunesuppression [21]. An alternative is "cyborgization", i.e. equipping the armless patient with the prosthetic hand. At present, the construction of a multi-joint anthropomorphic mechanical structure that can copy even very complicated movements of the human hand

© Springer International Publishing AG 2017
E. Oliveira et al. (Eds.): EPIA 2017, LNAI 10423, pp. 174–185, 2017.
DOI: 10.1007/978-3-319-65340-2_15

poses no problem. Also the motion control of such a structure to accomplish defined finger postures is well known. The basic problem lies however in controlling the movement of prosthetic hands so as to enable their users to grasp and manipulate objects dexterously [20].

At the decision level this control can be reduced to the recognition of the patient's intent on the basis of biosignals coming from the patient's body. Electrical potentials accompanying skeleton muscles (called EMG signals) are an example of such biosignals. Through the tensing of these muscles, the disabled person may express his/her intentions as to the workings of the prosthesis [3,9,18,24]. Nevertheless, reliable recognition of intended movement is a serious problem. A natural solution to overcome this difficulty and increase the efficiency of the recognition stage may be achieved through the following actions [16]:

1. by introducing the concept of simultaneous analysis of different types of biosignals which are the carrier of information about the performed hand movement – the fusion of electromyographic signals (EMG signals) and mechanomyographic signals (MMG signals) is considered in this study;
2. through improving the recognition method – authors propose to use the multiclassifier system with dynamic ensemble selection scheme [2].

Multiclassifier (MC) systems combine responses of a set of base classifiers. For the classifier combination two main approaches used are classifiers fusion and classifiers selection [13]. In the first method, all classifiers in the ensemble contribute to the decision of the MC system, e.g. through sum or majority voting. In the second approach, a single classifier is selected from the ensemble and its decision is treated as the decision of the MC system. The selection of classifiers can be either static or dynamic. In the static selection scheme a classifier is selected for all test objects, whereas the dynamic classifier selection (DCS) approach explores the use of different classifiers for different test objects [2]. Recently, dynamic ensemble selection (DES) methods have been developed which first dynamically select an ensemble of classifiers from the entire set (pool) and then combine the selected classifiers by majority voting rule [12]. In this way a DES based system takes advantage of both selection and fusion approaches. In most of the methods, the base classifiers are selected from the pool on the basis of their individual accuracy measure called competence in a local region of the feature space. These methods differ in algorithms for determining classifier competence and ways of defining the local regions [2,12,13,25,26,30]. Regardless of the interpretation, competence measure evaluates classifier ability to correct activity (correct classification) in a defined region.

In this paper a new method for calculating the competence of a classifier in the feature space is developed and applied to the classifying user's intent of upper-limb prosthesis motion based on EMG and MMG biosignals. The proposed competence measure evaluates both the local class-dependent probabilities of correct classification and probabilities of interclass misclassification using concept of Randomized Reference Classifier [26] and a local fuzzy confusion matrix [23]. Such idea of cross-competence measure allows the ensemble to exploit even activity of incompetent classifiers instead of removing them from the ensemble.

The paper arrangement is as follows. Section 2 includes the concept of prosthesis control system based on the recognition of patient's intention and provides an insight into biosignals acquisition procedure and the method of feature extraction. Section 3 presents the key recognition algorithm based on the multiclassifier system working in dynamic ensemble selection scheme with original concept of competence measure. The experiments conducted and the results with discussion are presented in Sect. 4. The paper is concluded in Sect. 5.

2   Bioprosthetic Hand Control System

The bioprosthesis control performed by recognizing patient's intention involves three stages:

1. acquisition of signals;
2. reduction of dimensionality of their representation;
3. classification of signals.

As already mentioned, in this study the fusion of electromyography (EMG) signals and mechanomyography (MMG) signals is the basis for recognition of patient's intent. Myopotentials (EMG signals) can be detected through the skin by means of surface electrodes located above selected muscles. EMG signals measured on skin are the superposition of electrical potentials generated by recruited motor units of contracting muscles [4,10]. The MMG signals are mechanical vibrations propagating in the limb tissue as the muscle contracts. They have low frequency (up to 200 Hz) and small amplitude and can be registered as a "muscle sound" on the surface of the skin using microphones [11].

After the acquisition stage, the recorded signals have the form of strings of discrete samples. Their size is the product of measurement time and sampling frequency. For a typical motion, that gives a record of size between 3 and 5 thousand of samples (time of the order of 3–5 s, and the sampling of the order of 1 kHz). This "primary" representation of the signals hinders the effective classification and requires the reduction of dimensionality. This reduction leads to a representation in the form of a signal feature vector.

Former experimental research showed [14–16,24] that the effective method as regards to the recognition error and the calculation costs in the biosignal analysis are the sequence of two techniques: autoregressive (AR) model and principal component analysis (PCA).

The AR model belongs to a group of linear prediction methods that attempt to predict an value y_n of a time series of data $\{y_n\}$ based on the previous values $(y_{n-1}, y_{n-2}, \ldots)$. Several estimators of AR coefficients are well known in the field of signal processing. In the experimental investigations we choose the Burg algorithm because of its many remarkable advantages (it does not apply window data, minimizes forward and backward prediction errors, gives high resolution for short data records, always produces a stable model) [22]. The Burg algorithm estimates the AR coefficients by fitting an auto-regressive linear prediction filter model of a given order to the signal.

Although as a classifier construction different methodological paradigms can be used, we suggest to use multiclassifier systems with the dynamic ensemble selection method using procedure of fusion/selection based on original competence measure. Details of the classification stage are presented in the next section.

3   Multiclassifier System

3.1   Preliminaries

In the multiclassifier (MC) system we assume that a set of trained classifiers $\Psi = \{\psi_1, \psi_2, \ldots, \psi_L\}$ called base classifiers is given. A classifier ψ_l is a function $\psi_l : \mathcal{X} \to \mathcal{M}$ from a feature space $\mathcal{X} \subseteq \mathcal{R}^d$ to a set of class labels $\mathcal{M} = \{1, 2, \ldots, M\}$. Classification is made according to the maximum rule

$$\psi_l(x) = i \Leftrightarrow d_{li}(x) = \max_{j \in \mathcal{M}} d_{lj}(x), \tag{1}$$

where $[d_{l1}(x), d_{l2}(x), \ldots, d_{lM}(x)]$ is a vector of class supports (classifying functions) produced by ψ_l. Without loss of generality we assume that $d_{lj}(x) \geq 0$ and $\sum_j d_{lj}(x) = 1$.

The ensemble Ψ is used for classification through a combination function which, for example, can select a single classifier or a subset of classifiers from the ensemble, it can be independent or dependent on the feature vector x (in the latter case the function is said to be dynamic), and it can be non-trainable or trainable [13].

In this paper, we propose MC systems which use a dynamic ensemble selection scheme and trainable combining methods based on a competence measure $c_{ij}(\psi_l|x)(i, j \in \mathcal{M})$ of each base classifier $(l = 1, 2, \ldots, L)$ evaluating the class-dependent competence (for $i = j$) and interclass (cross-) competence (for $i \neq j$) of classifier ψ_l at a point $x \in \mathcal{X}$. For training methods of combining base classifiers it is assumed that a validation set

$$V = \{(x_1, j_1), (x_2, j_2), \ldots, (x_N, j_N)\}; \ \ x_k \in \mathcal{X}, \ j_k \in \mathcal{M} \tag{2}$$

containing pairs of feature vectors and their corresponding class labels is available. In the MC systems developed in this study, combining algorithm is implemented at the classification function (support) level which allows to determine supports provided by the MC system to different classes, as a weighted sum of supports of base classifiers, namely:

$$d_j(x) = \sum_{l=1}^{L} \sum_{i=1}^{M} d_{li}(x) c_{ij}(\psi_l|x), \ j \in \mathcal{M}. \tag{3}$$

In the next section two methods for calculation of competences $c_{ij}(\psi_l|x)$ of base classifiers will be developed.

3.2   Competence Measures

A natural concept of competence measure $c_{ij}(\psi_l|x)$ is probability that object given by the feature vector x belonging to the j-th class is assigned by ψ_l to the ith class [27], namely:

$$c_{ij}(\psi_l|x) = P_l(i|j, x). \tag{4}$$

In other words, probabilities (4) denote class-dependent probabilities of correct classification (for $i = j$) and misclassification (for $i \neq j$). A high value of class-dependent competence $c_{ii}(\psi_l|x)$ denotes that classifier ψ_l is capable of providing the correct classification of objects from the ith class, whereas the high value of cross-competence $c_{ij}(\psi_l|x)$ clearly shows that the investigated classifier tends to misclassify objects from the jth class to the ith class. In the proposed method the above mentioned indicators can be utilized to correct the response of a classifier that tends to commit systematic errors.

Unfortunately, for deterministic base classifiers ψ_l probabilities (4) are equal to 0 or 1, unlike the randomized classifiers for which these probabilities belong to the interval $[0, 1]$ [1]. We do not accept, however, impractical assumption that base classifiers assign labels under a stochastic scheme because all classifiers used in real examples operate in a deterministic manner. For this reason, a direct approach to calculating probabilities (4) is not used in this study. Instead, indirect methods for solving this problem and fully utilizing the combining model (3) are applied. In the first approach classifier ψ_l is modeled by the equivalent randomized reference classifier (RRC). In the second approach we will use a local confusion matrix which is built from the validation objects creating fuzzy neighborhood of point x. Details are described in the next two subsections.

The Method Using Randomized Reference Classifier (MC1). The proposed method of evaluation of the probabilities (4) is based on the original concept of a hypothetical classifier called Randomized Reference Classifier (RRC). The RRC, originally introduced in [26], is a stochastic classifier defined using a probability distribution over the set of class labels $\mathcal{M}$. The RRC uses the maximum rule (1) and a vector of class supports $[\delta_{l1}(x), \delta_{l2}(x), \ldots, \delta_{lM}(x)]$ for the classification of object x, where the j-th support is a realization of a random variable (rv) $\Delta_{lj}(x)$. The probability distributions of the rvs are chosen in such a way that the following conditions are satisfied:

$$\Delta_{lj}(x) \in [0, 1], \quad \sum_{j \in \mathcal{M}} \Delta_{lj}(x) = 1, \tag{5}$$

$$E[\Delta_{lj}(x)] = d_{lj}(x), \quad j = 1, 2, \ldots, M, \tag{6}$$

where E is the expected value operator. From the above definition it follows that RRC can be considered as equivalent to the classifier ψ_l for the feature vector x since it produces, on average, the same vector of class supports as the modeled base classifier ψ_l.

Since the RRC performs classification in a stochastic manner, it is possible to calculate the probability of classifying a validation object x_k to the i-th class:

$$P_l^{(RRC)}(i|j_k, x_k) = Pr[\forall_{m=1,\ldots,M,\ k \neq i} \ \Delta_{li}(x_k) > \Delta_{lm}(x_k)]. \tag{7}$$

The formula (7) denotes class-dependent probability of correct classification (for $i = j_k$) or misclassification (for $i \neq j_k$) of RRC classifier $\psi_l^{(RRC)}$ at a validation point x_k.

The key element in the modeling presented above is the choice of probability distributions for rvs $\Delta_{lj}(x), j \in \mathcal{M}$ so that the conditions (5)–(6) are satisfied. In this study, the beta distribution is selected – the justification of such a choice can be found in [26] and furthermore the MATLAB code for calculating probabilities (7) was developed and it is freely available for download [28].

Since the RRC can be considered equivalent to the modeled base classifier ψ_l, it is justified to use the probability (7) as the competence $c_{ij_k}(\psi_l|x_k)$ of the classifier ψ_l at the validation point $x_k \in \mathcal{V}$, i.e.

$$c_{ij_k}(\psi_l|x_k) \approx P_l^{(RRC)}(i|j_k, x_k). \tag{8}$$

The competence values for the validation objects $x_k \in \mathcal{V}$ can be then extended to the entire feature space $\mathcal{X}$. To this purpose the following normalized Gaussian potential function model was used [26]:

$$c_{ij}(\psi_l|x) = \frac{\sum_{x_k \in \mathcal{V}:j_k=j} c_{ij_k}(\psi_l|x_k)exp(-dist(x, x_k)^2)}{\sum_{x_k \in \mathcal{V}:j_k=j} exp(-dist(x, x_k)^2)}, \tag{9}$$

where $dist(x, x_k)$ is the Euclidean distance between x and x_k.

The Method Using Local Fuzzy Confusion Matrix (MC2). In the second approach we will use confusion matrix for evaluation of probability (4). A confusion matrix gives the complete picture of correct and incorrect classification made by classifiers ψ_l for separate classes [6]. The rows (columns) correspond to the true classes (results of classification made by classifier ψ_l), as shown in Table 1.

Table 1. The multiclass confusion matrix of classifier ψ_l.

		Classification by ψ_l			
		1	2	$\ldots$	M
True class	1	$\varepsilon_{11}^{(\psi_l)}$	$\varepsilon_{21}^{(\psi_l)}$	$\ldots$	$\varepsilon_{M1}^{(\psi_l)}$
	2	$\varepsilon_{12}^{(\psi_l)}$	$\varepsilon_{22}^{(\psi_l)}$	$\ldots$	$\varepsilon_{M2}^{(\psi_l)}$
	$\vdots$	$\vdots$	$\vdots$		$\vdots$
	M	$\varepsilon_{1M}^{(\psi_l)}$	$\varepsilon_{2M}^{(\psi_l)}$	$\ldots$	$\varepsilon_{MM}^{(\psi_l)}$

The value $\varepsilon_{ij}^{(\psi_l)}$ is determined from validation set (2) as the following ratio ($|\cdot|$ is the cardinality of a set):

$$\varepsilon_{ij}^{(\psi_l)} = \frac{|\mathcal{V}_j \cap \mathcal{D}_i^{\psi_l}|}{|\mathcal{V}_j|}, \tag{10}$$

where $\mathcal{V}_j = \{x_k \in \mathcal{V} : j_k = j\}$ denotes the set of validation objects from the jth class and $\mathcal{D}_i^{\psi_l} = \{x_k \in \mathcal{V} : \psi_l(x_k) = i\}$ is the set of validation objects assigned by ψ_l to the ith class.

Since we want to estimate probabilities $P_l(i|j,x)$ at a point x, values of confusion matrix $\varepsilon_{ij}^{(\psi_l)}(x)$ should be calculated on the base of local (for x) validation objects. A typical method is to define a neighborhood of an object x and only validation objects belonging to this neighborhood are used to calculate $\varepsilon_{ij}^{(\psi_l)}(x)$. Such an approach, however, has a major drawback: the method is very sensitive to the size of the neighborhood. As the neighborhood size increases, the sense of "locality" concept decreases, and as this size decreases, the risk that $\varepsilon_{ij}^{(\psi_l)}(x) = 0$ increases. In order to avoid this problem, we define validation objects creating the neighborhood of the point x as a fuzzy set:

$$\mathcal{V}(x) = \left\{(x^{(k)}, \mu_{\mathcal{V}(x)}(x^{(k)})) : x^{(k)} \in \mathcal{V}\right\}, \tag{11}$$

whose membership function is equal to 1 for $x^{(k)} = x$ and decreases with increasing the distance between $x^{(k)}$ and x. In the further experimental investigations, the Gaussian membership function was applied:

$$\mu_{\mathcal{V}(x)}(x^{(k)}) = c \exp(-dist(x, x^{(k)})^2), \tag{12}$$

where $dist(x, x^{(k)})$ is the Euclidean distance and c denotes normalizing coefficient.

From (10), (11) and (12) directly results the formula for determining values of local confusion matrix:

$$\varepsilon_{ij}^{(\psi_l)}(x) = \frac{|\mathcal{V}_j \cap \mathcal{D}_i^{\psi_l} \cap \mathcal{V}(x)|}{|\mathcal{V}_j \cap \mathcal{V}(x)|}, \tag{13}$$

where $|\cdot|$ is the cardinality of a fuzzy set [17] and $\mathcal{V}_j$ and $\mathcal{D}_i^{\psi_l}$ are treated as fuzzy sets defined in (10) with membership function equal to 1. Finally, normalizing (13) we get estimation (4):

$$c_{ij}(\psi_l|x) = \frac{\varepsilon_{ij}^{(\psi_l)}(x)}{\sum_{j \in \mathcal{M}} \varepsilon_{ij}^{(\psi_l)}(x)}. \tag{14}$$

4   Experimental Investigations

4.1   Experimental Setup

Performance of the MC systems developed was evaluated in experiments using real data. The experiments were conducted in the Matlab environment using PRTools 4.1 and Signal Processing Toolbox.

In the recognition process of the grasping movements, 6 types of grips (tripoid, pinch, power, hook, column and mouse grip) were considered. Our choice is deliberate one and results from the fact that the control functions of simple bioprosthesis are hand closing/opening and wrist pronantion/supination, however for the dexterous hand these functions differ depending on grasped object [3] (Fig. 1).

Tripoid grip   Pinch grip   Power grip   Hook grip   Column grip   Mouse grip

Fig. 1. Types of grips.

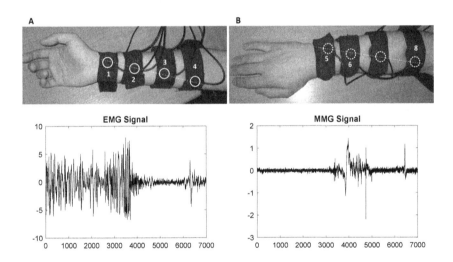

Fig. 2. The layout of the integrated sensors (EMG electrodes and MMG microphones) on the underside (A) and top side (B) of the forearm. Examples of EMG and MMG signals from channel 2.

The experiments were carried out on healthy persons. Biosignals were registered using 8 integrated sensors (containing EMG electrode and MMG microphone in one casing) located on a forearm (vide Fig. 2) and specially designed 16-channel measuring circuit with sampling frequency 1 kHz. For further processing the following sensors (channels) located above the most active muscles during grasping movements were selected [4]: 1 (sensors located above *pronator quadratus* muscle), 2 (*flexor digitorium supercialis*), 3 (*flexor digitorium profundus*), 5 (*extensor pollicis brevis*) and 8 (*supinator*).

The dataset used to test of proposed classification method consisted of 600 measurements, i.e. pairs EMG and MMG signals segment/movement class. Each segment lasted 6 s and was preceded with a 10 s break. The coefficients of AR function for different order of AR model ($p = 20, 50, 80$ per signal and per channel) were considered as the primary feature vector. Next, primary features were subjected to the PCA feature extraction procedure with the number of PC's determined by 95% of the total variation rule. The training and testing sets were extracted from each dataset using two-fold cross-validation. For combining the MC system, a two-fold stacked generalization method [29] was used. Three experiments were performed which differ in the biosignals used for classification (EMG signals, MMG signals, both EMG and MMG signals).

The experiments were conducted using heterogeneous ensemble with the following ten base classifiers [8]: (1–2) linear (quadratic) classifier based on normal distributions with the same (different) covariance matrix for each class, (3) nearest mean classifier, (4–6) k-nearest neighbors classifiers with $k = 1, 5, 15$, (7) naive Bayes classifier (8) decision-tree classifier with Gini splitting criterion, (9–10) feed-forward back-propagation neural network with 1 hidden layer (with 2 hidden layers).

In the experiment MC1 and MC2 systems were compared against six state-of-the-art multiclassifier systems: (1) The single best (SB) classifier in the ensemble [13]; (2) Majority voting (MV) of all classifiers in the ensemble [13]; (3) Dynamic classifier selection – local accuracy (LA) method [30]; (4) Dynamic ensemble selection – KNORA method (KE) [12]; (5) Randomized reference classifier (RRC) method [26,27]; (6) Multiclassifier with fuzzy inference system (MCF) [15].

4.2   Results and Discussion

Classification accuracies (i.e. the percentage of correctly classified objects) for methods tested in the experiments are listed in Table 2. The accuracies are average values obtained over 10 runs (5 replications of two-fold cross validation). Statistical differences between the performances of MC1 and MC2 systems and the six multiclassifier systems were evaluated using 5x2cv F test [7]. The level of p < 0.05 was considered statistically significant. In Table 2, statistically significant differences are given as upper indices of the method evaluated, e.g. for the dataset with p = 20 and EMG signals the MC1 system produced statistically better classification accuracies from SB, MV and LA methods.

Statistical differences in rank between multiclassifier systems were obtained using Friedman test with Iman and Davenport correction combined with a post hoc Holm stepdown procedure [5]. The average ranks and a critical rank difference calculated using a Bonferroni – Dunn test [5] are visualised in Fig. 3. The level of $p < 0.05$ was considered as statistically significant.

These results imply the following conclusions:

Table 2. Classification accuracies of classifiers compared in the experiment (description in the text). The best score for each dataset is highlighted. (p denotes the order of AR model).

p	Classifier/Mean accuracy [%]							
	SB	MV	LA	KE	RRC	MCF	MC1	MC2
	(1)	(2)	(3)	(4)	(5)	(6)	(7)	(8)
EMG signals								
20	77.2	75.5	74.3	79.8	**81.4**	78.8	80.1[1,2,3]	80.8[1,2,3,6]
50	79.9	80.5	80.7	**83.8**	81.7	80.1	83.2[1,2,3,5]	82.8[1,2,3,5]
80	84.0	83.2	81.7	82.6	85.3	83.1	**86.6**[1,2,3,4,6]	85.9[2,3,4,6]
Average	80.4	79.7	78.9	82.1	82.5	80.7	**83.3**	83.2
MMG signals								
20	45.8	47.3	48.8	50.9	49.9	48.4	51.4[1,2,6]	**51.8**[1,2,3,6]
50	47.9	48.8	47.9	51.6	50.6	49.6	**52.6**[1,2,3]	51.9[1,2,3]
80	52.2	51.2	50.1	57.3	**59.9**	55.6	58.6[1,2,3,6]	59.1[1,2,3,6]
Average	48.6	48.8	48.9	53.9	52.8	51.2	54.2	**54.3**
MMG and EMG signals								
20	84.5	85.8	84.7	**88.2**	86.5	85.5	87.8[1,3]	88.0[1,3,6]
50	86.4	87.6	86.9	90.3	89.5	90.2	90.4[1,3]	**91.5**[1,2,3]
80	90.7	91.1	91.9	92.7	94.6	93.6	94.2[1,2]	**94.9**[1,2,3]
Average	87.2	88.2	87.8	90.4	89.9	90.1	90.8	91.5
Av. rank	7.0	6.2	6.8	3.4	3.1	5.3	2.2	1.8

1. The MC1 and MC2 systems produced statistically significant higher scores in 60 out of 108 cases (9 datasets × 6 classifiers compared × 2 MC systems);
2. The MC1 (MC2) classifier:
   - for EMG signals outperformed, on average, the SB, MV, LA, KE, RRC and MCF systems by 2.9%, 3.6%, 4.4%, 1.2%, 0.8% and 2.6% (by 2.8%, 3.5%, 4.3%, 1.1%, 0.7% and 2.5%), respectively;
   - for MMG signals outperformed, on average, the SB, MV, LA, KE, RRC and MCF systems by 5.6%, 5.4% and 5.3%, 0.3%, 1.4% and 3.0% (by 5.7%, 5.5% and 5.4%, 0.4%, 1.5% and 3.1%), respectively;
   - for EMG and MMG signals outperformed, on average, the SB, MV, LA, KE, RRC and MCF systems by 3.6%, 2.6%, 3.0%, 0.4%, 0.9% and 0.7% (by 4.3%, 3.3%, 3.7%, 1.1%, 1.6% and 1.4%), respectively;
3. MC1 and MC2 methods have statistically higher average rank than MCF, MV, LA and SB methods;
4. The multiclassifier systems using both EMG and MMG signals achieved the highest classification accuracy for all datasets;
5. When the order of AR model increases then the accuracy of all methods investigated also increases.

Fig. 3. Average ranks of multiclassifier systems. Thick interval is the critical rank difference (2.686) calculated using the Bonferroni – Dunn test ($p < 0.05$).

5 Conclusion

The classic methods of analysis of biosignals in the bioprostheses control systems are widely discussed in the literature [10,11,19,24]. However, the classification stage still poses a challenge for researching new solutions enabling the reliable recognition of human intention. In this study a novel method for recognition of grasping movements is proposed. The method, combining base classifiers into multiclassifier system and taking into account the class and interclass competence of base classifiers, brings new possibilities to biosignal analysis. Results obtained in experimental investigations imply that it is worth trying solution that improves recognition efficiency.

The introduced approach constitutes the general concept of the human-machine interface, that can be applied for the control of a dexterous hand and an agile wheelchair as well as other types of prostheses, exoskeletons, etc. This, however, requires a further study, mainly in the experimental phase, which would allow to assess and verify the effectiveness of the adopted concept.

Acknowledgment. This work was supported by the statutory funds of the Dept. of Systems and Computer Networks, Wroclaw Univ. of Technology.

References

1. Berger, J.: Statistical Decision Theory and Bayesian Analysis. Springer, New York (1985). doi:10.1007/978-1-4757-4286-2
2. Britto, A., Sabourin, R., Oliveira, R.: Dynamic selection of classifiers a comprehensive review. Pattern Recogn. **47**, 3665–3680 (2014)
3. Carrozza, M., Cappiello, G., et al.: Design of a cybernetic hand for perception and action. Biol. Cybern. **95**, 626–644 (2006)
4. De Luca, C.: Electromyography. In: Webster, J.G. (ed.) Encyclopedia of Medical Devices and Instrumentation, pp. 98–109. Wiley, Hoboken (2006)
5. Demsar, J.: Statistical comparison of classifiers over multiple data sets. J. Mach. Learn. Res. **7**, 1–30 (2006)
6. Devroye, L.: A Probabilistic Theory of Pattern Recognition. Springer, New York (1996). doi:10.1007/978-1-4612-0711-5
7. Dietterich, T.: Approximate statistical tests for comparing supervised classification learning algorithms. Neural Comput. **10**, 1895–1923 (1998)
8. Duda, R., Hart, P., Stork, D.: Pattern Classification. Wiley, New York (2000)
9. Englehart, K., Hudgins, B.: A robust, real-time control scheme for multifunction myoelectric control. IEEE Trans. Biomed. Eng. **50**, 848–854 (2003)

10. Kakoty, M., Hazarika, S.: Towards electromyogram-based grasps classification. Int. J. Biomech. Biomed. Robot. **3**(2), 63–73 (2014)
11. Khushaba, R.: Application of biosignal-driven intelligent systems for multifunction prosthesis control. Ph.D. thesis, Faculty of Engineering and Information Technology, University of Technology, Sydney (2010)
12. Ko, A., Sabourin, N., Britto, A.: From dynamic classifier selection to dynamic ensemble selection. Pattern Recogn. **41**, 1718–1731 (2008)
13. Kuncheva, L.: Combining Pattern Classifiers: Methods and Algorithms. Wiley-Interscience, Hoboken (2004)
14. Kurzynski, M.: On a two-level multiclassifier system with error correction applied to the control of bioprosthetic hand. In: Proceedings of the 14th World Congress of Medical Informatics MEDINFO, p. 210 (2013)
15. Kurzynski, M., Wolczowski, A.: Multiclassifier system with fuzzy inference method applied to the recognition of biosignals in the control of bioprosthetic hand. In: Zeng, Z., Li, Y., King, I. (eds.) ISNN 2014. LNCS, vol. 8866, pp. 469–478. Springer, Cham (2014). doi:10.1007/978-3-319-12436-0_52
16. Kurzynski, M., Krysmann, M., et al.: Multiclassifier system with hybrid learning applied to the control of bioprosthetic hand. Comput. Biol. Med. **69**, 286–297 (2016)
17. Mamoni, D.: On cardinality of fuzzy sets. Int. J. Intell. Syst. Appl. **5**, 47–52 (2013)
18. Micera, C., Carpantero, J., Raspopovic, S.: Control of hand prostheses using peripheral information. IEEE Rev. Biomed. Eng. **3**, 48–68 (2010)
19. Oskoei, M., Hu, H.: Support vector machine-based classification scheme for EMG control applied to upper limb. IEEE Trans. Biomed. Eng. **55**, 1956–1965 (2008)
20. Peerdeman, B., Boere, D., et al.: Myoelectric forearm prostheses: state of the art from a user-centered perspective. J. Rehabil. Res. Dev. **48**, 719–738 (2011)
21. Ravindra, K., Ildstad, S.: Immunosuppressive protocols and immunological challenges related to hand transplantation. Hand Clin. **27**(4), 467–79 (2011)
22. Schloegl, A.: A comparison of multivariate autoregressive estimators. Sig. Process. **9**, 2426–2429 (2006)
23. Trajdos, P., Kurzynski, M.: A dynamic model of classifier competence based on the local fuzzy confusion matrix and the random reference classifier. Int. J. Appl. Math. Comput. Sci. **26**, 17–28 (2016)
24. Wolczowski, A., Kurzynski, M.: Human - machine interface in bio-prosthesis control using EMG signal classification. Expert Syst. **27**, 53–70 (2010)
25. Woloszynski, T., Kurzynski, M.: On a new measure of classifier competence applied to the design of multiclassifier systems. In: Foggia, P., Sansone, C., Vento, M. (eds.) ICIAP 2009. LNCS, vol. 5716, pp. 995–1004. Springer, Heidelberg (2009). doi:10.1007/978-3-642-04146-4_106
26. Woloszynski, T., Kurzynski, M.: A probabilistic model of classifier competence for dynamic ensemble selection. Pattern Recogn. **44**, 2656–2668 (2011)
27. Woloszynski, T., Kurzynski, M., et al.: A measure of competence based on random classification for dynamic ensemble selection. Inf. Fusion **13**, 207–213 (2012)
28. Woloszynski, T.: Matlab Central File Enchange (2010). http://www.mathwork.com/matlabcentral/fileenchange/28391-classifier-competence-based-on-probabilistic-modeling
29. Wolpert, D.: Stacked generalization. Neural Netw. **5**, 214–259 (1992)
30. Woods, K., Kegelmeyer, W., Bowyer, K.: Combination of multiple classifiers using local accuracy estimates. IEEE Trans. Pattern Anal. Mach. Intell. PAMI **19**, 405–410 (1997)

Classifying Heart Sounds Using Images of MFCC and Temporal Features

Diogo Marcelo Nogueira[1]([✉]), Carlos Abreu Ferreira[2], and Alípio M. Jorge[3]

[1] INESC TEC, Porto, Portugal
diogo.m.nogueira@inesctec.pt
[2] Instituto Politécnico do Porto and INESC TEC, Porto, Portugal
cgf@isep.ipp.pt
[3] FCUP-Universidade do Porto and INESC TEC, Porto, Portugal
amjorge@fc.up.pt

Abstract. Phonocardiogram signals contain very useful information about the condition of the heart. It is a method of registration of heart sounds, which can be visually represented on a chart. By analyzing these signals, early detections and diagnosis of heart diseases can be done. Intelligent and automated analysis of the phonocardiogram is therefore very important, to determine whether the patient's heart works properly or should be referred to an expert for further evaluation. In this work, we use electrocardiograms and phonocardiograms collected simultaneously, from the Physionet challenge database, and we aim to determine whether a phonocardiogram corresponds to a "normal" or "abnormal" physiological state. The main idea is to translate a 1D phonocardiogram signal into a 2D image that represents temporal and Mel-frequency cepstral coefficients features. To do that, we develop a novel approach that uses both features. First we segment the phonocardiogram signals with an algorithm based on a logistic regression hidden semi-Markov model, which uses the electrocardiogram signals as reference. After that, we extract a group of features from the time and frequency domain (Mel-frequency cepstral coefficients) of the phonocardiogram. Then, we combine these features into a two-dimensional time-frequency heat map representation. Lastly, we run a binary classifier to learn a model that discriminates between normal and abnormal phonocardiogram signals.

In the experiments, we study the contribution of temporal and Mel-frequency cepstral coefficients features and evaluate three classification algorithms: Support Vector Machines, Convolutional Neural Network, and Random Forest. The best results are achieved when we map both temporal and Mel-frequency cepstral coefficients features into a 2D image and use the Support Vector Machines with a radial basis function kernel. Indeed, by including both temporal and Mel-frequency cepstral coefficients features, we obtain sligthly better results than the ones reported by the challenge participants, which use large amounts of data and high computational power.

Keywords: Phonocardiogram · Electrocardiogram · Mel-frequency cepstral coefficients · Time features · Classification

© Springer International Publishing AG 2017
E. Oliveira et al. (Eds.): EPIA 2017, LNAI 10423, pp. 186–203, 2017.
DOI: 10.1007/978-3-319-65340-2_16

1   Introduction

Cardiovascular diseases (CVD) are the single leading cause of death worldwide. According to the estimates of the World Health Organization (WHO) in 2012, CVD account for approximately 17.5 million deaths worldwide, which corresponds to over 31% of all deaths globally. These facts alone show that CVD are a major global threat and any development to aid the prevention of such diseases is of great importance [24]. According to the latest statistics, 20% of people aged over 40 develop heart failure during their life. This condition is the number one reason for hospitalization among those over 65. Half of all patients die within 5 years of diagnosis, and each year heart failure costs the global economy $108 billion, with hospitalizations accounting for 60–70% of direct treatment costs. 14.9 million people in the EU and 5.7 million in the United States have heart failure; the impact on the rest of the world is not sufficiently documented [24].

A more pro-active approach involving low cost cardiac health screening of the general population can help the physician detect possible complications at an early stage. Currently, two effective cardiac screening methodologies are the Electrocardiogram (ECG) and echocardiogram exams but these can be expensive for mass screening and require technical expertise that is not always available. Despite remarkable advances in imaging technologies for the heart, the clinical evaluation of cardiac defects by auscultation has remained a main diagnostic method for congenital heart diseases. In experienced hands the method is effective, reliable, and cheap.

The auscultation of the heart and lungs with a stethoscope is often conducted on patients thought to have cardiac or pulmonary disease, before recommending additional diagnostic procedures, treatment, or no further action [15]. Because this process is simple, cheap, and quick to detect diseases, the stethoscope still maintains a key position in medicine in the modern era. However, auscultation is a subjective process that depends on the experience and hearing capability of the individual, a feature that may lead to a large variability in findings. The poor sensitivity of human hearing in the low frequency range of the heart sounds makes this task even more difficult. Also, the human hearing system is better at detecting frequency changes than intensity changes. The physical limitations of the human ear make it unable to analyze all the information contained in the acoustic signals of the heart [26].

Physically, a stethoscope covers a broad sound spectrum and the average frequency depends on the point of auscultation. It requires significant practice for a human ear to distinguish between them. The existence of methods that can automatically and successfully analyze heart signals, can be used as a diagnostic tool to help determine if an individual should be referred for expert diagnosis, specially in cases where access to clinicians and medical care is limited.

In this work, we develop a novel approach to classify heart sounds, which uses both temporal and Mel-frequency cepstral coefficients (MFCC) features. The main idea is to translate a 1D Phonocardiogram (PCG) signal into a 2D image that represents temporal and MFCC features. First we segment a PCG signal, using the ECG that was simultaneously recorded, to identify the S1 heart sound.

Second, we extract temporal and MFCC features from PCG signals. Third, we combine these features into a 2D image. Last, we run a binary classifier to classify each image as either being normal or abnormal. Our method is evaluated using ECG and PCG signals that were made available in the 2016 PhysioNet Computing in Cardiology Challenge [12,21].

The remainder of this paper is organized as follows. In Sect. 2, we present a brief description of ECG and PCG heart signals, stressing their main characteristics and how they relate to each other. In Sect. 3, we discuss the current challenges in the study of heart signals and the related work, including different methods and approaches that can be used to extract features and classify heart sounds. Section 4 introduces our methodology, and details each step of our procedure. In Sect. 5 we present and discuss the obtained results. At the end of the paper we present the main conclusions of this work.

2   Characteristics of ECG and PCG Heart Signals

The heart is one of the most important organs in our body. The heart beats continuously to pump oxygen and nutrient-rich blood throughout the human body to sustain life. A human heart is made of a strong muscle called myocardium, and is divided into chambers. The two upper chambers are known as atria while the two lower chambers are known as ventricles. The heart beats in regular intervals, controlled by the electrical pulses generated from the sinus node near the heart. This organ is susceptible to a variety of pathologies. One of the techniques used to detect these pathologies is the ECG, which consists in the recording of the variation of bioelectric potentials versus time of human heartbeats [5]. Another technique that can be used to verify the existence of pathologies is the PCG. During the squeezing of the blood from chamber to chamber, the valves keep the blood flowing smoothly in and out of the heart. This is done by automatically opening the valves, to let the blood flow from chamber to chamber, and closing the valves to prevent the backflow of blood [28]. PCG is a graphical representation of the waveform of heart sounds, which are generated by: (1) opening or closing of the heart valves, (2) flow of blood through the valve orifice, (3) turbulence created when the heart valves snap shut, and (4) rubbing of cardiac surfaces. The PCG creates a visual recording of these events and allows the detection of sub-audible heart-sounds and murmurs. This technique is very useful because it contains a great amount of physiological and pathological information regarding the human heart and vascular system.

2.1   ECG Signal

The ECG is a powerful diagnostic tool for heart disease. It can provide accurate information on the functional aspects of the heart and the cardiovascular system. The ECG signal is formed by a set of waves, such as the P-wave, representing the atrial depolarization, the QRS wave, which represents the depolarization of the ventricles [12], and the T-wave, which corresponds to the repolarization of

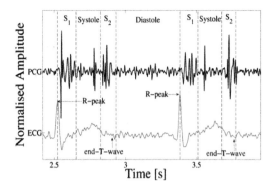

Fig. 1. Example of an ECG-labeled PCG, with the ECG and four states of the heart cycle (S1, Systole, S2, Diastole) shown. The R-peak and end-T-wave are labeled as reference for the approximate positions of S1 and S2, respectively [30].

the ventricles. The QT interval is the most important region for the detection of abnormality, each change that affects these characteristics represents a cardiac abnormality [12]. The ECG waveform is illustrated in the bottom of Fig. 1.

2.2 PCG Signal

The top of the Fig. 1 shows the heart sounds, composed by four different sounds: S1, S2, S3 and S4. The pumping action of a normal heart is audible by the 1st heart sound (S1) and the 2nd heart sound (S2). During systole, the atrioventricular valves are closed and the blood tries to flow back to the atrium, causing back bulging of the AV valves. This leads to vibration of the valves, the blood and the walls of the ventricles, and corresponds to the 1st heart sound. During diastole, the blood in the blood vessels tries to flow back to the ventricles, causing the semi lunar valves to bulge, but the elastic recoil of the arteries makes the blood bounce forward, thus leading to vibration of the blood, the walls and the ventricular valves, which produces the 2nd heart sound. S1 is a low-pitch sound with longer duration, whereas S2 is a high-pitch sound with a shorter duration. In normal situations, the S1–S2 interval (systole) is shorter than the S2–S1 interval (diastole). The 3rd heart sound (S3) is heard in the mid diastole due to the blood that fills the ventricles. The 4th heart sound (S4), also known as atrial heart sound, occurs when the atrium contracts and pumps blood to the ventricles. S4 appears with a low energy and is almost never heard by the stethoscope [11]. In addition to these components of the normal heart sounds, a variety of other sounds, such as heart murmurs, may be present in the cardiac signal. Murmurs can be benign (physiological) or abnormal (pathological), and are usually caused by turbulent blood-flow, which can happen inside or outside the heart. Abnormal murmurs can occur due to stenosis, which restricts the opening of a heart valve, or to regurgitation related with valves insufficiency, which allows backflow of blood following the partial closure of an inept valve.

2.3   Relationship Between ECG and PCG Signals

PCG can provide quantitative and qualitative information of heart sounds and murmurs. Studies on heart sound detection can be divided into two categories: ECG signal-dependent and ECG signal-independent. Our study is ECG signal-dependent. The opening and closing of the cardiac valves, and the sounds they produce, are the mechanical events of the cardiac cycle. They are preceded by the electrical events of the cardiac cycle. In Fig. 1 we plot part of both ECG and PCG signals to illustrate the relationship between them in the time domain. In this figure we can see that S1 occurs 0.04 s to 0.06 s after the onset of the QRS complex, and that S2 occurs towards the end of the T wave. Heart sound segmentation refers to the detection of the exact positions of the first (S1) and second (S2) heart sounds in a PCG. This is an essential step in the automatic analysis of heart sound recordings, as it allows the analysis of the periods between these sounds for the presence of clicks and murmurs. The segmentation becomes a difficult task if the PCG recordings are corrupted by in-band noise. In our work, we have a set of PCG signals with the corresponding ECG signals collected simultaneously. Therefore, we identify the start of the S1 using the ECG signal and then use this knowledge to segment the PCG. In particular, we use the Springer's segmentation algorithm [30] to identify the fundamental heart sounds (S1, Systole, S2 and Diastole) in the PCG waveform.

3   Current Challenges and Related Work

3.1   Current Challenges

As the quality and availability of PCG signals is no longer an issue, the development of appropriate algorithms that are able to detect heart diseases from heart sounds is an important challenge that has become the focus of work for many researchers. The ability to mathematically analyze and quantify the heart sounds represented on the PCG provides valuable information regarding the condition of the heart [25]. Thus, automated analysis and characterization of the PCG signal plays a vital part in the diagnosis and monitoring of valvular heart diseases. The main problems concerning the development of relevant techniques are the wide variety of distinguishable pathological heart sounds and the non-stationary characteristics of the PCG signals. Considering these issues, a question that can be addressed is how to increase the variety of distinguishable heart sounds while improving the performance of such systems in terms of reducing their computational complexity, without compromising their precision. PCG signal processing can be crudely divided into two main research areas. One is focused in the detection of events such as S1 and S2 to perform the segmentation of the PCG. The other deals with the detection of murmurs and, consequently, of cardiac pathologies [8].

3.2   Related Work

The segmentation process of PCG signals is a very important task to perform murmur detection and diagnosis of cardiac pathologies with computer analysis. Thus, it is essential that different components of the heart cycle can be timed and separated [10]. A large variety of algorithms that perform PCG segmentation have been presented in the literature. A solution for segmentation based in the time-domain characteristics of the PCG, was presented in [13], and another, based in the frequency-domain characteristics, in [17]. A threshold based on Shannon energy is set to detect peaks that correspond to S1 and S2 [16]. Correlation techniques have been used in [32], but this method may not perform well when the duration and the spectra of sound signal components show huge variations, making impossible to run this technique without user intervention.

In [23], as the heart sound and ECG signals are time varying, the Instantaneous Energy is computed to characterize the temporal behaviors of these signals. The purpose of the study is to perform heart sound segmentation based on the Instantaneous Energy of the ECG. Another important step in signal processing is feature extraction. If the features are not chosen properly, the performance of any classifier will be poor. The objective of the feature extraction procedure is to find the features from the available data and use them later for classification. These features were extracted from different analysis domains to ensure that the segments were described as thoroughly as possible. The analysis of heart sound is difficult to perform in the time domain because of noise interference and the overlapping of heart sound components. Thus, in many cases the processing of heart sound signals is done in the frequency domain. There are a large number of feature extraction algorithms available. These include the Fourier transform [19], the short time Fourier transform (STFT) [6], the time-frequency representation (TFR) [2], the MFCC [9] and the Discrete Wavelet Transform (DWT) coefficients [3]. However, the most widely used algorithms are the MFCC and the DWT. In this work we extract MFCC and time-frequency features from the signal.

After extracting the features from each signal, in a classification problem we need to learn a model that discriminates between normal and abnormal heart sounds. Most of the previous studies that learn models to classify heart sounds use artificial neural networks (ANN) or Support Vector Machines (SVM) [4]. In [14], Gupta et al. addressed the problem of distinguishing between two abnormal and one normal heart states. The methodology used by these authors uses Wavelet analysis of the PCG signal in combination with homomorphic filtering and K-means clustering method. The generalization accuracy of the proposed methodology was 97%. One of the first reported studies using neural networks for classification was presented by Barschdorff et al. [4]. These authors discussed the advantages of using neural networks over traditional classifiers, such as nearest neighbors. Spectral features obtained from short-term Fourier transform (STFT) analysis of the signal and mean values of corresponding sections of the signal envelope were used to train the neural network. Another algorithm that was widely used, and is known to generate highly accurate models, is the SVM classifier. An approach for heart sounds identification presented by Wu et al. reached a generalization accuracy of 95%. This approach uses wavelet transform to extract the envelope of the PCG signals [33]. Almost the same results were obtained by Jiang and Choi [34], who developed a system based in clustering algorithms for in-home use. However, this system was proven only by a case study. Another approach is the use of the tools and techniques of deep learning for the automated analysis of heart sounds [27]. In this paper, an algorithm was presented that accepts PCG waveforms as input and uses a deep convolutional neural network architecture to discriminate between normal and abnormal heart sounds.

4   Methodology

The methodology that we developed in this work is a novel approach to classify heart sounds. We use ECG and PCG collected simultaneously, to identify the fundamental heart sounds and thus segment the PCG signals more accurately. The main idea is to translate a 1D PCG signal into a 2D image that represents temporal and MFCC features. The methodology has four main steps:

– Segmentation of the PCG signal, identifying their four heart sounds states;
– Feature extraction of a group of 8 features in time domain, and MFCC in frequency domain;
– Transformation of the extracted features into two dimensional heat maps, which capture the time-frequency distribution of signal energy;
– Classification of the images generated, using different classifiers, distinguishing between normal and abnormal heat maps.

Each component is described below in detail. To better present each step of the methodology, we explore the dataset that was made available at the 2016 Physionet/Computing in Cardiology Challenge [21]. In this challenge the goal was to discriminate between normal and abnormal hearts using PCG and ECG signals.

4.1   Heart Sound Database

The challenge database provides a large collection of heart sound recordings, obtained from different real-world clinical and nonclinical environments. They include clean heart sounds but also very noisy recordings. The data were recorded from both normal and pathological subjects, and from both children and adults. We only use the training set A, which contains a total of 400 heart sound recordings (PCG signals lasting from 5 s to just over 120 s) and 400 ECG signals collected at the same time. The heart sound recordings were divided into two types: normal and abnormal heart sound recordings. The former were recorded from healthy subjects and the latter from patients with a confirmed cardiac diagnosis. These patients suffered from a variety of illnesses, but a more specific classification of the abnormal recordings was not provided. It is noteworthy that the number of normal recordings does not equal that of abnormal recordings, i.e., the dataset used is unbalanced. The distribution of the two classes in the dataset is approximately 70% of normal recordings and 30% of abnormal recordings. More detailed information about the dataset can be found in [21].

4.2   Segmentation

The first step of our method is to segment the PCG. In this work, the segmentation of the PCG was performed with the Springer's segmentation algorithm [30]. This algorithm is based on a logistic regression hidden semi-Markov model to predict the most likely sequence of states by incorporating information about the expected duration of each heart sound state. By applying this segmentation algorithm (which uses the ECG signals as reference, as explained above) to the PCG signals, we were able to identify the beginning and end of the four fundamental heart sound states (S1, Systole, S2 and Diastole). In our approach, we divide the original PCG signals into shorter segments. Using the information obtained with the segmentation algorithm, we selected the beginning of each heartbeat (S1) as a starting point for each segment that would be created. This was performed to ensure that sequences were aligned during classification. After the S1 heart sound was identified, we decided to create segments with a period of three seconds. We then extracted overlapping segments, and produced a total of 13404 segments of three seconds from the original 400 PCG signals. In Fig. 3 we can see the result of applying the segmentation algorithm.

4.3   Feature Extraction

After the segmentation step, we have a signal that is partitioned into several segments, with the heart sound states identified. Now we need to extract a set of features that describe each portion of the PCG signal.

In this step, two types of features are extracted from the heart sound signal. We extract a set of time domain features and MFCC features from the frequency domain. In the next lines we present the extracted features.

Time Features

After the segmentation of the PCG, and the identification of the four fundamental states of the heart cycle, some features were extracted. Currently, we are using eight time-domain features:

- Average duration of states S1;
- Average duration of states Systole;
- Average duration of states S2;
- Average duration of states Diastole;
- Average duration of the intervals RR;
- Ratio between the duration of the Systole and the RR period, of each heart beat;
- Ratio between the duration of the Diastole and the RR period, of each heart beat;

– Ratio between the duration of the Systole and the Diastole, of each heart
beat.

MFCC Features

We use the MFCC to extract features from the audio signal. The MFCC is a
linear representation of the cosine transforms of a short duration of logarithmic
power spectrum of the sound signal on a non-linear scale Mel frequency [20]. It
perceives frequency in a logarithmic way, inspired in the behavior of the human
ear. It is a powerful signal processing algorithm, widely used in the field of sound
recognition. The advantage of extracting MFCC parameters is that all features
of the sound signal are concentrated in the first coefficients, thus facilitating the
extraction task for operations in clustering algorithms or sound recognition [18].
Obtaining the MFCCs involves analyzing and processing the sound, according
to the following steps: pre-emphasis, windowing, fast Fourier transform (FFT),
Mel-filtering, nonlinear transformation, and discrete cosine transform (DCT).
The stages of MFCC coefficient extraction are shown in Fig. 2. The pre-emphasis
operation enhances the received signals to compensate for signal distortions. The
windowing operation divides a given signal into a sequence of frames. The FFT
operation is applied to the windowed signals for spectral analysis. The Mel-
filtering operation is designed based on human perception, and it integrates the
frequency compositions from one Mel-filter band into one energy intensity. The
non-linear transformation operation takes the logarithm of all Mel-filter band
intensities. The transformed intensities are then converted into MFCC using
DCT. The computation of the MFCC includes Mel-Scale filter-banks, an they
are computed as follows [22]:

$$m = 1127 log_e \left(\frac{f}{700} + 1 \right) \tag{1}$$

where f is the frequency in the linear scale and m is the resulting frequency in
Mel-Scale. The power spectral density (PSD) of the spectrum is mapped onto
the Mel-Scale by multiplying it with the filter-banks constructed earlier, and the
log of the energy output of each filter is calculated as follows [22]:

$$s[m] = log_e \left(\sum_{k=10}^{N-1} |X[k]|^2 H_m[k] \right) \tag{2}$$

Fig. 2. MFCC feature extraction process.

where $H_m[k]$ is the filter-banks and m is the number of the filter-bank. To obtain the MFCC, the discrete cosine transform (DCT) of the spectrum is computed [22]:

$$c[n] = \sum_{m=0}^{N-1} S[m] cos\left(\frac{\pi n}{M}\left(m - \frac{1}{2}\right)\right), n = 0, 1, 2....M \tag{3}$$

where M is the total number of filter banks.

In our case, in the windowing stage, we run overlapping sliding windows over the segments of three seconds that were created in the segmentation process. We chose a window length of 25 ms and a step size of 10 ms. By applying the described procedure, we calculated a total of 12 MFCC filterbanks per sliding window, which makes a total of 300 time frames for each signal of three seconds.

4.4   Transformation of Features in Images

At this stage, for each segment of three seconds of signal, we have a total of eight features extracted in the time domain and a collection of 3600 cepstral coefficients resulting from the 12 MFCC filterbanks and 300 time frames. We joined the two sets of features. To adjust the dimensions, zero padding was performed. The merge of the features produced an array with 12 rows and 301 columns.

Figure 3 illustrates one segment of three seconds from the original one-dimensional PCG waveforms, with the identification of the heart sound states calculated during signal segmentation. In addition, the heat map resulting from the conversion of the extracted features is also shown. The heat map has a total of 12 rows by 301 columns. The features from the time domain are in column number 301; the first 300 columns correspond to MFCC features. In these, the horizontal axis represents the sliding window and the vertical axis presents the 12 filterbank frequencies that were used in the calculation of the MFCC. We have also done some experiments, using the two feature sets separately, to evaluate the impact that their joint use has on the results.

4.5   Classification of Heart Sound Images

The aim of the classification procedure is to develop a rule whereby any new observation, represented by a feature vector, can be classified into one of the existing classes.

In this step, we run an algorithm to learn a classification model that is able to discriminate between normal and abnormal heart sounds. We learn the classification model by using the heart sound images obtained in the previous step.

There is a wide variety of classification methods applied in several areas, including the study of cardiac signals (ECG and PCG). Some of the classifiers used in this area are SVM [31], K-nearest neighbor (kNN) classifiers [22],

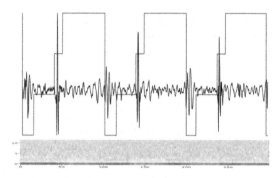

Fig. 3. Example of a PCG with the four states of the heart cycle (S1, systole, S2, diastole) identified (red line). MFCC heat map visualization of 3-s segment of heart sound data. (Color figure online)

Gaussian Mixture Model (GMM) [22], and several types of Neuronal Networks (NN) [7]. In our methodology, we study and evaluate several algorithms: the SVM, the Random Forest, the K-means Clustering and the Convolutional Neural Network (CNN), using as input parameters, the images created from the extracted features. While the CNN allows the use of images directly as an input parameter, for the other classifiers it is necessary to convert the image in a vector line, so that it can be used as an input parameter.

SVM

In our model, we used an SVM with a radial basis function (RBF) kernel. The RBF kernel has the formula:

$$K\left(x^{(i)}, x^{(j)}\right) = \phi(x^{(i)})^T \phi(x^{(j)}) \tag{4}$$

$$K\left(x^{(i)}, x^{(j)}\right) = exp\left(-\gamma \parallel x^{(i)} - x^{(j)} \parallel^2\right), \gamma > 0 \tag{5}$$

where the $x^{(i)}$ and $x^{(j)}$ represents two features vectors in some input space. The γ factor is a free parameter. In our method we adjust the γ parameter and the cost value, in order to optimize the results, avoiding falling in overfitting.

Convolutional Neural Networks

With the transformation of the extracted features into images, the CNN was chosen to perform the training image classifier, given their ability to automatically learn appropriate convolutional filters. We decided to train a CNN, using the features images as inputs. The architecture, and the parameters selected, were based on the work of Rubin et al. [27], who built a PCG signal classifier using deep convolutional neural networks.

Random Forest

The Random Forest is a classification method that works by creating an ensemble of decision trees at training time.

In our case, we compose a random forest with a number of trees and a number of variables randomly sampled as candidates at each split, in order to optimize the results, avoiding falling in overfitting.

K-Means Clustering

Cluster Analysis is a process of aggregating the objects into various groups on the basis of their similarities. K-Means algorithm is one of many methods used to perform clustering that is included in a group of unsupervised methods.

In this study, we tried to form two clusters, in order to divide the signals into the two existing classes, normal and abnormal. We used the Euclidean Distance method to measure the shortest distance between several signals. We also defined how many random sets were chosen, in order to optimize the results.

4.6   Evaluation Metrics

In the classification process, the 13404 images generated from the extracted features were classified. Once the dataset used was unbalanced, consisting of approximately 70% normal segments and 30% abnormal segments, we performed a 10-fold stratified cross validation. In a typical (k-fold) cross-validation method, a dataset S is first randomly partitioned into k equally-sized, disjoint subsets (folds) $S_1, S_2, ..., S_n$. Each k fold is then in turn used as the test set, while the remaining $(k - 1)$ folds are used as the training set. A classifier is then constructed from the training set, and its accuracy is evaluated on the test set. This process repeats k times, with a different fold used as the test set each time. The estimated true accuracy by this method is the average over the k folds. One distinct feature of cross-validation is that all the k test sets are disjoint, and thus each case in the original training set is tested once and only once. An extension of regular cross-validation is stratified cross-validation. In k-fold stratified cross-validation, a dataset S is partitioned into k folds such that each class is uniformly distributed among the k folds. The result is that the class distribution in each fold is similar to that in the original data set S. In this sense, the partition is "balanced" in terms of class distributions. In contrast, regular cross-validation randomly partitions S into k folds without considering class distributions. A possible scenario with regular cross-validation is that a certain class could be distributed unevenly (some folds contain more cases of the class than other folds). This distortion in class distributions can cause a less reliable accuracy estimation [35].

Given that the classification models are trained using the images generated from the segments of three seconds signal, it was necessary to group the predictions of the various segments to classify the original PCG signals. In the evaluation of the classification of the segments belonging to the same signal, a metric was used, in which only the signals with more than 60% of the segments classified as normal, would be classified as normal.

Once the normal PCG signals came from healthy subjects and the abnormal ones from patients with a confirmed cardiac diagnosis, the labels of the signals were assigned taking into account the patients' medical history, and not through the analysis of signals by a physician. This fact may lead to the existence of signals with the abnormal label that do not present the characteristics to be integrated in this class, in the whole signal studied, or in some of the segments of three seconds studied. By using this metric, we are considering that it is possible for an abnormal signal to contain segments of three seconds that are classified as normal. Different values were applied for this metric, and the best results were obtained for the 60%.

Equations (6), (7) and (8) show the sensitivity, specificity and overall metrics, respectively, which were used to evaluate the results. The measures were defined using True Positive (TP), True Negative (TN), False Positive (FP) and False Negative (FN):

$$Sensitivity = \frac{TP}{TP + FN} \tag{6}$$

$$Specificity = \frac{TN}{TN + FP} \tag{7}$$

$$Overall = \frac{Sensitivity + Specificity}{2} \tag{8}$$

5   Experimental Results

In this work we explore the dataset that was made available at Physionet databases. The goal is to discriminate between normal and abnormal hearts using PCG and ECG signals. We present a new approach, whose main idea is to translate a 1D PCG signal into a 2D image that represents temporal and MFCC features. After that, we use a binary classifier to learn a model that discriminates between normal and abnormal PCG signals. This algorithm was developed using the R statistical package. Next, we present and discuss the obtained results.

5.1   Results

During classification, the number of MFCC features to be used was treated as a hyper-parameter. Several tests were performed, with a different number of MFCC features, in order to optimize the classification results. Table 1 shows the results obtained with the different approaches, using 5 and 6 MFCC features, performed with the SVM, Random Forest (RF), K-means and CNN. The set of features composed by 5 MFCC and the TF, showed better results than the set composed by 6 MFCC and the TF (with the exception of CNN). Among the classification algorithms, the best results were obtained with SVM, followed by RF, K-means and CNN, in this order, as can be seen in Table 1.

Table 2 shows some results of the experiments where we studied the contribution of mapping temporal features to improve the results obtained with the MFCC features alone. In this table we present the results obtained with the classifiers SVM, RF, K-means and CNN, for two sets of features, one composed by 4 MFCC only and another composed by 4 MFCC and TF.

Table 1. Results obtained in the various tests performed.

Type of features	Classifier	Sensitivity	Specificity	Overall
5 MFCC + TF	SVM	0.9187	0.8205	0.8696
6 MFCC + TF	SVM	0.9081	0.8034	0.8558
5 MFCC + TF	RF	0.9789	0.4017	0.6903
6 MFCC + TF	RF	0.9823	0.3418	0.6621
5 MFCC + TF	K-means	0.7456	0.5556	0.6506
6 MFCC + TF	K-means	0.7420	0.5556	0.6488
5 MFCC + TF	CNN	0.8622	0.1538	0.5080
6 MFCC + TF	CNN	0.1343	0.9487	0.5415

Table 2. Results obtained, with or without inclusion of time features.

Type of features	Classifier	Sensitivity	Specificity	Overall
4 MFCC + TF	SVM	0.9647	0.7265	0.8456
4 MFCC	SVM	0.9435	0.7094	0.8264
4 MFCC + TF	RF	0.9788	0.4188	0.6988
4 MFCC	RF	0.9647	0.4017	0.6832
4 MFCC + TF	K-means	0.7951	0.4615	0.6283
4 MFCC	K-means	0.8021	0.4274	0.6147
4 MFCC + TF	CNN	0.5724	0.5812	0.5768
4 MFCC	CNN	0.5018	0.5641	0.5329

5.2   Analysis of the Results

As already mentioned, the number of MFCC features used during classification was treated as a hyper-parameter, and several experiments with a different number of MFCC have been performed. The best results obtained are presented on Tables 1 and 2. As can be seen in the tables, the best results were obtained with the SVM radial basis. The best result was obtained with a set of five MFCC features, together with the temporal features, with which a sensitivity of 0.9187, a specificity of 0.8205 and an overall of 0.8696 were obtained. With the RF and K-means classifiers, the results are not so good, because these classifiers have very low Specificity values, which consequently reduces the Overall. This was due to the high number of false positives returned by the classifier, as a consequence of this being the minority class of the dataset (approximately 30%), and the classifier having a lower recognition rate of the signals belonging to this class. Regarding the results obtained with the CNN, they fall below those obtained by Rubin et al. [27]. This can be related with the amount of data explored: in this work we were able to use only 10% of the dataset used by Rubin et al. As is well known, CNN performance is heavily related with the amount of data used to learn the network. Typically, if more data is used to train, the better the results will be [29]. In our work, we only used a small portion of the dataset due to the computational power that was available.

In Table 2 we present a set of results performed with the various classifiers, in which two types of features were used. In one case 4 MFCC were used together with the temporal features and in the other case only 4 MFCC were used without the temporal features. Analyzing the results, it is possible to conclude that the use of time features together with the MFCC, presents better results than using the 4 MFCC alone, with cases where the overall gain is approximately 0.04.

The overall scores for the top entries of the PhysioNet Computing in Cardiology challenge were very close [1]. The difference between the top place finisher overall (0.8602) and the 10th place (0.8263) was just approximately 0.04. Although the dataset we use is only part of the one used in the challenge, the class distribution is similar. Our best result is about 0.01 higher than the winner of the challenge. The use of time features, along with the MFCC, had a fundamental role in the obtained results, as it was demonstrated in the analysis of Table 2. Their presence led to an improvement of the results in all the classifiers used and, in the case of SVM, led to an improvement of approximately 0.02. Furthermore, our best performance was achieved using a single SVM radial basis, whereas other top place finishers of the challenge achieved strong classification accuracies with an ensemble of classifiers. In practical terms, a system that relies on only a single classifier, as opposed to a large ensemble, has the advantage of limiting the amount of computational resources required for classification.

6   Conclusions

We have used a SVM radial basis algorithm in the classification of heart sounds as normal or abnormal, obtaining an accuracy of approximately 86.97%. The approach included the segmentation of the heart signal, identifying the four states of the heart cycle, and creating three second signal segments. From these segments we extracted a group of MFCC features, which capture the time-frequency distribution of signal energy, and a group of eight temporal features. The group of features of each segment of three seconds were converted into an image, in the form of heat-map, which was the input to our classifier - a SVM radial basis. The performance of the model was evaluated and compared to other classifiers. The proposed approach outperforms all the other classifiers, achieving 86.97% accuracy in the binary classification task of identifying normal and abnormal heart sounds. Another classifier used was the CNN, which had worse results than the other classifiers. One possible cause for this is the small size of the dataset used, since this algorithm requires a large volume of data to converge. In the future we will investigate the usage of our methodology in larger datasets, and explore other types of features (wavelets). The analysis of the results showed that the unbalanced dataset might be problematic for identifying the minority class, and the results could be improved by collecting more training data, and by balancing the dataset. Furthermore, we intend to use CNN in larger datasets, in order to take full advantage of its ability.

Acknowledgments. This work is supported by the *NanoSTIMA Project: Macro-to-Nano Human Sensing: Towards Integrated Multimodal Health Monitoring and Analytics/NORTE-01-0145-FEDER-000016* which is financed by the *North Portugal Regional Operational Programme (NORTE 2020)*, under the *PORTUGAL 2020 Partnership Agreement*, and through the *European Regional Development Fund (ERDF)*.

References

1. Physionet Challenge 2016: Classification of Normal/Abnormal Heart Sound Recordings. https://www.physionet.org/challenge/2016/papers/
2. Avendaño-Valencia, L.D., Godino-Llorente, J.I., Blanco-Velasco, M., Castellanos-Dominguez, G.: Feature extraction from parametric time-frequency representations for heart murmur detection. Ann. Biomed. Eng. **38**(8), 2716–2732 (2010)
3. Balili, C.C., Sobrepena, M.C.C., Naval, P.C.: Classification of heart sounds using discrete and continuous wavelet transform and random forests. In: 2015 3rd IAPR Asian Conference on Pattern Recognition (ACPR), pp. 655–659, November 2015
4. Barschdorff, D., Bothe, A., Rengshausen, U.: Heart sound analysis using neural and statistical classifiers: a comparison. In: Proceedings of Computers in Cardiology, pp. 415–418, September 1989
5. Boussaa, M., Atouf, I., Atibi, M., Bennis, A.: ECG signals classification using MFCC coefficients and ANN classifier. In: 2016 International Conference on Electrical and Information Technologies (ICEIT), pp. 480–484, May 2016
6. Boutana, D., Benidir, M., Barkat, B.: Segmentation and identification of some pathological phonocardiogram signals using time-frequency analysis. IET Sig. Proc. **5**, 527–537 (2011)
7. Chen, T.E., Yang, S.I., Ho, L.T., et al.: S1 and S2 heart sound recognition using deep neural networks. IEEE Trans. Biomed. Eng. **64**(2), 372–380 (2017)
8. Choi, S., Jiang, Z.: Cardiac sound murmurs classification with autoregressive spectral analysis and multi-support vector machine technique. Comput. Biol. Med. **40**(1), 8–20 (2010)
9. Colonna, J., Peet, T., Ferreira, C.A., Jorge, A.M., Gomes, E.F., Gama, J.A.: Automatic classification of anuran sounds using convolutional neural networks. In: Proceedings of the Ninth International C* Conference on Computer Science and Software Engineering, C3S2E 2016, pp. 73–78. ACM (2016)
10. El-Segaier, M., Lilja, O., Lukkarinen, S., Slrnmo, L., Sepponen, R.: Computer-based detection and analysis of heart sound and murmur. Ann. Biomed. Eng. **33**(7), 937–942 (2005)
11. Ergen, B., Tatar, Y., Gulcur, H.O.: Time-frequency analysis of phonocardiogram signals using wavelet transform: a comparative study. Comput. Methods Biomech. Biomed. Eng. **15**(4), 371–381 (2012)
12. Goldberger, A.L., Amaral, L.A.N., Glass, L., Hausdorff, J.M., Ivanov, P.C., Mark, R.G., Mietus, J.E., Moody, G.B., Peng, C.K., Stanley, H.E.: Physiobank, physiotoolkit, and physionet: components of a new research resource for complex physiologic signals. Circulation **101**(23), e215–e220 (2000)
13. Groch, M.W., Domnanovich, J.R., Erwin, W.D.: A new heart-sounds gating device for medical imaging. IEEE Trans. Biomed. Eng. **39**(3), 307–310 (1992)
14. Gupta, C.N., Palaniappan, R., Swaminathan, S., Krishnan, S.M.: Neural network classification of homomorphic segmented heart sounds. Appl. Soft Comput. **7**(1), 286–297 (2007)

15. Hanna, I.R., Silverman, M.E.: A history of cardiac auscultation and some of its contributors. Am. J. Cardiol. **90**(3), 259–267 (2002)
16. Huiying, L., Sakari, L., Iiro, H.: A heart sound segmentation algorithm using wavelet decomposition and reconstruction. In: Proceedings of the 19th Annual International Conference of the IEEE Engineering in Medicine and Biology Society, vol. 4, pp. 1630–1633, October 1997
17. Iwata, A., Ishii, N., Suzumura, N., Ikegaya, K.: Algorithm for detecting the first and the second heart sounds by spectral tracking. Med. Biol. Eng. Comput. **18**(1), 19–26 (1980)
18. Kishore, K.V.K., Satish, P.K.: Emotion recognition in speech using MFCC and wavelet features. In: 2013 3rd IEEE International Advance Computing Conference (IACC), pp. 842–847, February 2013
19. Kumar, D., Carvalho, P., Antunes, M., Paiva, R.P., Henriques, J.: Heart murmur classification with feature selection. In: 2010 Annual International Conference of the IEEE Engineering in Medicine and Biology, pp. 4566–4569, August 2010
20. Lalitha, S., Geyasruti, D., Narayanan, R., Shravani, M.: Emotion detection using MFCC and Cepstrum features. Procedia Comput. Sci. **70**, 29–35 (2015)
21. Liu, C., Springer, D., Li, Q., Moody, B., Juan, R.A., Chorro, F.J., Castells, F., Roig, J.M., Silva, I., Johnson, A.E.W., Syed, Z., Schmidt, S.E., Papadaniil, C.D., Hadjileontiadis, L., Naseri, H., Moukadem, A., Dieterlen, A., Brandt, C., Tang, H., Samieinasab, M., Samieinasab, M.R., Sameni, R., Mark, R.G., Clifford, G.D.: An open access database for the evaluation of heart sound algorithms. Physiol. Meas. **37**(12), 2181 (2016)
22. Lubaib, P., Muneer, K.A.: The heart defect analysis based on PCG signals using pattern recognition techniques. Procedia Technol. **24**, 1024–1031 (2016)
23. Malarvili, M.B., Kamarulafizam, I., Hussain, S., Helmi, D.: Heart sound segmentation algorithm based on instantaneous energy of electrocardiogram. In: Computers in Cardiology, pp. 327–330, September 2003
24. Mozaffarian, D., Benjamin, E.J., Go, A.S., et al.: Heart disease and stroke statistics–2016 update. Circulation **133**(4), e38–e360 (2015)
25. Obaidat, M.S.: Phonocardiogram signal analysis: techniques and performance comparison. J. Med. Eng. Technol. **17**(6), 221–227 (1993)
26. Rangayyan, R., Lehner, R.: Phonocardiogram signal analysis: a review. Crit. Rev. Biomed. Eng. **15**(3), 211–236 (1987)
27. Rubin, J., Abreu, R., Ganguli, A., Nelaturi, S., Matei, I., Sricharan, K.: Classifying heart sound recordings using deep convolutional neural networks and mel-frequency cepstral coefficients. In: Computing in Cardiology Conference (CinC), pp. 813–816. IEEE (2016)
28. Santos, M.A.R., Souza, M.N.: Detection of first and second cardiac sounds based on time frequency analysis. In: Proceedings of the 23rd Annual EMBS International Conference, October 2001
29. Shi, W., Gong, Y., Wang, J.: Improving CNN performance with min-max objective. In: Proceedings of the Twenty-Fifth International Joint Conference on Artificial Intelligence, IJCAI 2016, pp. 2004–2010. AAAI Press (2016)
30. Springer, D.B., Tarassenko, L., Clifford, G.D.: Logistic regression-hsmm-based heart sound segmentation. IEEE Trans. Biomed. Eng. **63**(4), 822–832 (2016)
31. Rathikarani, V., Dhanalakshmi, P.: Automatic classification of ECG signal for identifying arrhythmia. Int. J. Adv. Res. Comput. Sci. Softw. Eng. **3**(9) (2013)
32. White, P.R., Collis, W.B., Salmon, A.P.: Time-frequency analysis of heart murmurs in children. In: IEE Colloquium on Time-Frequency Analysis of Biomedical Signals (Digest No. 1997/006), pp. 3/1–3/4 (1997)

33. Wu, J.B., Zhou, S., Wu, Z., Wu, X.M.: Research on the method of characteristic extraction and classification of phonocardiogram. In: 2012 International Conference on Systems and Informatics (ICSAI 2012), pp. 1732–1735, May 2012
34. Jiang, Z., Choi, S.: A cardiac sound characteristic waveform method for in-home heart disorder monitoring with electric stethoscope. Expert Syst. Appl. **31**, 286–298 (2006)
35. Zhang, Y.D., Yang, Z.J., Lu, H.M., Zhou, X.X., Phillips, P., Liu, Q.M., Wang, S.H.: Facial emotion recognition based on biorthogonal wavelet entropy, fuzzy support vector machine, and stratified cross validation. IEEE Access **4**, 8375–8385 (2016)

Discovering Interesting Associations in Gestation Course Data

Inna Skarga-Bandurova$^{(\boxtimes)}$ ⓘ, Tetiana Biloborodova ⓘ,
and Maksym Nesterov ⓘ

Volodymyr Dahl East Ukrainian National University, Severodonetsk, Ukraine
{skarga-bandurova,biloborodova}@snu.edu.ua

Abstract. Finding risk factors in pregnancy related to neonatal hypoxia is a challenging task due to the informal nature and a wide scatter of the data. In this work, we propose a methodology for sequential estimation of interestingness of association rules with two sets of criteria. The rules suggest that a strong relationship exists between the specific sets of attributes and the diagnosis. We set up a profile of the pregnant woman with a high likelihood of hypoxia of the newborn that would be beneficial to medical professionals.

Keywords: Data mining · Association rules · Interestingness measures · Gestation course data · Neonatal hypoxia

1 Introduction

Quality care throughout pregnancy, childbirth and postnatal period is a paramount task of obstetrics and gynecology. Despite significant progress in maternal health care in recent years, the etiology of certain diseases has not been fully explored. One such disease is hypoxia (s.a. antepartum fetal hypoxia, neonatal hypoxia or hypoxia of the newborn). Diagnosis of fetal hypoxia and neonatal hypoxia is based on the information provided by series of pregnancy-related examination, a thorough antenatal screening, ultrasonography observations, interview of the patient and a history assessment. However, distinguishing hypoxia using these clinical protocols remains a diagnostic challenge especially during the early stage of the disease. Medical research aimed at identifying causes and mechanisms of fetal hypoxia as well as early recognition the factors leading to hypoxia highly disagree on this point [1–5]. Furthermore, in the early stage, the most diseases offer better opportunities to be treated. Thus, the primary target is to improve our knowledge of different aspects of neonatal hypoxia.

Taking into account a large variety the causes of neonatal hypoxia, the actual task is grouping certain factors and finding critical combinations of parameters raise the risk of this condition. One way around this problem is to take advantage of the data mining technique and discover interesting associations in data.

The study is concentrated on extracting interesting rules from gestation course data by applying an additional measure of interestingness besides having well-known minimum support and confidence, useful for early diagnosis of neonatal hypoxia. We apply the associative rule mining technique to find combinations of parameters related to the risk factors in pregnancy allowing a judge the presence of a hypoxia of the newborn.

© Springer International Publishing AG 2017
E. Oliveira et al. (Eds.): EPIA 2017, LNAI 10423, pp. 204–214, 2017.
DOI: 10.1007/978-3-319-65340-2_17

The remainder of this paper is organized as follows. The second section provides a brief review of related works. The methodologies, materials and methods used in this work are described in section three. Here we discuss the approach used to obtaining and reducing association rules from the gestation course data. Experimental results with medical data sets are described in section four. Section five contains the conclusions of this paper and possible directions of future work.

2 Background and Related Work

Association rules are widely used for medical data since their introduction by Agraval et al. [6]. Detailed review of fundamental algorithms with current trends of association and frequent pattern mining for medical application, their advantages and disadvantages can be found in [7]. Association rule mining for the early diagnosis of Alzheimer's disease is discussed in [8]. Clinical decision support system (CDSS) for the treatment of encephalopathy using associative rules is provided in [9]. CDSS generate decisions on the basis of both clinical and physiological data applying association rule data mining algorithm and clustering algorithm. Its distinctive feature is a wide range of data on possible pathological conditions and the ability to provide assistance in making decisions in real time. Ordonez et al. [10] explored the idea of discovering association rules in medical data. In their study, Ordonez et al. presented two algorithms to mine association rules. Several medically important association rules are discussed as well as rules which are not interesting. In [11] a unified approach to quantify the association rules is proposed. Authors suggest a comprehensive definition of the interestingness of the rules. For rules with calculated importance, they used the property of anti monotonicity. The method of associative rule mining to refine existing rules and assessing the risk of drug side effects was described in [12]. To clarifying rules the sets of organism responses to a particular medication were used. To obtained (refined) rules the risk assessment of adverse effects on the body on particular drug was made. To this, the reliability indicators, the elevator, and the chi-square value (the significance of the association) were used.

Discovering interesting association rules in the medical domain often involve real challenges arise from their nature and the field of application. Rules and associations involve many items hard to interpret and generate a lot of outcomes. It is worthwhile noting that despite all the improvements in algorithms, the obtained association rules can either be too obvious, or contradict a priori knowledge, or contain redundant information [13]. The task of mining association rules is to generate minimal set of rules providing complete coverage of diagnostic signs with support and confidence greater or equal than some pre-specified thresholds of minimum support and minimum confidence, respectively.

3 Methodologies, Materials, and Methods

When searching for the interesting associations in gestation course data, we assume that signs of neonatal hypoxia are the frequently occurring sequences of indicators, markers, and indexes obtained during pregnancy-related examination recorded in pregnancy profile. Thus, our strategy is to find these indicators for neonatal hypoxia and reducing insignificant patterns in the results.

To achieve this goal, the process discovering interesting associations in gestation course data is divided into seven steps:

1. Selection the significant parameters related to the risk factors in pregnancy affecting the emergence of neonatal hypoxia;
2. Converting numerical data to nominal scale in accordance with the medical thresholds;
3. Mining associating rules and sampling rules for the examined pathology;
4. Pruning the number of candidates in compliance with the lift indicator;
5. Calculation interestingness of rules with respect to each other;
6. Reduction the number of rules in compliance with the quantitative measure of their interestingness;
7. Creating the profile of a pregnant woman with the risk of neonatal hypoxia.

3.1 Data Description

In current research we used real gestation course data of 186 pregnant women at the gestation age from 12 to 38 weeks: 81 datasets with neonatal hypoxia, 105 datasets without this pathology.

In our previous study [14] we selected the significant parameters related to the risk factors in pregnancy affect the emergence of neonatal hypoxia. In decreasing order of influence, they are: maturation of the placenta at 30 to 38 weeks, placenta thickness at 30 to 38 weeks, blood prothrombin index, amniotic fluid index (AFI) at 30 to 38 weeks, erythrocyte sedimentation rate (ESR) at 21 week, ESR at 30 week.

All quantitative data were converted to nominal scale in accordance with physical standards. As a result, the following gradations were obtained:

- placental maturity degree at 30 to 38 weeks: null (0), first (I), second (II), third (III);
- placenta thickness at 30 to 38 weeks: low (0–24 mm), normal (25–45 mm), high (over 46 mm);
- prothrombin index: four (IV), five (V), six (VI);
- AFI at 30 to 38 weeks: low (0–82 mm), normal (83–268 mm), high (over 269 mm);
- ESR at 21 week: low (0–5 mm/sec), normal (6–25 mm/sec), high (over 26 mm/sec);
- ESR at 30 week: low (0–4 mm/sec), normal (5–40 mm/sec), high (over 40 mm/sec).

3.2 Association Rule Mining for Gestation Course Data

The study was conducted with the R - a free software environment for statistical computing and graphics and R package arules [15].

For association rule mining we use Apriori algorithm [16] and to keep things simple, set the following rule evaluation metrics: min support 0.1 and min confidence 0.2.

On the first stage we obtained 473 rules and sorted them according to the target diagnosis - neonatal hypoxia, as a result 29 rules were formulated. Table 1 presents the best results achieved by Apriori algorithm.

In general case, association analysis algorithms generate a huge number of items and can produce up to hundreds of association rules. An association rule is an implication expression R: $X \rightarrow Y$, where X denoted antecedent and Y denotes consequent $X \cap Y = \emptyset$. Both X and Y are considered as a set of conjuncts of the form $c_1, c_2 \ldots, c_k$. The strength of the association rule is measured in terms of its support (s), confidence [17] and interestingness [10]. To demonstrate the interpretation of the rules obtained let's analyze rule 286. Support determines how often a rule is applicable to a given data set and gives us the ratio of number pregnant women with following items occur together: 'ESR indicators at week 21 of pregnancy = increased', 'the vertical size of the amniotic fluid on ultrasound scanning during 30–38 weeks of gestation = decreased', 'the thickness of the placenta on ultrasound scanning during 30–38 weeks of gestation = normal' with diagnosis = 'pathology' to the total number of pregnant women. Thus, we can see that there are 26 pregnancy women with a similar set of parameters.

The confidence determines how frequently items in set of consequences Y appear in cases containing antecedents X, this indicator shows us that the pathology is diagnosed in 59% of cases with the presence of increased ESR index at 21 weeks of pregnancy, a lowered vertical amniotic fluid size, and a normal placental thickness index during 30–38 weeks of pregnancy.

The lift indicates the probability of a newborn pathology in the case of all items mentioned above occur together. This probability for our data is 0.35 or 35%. More formally, lift computes the ratio between the confidence of rule and the support of the set in the rule consequent [18].

For pair of rule-candidates, binary variables R_1 and R_2 the lift is equivalent to interest factor, which is defined as follows:

$$I(R_1, R_2) = \frac{s(R_1, R_2)}{s(R_1) \cdot s(R_2)}. \tag{1}$$

The measure of interestingness in this case can be interpreted as follows:

$$I^1(R_1, R_2) \begin{cases} = 1, \text{ if } R_1 \text{ and } R_2 \text{ are independent,} \\ > 1, \text{ if } R_1 \text{ and } R_2 \text{ are positively correlated,} \\ < 1, \text{ if } R_1 \text{ and } R_2 \text{ are negatively correlated.} \end{cases} \tag{2}$$

Pruning the number of candidates in compliance with the lift indicator less than 1 gives us 18 rules-candidates instead of 29 with target diagnosis (see Fig. 1). The numbers of the graph nodes correspond to the numbers of the rules listed in Table 1.

Table 1. Support, confidence and lift values to the assigned associated rules

Rule no.	Antecedent (item name)	Support	Confidence	Lift
213	Placenta maturity at 30 to 38 weeks = 1	0.1344	0.6944	1.5946
214	Placenta maturity at 30 to 38 weeks = 1, Placenta thickness at 30 to 38 weeks = normal	0.1344	0.6944	1.5946
284	ESR at 21 week = high, AFI at 30 to 38 weeks = low	0.1398	0.5909	1.3569
286	ESR at 21 week = high, AFI at 30 to 38 weeks = low, Placenta thickness at 30 to 38 weeks = normal	0.1398	0.5909	1.3569
290	ESR at 21 week = high, ESR at 30 week = high, AFI at 30 to 38 weeks = low	0.1129	0.5833	1.3395
291	ESR at 21 week = high, ESR at 30 week = high, AFI at 30 to 38 weeks = low, Placenta thickness at 30 to 38 weeks = normal	0.1129	0.5833	1.3395
297	AFI at 30 to 38 weeks = low, Placenta thickness at 30 to 38 weeks = normal	0.2097	0.5735	1.3169
299	ESR at 30 week = high, AFI at 30 to 38 weeks = low, Placenta thickness at 30 to 38 weeks = normal	0.1290	0.5714	1.3121
306	AFI at 30 to 38 weeks = low	0.2150	0.5634	1.2937
312	ESR at 30 week = high, AFI at 30 to 38 weeks = low	0.1290	0.5581	1.2816
358	ESR at 30 week = high, Placenta thickness at 30 to 38 weeks = normal	0.2097	0.4937	1.1336
359	ESR at 21 week = high, ESR at 30 week = high, Placenta thickness at 30 to 38 weeks = normal	0.1667	0.4920	1.1299
361	ESR at 30 week = normal	0.1290	0.4898	1.1247
363	ESR at 21 week = high, Placenta thickness at 30 to 38 weeks = normal	0.2097	0.4875	1.1194
370	ESR at 30 week = high	0.2527	0.4700	1.0792
371	ESR at 21 week = high, ESR at 30 week = high	0.1989	0.4683	1.0755
373	Placenta thickness at 30 to 38 weeks = normal	0.3441	0.4571	1.0497
374	ESR at 21 week = high	0.2527	0.4563	1.0478
391	ESR at 21 week = normal, Placenta thickness at 30 to 38 weeks = normal	0.1075	0.4255	0.9771
403	ESR at 21 week = normal	0.1344	0.3968	0.9112
410	Placenta maturity at 30 to 38 weeks = 2, Placenta thickness at 30 to 38 weeks = normal	0.1236	0.3833	0.8802
414	Placenta maturity at 30 to 38 weeks = 2	0.1344	0.3788	0.8698
430	ESR at 21 week = high,	0.1075	0.3509	0.8057

(*continued*)

Table 1. (*continued*)

Rule no.	Antecedent (item name)	Support	Confidence	Lift
	Prothrombin index = 5, Placenta thickness at 30 to 38 weeks = normal			
431	ESR at 21 week = high, ESR at 30 week = high, Prothrombin index = 5	0.1129	0.3500	0.8037
440	ESR at 21 week = high, Prothrombin index = 5	0.1344	0.3333	0.7654
441	ESR at 30 week = high, Prothrombin index = 5	0.1290	0.3333	0.7654
442	ESR at 30 week = high, Prothrombin index = 5, Placenta thickness at 30 to 38 weeks = normal	0.1021	0.3333	0.7654
453	Prothrombin index = 5	0.1667	0.3039	0.6978
457	Prothrombin index = 5, Placenta thickness at 30 to 38 weeks = normal	0.1236	0.2949	0.6771

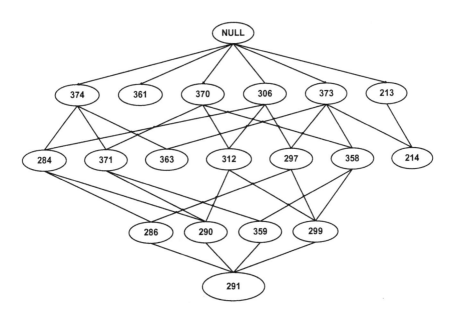

Fig. 1. Pruned set of candidates in compliance with the lift

3.3   Reducing Number of Rules

As it mentioned above, in medical applications a large number of rules are determined. In order to increase the information importance of rules, it is necessary to reduce their number and focus on potentially interesting ones. Further exploration of interestingness leads us to discovering different subjective and probabilistic measures of interestingness. To determine the interestingness of the rule, various probabilistic measures are used: support, confidence, Goodman-Kraskal, Pyatetsky-Shapiro, Laplace, etc. [19, 20]. In the present study, for reducing number of rules we applied three level technique proposed in [11] beginning with detection of deviations in data, then testing of differences among adjusted attributes and finally, quantifying the interestingness of association rules.

1. Detecting deviations in data is performed as follows.

The every conjunct cj from association rule set is represented in the form $<A = V>$, where A is an item name (attribute), Dom (A) is the domain of A, and I (value) $\in$ Dom (A). Degree of deviation is defined as deviation between two conjuncts $\Delta(c_i, c_j)$ and is calculated on the basis of the comparison between the items of the two conjuncts. For conjuncts c_i, c_j deviation of c_i with respect to c_j is defined as a Boolean function as follows:

$$\Delta(c_i, c_j) = \begin{cases} 0, \text{ if } A_i = A_j \text{ and } V_i = V_j, \\ 1, \text{ if } A_i = A_j \text{ and } V_i \neq V_j. \end{cases} \tag{3}$$

2. The differences among adjusted attributes can be calculated using the following formula:

$$\overline{d}(R_1, R_2) = \begin{cases} 0, & \text{if } |R_1| = |R_2| \forall c_i \in R_1, \exists c_j \in R_2, \text{ that } \Delta(c_i, c_j) = 0, \\ 1 & \forall c_i \in R_1, \neg\exists c_j \in R_2, \text{ that } \Delta(c_i, c_j) = 1, \\ \dfrac{\sum\limits_{c_i \in R_1, c_j \in R_2} \min\Delta(c_i, c_j)}{|R_1|}, & \text{otherwise,} \end{cases} \tag{4}$$

where R_1 and R_2 are considered as two sets of conjuncts c_i and c_j.

Parameter value $\overline{d} = 0$ indicates that R_1 and R_2 are identical, $\overline{d} = 1$ indicates the maximum deviation between rule sets, and the other $\overline{d}$ values between 0 and 1 are defined as a transient deviation.

3. Quantifying the interestingness of association rules

Let $R_1: X_1 \rightarrow Y_1$ and $R_2: X_2 \rightarrow Y_2$ be two association rules, then interestingness of a rule R_1 with respect to the rule R_2 is calculated as follows:

$$I^{II}(R_1, R_2) = \begin{cases} 0, & \text{if } \overline{d}(X_1, X_2) = 0 \text{ and } \overline{d}(Y_1, Y_2) = 0, \\ \left(\min\limits_{S \in R} \overline{d}(X_1, X_2) + \overline{d}(Y_1, Y_2)\right)/2, & \text{if } \overline{d}(X_1, X_2) \geq \overline{d}(Y_1, Y_2), \\ \left(\overline{d}(X_1, X_2) + \min\limits_{S \in R} \overline{d}(Y_1, Y_2)\right)/2, & \text{if } \overline{d}(X_1, X_2) < \overline{d}(Y_1, Y_2), \\ 1, & \text{if } \overline{d}(X_1, X_2) = 1 \text{ and } \overline{d}(Y_1, Y_2) = 1. \end{cases} \tag{5}$$

According to formula (5), $I^{II} = 0$ indicates that R_1 and R_2 are identical, $I^{II} = 1$ denotes maximum deviation between R_1 and R_2. Other cases indicate different deviations in the interestingness of association rules. To select interesting rules the user should specify the threshold of their interestingness. The anti-monotone property based on the threshold of the measure of interest can be applied to reduce the dimension of the resulting rule set. The anti-monotone property is that the measure of the interest of any set of elements should not exceed the minimal measure of interest of any of its subsets. This property greatly facilitates the mining rules.

4   Findings and Study Outcome

Taking all these point together, we calculated the interestingness of the associative rules for the diagnosis of hypoxia of the newborn with a threshold of interest equal to 0.2. Within the accuracy of observation for gestation course data of 186 pregnant women with 81 datasets with neonatal hypoxia, the following results were obtained.

The deviation in data at the first level for simple one-element rules 213, 306, 361, 370, 373, 374 is equal to 1. The deviation of the consequences is equal to 0.

The difference among adjusted attributes at the second level is 0.5, and the deviation of the consequences is 0.

Calculations on the third level give us the interestingness of association rules 213, 306, 361, 370, 373, 374 is equal to 0.25, i.e. above the threshold of interest and therefore these rules are considered as interesting.

The interestingness of the rules 214, 284, 297, 312, 358, 363, 371 for two-element rule sets is 0.25.

Three-element rules 286, 290, 299 have an interest of 0.33, and three-element rule 359 has an interest of 0.165, i.e. less than the assigned threshold of interestingness. Thus, all rules with interestingness less than the minimum assigned value 0.2 are considered as not interesting, and conformably to the property of anti-monotone, all subsets of these sets are not interesting either and can be excluded from further consideration. In Fig. 2 the rules that were excluded are highlighted by a grey background.

As a result, the total number of association rules was reduced to 16. Based on these rules, we created a profile of pregnant women with a high likelihood of hypoxia of the newborn, shown in Table 2.

It may be concluded that the combination of the objective measures with the subjective measure of interestingness makes it possible to improve the results in quantifying the interestingness of rules and to discover associations among attributes which characterize the patterns of normal and pathology diagnosis and to make use of them for the early diagnosis of neonatal hypoxia. These findings warrant further application and development of data mining techniques for medical informatics.

In spite of positive trends observed, a number of topics need for adjustment and special consideration such as sample size, algorithms for selecting the significant parameters related to the risk factors in pregnancy, accounting for missing values in datasets and many others. Another important thing here is the fact that interestingness is genuinely human construct and strongly depended from the context, which cannot be tackled automatically, hence a human-in-the-loop [21, 22] should be taken into consideration.

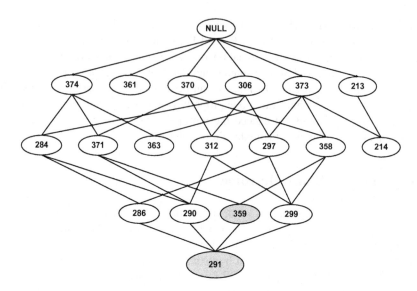

Fig. 2. A reduced number of rules in compliance with their interestingness

Table 2. Profile of a pregnant woman with a threat of hypoxia in a newborn

Item name (attribute)	Item values	Normal limits
ESR at 21 week of pregnancy (mm/sec)	26–69	25
ESR at 30 week of pregnancy (mm/sec)	4–69	30–35
Placental maturity at 30 to 38 weeks (grade)	I	I–II
Placenta thickness at 30 to 38 weeks (mm)	25–45	25–45
AFI at 30 to 38 weeks (mm)	269–306	82–268

5 Conclusions and Future Work

Our research is aimed at improving association rule mining technique in the medical domain. In this work, we have proposed a methodology for sequential estimation of interestingness of association rules and applied two sets of criteria for evaluating the quality of association rules. The first set of criteria consists of objective interestingness measure based on the statistical indicators as support, confidence, and lift. The second set of criteria involves subjective measures of interestingness based on quantifying the interestingness of association rules. A three-level procedure for reducing the number of association rules and sifting through the candidates to identify the most interesting rules has been performed.

The hybrid framework to association rule mining has been tested on real gestation course dataset. Based on the results, we set up a profile of pregnant women with a high likelihood of hypoxia in the newborn and obtained encouraging results. Two points are worth noting about the effects of using this approach. There is a possibility of inaccuracy in results, due to a small sample size. The research result requires a medical expert assessment for determining the practical value of the rules obtained. Nevertheless, results bring us to the conclusion that this approach offers hope to improve our knowledge about latent signs of neonatal hypoxia.

References

1. Seikku, L., Rahkonen, L., Tikkanen, M., Hämäläinen, E., Rahkonen, P., Andersson, S., Teramo, K., Paavonen, J., Stefanovic, V.: Amniotic fluid erythropoietin and neonatal outcome in pregnancies complicated by intrauterine growth restriction before 34 gestational weeks. Acta Obstet. Gynecol. Scand. **94**(3), 288–294 (2015)
2. Martinez-Biarge, M., Diez-Sebastian, J., Wusthoff, C.J., Mercuri, E., Cowan, F.M.: Antepartum and intrapartum factors preceding neonatal hypoxic-ischemic encephalopathy. Pediatrics **132**(4), e952–e959 (2013)
3. Mertsalova, O.V.: Perinatal hypoxic injuries of fetal CNS in high-risk pregnant women (diagnosis, prognosis of outcomes, optimization of pregnancy and delivery management) (2002)
4. Antonucci, R., Porcella, A., Pilloni, M.D.: Perinatal asphyxia in the term newborn. J. Pediatr. Neonatal Individ. Med. **3**(2), e030269 (2014)
5. Hypoxic-Ischaemic Encephalopathy (HIE). Queensland Clinical Guidelines (2016)
6. Agrawal, R., Imielinski, T., Swami, A.: Mining association rules between sets of items in large databases. In: ACM SIGMOD Conference, pp. 207–216 (1993)
7. Kumar, K.P., Arumugaperumal, S.: Association rule mining and medical application: a detailed survey. Int. J. Comput. Appl. **80**(17), 0975–8887 (2013)
8. Chaves, R., Gorriz, J.M., Ramirez, J., Illan, I.A., Salas-Gonzalez, D., Gomez-Rio, M.: Efficient mining of association rules for the early diagnosis of Alzheimer's disease. Phys. Med. Biol. **56**, 6047–6063 (2011)
9. Cheng, C.-W., Chanani, N., Enugopalan, J., Maher, K., Wang, M.D.: icuARM - an ICU clinical decision support system using association rule mining. IEEE J. Transl. Eng. Health Med. **1**, 4400110 (2013)
10. Ordonez, C., Santana, C.A., de Braal, L.: Discovering interesting association rules in medical data. In: ACM DMKD Workshop, pp. 78–85 (2000)
11. Kaur, H., Wasan, S.K., Al-Hegami, A.S., Bhatnagar, V.: A unified approach for discovery of interesting association rules in medical databases. In: Perner, P. (ed.) ICDM 2006. LNCS, vol. 4065, pp. 53–63. Springer, Heidelberg (2006). doi:10.1007/11790853_5
12. Reps, J.M., Aickelin, U., Ma, J., Zhang, Y.: Refining adverse drug reactions using association rule mining for electronic healthcare data. In: IEEE International Conference on Data Mining Workshop, pp. 763–770 (2014)
13. Simovici, D.A.: Data Mining of Medical Data: Opportunities and Challenges in Mining Association Rules (2012). www.cs.umb.edu/~dsim/papersps/dmmd.pdf
14. Skarga-Bandurova, I., Biloborodova, T.: Exploratory data analysis to identifying meaningful factors of hypoxic fetal injuries. Inf. Model. **44**(1216), 122–135 (2016). Herald of the NTU "KhPI". NTU "KhPI", Kharkov. doi:10.20998/2411-0558.2016.44.09
15. Hahsler, M., Grun, B., Hornik, K., Buchta, C.: Introduction to arules – a computational environment for mining association rules and frequent item sets (2005). http://www.lsi.upc.edu/~belanche/Docencia/mineria/Practiques/R/arules.pdf
16. Hegland, M.: The apriori algorithm – a tutorial. WSPC/Lect. Notes Ser. **9**(7) (2005). http://www2.ims.nus.edu.sg/preprints/2005-29.pdf

17. Doddi, S., Marathe, A., Ravi, S.S., Torney, D.C.: Discovery of Association Rules in Medical Data. http://citeseerx.ist.psu.edu/viewdoc/download?doi=10.1.1.198.4047&rep=rep1&type=pdf
18. Zhao, Y., Zhang, C., Cao, L.: Post-Mining of Association Rules: Techniques for Effective Knowledge Extraction. Information Science Reference (2009)
19. Masood, A., Ouaguenouni, S.: Probabilistic measures for interestingness of deviations – a survey. Int. J. Artif. Intell. Appl. **4**, 1 (2013)
20. Billing, V.A.: Association rule mining for medical diagnostics. Softw. Solut. Syst. **2**, 146–157 (2016)
21. Holzinger, A.: Interactive machine learning for health informatics: when do we need the human-in-the-loop? Brain Inf. **3**(2), 119–131 (2016)
22. Yildirim, P., Ekmekci, I.O., Holzinger, A.: On knowledge discovery in open medical data on the example of the FDA drug adverse event reporting system for alendronate (fosamax). In: Holzinger, A., Pasi, G. (eds.) HCI-KDD 2013. LNCS, vol. 7947, pp. 195–206. Springer, Heidelberg (2013). doi:10.1007/978-3-642-39146-0_18

Artificial Intelligence in Power and Energy Systems

Severity Estimation of Stator Winding Short-Circuit Faults Using Cubist

Tiago dos Santos[1,3]([✉]), Fernando J.T.E. Ferreira[2], João Moura Pires[1], and Carlos Viegas Damásio[1]

[1] Department of Computer Science, NOVA-LINCS,
Universidade Nova de Lisboa (FCT/UNL), Lisbon, Portugal
tmd.santos@campus.fct.unl.pt, tiagomiguel.santos@altran.com,
{jmp,cd}@fct.unl.pt
[2] Department of Electrical and Computer Engineering,
Institute of Systems and Robotics, University of Coimbra, Coimbra, Portugal
ferreira@deec.uc.pt
[3] Altran Portugal, Lisboa, Portugal

Abstract. In this paper, an approach to estimate the severity of stator winding short-circuit faults in squirrel-cage induction motors based on the Cubist model is proposed. This is accomplished by scoring the unbalance in the current and voltage waveforms as well as in Park's Vector, both for current and voltage. The proposed method presents a systematic comparison between models, as well as an analysis regarding hyper-parameter tunning, where the novelty of the presented work is mainly associated with the application of data-based analysis techniques to estimate the stator winding short-circuit severity in three-phase squirrel-cage induction motors. The developed solution may be used for tele-monitoring of the motor condition and to implement advanced predictive maintenance strategies.

Keywords: Fault diagnosis · Induction motor · Inter-turn short-circuit · Severity estimation · Machine learning · Regression · Cubist

1 Introduction

The three-phase squirrel-cage induction motor (SCIM) is the most used kind of electric motor due to its relatively low cost, good efficiency and high availability - representing about 85–90% of the electric motors installed in the industry [1]. Although the probability of breakdowns of electric motors is very low [2], these motors are critical to the industry. Since an unexpected failure can have high costs associated [3], the investment in maintenance practices that improve the efficiency and availability of electrical motors is very attractive to the industry. Stator winding short circuits are the most frequent electrical faults, forming 26% of the faults in electrical motors and in low power motors can go up to 90% [3].

© Springer International Publishing AG 2017
E. Oliveira et al. (Eds.): EPIA 2017, LNAI 10423, pp. 217–228, 2017.
DOI: 10.1007/978-3-319-65340-2_18

1.1   Stator Winding Short-Circuits

The SCIM, illustrated in Fig. 1, can be mainly decomposed in a stator and a rotor. The stator is composed by coils, each coil having a number of turns, which generates a rotating magnetic field that makes the rotor rotate.

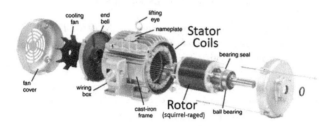

Fig. 1. A three-phase squirrel-cage induction motor. From: goo.gl/M8J6Ax

Short-circuits are phenomenona that can occur in the stator windings in three forms: inter-turn short circuit, inter-winding short circuit and earth fault. Following the scheme in Fig. 2, an inter-turn short-circuit fault is one such as the one that is happening in the Phase C's winding. These faults appear between the turns of the same coil, and therefore the faulty current is not much.

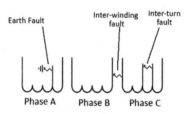

Fig. 2. Types of insulation faults.

This small faulty current is enough to start degrading the surrounding turns (due to thermal and electromagnetic stress), increasing the faulty current and letting the fault evolve to an inter-winding fault, where an adjacent winding (Phase B's winding) of the faulty winding (phase C's winding) starts to degrade. This fault will decrease the created magnetic field, which will deteriorate the motor's efficiency since it will now produce less mechanical energy. If not timely detected, it can degenerate into an earth short-circuit (also shown in Fig. 2). It is known that the time between the onset of the fault and a degradation that causes the motor to enter in fault state depends mainly on the initial number of shorted turns and the initial fault loop resistance, among others factors.

1.2 Stator Winding Short-Circuit Detection and Estimation

It is possible to detect stator winding short-circuits through model based or data based approaches, or even a combination of both [4]. A data based approach provides several advantages over model based approaches, such as non-ideal assumptions about the motor, learning of the sensors behavior [5] and can be used to classify or estimate the state of the motor without the need of complex physical models [4]. The problem of detecting Stator Winding Short Circuit faults is vastly studied in the literature, where both model based [6,7] as well as data based strategies are proposed [8–10].

Nevertheless, techniques to complement the detection of the Stator Winding Short-Circuit by estimating its severity are still limited. The simple detection of the fault is not enough, once it does not provide any indication of the fault's degradation and, *per si*, does not allow for an adequate and realistic maintenance plan. Therefore, it is important to achieve an early estimation of the severity of the Stator Winding Short-Circuit.

To approach the problem of Stator Winding Short-Circuit's severity estimation, [11] proposed a model-based approach to estimate the percentage of shorted turns (μ) and the value of the winding shorted portion's insulation resistance (r_f). This is done by measuring the current and voltage, calculate the negative sequence component both for current and voltage and the two target variables (μ and r_f) are derived from the estimation of one parameter by means of using an equality constraint on fault parameters and a nonlinear Kalman Filter. The authors test the proposed methodology with short-circuits with a percentage of shorted-turns between 10% and 16%, and a r_f between $20\,\Omega$ and $10\,\Omega$.

In [12,13], a model-based approach is proposed where the percentage of shorted turns is estimated. To achieve that, [12] measures the currents and voltages in the motor's terminal box (1.4 kHz sample frequency) and a model of a motor in short-circuit state is derived. Using Linear Matrix Inequalities theory and an observer, the percentage of shorted turns is estimated (as well as other properties). In [13], a model for short-circuit is derived and by estimating the model's parameters, the percentage of shorted turns is estimated.

In [14], the authors derive a model based strategy based on a dynamic Induction Motor model, where through the sequence component analysis it is possible to estimate a severity factor which is given by Eq. 1, where I_{nom} is the nominal current of the motor, and $\mu_{dq}i_f$ is the obtained fault signal.

$$SI = \frac{|\mu_{dq}i_f|}{\sqrt{2}I_{nom}} \tag{1}$$

In [14], the authors test the proposed methodology with short-circuits in phase A of the motor. The emulated short-circuits are of two types: 3 shorted turns of the phase winding (which winding contains 300 turns) and 3 shorted turns with a very low faulty current. The authors show that the proposed severity index estimation is robust for such cases.

1.3 Proposed Method

In this work, which is an extension of the work developed in [10], a data based approach is proposed where a model is developed using the Cubist algorithm to estimate a severity factor that depends on the percentage of shorted turns (per phase) and the percentage of faulty current (per rated current). The input for the Cubist is the result of a feature extraction process that takes place in the raw data, as well as in the d-q space. The d-q space is the output space of the Park's transformation function, which is explained in Subsect. 3.2. In the d-q space, by applying Principal Component Analysis (PCA), the components are used to score the unbalance. The Cubist model was chosen after a systematic comparison with other models, and went through a process of fine-tunning. To acquired the data, several experiments were made to emulate different short-circuits. To do so, a special motor was used to generated the short-circuit data while a data logger monitored the line currents and voltage of the motor.

1.4 Outline

The presented paper is structured in the following way - Sect. 2 describes the data generation process, presents the available data for this work and explains the proposed severity index; Sect. 3 shows the proposed extracted features in the raw space as well as in the d-q space, explains the process used to take into account the variations of the supply current; Sect. 4 presents the experiments done as well as the evaluation process to choose the proposed Cubist model; Sect. 5 presents the authors' conclusion of the presented work.

2 Data Generation Process

For the experiments, a special 400-V, 50-Hz, 4-pole, 2.2-kW delta-connected SCIM (nominal current of 4.5 A), with reconfigurable stator windings through external access to the terminals of all the coils was used. The stator core has 36 slots, and the stator winding has two sets of coils, each with 6 coils per phase.

The currents and line-to-neutral voltages waveforms of the three phases (R, S and T; 50-Hz), have been acquired at a 1-kHz sampling rate (which is relatively low), using a commercial datalogger (InMonitor). Each minute, five cycles are acquired and from those cycles an averaged cycle is computed - resulting on 20 points, representing 20 ms. The average waveform is a way to mitigate some noise and/or interference transients during the data acquisition process. The averaged cycle is sent via Wi-Fi to a database, where the data is finally recorded.

To emulate the stator winding short-circuits, an external resistance has been connected to the external terminals. Data have been collected for different motor states, namely, healthy with and without load, 2.5-A short-circuit on all the paired coil terminals in each phase, with and without load, and 1.5-, 1.0-, 0.25-A short-circuits in one coil of a given phase. Table 1 shows the number of cycles generated given the phase in fault, the number of coils in fault, the fault current and the motor condition. When one coil is short-circuited (total of 50 turns) it represents a short-circuit of 16.7% of the total number of turns per phase (total of 300 turns), whereas when half a coil is short circuited (total of 25 turns) it represents a short-circuit of 8.3% of the total number of turns per phase. Table 1 presents the severity index for the generated data.

Table 1. Proposed severity index (SI) in the generated data given the shorted turns and short circuit (SC) current, plus the number of cycles per severity.

Shorted turns	0	25	50	50	50	50	50
Shorted turns (%)	0	0.083	0.167	0.167	0.167	0.167	0.167
SC current (A)	0	2.5	2.5	2.0	1.5	1.25	0.25
SC current (%)	0	0.556	0.556	0.444	0.333	0.277	0.056
SI	0	0.354	0.396	0.333	0.271	0.239	0.115
Number of cycles	531	122	880	37	46	45	43

As referred in Subsect. 1.1, the two main contributors for the degradation of the fault are the number of shorted turns and the fault loop resistance (which is related to the short-circuited current). Therefore, we proposes a severity index which is composed by the percentage of shorted turns given the total of turns per phase (50%) and the percentage of generated faulty current given the rated current of the motor (50%), as stated in Eq. 2 - where SI is the Severity Index, STP is Shorted Turns Percentage and SCC is Short Circuit Current (A).

$$SI = STP * 0.5 + SCC * 0.5 \tag{2}$$

A projection of the raw data over time can be seen in Fig. 3, where Fig. 3a shows the current of a healthy motor's cycle (with a duration of 0.02 s). When the motor is healthy, any phase of the three-phase current system has approximately the same peak value and approximately the same distance between the adjacent phases - condition which is known by a balance in the phases of the current. An unbalance condition appears when the motor presents a stator short-circuit, as it is shown in Fig. 3b. Comparing Fig. 3a and b, it is possible to observe the existence of an unbalance on the phases in Fig. 3b.

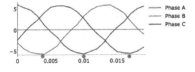   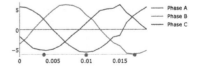

(a) Healthy cycle current   (b) Short-circuited cycle current

Fig. 3. Performance on validation and test set.

3   Feature Extraction

Before extracting any feature, each signal (current phase A, B, C and voltage A, B, C) is normalized by the nominal value of the motor. This normalization allows for a certain generalization to estimate the severity for other machines of the same power type. The averages are a way to take into account the variations of the supply current which may happen due to external factors.

The features that will be extracted are: **(a)** the first Principal Components (PC) coordinates both for current and voltage in d-q space, **(b)** eccentricity for both current and voltage in d-q space using the two PCs, **(c)** averages of the previous 6 record's first PC coordinates of the current and voltage in d-q space, **(d)** averages of the previous 6 records's eccentricity of the PCs of the current and voltage in d-q space, **(e)** score of the three phase currents and voltages unbalance, **(f)** average of the RMS current and voltage phases' value, **(g)** average of the previous 6 records's score of the three phase currents and voltages unbalance, **(h)** root mean square value for each phase current and voltage, and **(i)** averages of the RMS value of the previous 6 records for each phase current and voltage.

3.1   Raw Data

The features obtained from the raw data are **(e)**–**(i)**, forming a total of 18 features. To score the three-phase unbalance (for currents and voltages), the current RMS value for each phase (I_A, I_B, I_C) is calculated and then the current unbalance was calculated according to (3).

$$unb_I = \left(\frac{max\left(|I_A - avg|, |I_B - avg|, |I_C - avg|\right)}{avg} \right)$$
$$avg = \frac{I_A + I_B + I_C}{3} \tag{3}$$

3.2   Park's Vector

For each record, the Park's Transform is applied to the currents and voltages, resulting into the Park's Vector, which, over an entire period, results into a circle (symmetrical condition) or an ellipse containing some ripple (asymmetrical condition). The instantaneous values of the direct (d) and quadrature (q) vectors, i_d and i_q, resulting from the application of the Park Transform to the instantaneous values of the three line currents, i_a, i_b and i_c, are given by:

$$\begin{cases} i_d = \sqrt{\frac{2}{3}}i_a - \sqrt{\frac{1}{6}}i_b - \sqrt{\frac{1}{6}}i_c \\ i_q = \sqrt{\frac{1}{2}}i_b - \sqrt{\frac{1}{2}}i_c \end{cases} \tag{4}$$

This is an intermediate step so that the PCA can be applied. In the Park's Vector there are several characteristics that allow the determination of several short-circuit faults. From the resultant ellipse's format, it is possible to associate its eccentricity (Fig. 4) with the severity of the fault.

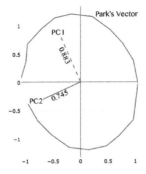

Fig. 4. Principal components of the Park's Vector with eigen-value (d-q space).

3.3 PCA Transform

The features obtained from the d-q space are **(a)–(d)**. PCA is a widely used method (a linear orthogonal transformation) which yields directions of maximum variance. For this reason, this method is normally employed for dimension reduction, given that the directions that have a greater data variance are those that describe better the data.

As a result, PCA is able to provide the main directions of the given data on the space-vector and, when applied to the elliptical form of the Park's Vector, the two first components correspond to the major and minor axis (as shown in Fig. 4). From here, an unbalance score is calculated as an eccentricity:

$$score = 1 - e_2/e_1 \tag{5}$$

where e_2 is the eigen-value of the second principal component and the e_1 is the eigen-value of the first principal component.

4 Modeling and Evaluation

The modeling and evaluation were made using R (version 3.3.1) under macOS Sierra. The caret [15] package (version 6.0-73) was used since it simplifies the task of experimenting a set of models and simplifies the interface of the training pipeline. The modeling stages consisted on selecting the better candidates from a set of selected models (Sect. 4.2) and only the best two of this stage were further analyzed (Sect. 4.3). After the training stage, the two models are evaluated in both validation set and test set.

4.1 Cubist

The Cubist is a rule-based regression model which follows the principles of an M5 Model Tree [16]. A tree is grown and in the leaf nodes, instead of classes or values, they contain a linear regression model which is based on the predictors used in the activation path of the rule. Also, each intermediate node also has a linear regression model with the predictors that were activated from the root until the node. These regressions are used to smooth the results, which are taken into account together with the leaf node's linear regression model result.

The final result of the Cubist can also be adjusted by the k parameter, which indicates that the result should be averaged with the k most identical instances in the training set. The technique used to identify the most similar instances in the training set is the k-NN, where the Manhattan distance is used [17].

The Cubist model can also make use of the boosting strategy, which is an ensemble technique that can reduce both bias and variance. This strategy consists on iteratively learning weak classifiers of the same model with respect to a dataset, where the next model's learning will depend on the performance of the previous model - points where the previous model had a higher error associated will be more important than the others for the next model. When weak learners are joined, they are typically weighted in a way that is usually related to the weak learner's performance - low performance learners have low weight, while high performance learners have high weights. To output the result, the Cubist with ensemble calculates an average of the learners as the final result.

4.2   Selecting Promising Models

An experiment to study the performance of a set of models was assessed. The chosen models for this experiment were k-NN, Stochastic Gradient Boosting, Random Forest, Cubist, Support Vector Machine (SVM) with Radial Basis Function Kernel and Artificial Neural Networks (ANN). Since the goal is not to study a final model but rather have a general perception of the models' performance, the train process was a rather simple one. The dataset was randomly split in train set (70%) and test set (30%), and for each train model a bootstrap resample with 10 repeats was considered.

The k-NN parameters were combinations of $k = [15, 31, 49]$, $distance = [0.5, 1, 2]$ and $kernel =$ [rectangular, gaussian, cosine]. The Stochastic Gradient Boosting parameters were combinations of $n.trees = [100, 150, 250]$, $interac.deep = [1, 3, 10]$, $reduction.stepsize = [0.1, 0.5, 1]$ and $min.observs = [10, 15, 30]$. The Random Forest parameters were combinations of $n.trees = 500$ and $mtry = [1..10]$. The Cubist model parameters were combinations of $neighbors = [1, 3, 6, 9]$ and $committes = [1, 20, 35, 50, 80, 90, 100]$. The SVM parameters were combinations of C= $[0.5, 1, 4, 8, 32, 128]$ and $sigma = [0.01, 0.02, 0.06, 0.1]$. The ANN parameters were combinations of $hidden.size = [2, 8, 10, 14, 16]$ and $decay = [0, 0005, 0, 001, 0, 002, 0, 005, 0, 01]$.

To evaluate the performance of the model's instances, two metrics were used: Mean Absolute Error (MAE, Eq. 6) and Root Mean Square Log Error (RMSLE, Eq. 7). In both equations n is the size of the sample, $\hat{y}$ is the estimated value and y is the true value.

$$MAE = \frac{\sum_{i=1}^{n} |y - \hat{y}|}{n} \tag{6}$$

$$RMSLE = \sqrt{\frac{\sum_{i=1}^{n}(log(\hat{y}+1) - log(y+1))^2}{n}} \qquad (7)$$

In this experiment, it was noticeable that the great majority of instances of Cubist and k-NN were systematically better than the rest of the models, and therefore the chosen models for further study were the Cubist and k-NN.

4.3   Model Training

After the pre-selection of two machine learning models, another assessment regarding the influence of meta-parameters in the models (resample technique used, chosen metric to chose the best model during the resample process, type of preprocess applied to data) was made. The data was randomly divided in train set (50%), validation set (20%) and test set (30%).

The tested pre-process techniques were Yeo-Johnson Transformation, center, scale, range, Box-Cox Transformation and Spatial Sign Transform.

The Spatial Sign transformation is a multidimensional normalization which is defined as follows:

$$x^{*spa-sign} = \begin{cases} \dfrac{x}{||x||} & \text{if } x \neq 0 \\ 0 & \text{if } x = 0 \end{cases} \qquad (8)$$

where $x^{*spa-sign}$ represents the transformed vector by the spatial sign transformation, x is the input vector that represents the instance, and $||x||$ represent the vector's euclidean norm. This transformation has an output domain of $[0, 1]$ [18].

The tested resample techniques were bootstrap (50 and 25 repeats), bootstrap632 (50 and 25 repeats), repeated cross validation (6 folds and 10 repeats; 3 folds and 10 repeats), cross validation (6 and 3 folds). The tested metrics during the resample process were MAE (Eq. 6) and RMSLE (Eq. 7). The Cubist and k-NN parameters were the same as the previous experiment.

4.4   Evaluation

After training the two models with all the configurations, they were evaluated in both validation and test set by using MAE and RMSLE. Figure 5 shows an overview of the models' performance on the validation set.

Figure 5 is composed by two rows and two columns - the first row for the RMSLE and the second row MAE; the first column for Cubist and the second column for k-NN. It is possible to verify that, in Fig. 5, the best k-NN instance is better than the best Cubist instance, either for MAE as well as for RMSLE.

Regarding MAE, it is noticeable that for all the pre-process techniques, the best k-NN instance is better than the best Cubist instance - being the best Cubist instance associated with the Spatial Sign Transform. It is also shown that the k-NN scores a lower MAE but an equivalent RMSLE when comparing to the Cubist with a Spatial Sign Transform.

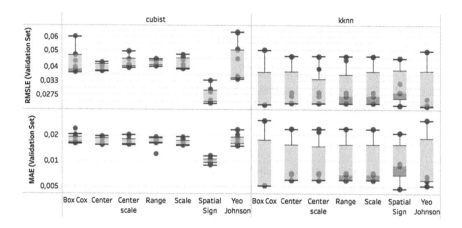

Fig. 5. K-NN and Cubist performance on validation set (MAE and RMSLE).

Regarding RMSLE, the only pre-process that leads the Cubist to a performance close to the k-NN is the Spatial Sign Transformation, whereas the k-NN presents instances that can achieve low RMSLE independent of the pre-process.

This means that most of the time the k-NN will produce an estimate that is closer to the truth than the Cubist estimation, but there are times where the k-NN estimate will be way further away than the Cubist. In other words, in this dataset the Cubist model have a more reliable estimation than the k-NN due to the error-variation in the estimation, as it can be seen in Fig. 6.

Figure 6 shows the predictions of the Cubist (Fig. 6(a)) and k-NN (Fig. 6(b)) for the validation set. In this figure the miss-estimations of the k-NN are noticeable higher than the miss-estimations of the Cubist, in spite of the Cubist present more miss-estimations than the k-NN - making the error-variation of the k-NN higher than the Cubist's.

In the test set results, the same observation was made regarding the error-variation in the estimation between the Cubist with Spatial Sign Transformation and any k-NN group. It was noticeable that both MAE and RMSLE of test set are a little higher when compared to the MAE and RMSLE of the validation set. At this point, it can be concluded that the Spatial Sign Transformation is the transformation that brings better results both for Cubist and for k-NN models.

After inspecting the parameters of the best models given the Spatial Sign Transformation, it was possible to notice that the resample technique was indifferent. Regarding the metric used during resample, there was a slight incidence of MAE metric over the other, but all of the tested metrics appeared.

Regarding model parameter configuration for k-NN model, only instances with a rectangular kernel appeared, all of them with the $k = 49$ and the distance parameter were whether 0.5 or 2.

Regarding model parameter configuration for Cubist, there great majority of the instances had a committee quantity greater than 30, existing some instances

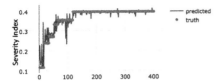 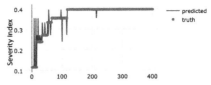

(a) Cubist performance for validation and test set.   (b) K-NN performance for validation and test set.

Fig. 6. Performance on validation and test set.

with a committee quantity of 1 and 10. The number of neighbors varied from 1 to 9, with no visible incidence.

At the end of the evaluation process, the Cubist model is chosen due to two factors: it presents an ensemble model, and therefore is more robust than the k-NN, and due to the observation that when the k-NN miss-estimate the predictions, those miss-estimations are way worse than the Cubist's miss-estimations. At the end of the day, the Cubist model predictions will present a lower error-estimate variation than the ones predicted by k-NN which can be seen in Fig. 6.

5   Conclusions

This work presents a practical way for industrial condition monitoring, given that the goal is to apply the presented method to thousands of motors to complement the detection of stator-winding inter-turns short-circuit detection. The data-based nature of the proposed technique makes it a good fit for the industrial scale, and the shown robustness of the estimation of the proposed severity index allows for a severity fault monitoring which can provide early insights on the state of the motor, allowing to a timely maintenance plan. It is important to remind that the emulated short-circuits were generated with and without load.

The presented work can be improved by acquiring data associated with undervoltage, overvoltage and unbalanced voltage conditions. A database of more motors presenting a more vast short-circuits severity would also be beneficial to ensure the robustness of the estimator.

Acknowledgments. This work has been supported by FCT - Fundação para a Ciência e Tecnologia MCTES, UID/CEC/04516/2013 (NOVA LINCS).

References

1. Ferreira, F.J.T.E., Cruz, S.M.A.: Visão geral sobre selecção, controlo e manutenção de motores de indução trifásicos: Manutenção 101, 46–53 (2009)
2. Motor Reliability Working Group: Report of Large Motor Reliability Survey of Industrial and Commercial Installations, Part 3: IEEE Transactions on Industry Applications, Vol. IA-23, No. I, January/February (1987)

3. Albrecht, P.F., Appiarius, J.C., McCoy, R.M., Owen, E.L., Sharma, D.K.: Assessment of the reliability of motors in utility applications - updated. IEEE Trans. Energy Convers. **EC-1**(1) (1986)
4. Riera-Guasp, M., Antonino-Daviu, J.A., Capolino, G.A.: Advances in electrical machine, power electronic, and drive condition monitoring and fault detection: state of the art. IEEE Trans. Ind. Electron. **62**(3), 1746–1759 (2015)
5. Janakiraman, V.M.: Machine Learning for Identification and Optimal Control of Advanced Automotive Engines. The University of Michigan, Ann Arbor (2013)
6. Pires, V.F., Foito, D., Martins, J.F., Pires, A.J.: Detection of stator winding fault in induction motors using a motor square current signature analysis (MSCSA). In: 2015 IEEE 5th International Conference on Power Engineering, Energy and Electrical Drives (POWERENG) (2015)
7. Mohamed, S., Ghoggal, A., Guedidi, S., Zouzou, S.E.: Detection of inter-turn short-circuit in induction motors using Park-Hilbert method. Int. J. Syst. Assur. Eng. Manag. **5**(3), 337–351 (2014)
8. Patel, R.A., Bhalja, B.R.: Condition monitoring and fault diagnosis of induction motor using support vector machine. Electr. Power Compon. Syst. **44**(6), 683–692 (2016)
9. Jawadekar, A., Paraskar, S., Jadhav, S., Dhole, G.: Artificial neural network-based induction motor fault classifier using continuous wavelet transform. Syst. Sci. Control Eng.: Open Access J. **2**(1), 684–690 (2016)
10. dos Santos, T., Ferreira, F.J.T.E., Pires, J.M., Damásio, C.V.: Stator winding short-circuit fault diagnosis in induction motors using random forest. In: Proceedings of the 11th IEEE International Electric Machines and Drives Conference, DISC, Miami, FL, United States, May 2017
11. Nguyen, V., Wang, D., Seshadrinath, J.: Fault severity estimation using nonlinear kalman filter for induction motors under inter-turn fault (2016)
12. Kallesøe, C.S., Vadstrup, P., Due, P., Vej, J.: Observer based estimation of stator winding faults in delta-connected induction motors, a LMI approach, pp. 2427–2434 (2006)
13. Bachir, S., Tnani, S., Trigeassou, J., Champenois, G.: Diagnosis by parameter estimation of stator and rotor faults occurring in induction machines (2006)
14. De Angelo, C.H., Bossio, G.R., Giaccone, S.J., Valla, M.I., Solsona, J.A., García, G.O.: Online model-based stator-fault detection and identification in induction motors **56**(11), 4671–4680 (2009)
15. Kuhn, M.: The caret Package. https://topepo.github.io/caret/
16. Quinlan, J.R.: Learning with continuous classes. In: Proceedings of the 5th Australian Joint Conference on Artificial Intelligence, Singapore (1992)
17. Kuhn, M., Johnson, K.: Applied Predictive Modeling. Springer, Heidelberg (2013)
18. Serneels, S., De Nolf, E., Van Espen, P.J.: Spatial sign preprocessing: a simple way to impart moderate robustness to multivariate estimators. J. Chem. Inf. Model. **46**(3), 1402–1409 (2006)

Estimating Energy Consumption in Evolutionary Algorithms by Means of FRBS

Towards Energy-Aware Bioinspired Algorithms

Josefa Díaz Álvarez[1], Francisco Chávez de La O[1(✉)],
Juan Ángel García Martínez[1], Pedro Ángel Castillo Valdivieso[2],
and Francisco Fernández de Vega[1]

[1] Universidad de Extremadura, Badajoz, Spain
{mjdiaz,fchavez,jangelgm,fcofdez}@unex.es
[2] ETSI Informática, Universidad de Granada, Granada, Spain
pacv@ugr.es

Abstract. During the last decades, energy consumption has become a topic of interest for algorithm designers, particularly when devoted to networked devices and mainly when handheld ones are involved. Moreover energy consumption has become a matter of paramount importance in nowadays environmentally conscious society. Although a number of studies are already available, not many have focused on Evolutionary Algorithms (EAs). Moreover, no previous attempt has been performed for modeling energy consumption behavior of EAs considering different hardware platforms. This paper thus aims at not only analyzing the influence of the main EA parameters in their energy related behavior, but also tries for the first time to develop a model that allows researchers to know how the algorithm will behave in a number of hardware devices. We focus on a specific member of the EA family, namely Genetic Programming (GP), and consider several devices when employed as the underlying hardware platform. We apply a Fuzzy Rules Based System to build the model that allows then to predict energy required to find a solution, given a previously chosen hardware device and a set of parameters for the algorithm.

Keywords: Green computing · Energy-aware computing · Performance measurements · Evolutionary algorithms

1 Introduction

In the age of communications, a growing environmental awareness has permeated computer science, and green computing has arise to address environmental problems associated with power consumption [1]. The demand for data center capacity has grew tremendously over the last decade. Thus, big companies and public institutions try to always increase computing performances, which produce a growth in power consumption due to both the computer systems and cooling equipment that supports their clients' IT gear.

© Springer International Publishing AG 2017
E. Oliveira et al. (Eds.): EPIA 2017, LNAI 10423, pp. 229–240, 2017.
DOI: 10.1007/978-3-319-65340-2_19

In this light, power consumption as well as the overheating are two big problems to be solved. But this problem is not only present in large computing facilities; it is also present in desktop, ephemeral handheld and wearable systems, were frequently algorithms must be tunned up to save as much energy as possible, so that device can run for longer without recharging. Thus, although desktop and ephemeral systems are generally suitable to run almost any kind of algorithm, they are frequently disregarded when the energy consumption is taken into account.

Evolutionary Algorithms (EAs), which are very successful solving complex optimization problems, have also been recently run on these kind of devices [2]. Given their stochastic nature, the effort and time required to find solutions are proportional to the difficulty of the problem, the size of their search space, and the parameters value we may choose: a poor selection of parameters involved may make exponentially grow times to solution and thus energy consumption. But both values are also dependent on hardware platform involved: memory capacity and management, instruction set architecture, etc., directly determines both performance and energy consumption for any algorithm that may be run.

Therefore, estimating the energy required to find solutions of quality will contribute to find an informed compromise between solutions quality and time and energy consumption. Although the relevance of the topic has already been acknowledged [2], to the best of our knowledge this is the first time a model is developed for energy consumption in EAs that takes into account their main parameters and underlying hardware.

Thus the main contribution of this paper is the application a Fuzzy Rule Based System to the modeling of energy consumed by an EA, particularly Genetic Programming, when looking for solutions. A preliminary model is developed and tested.

The rest of the paper is organized as follows: Sect. 2 describes previous works on the area; Sect. 3 describes the experiments performed and Sect. 4 shows the results obtained. Finally, we summarize our conclusions in Sect. 5.

2   Energy Efficiency and Evolutionary Algorithms

The literature reflects the interest of the scientific community in the energy efficiency. Last decade has been an engine of scheduling algorithms, where the goal is optimizing the energy consumption. New algorithms have been developed for the *Dynamic speed scaling* technique [3,4], where tasks are scheduled to customized frequencies to reduce energy consumption and overheating. *Dynamic Voltage and Frequency Scaling* (DVFS) and *Earliest- Deadline-First with Virtual Deadlines* (EDF-VD) scheduling techniques are integrated [5] to design an optimal algorithm for reducing energy consumption in mixed-criticality systems (Real Time).

Regarding EAs, many scientific areas have took advantages because its flexibility to solve a large number of optimization problems. The growing concern for environmental issues has put the spotlight on renewable and sustainable energy.

Recently optimization works address energy optimization applying Genetics Algorithms (GAs) such as the optimization and modeling of the power threshold at which car engine is turned on [6]. The model is based on vehicle fuel-rate, battery state of charge and driveline power demand. In [7] a multi-objective optimization model is proposed to help designers in green building design. The model is able to dynamically predict the energy consumption and thermal comfort status of residential buildings. On the other hand, the energy awareness not only affects large infrastructures; power consumption is the main concern for mobile devices, mainly battery-powered. Also for these kind of devices, EAs have been employed to find how to reduce power consumption. For instance, in [8] a multi-objective algorithm (NSGA-II) was employed to find cache configurations that reduce power consumption and the execution time [8].

However, previously mentioned works consider EAs as a tool to improve the energy efficiency when facing a given problem and they do not take into account the energy that the EA may consume.

In this context, a preliminary work has been recently published [9] which addresses the problem of measuring the energy consumed by the EA, particularly GP, and analyzes the algorithm behavior when a well-known benchmark problem, the multiplexer, is running. Experimental tests were carried out in different devices such as laptop, including a macbook, blade systems, tablets, and Raspberry-Pi. The purpose was to determine the relationship between the main parameters of the algorithm and power consumption, and also with respect to the particular hardware device, when a solution is looked for. As a conclusion, devices like Raspberry-Pi or tablets were seen as more energy efficient, at least for the problem analyzed.

Although studies about the time or number of generations required to find solutions has been a topic of interest since the nineties, and Koza was one of the first to propose how to predict it from a given set of parameters [10], and there certainly exists a relationship between time and energy required to run an algorithm, in [9] some non-linearities were described which affects the energy required to run the algorithm, which are related to hardware features and parameters selected. These components, that are influenced, by cache memory management, for instance, are simply hidden to time to completion models that only takes into account algorithm parameters, given that hardware features are not part of those models.

In this paper we focus on relationship between the GP algorithm and their main parameters and the hardware device we may use to run the algorithm. The goal is thus to test a number of hardware devices, making a parameter sweep. Thus, a large number of runs are launched, and then a model is built based on the well-known fuzzy logic proposed by Zadeh [11]. We have used a Fuzzy Rule-Based System (FRBS) called METSK-HD [12], which is based on Takagi-Sugeno-Kang (TSK) type [13,14].

3 Methodology

This research work tries to develop a first energy consumption estimation model for EAs, particularly GP algorithm. This section details how experimental tests have been carried out in order to define the interconnection among components involved in an optimization algorithm through GP. In the following subsections, the algorithm setting Sect. 3.1, computational platforms Sect. 3.2 and the predictive system Sect. 3.3 are presented.

3.1 Algorithmic Setting

To design this first energy consumption estimation model, a well known GP problem has been selected (multiplexer-6). The multiplexer program emulates the behavior of this electronic component. In the case of a 6 bits multiplexer, 2 bits are associated with the address entries and the other 4 bits with the data entries. An implementation in C programming language has been used as it is one of the most popular languages for implementing EAs algorithms.

Although EAs are stochastic programs, which are useful to solve complex optimization problems, the impact of some decisions related to the language implementation can affect to the computational efficiency of the algorithm [15] and, hence to the energy consumption, which is the goal of this paper. Regarding the problem at hand, we have addressed the 6-bits multiplexer problem. Functions and terminal sets are the standard ones described by Koza [10]. Regarding the implementation, the well known lilgp[1] implementation in C language has been used.

Considering the impact of the main EAs parameters have on performance and, hence the influence on the energy consumption until a optimal solution is reached, we have defined a set of values to the main GP algorithm parameters, which can be viewed in Table 1. Regarding the termination condition, all tests must be completed to obtain the highest accuracy, and to ensure the relationship between defined parameters and the energy consumption.

Table 1. Main GP parameters. A total number of 1716 combinations were tested (Max length and Max depth are directly related).

Generations	10, 20, 40, 60, 80, 100, 150, 200, 300, 400 and 500
Population sizes	50, 60, 70, 80, 90, 100, 120, 140, 160, 180, 200, 250, 300, 400, 450, 500, 600, 700, 800, 900, 1000
Max depth	3, 5, 6, 7, 8, 9
Max length	10, 32, 64, 128, 256, 512
Crossover probability	0.9
Mutation probability	0.1

---

[1] http://garage.cse.msu.edu/software/lil-gp/.

As previously mentioned, the stochastic nature of EAs has led us to run each individual experiment 30 times. The algorithm performance is calculated as the average of 30 runs. Because different hardware platforms are considered, these runs have been set up with the same 30 different random seeds. Thus, all of the runs are exactly the same in every platform, when considering high level operations defined in the high level programming language.

On the other hand, given the goal is to design an energy consumption estimation model, we are interested in the average energy consumption for the 30 runs in order to establish an accurate relationship. Thus, the algorithms are configured to finish when the optimal solution is found.

3.2   Computational Platforms

Three computational platforms have been tested, i.e., raspberry pi, tablet and laptop. Table 2 provides the details for the hardware architectures and operating systems used. Tackling a given optimization problem, the optimization algorithm cannot be considered completely isolated from the hardware device in which it is executed, neither from the operating system. Hardware features such as processor speed, instruction set architecture and operating system are not addressed in this work. Nevertheless, these differences may influence future decision on the preferred hardware and operating system for the algorithms.

However, each device has a specifications for power consumption in *watt-hour*, which is the unit of electrical measurement. Given we are interested in the energy consumption of the algorithm on different hardware platform, we have taken it into account in order to measure the energy consumption. We take watts per hour values when devices are at a peak load. Watt-hour for each device is specified in Table 2.

Table 2. Devices

Device	Processor	Cores	RAM	OS	Watt-hour
raspberry pi	Cortex-A7 900 MHz	4	1 GB	Raspbian GNU/Linux 7	12.5
tablet	Samsung Galaxy Tab 3 SM-T311, Exynos 4212 1.5 GHz	2	1.5 GB	Android 4.4.2 (kernel 3.0.31)	14.8
laptop	Intel(R) Core(TM) i5-2450 M 2.5 GHz	4	8 GB	Ubuntu 12.04.5 LTS	75

We must admit that we can deactivate particular services such as wifi, bluetooth and hdmi connection, even leds on the board, etc. in order to reduce the device power consumption. In this work, we consider all components are enabled and devices are plugged while the algorithm is running.

Once running conditions are set up, the algorithm for the problem described above is launched. As above mentioned, for each different combination of the first three parameters described in Table 1, the algorithm is run 30 times and the average time is computed and stored in a log file to be further processed. Average energy consumption is calculated according to (1) for each combination, based on its average execution time.

$$Energy = Power \times Time \tag{1}$$

where Joule, Watts and Seconds are the units for energy, power and time, respectively. As soon as the capture data phase has been completed, the main problem is to identify the interconnection among given parameters, which is address in the following subsection.

3.3 Predictive System

In order to estimate the energy consumption on the basis of the algorithm parameters, it must be firstly found the degree of relationship among them. This information is crucial to define an energy consumption predictive function. In this work, we present an Energy Consumption Predictive Model (ECPM) by using a TSK FRBS called METSK-HD [12] to generate the Rules Database (RB) and the Knowledge Base (KB) which allow us to predict the energy consumption of the algorithm studied. The results presented in [12] demonstrate that the TSK FRBS improves the accuracy where a high-dimensional and large-scale regression datases have been used. In the problem described in this paper, we are working with four input variables: number of generations (Gen), population size (PS), max tree depth (TD), max length (ML), and one output variable energy (E).

A FRBS is composed by a KB and a RB. The KB is formed by the well-known Membership Functions (MF). On the other hand, the RB is formed by rules with an antecedent and a polynomial function of the input variables in the consequent. Due to this rule structure the system losses interpretability, unlike Mandani systems [16,17], where the consequent is a more simple expression dependent of the linguistics variables. The rules used in a TSK FRBS Sect. 3.3 present the following structure:

IF X_1 is A_1 and ... and X_n is A_n
then Y = p_1 x X_1 + .. + p_n x X_n + p_0

where X_i are the system input variables, Y is the system output variable, p_i are real-values coefficients and A_i are fuzzy sets.

If we consider m rule in the KB the output of TSK system is computed as the weighted average of the individual rule output $Y_i, i = 1...m$:

$$\frac{\sum_{m}^{i=1} h_i \cdot Y_i}{\sum_{m}^{i=1} h_i} \tag{2}$$

with $h_i = T(A_1(x_1), ..., A_n(x_n))$ being the matching degree between the antecedent part of the ith rule and the current system inputs $x = (x_1, ..., X_n)$, and with T being a t-norm.

TSK FRBSs have been applied successfully to a large quantity of problems. The main advantage of these kinds of systems is the fact that they present a compact system equation for estimating the parameters p_i using classical methods, and obtaining an accurate system, which can be very useful for accurate fuzzy modeling.

An ad-hoc TSK FRBS implementation is unviable when we work with large or the high-dimensional data sets. In this kind of problems, it is necessary an automatic process to learn the KB and RB. Due to the high complexity of the search space involved, it is used different stages. However, both parts (KB and RB) should be learning and optimized together. Different techniques have been used, but the Genetic Fuzzy Systems (GFS) [18] has the best results. EAs are able to learn the antecedents and consequents of the rules system together, and to optimize the MF of the KB. Figure 1 shows the summary of the optimization process of TSK FRBS.

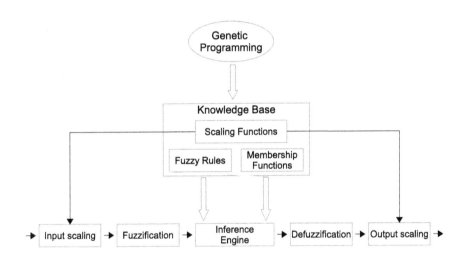

Fig. 1. Summary of the optimization process.

This process is divided in two stages. In the first stage, the initial Data Base (DB) based on a fuzzy grid in order to obtain zero-order TSK candidate rules, is learned. The second stage applies an advanced post-processing for fine scatter-based evolutionary tuning of MFs combined with a rule selection. Figure 2 shows the process described previously.

4   Results

A described in the previous section, a C implementation of the well known GP multiplexer-6 problem has been used.

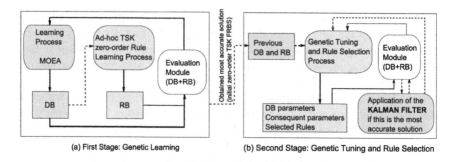

(a) First Stage: Genetic Learning   (b) Second Stage: Genetic Tuning and Rule Selection

Fig. 2. TSK FRBS optimization process.

The algorithms have been parameterized with a defined set of number of generations, population sizes, max tree depth and maximum length. Once this first phase has been completed, we obtain the energy consumption for the different parametrizations options of the problem. As we expected, devices such as raspberry pi and tablet have quite long time requirements. Despite these devices are not designed to run EAs, they are considerably useful to non-standard distributed models [19].

Once the energy consumption values are collected we need to obtain the prediction model by means of the FRBS describe in Sect. 3.3. The predictive model is obtained along a tuned process divided in 2 steps, training and test phase. We need to obtain 3 different predictive models, one for each platform.

First experiments have been done through a FRBS, having obtained a high hit rate. Generally, obtained values are close to the original ones, which are provided to the training phase. Figure 3 shows the prediction obtained by the preliminary *ECPM* for the multiplexer-6 problem running on laptop (Fig. 3a), raspberry pi (Fig. 3b) and tablet(Fig. 3c). The X axis represents the 200 test samples provided to the FRBS to be predicted. The Y axis shows the Squared Error (SE) between the original energy values and predicted energy values, $((original\_value - predicted\_value)^2)$.

As we can see in the predicted values, along the tests performed, they are close to the original values, so these are promising results to continue working in the same direction. However, as we can see in Fig. 3 there are some values that have a larger error in the prediction. These values present a higher SE compared with the rest of the samples and they must be studied. Table 3 shows the three highest values for each platform. As can be seen, input variables values are among the highest values, which correspond to a higher energy consumption. Although, theses samples obtain the highest SE with respect to rest of predictions, we can observe that these values are very small, which allows us to affirm that the predictive model fits very well to the real energy values, for the platforms studied. The lack of precision may be due to fewer values available for the learning phase at the upper range values. A larger number of samples in the upper values would help the learning phase and reduce these differences.

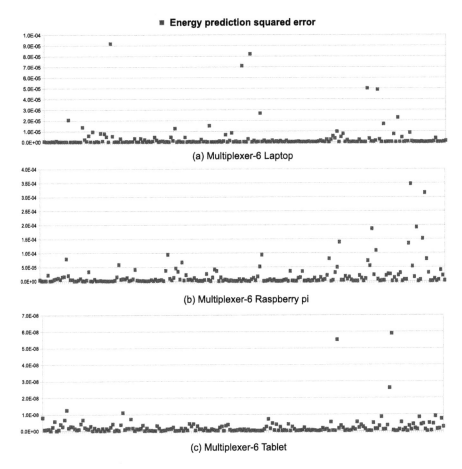

Fig. 3. Energy prediction. Multiplexer-6 problem in laptop (a) raspberry pi (b) and tablet (c) The axis X represents each test samples provided to the FRBS to be predicted.

Table 3. Study of the three highest values with the highest SE for each platform

Device	Generation	Pop. size	Max tree depth	Max length	SE
laptop	100	1000	9	512	9.18E-05
	500	800	6	64	7.12E-05
	200	900	9	512	8.21E-05
raspberry pi	300	450	6	64	3.47E-04
	300	900	3	10	1.92E-04
	300	1000	9	512	3.15E-04
tablet	100	450	3	10	5.52E-08
	150	700	9	512	2.60E-08
	150	900	9	512	5.89E-08

Regarding the quality of the predictions reached, Table 4 shows information related to the number of rules generated by the FRBS, MSE and the Root Mean Squared Error (*RMSE*) (fitness function in the FRBS optimization process). The FRBS applied proposes a number of rules, to carry out the prediction. The maximum number of rules that the FRBS will obtain is 100 rules by default, although a lower value can be defined. If the algorithm is not able to propose a lower number of rules, this maximum value is established. In the predictive models obtained for each platform, the number of rules is high and the system interpretability is lost. On the other hand, the FRBS can eliminate input variables if theses variables are not necessary to optimize the predictive model, however the model obtained have not eliminated any input variable. Although different techniques can be found to reduce that number [20], this is not the goal of this preliminary *ECPM*. The following expression shows us a particular TSK fuzzy rule sample Listing 1.1 for one of the predictive models obtained:

Listing 1.1. TSK fuzzy rule sample

```
IF
   POP_SIZE    IS  -227.762520279924  54.578010373498  377.336251766050 AND
   MAX_GEN     IS  -275.994420676138  64.816048292874  239.764866808436 AND
   MAX_LENGTH  IS  -116.652906027707  -5.790474603268  197.978884120633 AND
   MAX_DEPTH   IS     1.093684257844   2.958056048254    4.223114574969
THEN
   J = (-0.000000972185) x POP_SIZE + (-0.000002470696) x MAX_GEN +
       0.001331033469 x MAX_NODOS + 0.000399310185 x MAX_DEPTH +
       0.000133103397
```

Table 4. Summary of experimental test for the Multiplexer-6 GP problem on three different devices. Number of rules *FR* generated by the FRBS, the Mean Squared Error (*MSE*) and the Root Mean Squared Error (*RMSE*)

Device	FR	MSE	RMSE
laptop	85	1.68E-06	1.30E-03
raspberry pi	80	9.31E-06	3.05E-03
tablet	78	1.20E-09	3.46E-05

5   Conclusions

We have presented a preliminary energy estimation model, which is especially aimed at EAs, in particular, GP algorithms. To implement this model we have applied a Fuzzy Rule Based System that is able to predict the energy consumption by using an inference engine. We have addressed the multiplexer-6 problem and we have used `lilgp` as a well known C implementation for the GP algorithms. Experimental tests have been carried out on three different hardware platforms: raspberry pi, laptop and tablet, where a different operating system is running: *Raspbian, Ubuntu* and *Android*.

In this preliminary model, we have obtained one model for each hardware platform addressed. Results show this first Energy Consumption Predictive Model has a low error in the prediction phase, on three tests performed. As it is expected, the main parameters of the GP the algorithm must have a considerable influence on the energy consumption. The Energy Consumption Predictive Model has good predictions in general, however the model obtains differences, but non significative, for the samples with the parameters describe above.

The main conclusion we may draw from the results is that this first FRBS model is able to correctly estimate the energy consumption of EAs on different devices. This may be useful in the future to select the preferred hardware, and decide beforehand the parameters to be employed if an upper limit for the energy devoted to solve the problem is established. The model would allow to compare several settings before launching the run.

Although we presents a preliminary model which is based on a single GP problem, the results obtained allows as to foresee the interest of the approach. We hope to run extended set of experiments in the future, considering different problems and other algorithms from the EA family.

Acknowledgements. We acknowledge support from Spanish Ministry of Economy and Competitiveness and European Regional Development Fund (FEDER) under project EphemeCH (TIN2014-56494-C4-{1,2,3}-P), and Junta de Extremadura FEDER, project GR15068.

References

1. de Vega, F.F., Pérez, J.I.H., Lanchares, J.: Parallel Architectures and Bioinspired Algorithms, vol. 122. Springer, Heidelberg (2012)
2. Cotta, C., Fernández-Leiva, A., de Vega, F.F., Chávez, F., Merelo, J., Castillo, P., Bello, G., Camacho, D.: Ephemeral computing and bioinspired optimization - challenges and opportunities. In: 7th International Joint Conference on Evolutionary Computation Theory and Applications, Lisboa, Portugal, pp. 319–324. Scitepress (2015)
3. Albers, S.: Algorithms for dynamic speed scaling. In: Schwentick, T., Dürr, C. (eds.) 28th International Symposium on Theoretical Aspects of Computer Science (STACS 2011). Leibniz International Proceedings in Informatics (LIPIcs), vol. 9, pp. 1–11. Schloss Dagstuhl-Leibniz-Zentrum fuer Informatik, Dagstuhl (2011)
4. Kumar, G., Shannigrahi, S.: New online algorithm for dynamic speed scaling with sleep state. Theor. Comput. Sci. **593**, 79–87 (2015)
5. Huang, P., Kumar, P., Giannopoulou, G., Thiele, L.: Energy efficient DVFS scheduling for mixed-criticality systems. In: 2014 International Conference on Embedded Software (EMSOFT), pp. 1–10, October 2014
6. Chen, Z., Mi, C.C., Xiong, R., Xu, J., You, C.: Energy management of a power-split plug-in hybrid electric vehicle based on genetic algorithm and quadratic programming. J. Power Sources **248**, 416–426 (2014)
7. Yu, W., Li, B., Jia, H., Zhang, M., Wang, D.: Application of multi-objective genetic algorithm to optimize energy efficiency and thermal comfort in building design. Energy Build. **88**, 135–143 (2015)

8. Álvarez, J.D., Risco-Martín, J.L., Colmenar, J.M.: Multi-objective optimization of energy consumption and execution time in a single level cache memory for embedded systems. J. Syst. Softw. **111**, 200–212 (2016)
9. de Vega, F.F., Chávez, F., Díaz, J., García, J.A., Castillo, P.A., Merelo, J.J., Cotta, C.: A cross-platform assessment of energy consumption in evolutionary algorithms. In: Handl, J., Hart, E., Lewis, P.R., López-Ibáñez, M., Ochoa, G., Paechter, B. (eds.) PPSN 2016. LNCS, vol. 9921, pp. 548–557. Springer, Cham (2016). doi:10. 1007/978-3-319-45823-6_51
10. Koza, J.R.: Genetic Programming: On the Programming of Computers by Means of Natural Selection. MIT Press, Cambridge (1992)
11. Zadeh, L.: Fuzzy sets. Inf. Control **8**(3), 338–353 (1965)
12. Gacto, M., Galende, M., Alcalá, R., Herrera, F.: METSK-HDe: a multiobjective evolutionary algorithm to learn accurate tsk-fuzzy systems in high-dimensional and large-scale regression problems. Inf. Sci. **276**, 63–79 (2014)
13. Sugeno, M., Kang, G.: Structure identification of fuzzy model. Fuzzy Sets Syst. **28**(1), 15–33 (1988)
14. Takagi, T., Sugeno, M.: Fuzzy identification of systems and its applications to modeling and control. IEEE Trans. Syst. Man Cybern. **1**, 116–132 (1985)
15. Nesmachnow, S., Luna, F., Alba, E.: An empirical time analysis of evolutionary algorithms as C programs. Softw. Pract. Exp. **45**(1), 111–142 (2015)
16. Mamdani, E.H.: Application of fuzzy logic to approximate reasoning using linguistic synthesis. IEEE Trans. Comput. **C−26**(12), 1182–1191 (1977)
17. Mamdani, E., Assilian, S.: An experiment in linguistic synthesis with a fuzzy logic controller. Int. J. Man-Mach. Stud. **7**(1), 1–13 (1975)
18. Herrera, F.: Genetic fuzzy systems: taxonomy, current research trends and prospects. Evol. Intel. **1**(1), 27–46 (2008)
19. García-Valdez, M., Trujillo, L., Merelo, J.J., de Vega, F.F., Olague, G.: The evospace model for pool-based evolutionary algorithms. J. Grid Comput. **13**(3), 329–349 (2015)
20. Balasubramaniam, J.: Conditions for inference invariant rule reduction in frbs by combining rules with identical consequents. Acta Polytech. Hung. **3**(4), 113–143 (2006)

Application of Robust Optimization Technique to the Energy Planning Problem

Saulo C. de A. Ferreira$^{(\boxtimes)}$, Jerson dos S. Carvalho, Leonardo W. de Oliveira,
Taís L.O. Araújo, Edimar J. de Oliveira, and Marina B.A. Souza

Department of Electrical Engineering, Federal University at Juiz de Fora (UFJF),
Juiz de Fora, MG, Brazil
{saulo.custodio,jerson.carvalho,tais.lacerda2011,
marina.borges}@engenharia.ufjf.br,
{leonardo.willer,edimar.oliveira}@ufjf.edu.br

Abstract. The present work proposes an approach based on the application of the robust optimization technique named column-and-constraint generation (C&CG), for solving the problem of energy planning comprising the minimization of the thermoelectric dispatch cost during a daily operation of a system with wind and hydraulic generation. In order to define the hourly dispatch of thermoelectric generation, the approach considers a history of flow for the hydraulic generation, as well as uncertainties over the wind behavior in the wind power plant. Thus, the short-term energy planning is defined by taking into account the wind stochastic through the concept of uncertainties. As solving proposal, linear programming with a robust optimization (RO) mathematical technique through the C&CG algorithm is used. This method is applied to divide the global problem into wind speed uncertainties scenarios.

Keywords: Energy planning · Robust optimization · C&CG

1 Introduction

Brazil is a country whose electricity production is historically based on two main sources, the prevalent hydropower resource due to its availability and the complementary power from thermoelectric plants, most of which operate only in times of low hydro offer in face of unfavorable hydrological scenarios. In this way, the Brazilian energy system is called hydrothermal [1]. However, with the increasing demand for electricity and the importance of environmental issues, it is necessary to complement the hydrothermal system with renewable sources such as solar, wind and biomass. Thus, it becomes necessary to invest in researches for the electricity sector in order to obtain a more mixed and renewable energy matrix [2].

The investments in energy researches have been focused on the development of renewable sources to make the electric sector less susceptible to crises as well as to reduce environmental impacts [3]. Brazil has a potential for wind power

© Springer International Publishing AG 2017
E. Oliveira et al. (Eds.): EPIA 2017, LNAI 10423, pp. 241–252, 2017.
DOI: 10.1007/978-3-319-65340-2_20

generation, for instance, in the northeastern region that has half of the whole country capacity, in addition to some places of the South and Southeast regions [4,5]. In this scenario of research that comprises different sources, optimization methods have been proposed, some of them by handling the problem of thermal generation unit's commitment in systems that also rely on other forms of energy use.

The problem of commissioning thermoelectric units has the purpose of defining generation dispatch that minimizes the cost of operating a system. In order to define this dispatch, it is necessary to consider the uncertainties arising from each generation source [6,7]. Therefore, robust optimization methods, such as the mathematical decomposition technique of Benders and the algorithm of Column-and-Constraint Generation have been developed.

Due to the applicability of the Benders mathematical decomposition to RO problems, studies to reduce the computational cost of the energy planning problem and the number of Benders cuts can be found in the literature, such as [8–10]. The C&CG algorithm consists of a solving procedure similar to the dual Benders method, but with differences in the strategy of cuts generation [8]. The C&CG generates constraints for the decision variables from uncertainty scenarios in a dynamic way, instead of constraints based on the dual solution of subproblems as the Benders method.

The C&CG method was developed by Zhao and Zeng [9] to solve an energy planning problem with an intermittent wind power source. Zeng and Zhao [10] and Zhao [8] compared the C&CG with the dual Benders method, and proved that the first is suitable for RO and provides a convergence with fewer iterations between the subproblems resulting from the decomposition. The C&CG is not conceptually stochastic, but rather deterministic and based on sets [11]. The objective of the method is to determine a solution that is feasible for any uncertainty hypothesis in a given set. The diverse applicability [12] and computational efficiency makes the C&CG useful in several areas [13].

Against this background, the present work proposes the application of the C&CG method to efficiently solve the problem of short-term energy planning, through the commissioning of thermoelectric units via robust optimization for a system that also has wind and hydraulic energy sources. As in the work of Zhao and Zeng [9], the uncertainties considered in the RO problem refer to the intermittent wind speed, but the wind power is modeled as a function of such uncertainties in the proposed algorithm. In order to minimize the operational cost, the proposed algorithm determines the dispatch of thermoelectric generators for a daily operating horizon. The main contribution is to model the wind power as a polyhedral uncertainty set from the wind speed uncertainty set and a practical power curve. In addition, the representation of ramp constrains in thermoelectric commissioning and the inclusion of hydraulic generation in the RO problem via C&CG are also contributions of the present work.

2   Problem Formulation

2.1   C&CG Algorithm

The C&CG method consists of a mathematical technique that seeks to enable the operation of a system subject to uncertainties, even for the worst operating condition [9]. Similar to the mathematical decomposition of Benders, the C&CG algorithm divides the original problem into two subproblems named master and slave. The difference lies in the cutting strategy, which is the scheme used to generate new constraints to lead the optimization process to a robust solution. According to Zeng and Zhao [10], C&CG finds the solution with a smaller number of iterations in relation to the Benders technique, resulting in higher computational efficiency. The algorithm generates new constraints with the decision variables at each iteration and adds them to the master subproblem until the convergence condition is reached.

The C&CG method can be applied to linear and non-linear problems. As the planning problem proposed in the present work is linear, the generic optimization model 1 is used to explain this method.

$$
\begin{aligned}
&Min_y \ c^T y \ + \ Max_{u \in U} Min_{x \in F(y,u)} b^T x \\
&subject \ to: \\
&Ay \ \geq \ d \ \forall y \ \in \ S_y \\
&F(y,u) \ = \ \{x \in S_x \ /Gx \ \geq \ h - Ey - Mu\} \\
&u \ \in \ U, S_y \ \subseteq \ R^n_+, S_x \ \subseteq \ R^n_+
\end{aligned}
\tag{1}
$$

Where:

y, x	Decision variables of the master and slave subproblems, respectively;
c, b	Costs associated with the decision variables x and y, respectively;
A, G, E, M	Matrices of the linear constraints;
d, h	Vectors of the linear constraints;
U	Set of variables that model the uncertainties of the problem.

The global optimization problem is given by generic formulation 1. As mentioned above, the C&CG method resembles the Benders decomposition technique with regard to the division of the global problem into two subproblems, master and slave, the former being formulated as in 2 [10].

$$
\begin{aligned}
&Min_y \ c^T y \ + \ \alpha \\
&subject \ to: \\
&Ay \ \geq \ d \ \forall y \ \in \ S_y \\
&\alpha \ \geq \ 0
\end{aligned}
\tag{2}
$$

Where α is the expected cost for the second subproblem. In the master subproblem, the uncertainty scenarios are not represented in an explicit way and their impact on the cost of the global problem is given by the variable α.

In turn, the slave subproblem is formulated as its dual form in the C&CG solving method. In terms of objective function, although the same numerical result of the corresponding primal problem is reached, the dual formulation allows the cost of the subproblem to be minimized while maximizing the uncertainty. This procedure leads to the worst case scenario for the RO. The slave subproblem can be modeled as formulation 3.

$$Max_{u,\pi}(h - Ey^* - Mu)^T \pi$$
$$subject\ to:$$
$$G^T \pi \leq b \quad (3)$$
$$u \in U, \pi \geq 0$$

Formulation 3 represents the slave subproblem in its dual form [10] where y^* is the optimal value of the master subproblem decision variables and π represents the dual variables. Thus, from the optimal value of the decision variables y^*, the maximum value of uncertainty can be find, which consists of the worst operating scenario. From this point, the lower and upper limits of the objective function for the overall problem are determined by Eqs. 4 and 5, respectively [10]. Convergence is achieved when the difference between them is less than a prespecified tolerance. Otherwise, the cut represented by Eqs. 6, 7 and 8 [10] are added to the master subproblem for a new run.

$$c^T y^* + \alpha^* \quad (4)$$

$$c^T y^* + (h - Ey^* - Mu^*)^T \pi^* \quad (5)$$

$$b^T x^l - \alpha \leq 0, \forall l \leq k \quad (6)$$

$$Ey + Gx^l \geq h - Mu_l^*, \forall l \leq k \quad (7)$$

$$x^l \in S_x, \forall l \leq k \quad (8)$$

Where:
k *Total number of cuts;*
l *Current iteration index;*
u_l^* *Uncertainty value u obtained from the slave subproblem in iteration l.*

It is observed that the value of u_l^* obtained from the slave subproblem is required for obtaining the cut. In addition, it can be verified that new variables x^l are created with each cut l, which increases the number of variables. This increase is offset by the reduction in the number of iterations between the two subproblems, compared to the Benders technique. The flowchart of the C&CG algorithm is shown in Fig. 1 and its main steps are described hereafter.

Step 1 - Master subproblem: Obtains the value of the decision variables y^* that make the system operation feasible even for the worst case of the uncertainty set. It is observed that for $m = 1$, there is no information on the cost of the second subproblem (α) associated with the uncertainties. Thus, in the first iteration, the solution obtained from the master subproblem only satisfies the constraints of formulation 2.

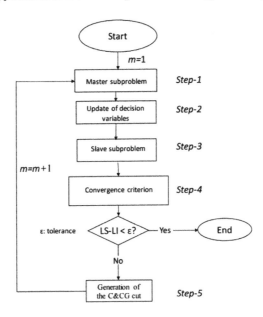

Fig. 1. Flowchart of the C&CG algorithm

Step 2 - Update of decision variables: The y^* variables found in the master subproblem are provided to the slave subproblem as parameters.

Step 3 - Slave subproblem: This subproblem, formulated in its dual form, determines the value of the variables x and the uncertainty u, for every scenario of the set U.

Step 4 - Convergence criterion: Given by the difference between the lower and upper limits of Eqs. 4 and 5, respectively. It should be less than the prespecified tolerance, meaning that the forecast of the slave subproblem cost, associated with uncertainty, is sufficiently close to its actual value.

Step 5 - C&CG cut: If convergence is not achieved, the cut is assembled according to Eqs. 6, 7 and 8, which are included in the master subproblem for a new run.

2.2   Application of C&CG to the RO Problem for Energy Planning

The energy planning problem has as the objective determining the power dispatch of each generating unit that meets demand efficiently with the lowest possible cost. The constrains on each unit vary according to the primary source and the features inherent to each energy conversion process. Among the generation sources, wind turbines introduce uncertainty in the planning and operation due to the behavior of winds, which impacts on the problem solution [14].

In order to minimize the total cost for meeting the load demand, the global RO problem can be formulated by objective function 9 and constrains 10 to 16.

$$Min \sum_{t=1}^{T} (\sum_{i=1}^{n_T} r_i Pterm_{i,t} + \sum_{j=1}^{n_E} s_j Pe_{j,t} + \sum_{m=1}^{n_H} u_m V_{V_{m,t}} + z_t Pdef_t) \quad (9)$$

subject to:

$$\sum_{i=1}^{n_T} Pterm_{i,t} + \sum_{j=1}^{n_E} Pe_{j,t} + \sum_{m=1}^{n_H} \rho_m V_{T_{m,t}} + Pdef_t = Pload_t, \ \forall t \in T \quad (10)$$

$$V_{f_{m,t}} + V_{T_{m,t}} + V_{V_{m,t}} = V_{0_{m,t}} + A_{f_{m,t}}, \ \forall m \in n_H, \forall t \in T \quad (11)$$

$$Pterm_{i,t} - 1.1 Pterm_{i,t-1} \leq 0, \ \forall i \in n_T, \ \forall t = 2,3,...,T \quad (12)$$

$$Pterm_{i,t} - 0.9 Pterm_{i,t-1} \geq 0, \ \forall i \in n_T, \ \forall t = 2,3,...,T \quad (13)$$

$$Pterm_{i,t} \geq 0; \ Pdef_t \geq 0; \ V_{V_{m,t}} \geq 0, \ \forall i \in n_T, \ \forall m \in n_H, \forall t \in T \quad (14)$$

$$k_{m,t} \geq V_{f_{m,t}} \geq 0; \ g_{m,t} \geq V_{T_{m,t}} \geq 0, \ \forall i \in n_T, \ \forall m \in n_H, \forall t \in T \quad (15)$$

$$\underline{Pe_{j,t}} \leq Pe_{j,t} \leq \overline{Pe_{j,t}}, \ \forall j \in n_E, \forall t \in T \quad (16)$$

Where:

T	*Planning horizon;*
n_T, n_E, n_H	*Numbers of thermal generators, wind turbines and hydroelectric units respectively;*
$Pterm_{i,t}$	*Power generated by thermal unit i in period t;*
$Pe_{j,t}$	*Power generated by wind unit j in period t;*
$V_{V_{m,t}}$	*Volume discharged by hydroelectric power station m in period t;*
$Pdef_t$	*Power deficit in period t;*
r_i	*Unit cost of thermoelectric unit i;*
s_j	*Unit cost of wind unit j;*
u_m	*Unit cost established for the volume discharged by hydroelectric unit m;*
z_t	*Unit cost of energy deficit in period t;*
$Pload_t$	*Load demand in period t;*
$V_{T_{m,t}}$	*Water turbined by hydroelectric unit m in period t;*
ρ_m	*Productivity of a hydroelectric plant that links the turbined water to the generated power;*
$V_{0_{m,t}}, V_{f_{m,t}}$	*Initial and final volumes of hydroelectric unit m in period t, respectively;*
$A_{f_{m,t}}$	*Water inflow for hydroelectric unit m reservoir at hour t;*
$k_{m,t}, g_{m,t}$	*Limits of final and turbined volumes, respectively, for hydroelectric unit m in period t;*
$\underline{Pe_{j,t}}, \overline{Pe_{j,t}}$	*Lower and upper limits of wind power in period t, respectively.*

Constraint 10 establishes the power balance of the system, i.e., the total generated power must be equal to the demand power added to the deficit for each period of the planning horizon. The water balance is represented by constraint 11, where from the second period onwards, the initial volume $V_{0_{m,t}}$ is equal to the final one of the previous period, $V_{f_{m,t-1}}$. In the first period, $V_{0_{m,t}}$ is the volume stored by plant m at the beginning of the planning horizon. Ramp constrains 12 and 13 represent a maximum variation of 10% in the power from each thermoelectric unit between two consecutive periods. Finally, constraints 14 to 16 define the limits of the optimization model variables, and constraint 16 is related to the set of uncertainties.

2.3   Application of the C&CG Technique

The application of the C&CG technique to the energy planning problem, as proposed in the present work, involves the division of the global problem into the master and slave subproblems as previously described. The master subproblem optimizes the power supplied by the thermoelectric units, $Pterm_{i,t}$, in order to minimize the cost of dispatch and to enable the system operation subject to all possible wind scenarios. In this way, the master subproblem can be written as follows:

$$
\begin{aligned}
&Min \sum_{t=1}^{T}(\sum_{i=1}^{n_T} r_i Pterm_{i,t}) + \alpha \\
&subject\ to: \\
&Pterm_{i,t} - 1.1 Pterm_{i,t-1} \leq 0,\ \forall i \in n_T,\ \forall t = 2,3,...,T \\
&Pterm_{i,t} - 0.9 Pterm_{i,t-1} \geq 0,\ \forall i \in n_T,\ \forall t = 2,3,...,T
\end{aligned}
\tag{17}
$$

The slave subproblem seeks to maximize the uncertainty, whose objective is to identify the worst case for the system operation within the set of uncertainties. The identification of the worst case is required so that the RO can enable the operation through all the possible scenarios. If the problem does not converge, one option is to reduce the planning horizon.

$$
Max \sum_{t=1}^{T} \sum_{m=1}^{n_H} (V_{0_{m,t}} + A_{f_{m,t}})\lambda_{m,t} + (Pload_t - \sum_{i=1}^{n_T} P^*_{term_{i,t}} - \sum_{j=1}^{n_E} Pe_{j,t})\tau_t
$$

$$
+ \sum_{m=1}^{n_H} (-k_{m,t}\beta_{m,t} - g_{m,t}\Psi_{m,t})]
\tag{18}
$$

subject to:

$$
\tau_t \leq z_t,\ \forall t \in T
\tag{19}
$$

$$
\rho_m \tau_t + \lambda_{m,t} - \Psi_{m,t} \leq 0,\ \forall m \in n_H,\ \forall t \in T
\tag{20}
$$

$$
\lambda_{m,t} - \lambda_{m,t+1} - \beta_{m,t} \leq 0,\ \forall m \in n_H,\ \forall t = 1,2,...,T-1
\tag{21}
$$

$$\lambda_{m,t} - \beta_{m,t} \leq 0, \ \forall m \in n_H, \ \forall t = T \tag{22}$$

$$\lambda_{m,t} \leq u_{m,t}, \ \forall m \in n_H, \ \forall t = T \tag{23}$$

$$\underline{Pe_{j,t}} \leq Pe_{j,t} \leq \overline{Pe_{j,t}}, \ \forall j \in n_E, \ \forall t \in T \tag{24}$$

Where:

λ Dual variables related to water balance constraints;
τ Dual variables referring to power balance constraints;
β Dual variables referring to channeling constraints of final volume;
Ψ Dual variables referring to channeling constraints of turbinated water.

The dual variables λ and τ can be positive or negative since both are associated with equality constraints. β and Ψ are greater than or equal to zero because they come from inequality constraints. It is also worth noting that the value of P_{term}^* from the master subproblem solution is required in the slave subproblem. With respect to the objective function, the term $V_{0_{m,t}}$ is not included for $t = 1$. In the other periods, the λ coefficient will be only the affluence, due to the fact that the initial volume is equal to $V_{f_{m,t-1}}$, decision variable of the primal slave subproblem. The dual slave subproblem resulting from the decomposition is notably nonlinear despite the linear feature of the original problem. However the introduction of the nonlinearity is needed to obtain a robust solution. If its convergence is not achieved, the cut is assembled according to 6 to 8 and added to the master subproblem. For the planning problem, the cuts are formulated as follows.

$$\sum_{t=1}^{T} \left(\sum_{m=1}^{n_H} u_m V_{V_{m,t}^l} + z_t Pdef_t^l \right) - \alpha \leq 0 \tag{25}$$

$$\sum_{i=1}^{n_T} Pterm_{i,t} + \sum_{m=1}^{n_H} \rho_m V_{T_{m,t}^l} + Pdef_t^l = Pload_t - \sum_{j=1}^{n_E} Pe_{j,t}^*, \ \forall t \in T \tag{26}$$

$$V f_{m,t}^l + V_{T_{m,t}^l} + V_{V_{m,t}^l} = V_{0_{m,t}} + Af_{m,t}, \ \forall m \in n_h, \ \forall t \in T \tag{27}$$

$$Pdef_t^l \geq 0; \ V_{V_{m,t}^l} \geq 0, \ \forall m \in n_H, \ \forall t \in T \tag{28}$$

$$k_{m,t} \geq V f_{m,t}^l \geq 0; \ g_{m,t} \geq V_{T_{m,t}^l} \geq 0, \ \forall m \in n_H, \ \forall t \in T \tag{29}$$

At each iteration between the decomposition subproblems, new variables and constraints are included in the master subproblem, which reduces the search space and allows the algorithm to find the solution more efficiently. It is also noted that the cut uses the value of $Pe_{j,t}^*$ obtained from the solution of the slave subproblem of the last iteration.

3   Results and Discussions

With the purpose of evaluating the application proposed in the present work, a power system modeled as a single bus that has a hydroelectric plant, a thermoelectric unit and a wind power turbine is used. The objective of the RO problem is to minimize the cost of dispatching the thermoelectric unit due to its fuel consumption and environmental impact, for a daily operating horizon. The simulation was performed in the MATLAB software version 2016. For solving the master subproblem, which consists of a linear and continuous mathematical programming, the *linprog* toolbox was used. In turn, the toolbox *fmincon*, proper for nonlinear and continuous programming, was used for the slave subproblem. The system parameters are:

- Thermoelectric generation: capacity of 100 kW and cost of R\$30 per kW;
- Hydroelectric generation: maximum turbined volume of 300 hm^3/h, maximum storage volume of 400 hm^3, penalization for discharged volume of R\$0,01 per hm^3 and productivity of 1 kW/hm^3/h;
- Deficit cost of R\$200 per kW;
- Daily scenario of water inflow and demand given by Table 1;
- Wind generation: uncertainty given by two daily wind speed scenarios. The wind values are converted into power by using a linear approximation function that provides the lower and upper limits for the wind generation at each hour of the day [6,15], according to Table 2. The linearization of the power generation function seeks to simplify the model and easy the robust optimization application, although the proposed technique allows the using of a nonlinear function. The rated power of the wind generator is 30 kW.

Table 1. Inflows and demands over the 24-h horizon

Hour	Water inflow (hm^3)	Demand (kW)	Hour	Water inflow (hm^3)	Demand (kW)	Hour	Water inflow (hm^3)	Demand (kW)
1	211.64	260	9	211.64	265	17	211.64	390
2	191.00	260	10	191.00	270	18	191.00	385
3	211.64	260	11	211,64	285	19	211,64	370
4	191,00	260	12	191,00	300	20	191,00	340
5	211,64	260	13	211,64	310	21	211,64	310
6	191,00	260	14	191,00	320	22	191,00	270
7	211,64	260	15	211,64	350	23	211,64	250
8	191,00	265	16	191,00	370	24	191,00	230

From the power limits of Table 2, the proposed application defines the polyhedral set of uncertainties, similar to Zhao and Zeng [9], but in the present work

Table 2. Lower and upper wind power limits in the 24-h horizon

Hour	Min. power (kW)	Max. power (kW)	Hour	Min. power (kW)	Max. power (kW)	Hour	Min. power (kW)	Max. power (kW)
1	8.43	13.56	9	0.20	30.00	17	20.44	30.00
2	0	6.43	10	0	1.24	18	6.29	11.82
3	4.68	4.84	11	1.18	23.08	19	12.77	21.66
4	22.23	25.06	12	2.25	16.73	20	1.91	9.79
5	0	7.69	13	9.77	21,89	21	1.18	10.51
6	6.95	12.66	14	4.88	17.57	22	10.27	22.56
7	0	3.79	15	9.17	14.08	23	7.80	10.09
8	9.51	15.26	16	2.50	10.24	24	0	17.92

for the wind power. This procedure ensures the robustness of the method. The polyhedral set is defined by constraints 30 to 34, where Pe_t is the wind power in period t, and $Pe_{t,min}$ and $Pe_{t,max}$ are the lower and upper power limits in t, respectively, according to Table 2.

$$Pe_{t,min} \leq Pe_t \leq Pe_{t,max}, \ 1 \leq t \leq 24 \tag{30}$$

$$Pe_1 + Pe_2 + Pe_3 + Pe_4 + Pe_5 + Pe_6 \geq 63.22 \tag{31}$$

$$Pe_7 + Pe_8 + Pe_9 + Pe_{10} + Pe_{11} + Pe_{12} \geq 81.09 \tag{32}$$

$$Pe_{13} + Pe_{14} + Pe_{15} + Pe_{16} + Pe_{17} + Pe_{18} \geq 95.04 \tag{33}$$

$$Pe_{19} + Pe_{20} + Pe_{21} + Pe_{22} + Pe_{23} + Pe_{24} \geq 83.28 \tag{34}$$

Regarding the uncertainty set, a 10% margin on wind power capacity was used. After the parameters definition, the master and slave subproblems are modeled with the inclusion of constraints 30 to 34 in the slave subproblem for the uncertainty representation, by maintaining its primal form according to Zeng and Zhao [10].

The optimal solution was found after four iterations between the subproblems, through three sets of cuts with a computational time of 9.75 s. Table 3 presents the evolution of the lower and upper limits of the C&CG algorithm considered as the convergence criterion. It can be observed that the optimal cost is R\$55, 638.26. Table 4 shows the optimal dispatch obtained for the thermoelectric generation.

Table 3. Evolution of the C&CG lower and upper limits

Iteration	Lower limit LI (R)	Upper limit LS (R)
1	0	359.136,51
2	55.620,40	55.832,64
3	55.636,99	55.645,46
4	55.638,26	55.638,26

Table 4. Optimum solution obtained by C&CG for thermoelectric dispatch

Hour	Thermal power (kW)	Hour	Thermal power (kW)	Hour	Thermal power (kW)
1	58.29	9	80.88	17	100.00
2	58.81	10	85.82	18	92.64
3	60.13	11	90.78	19	83.37
4	62.17	12	95.37	20	75.04
5	64.88	13	97.82	21	67.53
6	68.16	14	100.00	22	60.78
7	71.97	15	100,00	23	54.70
8	76.23	16	100,00	24	49.23

4   Conclusions

The present work presented the application of a robust optimization method for the energy planning considering uncertainties about wind generation. The objective is to minimize the cost of thermoelectric dispatch in a system that also has hydraulic and wind generation. The treatment of the polyhedral set of uncertainties differs from the literature by explicit modeling of wind power uncertainty from wind speed scenarios. The solution obtained enables the operation of the energy system for each scenario considered. The inclusion of ramp constrains and hydraulic generation in the robust optimization problem also characterizes an innovative contribution of the work. The results demonstrate the applicability of the C&CG method for the robust optimization of energy systems. Based on the results, the inclusion of uncertainties over demand and other generation sources will be investigated as future work, as well as variations in the level of uncertainties of the polyhedral set.

Notice that the representation of more than one thermal units does not include additional complexity to the uncertainty representation, because the polyhedral model is not affected by the number of generating units. Moreover, the network constraints can be included in the optimization approach, but it is not in the scope of the present work and will be investigated in future works.

Acknowledgments. The authors would like to thank CNPq, CAPES, FAPEMIG and INERGE for supporting this research.

References

1. EPE – Empresa de Pesquisa Energética: Aspectos Fundamentais de Planejamento Energético, December 2005
2. da Silva, D.M., Vila, C.U.: Estudo comparativo de metodologias computacionais na modelagem da geração eólica no despacho hidrotérmico. In: Conferência Internacional de Energias Inteligentes, SmartEnegy 2016, Curitiba, Brazil, November 2016
3. Bouffard, F., Galiana, F.D.: Stochastic security for operations planning with significant wind power generation. In: 2008 IEEE Power and Energy Society General Meeting-Conversion and Delivery of Electrical Energy in the 21st Century, pp. 1–11. IEEE (2008)
4. Dias, B.H., Marcato, A.L.M., Souza, R.C., Soares, M.P., Silva, I., Brandi, R.B.S., Ramos, T.P., Tomim, M.A., de Oliveira, E.J.: Processamento paralelo e algoritmo de fechos conexos na programao dinmica estocástica aplicada ao planejamento da operação de sistemas hidrotérmicos. In: Anais do XVIII 2010 CBA, Bonito. OPEC, pp. 3931–3938 (2010)
5. Loken, E.: Use of multicriteria decision analysis methods for energy planning problems. Renew. Sustain. Energy Rev. **11**(7), 1584–1595 (2007)
6. Ferreira, S., de Oliveira, L.W., Mayrink, S., de Oliveira, E.J., Borges, M.B.A.: Otimização de sistemas de potência com geração renovável considerando cenários operativos. In: Anais do XLVIII 2016 SBPO, Sociedade Brasileira de Pesquisa Operacional, p. 3318 (2016)
7. Silva, J.C., Júnior, G.C., Vinhal, C.D.: Aplicação de otimização multiobjetivo por enxame de partículas no planejamento energético de sistemas hidrotérmicos. In: Anais do Computer on the Beach, pp. 148–157 (2013)
8. Zeng, B.: Solving two-stage robust optimization problems by a constraint-and-column generation method. University of South Florida, FL, Technical report (2011)
9. Zhao, L., Zeng, B.: Robust unit commitment problem with demand response and wind energy. In: 2012 IEEE Power and Energy Society General Meeting, pp. 1–8. IEEE (2012)
10. Zeng, B., Zhao, L.: Solving two-stage robust optimization problems using a column-and-constraint generation method. Oper. Res. Lett. **41**(5), 457–461 (2013)
11. Xiao, S., Li, Y., Rotaru, M., Sykulski, J.K.: Six sigma quality approach to robust optimization. IEEE Trans. Magn. **51**(3), 1–4 (2015)
12. Gabrel, V., Lacroix, M., Murat, C., Remli, N.: Robust location transportation problems under uncertain demands. Discret. Appl. Math. **164**, 100–111 (2014)
13. Bertsimas, D., Brown, D.B., Caramanis, C.: Theory and applications of robust optimization. SIAM Rev. **53**(3), 464–501 (2011)
14. de Oliveira, E., Rodrigues, M., Dias, B., de Oliveira, L., Junior, I., et al.: Security constraints for wind power operation. In: 2015 IEEE Eindhoven PowerTech, pp. 1–6. IEEE (2015)
15. Maria, T.C., Oliveira, L.W.: Planejamento de geração eólica em sistemas de distribuição com representação de regime de ventos. In: Anais do VI 2016 SBSE, Natal, FUNPEC (2016)

EnAPlug – An Environmental Awareness Plug to Test Energy Management Solutions for Households

Luis Gomes[(✉)], Filipe Sousa, and Zita Vale

GECAD – Research Group on Intelligent Engineering and Computing for
Advanced Innovation and Development, Institute of Engineering – Polytechnic
of Porto (ISEP/IPP), Rua Dr. António Bernardino de Almeida,
431, 4249-015 Porto, Portugal
{lufog, ffeso, zav}@isep.ipp.pt

Abstract. The present paper presents a new kind of Smart Plug that covers the needs of power systems R&D centers. EnAPlug, described in this paper, enables the monitor and control of loads, as a normal Smart Plug. However, it has a great benefit in comparison with a normal Smart Plug, the EnAPlug allows the integration of a variety of sensors so the user can understand the load and the surrounding environment (using a set of sensors that better fit the load). The sensors are installed in the load itself, and must have a clear fit to the load. The paper presents a demonstration of an EnAPlug used in a refrigerator for a demand response event participation, using the sensor capability to measure important values, such as, inside temperature.

Keywords: Demand response participation · Multi-agent system · Smart plug

1 Introduction

The power system paradigm has been changing in the last years and will continue to change in future years, resulting in the appearance of smart grids [1]. The centralization of generation will end, appearing decentralized generation [2]. The end-consumers will be incentivized to actively participate in smart grids, in a win-win situation, changing completely their roles in today's paradigm [3]. One of the aspects of smart grids is the integration of microgrids.

The proliferation of microgrids started using use cases around the world [4, 5], and now this concept can be seen and analyzed in real scenarios. The transaction from scientific concepts towards real implementations, such as [6], is a positive step enabling the validation of theoretical methodologies in real and uncontrollable environments.

The present work has been developed under the EUREKA - ITEA2 Project M2MGrids (ITEA-13011), Project SIMOCE (ANI|P2020 17690), and has received funding from FEDER Funds through COMPETE program and from National Funds through FCT under the project UID/EEA/00760/2013 and SFRH/BD/109248/2015.

© Springer International Publishing AG 2017
E. Oliveira et al. (Eds.): EPIA 2017, LNAI 10423, pp. 253–259, 2017.
DOI: 10.1007/978-3-319-65340-2_21

Other important aspect for smart grid successful implementations is the application of Demand Response (DR) programs to give an active role to the small and medium players (usually households or small offices) [7]. The use of DR programs brings clear advantages to smart grids and microgrids [8]. Some use of DR can be found in [9]. Nevertheless, to increase DR dissemination and to promote the appearance of new programs, automatic and intelligent responses must be implemented in the consumer side, specially the small and medium players.

The application of Smart Homes such as in [10, 11], brings advantages for energy management inside the households, but must important, can increase the DR programs participation using intelligent response methodologies. The development and application of autonomous and intelligent methodologies, for DR users' response, must consider the users impact (particularly the negative impact provoked).

2 Background of the Proposal

To implement a Smart Home, monitoring and controlling units are needed, such as, Smart Plugs. At this moment is possible to find a significant number of Smart Plugs available on the market. However, must of them had limitations, such as: not having monitoring; or just monitors the current; or having a closed system without any API.

The use of Smart Plugs in R&D centers can be done using software like Home Assistant[1]. This is an open source software that aggregates various Internet of Things (IoT) devices into a unique system, while provides a RESTFul interface to monitor and control devices. However, if the R&D center intention is to study intelligent methodologies in the energy management of the household (for instance, to participate in DR programs), more data and new types of intelligent load control are needed. And for this situation, there is not a suitable Smart Plug in the market.

This paper presents the Environmental Awareness Plug (EnAPlug), a Smart Plug that can be easily developed in R&D centers fulfilling the center needs and proposes. EnAPlug combines actuators to control the load, and sensors, to monitor not only the load status and energy but also the environment that surrounds the load.

3 Environmental Awareness Plug

EnAPlug was idealized and developed for R&D centers that have a need to test energy management solutions in households. The development of EnAPlug enables R&D centers to overcome the limitations of the Smart Plugs available on the market, with a costume made solution with context awareness capabilities. EnAPlug can also be used outside R&D centers for load monitoring and control, enabling a context awareness monitoring of a specific energy resource, for instance, our home kitchen oven.

---

[1] https://home-assistant.io/.

The premises of EnAPlug was to build a modular plug that can work with several actuators and sensors while being open for other systems. For this reason, the control and monitor of EnAPlug is open and can be accessible with GET and POST requests.

Figure 1 shows EnAPlug overall architecture. The light blue block that identifies the microcontroller was implemented using an Arduino Mega 2560 R3, nonetheless other microcontrollers can be used. The microcontroller is the processing unit of EnAPlug and has the following requirements: a serial communication port; at least 1 digital output for the load control; the capability to have TCP/IP connection (using a compatible module); and some digital and analog inputs for sensors (it can also provide communication protocols, such as, I2C).

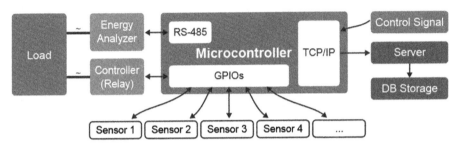

Fig. 1. EnAPlug overall architecture (Color figure online)

The yellow blocks are connected to the 230 V/AC. The Energy Analyzer must be compatible with Modbus/RTU protocol. This requirement will enable the microcontroller to communicate with the energy analyzer using a simple MAX485 component that converts serial communications into RS-485 communications, and vice-versa. The Controller block can be a relay, providing on/off control, or other kind of control, such as, a dimmer. For this paper, it will be used a relay with a 5 V/DC coil. The orange block represents the load that we want to monitor and control.

The green and red blocks are external blocks of EnAPlug and are connected using the TCP/IP connection available in EnAPlug. The Control Signal is made using a socket connection to the microcontroller IP on port 80. The Server block is an external server that receives JSON messages and save them in a SQL Server database. The period of storages is defined by EnAPlug.

The sensors blocks are the sensors connected to the Microcontroller that are suitable for the measured load. The idea of the sensors is to give a better knowledge about the measuring Load. For instance, if the intention is to monitor and control a lamp, it is recommended to use a movement sensor and a clarity sensor. The sensors placed must increase the knowledge regarding the load and its context. If we know the load context is possible to perform an intelligent control.

EnAPlug is a device that understand their environment, enabling an intelligent and a more efficient control. However, the environment awareness capability is only possible with the right sensors. For instance, if the goal is to measure a television, a temperature sensor is not adequate. Therefore, to understand a television more appropriated sensors should be chosen, such as, presence, clarity and noise sensors.

4   Demonstration

For this demonstration, EnAPlug was integrated in the Multi-Agent Smart Grid Platform (MASGriP) [12]. MASGriP has the capability to represent small and medium players in a microgrid scenario. For this scenario MASGriP will be used as a connected microgrid with three players, representing our R&D buildings (Fig. 2). This representation of MASGriP can be seen in works, such as, [6, 13–15]. In our R&D center, namely building N, two EnAPlugs were installed and connected to its representative agent:

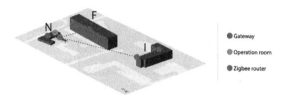

Fig. 2.   GECAD MASGriP configuration

- EnAPlug for refrigerator (Fig. 3) – for this EnAPlug is used on/off control of the entire refrigerator (including the inside lamp), an energy analyzer to monitor power, reactive power, voltage and current and four sensors: inside temperature and humidity sensor; an outside temperature sensor; and a door opener detector using a clarity sensor;

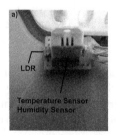
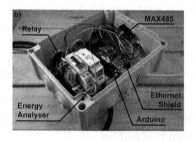

Fig. 3.   EnAPlug installed in the refrigerator: (a) inside sensors, (b) EnAPlug, (c) User interface

- EnAPlug for water heater – for this EnAPlug is used a temperature sensor to monitor the water temperature, an on/off controller. The stored energy readings are power, reactive power, voltage and current.

EnAPlug readings, from the energy analyzer and from the sensors, are stored in a database each five seconds. A MASGriP agent, that represents building N, uses that data for energy management and gives direct control signals to the EnAPlug.

An external DR event was trigger in MASGriP from 05:00 p.m. to 06:00 p.m.. The event demands to turn off of the refrigerators within this hour. In Fig. 4 is shown the results of the refrigerator connected to EnAPlug, where is visible the DR event and the turn off the refrigerator.

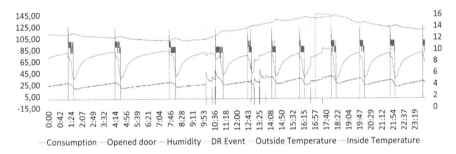

Fig. 4. Refrigerator readings between 00:00 a.m. and 23:59 p.m. (Color figure online)

During the day is possible to see, in Fig. 4, the refrigerator light turning on (peaks in blue line of consumptions) when the door is open (red line below). During the event EnAPlug detects an open door but there is no increase of consumption, meaning that the light was off. The inside temperature (purple line) was stable and did not increase beyond the refrigerator limit. The DR event was a success as we can see using the consumption line and the inside temperature line. The EnAPlug can detect dangerous situations, such as, the increase of inside temperature and turn the refrigerator back on in an emergency. In this case, the situation was controlled and no damage was made. The results show that after DR event, when the refrigerator was turned on again, the motor started immediately to decrease the inside temperature.

In Fig. 5 is shown the water heater during 24 h. The temperature sensor is placed outside the water heater (for security reasons), glued in the water pipe. The consumption and the temperature increases when the water heater turned on (06:45). The temperature also increases when a person uses hot water (08:30).

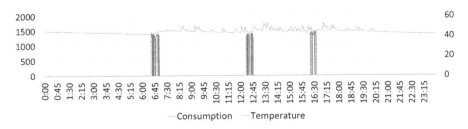

Fig. 5. Water heater readings between 00:00 a.m. and 23:59 p.m.

5   Conclusions

The use of smart plugs can be included in demand side management systems. However, the information provided by the smart plugs, available on the market, are limited because they don't understand the load context, making it difficult to execute intelligent energy management algorithms.

The use of EnAPlug brings advantages for R&D centers regarding load study and analysis. For power systems, EnAPlug has the advantage of environmental and contextual awareness that can be used for intelligent algorithms. EnAPlug is dynamic and easy to use in a R&D center, enabling the sensing, monitoring and control of energy loads. It is a possibility, demonstrated in the present paper, to use EnAPlugs in a multi-agent system for power system simulation.

The main contribution of this paper is the demonstration of a truly smart plug with environment awareness capabilities for energy management.

References

1. Dimeas, A.L., Hatziargyriou, N.D.: Operation of a multiagent system for microgrid control. IEEE Trans. Power Syst. **20**, 1447–1455 (2005)
2. Kirschen, D.: Demand-side view of electricity markets. IEEE Trans. Power Syst. **18**(2), 520–527 (2003)
3. Yan, Y., Qian, Y., Sharif, H., Tipper, D.: A survey on smart grid communication infrastructures: motivations, requirements and challenges. IEEE Commun. Surv. Tutor. **15**(1), 5–20 (2013)
4. Washom, B., Dilliot, J., Weil, D., Kleissl, J., Balac, N., Torre, N., Richter, C.: Ivory tower of power: microgrid implementation at the University of California, San Diego. IEEE Power Energy Mag. **11**(4), 28–32 (2013)
5. Stamp, J.: The SPIDERS project - smart power infrastructure demonstration for energy reliability and security at US military facilities. In: 2012 IEEE PES Innovative Smart Grid Technologies (ISGT), Washington, DC, p. 1 (2012)
6. Gomes, L., Silva, J., Faria, P., Vale, Z.: Microgrid demonstration gateway for players communication and load monitoring and management. In: 2016 Clemson University Power Systems Conference (PSC), Clemson, SC, pp. 1–6 (2016)
7. Faria, P., Vale, Z.: Demand response in electrical energy supply: an optimal real time pricing approach. Energy **36**(8), 5374–5384 (2011)
8. Siano, P.: Demand response and smart grids - a survey. Renew. Sustain. Energy Rev. **30**, 461–478 (2014)
9. Gomes, L., Faria, P., Fernandes, F., Vale, Z., Ramos, C.: Domestic consumption simulation and management using a continuous consumption management and optimization algorithm. In: IEEE PES T&D Conference and Exposition, Chicago, IL, USA, pp. 1–5 (2014)
10. Tsui, K.M., Chan, S.C.: Demand response optimization for smart home scheduling under real-time pricing. IEEE Trans. Smart Grid **3**, 1812–1821 (2012)
11. Fernandes, F., Carreiro, A., Morais, H., Vale, Z., Gastaldello, D.S., Amaral, H.L.M., Souza, A.N.: Management of heating, ventilation and air conditioning system for SHIM plat-form. In: IEEE PES Innovative Smart Grid Technologies Latin America (ISGT LATAM), Montevideo, pp. 275–280 (2015)

12. Morais, H., Vale, Z., Pinto, T., Gomes, L., Fernandes, F., Oliveira, P., Ramos, C.: Multi-agent based smart grid management and simulation: situation awareness and learning in a test bed with simulated and real installations and players. In: 2013 IEEE Power & Energy Society General Meeting, Vancouver, BC, pp. 1–5 (2013)
13. Gomes, L., Fernandes, F., Faria, P., Silva, M., Vale, Z., Ramos, C.: Contextual and environmental awareness laboratory for energy consumption management. In: 2015 Clemson University Power Systems Conference (PSC), pp. 1–6 (2015)
14. Gomes, L., Lefrançois, M., Faria, P., Vale, Z.: Publishing real-time microgrid consumption data on the web of Linked Data. In: 2016 Clemson University Power Systems Conference (PSC), pp. 1–8 (2016)
15. Vinagre, E., Gomes, L., Vale, Z.: Electrical energy consumption forecast using external facility data. In: 2015 IEEE Symposium Series on Computational Intelligence, pp. 659–664 (2015)

Flower Pollination Algorithm Applied to the Economic Dispatch Problem with Multiple Fuels and Valve Point Effect

Rafael Ochsendorf G. Souza, Ezequiel Silva Oliveira,
Ivo Chaves Silva Junior$^{(\boxtimes)}$, André Luís Marques Marcato,
and Marcos T.B. de Oliveira

Department of Electrical Engineering, Federal University of Juiz de Fora (UFJF),
Rua José Lourenço Kelmer, s/n – Martelos, Juiz de Fora, MG, Brazil
{rafael.ochsendorf,ezequiel.silva,
oliveira.marcos}@engenharia.ufjf.br,
{ivo.junior,andre.marcato}@ufjf.edu.br

Abstract. Due to the high importance of economic dispatch in planning and operating electric power systems, new methods have been researched to minimize the costs of power generation. To calculate these costs, the power generation of each thermal unit must be evaluated. When a thermal unit is modelled considering real world constraints, such as multiple fuels and valve point effect, traditional optimization methods are inefficient due to the nature of the cost function. This paper shows a study of a metaheuristic method, based on flower pollination to search for satisfactory results for economic dispatch. The results obtained are compared with results from other authors, with the purpose of evaluating how efficient the technique presented here is.

Keywords: Economic dispatch · Metaheuristic · Multiple fuels

1 Introduction

Electrical power systems attempt to supply the demand with the minimal possible cost. This is the Economic Dispatch (ED) problem, that aims to minimize the costs through allocating the power generated among thermal units to minimize this cost.

Economic Dispatch is a nonlinear, mixed integer programming problem where the function that describes the costs to generate power is usually approximated by a quadratic function [1]. Formerly, the ED problem has been solved through multiple optimization techniques considering that the cost function is a convex function, which largely simplifies the problem [1, 2].

In reality, however, when it is considered that a thermal unit can work with multiple fuels and that the valve point effect will happen, the cost function becomes non-convex. With that being said, classic optimizations methods that have been previously used to solve this problem become inefficient. When the cost function is considered as a non-convex function, the ED problem becomes much more complex to be solved, and metaheuristics methods show up as interesting alternatives to deal with this problem.

The original version of this chapter was revised: The name of the fifth author was corrected. The correction to this chapter is available at https://doi.org/10.1007/978-3-319-65340-2_72

© Springer International Publishing AG 2017
E. Oliveira et al. (Eds.): EPIA 2017, LNAI 10423, pp. 260–270, 2017.
DOI: 10.1007/978-3-319-65340-2_22

Several methods have been previously applied to ED, such as Genetic Algorithm [3], Differential Evolution [4], Q-Learning [5], Particles Swarm [6], and even modified or hybrids techniques.

Bioinspired optimization techniques perform well and seem to be more and more promising. Therefore, these methods have been frequently applied to engineering problems and have often found great results.

In this context, a new metaheuristic method was developed by Yang [7] and has been applied to solve multiple engineering problems, including economic dispatch [8, 9].

This paper performs an analysis of results obtained through the application of flower pollination algorithm (FPA) to the economic dispatch problem, and the results obtained are compared with other results that can be found in the literature to validate FPA's viability. This analysis contributes to understand how efficient FPA is when applied to the ED problem, and encourages further investigation of FPA when applied to different cases, given that the solutions found in this paper were good.

2 Modelling of Economic Dispatch

Economic Dispatch Problem consists of an optimization problem that aims to minimize the total cost of fuel needed to supply the demand, considering operation constraints.

Therefore, the problem consists of minimizing a function (F_T), that represents the total cost of power generation, including every thermal unit in the system. Two other restrictions are part of this problem, one of them being the physical limit that every generator has: It needs to generate powers within its limits (the maximum and minimum power that every generator can handle) and the other constraint is given by the fact that the power generated must be equal to the demand. Therefore, the problem can be modelled by the following equations:

$$Minimize\ F_T = \sum_{i=1}^{N} F_i(P_i) \tag{1}$$

Subject to:

$$\sum_{i=1}^{N} (P_i) = P_D \tag{2}$$

$$P_i^{min} \leq P_i \leq P_i^{max} \tag{3}$$

Where:

F_T: Total generation cost;
F_i: Cost to generate power by generator i;
P_i: Active power generated by generator i;
P_D: Total system demand;

P_i^{min}: Minimum power output by generator i;
P_i^{max}: Maximum power output by generator i;
N: Total number of generators in the system;

In the upcoming subsection, the classic model of this problem is described, which approximates the cost function to a quadratic function.

2.1   Classic Models

In this case, the cost function is simply approximated by a quadratic function, which can be seen below:

$$F_i(P_i) = a_i + b_i P_i + c_i P_i^2 \tag{4}$$

Where a_i, b_i and c_i are costs coefficients related to generator i.

The restrictions to the classic model are represented by Eqs. (2) and (3). Equation (2) refers to the power balance of the system, when power loss is considered 0. Equation (3) refers to the minimum and maximum power output a generator can have due to its physical limitations.

2.2   Real World Restrictions

When considering real world restrictions, a few facts should be considered to properly solve the Economic Dispatch problem. These considerations increase the problem complexity. Valve point effect and the possibility for a thermal unit to operate with multiple fuels are explained below.

1. Valve Point: This is a real-world restriction, which happens when the valve is opened to control the temperature inside a turbine or boiler [10]. This affects the total fuel consumed by the system, given that the temperature drops and it takes some time until it goes up again to the ideal temperature in terms of performance. This effect creates ripples in the cost function. The cost function therefore can be represented by the following equation:

$$F_i(P_i) = a_i + b_i P_i + c_i P_i^2 + \alpha_i \left| e_i \sin \left(f_i \left(P_i^{min} - P_i \right) \right) \right| \tag{5}$$

Where:

a_i, b_i and c_i are costs coefficients related to generator i.
e_i and f_i are coefficients that represent the valve point for generator i;
α_i is a binary number that can turn the valve point on and off for generator i;

As a result of the valve point effect, the cost function becomes a non-convex function, with multiple minimum and maximum local points, increasing the complexity of the problem.

2. Multiple Fuels: The type of fuel consumed by a thermal unit directly effects its operating costs. With that being said, the coefficients a_i, b_i and c_i that were present in Eqs. (4) and (5) are different for every type of fuel. The ED problem must find which fuel every thermal unit should use to minimize the system's cost. Therefore, when it is considered that every generator has the possibility to consume multiple fuels, Eq. (5) can be changed into the following equation:

$$F_i(P_i) = \begin{cases} a_{i1} + b_{i1}P_i + c_{i1}P_i^2 + \alpha_i|e_{i1}\sin(f_{i1}(P_i^{\min} - P_i))| \ (I) \\ a_{i2} + b_{i2}P_i + -c_{i2}P_i^2 + \alpha_i|e_{i2}\sin(f_{i2}(P_{i1} - P_i))| \ (II) \\ \quad\vdots \\ a_{inc} + b_{inc}P_i + c_{inc}P_i^2 + \alpha_i|e_{inc}\sin(f_{inc}(P_{i(nc-1)} - P_i))| \ (III) \end{cases}$$
(6)

Where Eq. (1) refers to the costs using fuel type I, Eq. (2) refers to the costs using fuel II, and Eq. (3) generalizes the cost function for nc available fuel types, where nc is the total number of fuels available for generator i.

3 Flower Pollination Algorithm

This paper uses FPA to find the optimal solution for the ED problem. This algorithm is based on flower evolution, which has been an ongoing process on our planet for at least 125 million years [11]. According to [11], FPA has four main rules:

1. Biotic pollination (done by animals, insects and birds) and cross pollination are global pollination (global search), and move in a way that can be described by Levy's flight.
2. For local pollination (local search), self-pollination and abiotic pollination are considered.
3. Biotic pollination may develop flower constancy, this is related to the probability of similar flowers reproducing.
4. The search for new solutions through local or global solutions is defined by a parameter $p \in [0, 1]$. In this paper, the value for this parameter was set to 0.6.

The four rules above, created by [11] define the search mechanism done through FPA. Those rules can furthermore be transformed into mathematics equations, so the search for the optimal solution is described by the equations below:

For biotic or cross-pollination:

$$x_i^{t+1} = x_i^t + L(x_i^t - g*)$$
(7)

Where:

x_i^t: Solution vector for iteration t.
$g*$: Best solution found so far.
L: Step vector which obeys Levy's Flight.

For abiotic pollination, the following equation is applied:

$$x_i^{t+1} = x_i^t + \epsilon\left(x_j^t - x_k^t\right) \tag{8}$$

Where:

x_j^t, x_k^t: Pollens for different flowers of same species.
ϵ: A random number between 0 and 1, which represents a random, local search for a new flower.

Therefore, according to [11], the following pseudo code represents the search mechanism done by FPA:

```
Define objective function, minimize or maximize f(x), x =
(x₁, x₁, ..., xₐ)
Initialize a population containing n flowers with random
solutions.
Define the switch probability parameter p ∈ [0,1].
Search for the best solution g* within the initial solu-
tion.
Define when the algorithm should stop, such as the max
number of iterations t.
While (t < Max number of iterations)
   For i = 1 until n
      Get a random number between 0 and 1, rand.
         If rand < p
            Draw a step vector L which obeys Levy's flight.
            Perform global pollination through equation (7)
         Else
            Draw a random number ϵ between 0 e 1.
            Perform local pollination through equation (8)
         End if
      Evaluate new solutions.
      If new solutions are better, update the population
with the new solution.
   End for
End while
Print best solution found by the algorithm
```

4 Study of Case and Results Analysis

Guided by the pseudo code developed by [11] shown in the previous section, the method has been applied to solve the economic dispatch problem considering valve point effects and multiple fuels, through the software MATLAB. The method was applied to systems with different demands, allowing further observation of this method's performance applied to problems of this nature.

Initially, it is needed to define the input parameters, n and p. Since these parameters may affect how the method performs, multiple settings were tested, by changing the value of p from 0,1 to 0,9 with a step of 0,1, and with the numbers of flowers n increasing from 2 to 25 with a step of 1. For each setting presented above, FPA was applied to the system presented in [5], which has been solved by several different methods before. The stopping criteria was defined as 1.500 iterations, and the best results were found with $n = 20$ and $p = 0,6$. This system consists of 10 thermal units and a load of 2.700 MW, with valve point effect. The details such as the value of the coefficients of each thermal unit and the minimum and maximum power that can be generated can be found in [5].

Now that the parameters have successfully been defined, FPA's performance was tested by applying it to the aforementioned system. The results will be compared with other results previously found in the literature. The best quality result found by the method is shown in Table 1:

Table 1. Results obtained through FPA for a system with 2.700 MW and valve point.

Thermal unit	Fuel type	Power generated (MW)	Generation costs ($/h)
1	1	185,6290	28,1811
2	3	205,8662	35,0194
3	2	358,4885	88,2373
4	3	230,8607	43,4672
5	1	276,3482	71,2064
6	3	230,8607	43,4087
7	1	282,2848	69,7562
8	3	230,8607	43,3705
9	3	414,3451	111,7990
10	1	284,4559	74,8832
Total		2.700	609,1843

Figure 1 shows the convergence to the best solution for the case above:

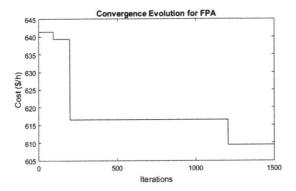

Fig. 1. Convergence Evolution for ED problem using FPA.

The algorithm converged after 1.207 iterations. The best solution found can be compared to other techniques, as shown in Table 2:

Table 2. Comparison between results found through FPA and other methods for case I.

Method	Minimum costs ($/h)
CGA-MU [3]	624,7193
IGA-MU [3]	624,5178
NPSO-LRS [12]	624,1273
APSO[1] [13]	624,0145
APSO[2] [14]	623,9099
CBPSO-RVM [15]	623,9588
DE [4]	623,8900
EDE [4]	623,8300
Q-learning [5]	624,3116
Trelea-PSO [1]	606,1120
FPA	609,1843

According to Table 2, FPA had better results than most other methods, with the only exception being Trelea-PSO. However, it is still interesting to study FPA's performance as a whole. With that mind, the previous method was applied to the system 100 times, each time containing 1.500 iterations. Each set of 1.500 iterations took approximately 68 s to be completed.

This analysis allows us to easily obtain the minimum, average and maximum values found through FPA, and study how the results were distributed. The following Table shows the minimum, average and maximum values found through FPA:

Table 3. Maximum, average and minimum values of solutions found through FPA.

Maximum value	653,4226
Average value	629,5662
Minimum value	609,1843

The distribution of the solutions that were found more than once can be found in Table 4:

Since this method doesn't guarantee that the solution will always converge to the same result and there is a big number of different results, it can be interesting to have a further investigation on how the results were distributed. Therefore, a boxplot can be a strong analytical tool to evaluate the method's performance. Figure 2 shows a boxplot of the results previously found.

Table 4. Distribution characteristics for FPA applied to the ED problem.

Method	Number of repetitions
609,1843	2
612,4748	2
612,5925	2
617,5620	2
618,0723	2
618,1887	2
618,7902	3
623,4816	2
631,1166	2
633,2846	2
637,4722	2
639,5037	3
639,7629	2
Different solutions found	85

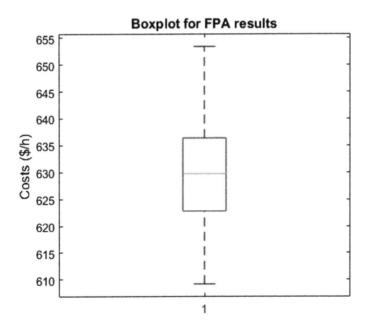

Fig. 2. Distribution of the results found through FPA seen through a boxplot.

Through Fig. 2, several conclusions can be made, such as:

1. The lower quartile, which splits off the lowest 25% results, contains results ranging from 609,1843 to 622,7585.
2. The upper quartile, which splits off the highest 25% results, contains results ranging from 636,391 to 653,4226.

3. Based on observations 1 and 2, 50% of the results can be found between 622,7585 and 653,4226.
4. After running the code 100 times, the median was equal to 629,7428, which is a result that is very close to the average value previously found in Table 3. Not only that, but this value is close to the best solution found by several methods, as seen in Table 2.
5. The standard deviation of the 100 simulations was 9,3876.

Given that this method has had very positive results, it now can be applied to other systems to validate its efficiency. With that in mind, FPA was applied to two other scenarios. They are the same system that was previously studied, but the power demanded is different and there is no valve point effect. These systems were chosen because they were previously studied by other authors, and therefore we have results to compare with. The results are shown in Table 5:

Table 5. Comparison of results found through FPA for systems with 2.500 MW and 2.600 MW with no valve point.

2.500 MW		2.600 MW	
Method	Minimum costs ($/h)	Method	Minimum costs ($/h)
HNUM [17]	526,700	HNUM [17]	574,030
HNN [18]	526,130	HNN [18]	574,260
MPSO [19]	526,239	MPSO [19]	574,381
DE [20]	526,239	DE [20]	574,381
EALHN [21]	526,239	EALHN [21]	574,381
Trelea-PSO [1]	511,044	Trelea-PSO [1]	556,659
FPA	522,007	FPA	561,971

As seen in Table 5, once again FPA performed better than most methods, with the only exception being Trelea-PSO. The results obtained through FPA for the systems above can be seen with more details in Table 6:

Table 6. Power generated per thermal unit and costs for systems with 2.500 MW and 2.600 MW with no valve point effect.

TU	Fuel type		Power gen. (MW)		Costs ($/h)	
–	2.500 MW	2.600 MW	2.500 MW	2.600 MW	2.500 MW	2.600 MW
1	2	2	218,0949	219,9845	42,9339	43,8965
2	3	3	184,2068	196,2621	26,9530	30,8913
3	2	2	353,9263	356,1525	85,7799	86,9747
4	3	3	225,5379	231,8897	41,3901	43,7836
5	1	1	217,8836	237,4385	45,4987	53,2824
6	3	3	225,5379	231,8897	41,3901	43,7836
7	1	1	227,6640	246,2935	46,1413	53,4473
8	3	3	225,5379	231,8897	41,3901	43,7836
9	3	3	393,9547	401,4975	102,0699	105,6054
10	1	1	227,6558	246,7023	48,4591	56,5227
Total			2.500 MW	2.600 MW	522,0068	561.9712

The distribution of the results for the cases above were very similar to the first system studied.

Comparing Tables 6 and 1, it is possible to observe that the best solution found without the valve point included had the same fuel types for every thermal unit. However, the same cannot be said when the valve point is included. This occurs because the cost function changes drastically with the addition of the valve point effect, as it has been discussed previously in Sect. 2. The valve point effect further increases the complexity of the problem, given that the amount of minimum and maximum local points is greatly increased when it is considered.

5   Conclusions

The method presented in this paper solves ED problems efficiently. A real-world approach was taken while applying the method, respecting the consequences caused by valve point effect (in the first system studied) and multiple fuels (for every system). Given that the function that has to be minimized becomes a non-convex function, metaheuristic methods seem to be a very interesting approach to solve this problem, and FPA was able to achieve outstanding results. Furthermore, the algorithm presented here still has room for improvement.

With that in mind, this paper encourages further studies in this area. This method could be applied to larger scale real systems to verify its behavior when applied to different cases. Given that the method didn't have a high convergence ratio, it would certainly be very interesting to see if it would still be as efficient as it was so far. It is possible that the low convergence ratio could be a difficulty found by the method when applying it to bigger systems. However, this aspect could be improved by using hybrid versions of this method to improve the convergence ratio.

Furthermore, another consideration would be studying this method when transmission system constraints are taken into account. This would raise the complexity of the problem significantly, given that even the location of each thermal unit will impact in the problem.

Acknowledgments. The authors would like to thank INERGE (Instituto Nacional de Energia Elétrica), GOHB (Grupo de Otimização Heurística Bioinspirada) and FCT (Fundação Centro Tecnológico de Juiz de Fora) for the support given throughout the development of this paper, which made it possible.

References

1. Oliveira, E.S., Silva Junior, I.C., de Oliveira, L.W., Dias, B.H., Oliveira, E.J.: Non-convex Economic Dispatch using Trelea Particle Swarm Optimization. PowerTech, Eindhoven (2016)
2. Wood, A.J., Wollenberg, B.F.: Power Generation, Operation, and Control, 2nd edn. Wiley, Hoboken (1996)

3. Chiang, C.-L.: Improved genetic algorithm for power economic dispatch of units with valve-point effects and multiple fuels. IEEE Trans. Power Syst. **20**(4), 1690–1699 (2005)
4. Sayah, S., Hamouda, A.: Nonsmooth economic power dispatch through an enhanced differential evolution approach. In: 2012 International Conference on Complex Systems (ICCS), pp. 1–6 (2012)
5. Abouheaf, M., Haesaert, S., Lee, W.-J., Lewis, F.: Approximate and reinforcement learning techniques to solve non-convex economic dispatch problems. In: Multi-Conference on Systems, Signals Devices (SSD), pp. 1–8 (2014)
6. Gaing, Z.-L.: Particle swarm optimization to solving the economic dispatch considering the generator constraints. IEEE Trans. Power Syst. **18**(3), 1187–1195 (2003)
7. Yang, X.-S.: Flower pollination algorithm for global optimization. In: Unconventional Computation and Natural Computation 2012, pp. 240–249 (2012)
8. Prathiba, R., Moses, M.B., Sakthivel, S.: Flower pollination algorithm applied for different economic load dispatch problems. Int. J. Eng. Technol. (IJET) **6**(2), 1009–1016 (2014)
9. Sarjiya, S., Putra, P.H., Saputra, T.A.: Modified flower pollination algorithm for nonsmooth and multiple fuel options economic dispatch. In: 8th International Conference on Information Technology and Electrical Engineering (ICITEE) (2016)
10. Oliveira, E.S.: Metaheurísticas aplicadas ao problema do despacho econômico de energia elétrica. Master's Degree final paper. Universidade Federal de Juiz de Fora (2015)
11. Yang, X.S., Karamanoglu, M., He, X.: Multi-objective flower algorithm for optimization. In: International Conference on Computational Science (ICCS), Procedia Computational Science, pp. 861–868 (2013)
12. Selvakumar, A.I., Thanushkodi, K.: A new particle swarm optimization solution to nonconvex economic dispatch problems. IEEE Trans. Power Syst. **22**(1), 42–51 (2007)
13. Selvakumar, A.I., Thanushkodi, K.: Anti-predatory particle swarm optimization: solution to nonconvex economic dispatch problems. Electr. Power Syst. Res. **78**(1), 2–10 (2008)
14. Panigrahi, B., Pandi, V.R., Das, S.: Adaptive particle swarm optimization approach for static and dynamic economic load dispatch. Energy Convers. Manag. **49**(6), 1407–1415 (2008)
15. Lu, H., Sriyanyong, P., Song, Y.H., Dillon, T.: Experimental study of a new hybrid PSO with mutation for economic dispatch with non-smooth cost function. Int. J. Electr. Power Energy Syst. **32**(9), 921–935 (2010)
16. Bhattacharya, A., Chattopadhyay, P.: Hybrid differential evolution with biogeography-based optimization for solution of economic load dispatch. IEEE Trans. Power Syst. **25**(4), 1955–1964 (2010)
17. Lin, C., Viviani, G.: Hierarchical economic dispatch for piece-wise quadratic cost functions. IEEE Trans. Power Syst. **6**, 1170–1175 (1984)
18. Park, J., Kim, Y., Eom, I., Lee, K.: Economic load dispatch for piecewise quadratic cost function using hopfield neural network. IEEE Trans. Power Syst. **8**(3), 1030–1038 (1993)
19. Park, J.-B., Lee, K.-S., Shin, J.-R., Lee, K.Y.: A particle swarm optimization for economic dispatch with nonsmooth cost functions. IEEE Trans. Power Syst. **20**(1), 34–42 (2005)
20. Noman, N., Iba, H.: Differential evolution for economic load dispatch problems. Electr. Power Syst. Res. **78**(8), 1322–1331 (2008)
21. Vo, D.N., Ongsakul, W.: Economic dispatch with multiple fuel types by enhanced augmented lagrange hopfield network. Appl. Energy **91**(1), 281–289 (2012)

Dynamic and Static Transmission Network Expansion Planning via Harmony Search and Branch & Bound on a Hybrid Algorithm

Luiz E. de Oliveira[1]($\boxtimes$) ⓘ, Francisco D. Freitas[1] ⓘ,
Ivo C. da Silva Jr.[2], and Phillipe V. Gomes[3] ⓘ

[1] Electrical Engineer Postgraduate Program, Department of Electrical
Engineering, University of Brasília (UnB), Brasília, DF 70910-900, Brazil
`luiz.eduardo@engenharia.ufjf.br`, `ffreitas@ene.unb.br`
[2] Electrical Engineer Postgraduate Program, Department of Electrical
Engineering, Federal University of Juiz de Fora (UFJF),
Juiz de Fora, MG 36081-900, Brazil
`ivo.junior@ufjf.edu.br`
[3] INESC TEC, Department of Electrical and Computer Engineering,
Faculty of Engineering, University of Porto, Porto, Portugal
`phillipe.gomes@fe.up.pt`

Abstract. This work presents a method based on metaheuristics to solve the problem of Static (STNEP) and Dynamic (DTNEP) Transmission Network Expansion Planning in electrical power systems. The result of this formulation is mixed-integer nonlinear programming (MINLP), where the difficulties are intensified in the DTNEP by the temporal coupling. Therefore, a methodology was developed to reach the solution in three different stages: The first one is responsible for obtaining an efficient set of best candidate routes for the expansion; the metaheuristic optimization process, Harmony Search (HS), is used to find STNEP's optimal solution and its neighborhood that provides a DTNEP candidate zone; lastly, a hybrid algorithm that mixes the HS and Branch & Bound (B&B) concepts is adapted to provide the optimal DTNEP. In this study, the lossless linearized modeling for load flow is used as a representation of the transmission network. Tests with the Garver and southern Brazilian systems were carried out to verify the performance method. The computational time saving for the STNEP and DTNEP prove the efficacy of the proposed method.

Keywords: Dynamic Transmission Expansion Planning · Constructive Heuristic Algorithms · Harmony Search · Branch & Bound

1 Introduction

Brazil is a country that has one of the most renewable and cleanest energy matrixes in the world: about 42%, according to [1]. Due to the high potential of its watersheds, when considering only the product of electric energy, reference [2] cites the country as second in sustainable power generation, reaching 96% of its generation. As a

© Springer International Publishing AG 2017
E. Oliveira et al. (Eds.): EPIA 2017, LNAI 10423, pp. 271–282, 2017.
DOI: 10.1007/978-3-319-65340-2_23

consequence, the country is near Norway's sustainable consumption which reaches an incredible mark of 100%. However, these renewable sources are generally far from the main centers of consumption, thus increasing the complexity of the National Inter-connected System (SIN). This fact requires an accurate analysis of the different strategies to expand the electric system. Thus, Transmission Network Expansion Planning (TNEP) arises to minimize the cost of investment in the electric system, supplying the expected demand for a planning horizon as in [3, 4].

In general, TNEP can be classified as Static (STNEP) and Dynamic (DTNEP) according to the planning horizon. The static view is a simplistic approach that con-siders only one future stage in the planning horizon and demonstrates to the planner just "which" reinforcements are needed and "where" they should be installed [5]. On the other hand, the dynamic view gives important information to the planner about "when" these reinforcements should be allocated in the network, resulting in a more robust and effective response. In addition to the difficulties present in the static model, the temporal consideration causes the problem to grow exponentially, leading the dynamic models to require a great computational effort, according to [6, 7].

The computational advancements of the past decades have enabled engineers and planners to research and determine robust and effective solutions to such problems. The use of metaheuristics to solve this type of problem fits perfectly into these problem's descriptions. It is applied to give answers to problems to which there is little infor-mation about and/or how the optimal solution looks like is not known. In systems where the combinatorial explosion of possible solutions is detected, bio-inspired metaheuristics have become tools of utmost importance as in [4].

Taking into account the above information, this work presents a model based on the metaheuristic Harmony Search (HS) associated to constructive heuristic methods for STNEP solution. For the DTNEP, we chose to use HS in association with Branch & Bound (B&B) in the dynamic distribution of the best paths.

The paper is organized as follows. Section 2 describes a modeling of the trans-mission network expansion problem. In Sects. 3 and 4, in this sequence, there is a robust elucidation about optimization techniques: Harmony Search and Branch & Bound. In Sect. 5 the proposed method is presented. In all stages of the problem solving process modeled in Sect. 2, the transmission network is represented by the linearized load flow model. The performance of these models through the tests with the Garver and the Brazilian South systems, together with the comparisons to the literature, is presented in Sect. 6. The conclusions can be found in Sect. 7.

2   Transmission Network Expansion Planning

The DTNEP can be formulated as a mixed-integer nonlinear programming problem, whose solution aims to minimize the cost of investment on transmission systems by satisfying all of the following constraints: active power balance; Expansion Parameter, PE_{ij}^t; load shedding restrictions. The STNEP can be modeled using the same mathe-matical formulation as DTNEP except for t fixed at the last stage of the planning horizon.

$$Min \sum_{t=1}^{nt} \left(\sum_{d=1}^{nbar} C_d^t \cdot def_d^t + \sum_{(i,j) \in C} C_{ij}^t \cdot PE_{ij}^t \right) \tag{1}$$

subject to,

$$\sum_{t=1}^{nt} \left(g_i^t - \sum_{j \in \Omega i} fe_{ij}^t - \sum_{j \in \Omega i} fc_{ij}^t \cdot PE_{ij}^t \right) = Dem_i^t \tag{2}$$

$$fe_{ij}^t = \gamma_{ij} \cdot \theta_{ij}^t, \qquad \forall (i,j) \in E \tag{3}$$

$$fc_{ij}^t = \gamma_{ij} \cdot \theta_{ij}^t \cdot PE_{ij}^t, \qquad \forall (i,j) \in C \tag{4}$$

$$\left| f_{ij}^t \right| \le \overline{f_{ij}}, \qquad \forall (i,j) \in E, C \tag{5}$$

$$\underline{g_i^t} \le g_i^t \le \overline{g_i^t} \tag{6}$$

$$0 \le def_i^t \le Dem_i^t \tag{7}$$

$$\overline{Exp_{ij}^{t-1}} - PE_{ij}^t = \overline{Exp_{ij}^t} \tag{8}$$

$$0 \le PE_{ij}^t \le \overline{Exp_{ij}^t}, \qquad \forall (i,j) \in C \tag{9}$$

$$C_{ij}^t = \frac{C_{ij}^0}{(1+tx)^{(t-t_0)}}, \qquad \forall (i,j) \in C \tag{10}$$

where nt is the number of stages; $nbar$ is the number of buses; C_d^t is the cost of energy deficit; C_{ij}^t is the present-time cost of investment of the branch $i{-}j$ at stage t; def_d^t is the energy deficit; PE_{ij}^t is the expansion parameter of the branch $i{-}j$ at stage t; g_i^t is the generation of the bus i at stage t; Dem_i^t is the demand of the bus i at stage t; fe_{ij}^t is the power flow on the existent branch $i{-}j$ at stage t; fc_{ij}^t is the power flow in the candidate branch $i{-}j$ at stage t; γ_{ij} is the susceptance of the branch $i{-}j$; θ_{ij}^t is the angular shift between buses $i{-}j$; C is the set of the expansion candidate routes; E is the set of existent branchs; tx is the annual interest rate.

The objective function described in (1) aims to minimize the TNEP investments and the energy deficit costs for each stage of the planning horizon. The deficit generation has a high cost of operation and can be interpreted as a fictional generation of active power inserted into each bus to ensure system feasibility.

TNEP's problems are usually represented by linear load flow models as in [4, 5, 7, 8]. This modeling is described by (2), (3), (4), (5), (6) and (7). It allows simplicity, less computational effort and acceptable accuracy in accordance with Kirchhoff's laws on the active power balance of each stage.

The expansion parameter, PE_{ij}^t, is a discrete variable associated to each candidate route that represents the planner's decision to construct or not certain circuits on every TNEP. After defining PE_{ij}^t, it is necessary to update the maximum expansion limit for the next stage on each route as defined in (8) and (9). The present cost of investment for each candidate route is obtained by (10) considering tx as the annual interest rate.

3 Harmony Search

Inspired by the musical improvisation process of a jazz trio, where each musician seeks the perfect harmony for the group, the Harmony Search (HS) metaheuristic optimization process is ruled by the same vision of music as the pursuit of the perfect state of harmony. This idea is analogous to the search for optimality in a mathematical optimization process. According to the metaheuristics already known [9], HS does not require gradient information or a feasible starting point. In this paper, the authors chose to use HS due to its mathematical flexibility and simplicity. For a better understanding of the method, the stages involved in the HS process are detailed in the following subsections.

3.1   Problem Initialization and Algorithm Parameters

It is necessary to specify the optimization problem by an objective function and its restrictions. As an example, we can apply the equations presented in Sect. 2. Furthermore, as demonstrated in [10], the stop criterion, the Harmonic Memory Consideration Rate (HMCR), the Pitch Adjustment Rate (PAR), Bandwidth (*lb*) and Harmonic Memory Size (HMS) are the parameters to be set for HS initialization. The Harmonic Memory is initialized with HMS random vectors whose lengths corresponding to the n decision variables, i.e., $HM_{HMS \cdot n}$.

To use the HM more effectively, the programmer must assign HMCR $\in [0, 1]$. If this rate is too small, the algorithm will rarely consult HM, resulting in a long time for convergence. On the other hand, if HMCR is extremely high (near 1), almost always, the harmonies to be used will come from HM, which will potentially increase the probability to converge to a local optimum. As HMCR, PAR is a continuous parameter that usually does not work close to its limits. If PAR is very small, rarely will HM solutions be adjusted and the only way to obtain new solutions will be through randomization. On the other hand, if the PAR is too high, the algorithm may not fully converge due to the lack of communication between the solutions.

3.2   The Searching Process

The generation of the new harmony vector, x', can be explained in more detail with the help of the musical improvisation process. The new song or solution vector $x' = x_1^t, x_2^t, \ldots, x_n^t$ could be generated by any skilled musician based on these three following rules: (i) compose new or random notes; (ii) play any famous piece of music exactly, from memory; (iii) play something similar to a known piece (thus adjusting the pitch slightly). In an optimization process these options are respectively: (i) randomness, (ii) use of harmonic memory through collective intelligence, and (iii) pitch adjustments [10]. In case the algorithm chooses to fit a known solution, an adequate *lb* is the key for the convergence of the method, according to (11).

$$x_i^t = x_i^{t-1} \pm lb \cdot rand \qquad (11)$$

At this point, the algorithm uses the fitness function to measure the attractiveness of the new solution to the objective function. If the new harmony is better than the worst HM solution, then this new vector is included in HM.

As the final action of iteration, the algorithm will test whether the stop criterion has been satisfied. In case of failure, it will improvise a new harmony, i.e., a new repetition of the searching process will begin. At the end of the optimization process, with the stopping criterion satisfied and the convergence of the method verified, the algorithm returns a probable global optimum.

4 Branch and Bound

Among the complete algorithms, a strategy known as Branch & Bound, whose origin goes back to the fifties, is commonly used to solve complex combinatorial optimization problems [11]. In short, B&B divides the initial problem (STNEP) into N subproblems (N stages) to simplify the (dynamic) optimization process. Furthermore, its capability of learning throughout the optimization process and insert restrictions by itself to speed up the conquest of the best solution has made B&B algorithm the perfect candidate for mining the optimal DTNEP from STNEP solutions.

The value of any feasible DTNEP solution is better than the static solution. In this study, a HS initialization algorithm is used to start B&B from a sub-optimal solution and increase its effectiveness. Infeasible solutions are not accepted by the method. As an example, the insertion of any i−j branch in any stage that disrespects the system constraints will not result in a feasible DTNEP. The problem only reaches the stopping criterion when the N subproblems are visited by the algorithm, i.e., every year of planning, B&B prunes every dead (infeasible) or infected (very expensive) branch of the solution tree and allows the growth of the good (feasible and the cheapest planning) branches until the end of the planning horizon.

5 Proposed Method

STNEP can be formulated as a mixed-integer nonlinear problem. Furthermore, temporal coupling must be considered in DTNEP. Figure 1 illustrates the flowchart of the proposed method, which is divided into three main blocks to reduce these mentioned difficulties and help to solve the problem: in the first one, a Constructive Heuristic Algorithm (CHA) is responsible for finding the relevant routes and reducing the sample space; the 2nd block solves STNEP and provides the next stage with an Optimal Static Region (OSR); in the last stage, the hybrid HS-B&B algorithm makes the DTNEP of all STNEP solutions from the OSR to find the optimal DTNEP solution.

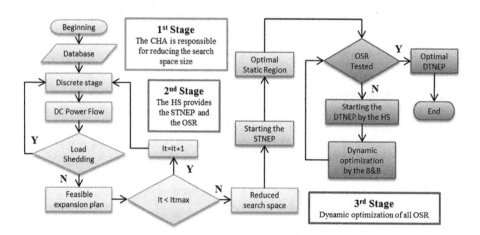

Fig. 1. Flowchart of the proposed method: CHA (blue); Static Stage (purple); Dynamic Stage (orange) (Color figure online)

5.1   Constructive Heuristic Algorithm

In [7], a CHA was proposed whose sensitivity analysis was based exclusively on the loading rate, Ψ_{ij}, of feasible plans. In this study, the CHA couples the previous study to an analysis of the Lagrange multipliers data, λ_{ij}, on infeasible plans.

Firstly, the new CHA tests numerous discrete solutions without bias for the last stage of the planning, where demands are greater. For each load shedding, i.e., infeasible STNEP, the Lagrange multipliers are collected and the CHA tries another discrete STNEP. When the CHA offers a feasible STNEP resulting in no load shedding of DC power flow, one interaction is counted. From there, it is possible to conclude that either in a feasible STNEP or in an infeasible STNEP, every expanded route is observed and analyzed. The larger the system, the greater the probability of infeasible STNEP is, i.e., the greater the range of tests the program will execute.

After reaching the upper bound iterations number, *itmax*, defined by the planner and testifying that CHA has tested at least once each of the branches in an infeasible expansion planning, the CHA will infer and will calculate the mean and variance from load rating data and Lagrange Multipliers data. Those candidate routes that obtain above average plus variance results are raised to the reduced and relevant hall of the best candidate routes for the expansion.

This set of picked routes is very important and relevant because it reduces exponentially the sample space, as observed in (12) and (13) for STNEP and DTNEP, respectively. For any solution method, a reduced set of candidate routes aggregates efficiency to the solution of the TNEP problem, thus becoming an attractive area of study and research.

$$(X_{\mathrm{max}} + 1)^{N-ex} \tag{12}$$

$$\left(\frac{(nt + X_{\mathrm{max}})!}{(nt!) * (X_{\mathrm{max}}!)} \right)^{N-ex} \tag{13}$$

where N is the initial number of candidate routes; ex is the number of excluded routes; X_{max} is the maximum expansions allowed per route; nt number of planning stages.

5.2   Static Expansion Planning

Since the set of relevant routes is defined, the algorithm passes to the static optimization process lead by HS, the metaheuristic presented in Sect. 3. In this study, an initialization algorithm was incorporated to increase the efficiency of the static optimization region.

Initialization Algorithm

The Harmonic Memory is initialized with the worst feasible answers as possible: the maximum limit of expansion for each route. So, the initialization algorithm refines these initial solutions and randomly reaches local minimums for each HM previous solution. How? A candidate branch is withdrawn and the feasibility of the N−1 solution is checked. If it is a feasible STNEP, the route is changed and another one is removed in succession until it is faced with a infeasible STNEP. Then, HS returns the last withdrawn branch to the solution and keeps observing the other routes until all of them are on its lower bound for a feasible STNEP: local minimums.

Static Optimization Process

After initializing the optimization process starting from satisfactory solutions, the HS keeps looking for the optimal STNEP, taking into account the power balance, load shedding and discretization of the expansion parameters. To avoid stagnation in circles, this method was enhanced to recognize a tested solution and to not waste time testing it again, which increased the efficiency of the same even more.

Contrary to what is conventionally done in the optimization process, that is, seeking for only one optimal solution, in this methodology the HS is modified to find not only a single Optimal Static Solution (OSS), but also to provide an Optimal Static Region (OSR) to be refined in the dynamic part of the methodology. That is, OSR will provide the best STNEPs for the dynamic expansion. This optimal zone concept is empirically given by (14), which defines that OSR are those solutions near OSS.

$$OSS \le OSR \le OSS.(1 + tx) \tag{14}$$

5.3   Dynamic Expansion Planning

The dynamic optimization is the last stage on the flowchart of the proposed method. In this stage, the hybrid algorithm HS-B&B finds the optimal DTNEP of all OSR respecting the temporal coupling and avoiding the possible load shedding.

To find the best DTNEP distribution of all OSR, the HS-B&B algorithm is initialized prioritizing the cheaper routes and delaying the construction of the more expensive routes. When two or more routes has the same cost of investment, the one with the highest loading rate is prioritized.

With a good starting solution in hand, the B&B starts to search for the optimal solution that may have escaped from this initialization technique. Since the HS provides a good DTNEP response for B&B, it becomes easier to prune not only the dead branches of the trees (OSR), but also the infected ones. That is, when the hybrid HS-B&B works, the algorithm prunes not only the infeasible dynamic planning but also the expensive ones too. This technique allows robustness (B&B) and efficiency (HS) in the dynamic step of the proposed method. After all OSR is tested, the method compares the possible DTNEPs to find the best solution, i.e., the optimal DTNEP.

6 Results and Discussion

In this section the tests are performed with the IEEE Garver test system [8], and with the Brazilian Southern system model [14][1]. In both cases, the stagnation of the algorithm was used as a stopping criterion. The STNEP found in [4, 12] as well as the DTNEP from [13] were compared to these results.

For both systems, 10 years was considered, i.e., 10 stages for the planning horizon; the annual rate of interest, $tx = 10\%$; the first-year demand equivalent to 50% of the final demand and linear growth; 1 MW was the maximum load shedding allowed; maximum load runoff equivalent to nominal. When the systems data is changed, it will be shown on the test descriptions and/or on the Table 1.

All the tests were realized using MATLAB 7.9.0 R2009B on the same Dell laptop with the following characteristics: Intel core i5-480 M, 2.67 GHz and 6.0 GB of RAM. Although there were different possible configurations, to reduce the computational effort and to save time, both systems were tested using the CHA. The minimum, maximum and media runtime for all these tests are presented in Table 2.

6.1 Garver System

Originally proposed by [8], this system, with 6 bus, 6 existing branches, 15 candidate branches and a total demand of 760 MW in the last stage, although small, illustrates the greatest difficulties encountered in solving the DTNEP problem. For example, the combinatorial explosion of solutions as expressed by (13).

To ease the computational effort in solving the problem, it is strongly recommended to apply the CHA and refine the candidate routes. Figure 2 shows the CHA effect on the sample. From the CHA based on the average loading rate, Ψ_{ij}, of all the inserted routes on feasible planning, it was possible to note relevance in routes 1-2, 1-6, 2-3, 3-5 and 4-6. On the other hand, when the CHA favors the analysis of the Lagrange multipliers

---

[1] More information about transmission expansion planning and both systems specifications can be found at https://sites.google.com/engenharia.ufjf.br/portfolioengenharia/pesquisa.

data, λ_{ij}, branches 1-2 and 1-6 were considered irrelevant. However, it was decided to join these sets to ensure robustness in the method.

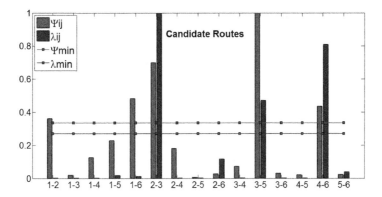

Fig. 2. Set of relevant routes for the Garver System defined by the CHA

After 300 simulations, the static block of optimization found the OSS in the literature: US$110M, allowing redispatch in generation; and US$200M without redispatch. The algorithm obtained success in 98.3% and 95.8%, respectively.

The yearly result of the DTNEP for the Garver system is shown on Table 1. Note that when three reinforcements were considered as the maximum limit of expansion per route, the total dynamic investment, avoiding the load shedding, is equivalent to US$81.896M. For $X_{max} = 2$, the best DTNEP found is US$87.948M of cost of investment. In the same order, the DTNEP using the same annual interest rate saving approximately 25.6% and 32.3% of expenses in relation to their STNEP. Still on the $X_{max} = 2$ case, the optimal DTNEP proposed in this work reached better results than those previously known in the literature [13].

Compared to [4, 12], the enhancement made on CHA and the initialization algorithm in parallel to the repetitions control technique on STNEP accelerated exponentially the effectiveness of the method as shown in Table 2.

6.2   The Southern Brazilian System

This real referred system was originally formed by 46 bus and 11 of them are insulated; 66 circuits in the base topology; 79 candidate paths and 6880 MW as expected demand. Initially proposed in [14], the Southern system has been widely used to validate results of new methods and purposes on the TNEP problem as studied by [4, 12].

For this system the best STNEP for $X_{max} = 3$ without generation redispatch has a total cost of investment of US$154.42M, corresponding to the addition of 16 new circuits. They are: 05-06 (2); 06-46 (1); 19-25 (1); 20-21 (1); 24-25 (2); 26-29 (3); 28-30(1); 29-30 (2); 31-32 (1); 42-43 (2). When the redispatch is allowed, for $X_{max} = 3$, the solution found is the same as the known literature US$70.289M, as in [4, 13].

Taking into account that the maximum loading assumed by the transmission lines was the nominal, 1 MW as the maximum load shedding allowed and maximum two reinforcements per route, this proposed method found US$42.524 to be the optimal DTNEP, according to Table 1. Such planning diverges from the US$38.94M found in [13]. However, when simulating the expansions proposed in [13], including the manual insertion of the reinforcements provided in their respective stages, in the 5th year a load shedding of more than 1 MW was observed in bus 9. It is highlighted that 1 MW is the Maximum cut-off value normally used in the specialized literature [5, 7, 12, 14] and therefore adopted in this work.

Table 1. Cost of investment comparation

Method	HS-B&B		HS-B&B		Lagrange		HS-B&B		Lagrange	
Static Invest.	Garver $X_{max} = 3$ US$110M		Garver $X_{max} = 2$ US$130M		Garver $X_{max} = 2$ US$130M		South $X_{max} = 3$ US$70.289M		South $X_{max} = 3$ US$70.289M	
Year	Routes	C_{ij}^t	Routes	C_{ij}^t	Routes	C_{ij}^t	Routes	C_{ij}^t	Routes	C_{ij}^t
1	4-6	30.00	2-3	20.00	2-3	20.00	–	–	–	–
2	–	–	–	–	–	–	–	–	–	–
3	–	–	3-5	16.53	3-5	16.53	20-21	6.75	20-21	6.75
4	4-6	22.54	–	–	4-6	22.53	–	–	–	–
5	–	–	4-6	20.49	–	–	5-6 6-46	16.52	5-6 13-20	6.07
6	3-5	12.42	–	–	–	–	–	–	6-46	9.93
7	4-6	16.93	4-6	16.93	4-6	16.93	42-43	4.62	42-43	4.61
8	–	–	–	–	–	–	5-6 20-21 20-23	11.61	5-6 13-20 20-23	7.77
9	–	–	2-6	14.00	2-6	14.00	–	–	20-21	3.81
10	–	–	–	–	–	–	13-20	3.02	–	–
Dynamic Invest.	US$81.892M		US$87.948M		US$89.99M		US$42.524M		US$38.94M	

The southern Brazilian system was simulated fifty times in each configuration. The required time on the Dynamic (DP) and Static Planning (SP) is presented in Table 2. When HS-B&B is compared to Particle Swarm Optimization (PSO) presented in [4] and to Bat Algorithm (BA) results found in [12], for both tested systems, the fastest STNEP provided by the hybrid HS-B&B algorithm converged to the optimal solution quicker than the BA and PSO. In some cases even the worst HS-B&B solution showed faster results than those compared to the metaheuristics. The great surprise is the runtime for the DTNEP southern Brazilian System. The Lagrange method used in [13], requires approximately three times more than HS-B&B to reach the optimal solution.

Table 2. Runtime comparison of all the different configurations tested for the systems

System	Redispatch	SP	DP	HS-B&B	Lagrange (mean)	BA (mean)	PSO (mean)
Garver $X_{max} = 3$	Not allowed	X		min 35 s max 124 s mean 102 s	–	165 s	192 s
Garver $X_{max} = 2$	Yes	X		min 17 s max 25 s mean 19 s	–	–	–
Garver $X_{max} = 2$	Yes		X	min 20 s max 30 s mean 24 s	–	–	–
Garver $X_{max} = 3$	Yes	X		min 19 s max 53 s mean 28 s	–	125 s	160 s
Garver $X_{max} = 3$	Yes		X	min 17 s max 24 s mean 20 s	–	–	–
South $X_{max} = 3$	Not allowed	X		min 351 s max 1030 s mean 562 s	–	–	1626 s
South $X_{max} = 3$	Yes	X		min 207 s max 690 s mean 303 s	–	278 s	992 s
South $X_{max} = 3$	Yes		X	min 499 s max 720 s mean 586 s	34 min 42 s or 2082 s	–	–

7 Conclusion

In this work, an enhancement is proposed to the method presented in [7] resulting in a hybrid HS-B&B algorithm most capable of solving the Dynamic Transmission Network Expansion Planning (DTNEP). As innovations, it is possible to list: the CHA was upgraded and uses not only the load rating to find the relevant routes but also information from Lagrange Mutipliers; the static stage was equipped with a logical to avoid test repetitions; the B&B insertion in the dynamic stage also allowed robustness and efficacy in the methodology. It can be seen when the time required to find an optimal solution is compared to other optimization techniques. In most cases the proposed method was faster than BA, PSO and the Lagrange method. Even in the worst cases, HS-B&B has shown an acceptable runtime.

Besides time saving, the proposed method also reached the known Optimal Static Solution (OSS) for both cases. Regarding the DTNEP, generally, 1 MW is the maximum load-shedding allowed in TNEP studies, as in [3, 4, 6, 8, 15] and therefore adopted in this work. Unfortunately, the solution obtained in [13] contemplates a load shedding higher than the maximum 1 MW tolerated in literature, thereby, making a comparison of the results impossible.

HS-B&B found the optimal solution in both tested systems and surpassed the expected results for computation time for the STNEP and DTNEP, thereby, proving the efficacy and robustness of the proposed method.

Lastly, it is possible to highlight some topics that will serve as a continuation of the present work: increase the CHA efficiency and test it on larger systems; insertion of losses in the transmission network; AC power flow analysis; and inclusion of uncertainties in generation and load.

Acknowledgments. The authors would like to thank to FAPDF, CAPES/CNPQ and Portfólio Engenharia for the financial support.

References

1. Portal Brasil. http://www.brasil.gov.br/meio-ambiente/2015/11/energia-renovavel-represen ta-mais-de-42-da-matriz-energetica-brasileira. Accessed 28 Apr 2017
2. EIA. https://www.eia.gov/beta/international. Accessed 28 Apr 2017
3. Villajuan Montes, C.V.: Modelos de Programação Linear Inteira Mista para Resolver Problemas de Planejamento de Expansão e de Operação de Sistemas de Transmissão de Energia Elétrica. M.Sc. UNESP, Ilha Solteira (2016)
4. Mendonça, I.M.: Identificação de Rotas Relevantes para o Planejamento Estático da Expansão de Sistemas de Transmissão de Energia Elétrica. Ph.D. UFJF, Juiz de Fora (2016)
5. Ribeiro, L.Y.O.: Análise do Planejamento Multi-etapa da Expansão da Transmissão de Sistemas Regionais. B.Sc. UFRJ, Rio de Janeiro (2017)
6. Rocha, M.J.C.: Transmission expansion planning, a multiyear approach considering uncertaintes, Ph.D. FEUP, Porto (2011)
7. De Oliveira, L.E., Mendonça, I.M., Da Silva Jr., I.C., Rosa, F.P.O.: Planejamento Dinâmico da Expansão de Transmissão de Sistemas Elétricos de Potência Utilizando o Algoritmo de Otimização Harmony Search, Anais do XX Congresso Brasileiro de Automática, Belo Horizonte, pp. 1761–1768 (2014)
8. Garver, L.L.: Transmission network estimation using linear programming. IEEE Trans. Power Appar. Syst. **PAS-89**(7), 1688–1697 (1970)
9. Yang, X.S.: Nature-Inspired Metaheuristic Algorithms, 2nd edn. Luniver Press, University of Cambridge, Cambridge (2010)
10. Assad, A., Deep, K.: Applications of harmony search algorithm in data mining: a survey. In: Pant, M., Deep, K., Bansal, J.C., Nagar, A., Das, K.N. (eds.) SocProS 2015. AISC, pp. 863–874. Springer, Singapore (2016). doi:10.1007/978-981-10-0451-3_77
11. Pessoa, T.C.: Estratégias Paralelas Inteligentes para o Método Branch-And-Bound Aplicadas ao Problema do Caixeiro Viajante. M.Sc. UECE, Fortaleza (2012)
12. Arêdes, C., Da Silva Jr., I.C., Mendonça, I.M., Dias, B.H., Oliveira, L.W.: Planejamento Estático da Expansão de Sistemas de Transmissão de Energia Elétrica Via Ecolocalização (2014)
13. Poubel, R.P.B.: Planejamento Dinâmico da Expansão de Sistemas de Transmissão de Energia Elétrica. M.Sc. dissertation. UFJF, Juiz de Fora. (2012)
14. Pereira, M.V., Pinto, L.M.: Application of sensitivity analysis of load supplying capability to interactive transmission expansion planning. IEEE Trans. Power Appar. Syst. **PAS-104**(2), 381–389 (1985)
15. Binato, S.: Expansão Ótima de Sistemas de Transmissão através de Decomposição de Benders e Técnicas de Planos Cortantes. Ph.D. COPPE – UFRJ, Rio de Janeiro (2000)

Nord Pool Ontology to Enhance Electricity Markets Simulation in MASCEM

Gabriel Santos[1(✉)], Tiago Pinto[2], Isabel Praça[1], and Zita Vale[1]

[1] GECAD - Research Group on Intelligent Engineering and Computing for Advanced Innovation and Development, Institute of Engineering - Polytechnic of Porto (ISEP/IPP), Rua Dr. António Bernardino de Almeida, 431, 4200-072 Porto, Portugal
{gajls,icp,zav}@isep.ipp.pt
[2] BISITE Research Group - University of Salamanca,
Calle Espejo, s/n, 37007 Salamanca, Spain
tpinto@usal.es

Abstract. This paper proposes the use of ontologies to enable information and knowledge exchange, to test different electricity market models and to allow players from different systems to interact in common market environments. Multi-agent based software is particularly well fitted to analyse dynamic and adaptive systems with complex interactions among its constituents, such as the complex and dynamic electricity markets. The main drivers are the markets' restructuring and evolution into regional and continental scales, along with the constant changes brought by the increasing necessity for an adequate integration of renewable energy sources. An ontology to represent the concepts related to the Nord Pool Elspot market is proposed. It is validated through a case study considering the simulation of Elspot market. Results show that heterogeneous agents are able to effectively participate in the simulation by using the proposed ontologies to support their communications with the Nord Pool market operator.

Keywords: Electricity markets · Multi-agent simulation · Nord Pool Elspot market · Semantic interoperability

1 Introduction

Real-world restructured electricity markets (EM) are sequential open-ended games with multiple participants trading for electric power. EM are extremely complex and dynamic environments due to their restructuring and evolution into regional and continental scale markets, along with the constant changes brought by the increasing necessity for an adequate integration of renewable energy sources [1,2].

With this restructuring EM became more competitive, posing new challenges to its participants and regulators, forcing them to rethink their behaviour and market strategies. Regulators need to experiment new market rules to detect inefficiencies before implementing them. Market players are very interested to understand its behaviour and operation to maximize their profits [1,3].

© Springer International Publishing AG 2017
E. Oliveira et al. (Eds.): EPIA 2017, LNAI 10423, pp. 283–294, 2017.
DOI: 10.1007/978-3-319-65340-2_24

Decision support simulation tools to address the new challenges became essential to these entities. Simulation and Artificial Intelligence techniques are required under this context. Simulators in this area must be able to deal with the dynamic and rapid evolution of EM and adopt new models and constraints of the market, providing players with adequate tools to adapt themselves to this changing environment. Multi-agent based simulators are particularly well suited for the analysis of complex interactions in dynamic and complex systems such as the EM [3].

Some of the main advantages that multi-agent approaches provide are the facilitated inclusion of new models, market mechanisms, player types, and different types of interactions [4]. In this domain some reference modelling tools have emerged, such as AMES (Agent-based Modelling of Electricity Systems) [5], EMCAS (Electricity Market Complex Adaptive System) [6] and MASCEM (Multi-Agent Simulator of Competitive Electricity Markets) [7,8].

MASCEM [7,8] is a modelling and simulation tool developed to study the complex and restructured EM. It supplies players with simulation and decision-support resources, providing them with competitive advantage in the market. It's multi-agent architecture models EM's complex entities, with their distinct characteristics, aims, and interactions.

Although several works have confirmed the adequate applicability of multi-agent simulation to the study of EM, they have a common limitation: the lack of interoperability between the various systems to allow the exchange of information and knowledge, to test different market models and to allow market players from different systems to interact in common market environments. Current tools are directed to the study of different EM mechanisms and to the analysis of the relationships between market entities, but they do not enable the interoperability with external systems.

These limitations point out the need for the interaction between agent-based simulators in the scope of EM. These simulators could gain significant added value by sharing their knowledge and market models with other agent societies. Such tools would provide the means for an actual improvement in current EM studies and development [9,10]. To overcome this issue the *Electricity Markets Ontology* (EMO) has been proposed in [11].

This article introduces the *Nord Pool Ontology* (NPO), an extension from EMO [11], developed to provide MASCEM with interoperability in the simulation of Nord Pool Elspot market.

After this introductory section, Sect. 2 presents related work on multi-agent interoperability, Nord Pool Spot market model, and agent-based EM simulation. Section 3 introduces the *Nord Pool Ontology* and Sect. 4 features a case study based on real data. Finally, Sect. 5 exposes the most relevant conclusions.

2 Related Work

Accordingly to the Foundation for Intelligent Physical Agents (FIPA), multi-agent systems should be able to interoperate. However, it does not mean that agents are able to exchange any useful information due to the use of different languages and vocabularies, specific to each domain, developer team and development platform [7]. It is required that they share a common vocabulary so the messages may be interpreted correctly among agents. Ontologies are used to this end, enabling the standardization of communications and interpretation of concepts between independent systems [7,11].

2.1 Multi-agent Interoperability

There are inherent difficulties in the integration of independently developed agent-based systems, especially to access and map private ontologies. This work has the purpose of disseminating the development of interoperable multi-agent simulators in the EM research area, enabling knowledge exchange between them in order to take full advantage of their functionalities, and promoting the adoption of a common semantic that enables the communication between heterogeneous systems. For that purpose EMO has been proposed [11]; a general ontology that gathers the main concepts of EM, so that it can be imported and extended by lower-level domain ontologies, facilitating mappings between them and the share of knowledge between systems.

EMO incorporates abstract concepts and axioms referring to the main existing EM, with the aim of being as inclusive as possible in order to be extended and reused in the development of market specific ontologies. It was kept as simple as possible to facilitate its reuse and extension independently of the market's features and/or rules. However, some markets' constraints were also defined, given that the suggested ontologies were developed considering its use by agent based simulation tools.

It is publicly available[1] to third-party developers who wish to reuse or extend it for new agent-based EM simulation tools; or even to integrate their agent-based simulators with MASCEM, taking advantage of its simulation capabilities and market models.

Two additional modules have been developed to enable semantic communications between the market operator and player agents [12]: (i) the *Call for Proposal* (CFP) ontology and (ii) the *Electricity Markets Results* (EMR) ontology. EMO defines the main concepts and axioms of EM, while CFP and EMR ontologies define *Requests*, *Responses* and *Informs* enabling a semantic interaction between the participating agents. CFP and EMR ontologies are also available online[2]. Further details about them can be found in [12].

2.2 Nord Pool Elspot Market

The Elspot market from Nord Pool is an auction based market, where both buyers and sellers present offers (symmetrical pool). The offers must be contained

---

[1] http://www.mascem.gecad.isep.ipp.pt/ontologies/electricity-markets.owl.
[2] http://www.mascem.gecad.isep.ipp.pt/ontologies/call-for-proposal.owl,
    http://www.mascem.gecad.isep.ipp.pt/ontologies/electricity-markets-results.owl.

in the price range set by Nord Pool Spot. Elspot enables three types of offers [13], namely:

- **Hourly Orders**: simple orders, which may contain up to 64 combinations of price/amount of energy for each hour of the auction;
- **Block Orders**: with the purpose of connecting various periods. The offer is accepted in all periods or is rejected altogether. These present a lower priority when compared to simple orders.
- **Flexible Hourly Orders**: give the opportunity to present sale offers only, without indicating a specific period for the same, *i.e.* these volumes can be transacted in any period of the day, depending on the offer price, and on the necessities of the market for each period.

Nord Pool [13,14], supports the submission of *Flexible hourly orders* in addition to *Block orders*. The supported *Block orders* intend to connect several periods on an all-or-none basis, meaning that the order is accepted in all periods or rejected altogether. *Block orders* have low priority when compared with *Hourly orders*. In turn, a *Flexible hourly order* is a single sale offer (purchases are not allowed) where sellers specify only the price and amount of energy to trade. The period is not indicated as this type of order is accepted in any period of the day, depending on the optimization of the overall socio-economic welfare of the market.

For flexible offers, trading occurs in the same way as with the hourly orders, and these deals will apply in the period when its use maximizes the overall market's social welfare. Regarding the block offers, they will be accepted if the market price of all periods in which the block applies is equal to, or higher than, the price of the block bid, for selling offers; or if the market price of the block periods is equal to, or less than, the price of the block, for purchasing bids. This condition is called *fill-or-kill*.

2.3 MASCEM Overview

MASCEM [7,8] is a modelling and simulation tool developed to study and simulate EM operation. It models the main market entities and their interactions. Medium/long-term gathering of data and experience is also considered to support players' decisions in accordance with their characteristics and goals. The main market entities are implemented as software agents, such as: market and system operators, buyer and seller agents (consumers, producers and/or prosumers), and aggregators. Figure 1 illustrates MASCEM's multi-agent model.

The Market Operator regulates pool negotiations by validating and analysing the players' bids depending on the type of negotiation, and determines the market price, the accepted and refused bids, and the economical dispatch that will be sent to the System Operator.

The System Operator examines the technical feasibility from the power system point of view and solves congestion problems that may arise. Is responsible for the system's security as well as to assure that all conditions are met within the system.

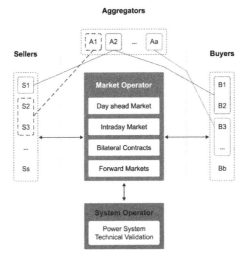

Fig. 1. MASCEM's multi-agent model [11]

Buyer and Seller agents are the key elements of EM. A Buyer agent may be a consumer or distribution company which participates in the EM in order to buy certain amounts of power. On the other hand, a Seller agent may simulate electricity producers or other entities able to sell energy in the market.

Aggregators, represent alliances of small independent players, enabling their participation in the wholesale EM and to compete with big players. They manage their aggregates' information and are seen from the market's point of view as buyer or seller agents.

The main types of negotiations normally present in EM included in MASCEM are: day-ahead and intraday pool (symmetric or asymmetric, with or without complex conditions) markets, bilateral contracts and forward markets. By selecting a combination of these market models, it is also possible to perform hybrid simulations.

For each scenario, the user must input the market and market type to simulate, the number of simulation days, the number of participating players and their strategies considering each type of agent, with their own decision-support resources, assuring them competitive advantage in the market. MASCEM allows the simulation of three of the main European EM: MIBEL[3], EPEX[4] and Nord Pool[5].

---

[3] http://www.mibel.com/.

[4] https://www.epexspot.com/.

[5] http://www.nordpoolspot.com/.

3   Nord Pool Ontology

The Nord Pool Ontology (NPO) imports EMO, extending its concepts and including some new classes, object and data properties. It is publicly available for reuse and extension[6]. Figure 2 highlights the classes (in yellow), object (in blue), and data properties (in green) included in NPO.

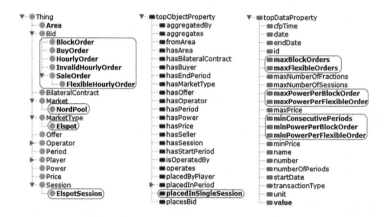

Fig. 2. *Nord Pool Ontology* classes, object and data properties (Color figure online)

NPO extends only concepts from EMO. The **BLockOrder**, **BuyOrder**, **HourlyOrder**, **InvalidHourlyOrder** and **SaleOrder** concepts are extended from **EMO:Bid**; in the same way as **NordPool**, **Elspot** and **ElspotSession** extend from **EMO:Market**, **EMO:MarketType** and **EMO:Session**, respectively. It is also possible to observe in Fig. 2 the **FlexibleHourlyOrder** concept (on the left column), included as a subclass of **SaleOrder**, meaning that it is only allowed as a sale bid. A new object property - placedInSingleSession - and seven new data properties (maxBlockOrders, maxFlexibleOrders, maxPowerPer BlockOrder, maxPowerPerFlexibleOrder, minConsecutivePeriods, minPowerPer BlockOrder and minPowerPerFlexibleOrder) were also included.

Figure 3[7] exposes the classes, object properties and data properties of NPO. The EMO's concepts are illustrated in yellow, and the prefix *"EMO:"* identifies EMO's object and data properties. The object properties of both EMO and NPO are identified in blue. As is possible to observe, in NPO, the **EMO:Area** is redefined including the new seven data properties of NPO.

NPO is used by players willing to participate in **Elspot** simulations through its market operator. Tables 1, 2 and 3 provide the description logic[8] (DL) syntaxes of its object and data properties, and classes. Similarly to EMO, NPO has expressiveness *ALCHIQ(D)* [11].

---

[6] http://www.mascem.gecad.isep.ipp.pt/ontologies/nordpool.owl.

[7] http://www.mascem.gecad.isep.ipp.pt/ontologies/paper/epia/17/npo.png.

[8] http://www.obitko.com/tutorials/ontologies-semantic-web/owl-dl-semantics.html.

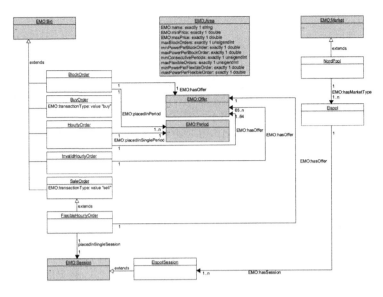

Fig. 3. *Nord Pool Ontology* (Color figure online)

Table 1. *Nord Pool Ontology* object property DL syntax

Object Property
placedInSingleSession $\sqsubseteq R$
$\top \sqsubseteq \, \leq 1$ placedInSingleSession

Table 2. *Nord Pool Ontology* data properties DL syntax

Data Properties	
maxBlockOrders $\sqsubseteq \cup$ $\top \sqsubseteq \, \leq 1$ maxBlockOrders	maxFlexibleOrders $\sqsubseteq \cup$ $\top \sqsubseteq \, \leq 1$ maxFlexibleOrders
maxPowerPerBlockOrder $\sqsubseteq \cup$ $\top \sqsubseteq \, \leq 1$ maxPowerPerBlockOrder	maxPowerPerFlexibleOrder $\sqsubseteq \cup$ $\top \sqsubseteq \, \leq 1$ maxPowerPerFlexibleOrder
minPowerPerBlockOrder $\sqsubseteq \cup$ $\top \sqsubseteq \, \leq 1$ minPowerPerBlockOrder	minPowerPerFlexibleOrder $\sqsubseteq \cup$ $\top \sqsubseteq \, \leq 1$ minPowerPerFlexibleOrder
minConsecutivePeriods $\sqsubseteq \cup$ $\top \sqsubseteq \, \leq 1$ minConsecutivePeriods	

Table 3. *Nord Pool Ontology* classes DL syntax

Classes
Area ⊑ **EMO:Area** ⊓ 1 maxBlockOrders ⊓ 1 maxPowerPerBlockOrder ⊓ 1 minPowerPerBlockOrder ⊓ 1 minConsecutivePeriods ⊓ 1 maxFlexibleOrders ⊓ 1 maxPowerPerFlexibleOrder ⊓ 1 minPowerPerFlexibleOrder
BuyOrder ⊑ **EMO:Bid** ⊓ EMO:transactionType "buy"
SaleOrder ⊑ **EMO:Bid** ⊓ EMO:transactionType "sell"
BlockOrder ⊑ **EMO:Bid** ⊓ ∃ EMO:hasOffer 1 **EMO:Offer** ⊓ ∃ EMO:placedInPeriod 1 **EMO:Period**
HourlyOrder ⊑ **EMO:Bid** ⊓ ∃ EMO:hasOffer ≤ 64 **EMO:Offer** ⊓ ∃ EMO:placedInSinglePeriod 1 **EMO:Period**
InvalidHourlyOrder ⊑ **EMO:Bid** ⊓ ∃ EMO:hasOffer ≥ 65 **EMO:Offer**
FlexibleOrder ⊑ **SaleOrder** ⊓ ∃ EMO:hasOffer 1 **EMO:Offer** ⊓ ∃ placedInSingleSession 1 **EMO:Session**
ElspotSession ⊑ **EMO:Session**
Elspot ⊑ **EMO:MarketType** ⊓ ∃ EMO:hasSession **ElspotSession**
NordPool ⊑ **EMO:Market** ⊓ ∃ EMO:hasMarketType **Elspot**

The **Area** is redefined to include new data properties related with the Nord Pool Elspot EM, namely maxBlockOrders, maxPowerPerBlockOrder, minPowerPerBlockOrder, minConsecutivePeriods, maxFlexibleOrders, maxPowerPerFlexibleOrder and minPowerPerFlexibleOrder. Each area determines these values considering its particular constraints. On the other hand, enabling a greater flexibility of parameterizations enables more valuable and richer simulations.

BuyOrder and **SaleOrder** are subclasses of **EMO:Bid**, being defined by the transactionType data property, which is equal to "buy" or "sell" respectively. **BlockOrder** is also subclass of **EMO:Bid** but only comprises an **EMO:Offer** valid for an interval of **EMO:Period**s, using the EMO:hasOffer and EMO:placed-InPeriod respectively.

The **HourlyOrder** is also subclass of **EMO:Bid** but including a maximum number of 64 **EMO:Offer**s; and it only can be related to a **EMO:Period**, making use of the EMO:placedInSinglePeriod *Functional*[9] object property. In turn, an **InvalidHourlyOrder** is defined as a **EMO:Bid** with 65 or more **EMO:Offer**s.

The **FlexibleHourlyOrder** is subclass of **SaleOrder** and only accepts one **EMO:Offer** which can be only assigned to a **EMO:Session**, using the object properties EMO:hasOffer and placedInSingleSession, respectively. The placedInSingleSession object property is also *Functional*. The **FlexibleHourly-Order** may be seen as a complex condition only available for sellers, similarly to

---

[9] A functional property is a property that only relates the same subject to one single object/value.

the day-ahead complex conditions of MIBEL, which are only allowed for seller agents[10].

The **ElspotSession** is subclass of **EMO:Session**; and **Elspot** is subclass of **EMO:MarketType**, including the **ElspotSession** using the object property EMO:hasSession. The **NordPool** concept is subclass of **EMO:Market** and includes the **Elspot** market type with the object property EMO:hasMarketType.

The next section presents a case study to demonstrate NPO's use to support players' participation in Elspot market.

4   Case Study

The case study is based on a scenario generated by RealScen (Realistic Scenarios Generator) [15], using real data extracted from several European market operators, with the tool [16]. The scenario was created with the intention of representing the Nord Pool Elspot market reality through a summarized group of players, considering data of 25th July 2012. It includes 41 buyers and 41 sellers, resulting in a total of 82 players.

As the simulation starts, MASCEM's Main Agent reads the input file to generate the involved players and their knowledge base (KB) files. After being created, each agent receives a message from MASCEM's Main Agent with its KB represented in RDF/XML[11].

```
1   <?xml version="1.0" encoding="UTF-8" standalone="no"?>
2   <rdf:RDF
3     xmlns:cfp="http://www.mascem.gecad.isep.ipp.pt/ontologies/call-for-proposal.owl#"
4     xmlns:emo="http://www.mascem.gecad.isep.ipp.pt/ontologies/electricity-markets.owl#"
5     xmlns:nordpool="http://www.mascem.gecad.isep.ipp.pt/ontologies/nordpool.owl#"
6     xmlns:owl="http://www.w3.org/2002/07/owl#"
7     xmlns:rdf="http://www.w3.org/1999/02/22-rdf-syntax-ns#"
8     xmlns:rdfs="http://www.w3.org/2000/01/rdf-schema#"
9     xmlns:xsd="http://www.w3.org/2001/XMLSchema#"
10    xml:base="http://www.mascem.gecad.isep.ipp.pt/ontologies/">
11    <rdf:Description rdf:about="nordpool.owl#iMO-NORDPOOL_2012_07_25">
12      <emo:name>NORDPOOL 2012 07 25</emo:name>
13      <rdf:type rdf:resource="electricity-markets.owl#MarketOperator"/>
14    </rdf:Description>
15    <rdf:Description rdf:about="nordpool.owl#iPrice1-P22-ElspotSession2012-07-25-0">
16      <emo:value rdf:datatype="http://www.w3.org/2001/XMLSchema#double">9.86
        </emo:value>
17      <emo:unit>EUR</emo:unit>
18      <rdf:type rdf:resource="electricity-markets.owl#Price"/>
19    </rdf:Description>
```

Fig. 4. Proposal sent by Seller 22

The market session begins with the market operators sending the call for proposals (CfP) to all registered players. After, each player queries its KB in

---

[10] http://www.omie.es/en/home/markets-and-products/electricity-market/our-electricity-markets/daily-market.

[11] XML syntax to represent a Resource Description Framework (RDF) graph.

order to send its proposal to the market operator. Figure 4 shows a snippet of
the market proposal sent by Seller 22. The complete version is available online[12].

After receiving all the proposals and validating incoming offers, the market
operator analyses the bids, executes the market algorithm, and generates the result
RDF/XML files to be sent to the participating players. Figure 5 presents the result
sent by the market operator to Seller 22 (in RDF/XML); also available online[13].

```
1    <?xml version="1.0" encoding="UTF-8" standalone="no"?>
2    <rdf:RDF
3      xmlns:emo="http://www.mascem.gecad.isep.ipp.pt/ontologies/electricity-markets.owl#"
4      xmlns:emr="
       http://www.mascem.gecad.isep.ipp.pt/ontologies/electricity-markets-results.owl#"
5      xmlns:nordpool="http://www.mascem.gecad.isep.ipp.pt/ontologies/nordpool.owl#"
6      xmlns:owl="http://www.w3.org/2002/07/owl#"
7      xmlns:rdf="http://www.w3.org/1999/02/22-rdf-syntax-ns#"
8      xmlns:rdfs="http://www.w3.org/2000/01/rdf-schema#"
9      xmlns:xsd="http://www.w3.org/2001/XMLSchema#"
10     xml:base="http://www.mascem.gecad.isep.ipp.pt/ontologies/">
11     <rdf:Description rdf:about="electricity-markets-results.owl#iFlexibleResult-2">
12       <emo:hasPrice rdf:resource=
         "electricity-markets-results.owl#iMarketPrice-FlexibleResult-2"/>
13       <emo:hasPower rdf:resource=
         "electricity-markets-results.owl#iTradedPower-FlexibleResult-2"/>
14       <emr:periodNumber rdf:datatype="http://www.w3.org/2001/XMLSchema#unsignedInt">2
         </emr:periodNumber>
15       <rdf:type rdf:resource="electricity-markets-results.owl#FlexibleResult"/>
16     </rdf:Description>
17     <rdf:Description rdf:about=
         "electricity-markets-results.owl#iTradedPower-FlexibleResult-11">
18       <emo:unit>MW</emo:unit>
19       <emo:value rdf:datatype="http://www.w3.org/2001/XMLSchema#double">0.0</emo:value>
20       <rdf:type rdf:resource="electricity-markets-results.owl#TradedPower"/>
21     </rdf:Description>
```

Fig. 5. Result sent to Seller 22 by Elspot's market operator

Figure 6 illustrates the market result for Seller 22. In this market, Seller 22
uses three flexible hourly orders. These flexible hourly orders (available only
to seller agents), allow the players to specify a fixed price and volume. The
hour is not specified. The order will be accepted in the hour that optimizes the
socioeconomic welfare of the market. In this scenario three orders were submitted
with the volume of 2000 MWh each, all at the same price of 40€/MWh.

It is possible to observe from the chart of Fig. 6 that during the first twenty
one periods none of the orders was accepted although bid price being below the
established market price. The light yellow bars indicate a total of 6000 MWh of
unsold energy during these periods (referring to the total of the three flexible
offers, of 2000 MWh each). All flexible hourly orders were accepted in the 22nd
period. Only the block orders were unsatisfied in all of the 24 hourly periods.
As mentioned before, the condition for the acceptance of each (or all) flexible
offer(s) is not only the proposed bid price, but also the maximization of the
socioeconomic welfare of the market session, from the market operator's perspective. Additionally, the use of the proposed ontology allows inferring market
rules from the contained information. Taking these rules into account, behaviours
can be modelled and adapted.

---

[12] http://www.mascem.gecad.isep.ipp.pt/ontologies/paper/epia/17/proposal.rdf.
[13] http://www.mascem.gecad.isep.ipp.pt/ontologies/paper/epia/17/result.rdf.

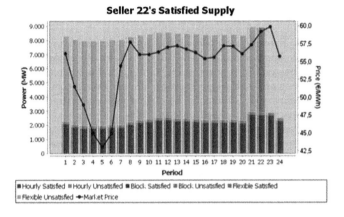

Fig. 6. Result achieved by Seller 22 (Color figure online)

5   Conclusions

This work disseminates the development of interoperable multi-agent simulators in the EM research area, thus enabling knowledge exchange between them in order to take full advantage of their functionalities, and promoting the adoption of a common semantic that enables the communication between these systems.

Opening the simulation environment to other systems enables the integration of different market models and allows agents, from heterogeneous systems, to be able to interact in joint simulations. For such, it is mandatory that the messages exchanged by the involved agents may be properly interpreted. The realism and depth of EM and power systems' studies can benefit in a large scale from the cooperation between the different platforms.

The *EMO* has been developed to achieve systems interoperability. It is the base ontology from which other domain specific ontologies were extended, such as the *CFP*, *EMR* and *NPO*. The first two are common ontologies for EM operation, while the last one is related to the Nord Pool EM model included in MASCEM. The developed ontologies are publicly available to be easily reused and extended by ontology engineers EM scope.

The integration of the proposed ontologies provides an enhanced platform to study and explore the implications and consequences of new and already existing approaches in EM. The presented case study illustrates the use and usefulness of the developed module, being given emphasis to the communications exchanged between agents instead of the achieved market's results.

Acknowledgments. This work has received funding from the European Union's Horizon 2020 research and innovation programme under the Marie Sklodowska-Curie grant agreement No. 641794 (project DREAM-GO) and from FEDER Funds through COMPETE program and from National Funds through FCT under the project UID/EEA/00760/2013.

294 G. Santos et al.

References

1. Sioshansi, F.P.: Evolution of Global Electricity Markets-New Paradigms, New Challenges, New Approaches, pp. 645–677. Academic Press, Amsterdam (2013)
2. Sharma, K.C., Bhakar, R., Tiwari, H.P.: Strategic bidding for wind power producers in electricity markets. Energy Convers. Manag. **86**, 259–267 (2014)
3. Meeus, L., Purchalaa, K., Belmans, R.: Development of the internal electricity market in Europe. Electr. J. **18**(6), 25–35 (2005)
4. Santos, G., et al.: Multi-agent simulation of competitive electricity markets: autonomous systems cooperation for European market modelling. Energy Convers. Manage. **99**, 387–399 (2015)
5. Li, H., Tesfatsion, L.: Development of open source software for power market research: the AMES test bed. J. Energy Mark. **2**, 111–128 (2009)
6. Koritarov, V.: Real-world market representation with agents: modeling the electricity market as a complex adaptive system with an agent-based approach. IEEE Power Energy Mag. **2**, 39–46 (2004)
7. Santos, G., Pinto, T., Praça, I., Vale, Z.: MASCEM: optimizing the performance of a multi-agent system. Energy **111**, 513–524 (2016)
8. Praça, I., Ramos, C., Vale, Z., Cordeiro, M.: MASCEM: a multi-agent system that simulates competitive electricity markets. IEEE Intell. Syst. **18**, 54–60 (2003)
9. Alvarado-Pérez, J.C., Peluffo-Ordóñez, D.H., Therón, R.: Bridging the gap between human knowledge and machine learning. Adv. Distrib. Comput. Artif. Intell. J. **4**(1) (2015). Salamanca University Press Journal
10. Frikha, M., Mhiri, M., Gargour, F.: A semantic social recommender system using ontologies based approach for tunisian tourism. Adv. Distrib. Comput. Artif. Intell. J. **4**(1) (2015). Salamanca University Press Journal
11. Santos, G., Pinto, T., Vale, Z., Praça, I., Morais, H.: Enabling communications in heterogeneous multi-agent systems: electricity markets ontology. Adv. Distrib. Comput. Artif. Intell. J. (ADCAIJ) **5**(2) (2016). Salamanca University Press Journal
12. Santos, G., Pinto, T., Praça, I., Vale, Z.: An interoperable approach for energy systems simulation: electricity market participation ontologies. Energies **9**(11), 878 (2016)
13. Nord Pool Spot - Trading, Day-ahead market Elspot (2017). http://www.nordpoolspot.com/TAS/Day-ahead-market-Elspot/. Accessed Apr 2016
14. Fernandes, R., Santos, G., Praça, I., Pinto, T., Morais, H., Pereira, I.F., Vale, Z.: Elspot: nord pool spot integration in MASCEM electricity market simulator. In: Corchado, J.M., et al. (eds.) PAAMS 2014. CCIS, vol. 430, pp. 262–272. Springer, Cham (2014). doi:10.1007/978-3-319-07767-3_24
15. Teixeira, B., Silva, F., Pinto, T., Praça, I., Santos, G., Vale Z.: Data mining approach to support the generation of realistic scenarios for multi-agent simulation of electricity markets. In: 2014 IEEE Symposium on Intelligent Agents (IA) at the IEEE SSCI 2014. IEEE Symposium Series on Computational Intelligence, Orlando, Florida, USA, pp. 9–12, December 2014
16. Pereira, I.F., Sousa, T.M., Praça, I., Freitas, A., Pinto, T., Vale, Z., Morais, H.: Data extraction tool to analyse, transform and store real data from electricity markets. In: Omatu, S., Bersini, H., Corchado, J.M., Rodríguez, S., Pawlewski, P., Bucciarelli, E. (eds.) Distributed Computing and Artificial Intelligence, 11th International Conference. AISC, vol. 290, pp. 387–395. Springer, Cham (2014). doi:10.1007/978-3-319-07593-8_45

Electricity Rate Planning for the Current Consumer Market Scenario Through Segmentation of Consumption Time Series

Alfredo Vellido$^{(\boxtimes)}$ and David L. García

Department of Computer Science, Universitat Politècnica de Catalunya,
08034 Barcelona, Spain
avellido@cs.upc.edu

Abstract. The current European legislation requires households the installation of smart metering systems. These will eventually allow electric utilities to gather richly detailed data of consumption. In this scenario, the implementation of data mining procedures for actionable knowledge extraction could be the key to competitive advantage. These may take the form of market segmentation using clustering techniques for the identification of customer behaviour patterns of electricity consumption that could justify the definition of tailored tariffs. In this brief paper, we show that the combination of a standard clustering algorithm with a similarity measure specifically defined for non-i.i.d. data, namely Dynamic Time Warping, can reveal an actionable segmentation of a real consumer market, combining business criteria and quantitative evaluation.

Keywords: Time series · Dynamic Time Warping · x-Means · k-Shape · Electric utility · Load curves · Tariff personalization

1 Introduction

Following the process of deregularization of the Spanish energy markets that took place in 1997, the main challenge electric utilities nowadays face is the implementation of a feasible hourly rating system. With a system in operation since January 2016, Spain has pioneered the process of billing electricity customers depending on both their hourly electricity consumption and the price of the electricity at that same time interval. In order to make this possible, customers must have digital smart meters integrated in the system.

At the time of writing, more than 11 million Spanish households already have this kind of smart meters installed, and the authorities aim to replace all remaining standard electricity meters before 2018 [1]. This must be understood in the context of the global introduction of smart meters in European countries, which is not just the result of technological evolution but, mostly, a process associated with the application of EU legislation: The EU directive 2006/32/EC [2],

© Springer International Publishing AG 2017
E. Oliveira et al. (Eds.): EPIA 2017, LNAI 10423, pp. 295–306, 2017.
DOI: 10.1007/978-3-319-65340-2_25

in particular, enforces that, by 2020, at least 80% of households should have smart metering systems installed.

In this rapidly evolving scenario, electricity supply is quickly turning into a data-rich environment that justifies the implementation of data mining procedures. One instantiation of data analysis in this market is its segmentation using clustering techniques [3] for the identification of homogeneous customer behaviour patterns of electricity consumption. Such clustering-based segmentation process can lead to the definition of tariffs specifically tailored to given electricity consumption prototypical patterns. In the immediate future, such level of tariff personalization might be one of the few ways for electric utilities to retain a competitive advantage against competitors in a liberalized market.

For this paper, we investigated different strategies for the clustering of the hourly consumption curves (for a residential market) of customers of one of the main Spanish electric utilities. A sample of over two thousand customers with regular electrical consumption was used in our experiments to group them according to the similarity of their consumption profiles as a basis for the segmentation of their market. First, we used the standard k-Means algorithm with Dynamic Time Warping (DTW) as a measure of distance between consumption time series; this is a technique that has already provided useful results in this domain [4,5]. The x-Means clustering algorithm [6] was then used to estimate the optimal number of clusters for data partitioning, starting from the previously obtained solution as validated by market experts. Second, we applied k-Shape [7], a novel method for time series clustering, for comparison.

2   Electricity Consumption Customer Data

The data available for this study consists of records of hourly electricity consumption from December 1st, 2013 to November 30th, 2014. The database includes a sample of 2,030 customers with a consumption of over 50 kWh for each month of the year, a threshold selected by domain experts as the minimum consumption amount to be considered significant. Additionally to the consumption data, we have, for each customer, information on their current type of tariff and the geographical location (autonomous community and province). Finally, and in order to analyze the obtained results in business terms, the hourly energy cost for the same period of time is also available.

An additional issue to take into account is data normalization, so that different customers can be properly compared from the distribution of his consumption over time, not its magnitude. Therefore, a method able to preserve the shape of the consumption curve is required. The simple data normalization in our experiments consisted on dividing each value of hourly consumption by the total daily consumption of the customer.

3   Methods

3.1   Dynamic Time Warping

Dynamic Time Warping (DTW) provides a similarity measure between two temporal sequences, calculating the optimal match among them with certain restrictions [10]. The sequences are warped non-linearly in the time dimension to determine a measure of their similarity that is independent of certain non-linear variations in the time dimension. The parameter that rules the maximum distance (in terms of time) that can separate a possible match between two points from different time series (i.e. admissible warping level) is called *warping window* parameter (w). Hence, a DTW algorithm with a w value of 0 will behave as if we are using Euclidean distance to compute similarities because no distortion in the time-axis is allowed. This similarity can thus be used in classical clustering or classification algorithms. Centroid estimation though, becomes a problem. For the Euclidean distance, finding a centroid is as simple as calculating the arithmetic mean of each attribute over the data. For DTW, though, the arithmetic mean will not yield a centroid with minimum DTW distance to all data instances. That is why it is necessary to use DTW Barycenter Averaging (DBA) [8], an iterative algorithm which converges to the real centroid of time series measured with DTW. For the readers' benefit, further details about DTW can be found, for instance in [9]. DTW has already shown promise in the field of electricity consumption cluster analysis [4,5].

The k-Means algorithm consists of two steps that are iteratively repeated until converge occurs: the first step assigns each series to a cluster according to the distance to the centroids (it is here where we substitute the standard Euclidean distance by the DTW distance). In the second step, cluster centroids are updated by averaging the instances (series) assigned to each one. For this process, DBA is used instead of a regular arithmetic mean.

3.2   X-Means

Unlike the standard k-Means algorithm, one of its extensions, namely x-Means [6], was designed to provide an estimation of the most appropriate number of clusters. To do so, it evaluates a range of possible values for the number of clusters, starting with the lowest, and adding extra clusters iteratively until it reaches the maximum number set.

The algorithm starts from a regular k-Means, with as many clusters as the lower bound of the range of clusters to test (in our experiments, reported next, with the k-Means clusters validated by domain experts). A further k-Means process is carried out in each one of the clusters, splitting each of them in two. Both prior and posterior solutions are evaluated using the Bayesian Information Criterion (BIC). Then, if the split yields a higher BIC, it is preserved. The process is repeated until the maximum established number of clusters is reached or when splits do not improve results significantly any longer. Once the whole process is concluded, the BIC is calculated for each of the global cluster solutions obtained in the process and the best one is selected.

3.3   K-Shape

The k-Shape algorithm was recently developed as a domain-independent, accurate, and scalable clustering method for time series clustering, using a distance measure that is invariant to scaling and shifting. It is a centroid-based clustering method that is able to preserve the *shape* of the temporal sequences. It is inspired on k-Means, and it therefore consists of two main steps, namely time series shape similarity calculation for cluster assignment, and time series shape extraction to obtain centroids. Just as k-Means, these two steps are repeated iteratively until a convergence criterion is met.

As a distance measure, this algorithm proposes a method able to handle distortions in amplitude and phase, a normalized version of the cross-correlation measure. This measure is widely used for signal and image processing, but has been mostly ignored for time series comparison. The Cross-correlation is a statistical measure with which it is possible to determine similarity between two sequences even if they are not properly aligned. It considers all possible shifts among both series and calculates the scalar product of each shift, producing a cross-correlation sequence. This is defined as:

$$CC_w(\boldsymbol{x}, \boldsymbol{y}) = R_{w-m}(\boldsymbol{x}, \boldsymbol{y}), w \in 1, 2, \ldots, 2m - 1 \tag{1}$$

Where w is the shift, $\boldsymbol{x}$ and $\boldsymbol{y}$ are the signals, m is their length, and R_{w-m} is computed as:

$$R_k = \begin{cases} \sum_{l=1}^{m-k} x_{l+k} \cdot y_l, & k \geq 0 \\ R_{-k}(\boldsymbol{x}, \boldsymbol{y}), & k \leq 0 \end{cases} \tag{2}$$

The point where this sequence is maximized is the optimal shifting among the sequences. This is a similarity measure, though, not a distance. The Shape-based distance (SBD) is defined as an inverse of the normalized cross-correlation measure:

$$SBD(\boldsymbol{x}, \boldsymbol{y}) = 1 - \max_w \left(\frac{CC_w(\boldsymbol{x}, \boldsymbol{y})}{\sqrt{R_0(\boldsymbol{x}, \boldsymbol{x}) \cdot R_0(\boldsymbol{y}, \boldsymbol{y})}} \right) \tag{3}$$

Then, time series shape extraction entails finding a series that minimizes the distance to all the instances of the cluster, that is:

$$\boldsymbol{\mu}_k = \arg\min_{\boldsymbol{\mu}_k} \sum_{\boldsymbol{x} \in P_k} SBD(\boldsymbol{x}, \boldsymbol{\mu}_k), \tag{4}$$

which is equivalent to the maximization of the normalized cross-correlation measure from the centroid to each sequence:

$$\boldsymbol{\mu}_k = \arg\max_{\boldsymbol{\mu}_k} \sum_{\boldsymbol{x} \in P_k} \left(\frac{\max_w CC_w(\boldsymbol{x}, \boldsymbol{\mu}_k)}{\sqrt{R_0(\boldsymbol{x}, \boldsymbol{x}) \cdot R_0(\boldsymbol{\mu}_k, \boldsymbol{\mu}_k)}} \right)^2 \tag{5}$$

Through some mathematical analysis, this problem can be reduced to a well-known problem called maximization of the Rayleigh quotient.

4   Experiments

Each customer in the original database is represented by an electricity consumption vector of length $8,760$, corresponding to each hour of the available year period. From a preliminary exploration of this database, a few general patterns clearly emerged: seasonality was observed, with neatly differing patterns for the spring-summer and autumn-winter periods (mostly due to variation in usage of air conditioning and heating systems). Focusing in detail on the behaviour of each client during the year, we found that their pattern is almost identical month by month; most of them ($65,6\%$) experiences zero or one changes of pattern, mainly due to seasonality factors. And, moreover, the ones that experience two or more jumps they do it among similar patterns.

Differences were also evident when comparing weekends/holidays and working days. Given that the aim of this paper is finding out about the feasibility of a clustering strategy as the basis for the design of tailored tariffication plans, we decided to restrict our experiments to the daily series of the working days of a single month, namely July 2014, leaving the investigation of seasonality and working vs. non-working periods effects for future research.

Furthermore, consumption in working days was found, for each customer, to be very homogeneous across the month, as the hourly variation of consumption for more than 90% of customers does not deviate more than a 5% from their month average in 20 out of 24 hours, during at least 20 of the working days of a given month. For this reason, instead of using the complete month vector, we used the daily consumption average over a month (a vector of 24 elements) for each customer. Several experiments were performed, described next:

I. Customer clustering was first carried out using the k-Means algorithm, with DTW as the measure of distance between series. Experiments with values of k from 2 to 7 were performed. The limit of seven was imposed because a higher number of clusters would not make sense from a business point of view, given that too high a number of different tariffs was not considered practical by the utility market experts. Each of the segmentation solutions was assessed by these domain experts, and the selection of the most adequate number of clusters (i.e. segments) was made on the basis of this assessment, which also took into account the hourly energy cost, estimated as:

$$\bar{c}_k = \frac{1}{N_k} \sum_i^{N_k} c \cdot x_{ki}, \quad k = 1, \ldots, K \tag{6}$$

where N_k is the number of instances in cluster k and c is the mean hourly energy cost for July, 2014.

II. Once the optimal number of clusters was chosen, we performed a detailed analysis of the impact in the variation of the window parameter (w) in the DTW phase over the final clustering result. The higher the window parameter, the more time distortion of the consumption series we allow in order to find matches with other curves. We finally used these experiments to decide the optimal size of the window parameter.

III. The solution chosen by the experts was then fed to the x-Means algorithm. With this, we aimed to test if there was also a quantitative criterion to either support the decision of the experts, or suggest a further partition of the data. This can be done because x-Means uses BIC to assess the most adequate cluster partition. These results were further evaluated using the hourly energy cost described in the previous paragraph, in order to find out whether the estimation provided by this algorithm was also useful from a business viewpoint.

IV. Finally, the experiments in I were replicated using the k-Shape algorithm to compare the performance of the algorithms in terms of business applicability, allowing the choice of the most appropriate one.

In all the experiments, the obtained results were analyzed by the domain experts taking into account the shapes of the cluster centroids, as well as their interpretability, the distribution of customers across clusters and their economical significance. To enhance the interpretability of the resulting clusters, the mean curve of the energy consumption is shown for each cluster in the results reported next.

4.1   Results and Discussion

I. The results of the application of k-Means with DTW to the clustering of the pre-processed data are shown in Fig. 1. The six plots correspond to each one of the clustering solutions with $k = 2, \ldots, 7$. These clusters were studied by domain experts to assess their business interpretability and applicability for tariff personalization. Additionally, the highest energy cost differential among the clusters was calculated, as a measure of the inter-cluster economic heterogeneity. Both results are shown in Table 1 and, according to them, experts chose the optimal number of clusters to be five, as the corresponding segmentation offers very good business interpretability, while achieving a high cost differential among clusters. Although this differential is even higher for the 7 clusters solution, the size of the smallest cluster is too small for practical tariff personalization purposes.

Table 1. General characteristics of the different cluster solutions obtained through k-Means with DTW. The distribution shows the proportion of the data for the biggest and smallest clusters.

# of clusters	Business interpretability	Distribution	ΔCost
2	Poor	84.4%/15.6%	2.3%
3	Good	67.3%/3.5%	4.7%
4	Good	43.6%/6.0%	5.8%
5	Very good	43.4%/3.5%	11.4%
6	Very good	32.4%/3.2%	11.3%
7	Good	31.2%/1.1%	14.9%

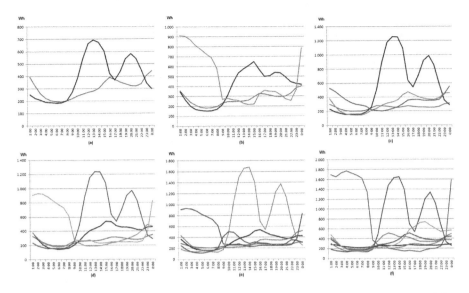

Fig. 1. Results of the clustering performed by k-Means with DTW distance. (a) 2 clusters, (b) 3 clusters, (c) 4 clusters, (d) 5 clusters, (e) 6 clusters, (f) 7 clusters.

The selected clustering solution is shown in more detail in Fig. 2, accompanied with a summary of the cluster characteristics in Table 2. This table includes the resulting customer segments, labeled for commercial purposes, together with the cluster relative size and the mean energy cost for each cluster. The algorithm, even if simple, provides useful and actionable results from a business perspective, as it allows to define five different tariffs with significant economic differential.

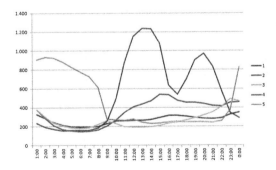

Fig. 2. Five-cluster solution selected by the domain experts, shown in more detail.

II. Once the first experiment led us to an optimal number of clusters of five, we check if an eventual variation of the window parameter (w) in the DTW algorithm would lead us to a better result. In order to do so, we repeat a five-cluster segmentation varying this parameter w from 1 to 6. As visible from Fig. 3,

Table 2. Labels assigned to each of the clusters in the expert-selected solution, together with the relative size of each cluster and their average energy cost.

# of clusters	Label	Distribution	Cost (c/kWh)
1	Homogeneous consumption	43.35%	5.73
2	Consumption from noon	37.34%	5.92
3	Evening consumption	9.75%	5.75
4	Meal times double peak	6.11%	5.99
5	Nighttime consumption	3.45%	5.38

the final cluster centroids vary depending on the value of this factor, and the most unstable is the one that explains the nighttime consumption pattern. This can be explained by the fact that clients with a "polarized behaviour" during the day (important *peaks* and *valleys*, as in the case of nighttime consumption segment) tend to be attracted by smoothed centroids. Further, this absorption is aggravated for clusters with few clients, because the change of their cluster assignations entails a significant variation of their centroids.

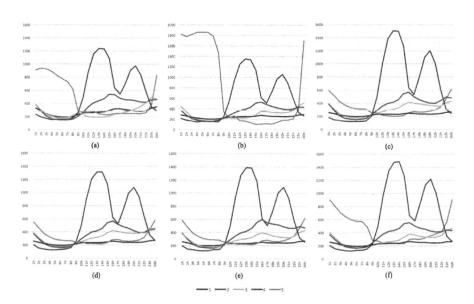

Fig. 3. Consumption centroids of 5-cluster segmentation, varying the warping window size. (a) $w = 1$, (b) $w = 2$, (c) $w = 3$, (d) $w = 4$, (e) $w = 5$, (f) $w = 6$.

In Fig. 3(b) the effect explained above takes place: the nighttime consumption cluster appears with a rise in areas of high values but, in contrast, the cluster size diminishes from 124 clients (using $w = 1$) to 23 (using $w = 2$). Although the second result could seem better in terms of clustering quality, it makes no sense from a business point of view, because of its extremely small size. In the end, the warping window parameter was set to a value of 1.

III. This 5-cluster solution with a DTW warping window parameter set to 1 is now used as the basis for refinement using x-Means. We investigate if the BIC and cost criteria previously described justify any further split of the segments. Figure 4 displays the values of BIC as the number of clusters increase. Results for up to 22 clusters are shown. Higher BIC values indicate a better solution. The best one would thus be one with 19 clusters. As previously mentioned, though, a solution with too many sparsely populated clusters is useless from the business point of view, as seen in Table 3 where the last 8 clusters consist of less that 2% of the customers, and because their small differences in cost would not justify differentiated marketing actions.

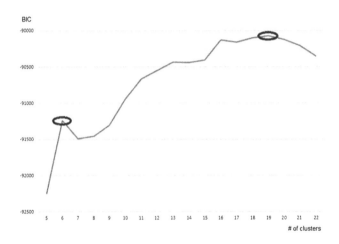

Fig. 4. BIC values for x-Means solutions of up to 22 clusters using the previously validated 5-cluster solution as a starting point. Two solutions are highlighted: that with the highest BIC value although impractical from a tariffication viewpoint, and that with an appropriate compromise between BIC, cost and real applicability.

Table 3. Cluster sizes for the optimal solution estimated by x-Means.

Cluster	1	2	3	4	5	6	7	8	9
Size	21.3%	16.3%	11.4%	10.8%	8.0%	6.1%	5.4%	4.9%	4.1%

10	11	12	13	14	15	16	17	18	19
3.2%	3.0%	1.5%	1.2%	1.0%	1.0%	0.4%	0.2%	0.1%	0.1%

According to the BIC values, a 6-cluster solution seems to be the best practical choice. Each sub-figure in Fig. 5 shows the result of splitting each of the five

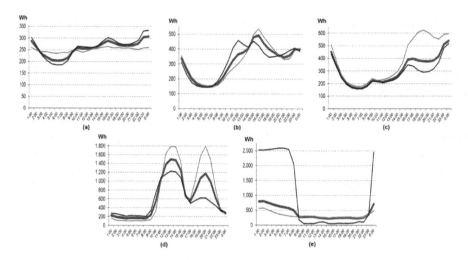

Fig. 5. Results of the splits performed by the x-Means algorithm over 5 clusters. Each subplot corresponds to a cluster, the thick line representing the original centroid of the cluster and the thin lines representing the two new centroids obtained. (a) Homogeneous consumption (b) Consumption from noon (c) Consumption at eve (d) Double peak at afternoon (e) Consumption at early morning.

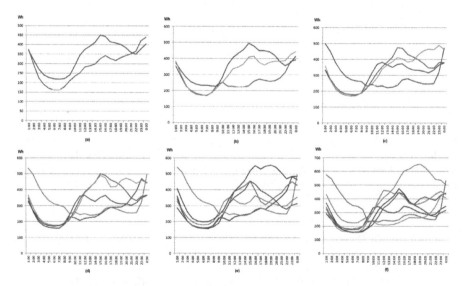

Fig. 6. Results of the clustering performed by the k-Shape algorithm. (a) 2 clusters (b) 3 clusters (c) 4 clusters (d) 5 clusters (e) 6 clusters (f) 7 clusters.

clusters in the initial solution, so as to obtain a sixth one. Table 4 gathers the results of the increment of BIC generated by each split. All of them are positive, but the splitting of cluster 5 is shown to provide the greatest advantage. This is confirmed by the $\Delta Cost$ values, all of which are rather small, with the exception of that for cluster 5 (consumption at early morning). Despite the sub-clusters resulting from cluster 5 splitting being very sparse, their consumption profile is so characteristic (extremely high nighttime consumption) that the definition of such further segments was deemed useful from a tariffication standpoint.

Table 4. Evaluation of the x-Means cluster splits, using the BIC and cost criteria.

	Cluster 1	Cluster 2	Cluster 3	Cluster 4	Cluster 5
ΔBIC	10	123	184	57	381
ΔCost	0.88%	0.23%	0.97%	1.68%	8.99%

Table 5. Validation of the different clustering results obtained through k-Shape. The distribution shows the proportions of the biggest and smallest clusters.

# of clusters	Business interpretability	Distribution	ΔCost
2	Bad	54.5%/45.6%	0.2%
3	Poor	39.5%/25.6%	1.0%
4	Good	35.5%/17.9%	3.6%
5	Good	25.7%/15.0%	3.9%
6	Poor	22.0%/12.7%	4.5%
7	Poor	19.2%/11.4%	4.9%

IV. Finally, the previous results where compared to those obtained using the k-Shape algorithm. The latter are shown in Fig. 6. Again, each sub-figure corresponds to the k clusters, with $k = 2, \ldots, 7$, found by the algorithm. When compared with the results of k-Means with DTW, the clusters are far more similar to each other. The evaluation summarized in Table 5 indicates that the business interpretability of the results is far worse and the differential of cost, lower. Moreover, the customer distribution per cluster shows a small difference between the sizes of the biggest and smallest clusters, meaning that all the clusters have a similar size. This would imply a uniform distribution of customers per segment, which is unlikely in a real market, according to expert opinion. Considering all this, it can be argued that the use of k-Means with DTW is more suitable for the realization of profitable customer personalized tariffs.

5   Conclusion

The "personalization" of electricity tariffs can be made operational as market segmentation, implemented through data clustering techniques. Household electricity consumption data comes in the form of time series and, therefore, clustering techniques that cater specifically for this type of data must be used. Some of these have been tested in this paper. We have stressed the fact that the results of the application of clustering for the problem at hand should be evaluated not only according to internal quantitative measures but also in terms of business practical actionability. The use of a similarity measure suitable for time series, namely DTW, as the basis for a k-Means-based clustering has been shown to yield a solution to the problem of tariff personalization that is more convincingly practical than the one provided by the more sophisticated k-Shapes algorithm. The refinement of the solution selected by experts has been only slightly refined using the x-Means algorithm, providing further indication of the adequacy of the original solution. These preliminary experiments with a simplified version of the originally available data should be understood as a proof of concept to lay the ground for more ambitious experiments.

References

1. Orden IET/290/2012, de 16 de febrero, por la que se modifica la Orden ITC/3860/2007, de 28 de diciembre, por la que se revisan las tarifas eléctricas a partir del 1 de enero de 2008 en lo relativo al plan de sustitución de contadores. https://www.boe.es/diario_boe/txt.php?id=BOE-A-2012-2538
2. The European Parliament and The Council of the European Union: Directive 2006/32/EC of the European Parliament and of the Council on Energy End-Use Efficiency and Energy Service and Repealing Council Directive 93/76/EEC (2006)
3. Flath, C., Nicolay, D., Conte, T., van Dinther, C., Filipova-Neumann, L.: Cluster analysis of smart metering data. Bus. Inf. Syst. Eng. **4**(1), 31–39 (2012)
4. Alzate, C., Sinn, M.: Improved electricity load forecasting via kernel spectral clustering of smart meters. In: Proceedings of the IEEE 13th International Conference on Data Mining (ICDM 2013), pp. 943–948. IEEE (2013)
5. Lines, J., Bagnall, A., Caiger-Smith, P., Anderson, S.: Classification of household devices by electricity usage profiles. In: Yin, H., Wang, W., Rayward-Smith, V. (eds.) IDEAL 2011. LNCS, vol. 6936, pp. 403–412. Springer, Heidelberg (2011). doi:10.1007/978-3-642-23878-9_48
6. Pelleg, D., Moore, A.: X-means: extending K-means with efficient estimation of the number of clusters. In: Langley, P. (ed.) ICML 2000. Morgan Kaufmann, San Francisco, pp. 727–734 (2000)
7. Paparrizos, J., Gravano, L.: k-Shape: efficient and accurate clustering of time series. SIGMOD Rec. **45**(1), 69–76 (2016)
8. Petitjean, F., Forestier, G., Webb, G.I., Nicholson, A.E., Chen, Y., Keogh, E.: Faster and more accurate classification of time series by exploiting a novel dynamic time warping averaging algorithm. Knowl. Inf. Syst. **47**(1), 1–26 (2016)
9. Senin, P.: Dynamic time warping algorithm review. Technical report, Information and Computer Science Department, University of Hawaii at Manoa Honolulu, USA, pp. 1–23 (2008)
10. Berndt, D.J., Clifford, J.: Using dynamic time warping to find patterns in time series. In: KDD Workshop. vol. 10, no. 16 (1994)

Artificial Intelligence in Transportation Systems

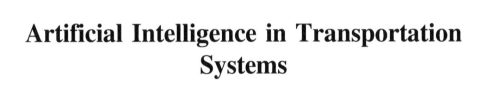

Towards Dynamic Rebalancing of Bike Sharing Systems: An Event-Driven Agents Approach

Jeremias Dötterl[1]([✉]), Ralf Bruns[1], Jürgen Dunkel[1], and Sascha Ossowski[2]

[1] Computer Science Department, Hannover University of Applied Sciences and Arts, Hannover, Germany
{jeremias.doetterl,ralf.bruns,juergen.dunkel}@hs-hannover.de
[2] CETINIA, University Rey Juan Carlos, Madrid, Spain
sascha.ossowski@urjc.es

Abstract. Operating a Bicycle Sharing System over some time without the operator's intervention causes serious imbalances, which prevents the rental of bikes at some stations and the return at others. To cope with such problems, user-based bicycle rebalancing approaches offer incentives to influence the users' behavior in an appropriate way. In this paper, an event-driven agent architecture is proposed, which uses Complex Event Processing to predict the future demand at the bike stations using live data about the users. The predicted demands are used to derive situation-aware incentives that are offered by the affected stations. Furthermore, it is shown how bike stations cooperate to prevent that they outbid each other.

1 Introduction

Bike Sharing Systems (BSS) have become increasingly popular in recent years offering bicycles for collaborative use. They allow users to rent bikes temporarily for exploring the city or commuting to their workplaces. In general, BSS reduce air pollution, traffic congestion and demand for parking space. Popular examples for BSS are Vélib' in Paris and CitiBike in New York City. Most BSS provide the same infrastructure, which we also assume in the following: The systems are equipped with fixed docking stations, where users rent and return the bikes.

A key issue in operating a BSS is fleet management. Due to asymmetric demands, some stations tend to run out of bikes, whereas others get completely occupied. Such stations are problematic as they hinder the bicycle flow of the BSS and thus reduce the customers' satisfaction and the operator's benefits. BSS operators use different strategies to avoid such situations. Currently, most systems redistribute bikes by transporting them with trucks between affected stations.

In this paper, we present an innovative *user-based bicycle rebalancing approach* that offers incentives to users to influence their behavior: the incentives should encourage users to return their bikes at appropriate stations causing a positive effect on the overall system balance. Our approach is based on an

© Springer International Publishing AG 2017
E. Oliveira et al. (Eds.): EPIA 2017, LNAI 10423, pp. 309–320, 2017.
DOI: 10.1007/978-3-319-65340-2_26

event-driven agent architecture, which takes live data of the users into account for predicting the future demand at the stations. Furthermore, the stations are cooperating to prevent that they outbid each other.

The paper is structured as follows: in the next section we briefly introduce the bicycle rebalancing problem. In Sect. 3, first we explain the general idea of our rebalancing approach. Then, the event-driven agent architecture is presented and the two different agent types are discussed in detail. In particular, we show how agents exploit live data to predict user demand and how agent coordination works for incentive-based repositioning. Section 4 presents some related work. Finally, Sect. 5 gives some concluding remarks.

2 Bicycle Rebalancing Problem

Every BSS with a fixed number of stations is inevitably confronted with the *Bicycle Rebalancing Problem* [3]. Operating the BSS over some time without the operator's intervention causes serious imbalances at some stations:

- *Exhaustion*: Some stations become empty quickly, which prevents further bike rentals.
- *Congestion*: Other stations tend to fill-up quickly preventing bike returns.

We can identify different causes for an asymmetric demand yielding imbalanced stations:

- *Inherent causes*, e.g., the city topography: Stations located on a hill experience a lack of bikes more frequently, because typically users are reluctant to ride to up-hill stations to return their bikes there.
- *Temporary causes*, e.g., commuter traffic [6,13]: In the morning, users commute from the residential areas in outer zones to their workplaces in the city. In the evening an inversion of demand occurs, when they commute back home.

Imbalanced stations have negative effects on the BSS's service level, which can be defined as the fraction of potential customers that have to be declined [11]. A drop of the service level below a certain threshold may not only reduce the customers' satisfaction and the operator's revenues, but may also violate service level agreements promised by the BSS operator (see, e.g., [16]).

Repositioning is a mechanism to deal with imbalanced BSS stations: bikes are moved from congested towards exhausted stations. Two different repositioning strategies can be distinguished:

- *Operator-Based Repositioning*: A BSS service team repositions bikes with trucks. This approach is effective as many bikes can be relocated at once with a single truck. Unfortunately, operator-based repositioning is costly and conflicts the idea of BSS as an environment-friendly transportation alternative [4,13].

- *User-Based Repositioning*: Instead of BSS staff, the BSS users themselves rebalance the system. In exchange for incentives (e.g., a discount on the trip price), the users of the system perform repositioning activities that are beneficial for the balance of the BSS. Users are incentivized to return their bikes to (nearly) exhausted stations and to rent from (nearly) congested stations in order to achieve a self-sustaining system. User-based repositioning has a low carbon footprint and the potential to reduce costs for the BSS.

A hybrid approach, which combines both repositioning modes, is possible and comes with the corresponding trade-offs.

3   Dynamic Rebalancing with Event-Driven Agents

3.1   General Idea: Situation-Aware Rebalancing Using Live Data

We propose a novel dynamic and user-based rebalancing approach for BSS. Our approach achieves situation awareness by incorporating *live data* about the users' current locations and behaviors into the rebalancing process. Stations continuously monitor their current state and the users' behavior in their environment to identify rebalancing opportunities. We suggest a user-based repositioning approach that applies two subsequent steps:

1. *Demand Prediction*: the future demand at BSS stations is used to react in a proactive way on foreseen critical situations. It can be inferred by analyzing the users' current situations as well as historical data.
2. *Incentive-Based Repositioning*: Bike stations cooperate when offering appropriate incentives to the users for avoiding critical imbalances. We consider an incentive scheme that grants discounts on trip prices, i.e. users who return a bike to a station that is experiencing a bike shortage have to pay less for this particular trip.

Demand Prediction: Demand prediction requires precise knowledge about the current state of the BSS and is based on appropriate live data.

- *Live Situation*: Stations have to know their current occupancy and the users' situation to predict near-future demand. The current occupancy of the stations can be derived directly using the available data about the bike rentals and bike returns. The situations of BSS users are analyzed by monitoring the live data of the built-in sensors of their smartphones that provide data such as GPS position and velocity.
- *Proximity Area*: A station is not interested in far away but in nearby users who are candidates for returning a bike. Therefore, each station keeps track of its own proximity area, which contains all users who can reach the station within a certain time frame, e.g. 30 min. Whether a user can reach the station within the time frame depends on his/her current location and movement behavior (e.g., average speed). Figure 1 illustrates the proximity areas of two stations

s_1 and s_2 with the users Alice, Bob, Carol and Dave, who are members of different proximity areas depending on their locations and velocities. Members of a station's proximity area are potential recipients of incentive offers in case the station intends to increase its occupancy. Whenever a user enters a station's proximity area, the station determines whether to offer an incentive to the user.

- *Predictive State*: Based on the live data, each station predicts its near-future occupancy (high, medium, low) to proactively prevent exhaustions and congestions. For the computation of the predictive state, the station considers the current members of its proximity area as candidates of a future bike return. Whenever a station's situation changes, the station re-evaluates its predictive state. Situation changes are caused by rentals and returns or by users entering and leaving the station's proximity area.

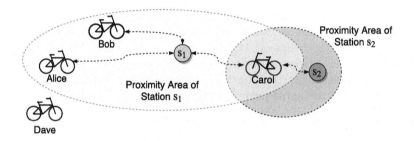

Fig. 1. Proximity area of bike stations

Incentive-Based Repositioning: For implementing user-based repositioning, a station may send incentive offers to nearby users.[1] The incentives should encourage users to return their bikes at appropriate stations causing a positive effect on the overall system balance.

- *Station Neighborhood*: Each station has knowledge about its neighborhood, a set of other stations that are located near that particular station. Whenever a station determines an incentive value, it also considers the interests of its neighbors. Stations that do not want to receive further bikes have to rely on their neighbors to attract these bikes instead (by offering appropriate incentives).
- *Cooperation*: Because the stations do all belong to the same BSS operator, they do not compete but cooperate with each other, with the common goal of a balanced BSS. If a sufficient number of users can be convinced to return their bikes at an appropriate station, the system rebalances itself without (or with minimal) additional operator-based rebalancing efforts.

---

[1] Users are notified about incentives with an acoustical signal so that they do not have to constantly watch their smartphones and can concentrate on the traffic.

3.2   Event-Driven Agent Architecture for Bicycle Rebalancing

For the realization of our approach, we present an abstract multi-agent architecture shown in Fig. 2, which consists of two different agent types: User Agents (UA) and Station Agents (SA).

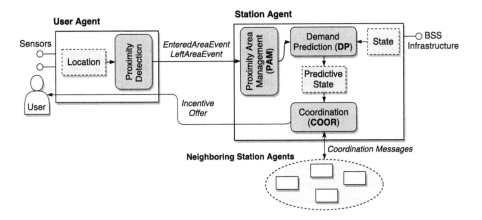

Fig. 2. Bicycle rebalancing architecture with event-driven agents

User Agents (UA) run on the users' personal smartphones and are responsible for detecting the users' proximities to the stations. The UA continuously analyzes the location data provided by the smartphone's GPS sensor. Based on this location data, the UA infers the user's movement behavior, mainly the user's average speed. Based on the user's current location and movement behavior, the UA computes the user's temporal distance to the nearby stations. If the temporal distance is below a certain time threshold, e.g. 30 min, then the user must have entered the proximity area of a station.

The UA notifies the corresponding SA by the event message: EnteredArea Event. Leaving a proximity area is indicated by a LeftAreaEvent event message. Through this event notifications, the SAs are always aware of the *live situations* of the users.

Furthermore, the UA receives incentive offers from the SAs and displays them to the user.

Station Agents (SA) act on behalf of the individual stations. Each SA aims to satisfy the interests of the station it represents (considering the interests of the stations in its neighborhood). The SA listens to event notifications from nearby UAs and handles the events according to the *incentive process* introduced above in Sect. 3.1: Whenever a user enters or leaves the station's proximity area, the SA:

   1. updates its knowledge about the station's proximity area and
   2. recomputes its predictive state.

Furthermore, for each user who enters the station's proximity area, the SA:

3. determines an incentive (in coordination with its neighbors) and
4. if an incentive should be offered, notifies the user by sending the offer to the user's UA.

Below, we introduce the components of UA and SA in detail. Let S denote the set of all stations in the BSS. Each station $s_i \in S$ has a fixed capacity $cap_i \in \mathbb{N}$ and a variable occupancy $occ_i \in \{0, \ldots, cap_i\}$. Furthermore, let U denote the set of users.

In the following, we observe the interaction of the UA of a particular user $u \in U$ and the SA of a particular station $s_i \in S$. User u is riding a bike through the city, which he/she has rented from one of the stations earlier.

Proximity Detection. The *Proximity Detection* is the most sophisticated part of the UA. It monitors the temporal distance of u to each of the stations $s \in S$. For this purpose, it uses *Complex Event Processing (CEP)* to analyze the stream of location data provided by the smartphone's GPS sensor.

CEP is a software technology for analyzing massive event streams in real-time [8]. CEP rules written in a declarative event processing language (EPL) can detect event patterns in a data stream. CEP is the key technology in order to deliver live data about the users behavior in real-time to the SAs, see also [2].

The following three exemplary CEP rules illustrate some part of the proximity detection process. The first rule has the task to find out if a user has changed his/her position. The rule considers two subsequently occurring *GPS events* and assigns the alias names g1 and g2 to them.

```
rule: "new user position"
CONDITION GPS-Evt AS g1  ->  GPS-Evt AS g2
          AND (Geo.isDifferent(g1,g2))
ACTION    new PositionEvt(g2)
```

The sequence operator -> denotes the temporal sequence of events. The newer *GPS event* g2 is only relevant for further processing if the user location has changed considerably. Therefore, it is checked if the two GPS locations differ significantly by using a service isDifferent(..) provided by the class Geo that implements spatial operations. The generation of a new *Position event* signalizes the location change.

The average speed of the movement of a user can be calculated by aggregating all *Position events* within the last five minutes and determining the average of the measured distinct speed values. The speed is determined by a method getSpeed(..) that is provided by the GPS sensors. A corresponding *Moving event* is generated by the following CEP rule.

```
rule: "average speed of movement"
CONDITION PositionEvt AS p
          AND avg(p.getSpeed()).within:batch(5 min) AS avgSpeed
ACTION    new MovingEvt(p.userID, p.pos, avgSpeed)
```

The subsequent CEP rule monitors the temporal distance between the user to each station. From the current location and speed, the Proximity Detection can estimate which stations the user can reach within a certain time frame. For every new *Moving event* the rule checks if any proximity area of a station is affected by the movement.

```
rule:"entering proximity area"
CONDITION MovingEvt AS m
          AND (Geo.distance(m.pos, station.pos)/m.avgSpeed) < 0.5
ACTION    new EnteredAreaEvent(m.userID, station.ID)
```

Again a service `distance(..)` provided by the class `Geo` is used to determine the spatial distance between user and station. This spatial distance is divided by the average speed of the user and if the resulting temporal distance is less than 30 min, then the user has entered the proximity area of a SA.[2] In this case a new `EnteredAreaEvent` is generated and submitted to the SA of the corresponding station, see Fig. 2.[3]

Proximity Area Management (PAM). The PAM is a component of the SA and listens to event notifications it receives from the UAs. The PAM uses these events to keep track of the station's proximity area. Whenever a `EnteredAreaEvent` or `LeftAreaEvent` is received, the PAM updates its knowledge base accordingly.

More formally, the PAM of station $s_i \in S$ maintains set $B_i \subseteq U$, which contains all users $u \in U$ that are currently members of the proximity area of station s_i. The PAM provides set B_i to the Demand Prediction (DP) component.

With the arrival of the `EnteredAreaEvent` that reports the proximity of user u, the PAM of s_i adds u to the set B_i. Furthermore, the Demand Prediction (DP) is invoked with the updated set B_i.

Demand Prediction (DP). The DP estimates the stations near-future demand in order to proactively prevent exhaustions and congestions. A station's predictive state captures the station's estimated occupancy in the near future, expressed as a categorical value

$$predState_i \in \{low, medium, high\}$$

The predictive state $predState_i$ is computed by the prediction function

$$predictState(occ_i, nb_i)$$

which operates on the station's occupancy occ_i and the number of users in the station's proximity area $nb_i = |B_i|$.

The prediction function can be derived by various approaches:

---

[2] Of course, it also has to be regarded if the user is already a member of this proximity area.

[3] The leaving of a proximity area has to be treated accordingly and is indicated by a `LeftAreaEvent`.

- *Machine Learning* approaches can learn the function by applying supervised learning.
- A simple statistical approach can be used, e.g.,

$$predictState(occ_i, nb_i) = state(occ_i + prob_{return} * nb_i \\ - n_{rental}, cap_i)$$

- $prob_{return}$: percentage of the bikes in the proximity area returned to station s_i in the considered time interval
- n_{rental}: average number of bikes rented in the time interval
- *state* function: maps a concrete occupancy value to one of the three categorical values *low*, *medium*, *high*. A possible state function could be defined as follows:

$$state(occ_i, cap_i) = \begin{cases} low & \text{if } (occ_i/cap_i) < 0.2 \\ medium & \text{if } 0.2 \leq (occ_i/cap_i) < 0.8 \\ high & \text{if } (occ_i/cap_i) \geq 0.8 \end{cases}$$

Note that there are various ways to estimate $prob_{return}$ and n_{rental}.

In our setting, the DP recomputes $predState_i$ and forwards it to the Coordination (COOR) component.

Coordination (COOR). The COOR component determines an appropriate incentive value for a nearby user, considering its own predictive state $predState_i$ as well as the predictive states of its neighbor stations.

To decide whether the user should be offered an incentive, it is not sufficient to only consider the own predictive state of station s_i. If s_i wants to attract the bike of the nearby user, it can offer a high incentive value (= offer a high discount on the trip price). But if s_i wants to reduce its occupancy, it has to rely on its neighboring stations to attract the bike instead. Therefore, stations also have to consider the predictive states of their neighbors in order to choose their incentive values in a way, which also are in the interest of the neighbor stations.

For each station s_j we define its neighborhood

$$N_j = \{s \mid s \in S \wedge s \neq s_j \wedge distance(s_j, s) \leq radius_j\}$$

where the *distance* function computes the geographical distance between two stations and $radius_j$ defines the neighborhood radius for station s_j. For simplicity, for each station s_j we choose the value $radius_j$ so that $|N_j| = 2$, i.e. every station has exactly two neighbors.

COOR of station s_i uses its personal predictive state $predState_i$ and the predictive states of its neighbor stations

$$\bigcup_{n \in N_i} predState_n$$

to decide whether to offer an incentive to the user. In our setting in which every station has exactly two neighbors, the station can use a simple decision table to determine the incentive values.

In Fig. 3, an example scenario is shown, in which the user is member of the proximity areas of the stations s_1, s_2, and s_3. The stations s_4 and s_5 are not reachable for the user within the time frame of 30 min. Each of the stations s_1 to s_5 has a predictive state. Furthermore, each station knows the predictive state of its two neighbor stations.

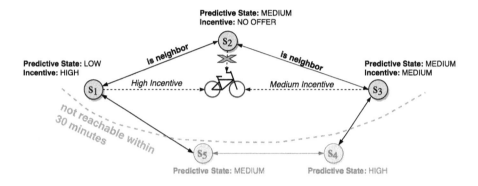

Fig. 3. Example scenario for incentive determination

In the given scenario, station s_1 suffers from exhaustion (or expects an exhaustion in the near future), while its neighbors s_2 and s_5 both have a medium predictive state. In accordance with the decision table in Fig. 4, station s_1 offers a high incentive (see row 4). Station s_3, on the other hand, offers a medium incentive (row 11). Station s_3 itself has a medium predictive state and does not want to increase its occupancy. However, station s_4 (a neighbor of s_3) suffers from congestion and wants to decrease its occupancy. Therefore s_3 offers a medium incentive to make itself a more attractive destination in comparison to

	predictive state of current station S_x	predictive states of neighboring stations S_{n1} and S_{n2}		decision for current station S_x
1	low	low	low	no offer (no competition)
2	low	low	medium	medium incentive
3	low	low	high	medium incentive
4	low	medium	medium	high incentive
5	low	medium	high	high incentive
6	low	high	high	high incentive
7	medium	low	low	no offer
8	medium	low	medium	no offer
9	medium	low	high	medium incentive
10	medium	medium	medium	no offer
11	medium	medium	high	medium incentive
12	medium	high	high	high incentive
13	high	(any)	(any)	no offer

Fig. 4. Decision table for incentive determination.eps

s_4. Ideally, this reduces the number of bike returns at s_4, whereas bike rentals take place at the usual rate. Thus, we expect that s_4 will achieve balance in the near future.

4   Related Work

With the recent emergence of large-sized BSS in cities all over the world [14], BSS are starting to become a popular research topic [5]. The bicycle rebalancing problem poses a relevant problem that BSS operators face in their day-to-day business [9] and therefore it has become the focus of different research efforts [7,12]. Thereby, lots of research focuses on the static rebalancing problem. Traditionally, BSS operators employ service staff who reposition bicycles with trucks. Recently, different user-based rebalancing solutions have been proposed.

Singla et al. [15] present a system architecture for a user-based rebalancing of BSS. The proposed architecture consists of a smartphone app over which the users can request target stations (start and destination) for their journey. On request, the system recommends the user a target station together with a price, which is determined by a dynamic pricing mechanism. The prices are dynamically adapted to the current system status, the user's location, near-future demand, available budget, and information about prior interactions with the user. Compared to the system of Singla et al., in our system incentives are not computed by a central pricing instance. Instead, incentives are offered in a decentralized way by the station agents, which represent the different stations' interests. Furthermore, our system does not recommend one single target station on request, but pro-actively assigns incentive values to all stations that are reachable for the user within the near future. This means, we designed a location-aware system that informs users about suitable target stations nearby. Thus, the user does not only have the choice between his initially intended destination and one alternative, but has a variety of stations to choose from.

Similar to our agent-based approach, Papanikolaou and Larson [10] present a new operational model for mobility-on-demand systems. In the proposed Market Economy of Trips (MET), users of the BSS act as buyers and sellers who buy bikes from one station (bike rental) and sell it to another (bike return). The stations act as traders, which buy bikes from users and resell them to others. Thereby, the start and end station determine the trip price dynamically in order to influence the bicycle trips in way that is beneficial for the balance of the BSS. Like in our approach, in the MET stations are (represented by) autonomous entities that determine trip prices based on their personal interests. The major difference between the two approaches is that we consider a pricing scheme based on trip discounts, which is realized by cooperative stations (station agents). The MET determines trip prices freely and unbound from a fixed default price and aims to maximize the bicycle flow with the help of competitive stations.

Reiss and Bogenberger [13] propose a rebalancing approach for free-floating BSS (like the one in Munich, Germany), which allow users to drop their bikes at arbitrary publicly accessible places within a designated operating area. The authors suggest a hybrid rebalancing strategy, in which user-driven and operator-driven rebalancing are combined. The repositioning is performed according to a pre-computed demand model, which tries to predict the future demand at different areas in the city at different times of the day. Because the demand model operates only on historical data, it cannot react to short-term changes. For our system, we envision a dynamic demand prediction method that also considers live data, i.e. the current station occupancies and the nearby users.

Aeschbach et al. [1] present a set of different control strategies for user-driven rebalancing. These control strategies define how the system interacts with the users to achieve a rebalanced BSS. By evaluating the different strategies with a simulation, they conclude that preemptive strategies are more effective than reactive strategies. This means that rebalancing efforts should already be undertaken before the involved stations become completely full or empty. This is realized in our system because the SAs already try to attract bikes when the occupancy falls below a certain threshold. Our control strategy differs from the ones described by Aeschbach et al. Instead of determining one specific alternative station, our approach is aware of the users' current locations and continuously recommends them new possible destination stations.

5   Conclusion

In BSS, an efficient rebalancing of bikes requires up-to-date information about the BSS's overall operational state. In this paper, we introduced a new dynamic and user-based bicycle rebalancing approach that incorporates the current situation of the users into the decision making process.

The proposed novel event-driven agents architecture enables the automatic determination of situation changes of BSS users, which are immediately propagated to the affected bike stations. Situation awareness is achieved by continuously analyzing the built-in smartphone sensors in order to derive the current state of the users. The proposed event-driven agents concept provides effective data fusion of live data and enables (almost) real-time operations.

Currently, we are developing a prototypical implementation of our approach, which we plan to evaluate with a simulation.

In future work, we intend to investigate a more sophisticated demand prediction that predicts the trip destination of a certain user. This could be achieved by supervised learning from user-specific training data.

References

1. Aeschbach, P., Zhang, X., Georghiou, A., Lygeros, J.: Balancing bike sharing systems through customer cooperation - a case study on london's barclays cycle hire. In: 2015 54th IEEE Conference on Decision and Control (CDC), pp. 4722–4727. IEEE, December 2015

2. Billhardt, H., Lujak, M., Ossowski, S., Bruns, R., Dunkel, J.: Intelligent event processing for emergency medical assistance. In: Proceedings of the 29th Annual ACM Symposium on Applied Computing, SAC 2014, pp. 200–206. ACM, New York (2014)

3. Contardo, C., Morency, C., Rousseau, L.-M.: Balancing a dynamic public bike-sharing system. Technical report, CIRRELT (2012)

4. DeMaio, P.: Bike-sharing: history, impacts, models of provision, and future. J. Public Transp. **12**(4), 3 (2009)

5. Fishman, E., Washington, S., Haworth, N.: Bike share: a synthesis of the literature. Transport Rev. **33**(2), 148–165 (2013)

6. Froehlich, J., Neumann, J., Oliver, N.: Sensing and predicting the pulse of the city through shared bicycling. In: Proceedings of the 21st International Joint Conference on Artifical Intelligence, IJCAI 2009, pp. 1420–1426. Morgan Kaufmann Publishers Inc., San Francisco (2009)

7. Di Gaspero, L., Rendl, A., Urli, T.: Balancing bike sharing systems with constraint programming. Constraints **21**(2), 318–348 (2016)

8. Luckham, D.: The Power of Events: An Introduction to Complex Event Processing in Distributed Enterprise Systems. Addison-Wesley, Reading (2002)

9. Nair, R., Miller-Hooks, E., Hampshire, R.C., Bušić, A.: Large-scale vehicle sharing systems: analysis of vélib'. Int. J. Sustain. Transp. **7**(1), 85–106 (2013)

10. Papanikolaou, D., Larson, K.: Constructing intelligence in point-to-point mobility systems. In: 2013 9th International Conference on Intelligent Environments, pp. 51–56. IEEE, July 2013

11. Pfrommer, J., Warrington, J., Schildbach, G., Morari, M.: Dynamic vehicle redistribution and online price incentives in shared mobility systems. IEEE Trans. Intell. Transp. Syst. **15**(4), 1567–1578 (2014)

12. Rainer-Harbach, M., Papazek, P., Hu, B., Raidl, G.R.: Balancing bicycle sharing systems: a variable neighborhood search approach. In: Middendorf, M., Blum, C. (eds.) EvoCOP 2013. LNCS, vol. 7832, pp. 121–132. Springer, Heidelberg (2013). doi:10.1007/978-3-642-37198-1_11

13. Reiss, S., Bogenberger, K.: Optimal bike fleet management by smart relocation methods: combining an operator-based with an user-based relocation strategy. In: 19th IEEE International Conference on Intelligent Transportation Systems, ITSC 2016, Rio de Janeiro, Brazil, 1–4 November 2016, pp. 2613–2618 (2016)

14. Shaheen, S., Guzman, S., Zhang, H.: Bikesharing in Europe, the Americas, and Asia. Transp. Res. Rec.: J. Transp. Res. Board **2143**, 159–167 (2010)

15. Singla, A., Santoni, M., Bartók, G., Mukerji, P., Meenen, M., Krause, A.: Incentivizing users for balancing bike sharing systems. In: Proceedings of the Twenty-Ninth AAAI Conference on Artificial Intelligence, AAAI 2015, pp. 723–729. AAAI Press (2015)

16. Transport for London. Cycle hire contracts. service level agreements (2009). https://tfl.gov.uk/corporate/publications-and-reports/cycle-hire-contracts. Accessed 21 Feb 2017

Mobility Mining Using Nonnegative Tensor Factorization

Hamid Eslami Nosratabadi[(⊠)], Hadi Fanaee-T, and Joao Gama

LIAAD-INESC TEC, Rua Dr. Roberto Frias, 4200-465 Porto, Portugal
hamid.e.nosratabadi@fc.up.pt, hadi.fanaee@fe.up.pt,
jgama@fep.up.pt

Abstract. Mobility mining has lots of applications in urban planning and transportation systems. In particular, extracting mobility patterns enables service providers to have a global insight about the mobility behaviors which consequently leads to providing better services to the citizens. In the recent years several data mining techniques have been presented to tackle this problem. These methods usually are either spatial extension of temporal methods or temporal extension of spatial methods. However, still a framework that can keep the natural structure of mobility data has not been considered. Non-negative tensor factorizations (NNTF) have shown great applications in topic modelling and pattern recognition. However, unfortunately their usefulness in mobility mining is less explored. In this paper we propose a new mobility pattern mining framework based on a recent non-negative tensor model called BetaNTF. We also present a new approach based on interpretability concept for determination of number of components in the tensor rank selection process. We later demonstrate some meaningful mobility patterns extracted with the proposed method from bike sharing network mobility data in Boston, USA.

Keywords: Mobility mining · Nonnegative tensor factorization · BetaNTF

1 Introduction

Extracting mobility patterns has been recently studied in the context of spatial data mining. It has lots of applications in urban planning, scheduling and public transportation. In the recent decade several data mining techniques have been exploited for addressing this problem. For instance, [5] used Markov models to tackle the problem of predicting next locations. In [20] the authors exploited association rules to extract patterns for tourist attraction problem. In [21] a heuristic method is proposed based on data mining which consider the trajectory of a focal tourist and the movements of past visitors. However, in neither of these works the spatiotemporal structure of traffic data is considered simultaneously.

Tensor decompositions are one of models that can naturally capture and model the spatiotemporal variance of traffic data. They are recently applied for solving many problems in relevant areas such as traffic flow prediction [2], data compression of urban traffic data [1], clustering and prediction of temporal evolution of global urban network [6], traffic speed data imputation [10], estimation of missing traffic volume [11, 14–18],

© Springer International Publishing AG 2017
E. Oliveira et al. (Eds.): EPIA 2017, LNAI 10423, pp. 321–330, 2017.
DOI: 10.1007/978-3-319-65340-2_27

and traffic volume data outlier recovery [19]. However, to the best of our knowledge, Non-negative Tensor Factorization (NNTF) has never been applied to the mobility pattern extraction problem. This is while NNTF has been successfully applied to problems related to topic modelling [3] for extracting topic models from the text corpus. Our main objective in this work is to extend the application of NNTF from topic modelling to extract mobility patterns from dynamic traffic data.

Our initial empirical evaluation with traditional NNTF models such as CP-NLS [12, 13] against the recent method, BetaNTF [4] indicates the better performance of BetaNTF. The BetaNTF algorithm first time was developed in signal processing for blind source separation.

Our main objective in this work is to extract interesting, meaningful mobility patterns from bike sharing network data using BetaNTF model. The data being generated in bike sharing networks naturally has a tensor structure of "Origin x Destination x Time". That is why it is quite relevant to be analyzed with tensor decomposition models. However, one of the important problems in applying tensor decomposition models is how to determine the number of components. This becomes more difficult in pattern extraction since not only the model should be accurate but also it should be interpretable. To solve this problem, for the first time we introduce a new mechanism based on the interpretability of patterns for determining number of components. To summarize, our contributions include:

- For the first time we extend the ideas in topic modelling based on non-negative tensor factorization to the problem of mobility pattern mining.
- We apply BetaNTF a recent non-negative tensor decomposition algorithm (based on CP structure) for extracting patterns.
- We propose a new approach based on interpretability for determining of number of components in the BetaNTF model.
- We evaluate our proposal on a real-world bike sharing data set and provide realistic evidences regarding the validity of extracted patterns.

The rest of the paper is organized as follows. Details of the proposed method is presented in Sect. 2. Section 3 describes the experimental setup, data set and the empirical results. Section 4 gives the results. The last section concludes the exposition presenting the final remarks.

2 Methodology

The overall picture of our methodology is illustrated in Fig. 1. In the following section each of these components will be described in more details.

2.1 Tensor Transformation

The raw mobility data normally is presented in the format of transactional database. Each row usually contains information regarding the origin and destination of travel and also the timestamp when the travel is started and ended. A pre-processing step is

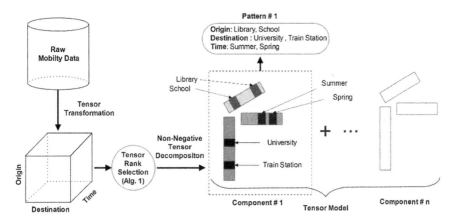

Fig. 1. Cartoon of the proposed method

required to transform this kind of databases to tensor format. A list of distinct stations and days is first retrieved and then we count number of performed travels between origin/destination stations during various day intervals. This can be carried out via group queries on the database. For instance, a query like "Count number of travels from station S#1 to station S#2 in day#3" constitutes a triplet of X $(1,2,3) = 15$ in the third-order tensor. 15 in the example is one of the elements of the tensor and is the number of travels from station 1 to station 2 in day 3. Given the count for all possible triplets we can generate the full tensor of "Origin x Destination x Time" (ODT) which will be later used in analysis step.

2.2   Nonnegative Tensor Factorization

Non-negative tensor decompositions are considered more suitable than regular decomposition models for analysis of visual and count data (which is the case here). The reason is that in the non-negative models the elements in factor matrices have the non-negativity restriction which is more interpretable. In the case of mobility data for instance, negative values in the factor matrices cannot be justified with existing physical reality. Because, we cannot find any negative number of travels between the stations. In this step we apply BetaNTF decomposition on the ODT tensor and retrieve the factor matrices. Note that BetaNTF is from the CP/PARAFAC family, therefore the decomposed space will include three factor matrices respectively for "origin", "destination" and "time" dimensions. BetaNTF instead of using Alternating Least Squares technique [9] which is used in the majority of algorithms fits the tensor model by using beta-divergence as the cost-functions.

2.3   Rank Selection Based on Interpretability

One of the difficult problem in tensor decomposition or in general in latent models is how to choose the number of components (or latent variables). This situation gets worse in the application of mobility pattern mining where the quality of extracted patterns is directly related to the chosen number of components. The common techniques for determining number of components are automatic methods such as triangle technique [8] (i.e. ranktest in Tensorlab) which are mostly used in the literature. But the problem is that this type of techniques only considers the trade-off between accuracy and simplicity. In the mobility pattern mining another factor gets importance which is interpretability. In order to solve this issue, we propose a new rank selection methodology which selects the tensor rank by considering the trade-off between the number of distinct extracted patterns and the model simplicity. Our proposed algorithm for rank selection is demonstrated in Algorithm 1. We first apply BetaNTF with R number of components varying from 1 to Max R on input X tensor. Next, we extract patterns using methodology described in Sect. 2.4. Then we generate a table (See Table 1 for example) including a list of distinct number of discovered areas (c1) and number of patterns with different origin and destination zones (c2) and maximize c1 and c2 while minimize R. The logic behind this method that R is chosen as suitable number of components when its corresponding model covers more various distinct patterns while keeps the model as simple as possible.

Table 1. Dispersion of the obtained pattern from R = 1 to R = 15

R	The number of encompassed area	The number of distinct area
1	2	0
2	2	1
3	3	2
4	3	4
5	5	5
6	4	5
7	4	6
8	3	4
9	4	4
10	5	8
11	6	11
12	3	7
13	2	12
14	3	9
15	4	8

2.4   Pattern Extraction

There exists almost no work in the literature that provides a solution for automatic extraction of patterns (or topic models) from the decomposed tensor space. Usually the patterns are extracted by visual inspection of components. In this paper for the first time we propose an automatic mechanism for extraction of patterns from the factor matrices obtained from the decomposition model. Our proposed approach is as follows. Decomposition of ODT tensor (let's say with size of $N \times M \times K$) with R number of components gives us three factor matrices of size $N \times R$ (origin dimension), $M \times R$ (destination dimension) and $K \times R$ (time dimension). The set including the first column of $N \times R$ and $M \times R$ and $K \times R$ matrices constitutes the first pattern (see Fig. 1). Likewise, the second pattern can be built by the second columns of these matrices. Now we only need to find the elements with highest weights in these factor matrices. We tested three strategies for doing this, with z-score, with top N items and finally top N percentage. It seems that top N percentage gives a more interpretable results. Besides, choosing sigma threshold for z-score method was a bit difficult when there is a big difference between sizes of dimensions. So we select the top N% of items in the first column of factor matrices corresponding to each dimension and then generate a triplet of indices related to that weights. For example, suppose that the corresponding weight for *Central Station* in the origin dimension is selected as Top 1 and weight for *City park* is the highest weight in factor matrix of destination dimension. Also suppose that the weight for 2013-09-23 is the maximum weight among all in the first column of "time" factor matrix. A triplet like {O:"Central Station", D:" City Park", T: "2013-09-23"} would be outputted as the first extracted pattern.

We also relate the extracted temporal components to days of the week, holiday, month, season, and so forth to find the temporal dimension of patterns.

Algorithm (1) Tensor rank selection based on interpretability

```
Input: X (Origin × Destination × Time tensor), Max R
Output: determining of the best R rank
1 For R=1 to Max R
2 Apply BetaNTF on X given R
3 Extract patterns using the methodology described in
section 2.4
4 c1 ← number of distinct zones
5 c2 ← number of distinct areas with different origin
and destinations
6 End
7 Selected R ← Maximize c1,c2 and Minimize R
```

3 Experimental Evaluation

In this section we begin by describing the dataset and then explain the configuration used for experiments. Afterwards we demonstrate the obtained results.

3.1   Dataset

Boston bike-sharing data set has been extracted from hub-way data challenge 2013 [7]. It includes a historical usage log of all transactions in the network from 2011-07-28 to 2012-10-01, exclusive to the system's off-days in the winter, a total of 327 days. There are also 95 stations in total. After creating adjacency matrices for each day, the generated ODT traffic tensor will be in size $95 \times 95 \times 327$.

3.2   Experimental Setting

These configurations are used in the experiments. Max $R = 15$ is chosen in the Algorithm 1. The Selected R is chosen as 11 after generating Table 1 by taking into account the trade-off between simplicity of model and maximization of number of distinctive patterns and areas. Number of iterations in BetaNTF algorithm is set as 70. We also set Itakura-Saito cost function [22] in the BetaNTF algorithm. The N in the Top N% weight selection is set as 3 based on trial and error.

3.3   Results

In this section we will demonstrate the mobility patterns extracted from the Boston bike sharing dataset (Figs. 2, 3, 4, 5, 6, 7, 8, 9, 10, 11 and 12). In all figures, the λ value according to each component are shown. λ is obtained after normalization of decomposed tensor and has similar meaning as eigenvalue in matrix factorization. The component with higher lambda is more important. In our experiment the first and last λ are obtained respectively as 289 and 36.

Among the discovered patterns, Boston South Station and Boston North station are the main hotspots among than the others. Boston North station is surrounded by TD garden (multi-purpose arena) which seems to be related to sport and entertainment events. Boston south station also seems to be the transit hub as is surrounded by many transit stations. In terms of the time dimension, Tuesday and Wednesday in summer, especially in the month of August have appeared more frequently and probably play an important role in creating more diverse patterns.

In all figures, the red label marker specifies the point of destination, the green label marker displays the origin and the gray one demonstrates those points that origin and destination are overlapped. In the following we describe each extracted pattern in more details.

Pattern#1: In the first pattern (Fig. 2) we observe two origin and two destination areas that demonstrate a mobility flow from two main stations in Aquarium and Arlington to Boston North Station and Boston South Station, one of two main transit hubs. This can be related to sport and entertainment events where people tend to use more bikes to transit from point of interests such as TD Garden and Boston Common. This temporal component reveals that this pattern is more frequent on Tuesdays and Wednesdays (working days) in the summer (months of July, August and September).

Pattern#2: In this pattern which is shown in Fig. 3, we can see a mobility link between North End Area which contains variety of tourist attractions to Boston South Station. This pattern also temporally occurs Saturdays and Sundays (weekend) in the seasons of spring and summer, in particular months of May, June, July and August. This pattern probably is related to weekend trips to point of interests and restaurants.

Pattern#3: Interesting mobility flow can be observed in this pattern (Fig. 4) between two transit hubs of Boston South Station and Boston North station. The peak in the temporal component is related to month of August, so probably it uncovers a transit pattern of tourists who move between these two stations.

Pattern#4: This pattern (Fig. 5) probably demonstrates the mobility behavior of youth in Harvard medical school and Boston Sport club which also might be the central point for bikers. Temporally this pattern is more seen on Mondays and Wednesdays (working days) in the spring and summer, in particular months of July and August.

Pattern#5: The fifth pattern corresponds to a mobility flow originated in Downtown Crossing and Boston south Station approaching TD Garden and North End (Fig. 6) during Mondays and Wednesdays (working days) in the summer, especially on August and September.

Pattern#6: This pattern demonstrates the bi-directional mobility in the area close to Star Market and Portsmouth Playground (Fig. 7) which temporally occurs on Wednesdays and Sundays in holidays in the working days in spring and summer, especially in April and July.

Pattern#7: The spatial and temporal component of this pattern seems to be related to the mobility of students of MIT campus during the working days, especially in period of school opening in September. It seems students arriving from the north and south rent/leave the bikes at three close stations nearby the MIT campus (Fig. 8).

Pattern#8: This pattern (Fig. 9) seems to be related to shopping mobility between W Newton St. where there is a shopping center nearby and Dartmouth St which is more frequent on beginning of the week (Monday and Tuesday) in the Summer, especially in months of June and July.

Pattern#9: This pattern (Fig. 10) reveals a mobility flow from Downtown Crossing area to two origins at TD Garden (Boston North Station) and North End which is more frequent on Mondays and Thursdays (Working days) in the summer and autumn, especially in August and September.

Pattern#10: The stations appeared in this pattern are nearby stations to Boston University (Fig. 11). Apparently this reflects the mobility of Boston University's students. The temporal component also shows that this is a frequent pattern during the Tuesdays (working days) in the months of August and September.

Pattern#11: This pattern (Fig. 12) includes two destinations close to Massachusetts college of Pharmacy and Boston children's Hospital and two origins close to Boston Public Librar. It seems there is a link between these points during Wednesdays and Thursdays (working days) in the spring and summer, especially in June and July.

Fig. 2. Pattern#1,
λ = 289.68

Fig. 3. Pattern#2,
λ = 272.68

Fig. 4. Pattern#3, λ = 186.95

Fig. 5. Pattern#4, λ = 180.64

Fig. 6. Pattern#5,
λ = 138.23

Fig. 7. Pattern#6,
λ = 136.42

Fig. 8. Pattern#7,
λ = 129.10

Fig. 9. Pattern#8, λ = 125.24

Fig. 10. Pattern#9,
λ = 95.93

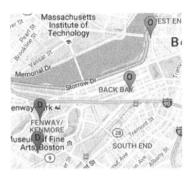

Fig. 11. Pattern#10, $\lambda = 75.33$ **Fig. 12.** Pattern#11, $\lambda = 36.02$

4 Conclusion

We extend the application of Non-negative tensor factorization from topic modelling and pattern recognition to mobility pattern mining. In particular, we demonstrate that the recent technique, BetaNTF which was originally developed for bling source separation has quite good potential for mobility pattern mining. We for the first time present a new technique for choosing number of components based on the provided interpretability. By applying our method on the real-world mobility data of Boston bike sharing network we provide some evidences of mobility behaviors that justify the usefulness of the proposed methodology. Some of the patterns such as mobility patterns of students close to the university campuses, or mobility close to shopping centers or tourist mobility makes sense and confirms the validity of patterns.

Acknowledgements. This research was carried out in the framework of the project "TEC4-Growth – RL SMILES – Smart, mobile, Intelligent and Large Scale Sensing and analytics NORTE-01-0145-FEDER-000020" which is financed by the north Portugal regional operational program (NORTE 2020), under the Portugal 2020 partnership agreement, and through the European regional development fund. The authors thank Antoine Liutkus for providing the code for BetaNTF and Huway Company for providing the dataset.

References

1. Asif, M., et al.: Data compression techniques for urban traffic data. In: 2013 IEEE Symposium on Computational Intelligence in Vehicles and Transportation Systems (CIVTS) (2013)
2. Abadi, A., Tooraj, R., Petros, A.: Ioannou.: traffic flow prediction for road transportation networks with limited traffic data. IEEE Trans. Intell. Transp. Syst. **16**(2), 653–662 (2015)
3. Bader, B.W., Berry, M.W., Broene, M.: Discussion tracking in enrron email using PARAFAC. In: Berry, M.W., Castellanos, M. (eds.) Survey of Text Mining II, pp. 147–163. Springer, London (2008)

4. Cichocki, A., et al.: Non-negative tensor factorization using alpha and beta divergences. In: 2007 IEEE International Conference on Acoustics, Speech and Signal Processing-ICASSP 2007, vol. 3. IEEE (2007)
5. Chen, M., Xiaohui, Y., Yang, L.: Mining moving patterns for predicting next location. Inf. Syst. **54**, 156–168 (2015)
6. Han, Y., Fabien, M.: Analysis of large-scale traffic dynamics in an urban transportation network using non-negative tensor factorization. Int. J. Intell. Transp. Syst. Res. **14**(1), 36–49 (2016)
7. http://hubwaydatachallenge.org/
8. Castellanos, J.L., Gomez, S., Guerra, V.: The triangle method for finding the corner of the L-curve. Appl. Numer. Math. **43**(4), 359–373 (2002)
9. Carroll, J.D., Chang, J.J.: Analysis of individual differences in multidimensional scaling via an N-way generalization of "Eckart-Young" decomposition. Psychometrika **35**, 283–319 (1970)
10. Ran, B., et al.: Traffic speed data imputation method based on tensor completion. Comput. Intell. Neurosci. **2015**, 22 (2015)
11. Ran, B., et al.: Estimating missing traffic volume using low multilinear rank tensor completion. J. Intell. Transp. Syst. **20**(2), 152–161 (2016)
12. Sorber, L., van Marc, B., de Lieven, L.: L.: Optimization-based algorithms for tensor decompositions: canonical polyadic decomposition, decomposition in rank-(L_r, L_r,1) terms, and a new generalization. SIAM J. Optim. **23**(2), 695–720 (2013)
13. Sorber, L., van Marc, B., de Lieven, L.: Unconstrained optimization of real functions in complex variables. SIAM J. Optim. **22**(3), 879–898 (2012)
14. Tan, H., et al.: A tensor-based method for missing traffic data completion. Transp. Res. Part C: Emerg. Technol. **28**, 15–27 (2013)
15. Tan, H., et al.: Low multilinear rank approximation of tensors and application in missing traffic data. Adv. Mech. Eng. **6**, 157597 (2014)
16. Tan, H., et al.: Traffic volume data outlier recovery via tensor model. Math. Prob. Eng. **2013**, 164810 (2013)
17. Tan, H.: Traffic missing data completion with spatial-temporal correlations. Department of Civil and Environmental Engineering, University of Wisconsin-Madison (2014)
18. Tan, H., et al.: A new traffic prediction method based on dynamic tensor completion. Procedia-Soc. Behav. Sci. **96**, 2431–2442 (2013)
19. Tan, H., et al.: Correlation analysis for tensor-based traffic data imputation method. Procedia-Soc. Behav. Sci. **96**, 2611–2620 (2013)
20. Versichele, M., et al.: Pattern mining in tourist attraction visits through association rule learning on Bluetooth tracking data: a case study of Ghent. Belg. Tour. Manag. **44**, 67–81 (2014)
21. Zheng, W., Xiaoting, H., Yuan, L.: Understanding the tourist mobility using GPS: where is the next place? Tour. Manag. **59**, 267–280 (2017)
22. Itakura, F., Saito, S.: Analysis synthesis telephony based on the maximum likelihood method. In: Proceedings of 6th of the International Congress on Acoustics, pp. C–17–C–20, Los Alamitos. IEEE (1968)

Machine Learning for Pavement Friction Prediction Using Scikit-Learn

Pedro Marcelino[1](✉), Maria de Lurdes Antunes[1], Eduardo Fortunato[1], and Marta Castilho Gomes[2]

[1] LNEC, Lisbon, Portugal
pmarcelino@lnec.pt
[2] IST, Lisbon, Portugal

Abstract. During the last decades, the advent of Artificial Intelligence (AI) has been taking place in several technical and scientific areas. Despite its success, AI applications to solve real-life problems in pavement engineering are far from reaching its potential. In this paper, a Python machine learning library, scikit-learn, is used to predict asphalt pavement friction. Using data from the Long-Term Pavement Performance (LTPP) database, 113 different sections of asphalt concrete pavement, spread all over the United States, were selected. Two machine learning models were built from these data to predict friction, one based on linear regression and the other on regularized regression with lasso. Both models showed to be feasible and perform similarly. According to the results, initial friction plays an essential role in the way friction evolves over time. The results of this study also showed that scikit-learn can be a versatile tool to solve pavement engineering problems. By applying machine learning methods to predict asphalt pavements friction, this paper emphasizes how theory and practice can be effectively coupled to solve real-life problems in contemporary transportation.

Keywords: Machine learning · Pavement engineering · Friction prediction · Scikit-learn · Python

1 Introduction

Recent advances in Artificial Intelligence (AI) and its specific approaches, such as machine learning, fostered the application of these techniques in different areas of science and engineering, as a way to solve practical problems. However, the number of studies on machine learning applications for pavement engineering problems is scarce. This suggests that the potential of these powerful tools is not being used by pavement engineers.

In this paper, a contribution is given to fill the gap between machine learning and pavement engineering, by the application of a general purpose machine learning toolbox, scikit-learn, for friction prediction in asphalt pavements.

Friction plays an important role in road safety, as studies show that roads with high friction are less prone to accidents [1]. Over long-term, with the deterioration process of the infrastructure, friction tends to decrease, leading to maintenance and rehabilitation

© Springer International Publishing AG 2017
E. Oliveira et al. (Eds.): EPIA 2017, LNAI 10423, pp. 331–342, 2017.
DOI: 10.1007/978-3-319-65340-2_28

needs. Reliable and accurate predictions of friction are then essential to increase the effectiveness of maintenance planning in infrastructure management. Using data collected by road administrations to develop the prediction models, true data-driven preventive maintenance policies can be established.

Since this paper pretends to show how machine learning can be applied in pavement engineering, it focus on the development of a working end-to-end pipeline, using scikit-learn and other Python libraries, that could be analysed from the engineering perspective and that could motivate readers to build their own analysis. For a more conceptual introduction to machine learning methods, see Hastie et al. [2] and Murphy [3].

2 Scikit-Learn Concepts

Scikit-learn [4] is a Python library that integrates a set of state-of-the-art machine learning algorithms. This library allows non-machine learning experts to apply many well-known machine learning algorithms. The easy-to-use interface and the integration with Python fostered the use of scikit-learn across different academic and industry fields. Although there are other learning packages than scikit-learn (e.g. statsmodels [5]), none seems to have so many machine learning tools as it.

To be a generic purpose library, scikit-learn is based on a convention that intends to turn it domain-independent. Thus, all objects and algorithms work with input data in the form of 2D arrays (samples x features) and share the following uniform set of methods:

- **Estimators**, to fit models from data. The estimator interface applies a *fit* method to model parameters, allowing them to learn from training data. All supervised and unsupervised learning algorithms on scikit-learn are available as objects that implement this interface.
- **Predictors**, to make predictions for new data. In addition to the *fit* method, the estimator interface also provides a *predict* method that takes an array as input and makes predictions for each sample based on the estimated model.
- **Transformers**, to convert data between different representations. In some learning algorithms, it is common to modify data before using it. For this reason, scikit-learn has estimators with the *transform* method.

The main objective of any machine learning application is to generalize beyond the examples given in the input data set. To do so, it is necessary to be aware of problems like overfitting [3] and develop reliable metrics to evaluate estimators and set hyper-parameters (parameters that express higher level properties of the model, typically fixed before the fitting process begins).

To evaluate estimators in a reliable way, the cross-validation technique can be applied. This iterative technique is based on fitting the model on a fraction of the data, the training set, and testing it on the left-out unseen data, the test set. There are several cross-validation strategies. The one followed in this paper is described in Sect. 4.3.

Cross-validation also plays an important role in the optimization (tuning) of hyperparameters. Considering a given model, cross-validation can be used on various test sets, in order to assess the hyperparameters value that leads to the best average score. This procedure can be done in scikit-learn using the GridSearchCV estimator. It takes as inputs an estimator and a set of hyperparameters defined by the user. Then, cross-validation scores are computed for all hyperparameters combination to choose the best one. Further details about how hyperparameters were tuned in this paper can be found in Sect. 4.3.

Python is a high-level programing language that offers a wide variety of libraries designed for scientific research. In this study, besides scikit-learn, other scientific Python libraries like NumPy [6], Matplotlib [7], and Pandas [8] were also used.

3 Pavement Friction

Wet pavement friction is a measure of the road contribution to the tire/road friction when the pavement surface is wet. This property is measured under specified and standardized conditions, in order to ensure that the contribution that the road provides to tire/road friction can be isolated [9]. In this study, both terms 'wet pavement friction' and 'skid resistance' are used interchangeably, as it is common in literature and practice [10].

The skid resistance of an asphalt pavement plays an important role on road safety. Studies show that crashes and skid have a linear relationship, as well as that the risk of accident increases when the skid resistance is below certain threshold values [1].

The integration of reliable prediction models is essential to improve skid resistance management, ensuring safety conditions and efficient allocation of resources.

Pavement skid resistance can decrease over time. Since predicting the evolution of skid resistance is fundamental to ensure proper planning and management methodologies, several previous studies investigated these issues and empirical models were developed from laboratory observation and field survey.

A study conducted by Prowell et al. (as cited in Wilson [11]) developed a simplified general model for skid resistance variation during the service life of a pavement. This model is shown in Fig. 1.

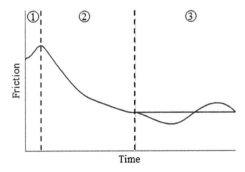

Fig. 1. Simplified general model for skid resistance evolution (adapted from Wilson [11]).

According to this model, there are three stages of variation in skid resistance:

1. **Initial roughening phase.** Initial values of skid resistance are low, probably due to bitumen coating the aggregate. However, the initial wear induced by traffic action, lead to bitumen removal. This will expose and roughen the aggregate's surface, thus increasing the skid resistance.
2. **Polishing phase.** Over time, traffic action induces significant modifications of the surface texture. After a certain point, skid resistance starts to decrease due to the smoothing and polishing actions under a permanent exposure to traffic loads.
3. **Equilibrium phase.** The equilibrium phase is reached when a stable cyclical variation of skid resistance starts to occur. This variation follows a seasonal pattern, with low skid resistance in the summer months and high skid resistance over winter months.

A number of studies support this model. In New Zealand, Cenek et al. [12] studied over a 10-year period the variation of skid resistance. During this period, skid resistance measurements were taken every three months and the results followed the simplified general model already presented.

Also, a study conducted by Chen et al. [13] analysed eight years of observations, showing that, in most cases, skid resistance of a pavement will slightly increase shortly after becoming open to traffic and then decrease for several years, before it finally reaches an equilibrium phase. According to the same study, several other references confirm that the evolution of skid resistance of pavement can be described by the simplified general model.

Depending on the study, different durations are proposed for each of the three phases of the model. Cenek et al. [12] consider that the initial roughening phase lasts up to one year and that the polishing phase should take between four to five years. In contrast, Chen et al. [13] considers that the initial roughening phase can last between six months to two years, while the polishing phase lasts between three to six years.

The model proposed in this study aims to predict friction during the polishing and equilibrium phases.

4   Application to the Case Study

4.1   Data Preparation: From LTPP Database to a Data Matrix

The Long-Term Pavement Performance (LTPP) database was used to develop a friction prediction model based on real data.

The LTPP database is an extensive data set that has been collected since 1987 in in-service highways all over the United States and Canada. It has information on pavement performance (e.g. pavement surface friction measurements) as well as on the different factors affecting its performance, such as precipitation, traffic, temperature, subgrade soil, or maintenance practices [14].

In this study, 113 different sections of asphalt concrete pavement, spread all over the United States, were selected. Although the LTPP database provides large amounts of data, friction monitoring data is available only in some road sections because its collection is voluntary. Since surface friction is the output, it will play a critical role in the design of the data set.

The surface friction data in LTPP database consists of measurements taken by several types of friction testers. Only road sections using the locked wheel skid trailer mounted with ribbed tire [15] were selected in this study. This selection corresponds to the maximum number of data points and avoids equipment/method related bias. The locked wheel friction measuring devices provide a coefficient of friction, which is reported as friction number or skid number [10]. The friction number is the ratio between the measured horizontal force at the tire-pavement interface and the normal force on the tire when the tire is fully locked. Friction data of each section was checked for practicality/consistency and filtered out according to the recommendations in the literature [16, 17].

Surface friction is affected by various factors, like traffic, environmental conditions and pavement surface characteristics [18]. Some of these factors are available in the LTPP database. For the purposes of this study, a selection of them was conducted considering the literature and the authors' experience:

- **Average monthly temperature** (MEAN_MON_TEMP_AVG) (degrees C). Temperature is one of the environmental factors that can affect pavement surface friction. According to a study conducted by Ahammed and Tighe [19], although surface friction variation can be estimated from pavement surface temperature or ambient temperatures, ambient temperature is slightly better correlated with surface friction values. Consequently, air temperature at time of testing was used.
- **Total monthly precipitation** (TOTAL_MON_PRECIP) (mm). Precipitation is another environmental factor that can affect friction, in particular because precipitation tends to remove lubricating agents and contaminants from the roadway surface [20]. Data from the month previous to the friction measurement was used to consider the effect of precipitation.
- **Accumulated traffic** (ACCUM_KESAL_YEAR) (kESAL/year). Traffic action tends to polish the aggregates of the surface. This makes them slipper, reducing pavement friction. To consider the effect of traffic over time, the average Equivalent Single Axle Load (ESAL) per year was used. Values were converted to kESAL/year units, which is the same as 1,000 ESAL/year. Since the LTPP database only reports yearly values, the accumulated traffic was computed as the mean kESAL/year times the pavement service life in years.
- **International Roughness Index** (IRI) (m/km). This index evaluates pavement roughness. Its inclusion was based on a study conducted by Fuentes et al. [21]. This study considers that pavement friction evaluation should incorporate the effects of pavement roughness, as described by IRI.
- **Initial friction number** (FN_0) (FN). The initial friction number intends to represent the friction number immediately after the initial roughening phase. Since the model is representative of skid evolution during polishing and equilibrium phases, for prediction purposes, the initial friction number corresponds to the initial conditions of the pavement. Based on the values proposed by Cenek et al. [12], it was considered that all the friction numbers measured up to one year after the opening of the road to traffic belonged to the initial roughening phase. In each section, the maximum of these values was considered to be the initial friction number.

Data referring to these factors was pre-processed into a format that could be read by scikit-learn. Accordingly, a data matrix (X) with all the factors mentioned above was created, and the friction number (FN) was defined as the target variable to predict (y).

One important note regarding data preparation is related with how maintenance and rehabilitation (M&R) actions were took into account. Several M&R actions affect pavement surface characteristics. If these actions improve surface friction characteristics, the model should be able to consider this effect. Accordingly, it was defined that the pavement would recover its initial characteristics if some specific M&R actions occurred. This means that friction measurements up to one year after those M&R actions belong to the initial roughening phase. The set of M&R actions that can improve surface friction characteristics was chosen according to the authors' knowledge.

This study carried out a comprehensive data analysis. The framework presented in Hair et al. [22] was followed to evaluate missing data, to identify outliers, and to test for the assumptions underlying most multivariate techniques. Various graphical techniques (e.g. histograms, scatter plots, heat maps) were used to examine both the individual variables and the relationships among them. The main results of the data analysis are then mentioned.

In what regards the evaluation of missing data, the problem was addressed considering only the pavement sections in which the data was complete. All the pavement sections with missing data were excluded from the analysis.

To identify outliers, data values were converted to standard scores with mean of 0 and a standard deviation of 1. All the values falling at the outer ranges, high or low, of the standard normal distribution were defined as outliers. Since the sample had more than 80 observations, the threshold value considered was 4 [22]. Two outliers were then identified and removed.

Finally, the assumptions underlying the regression analysis were tested. According to Harrell [26], it is necessary to verify the assumptions of linearity and additivity. From the several methods proposed to verify these assumptions, the critical examination of the residual plots was chosen. Thus, simple regression analysis was performed for all inputs and the residuals were examined, looking for systematic patterns that could indicate nonlinear relationships. As a result of this analysis, the ACCUM_KESAL_YEAR predictor was transformed. A log transformation was applied to this predictor, which led to the spread of the residual distribution as presented in Fig. 2. From the engineering

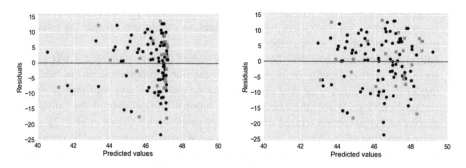

Fig. 2. Residual plots before (left) and after (right) the data transformation.

perspective, this transformation makes sense, since no road can have an infinite growth of traffic. Consequently, it is reasonable to think that after some years, the ACCUM_-KESAL_YEAR tends to converge asymptotically to a limit.

4.2   Friction Prediction Models

Friction prediction is a supervised learning problem, since inputs are used to predict the value of an output. In this specific case, the inputs are those already described in data matrix X, while the output y is FN. As y takes continuous values, the learning problem is known as regression [2].

Scikit-learn has several regression methods available. This study used linear regression and regularized regression with lasso. Such regression strategies are simple yet interpretable when used on pavement engineering data.

The linear regression model assumes that the regression function $E(Y \mid X)$ is linear in the inputs $X_1, \ldots, X_p$, having the following form:

$$f(X) = \beta_0 + \sum_{j=1}^{p} X_j \beta_j \tag{1}$$

Here the β_j's are unknown parameters or coefficients and the variables X_j are quantitative inputs.

The ordinary least squares method is a common solution to estimate the parameters β. In this method, the coefficients $\beta = (\beta_0, \beta_1, \ldots, \beta_p)^T$ are chosen to minimize the residual sum of squares:

$$RSS(\beta) = \sum_{i=1}^{N} (y_i - f(x_i))^2 = \sum_{i=1}^{N} \left(y_i - \beta_0 - \sum_{j=1}^{p} x_{ij} \beta_j \right)^2 \tag{2}$$

where y_i represents the target variable.

As an alternative, a regularized regression with lasso can be used. The regularized regression with lasso is a shrinkage method, which imposes a penalty to the regression coefficients, shrinking their size. In general, the shrinkage of the regression coefficients reduces the variance of the predicted values. This leads to the improvement of the overall prediction accuracy, even if some sacrifice in bias occurs [2].

The lasso estimate is defined by:

$$\hat{\beta}^{lasso} = argmin_{\beta} \left\{ \frac{1}{2} \sum_{i=1}^{N} \left(y_i - \beta_0 - \sum_{j=1}^{p} x_{ij} \beta_j \right)^2 + \lambda \sum_{j=1}^{p} |\beta_j| \right\} \tag{3}$$

where λ is the parameter that controls the amount of shrinkage. Larger values of λ correspond to a greater amount of shrinkage.

One particular aspect of lasso is that it will cause some of the coefficients to be exactly zero. In this sense, lasso works as a regularization and selection method. This was the main reason behind the choice of lasso. Being an engineering case, it is important to be able to interpret the model. Choosing the smaller subset of predictors that exhibit the strongest effects is a way to achieve that.

4.3   Model Selection ad Assessment

Model selection and model assessment are important processes in machine learning, as they select model's level of flexibility (model selection) and evaluate its performance (model assessment). This means that these processes are essential to tune hyperparameters, in order to select the best-performing model from a given hypothesis space, and to compare different models, enabling the choice of the model that has the best generalization performance.

There are several approaches for model assessment and selection, many of them discussed in Hastie et al. [2]. According to Stone [23], cross-validation is a viable option for model selection and assessment. However, different cross-validation approaches should be used because the process of model selection is different from the process of model assessment. This distinction is important to avoid a tendency found in the literature to report the cross-validation error found during the model selection as the assessed model performance [24]. In this sense, Varma and Simon [25] suggested the use of nested cross-validation as an unbiased estimate of the true error.

Accordingly, this study applied a nested cross-validation. A typical 5-fold cross-validation [2] was used and the error metric considered was the coefficient of determination (R^2). The R^2 is a value that measures the proportion of variance that can be explained by the regression model. Its best possible value is 1.

5   Discussion of Results

Table 1 shows the equations resulting from each model, as well as the R^2 values. Also, it is provided in Fig. 3 the plot of residuals to provide a visual assessment of the errors.

Table 1. Equations and R^2 values for each model.

Model	Equation	R^2
Linear regression	FN = 0.011 TOTAL_MON_PRECIP − 0.117 MEAN_MON_TEMP_AVG + 0.062 ACCUM_KESAL_YEAR + 0.869 FN_0−5.573 IRI	0.574
Regularized regression with lasso	FN = 0.010 TOTAL_MON_PRECIP − 0.131 MEAN_MON_TEMP_AVG + 0.827 FN_0	0.583

One of the first aspects standing out from the results is the exclusion of IRI and ACCUM_KESAL_YEAR from the regularized regression with lasso. This means that the proportion of variance that these variables explain in the regularized regression model is reduced.

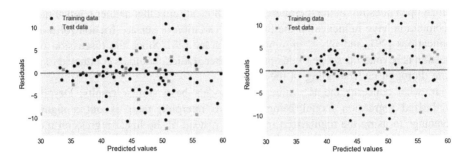

Fig. 3. Residual plots for linear (left) and regularized (right) regression.

From the engineering perspective, the exclusion of IRI was somehow expected. Although friction is related with pavement roughness [27], the texture wavelengths that affect the tire/pavement interaction are usually between 10^{-6} m and 10^{-1} m [10]. These wavelengths correspond to a finer-scale texture than IRI, which measures wavelengths larger than 100 m. A better option would be the inclusion of microtexture (wavelengths between 10^{-6} and 10^{-3} m) and microtexture (wavelengths between 10^{-3} and 10^{-1} m) in the model. That was not possible because few sections of the LTPP database include that information.

Regarding the exclusion of ACCUM_KESAL_YEAR, it is difficult to find a reasonable engineering explanation. Traffic is supposed to be one of the main factors motivating friction changes over time. Its action tends to polish the aggregates and makes them slipper. One possible explanation for this result may be the method used to determine ACCUM_KESAL_YEAR. As said before, this variable resulted from the multiplication of the mean kESAL/year by the number of years in service of the pavement. This is an approximated method that could be refined at the expense of an increased computational cost. Further studies concerning this result should be conducted.

The regularized regression model shows that FN_0 is the input that influences the most the FN. This means that the initial friction number affects significantly the change of friction over time. From an engineering standpoint, this is a reasonable result as it makes sense to think that different initial conditions can led to different deterioration rates. In road pavements, several contract documents are specific in friction requirements on work acceptance. According to the results, the definition of the threshold relative to the initial friction number should be a concern of road agencies, as any improvement in its determination can have an important impact in the infrastructure performance.

Coefficients related to environmental factors (MEAN_MON_TEMP_AVG and TOTAL_MON_PRECIP) show that temperature has a larger influence than precipitation. FN seems to increase with larger values of precipitation and decrease when temperatures are lower. These results are in line with the studies conducted by Song et al. [28], which reported a similar qualitative relationship between these variables.

When compared with the FN_0 coefficient, both environmental factors have reduced relevance. The way environmental factors affect skid evolution over time is still an open question in the literature, with authors arguing that neither temperature nor precipitation have influence on the long-term variation in surface friction for practical applications [29], and others arguing the contrary [28]. Since the discussion of this question is beyond the scope of this paper, further studies should be conducted to gain a more thorough understanding of the issue.

In what concerns the R^2 value, both models have similar results. Despite the regularized regression model being easier to interpret, there is not a significant advantage in using the regularized regression instead of the linear regression model.

The residual plots of both models show the residuals falling randomly, with relatively equal dispersion about zero and no strong tendency to be either greater or less than zero. This indicates that basic assumptions in multiple regression analysis are met.

The values reported for R^2 are far from perfect. However, it is important to remember that the models developed in this study learned from a real data set, which did not consider any specific selection of sections that could contribute for an improvement of the results. The models resulted from a pure data set, in a predictive analytics approach that can be considered closer to a big data approach than to a traditional one. Moreover, due to the lack of information in the LTPP database, some inputs that, according to the literature, could have a significant influence in skid resistance, like the pavement surface characteristics, were not considered. In this sense, it is believed that further data gathering can improve the results achieved in this study.

6 Conclusions

This paper uses a real case to illustrate how machine learning techniques can be applied to pavement engineering data using the scikit-learn Python toolkit. Supervised learning was applied to predict friction in asphalt pavements. Using scikit-learn, the Python code necessary to perform machine learning tasks is straightforward. The main challenges lie in pre-processing the data properly, choosing the right model for the problem, and interpreting the results, which are typically the tasks that can benefit from the engineering knowledge.

It was concluded that the initial friction number is an important input for the prediction of friction number over time. This is an important result regarding the definition of the maintenance policies, since friction number upon work acceptance is usually defined in contract documents. Accordingly, any refinements to the thresholds considered in those documents can contribute for better policies.

Other conclusions of this study are related to the need of acquiring additional data or considering other machine algorithms to improve the results achieved. The solution presented in this paper is limited by the data available in the LTPP database, which left out of the model several variables that are known to be related with friction. Moreover, only linear regression and regularized regression with lasso was explored in this study. For example, the application of random forests could turn the results of the study more comprehensive, as random forests are a non-linear approach. Further studies will be conducted in these matters, leveraging the structured scikit-learn approach proposed in this study.

The example discussed in this paper shows the potential of statistical learning applications to data-driven maintenance policies. By analysing data collected on pavements submitted to real use conditions, the prediction models developed in this paper have a practical relevance that laboratorial or theoretical models cannot achieve. Since better predictive models lead to cost-effective and timely maintenance practices, this study is a good example of how cutting-edge AI technologies can be effectively developed and applied to improve the sustainability of the transport systems.

References

1. Wallman, C.G., Åström, H.: Friction Measurement Methods and the Correlation Between Road Friction and Traffic Safety. VTI, Sweden (2001)
2. Hastie, T., Tibshirani, R., Friedman, J.J.H.: The Elements of Statistical Learning. Springer, Heidelberg (2001)
3. Murphy, K.: Machine Learning: A Probabilistic Perspective. MIT Press, Cambridge (2012)
4. Pedregosa, F., Varoquaux, G., Gramfort, A., Michel, V., Thirion, B., Grisel, O., Blondel, M., Prettenhofer, P., Weiss, R., Dubourg, V., Vanderplas, J., Passos, A., Cournapeau, D., Brucher, M., Perrot, M., Duchesnay, É.: Scikit-learn: machine learning in python. J. Mach. Learn. Res. **12**, 2825–2830 (2011)
5. Seabold, S., Perktold, J.: Statsmodels: econometric and statistical modeling with python. In: Proceedings of the 9th Python in Science Conference, vol. 57, Austin (2010)
6. Van der Walt, S., Colbert, S.C., Varoquaux, G.: The numpy array: a structure for efficient numerical computation. Comput. Sci. Eng. **13**, 22–30 (2011)
7. Hunter, J.D.: Matplotlib: a 2D graphics environment. Comput. Sci. Eng. **9**, 90–95 (2007)
8. McKinney, W.: Python for Data Analysis. O'Reilly, Springfield (2012)
9. Kane, M., Scharnigg, K.: D10: report on different parameters influencing skid resistance, rolling resistance and noise emissions. Technical report, TYROSAFE project (2009)
10. Henry, J.J.: Evaluation of pavement friction characteristics a synthesis of highway practice. In: NCHRP synthesis 291. Transportation Research Board (2000)
11. Wilson, D.J.: The effect of rainfall and contaminants on road pavement skid resistance. Research report, New Zealand Transport Agency (2013)
12. Cenek, P.D., Alabaster, D.J., Davies, R.B.: Seasonal and weather normalisation of skid resistance measurements. Research report, Transfund New Zealand (1999)
13. Chen, X., Dai, S., Guo, Y., Yang, J., Huang, X.: Polishing of asphalt pavements: from macro- to micro-scale. J. Test. Eval. **44**(2), 882–894 (2015)
14. Long-Term Pavement Performance (LTPP) Database. LTPP InfoPave (2017). https://infopave.fhwa.dot.gov. Accessed Feb 2017
15. Standard, A.S.T.M.: Standard test method for skid resistance of paved surfaces using a full-scale tire. ASTM International, West Conshohocken (2009)
16. Titus-Glover, L., Tayabji, S.D.: Assessment of LTPP friction data. Technical report, Federal Highway Administration (1999)
17. Rada, G.: SHRP-LTPP monitoring data: five-year report. Technical report, Strategic Highway Research Program (1994)
18. Hall, J.W., Smith, K.L., Titus-Glover, L.: Guide for pavement friction. Technical report, Transportation Research Board (2009)
19. Ahammed, M.A., Tighe, S.L.: Early-Life, long-term, and seasonal variations in skid resistance in flexible and rigid pavements. Trans. Res. Rec. **2094**(1), 112–120 (2009)

20. Saito, K., Henry, J.J.: Mechanistic model for predicting seasonal variations in skid resistance. Trans. Res. Rec. **946**, 29–37 (1983)
21. Fuentes, L., Asce, M., Gunaratne, M., Hess, D.: Evaluation of the effect of pavement roughness on skid resistance. J. Trans. Eng. **136**(7), 640–653 (2010)
22. Hair, J.F., Black, W.C., Babin, B.J., Anderson, R.E.: Multivariate Data Analysis. Pearson, London (2014)
23. Stone, M.: Cross-validatory choice and assessment of statistical predictions. J. R. Stat. Soc. **36**(2), 111–147 (1974)
24. Krstajic, D., Buturovic, L.J., Leahy, D.E., Thomas, S.: Cross-validation pitfalls when selecting and assessing regression and classification models. J. Chem. Inf. **6**(10), 1–15 (2014)
25. Varma, S., Simon, R.: Bias in error estimation when using cross-validation for model selection. BMC Bioinf. **7**, 1–8 (2006)
26. Harrell, F.E.: Regression Modeling Strategies. Springer, Heidelberg (2015)
27. Flintsch, G., McGhee, K., Izeppi, E.L., Najafi, S.: The Little Book of Tire Pavement Friction. Pavement Surface Properties Consortium (2012)
28. Song, W., Chen, X., Smith, T., Hedfi, A.: Investigation of hot mix asphalt surfaced pavements skid resistance in Maryland state highway network system. In: TRB 85th Annual Meeting (2006)
29. Ahammed, M.A., Tighe, S.L.: Effect of short-term and long-term weather on pavement surface friction. Int. J. Pavement Res. Technol. **3**(6), 295–302 (2010)

Optimising Cyclic Timetables with a SAT Approach
EPIA 2017

Gonçalo P. Matos[1,2]([✉]), Luís Albino[2], Ricardo L. Saldanha[2],
and Ernesto M. Morgado[1,2]

[1] Instituto Superior Técnico, Av. Rovisco Pais, 1, 1049-001 Lisbon, Portugal
{goncalo.p.matos,ernestomorgado}@tecnico.ulisboa.pt
[2] SISCOG, Sistemas Cognitivos SA, Campo Grande 378 - 3,
1900-097 Lisbon, Portugal
{goncalo.matos,lmalbino,rsaldanha,emorgado}@siscog.pt

Abstract. This paper describes the preliminary results of an ongoing research on cyclic railway timetabling, namely on optimising timetables with respect to travel time using Boolean Satisfiability Problem (SAT) approaches.

Some works already done in the field of railway timetables propose solutions to the optimisation problem using Mixed Integer Linear Programming (MILP) and SAT. In this work, we propose a binary search procedure which uses a SAT solver to get *global* minimum solutions with respect to travel time, and a procedure which is being developed to compute a better upper bound for the solution value and speed up the search process.

Finally, we present some promising preliminary results which show that our approach applied to real world data performs better than existing SAT approaches and a state-of-the-art MILP approach.

Keywords: Cyclic railway timetabling · Optimisation · Travel time · Periodic Event Scheduling Problem · SAT

1 Introduction

Railway timetabling is a major step in the overall process of planning the operations in a railway network, and is closely related to other planning activities such as line planning, and rolling stock and crew scheduling.

In this work, we focus on cyclic railway timetabling. In a cyclic timetable, each event (e.g. a train departure from a certain station) scheduled for some time instant actually occurs recurrently at that same instant, at each cycle time (e.g. every hour).

Several major train operators use cyclic timetables because they have several advantages [15]. They can be easily memorized by passengers, as they only need

© Springer International Publishing AG 2017
E. Oliveira et al. (Eds.): EPIA 2017, LNAI 10423, pp. 343–354, 2017.
DOI: 10.1007/978-3-319-65340-2_29

to know the minutes of the hour of the departures from their favorite origins to their favorite destinations, and they can be represented compactly.

From a planning perspective, cyclic timetables are also useful because the planner only needs to consider one time period (with possibly some adjustments).

Concerning cyclic timetables, one can be interested in finding a feasible timetable or an optimised one, according to some criteria. Henceforth, we will refer to these problems as Cyclic Timetable Satisfaction Problem (CTSP) and Cyclic Timetable Optimisation Problem (CTOP), respectively.

Over the last years, several approaches were studied for modeling and solving either the CTSP or the CTOP, namely constraint propagation, MILP, heuristically-guided search and genetic algorithms. A well-known approach for modeling the CTSP, called the Periodic Event Scheduling Problem (PESP), was introduced by Serafini and Ukovich [16].

Since PESP models were proposed, several approaches were used to solve the problem with increasing success. Recent works ([6,8,11]) suggest that SAT is currently the best known method for solving the PESP and the CTSP. The SAT problem is to decide whether a propositional formula is *satisfiable* or not. Essentially, the PESP problem is encoded as a propositional formula and solved using a state-of-the-art SAT solver.

Besides solving the CTSP, which is challenging *per se*, solving the CTOP with several objectives such as minimizing travel time or maximizing robustness[1] is also an area of interest. Recent works ([9,15]) have been done in this area, some of which also used SAT approaches ([3–5]).

This paper presents an ongoing research which is being performed in the context of a Master's thesis [14] at Instituto Superior Técnico, the University of Lisbon engineering faculty, and SISCOG[2], a portuguese software company specialized in solutions for creating and updating operational plans of companies that provide regular transportation services, such as passenger railway operators and metro systems.

Tackling real-world, large-sized timetabling problems (instead of merely small academic instances) is a major goal of this work. By working on this domain, SISCOG has access to timetable data and one of SISCOG Suite products, ONTIME, deals with the railway timetabling problem. Hence, the work being developed will be integrated on this product in order to improve it.

As discussed previously, SAT is currently a promising approach to solve the CTSP with good results already achieved both in generating feasible timetables and finding conflicts. Thus, this approach is being followed in this work. However, instead of solving the CTSP, we intend to solve the CTOP with SAT to get an optimal solution.

Regarding the optimisation of timetables, the work done so far used MILP ([15]) or constraint satisfaction ([9]), among other approaches. MaxSAT—a SAT based approach focused on the weighted maximisation of satisfied clauses—was

---

[1] A robust timetable is a timetable that does not tend to become disrupted when subject to perturbations.

[2] SISCOG - Sistemas Cognitivos, SA (http://www.siscog.eu).

already applied for minimization of the violations in infeasible instances ([4]), and for optimising cyclic timetables with respect to the passengers' routes ([3]). Even though there has been a remarkable progress in solving the CTOP, we believe that the potential of SAT approaches is not yet fully explored.

In particular, we are interested in optimising the travel time (a linear objective function defined in [15]) using incremental calls to a SAT solver. We propose a binary search procedure using a SAT solver to get optimal solutions for timetables, and an algorithm designed for computing a better upper bound for the solution value and for speeding up the search process. We believe that iteratively calling a SAT solver, with the help of a procedure for computing a good upper bound for the objective value, and performing a binary search may reduce the number of SAT solver calls and lead to better performances than using a MaxSAT solver.

We intend to evaluate the performance of our solution by comparing the achieved results - both in terms of objective value and computational time - with the ones obtained with existing tools in ONTIME (which are based on a MILP approach described in [15]) and with a MaxSAT approach as well.

On Sect. 2, some background on cyclic timetabling and other two related problems - the already mentioned PESP and SAT - is given first. On Sect. 3, a method to encode a PESP into SAT is presented, as well as the state-of-the-art on railway timetable optimisation. Sections 4 and 5 describe respectively the proposed solution for this problem and some preliminary and promising results which show that our approach applied to real world data performs better than the integer linear programming approach incorporated in ONTIME. Finally, we present the conclusions (Sect. 6).

2   Definitions

2.1   The Periodic Event Scheduling Problem (PESP)

The Periodic Event Scheduling Problem (PESP) was introduced by Serafini and Ukovich [16] as a formulation for a cyclic scheduling problem. The PESP is *NP-complete* for fixed $T \geq 3$ [15].

This formulation considers the concept of *event*, which can be a train departure (arrival) from (to) a network node (e.g. a railway station). The goal is to find a schedule for a set of such periodically recurring events, subject to a set of constraints under periodic time windows. The constraints force the time elapsed between two recurring events to be inside a periodic time window.

The PESP formulation also considers a cycle time T for which a schedule has to be created.

A formal definition, as stated by Peeters [15], is the following:

Definition 1 (PESP). *Given a set N of events, a set $A \subseteq N \times N$, a cycle time T, and time windows $[l_{ij}, u_{ij}]$ for all $(i,j) \in A$, the Periodic Event Scheduling Problem is to find a periodic schedule $v_i \in [0, T[, i \in N$, satisfying:*

$$(v_j - v_i) \bmod T \in [l_{ij}, u_{ij}] \text{ for all } (i,j) \in A, \tag{1}$$

or to conclude that no such schedule exists.

The previous Equation is usually abbreviated as

$$(v_j - v_i) \in [l_{ij}, u_{ij}]_T \text{ for all } (i, j) \in A. \tag{2}$$

Therefore, the PESP considers a decision problem.

The PESP can also be represented in a graph, whose nodes are the events to be scheduled and whose edges represent the constraints between events, with an associated periodic time window. This graph is known as the Periodic Event Network (PEN).

2.2   The SAT Problem

A propositional formula is composed of propositional (boolean) variables and a set of connectives: conjunction ($\wedge$) and disjunction ($\vee$), which are binary connectives, and negation ($\neg$), which is unary. A variable or its negation is called a *literal*, whereas a disjuntion of literals is called a *clause*.

The Boolean Satisfiability Problem (SAT) is to decide whether a propositional formula is *satisfiable* or not. If a formula is satisfiable then there is an assignment (called *interpretation*) to its boolean variables which verifies the formula, that is, makes it have the value *true*. In that case, such an interpretation is called a *model* for the formula. If, otherwise, the formula is not satisfiable, we usually say that the problem is UNSAT.

A generalization of the SAT problem exists, called Maximum Satisfiability Problem (MaxSAT). The MaxSAT is the problem of determining an assignement that maximizes the number (or the *weighted* sum) of the satisfied clauses in a propositional formula (usually one which is unsatisfiable. The SAT problem is *NP-complete* [1], and so is MaxSAT [2].

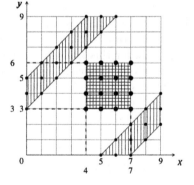

Fig. 1. Feasible (striped) and infeasible (white) regions for constraint $[3, 5]_{10}$ between events x and y. The gridded square shows an infeasible rectangle. The generated clause for this rectangle, according to Eq. 4, is $(\neg q_{x,7} \vee q_{x,3} \vee \neg q_{y,6} \vee q_{y,2})$. *Figure reproduced from* [11].

3   Related Work

3.1   From PESP to SAT

Several methods exist in the literature to convert any Constraint Satisfaction Problem (CSP) into SAT in order to solve it with a state-of-the-art SAT solver.

After all, a PESP is also a CSP, and hence several methods were already proposed to model and solve PESPs using SAT solvers. These methods are called *encodings*.

Furthermore (as of 2016), the currently best performing PESP solver is SAT-based ([6,8,11]). So, in this work, we will also encode and solve our PESP instances with SAT.

The Order Encoding. In this approach, we assume that the domains of all variables are finite and ordered. The description presented here is based on [6,11].

Let x be an event. In the concrete case of the PESP, all variables (events times) have domain $[0, \ldots, T]$, so we can encode event x as:

$$encode\_ordered : x \mapsto \left(\neg q_{x,-1} \wedge q_{x,T-1} \bigwedge_{i \in [0,T-1]} (\neg q_{x,i-1} \vee q_{x,i})\right) \tag{3}$$

with $\forall i \in [l, u-1] : q_{x,i}$ being a propositional variable such that $q_{x,i}$ represents the proposition $v_x \leq i$.

To encode the constraints, we exclude rectangular regions which contain infeasible pairs of starting times for each pair of events (see Fig. 1).

In order to encode a constraint, we can calculate the set of all of its infeasible rectangles using an auxiliary function ζ described in [6]. Then, for each excluded rectangle $r = ([x_1, x_2] \times [y_1, y_2])$ related with the constraint between the pair of events $(x, y) \in A$, we apply the function:

$$encode\_ordered\_rec : x, y, ([x_1, x_2] \times [y_1, y_2]) \mapsto (\neg q_{x,x_2} \vee q_{x,x_1-1} \vee \neg q_{y,y_2} \vee q_{y,y_1-1}) \tag{4}$$

So the complete PESP model is translated into SAT applying the previous functions to all event nodes and edges of the PEN:

$$\bigwedge_{i \in N} encode\_ordered(i) \bigwedge_{(i,j) \in A} \bigwedge_{r \in \zeta(l_{ij}, u_{ij})} encode\_ordered\_rec(i, j, r) \tag{5}$$

Großman shows [6] that it is possible to extract exactly one starting time for each event x given an interpretation I returned by the SAT solver, with respect to the previous encoding, using the function:

$$x = \xi_x(I) = \begin{cases} k & k \in [l, u-1] : q_{x,k-1}^I = false \wedge q_{x,k}^I = true \\ u & k = u : q_{x,u-1}^I = false \end{cases} \tag{6}$$

3.2 Timetable Optimisation

As explained in the introduction, besides finding a feasible schedule for a railway network (which is *per se* a challenging problem), one may be interested in optimising the generated timetable with respect to some objective function.

In [15], Peeters presents three objective functions, and solves the problem using *cycle bases* and *cutting planes*, with the *Cycle Periodicity Formulation*

(CPF) also introduced in that work. These objective functions depend on *process times* (or tensions), rather than event times, which can be defined, given the events v_i and v_j, as:

$$x_{ij} = v_j - v_i + Tp_{ij} \qquad (7)$$

where p_{ij} is an integer decision variable.

Passenger Travel Time. One of the objective functions presented in [15], which will be the main reference for this paper, is minimizing the passenger travel time. Connection and dwell times influence the total passenger trip time. Each minute of dwell above the minimum dwell time adds to the minimum possible travel time. So, these excess connection and dwell times are given by $(x_{ij} - l_{ij})$. If we define a weight w_{ij} for the objective function, we want to minimize

$$\sum_{(i,j) \in A} w_{ij}(x_{ij} - l_{ij}) \qquad (8)$$

In [3], Gattermann and Nachtigall addressed the approach of integrating passenger routes in the timetabling problem, so that the timetable is generated and optimised taking into account the paths that passengers will most probably choose given that current timetable.

They model the problem as a *partial weighted MaxSAT* problem, using the order encoding as proposed in [8], and aim to maximize the speedup of the passengers routed along their shortest paths according to travel time. In a sense, their objective function tries to minimize the passengers' travel time taking into account the passenger chosen routes, while our approach aims to minimize the total travel time of the timetable.

Gattermann et al. use auxiliary variables $\tau_{ij}^k \in \{0, 1\}$, $k \in \{0, \ldots, u_{ij} + 1\}$ for all arcs $(i, j) \in A$, which determine if $v_j - v_i + p_{ij}T \geq k$ holds. They also write a set of clauses ensuring the consistency of the relation of these variables, as in the order encoding.

The length of an activity can then be expressed as the sum of the τ_{ij}^k variables:

$$v_j - v_i + Tp_{ij} = \sum_{k=1}^{u_{ij}} \tau_{ij}^k \qquad (9)$$

Since they model the problem as MaxSAT, all the clauses appearing in the objective get their respective weight from the objective function and all other clauses which are needed to model the constraints get weight ∞, that is, they always have to be fulfilled.

In [7], a useful graph is shown which summarizes the possible approaches to optimisation in cyclic timetabling:

– One approach is to use a SAT solver to get an initial solution, and then feed a MILP solver with it.
– Another one is to use a MaxSAT solver.

– The third one is to iteratively call a SAT solver, guided by some heuristic. In [7], Großmann states that the heuristic they used in this latter approach only provides a local minimum, whereas the other approaches provide a global minimum.

According to [7], the MaxSAT method seems promising with respect to objective value and computation time, when compared to the MILP approach. Nevertheless, the heuristic tends to get better solutions faster.

4   Solution Architecture

4.1   Architecture Overview

The solution that we propose is to optimise the travel time using a SAT solver.

In order to do so, the first step is to model the linear objective functions (in this case, the Eq. 8) in propositional formulas written in clausal form, so that they can be given to a SAT solver. Furthermore, a SAT solver works as an oracle whose output is whether the provided formula is satisfiable or not, so we cannot ask it to minimize or maximize an objective function directly. Instead, we need to formulate the optimisation problem as a satisfaction query and rely on multiple calls to the SAT solver.

The base idea of our approach is the following. If we want to minimize an objective function in the form

$$\sum_l w_l \cdot x_l \tag{10}$$

where x_l are propositional variables and w_l are weights associated with each variable, then we model the function as a constraint instead:

$$\sum_l w_l \cdot x_l \leq C \tag{11}$$

being C an integer constant. Then, we apply the procedure described in Algorithm 1.

Several methods exist in the literature to model sums like this in propositional formulas, named pseudo-boolean constraints, so the research and choice of one such method will also be part of this work. One of those methods that we already tested and provided promising results is the Generalized Totalizer Encoding [10].

The difference between our approach and the binary heuristic described by Großmann in [4,7] is that our method will provide us the global optimal solution. This is due to the way we encode the objective function in a propositional formula. While in [4] in each step of the binary heuristic the upper bound *for each constraint* is reduced by 1 time unit, our approach uses a single constant C representing the total sum of the objective function. Hence, when we increase or reduce 1 unit in the constant C we are not imposing which constraints will be affected, we just let the solver find a solution possibly modifying some event times such that the total sum is reduced by the required amount.

Algorithm 1. Minimize $\sum_l w_l \cdot x_l \leq C$ by binary search

---

Require: A SAT formula F containing the encoding of PESP and $\sum_l w_l \cdot x_l \leq C$.
Require: Initial LB and UB.
1: **procedure** OPTIMISE_BINARY($F, initial\_LB, initial\_UB$)
2:     $LB \leftarrow initial\_LB$
3:     $UB \leftarrow initial\_UB$
4:     $M \leftarrow$ UNSAT
5:     **while** $LB \leq UB$ **do**
6:         $C \leftarrow \frac{LB+UB}{2}$
7:         Update value of C in $\sum_l w_l \cdot x_l \leq C$ inside the SAT formula F.
8:         **if** SAT(F) **then**   ▷ Call SAT solver
9:             $M \leftarrow$ model for F
10:             $C' \leftarrow$ cost of solution M
11:             $UB \leftarrow C' - 1$
12:         **else**
13:             $LB \leftarrow C + 1$
14:         **end if**
15:     **end while**
16:     **return** M
17: **end procedure**

On the other hand, we believe that our approach with iterative calls to a SAT solver may outperform the approach described in [7] of using a MaxSAT solver in the sense that our method is guided with knowledge from the problem (the lower and upper bounds for C and the binary search procedure), whereas a generic MaxSAT solver does not know the domain of the problem it is solving. Our specialized method does not modify existing clauses nor it removes any variables or clauses between SAT calls (we just add new clauses and fix the values of some variables in order to define the value for C), so we can avoid re-encoding the whole problem for each iteration and we also benefit from the lemmas (conflicts) learned by the SAT solver in previous calls.

The solution architecture we propose may be summarized in Algorithm 2:

4.2   Encoding the Objective Function

As already mentioned our objective function is the total travel time. To simplify the following discussion, we will assume that all weights are unitary, i.e., $w_{ij} = 1$ in Eqs. 8 and 11.

We followed an approach based on [3].

We add auxiliary variables $\hat{\tau}_{ij}^k \in \{0,1\}$, for all constraints $(i,j) \in A$ and $k \in \{0,\ldots,u_{ij} - l_{ij}\}$, representing the following proposition: the *difference* between the tension x_{ij} and the lower bound l_{ij} for the constraint is greater or equal than k.

Then, we impose order encoding constraints on these new variables:

$$(i,j) \mapsto (\hat{\tau}_{ij}^0 \wedge \neg\hat{\tau}_{ij}^{u_{ij}+1} \bigwedge_{k \in \{1,\ldots,u_{ij}+1\}} (\neg\hat{\tau}_{ij}^k \vee \hat{\tau}_{ij}^{k-1})) \tag{12}$$

Algorithm 2. Optimise a cyclic timetable with SAT
Require: A PESP problem P.

```
 1: procedure OPTIMISE_TIMETABLE(PESP P)
 2:     Represent P in a PEN graph G.
 3:     G' ← compact the graph G.                          ▷ Using ONTIME
 4:     F ← order_encode(G')
 5:     if SAT(F) then                                     ▷ Call SAT solver
 6:         C ← compute initial UB for P                   ▷ See Sect. 4.3
 7:         F' ← F ∪ order_encode(∑_l w_l · x_l ≤ C)
 8:         M ← optimise_binary(F', 0, C)                  ▷ See Algorithm 1
 9:         return Decoded optimised timetable from M
10:     else
11:         return "Infeasible"
12:     end if
13: end procedure
```

and encode the following implications as clauses:

$$(v_j - v_i - l_{ij} + T \cdot p_{ij} \geq k) \implies \hat{\tau}_{ij}^k$$

$$\iff (v_j - v_i - l_{ij} + T p_{ij} < k) \vee \hat{\tau}_{ij}^k \qquad (13)$$

$$\iff (v_j - v_i + T \cdot p_{ij} \in [l_{ij}, k + l_{ij} - 1]) \vee \hat{\tau}_{ij}^k$$

Notice that the first part of the disjunction in Eq. 13 is just another typical PESP constraint, which we encode in the *order encoding* in the same way as any other original PESP constraint.

So, we want to minimize:

$$\sum_{(i,j) \in A} (x_{ij} - l_{ij}) = \sum_{(i,j) \in A} \left(\sum_{k=1}^{u_{ij} - l_{ij}} \hat{\tau}_{ij}^k \right) \qquad (14)$$

We can encode this objective into a single pseudo-boolean formula as seen in Eq. 11, where the l indexes correpond to (i, j, k) triples, the weights w_l are assumed to be 1 in our simplified approach, and the x_l variables in Eq. 11 are replaced by the variables $\hat{\tau}_{ij}^k$ in our encoding. Then, we apply Algorithm 1.

4.3   Computing the Initial Upper Bound (UB)

In order to reduce the number of required iterations during the binary search, we developed a procedure which computes a better initial UB for the objective function.

The simplest (and initial) UB is the sum of the upper limits of the constraint windows for all weighted constraints in the problem, which can be easily proved to be always greater than or equal to the value of an optimal solution.

In order to improve this UB (i.e., lower its value) without losing optimality, we perform a sequence of SAT calls where we progressively impose tighter windows for the weighted constraints until the problem has no solution.

In order to do so, in the first iteration we fix the value *false* for the highest $\hat{\tau}$ variable for each event pair. By fixing this variable, we are reducing in 1 unit the upper limit of the window for each constraint.

In the next iterations, we progressively fix more $\hat{\tau}$ variables with the value *false*, reducing one more unit in each constraint window at each iteration.

We stop once we get an UNSAT answer from the SAT solver. In that moment, we can no longer tighten the constraints, and the previous SAT solution is the best we can get following this method (note that it is a local minimum). We return the objective value of that previous solution as the best known UB. Note that it is never lower than the value of an optimal solution, as we found at least one solution with that value, so we do not lose feasibility nor the global optimum.

If, otherwise, we can fix all the $\hat{\tau}$ variables and still get a SAT answer, then the algorithm could luckily find the optimal solution (whose cost is zero) and we do not even need to perform the binary search.

Besides lowering the initial UB, one of the biggest advantages of using this procedure before performing the binary search is the fact that all the lemmas learned by the SAT solver during these iterations are kept and can be used to improve the performance of the solving process later.

5   Preliminary Results

We applied the described SAT algorithms to real world data from a major European passenger railway operator and a major US metro system. Each problem is characterized in Table 1 by the number of departure/arrival events, the total number of constraints and the number of constraints with costs (which are relevant for the optimisation problem).

Table 1 also shows the execution times for finding an optimal solution (SAT TIME). To evaluate the performance of our method, we compared them with the execution time needed for the MILP model[3] used in ONTIME to find an optimal solution (MILP TIME), and also with the execution time needed for a MaxSAT approach based[4] on [3] (MaxSAT TIME). In Table 1, the execution time entries with a + represent runs which took more than a time limit that we imposed.

The tests were run on a machine with an Intel Core i7-3770 CPU @ 3.40 GHz and 16 GB of RAM. We used the SAT solver Glucose 4.0, the MaxSAT solver open-wbo [13] and the MILP solver CPLEX 12.5.1.

The results show that our approach outperforms CPLEX in most of the problems. For several of them, we could even stop the execution of CPLEX after a couple of hours without having found any solution at all, while our SAT based approach found the optimal solution in just seconds. The bad results of the MILP solver may be due to poor lower bounds.

---

[3] Based on [15].

[4] We formulated in MaxSAT our optimisation problem, which differs from the one in [3] for not taking into account the passenger routes but optimising the whole timetable instead.

Table 1. Results on real world data.

Problem name	Events	Constraints total	Edges with cost	SAT					MaxSAT		MILP		
				Variables	Clauses	Value	Gap %	TIME	Value	TIME	Value	Gap %	TIME
R1	8389	69348	879	538996	2355813	39601	0	00:13:00	-	05:00:00 +	39601	0	00:03:11
R2	8395	69348	874	478911	5868372	38873	15.59	02:51:00	-	05:00:00 +	-	-	08:00:00 +
M1_24	916	2122	445	129239	1319816	0	0	00:00:01	0	00:00:06	0	0	00:00:02
M2_48	1922	8410	966	215439	2503581	0	0	00:00:03	0	00:00:15	0	0	00:05:47
M3_80	3320	22316	1610	258844	3184876	0	0	00:00:09	0	00:00:30	-	-	02:00:00 +
M4_96	3984	31761	1932	258844	3184876	0	0	00:00:14	0	00:00:40	-	-	02:00:00 +
M5_112	4648	42861	2254	301944	3910677	0	0	00:00:23	0	00:00:52	-	-	02:00:00 +
M6_120	4980	49037	2415	323494	4315058	0	0	00:00:18	-	02:00:00+	-	-	02:00:00 +

Furthermore, the results also suggest that our approach outperforms an equivalent MaxSAT approach, since the execution times were lower for all problems with no exception and there were problems for which the MaxSAT approach could not find a solution in several hours.

6   Conclusions

In this work, we focus on optimising cyclic railway timetables.

Firstly, the state of the art with respect to solving the PESP using SAT and other approaches was studied and presented in Sect. 3.

We concluded with this initial research that SAT is currently a promising approach to solve the PESP with good results already achieved both in generating feasible timetables and finding conflicts. Therefore, this approach will be followed in the remaining of this work.

Regarding the optimisation of timetables, the work done so far by other researchers was mainly through MILP and constraint satisfaction. Some recent works with MaxSAT also showed promising results. The method we propose, however, innovates in the sense that we model and optimise timetables with respect to travel time using only incremental SAT calls, while still getting *global* minimum solutions.

Some preliminary results show that our new approach already outperforms the best approaches that ONTIME had before, namely the one that used CPLEX, and also an equivalent MaxSAT formulation of the problem, hence supporting our thesis that an informed SAT approach may perform better than a general MaxSAT one.

References

1. Cook, S.A.: The complexity of theorem-proving procedures. In: Proceedings of the Third Annual ACM Symposium on Theory of Computing, pp. 151–158 (1971)
2. El Halaby, M.: On the computational complexity of MaxSAT. In: Electronic Colloquium on Computational Complexity (ECCC), vol. 23, p. 34 (2016)

3. Gattermann, P., Nachtigall, K.: Integrating passengers' routes in periodic timetabling: a SAT approach. In: 16th Workshop on Algorithmic Approaches for Transportation Modelling, Optimization, and Systems (ATMOS 2016), vol. 54, no. 3, pp. 1–15 (2016)

4. Gro, P., Opitz, J., Wei, R.: On resolving infeasible periodic event networks. In: Proceedings of the 13th Conference on Advanced Systems in Public Transport (CASPT 2015) (2015)

5. Großmann, P., Weiss, R., Opitz, J., Nachtigall, K.: Automated generation and optimization of public railway and rail freight transport time tables. MTM **5**, 23–26 (2012)

6. Großmann, P.: Polynomial reduction from PESP to SAT. Technical report (2011)

7. Großmann, P.: Satisfiability and optimization in periodic traffic flow problems. Ph.D thesis, TU Dresden (2016)

8. Großmann, P., Hölldobler, S., Manthey, N., Nachtigall, K., Opitz, J., Steinke, P.: Solving public railway transport networks with SAT. Technical report, TU Dresden (2011)

9. Ingolotti, L., Lova, A., Barber, F., Tormos, P., Salido, M.A., Abril, M.: New heuristics to solve the "CSOP" railway timetabling problem. In: Ali, M., Dapoigny, R. (eds.) IEA/AIE 2006. LNCS, vol. 4031, pp. 400–409. Springer, Heidelberg (2006). doi:10.1007/11779568_44

10. Joshi, S., Martins, R., Manquinho, V.: Generalized totalizer encoding for pseudo-boolean constraints. In: Pesant, G. (ed.) CP 2015. LNCS, vol. 9255, pp. 200–209. Springer, Cham (2015). doi:10.1007/978-3-319-23219-5_15

11. Kümmling, M., Großmann, P., Nachtigall, K., Opitz, J., Weiß, R.: A state-of-the-art realization of cyclic railway timetable computation. Public Transp. **7**(3), 281–293 (2015)

12. Martins, R., Joshi, S., Manquinho, V., Lynce, I.: Incremental cardinality constraints for MaxSAT. In: O'Sullivan, B. (ed.) CP 2014. LNCS, vol. 8656, pp. 531–548. Springer, Cham (2014). doi:10.1007/978-3-319-10428-7_39

13. Martins, R., Manquinho, V., Lynce, I.: Open-WBO: a modular MaxSAT solver'. In: Sinz, C., Egly, U. (eds.) SAT 2014. LNCS, vol. 8561, pp. 438–445. Springer, Cham (2014). doi:10.1007/978-3-319-09284-3_33

14. Matos, G.P.: Optimisation of periodic train timetables. Master's thesis project, Technical report, Instituto Superior Técnico, Lisbon, Portugal (2017)

15. Peeters, L.W.P.: Cyclic railway timetable optimization. Trail thesis series 22 (2003)

16. Serafini, P., Ukovich, W.: A mathematical model for periodic scheduling problems. SIAM J. Discrete Math. **2**, 550–581 (1989)

Transportation in Social Media: An Automatic Classifier for Travel-Related Tweets

João Pereira[1,2]([✉]), Arian Pasquali[3], Pedro Saleiro[1,2], and Rosaldo Rossetti[1,2]

[1] FEUP, Universidade do Porto, Porto, Portugal
{joao.filipe.pereira,pssc,rossetti}@fe.up.pt
[2] LIACC, Universidade do Porto, Porto, Portugal
[3] INESC TEC, Universidade do Porto, Porto, Portugal
arrp@inesctec.pt

Abstract. In the last years researchers in the field of intelligent transportation systems have made several efforts to extract valuable information from social media streams. However, collecting domain-specific data from any social media is a challenging task demanding appropriate and robust classification methods. In this work we focus on exploring geo-located tweets in order to create a travel-related tweet classifier using a combination of bag-of-words and word embeddings. The resulting classification makes possible the identification of interesting spatio-temporal relations in São Paulo and Rio de Janeiro.

Keywords: Geo-located Twitter · Transportation · Text classification

1 Introduction

Social media data is still in the process of maturation regarding its use in the transportation and mobility fields. Users tend to publicly share events in which they participate, as well as the ones related to the operation of the transportation network, such as accidents and other disruptions. The exploration of social media data brings particular advantages, under virtually no cost, such as real-time data and content authenticity due to its human generated nature. In the domain of transportation, social media data analysis can produce valuable insights to support traffic management and control, human mobility, shared services, and policy making studies.

The main goal of this work lies upon the development of an automatic system capable of discriminating travel-related tweets from a stream of geo-located tweets. However, extracting accurate knowledge from social media content is still challenging. Social media texts are usually short, informal, with a lot of abbreviations, jargon, slang and idioms, being such characteristics the biggest challenges to surpass regarding text analysis.

We take advantage of recent developments on neural language models [1], and train continuous word representations, the so called word embeddings, from two streams of geo-located tweets in São Paulo and Rio de Janeiro, comprising

© Springer International Publishing AG 2017
E. Oliveira et al. (Eds.): EPIA 2017, LNAI 10423, pp. 355–366, 2017.
DOI: 10.1007/978-3-319-65340-2_30

more than 8 millions tweets. These word embeddings representations are able to capture syntactic and semantic relations between words in tweets that are useful in the context of transportation (e.g. "ônibus" and "busão").

Consequently, we combine bag-of-embeddings and standard bag-of-words to learn a binary classifier of travel/non-travel tweets classification. We train and evaluate our model using a new hand-coded gold standard specifically created for this work. We applied the resulting classifier to both streams of geo-located tweets and obtained interesting spatio-temporal relations on both cities, demonstrating the usefulness of travel-related filtering on streams of geo-located tweets.

The remainder of this paper is organised as follows. In Sect. 2, we present some of the related work already done in the area. The methodology behind the collection of geo-located tweets, as well as, its exploratory analysis are detailed in Sect. 3. In Sect. 4, we describe our approach, the processing steps applied to our data and the features selection. The experimental set up is presented in Sect. 5, while the results of our experiences and their discussion are presented in Sect. 6. We draw conclusions and highlight main contributions in Sect. 7, alongside some suggestions for further developments in this project.

2 Related Work

Classification models applied to Twitter data were already proposed and tested in different areas of study, ranging from sentiment analysis for political data science [2,3] to predict stock market fluctuations [4], or to predict content popularity on Twitter [5]. Recently, the research community has realised the potential of using social media data to study the various dimensions of transportation systems, including mobility, travel purpose and different modes of transport and their interactions [6,7]. In the work by Ulloa et al. [8], authors proposed a domain-agnostic framework capable of extracting relevant informations from real-time Twitter data in the field of transportation.

Kurkcu et al. [9] use geo-located tweets to try and discover human mobility and activity patterns. The subject of transport modes was explored by Maghrebi et al. [10] in the city of Melbourne, Australia. From a dataset of 300,000 geo-located tweets, authors tried to extract tweets related to several modes of transport using a keyword-based search method.

Additionally, there were also different efforts focused on the tracking of accidents using Twitter social media data. Mai and Hranac [11] tried to establish a correlation between the California Highway Patrol incident reports and the increased volume of tweets posted at the time they were reported. On the other hand, Rebelo et al. [12] implemented a system capable of extract and analyse events related to road traffic, coined TwitterJam. In that study, authors also used geo-located tweets that were already confirmed as being related to events on the roads and compared their counts with official sources.

Some authors have also worked towards extracting travel-related content from tweets. For instance, Carvalho et al. [13] created a travel-related classifier, whose training set had the particularity of being unbalanced, since the percentage of tweets known to be travel-related was very low. Authors reported that using a bootstrapping strategy with linear Support Vector Machines (SVM) in combination with vectorized messages, such as unigram bag-of-words, the performance results were increased. On another work, Kuflik et al. [14] proposed a framework to automatically extract and analyse transport-related tweets, in which the filter process was carried out through classification models.

3 Data

The data used for this study was collected using Twitter's Streaming API through a Python library (Tweepy[1]). The library was configured with the'locations' filter activated, whose main purpose is to allow the retrieval of all tweets within a defined bounding-box. Such a bounding-box is a rectangle obtained by two coordinate pairs (latitude and longitude, for the South-West point and the North-East point), as illustrated in Figs. 1 and in 2. The selected target scenarios in this study are the two largest and most active Brazilian cities on Twitter, namely Rio de Janeiro and São Paulo, both capitals of states with the same names, abbreviated by RJ and SP, respectively.

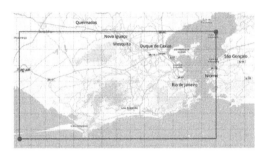

Fig. 1. Rio de Janeiro   **Fig. 2.** São Paulo

Messages were collected for a period of one whole month, between days March 12 and April 12, 2017, and the resulting datasets sum up a total of 5.3M and 2.4M tweets for RJ and for SP, respectively.

3.1 Collecting Geo-Located Tweets

As we referred above, the data was collected using a bounding-box-based filter; however, we detected that not all tweets were located inside the defined bounding-boxes. Indeed, the documentation of the Twitter Streaming API mentions that the locations filter has two possible heuristics[2]: (1) if the coordinates field is populated, the values there will be tested against the bounding-box; (2) if the coordinates field is empty but place is populated, the region defined in place is checked for intersections against the locations bounding-box. Any overlapping areas will yield a positive match.

---

[1] http://www.tweepy.org/.

[2] https://dev.twitter.com/streaming/overview/request-parameters#locations.

Table 1. Datasets composition (10^6)

City	All	PT	Non-PT	Inside bounding-box	Outside bounding-box	PT and inside bounding-box
Rio de Janeiro	6,175	5,355	0,819	4,327	1,848	3,749
São Paulo	2,934	2,444	0,490	2,016	0,918	1,672

The first heuristic only happens if a user is able/willing to tag a post with his precise geo-location associated with it; otherwise, the user can tag the post associated with a place, selected from a list provided by Twitter, in which case the second heuristic applies. Considering the *place* field in a tweet is composed by a bounding-box, if any piece of it overlaps the bounding-box used in the filter process, then a positive match is yielded and the tweet is retrieved. For example, if a tweet has a place such as Brazil and our filter bounding-box is defined for Rio de Janeiro, all tweets from place Brazil will be in our dataset, regardless the fact some tweets are posted elsewhere, such as in the city of Manaus, very far away from Rio de Janeiro. To solve this matching problem, we used the default Twitter bounding-boxes for RJ and SP to check whether a certain place is or is not inside the desired area. For tweets which field *coordinates* was empty, we calculate the centre of the bounding-box and use that Only tweets whose field *language* was Portuguese (PT) were considered. The final composition of our dataset is presented in Table 1.

3.2 Exploratory Data Analysis

In order to gain better insight into the composition of our datasets, several analysis were performed so as to understand what were the most active hours of the day and days of the week in terms of geo-located tweets, as well as the most mentioned *hashtags* and used words in their contents. This exploratory analysis was performed over the tweets in Portuguese (7.8M tweets).

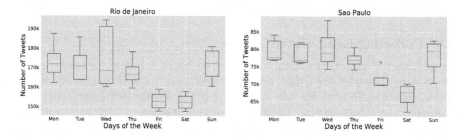

Fig. 3. Frequency of tweets for each day of the week

Figure 3 illustrates the volume of tweets per day of the week collected during the month of the study. An interesting point to enhance is the difference between the volumes of geo-located tweets of the two cities. According to IBGE (*Instituto Brasileiro de Geografia e Estatística*) statistics, Rio de Janeiro[3] has 6.5M habitants, half of the population of the city of São Paulo[4] which has 12M citizens.

On the other hand, our datasets of geo-located tweets comprises 98 K distinct users posting geo-located tweets in Rio de Janeiro, while São Paulo only has 78k. In terms of total geo-located tweets, Rio de Janeiro doubles the number of tweets in São Paulo. Such difference in the volume of the datasets can arise several questions about why geo-located Twitter activity in RJ is more intense than SP.

As we observe in Fig. 4, it is possible to establish correlation between the Power law distribution and the frequency of tweets per user in our datasets. The notable long tail shows us the existence of a large number of occurrences of users whose activity on Twitter is much lower. Such correlation is strongly supported by the number of users that have less than 10 tweets posted in the month of data - 51.7k and 51.5k for RJ and SP, respectively. This values represent more than 60% of the users in both cities, while 35% of the remaining users belong to the interval of users that have posted 10–100 tweets. Only a few percentage of users had posted more than 100 tweets.

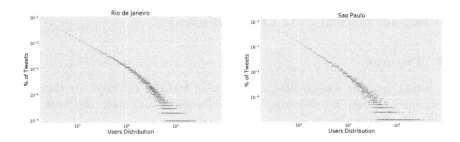

Fig. 4. Distribution of users per number of tweets

4   Classifying Travel-Related Tweets

The main goal of this work is to support the characterisation of travel-related tweets in Rio de Janeiro and in São Paulo. Considering the volume of the collected data, it was then necessary to automatically identify tweets whose content somehow suggests to be related to the transportation domain. Conventional approaches would require us to specify travel-related keywords to classify such tweets. On the contrary, our approach consisted in training a classifier model to automatically discriminate travel-related tweets from non-related ones.

One big challenge always present in text analysis is the sparse nature of data, which is especially the case in Twitter messages. Conventional techniques such as

---

[3] http://cod.ibge.gov.br/493.
[4] http://cod.ibge.gov.br/E4X.

Bag-of-Words tend to produce sparse representations, which become even worse when data is composed by informal and noisy content.

Word embeddings, on the other hand, is a text representation technique that tries to capture syntactic and semantic relations from words. The result is a more cohesive representation where similar words are represented by similar vectors. For instance, *"taxi"/"uber"*, *"bus/busão/ônibus"*, *"go to work"/"go to school"* would yield similar vectors respectively. We are particularly interested in exploring the characteristics of word embeddings techniques to understand to which extent it is possible to improve the performance of our classifier to capture such travel-related expressions.

4.1   Data Preparation

Each tweet of our training and test sets was submitted to a small and basic group of pre-processing operations, as detailed below.

- **Lowercasing:** Every message presented in a tweet was converted into lowercase;
- **Transforming repeated characters:** Sequences of characters repeated more than three times were transformed, e.g. "loooool" was converted to "loool";
- **Cleaning:** Removing URLs and user mentions.

4.2   Features

We established the use of different groups of features to train our classification model, namely bag-of-words, bag-of-embeddings and both combined. Such groups are detailed below.

- **Bag-of-words (BoW):** This group of features was obtained using unigrams with standard bag-of-words techniques. We considered the 3,000 most frequent terms across the training set excluding the ones found in more than 60% of the documents;
- **Bag-of-embeddings (BoE):** We created bag-of-embeddings using *paragraph2vec* [15]. This method is capable of learning distributed representations of words, each word being represented by a distribution of weights across a fixed number of dimensions. Authors have also proved [16] that this kind of representation is robust when encoding syntactic and semantic similarities in the embedding space. We trained 10 iterations over the whole Portuguese dataset using a context window of value 2 and feature vectors of 100 dimensions. We then took the corresponding embedding matrix to yield the group of features fed into our classification routine.
- **Bag-of-words plus Bag-of-embeddings:** We horizontally combined both the above matrices into a single one and used it as a single group of features.

5   Experimental Setup

In this section we describe the strategy chosen to create the training and test sets in order to conduct our study. The experimental classification models, their tuning parameters, as well as the evaluation metrics to measure their performance are also discussed.

5.1   Training and Test Sets

The construction of the training and test sets followed a traditional approach. We thus tried to select balanced training sets, to which it was necessary to identify tweets that could possibly be travel-related. We were inspired by a strategy used in the study by Maghrebi et al. [10], which consists in searching tweets from a collection using specific travel terms and regular expressions. Using the correspondent terms for each mode of transport - (Bike) *bicicleta, moto*; (Bus) *onibus, ônibus*; (Car) *carro*; (Taxi) *taxi, táxi*; (Train) *metro, metrô, trem*; (Walk) *caminhar* - combined with the regular expression $space + term + space$, we found about 30,000 tweets. From this subset, we randomly selected a small sample of 3,000 tweets to manually confirm they were indeed related to travel topics. After this manual annotation we selected 2,000 tweets and used them as positive samples in the training dataset.

In order to select negative samples for the training dataset we randomly selected 2,000 tweets and also manually verified their content to assure that they were not travel-related. Finally, our training set was composed by 4,000 tweets, from which 2,000 were travel-related and 2,000 were not. We selected 1,000 tweets randomly that were not present in the training set so as to build the test set, and then manually classified them as travel-related or non-travel-related. In the end, 71 tweets were found to be travel-related and whereas 929 were not.

5.2   Classification

Support Vector Machines (SVM), Logistic Regression (LR) and Random Forests (RF) were the classifiers used in our experiences. The SVM classifier was tested under three different kernels, namely *rbf*, *sigmoid* and *linear*; the latter proved to obtain the best results.

The LR classifier was used with the standard parameters, whereas the RF classifier used 100 trees in the forest. The gini criterion and the maximum number of features were limited to those as aforementioned in Sect. 4.2, in the case of the RF classifier.

5.3   Evaluation Metrics

To evaluate the performance of the classifiers in our experiences we used five different metrics. Firstly we compute a group of three per-class metrics, namely precision, recall and the F1-score. Bearing in mind this study considers a binary classification, metrics were associated with the travel-related class only, i.e. the positive class. The ROC (Receiver operating characteristic) curve gives us the TPR (True positive rate) and the FPR (False positive rate) for all possible variations of the discrimination threshold. Through the ROC curve, we compute the area under the curve (AUC) to see what was the probability of the classifier to rank a random travel-related tweet higher than a random non-related one.

6   Results and Analysis

In this section we present the results obtained in the experimental setup. A comparison of different learning algorithms using the features mentioned in Sect. 4.2 is provided as so some analysis on tweets classified as travel-related.

6.1   Results

Table 2 presents the results obtained using the different features combination for our test set composed by 1,000 tweets manually annotated. According to the evaluation metrics we conclude that the bag-of-word and bag-of-embeddings combined produced better classification models. The model produced by the Linear SVM performed slightly better than the LR and the RF. Interesting to note is that BoW features have influence on the precision scores obtained from our results, producing more conservative classifiers. Regarding the recall results, we can see that the Logistic Regression using only bag-of-embeddings features was the model with best results; perhaps if the precision is taken into consideration, the same conclusions will not be possible. Analysing the scores provided in Table 2, the best model under the F1-score was the Linear SVM, with a score of 0.85.

Table 2. Travel-related classifiers results.

Classifier	Features	Precision	Recall	F1-score
Linear SVM	BoW	1.0	0.6761	0.8067
	BoE	0.4338	0.8309	0.5700
	BoW + BoE	**1.0**	**0.7465**	**0.8548**
Logistic regression	BoW	1.0	0.6338	0.7759
	BoE	0.4444	0.8451	0.5825
	BoW + BoE	1.0	0.6761	0.8067
Random forest	BoW	1.0	0.6338	0.7759
	BoE	0.2298	0.8028	0.3574
	BoW + BoE	1.0	0.6338	0.7759

6.2   Analysis

The performance of all three classifiers is illustrated using the ROC Curve in Fig. 5. The area under the curve of the Receiver Operating Characteristic (AUC) was very similar for both the Logistic Regression and the Linear SVM models. The results obtained from the Random Forest model were not so promising as expected.

After the selection of our classification model, we decided to classify all the Portuguese dataset and draw some statistics from the results. The trained Linear SVM classifier was used to predict whether tweets were travel-related or not, since it was the model presenting the best score under the F1-score metric (as shown in Table 2). From a total of 7.8M tweets, our classifier was able identified 37,300 travel-related entries.

Figure 6 depicts the distribution of travel-related tweets over the days of the week. We can see that the first three business days (Monday, Tuesday and Wednesday) are the ones on which the Twitter activity is higher for both cities.

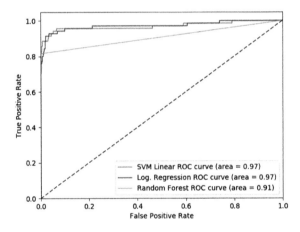

Fig. 5. ROC curve of SVM, LR and RF experiences

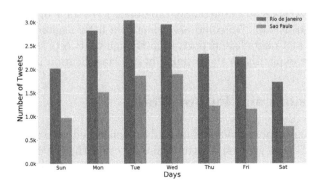

Fig. 6. Positive predicted tweets per day of week

Fig. 7. Rio de Janeiro Heatmap of the positive tweets

In order to understand the spatial distribution of travel-related tweets we generated a heatmap for both cities. We calculate the centre of the bounding-box attached to the tweets which field *coordinates* was empty. From the heatmap of RJ, illustrated in Fig. 7, it is possible to identify that some agglomerations of tweets are located at Central do Brasil, Cidade Nova and Triagem train stations, as well as at Uruguaiana, Maracanã and Carioca metro stations. The Rio-Niterói bridge, connecting Rio de Janeiro to Niterói, as well as the piers on both sides also presented considerable clouds of tweets classified as travel-related.

The heatmap for the city of SP was also an interesting case to observe. Almost every agglomeration matched some metro or train station. Estação Brás, Tatuapé, Belém, Estação Paulista, Sé, Liberdade were some of the stations highlighted in the heatmap. We could also identify a little agglomeration of travel-related tweets at Congonhas airport, even though no tweets seemed to mention the word *plane* explicitly in the training of our classification model.

7   Conclusions and Future Work

The methodology reported across our study is concerned with the problem of the construction of a fine-grained Twitter training set for the travel domain and also the automatic identification of travel-related tweets from a large scale corpus. We combined different word representations to verify whether our classification model could learn relations between words at both syntactic and semantic levels.

After using standard techniques such as bag-of-words and bag-of-embeddings, we have used them combined yielding results that showed that these different groups of features can complement each other.

The future directions for our research will include the application of unsupervised topic modelling algorithms to the non-related subset given by our classifier. This extension to our approach will validate the classification performance of our model by analysing different non-travel-related content within the subset, making it possible to identify topics such as tourism, business, night life, among others. We also plan to experiment with more sophisticated preprocessing routines and analysis to improve the quality of our data so as to verify what effect these preparation phases will have on the results obtained.

Another important work to pursue in the future is to correlate the results of this study with official sources of transportation agencies relatively to traffic congestions and other events on the transportation network, including all modes of transports and their integration interfaces. This kind of association will be useful both to validate the proposed approach as well as to improve the inference process and knowledge extraction. The automatic classifier herein presented will then be integrated into data fusion routines to enhance transportation supply and demand prediction processes alongside other sensors and sources of information.

Acknowledgements. This work was partially supported by Project "TEC4Growth - Pervasive Intelligence, Enhancers and Proofs of Concept with Industrial Impact/ NORTE-01-0145-FEDER-000020".

References

1. Mikolov, T., Sutskever, I., Chen, K., Corrado, G.S., Dean, J.: Distributed representations of words and phrases and their compositionality. In: NIPS (2013)
2. Saleiro, P., Amir, S., Silva, M., Soares, C.: Popmine: tracking political opinion on the web. In: 2015 IEEE International Conference on Computer and Information Technology; Ubiquitous Computing and Communications; Dependable, Autonomic and Secure Computing; Pervasive Intelligence and Computing (CIT/IUCC/DASC/PICOM), pp. 1521–1526. IEEE (2015)
3. Saleiro, P., Gomes, L., Soares, C.: Sentiment aggregate functions for political opinion polling using microblog streams. In: Proceedings of the Ninth International C* Conference on Computer Science & Software Engineering, pp. 44–50. ACM (2016)
4. Saleiro, P., Rodrigues, E.M., Soares, C., Oliveira, E.: FEUP at SemEval-2017 task 5: predicting sentiment polarity and intensity with financial word embeddings. In: Proceedings of the 11th International Workshop on Semantic Evaluation (SemEval-2017), pp. 895–899. Association for Computational Linguistics, Vancouver, August 2017
5. Saleiro, P., Soares, C.: Learning from the news: predicting entity popularity on Twitter. In: Boström, H., Knobbe, A., Soares, C., Papapetrou, P. (eds.) IDA 2016. LNCS, vol. 9897, pp. 171–182. Springer, Cham (2016). doi:10.1007/978-3-319-46349-0_15

6. Kokkinogenis, Z., Filguieras, J., Carvalho, S., Sarmento, L., Rossetti, R.J.F.: Mobility network evaluation in the user perspective: real-time sensing of traffic information in Twitter messages. In: Advances in Artificial Transportation Systems and Simulation, pp. 219–234 (2015)

7. Rashidi, T.H., Abbasi, A., Maghrebi, M., Hasan, S., Waller, T.S.: Exploring the capacity of social media data for modelling travel behaviour. Transp. Res. Part C: Emerg. Technol. **75**, 197–211 (2017)

8. Ulloa, D., Saleiro, P., Rossetti, R.J., Silva, E.R.: Mining social media for open innovation in transportation systems. In: 2016 IEEE 19th International Conference on Intelligent Transportation Systems (ITSC), pp. 169–174. IEEE (2016)

9. Kurkcu, A., Ozbay, K., Morgul, E.F.: Evaluating the usability of geo-located twitter as a tool for human activity and mobility patterns: a case study for New York city. In: Transportation Research Board 95th Annual Meeting, no. 16–3901 (2016)

10. Maghrebi, M., Abbasi, A., Waller, S.T.: Transportation application of social media: travel mode extraction. In: 2016 IEEE 19th International Conference on Intelligent Transportation Systems (ITSC), pp. 1648–1653. IEEE (2016)

11. Mai, E., Hranac, R.: Twitter interactions as a data source for transportation incidents. In: Proceedings of Transportation Research Board 92nd Annual Meeting, no. 13–1636 (2013)

12. Rebelo, F., Soares, C., Rossetti, R.J.F.: TwitterJam: identification of mobility patterns in urban centers based on tweets. In: 2015 IEEE First International Smart Cities Conference (ISC2), pp. 1–6. IEEE (2015)

13. Carvalho, S., Sarmento, L., Rossetti, R.J.F.: Real-time sensing of traffic information in Twitter messages. In: 2010 13th International IEEE Conference on Intelligent Transportation Systems (ITSC 2010) 4th Workshop on Artificial Transportation Systems and Simulation (ATSS), Funchal, Portugal, 19–22 September 2010, pp. 1–4 (2010)

14. Kuflik, T., Minkov, E., Nocera, S., Grant-Muller, S., Gal-Tzur, A., Shoor, I.: Automating a framework to extract and analyse transport related social media content: the potential and the challenges. Transp. Res. Part C: Emerg. Technol. **77**, 275–291 (2017)

15. Le, Q., Mikolov, T.: Distributed representations of sentences and documents. In: Proceedings of the 31st International Conference on Machine Learning (ICML-14), pp. 1188–1196 (2014)

16. Mikolov, T., Yih, W.-T., Zweig, G.: Linguistic regularities in continuous space word representations. In: HLT-NAACL, vol. 13 (2013)

Artificial Life and Evolutionary Algorithms

A Meta-Genetic Algorithm for Hybridizing Metaheuristics

Ahmed Hassan[(✉)] and Nelishia Pillay

University of KwaZulu-Natal, Pietermaritzburg 3209, South Africa
ahmedhassan@aims.ac.za, pillayn32@ukzn.ac.za

Abstract. The research presented in this paper forms part of the initiative aimed at automating the design of intelligent techniques to make them more accessible to non-experts. This study focuses on automating the hybridization of metaheuristics and parameter tuning of the individual metaheuristics. It is an initial attempt at testing the feasibility to automate this design process. A genetic algorithm is used for this purpose. Each hybrid metaheuristic is a combination of metaheuristics and corresponding parameter values. The genetic algorithm explores the space of these combinations. The genetic algorithm is evaluated by applying it to solve the symmetric travelling salesman problem. The evolved hybrid metaheuristics are found to perform competitively with the manually designed hybrid approaches from previous studies and outperform the metaheuristics applied individually. The study has also revealed the potential reusability of the evolved hybrids. Based on the success of this initial study, different problem domains shall be used to verify the automation approach to the design of hybrid metaheuristics.

Keywords: Metaheuristics · Hybrid metaheuristics · Meta-genetic algorithm

1 Introduction

Hybrid metaheuristics have proven to be effective at solving combinatorial optimization problems [4, 27]. However, designing hybrid metaheuristics is a very challenging task [4, 27] involving various critical design decisions, including which metaheuristics to combine, how to combine these and which parameter values to use for each metaheuristic. The research presented in this paper aims at investigating the possibility of automating these design decisions.

A genetic algorithm is used to automate these design decisions. The metaheuristics are combined linearly and each chromosome is a sequence of metaheuristics, with each gene containing a character representing a metaheuristic and the relevant parameter values for that metaheuristic. A steady-state genetic algorithm employing tournament selection, crossover and mutation is used to explore the space of metaheuristics and their parameter values. The metaheuristics comprising the chromosomes include iterated local search, tabu search, simulated annealing and a memetic algorithm.

© Springer International Publishing AG 2017
E. Oliveira et al. (Eds.): EPIA 2017, LNAI 10423, pp. 369–381, 2017.
DOI: 10.1007/978-3-319-65340-2_31

The automatically designed hybrid metaheuristics (ADHMs) evolved by the meta-genetic algorithm (MGA) are evaluated using the symmetric traveling salesman problem (TSP) and their performance is compared to manually designed hybrid approaches. The ADHMs are found to be very competitive to the manually designed approaches. The ADHMs are also found to outperform the metaheuristics when they are used separately. The main contributions of this research are:

- This study has shown a simple, yet effective, approach to the automation of hybrid metaheuristics. This has been illustrated using the symmetric traveling salesman problem, however the approach can be applied to solving any combinatorial optimization problem; see Sect. 7.
- The research has shown the potential of automating the design of hybrid metaheuristics. The approach performs competitively with carefully crafted, manually designed hybrid heuristics. The approach is also found to have better performance than the standard metaheuristic when applied individually.

The rest of the paper is organized as follows. In Sect. 2, the motivation of the paper is stated. Section 4 describes the proposed meta-genetic algorithm. The experimental setup is specified in Sect. 5. In Sect. 6, the results are presented and discussed. Section 7 provides the conclusion and the future work.

2   Motivation

The best known results in many optimization problems are found by hybrid metaheuristics [27]. The design of hybrid metaheuristics is challenging, requiring expert knowledge in algorithm design, data structures and statistics [4]. The design of metaheuristics involves many hard-to-make design choices such as whether to use a single method or to hybridize a number of methods; which methods/components to include; how to synthesize the hybridization; how to prune the space of all possible design choices; how to configure the hybrid method and/or each of its components. The main aim of this research is to investigate the possibility of automating this design process which will give researchers the time to focus on other aspects, with a long-term goal of providing tools for non-experts to use, hence facilitating multidisciplinary research.

Analogous to the way experts come up with hybrid solvers, in this paper the design phase is separated from the application phase. The design phase involves designing a hybrid metaheuristic for solving a particular optimization problem. In the application phase, the algorithm crafted in the design phase is applied to the optimization problem at hand. The design phase is usually conducted manually by the researcher. In this study we investigate automating this process thereby relieving the researcher from carrying it out manually.

Please note that the aim of this research is not to compete with or improve on the state of the art techniques for solving a particular problem. The main focus is to show how the design process can be automated and to investigate the difference in performance of the automatically designed and manually designed hybrid metaheuristics, with the aim of producing hybrids that perform at least as good as the manually designed hybrids.

3   Related Work

The automation of the design of metaheuristics is tackled from many aspects using different approaches: algorithm selection [25], algorithm portfolios [15], reactive search [2], automatic algorithm configuration [18] and hyper-heuristics [5].

In a narrower sense, prior work includes that of Adriaensen et al. [1] in which a focused ILS is used for automating hyper-heuristics. Kanda et al. [19] use meta-learning to choose, based on the problem features, the most effective metaheuristic. Bhanu and Gopalan [3] use a great deluge hyper-heuristic to control a set of hybrid genetic algorithms. Grobler et al. [16] use a selection hyper-heuristic to manage a number of population-based metaheuristics. Maashi et al. [21] use a choice function hyper-heuristic to intelligently select the most appropriate multi-objective evolutionary algorithm at each point of solving the problem. Pillay [24] uses an evolutionary algorithm hyper-heuristic to evolve sequences of classical artificial intelligent search methods.

To the best of our knowledge, this the first study which uses a multipoint metaheuristic to automatically hybridize and tune single point and population-based metaheuristics. The success of using genetic algorithms for parameter tuning in evolutionary algorithms [13] as well as determining the control flow in evolutionary algorithms [11] motivates the use of the genetic algorithm in this paper. Please note that the subject of this work is to hybridize metaheuristics; not to select the most suitable metaheuristic based on the instance features.

4   Meta-genetic Algorithm for Hybridizing Metaheuristics

The MGA is a steady state genetic algorithm evolving a population of metaheuristic hybrids consisting of the standard metaheuristics (SMHs); namely, simulated annealing (SA), tabu search (TS), iterated local search (ILS) and a memetic algorithm (MA). Along with finding appropriate metaheuristic hybrids, the MGA also finds suitable parameter settings for the SMHs in an online fashion.

4.1   Standard Metaheuristics

Please refers to [14] for the description of the SMHs used in this paper. The details that are specific to our implementation are only presented here.

ILS: The perturbation of the ILS is done by executing random moves for a number of times determined by the perturbation strength. The local search used by the ILS is the best improvement local search which makes the best move at each step and stops when there is no further improvement. The acceptance criterion accepts improving moves only.

TS: The TS used in this paper is the best improvement tabu search which makes the best non-tabu move at each iteration. A move is allowed by the aspiration criterion if it is the best move seen so far in the neighborhood and it produces a solution better than the best solution. The tabu list is ruled by: first enters, first leaves. The tabu condition is defined in Sect. 5.2.

SA: The temperature decreases geometrically, i.e. $T_{k+1} = c \times T_k$ where $c \in (0, 1)$ is the cooling rate. The length of the repetition schedule is equal to the size of the neighborhood. The probability function is defined as:

$$\Pr(s, s', T) = \exp\left(\frac{-100 \times [f(s') - f(s)] / f(s')}{T}\right),$$

where $f(.)$ denotes the objective function, T denotes the temperature and s is the current solution and s' is a candidate solution.

MA: The MA is a steady state genetic algorithm combined with local search. At each generation, the maximum preservative crossover operator [22] is used to produce one offspring. Then, the local search is applied to the offspring. The worse individual in the population is replaced by the offspring if the offspring is better. The local search is the first improvement local search which makes the first improving move it finds and stops when there is no further improvement.

4.2   Chromosome Representation and Initial Population Generation

The chromosomes are represented by strings of the form $h_1 : s_1, h_2 : s_2,$ ...,$h_n : s_n$ where n is the chromosome length and each gene is of the form $h_i : s_i$ for i = 1, 2, ..., n where h_i can be simulated annealing S, tabu search T, iterated local search I, or the memetic algorithm M and s_i is the specification for running h_i. For instance, if h_i is the tabu search T, then s_i could be (10, 75) which means running the tabu search for 10 iterations and the length of tabu list is 75. An example of a chromosome is M:(50,100,2),S:(45, 0.5, 0.95) which is interpreted as running the memetic algorithm for 50 generations with a population of size of 100 and a tournament of size 2 followed by running simulated annealing with an initial temperature of 45, a final temperature of 0.5 and a cooling rate of 0.95.

The chromosomes of the initial population are created at random where each gene is created by selecting one of the SMHs along with its parameters at random. The parameters are chosen from predetermined ranges. The length of each chromosome is also randomly chosen. The shortest chromosome is of length one and the longest chromosome is bounded by a limit. Duplicates are not allowed in the initial population.

4.3   Fitness Evaluation and Selection

The fitness of each chromosome is calculated by executing the specified SMH at each gene using the corresponding specification. Each chromosome is evaluated on one problem instance. All elements of a population are applied to the same initial solution of the same problem instance. The execution of the chromosomes is handled sequentially, i.e. once the execution of a gene ends, the execution of the subsequent gene starts using the output of the preceding gene as an input. The execution of the chromosome is terminated once an optimal solution is found or until the last gene is executed. The fitness of the chromosome is the cost of the best solution found by the chromosome. To facilitate the transition from one gene to the next, the best solution found by the preceding gene is passed to the subsequent gene if it encodes a single point search. When the subsequent gene encodes a population-based method, seventy percent of the initial population is made of randomly created solutions and the rest of the population is comprised of the solutions created by the preceding genes inserted with equal proportions.

Tournament selection is used which involves choosing a few individuals at random from the population which compete based on fitness. The fittest individual is the winner of the tournament. The winner of the tournament is used to create offspring.

4.4 Regeneration

The crossover operator is used to produce the offspring. Two crossover points are chosen independently at random in both parents and the chromosomal substrings are swapped at the crossover points so that two offspring are generated. Then the offspring are mutated at one gene chosen at random. The mutation is done by choosing a SMH along with its parameter values at random. The two fittest individuals out of the two parents and the two offspring survive and they are inserted into the next generation.

5   Experimental Setup

5.1 Evaluation of the MGA

The symmetric TSP is used to evaluate the performance of the proposed MGA. The TSP has been used extensively to benchmark newly proposed methods due to its rich complexity and wide applications.

The proposed MGA is an automated approach for designing metaheuristic hybrids and thus it is compared to recently proposed manually designed hybrid systems; namely, the method of Wu et al. [28] (GCGA), the method of Créput and Koukam [7] (MSOM), the method of Chen and Chien [6] (GSAACPSO) and the two methods of Lin et al. [20] (AHSATS-DCM and AHSATS-2OPT).

The problem set consists of 30 problem instances chosen from TSPLIB.[1] The number of cities in these instances ranges from 51 to 724. It is worth noting that although instances of these sizes can be solved up to optimality using exact techniques, they are still challenging for recent hybrid metaheuristics and approximate hybrid methods; see for instance [9, 23, 26]. Furthermore, the aim of the proposed study is not to develop a specialized large-scale TSP solver.[2]

---

[1] http://comopt.ifi.uni-heidelberg.de/software/TSPLIB95/.
[2] Large-scale TSP solvers require special data structures and heuristics [17] which falls out of the scope of this study.

5.2   TSP Specific Details

The solutions are tours represented as permutations of integers where each city is identified by a unique number from 0 to $n - 1$ assuming there are n cities. The initial solutions are created uniformly at random using the algorithm of Durstenfeld [12]. The length of tours is calculated as specified in the TSPLIB. The 2-opt operator [8] is used to facilitate the transition from one solution to a neighboring solution during the search. The perturbation of the ILS described in Sect. 4.1 is done by executing random 2-opt moves determined by the perturbation strength. The tabu condition of the TS described in Sect. 4.1 is based on the 2-opt moves. A 2-opt move is declared tabu if both cities involved in the 2-opt move are in the tabu list.

5.3   Parameter Settings

The parameter values of the SMHs are chosen by the MGA from specific ranges. The ranges are chosen to be wide enough to give the MGA the flexibility of determining the appropriate values for each parameter. The ranges of the parameters for each SMH are documented online.[3]

5.4   Experiments

There are three experiments conducted.

Experiment I: The main aim of Experiment I is to compare the automated design with the manual design. The automatically designed hybrid metaheuristics evolved by the MGA are compared to the manually designed approaches mentioned in Sect. 5.1 in terms of the best and the average performance. Please note that there is a clear separation between the design phase and the application phase; thus, unlike the hyper-heuristic studies [5], the MGA replaces the human designer and thus it is not directly compared with the published methods; rather, the performance of the hybrid metaheuristics that are designed by the MGA is compared with the performance of the manually designed hybrid methods. The Friedman test is used to detect whether there are significant differences in the performance of the ADHMs and the other methods. Then, the Wilcoxon signed ranks test is used to perform the pairwise comparisons involving the ADHMs and the manually designed approaches. The Holm procedure is used to control the family-wise error associated with multiple comparisons.

Experiment II: The aim of Experiment II is to compare the performance of the hybrid solvers to the individual metaheuristics, i.e. the TS, ILS, SA and MA. Each metaheuristic is tuned automatically offline using Iterated Race for Automatic Algorithm Configuration (irace).[4] The details of the offline parameter tuning can be found online.[5] The performance of the evolved hybrid metaheuristics is

---

[3] https://www.dropbox.com/s/2cyeywtxvd56rjr/parameter_settings.rtf?dl=0.

[4] http://iridia.ulb.ac.be/irace/.

[5] https://www.dropbox.com/s/01imrwvtc48ce18/offline_tuning.rtf?dl=0.

compared to each of the metaheuristics individually applied to solve the problem instance. The Friedman test and the Holm procedure are used.

Experiment III: This experiment is an initial investigation of the reusability of the ADHMs. A set of 22 instances is used. The instances are divided into "hidden" and "seen" instances. The hidden instances are grouped into two classes: ClassA comprised of 10 instances with sizes less than 300 cities and ClassB comprised of 10 instances with sizes larger than 300 cities. For each class, one "seen" instance is used by the MGA to evolve a hybrid solver. Then, that hybrid solver is used to solve all the hidden instances belonging to the corresponding class. The best and average objective value over 30 runs are used to evaluate the performance of the hybrid solvers on the hidden instances.

5.5   Implementation Platform

The simulations are run on a cluster consisting of Intel 5th generation CPUs (2.6 GHz). The cluster is interconnected with FDR 56 GHz InfiniBand. The OS is CentOS 7.0. The programming language is the OpenJDK Java version 1.7.0_111.

6   Results and Discussion

6.1   Experiment I

In Experiment I, the performance of the ADHMs is compared to that of the manually designed approaches. The best and the mean performance of the ADHMs over 30 independent runs are shown in Table 1. For each method shown in the table, the first column gives the percentage deviation of the best solutions from the best known solutions where the percentage deviation (denoted by Δ) of a solution S from the best known solution S^* is defined as

$$\Delta = 100 \times \frac{S - S^*}{S^*}. \tag{1}$$

The second column gives the mean performance. The third column gives the runtime measured in seconds. From Table 1, the ADHMs find the best known solutions for 22 instances out of 30. The ADHMs perform better in terms of both the best and mean performance compared to GCGA, MSOM, GSAACPSO; perform slightly better than AHSATS-2OPT in terms of the best performance and slightly worse in terms of the mean performance; perform equally with the AHSATS-DCM in terms of the best performance and slightly worse in terms of the mean performance.

The statistical analysis is used to detect whether the differences in the performance of the ADHMs and the other published methods are significant. The Friedman test is used. The average rankings computed by the Friedman test are AHSATS-CDM: 1.53, AHSATS-2OPT: 2.22, ADHMS: 2.25, GSAACPSO: 4.06, MSOM: 5.44 and GCGA: 5.5. High ranks correspond to poor performance. The Friedman

Table 1. Comparison of the performance of the ADHMS with previously published work. BKS stands for the best known solution.

Instance	BKS	MGA			AHSATS-DCM			AHSATS-2opt			GSAACPSO			MSOM			GCGA		
		Δ*	Mean	T	Δ*	Mean	T	Δ*	Mean	T	Δ*	Mean	T	Δ*	Mean	T	Δ*	Mean	T
eil51	426	0	426	0.2	0	426	2.7	0	426	4.9	0.23	427.27	-	1.64	435.12	0.25	0.23	430	0.98
berlin52	7542	0	7542	0.7	0	7542	4.6	0	7542	5.1	0	7542	-	0	7693.59	0.3	-	-	-
eil76	538	0	538	0.5	0	538	4.3	0	538	7.7	0	540.2	-	2.04	553.49	0.39	2.23	551	2.42
kroA100	21282	0	21282	2.4	0	21282	4.7	0	21284.33	10	0	21370.47	-	0.24	21524.61	0.53	0.05	21543	2.57
kroB100	22141	0	22159	4.2	0	22160.5	5.1	0	22160.67	10	0	22282.87	-	0.92	22528.47	0.52	0.24	22542	2.55
kroC100	20749	0	20762	2.2	0	20749	4.4	0	20749.33	10.3	0	20878.97	-	0.32	20896.32	0.5	0.32	21025	2.88
kroD100	21294	0	21315	1.2	0	21294	4.9	0	21294	9.5	0.07	21620.47	-	0.8	21536.75	0.51	1.22	21809	2.53
kroE100	22068	0	22111	2.1	0	22213.17	5.3	0	22125.2	10.1	0	22183.47	-	1.12	22507.15	0.52	0.24	22379	2.53
rd100	7910	0	7928	1.5	0	7910	4.6	0	7910	9.7	0	7987.57	-	0.99	8119.62	0.5	0.96	8031	2.55
eil101	629	0	632	3.3	0	629	5.6	0	629	10.1	0.16	635.23	-	2.07	648.81	0.51	1.59	646	2.22
lin105	14379	0	14379	1.8	0	14379	5.5	0	14382.67	11.1	0	14406.37	-	0	14427.89	0.55	0.56	14544	2.55
pr124	59030	0	59034	3.7	0	59037.67	5.6	0	59030	12.6	-	-	-	0.26	59927.26	0.62	0	59141	4.23
bier127	118282	0	118369	3.2	0	118291.5	15.2	0	118322.17	17.6	0	119421.83	-	1.25	121570.24	0.8	0.91	120412	2.52
ch130	6110	0	6153	5.4	0	6113.17	5.2	0	6119.83	12.6	0.51	6205.63	-	0.8	6282.91	0.66	-	-	-
pr136	96772	0.02	97168	8.8	0.01	96946.83	5.5	0.15	96984.17	13.1	-	-	-	0.73	99771.93	0.76	0.47	99505	3.02
pr144	58537	0	58537	5.3	0	58581.17	6.2	0	58563.5	13.8	-	-	-	-	-	-	0	58560	4.26
ch150	6528	0	6546	5.5	0	6550	6.3	0.32	6553.33	15.6	0	6563.7	-	1.67	6720.58	0.78	-	-	-
kroA150	26524	0	26567	7.8	0	26536	6.3	0	26548.5	15.9	0	26899.2	-	1.64	27248.11	0.76	1.4	27298	3.83
kroB150	26130	0	26168	8.9	0.01	26156.67	6.7	0.02	26173.33	15.8	0	26448.33	-	0.74	26550.69	0.77	1.63	26682	3.58
pr152	73682	0	73741	5.5	0	73754.67	6.7	0	73825	16	-	-	-	1.57	75597.73	0.89	0.19	74582	4.19
d198	15780	0.14	15826	20.1	0.07	15800.33	57.8	0.07	15805.33	56.9	-	-	-	-	-	-	1.01	16084	3.78
kroA200	29368	0	29432	13.2	0.05	29498	8.5	0	29466.33	20.7	0.05	29738.73	-	1.08	30014.1	1.06	1.33	29910	4.48
kroB200	29437	0.04	29577	7.3	0	29469.33	8.1	0.03	29488.5	20.4	0.35	30035.23	-	1.82	30590.93	1.07	2.09	30627	4.55
pr226	80369	0	80399	30.1	0	80577.67	24.1	0.12	80702.67	35.3	-	-	-	-	-	-	0.35	80969	8.08
pr264	49135	0	49283	11.9	0	49135	14.8	0	49142.5	28.2	-	-	-	-	-	-	0.62	50344	8.64
pr299	48191	0.11	48562	11.2	0	48251.83	12.1	0	48225.83	31.6	-	-	-	-	-	-	4.11	50812	5.37
lin318	42029	0.3	42582	29.2	0.35	42301.83	12.5	0.28	42375.5	34.1	1.09	43002.9	-	3.63	44344.8	1.86	3.74	44191	5.48
rd400	15281	0.52	15568	69.1	0.09	15339.33	15.5	0.18	15363.33	43.2	-	-	-	-	-	-	6.11	16420	5.6
pr439	107217	0.2	108000	86.7	0.16	108039.17	27.3	0.31	108808.83	47.6	-	-	-	-	-	-	5.19	113787	4.64
rat575	6773	2.24	6973	86.1	0.27	6812.5	24.2	0.5	6822.17	60.1	1.74	6933	-	4.3	7143.48	3.62	-	-	-

statistic is 69.26 and the p-value is $4.86E^{-11}$ which strongly suggests there is at least two methods with significantly different performance [10]. The Holm procedure is used to control the family-wise error associated with multiple comparisons. The p-values, the adjusted p-values and the adjusted significance levels computed by the Holm procedure are documented online.[6] The pairwise compariosns reveal that the ADHMs achieve statistically significant improvement over GCGA, MSOM, GSAACPSO. However, the difference in the performance of the ADHMs and (AHSATS-2OPT and AHSATS-DCM) is not statistically significant.

6.2 Experiment II

The second experiment evaluates the performance of the ADHMs in comparison with the individual SMH tuned using the irace package. For each problem instance, the SMH is run for the same amount of time required for the execution of the ADHMs. The results are averaged over 30 independent runs. The percentage deviations of the mean performance of the SMHs and the ADHMs from the best known solutions are shown in Table 2 which demonstrates the superior performance of the ADHMs. The Friedman test is used to detect whether performance of the ADHMs and the SMHs is significantly different. The average rankings of

Table 2. The percentage deviation of the mean solutions from the optimal solutions.

Instance	ADHMs	SA	TS	ILS	MA	Instance	ADHMs	SA	TS	ILS	MA
eil51	0	9.35	2.13	0.52	1.22	ch150	0.28	2.74	4.99	0.72	1.24
berlin52	0	1.91	0.63	0	0.46	kroA150	0.16	2.4	5.91	0.21	1.06
eil76	0	6.4	1.12	0.35	0.45	kroB150	0.15	2.23	6.04	0.23	1.45
kroA100	0	1.13	3.65	0.01	0.48	pr152	0.08	4.86	3.02	0.18	0.76
kroB100	0.08	1.94	4.51	0.2	0.63	d198	0.29	1.54	1.45	0.23	0.97
kroC100	0.06	1.84	4.92	0.85	0.92	kroA200	0.22	3.18	7.31	0.29	1.43
kroD100	0.1	4.14	5.14	1.89	0.98	kroB200	0.48	3.77	8.07	0.69	1.79
kroE100	0.19	1.96	3.42	1.49	0.98	pr226	0.04	1.49	4.3	0.14	0.8
rd100	0.23	3.34	5.02	2.27	1.01	pr264	0.3	19.37	5.6	0.93	1.5
eil101	0.48	3.12	1.81	1.34	1.56	pr299	0.77	5.15	8.63	1.05	2.26
lin105	0	2.35	3.02	0.83	0.64	lin318	1.32	4.3	6.43	1.38	1.88
pr124	0.01	1.31	2.2	0.38	0.26	rd400	1.88	2.84	7.69	1.48	2.1
bier127	0.07	3.09	4.52	1.08	0.58	pr439	0.73	3.13	8.02	0.97	1.38
ch130	0.7	2.47	6.31	1.03	1.29	pcb442	1.75	2.91	6.06	1.87	2.4
pr136	0.41	2.64	3.47	0.8	1.39	rat575	2.95	5.96	8.93	2.5	3.48
pr144	0	2.99	2.8	0.07	0.12	-	-	-	-	-	-

---

[6] https://www.dropbox.com/s/0c7gtcijdlbx5w4/stat_analysis.rtf?dl=0.

the methods are ADHMs: 1.11, ILS: 2.08, MA: 2.80, SA: 4.26 and TS: 4.75. Which indicates that the ADHMs are the best. The Friedman statistic is 112.35 and the p-value is $7.18E^{-11}$ which indicates the differences are significant. The unadjusted p-values are computed from the Friedman rankings. The Holm procedure is used. The results of the statistical analysis is documented online.[7] All the pairwise comparisons are found to be significant which indicates that the ADHMs outperform each of the SMHs when used individually.

6.3   Experiment III

The third experiment tests the reusability of the evolved hybrid solvers by evaluating the performance of hybrid solvers evolved for seen instances on hidden instances. The hidden instances are divided into two classes (ClassA & ClassB) as mentioned in Sect. 5.4. For each class, a training instance is chosen and a hybrid solver is evolved for it. Then, the performance of the hybrid solver is tested on the hidden instances belonging to that class. The best and the mean performance over 30 runs are used to verify the quality of the "trained" solvers on the hidden instances. The results are shown in Table 3 in which Δ^* and Δ represent the percentage deviations from the best known solutions of the best and mean solutions respectively. In the table, `ch130` and `rd400` are the training instances.

Table 3. The percentage deviation from the best known solutions of the best and the mean performance of the hybrid solvers applied to the hidden instances.

ClassA				ClassB			
Instance	Δ^*	Δ	QL	Instance	Δ^*	Δ	QL
berlin52	0	0	0	lin318	0.1	0.83	−0.48
kroA100	0	0.01	0.01	rd400	-	-	-
kroC100	0	0.03	−0.03	fl417	0.32	0.65	0.22
ch130	-	-	-	pr439	0.17	1.03	0.6
ch150	0	0.34	0.06	pcb442	1.03	1.75	0.26
kroB150	0	0.37	0.23	d498	0.95	1.81	0.3
kroA200	0	0.35	0.13	u574	1.3	2.35	0.8
kroB200	0	0.71	0.23	rat575	1.96	2.78	0.11
pr226	0	0.21	0.18	p654	0.37	0.56	0.13
pr264	0	0.41	0.11	d657	1.32	2.11	0.31
pr299	0.02	0.68	−0.09	u724	1.33	2.32	0.27

---

[7] https://www.dropbox.com/s/0c7gtcijdlbx5w4/stat_analysis.rtf?dl=0.

From Table 3, the "trained" ADHM finds the best known solution for 9 instances out of 10 for ClassA. For ClassB, the deviation of best solution found by the trained solver is less than 2%. The fourth column (QL) is the quality loss which is the difference between the mean performance of the trained ADHMs and the actual ADHMs evolved for each of the hidden instances. A negative difference indicates that the trained ADHMs perform better. In general, the quality loss is less than 1% which implies that the trained ADHMs are reusable since there is not much deterioration in their performance. It is worth noting that by combining Tables 1 and 3 that the trained ADHMs perform better than GCGA, MSOM and GSAACPSO and perform slightly worse than AHSATS-DCM and AHSATS-2OPT. In particular, the difference in the mean performance of the trained ADHMs and the AHSATS-DCM (the best performer) is less than 1% for ClassA and less than 2% for ClassB (except for `rat575`). This demonstrates that the trained ADHMs are competitive to the manually crafted hybrid metaheuristics.

7   Conclusion and Future Work

The research presented in this paper is an initial attempt to ascertain the feasibility of automating the design of hybrid metaheuristics. The paper illustrates how a meta-genetic algorithm can be used to hybridize metaheuristics and dynamically tune the parameters of the individual metaheuristics. The study has revealed the potential of automating the design of metaheuristics. The evolved hybrids were found to perform competitively with manually designed hybrids and perform better than the metaheuristics applied individually. The evolved hybrid solvers were also found to be reusable. The meta-genetic algorithm is readily applicable to other domains. Technically, only three aspects need to be changed in order to apply the meta-genetic algorithm to a new problem domain: the representation of the solution; the problem-specific heuristic (the move operator) and the objective function.

Given the success in this initial study, future research will be conducted to extend this work further. In this study, the metaheuristics were combined linearly. In future work, other mechanisms for combining the metaheuristics will be investigated on different problem domains.

References

1. Adriaensen, S., Brys, T., Nowé, A.: Designing reusable metaheuristic methods: a semi-automated approach. In: 2014 IEEE Congress on Evolutionary Computation (CEC), pp. 2969–2976. IEEE (2014)
2. Battiti, R., Brunato, M., Mascia, F.: Reactive Search and Intelligent Optimization, vol. 45. Springer Science & Business Media, Heidelebrg (2008)
3. Bhanu, S.M.S., Gopalan, N.: A hyper-heuristic approach for efficient resource scheduling in grid. Int. J. Comput. Commun. Control **3**(3), 249–258 (2008)
4. Blum, C., Puchinger, J., Raidl, G.R., Roli, A.: Hybrid metaheuristics in combinatorial optimization: a survey. Appl. Soft Comput. **11**(6), 4135–4151 (2011)

5. Burke, E.K., Gendreau, M., Hyde, M., Kendall, G., Ochoa, G., Özcan, E., Qu, R.: Hyper-heuristics: a survey of the state of the art. J. Oper. Res. Soc. **64**(12), 1695–1724 (2013)
6. Chen, S.M., Chien, C.Y.: Solving the traveling salesman problem based on the genetic simulated annealing ant colony system with particle swarm optimization techniques. Expert Syst. Appl. **38**(12), 14439–14450 (2011)
7. Créput, J.C., Koukam, A.: A memetic neural network for the euclidean traveling salesman problem. Neurocomputing **72**(4), 1250–1264 (2009)
8. Croes, G.A.: A method for solving traveling-salesman problems. Oper. Res. **6**(6), 791–812 (1958)
9. Deng, W., Chen, R., He, B., Liu, Y., Yin, L., Guo, J.: A novel two-stage hybrid swarm intelligence optimization algorithm and application. Soft. Comput. **16**(10), 1707–1722 (2012)
10. Derrac, J., García, S., Molina, D., Herrera, F.: A practical tutorial on the use of nonparametric statistical tests as a methodology for comparing evolutionary and swarm intelligence algorithms. Swarm Evol. Comput. **1**(1), 3–18 (2011)
11. Dioşan, L., Oltean, M.: Evolutionary design of evolutionary algorithms. Genet. Program Evolvable Mach. **10**(3), 263–306 (2009)
12. Durstenfeld, R.: Algorithm 235: random permutation. Commun. ACM **7**(7), 420 (1964)
13. Eiben, Á.E., Smit, S.K.: Evolutionary algorithm parameters and methods to tune them. In: Hamadi, Y., Monfroy, E., Saubion, F. (eds.) Autonomous Search, pp. 15–36. Springer, Heidelberg (2011). doi:10.1007/978-3-642-21434-9_2
14. Gendreau, M., Potvin, J.: Handbook of Metaheuristics. International Series in Operations Research & Management Science. Springer, Heidelberg (2010)
15. Gomes, C.P., Selman, B.: Algorithm portfolios. Artif. Intell. **126**(1), 43–62 (2001)
16. Grobler, J., Engelbrecht, A.P., Kendall, G., Yadavalli, V.: Alternative hyper-heuristic strategies for multi-method global optimization. In: IEEE Congress on Evolutionary Computation, pp. 1–8. IEEE (2010)
17. Helsgaun, K.: An effective implementation of the lin-kernighan traveling salesman heuristic. Eur. J. Oper. Res. **126**(1), 106–130 (2000)
18. Hutter, F., Hoos, H.H., Stützle, T.: Automatic algorithm configuration based on local search. AAAI **7**, 1152–1157 (2007)
19. Kanda, J., de Carvalho, A., Hruschka, E., Soares, C., Brazdil, P.: Meta-learning to select the best meta-heuristic for the traveling salesman problem: a comparison of meta-features. Neurocomputing **205**, 393–406 (2016)
20. Lin, Y., Bian, Z., Liu, X.: Developing a dynamic neighborhood structure for an adaptive hybrid simulated annealing-tabu search algorithm to solve the symmetrical traveling salesman problem. Appl. Soft Comput. **49**, 937–952 (2016)
21. Maashi, M., Özcan, E., Kendall, G.: A multi-objective hyper-heuristic based on choice function. Expert Syst. Appl. **41**(9), 4475–4493 (2014)
22. Mühlenbein, H., Gorges-Schleuter, M., Krämer, O.: Evolution algorithms in combinatorial optimization. Parallel Comput. **7**(1), 65–85 (1988)
23. Osaba, E., Yang, X.S., Diaz, F., Lopez-Garcia, P., Carballedo, R.: An improved discrete bat algorithm for symmetric and asymmetric traveling salesman problems. Eng. Appl. Artif. Intell. **48**, 59–71 (2016)
24. Pillay, N.: Intelligent system design using hyper-heuristics. S. Afr. Comput. J. **56**(1), 107–119 (2015)
25. Rice, J.R.: The algorithm selection problem. Adv. Comput. **15**, 65–118 (1976)

26. Saenphon, T., Phimoltares, S., Lursinsap, C.: Combining new fast opposite gradient search with ant colony optimization for solving travelling salesman problem. Eng. Appl. Artif. Intell. **35**, 324–334 (2014)
27. Talbi, E.G.: A taxonomy of hybrid metaheuristics. J. Heuristics **8**(5), 541–564 (2002)
28. Wu, C., Liang, Y., Lee, H.P., Lu, C.: Generalized chromosome genetic algorithm for generalized traveling salesman problems and its applications for machining. Phys. Rev. E **70**(1), 016701 (2004)

Econometric Genetic Programming in Binary Classification: Evolving Logistic Regressions Through Genetic Programming

André Luiz Farias Novaes[1]($\boxtimes$), Ricardo Tanscheit[2],
and Douglas Mota Dias[3]

[1] Informatics Department, University of Lisbon, Lisbon, Portugal
andrelfnovaes@gmail.com
[2] Electrical Engineering Department, PUC-Rio, Rio de Janeiro, RJ, Brazil
ricardo@ele.puc-rio.br
[3] Electronics and Telecommunications Engineering Department,
UERJ, Rio de Janeiro, RJ, Brazil
douglasmota.uerj@gmail.com

Abstract. Logistic Regression and Genetic Programming (GP) have already been compared to each other in classification tasks. In this paper, Econometric Genetic Programming (EGP), first introduced as a regression methodology, is extended to binary classification tasks and evolves logistic regressions through GP, aiming to generate high accuracy classifications with potential interpretability of parameters, while uses statistical significance as a feature-selection tool and GP for model selection. EGP-Classification (or EGP-C), the name of this proposed EGP's extension, was tested against a large group of algorithms in three cross-sectional datasets, showing competitive results in most of them. EGP-C successfully competed against highly non-linear algorithms, like Support Vector Machines and Multilayer Perceptron with Back Propagation, and still allows interpretability of parameters and models generated.

Keywords: Genetic programming · Binary classification · Logistic regression · Model selection

1 Introduction

Logistic Regression (LR or logit regression) and Genetic Programming (GP) have already been compared to each other in classification tasks [1–3].

The work on [4] is pioneer in evolving LR models through GP. As they state, their approach merges the ability of LR to deal with dichotomous data and provide quantitative results with the optimization characteristic of GP to search the entire hypothesis space for the "most fit" hypothesis. GP modifies, using an iterative trial and error process, LR models formed by vegetation indices built from basic function blocks defined in the function and terminal sets. Each candidate model is refined with a stepwise backward elimination using the level of significance associated with Chi-square test of each term and then evaluated based on the fitness function which is

© Springer International Publishing AG 2017
E. Oliveira et al. (Eds.): EPIA 2017, LNAI 10423, pp. 382–394, 2017.
DOI: 10.1007/978-3-319-65340-2_32

defined by the model's Kappa statistics and the number of terms in the model. Figure 1 shows a possible individual generated by its algorithm.

Kaizen Programming (KP) [18] is an interesting evolutionary tool based on concepts of continuous improvement from Kaizen methodology, which was successfully tested against traditional SR benchmark functions. In [19], KP was coupled with LR models to extract useful features from a widely studied credit scoring dataset, aiming at improving the prediction performance of LR.

EGP, which was first introduced in [5] for regression tasks and tested against traditional feature-selection econometric algorithms, is carefully constructed considering econometric theory on cross-sectional datasets, aiming to generate high accuracy regressions with potential interpretability of parameters.

EGP is now extended to binary classification tasks, evolving logistic regressions through GP, aiming to improve the approach proposed by its predecessors, [4, 19], particularly on interpretation of parameters. Predictors 1, 2 and 3, in Fig. 1, when components in a logit model, offer just a few or even none interpretation of parameters. To perceive this, it is sufficient to try an interpretation on $(B_5B_3)/(B_3 + B_1)$, a coefficient in a LR model of [4]. EGP-C uses just polynomials in the $X\beta$ part of LR and to see why this kind of approach is beneficial to parameter interpretation, see [6]. EGP-C is interpretation-oriented and also aims to generate high accuracy models.

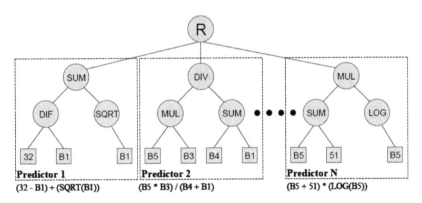

Fig. 1. Example of a proposed candidate model representation for the GP and LR integrated model. (Source: [4])

This paper is organized as follows: Sect. 2 describes the elements of econometrics used by EGP-C: there is no intention to fully exhaust the theme; justification on these elements is presented when necessary. Section 3 succinctly describes EGP-C. Sections 4 proposes experiments and discuss results. Conclusion is done in Sect. 5, with mention to future work.

2   Econometrics

2.1   Logistic Regression, Maximum Likelihood, Newton's Method

The Logistic Regression (LR) aims to model P_t, the conditional probability of $y_t = 1$ to X, with $t \in [1, n]$. Only possible outcomes for y_t are 0 or 1. The matrix $X = [x_1 \ldots x_i \ldots x_k]$ is constructed by x_i $n \times 1$ vectors, $i \in [1, k]$. Mathematically:

$$P_t \equiv \Pr(y_t = 1 | X) = E(y_t | X) \tag{1}$$

Multiple linear regressions are inadequate to model (1) and [7] shows the reason. Logit or probit models [8] are well recognized methods for binary classification tasks. Both methods consist of modelling $E(y_t | X)$ with a transformation function, $F(x)$, applied to an index function, $h(X_t, \beta)$:

$$E(y_t | X) = F(h(X_t, \beta)) = F(X_t \beta) \tag{2}$$

with $h(X_t, \beta) = X_t \beta$. The expected value $E(y_t | X)$ is a typical cumulative probability distribution, a monotonically growing linear transformation that maps from the real line to $[0, 1]$, with properties $F(-\infty) = 0$, $F(\infty) = 1$ and $(\partial F(x)/\partial x) > 0$.

Logit and probit models are usually preferred over other econometric classification models mainly due linearity on $h(X_t, \beta)$. For probit regressions, $E(y_t | X) = \phi(X_t \beta)$, the cumulative normal probability distribution, which has not closed formula but is easily calculated numerically. For the logit regression:

$$E(y_t | X) = \Lambda(X_t \beta) = \frac{e^{X_t \beta}}{1 + e^{X_t \beta}} \tag{3}$$

which has closed formula. $\Lambda(X_t \beta)$ is called logistic function.

Maximum Likelihood (ML) is commonly used to estimate $\widehat{\beta}$ on (3) [9]. ML estimation proposes the maximization of the ML function, which gives the likelihood of the sample y to be observed as realizations of n independent Bernoulli random variables. The vector $\widehat{\beta}$ is the solution of this maximization, which usually occurs on the logarithm of ML function, because it involves a sum instead of a product:

$$l(y, \beta) = \sum_{t=1}^{n} [y_t \log(\Lambda(X_t \beta)) + (1 - y_t) \log(1 - \Lambda(X_t \beta))] \tag{4}$$

which is globally concave whenever $\log(\Lambda(X_t \beta))$ and $\log(1 - \Lambda(X_t \beta))$ are concave functions of X_t: in such case, $\widehat{\beta}$ is unique. However, [10] states that the presence of non-linear elements, crossed feature terms (like $x_3 x_{11}^2$), will not permit oneness of $\widehat{\beta}$. First order conditions of (4) are:

$$\sum_{t=1}^{n} (y_t - \Lambda(X_t \widehat{\beta})) X_{ti} \tag{5}$$

Conditions in (5) are just solved numerically, due non-linearity in parameters $\widehat{\boldsymbol{\beta}}$, and Newton's Method (NM) is an interactive method that possibly solves it, performing as follows:

$$\boldsymbol{\beta}^{(s+1)} = \boldsymbol{\beta}^{(s)} - \boldsymbol{H}^{-1}\left(\boldsymbol{\beta}^{(s)}\right)\nabla l\left(\boldsymbol{\beta}^{(s)}\right) \tag{6}$$

with $\boldsymbol{H}$ the Hessian Matrix and ∇l the gradient of $l(\boldsymbol{\beta})$. Even if there is no global maximum for $l(\boldsymbol{\beta})$, [11] guarantees it always increases by NM.

2.2   Hypothesis Test

Hypothesis Test (HT) is applied in EGP-C in the same way it is applied in EGP and it is only possible due satisfiability of three regularity conditions, as described in [12]. Under these conditions and n sufficiently large, the following verifies:

$$\widehat{\boldsymbol{\beta}} \xrightarrow{d} N\left(\boldsymbol{\beta}, [I(\boldsymbol{\beta})]^{-1}\right) \tag{7}$$

$$\frac{\widehat{\beta}_i - \beta_i}{SE\left(\widehat{\beta}_i\right)} \sim N(0, 1) \tag{8}$$

with $I(\boldsymbol{\beta})$, the Fisher Information, equals to σ_{β}^2, the asymptotic variance. For a brief review on HT and how it is applied in EGP, see [5].

3   Econometric Genetic Programming – Classification: EGP-C

EGP-C is the EGP algorithm applied to classifications tasks, when logit models are evolved. The main difference between EGP and EGP-C lies in Accuracy and related metrics, showed in Sect. 3.3.

EGP-C evolves models in format of (3) through GP, which is responsible for model selection. GP is mainly based in [13] configuration.

3.1   Representation

Individuals are multigenic. Any constant in any program comes from NM in (6), i.e. there are no ephemeral constants. The terminal set, namely Ω, is purely composed by variables. The primitive set, namely ϑ, is composed just by variables and operations of sum and multiplication, due $X\beta$ format.

Search space for EGP-C is the number of models, n_{mod}, which is function of the number of regressors created for an individual, n_{reg}.

$$n_{reg} = \sum_{q_{var}=1}^{K} \frac{(K-1+q_{var})!}{(K-1)!q_{var}!} \tag{9}$$

$$n_{mod} = \sum_{q_{reg}=1}^{n_{reg}} \frac{n_{reg}!}{(n_{reg}-q_{reg})!} \tag{10}$$

In (9), q_{var} is the number of variables on Ω necessary to create a regressor; in (10), q_{reg} is the number of regressors required to build a model. (9) is the sum of possible combinations with repetitions, q_{var} to q_{var}. (10) is the sum of possible arrangements of n_{reg} regressors, q_{reg} to q_{reg}. Supposing $K = 3$ for a particular dataset, n_{mod} rounds 10^{17}.

3.2   Initial Population

EGP-C uses a probabilistic version of ramped half-and-half method. Figure 2 shows a possible individual generated by EGP-C.

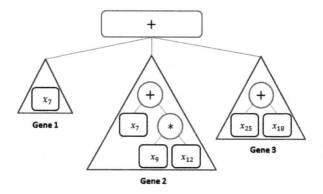

Fig. 2. A possible individual generated by EGP-C.

Set Ω is composed by K features (independent variables). Every individual has its own set of regressors, forming its own X, composed by simple or combined elements of Ω. As an example, it is possible that x_1, $x_3 x_{11}^2$ and $x_3 x_4 x_6$ are regressors of a particular individual, formed by features x_1, x_3, x_4, x_6 and x_{11}.

3.3   Accuracy

In EGP, RMSE is the objective function and $\overline{R}^2$ is used to compare models. In EGP-C, the percentage of correctly classified instances ("%_corr") has been chosen as objective function (accuracy measure), due benchmarks were evaluated using such metric. Experiments and Results will fully describe the comparison methodology.

To calculate accuracy in an EGP-C individual, the following procedure needs to be done (Fig. 3).

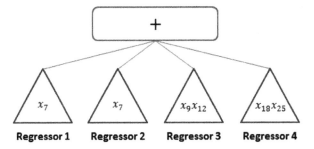

Fig. 3. The multigenic individual is written as a set of regressors. Repetitions will be discarded.

EGP-C will solve (5) for $X\beta = \beta_1 x_7 + \beta_2 x_9 x_{12} + \beta_3 x_{18} x_{25}$. If any of the regressors are not statistically significant, they will be removed from (5). In sequence, (6) is recalculated just with statistically significant regressors from (5). %_corr is finally calculated using $\widehat{\beta}$ after these steps. This routine is traditional in econometric studies, ensuring statistical significance over a determined significance level α. Modifications described are necessary just for accuracy calculation, therefore individuals will keep their multigene structure to mutation, crossover and elitism (Fig. 4).

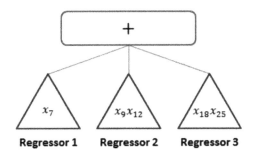

Fig. 4. Individual ready for accuracy calculation.

EGP-C does not estimate on genes, just on regressors, by two main reasons: possible multicollinearity problem, interfering on HT for β_i, and lack of interpretation for $\widehat{\beta}_i$ when it is related to a gene.

3.4   Selection

Tournament selection with $n_{tourn} = 7$ and repetitions allowed, with a variation on lexicographic parsimony pressure of [14], is used. Individuals with a large number of statistically significant regressors will be preferred over others with a few number, in the same range of fitness. Therefore, EGP-C is parsimonious in its nature, because it avoids the individuals with a large amount of *introns* (in this case, non statistically significant regressors).

3.5   Mutation, Crossover and Elitism

Types of mutation used: traditional mutation proposed by [15] and mutation by regressors' substitution. Types of crossover used: intergenic and intragenic crossovers. Mutation and crossover rates vary through evolution following automatic adaptation of operators as described in [16]. Elitism rate is set to 5% of individuals by generation.

3.6   Tools and Parameters

EGP-C is implemented through a modification on GPTIPS, a *Matlab* toolbox, presented in [17]. Information on EGP-C parameters are shown in Table 1.

Table 1. EGP-C Parameters

Parameters	
- Population size	150
- Generations	50
- Maximum gene depth	5
- Maximum number of genes by individual	5
- Probability of traditional mutation [15]	95%.
- Probability of intragenic crossover	50%.
- Threshold for classification in LR	$E(y_t|X) = 0.5$

4   Experiments and Results

EGP-C can be used in different forms, e.g. for model selection or interpretation of parameters. For the reasoning of this article, EGP-C was submitted to generate high accuracy models, with potential interpretability of parameters, and tested against a large group of algorithms in three classification cross-sectional datasets, namely: "Breast Cancer **Wisconsin** (Original) Data Set"; "Pima Indians **Diabetes** Data Set"; "**Ionosphere** Data Set". All information on datasets can be found in UCI Machine Learning Repository [20].

To fully test EGP-C's capability to generate high accuracy models, a generous list of algorithms to compare it was required. The Computational Intelligence Laboratory in Informatics' Department of Nicolaus Copernicus University holds results on a list of algorithms for datasets used in this article. Their comparison methodology is based on a 10-fold cross validation on the entire dataset and that is the reason EGP-C is evaluated in the same manner. Authors of each algorithm are responsible for every result divulgated at Computational Intelligence Laboratory in Informatics' Department of Nicolaus Copernicus University domain [21].

Tables 2, 3 and 4 present the results. Results for EGP-C are identified as "EGP-Classification" in Tables. Algorithms are ordered by %_corr, the percentage of correct hits, while standard deviation works as the next sorting criteria.

Table 2. Results for Wisconsin Dataset

Position	Algorithm	% of correct hits ± standard deviation	Reference
1	NB + kernel est	97,5 ± 1,8	WD, WEKA, 10×10CV
2	SVM (5xCV)	97,2	Bennet and Blue
3	kNN with DVDM distance	97,1	our (KG)
4	GM k-NN, k = 3, raw, Manh	97,0 ± 2,1	WD, 10×10CV
5	GM k-NN, k = opt, raw, Manh	97,0 ± 1,7	WD, 10CV only
6	VSS, 8 it/2 neurons	96,9 ± 1,8	WD/MK; 98.1% train
7	FSM-Feature Space Mapping	96,9 ± 1,4	RA/WD, a = .99 Gaussian
8	Fisher linear discr. anal	96,8	Ster, Dobnikar
9	MLP + BP	96,7	Ster, Dobnikar
10	MLP + BP (Tooldiag)	96,6	Rafał Adamczak
11	LVQ	96,6	Ster, Dobnikar
12	kNN, Euclidean/Manhattan f.	96,6	Ster, Dobnikar
13	SNB, semi-naive Bayes (pairwise dependent)	96,6	Ster, Dobnikar
14	**EGP-Classification**	**96,43 ± 2,88**	
15	SVM lin, opt C	96,4 ± 1,2	WD-GM, 16 missing with −10
16	VSS, 8 it/1 neuron!	96,4 ± 2,0	WD/MK, train 98.0%
17	GM IncNet	96,4 ± 2,1	NJ/WD; FKF, max. 3 neurons
18	NB - naive Bayes (completly independent)	96,4	Ster, Dobnikar
19	SSV opt nodes, 3CV int	96,3 ± 2,2	WD/GM; training 96.6 ± 0.5
20	IB1	96,3 ± 1,9	Zarndt
21	DB-CART (decision tree)	96,2	Shang, Breiman
22	GM SSV Tree, opt nodes BFS	96,0 ± 2,9	WD/KG (beam search 94.0)
23	LDA - linear discriminant analysis	96	Ster, Dobnikar
24	OC1 DT (5xCV)	95,9	Bennet and Blue
25	RBF (Tooldiag)	95,9	Rafał Adamczak
26	GTO DT (5xCV)	95,7	Bennet and Blue
27	ASI - Assistant I tree	95,6	Ster, Dobnikar
28	MLP + BP (Weka)	95,4 ± 0,2	TW/WD
29	OCN2	95,2 ± 2,1	Zarndt
30	IB3	95,0 ± 4,0	Zarndt
31	MML tree	94,8 ± 1,8	Zarndt

(continued)

Table 2. (*continued*)

Position	Algorithm	% of correct hits ± standard deviation	Reference
32	ASR - Assistant R (RELIEF criterion) tree	94,7	Ster, Dobnikar
33	C4.5 tree	94,7 ± 2,0	Zarndt
34	LFC, Lookahead Feature Constr binary tree	94,4	Ster, Dobnikar
35	CART tree	94,4 ± 2,4	Zarndt
36	ID3	94,3 ± 2,6	Zarndt
37	C4.5 (5xCV)	93,4	Bennet and Blue
38	C4.5 rules	86,7 ± 5,9	Zarndt
39	Default, majority	65,5	–
40	QDA - quadratic discr anal	34,5	Ster, Dobnikar

Table 3. Results for Diabetes Dataset

Position	Algorithm	% of correct hits ± standard deviation	Reference
1	Logdisc	77,7	Statlog
2	IncNet	77,6	Norbert Jankowski
3	DIPOL92	77,6	Statlog
4	Linear Discr. Anal.	77,5 − 77,2	Statlog; Ster & Dobnikar
5	SVM, linear, C = 0.01	77,5 ± 4,2	WD-GM, 10XCV averaged 10x
6	SVM, Gauss, C, sigma opt	77,4 ± 4,3	WD-GM, 10XCV averaged 10x
7	**EGP-Classification**	**76,95 ± 6,00**	
8	SMART	76,8	Statlog
9	GTO DT (5xCV)	76,8	Bennet and Blue
10	kNN, k = 23, Manh, raw, W	76,7 ± 4,0	WD-GM, feature weighting 3CV
11	kNN, k = 1:25, Manh, raw	76,6 ± 3,4	WD-GM, most cases k = 23
12	ASI	76,6	Ster & Dobnikar
13	Fisher discr. analysis	76,5	Ster & Dobnikar
14	MLP + BP	76,4	Ster & Dobnikar
15	MLP + BP	75,8 ± 6,2	Zarndt
16	LVQ	75,8	Ster & Dobnikar
17	LFC	75,8	Ster & Dobnikar

(*continued*)

Table 3. (*continued*)

Position	Algorithm	% of correct hits ± standard deviation	Reference
18	RBF	75,7	Statlog
19	NB	75,5 − 73,8	Ster & Dobnikar; Statlog
20	kNN, k = 22, Manh	75,5	Karol Grudziński
21	MML	75,5 ± 6,3	Zarndt
22	FSM stand. 5 feat.	75,4 ± 4,9	WD, 10x10 test, CC > 0.15
23	SNB	75,4	Ster & Dobnikar
24	BP	75,2	Statlog
25	SSV DT	75,0 ± 3,6	WD-GM, SSV BS, node 5CV MC
26	kNN, k = 18, Euclid, raw	74,8 ± 4,8	WD-GM
27	CART DT	74,7 ± 5,4	Zarndt
28	CART DT	74,5	Stalog
29	DB-CART	74,4	Shang & Breiman
30	ASR	74,3	Ster & Dobnikar
31	FSM standard	74,1 ± 1,1	WD, 10x10 test
32	ODT, dyadic trees	74,0 ± 2,3	Blanchard
33	Cluster means, 2 prototypes	73,7 ± 3,7	MB
34	SSV DT	73,7 ± 4,7	WD-GM, SSV BS, node 10CV strat
35	SFC, stacking filters	73,3 ± 1,9	Porter
36	C4.5 DT	73	Stalog
37	C4.5 DT	72,7 ± 6,6	Zarndt
38	Bayes	72,2 ± 6,9	Zarndt
39	C4.5 (5xCV)	72	Bennet and Blue
40	CART	72,8	Ster & Dobnikar
41	Kohonen	72,7	Statlog
42	C4.5 DT	72,1 ± 2,6	Blanchard (average in 100 runs)
43	kNN	71,9	Ster & Dobnikar
44	ID3	71,7 ± 6,6	Zarndt
45	IB3	71,7 ± 5,0	Zarndt
46	IB1	70,4 ± 6,2	Zarndt
47	kNN, k = 1, Euclides, raw	69,4 ± 4,4	WD-GM
48	kNN	67,6	Statlog
49	C4.5 rules	67,0 ± 2,9	Zarndt

Table 4. Results for Ionosphere Dataset

Position	Algorithm	% of correct hits ± standard deviation	Reference
1	3-NN + simplex	98,7	Our own weighted kNN
2	VSS 2 epochs	96,7	MLP with numerical gradient
3	3-NN	96,7	KG, GM with or without weights
4	IB3	96,7	Aha, 5 errors on test
5	1-NN, Manhattan	96	GM kNN (our)
6	MLP + BP	96	Sigillito
7	SVM Gaussian	94,9 ± 2,6	GM (our), defaults, similar for C = 1 − 100
8	C4.5	94,9	Hamilton
9	3-NN Canberra	94,7	GM kNN (our)
10	RIAC	94,6	Hamilton
11	C4 (no windowing)	94	Aha
12	C4.5	93,7	Bennet and Blue
13	SVM	93,2	Bennet and Blue
14	Non-lin perceptron	92	Sigillito
15	FSM + rotation	92,8	our
16	1-NN, Euclidean	92,1	Aha, GM kNN (our)
17	DB-CART	91,3	Shang, Breiman
18	Linear perceptron	90,7	Sigillito
19	OC1 DT	89,5	Bennet and Blue
20	CART	88,9	Shang, Breiman
21	SVM linear	87,1 ± 3,9	GM (our), defaults
22	**EGP-Classification**	**86,9 + 5,21**	
23	GTO DT	86	Bennet and Blue

EGP-C was competitive in Wisconsin and Diabetes datasets, performing in 14th (40 algorithms in total) and 7th (49 in total), respectively. Support Vector Machines (SVMs) and Multilayer Perceptron with Back Propagation (MLP + BP), which are highly non-linear in structure, using more complex non-linear functions like trigonometric ones, presented results just a little better than EGP-C (in average, 0.5% above). Additionally, SVMs and MLP + BP permits low or none interpretability of parameters.

In logit models, the coefficient $\widehat{\beta}_i$ can be interpreted as the effect of a unit of change in x_i on the predicted logits with other regressors considered constants in the model. (11) is a model generated by EGP-C.

$$\frac{e^{-7.12 + 0.14x_4 - 0.25x_6}}{1 + e^{-7.12 + 0.14x_4 - 0.25x_6}} \tag{11}$$

with $X\beta = -7.12 + 0.14x_4 - 0.25x_6$. The effect on the odds of a 1-unit increase in x_4 is $e^{0.14} = 1.15$, meaning the odds of an instance to be classified as $y_t = 1$ increase approximately 15% when x_4 is added by one unit (of x_4), regardless of the x_6 value.

In Ionosphere dataset, EGP-C was not competitive. Ionosphere has a binary attribute with 89.17% of its values equals to 1 and the rest, 10.83%, equals 0. When combining features to generate regressors, this attribute (suppose it is x_1) can easily form a regressor that is collinear with other. For example, x_1 and x_1^2 composing the same individual. In such cases, X has not full rank and thus the variant of NM used to solve (5) will fail to find a maximum (even it is local) to (4), because this version of NM has not a protection against linear dependent columns. That is why EGP-C, in some circumstances like highly unbalanced datasets, is purposely set to do not generate too large individuals, consequently compromising accuracy. EGP-C controls individuals' growth by parsimoniously regulating GP parameters as population size, number of generations or maximum gene height for trees.

5   Conclusion and Future Work

EGP-C was successful in achieving its objective of generating high accuracy logit models. Although non-linear, logit models generated by EGP-C hold a linear portion on its structure, $X\beta$, which permits potential interpretability of parameters.

Future work points out in designing EGP for time series forecast. High collinearity between columns of X requires a distinct approach to prediction, depending on the model someone is interested in.

References

1. Nourani, V., Pradhan, B., Ghaffari, H., Sharifi, H.: Landslide susceptibility mapping at Zonouz plain, Iran using genetic programming and comparison with frequency ratio, logistic regression, and artificial neural network models. Commun. J. Int. Soc. Prev. Mitig. Nat. Hazards **71**(1), 523–547 (2014)
2. Ritchie, M.D., Motsinger, A.A., Bush, W.S., Coffey, C.S., Moore, J.H.: Genetic programming neural networks: a powerful bioinformatics tool for human genetics. Commun. Appl. Soft Computing J. **7**(1), 471–479 (2007)
3. Ong, C.-S., Huang, J.-J., Tzeng, G.-H.: Building credit scoring models using genetic programming. Commun. Expert Syst. Appl.: Int. J. **29**(1), 41–47 (2005)
4. Momm, H.G., Easson, G., Kuszmaul, J.: Integration of logistic regression and genetic programming to model coastal Louisiana land loss using remote sensing. In: Proceedings of the American Society for Photogrammetry and Remote Sensing 2007 Annual Conference, ASPRS 2007, Tampa, FL, USA (2007)
5. Novaes, A.L.F., Tanscheit, R., Dias, D.M.: Programação Genética Econométrica Aplicada a Problemas de Regressão em Conjuntos de Dados Seccionais. In: Proceedings of XIII Encontro Nacional de Inteligência Artificial, ENIAC 2016, Recife, PE, Brazil (2016)
6. Wooldridge, J.: Introductory Econometrics: A Modern Approach, 4th edn. Cengage Learning, Boston (2009)

7. Novaes, A.L.F.: Programação Genética Econométrica: uma Nova Abordagem para Problemas de Regressão e Classificação em Conjuntos de Dados Seccionais. Master's thesis. Pontifícia Universidade Católica do Rio de Janeiro (PUC-Rio), Rio de Janeiro, Brazil (2015)
8. Hastie, T., Tibshirani, R., Friedman, J.: The Elements of Statistical Learning, 1st edn. Springer New York Inc., New York (2001)
9. Davidson, R., MacKinnon, J.: Estimation and Inference in Econometrics, 1st edn. Oxford University Press, Oxford (1993)
10. Pratt, J.W.: Concavity of the log likelihood. J. Am. Stat. Assoc. **76**(1), 103–106 (1981)
11. Murray, W.: Newton-Type Methods. 1st edn. Stanford (2010)
12. Greene, W.H.: Econometric Analysis, 7th edn. Prentice Hall, Upper Saddle River (2011)
13. Poli, R., Langdon, W.B., McPhee, N.F.: A Field Guide to Genetic Programming, 1st edn. Lulu Enterprises, Raleigh (2008)
14. Luke, S., Panait, L.: Lexicographic parsimony pressure. In: Proceedings of the 2002 Conference on Genetic and Evolutionary Computation, GECCO 2002, pp. 829–836. ACM, San Francisco (2002)
15. Koza, J.R.: Genetic Programming: On the Programming of Computers by Means of Natural Selection (Complex Adaptive Systems), 1st edn. The MIT Press, Cambridge (1992)
16. Silva, S., Almeida, J.: Gplab – a genetic programming toolbox for matlab. In: Proceedings of the Nordic MATLAB Conference, pp. 273–278 (2003)
17. Searson, D.P., Leahy, D.E., Willis, M.J.: GPTIPS: an open source genetic programming toolbox for multigene symbolic regression. In: Proceedings of The International Multiconference of Engineers and Computer Scientists 2010, IMECS 2010, Hong Kong, pp. 77–80 (2010)
18. De Melo, V.V.: Kaizen programming. In: Proceedings of the 2014 Conference on Genetic and Evolutionary Computation, GECCO 2014, pp. 895–902. ACM, New York (2014)
19. De Melo, V.V., Banzhaf, W.: Improving logistic regression classification of credit approval with features constructed by Kaizen programming. In: Proceedings of the 2016 Conference on Genetic and Evolutionary Computation, GECCO 2016, pp. 61–62. ACM, New York (2016)
20. UCI Machine Learning Repository. University of California, School of Information and Computer Science, Irvine, CA. http://archive.ics.uci.edu/ml. Accessed 24 Feb 2015
21. Datasets used for classification: comparison of results. Nicolaus Copernicus University, Department of Informatics, Computational Intelligence Laboratory, Toruń, Poland. http://www.springer.com/lncs. Accessed 24 Feb 2015

GAVGA: A Genetic Algorithm for Viral Genome Assembly

Renato R.M. Oliveira[1,2(✉)] ⓘ, Filipe Damasceno[2], Ronald Souza[2],
Reginaldo Santos[1,3] ⓘ, Manoel Lima[1], Regiane Kawasaki[2],
and Claudomiro Sales[1,2,3] ⓘ

[1] Computer Science Graduate Program (PPGCC), UFPA, Belém, Pará, Brazil
renato.oliveira@icen.ufpa.br
[2] Laboratory of Bioinformatics and High-performance Computing (LaBioCAD),
UFPA, Belém, Pará, Brazil
[3] Laboratory of Applied Electromagnetics, UFPA, Belém, Pará, Brazil

Abstract. Bioinformatics has grown considerably since the development of the first sequencing machine, being today intensively used with the next generation DNA sequencers. Viral genomes represent a great challenge to bioinformatics due to its high mutation rate, forming quasispecies in the same infected host. In this paper, we implement and evaluate the performance of a genetic algorithm, named GAVGA, through the quality of a viral genome assembly. The assembly process works by first clustering the reads that share a common substring called seed and for each cluster, checks if there are overlapping reads with a given similarity percentage using a genetic algorithm. The assembled data are then compared to Newbler, SPAdes and ABySS assemblers, and also to a viral assembler such as VICUNA, which confirms the feasibility of our approach. GAVGA was implemented in python 2.7+ and can be downloaded at https://sourceforge.net/projects/gavga-assembler/.

Keywords: Assembly · Genetic algorithms · Viral · Genomes

1 Background

Bioinformatics is currently in high growth, starting with the emergence of the first DNA sequencing and assembly methods [1]. At that time, the genome of thousands of microorganisms was assembled and stored in public databases. Genome assemble, sequence alignment, genome binning and gene prediction are some of the many goals that can be achieved through computational methods such as data mining, machine learning and clustering techniques [2, 3].

Many of the analysis done to an organism through Bioinformatics starts by obtaining its DNA (whole genome) through sequencing techniques. There is still no method capable of extracting the whole genome of a microorganism. To solve this problem, the DNA is randomly divided into several small fragments, which are sequenced and then assembled to obtain the complete and original genome. These fragments (reads) are grouped, if they share common nucleotide information, in structures called contigs, which can be also grouped in a bigger structure called

© Springer International Publishing AG 2017
E. Oliveira et al. (Eds.): EPIA 2017, LNAI 10423, pp. 395–407, 2017.
DOI: 10.1007/978-3-319-65340-2_33

scaffolds. The different ways to perform the assembly of these reads constitute an algorithmic problem known as fragments assembly [1]. The assembly softwares assume one of the two well-known methods for assembling datasets of reads: OLC (Overlap - Layout - Consensus) and de-Bruijn Graph (kmers), which use Hamiltonian and Eulerian Graphs, respectively [4].

Viral infections are leading the cause of death worldwide for many years (http://www.who.int/mediacentre/factsheets/fs310/en/). Despite all the advances in sequencing technologies and downstream analysis, viral genomes are still difficult to analyze due to its high genome mutation rate, causing the constitution of a diverse (genetically heterogeneous) population while infecting a single host [5]. To harbor this problem, many viral genome assembler were developed. VICUNA [6] is OLC-based and generates consensus assemblies by first clustering the reads that present some similarity by using min hashes. Then the contigs formed by the initial clusters are merged to generate the final output. IVA [7] is an iterative kmer assembler which chooses the most abundant kmer seed (k) among the reads, map all the reads to k and assemble them, generating a contig. This process is repeated until no more read can be mapped to form new contigs or no new seed can be made. PRICE [8] works similarly to IVA, using a seed from a local reference genome instead of using from the input data. VirusTAP [9] is a web pipeline for viral genome assembly which gathers a whole set of tools, aiming to generate results with high accuracy from either genome or metagenome (environmental sample) data. These known viral genome assemblers have some limitations regarding to the sequencing technology and the amount of data that they accept to generate an accurate assembly. VICUNA only assemble a high number of single-end reads and Illumina paired-end reads. IVA can only assemble paired-end reads in a high quantity. PRICE demands a reference seed, discarding the possibility of assembling an unknown viral genome. VirusTAP only accepts Illumina paired-end reads. These questions regarding the use of some viral assemblers only with data with paired-end and specific sequencing machine reads end up limiting some groups of pursuing their researches.

Regarding to optimization problems, Genetic Algorithm (GA), an evolutionary technique from artificial intelligence, is currently presenting good results. GAs can find a feasible solution in a large feature space of assembly possibilities. In this paper, we present GAVGA–A Genetic Algorithm for Viral Genome Assembly, which is mainly based on the core concepts of the OLC technique, along with the concepts of clustering and genetic algorithms to assemble genomes. GAVGA can assemble paired (see Data Preprocessing Section) and single-end reads.

In [10], the authors show that OLC technique can be divide into overlap detection, fragments layout and decision of the consensus sequence. The overlap detection step finds a region with minimum similarity between two reads. Figure 1a shows an example of overlapping regions between two sequences. Considering the sequences AGA, GAT, TCG and GAG, Fig. 1b shows the overlap graph that represent them. After the overlap graph creation, we proceed to the discovery of paths in the graph (Fragments Layout step), where we should discover a Hamiltonian path, which is the one that visits each node in a graph only once [11, 12], i.e. the one with the highest sum of the edges weights. After finding the best Hamiltonian Path, we initiate the last step of the OLC technique, the Consensus, where the chosen Hamiltonian Path reconstructs the assembled sequence.

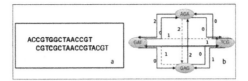

Fig. 1. Overlap between two reads and an overlap graph. (a) Overlap between two reads. The black nucleotides indicate similarity while the red one indicates a mismatch. (b) Overlap graph, where each node is a read to be assembled and the edges between two nodes indicate the size of the overlap found. The green dashed lines represent a Hamiltonian path in the graph. (Color figure online)

Although widely used, the OLC technique has some disadvantages. The Hamiltonian Path Problem is NP-Hard when it comes to an optimization problem, but it is NP-Complete when it comes to a decision problem and there are no efficient algorithms to solve this problem yet [13, 14]. Furthermore, the OLC technique is not suitable for sequences with many repeated reads.

2   Implementation

GA is a search and optimization stochastic technique based on Darwin's natural and genetic selection theory [15]. According to Darwin, along the generations of a population, individuals who are better adapted to the environment are more likely to perpetuate their genetic code by reproducing with others well-adapted individuals. However, this better adaptation can be worsened (or improved) if this individual suffers genetic mutation. Thus, through the selection principle, individuals who are better adapted to an environment will more likely survive, so that the population will evolve, always through adaptation.

Computationally, we consider the environment as an optimization problem and the individual as a possible solution, where the goal is to find the individual who is more adapted to the environment (the solution that better solve the problem). An individual is represented by a chromosome, which contains the coding (genotype) of a possible solution (phenotype) for a specific problem. The chromosomes are generally implemented as lists or vectors where each vector position of the list is named genes and the possible values of a gene are named alleles [15]. Selection, reproduction (crossover) and mutation processes are also represented computationally and they will be seen in more details as it follows.

3   Data Preprocessing

The downloaded data is in the SRA (Short Reads Archive) file format, in which reads obtained from a sequencer are provided by NCBI [16]. GAVGA needs a FASTQ file as input to run properly. Thus, the SRA file must be converted to the FASTQ format through the SRAToolkit [17]. As the data consists of paired-end reads, PEAR [18] was used to merge the reads to obtain a single read for each pair.

After sequencing, the rawdata generally presents contaminant reads from the host. We used BioBloom [19] to screen the data and remove the contaminants. The PRINSEQ [20] tool was used to trim the 5' and 3' bases with bad. As some of the raw reads might have bad quality, they are first trimmed, discarding bases of the reads that had a quality value below PHRED 20 and discarding the reads that had less than 20 bp (base pairs).

After trimming, we used Fastx Toolkit (http://hannonlab.cshl.edu/fastx_toolkit/) to filter the reads that had less than 80% of the bases with a quality below 20 PHRED.

4   GAVGA Operators and Components

GAVGA was implemented in Python and can be used in any operational system supporting Python 2.7+. First, the input reads are clustered in groups that share a common seed. In this process, the algorithm randomly takes one read of the dataset and all its seeds are extracted, i.e., all its substrings of a fixed length (default is 16). Then, any read from the whole dataset that share at least one of the extracted seeds will be grouped, forming clusters. If a cluster contains less than 10 reads or if a read does not share at least one seed, they are gathered in a cluster called remaining reads.

The chromosome is represented by a vector of strings with n positions, where each position stores a read from the input file. Figure 2a shows a simple file (input reads) containing only 5 small reads and how a chromosome is represented with such information (Fig. 2b).

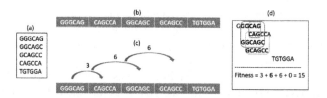

Fig. 2.   (a) Text file containing 5 reads extracted from a fictional microorganism. (b) Chromosome Representation, where each chromosome gene is a read from the file in Fig. 2a. (c) Assembly process of a chromosome and its fitness calculation. If the reads from two adjacent genes i and $i + 1$ are assembled, then the gene $i + 2$ will have to overlap to the result of the assembled genes i and $i + 1$. (d) Assembled sequence for the chromosome in Fig. 2b.

Each cluster initially formed will represent a population in the GA. To create a population of chromosomes (generate population), reads that compose the chromosomes genes are randomly chosen with no repetition. The number of chromosomes represents the size of population. This is a parameter of the GA and must be chosen a priori.

To obtain the information represented in the chromosome of Fig. 2b, the total sum of the overlaps between adjacent reads (genes) is calculated (calculate fitness). This sum value is the fitness of the chromosome and the algorithm below demonstrates its calculation:

```
1.  total_sum=0
2.  num_genes=number of genes of a chromosome
3.  gene0 = chromosome[0]
4.  i=1
5.  while i < num_genes do{
6.          gene1 = chromosome[i]
7.      If has_overlap(gene0, gene1):
8.              total_sum+=overlap(gene0, gene1)
10.             gene0 = overlap_contig(gene0, gene1)
11.     else:
12.             gene0 = chromosome[i]
13.         i++
14. fitness = total_sum
```

Being i a position of the gene in the chromosome that ranges from 0 to the total of genes that compound a chromosome, if there is overlap between the gene i with the gene $i + 1$ (line 7), then the overlap length is summed to the total overlap length of the read (line 8). It is also evaluated if there is overlap between the contig resulted from the previous genes (line 10) with the gene $i + 2$. This process is repeated until it reaches the last gene of the chromosome.

GAVGA identifies if a chromosome is better than another (i.e. if one solution is better than another) by comparing their fitness. The higher the fitness, the better is the overlapping performance, resulting in a good assembly. In Fig. 2d, for example, the fitness from the chromosome in the Fig. 2c is calculated.

In the *parents selection* step, the chromosome with the best fitness values that may generate good solutions as offspring are selected. This selection is made by tournament, an approach where t (adjustable value) chromosomes are selected and the chromosome who has the best fitness among them is selected as a future parent. This process is repeated until it reaches a number of chromosomes equal to 40% of the population. This percentage is typical of the Steady-State approach [21], where is not the whole population that is replaced by new chromosomes, but only part of it.

After Parents Selection, the crossover process is initiated, where chromosomes selected as parents will be randomly chosen in pairs to generate an offspring. Given a probability Pc that two chromosomes will recombinate, there will be an exchange of genes between those two chromosomes, thus creating two new chromosomes with new information coming from their parents. Figure 3a demonstrates the crossover process between two chromosomes. A random cutoff point is chosen for both parent, as indicated by the vertical lines. Genes before the cutoff point are passed to the offspring, and the other remaining information is populated with genes from the other chromosome, without reads repetition. The second child is generated in the same way (Fig. 3b). The offspring is submitted to a *mutation* process, where genes are permuted with a given probability Pm. Figure 3c shows how the mutation occurs in GAVGA, when two genes of a chromosome are chosen at random. These genes are permuted, as demonstrated in Fig. 3d, then generating a new chromosome (Fig. 3e).

The population of the next generation is formed by an elitist selection. All chromosomes from the previous generation and the offspring generated are sorted according to their fitness. If c children chromosomes were generated, so the c chromosomes with the worst fitness are removed from the population and the remaining are passed to the next generation.

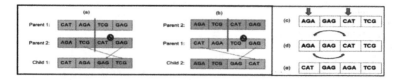

Fig. 3. (a) Crossover process. Parents 1 and 2 have different sizes. One point crossover is selected in the first parent, so the first child can be created. (b) One point is selected in the second parent so the second child can be created. The generated offspring cannot harbor repeated reads. (c) Chromosome Mutation. Two genes of a chromosome are chosen at random. (d) These genes are swapped. (e) A new chromosome is generated.

Traditionally, there are some others required parameters for a GA: Population size is the number of chromosomes that will represent possible solutions to the problem that is intended to optimize or solve; Number of generations is the maximal number of iterations that the process of selection, crossover, mutation and assessment will be performed.

The crossover rate was in the range of 0.6 to 0.9 and the mutation rate was in the range of 0.3 to 0.6. These values are interpreted as ranges due to the application of Rechenberg strategy where the crossover and mutation probabilities are increased or decreased during the execution of the algorithm, by approaching or not to optimal solutions [22]. For example, if 1/5 of the offspring has a fitness value better than the individuals from the current generation, it means that the optimal solution (local or global) is distant to be found and the operators' rate must be increased, thus accelerating the convergence of the algorithm. Otherwise, the operators' rate is decreased, because it means that the optimal solution is close of being found.

The parameters regarding to population size, mutation and crossover rate, minimum overlap length, minimum overlap similarity, maximal number of generations, tournament ring and number of executions can all be set in the configuration file that follows GAVGA.

The comparison of GAVGA results to the other assembling softwares' is given by means of measuring the largest contig, the total basepairs and the total contigs obtained by each software, as well as the similarity percentage when aligning the results to the reference genome using BLAST [23]. The larger the contig, higher the similarity percentage and lower the total of contigs, the better.

4.1   Related Works

In [24] a GA is used to perform the genome assembly, where the chromosome representation was done by using a set of bits that represent an index of a read to be assembled. Parsons considered the fitness function as the amount of all the overlap lengths between the reads that composed a chromosome. The chromosome representation used by [25] was of several of chromosomes with only two genes that were used as index to the reads to be assembled. Besides, the fitness function was also the overlap length between the two reads. In this case, the whole solution was represented by all the population, and not by the chromosome. Another similar work can be found in [26–28].

The problem found in these works is that they only executed their algorithms with no more than 1,049 reads, not being clear if their algorithms would be able to assemble data that are usually ten times higher.

5 Results and Discussion

This paper presents a genetic algorithm able to assemble genomes. To evaluate GAVGA results we used 2 datasets, one with real reads extracted from the Human Immunodeficiency Virus 1, downloaded from NCBI under the accession number ERR846528, and the other one with simulated reads from Herpesvirus genome, using ART (version 2.6.0) [29] to simulate a 454 sequencing. We opted to perform a simulation using the 454 sequencing only to show that GAVGA is able to deal with different sequencing error models. We compared the GAVGA results to Newbler (Roche Products), SPAdes [30] and ABySS [31] results and as we are assembling viral genomes, we also compared to VICUNA assembler. VirusTAP pipeline and IVA were not executed because they require a specific sequencing technology, so we opted by only comparing to softwares that can assemble non-specific sequencing technology data. All the tools were executed under only one processing thread with shared memory.

5.1 Real Dataset

The file for the real reads contained 13,221 paired-end sequences extracted by a Illumina MiSeq sequencing. After preprocessing, there was 6,891 remaining reads, totalizing 1,173,484 bp (1.2 Mbases), meaning a good coverage of 130X, assuming that the HIV reference genome has 9,000 bp.

Newbler, GAVGA and VICUNA had the minimum overlap length and minimum overlap similarity configured to 40 bp and 90%, respectively. SPAdes and ABySS had their kmer value configured to 41 so that the overlap between kmers state in 40 bp.

GAVGA is a stochastic algorithm, so we recommend setting the number of runs to >1, to the algorithm combine the contigs of each run, improving the final results. To increase the confidence of the algorithm, it was executed 5 times in a quad-core computer with 8 GB RAM and a 3.10 GHz Intel core i5 CPU, running Ubuntu 14.04. The data presented in Table 1 shows the average results obtained in five executions of GAVGA with three different population sizes (2, 6 and 10 individuals). As Newbler, SPAdes, ABySS, and VICUNA use deterministic algorithms, they were only executed 1 time.

GAVGA was executed with 3 different population sizes. The results on Table 1 show that even with a population size of only 2 individuals, GAVGA reaches good results. From now on, we are considering the results obtained with 2 individuals in the population. The number of contigs obtained by Newbler (3 contigs) were still better than those obtained by GAVGA (mean of 105 contigs) and the other assemblers. In the other hand, GAVGA obtained a total of contigs lower than SPAdes (131 contigs), ABySS (149 contigs) and VICUNA (143 contigs). GAVGA presents a standard

Table 1. Statistical results of GAVGA, Newbler, SPAdes, ABySS and VICUNA assemblers on a real dataset. The results for each assembler are shown in the table regarding to the total of contigs generated, the largest contig encountered and the total bases of the final contigs.

Assembler	Total of contigs	Largest contig (bp)	Total bases (bp)
GAVGA (pop size = 2)	105 ± 3.93	9004.2 ± 471.70	49930.2 ± 3945
GAVGA (pop size = 6)	98 ± 1.41	9000.2 ± 488.73	46501.6 ± 4634.9
GAVGA (pop size = 10)	100.2 ± 2.48	8443 ± 1211.44	48799.2 ± 2456.42
Newbler	3	9077	9828
SPAdes	131	4543	13001
ABySS	149	3962	18007
VICUNA	143	439	22605

deviation in its results because it is a stochastic algorithm, that explain why we executed it 5 times (a very common approach while evaluating a GA approach).

In addition, the length of the largest contig obtained by GAVGA (9,228 bp) during the 5 executions was 151 bp larger than the largest contig obtained by Newbler (9,077 bp) and considerably larger than the largest contigs obtained by the other assemblers. Also, the genetic information of the contigs obtained by GAVGA, as well as the other assemblers, was correct, as demonstrated in Fig. 4 when performed a BLAST alignment using the largest contig obtained by each assembler against the NCBI database of Human Immunodeficiency Virus. The information presented in Fig. 4 shows that GAVGA correctly assembled the reads.

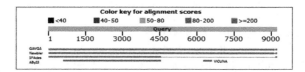

Fig. 4. BLAST alignment of the greatest contig obtained by GAVGA against the NCBI HIV Genome Database. The contig had an alignment of 90% similarity and 100% covered, indicating that the contig was well assembled by GAVGA.

In Fig. 5 is demonstrated how the solutions found by GAVGA converged to its final solutions. To show the convergence tendency, we chose to analyze the first population created in the clustering phase, which is formed by 2 individuals with 626 genes (reads) each.

When every population converge to an optimal solution, the algorithm assembles the best individual, resulting in optimal contigs. The resulting contigs from each population are joined and re-clustered into new populations. This process repeats until there is no more convergence in any population. Figure 6 shows the amount of contigs at each reclustering process (era) done by GAVGA while assembling the real dataset with population size = 2.

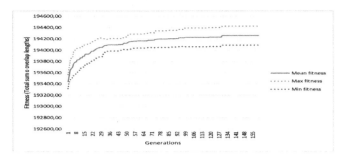

Fig. 5. Mean fitness of five executions of GAVGA. The graphic shows the convergence's tendency of the genetic algorithm.

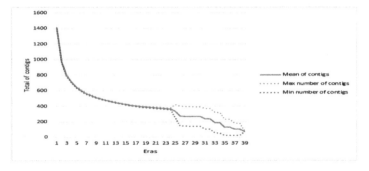

Fig. 6. Convergence of the total of contigs in each era of clustering done by GAVGA. The graphic considers five executions of the GA while assembling the real dataset with population size = 2.

5.2   Simulated Dataset

To simulate the 454 sequencing of Human Herpesvirus 1 (152,222 bp), we downloaded its genome from NCBI under the accession number NC_001806.2. We simulated the sequencing using ART simulator, choosing the sequencing technology as being 454 GS FLX, the coverage of sequencing as 20X, generating 10,724 single-end reads.

The test parameters were the same used and demonstrated in session 3.1. The results of GAVGA and the other assemblers are demonstrated in Table 2. GAVGA was also executed with 3 different population sizes while assembling the simulated dataset.

The results on Table 2 show that with a population size of 6 individuals, GAVGA reaches good results. From now on, we are considering GAVGA results obtained with 6 individuals in the population. The number of contigs obtained by Newbler (3 contigs) were slightly better than those obtained by GAVGA (mean of 9 contigs) and the other assemblers. In the other hand, GAVGA obtained a total of contigs considerably lower than SPAdes (38 contigs), ABySS (111 contigs) and VICUNA (411 contigs). In addition, the length of the largest contig obtained by GAVGA (149,400 bp) during the

Table 2. Statistical results of GAVGA, Newbler, SPAdes, ABySS and VICUNA assemblers on a simulated dataset. The results for each assembler used are shown in the table regarding to the total of contigs generated, the largest contig encountered and the total bases of the final contigs. As we are assembling a simulated dataset, now we can calculate the similarity of the contigs and the coverage against the reference genome.

Assembler	Total of contigs	Largest contig (bp)	Total bases (bp)	Largest contig similarity to reference (%)	Reference coverage (%)
GAVGA (pop size = 2)	11.6 ± 1.81	128707 ± 11059.4	213890.8 ± 45929.9	98 ± 0	90 ± 8.21
GAVGA (pop size = 6)	9 ± 2.12	135109 ± 15126.35	208496.6 ± 49701.5	98 ± 0	93 ± 8.21
GAVGA (pop size = 10)	7.6 ± 1.67	133101.2 ± 11216.7	209612 ± 52756.2	98 ± 0	93 ± 8.21
Newbler	3	107952	136387	99	70
SPAdes	38	54680	137498	99	35
ABySS	111	28397	139986	99	18
VICUNA	411	436	63974	100	0.2

5 executions was almost (99%) the whole Human Herpesvirus 1 genome and 41,448 bp larger than the largest contig obtained by Newbler (107,952 bp) and considerably larger than the largest contigs obtained by the other assemblers. Also, the genetic information of the contigs obtained by GAVGA, as well as the other assemblers, was correct, as demonstrated in Fig. 7 when performed a BLAST alignment using the largest contig obtained by each assembler against the reference genome of Human Herpesvirus 1. The information presented in Fig. 7 shows that GAVGA correctly assembled the simulated reads and almost obtained the whole Herpesvirus genome, showing its feasibility while assembling a genome.

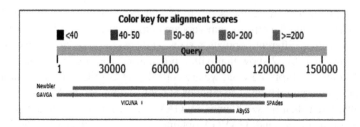

Fig. 7. BLAST alignment of the largest contigs against the Human Herpesvirus 1 reference genome. The longest contigs obtained by GAVGA, Newbler, SPAdes, ABySS and VICUNA are aligned against the Herpesvirus genome.

6 Conclusions

Many assembly softwares are available to the Bioinformatics community to be used in the assembly of microorganisms' genomes. In particular, we have a big variety of viral genome assemblers that focus in the high mutation rate of the viral DNA in order to solve problems regarding to the high diverse population of one single virus in a single host. The problem is that many of this viral assemblers softwares are very difficult to use and can only be applied on data with a high number of single-end and Illumina paired-end reads.

This paper presented GAVGA, a Genetic Algorithm for Viral Genome Assembly that could assemble single and paired-end reads (Data Preprocessing session), despite the sequencing technology used. Different from other state of the art assembler that construct a graph to assemble reads into a genome, we demonstrated how a genetic algorithm can also be used to do so. The results in the tests with either real or simulated dataset showed that GAVGA obtained contigs longer than the contigs obtained by the other softwares. Besides, GAVGA contigs were also very similar to its references genomes, showing that the algorithm assembled the reads correctly. None of the related works with genetic algorithms for genome assembling attempted to assemble the same amount of reads that we used as input in this paper.

In a further version of GAVGA we intend to implement its code using CUDA, allowing the algorithm to process each population (cluster of reads) in parallel using hundreds of threads simulated by a Graphics Processing Unit (GPU). Besides, we also will optimize the genetic operators and implement parallelization by CPU's threads, including future tests in order to decrease the variance of GAVGA results. We recommend using GAVGA in the assembling of small genomes such as viral ones and it can be downloaded at https://sourceforge.net/projects/gavga-assembler/.

References

1. Nagarajan, N., Pop, M.: Sequence assembly demystified. Nat. Rev. Genet. **14**(3), 157–167 (2013)
2. Palmer, L.E., Dejori, M., Bolanos, R., Fasulo, D.: Improving de novo sequence assembly using machine learning and comparative genomics for overlap correction. BMC Bioinform. **11**(1), 33 (2010)
3. Goés, F., Alves, R., Corrêa, L., Chaparro, C., Thom, L.: Towards an ensemble learning strategy for metagenomic gene prediction. In: Campos, S. (ed.) BSB 2014. LNCS, vol. 8826, pp. 17–24. Springer, Cham (2014). doi:10.1007/978-3-319-12418-6_3
4. Peltola, H., Söderlund, H., Tarhio, J., Ukkonen, E.: Algorithms for some string matching problems arising in molecular genetics. In: IFIP Congress, pp. 59–64 (1983)
5. Henn, M.R., Boutwell, C.L., Charlebois, P., Lennon, N.J., Power, K.A., Macalalad, A.R., Zody, M.C.: Whole genome deep sequencing of HIV-1 reveals the impact of early minor variants upon immune recognition during acute infection. PLoS Pathog. **8**(3), e1002529 (2012)
6. Yang, X., Charlebois, P., Gnerre, S., Coole, M.G., Lennon, N.J., Levin, J.Z., Henn, M.R.: De novo assembly of highly diverse viral populations. BMC Genom. **13**(1), 475 (2012)

7. Hunt, M., Gall, A., Ong, S.H., Brener, J., Ferns, B., Goulder, P., Otto, T.D.: IVA: accurate de novo assembly of RNA virus genomes. Bioinformatics **31**(14), 2374–2376 (2015)

8. Ruby, J.G., Bellare, P., DeRisi, J.L.: PRICE: software for the targeted assembly of components of (Meta) genomic sequence data. G3: Genes Genomes Genet. **3**(5), 865–880 (2013)

9. Yamashita, A., Sekizuka, T., Kuroda, M.: VirusTAP: Viral genome-targeted assembly pipeline. Frontiers in microbiology **7**, 32 (2016)

10. Gusfield, D. Algorithms on strings, trees and sequences: computer science and computational biology. Cambridge university press (1997)

11. Szwarcfiter, J.L.: Grafos e algoritimos computacionais, 2nd edn. Rio de Janeiro (1998)

12. Hoffman, A.J., Wolfe, J., Garfinkel, R.S., Johnson, D.S., Papadimitriou, C.H., Gilmore, P.C., Golden, B.L.: The Traveling Salesman Problem: A Guided Tour of Combinatorial Optimization. Wiley, Hoboken (1986)

13. Bertossi, A.A.: The edge Hamiltonian path problem is NP-complete. Inf. Process. Lett. **13** (4–5), 157–159 (1981)

14. Héam, P.C., Hugot, V., Kouchnarenko, O.: The emptiness problem for tree automata with at least one global disequality constraint is NP-hard. Inf. Process. Lett. **118**, 6–9 (2017)

15. Davis, L.: Handbook of Genetic Algorithms. Van Nostrand Reinhold, New York (1991)

16. NCBI Illumina MiSeq paired end sequencing of Human Immunodeficiency Virus 1. http://www.ncbi.nlm.nih.gov/sra/?term=ERR846528. Accessed 15 Apr 2017

17. Sherry, S.: NCBI SRA Toolkit technology for next generation sequence data. In: Plant and Animal Genome XX Conference (2012)

18. Zhang, J., Kobert, K., Flouri, T., Stamatakis, A.: PEAR: a fast and accurate Illumina Paired-End reAd mergeR. Bioinformatics **30**(5), 614–620 (2014)

19. Chu, J., Sadeghi, S., Raymond, A., Jackman, S.D., Nip, K.M., Mar, R., Birol, I.: BioBloom tools: fast, accurate and memory-efficient host species sequence screening using bloom filters. Bioinformatics **30**(23), 3402–3404 (2014)

20. Schmieder, R., Edwards, R.: Quality control and preprocessing of metagenomic datasets. Bioinformatics **27**(6), 863–864 (2011)

21. Vavak, F., Fogarty, T.C.: Comparison of steady state and generational genetic algorithms for use in nonstationary environments. In: Proceedings of IEEE International Conference on Evolutionary Computation, pp. 192–195. IEEE (1996)

22. Rechenberg, I.: Evolution Strategy: Optimization of Technical systems by means of biological evolution. Fromman-Holzboog, Stuttgart, 104 (1973)

23. Altschul, S.F., Gish, W., Miller, W., Myers, E.W., Lipman, D.J.: Basic local alignment search tool. J. Mol. Biol. **215**(3), 403–410 (1990)

24. Parsons, R.J., Forrest, S., Burks, C.: Genetic algorithms, operators, and DNA fragment assembly. Mach. Learn. **21**(1), 11–33 (1995)

25. Fraga, J.S. Algoritmos genéticos e o problema de montagem de reads (Master's thesis) (2014)

26. Kikuchi, S., Chakraborty, G.: Heuristically tuned GA to solve genome fragment assembly problem. In: IEEE Congress on Evolutionary Computation, CEC 2006. pp. 1491–1498. IEEE (2006)

27. Indumathy, R., Maheswari, S.U.: Nature inspired algorithms to solve DNA fragment assembly problem: a survey. Int. J. Bioinform. Res. Appl. **2**(2), 45–50 (2012)

28. Hughes, J., Houghten, S., Mallen-Fullerton, G. M., Ashlock, D.: Recentering and restarting genetic algorithm variations for dna fragment assembly. In: 2014 IEEE Conference on Computational Intelligence in Bioinformatics and Computational Biology, pp. 1–8. IEEE (2014)

29. Huang, W., Li, L., Myers, J.R., Marth, G.T.: ART: a next-generation sequencing read simulator. Bioinformatics **28**(4), 593–594 (2012)
30. Bankevich, A., Nurk, S., Antipov, D., Gurevich, A.A., Dvorkin, M., Kulikov, A.S., Pyshkin, A.V.: SPAdes: a new genome assembly algorithm and its applications to single-cell sequencing. J. Comput. Biol. **19**(5), 455–477 (2012)
31. Simpson, J.T., Wong, K., Jackman, S.D., Schein, J.E., Jones, S.J., Birol, I.: ABySS: a parallel assembler for short read sequence data. Genome Res. **19**(6), 1117–1123 (2009)

Cartesian Genetic Programming in an Open-Ended Evolution Environment

António Simões, Tiago Baptista[✉], and Ernesto Costa

CISUC, Department of Informatics Engineering,
University of Coimbra, Coimbra, Portugal
ajsimoes@student.dei.uc.pt, {baptista,ernesto}@dei.uc.pt

Abstract. In this paper we describe and analyze the use of the Cartesian Genetic Programming method to evolve Artificial Neural Networks (CGPANN) in an open-ended evolution scenario. The issue of open-ended evolution has for some time been considered one of the open problems in the field of Artificial Life. In this paper we analyze the capabilities of CGPANN to evolve behaviors in a scenario without artificial selection, more specifically, without the use of explicit fitness functions. We use the BitBang framework and one of its example scenarios as a proof of concept. The results obtained in these first experiments show that it is indeed possible to evolve CGPANN brains, in an open-ended environment, without any explicit fitness function. We also present an analysis of different parameter configurations for the CGPANN when used in this type of scenario.

Keywords: Artificial life · Multi-agent systems · Open-ended evolution · Neuroevolution · Cartesian genetic programming

1 Introduction

In Artificial Life research, the issue of open-ended evolution has been considered, for some time, one of its open problems [4]. A definition of open-ended evolution has not yet gathered consensus. Nonetheless, one of the properties of open-ended systems that is generally agreed upon is that of the continuous production of novel forms [12]. The requirements to achieve open-ended evolution in artificial systems has long been studied, although, again, a definite answer has not been agreed upon. A recent overview of the research on open-ended evolution, its definitions and requirements can be found in [1,15]. One of these requirements that has been considered by several authors is that of the lack of notion of better individual [2,5]. This notion of better individual is central in most evolutionary algorithms, and is quantified by using fitness functions. As such, considering this requirement for open-ended evolution, we need to remove the fitness from the systems. In this paper, we analyze the feasibility of using the Cartesian Genetic Programming (CGP) algorithm [10,11] in such an open-ended evolution setting. More specifically, we will use the Cartesian Genetic Programming encoded Artificial Neural Networks (CGPANN) variant of CGP [19].

© Springer International Publishing AG 2017
E. Oliveira et al. (Eds.): EPIA 2017, LNAI 10423, pp. 408–420, 2017.
DOI: 10.1007/978-3-319-65340-2_34

In 1943, McCulloch and Pitts [9] proposed a simple computational model for a neuron. An artificial neuron is composed of several weight inputs to whom an activation function is applied to determine the corresponding output. Linking several neurons we obtain an Artificial Neural Network (ANN). There are many types of ANNs, depending on the topology (how neurons are connected), the activation function (how the output is computed based on its weight inputs) and on the learning algorithm (how the weights can be modified). ANNs have been applied successfully to many classes of problems, e.g., pattern recognition. One of the main difficulties of ANNs is the definition of both the weight and the topology. Without surprise over the years different approaches were proposed to solve the design issue. One of these approaches is called Neuro Evolution (NE), where an Evolutionary Algorithm (EA) is used to evolve the weights and/or the topology of neural networks. One of the advantages of these methods is being especially suited to problems without precise fitness functions [22]. As we are considering an evolutionary system without any fitness function, Neuro Evolution appears to be a good fit.

The earlier NE methods of the 90's were limited to the evolution of the connections' weights until a reasonable solution was reached [7,22]. Later on, in 2002, Stanley and Miikkulainen [14] argued that the topology of a network affects its performance but heuristic approaches were not needed to find the appropriate topology for a given problem. Instead they proposed an algorithm called Neuro Evolution of Augmented Topologies (NEAT) [13]. NEAT is an EA that evolves both the weights and the topology starting from a population of feed forward ANNs, initially without any hidden layer. The coding is direct and the mutation operators consisted in altering the weights of the connections, adding a connection between two nodes that are not connected, adding nodes, deleting nodes or deleting connections. More recently, Turner and Miller used CGP to encode ANNs, having tested the method in benchmark optimization and machine learning problems [16,19], with promising results.

The use of Neuro Evolution in the context of open-ended evolution is not new. In his PhD Thesis Stanley [13] talks about applying NeuroEvolution methods to open-ended problems where he states that the capability of producing evolving topologies can produce novelty and complexity within the simulation which are the critical behavioral hallmarks studied in OEE [15]. Also, Channon used NE to evolve the brains of agents in an open-ended environment in his framework Geb [6] where he states that he used NeuroEvolution with the aim of achieving sufficient genetic neutrality.

In this paper we will focus on a specific method of NE that uses the CGP [10,11] evolutionary algorithm to evolve the topology and weights of a neural network (CGPANN [8,16]) in an open-ended evolution environment. We will use the BitBang framework [2,3] as a test-bed. This is a multi-agent framework especially suited for open-ended evolution simulations. In the base framework, the agents use a rule list as their brain, but it is fairly easy to change this with different algorithms. In this case, we will use CGPANN to encode neural networks that will be used as the brain of the agents. We will also use one of the environments used in [2] to test the BitBang framework. In this environment, agents evolve foraging capabilities, using no explicit fitness function. We will use this as a first test of the application of CGPANN to an evolutionary system where no fitness function is used.

The rest of the paper is organized as follows. In Sect. 2, we introduce the BitBang framework that we will use to do the experiments. Next, we will further detail the CGP algorithm, in Sect. 3, and the CGPANN approach, together with the experimental settings used in the simulations, in Sect. 4. We will then present and discuss the results (Sect. 5), and finally draw some conclusions and present future work (Sect. 6).

2   BitBang Framework

As mentioned earlier, we will use the BitBang framework [2] (named after the big bang theory), as a simulation environment to test the use of CGP in an open-ended evolution scenario. Implementing a modern autonomous agent model, this framework has roots in Artificial Life systems and Complexity Science. The simulated world is composed of entities. These can either be inanimate objects that are designated as *things*, or entities that have reasoning capabilities and power to perceive and affect the world—the *agents*. Both have traits that characterize them, such as color, size, or energy—the *features*. The agents communicate with, and change the environment using *perceptions* and *actions*, taking decisions using the *brain*.

In the model used by the framework, there is no definition of a simulation step, and there is no type of centralized control. As such, the simulation can be thought of as being asynchronous. The agents will independently perceive, decide, and act. Moreover, there is no evolutionary mechanism included in the definition of the model, since evolution is essentially implemented as an action. That is accomplished by giving the agents the capability of reproduction. Again, there is no central control bound to this process. The agents choose when to reproduce and with what other agent to reproduce with. In addition, there is no explicit fitness function. The agents die due to lack of resources, predators, age, or any other mechanism implemented in the world. To have a more in-depth view of the conceptual model and architecture of BitBang, refer to the full description of the framework in [2].

The BitBang Framework was chosen mostly due to its modular architecture, making it easy to plug-in a new brain algorithm, and test on already implemented environments. Also, its generic architecture will allow the initial test with a simple environment, and later move on to more complex experiments. As mentioned earlier, we will use one of the environments described by the authors of BitBang (the Foragers scenario [2]) as a first test.

In the experimental setup we will describe further the scenario implemented and how we combine the perceptions and actions of this scenario with the CGPANN brain.

3   Cartesian Genetic Programming

Cartesian Genetic Programming (CGP) [10,11] is a type of Genetic Programming (GP) method based on the separation of the genotype (a structured vector of integers) from the phenotype (an acyclic graph). An important characteristic of CGP, besides the indirect encoding scheme, is the fact that not all elements of the genotype are necessarily expressed in the phenotype, i.e., some of the nodes of the final graph and the corresponding connections will be inactive. CGP's genotype is composed by Function genes (F_i), Connection genes (C_i) and Output genes (O_i) (see Fig. 1).

The Function genes represent the function operating at each node of the graph and they can be any mathematical or logical function (e.g., ADD, SUB, Sigmoid, Step). The Connection genes represent the inputs of a node. The Output genes determine the output of the network.

The topology in CGP itself is constrained by a maximum number of nodes but it can be modified by activating or deactivating nodes due to mutation of the elements in the genotype. The inactive nodes are the ones that do not have a direct or indirect connection to an output node. This way CGP performs a very effective search on the space of possible topologies, trying to find the best structure for the problem at hand.

The mutation operator used in CGP is typically only a point mutation operator. This operator works as follows: first determine the number of genes to mutate (total size of the chromosome time the mutation rate); for each to mutate, choose a random one form the chromosome, and change its value to a new valid allele for that gene depending on the type of gene (function, connection or output). No crossover operators are typically used.

CGP uses an Evolutionary Algorithm called $(1+\lambda)$-Evolutionary Strategy typically with $\lambda = 4$. From a population of one individual λ offspring are generated by mutation. From the $(1+\lambda)$ individuals we choose the best one and repeat

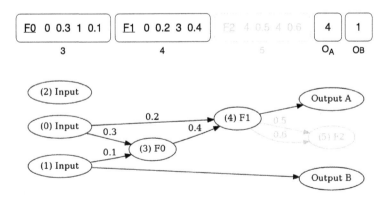

Fig. 1. Example of a CGPANN genotype and the corresponding phenotype where the Active genes are represented in black and the Inactive genes are represented in grey.

the process of reproduction with variation until we reach a stopping condition (e.g. number of evaluations).

CGPANN is a Topology and Weight Evolving Artificial Neural Network (TWEAN) method developed and analyzed by Khan et al. [8] and later on implemented and analyzed in greater detail by Turner and Miller [16,19]. This method uses most of the same architecture as CGP, with only the following changes: the function set used is restricted to those usual in ANN (e.g. sigmoid), and an extra gene is added to each connection to represent the weights. In Fig. 1, we can see that the genotype incorporates the weights in the connection by adding a weight gene in the genotype.

Cartesian Genetic Programming has been shown to have a number of interesting properties, like the Neutral Genetic Drift phenomenon [20,21], or its resilience to bloat [17]. Moreover the possibility of evolving both topology and weights of an ANN, make it a good candidate to be used in an open-ended evolution setting.

4   Experimental Setup

In this section we describe the experimental setup used to test the CGPANN method used as a brain of agents in the BitBang Framework. To accomplish these experiments we used the CGP library (described in [18]) and the BitBang Framework (described in [2,3]). The specific simulated environment used was the one described by the authors of BitBang in [2]. In that work, a rule list was used as the brain of agents. We will make an effort to change as little form the original simulations as possible, changing only the parameters that are related to the new brain used.

In this Foraging scenario the agents need to evolve foraging skills to be able to live and reproduce. The world is a 2D world where the agents and resources are placed. The terrain is a square. This area restricts the placement of agents and resources, but does not restrict the movement of the agents. The world is infinite, i.e., an agent can move past the boundaries of the populated terrain. Initially, the field is populated with a configured amount of randomly placed resource items. These are periodically replenished (at fixed intervals) so that the total food count is maintained. The number of resources available is configurable to be able to fine tune the system so as to allow agents to survive but also provide enough evolutionary pressure.

On initialization, the world is populated with randomly placed, and randomly generated agents. At this time, it is highly probable that the agents will not execute the reproduction action, either by not choosing it, or because they don't have enough energy to reproduce. To keep the population alive, whenever the number of agents in the world falls bellow a given threshold, new agents are created. If there are live agents in the environment, one will be picked for reproduction, otherwise a new random agent is created. Note that, as stated in the Introduction, there is no explicit fitness function, so the agent chosen for reproduction will be randomly selected from the population of live agents.

The scenario is thus composed of two entities: resource items and one type of agent. The agents have 3 features: **Energy**, the current level of energy (when it reaches 0 the agent dies), **Metabolic Rate**, current consumed energy per time unit and **Birth Date**, the time when the agent was created.

The agents Perceptions are: **Energy**, the agent's perception of its own energy, **Resource Location**, a numerical value that indicates the nearest resource within the vision (0 - No Resource near; 1 - Resource located to the left of the agent; 2 - Resource located to the right of the agent. 3 - Resource located in front of the agent) and **Reach Resource**, binary value that indicates if the agent has a resource that is in range for eating.

The agents actions are: **Movement**, 3 movement actions (Forward, Rotation to the right and Rotation to the left), **Eat**, the agent consumes a resource within its range replenishing an amount of energy, and **Reproduce**, this action allows the agent to reproduce itself. The reproduction implemented is asexual. When the action is executed, a new agent is created and placed in the world. The new agent will be given a brain that is a mutated version of its parent's brain. The action will also transfer energy from the parent to the offspring. The amount of energy consumed in the action is the sum of the initial energy for the new agent and a configurable fixed cost.

In Table 1 we present the configuration values used for the experiments conducted. We only show the parameters that are specific to these experiments. The rest of the configuration values were set to those from the original rule list implementation, presented in [2].

Table 1. Foraging configurations values

Parameter	Values
Time limit	100 000
Number of nodes	5; 10; 100; 1000
Arity	5
Mutation rate	0.01; 0.05; 0.1
Mutation operator	Point mutation
Weights	$[-1; 1]$

To connect the agent's perceptions to the CGPANN brain, and the its outputs to the agent's actions we created three different transformation methods.

The first method (Binary) transforms the numerical value of the perceptions into a binary representation and the output is retrieved as a binary value that indicates the position in a vector of actions (considering that if the output is greater than 0.5 its consider a 1).

The second method (Max Value) we transform the numerical value of the perceptions and we normalize its value into the range of 0 to 1. The output is directly mapped to the actions and the action chosen is the one that has the highest activation value.

In the third method (Threshold) we transform the perceptions in the same way as in the Max Value method. The activation of an action happens when the corresponding output has a higher value than a given threshold (in this case 0.5). This allows the agents to choose more than one action to execute at the same time.

5   Results

In the first analysis we experimented with a small architecture for the network using 10×5 (nodes x arity) network, Point Mutation with the probability values equals 0.01 and using the Threshold method. In Fig. 2 we can see that the agents can evolve sustainable foraging around 2010 time units and a sustainable reproduction around 10885 time units.

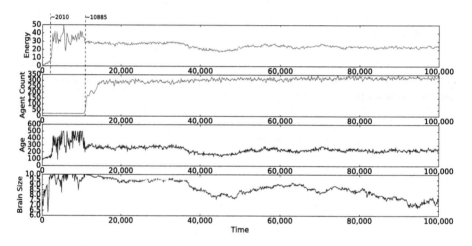

Fig. 2. Plot of the evolution of average gatherer energy, number of agents, average age and brain size of one of the simulations.

Upon further analysis we can see that when they start foraging the average age and the average energy starts to rise and when they start to reproduce both start to decline. This behavior occurs because more agents start to evolve capable foraging abilities leading then to survive longer and start reproducing. The reproduction of agents affects the world by introducing more and more agents, therefore leaving less resources to gather. This creates a pressure to evolve even further. From the pressure the lesser evolved agents die creating the behavior seen in the figure.

In the following test we look at the time that it took to evolve both foraging and reproductive behaviors in a sustainable way. For this we looked at the different types of methods created to implement the CGPANN in the scenario, different sizes of networks and different values of mutation (displayed in Fig. 3).

For the experiments presented next, we ran 30 independent simulations for each configuration of the parameters. To analyze the results from the various parameter configuration variations, we determined the statistical significance of the null hypothesis of no difference for each set of experiments using Kruskal-Wallis ANOVAs with $\alpha = 0.05$. If a significant difference in one of these sets of experiments was found, further pairwise Mann-Whitney U tests with Holm's p-value adjustment were conducted. These non-parametric tests were chosen because the data is not guaranteed to follow a normal distribution, and runs are independent and non-related.

In Fig. 3(a) and (b), we test the three different transformation methods for the connections from perceptions to inputs and outputs to actions. We show the time to evolve foraging and reproduction abilities using these methods with a 10×5 network and 0.05 of mutation value. With p-values equal to 3.82e−13 and 2.20e−13 for foraging and reproduction respectively, we can see that there is a significant difference between the methods. Further pairwise testing, shown in Table 2, lets us see that the Binary method produces worse results than the other two methods. The resulting outcome is caused by the mapping not encoding all variations of the outputs. The reason for this is there are 5 outputs and the binary equivalent to 5 is 101 leaving 2 non mapped representations (110, 111). As for the other two methods the results are due to the fact that the number of inputs and outputs are smaller than the ones used in the Binary method producing the observed outcome.

Table 2. Pairwise comparisons: time of evolution for foraging and reproduction for different transformation methods.

Task	Methods	Threshold	MaxValue
Foraging	MaxValue	1.00	-
	Binary	4.04e-10	6.93e-10
Reproduction	MaxValue	0.72659	-
	Binary	6.94e-10	4.05e-10

In Fig. 3(c) and (d) we used different values of nodes to observe different sizes in the network and the outcome in their evolution. Using a the same parameters of arity and mutation value we can see that 10 nodes have better results on average to evolve reproduction behavior. With a p-value equals 2.40e−11 and 1.33e−18 for foraging and reproduction respectively we can observe that there is a significant difference between values of nodes. Observing Table 4 revels us that increasing the size of the network produces worse results. Increasing the node size implies that more time is needed for an network capable of producing foraging and reproduction abilities. The same outcome happens when we increase the arity. This is because increasing the node size and the arity value produces a larger network where the evolutionary process takes more time to evolve a network suited to develop foraging and reproductive behaviors.

Evolution of Foraging

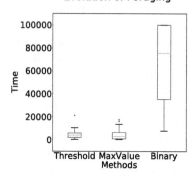

(a) Time to evolve foraging using different type of input-output methods.

Evolution of Reproduction

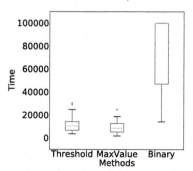

(b) Time to evolve reproduction using different type of input-output methods.

Evolution of Foraging

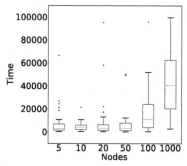

(c) Time to evolve foraging using different brain sizes

Evolution of Reproduction

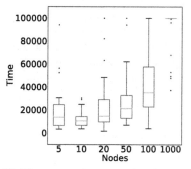

(d) Time to evolve reproduction using different brain sizes

Evolution of Foraging

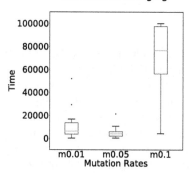

(e) Time to evolve foraging using different mutation values

Evolution of Reproduction

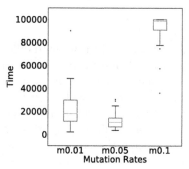

(f) Time to evolve reproduction using different mutation values

Fig. 3. Box plots of times to evolve foraging and reproductive behaviors.

In a further analysis we look at the number of active nodes after the agents started reproducing Table 3, in this we found that the number of active nodes is less than half of the maximum number of nodes except for the maximum of nodes equal to 5. These results implies that the small CGPANN networks that are capable of evolving faster than the larger ones.

Table 3. Average active nodes and standard deviation found after the evolution of reproduction.

Nodes	Avg. active nodes	Standard deviation
5	3.97	0.45
10	6.38	1.17
20	11.25	2.30
50	23.72	5.38
100	46.41	6.05
1000	323.11	27.45

Table 4. Pairwise comparisons: time of evolution for foraging and reproduction for different node values.

Task	Nodes	5	10	20	50	100
	10	1.00	-	-	-	-
	20	1.00	1.00	-	-	-
Foraging	50	1.00	1.00	1.00	-	-
	100	0.28593	0.08888	0.28593	0.08888	-
	1000	1.76e-06	4.22e-08	1.76e-06	5.29e-07	0.00121
	10	1.00	-	-	-	-
	20	1.00	0.67306	-	-	-
Reproduction	50	0.67306	0.00392	1.00	-	-
	100	0.00091	9.47e-07	0.00996	0.12550	-
	1000	3.37e-09	1.08e-09	1.78e-08	2.01e-08	2.59e-07

In Fig. 3(e) and (f) similarly to the experiments done before we use different values of mutation. Tested with a 10×5 network and the Threshold method. We can observe that the best value of mutation is 0.05. Looking at the p-values for foraging (p value $= 3.21e-12$) and reproduction (p value $= 2.38e-14$) we see there is a significance difference between different values. In Table 5 we can see that 0.05 has a faster evolution of foraging and reproduction. Upon further analysis to the average agent count we discovered that using 0.05 for the mutation value produced fewer agents that other two values (0.01 and 0.1). The argument for this results is that using a 0.05 for the mutation value results in faster evolution but produces a sub-optimal solution but further analysis to the evolution is needed to verify this claim.

Table 5. Pairwise comparisons: time of evolution for foraging and reproduction for different mutation values.

Task	Mutation value	0.01	0.05
Foraging	0.05	0.07977	-
	0.1	6.29e-10	2.84e-09
Reproduction	0.05	0.00685	-
	0.1	6.29e-10	2.71e-10

Comparing the two brain methods, one used in this paper (CGPANN) and the other seen in [2] (Rule List), we did not find any significant difference in both evolution of foraging and evolution of reproduction. The resulting p-values are 0.40769 for foraging and 0.15154 for reproduction.

6   Conclusion

In these experiments we can clearly see that the CGPANN method can produce networks that are capable of evolving both foraging and reproduction behaviors in a sustainable way. This provides us with a first indication that CGPANN can be applied to this type of scenario, and that it is able to evolve without any explicit fitness function. We believe these results are promising, and lay the foundations to further test and analyze the use of CGPANN for open-ended evolution research.

In this study we tested a number of parameters of CGPANN. However, more experiments are needed, specifically to test how the system behaves with larger networks, and given more time to evolve.

Comparing these results to the ones in [2] we can not see further improvements in the evolved behaviours, only on the time that it took to produce foraging and reproduction behaviors. The scenario is a simple scenario, where no further behaviours are available to the agents, and served as a first test of the use of CGPANN in this setting. We should now move on to more complex environments and agent capabilities, to further test if the use of this brain algorithm does enable more complex behaviours to evolve, where other algorithms failed to do so.

References

1. Banzhaf, W., Baumgaertner, B., Beslon, G., Doursat, R., Foster, J.A., McMullin, B., de Melo, V.V., Miconi, T., Spector, L., Stepney, S., White, R.: Defining and simulating open-ended novelty: requirements, guidelines, and challenges. Theory Biosci. **135**(3), 1–31 (2016)
2. Baptista, T.: Complexity and emergence in societies of agents. Ph.D. thesis, University of Coimbra, Coimbra, July 2012
3. Baptista, T., Menezes, T., Costa, E.: Bitbang: a model and framework for complexity research. In: Proceedings of the European Conference on Complex Systems 2006, Oxford, UK, p. 73, September 2006

4. Bedau, M.A., McCaskill, J.S., Packard, N.H., Rasmussen, S., Adami, C., Green, D.G., Ikegami, T., Kaneko, K., Ray, T.S.: Open problems in artificial life. Artif. Life **6**(4), 363–376 (2000)
5. Channon, A.: Three evolvability requirements for open-ended evolution. In: Maley, C.C., Boudreau, E. (eds.) Artificial Life VII Workshop Proceedings, Portland, USA, pp. 39–40 (2000)
6. Channon, A.: Unbounded evolutionary dynamics in a system of agents that actively process and transform their environment. Genet. Program. Evolvable Mach. **7**(3), 253–281 (2006)
7. Floreano, D., Durr, P., Mattiussi, C.: Neuroevolution: from architectures to learning. Evol. Intell. **1**, 47–62 (2008)
8. Khan, M.M., Khan, G.M., Miller, J.F.: Evolution of neural networks using Cartesian genetic programming. In: IEEE Congress on Evolutionary Computation, pp. 1–8, July 2010
9. McCulloch, W., Pitts, W.: A logical calculus of ideas immanent in nervous activity. Bull. Math. Biophys. **5**(3), 115–133 (1943)
10. Miller, J.F. (ed.): Cartesian Genetic Programming. Natural Computing Series, 1st edn. Springer, Heidelberg (2011)
11. Miller, J.F., Thomson, P.: Cartesian Genetic Programming. Genet. Program. **10802**(3), 121–132 (2000)
12. Standish, R.K.: Open-ended artificial evolution. Int. J. Comput. Intell. Appl. **3**(2), 167–175 (2003)
13. Stanley, K.O.: Efficient evolution of neural networks through complexification. Ph.D. thesis, The University of Texas at Austin, November 2004
14. Stanley, K.O., Miikkulainen, R.: Efficient reinforcement learning through evolving neural network topologies. In: Proceedings of the Genetic and Evolutionary Computation Conference (GECCO-2002), San Francisco, US, p. 9 (2002)
15. Taylor, T., Bedau, M.A., Channon, A., Ackley, D., Banzhaf, W., Beslon, G., Dolson, E., Froese, T., Hickinbotham, S., Ikegami, T., McMullin, B., Packard, N., Rasmussen, S., Virgo, N., Agmon, E., Clark, E., McGregor, S., Ofria, C., Ropella, G., Spector, L., Stanley, K.O., Stanton, A., Timperley, C., Vostinar, A., Wiser, M.: Open-ended evolution: perspectives from the OEE workshop in York. Artif. Life **22**(3), 408–423 (2016)
16. Turner, A.: Evolving artificial neural networks using Cartesian genetic programming. Ph.D. thesis, University of York, York, September 2015
17. Turner, A., Miller, J.F.: Cartesian genetic programming: why no bloat? In: 2013 Proceedings of the Thirty-third SGAI International Conference on Artificial Intelligence, pp. 193–204 (2014)
18. Turner, A., Miller, J.F.: Introducing a cross platform open source Cartesian genetic programming library. Genet. Program. Evolvable Mach. **16**, 83–91 (2015)
19. Turner, A.J., Miller, J.F.: Cartesian genetic programming encoded artificial neural networks: a comparison using three benchmarks. In: Proceedings of the 15th Annual Conference on Genetic and Evolutionary Computation, GECCO 2013, NY, USA, pp. 1005–1012 (2013). http://doi.acm.org/10.1145/2463372.2463484
20. Vassilev, V.K., Fogarty, T.C., Miller, J.F.: Smoothness, ruggedness and neutrality of fitness landscapes: from theory to application. In: Ghosh, A., Tsutsui, S. (eds.) Advances in Evolutionary Computing. Natural Computing Series, pp. 3–44. Springer, Berlin (2003). doi:10.1007/978-3-642-18965-4_1

21. Vassilev, V.K., Miller, J.F.: The advantages of landscape neutrality in digital circuit evolution. In: Miller, J., Thompson, A., Thomson, P., Fogarty, T.C. (eds.) ICES 2000. LNCS, vol. 1801, pp. 252–263. Springer, Heidelberg (2000). doi:10.1007/3-540-46406-9_25
22. Yao, X.: Evolving artificial neural networks. In: Proceedings of the IEEE, pp. 1423–1447, February 1999

A Genetic Algorithm Approach for Static Routing and Wavelength Assignment in All-Optical WDM Networks

Diego Bento A. Teixeira[1,2(✉)], Cassio T. Batista[1(✉)],
Afonso Jorge F. Cardoso[2], and Josivaldo de S. Araújo[1]

[1] Federal University of Pará (UFPA), Belém 66075-110, Brazil
diegoaires@gmail.com, {cassiotb,josivaldo}@ufpa.br
[2] Brazilian Agricultural Research Corporation (Embrapa), Belém 66095-903, Brazil
ajfcardoso@gmail.com

Abstract. In order to transmit data efficiently over an optical network, many routing and wavelength assignment (RWA) algorithms have been proposed. This work presents a genetic algorithm that aims at solving the RWA problem, which consists of choosing the most suitable lightpath (i.e., a combination of a route and a wavelength channel) between a source-destination pair of nodes in all-optical networks. A comparison to some already known approaches in terms of blocking probability was made. Results show a reasonable performance, since the average blocking probability achieved by the genetic algorithm was lower than or relatively equivalent to the standard approaches compared.

Keywords: Genetic algorithm · Routing and wavelength assignment · WDM optical networks

1 Introduction

Quality of service and speed have always been crucial factors regarding the performance of communication networks. With today's international, geographical integration of people, business, commerce, etc., the hunger for large bandwidths has become another item in the list of needs, which makes optical networks a great solution for all those demands. Besides, the amount of bandwidth per fiber can significantly be increased by the wavelength division multiplexing (WDM) technology, which allows optical nodes to transmit signals on different wavelength channels over the same fiber link [2].

Similarly to electronic networks, a path must be calculated in order to transmit data between nodes of a WDM network. However, since the latter expands multiple optical channels through its links, a wavelength must also be allocated for the chosen path. The term "routing and wavelength assignment" (RWA) refers to a classic problem in wavelength routed, optical WDM networks, whose goal is to provide a good combination of a route and a wavelength for each connection in order to establish a communication.

© Springer International Publishing AG 2017
E. Oliveira et al. (Eds.): EPIA 2017, LNAI 10423, pp. 421–432, 2017.
DOI: 10.1007/978-3-319-65340-2_35

The RWA problem has extensively been studied by many researchers. Most works focuses on WDM networks with dynamic traffic [1,10], in which the allocation of network resources to connections is done in real time, with no prior information about the overall state of the network. Other researchers, on the other hand, have proposed solutions regarding the static traffic [8,15], where the network overall, current state is known in advance.

Despite some algorithms have already been consolidated as state-of-the-art for routing (such as Dijkstra and Bellman-Ford) as well as for the wavelength assignment subproblem (first-fit, random-fit, etc.), alternative methods to compute the best match between routes and wavelengths usually offer singular advantages. Since the RWA itself is a NP-complete problem, genetic algorithms have often been used to solve it [3,14]. A genetic algorithm (GA) is an optimization technique used to solve problems through a process that mimics biological evolution. It is commonly used when standard heuristic approaches are either too much expensive to be applied or cannot be applied at all.

This work proposes a GA approach to compute the best lightpath (which comprises the best match between a route and a wavelength) between source-destination (SD) pairs of nodes of the U.S. National Science Foundation (NSF) network topology, simulated as a WDM all-optical network with static traffic. The remainder of the paper is divided as follows. An overview about concepts regarding the RWA problem and genetic algorithms is given in Sect. 2. Section 3 shows details of the proposed GA, while comparison environment and results are discussed in Sect. 4. Finally, Sect. 5 presents the conclusions and plans for future works.

2   Background

This section formulates the RWA problem and addresses the concepts of genetic algorithms. An overview of some techniques used to solve both RWA subproblems is given, emphasizing the approaches used on our simulation.

2.1   RWA Problem in WDM Networks

In WDM networks, a number of optical carriers is multiplexed into a single optical fiber using various, different wavelengths. For all-optical WDM networks, also called transparent networks, two intrinsic constraints arise: the wavelength-continuity constraint, which states that the same wavelength must be used on each and every physical fiber link of a traversed path [16]; and the distinct wavelength constraint, which says that two connections must not use the same wavelength on the same fiber link [9]. Both constraints occur due the absence of opto-electro-opto converters on the nodes of all-optical networks, which means the signal remains in the optical domain throughout all communications. Analogously, those restrictions are not considered on opaque networks because, unlike transparent networks, its intermediate nodes do perform optoelectronic conversion before forwarding packets [6].

The routing and the wavelength assignment subproblems, together, compose the RWA problem in WDM networks. Given a fixed number of wavelengths per link and a set of connection requests, a RWA algorithm for static traffic must maximize the number of optical connections established on the network [16] while attempting to minimize the total number of wavelengths used [11].

Routing. The routing subproblem itself can be classified into three types: fixed routing, fixed-alternate routing and adaptive routing [12].

– Fixed routing: given a source-destination pair of nodes, the same predetermined route, typically the shortest one, is always chosen. Dijkstra's algorithm is the main example of the fixed routing approach.
– Fixed-alternate routing: a set of routes is kept in a routing table instead of a single route for each SD pair. Yen's algorithm, also known as K-shortest path algorithm, is an example of fixed-alternate routing.
– Adaptive routing: the route for a SD pair is calculated dynamically based on the current configuration of all connections in progress on the network. An example of this technique is the least-congested routing algorithm, which chooses a path with more wavelengths available per link [5].

Wavelength Assignment. The wavelength assignment subproblem can be solved through many approaches, such as greedy coloring, first-fit, random-fit, most-used, least-used, etc [16]. This section highlights only the first two algorithms aforesaid, since both were used during the simulations.

– Greedy coloring: the same wavelength (color) is assigned to as many lightpaths as possible before moving to the next wavelength. This can be done by a sequential graph-coloring algorithm, which is normally preceded by a vertex ordering strategy, such as largest-first or smallest-last.
– First-fit: the wavelengths are sorted by weight in ascending order and then the first available one is picked. First-fit requires no global information and has a low computational overhead since it does not need to search the entire space if a low-weighted wavelength is ready to be used.

2.2   Genetic Algorithm

Genetic algorithms [7] are generalized methods of search and optimization inspired by Darwin's Evolution Theory. Within this context, a population of individuals, also called chromosomes, is created as potential solutions to the problem. Each chromosome is submitted to genetic operators, such as selection, crossover and mutation, which either modify the current individuals or generate new ones into the population. The main idea behind GAs is to apply a fitness function to each chromosome in order to evaluate them for finally choosing, after some number of generations, among the fittest individuals—which have higher chances to be the best ones, since they have survived along the process —, the most suitable solution to the problem.

3   Proposed Genetic Algorithm

The structure of the proposed GA is mainly based on [13]. The chromosome encoding and genetic operators such as selection, crossover and mutation are detailed below. The evaluation step itself, exclusively, is mostly based on [4].

3.1   Chromosome

The chromosomes represent distinct paths between a fixed source-destination pair of routers. Each gene stores an index that represents a router in the network. The alleles are positive integer numbers ranging from 0 up to 13, which is the maximum router index in the NSF network. For example, three chromosomes C_1, C_2 and C_3 belong to the population if the respective routes R_1, R_2 and R_3 are valid paths in the network. They are coded as lists, as shown below:

$C_1 = R_2 = [0\ 2\ 8\ 9\ 12]$
$C_2 = R_2 = [0\ 5\ 10\ 12]$
$C_3 = R_3 = [0\ 1\ 3\ 4\ 9\ 12]$

Therefore, the routing subproblem is solved by just initializing a population of individuals. The algorithm used to generate random, valid paths is given according to the following enumerated steps:

1. Start at the source node (e.g., 0);
2. Choose one of the nodes adjacent to the current node. This choice must be random and all nodes must be chosen with equal probability;
3. If the chosen node is not part of the chromosome yet, mark it as the next node in the path. Otherwise, choose another one;
4. Repeat step 2, always using the next node as the current one;
5. Follow the algorithm until the destination node (e.g., 12) is found.

3.2   Evaluation

The first step of the evaluation routine is about the wavelength assignment problem under the wavelength-continuity and the distinct wavelength constraints (as discussed on Sect. 2). Both conditions are met by using a general objective function (GOF) [4], which was developed considering only static traffic. This function, shown in Eq. 1, ensures a communication with minimal restrictions in WDM networks by not taking power, distance and optoelectronic conversion constraints into consideration.

$$L(R_j, \lambda_x) = \frac{\sum_{i=1}^{n} (w_{\lambda_x})_i}{w_{\lambda_x} \sum_{i=1}^{n} l_i} \tag{1}$$

In short terms, the GOF defines a label L for the lightpath defined by a specific route R_j when a specific wavelength λ_x is used. When $L = 1$, the wavelength

is available over all links l of the route, which means that no wavelength converters must be used to establish a connection between the source and destination
nodes. Any value $L < 1$, however, means at least one wavelength-converter must
be used on that lightpath in order to communicate the SD pair. Notice that
lower wavelength indexes have lower weights w_{λ_x} as well.

A simulation of the computation of the labels for hypothetical routes R_1, R_2
and R_3 is shown below. The NSF network is assumed to have four channels or
wavelengths on each link, represented by λ_1, λ_2, λ_3 and λ_4. A missing wavelength
on a specific link means that it is being used in another lightpath.

Analysing the labels computed by GOF for the route $R_1 = [0\ 2\ 8\ 9\ 12]$, shown
in Fig. 1, we can notice that λ_1 is the only wavelength that is available on all
links of the path, which agrees with the label $L(R_1, \lambda_1) = 1$.

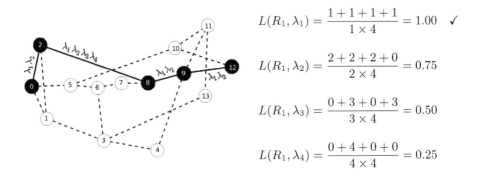

$$L(R_1, \lambda_1) = \frac{1+1+1+1}{1 \times 4} = 1.00 \quad \checkmark$$

$$L(R_1, \lambda_2) = \frac{2+2+2+0}{2 \times 4} = 0.75$$

$$L(R_1, \lambda_3) = \frac{0+3+0+3}{3 \times 4} = 0.50$$

$$L(R_1, \lambda_4) = \frac{0+4+0+0}{4 \times 4} = 0.25$$

Fig. 1. Route $R_1(C_1)$

Figure 2 highlights the route $R_2 = [0\ 5\ 10\ 12]$. It can be seen that none of
the wavelengths is available on all links of the path, which is confirmed by the
labels $L(R_2, \lambda_x) < 1$, $\forall x$.

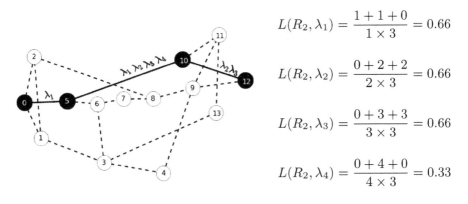

$$L(R_2, \lambda_1) = \frac{1+1+0}{1 \times 3} = 0.66$$

$$L(R_2, \lambda_2) = \frac{0+2+2}{2 \times 3} = 0.66$$

$$L(R_2, \lambda_3) = \frac{0+3+3}{3 \times 3} = 0.66$$

$$L(R_2, \lambda_4) = \frac{0+4+0}{4 \times 3} = 0.33$$

Fig. 2. Route R_2 (C_2)

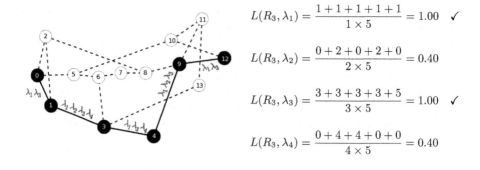

$$L(R_3, \lambda_1) = \frac{1+1+1+1+1}{1 \times 5} = 1.00 \quad \checkmark$$

$$L(R_3, \lambda_2) = \frac{0+2+0+2+0}{2 \times 5} = 0.40$$

$$L(R_3, \lambda_3) = \frac{3+3+3+3+5}{3 \times 5} = 1.00 \quad \checkmark$$

$$L(R_3, \lambda_4) = \frac{0+4+4+0+0}{4 \times 5} = 0.40$$

Fig. 3. Route R_3 (C_3)

The route $R_3 = [0 \; 1 \; 3 \; 4 \; 9 \; 12]$, on the other hand, has two wavelengths available on all links along the path: λ_1 and λ_3, as shown in Fig. 3. When more than one wavelength is available per link, the GA chooses the one with lower weight, which is based on the first-fit procedure. In other words, in this case, λ_1 would be chosen over λ_3 because $w_{\lambda_1} < w_{\lambda_3}$.

In addition to the GOF label, two more parameters are used for choosing the best chromosome. Those criteria will be detailed at Sect. 3.3.

3.3   Selection

The selection operator defines which individuals must reproduce. The tournament selection technique was used, where k individuals are randomly chosen and the one with higher fitness value is picked as the first parent chromosome. The same process is repeated for choosing the second parent. The crossover rate P_c defines the percentage of individuals that are selected to reproduce.

In the simulations of Sect. 3.2, both routes R_1 and R_3 have available wavelengths over all links of their respective paths. The GA would consider, however, R_3 as being better than R_1, since R_3 has two wavelengths available, while R_1 has just one. In other words, even though R_3 is longer than R_1, the former is still least congested than the latter, which agrees with the adaptive routing concept. In case of a tie in the congestion criteria (let's say R_1 had two wavelengths available on each link, as well as R_3), the selection step would choose the route with lowest wavelength-available weight w_λ.

An insertion sort algorithm was configured to sort the chromosomes according to the criteria aforementioned, summarized as follows. Given that the routes/chromosomes have at least one channel free, which is verified by the GOF algorithm:

1. Sort them on descending order by the number of wavelengths available on the entire path. In other words, the least congested path comes first;
2. If there is a tie on the number of λ available, the selection follows the first-fit procedure by choosing the route whose channel has lower weight w_λ;

3. In case of a second tie, now on the weight of the wavelengths available, the route with the least number of hops is chosen, which means the GA gives priority to the shortest path.

3.4   Crossover

Crossover is the process of exchanging genes between individuals. It is expected that, at each new generation, the offspring adapts to the environment as well as or even better than its parents. A one-point crossover was used, in which a common router (gene) between two parent routes C_{parent_1} and C_{parent_2} is chosen as crossover point. Two offspring C_{off_1} and C_{off_2} are then generated, each one receiving parts from both parents. The following example shows the crossover operation. Given that $\underline{8}$ is the parents' common router chosen as crossover point:

$C_{parent_1} = [0\ 5\ 6\ 7\ \underline{8}\ 9^*\ 12]$
$C_{parent_2} = [0\ 2\ \underline{8}\ 9^*\ 11\ 10\ 12]$
$C_{off_1} = [0\ 5\ 6\ 7\ \underline{8}\ 9\ 11\ 10\ 12]$
$C_{off_2} = [0\ 2\ \underline{8}\ 9\ 12].$

If there is more than one common router (such as the index 9^* in the example above), the crossover point is randomly chosen, with equal probability, among all the common routers. On the other hand, if there is no common router between the parents, the chromosomes do not cross and no offspring is generated. An offspring is also discarded if it has the same router index on both parts received from each of its parents.

3.5   Mutation

The mutation operator is applied in order to keep the diversity of the population and to prevent premature convergence. Based on a mutation probability value P_m, a random gene g is chosen from a chromosome $C_{original}$ as a single mutation point, and a new fresh route is created from g to the destination node, producing a new chromosome $C_{mutated}$ as well. In the following example, $g = \underline{7}$ is the router index chosen as mutation point, and a new route from 7 to 12 is created, which is composed by the router indexes $r_1, r_2, ..., r_n$.

$C_{original} = [0\ 5\ 6\ \underline{7}\ 8\ 9\ 12]$
$C_{mutated} = [0\ 5\ 6\ \underline{7}\ r_1\ r_2\ ...\ r_n\ 12]$

If there is no way to build a new fresh route, the mutation is not performed and the chromosome $C_{original}$ returns to the population.

4   Simulation Scenario and Results

The genetic algorithm was compared to standard techniques consisting of a combination of routing algorithms with wavelength assignment algorithms, as shown in Fig. 4. Two shortest path algorithms were used for the routing subproblem: Dijkstra and Yen, which represent the fixed and fixed-alternate routing schemes, respectively. The latter is a generalization of Dijkstra's algorithm (which computes only a single shortest path) to compute the K-shortest paths between a pair of nodes. First-fit and greedy coloring heuristics were applied to solve the wavelength assignment subproblem. Notice that the auxiliary graph $H(V,E)$ is a dependence required by the sequential graph-coloring algorithm [16].

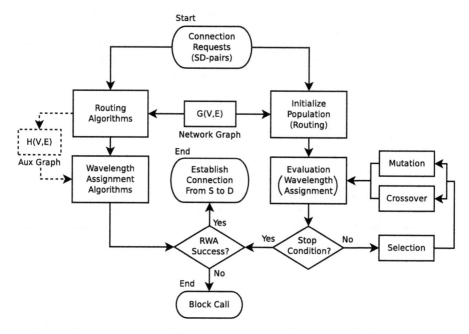

Fig. 4. A genetic algorithm (right side) was compared to already known RWA techniques (left side).

4.1 Simulation

The simulations were run as a Python program. A MATLAB toolbox[1] for WDM networks was adapted to Python in order to generate loads on all links of the network. Shortest path algorithms and sequential greedy coloring heuristic with largest-fit vertex ordering strategy were implemented using NetworkX[2] software package. The number of alternate routes returned by Yen's algorithm was $K = 2$.

The minimum number of generations of the GA was set to 35 and the maximum to 80. Population size was set to 30. Selection's tournament size was defined as $k = 3$. Mutation and crossover rate were set to $P_m = 0.02$ and $P_c = 0.50$, respectively. Before the 20th generation, if the best individual has not

---

[1] https://www.mathworks.com/matlabcentral/fileexchange/4797.
[2] https://networkx.github.io/.

been changed along 10 previous consecutive generations, the selection pressure is reduced by (i) increasing the mutation rate to $P_m = 0.20$, which is further restored by dividing it by 2 at each 5 next generations; (ii) and reducing the tournament size to $k = 2$, further restoring it by incrementing after each 10 next generations. If the fitness value of the best individual does not change over 15 consecutive generations after the 20th, the GA stops and returns the fittest chromosome.

The load L_E on the network was increased from 1 up to 30 Erlangs. The amount of traffic was modeled by a Poisson distribution. Node 0 of NSF network was chosen as source node for all connection requests. Similarly, node 12 was chosen as the destination node. The interarrival times between connections are exponentially distributed, as well as the time a connection occupies the network resources (holding time). Given a load L_E, in Erlangs, the blocking probability $\overline{B}_p$ can be computed as an average of the ratio between the number of blocked calls N_{bc} and the number of calls arrived N_{ca}, as shown in Eq. 2:

$$\overline{B}_p(L_E) = \frac{1}{N_s} \times \sum_{i=1}^{N_s} \frac{N_{bc}(L_E)_i}{N_{ca}(L_E)_i} \qquad (2)$$

A total of $N_s = 20$ simulations was performed, each one with the number of iterations set to 500. The National Science Foundation network topology, a 14-node network with bidirectional links, previously shown in Figs. 1, 2 and 3, was adopted in our simulation. Since only wavelength-continuity and distinct wavelength constraints were considered, the distance between optical nodes was not taken into consideration.

4.2   Results

Figure 5 shows the blocking probability over a 4-channel NSF network topology. Despite all five curves equally converge to similar points while the load over the links is increased, the difference between the fixed routing (i.e. Dijkstra) and both fixed-alternate and adaptive routing approaches (Yen and GA, respectively) can be seen right at the outset, being emphasized onwards. Notice that the curves of Dijkstra's algorithm often overlap, no matter which wavelength assignment algorithm is being used. With a load of 30 Erlangs, by the way, fixed routing approaches reached a blocking probability value of approximately 87%.

Fixed-alternate and adaptive routing methods also achieved a similar performance among themselves, since their curves overlap in most points. Even so, it can be seen that the proposed GA has had a slightly better performance, since its curve happens to be below all others after the sixteenth load value. For other values of load the performance achieve for GA and Yen's algorithm can be considered equivalent. Graph coloring and first-fit heuristics also achieved similar performance when used with Yen's routing approach, but the former, represented by the square-marked curve, has blocked a little more calls than first-fit at load values of 17 and from 20 to 26 Erlangs. At 30 Erlangs, Yen's algorithm reached 73% of blocking probability, while GA achieved approximately 71%.

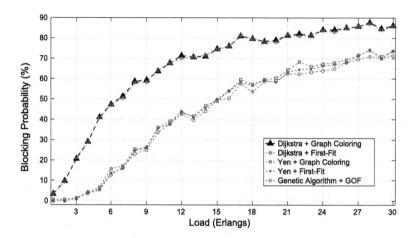

Fig. 5. Blocking probability with 30 Erlangs over a 4-channel network.

The situation happens to be the same for a 8-channel network, as shown in Fig. 6. Dijkstra's algorithm has had, again, the worst results when compared to Yen's algorithm and GA after three Erlangs. Still, fixed routing curves for both graph coloring and first-fit wavelength assignment heuristics also overlap, having approximately 71% of blocked calls with 30 Erlangs.

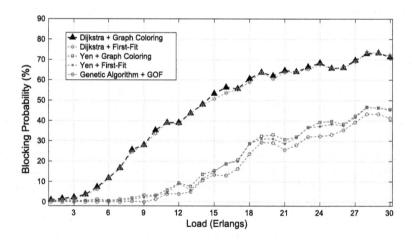

Fig. 6. Blocking probability with 30 Erlangs over an 8-channel network.

For alternate routing, first-fit achieved a slightly better performance than graph coloring, both using Yen's algorithm as routing scheme. However, the two curves overlap in most points, which is not the case of GA's curve. Here, the genetic algorithm has clearly achieved the best performance, where the circle-marked curve stays below all others after a load of eight Erlangs. For 30 Erlangs, the GA achieved a percentage of 41% of blocked calls, while Yen's algorithm with both first-fit and graph coloring achieved 46%, approximately.

4.3 Discussion

Based on the results of the simulations, it can be inferred that the performance of RWA algorithms is strongly related to the routing subproblem. Since fixed routing algorithms return only a single route for any connection request, the performance was expected to be poor, as already stated on [16], which results in high blocking probabilities across all network loads.

Fixed-alternate routing proved to be a good solution, as it considerably reduced blocking probabilities. Even with as few as two alternate paths, the number of allocated calls was significantly increased. However, since Yen's algorithm does not return alternate paths that are link-disjoint[3], the proposed genetic algorithm can be considered a suitable solution. The GA exploits the availability of wavelengths over all links of many routes by using GOF algorithm combined with the least-congested adaptive routing approach. This technique has proven to achieve a reasonably better performance than both fixed and fixed-alternate routing in the number of established connections.

5 Conclusion and Future Work

This paper presented a new genetic algorithm (GA) approach to solve the routing and wavelength assignment (RWA) problem in all-optical networks with static traffic. Simulation results showed that the GA performed slightly better than the standard approaches for both routing, such as fixed (Dijkstra) and fixed-alternate routing (Yen), and wavelength assignment subproblems (graph coloring and first-fit) in terms of blocking probability. Plus, evolutionary algorithms are often a good choice for solving non-polynomial problems.

While the main focus of research nowadays is at wavelength-convertible networks with dynamic traffic, this solution addresses the static traffic with no optoelectronic conversion, thus considering only the intrinsic restrictions of transparent networks, namely the wavelength-continuity and the distinct wavelength constraints. This was accomplished by using a general objective function (GOF) as basis for evaluating a set of paths coded as chromosomes in the GA.

As future work, the GOF algorithm should be used as fitness function for other evolutionary approaches such as evolutionary strategy and particle swarm optimization, always comparing the results with the proposed GA. Additionally, since the GOF was specifically developed to be applied over networks with static traffic, a second work is to replace GOF by another fitness function, so the same genetic algorithm model proposed here can be used to solve the RWA problem for both static and dynamic traffics. Lastly, a third work is to apply a traffic model considering random source and destination pairs of nodes, since the blocking probability was mainly computed considering a single source node.

---

[3] Two paths are link disjoint if they do not share any link.

References

1. Balasis, F., Wang, X., Xu, S., Tanaka, Y.: Dynamic physical impairment-aware routing and wavelength assignment in 10/40/100 Gbps mixed line rate optical networks. In: 16th International Conference on Advanced Communication Technology, pp. 343–351 (2014)
2. Banerjee, N., Mehta, V., Pandey, S.: A genetic algorithm approach for solving the routing and wave-length assignment problem in WDM networks. In: 3rd IEEE/IEE International Conference on Networking ICN-2004, pp. 70–78 (2004)
3. Bisbal, D.: Dynamic routing and wavelength assignment in optical networks by means of genetic algorithms. Photonic Netw. Commun. 7(1), 43–58 (2015)
4. Cardoso, A.J.F., Costa, J., Francês, C.R.L.: A new proposal of an efficient algorithm for routing and wavelength assignment in optical networks. J. Commun. Inf. Syst. 25(1), 11–18 (2010)
5. Chatterjee, B.C., Sarma, N., Oki, E.: Routing and spectrum allocation in elastic optical networks: a tutorial. IEEE Commun. Surv. Tutor. 17(3), 1776–1800 (2015)
6. Ellinas, G., Labourdette, J.-F., Walker, J., Chaudhuri, S., Lin, L., Goldstein, E., Bala, K.: Network control and management challenges in opaque networks utilizing transparent optical switches. IEEE Commun. Mag. 42(2), s16–s24 (2004)
7. Goldberg, D.E.: Genetic Algorithms in Search. Optimization and Machine Learning, 1st edn. Addison-Wesley Longman Publishing Co. Inc., Boston (1989)
8. Li, Y., Dai, H., Shen, G., Bose, S.K.: Adaptive FEC-based lightpath routing and wavelength assignment in WDM optical networks. Opt. Switch. Netw. 14, 241–249 (2014)
9. Randhawaa, R., Sohalb, J.S.: Static and dynamic routing and wavelength assignment algorithms for future transport networks. Optik 121, 702–710 (2010)
10. Sakthivel, P., Sankar, P.K.: Dynamic multi-path RWA algorithm for WDM based optical networks. In: International Conference on Electronics and Communication Systems (ICECS), pp. 1–5 (2014)
11. Varela, G.N.: Ant colony optimisation for virtual-wavelength-path routing and wavelength allocation. In: Proceedings of the 1999 Congress on Evolution Computer, pp. 1809–1816 (1999)
12. Wason, A., Kaler, R.S.: Wavelength assignment problem in optical WDM networks. Int. J. Comput. Sci. Netw. Secur. 7(4), 27–31 (2007)
13. Yussof, S., Razali, R.A., See, O.H., Ghapar, A.A., Din, M.M.: A coarse-grained parallel genetic algorithm with migration for shortest path routing problem. In: Proceedings of the 11th IEEE International Conference on High Performance Computing and Communication, pp. 615–621 (2009)
14. Zakouni, A., Luo, J., Kharroubi, F.: Genetic algorithm and tabu search algorithm for solving the static manycast RWA problem in optical networks. J. Comb. Optim. 33(2), 726–741 (2016)
15. Zakouni, A., Luo, J., Kharroubi, F.: Random optimization algorithm for solving the static manycast RWA problem in optical WDM networks. In: 2016 International Conference on Information and Communication Technology Conversion, pp. 640–645 (2016)
16. Zang, H., Jue, J.P., Mukherjee, B.: A review of routing and wavelength assignment approaches for wavelength-routed optical WDM networks. Opt. Netw. Mag. 1(1), 47–60 (2000)

Business Applications of Artificial Intelligence

A Recommender Model of Teaching-Learning Techniques

Dulce Mota[1,3,5(✉)], Luis Paulo Reis[2,4], and Carlos Vaz de Carvalho[3,5]

[1] FEUP – Faculty of Engineering, University of Porto, Porto, Portugal
mdm@isep.ipp.pt
[2] EEUM/DSI – School of Engineering, University of Minho, Braga, Portugal
lpreis@dsi.uminho.pt
[3] ISEP – School of Engineering, Polytechnic of Porto, Porto, Portugal
cmc@isep.ipp.pt
[4] LIACC – Artificial Intelligence and Computer Science Lab, Porto, Portugal
[5] GILT – Games, Interaction and Learning Technologies, Porto, Portugal

Abstract. Learning contents creation supported on computer tools has triggered the scientific community for a couple of decades. However, teachers have been facing more and different challenges, namely the emergence of other delivery learning approaches besides the traditional educational settings, the diversification of the student target population, and the recognition of different ways of learning. In education domain, diverse recommender systems have been developed so far for recommending learning activities and more specifically, learning objects. This research work is focused on teaching-learning techniques recommendation to assist teachers by providing them recommendation about which teaching-learning techniques should scaffold teaching-learning activities to be carried out by students. This paper presents a recommender model sustained in diverse elements, namely, a hybrid recommender system, an association rules mechanism to infer possible combinations of teaching-learning techniques, and collaborative work among several actors in education. An evaluation is carried out and the preliminary results are very encouraging, revealing that teachers seem very enthusiastic and motivated to rethink their teaching-learning techniques when designing teaching-learning activities.

Keywords: Recommender systems · Ontologies · Association rules · Learning design

1 Introduction

The design of teaching-learning activities (TLAs) encompasses a very demanding challenge for educators considering currently challenges that education settings are facing to. First, the traditional education settings are no longer the unique teaching-learning delivery mode for which the widespread innovations of Information and Communication Technologies (ICT) have contributed greatly. Then, the target population of students is becoming more diversified as a consequence of many factors of the contemporary society, for example, immigration and unemployment. Finally, recent human learning theories as well as human intelligence theories have also contributed

© Springer International Publishing AG 2017
E. Oliveira et al. (Eds.): EPIA 2017, LNAI 10423, pp. 435–446, 2017.
DOI: 10.1007/978-3-319-65340-2_36

significantly to better understand how individuals learn. The proposed model assumes that a TLA encompasses two main branches. On the one hand, common features inherent to teaching-learning context, for example, subject, learning goals, target population, difficulty level, and, on the other hand, the teaching-learning technique (TLT), or techniques, which serves as a scaffold for the TLA execution. This way, a very same TLA may be performed by means different TLTs. There are a huge amount of teaching-learning techniques, for example, Brainstorming, Concept Mapping, Jigsaw, Role Playing, and Debate. When designing TLAs, the main problem that teachers face to is how diversify and adapt TLTs taken into account the TLAs' goals and the student population' interests and needs as well. This issue has driven this research work, which has contributed to devise a recommender model for TLTs. This model is sustained in diverse elements, namely, a hybrid recommender system, an association rules mechanism to infer possible combinations of teaching-learning techniques, and collaborative work among several actors in education.

The remainder of this paper is structured as follows: Sect. 2 introduces the Learning design subject. Then, a brief review on recommender systems as well as on computational ontologies is described in Sect. 3. Section 4 is devoted to describe the proposed recommender model of teaching-learning techniques. Finally, Sect. 5 presents the main conclusions and proposals for further research directions.

2 Learning Design Overview

Important achievements have emerged in both Educational Psychology and Information and Communication technologies since last century, which have contributed significantly to diverse revisions and adaptations in different education practices, namely instructional design, curriculum development, organizational learning, and special education. In addition, it is a straightforward thought that traditional educational settings are no longer the unique approach to learn. The Internet and, particularly, the Web, have already given a huge boost for that purpose [1]. Among other potentialities, the Web can promote diverse adaptations, for instance, it can be configured to different learning perspectives (for example, Social Cognitive, Information Processing and Constructivism), to different delivery approaches (namely, blended learning and distance learning), to the context (more formal or more informal), taking into account the beliefs, values, motivations and social representation [2].

Consequently, rethinking pedagogy and learning has become an emerging challenge for the 21st century [3] in order to, on the one hand, contribute to minimize the gap between recent research work regarding learning theories and the teaching practices, and, on the other hand, to design adaptive learning contents and, not less important, to adapt and diversify TLTs taking into account the learning environments specificities. In addition, there are other relevant matters that deserve special attention as well, namely reusing, sharing and interoperability of learning material across different platforms.

2.1 Definitions

Learning design can be introduced as follows: "it aims at providing teachers with a framework capable to bridge the gap between rich, descriptive models and technologies, and the everyday practice and understanding of teachers" [4]. According to Koper [5], learning design is described: "as the application of learning design knowledge when developing a concrete unit of learning (UOL), e.g. a course, a lesson, a curriculum, a learning event". The meaning of learning design knowledge can be transmitted by a series of prescriptive rules with the following format: "if situation, then method".

In practice, a learning design takes a form of a TLA to be carried out by students in a specific learning scenario. The TLA concept can be described as "a specific interaction of learner(s) with other(s) using specific tools and resources, orientated towards specific outcomes" [6].

As for the design of TLAs diverse aspects should be reflected on, which can be separated into two classes: the educational context and the design context [7]. Basically, the former embraces pedagogical practices, delivery means and technological aspects, whereas the latter is devoted to design tools, frameworks that teachers may use to design learning scenarios in order to fulfill an acknowledged set of important features, namely, accessibility, adaptability, interoperability, sharing and reuse of e-contents, including teaching-learning activities.

2.2 Embedding Advanced Features in Design Tools

At present, it can be stated that there is a considerable amount of design tools [7] for teaching-learning activities creation. In general, they are embedded with some type of pedagogical capabilities, for example, design patterns, and textual/graphical design facilities. To help teachers through the design process, some of these tools provide extra information to guide them into good pedagogical decisions. However, it is very difficult to find design tools that can make partially or fully automatic recommendations to help teachers in deciding, for example, which teaching-learning method/technique/strategic best suits to a specific learning activity taking into account the environment specificities. Although recommendation mechanisms started to be currently in educational applications/platforms for recommending, for example, learning contents, learning activities, in the particular case of design tools it is a flourishing field.

In addition, in terms of data management for recommendation purpose, the ontological engineering approach has also received special emphasis ultimately. Its popularity can be attributed to the fact that a computational ontology provides a shared and common understanding of a specific domain that can enable communication between people and software applications [8].

3 Recommender Systems and Computational Ontologies Overview

3.1 Recommender Systems

The research area of Recommender Systems (RSs) can be traced to the fields of Information Retrieval (IR), Machine Learning (ML) and Decision Support Systems

(DSS), however, these particular systems have emerged as a research field of their own for the last two decades [9].

RSs can be defined as software tools and techniques providing users with suggestions for items a user may wish to utilize [10]. Two preliminary models can be pointed out regarding RSs: *prediction version of problem* and *ranking version of problem* [11]. The former is devoted to predict the rating for a user-item combination. It is assumed that training data is available, indicating user preferences for items. The latter aims at determining the top-k items for a particular user, or the top-k users to target for a particular item. There are diverse taxonomies connected to RSs [12–15].

Recommender systems have been included in several software applications for recommending "items" sourcing in different goals, for example, books, movies, news, friends (diverse examples can be found in [11]). Other domains, such as robotic soccer [16], and in education RSs are achieving a particular relevance. In [17] it is proposed a system (supported in collaborative filtering and knowledge based techniques) to recommend activities and resources that help students in achieving competence levels throughout an online or blended course. Imran et al. [18] integrated a recommender system into a learning management system named PLORS, for recommending which learning objects within a course are more useful for learners. Association rule mining along with a neighborhood algorithm are part of the recommender mechanism. In [19] it is proposed a recommender system which helps a user to find educational resources that are most appropriate to his/her needs and preferences. A multi-agent architecture (BDI- Belief, Desire, Intention) is used, being a dedicated agent responsible for making a flexible contend-based retrieval as well as providing an ordered list of the resources that better meet the user profiles data.

3.2 Computational Ontologies in the Education Domain

The application of ontologies to learning technology has made openly available formal representation schemas for activity sequences and learning resource descriptions, based on evolved standards [20]. An important benefit can be reported to recommendation facilities. Mizoguchi et al. [21] have developed an ontological solution to respond to three main challenges, namely, to make computers "understand" a variety of learning/instructional theories; to "utilize" such theories to develop learning scenarios conducted by instructional designers; and to make it possible to share learning scenarios created in standard technology compliant formats. To that purpose, they developed the OMIBUS ontology, which was constructed to cover different learning/instructional theories, and it is used to assist teachers in planning lessons. Vesin et al. [22] have developed an ontology-based architecture with a recommendation strategy in Java Tutoring System. Such architecture supports adaptive and personalized tutoring relying on Semantic Web standards and related technologies. ORLM ontology [23] provides learning material recommendation aligned to the student's learning styles combining personal needs with preferences. This personalized approach has been used in Intelligent Tutoring Systems and Hypermedia Adaptive Systems yet using different implementations. In general, the ontology approach provides more accurate definitions and extendable capabilities as well. Yu et al. [24] propose an ontology to model diverse knowledge, namely learner context, content and knowledge about the domain being learned. The main goal is to provide a personalized, complete and augmented learning program for the learner being delivered by an automatic recommender system. Amorim et al. [25] developed an ontology to represent the semantics of the IMS Learning Design specification to cope with the expressiveness limitations found on the current XML-Schema implementation of the IMS LD conceptual model. In [26] an ontological solution is proposed for modelling learning outcomes. They adopted the "ABCD" model to create learning outcomes using the revised Bloom taxonomy for their classification. Sicilia et al. [20] describe the foundations of using ontologies for instructional-design theories modelling. These theories are modelled as collections of methods represented as a combination of rules and concept constraints that express the recommendation imposed by those theories on the final arrangement of activities and learning resources. Draganidis et al. [27] developed an ontology-based application for competency management and learning paths. Cassel [28] devises an ontology of all computing disciplines for generating computing curricula, at level of both society recommendations and individual program curriculum review and development. In [29] it is presented an ontology containing information on various disabilities encountered in higher education. The main goal is to provide suitable learning resources for students with specific needs. The LOCO-Cite ontology is part of the LOCO (Learning Object Context Ontologies) ontological framework, and serves as an integration point of other types of learning-related ontologies such as user model ontology, an ontology of learning design, and a content structure ontology. The main goal consists in enabling personalized feedback to teachers to rethink the content and the structure of online courses helping, in this way, customise the courses to the students' needs [30].

Next section presents the proposed recommender model for teaching-learning techniques to assist teachers in designing teaching-learning activities to be carried out by students.

4   The Recommender Model

4.1   Definitions

A core concept of the proposed model is the teaching-learning technique one. It can be defined as "a fined grained instantiation of a method that scaffolds a sequence of unambiguous steps to accomplish a settled goal for supporting a teaching-learning activity." Following this definition, it should be highlighted that the same teaching-learning technique may be used for various teaching-learning activities as it provides the guidance, i.e., a sequence of predefined steps/tasks to be carried out, and therefore it is not the proper learning content.

A TLT embraces two types of data/components. On the one hand, the technique analytics, and on the other hand, the sequence of tasks to be carried out, i.e., the TLT or sequences of them. The former includes data for describing the educational context a particular technique is more suited to, for example, type of interaction (class based, one to may, one to one, among others), type of delivery (face-to-face, blended, among others), student/class motivational level, student/class performance level, resolution scope (open-ended and close-ended), and teaching-learning objectives (LOs). For a same attribute, it can be assigned different values. In turn, the sequence of tasks describes the scaffold structure to be fulfilled with tasks descriptions in order to be carried out by all participants during the TLA execution.

For the purpose of this research work, a teaching-learning activity is described as: "A teaching-learning activity is an educator construction of what other participants should be engaged in to attain specific goals supported by one or more specific teaching-learning techniques, taking into account the specificities of the educational context including diversity and participants' particularities." In this particular context, the term *educator* was chosen instead of teacher on purpose, to emphasize that besides teachers, other actors can also be responsible for TLAs creation. Following the same reasoning of TLT modeling, the TLA data embraces a set of attributes associated to the teaching-learning context, and a set of tasks, which are sourced in one TLT, at least. In contrast to the TLT modeling, in a TLA it is not allowed most attributes be multi-instantiated. For example, for the resolution scope attribute, the teacher only can chose either *open ended* or *close ended*, not both at the same time.

4.2   Recommender Model Description

Conceptualization

The recommender model is anchored in three core characteristics: a hybrid recommender mechanism for ranking TLTs, an association rules mining mechanism to infer complementary combinations of TLTs, and collaborative work among several actors in education each one with specific competencies.

Starting with the hybrid recommendation approach, it comprises filtering and ranking methods supported on data obtained from two different data sources. On the one hand, past TLAs designed by teachers. These TLAs include the TLTs that teachers chose from a provided list of recommended TLTs. On the other hand, TLTs instances are obtained by means OTILIA ontology [31]. The teachers' behaviour regarding past TLTs' selection takes the form of implicit rating, as opposed to explicit rating, which could be provided by teachers on the bases of explicitly ratings. This way, a mixed of a collaborative and a knowledge-based approach was followed.

Regarding the association rules mining mechanism it aims at producing sequences of two or more TLTs for a particular TLA. As already explained, a TLA may need two or more TLTs to be performed. Therefore, the mining mechanism has an important role in this regard facilitating the construction of relationships among TLTs. For that purpose, the association rule mining algorithm APRIORI [32, 34] was chosen. Other related algorithms will also be tested subsequently [33].

Finally, the collaborative work characteristic takes into account specific competencies from four main actors: the educational psychologist, the scholar psychologist, the ontology engineer and the teacher. Briefly, the educational psychologist contributes with the high level knowledge in order to describe teaching-learning techniques along with the rules to be applied in real educational contexts. The scholar psychologist, and can exist several of them, is responsible for instantiating teaching-learning techniques.

Once the scholar psychologist is responsible for instantiating TLTs, which will be kept into the ontology for recommendation purpose, this data source minimize the "cold-start" problem assigned usually to collaborative and contend-based recommender systems. In turn, the ontology engineer needs to implement and maintain the ontology in close collaboration with psychologists. Finally, the teacher is devoted to design teaching-learnings activities. The full recommendation procedure is explained next.

Recommendation Algorithm

The proposed approach for recommending TLTs encompasses the following main phases: (1) Read the feature values of the current TLA (TLAcr - the one for which the recommendation of TLTs is the target); (2) Search/filter for stored TLAs that match a specific criteria (apply criteria A - further details in this section). (3) After being extracted the LOs from each filtered TLA a similarity calculation is performed taken into account the LOs features values sourced in the TLAcr and each filtered TLT. The resulting list is ordered and displayed to the teacher afterwards. (4) Meanwhile, a query is performed to obtain TLTs from the ontology that match a specific criteria (apply criteria B - further details in this section); (5) LOs from each TLT obtained in the previous step are compared to the ones of the TLAcr, and a similarity calculation is performed (identical to the one in step 3). A default TLA is created for each filtered TLT. (6) Sort all TLAs obtained in previous steps (further details in this section); (7) Construct association rules to obtain other combinations of TLTs based on the ordered list obtained in the previous step. Figure 1 illustrates the main phases of the proposed recommendation algorithm.

Before explaining the mentioned criteria as well as the calculation of the similarity score, the characterization of relevant entities are presented. As for the TLA entity, it can be characterized as a set (A) of n attributes:

$$A = \{A_1, A_2, \ldots, A_k, A_{k+1} \ldots, A_n\} \, where \, n > 0$$

where the most prominent attributes are the learning objectives (LOs) and the TLTs' that are connected to. The attributes from 1 to k are part of the learning context component, whereas positions greater than k belong to the structural component of the TLA. This component keeps the sequence of tasks to be carried out by students, in sum, the TLTs themselves. Let A_k be a set of learning objectives of a TLA_i and A_{k+1} a set of TLTs.

$$A_k = \{lo_{i,1}, lo_{i,2}, \ldots, lo_{i,p}\}, A_{k+1} = \{tlt_{i,1}, tlt_{i,2}, \ldots, tlt_{i,q}\} \, where \, p > 0, q > 0$$

Regarding criteria A, the system searches all stored TLAs, for which the attributes of the context component do exact matching with the exception of the learning objectives. The latter are used to calculate the similarity score. The main difference between criteria A and B is concerned to the fact that a TLT is configured to match diverse feature values for a very same attribute. For example, a specific TLT can be devised to be executed both in face to face and blended mode. However, when a teacher characterizes the learning context for a TLA s/he can only choice one of the provided modes.

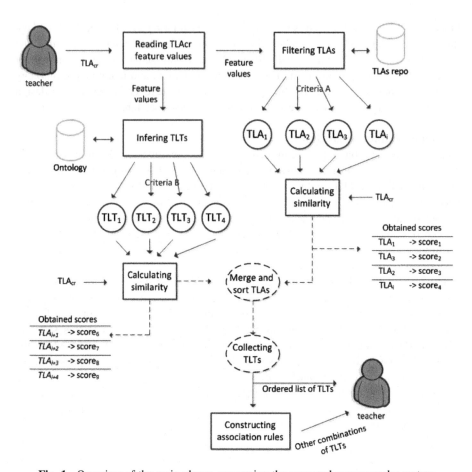

Fig. 1. Overview of the main phases concerning the proposed recommender system

As for the similarity method, first it is computed the similarity matrix (B) for each pair (TLA_{cr}, TLA_i) (see Fig. 2). Then, to calculate the final similarity score between TLA_{cr} and TLA_i, it is used the expression (1). The Jaccard' coefficient is part of the calculation. Then, it is added the a value for sorting purpose. The resulting scores for all TLAs are then sorted in descending order, and therefore the TLAs with higher scores will come first. After this phase, it is necessary to collect the TLTs included in each TLA, in the same order, and a list of TLTs can be provided to the teacher. Meanwhile, the algorithm proceeds to the final phase, where APRIORI algorithm is used to construct relevant rules, i.e., combination of TLTs worked in the previous steps. This way, the system can try to find significant rules, which can be viewed as additional information to teachers facilitating, this way, informed decisions.

$$Sim(TLA_{cr}, TLA_i) = a + \frac{a}{a+b+c} \qquad (1)$$

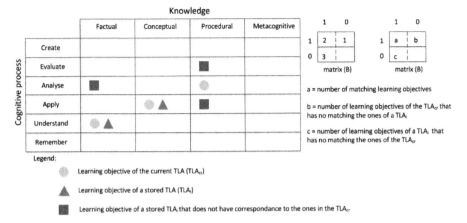

Fig. 2. Illustration of a matching procedure between LOs sourcing in the current TLA and a TLA (TLA$_i$) stored in the repository

In Fig. 3 it is presented an output regarding TLTs recommendations.

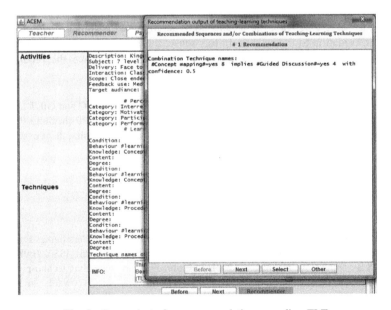

Fig. 3. Screenshot of a recommendation regarding TLTs

The proposed model is now in an evaluation stage by means a qualitative methodology, which combines a semi-structured paper questionnaire, an experiment using the developed prototype, and observation. Teachers of 3rd cycle and secondary education were randomly selected to participated in this process. Despite this stage is not yet completed, it can be stated based on the results obtained so far, teachers are very enthusiastic about it. So far, the usefulness and innovative characteristics of the recommender model are highlighted.

Next section presents the conclusions and future research work directions.

5 Conclusion

This paper describes a recommender model which provides suggestions to teachers of teaching-learning techniques to be integrated in teaching-learning activities. The underlined motivation is driven by diversification and adaptability trends in order to engage a larger student' population in performing TLAs. Therefore, teachers can experiment novel TLTs they might not be able to otherwise. Moreover, different ways of learning have more chances to be covered.

A hybrid recommender mechanism for ranking TLTs was described which uses a similarity metric based on special features of TLAs, namely, learning objectives. In addition, it is applied an association rules mining mechanism to infer complementary combinations of TLTs. Collaborative work among several actors in education context comprises another strategy of the proposed model.

In the near future, it is envisioned to follow a more interactive process to expand or refine the system recommendations without undermining teacher's expectations when designing a TLA. This way, the teacher may be engaged in guided dialogues giving valuable information to the system. In this sense, the next major focus of the research work is the study of query argumentation strategies to improve the recommender performance.

Acknowledgments. This research has been supported in part by LIACC and GILT labs. At an earlier stage, the PROTEC advanced program of the responsibility of IPP (Instituto Politécnico do Porto) was conceived to support teachers rolled in PhD courses releasing them from teaching work.

References

1. Collis, B.: Tecnología de la Información en la Educación Superior: Paradigmas Emergentes. In: Revista de Universidad y Sociadad del Conocimiento 2(2) (2006). ISSN 1698-580X
2. Dias, S.B., Diniz, J.A., Hadjileontiadis, L.J.: Embracing and embedding techno-pedagogical strategies. In: Dias, S.B., Diniz, J.A., Hadjileontiadis, L.J. (eds.) Towards an Intelligent Learning Management System Under Blended Learning, vol. 59, pp. 35–51. Springer, Heidelberg (2014). doi:10.1007/978-3-319-02078-5_3
3. Sharpe, R., Beetham, H., Freitas, S.: Rethinking learning for a digital age: how learners are shaping their own experiences. In: Sharpe, R., Beetham, H., Freitas, S. (eds.) Taylor & Francis Group, Routledge (2010). ISBN 978-0-415-87543-1
4. Cameron, L.: How learning design can illuminate teaching practice. In: The Future of Learning Design Conference, Paper 3, 10 December (2009). http://ro.uow.edu.au/fld/09/Program/3. Accessed May 2011

5. Koper, E.J.R.: An introduction to learning design. In: Koper, R., Tattersall, C. (eds.) A Handbook on Modelling and Delivering Networked Education and Training, pp. 3–20. Springer, Berlin (2005). doi:10.1007/3-540-27360-3_1. ISBN 3-540-22814-4

6. Beetham, H.: An approach to learning activity design. In: Beetham, H., Sharpe, R. (eds.) Rethinking Pedagogy for a Digital Age. Designing and Delivering e-learning, Taylor & Francis Group, Routledge (2007). ISBN 978-0-415-40874-5

7. Mota, D., Reis, L.P., Carvalho, C.V.: Design of learning activities – pedagogy, technology and delivery trends. EAI Endorsed Trans. e-Learning **14**(4), e5 (2014)

8. Fensel, D.: Ontologies: A Silver Bullet for Knowledge Management and Electronic Commerce. Springer, Heidelberg (2001). ISBN 978-3-662-04398-1

9. Jannach, D., Zanker, M., Ge, M., Gröning, M.: Recommender systems in computer science and information systems - a landscape of research. In: Huemer, C., Lops, P. (eds.) E-Commerce and Web Technologies. EC-Web 2012. LNBIP, vol. 123, pp. 76–87. Springer (2012). doi:10.1007/978-3-642-32273-0_7

10. Ricci, F., Rokach, L., Shapira, B.: Introduction to recommender systems. In: Ricci, F., Rokach, L., Shapira, B., Kantor, P. (eds.) Recommender Systems Handbook, pp. 1–35. Springer, Heidelberg (2011). doi:10.1007/978-0-387-85820-3_1

11. Aggarwal, C.: Recommender Systems: The Textbook. Springer International Publishing, Switzerland (2016). ISBN 978-3319296579

12. Burke, R.: Hybrid recommender systems: survey and experiments. User Model. User-Adapted Interact. **12**(4), 331–370 (2002)

13. Pazzani, M., Billsus, D.: Content-based recommendation systems. In: Brusilovsky, P., Kobsa, A., Wolfgang, N. (eds.) The Adaptive Web - Methods and Strategies of Web Personalization. LNCS, vol. 4321, pp. 325–341. Springer, Heidelberg (2007). doi:10.1007/978-3-540-72079-9_10

14. Schafer, J., Frankowski, D., Herlocker, J., Sen, S.: Collaborative filtering recommender systems. In: Brusilovsky, P., Kobsa, A., Wolfgang, N. (eds.) The Adaptive Web - Methods and Strategies of Web Personalization. LNCS, vol. 4321, pp. 291–324. Springer, Heidelberg (2007). doi:10.1007/978-3-540-72079-9_9

15. Ekstrand, M., Riedl, J., Konstan, J.: Collaborative filtering recommender systems. Hum.-Comput. Interact. **4**(2), 81–173 (2010)

16. Abreu, P., Silva, D., Almeida, F.: Improving a simulated soccer team's performance through a memory–based collaborative filtering approach. Appl. Soft Comput. **23**, 180–193 (2014). Elsevier

17. Chavarriaga, O., Florian-Gaviria, B., Solarte, O.: A recommender system for students based on social knowledge and assessment data of competences. In: Rensing, C. et al. (eds.) EC-TEL 2014. LNCS, vol. 8719, pp. 56–69. Springer, Heidelberg (2014). doi:10.1007/978-3-319-11200-8_5

18. Imran, H., Belghis-Zadeh, M., Chang, T., Kinshuk, G.S.: PLORS: a personalized learning recommender system. Vietnam J. Comput. Sci. **3**(1), 3–13 (2016). Springer

19. Casali, A., Gerling, V., Deco, C., Bender, C.: A recommender system for learning objects personalized retrieval. Educational recommender systems and technologies: practices and challenges.Educational. In: Santos, O., Boticario, J. (eds.) Recommender Systems and Technologies: Practices and Challenges, pp. 182–201 (2011). ISBN 978-1613504895

20. Sicilia, M.-Á., Lytras, M., Sánchez-Alonso, S., García-Barriocanal, E.: Modeling instructional-design theories with ontologies: using methods to check, generate and search learning designs. Comput. Hum. Behav. **27**, 1389–1398 (2011)

21. Hayashi, Y., Bourdeau, J., Mizoguchi, R.: Using ontological engineering to organize learning/instructional theories and build a theory-aware authoring system. Artif. Intell. Educ. **12**(2), 211–252 (2009)

22. Vesin, B., Ivanović, M., Klašnja-Milićević, A., Budimac, Z.: Ontology-based archiecture with recommendation strategy in Java tutoring system. Comput. Sci. Inf. Syst. **10**(1), 237–261 (2013)
23. Valaski, J., Malucelli, A., Reinehr, S.: Recommending learning materials according to ontology-based learning styles. In: Proceedings of International Conference on Information Technology and Application, pp. 71–75 (2011)
24. Yu, Z., Nakamura, Y., Jang, S., Kajita, S., Mase, K.: Ontology-based semantic recommendation for context-aware e-learning. In: Indulska, J. et al. UIC 2007. LNCS, vol. 4611, pp. 898–907. Springer, Heidelberg (2007). doi:10.1007/978-3-540-73549-6_88
25. Amorim, R., Lama, M., Sánchez, E., Riera, A., Vila, X.: A learning design ontology based on the IMS specification. Educ. Technol. Soc. **9**(1), 38–57 (2006)
26. Kalou, A., Solomou, G., Pierrakeas, C., Kameas, A.: An ontology model for building, classifying and using learning outcomes. In: IEEE International Conference on Advanced Learning Technologies, pp. 61–65. IEEE Computer Society (2012)
27. Draganidis, F., Chamopoulou, P., Mentzas, G.: A semantic web archiecture for integrating competence management and learning paths. J. Knowl. Manag. **12**(6), 121–136 (2008)
28. Cassel, L.: Using a computing ontology in curriculum development. In: Dicheva, D., Mizoguchi, R., Greer, J. (eds.) Semantic Web Technologies for e-Learning, pp. 44–56. IOS Press (2009)
29. Nganji, J., Brayshaw, M., Tompsett, B.: Ontology-based e-learning personalisation for disabled students in higher education. Innov. Teach. Learn. Inf. Comput. Sci. **10**(1), 1–11 (2011)
30. Javanović, J.: Generating context-related feedback for teachers. Int. J. Technol. Enhanced Learn. **1**(1/2), 47–69 (2008)
31. Mota, D., Reis, L.P., Carvalho, C.V.: OTILIA – an architecture for the recommendation of teaching-learning techniques supported by an ontological approach. In: Proceedings of the 44th IEEE Frontiers in Education Conference, Madrid, Spain, pp. 22–25 (2014)
32. Agrawal, R.: Mining association rules between sets of items in large databases. In: Proceeding of the 1993 ACM SIGMOD Conference, Washington, pp. 207–216 (1993)
33. More, N.: Recommenation of books using improved apriori algoritm. Int. J. Innov. Res. Sci. Technol. **1**(4), 80–82 (2014)
34. Sá, C., Soares, C., Jorge, A.M., Azevedo, P., Costa, J.: Mining association rules for label ranking. In: Huang, J.Z., Cao, L., Srivastava, J. (eds.) PAKDD 2011, vol. 6635, pp. 432–443. Springer, Heidelberg (2011). doi:10.1007/978-3-642-20847-8_36

Credit Scoring in Microfinance Using Non-traditional Data

Saulo Ruiz[1(✉)], Pedro Gomes[1], Luís Rodrigues[1], and João Gama[2]

[1] Seedstars, Geneva, Switzerland
{saulo,pedro,luis}@seedstars.com
[2] Laboratory of Artificial Intelligence and Decision Support,
University of Porto, Porto, Portugal
jgama@fep.up.pt

Abstract. Emerging markets contain the vast majority of the world's population. Despite the huge number of inhabitants, these markets still lack a proper finance infrastructure. One of the main difficulties felt by customers is the access to loans. This limitation arises from the fact that most customers usually lack a verifiable credit history. As such, traditional banks are unable to provide loans. This paper proposes credit scoring modeling based on non-traditional data, acquired from smartphones, for loan classification processes. We use Logistic Regression (LR) and Support Vector Machine (SVM) models which are the top performers in traditional banking. Then we compared the transformation of the training datasets creating boolean indicators against recoding using Weight of Evidence (WoE). Our models surpassed the performance of the manual loan application selection process, loans granted through the models criteria presented fewer overdues, also the approval criteria of the models increased the amount of granted loans substantially. Compared to the baseline, the loans approved by meeting the criteria of the SVM model presented -196.80% overdue rate. At the same time, the approval criteria of the SVM model generated 251.53% more loans. This paper shows that credit scoring can be useful in emerging markets. The non-traditional data can be used to build algorithms that can identify good borrowers as in traditional banking.

Keywords: Credit scoring · Microfinance · Logistic regression · Support vector machine · Emerging markets

1 Introduction

Finance in emerging markets is an exciting and growing market that is distinct from what one can find in developed countries. Even though studies show that 85% of the world population is in emerging markets [2], they still lack a proper finance infrastructure. According to the World Bank, it is estimated that there are 2.5 billion unbanked adults who lack access to financial services [1]. From these financial services, loans are the most relevant and more requested services. In emerging markets, customers cannot rely on banks to have access to

© Springer International Publishing AG 2017
E. Oliveira et al. (Eds.): EPIA 2017, LNAI 10423, pp. 447–458, 2017.
DOI: 10.1007/978-3-319-65340-2_37

credit as they usually lack a verifiable credit history. Microfinance Institutions (MFI) target these customers, by providing local access to basic financial services. However, due to the risks involved with this kind of service, MFI's loan process tends to be slow and cumbersome. Customer requests frequently include an identification card, employment letter, utility bills, loan application letter, or guarantors. Although it is a common practice to require this type of information in developed economies, most customers in emerging markets do not have them. Furthermore, MFI apply high interest rates which can directly affect the utility of this service. These factors reduce significantly the number of customers that can apply for a loan.

Digital technologies bring a new dynamic to the finance market in emerging markets. Smartphone adoption in these markets is approaching the numbers of developed economies [15] and new fintech solutions for unbanked people are surfacing. In the recent years, several companies proposed loan products across emerging markets where one can use a simple mobile app to apply for a loan [9]. By being more flexible than MFI, they can target different customers. However, challenges in customer classification and eligibility for a loan arise. Credit scoring has been the way to go in traditional credit institutions, and normally rely on reliable user data such as his credit history. These new loan products lack access to traditional data. They only have access to input from customer and data collected from their smartphones, such as call logs, Short Message Service (SMS) logs, apps installed and social network relationships.

This paper proposes credit scoring modeling based on non-traditional-data and aims to help with loan classification processes of these companies. Better classification will result in a bigger investment in loan products in these markets. Loans will help unbanked adults to invest in their personal and professional endeavors, which will eventually lead to new opportunities and better quality of life.

The remainder of this paper is organized as follows. In the next section, we will revise related work on credit scoring. Section 3 presents the datasets used in the experiments. Section 4 describes the methodology used in the experiments. Section 5 present the results of the credit scoring model experiments. Conclusions and the outlook of this approach are highlighted in the Sect. 6.

2   Related Work

In the early 2000s Mark Schreiner, who can be considered as one of the main contributors of credit scoring for microfinance, started using structured databases for building models that can be replicated. This work on structured databases was implemented mostly for MFIs located in Latin America. Credit scoring models of Schreiner were based on scorecards that include details from customer, loan, and loan officer. The scorecard system showed positive results, however, it was difficult to implement since loan officers had to do the process manually to fill the scorecard. In some cases the loan officer even had to visit the customer in order to validate some information such as household goods. These models can be seen on [17–19]. Schreiner proved to MFIs that credit scoring could work for their institutions. His approach worked both with non-traditional variables and also with financial system information from the bureaus. Despite the promising results of his models, Schreiner concluded that due to the high difficulty of implementation and low added value, these models were not able to replace the loan officers with an automated process.

Some emerging markets use mobile money. This form of *money* refers to payment services operated in financial regulation and performed from or via a mobile device. This system, provided by a Mobile Network Operator (MNO), works like a bank account for the user. It allows several types of financial transactions, for example, bills payment and money transfer. These transactions generate the same type of data that a savings account in a traditional bank would generate. The use and coverage of mobile money is a growing trend, as in 2005, only 5 emerging markets supported this technology which has spread already to two-thirds (92) of emerging markets [12]. However, not only more MNOa are providing these services in different countries, but also the individuals in those countries are using the service more often for their different financial needs. Also, the number of active users is on constant growth, going from one million active accounts in 2008 to 174 million at the end of 2016 [12]. People in emerging markets are embracing this service to meet their financial needs.

During the past year, MNOs processed around 30,000 transactions per minute [12]. The number of transactions per year grew from 1.2 billion transactions to 268 billion over the last decade. From these transactions, 68.7% are Peerto-Peer (P2P) transactions and 12.5% are bill payment transactions. The vast proportion of P2P transactions is due to the way some small businesses operate. Instead of using cash or credit card, a person can buy fish to a local fish shop and pay by transferring from the mobile money account of the customer to the mobile money account associated with the fish shop. The bills payment transaction works the same as in developed and more mature markets. For example, a customer subscribes to a service, such as electric or telecommunication service. Bill payments can provide better insights about the acquisition level of the customers. Even if the P2P transactions can be used to acquire goods, it is not exclusive to such use. The data from these kinds of transactions can be shared between the MNO and a financial services company.

Companies like M-Shwari [7] and InVenture (today known as Tala) [9] have built services on top of mobile money to offer mobile savings and mobile credit. Mobile money data is a useful variable to discriminate among defaulters and non-defaulters. Nonetheless, the use of MNO data limits the ability of a business to grow since some of the emerging markets have a relatively low penetration of mobile money service [11]. On the other hand, companies like Lenddo [22] and Wonga [10] focus more on the social media footprint. This approach is useful to evaluate customers with medium to high presence on the social media since is based on *likes*, *friends* and *shares* [8]. On the flip side, it struggles to discriminate when low or no information on social media is available, which can be the case in rural areas.

Other companies in the same sector claim to use machine learning on their evaluation pipeline. Based on their operational description, Kreditech [13], Branch.co [5] and Cignifi [6] state that the use of machine learning is core on their loan evaluation process.

A more similar case to ours is the MobiScore approach [16]. This approach is based on customers demographics and device logs as we intend to do. The main difference is that MobiScore studies the default for credit cards while we focus on short-term micro loans. The MobiScore proved that a scoring model trained with mobile network usage data could be useful to estimate the financial risk of a person. Macroeconomic variables can also be a factor to consider when lacking formal sources of financial data. The case presented in [4] proposes the integration of macroeconomic variables to build a reliable scoring model. The models include variables like rate of annual change of Gross Domestic Product (GDP) during loan term and rate of annual change in the cost of electricity during the loan term. These models performed better in terms of misclassification than the classic approach.

Regardless the primary source of data (social/online, mobile or MNO), MFIs have been benefited from these new technologies, they now can create a branchless structure. With this new structure, MFIs solved two issues. First, MFIs have now better criteria to evaluate their customers. And second, the enormous cost of brick and mortar schema was eliminated. For more about branchless banking see [14].

3   Datasets

This section describes the datasets used to understand the behavior of our customers. Two datasets are used for experimentation. Even though both have the same features, the transformation process and selection process are different. The first dataset, hereinafter called dataset A, covers all the first loan granted to the customers. Only the completed loans were considered, meaning that only paid loans and loans which have passed their respective due date were used. The second dataset, from now on called dataset B consists of all loans granted and not only the first loan of each customer. As in dataset A, only completed loans were considered when generating this dataset.

Both datasets combine demographics of customers, personal information, loan details, mobile network usage and mobile features. We also included the performance of the loan (overdue or not) which is the target of prediction. In our scenario, a Non-Performing Loan (NPL) is a loan that has passed more than 3 days after due date and has not been entirely repaid. Therefore this loan is considered as an overdue in the dataset and marked with 1 in the target variable. The dataset A consists of 38.5% overdue loans and 61.5% paid on time loans. Dataset B contents 43.5% overdue loans and 56.5% paid on time loans. The summarized variables on both datasets use a 30 days window, using the previous 30 days from the moment of the loan application.

The variables can be grouped by source. First, we focus on personal information of the customer. This personal information, including demographics, is collected when the customer opens the mobile app for the first time. In this first interaction with our service, the user also needs to fill a profile. Some of the variables in the profile can be changed later on, e.g. employment status. This information can provide better insights about the acquisition level of the customers. Some variables refer to the goods the customers have (e.g., house, car) and go to their employment status. It also collects information about the dependents of the customer thought marital status and number of children. This type of data has been considered since the building of scorecards [18] to the use of advanced classification techniques as shown in [4, 16, 23], among others.

We also collected mobile phone network usage variables. These variables capture whenever the customer uses one of the services provided by the MNO, e.g. incoming or outgoing calls, SMS, etc. [3] show that having a service of a given MNO can have an impact when building a scoring model. The hypothesis is that high tier customers will relate with high tier MNO. From mobile phone, we also collect system information, e.g. mobile applications installed. With the categories of the applications installed in the device, we can create a complete profile of the customers. The applications installed work as the *"likes"* and *"shares"* presented in [8]. Providing an idea of the real interests of the customers.

Finally, we add loan characteristics and conditions: length, amount, and purpose of the loan.

Table 1. Table of features considered on datasets.

Features considered on datasets grouped by source		
Personal information	MNO and device features	Loan characteristics
Age	Airtime	Loan amount
Gender	Airtime top ups	Loan length
Marital status	Number of calls	Loan reason
Education level	Number of SMS	
Number of children	Device brand	
Employment status	Last mobile update	
Ownership of house	Number of apps installed	
Monthly income		

Table 1 shows in detail the list of the features used. This list presents only the core variables, we combine some of this features to create more meaningful variables, e.g. amount requested divided by monthly income became the *"debt ratio"*.

4   Comparing Two Different Representations for the Credit Scoring Problem

As presented in the Sect. 3, the target variable is a binary variable where 1 means overdue and 0 means paid on time. The classification task was modeled using supervised learning algorithms. Each entry will be processed to generate an output V which will be the estimated probability of going overdue.

We performed an experiment using each dataset. The main differences between both datasets were the variable selection procedure and the transformation method used.

4.1   First Experiment: Boolean Indicators

For the first experiment, we used dataset A. The dataset was extended by transforming the categorical variables into several dummy (binary) variables. For variables with N categories we generated N−1 new variables, e.g. "Gender": 'Male','Female' was turned into "Male": '1','0'. Date type variables were transformed into time unit elapsed since the date referenced, e.g. date of birth turned into age.

After converting the dataset, we applied an information gain ranker to select the variables that contribute to the classification task and drop those variables that create noise. Then, we applied supervised learning algorithms to the transformed dataset to build the models.

The two primary classification methods that we tested in this experiment were: Logistic Regression (LR) and Support Vector Machine (SVM). Not only LR and SVM performed better in terms of Area under Receiver Operating Characteristic (AUROC) but also these models make no assumption on the distribution of data, meaning they are quite tolerant to the input received [21]. We used 10-fold cross-validation to test the performance of the dataset. Our main metrics of evaluation were accuracy and approval rate. We choose these metrics so we can compare baseline set in the previous evaluation process. In our use case, we preferred to reduce the accuracy of the prediction of good borrowers in order to have better predictions in the overdue class. For each algorithm, we used grid-search for setting the hyper-parameters in order to optimize the evaluation measures. The output for each loan Vi was then transformed into a probability Pi following the expression:

$$P_i = \frac{e^{V_i}}{e^{V_i} + 1} \tag{1}$$

The models were applied to the new incoming loan applications on which the probability P for each new application was computed by the model and compared with a given threshold. Only applications from customers who applied for the first time and customers with only one paid loan before application were evaluated by the models.

4.2 Second Experiment: Implementing Weight of Evidence

The second experiment was based on dataset B. For this dataset, we used the Weight of Evidence (WoE) coding of variables. The WoE focuses on the odds ratio. The WoE of a category C for an X variables is computed as:

$$WoE(X_C) = \left[ln \left(\frac{TotalGoods(X_C)}{TotalBads(X_C)} \right) \right] * 100 \tag{2}$$

In Eq. 2, TotalGoods(X_C) refers to the number of borrowers that paid on time for category C in variable X. The same concept applies to TotalBads(X_C) but considering the borrowers that went overdue. Note that the value of the WoE is 0 when both distributions good and bad are equal. It indicates that the category evaluated does not allow to differentiate between classes. Using the recoded dataset, we calculated the Information Value (IV) of each variable. The IV for a category C of a variable X with n number of categories is as follow:

$$IV(X_C) = \frac{WoE_{C_i}}{\sum_{i=1}^{n} WoE_{C_i}} \tag{3}$$

The IV for variable X is the sum of the IV of each category C of X. It can be calculated as:

$$IV(X) = \sum_{i=1}^{C} \left[(TotalGoods_i - TotalBads_i) * ln \left(\frac{TotalGoods(X_C)}{TotalBads(X_C)} \right) \right] \tag{4}$$

Following the calculation of IV for each variable, we then used the interpretation of the IV statistic presented in [20] to select the relevant variables. The rules used were:

When IV:

– Less than 0.02, the variable does not differentiate the Goods/Bads odds ratio.
– Between 0.02 to 0.1, the variable has only a weak relationship to the Goods/Bads odds ratio.
– Between 0.1 to 0.3, the predictor has a medium strength relationship to the Goods/Bads odds ratio.
– Equal 0.3 or higher, the predictor has a strong relationship to the Goods/Bads odds ratio.

We selected the variables with weak, medium and strong relationship to the Goods/Bads odds ratio and trained the models. In this experiment, we trained both algorithms based on dataset B with the WoE transformation. As before, we used grid-search for setting the hyper-parameters in order to optimize the evaluation measures and 10-fold cross-validation to measure the performance. The output for each loan Vi was transformed using Eq. 1 and then probability Pi of each application was compare to a given threshold. The models were applied to loan applications under the same criteria as the first experiment.

5   Analysis of Results

Our experiment results were compared to the baseline results. This baseline comprises the results of a relevant sample of loans that followed expert rules. To review the performance of the models, we need to compare the overdue rate. This rate represents the proportion of NPL over the total loans granted which met the approval criteria of the models. Only loans that passed their respective due date were considered. The length of both experiments was 40 days, but the experiments were performed in different time periods. The second experiment kicked off five days after the end of the first experiment.

Table 2. Improvements of models in relation to the baseline.

Models performance		
Model	Overdue rate	Approval rate
Experiment 1 LR	−26.45%	−4.33%
Experiment 1 SVM	442.19%	−91.91%
Experiment 2 LR	−115.50%	56.46%
Experiment 2 SVM	**−196.80%**	**251.53%**

In the first experiment, two algorithms were implemented, and A|B testing was used to select which model will evaluate the corresponding loan application. The number of the application was used to divide the population into two parts. This numbers is a sequence of natural numbers. Therefore, assigning the applications with odd application number to LR algorithm and the remaining (even application number) to the SVM algorithm. The overdue rate represented in the first experiment shows the performance of each application that met the approval criteria on the corresponding algorithm. In the second experiment, since only one algorithm was implemented, all the applications went through that algorithm.

The results shown in Table 2 compare the scoring models with the manual process. The manual process refers to the all applications received before the beginning of the first experiment. This process was based on expert criteria pipeline. From the manual process, we considered only applications from customers who applied for the first time and customers with only one paid loan before. We selected these applications in order to match the same population targeted by the models.

The two main indicators to compare are the overdue rate and the approval rate. We focused on these two indicators since they are the core of a stable and sustainable business model. A high overdue rate will make the business model unprofitable, while a low approval rate will not grant enough loans even to cover the operational costs.

First, we notice that both models of the first experiment failed to improve the overdue rate, increasing the costs of overdue. The LR from the first experiment

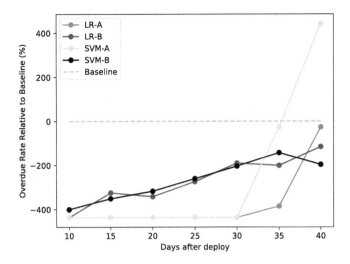

Fig. 1. Comparison of overdue rate relative to baseline by days after deployment.

allowed to grant more loans, however, the quality of the loans was poor. In Fig. 1, we compare the performance of the models in terms of classification error with real cases. The horizontal axis is the number of days after the deployment relative to the model under evaluation. Before the 30th day of deployment, both models trained with dataset A do not show overdue loans, this is because the approval rate of LR trained with dataset A (LR-A) and SVM trained with dataset A (SVM-A) was relatively low and just a few loans with less than 30 days of length were granted. However, after the loans granted by LR-A and SVM-A reached their respective due date, an increase in the overdue rate can be observed. Even if LR-A and SVM-A achieved a relatively good overdue rate, these models would not be suitable for the business due to lack of approval. The models approved less than the baseline with -4.33% and -91.91% decrease of the approval rate respectively.

Models trained with dataset B show a better behavior overall. They improve both the approval rate and the accuracy rate. As seen on Fig. 1, models based on dataset B are more stable on the overdue rate after the 30th day of deployment. These models are more constant and stable when compared to models created with dataset A. The approval rate for LR-A and SVM-A increased 56.46% and 251.53% respectively at the end of the experiments as seen in Fig. 2.

One of the main differences between the models, apart datasets of training, is the allocation of weights on the variables. Models trained with dataset A gave more weights to variables related to the customer profile and loans conditions. The profile data of the customer is filled by himself and cannot be verified. Furthermore, the conditions of the loans are capped to a specific value, meaning they can only make variations within a small interval.

On the other hand, models trained with dataset B allocated more weights in variables related to historical data of the mobile phone of the customer. These

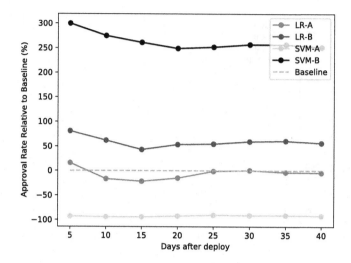

Fig. 2. Comparison of approval rate relative to baseline by days after deployment.

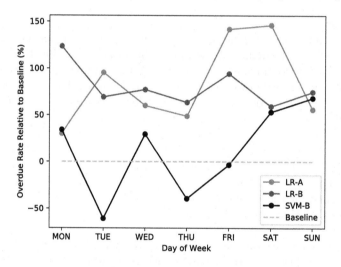

Fig. 3. Overdue rate relative to baseline by day of the week.

variables present a better profile of the customer and are more reliable, as the customer is not aware of its collection and/or cannot easily be forged. Both models trained with dataset B already surpassed the performance of the manual loan application selection process.

While analyzing the performance of the models, we noticed trends related to the nonpayment of the loans. As seen in Fig. 3, in general, the overdue rate tends to rise as the week progresses. This trend is also present in SVM trained with dataset B (SVM-B) which was the best model so far. LR-A also shows higher overdue rate in the last days of the week but concentrated on Friday and

Saturday. LR trained with dataset B (LR-B) shows less variation among the week days. We did not consider SVM-A in this analysis due to the low number of approved loans with this model.

6 Conclusions

As we have shown in the previous section, the use of credit scoring can be a useful tool to grant loans in emerging markets. Even though the first experiment did not succeed as expected, both models trained with dataset B and the WoE recoding, proved to be better than baseline in both metrics used for evaluation. Loans evaluation with LR-B and SVM-B models not only improved the overdue rate and the approval rate but also optimized the time of the loan approval pipeline.

There is a two months gap between the training of the models used in the first experiment and the deployment of this experiment. We believe this gap of time may have affected the result for these models.

For future work, we will focus in using trends on the macroeconomic environment. We believe this can be a determining factor in the performance of the credit scoring in emerging markets. Furthermore, we will study the predictive power of models with different time windows and models with streaming data as the learning base. Since emerging markets present such a dynamic behavior, maybe a dynamic model would present better performance than the one achieved with static data. Both LR-B and SVM-B need to be studied for a longer period. We intend to analyze trends in the relation of the due date of the loan and the corresponding day of the month.

References

1. Bank, W.: Financial inclusion: Helping countries meet the needs of the under-banked and under-servedk (2013). http://www.worldbank.org/en/results/2013/04/02/financial-inclusion-helping-countries-meet-the-needs-of-the-underbanked-and-underserved. Accessed 30 Apr 2017
2. Barnes, P.: E-commerce in emerging markets: the biggest growth opportunity (2016). http://marketrealist.com/2016/12/emerging-markets-better-demographics/. Accessed 28 Apr 2017
3. Biçer, I., Sevis, D., Bilgic, T.: Bayesian credit scoring model with integration of expert knowledge and customer data. In: International Conference 24th Mini EURO Conference âĂIJContinuous Optimization and Information-Based Technologies in the Financial SectorâĂİ (MEC EurOPT 2010), pp. 324–329. Vilnius Gediminas Technical University Publishing House "Technika" (2010)
4. Blanco, A., Pino-Mejías, R., Lara, J., Rayo, S.: Credit scoring models for the microfinance industry using neural networks: evidence from peru. Expert Syst. Appl. **40**(1), 356–364 (2013)
5. Branch.co: Social impact drives our work (2017). https://branch.co/how_we_work. Accessed 30 Apr 2017
6. Cignifi: cignifi technology (2017). http://cignifi.com/technology/. Accessed 30 Apr 2017

7. Cook, T., McKay, C.: How m-shwari works: the story so far. Consultative Group to Assist the Poor (CGAP) and Financial Sector Deepening (FSD) (2015)
8. De Cnudde, S., Moeyersoms, J., Stankova, M., Tobback, E., Javaly, V., Martens, D., et al.: Who cares about your facebook friends? Credit scoring for microfinance. Technical report (2015)
9. Fifer Mandell, A., Strawther, M., Zhu, J.: Inventure: building credit scoring tools for the base of the pyramid (2015)
10. Harkness, T.: Big Data: Does Size Matter? Bloomsbury USA (2016). https://books.google.pt/books?id=oW0dswEACAAJ
11. Katakam, A., Frydrych, J., Murphy, A., Naghavi, N.: State of the industry 2015: mobile money (2015)
12. Katakam, A., Frydrych, J., Murphy, A., Naghavi, N.: State of the industry on mobile money: decade edition: 2006–2016 (2016)
13. Kreditech: kreditech - what we do (2017). https://www.kreditech.com/what-we-do/. Accessed 30 Apr 2017
14. Pickens, D., Porteous, D., Rotman, S.: Scenarios for Branchless Banking in 2020. CGAP, Washignton, DC (2009)
15. Poushter, J.: Financial inclusion: helping countries meet the needs of the under-banked and under-servedk (2016). http://www.pewglobal.org/2016/02/22/smartphone-ownership-and-internet-usage-continues-to-climb-in-emerging-.economies/. Accessed 30 Apr 2017
16. San Pedro, J., Proserpio, D., Oliver, N.: Mobiscore: towards universal credit scoring from mobile phone data. In: International Conference on User Modeling, Adaptation, and Personalization, pp. 195–207. Springer (2015)
17. Schreiner, M.: A scoring model of the risk of costly arrears for loans from affiliates of women's world banking in Colombia. Women's World Banking (2000)
18. Schreiner, M.: The risk of exit for borrowers from a microlender in bolivia. Washington University in St. Louis, Center for Social Development (1999). http://gwbweb.wustl.edu/users/schreiner
19. Schreiner, M., et al.: A scoring model of the risk of costly arrears at a microfinance lender in bolivia. Washington University in St. Louis, Center for Social Development (1999). http://gwbweb.wustl.edu/users/schreiner
20. Siddiqi, N.: Credit Risk Scorecards. Developing and Implementing Intelligent Credit Scoring. Wiley, Hoboken (2006)
21. Sousa, M.R., Gama, J., Brandão, E.: A new dynamic modeling framework for credit risk assessment. Expert Syst. Appl. **45**, 341–351 (2016)
22. Stewart, J.: Systems and methods for using online social footprint for affecting lending performance and credit scoring, US Patent 8,694,401, 8 Apr 2014
23. Van Gool, J., Verbeke, W., Sercu, P., Baesens, B.: Credit scoring for microfinance: is it worth it? Int. J. Financ. Econ. **17**(2), 103–123 (2012)

Intelligent Robotics

Approach for Supervising Self-localization Processes in Mobile Robots

P.C.M.A. Farias[1,3]([✉]), Ivo Sousa[1], Héber Sobreira[1],
and António Paulo Moreira[1,2]

[1] INESC-TEC, Rua Dr. Roberto Frias, 4200-465 Porto, Portugal
{ivo.e.sousa,heber.m.sobreira}@inesctec.pt, amoreira@fe.up.pt
[2] Faculty of Engineering, University of Porto,
Rua Dr. Roberto Frias, 4200-465 Porto, Portugal
[3] Polytechnic School, Federal University of Bahia,
Rua Aristides Novis, Salvador 40210-630, Brazil
paulo.farias@ufba.br

Abstract. In this paper it will be presented a proposal of a supervisory approach to be applied to the global localization algorithms in mobile robots. One of the objectives of this work is the increase of the robustness in the estimation of the robot's pose, favoring the anticipated detection of the loss of spatial reference and avoiding faults like tracking derail. The proposed supervisory system is also intended to increase accuracy in localization and is based on two of the most commonly used global feature based localization algorithms for pose tracking in robotics: Augmented Monte Carlo Localization (AMCL) and Perfect Match (PM). The experimental platform was a robotic wheelchair and the navigation used the sensory data from encoders and laser rangers. The software was developed using the ROS framework. The results showed the validity of the proposal, since the supervisor was able to coordinate the action of the AMCL and PM algorithms, benefiting the robot's localization system with the advantages of each one of the methods.

Keywords: Localization supervision · Fault detection · AMCL · Perfect match · Mobile robots · Robotic wheelchairs

1 Introduction

Self-localization is one of the most fundamental problems in mobile robotics, and it is of utmost importance that it can be done robustly and reliably. If the robot is not aware of its pose at every moment, it will not be able to perform the assigned tasks properly and may even generate high risk situations for people and equipment damage.

In order to avoid possible loss of tracking or anomalous situations during the robot navigation, it was developed a supervisor system to integrate more than one localization approach. Generally speaking, the idea is to coexist two or more distinct global self-localization methods (already using odometry) that will be

© Springer International Publishing AG 2017
E. Oliveira et al. (Eds.): EPIA 2017, LNAI 10423, pp. 461–472, 2017.
DOI: 10.1007/978-3-319-65340-2_38

running in parallel, and each of these algorithms returns an estimated position at a given time instant.

The supervisory program receives some performance indicators from each one of the localization algorithms, using this information to infer the quality of their estimation and their respective confidence. By having more than one localization approach based on different methods, it is possible to complement each other and take advantage of their best features at different times and environments. As an example, if one of the methods starts to derail, because of some environment disturbances (e.g., total or partial sensor occlusion on crowded environments), its performance indicators will start signal a low quality pose estimation, which could be used to indicate an abnormal situation. Using this failure information, the supervisor can act accordingly by correcting the faulty algorithm, or in a more extreme case, stop the robot and start a recovery mechanism when all localization methods are giving poor indicators.

In this work, two localization algorithms, AMCL and Perfect Match, were employed. The AMCL algorithm [1] has a widespread use in the robotics community, and its robustness is one of its strongest characteristics. The Perfect Match was initially described in [2] and adapted to the case under study from work [3]. This method, in comparison with the AMCL, stands out for its greater precision in pose estimation and its computational lightness. In order to combine the characteristics of the two localization methods, a performance index based supervisor system was developed, which evaluates the quality of the AMCL and Perfect Match estimates. The algorithm that provides the best localization estimate is used as a reference for the correction of the other, which is momentarily worse performing.

The lack, by both the algorithms, of an estimate that meets the requirements established by the supervisor may indicate that robot has completely lost its spatial reference, and should trigger the global localization procedure.

This approach was tested with data collected from a robotic wheelchair, which has a low-cost laser located at a small height. These factors make navigation critical, since the data collection is subject to the presence of outliers (furniture, people passing around) and occlusions. This scenario can benefit greatly from a more robust navigation system.

2   Related Work

Navigation in crowded and full of obstacles spaces, offers an additional degree of difficulty to the robot localization system. Platforms aimed to operate in this kind of environment, like tourist sites, fairs, hospitals, etc., must be robust to operate safely. In this work, the experimental platform is a wheelchair with autonomous navigation based on odometry and 2D LRF (Laser Range Finder), which operates in environments such as described.

In [4,5], there is a description of the most basic aspects in the robot localization problem: Global Localization, Position Tracking and Robot Kidnapping. The first two points have been the subject of intense discussion, with several algorithms already established and stable. The detection of robot kidnapping, or similarly, the recognition when the robot is lost, can be benefited by the implementation of a supervision system, which monitors the potential failure situations.

There are also solutions like in [6], which addresses the problem reinforcing the robust localization algorithms. In this case, by using visual place recognition along with the LRF to recover the system from possible errors in the localization.

The work presented in [7] show an approach to enhance the precision in localization using natural landmarks, applied to the industrial environment. The paper shows a combination of three algorithms, in order to meet the precision requirements established by the industry standards. They are applied sequentially: first the AMCL, then the ICP (Iterative Closest Point) [8] scan matching and finally a solution refinement method based on Discrete Fourier Transform. Each step improves the estimation of the previous algorithm, and an accuracy better than 1 cm and 0.5° was reported. The method was tested with forklifts performing docking maneuvers in an industrial warehouse.

Inspired by the previous research, the present work seeks to broaden the investigation of the tracking derail problem. To explore strategies for the early identification of the loss of spatial reference by the robot and to improve the accuracy of the pose estimation, two localization methods were used (AMCL and Perfect Match) coordinated by a supervisory system.

3   AMCL and Perfect Match Algorithms

The AMCL is a multi-hypothesis model, which calculates a set of estimates of the robot's pose, or particles, assigning them weights (probabilities) and selecting the one that had greater weight as being the most probable particle that represents the current position of the robot.

This method, despite of the known advantages in terms of robustness and localization efficiency, has the disadvantage of making the algorithm heavier and computationally slow as the number of calculated estimates increases.

The odometry has a very important role in the filter, being responsible in a first phase for the propagation of the robot's pose, before the attribution of weights to the particles in the sensorial phase of the model.

Thus, non-modeled odometry faults can lead to loss of pose tracking even using a high number of particles.

Although the particle filter uses the laser sensory data, that are used to assign a weight to each of the particles, if there are no samples near the correct location of the robot, these data will not contribute to the recovery of the pose estimate [1].

On the other hand, the Perfect Match algorithm uses a map matching technique to estimate one pose of the robot based on the laser data. The integration of odometry data in Perfect Match has mainly the objective of preventing the algorithm's output from oscillating or drastically "jumping" from one place to another, allowing a better pose tracking. Thus, this method exhibits a great dependence on the quality of the sensory data and on the geometric character-istics of the map, presenting a considerable sensitivity to spurious information. To increase its robustness, outliers rejection filters were introduced [3], which improved the performance of the method.

As these two algorithms are based on different paradigms, each with their strong points and weaknesses, it may be advantageous to use both in parallel to increase the robustness of the robot's localization problem.

4   Robot Platform

The experimental platform to data collect was a WMRA (Wheelchair Mounted Robotic Arms) shown in Fig. 1. It is important to note that in this study, the platform was only used as a mobile robot, and that the robotic manipulator was not part of the scope of work.

The robot has two LRF units. The lower laser (URG-04LX-UG01) is used to navigation and obstacle detection. The top laser (Hokuyo UST-10LX), with higher resolution, is used to provide the ground truth to the localization algo-rithms. The wheelchair is also equipped with an RGB-D camera and an IMU, which can be integrated into the supervision system in the future.

Fig. 1. Wheelchair prototype.

5   Proposed Algorithm for the Localization Supervision

The experimental conditions of interest for the wheelchair data collecting are the use of a low cost front laser located at low height. Considering this scenario, it is important to have the localization and supervision algorithms as robust and reliable as possible.

The main objective of this approach, considering the practical application of this particular case (i.e., an autonomous wheelchair carrying a disabled person) is that the robot never gets lost. In case this happens, the supervisor should detect the faulty situation and stop the wheelchair, launching some recovery procedure to regain the robot's correct pose, using a global localization method.

As presented in [9], the Perfect Match algorithm had its functionality extended in order to be used as a more robust global localization algorithm and to be applicable in other types of scenarios, besides the RoboCup Midsize league [2].

One of these features was the inclusion of two outlier rejection filters, to get rid of the laser scan points that do not correspond to features in the map previously created. This spurious data is generated by temporary or mobile entities, like people circulating in the shared space of the robot, tables, chairs, boxes in the ground, etc. This information don't contribute to the robot's self-localization, and acts as a disturbing noise in the process.

The use of two consecutive filters with different thresholds, instead of only one filter with a more demanding value, has improved the performance of the algorithm. This due to the fact that, in a first filtering stage if the algorithm does not have a good robot pose estimate, one can discard a considerable number of points that do not really correspond to outliers. This two-stage outlier filtering provided a more judicious rejection procedure.

Therefore, if there are few data points remaining after rejection of outliers, it can be inferred a low confidence level in the estimation made by the algorithm. It is also possible to establish a lower threshold to indicate that the robot has lost its spatial reference.

Another established performance index is the cost function value of the optimization algorithm that is used by Perfect Match, which is given by:

$$E = \sum_{i=1}^{n} E_i, \ with \ E_i = 1 - \frac{L_c^2}{L_c^2 + error_i^2} \qquad (1)$$

This value is found after calculating the cost function for each laser point i. The L_c parameter is adjusted to discard points with large error.

From these two performance indicators, the pose estimate quality from the Perfect Match algorithm can be deduced, detecting failures or the beginning of a localization loss.

The AMCL is used in parallel, and outputs the estimated pose and a covariance matrix. Through the covariance matrix, the quality of the estimation of the algorithm is analyzed, being the main performance indicator to detect anomalous situations in the AMCL process.

$$AmclCov_{Norm} = \begin{bmatrix} \dfrac{\text{var}(x)}{Err_d{}^2} & \dfrac{\text{cov}(x,y)}{Err_d{}^2} & \dfrac{\text{cov}(x,\theta)}{Err_d Err_o} \\[2mm] \dfrac{\text{cov}(x,y)}{Err_d{}^2} & \dfrac{\text{var}(y)}{Err_d{}^2} & \dfrac{\text{cov}(y,\theta)}{Err_d Err_o} \\[2mm] \dfrac{\text{cov}(x,\theta)}{Err_d Err_o} & \dfrac{\text{cov}(y,\theta)}{Err_d Err_o} & \dfrac{\text{var}(\theta)}{Err_o{}^2} \end{bmatrix} \quad (2)$$

First, the covariance matrix is normalized as presented in Eq. (2), in which Err_d and Err_o are the maximum allowed error for distance and orientation, respectively. Then, the highest eigenvalue $(maxVar)$ of the covariance matrix (2) is calculated and the following condition is checked: $2\sqrt{maxVar} > 1$.

If this condition evaluates to true, the covariance matrix is bigger than the predefined thresholds for distance error and orientation error, thus indicating a possible faulty state.

The main function of the supervisory algorithm is to take each of these performance indicators into account and make decisions accordingly. The AMCL is a very robust algorithm, being difficult to get completely lost, which is useful for correcting the Perfect Match estimate if it starts to diverge. The Perfect Match was included as a way to refine and improve the accuracy given by AMCL that is usually less precise and has a worse repeatability. And since AMCL is an algorithm that already introduces a considerable overhead in processing time, the inclusion of Perfect Match has no negative performance impact.

The supervisor monitors the pose estimates and performance indexes of AMCL and Perfect Match. When there is a large discrepancy between the pose values, the method with the best indicative of accuracy is used to correct the other. For the case in which both algorithms estimates a pose sufficiently close to each other, the supervisor doesn't make any corrections and the pose given

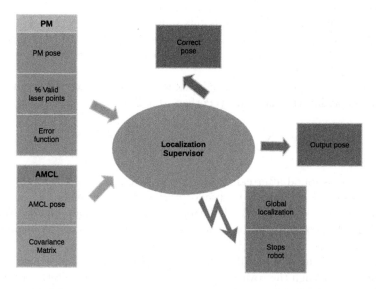

Fig. 2. Inputs and outputs of the supervisory algorithm.

by Perfect Match is maintained, considering that it will give a more refined estimation than the AMCL. Except when the two methods show low performance indicators, albeit with similar pose estimates. This may indicate a situation where the robot is totally lost, and it has to stop for security reasons, launching some global localization in order to retrieve the its correct pose (Fig. 2).

6   Experimental Setup

The data from the top LRF was used to establish the groundtruth, with the pose estimate calculated by the Perfect Match algorithm. This sensor was mounted in a higher height (1.80 m), thus avoiding disturbances in the localization process.

The developed software (e.g. supervisor, trajectory controller, Perfect Match node, hardware abstraction layer) followed the the ROS [10] framework guidelines. Some standard ROS nodes were also used, such as the AMCL package [11].

A trajectory was defined to traverse a large room ($\approx 10.0 \times 7.0$ m) and a long corridor ($\approx 18.0 \times 2.5$ m). The section of the trajectory located in the room had a large number of objects not belonging to the original map (outliers), and the trajectory segment in the corridor was defined with a smaller amount of spurious information. The results were analysed using the two localization algorithms in conjunction with the supervisor, getting the laser sensory data from the lower LRF.

In order to minimize the frame offset between the groundtruth and the pose estimates, only the map created by the top laser was used, even for the laser sensory data from the lower laser. This makes the comparison between the groundtruth and the global localization methods much more precise, but harms the localization algorithms when using the lower laser data, mainly because of the non existing features in that map, which are only visible at lower heights. As we are trying to test the robustness of these algorithms in difficult conditions (e.g., great number of outliers, dynamic environments), this is another handicap added to our analysis, to prove the viability of our approach.

The predefined path was autonomously navigated by the wheelchair, while all the sensor data (lasers and odometry) was acquired, as well as the groundtruth pose. Some datasets were registered, in which the robot performed the same path in different conditions: with people passing in front of the laser, disturbing the measurement process putting a board close to the walls, forcing the robot to stop by activating the safety laser. The datasets were also recorded without any disturbances, besides the objects already present in the room.

Using the recorded experiment data, the localization and supervisor algorithms were run offline, by using the lowerlaser data from those datasets.

7   Results

To evaluate the quality of the supervisor approach, experiments were performed to measure the accuracy and repeatability of both algorithms, as well as some examples of the supervisor action in correcting position estimates.

For the precision analysis, it was calculated the average distance and orientation errors in relation to groundtruth, in the room and in the corridor for all our datasets. Some of the data acquisitions runs were disturbed, to force an increase in the number of outliers. The results are shown in Tables 1 and 2.

Table 1. Precision analysis - Room

Room			
	Mean absolute error	AMCL	PM
Position (m)	With forced outliers	0.1968	0.1952
	Without forced outliers	0.1646	0.1410
Orientation (degrees)	With forced outliers	6.9176	6.8977
	Without forced outliers	1.7407	1.4623

Table 2. Precision analysis - Corridor

Corridor			
	Mean absolute error	AMCL	PM
Position (m)	With forced outliers	0.1247	0.1178
	Without forced outliers	0.0912	0.0678
Orientation (degrees)	With forced outliers	4.6948	3.3525
	Without forced outliers	2.8768	1.2752

In comparison with AMCL, the Perfect Match algorithm has revealed a lower error overall, with a better performance in the corridor, where the number of outliers was lower than in the room. In the room conditions, AMCL is normally more appropriate because of its higher robustness to outliers, when Perfect Match reveals a better overall performance when the environment is more structured and have less outliers.

From the data in the table it can also be inferred that the Perfect Match is more sensitive to an increase of outliers than the AMCL. Whenever additional noise elements were introduced, such as people walking around or partial obstruction of the laser field of vision, the performance of Perfect Match worsened more than the AMCL.

In order to analyze the repeatability of the Perfect Match and the AMCL algorithms in the pose estimation, for the same reference path, consecutive executions of the same trajectory were conducted. In each experiment performed, the initial pose of each algorithm was slightly altered from the exact value. The error was calculated from the euclidean distance of the poses estimated for each of these experiments runs.

Figure 3 shows the position error time evolution for each localization algorithm. The experiments were performed in the corridor scenario. It was found a mean position error of $\mathbf{E_{AMCL}} = \mathbf{0.026}$ **m** and $\mathbf{E_{PM}} = \mathbf{0.002}$ **m**, for the AMCL and Perfect Match, respectively.

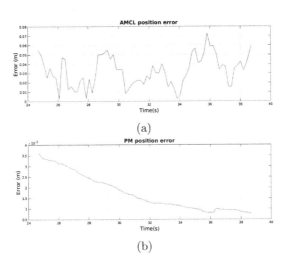

(a)

(b)

Fig. 3. (a) AMCL error. (b) PM error.

The Figs. 4 and 5 show some RVIZ screenshots with the supervisor in operation. The black an blue arrows represent the grondtruth and Perfect Match pose estimate, respectively. The red cloud represents the AMCL particles.

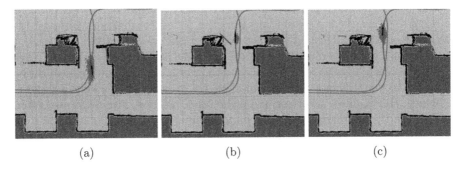

(a)   (b)   (c)

Fig. 4. (a) Both algorithms are well localized in relation to the groundtruth (black arrow). (b) Perfect Match (blue arrow) starts to get lost. (c) The supervisor corrects the Perfect Match pose based on the AMCL pose estimation (red particles). (Color figure online)

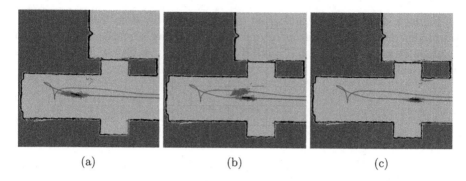

(a)   (b)   (c)

Fig. 5. (a) Both algorithms are well localized in relation to the groundtruth (black arrow). (b) AMCL (red particles) starts to diverge from the correct robot's pose and the covariance matrix gets abnormally high. (c) The supervisor corrects the AMCL pose based on the Perfect Match estimation (blue arrow). (Color figure online)

As it is possible to observe in the sequence of Fig. 4, Perfect Match (represented by the blue arrow) started to diverge, mainly because of the lack of valid laser points related to the high number of outliers in the room. By detecting this anomalous situation, the supervisor corrected its pose with the current AMCL estimate, which resulted in its successful recovery, avoiding the robot's loss.

In another experiment run showed in Fig. 5, when the robot was moving in the corridor the correction was reversely made, as the PM corrected the AMCL pose when it was going to diverge and lose its correct pose tracking.

8   Conclusions

In this article it was proposed the development of a supervisor system to localization algorithms, used in wheelchair autonomous navigation. The system aims to bring together the strongest characteristics of two localization methods: the robustness of the AMCL and the best accuracy of Perfect Match.

The supervisor operates by monitoring some performance indices of each algorithm. These criteria were established to infer the quality of the localization and to detect in advance that the method being analyzed is losing its spatial reference, and requires a correction by the other method, if it performs better. In case the two methods have poor performance, which can indicate the total loss of reference, a global location algorithm is triggered.

The wheelchair uses two lasers for localization. The top laser, with higher resolution, was used as groundtruth. The lower laser was used for navigation and safety. This creates a more restrictive operating condition, since the lower laser is more subject to outliers, in addition to having lower resolution.

The positive results, even with this unfavorable scenario, indicate the success of the approach. Also, experiments were performed to verify the accuracy of the algorithms in following a predefined trajectory. The robot's localization estimation, given by both algorithms and under the action of the supervisor, was compared with the groundtruth data. In two scenarios with different characteristics regarding the number of outliers, the wheelchair was able to keep navigating even in critical cases.

Another measure was the repeatability of the localization algorithms, which was evaluated by having the robot traverse the same trajectory several times, with slight perturbations at the starting point. Both managed to deal with the disturbances on the initial position of the navigation, and the Perfect Match presented an error about ten times smaller than the AMCL. In addition, some screenshots were placed showing the action of the supervisor in critical sectors of the trajectory.

As a future development, it is intend to add other sensors to the localization algorithms. In addition to the encoders, used for odometry, and LRF that have served as the data source for this work, the wheelchair has an Inertial Measurement Unit (IMU) and an RGB-D camera. Fusing the data from these other sensors can improve the wheelchair pose estimation and facilitate early detection of spatial reference loss.

Another future development perspective of this work is in the global localization procedure that should to be launched when both algorithms are lost. In addition to the AMCL that can be used for global localization, it is intended to investigate a muti-hypothesis approach applied to the Perfect Match algorithm.

Acknowledgement. Project "TEC4Growth - Pervasive Intelligence, Enhancers and Proofs of Concept with Industrial Impact/NORTE-01-0145-FEDER-000020" is financed by the North Portugal Regional Operational. Programme (NORTE 2020), under the PORTUGAL 2020 Partnership Agreement, and through the European Regional Development Fund (ERDF).

P.C.M.A. Farias (CNPq-Brazil research fellow) acknowledge support from CNPq/CsF PDE 233517/2014-6 for providing a scholarship.

References

1. Dellaert, F., Fox, D., Burgard, W., Thrun, S.: Monte carlo localization for mobile robots. In: Proceedings 1999 IEEE International Conference on Robotics and Automation (Cat. No. 99CH36288C), vol. 2, pp. 1322–1328 (1999)
2. Lauer, M., Lange, S., Riedmiller, M.: Calculating the perfect match: an efficient and accurate approach for robot self-localization. In: Bredenfeld, A., Jacoff, A., Noda, I., Takahashi, Y. (eds.) RoboCup 2005. LNCS, vol. 4020, pp. 142–153. Springer, Heidelberg (2006). doi:10.1007/11780519_13
3. Sobreira, H., Pinto, M., Moreira, A.P., Costa, P.G., Lima, J.: Robust robot localization based on the perfect match algorithm. In: Moreira, A.P., Matos, A., Veiga, G. (eds.) CONTROLO 2014. LNEE, vol. 321, pp. 607–616. Springer, Cham (2015). doi:10.1007/978-3-319-10380-8_58
4. Carlone, L., Bona, B.: A comparative study on robust localization: fault tolerance and robustness test on probabilistic filters for range-based positioning. In: 2009 International Conference on Advanced Robotics, pp. 1–8, June 2009

5. Llarena, A., Savage, J., Kuri, A., Escalante-Ramírez, B.: Odometry-based viterbi localization with artificial neural networks and laser range finders for mobile robots. J. Intell. Robot. Syst. **66**(1), 75–109 (2012). http://dx.doi.org/10.1007/s10846-011-9627-8

6. Pérez, J., Caballero, F., Merino, L.: Enhanced monte carlo localization with visual place recognition for robust robot localization. J. Intell. Robot. Syst. **80**(3), 641–656 (2015). http://dx.doi.org/10.1007/s10846-015-0198-y

7. Vasiljevi, G., Mikli, D., Draganjac, I., Kovai, Z., Lista, P.: High-accuracy vehicle localization for autonomous warehousing. Robot. Comput.-Integr. Manuf. **42**, 1–16 (2016). http://www.sciencedirect.com/science/article/pii/S0736584515300314

8. Censi, A.: An ICP variant using a point-to-line metric. In: 2008 IEEE International Conference on Robotics and Automation, pp. 19–25, May 2008

9. Pinto, M., Sobreira, H., Moreira, A.P., Mendona, H., Matos, A.: Self-localisation of indoor mobile robots using multi-hypotheses and a matching algorithm. Mechatronics **23**(6), 727–737 (2013). http://www.sciencedirect.com/science/article/pii/S0957415813001281

10. Quigley, M., Conley, K., Gerkey, B., Faust, J., Foote, T., Leibs, J., Wheeler, R., Ng, A.Y.: ROS: an open-source robot operating system. In: ICRA Workshop on Open Source Software, vol. 3, p. 5 (2009)

11. ROS: Adaptive monte carlo localization approach (2017). http://wiki.ros.org/amcl. Accessed 24 Mar 2017

Autonomous Interactive Object Manipulation and Navigation Capabilities for an Intelligent Wheelchair

Nima Shafii[1]([✉]), P.C.M.A. Farias[1,2], Ivo Sousa[1], Heber Sobreira[1],
Luis Paulo Reis[3], and Antonio Paulo Moreira[1]

[1] INESC Technology and Science, Faculty of Engineering,
University of Porto, Rua Dr. Roberto Frias, Porto, Portugal
nshafii@inesctec.pt, paulo.farias@ufba.br
[2] Polytechnic School, Federal University of Bahia, Rua Aristides Novis, Salvador,
Brazil
[3] Departamento de Sistemas de Informao, Universidade do Minho, Guimares,
Portugal

Abstract. This paper aims to develop grasping and manipulation capability along with autonomous navigation and localization in a wheelchair-mounted robotic arm to serve patients. Since the human daily environment is dynamically varied, it is not possible to enable the robot to know all the objects that would be grasped. We present an approach to enable the robot to detect, grasp and manipulate unknown objects. We propose an approach to construct the local reference frame that can estimate the object pose for detecting the grasp pose of an object. The main objective of this paper is to present the grasping and manipulation approach along with a navigating and localization method that can be performed in the human daily environment. A grid map and a match algorithm is used to enable the wheelchair to localize itself using a low-power computer. The experimental results show that the robot can manipulate multiple objects and can localize itself with great accuracy.

1 Introduction

Wheelchair Mounted Robotic Arms (WMRA) are designed to help elderlies and patients with disabilities in the performance of their activities of daily living (ADL) [6,10]. These activities involve reaching for every day household objects and manipulating them. Most system designed for performing these tasks are still based on the teleoperation in which the user control the wheelchair and the arm with a joystick or a similar type of devices [7]. With the larger need to have such systems, the WMRA needs to achieve more autonomy. For example, Tanaka et al. [17] showed that an WMRA can assist a patient by grasping a cup object and bring it to the user's mouth. However, the capabilities of a WMRA should be improved to be able to perform ADL scenarios autonomously, for example consider an ADL scenario where a disabled user aims to pick up a box of medicine from the table using an WMRA. This task can be separated

© Springer International Publishing AG 2017
E. Oliveira et al. (Eds.): EPIA 2017, LNAI 10423, pp. 473–485, 2017.
DOI: 10.1007/978-3-319-65340-2_39

in two main components: the WMRA must navigate the wheelchair near the table. Second, the robotic arm must grasp the medicine box and manipulate it to the user. In this paper, we present localization, object detection, grasping and manipulation approaches which enables a WMRA to perform the mentioned task autonomously. The proposed WMRA can help the patients with leg disability who cannot walk nor cannot stand up.

Regarding the object manipulation task, finding an appropriate grasp pose is still a challenging problem since small errors in estimating the pose of an object can cause a failed grasp. Grasp approaches try to solve the problem of finding a grasp configuration (i.e., robot arm position and orientation) that ensures the stability of the grasped object during a manipulation task. Researchers have explored data-driven approaches, that can directly map from vision to action. Numerous approaches in this direction have been presented for robotic object grasping and manipulation. They can be categorized in two different groups based on the prior knowledge that the robot has about grasping the object. The first group is grasping approaches for a known object. In these approaches, a database provides grasp hypotheses, then the robot finds an appropriate grasp pose by approximating the object's 3D pose and then filtering the hypotheses based on reachability [1]. The major drawback of these approaches is that preparing models for all possible objects is practically impossible. The second weakness of these approaches is originated from the fact that the objects cannot be assumed totally known to the robot since the objects are generally only partially visible.

The ideal arm robot mounted on the wheelchair should be able to grasp new objects while it is operating in the household environment. To do this, the robot should be capable of grasping novel objects without knowing any previous experiment about them (i.e. grasping unknown objects). In grasp approaches for unknown objects usually some heuristics are used to relate the structures extracted from the object's partial view to the grasp candidates [4,5]. These approaches relies on detecting the unknown object with considering some assumptions such as the object is on the flat trains. Although the work in [4] has shown rather reliable results, but they are sensitive to the performance of the object detection.

In this paper, we present an approach for grasping unknown objects, including different household objects, like bowls and dishes. We also present a method in which the robot first detects the tabletop object robustly, enabling the detection of tiny objects e.g. pen. The pose of the detected object is estimated by calculating a Local Reference Frame (LRF). Based on the calculated LRF, we present several new heuristics which enable the robot to grasp unforeseen objects and rather challenging objects like dishes. As a result, we will show that the robot can grasp several different household objects. In a scenario using an WMRA, we also show that our approach for object grasping and manipulation can deliver household objects to the patient.

Regarding the robot's global localization problem, it is important to adequate the approach with the application scenario of this project, the autonomous wheelchairs. Therefore, the focus is mainly on localization algorithms which are based on environmental natural contours, as they give better flexibility and discard the need of changing or adapting the target environment in which the wheelchair will operate. One of the most well known localization algorithms for this context is AMCL (Augmented Monte Carlo Localization), described in [18]. It uses a different number of particles according with the estimated pose uncertainty and furthermore it adds an approach to solve the global localization problem, i.e. in absence of an initial pose. As its main disadvantage, this method demands a higher computational effort for an increased quality of pose estimation. Alternatively, there is the map-matching localization approach, in which we highlight the Perfect Match (PM) algorithm, originally presented by Lauer et al. [8], as being a very lightweight method with a good performance. Sobreira et al. [15] recently expanded this algorithm for laser sensor data and added functionalities using outlier filters to increase its robustness. Also in the field of map-matching algorithms, there is ICP (Iterative Closest Point) [2] which has an high computational cost in order to search between the two sets of points previously to the optimization phase. A comparison study between these two map-matching algorithms showed that the Perfect Match has the best performance in all tested fields compared to its counterparts [16]. In this work, we present an approach based on PM for performing the navigation and localization tasks. This approach is implemented in an Raspberry Pi Single Board Computer (SBC), and therefore it is of utmost importance that the localization algorithm is as light as possible, ensuring the choice of PM algorithm.

The remainder of this paper is organized as follows: Sect. 2 presents a the architecture of our WMRA as well as the designed human-robot interaction interface. Section 3 describes the detailed methodologies used for object detection and presents our approach for grasping and manipulating unknown objects. The detailed methodologies used for robot localization and navigation are presented in Sect. 4. The evaluation of the system for both object manipulation and robot navigation capabilities are presented and discussed in Sect. 5; and finally conclusions and future work are presented in Sect. 6.

2   Platform Architecture

The overall WMRA architecture is shown in Fig. 1. The developed WMAR is based on a Vassilli wheelchair, model Evolution, adapted for the objective of autonomous navigation. The wheelchair is powered by a 24 V battery and has a pair of DC motors coupled to quadrature encoders. A Roboteq SDC2130 controller board is included for motor control and encoder reading. The controller board has a 32-bit microprocessor, which implements the algorithms used for closed loop speed control. The system uses two scanning lasers manufactured by Hokuyo. The lower laser, model URG-04LX-UG01, with 240° field of view, is used for safety and obstacle avoidance. The Hokuyo UST-10LX top laser is used for mapping and localization. It has 270° of scan angle and is positioned at a height of 1.80 m. In addition to odometry and laser scanning, the wheelchair is also equipped with a 9 DOF Inertial Measurement Unit (IMU), which utilizes an Extended Kalman Filter to combine the data from the magnetometer, accelerometer and rate gyro sensor and provide altitude and heading estimates. Integrated with the robotic manipulator system there is a RGB-D camera, which can be used also to provide visual odometry information. The processing stack is based on ROS [13] nodes (Indigo version). The nodes responsible for navigation (control and user interface) runs on two Raspberry Pi SBC, with Jessie Raspbian installed. The motor controller board, the two lasers, the IMU, and a wireless joystick for teleoperation are all connected to the Raspberry Pi units. At the moment, the object manipulation and perception nodes are executed by a portable computer, for performance reasons. Some of the most relevant ROS nodes were developed by the group. For example, the motor controller driver, the trajectory controller and the Perfect Match [8] based localization module were written in C^{++} to meet the project needs. The arm mounted on the wheelchair is Robotis Manipulator-h which has 6 Degrees of Freedom (DoF). A 3-Finger electric gripper is custom designed using FESTO FinGripper fingers.

2.1   Scenario Description

This prototype was developed with the purpose of allowing the displacement in indoor environments and manipulation of objects, enabling people with some type of motor impairment to perform their ADL. The typical application scenario is the definition, by the user, of some position goal within the mapped region, through a touchscreen interface. The map is shown by a browser, using the Rosbridge ROS package, and the person driving the wheelchair can indicate the robot final position and orientation. The navigation system is able also of following a predefined trajectory. Then, after

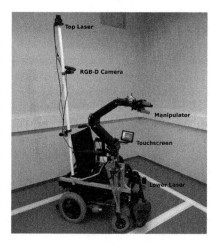

Fig. 1. Wheelchair prototype.

approaching a flat surface where objects of interest are located, the user can select the target object through the RVIZ ROS package.

2.2   User Interface

For grasping and robot navigation capabilities, a user interface is designed to be used by the patient that has leg or back impairment. The navigation user interface currently consists of a Raspberry Pi touch display, where a pre-calculated environment map is shown by a web browser, connected with the ROS node stack through Rosbridge. The user can choose the desired robot position and orientation (pose goal) simply by indicating on the screen the new wheelchair pose. To indicate the object to be grasped by the manipulator, the cloud of points obtained by the RGB-D camera is shown on the display through the RVIZ. The user can then indicate on the display which one is the target by touching on the point near to the object on the screen.

3   Object Detection and Manipulation

An object detection module was developed to detect objects on the table and to extract their point cloud. The point cloud captured by a Asus Xtion is the input. The captured point cloud is processed using several functionalities of the Point Cloud Library (PCL) [14]. The density of the point cloud is reduced using the voxelization method from PCL, where voxel size is $1\,\mu m^3$. First, the captured point clouds are transferred from the camera reference frame to the *arm base* frame. In order to detect the table-top objects, a table is detected by finding the dominant plane in the point cloud using a RANSAC algorithm. For extracting the table-top point clouds, the table points are segmented out from the point cloud. Several studies have used RANSAC to detect the table [3,9], but since the depth data has white noise and outliers, the outliers in Z direction can influence the table detection performance and some points on the table were not detected. In order to remedy this issue, the points above the table were removed using a filter threshold. In other works usually this threshold has been assigned statically big such that the robot could not recognize the tiny objects laid on the table. In this work in order to detect table points robustly, first by assuming that the table points have normal distribution, the mean and the standard deviation of the Z positions of the table points are estimated. Then, the table-top points that their height above the table mean are less than two times of the standard deviation are removed. By using this method, the table-top points that do not belong to the objects are detected robustly and our robot can recognize the tiny object such as pen as it is shown in Fig. 2.

Fig. 2. Grasping from the side: The proper grasp pose (black square). The grasp poses (red squares) are rejected. (Color figure online)

Afterwards, the table-top point cloud is segmented into individual clusters, as object candidates, using Euclidean clustering algorithm. If the number of points in a cluster is bigger than fifty, the cluster is assumed as a detected object. The average of the points of the cluster are calculated as the position of the detected objects. Then, The object which is nearest to the position reported by the user interface module is considered as the target object that to be grasped. The point cloud of the target object is used in the grasp pose detection approaches. In the next section, the approach to detect the grasp pose will be explained.

3.1 Grasp Pose Detection

In our approach for detecting the grasp pose, the first processing step on every individual point cloud given by the object detection module is to compute a LRF, i.e. a local, object-centric coordinate system. Since, the vertical direction (gravity direction) is always treated specially, therefore the Z axis is assigned to the direction that is perpendicular to the table. The X and Y axis must be calculated to construct the reference frame. For this purpose, the X axes is calculated using Principal Component Analysis (PCA) on the point cloud given by the object detection module. Since we assumed that the Z axis is perpendicular to the table, all points of the object are projected on the table. In this case, PCA computes the axes of minimum and maximum variance in the horizontal plane. Then, the axis with maximum variance is allocated to the X axis.

To calculated the PCA, firstly, the centroid of the point cloud is calculated by the equation $\mathbf{centroid} = \frac{1}{n}\sum_{i=1}^{n} p_i$, where $\mathbf{p}_i = \{p_x, p_y\}$ is the projected point cloud, and $\mathbf{centroid} = \{centroid_x, centroid_y\}$. The normalized covariance matrix, $\mathbf{Q}$, of the object is constructed using the Eq. 1.

$$\mathbf{Q} = \frac{1}{n}\sum_{i=1}^{n}(\mathbf{p}_i - \mathbf{centroid})(\mathbf{p}_i - \mathbf{centroid})^T, \tag{1}$$

Then, the eigenvalue decomposition is performed on the $\mathbf{Q}$ using the Eq. (2). The Λ is a diagonal matrix of the eigenvalues $\{\lambda_1, \lambda_2\}$ and $\mathbf{U}$ contains the two corresponding eigenvectors $\{\mathbf{u}_1, \mathbf{u}_2\}$. The eigenvalues of $\mathbf{Q}$ are positive and the eigenvectors are orthogonal. The eigenvector $\mathbf{u}_1$ which has the maximum eigenvalues is assigned to the X axis.

$$\mathbf{QU} = \Lambda\mathbf{U}, \tag{2}$$

Afterwards, the Y axes can be calculated by the outer product of Z and X axis. Since the sign of the first eigenvector $\mathbf{u}_1$ is ambiguous, the orientation of the eigenvector can be changed $180°$ between the different experiments. To solve the sign disambiguation, first the ψ orientation of the LRF are calculated using $\psi = \arctan 2(y, x)$. If the $\psi \in [-\pi/2, \pi/2]$ the X sign calculated becomes positive and the frame constructed is assigned to the LRF of the object. Otherwise, the sign calculated becomes negative, the reference frame is rotated around the Z axes $180°$ to construct the LRF.

For producing the bounding box of the object, the point cloud of the object, $\mathbf{O}$, is transformed by the orientation of the LRF, and the dimensions of the bounding box for each axis is specified by computing the minimum and maximum in the direction of the axis. Since the object is partially visible, the center of the object's bounding box is used as a proxy for the true Center of Mass (CoM).

The shape informations derived from partial 3D view (i.e. LRF, bounding box and its center) are used with some heuristic to select the grasp pose. In this study, we assume that it is possible to select grasp pose for different household objects by only using constructed LRF and different set of heuristics in the form of three grasp strategies. The heuristics are defined as follow:

Grasping from the Top: In this grasp strategy, it is assumed that the object is only approached by the robot along the z-axis (perpendicular to the surface) while the gripper closing direction is aligned with the y-axis. Thus, in order to find the suitable grasp pose on the object, it is only needed to find the grasp position on x-axis. To do that, first, object points are projected onto the xy-plane. Then, the points are clustered using equally sized interval along x-axis. Each cluster indicates one grasp candidate, and for each one, the maximum and minimum of the positions of points along y-axis indicate the grasp width. In order to select proper grasp candidate, since grasping around the center of mass of an object is preferable, first the cluster around the origin will be analyzed. This grasp minimizes the torque about the gripper axis due to the objects weight. If the grasp width of the selected candidate is bigger than gripper size (i.e. 13 cm) and does not fit into the robot's gripper, the other grasp candidates will be analyzed. The grasp candidates are then sorted based on how much their grasp width fits to the robot's palm. The size of palm of the our designed gripper arm is 8 cm. Note, the grasp candidates that reach to the maximum and minimum of the x-axis are rejected. Figure 3 (*left*) shows the process of the top grasps approach.

Fig. 3. (a) Grasping from the top, (b) Grasping from the side: the projected objects' points are analyzed to select the proper grasp pose (black square). The bad grasp poses (red squares) are rejected. (Color figure online)

Grasping from the Side: according to this grasp strategy, the object is approached in the horizontal plane, along the y-axis while negative y is used as approach direction and the gripper closing direction is aligned with the x-axis. In this case, the proper grasp position along z-axis should be found. To do that, first, object points are projected onto the xz-plane, then multiple grasps candidate are generated by sampling along the z-axis with equal interval size. If the size of grasp width of the candidate around the center of the bounding box fits inside the gripper, this grasp candidate will be selected. If not, other sampled grasp candidates are ranked based on how much they are fit inside the gripper. The grasp candidates located in limits of the z-axis are then rejected. The grasp candidate with highest rank will be selected. The process of the grasp selection using the horizontal side strategy is depicted in Fig. 3 (*right*).

Grasping from the Edge: In this strategy, the object is approached in the direction of the grasp line created from the object edge to the center of the bounding box. The gripper closing direction is aligned with the z-axis. This grasp strategy is designed to be used in grasping flat objects that are only graspable from their edge such as bowls and dishes. In this strategy, the proper grasp position along y-axis should be inferred. Since the robot will grasp the edge of the object, the desirable grasp point is around the edge of the object should be detected. To do that, first, object points are projected onto the yz-plane, then, the grasp candidate has the smallest grasp width is selected as selected as the objects edge. In this case The grasp candidates located in limits of the x-axis mostly are selected. Figure 4 shows the grasp point selection process and the grasp orientation line calculated using this strategy.

Fig. 4. Grasping from the edge: The proper grasp pose (black square), The grasp orientation line (White line).

In our grasp methodology, first, one of the proposed grasp strategies is selected based on the size of the bounding box of the object. To do that the following rules are presented bellow, here $||$ denotes the size of the bounding box.

Algorithm 1. rule of grasp strategy selection

---

if $|z - axis| > |x - axis|$ **and** $|z - axis| > |y - axis|$ **and** $|x - axis| < grippersize$ **then**
    perform grasping from the side
else if $|y - axis| > |z - axis|$ **and** $|x - axis| < grippersize$ **then**
    perform grasping from the top
else
    perform grasping from the edge
end if

3.2   Object Manipulation

For executing a grasp, the robot is commanded to perform actions based on the calculated grasp position and orientation. To control the robots gripper pose, an inverse kinematics module based on a geometric approach is developed using the work in [12]. An spline based approach is also developed to generate the path trajectory of the gripper.[1]

As a grasping scenario, first the robot is commanded to go to a pregrasp position that is 9 cm behind the grasp point along with the grasp orientation. When the pregrasp pose is reached, then the robot approaches the grasp point and then closes the fingers. Whenever the object is grasped, the robot picks up the object and navigates it to the predefined placing position near to the patient.

4   Localization and Autonomous Navigation

In terms of localization we used the Perfect Match algorithm based on the article [15] which implements a set of improvements and extends the original approach [8] to other type of applications, using lasers as an alternative to cameras. In this implementation, instead of using a fixed number of iterations for the RPROP optimization algorithm, a maximum number of cycles is defined or, in case the method converges to an error value of less than one defined threshold, the algorithm stops.

In this algorithm the vehicle pose is computed using 2D distance points from the surrounding environment. These points are acquired with the laser, and are matched with the map previously computed. Therefore, the vehicle pose is calculated by minimizing the fitting error between the data acquired and the computed map. Through the map occupancy grid it is possible to obtain the distance and gradient matrices. The distance matrix at each cell gives the distance to the closest obstacle. There are two gradient matrices, one in the x direction and the other in the y direction. The first gives the direction variation of the distance matrix with the variation of the x position. The second shows the direction variation with the y position variation.

A preprocessing step for the received laser data was also defined, to cope with the presence of outliers. The idea was to reject the more distant points to the nearest obstacle on the map, indicating the presence of people or objects. In reality, the outliers rejection procedure is performed twice. First, using a less demanding maximum distance, the points more distant than a threshold were discarded and the RPROP executed; in the second time, using the result of the previous process, a more demanding distance value was used and the RPROP algorithm was run again, obtaining the final result. This approach avoids the algorithm discarding a considerable number of points that do not really correspond to outliers. In addition to the described functionalities, the implementation allows to assign different weights to the points detected by the laser, according to their distance to the robot. For pose control, one can use free navigation with obstacle avoidance, or a predefined parametric trajectory. For the case of autonomous navigation of a wheelchair transporting a disabled person, it's better to use the free navigation approach, increasing the flexibility of the path the robot is following.

---

[1] Their code is available at https://github.com/nshafii/inesc_robotis_arm.

5   Results

This section presents the results of the two presented approaches for object grasping and autonomous navigation. Finally, in a ADL scenario, we will show that our WMRA uses these two capabilities to help a patient.

5.1   Object Manipulation and Grasp Evaluation

It is common to evaluate the quality of robotic grasps using simulators such as GraspIt! [11] that can execute grasps using perfect knowledge of the object and its environment. However, simulating and evaluating all possible combinations of object model and gripper contacts is computationally hard to deal with. Because of that the proposed methodology can only be verified empirically. We evaluate our grasp methodology by testing grasping scenarios on a real robot.

In our designed grasp evaluation scenarios, after the WMRA moved to a predefine place near to the table, the manipulator is instructed to pick-up an object using the proposed grasp methodology. After picking up the object, the robot carries the object to the placing position to see if the object slips due to bad grasp or not. A particular grasp is considered as success if the robot performed the scenario successfully. We analyzed the performance of our approach to grasp the household objects by evaluating the success rate. In our designed scenarios, 14 household objects were used which can be seen in Fig. 5.

Fig. 5. The 14 objects that are used in our grasp evaluation.

As a testing scenario, the objects were placed in different orientations. In each experiment, an object was first put in the orientation shown by the object view in the Fig. 5 and robot tried to grasp it. Afterwards, we rotated the object about 60° for six times and repeated the scenario to test all viewpoints of the object. Therefore, each object was tested to be grasped by the robot 6 times, and 84 grasp trails were performed to complete the whole experiments. In these experiments, the robot could perform 72 successful grasps meaning the overall success rate was about 85%. It has observed that the robot could grasp all objects by using the proposed strategies, and the failures mainly caused due to the lack of manipulability rather than the selecting bad grasp poses. A video is available online which shows the performance of our grasping on some the test objects[2].

5.2   Localization and Navigation Results

All the navigation was performed using the top laser range finder. In Fig. 6 the yellow points represent the raw laser data, and the green ones are the remaining points after the outlier rejection filter action. These are the points effectively used by the Perfect Match algorithm to estimate the robot pose. For testing purposes, a parametric trajectory represented by the red line in Fig. 6 was predefined in order to test if the localization algorithm was working correctly, verifying if the results were consistent and precise enough so that the wheelchair could follow the path during several hours even in the presence of outliers. The figure shows a good agreement between the desired trajectory and wheelchair pose estimation, represented by the black arrow. It is also possible to see in Fig. 6 the well fitted laser scans points overlapping the environmental map, which indicates that the localization algorithm has a good pose estimation for the robot. An analysis of the fitting error was performed with the experimental dataset, in order to evaluate the quality of the robot pose estimation. The Perfect Match algorithm had an average of 5 mm in the pose error estimation (and a maximum of 12 mm error), even in the presence of outliers. The error was calculated by the difference between the fixed map and the laser points data.

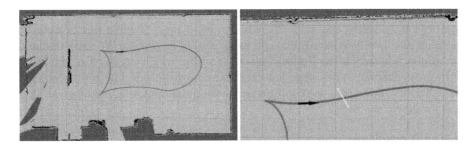

Fig. 6. (a) Perfect Match's good pose estimation (black arrow) following a predefined trajectory, in RVIZ. (b) Outliers rejection (yellow dots) in presence of an unexpected object detected by the laser scan. (Color figure online)

In Fig. 6 there's an example of the outlier rejection filter excluding the laser points (corresponding to an unexpected object) from the optimization algorithm and therefore avoiding the mismatching (or divergence) of the Perfect Match pose estimation. The figure shows a zoomed section of the map, highlighting the action of the outlier rejection filter. An artificial obstacle was introduced to

---

[2] https://www.dropbox.com/sh/8tt42g2obbvrhcb/AABDjCTIrcJ5izO0MlEgvK4_a?
dl=0.

occlude the laser beam, intending to degrade the quality of the pose estimate. The outlier filter was able to cope with the data noise, rejecting it. In the figure the obstacle is represented as a yellow line, meaning that it wasn't used by the Perfect Match algorithm.

5.3 Demonstration

Considering the described autonomous navigation and object manipulation apparatus, the developed prototype can be applied to a domestic scenario, to assist an elderly or handicapped person in their ADL. The user must first determine the desired positioning for the wheelchair, in order to place the objects to be manipulated within the operating region of the robotic manipulator. With the robotic arm positioned, the user indicates the wanted object, which is then picked up by the manipulator. Once the object is gripped, it can be moved to another site, or returned to the user. A video in https://youtu.be/hWtmkmWqUgY shows the robot functionality during this demonstration.

6 Conclusions

This paper presents our wheelchair mounted robotic arm system which enables a patient to navigate to different places, pickup and manipulate objects. In order to enable the robot to perform tasks, we present two methodologies; first one to detect and manipulate unknown objects, the second one to localize and navigate the robot. In the object manipulation approach the robot could detect table-top objects robustly and infer the proper grasp pose of unknown objects by calculating a local reference frame and using a set of heuristics. We also presented an approach based on the Perfect Match algorithm which can localize the robot with great accuracy and using low computation overhead. The results showed the efficiency of the proposed approaches both in manipulating unknown objects and localizing the robot.

Acknowledgements. This work is financed by the ERDF European Regional Development Fund through the Operational Programme for Competitiveness and Internationalisation - COMPETE 2020 Programme, and by National Funds through the FCT Fundao para a Cilncia e a Tecnologia (Portuguese Foundation for Science and Technology) within project POCI-01-0145-FEDER-006961. P.C.M.A. Farias acknowledge support from CNPq/CsF PDE 233517/2014-6 for providing a scholarship.

References

1. Bohg, J., Morales, A., Asfour, T., Kragic, D.: Data-driven grasp synthesisa survey. IEEE Trans. Robot. **30**(2), 289–309 (2014)
2. Censi, A.: An ICP variant using a point-to-line metric. In: IEEE International Conference on Robotics and Automation, ICRA 2008, pp. 19–25. IEEE (2008)

3. Holz, D., Holzer, S., Rusu, R.B., Behnke, S.: Real-time plane segmentation using RGB-D cameras. In: Röfer, T., Mayer, N.M., Savage, J., Saranlı, U. (eds.) RoboCup 2011. LNCS, vol. 7416, pp. 306–317. Springer, Heidelberg (2012). doi:10.1007/978-3-642-32060-6_26

4. Hsiao, K., Chitta, S., Ciocarlie, M., Jones, E.G.: Contact-reactive grasping of objects with partial shape information. In: 2010 IEEE/RSJ International Conference on Intelligent Robots and Systems (IROS), pp. 1228–1235. IEEE (2010)

5. Kasaei, S.H., Shafii, N., Lopes, L.S., Tomé, A.M.: Object learning and grasping capabilities for robotic home assistants. LNCS, vol. 9776. Springer, Cham (2016)

6. Kim, D.J., Wang, Z., Paperno, N., Behal, A.: System design and implementation of UCF-MANUS an intelligent assistive robotic manipulator. IEEE/ASME Trans. Mechatron. **19**(1), 225–237 (2014)

7. Ktistakis, I.P., Bourbakis, N.G.: A survey on robotic wheelchairs mounted with robotic arms. In: 2015 National Aerospace and Electronics Conference (NAECON), pp. 258–262. IEEE (2015)

8. Lauer, M., Lange, S., Riedmiller, M.: Calculating the perfect match: an efficient and accurate approach for robot self-localization. In: Bredenfeld, A., Jacoff, A., Noda, I., Takahashi, Y. (eds.) RoboCup 2005. LNCS, vol. 4020, pp. 142–153. Springer, Heidelberg (2006). doi:10.1007/11780519_13

9. Library, P.C.: Plane model segmentation documentation (2017). pointclouds.org/documentation/tutorials/planar_segmentation.php. Accessed 10 Feb 2017

10. Maheu, V., Archambault, P.S., Frappier, J., Routhier, F.: Evaluation of the JACO robotic arm: clinico-economic study for powered wheelchair users with upper-extremity disabilities. In: 2011 IEEE International Conference on Rehabilitation Robotics (ICORR), pp. 1–5. IEEE (2011)

11. Miller, A.T., Allen, P.K.: Graspit! a versatile simulator for robotic grasping. IEEE Robot. Autom. Mag. **11**(4), 110–122 (2004)

12. Pinto, A.C.P.: Advanced Mobile Manipulation for Logistics in Hospitals or Laboratories (2016)

13. Quigley, M., Conley, K., Gerkey, B., Faust, J., Foote, T., Leibs, J., Wheeler, R., Ng, A.Y.: ROS: an open-source robot operating system. In: ICRA Workshop on Open Source Software, vol. 3, p. 5 (2009)

14. Rusu, R.B., Cousins, S.: 3D is here: point cloud library (PCL). In: 2011 IEEE International Conference on Robotics and Automation (ICRA), pp. 1–4. IEEE (2011)

15. Sobreira, H., Pinto, M., Moreira, A.P., Costa, P.G., Lima, J.: Robust robot localization based on the perfect match algorithm. In: Moreira, A.P., Matos, A., Veiga, G. (eds.) CONTROLO 2014. LNEE, vol. 321, pp. 607–616. Springer, Cham (2015). doi:10.1007/978-3-319-10380-8_58

16. Sobreira, H., Rocha, L., Costa, C., Lima, J., Costa, P., Moreira, A.P.: 2D cloud template matching-a comparison between iterative closest point and perfect match. In: 2016 International Conference on Autonomous Robot Systems and Competitions (ICARSC), pp. 53–59. IEEE (2016)

17. Tanaka, H., Sumi, Y., Matsumoto, Y.: Assistive robotic arm autonomously bringing a cup to the mouth by face recognition. In: 2010 IEEE Workshop on Advanced Robotics and its Social Impacts (ARSO), pp. 34–39. IEEE (2010)

18. Thrun, S., Burgard, W., Fox, D.: Probabilistic Robotics. Intelligent Robotics and Autonomous Agents. MIT Press, Cambridge (2005)

Feedbot - A Robotic Arm for Autonomous Assisted Feeding

Catarina Silva[1(✉)], Jayakorn Vongkulbhisal[1,2], Manuel Marques[1],
João Paulo Costeira[1], and Manuela Veloso[2]

[1] ISR - IST, Universidade de Lisboa, Lisboa, Portugal
catarina.cruz.csilva@gmail.com, {jvongkul,manuel,jpc}@isr.ist.utl.pt
[2] Carnegie Mellon University, Pittsburgh, PA, USA
mmv@cs.cmu.edu

Abstract. The act of assisted feeding is a challenging task that requires
a good reactive planning strategy to cope with an unpredictable environment. It can be seen as a tracking task, where some end effector must
travel to a moving goal. This work builds upon state of the art algorithms, such as Discriminative Optimization, making use of a Kinect
camera and a modular robotic arm to implement a closed form system
that performs assisted feeding. It presents two different approaches: the
use of a variable rate function for updating the trajectory with information on the moving goal, and the definition of different risk regions that
will shape a safer trajectory.

Keywords: Assistive technology · Discriminative Optimization ·
Robotics

1 Introduction

In the caregiving setting, robots are increasingly being used to assist people with
physical disabilities. This new work paradigm is of particular interest for vital
tasks, such as assisted feeding, which is the act of feeding people who can not do
it by themselves. In these scenarios, assistive robots can provide independence
and improve the quality of life of the individuals.

The great majority of these systems rely on some kind of remote control to
perform the required tasks, such as a standard joystick [1] or even innovative
brain-computer interface technologies [2]. Unlike most of the related work, which
implements open loop systems, this work integrates vision and control techniques
into a closed form system. To tackle the tracking challenge, we use a RGB-D
camera to perceive the 3D world, obtaining a continuous pose estimation of the
person's face through Discriminative Optimization [6], presented in Sect. 2.

For the path planning task, there are many efficient algorithms from
sampling-based planning algorithms to trajectory optimization algorithms. However, in this context, it is not possible to foresee the movement of the human,
which motivates the need for good reactive planning [4,5]. The work builds upon

© Springer International Publishing AG 2017
E. Oliveira et al. (Eds.): EPIA 2017, LNAI 10423, pp. 486–497, 2017.
DOI: 10.1007/978-3-319-65340-2_40

the existence of such reactive approaches, but focuses mainly on the perception and human interaction scope. To follow and approach a moving goal, we make use of a simple trajectory planning algorithm and a modular robotic arm presented in Sect. 3. To avoid jitter at larger distances, we propose a variable tracking rate in Sect. 3.2 that depends on the goal distance. Additionally, we take in consideration the particular task of assisted feeding, that the interaction is performed on a person's face. To prevent possible injury, we define areas with a higher risk, such as the person's eyes, which influences the trajectory in Sect. 3.1.

We present an experimental setup with a Kinect camera and a 5DoF robotic arm built with Hebi modules in Sect. 4. The preliminary results show that the system can accurately track and approach the goal.

2   Vision Based Tracking

The task of assisted feeding translates into the problem of getting the end effector of an arm into the mouth of a person. Hence, the target is not static, but moving in the 3D space over time with an unpredictable motion due to motor impairment. This motivates the need for fast and accurate tracking of the person's head. The problem is modeled as a point cloud registration problem, and solved with the presented Discriminative Optimization [6] method.

2.1   Point Cloud Registration

Given two sets of points $P \in \mathbb{R}^{(3 \times N_P)}$ and $Q \in \mathbb{R}^{(3 \times N_Q)}$, the goal of point cloud registration is to find a rigid transformation $\tau(Q)$, represented by a rotation matrix R and a translation vector T in Eq. (1), that aligns Q to P.

$$\tau(Q) = RQ + T \tag{1}$$

In this work, we define P as the model point cloud of the face we wish to track, and Q_t as the scene point cloud obtained at time step t. Our goal is to compute (R_t, T_t) that aligns a subset of points in the scene Q_t to the model in P.

2.2   Discriminative Optimization

Most methods for solving the point cloud registration problem rely on the minimization of a cost function, such as the Iterative Closest Point (ICP) [12] and Robust Point Matching [13]. It is well-known that these algorithms are prone to local minima under noise and outliers, which could lead to incorrect registration.

On the other hand, Discriminative Optimization (DO) [6] learns search directions from training data without relying on a cost function. It finds a sequence of updates in the search space that lead to stationary points corresponding to the desired solutions. By learning from data with noise, outliers, and occlusion, DO was shown to be more robust against these perturbations which are typically present in real scenarios.

DO operates by encoding the point clouds using a function $h : \mathbb{R}^d \times R^{N_Q} \rightarrow \mathbb{R}^{2N_P}$ into a feature vector (see [6] for the form of h), then mapping the feature to an update vector using a linear map $D_k \in \mathbb{R}^{(p \times f)}$, where $k = 1, 2, \ldots$ denotes the update step. Let $x_k \in R^d$ denotes the estimate at step k in search space, which in this case is the Lie algebra representing 3D rigid transformation ($d = 6$). The update step of DO can be expressed by Eq. (2).

$$\boldsymbol{x}_k = \boldsymbol{x}_{k-1} - D_k h(\boldsymbol{x}_{k-1}; Q_t) \tag{2}$$

Here, x_0 is set to identity transformation. The Sequence of Update Maps (SUM) $\{D_k\}_k$ is learned from training data. Starting from an initial estimate x_0, the learned SUM is used to update x_k to obtain the goal transformation x_*.

Training. Given a training set $\{(\boldsymbol{x}_0^{(i)}, \boldsymbol{x}_*^{(i)}, Q^{(i)})\}_{i=1}^N$, where $\boldsymbol{x}_0^{(i)}$ is the initial parameter, $\boldsymbol{x}_*^{(i)}$ ground truth parameters, and $Q^{(i)}$ the scene point cloud of training instance i, DO learns the SUM $\{D_k\}_k$ by sequentially applying the ridge regression in Eq. (3) where λ is a hyper-parameter.

$$D_{k+1} = \arg\min_{\tilde{D}} \frac{1}{N} \sum_{i=1}^N ||\boldsymbol{x}_*^{(i)} - \boldsymbol{x}_k^{(i)} + \tilde{D}h(\boldsymbol{x}_k^{(i)}; Q^{(i)})||^2 + \frac{\lambda}{2}||\tilde{D}||_F^2 \tag{3}$$

To learn the SUM, we require a training set of scene point clouds $Q^{(i)}$ as the face model under different poses $(R^{(i)}, T^{(i)})$ and perturbations. Instead of manually labeling several images, we generate a synthetic training dataset as shown in Fig. 1. The steps are as follows:

1. Take a frame with a "good" view of the face;
2. Detect the face using a regular face classifier;
3. Extract the depth point cloud corresponding to the obtained RGB area;
4. Apply clustering to the point cloud and keep larger cluster as the model P;
5. Sub-sample and normalize the point cloud to fit a $(1 \times 1 \times 1)$ box - we define S as the matrix that represents this transformation;
6. Apply randomly generated transformations $\{(R^{(i)}, T^{(i)})\}_{i=1}^N$ to P;
7. Add noise, outliers, and occlusion to obtain $Q^{(i)}$.

Inference. One challenge of DO happens when the scene Q has a large discrepancy from the model P, which may cause x_k to not converge to the desired estimate. However, in a tracking application, we have access to the previous pose, and we can use it to simplify the problem. Taking the previous estimates, R_{t-1}, T_{t-1} we can transform the scene as shown in Eq. (4).

$$\widetilde{Q_t} = R_{t-1}Q_t + T_{t-1} \tag{4}$$

Note that, in practice, since in training we normalized the model with the transformation S, we must also apply S to Q_t.

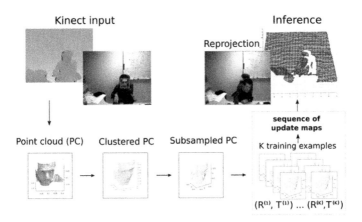

Fig. 1. DO training for the face tracking problem. The estimated pose is used to reproject the position and verify the pose.

With an adequate frame-rate for real-time applications, the transformed scene $\widetilde{Q}_t$ should be much closer to the model P, and thus the method should converge to the correct pose. The newly obtained estimates, $\widetilde{R}$ and $\widetilde{T}$, are then used to compute the transformation at time t by Eq. (5).

$$R_t = \widetilde{R}R_{t-1}, \quad T_t = \widetilde{R}T_{t-1} + \widetilde{T} \tag{5}$$

Once we obtain (R_t, T_t) that aligns Q to P, we inverse it to obtain (R', T') that aligns P to Q and provides the head pose in the camera coordinate system.

Initialization. In the previous sections, we take advantage of the sequential motion to provide accurate pose estimation in each frame. However, there is no previous estimate for the first frame, and this might lead to an initial error that propagates into the subsequent frames. Moreover, the inference can take a longer time to converge if the initial pose differs substantially from the correct pose.

To overcome this issue, we provide an initial estimate by replicating part of the training process. We obtain the first point cloud Q_1 as follows:

1. Detect the face using a regular face classifier;
2. Extract the depth point cloud corresponding to the obtained RGB area;
3. Subsample and normalize the point cloud to fit a $(1 \times 1 \times 1)$ box.

We then estimated the initial translation between the model P and Q_1, $T_0 = p_c - q_{1c}$, where p_c and q_{1c} are the centroids of P and Q_1 respectively. This estimate is used to initialize the registration in Eq. (4), where we use $R_0 = \mathbb{I}_3$ as the initial rotation. This allows DO to obtain to the correct pose without loss of efficiency. Figures 2a and b illustrate the advantages of the procedure.

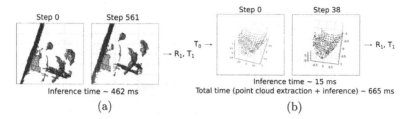

Inference time ~ 462 ms

(a)

Inference time ~ 15 ms
Total time (point cloud extraction + inference) ~ 665 ms

(b)

Fig. 2. Pose estimation inference: (a) Without initial estimate: it takes a large number of steps, and does not converge to the correct pose. (b) With initial estimate: the process converges to the correct pose in fewer steps

2.3   Goal Specification

The training procedure of the DO generates a 3D face model. It is then necessary to define the specific point that is to be used as goal for the end effector, as well as other points that might be of interest. These are selected manually in the tests. It is also possible to obtain a governing plane by applying Principal Component Analysis (PCA) on the template, as shown in Fig. 3. This can be used in the future to define a generic computation of the goal point, and it is also important to define the end effector orientation, in particular if the setup uses an arm with 6 DoF or more.

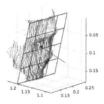

Fig. 3. Point cloud of the face model with a governing plane obtained with PCA. The normal vector of the plane is shown starting from the template centroid

3   Trajectory Planning and Control

The present work focuses on showing that the closed form system tracks and approaches the goal precisely with safe trajectories. To fulfill this purpose, a simple but fast trajectory generation approach is chosen that allows us to test some relevant features:

- Verify accuracy of closed form implementation on reaching the goal;
- Compare trajectories that update the tracking information with a fixed rate against a variable rate;
- Compare trajectories that approach the goal while considering risk areas against direct trajectories.

3.1   Trajectory Planning

We start by defining a trajectory in the 3D cartesian space, applying potential field methods to represent the goal as an attractive potential (a conical potential, in particular), and considered obstacles as repulsive potentials. Let $q = [x, y, z]$ be a point in a global reference frame, where the trajectories will be defined. Taking $q_{goal}^i = [x_{goal}^i, y_{goal}^i, z_{goal}^i]$ as the moving goal position at time i, and $q_{obs_k}^i = [x_{obs_k}^i, y_{obs_k}^i, z_{obs_k}^i]$ the position of obstacle k at time step i, then Eqs. (6) and (7) define the attractive and repulsive potentials acting over a point q in the global reference frame at time step i, where $D(q_1, q_2)$ is a distance function in space, such as the Euclidean Distance.

$$F_{att}^i = \frac{\epsilon_A}{D(q, q_{goal}^i)}(q_{goal}^i - q) \tag{6}$$

$$F_{rep_k}^i = \begin{cases} \epsilon_R(\frac{1}{D^*} - \frac{1}{D(q,q_{obs_k}^i)})\frac{1}{D^2(q,q_{obs_k}^i)}\Delta D(q, q_{obs_k}^i) & , if\, D(q, q_{obs_k}^i) \leq D^* \\ 0 & , if\, D(q, q_{obs_k}^i) > D^* \end{cases}$$

$$with \;\; \Delta D(q, q_{obs_k}^i) = \frac{(q - q_{obs_k}^i)}{D(q, q_{obs_k}^i)} \tag{7}$$

ϵ_A and ϵ_R are weights that factor in the attractive and repulsive components of the potential, respectively, and D^* is the range of obstacle influence. Combining the generated fields we get a vector that represents the direction in which the trajectory should move. A sequence of waypoints $\boldsymbol{P}^1, \boldsymbol{P}^2, \dots, \boldsymbol{P}^N$ is generated by using a fixed step. From these waypoints, the corresponding joint configurations $\boldsymbol{\Phi}^1, \boldsymbol{\Phi}^2, \dots, \boldsymbol{\Phi}^N$ are computed by applying a numerical optimization method for the inverse kinematics provided by the Hebi API. This method minimizes the angle displacement between the previous and goal configurations (see Sect. 4.1).

The motion throughout the trajectory waypoints should also prefer smoothness. Thus, to travel between waypoints, we apply a minimum jerk trajectory [8] by imposing smoothness conditions at each waypoint and a given set of intervals $\Delta t_1, \Delta t_2, \dots, \Delta t_N$. The method will output a trajectory function for each chunk i and each degree of freedom k:

$$T_i^k = a_0 + a_1 t + a_2 t^2 + a_3 t^3 + a_4 t^4 + a_5 t^5 \tag{8}$$

where the coefficients can be obtained by solving the linear system that results from the boundary conditions on position, velocity and, acceleration.

These trajectories are, however, optimized separately, and rely on the boundary conditions and on the intervals to be known. For this purpose, the three cubic method [7] was used, since it not only allows computing the minimum required time, taking into account the dynamic constraints of the system–joint velocity and acceleration limits–, but also provides boundary conditions for each waypoint through a simple cubic spline interpolation. The method computes two minimum intervals for each joint, one limited by the velocity constraint and the other by the acceleration constraint.

$$
\begin{cases}
\Delta T^k_{v_{min}} = 1.6 \frac{|q^k_1 - q^k_0|}{\dot{q}^k_{max}} & \text{(velocity constraint)} \\
\Delta T^k_{a_{min}} = \sqrt{6.4 \frac{|q^k_1 - q^k_0|}{\ddot{q}^k_{max}}} & \text{(acceleration constraint)}
\end{cases}
\tag{9}
$$

The interval ΔT^i is obtained by taking the maximum for all degrees of freedom of $\Delta T^k_{v_{min}}$ and $\Delta T^k_{a_{min}}$. This assures no dynamic constraint is violated for any joint. We then use the defined intervals to perform a cubic spline interpolation that returns a global trajectory, from which each waypoint boundary conditions will be computed.

Note that the global trajectory could be used to perform the desired path. However, experimental results showed that the minimum jerk trajectory, although using the interpolated values as boundary conditions, followed smoother paths. The procedure can be summarized in the following steps:

1. Generate waypoints in 3D space with potential field methods;
2. Use inverse kinematics to compute waypoints in configuration space;
3. Calculate minimum time interval for each chunk;
4. Use spline interpolation to get boundary conditions;
5. Compute minimum jerk trajectory between each pair of waypoints.

3.2   Update Rate

For this application, we propose that there is a smaller necessity for updating rapidly the trajectory while distance to the goal is large (obstacle collision should always be checked as often as possible). Thus, we propose a variable update rate as a simple linear function with saturation for both very small and very large distances, defined as ΔT_u in Eq. (10). The saturation values are set to T_u^- for distances lower than d^-, and T_u^+ for those higher than d^+.

$$
\Delta T_u = \begin{cases}
T_u^- & , if \, d < d^- \\
\frac{T_u^+ - T_u^-}{d^+ - d^-}(d - d^-) + T_u^- & , if \, d^- \le d \le d^+ \\
T_u^+ & , if \, d > d^+
\end{cases}
\tag{10}
$$

4   Implementation

4.1   Hebi Arm

To test the closed form system, we chose a robotic arm composed of Hebi modules [10], shown in Fig. 4. There are two types of modules: revolution joints and hard links. In this experimental setup, the arm has 5 DoFs. The modules can be controlled through an API that is able to receive feedback from the module's state and to send commands with the desired positions, velocities and torques of each joint.

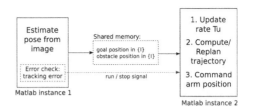

Fig. 5. Current Implementation

Fig. 4. Hebi robotic arm
with 5 DoFs

In testing, we used a control scheme with three summed parallel PIDs, one
for each command (position, velocity, and torque).

At each time step t_i, a command is sent with the desired position and a
gravity compensating torque, computed with the API, to each joint. This allows
an accurate actuation of the sent commands.

All measures of the arm are given with respect to a reference frame defined
by its first joint. Throughout the work, this reference frame is used as a global
reference frame ($\{I\}$).

4.2 Kinect

To perform the template tracking and pose extraction with DO, the implementation is done with a Kinect 360. Any measure provided by the template tracking
algorithm is retrieved in the camera's reference frame ($\{C\}$). These have to be
transformed into the global reference frame to be fed to the trajectory planner.
Hence, every time the camera is re-positioned, it is necessary to find the correct
transformation from $\{C\}$ to $\{I\}$.

The process used is the following: a board of aruco markers [9], with an associated reference frame $\{A\}$, is placed in a known location in the global reference
frame, transformation we define by $(R_{\{A\}}^{\{I\}}, T_{\{A\}}^{\{I\}})$. Then, using the visual markers' library we obtain $(R_{\{C\}}^{\{A\}}, T_{\{C\}}^{\{A\}})$ from $\{C\}$ to $\{A\}$. The final transformation
is given by the expression in (11). The use of aruco markers is limited only to
the calibration process. A different method for calibration can be used, making
the markers obsolete.

$$\boldsymbol{x}_{\{I\}} = R\,\boldsymbol{x}_{\{I\}} + T,\; with \quad \begin{cases} R = R_{\{A\}}^{\{I\}} R_{\{C\}}^{\{A\}} R_i \\ T = R_{\{A\}}^{\{I\}} R_{\{C\}}^{\{A\}} T_i + R_{\{A\}}^{\{I\}} T_{\{C\}}^{\{A\}} + T_{\{A\}}^{\{I\}} \end{cases} \tag{11}$$

4.3 Program Flow

The logic described in the previous sections is implemented in MATLAB^{TM},
since both the Hebi API and the DO base code are provided already in this

language. The program flow is shown in Fig. 5, where the tracking information is shared between instances. This implementation allows testing the desired characteristics of the system, but it is missing a better setup to test for the speed and re-planning performance. For this purpose we suggest a parallel implementation of steps 1, 2, and 3 in Fig. 5. The performance on this setup can be taken as a baseline for future approaches. To retrieve the Kinect input, the current implementation relies on libfreenect2 [11], an open source cross-platform driver for Kinect. The arm control is performed through the already mentioned Hebi API [10].

5   Results

This section presents an overview of the tests performed with the closed form implementation. To substitute the person's face, a styrofoam head was used. Both the mouth and the eyes location was selected manually. Starting from some position, the head was moved in all space directions, simulating a person's movement. A first set of tests was performed where the calibration from the camera reference frame to the global reference frame was obtained from a single aruco marker (Calib. 1), and a second set of tests used a planar board with 2×2 arucos (Calib. 1).

Table 1. General results for the closed form system

	Total	Inside	Outside	Success	Average norm error (m)
Calib. 1	77	36	41	47 %	.012
Calib. 2	69	62	7	90 %	.009

The results are shown in Table 1, where the average error of the end effector measured in the global frame is also presented. The error is computed from the commanded position and the actual position, obtained with a forward kinematics computation. We considered the end effector is inside the desired region if it is less than 1 cm away from the goal point.

The results emphasize the importance of calibrating properly the reference frames. In fact, with a proper calibration, the great majority of all tests were successful and reached the desired location. In particular, the tests that did not reached the desired region had a visibly smaller error than with the previous calibration. It is still necessary to improve the calibration process to verify these preliminary results. This supports the claim that the closed form system fulfills its goal.

5.1   Eyes as Risk Area

To test the impact of the use of the eye region as a risk area two sets of tests were performed: one where no obstacle is given to the trajectory generator, and one where a point representing each eye is used to compute the trajectory.

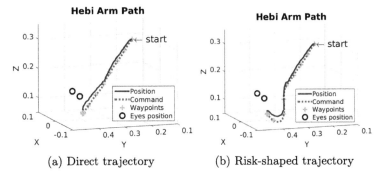

(a) Direct trajectory   (b) Risk-shaped trajectory

Fig. 6. Testing eyes as a risk area: the graphs show the desired and actual positions, the waypoints and the eyes' positions

Figures 6a and b show the resulting trajectories for a test of each of the described sets, respectively. It is visible that the trajectory's shape is deformed when the eyes are specified as a risk area, providing a safer path to the person's mouth.

5.2 Variable Rate vs. Fixed Rate

To test the impact of the proposed update rate function three sets of tests were performed: the first two sets used a fixed trajectory update rate, 0.5 s and 1 s, and the third set used the variable update rate function presented in equation (10) with $T_u^+ = 5\,\text{s}$, $T_u^- = 0.5\,\text{s}$, $d_u^+ = 1\,\text{m}$ and $d_u^- = 0.05\,\text{m}$. In both tests the styrofoam head was moving along the x axis and the approximation is done along the y and z axis.

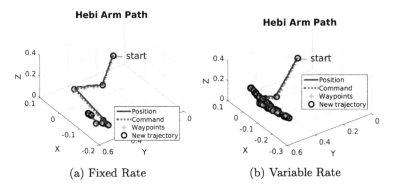

(a) Fixed Rate   (b) Variable Rate

Fig. 7. Testing rate functions: the graphs show the desired and actual positions, the followed waypoints and points where a new trajectory was computed

Figures 7a and b show the obtained trajectories for a test of the second set ($T_u = 1\,\text{s}$) and the third set (variable T_u), respectively. The trajectory with the variable rate only bends when the end effector is closer to the region where the styrofoam head was moving. This is desirable to the focused task, since it avoids unnecessary jitter caused by an unpredictable goal.

6   Conclusion

The work presents a closed form implementation of a visual servoed robotic arm to perform the task of assisted feeding. Using a simple trajectory planning approach that receives information from the environment through a Kinect camera, the preliminary results show that the end effector can be commanded to a moving goal while considering safety and smoothness criteria.

Two proposed methods to tackle the tracking and approximation problems entailed were presented. The results show that considering regions of risk in the interaction with an individual, the eyes in this particular case, shapes the trajectories in a way that increases safety. Moreover, using a variable update rate may avoid unnecessary jitter when dealing with an unpredictable target. Note that it is important to parametrize correctly all variables so the desired behavior is achieved but not overdone.

In the future, it is relevant to test the efficiency of the system components. For this purpose, a possible addition is to apply object detection with methods similar to [3], since the system already retrieves the necessary input, and to detail the behavior of the update function with respect to the goal and to the obstacles.

An important improvement to the system is the creation of automatic methods to calibrate the reference frames reliably and to define the goal and risk areas in a coherent manner between similar models. Also, since part of the captured environment is occupied by the robotic arm, an improvement to the work would be to encourage trajectories that minimize occlusion.

Lastly, a subsequent improvement to this system would be to add motion prediction techniques such as [14] to improve the response of the trajectory generation and, consequently, the system's efficiency in the task.

Acknowledgements. This work benefited greatly from professor Howie Choset's support, who provided access to the Hebi Modules used in this work. We also thank our colleagues from the biorobotics lab at CMU who provided valuable insights and expertise on these modules. This research was supported in part by Fundação para a Ciencia e a Tecnologia [UID/EEA/50009/2013]. Manuel Marques is partially supported by FCT project [IF/00879/2012].

References

1. Boucher, F.: From need to innovation [industrial activities]. IEEE Robot. Autom. Mag. **22**(3), 18–19 (2015)
2. Meng, J., et al.: Noninvasive electroencephalogram based control of a robotic arm for reach and grasp tasks. Sci. Rep. **6** (2016)

3. Fabrizio, F., De Luca, A.: Real-time computation of distance to dynamic obstacles with multiple depth sensors. IEEE Robot. Autom. Lett. **2**(1), 56–63 (2017)
4. Yoshida, E., Yokoi, K., Gergondet, P.: Online replanning for reactive robot motion: practical aspects. In: IEEE/RSJ IROS, pp. 5927–5933 (2010)
5. Kunz, T., Reiser, U., Stilman, M., Verl, A.: Real-time path planning for a robot arm in changing environments. In: IEEE/RSJ IROS, pp. 5906–5911 (2010)
6. Vongkulbhisal, J., De la Torre, F., Costeira, J.P.: Discriminative optimization: theory and applications to point cloud registration. In: IEEE CVPR (2017)
7. Tondu, B., Bazaz, S.A.: The three-cubic method: an optimal online robot joint trajectory generator under velocity, acceleration, and wandering constraints. Int. J. Robot. Res. **18**(9), 893–901 (1999)
8. Flash, T., Hogan, N.: The coordination of arm movements: an experimentally confirmed mathematical model. J. Neurosci. **5**(7), 1688–1703 (1985)
9. Garrido-Jurado, S., Muñoz-Salinas, R., Madrid-Cuevas, F.J., Marín-Jiménez, M.J.: Automatic generation and detection of highly reliable fiducial markers under occlusion. Pattern Recogn. **47**(6), 2280–2292 (2014)
10. Hebi API. http://hebirobotics.com/matlab/. Accessed 16 Mar 2017
11. Xiang, L., et al.: libfreenect2: Release 0.2 (2016). https://doi.org/10.5281/zenodo.50641
12. Besl, P.J., McKay, N.D.: A method for registration of 3-D shapes. IEEE Trans. Pattern Anal. Mach. Intell. **14**(2), 239–256 (1992)
13. Gold, S., Rangarajan, A., Lu, C., Mjolsness, E.: New algorithms for 2D and 3D point matching: pose estimation and correspondence. Pattern Recogn. **31**, 957–964 (1997)
14. Pérez-D'Arpino, C., Shah, J.A.: Fast target prediction of human reaching motion for cooperative human-robot manipulation tasks using time series classification. In: IEEE ICRA, pp. 6175–6182 (2015)

Improving and Benchmarking Motion Planning for a Mobile Manipulator Operating in Unstructured Environments

Andrea Tudico[1]($\boxtimes$), Nuno Lau[2], Eurico Pedrosa[2], Filipe Amaral[2], Claudio Mazzotti[1], and Marco Carricato[1]

[1] Department of Industrial Engineering, DIN, University of Bologna, Bologna, Italy
tudico.andrea@gmail.com, {claudio.mazzotti4,marco.carricato}@unibo.it
[2] Department of Electronics, Telecommunications and Informatics, IEETA, University of Aveiro, Aveiro, Portugal
{nunolau,efp,f.amaral}@ua.pt

Abstract. This paper presents the use, adaptation and benchmarking of motion planning tools that will be integrated with the KUKA KMR iiwa mobile robot. The motion planning tools are integrated in the robotic agent presented in [1]. The adaptation consists on algorithms developed to increase the robustness and the efficiency to solve the motion planning problems. These algorithms combine existing motion planners with a trajectory filter developed in this work. Finally, the benchmarking of different motion planners is presented. Three motion planning tasks with a growing level of complexity are taken in consideration for the tests in a simulation environment. The motion planners that provided the best results were RRTConnect for the two less complex tasks and PRM* for the most difficult task.

1 Introduction

Manufacturing systems that are designed for massive customizable production need productivity but also flexibility. In that context there is the need of new automation and robotics systems with artificial intelligence. Typically, industrial robots are used for repetitive tasks in a fixed working cell and the entire system is hardly reconfigurable. On the contrary, mobile robots equipped with lightweight robotic arms and sensors can work in an unstructured environment cooperating safely with humans and can be reprogrammed to perform different manipulation tasks, such as handling and transportation of objects and assembly operations.

The scope of this work is to solve the motion planning problem for the robotic arm of a mobile robot working in a unstructured environment integrating the motion planning instruments with the artificial intelligence of the robot and with the robot interface provided by the constructor.

The robot that is used in the project is based on the KUKA KMR iiwa (Fig. 1), that is a commercial mobile robot with a omnidirectional base. It is equipped with laser sensors and ultrasound sensors to detect obstacles, navigate

E. Oliveira et al. (Eds.): EPIA 2017, LNAI 10423, pp. 498–509, 2017.
DOI: 10.1007/978-3-319-65340-2_41

in the work space and localise the robot in the environment. The KUKA LBR iiwa is mounted on top of the base, it is a lightweight robotic arm suitable to work in contact with humans or to cooperate with them. The KMR is customized adding two stereo cameras, one mounted on the end-effector and one mounted on a pan-tilt mechanism. An overview of the whole system is reported in Fig. 1.

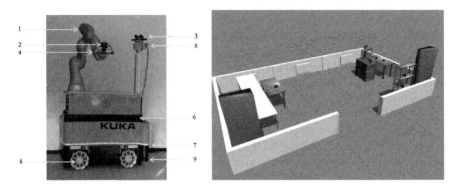

Fig. 1. Respectively KMR iiwa and a simulated environment. 1. Robotic arm (KUKA); 2. 2 RGB cameras fixed on the gripper; 3. 2 RGB cameras mounted on the pan/tilt base; 4. Gripper (SCHUNK); 5. Pan/tilt base (SCHUNK); 6. Ultrasound sensors (x8); 7. Coloured LED belt; 8. 4 Independent wheels; 9. 2 Laser scanners. Picture from [2]

The work space in which the robot has to move is characterized by several obstacles, such as tables and shelf. The robot has to work close to them and interact with objects that are placed on top of them in unknown positions. In most of the cases the object that is manipulated cannot be tilted. An example of a simulated workspace is reported in Fig. 1.

2   Related Work

The motion planning problem for a robotic arm consists in finding a trajectory, i.e. a sequence of joints positions, velocities and accelerations that take the robot from the initial to the final configuration respecting the physical and task restrictions. Thus, it can include the obstacle avoidance problem, i.e. the arm has to avoid collision with objects and with the robot itself during the movement, and it can consider constraints on the position and the orientation of the end-effector during the movement.

Cell decomposition and potential-field-based planners [3] are complete methods, thus if a feasible path exists they will find it, but they need an explicit representation of the geometry of the joints space, thus they have a high computational cost, and become inapplicable when the state space dimension grows.

Another approach is to use sample-based planners that are probabilistic complete. The sample planners are stochastic planners, i.e., for a given input, they can return different outputs, thus they lack repeatability. They are flexible, because they do not need any geometric representation of the joints space. They only need an algorithm for collision checking that can determine if a generic state of the robot is in collision or not with the environment, thus they can be applied to several workspaces and do not need to store a lot of information.

The sample-based planners can be divided in multiple query planners and single query planners. The first builds a roadmap, i.e. a graph of feasible paths that covers all the workspace and that can be used to solve planning problems with different start and final states. An example of this type of planner is the PRM [4]. On the contrary, the single query planners build directly a graph that connects the start and the final state, that can be used only to solve this planning problem. The basic single query algorithms are EST [5] and RRT [6], some of their variants are SBL [7] and SRT [8]. Moreover, there are the optimal version of PRM and RRT called PRM* and RRT* [9]. These planners try to find an optimal path according to a cost function, e.g. the length of the path. Moreover, there are BKPIECE and LBKPIECE [10] that, differently from the basic sample planners, guide the expansion of the tree using a discretization of the state space. LBKPIECE is a version of BKPIECE that uses lazy evaluation [11].

In the case of study, the motion planning problem includes also the obstacle avoidance problem, thus it is necessary to build a map of the environment using the sensor data.

There are several approaches to the mapping problem. The point clouds approach stores a large amount of measurement points, hence it is not memory efficient. The elevation maps [12] and the multi-level surface maps [13] are efficient, but do not represent unmapped areas and do not represent arbitrary 3D environments. Among the volumetric approaches, there is the OctoMap [14].

OctoMap uses a 3D occupancy grid mapping approach, i.e. it represents the occupied space, the free areas and the unknown areas using 3D voxels, i.e. cubic volumes that are obtained subdividing space with a grid.

3   Software Overview

The robot software was developed in ROS [15]. Solving the motion planning problem needs the use of motion planners and mapping function, thus we chose to use the MoveIt! library [16] that includes both of them.

MoveIt! is a ROS library, which allows the user to do the motion planning of his own robot using the open motion planning library (OMPL) [17], i.e. it can generate and execute a trajectory. MoveIt! takes into account the obstacle avoidance constraints, i.e. the planned path avoids collisions between the robot and the environment modelled with Octomap.

MoveIt! provides a graphical user interface (GUI) to interact with the simulated or real robot, to visualise the map of the environment and also to visualise the planned trajectory. The GUI is based on Rviz, that is a ROS tool suitable for general visualization. Fig. 2 presents an example of the graphical output provided in Rviz.

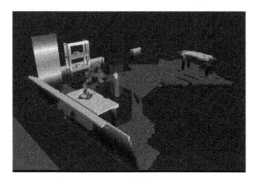

Fig. 2. Example of Rviz graphical output

In our approach we chose to integrate the functions of MoveIt! for planning and mapping in the high level artificial intelligence designed for the robot.

Simulators are useful to test the behaviour of the robot in a virtual reality instead of doing it with the real robot. Gazebo is a 3D robot simulator in complex indoor and outdoor environments. The environment and the hardware parts of the robot, its actuators and sensors are simulated in Gazebo.

4   Description of the Task

The SLC's task was performed at round A of the stage II of Challenge 2 of European Robotics Challenges project [18]. It consists in moving the robot inside an industrial-like environment to pick-up 5 SLCs from a table or a shelf and place them in a designated area of one of the tables. SLCs are small open boxes with various objects inside.

The main task can be subdivided in several sub-tasks that are solved with skills, i.e. ROS services that are called in the main program. The main skills are: move the platform from the current pose to the requested pose, move the arm from the current pose to the requested pose, pick-up an object from a table in the requested position, pick up an object from a shelf, place an object on a table, detect an object and extract his current pose using the stereo cameras information. The architecture of the robotic agent is the one presented in [1].

In the move-arm skill, in case there is no SLC attached to the gripper, the trajectory of the arm should be fast and free from collision, if there is a SLC attached to the gripper, the end-effector has to be maintained in a certain orientation along the planned path so that the content of the SLC does not fall down. In the skill that allows an object to be picked from a shelf, the arm has to move preventing itself or the SLC from impacting the shelf; this is a demanding task because the obstacles are very close.

5   Motion Planning Problem Resolution

There are two approaches to the motion planning problem: the first consists in finding the geometric path, i.e. a sequence of joint positions, and then a posteriori performing the time-parametrization; the second consists in finding directly the trajectory. In the case of study, the first approach is used because the challenge host provides a robot interface with several built-in functions to move the arm. The one that is used moves the arm through a geometric path that is given as an input, and the time-parametrization of the path is performed by the function.

Movelt! is used inside the skills to plan all movements. It generates a sequence of joint values that are given as inputs to the *move joint path* command of the robot interface that executes the trajectory. The skills that were chosen to implement and test our approach to the motion planning problem are the following:

- **Move Arm:** In this skill Movelt! is used to plan both with and without path constrains; different planners are chosen to solve the two cases. In the first case an algorithm was developed to increase the robustness of the motion planning.
- **Pick-up an object:** In this skill Movelt! is used to solve the motion planning problem and to insert a virtual box in the planning scene. Such a box allows the presence of the SLC attached to the end-effector to be considered in the motion planning.
- **Pick-up an object from a shelf:** In this skill Movelt! is used for both free and constrained planning.

5.1   Move-Arm

The *move_arm* skill is called to move the arm from the current pose to a target pose that is specified in the request that is sent by the main solver. The motion planning is done in different ways depending on if the SLC is attached to end-effector or not.

If the SLC is not attached to the arm, the motion planning problem is solved using Movelt! with the chosen sample planner. Often, in these cases, only one call of the motion planner is needed.

When a SLC is attached to the end-effector, path constraints are considered in the motion planning, i.e. the SLC has to be maintained in the same orientation that it has when it was grasped as explained in Sect. 4, with absolute tolerances for the rotation around the X, Y and Z axes equal to respectively, 0.5 rad, 0.5 rad and 2π rad. If the planning request includes orientation constrains, the solution provided by Movelt! is sometimes unfeasible, i.e. the planned path presents discontinuities in the joint values, that depend on the failure of the Inverse Kinematics solver. Thus Algorithm 1 was implemented to increase the robustness of the motion planning. The algorithm re-plans until the planning succeeds and then applies a filter to the planned path. The filter excludes the partial path that starts at a point of the path that correspond to discontinuities, i.e. the

---

Algorithm 1. Motion planning algorithm for constrained problems

---

Input: Current_state, Goal_state and Path_constrains;
Output: Solution_path;

---

while PLAN is not successful **do**
    Planned_path = PLAN(Current_state as the Start_state, Goal_state,
    Path_constrains);
end while
Filtered_path = PATH_FILTER(Planned_path);
Append the Filtered_path to the Solution_path;
while The Solution_path doesn't reach the Goal_state **do**
    while PLAN is not successful **do**
        Planned_path_2 = PLAN(last point of the Filtered_path as Start_state,
        Goal_state, Path_constraints);
    end while
    Filtered_path_2 = PATH_FILTER(Planned_path_2);
    Append the Filtered_path_2 to the Solution_path;
end while

---

difference between at least one of the joints values of the current point and the corresponding values of the previous point is over a discontinuity threshold that is considered acceptable. The output of the filter could be a path that doesn't reach the goal state, so in this case another plan is needed to complete the path.

The path filter eliminates from the output path of MoveIt! discontinuities and also, sets a minimum resolution for the path, called resolution threshold, discarding points that are too close. The path filter is presented in Algorithm 2. The functions that are called in the algorithm are:

- CONTINUITY_CHECK: Returns true if all the differences between the joint values of the current point and the corresponding joints values of the last point that was added to the output are below the discontinuity threshold.
- RESOLUTION_CHECK: Returns true if at least one of the differences between the joints values of the current point and the corresponding joint values of the last point that was added to the output is over the resolution threshold.

5.2   Pick-Up an Object

The *pick_object* skill is called to pick up a SLC from a table, in this skill MoveIt! is used to plan the movements that bring the arm over the SLC, then the SLC is approached with a vertical movement and finally it is vertically lifted and stopped a short distance over the table. When the skill is called, a virtual box that overlaps the SLC is inserted in the planning scene. Then, when the gripper grasps the SLC, the virtual object is attached to the end-effector and it is considered in the next motion planning performed by MoveIt!, so that the SLC does not hit the obstacles or the robot itself during the movement.

Algorithm 2. PATH FILTER

Input: Path, Discontinuity_threshold, Resolution_threshold;
Output: Filtered_path without discontinuities and without too close points;

---

for all Points of the Path **do**
   if The Point is not the first of the Path **then**
      if CONTINUITY_CHECK(Point, Filtered_path) **then**
         if RESOLUTION_CHECK(Point, Filtered_path) **then**
            Add the Point to the Filtered_path;
         end if
      end if
   else
      Add the Point to the output;
   end if
end for

5.3 Pick-Up an Object from a Shelf

The *pick_object_shelf* skill is called to pick up a SLC from a shelf. In this skill MoveIt! is used to plan the movements that bring the end-effector in the line of view of the SLC. In these cases, planning is performed with a sample planner, then the Cartesian planner is used to plan the necessary linear movement that bring the arm in the grasping pose. Finally, the SLC is grasped and the arm returns with a linear movement to the previous pose. The Cartesian planner generates a sequence of points in the workspace that are a discrete representation of the line segment that connects the start and the goal states. By using Inverse Kinematics, these points are transformed in the joint space. A virtual box that overlaps the SLC is inserted in the planning scene when the skill is called, then, when the gripper grasps the SLC the virtual object is attached to the end-effector.

6 Benchmarking of Motion Planners

This section presents the results of the motion planning by using our algorithms in a sample of three subtasks using different sample based motion planners taken from the OMPL library inside MoveIt! namely LBKPIECE, BKPIECE, PRM, EST, SBL, RRTConnect, PRM* and RRT*. The scope is to find the motion planners that are suitable to use inside our algorithms.

A sample of three subtasks with a growing level of difficulty is chosen to compare several settings (Fig. 3).

- The first motion planning problem is the easiest one because there are neither obstacles between the start and the final configuration nor path constraints to be considered.

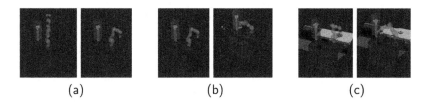

(a)   (b)   (c)

Fig. 3. Start and finish configurations of low, medium and high difficulty subtasks

– The second motion planning problem is of medium difficulty, because there are obstacles between the start and the final configuration, but there are no path constraints to be considered. The obstacle is the pan-tilt camera with also a virtual box that simulates the presence in the real robot of an area around the pan-tilt that cannot be reached by the arm to avoid that the camera is accidentally hit.
– The third motion planning problem is of high difficulty because there are obstacles between the start and the final configuration, there are path constraints to be considered and there is virtual box attached to the end-effector. The obstacle is the pan-tilt camera with the virtual box. The path constraints are on the orientation of the end-effector as explained in Sect. 5.1.

The three subtasks are chosen as different as possible to have a sample that covers all possible planning problems. For each subtask and setting, a sample of eight simulations is considered. The performance of the examined setting is assessed by the following metrics:

– **Total Planning Time:** The total time that is spent to solve the motion planning problem.
– **Length of the path:** Sum of the lengths of the line segments that connect the end-effector positions that correspond to the points of the planned path; this is an estimation of the length of the executed path.
– **Joints values variation:** The value of the index is obtained by summing the absolute values of the variations of the joint values from the first to the second point of the planned path, from the second to the third and continuing in the same way for all the points of the path.
– **Number of calls of the planner:** Number of times that the motion planner is called to solve the same motion planning problem. This index includes both the cases in which the planner is called again because the planning fails and the cases in which the planner is called again because after the filter application the path results incomplete.
– **Number of path points:** Number of points of the output path, each point is a set of joints values.

The planning is considered unsuccessful if the solution is not found after 60 s. The third metric provides an indirect raw measure of the time and energy needed to execute a movement.

Differently from all other planners, the optimal planners return an optimized solution by using the entire planning time specified in the input, so a preliminary analysis is conducted to find the input planning time for each planner. The lowest planning time that allows the planners to succeed are: 0.2 s for the PRM* and 1.75 s for the RRT*. The lowest planning time was found with an iterative method with a tolerance of 0.1 s. The PRM* is tested with a planning time of 0.2 s and 0.4 s, the RRT* is tested only with a planning time of 1.75 s.

The motion planning results using the different motion planners in the three subtasks are reported respectively in Tables 1, 2 and 3, in terms of mean and standard deviation throughout eight simulations.

Table 1. Results in terms of mean and standard deviation of eight simulations using the LBKPIECE, BKPIECE, PRM, EST, SBL, RRTConnect, PRM* and RRT* motion planners in the low-difficulty task

Planner	Success	Time (s)	Path length (m)	Joints variations (rad)	Num. of replans	Num. of points
LBKPIECE	100%	11.94 ± 3.44	1.27 ± 0.05	7.73 ± 3.72	1	14.62 ± 5.04
BKPIECE	100%	8.43 ± 2.96	1.43 ± 0.28	8.074 ± 4.01	1	13.5 ± 3.11
PRM	100%	0.56 ± 0.10	1.28 ± 0.06	6.91 ± 3.92	1	12.75 ± 3.01
EST	100%	1.67 ± 1.01	1.27 ± 0.06	7.38 ± 3.86	1	13.62 ± 3.02
SBL	100%	1.47 ± 0.74	1.33 ± 0.07	7.32 ± 4.46	1	13.25 ± 3.84
RRTConnect	100%	0.16 ± 0.03	1.32 ± 0.11	6.19 ± 3.94	1	12.25 ± 3.11
PRM* 0.2 s	100%	0.39 ± 0.10	1.30 ± 0.06	6.96 ± 3.92	1	12.75 ± 2.96
PRM* 0.4 s	100%	0.77 ± 0.09	1.26 ± 0.06	8.08 ± 3.96	1	13.75 ± 3.11
RRT* 1.75 s	75%	1.70 ± 0.04	1.54 ± 0.31	7.45 ± 4.60	1	16.33 ± 10.09

Table 2. Results in terms of mean and standard deviation of eight simulations using the LBKPIECE, BKPIECE, PRM, EST, SBL, RRTConnect, PRM* and RRT* motion planners in the medium-difficulty task

Planner	Success	Time (s)	Path length (m)	Joints variations (rad)	Num. of replans	Num. of points
LBKPIECE	100%	9.26 ± 1.58	0.97 ± 0.04	3.66 ± 1.44	1	11.88 ± 2.03
BKPIECE	100%	10.08 ± 2.75	1.18 ± 0.39	8.33 ± 4.88	1	23.38 ± 12.76
PRM	100%	0.38 ± 0.14	0.97 ± 0.04	3.35 ± 1.47	1	11.50 ± 2.07
EST	100%	2.79 ± 1.49	0.97 ± 0.04	3.57 ± 1.53	1	11.88 ± 2.03
SBL	100%	1.19 ± 0.43	1.06 ± 0.18	5.87 ± 3.98	1	15.50 ± 8.60
RRTConnect	100%	0.17 ± 0.04	1.20 ± 0.57	6.26 ± 3.87	1	15.25 ± 3.66
PRM* 0.2 s	100%	0.44 ± 0.16	1.12 ± 0.40	4.28 ± 1.80	1	13.13 ± 3.09
PRM* 0.4 s	100%	0.72 ± 0.11	0.97 ± 0.04	3.25 ± 1.52	1	11.50 ± 2.07
RRT* 1.75 s	75%	1.69 ± 0.05	0.98 ± 0.04	4.92 ± 2.49	1	14.50 ± 5.51

Table 3. Results in terms of mean and standard deviation of eight simulations using the LBKPIECE, BKPIECE, PRM, EST, SBL, RRTConnect, PRM* and RRT* motion planners in the high-difficulty task

Planner	Success	Time (s)	Path length (m)	Joints variations (rad)	Num. of replans	Num. of points
LBKPIECE	0%					
BKPIECE	37.5%	39.36 ± 15.84	1.16 ± 0.44	18.80 ± 9.65	3.67 ± 0.58	45.33 ± 28.10
PRM	100%	4.97 ± 6.45	1.06 ± 0.28	16.96 ± 4.87	3 ± 2.51	33.25 ± 9.65
EST	87.5%	17.93 ± 16.03	1.07 ± 0.10	17.63 ± 5.93	3.14 ± 2.55	30.86 ± 8.69
SBL	12.5%	20.03	1.46	13.74	1	14
RRTConnect	87.5%	1.45 ± 1.18	0.99 ± 0.07	15.51 ± 6.86	2.14 ± 1.35	34 ± 12.58
PRM* 0.2 s	75%	2.84 ± 2.57	1.32 ± 0.37	15.74 ± 8.46	9.33 ± 6.95	21.67 ± 10.84
PRM* 0.4 s	100%	1.77 ± 1.22	1.11 ± 0.26	13.46 ± 5.83	3.75 ± 2.61	22.13 ± 7.02
RRT* 1.75 s	75%	3.94 ± 0.84	0.93 ± 0.08	12.18 ± 3.08	2.5 ± 0.84	23.5 ± 7.01

6.1   Low Difficulty Subtask Results

In the low-difficulty subtask the main difference between the results of the different motion planners is the planning time, the fastest are the simplest ones, i.e. the RRTConnect and PRM planners. The PRM* algorithm is fast but slower than the previous ones and the solution in terms of quality (length of the path and joint variations) is not better than the others. Moreover, by increasing the planning time, the results in terms of quality do not improve enough to justify the major planning time. The RRT* is the only one that sometimes failed.

6.2   Medium Difficulty Subtask Results

In the medium-difficulty subtask, the results in terms of planning time are very similar to the ones in the low-difficulty subtask, hence the planners seem to deal well with collision restrictions. Differently from the low-difficulty subtask, in this case the different planners have different results in terms of quality. The best are LBKPIECE, PRM, EST and PRM* 0.4 s that have the lowest path lengths and joints variations. They also have the lowest standard deviations for the quality indexes, so that they are the best in terms of repeatability.

6.3   High Difficulty Subtask Results

The presence of path constraints, that is the main difference from the medium-difficulty subtask, significantly increases the complexity of the motion planning problem. In that case, the use of Algorithm 1 and of the path filter is needed because the trajectory planned by MoveIt! results unfeasible by using all the different planners. All planners need more time to find the solution, the planners have to be called more than once to find a path and the results in terms of quality is lower than the other cases. In fact, the joints variations are significantly higher than the ones in the medium-difficulty subtask, with the same start and final configurations. The path constraints reduce the dimension of the state space where the solution of the planning problem has to be found, so that the PRM and the PRM* (which, differently from the other planners, explore the entire state space) are more likely to find a solution. In fact, the PRM and the PRM* are the only ones that succeed in all simulations.

In terms of planning time, the best is RRTConnect, followed by the optimal planners and the PRM. The results of the PRM* improve by increasing the input planning time, because by using a planning time of 0.2 s, it needs to call the planner many times before it finds a solution. The PRM* with a planning time of 0.4 s gives the best results in term of both planning time and quality.

6.4   Discussion

By considering the results in the three subtasks, for the low and the medium difficulty subtasks the RRTConnect is chosen because it is the fastest and quality (length of the path, joints variations) is comparable with the one obtained by the other planners. For the high difficulty subtask, the PRM* with a planning time of 0.4 s gives the best results in terms of success rate and planning time; the quality of the output path is similar for the different planners.

7   Conclusions and Future Work

The developed motion planning tool is fast and robust, thus it can be applied in a real-time application. It is integrated in the artificial intelligence and with the interface of the mobile robot in a flexible way, thus it can be easily reused for a different task and a different robot, by simply changing the high level solver. RRTConnect is the best motion planner in the low and medium difficulty subtasks, whereas PRM* with a planning time of 0.4 s is the best motion planner for the high difficulty subtasks.

There are other motion planners that could be tested in the future to improve the obtained results in terms of quality of the path, planning time and repeatability. The Search-based motion planning (SBPL) solves two problems of the sample based planners. Given a problem, the solution of the planners is always the same for different calls of the solver, which is important when repeatability is necessary. Moreover, many of SBPL planners allow a trade off to be specified between the speed of the algorithm and the optimality of the solution in terms of path length. On the other hand, SBPL can be very slow in case of high dimensional problems. Example of Search-based motion planners are the A* [19] and ARA* [20].

The Stochastic Trajectory Optimization for Motion Planning (STOMP) [21] solves other two problems of the sample-based planners, i.e. it allows to find a smooth and not jerky trajectory and it allows an optimal trajectory to be found considering arbitrary criteria and constraints, such as the motors efforts.

Acknowledgment. This research was supported by European Union's FP7 under EuRoc grant agreement CP-IP 608849.

References

1. Pedrosa, E., Lau, N., Pereira, A., Cunha, B.: A skill-based architecture for pick and place manipulation tasks. In: Pereira, F., Machado, P., Costa, E., Cardoso, A. (eds.) EPIA 2015. LNCS, vol. 9273, pp. 457–468. Springer, Cham (2015). doi:10. 1007/978-3-319-23485-4_45

2. Niewada, V.: Development of an autonomous mobile robot. Final Year Internship Report, M.Sc., Robotics and Science for the Living, Imaging, Strasbourg University (2015)

3. Choset, H., et al.: Principles of Robot Motion: Theory, Algorithms, and Implementations. The MIT Press, Cambridge (2005)

4. Kavraki, L.E., et al.: Probabilistic roadmaps for path planning in high-dimensional configuration spaces. IEEE Trans. Robot. Autom. **12**, 566–580 (1996)

5. Hsu, D., et al.: Path planning in expansive configuration spaces. Int. J. Comput. Geom. Appl. **9**(4–5), 495–512 (1999)

6. Kuffner, J., et al.: RRT-connect: an efficient approach to single-query path planning. In: Proceedings of 2000 IEEE International Conference on Robotics and Automation, pp. 995–1001 (2000)

7. Snchez, G., et al.: A single-query bi-directional probabilistic roadmap planner with lazy collision checking. In: Tenth International Symposium on Robotics Research, pp. 403–417 (2001)

8. Erion, P., et al.: Sampling-based roadmap of trees for parallel motion planning. IEEE Trans. Robot. **21**(4), 597–608 (2005)

9. Karaman, S., et al.: Sampling based algorithms for optimal motion planning. Int. J. Robot. Res. **30**(7), 846–894 (2011)

10. Ucan, I.A., et al.: Kinodynamic motion planning by interior-exterior cell exploration. In: Workshop on the Algorithmic Foundations of Robotics, December 2008

11. Bohlin, R., et al.: Path planning using lazy PRM. In: Proceedings of IEEE International Conference on Robotics and Automation, ICRA 2000, vol. 1. IEEE (2000)

12. Hebert, M., et al.: Terrain mapping for a roving planetary explorer. In: Proceedings of IEEE International Conference on Robotics and Automation (ICRA) (1989)

13. Triebel, R., et al.: Multi-level surface maps for out-door terrain mapping and loop closing. In: Proceedings of IEEE/RSJ International Conference on Intelligent Robots and Systems (IROS) (2006)

14. Hornung, A., et al.: OctoMap: an efficient probabilistic 3D mapping framework based on octrees. Auton. Robot. **34**, 189 (2013). doi:10.1007/s10514-012-9321-0

15. http://www.ros.org/about-ros

16. http://moveit.ros.org/

17. http://ompl.kavrakilab.org/

18. http://www.euroc-project.eu

19. Hart, P.E., et al.: A formal basis for the heuristic determination of minimum cost paths. IEEE Trans. Syst. Sci. Cybern. **4**(2), 100–107 (1968)

20. Likhachev, M., et al.: ARA*: anytime A* with provable bounds on sub-optimality. In: Advances in Neural Information Processing Systems, pp. 767–774 (2003)

21. Kalakrishnan, M., et al.: STOMP: stochastic trajectory optimization for motion planning. In: ICRA 2011, pp. 4569–4574 (2011)

22. Domel, A., et al.: Autonomous pick and place operations in industrial production. In: 2015 12th International Conferece on Ubiquitous Robots and Ambient Intelligence (URAI), p. 356 (2015)

Knowledge Discovery and Business Intelligence

Exploring Resampling with Neighborhood Bias on Imbalanced Regression Problems

Paula Branco[1,2(✉)], Luís Torgo[1,2], and Rita P. Ribeiro[1,2]

[1] LIAAD - INESC TEC, Porto, Portugal
{paula.branco,ltorgo,rpribeiro}@dcc.fc.up.pt
[2] DCC - Faculdade de Ciências, Universidade do Porto, Porto, Portugal

Abstract. Imbalanced domains are an important problem that arises in predictive tasks causing a loss in the performance of the most relevant cases for the user. This problem has been intensively studied for classification problems. Recently it was recognized that imbalanced domains occur in several other contexts and for a diversity of types of tasks. This paper focus on imbalanced regression tasks. Resampling strategies are among the most successful approaches to imbalanced domains. In this work we propose variants of existing resampling strategies that are able to take into account the information regarding the neighborhood of the examples. Instead of performing sampling uniformly, our proposals bias the strategies for reinforcing some regions of the data sets. In an extensive set of experiments we provide evidence of the advantage of introducing a neighborhood bias in the resampling strategies.

1 Introduction

The class imbalance problem is well known and has been thoroughly studied [7,10]. This problem has important real world applications spanning from the medical to the meteorological or financial domains, among many others. In this type of predictive tasks, the goal of obtaining a model is hampered by the conjugation of: (i) the non-uniform preferences of the user; and (ii) the poor representation on the available data of the most important cases.

The study of the problem of imbalanced domains started with classification tasks, and in particular with two class problems. The majority of solutions for this problem is still concentrated in binary classification tasks. More recently, it was shown that the problem of imbalanced domains also arises in several other tasks, namely: regression, data streams or multi-target prediction tasks [3,8].

In this paper, we address the problem of imbalanced domains in regression, to which we will refer as the imbalanced regression problem. In a regression context, the continuous nature of the target variable brings an extra level of difficulty to the problem. Moreover, the definition of the more and less important values of the target variable is not as straightforward as in a classification tasks. We will refer to the less important cases in a data set as the normal cases, while rare/interesting cases will be the most important. To address imbalanced

© Springer International Publishing AG 2017
E. Oliveira et al. (Eds.): EPIA 2017, LNAI 10423, pp. 513–524, 2017.
DOI: 10.1007/978-3-319-65340-2_42

regression problems some proposals for pre-processing the given data set have been made (e.g. [17]). Still, as far as we know, no attempt was made for biasing the new data set taking into consideration the neighborhood of the examples.

The main goal of this paper is to study the impact of introducing a bias both in the generation of new synthetic cases and in the removal of cases considering the type of nearest neighbors (normal or rare) of each case. This bias can be introduced to either favor the "safer" and easier to learn cases (i.e., cases surrounded by cases of the same type), or to reinforce the "frontier" or harder to learn cases (i.e., cases whose nearest neighbors are mainly from a different type).

This paper is organized as follows. In Sect. 2 the problem definition is presented. Section 3 provides an overview of the related work. Our proposals are described in Sect. 4 and the results of an extensive experimental evaluation are discussed in Sect. 5. Finally, Sect. 6 presents the main conclusions.

2   Problem Definition

The problem of imbalanced domains occurs in the context of predictive tasks, where the goal is to obtain a model that approximates an unknown function $Y = f(\mathbf{x})$. To achieve this goal a training set $\mathcal{D} = \{\langle \mathbf{x}_i, y_i \rangle\}_{i=1}^{N}$ with N examples is used. When the target variable Y is continuous we face a regression task and when it is nominal we have a classification task.

Imbalanced regression problems are a particular class of regression tasks. In imbalanced regression the user preferences are not uniform across the target variable domain, i.e., the user assigns more importance to the predictive performance in some ranges of the target variable. Moreover, there is a poor representation of the most relevant ranges in the available training set $\mathcal{D}$. The conjunction of these two factors is the key source of problems, because it causes a performance degradation on the most important cases for the user. The learning algorithms are not able to focus on the most important ranges of the target variable due to the lack of examples in those ranges.

This setting is similar to the class imbalance problem where the most important class is under-represented in the given training set leading to a poor performance in the important class. Typically, when dealing with a class imbalance problem, the user simply states which is the important class without specifically quantifying how much each class is important. This becomes more complicated when dealing with multiclass imbalanced problems. In this case, there can be several important and less important classes and their importance may not be easy to define. The simple consideration of multiclass leads to an increased difficulty when dealing with this problem. Therefore, tackling an imbalanced regression problem implies an increased level of difficulty because the target variable has a potentially infinite number of values.

To address the problem of defining the target variable important ranges the notion of a **relevance function** was proposed by Torgo and Ribeiro [16] and Ribeiro [12]. The **relevance function**, $\phi : \mathcal{Y} \to [0, 1]$, maps the target variable domain into a scale of relevance, where 1 corresponds to the maximal relevance and 0 to the minimum relevance. The task of defining this relevance can be hard in regression problems. Ideally, a domain expert should provide this information. Although being the user responsibility to provide the relevance function, Ribeiro [12] proposed an automatic way for obtaining this information. Function $\phi(y)$ is estimated from the target variable domain distribution assuming that the rare and most extreme cases are the most relevant to the user, which is typically the case.

The relevance function values can be used to determine the sets of normal and rare values. To achieve this the user is required to set a threshold t_R on the relevance values. Given this threshold we can formally define the set of rare and relevant cases, $\mathcal{D}_R$, and the set of normal and uninteresting cases, $\mathcal{D}_N$, as follows: $\mathcal{D}_R = \{\langle \mathbf{x}, y \rangle \in \mathcal{D} : \phi(y) \geq t_R\}$ and $\mathcal{D}_N = \{\langle \mathbf{x}, y \rangle \in \mathcal{D} : \phi(y) < t_R\}$.

Let us consider, for instance, a regression problem where the target variable values represent the values of a sensor in a given machine. When the sensor indicates the most common value, typically there is not problem. However, when the sensor indicates extremely high or low values, then this can represent, for instance, a malfunction in the machine. These extreme values will be the most relevant for the user. Still, these values are usually under-represented in the data set because a normal functioning machine is expected for most of the time.

To handle imbalanced domains, it is required to take into account: (i) the performance evaluation issue; and (ii) the problem of biasing the learning algorithms towards the user preferences. Regarding the first issue, it has been shown that standard metrics are not suitable for this type of problems [3,12]. Therefore, new metrics were proposed for dealing with imbalanced domains in classification and also in regression, although fewer exist for the latter. A framework for obtaining precision and recall for imbalanced regression tasks was proposed in [12,14]. This framework is able to capture the key features of precision and recall measures defined for classification as well as the notion of numeric error needed in regression. In this paper we use the F_1-measure (F_1^{ϕ}) proposed in [1] that is based on the mentioned framework [12,14]. The contributions in this paper concern the second issue of biasing the learners towards the important rare cases. We explore the introduction of a bias linked with the cases neighborhood on existing pre-processing strategies for regression. This bias can be put forward in several different ways that we also study.

3   Related Work

As we have mentioned, most of the existing work regarding imbalanced domains is concentrated on binary classification tasks. More recently, solutions for this problem in other tasks began to appear. Pre-processing solutions are among the most commonly used because they act by changing the original data distribution, and therefore allow the use of any standard learning algorithm. Pre-processing methods for dealing with imbalanced domains mainly range between removing normal cases, including replicas of the rare cases, or generating new synthetic examples. These methods are efficient because they change the target variable distribution so that the learners focus on the rare and important examples. However, how this change should be carried out, is still an open research question.

The number of pre-processing strategies that has been proposed for classification tasks is extensive [3]. Still, for dealing with imbalanced regression only two pre-processing methods were proposed: random under-sampling [15,17] and smoteR [17]. These methods were initially proposed for dealing with class imbalance and were later adapted to a regression context. Random under-sampling is a simple method that changes the target variable distribution by randomly removing normal cases, i.e., cases with the less important target variable values. This way a better balance is achieved between rare (important) and normal (uninteresting) cases. A relevance function and a threshold are used to determine D_R and D_N. The method also requires setting a parameter that represents the reduction to be carried out in the normal cases. An adaption of the well-known SMOTE [4] algorithm was proposed for regression with the name of SMOTER [17]. This proposal combines the application of random under-sampling in the normal cases with the generation of new synthetic "smoted" examples from the rare cases. This method also depends on the definition of a relevance function for setting the rare and normal cases. The synthetic examples are generated through an interpolation strategy. The key idea is to build a new synthetic example by interpolating the features of two rare cases. The target variable value of the new case is determined as a weighted average of the target variable values of the two rare cases used. All rare cases are used in turn as seed examples. The user is also required to define the percentage of over and under-sampling to be carried out[1].

The most closely related proposal regarding the introduction of a bias in the generation of synthetic examples that takes into account each example neighborhood is the Adaptive Synthetic (ADASYN) method [6]. ADASYN was proposed for dealing with imbalanced classification. The key idea of this method is to use a density distribution for deciding the number of synthetic examples to generate for each original rare class case. A bias is introduced on the generation of new synthetic examples that favors the examples from the minority and important class cases that are closer to the decision border. With ADASYN, more synthetic examples are generated for the rare class cases that are harder to learn (i.e. with a larger number of neighbors from the normal class), while fewer new cases are generated for the easier examples.

4   Biasing Pre-processing Strategies

In this section we will describe our proposals regarding the introduction of a bias in resampling strategies for regression by considering the examples neighborhood. We propose two methods: one for adapting under-sampling and another for adapting an over-sampling strategy. These methods consider the neighborhood of each example for allowing the introduction of a bias on the resampling strategies. The methods proposed were tested on adaptations of two previously proposed strategies: random under-sampling and SMOTER. As mentioned before, random

---

[1] Further details regarding SmoteR algorithm can be obtained in [17].

under-sampling approach simply removes normal and uninteresting cases while SMOTER strategy combines under-sampling of normal cases with the generation of new synthetic rare cases. These strategies either uniformly select normal cases to be removed or generate new cases using uniformly each rare case. Our proposals for biasing under- and over-sampling allow to bias these strategies using the information of each case neighborhood.

The key idea of resampling with neighborhood bias is to inspect the examples nearest neighbors distribution in order to decide which normal cases should be removed with higher probability or which rare cases should be used more frequently as seed examples in the generation of new cases. We highlight that when applying an under-sampling strategy we are only interested in removing **normal cases** (i.e., examples in $\mathcal{D}_N$), while for over-sampling we are only concerned with increasing the **rare cases** (i.e., examples that belong to $\mathcal{D}_R$). Our proposals will bias the resampling strategies to achieve a non-uniform sampling that takes into consideration the distribution of the examples neighbors.

Let us begin with the definition of **frontier** and **safe** cases. An example $ex_i = \langle \mathbf{x}_i, y_i \rangle \in D_R$ (D_N) is as closer to the **frontier** as higher is the number of its k-nearest neighbors (kNN) that belong to D_N (D_R). An example $ex_i = \langle \mathbf{x}_i, y_i \rangle \in D_R$ (D_N) is as **safe** as higher is the number of its kNN that belong to D_R (D_N). This means that a rare case (belonging to D_R) having all its kNN belonging to D_N is as close as possible to the frontier. In this situation, the rare case is completely surrounded by cases from a different type (normal) and can be thought as an harder to learn case. On the other hand, a rare case is as safe as possible when all its kNN are also rare. This case can also be thought as an easy to learn case. We highlight that these notions apply in a similar way to both rare and normal cases. For introducing a bias in either under-sampling or over-sampling strategies the following two main variants may be considered: (i) **reinforce the frontier**, or harder to learn cases; and/or (ii) **reinforce the safe** or easier to learn cases. Both variants can be applied on the normal and on the rare cases, that is, we can reinforce the frontier cases either on the normal or the rare cases, and the same applies for reinforcing the safe cases.

When performing over-sampling, the variant that reinforces the frontier generates more synthetic examples for the cases having a larger number of normal nearest neighbors. On the other hand, when applying under-sampling to the normal cases, the frontier is reinforced when the examples with more rare neighbors are more likely to be kept. In both situations, the bias will favor the cases closer to the frontier. The key idea for reinforcing the safe cases is to bias the resampling in favor of these cases. When applying over-sampling, more synthetic cases should be generated for the examples with higher number of rare nearest neighbors. On the other hand, the application of under-sampling for reinforcing the safe cases assumes that normal cases having more rare neighbors should be more likely to be removed. Table 1 summarizes the application of variants described on the two unbiased resampling strategies used in this paper: random under-sampling and SMOTER.

Table 1. Summary of the resampling variants with neighborhood bias.

Acronym	Strat	Normal	Rare	Acronym	Strat	Normal	Rare
S._._	SmoteR	-	-	U._._	Undersamp	-	-
S.F.F	SmoteR	frontier	frontier	U.F._	Undersamp	frontier	-
S.F.S	SmoteR	frontier	safe	U.S._	Undersamp	safe	-
S.S.F	SmoteR	safe	frontier				
S.S.S	SmoteR	safe	safe				

Algorithms 1 and 2 show with more detail how our proposed variants for biasing the resampling strategies are obtained. We highlight that Algorithm 1 uses as input Bin_N: a subset of $\mathcal{D}_N$ with a given range of normal cases. This happens because it only makes sense to apply an under-sampling strategy to the normal cases. The same reasoning applies to the over-sampling strategy which we expect to be applied on rare cases. Therefore, in Algorithm 2 a subset $Bin_R \subseteq \mathcal{D}_R$ with a given range of rare cases is considered. Both Algorithms may be applied to one or more subsets of normal (Bin_N) or rare (Bin_R) cases. This can occur for instance on the rare cases when the user defines two relevant and distinct regions of the target variable values. In this case, the rare cases in $\mathcal{D}_R$ belong to two distinct bins, for instance, the cases with extreme low and high target variable values. When this occurs, the under-/over-sampling strategies should be applied in each bin separately. Algorithm 1 returns a data set $newD$ with an under-sampled with neighborhood bias Bin_N. Algorithm 2 returns a data set $newD$ with a new set of examples obtained from Bin_R with a neighborhood bias through a user provided over-sampling function $GenEx$.

We highlight that the decision of either reinforcing the frontier or the safe cases may not be trivial. In fact, the better option can be data dependent and several reasons may be pointed out for and against the two options. For instance, if we consider a data set having high levels of noisy examples, then, it is probably better to generate new rare examples based on the existing safe rare cases. However, if we have a data set with few noisy examples, then, the use of the frontier cases for obtaining new cases can be beneficial.

5   Experimental Evaluation

The main goal of our experiments is to assess the effectiveness of introducing a bias on the pre-processing strategies. We have selected 18 regression data sets from different domains whose main characteristics are described in Table 2. For each of these data sets we have obtained a relevance function through the automatic method proposed in [12]. This method assigns higher relevance to high and low extreme values of the target variable using the quartiles and the inter-quartile range of the target variable distribution[2]. We considered a threshold of

---

[2] Further details available in [12].

Algorithm 1. Under-sampling with neighborhood bias.

Input: $\mathcal{D}$ - original regression data set

　　　　Bin_N - subset of $\mathcal{D}$ with normal cases

　　　　$tgtNr$ - target number of examples to obtain in the new data set

　　　　k - nr of k nearest neighbors

　　　　Fr - logical value indicating if the reinforcement is applied to the

　　　　　　frontier (TRUE) or safe (FALSE) cases

Output: $newD$ - a new under-sampled data set

$KNNs \leftarrow kNN(Bin_N, D, k)$ // k-NN in set $\mathcal{D}$ of examples in Bin_N

$r \leftarrow$ vector of dimension $|Bin_N|$

foreach $x_i \in Bin_N$ **do**

　if $Fr = TRUE$ **then**

　　| $\Delta_i \leftarrow$ nr of KNNs of x_i that belong to Bin_N

　else

　　└ $\Delta_i \leftarrow$ nr of KNNs of x_i that do not belong to Bin_N

　└ $r_i \leftarrow \Delta_i/k$

$\hat{r} \leftarrow r/\sum_{i=1}^{|Bin_N|} r_i$

$newD \leftarrow$ sample $tgtNr$ examples from Bin_N with probability $\hat{r}$

return $newD$

0.8 on the relevance values in all data sets. To ensure the reproducibility of our results, all code, data sets used and main results are available in https://github. com/paobranco/NeighborhoodBiasResamplingRegression. All experiments were carried out in the R environment and we selected the three following types of learning algorithms: Multivariate Adaptive Regression Splines (MARS), Support Vector Machines (SVM) and Random Forests (RF). The learning algorithms, respective R packages and the used parameter variants are displayed in Table 3. We applied each of the 20 learning approaches (8 MARS + 6 SVM + 6 RF) to each of the 18 regression data sets using 9 resampling strategies. Thus 3240 ($20 \times 18 \times 9$) combinations were tested. All the resampling strategies were applied with the goal of balancing the rare and normal cases in the data sets. The 9 resampling strategies applied were as follows: (i) use the original data set without any preprocessing ("none"); (ii) apply the original SMOTER method without any bias; (iii) apply the original random under-sampling method; (iv) apply 4 variants of neighborhood bias with SMOTER; (v) apply two variants of neighborhood bias with under-sampling. Table 1 describes the resampling variants and acronyms used.

　　All the alternatives described were evaluated using the F_1^ϕ measure for regression referred in Sect. 2. We used $\beta = 1$, which means that the same importance is given to both precision and recall scores. The F_1^ϕ values were estimated through a 2×10 - fold cross validation process and the statistical significance of the observed paired differences was measured using the non-parametric Wilcoxon paired test. The experiments were carried out using the following R packages: *performanceEstimation* [13] for the experimental infra-structure; *uba*[3] for the

---

[3] Available at http://www.dcc.fc.up.pt/~rpribeiro/uba/.

Algorithm 2. Over-sampling with neighborhood bias.

Input: $\mathcal{D}$ - original regression data set

Bin_R - subset of $\mathcal{D}$ with rare cases

$tgtNr$ - number of new examples to generate in the new data set

k - nr of k nearest neighbors

Fr - logical value indicating if the reinforcement is applied to the
          frontier (TRUE) or safe (FALSE) cases

$GenEx$ - function for obtaining the new examples

Output: $newD$ - a data set containing the new examples

$KNNs \leftarrow kNN(Bin_R, \mathcal{D}, k)$ // k-NN in set $\mathcal{D}$ of examples in Bin_R

$\boldsymbol{r} \leftarrow$ vector of dimension $|Bin_R|$

foreach $x_i \in Bin_R$ **do**

   if $Fr = TRUE$ **then**

     | $\Delta_i \leftarrow$ nr of KNNs of x_i that do not belong to Bin_R

   else

     └ $\Delta_i \leftarrow$ nr of KNNs of x_i that belong to Bin_R

    $r_i \leftarrow \Delta_i / k$

$\hat{\boldsymbol{r}} \leftarrow \boldsymbol{r} / \sum_{i=1}^{|Bin_R|} r_i$

for $i = 1$ **to** $|Bin_R|$ **do**

   └ $g_i \leftarrow \hat{r}_i \times tgtNr$

$newD \leftarrow$ use $GenEx$ function to generate g_i new examples for each x_i.

return $newD$

---

relevance function and F_1^ϕ metric; and *UBL* [2] for the implementation of the random under-sampling and SMOTER resampling strategies.

We summarize the main results in Figs. 1 and 2. We provide the detailed results, as well as all the code and data sets used in https://github.com/paobranco/NeighborhoodBiasResamplingRegression. Figure 1 shows the number of best median F_1^ϕ scores across all strategies by learner type in all data sets tested, i.e., it counts the number of times each strategy (aggregated by none, original or with neighborhood bias) has the best overall F_1^ϕ score in each data set. Figure 2 shows the number of best median F_1^ϕ scores observed when taking into account only the scores inside each type of resampling strategy, i.e., for each strategy type we counted the number of times that each variant displayed the best score, considering only the scores obtained on those strategies.

The results presented show that there is an advantage on considering the new biased resampling strategies using the examples neighborhood. However, it is not straightforward which variant should be selected for each data set. This means that the resampling strategies with a neighborhood bias show an improved gain in F_1^ϕ when compared to the original resampling strategies. Still, we are not able to identify which is the biased strategy that has the best overall results on the 18 considered data sets. The scores obtained, although generally better with the introduction of bias in the resampling strategies, seem to be domain dependent in what concerns the reinforcement of the frontier or the safe cases.

Table 2. Data sets information by descending order of rare cases percentage. (*N*: nr of cases; *tpred*: nr predictors; *p.nom*: nr nominal predictors; *p.num*: nr numeric predictors; *nRare*: nr. cases with $\phi(y) > 0.8$; *%Rare*: *nRare/N*).

Data set	N	tpred	p.nom	p.num	nRare	% Rare	Data set	N	tpred	p.nom	p.num	nRare	% Rare
servo	167	4	2	2	34	0.204	a2	198	11	3	8	22	0.111
a6	198	11	3	8	33	0.167	fuelCons	1764	38	12	26	164	0.093
Abalone	4177	8	1	7	679	0.163	availPwr	1802	16	7	9	157	0.087
machCpu	209	6	0	6	34	0.163	cpuSm	8192	13	0	13	713	0.087
a3	198	11	3	8	32	0.162	maxTorq	1802	33	13	20	129	0.072
a4	198	11	3	8	31	0.157	bank8FM	4499	9	0	9	288	0.064
a1	198	11	3	8	28	0.141	ConcrStr	1030	8	0	8	55	0.053
a7	198	11	3	8	27	0.136	Accel	1732	15	3	12	89	0.051
boston	506	13	0	13	65	0.128	airfoil	1503	5	0	5	62	0.041

Table 3. Regression algorithms, parameter variants, and respective R packages used.

Learner	Parameter variants	R package
MARS	$nk = \{10, 17\}, degree = \{1, 2\}, thresh = \{0.01, 0.001\}$	**earth** [11]
SVM	$cost = \{10, 150, 300\}, gamma = \{0.01, 0.001\}$	**e1071** [5]
RF	$mtry = \{5, 7\}, ntree = \{500, 750, 1500\}$	**randomForest** [9]

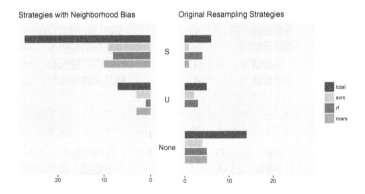

Fig. 1. Number of data sets with best median F_1^ϕ scores by learner and strategy type (S: SmoteR-based; U: undersampling-based).

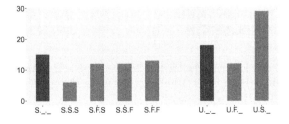

Fig. 2. Number of best median F_1^ϕ scores inside each type of resampling strategy.

Figure 3 show the total number of F_1^ϕ wins and losses (and significant wins/losses) for each resampling strategy against the baseline of using the original data set. The results were obtained with the Wilcoxon Signed Rank test for each data set with a significance level of 95%. Darker bars indicate significant wins/losses while lighter bars represent wins/losses without significance. These figures confirm that there is an advantage on considering the biased resampling strategies on imbalanced regression tasks. However, the results obtained are clearly dependent of the used learning algorithm. This is evident when comparing the results of Random Forest learner against the remaining learners.

We also compared the wins/losses of our proposed biased resampling strategies against the original resampling strategies. Figures 4 and 5 show the wins and losses of F_1^ϕ score of the neighborhood biased alternatives against respectively the SMOTER and random under-sampling strategies as baseline. The results of the comparison of the biased strategies against the SMOTER as baseline are not conclusive. Still, the S.F.S strategy that reinforces the safe rare cases and the frontier of the normal cases stands out. However, for the RF and MARS learners the original SMOTER strategy presents globally more wins. In the comparison against random under-sampling as baseline, the strategy that reinforces the frontier cases has more wins and significantly for all learners. This confirms that this biased strategy is preferable to the random under-sampling strategy.

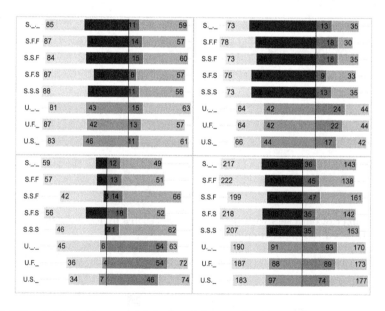

Fig. 3. Wins (left) and losses (right) of each learner (top left: MARS, top right: SVM, bottom left: RF and bottom right: Total) against using the original data set.

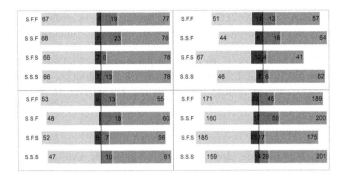

Fig. 4. Wins (left) and losses (right) of each learner (top left: MARS, top right: SVM, bottom left: RF and bottom right: Total) against the SMOTER strategy.

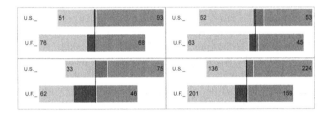

Fig. 5. Wins (left) and losses (right) of each learner (top left: MARS, top right: SVM, bottom left: RF and bottom right: Total) against the random under-sampling strategy.

6   Conclusions

In this paper we studied the introduction of a neighborhood bias on resampling strategies for dealing with the problem of imbalanced domains in regression tasks. The goal of introducing a bias in the pre-processing strategies is to avoid an uniform under-/over-sampling reinforcing some regions of the data sets at the expense of other regions. We use the information on the examples neighborhood to bias the resampling strategies towards the safe and/or frontier regions.

We show that there is a clear advantage when considering resampling strategies with a neighborhood bias. Moreover, the new strategies can easily be extended to other resampling strategies. The key contributions of this paper are: (i) the proposal of new resampling strategies that take into account the information on the examples neighborhood; (ii) test and compare our proposals against the baseline of not applying resampling and the original unbiased strategy.

As future work we plan to extend these approaches to imbalanced classification tasks, comparing the impact of reinforcing the safe/frontier cases in different data sets.

Acknowledgments. This work is financed by the ERDF European Regional Development Fund through the Operational Programme for Competitiveness and

Internationalisation - COMPETE 2020 Programme within project POCI-01-0145-FEDER-006961, and by National Funds through the FCT Fundação para a Ciência e a Tecnologia (Portuguese Foundation for Science and Technology) as part of project UID/EEA/50014/2013. P. Branco is supported by a Ph.D. scholarship of FCT (PD/BD/105788/2014). Prof. L. Torgo would also like to thank the support of Projects NORTE-01-0145-FEDER-000036 and UTAP-ICDT/CTM-NAN/0025/2014.

References

1. Branco, P.: Re-sampling approaches for regression tasks under imbalanced domains. Master's thesis, Department of Computer Science, Faculty of Sciences - University of Porto (2014)
2. Branco, P., Ribeiro, R.P., Torgo, L.: UBL: an R package for utility-based learning. arXiv preprint arXiv:1604.08079 (2016)
3. Branco, P., Torgo, L., Ribeiro, R.P.: A survey of predictive modeling on imbalanced domains. ACM Comput. Surv. (CSUR) 49(2), 31 (2016)
4. Chawla, N.V., Bowyer, K.W., Hall, L.O., Kegelmeyer, W.P.: SMOTE: synthetic minority over-sampling technique. JAIR 16, 321–357 (2002)
5. Dimitriadou, E., Hornik, K., Leisch, F., Meyer, D., Weingessel, A.: e1071: Misc Functions of the Department of Statistics (e1071), TU Wien (2011)
6. He, H., Bai, Y., Garcia, E.A., Li, S.: ADASYN: adaptive synthetic sampling approach for imbalanced learning. In: IEEE International Joint Conference on Neural Networks, pp. 1322–1328. IEEE (2008)
7. He, H., Garcia, E.A.: Learning from imbalanced data. IEEE Trans. Knowl. Data Eng. 21(9), 1263–1284 (2009)
8. Krawczyk, B.: Learning from imbalanced data: open challenges and future directions. Prog. Artif. Intell. 5, 1–12 (2016)
9. Liaw, A., Wiener, M.: Classification and regression by randomforest. R News 2(3), 18–22 (2002)
10. López, V., Fernández, A., García, S., Palade, V., Herrera, F.: An insight into classification with imbalanced data: empirical results and current trends on using data intrinsic characteristics. Inf. Sci. 250, 113–141 (2013)
11. Milborrow, S.: earth: Multivariate Adaptive Regression Spline Models. Derived from mda:mars by Trevor Hastie and Rob Tibshirani (2012)
12. Ribeiro, R.P.: Utility-based regression. Ph.D. thesis, Department Computer Science, Faculty of Sciences, University of Porto (2011)
13. Torgo, L.: An infra-structure for performance estimation and experimental comparison of predictive models in r. CoRR abs/1412.0436 (2014)
14. Torgo, L., Ribeiro, R.P.: Precision and recall for regression. In: Gama, J., Costa, V.S., Jorge, A.M., Brazdil, P.B. (eds.) DS 2009. LNCS, vol. 5808, pp. 332–346. Springer, Heidelberg (2009). doi:10.1007/978-3-642-04747-3_26
15. Torgo, L., Branco, P., Ribeiro, R.P., Pfahringer, B.: Resampling strategies for regression. Expert Syst. 32(3), 465–476 (2015)
16. Torgo, L., Ribeiro, R.P.: Utility-based regression. In: Kok, J.N., Koronacki, J., Lopez de Mantaras, R., Matwin, S., Mladenič, D., Skowron, A. (eds.) PKDD 2007. LNCS, vol. 4702, pp. 597–604. Springer, Heidelberg (2007). doi:10.1007/978-3-540-74976-9_63
17. Torgo, L., Ribeiro, R.P., Pfahringer, B., Branco, P.: SMOTE for regression. In: Correia, L., Reis, L.P., Cascalho, J. (eds.) EPIA 2013. LNCS, vol. 8154, pp. 378–389. Springer, Heidelberg (2013). doi:10.1007/978-3-642-40669-0_33

A Feature Selection Algorithm Based on Heuristic Decomposition

Luís Cavique[1]([⊠]) ⓘ, Armando B. Mendes[2] ⓘ,
and Hugo F.M.C. Martiniano[3] ⓘ

[1] MAS-BioISI, FCUL and Universidade Aberta, Lisbon, Portugal
luis.cavique@uab.pt
[2] Universidade dos Açores, Ponta Delgada, Portugal
armando.b.mendes@uac.pt
[3] BioISI, FCUL and Instituto Dr. Ricardo Jorge, Lisbon, Portugal
hfmartiniano@fc.ul.pt

Abstract. Feature selection is one of the most important concepts in data mining when dimensionality reduction is needed. The performance measures of feature selection encompass predictive accuracy and result comprehensibility. Consistency based feature selection is a significant category of feature selection research that substantially improves the comprehensibility of the result using the parsimony principle. In this work, the feature selection algorithm LAID, Logical Analysis of Inconsistent Data, is applied to large volumes of data. In order to deal with hundreds of thousands of attributes, a problem de-composition strategy associated with a set covering problem formulation is used. The algorithm is applied to artificial datasets with genome-like characteristics of patients with rare diseases.

Keywords: Data mining · Feature selection · Consistency measure · Set covering problem · Heuristic decomposition

1 Introduction

In feature selection two main objectives sustain the performance measures, the predictive accuracy and the result comprehensibility [12]. Some models do not take into account the predictive accuracy, and others, after reduction, tend to destroy the underlying semantics of the features. It would be highly desirable to find a theory that could not only reduce the number of features, but also preserve the data semantics.

In this context, Rough Set theory emerges as the desired tool by discovering the data dependencies and reducing the dimension. Rough Set theory was initially proposed as a tool to reason about vagueness and uncertainty in information systems by Pawlak [13] and later it was also proposed for attribute selection [14]. Rough Sets do not correct or exclude data inconsistencies, but rather for each class they determine a lower and an upper approximation.

In parallel, Peter Hammer's group [2, 8], with works in discrete optimization, developed LAD, Logic Analysis of Data. The key features of LAD are the discovery of the minimum number of attributes that are necessary for explaining all observations

© Springer International Publishing AG 2017
E. Oliveira et al. (Eds.): EPIA 2017, LNAI 10423, pp. 525–536, 2017.
DOI: 10.1007/978-3-319-65340-2_43

and the detection of hidden patterns in a dataset with two classes. An extension of the Boolean approach is needed when nominal non-binary attributes are used.

LAD and Rough Set approaches are a subset of filter models that aim to reduce the number of attributes of datasets using two phases: problem transformation and optimization. Their specificity is to keep the semantics of the data by removing only the redundant data.

By combining the two approaches, we proposed Logic Analysis of Inconsistent Data, LAID [5], which blends the best characteristics of both methods. The LAID method should deal with integer attributes associated with costs as in LAD, and be tolerant to inconsistency as in Rough Sets. The integration of both approaches is so close that LAID can be seen as a Rough Set extension.

One key area for application of the method is high-dimensional omics datasets, such as those generated by High-Throughput Sequencing (HTS) technologies. In the past few years, technological developments in this area have resulted in an astonishing growth of the amount of data produced, with a growth rate which doubles approximately every seven months.

The goal of this work is to solve a feature selection problem with a dataset involving two thousand observations and one million attributes. The performance measure is the comprehensibility of the solution, by achieving the minimum number of attributes with the maximum actionable knowledge that better explains the dataset to the final user. Most disease-related omics datasets are subject to restricted access, so artificial datasets with similar characteristics have been created.

This document extends previous works where LAID was presented [4, 5]. The novelty of this work includes the application of LAID to larger datasets and the development of a heuristic decomposition approach to the set covering problem.

This document is organized as follows. In Sect. 2, we present the related concepts of feature selection and heuristic decomposition. In Sect. 3, we present a three phase algorithm which finds the feature selection with minimum number of attributes. In Sect. 4, the computational results are shown. Finally, in the last section we draw some conclusions.

2   Related Work

This work combines the areas of attribute selection and problem decomposition. Consequently, in this section we introduce the related topics: feature selection and heuristic decomposition.

2.1   Feature Selection

Given that the time required to double information in the world is substantially decreasing every year, the motivation for feature selection is to reduce the dimensionality of the feature space. Surveys on feature selection methods can be found in [6, 12].

In feature selection, given thousands to millions of features, the goal is to select the most relevant ones. The performance measures have two main objectives, the predictive accuracy and the result comprehensibility. In this work we emphasize the comprehensibility of the results, as in Occam's razor principle that aims to obtain the simplest model, as opposed to the valuation of accuracy metrics.

We consider a dataset $D = \{O, X \cup C\}$ where $O = \{O_1, O_2, \ldots, O_n\}$ is a non-empty set of observations (instances or cases), $X = \{X_1, X_2, \ldots, X_m\}$ is a non-empty set of features (attributes or columns) and C is the class attribute.

In this short review we use the feature selection taxonomies reported in [12]. There are three basic models in feature selection: Filter, Wrapper and Hybrid model.

In the Filter model the most popular independent criteria are consistency measures, distance measures, information measures and dependency measures. In this sub-section the consistency measure and the distance measure are detailed because they are re-used in the document.

Using the consistency measure criteria, an inconsistency occurs when two or more observations have the same values in all attributes, but belong to different decision classes. This measure is used in algorithms that attempt to find the minimum number of features with the minimum number of inconsistencies. The well-known algorithm FOCUS [1] uses the concept of consistency, where irrelevant features are removed.

Distance measure criteria are applied in observations within the same class and in observations of diverse classes. In the same class, to obtain the disagreement value, the logic operator XOR is applied, where it returns True if $(O_x, X_a) \neq (O_y, X_a)$ and False otherwise. With diverse classes, the logic operator XOR can also be applied, where if $(O_x, X_a) \neq (O_y, X_a)$, feature X_a should be chosen because it differentiates the classes. Comparisons of observations within the same class measure the incoherence or noise of the feature. On the other hand, comparisons of observations between different classes measure how strong a feature is in the discrimination or separation of the classes. RELIEF algorithm [11] evaluates a feature subset based on the subtraction between the distance of observations in different classes and the distance of observations within the same class.

In the incremental or decremental process of feature selection, the information measure is given by the information gain from an added or removed feature.

The dependency measure of a feature is related to how important the correlation is between the feature and the class.

The Filter model is divided into two sequential steps. The feature selection step is executed before the learning phase of the prediction model, and there is no interaction between the selection and the prediction model.

The Wrapper model [9] is also divided into two steps, but with strong interaction between the feature selection step and the learning phase, where the results of the prediction are used as a criterion of feature choice.

Filter models are more intuitive and show better performance since they build the solution in a constructive process without iterations. On the other hand, they present the disadvantages of ignoring the modeling process. Consequently, most of the relevant features might not be adequate in the prediction model and the selection criterion is hard to estimate.

In the Wrapper models, the selection criterion is easy to estimate since the features are chosen by the prediction model, and therefore they are classified as model-aware as they incorporate the knowledge of the predictor. They also present the opposite disadvantages of the Filter models, which are computationally expensive and are less intuitive. The main disadvantage of this method is the increasing overfitting risk when the number of observations is insufficient. In other words, the Wrapper models do not identify statistical dependency, so the features might not be the most explanatory variables and therefore the model can lose its theoretical basis.

Hybrid methods have been proposed to reduce features in classification, where they try to combine the advantages of the two previous methods. The main disadvantage of the method is the significant low scalability when the feature number increases.

To sum up, in Filter methods, the selection criterion is hard to estimate, whereas Wrapper methods tend to destroy the underlying feature semantics.

In this work, a Filter model is implemented, which combines consistency and distance measures.

2.2   Heuristic Decomposition Approach

In order to solve a problem with hundreds of thousands of attributes, a Decomposition Heuristic should be introduced. In Linear Programming optimization some approaches can be mentioned such as Column Generation, Dantzig-Wolfe decomposition and Benders decomposition. A detailed introduction can be found in [3]. Decomposition is the act of breaking a large problem into sub-problems. Decomposition of a problem is possible if the structure of the problem is maintained. If problem A is separable into A^1, A^2, ..., A^k it can also run in a computer parallel environment, it is parallelizable.

Instead of minimizing the evaluation function f(A) the decomposition method minimizes the sub-problems $f(A^1)$, $f(A^2)$, ..., $f(A^k)$ and finally minimizes the master problem using function g(). Algorithm 1 presents the parallel version and Algorithm 2 the sequential version.

Algorithm 1: General Heuristic Decomposition (parallel version):
Input: sub-problems $A^{1..max\_k}$
1. solve the sub-problems:
sub-problem 1: y_1=minimize $f(A^1)$
sub-problem 2: y_2=minimize $f(A^2)$
...
sub-problem k: y_k=minimize $f(A^k)$
2. solve the master problem:
    master = minimize $g(y_1, y_2, ..., y_k)$

The sequential version of the decomposition heuristic, Algorithm 2, at each iteration updates the master problem, adding new information from the solved sub-problem.

Algorithm 2: General Heuristic Decomposition (sequential version):
Input: sub-problems $A^{1..max\_k}$
1. k=0
2. while not end condition
2.2.   k=k+1
2.1.   solve sub-problem: y_k = minimize $f(A^k)$
2.2.   solve master problem: master = minimize $g(master, y_k)$
3. end while

The decomposition principle can also be exploited in exact methods or in meta-heuristic methods [10]. Given the large number of attributes, a heuristic decomposition approach [15] is used in this work.

3   Logical Analysis of Inconsistent Data for Large Datasets

As stated before, in this work we propose a feature selection technique to deal with inconsistent data in large datasets. The inconsistent data is processed using the LAID method, to which we added a decomposition approach to manage large sets of attributes.

In Algorithm 3, we describe the LAID Algorithm with a decomposition technique. Firstly, to remove any inconsistency, we add a dummy binary variable named "je ne sais quoi", 'jnsq', since two observations with the same attributes that belong to different classes work against the consistency measure. In a second step, the Disjoint Matrix Generation $[A_{i,j}]$ and Cost Vector $[c_j]$ are created, where both are based on the definition of the distance measure. Finally, a Decomposition Heuristic for the Set Covering problem is applied. The algorithm can be specified as follows:

> **Algorithm 3:** LAID for Large Datasets
> Input: dataset D={O, X∪C} with binary variables
> Output: a subset of attributes with minimum cost
> 1. Check data inconsistencies and add dummy variable 'jnsq'
> 2. Disjoint Matrix Generation $[A_{i,j}]$ and Cost Vector $[c_j]$
> 3. Heuristic Decomposition for the Minimum Set Covering Problem

To exemplify the different steps of the algorithm a running example with six features and five observations is used.

3.1   Data Inconsistencies

Given the inconsistency of two observations O_a and O_b with the same values in all the attributes and belonging to different classes, a dummy binary variable "je ne sais quoi" [5] is added, assigning a value of 1 whenever the class = 1, or:

$$jnsq_a = \begin{cases} 1 & \text{if}(O_a = O_b) \text{ and}(\text{class}(O_a) \neq \text{class}(O_b)) \text{ and}(\text{class}(O_a) = 1) \\ 0 & \text{otherwise} \end{cases}$$

Instead of using the complex approximations of the Rough Sets to keep the data inconsistencies, LAID does not exclude the inconsistency by adding a dummy variable that allows the subsequent application of the other steps of the LAD method.

Given the dataset with six features $\{X_1, ..., X_6\}$ and five observations $\{O_1, ..., O_5\}$, the first step of LAID is verifying the existence of inconsistencies in the dataset. For each inconsistency the dummy variable 'jnsq' is assigned to 1 in class 1.

In Table 1 the dummy variable 'jnsq' is added in the last feature column in order to avoid data inconsistencies between observation O2 and O3, which present the same values for all the features.

Table 1. Variable 'je ne sais quoi' is added

Observation\feature	X_1	X_2	X_3	X_4	X_5	X_6	X_7 (jnsq)	Class
O_1	1	1	0	1	1	1	0	0
O_2	1	0	1	1	1	0	0	0
O_3	1	0	1	1	1	0	1	1
O_4	1	0	1	0	0	1	0	1
O_5	0	0	1	0	0	0	0	1

3.2   Disjoint Matrix Generation [$A_{i,j}$] and Cost Vector [C_j]

In the second step the Cost Vector [c_j] and Disjoint Constraints Matrix Generation [$A_{i,j}$] are created. Both, the Disjoint Matrix Generation [$A_{i,j}$] and Cost Vector [c_j] use the concept of distance measure for independent criteria in feature selection.

The Cost Vector [c_j] is obtained by adding the pair comparisons within the same class. This calculus is used to measure the general incoherence, or noise, of the feature j.

On the other hand, the Disjoint Matrix [$A_{i,j}$] is obtained by using the pair comparisons belonging to different classes. The disjoint matrix [$A_{i,j}$] for each attribute X_j and pair of observations (O_a, O_b), is defined as:

$$A_{i,j} = \begin{cases} 1 & \forall i : X_j(O_a) \neq X_j(O_b), \text{class}(O_a) \neq \text{class}(O_b), (O_a, O_b) \in O \times O \\ 0 & \text{otherwise} \end{cases}$$

The dimension of index i in matrix [$A_{i,j}$] depends on the constraint structure of dataset D. The upper bound of line i is $(n.(n-1))/2$ constraints due to the comparison of pairs of observations (O_a, O_b), where n is the number of observations. Each constraint results from the comparison of two different arbitrary observations O_a and O_b that belong to distinct classes. If one attribute j is different in the observations O_a and O_b the value of $A_{i,j}$ becomes value 1, denoting that at least one column (attribute) j must be maintained in order to differentiate the rows (constraint) i.

The cost vector [c_j] and the disjoint matrix [$A_{i,j}$] will be used as input in the Minimum Set Covering problem, where all constraints (or lines i) must be covered, at least once by some attributes.

Table 2 presents pairs of observations of the same class. For each observation the features of the same class should be equal in order to avoid disagreement. The sum of the disagreement of each feature is called cost and stored in the Cost Vector [c_j]. As stated before, for observations O_i and attributes X_j, the value of disagreement is given by the operator XOR that returns True if (O_x, X_a) $\neq$ (O_y, X_a) and False otherwise.

To obtain the disjoint matrix [$A_{i,j}$], for each observation the features of different classes should be different in order to discriminate. The number of lines generated in

Table 2. Cost vector $[c_j]$ shows the disagreement within the same class

Pairs same class	X_1	X_2	X_3	X_4	X_5	X_6	X_7 (jnsq)	Class
O_1,O_2		1	1			1		1
O_3,O_4				1	1	1	1	0
O_3,O_5	1			1	1		1	0
O_4,O_5	1					1		0
cost $[c_j]$	2	1	1	2	2	3	2	

$[A_{i,j}]$ is N.M, where N and M are the number of observations of class 0 and class 1, respectively. The value k_j corresponds to the number of lines covered for each feature j.

Table 3 presents the pairs of observations that belong to different classes, where the logic operator XOR can also be applied, since, if $(O_x, X_a) \neq (O_y, X_a)$, the feature X_a should be chosen because it distinguishes the two classes.

Table 3. Matrix $[A_{i,j}]$ shows the disjoint between different classes

Pairs different classes	X_1	X_2	X_3	X_4	X_5	X_6	X_7 (jnsq)
1 - O_1,O_3		1	1			1	1
2 - O_1,O_4		1	1	1	1		
3 - O_1,O_5	1	1	1	1	1	1	
4 - O_2,O_3							1
5 - O_2,O_4				1	1	1	
6 - O_2,O_5	1			1	1		
k_j	2	3	3	4	4	3	2

3.3 Heuristic Decomposition for the Minimum Set Covering Problem

In the third step of LAID a decomposition heuristic is applied to solve the Set Covering Problem. The optimization problem that finds the minimum number of columns that cover all the rows is the Set Covering problem and can be defined in binary programming as:

$$\text{minimize} \, f = \sum c_j . y_j$$
$$\text{subject to} \sum A_{i,j} . y_j \geq 1$$
$$\text{and } y_j \in \{0, 1\} \quad j = 1, \dots, m$$

In this sub-section, a greedy heuristic approach is used to solve the Minimum Set Covering problem, which reuses the algorithm proposed in [7].

In order to solve a problem with thousands of attributes, a Heuristic Decomposition for the Set Covering problem is applied. The matrix $[A_{i,j}]$ is divided into max_k sub-problems resulting in max_k sub-matrices $[A_{i,j}]^k$. Comparing this approach with meta-heuristics the sub-matrices correspond to different neighborhoods in Variable Neighborhood Search or to new regions in the diversification process of Tabu Search.

Algorithm 4 presents the heuristic decomposition for the minimum set covering problem. We consider the following notation:

k – iteration number
S – current solution
RS – repository of feasible solutions.

> **Algorithm 4:** Heuristic Decomposition for Set Covering Problem
> Input: sub-matrices $[A_{i,j}]^{1..max\_k}$
> Output: a subset of attributes with minimum cost
> 1. k=0, S = ∅
> 2. while not end condition
> 2.1. k=k+1
> 2.2. solve sub-problem: S = S + setCoverHeuristic $([A_{i,j}]^k)$
> 2.3. if S is feasible the
> 2.3.1.   RS=RS+S
> 2.3.2.   S = ∅
> 2.4. end_if
> 3. end_while
> 4. solve master problem: master = setCoverHeuristic $([A_{i,j}], [RS])$

The algorithm finds multiple feasible solutions in the iterative process, which are combined in the final step by solving the master problem. In this approach we use the same set covering heuristic for the sub-problems and for the master problem. The advantage is to have feasible solutions from the beginning. An alternative would be to select the best columns from the sub-problem and run the set covering heuristic in the master problem.

In this running example $f(c_j, k_j) = c_j/k_j$ and matrix $[A_{i,j}]$ is divided into two sub-matrices A1 and A2 in order to illustrate the decomposition technique. In Table 4 the sub-matrices of matrix $[A_{i,j}]$ and $f(c_j, k_j)$ are shown.

Table 4. Sub-matrices of matrix $[A_{i,j}]$

Features	X_1	X_2	X_3	X_4	X_5	X_6	X_7 (jnsq)
c_j	2	1	1	2	2	3	2
k_j	2	3	3	4	4	3	2
c_j/k_j	1	1/3	1/3	1/2	1/2	1	1
$[A_{ij}]^k$	A^1			A^2			

Since we have two sub-matrices A1 and A2 the sub-problem will run twice. In the first iteration from features $\{X_1, X_2, X_3\}$ solution $\{X_2, X_1\}$ is obtained with cost = 3. This solution is not admissible since there are 2 uncovered lines, line 4 and line 5.

In the second iteration from features $\{X_2, X_1\}$ from A1, plus $\{X_4, X_5, X_6, X_7\}$ from A2, the solution obtained is $\{X_2, X_4, X_7\}$. The current solution is admissible, since it covers all the lines of matrix $[A_{i,j}]$ and has cost = 5.

Given the subset $\{X_2, X_4, X_7\}$, in Table 5 the reduced dataset is presented. The number of features was reduced from 7 to 3 and the number of observations was also reduced from 5 to 4. Nearly all the combinations with 2 features are presented, with the exception of $X_2 = 1$ and $X_4 = 0$ because no observations occur.

Table 5. Reduced dataset

Observation\feature	X_2	X_4	X_7 (jnsq)	Class
O_1	1	1	0	0
O_2	0	1	0	0
O_3	0	1	1	1
O_4, O_5	0	0	0	1
No observations	1	0	0	?

4 Computational Results

To implement the computational results of this algorithm, some choices such as the computational environment, the performance measures and the datasets must be made.

The computer programs were written in C language and the GCC/Dev-C + + compiler was used. The computational results were obtained from an Intel Core Duo CPU 3.0 GHz processor with 4.0 GB of main memory running under the Windows 10 operating system. The INCD (National Infrastructure for Distributed Computing) services was used to run large datasets.

Two performance measures are used to evaluate results, the computational time and solutions quality. The quality is given by the cost of the set covering heuristic, where the minimum cost corresponds to the minimum number of attributes that better explain the dataset.

Since datasets with rare diseases information are subject to restricted access, we generated artificial datasets with similar characteristics. The dataset under study has 1,700 observations in the test group, with class 1, associated with rare disease patients, and 300 observations in the control group, with class 0, with people without the rare disease. In the original dataset the number of attributes is close to one million. The number of lines in the matrix $[A_{i,j}]$ is 510,000 (1,700 × 300) and the final dimension of the matrix is 510,000 × 1,000,000.

4.1 Computational Runtime

To study the performance of large matrices the time complexity should be take into account in order to estimate the total runtime.

For a two-class problem the number of observations are given by the tuple (O_0, O_1); (100, 100), (500, 500), (700, 700) and (1700, 300). The number of columns was tested from 100 to 5000 variables.

In the Decomposition Heuristic for the Set Covering Problem, for each sub-matrix $[A_{i,j}]^k$, the computational time is shown in Fig. 1, where a linear behavior can be found between runtime and the number of columns.

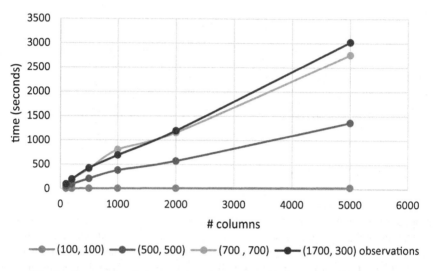

Fig. 1. Computational time varying the number of columns and observations

The total runtime for matrix $[A_{i,j}]$ with dimension 510,000 × 1,000,000, and k = 200, that is 200 sub-matrices $[A_{i,j}]^k$ of 510,000 × 5,000 each, can be estimated in 570,800 s, or approximately seven days. Since it is possible to decompose the problem, it can run in a computer parallel environment.

4.2   Quality of the Solutions

In the set covering problem a feasible (or admissible) solution is given when all the lines are covered for at least one chosen column.

The challenge of this work is to solve a feature selection problem with a dataset involving one million attributes. In the computational experiments performed with the artificial dataset with less than 1,000 columns, we verified that the admissibility of the solutions are found in 3 iterations at most, or in 3 sub-matrices $[A_{i,j}]^k$. For datasets with 5,000 columns, feasible solutions are found for each sub-matrix. Running 200 iterations, hundreds of possible good solutions are found and then used in the master step.

In the experiments, we found that each feasible solution includes between 50 to 100 columns, given the low density of the matrix. The minimum cost can be achieved from the set of solved sub-problems. Definitive quality assessment of the solutions must be evaluated by human specialists on rare diseases.

5   Discussion and Conclusions

Given the large datasets available in bioinformatics, the aim of this work is to present a feature selection method able to deal with thousands of observations and millions of attributes.

In feature selection two performance measures are considered: the predictive accuracy and result comprehensibility using the parsimony principle. The consistency measure is an important issue in the result comprehensibility. Thus, this document extends the previous work of the LAID algorithm, where the minimum number of attributes that better explain the dataset is found, achieving the maximal actionable knowledge. The novelty of this work includes the application of LAID to larger datasets and the development of a heuristic decomposition for the set covering problem.

In the set covering problem, the disjoint matrix $[A_{i,j}]$ and cost vector $[c_j]$ reuse the distance measure concept for the independent criteria in feature selection. Therefore, the algorithm combines consistency measure and the distance measure approaches. In the Decomposition Heuristic for the Set Covering Problem, the disjoint matrix is separable into sub-matrices $[A_{i,j}]^k$.

The algorithm finds multiple feasible solutions that are gathered in the master phase. The computational runtime for the feature selection with dimension 2,000 observations and 1,000,000 features are satisfactory.

The main conclusion of this study regarding the large volumes of data can be summarized considering two aspects: the algorithm and the data storage. The algorithm requires polynomial time complexity and separation of the problem to be parallelizable in a cloud environment. With respect to data storage, the in-memory access should be replaced by on-disk access to deal with large datasets.

In future work we plan to use data storage in HDF5 format. The Hierarchical Data Format, originally developed at the National Center for Supercomputing Applications, is designed to store and organize large amounts of data that can be accessed on-disk in multiple ways.

Acknowledgements. The first author would like to thank the FCT support UID/Multi/04046/ 2013. This work used the EGI infrastructure with the support of NCG-INGRID-PT (Portugal) and BIFI (Spain).

References

1. Almuallim, H., Dietterich, T.G.: Learning with many irrelevant features. In: Proceedings of 9th National Conference on Artificial Intelligence, pp. 547–552. MIT Press (1991)
2. Boros, E., Hammer, P.L., Ibaraki, T., Kogan, A., Mayoraz, E., Muchnik, I.: An implementation of logical analysis of data. IEEE Trans. Knowl. Data Eng. **12**(2), 292–306 (2000)
3. Boyd, S., Xiao, L., Mutapcic, A., Mattingley, J.: Notes on decomposition methods. Notes for EE364B, Stanford University, pp. 1–36 (2008)

4. Cavique, L., Mendes, A.B., Funk, M.: Logical analysis of inconsistent data (LAID) for a paremiologic study. In: Processing 15th Portuguese Conference on Artificial Intelligence, EPIA (2011)
5. Cavique, L., Mendes, A.B., Funk, M., Santos, J.M.A.: A feature selection approach in the study of azorean proverbs. In: Exploring Innovative and Successful Applications of Soft Computing. Advances in Computational Intelligence and Robotics (ACIR) Book Series, pp. 38–58. IGI Global (2013)
6. Chandrashekar, G., Sahin, F.: A survey on feature selection methods. Comput. Electr. Eng. **40**(1), 16–28 (2014)
7. Chvatal, V.: A greedy heuristic for the set-covering problem. Math. Oper. Res. **4**, 233–235 (1979)
8. Crama, Y., Hammer, P.L., Ibaraki, T.: Cause-effect relationships and partially defined Boolean functions. Ann. Oper. Res. **16**, 299–326 (1988)
9. John, G.H., Kohavi, R., Pfleger. K.: Irrelevant features and the subset selection problem. In: Proceedings of 11th International Conference on Machine Learning, ICML 1994, pp. 121–129 (1994)
10. Joncour, C., Michel, S., Sadykov, R., Sverdlov, D., Vanderbeck, F.: Column generation based primal heuristics. Electron. Notes Discret. Math. **36**, 695–702 (2010). Elsevier
11. Kira, K., Rendell, L.A.: The feature selection problem: traditional methods and a new algorithm. In: Proceedings of 9th National Conference on Artificial Intelligence, pp. 129–134 (1992)
12. Liu, H., Yu, L.: Toward integrating feature selection algorithms for classification and clustering. IEEE Trans. Knowl. Data Eng. **17**(4), 491–502 (2005)
13. Pawlak, Z.: Rough sets. Int. J. Comput. Inf. Sci. **1**, 341–356 (1982)
14. Pawlak, Z.: Rough Sets: Theoretical Aspects of Reasoning About Data. Kluwer Academic Publishers, Boston (1991)
15. Smet, P., Ernst, A., Vanden Berghe, G.: Heuristic decomposition approaches for an integrated task scheduling and personnel rostering problem. Comput. Oper. Res. **76**, 60–72 (2016)

Mining Rational Team Concert Repositories: A Case Study on a Software Project

Pedro Cunha[1(✉)], André Ferreira[1], and Paulo Cortez[2]

[1] Bosch Car Multimedia Portugal, S.A, 4705-820 Braga, Portugal
{fixed-term.pedro.cunha2,andre.ferreira2}@pt.bosch.com
[2] Department of Information Systems, ALGORITMI Centre,
University of Minho, 4804-533 Guimarães, Portugal
pcortez@dsi.uminho.pt

Abstract. Software repositories are key to support the development of software. In this article, we present a Mining Software Repositories (MSR) approach that considered a two-year software project repository, set using the Rational Team Concert (RTC) tool. Such MSR was designed in terms of three main components: RTC data extraction, RTC data mining and design of RTC intelligence dashboard. In particular, we focus more on the data extraction component, although we also present mining and dashboard outcomes. Interesting results were achieved, revealing a potential of the proposed MSR to improve the software project planning/development agility and quality.

Keywords: Software engineering · Data mining · Association rules

1 Introduction

Most software products are only possible by team collaboration. This is a direct result of the ever-growing complexity inherent to most software products. Software repositories are a fundamental element in the software development process allowing team members to share and store the result of their development efforts.

The term *software repository* is a wide-ranging term, applied to a large variety of relevant software development process entities. The most well-known repositories are source code repositories that provide source code version control features (e.g., git[1], SVN[2]). Source code version control tools provide not only a synchronization mechanism for software developers but also create a timeline of changes in the source code, allowing development teams to understand and track in detail the changes that result from implementing new and incremental product features. Other type of software repositories are bug or defect tracking repositories (e.g., Bugzilla[3]). These repositories allow a more effective and efficient management of product quality by supporting the efforts in testing and

---

[1] https://git-scm.com/.
[2] https://subversion.apache.org/.
[3] https://www.bugzilla.org/.

© Springer International Publishing AG 2017
E. Oliveira et al. (Eds.): EPIA 2017, LNAI 10423, pp. 537–548, 2017.
DOI: 10.1007/978-3-319-65340-2_44

removal of software defects. In advent of agile methodologies applied to software development, bug tracking systems evolved to issue management systems (e.g., Jira[4]), being these used as tools to support project management by allowing the creation and assignment of a set of additional issue types, that are used to document not only concepts relevant to project management (e.g., tasks) but also software engineering outcomes (e.g., features and software requirements). In this paper, IBM Rational Team Concert (RTC[5]) tool is used, which integrates under a single platform several software repository core aspects of version control and issue management systems.

Software repositories, such as RTC, typically store a vast and diverse amount of data, including direct results from the software engineering actions performed by developers and also complex inter-relations between developers and software engineering outcomes over the project lifetime. Such data translates and maintains relevant dependencies between actions and outcomes that are very difficult to track by a single person and that are quite relevant to understand how the software development evolves in a project. Mining these relations could potentially provide relevant knowledge for software teams to improve software processes. In particular, by understanding of cause-result relations of team actions. However, since a large amount of data is stored, the manual analysis of such data repository is prohibitive. Thus, several researchers have focused on using (semi-)automated approaches, leading to the Mining Software Repositories (MSR) concept [1]. In this paper, a MSR approach is presented being applied to an ongoing software project (as a case study). The goal of the case study was to extract valuable intelligence to guide software development decisions by the team in the scope of a software project. To achieve this goal, the focus was on three major steps: (i) retrieving RTC repository data; (ii) RTC data mining; and (iii) presenting RTC extracted knowledge using a friendly dashboard system.

Following this, a review of the related work will be presented in Sect. 2, being proceeded by the efforts related to the proposed MSR approach in Sect. 3. Finally, the conclusions are presented and discussed in Sect. 4.

2   Related Work

The concept of MSR to guide software development was first introduced by Hassan in 2005 [1], which applied a set of statistical and mathematical heuristics over data extracted from large open-source software repositories in order to identify a set of development process related issues. In 2008, the same author scrutinized the types of software development focus areas that gathered the most interest among researchers. Non-surprisingly, the prediction and understanding of defects were considered the preferential study facet [2]. More recently, in 2016, Farias et al. confirmed the preponderance of bug oriented studies within the MSR domain but also noticed a growth on other relevant issues, such as related with the developer or changes [3].

---

[4] https://www.atlassian.com/software/jira.
[5] http://www-03.ibm.com/software/products/en/rtc.

Since 2005, the usage of MSR approaches is increasing due to the steady growth and interest in software development support tools, repositories and the consequent inability to manually analyze all the data generated. In this section, we list a few examples. In 2005, the Dynamine system was presented, aiming to discover source code usage patterns, via the popular Apriori association rules algorithm, on large software systems and identify errors, by using version control repository data [4]. In 2010, Hribar and Duka presented an approach to assess the quality of software components using the k-Nearest Neighbors algorithm (KNN) and Fuzzy Logic [5]. More recently, in 2016, Sun et al. used Latent Dirichlet Allocation topic model detection to recommend interfaces for developers to reuse [6]. These studies exemplify that MSR can provide actionable insights related with software project development, thus aiding developers in their implementation and maintenance processes.

MSR is a more complex task when compared with standard data mining, where it is relatively easy to apply machine learning algorithms to tabular data via off-the-shelf solutions. In contrast, MSR works on semi-structured repository data and that often was not collected with mining in mind [2]. Thus, current MSR approaches require a substantial customization substantial effort, mainly set in terms of the design and implementation of the extraction of relevant repository data. We further note that the particular analysis of RTC repositories is a recent topic that has been scarcely researched. In 2011, Kwan et al. [7] studied RTC project development team coordination and its effects on software build success. In the same year, Biçer et al. [8] performed a MSR analysis over RTC aiming to build a defect prediction model using social network metrics. When compared with these two studies, this paper presents and focuses more on novel data extraction method, leading to a different set of analyzable attributes and business analysis scenarios. Similarly to [4], we adopt an association rule mining during the data modeling stage of our MSR.

3   Proposed MSR

In this paper, we present a MSR approach that includes three main components (detailed in next subsections): RTC repository extraction, RTC mining and dashboard decision support tool. As a case study, we selected an ongoing two-year software project, conducted by a team with around 15 developers and that is in its finishing stages. To support the development and maintenance of such project, a RTC repository was adopted, thus allowing to store interesting features that will consist in the raw data of our MSR. We further note that due to privacy and commercial issues, we can only provide limited details about the analyzed software project.

3.1   RTC Repository Data Extraction

RTC is an integrated lifecycle management environment that intends to keep track of the whole software process, from tasks definition to the submission of source code changes. The two core concepts of RTC are *changesets* and *workitems*. *Changesets* are sets of changes applied by developers to files or folders on a certain date. These *changesets* can be associated with the resolution or execution of a *workitem*. A *workitem* represents tasks to be performed by the team in the development process as well as bug reports and customer requirements. A *workitem* is created, modified and possibly resolved by an user at a certain date. It is also possible to define a target date for its resolution. We further note that RTC is widely adopted in projects created inside the software company, thus leading to an easier replication of the presented data extraction procedures to other projects, making possible to bridge a gap that is usually challenging within the MSR domain [2].

In general, the development is initiated by the requirement tracking phase. From the existing requirements, a set of development tasks is formulated, being these fulfilled by source code modifications. On a feature implementation scenario, visible at Fig. 1, the previously presented workflow maps into RTC objects as follows: **(1)** each requirement is represented as a Business Need *workitem* type; **(2)** a planned development task is described by the Task *workitem* type; **(3)** Source code changes are described by *changesets*.

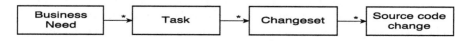

Fig. 1. Regular feature development workflow (UML domain model diagram; * means multiplicity)

RTC provides two official repository management APIs, in Java[6] and REST[7]. These methods for accessing RTC allow a larger spectrum of operations over the repository, being the Java API the one that allows a wider set of functionalities. Other options exist relying on Python[8]. Another possible approach at accessing RTC data would imply relying on existing migration tools such as rtc2Git[9] and rtc2Jira[10], into temporary git and Jira repositories, for which tools already exist that allow the conversion of the repositories' data into database records, by using CVSAnalY[11] or Bicho[12], for example. By default, a RTC repository also includes a web client to allow its users to visualize and query repository objects. For example, it is possible to define a query to obtain all the *workitems* of a certain project, allowing an exportation to a CSV file. The extraction of *changeset* objects is a topic that will receive more attention, since such data is not

---

[6] https://jazz.net/library/article/1229.

[7] https://jazz.net/wiki/bin/view/Main/ReportsRESTAPI.

[8] https://pypi.python.org/pypi/rtcclient.

[9] https://github.com/rtcTo/rtc2git.

[10] https://github.com/rtcTo/rtc2jira.

[11] https://github.com/MetricsGrimoire/CVSAnalY/.

[12] https://github.com/MetricsGrimoire/Bicho/.

obtainable as a formatted file, being its access only possible via a custom query result. This tool originates an additional set of data retrieval methodologies. The first is to perform a web crawling over the search result pages. It is also possible to identify which HTTP requests populate the search results pages and subsequently the *changeset* information page, in order to discover exploitable request patterns to obtain all the necessary information.

The main advantages of available APIs are the broad range of possible operations allowed on a repository. However, the large number of instances of these entities in the system increases the difficulty of effectively learning how to use such libraries. Moreover, when using APIs to obtain all *changesets* and *workitems* this may result in high computational resources consumption, possibly resulting into temporary service interruption. Furthermore, the use of already existing tools can be valuable by allowing a decrease in implementation effort necessary to retrieve data for analysis. Yet, the necessary time to obtain data depends on the repository size, which may result in a longer computational effort to retrieve all *changeset* data (see footnote 9). On the case of *workitem* retrieval, it is necessary that the *workitem* objects to retrieve are sequentially identified. Such precondition is not respected, after repository inspection, being this data access method deemed unfeasible. As such, use of web crawling or HTTP request exploiting is preferable, allowing a lower computational load on the server, corresponding to the load associated to render an information page in the web client. However, the automation level associated with these methods is limited, due to the necessity of manually updating the authorization cookies by logging in on the web client. Web crawling implies previous knowledge of the HTML page structure and, in this case, the search result pagination and the fact that this page relies on AJAX to fill the web client information increase the data extraction complexity. The utilization of HTTP request exploitation aims to accomplish a lower data extraction complexity due to the easy translation of the JSON responses into Java objects, as well as most of the request management process being almost totally programmatic, with the sole fault point being the user access cookies.

Table 1 summarizes the strengths and weaknesses of the RTC data access methods. Based on this, and having in mind that the data extraction engine must be computationally light, the usage of APIs was considered unfeasible. Thus, we opted the HTTP request exploitation access method, which presents a lower time overhead, when designing our functional data extraction module.

The developed data extraction engine retrieves attributes related with: *Workitems*, from a list of identifiers that are the result set of a previously developed query; and *Changesets*, using the unique *changeset* identifiers obtainable from the search result over all the *changesets* of the repository. The *changeset* search that is run at the web client can be tweaked to present a larger *changeset* quantity, until a maximum of 512 per page being controlled by their submission date. Unique *changeset* data is extractable using an identifier from the list of *changeset* search results. The *workitem* identifier retrieval is achievable via a

Table 1. Comparison between RTC data access methods

Access method	Advantages	Disadvantages
API	+ Possible operation range	− Very lengthy learning
	+ Authentication only needs to happen once	− Server shutdown susceptibility
Migration projects	+ Lower implementation effort	− Excessive data extraction time
		− Preconditions non-compliance
Web crawling	+ Lower computational load	− Authorization manual update
		− Page structure knowledge
		− Results pagination
		− AJAX populated page
HTTP requests	+ Lower computational load	− Authorization manual update
	+ High level of request automation	
	+ Easy response translation to Java objects	

RTC web client query, subsequently exporting its results to CSV, being these finally translated to the JSON format.

We first defined a data model for the RTC repository extraction. Such model includes a *RTCLog* object that contains two lists corresponding to the two core components of the RTC repository: *workitems* and *changesets*. A *workitem* is represented in the data model by its unique numeric identifier, its type (e.g., "Task", "Defect"), its priority and severity indexes, its resolution state (e.g., "Open", "In Progress", "Resolved"), as well as a textual summary and description, storing also information about the user that created, last modified, and resolved the *workitem*. Also, it includes temporal data related to the creation, last modification, resolution and target dates. A *workitem* also stores the identifiers of related *workitems*. A *changeset* instance records the unique textual identifier, its author, the creation date, the comment associated with it, the list of *workitem* identifiers, expressing logged work on a running task or defect. Moreover, a *changeset* has its list of changes performed on files or folders. Each change has its unique identifier, the path to the file or folder, the type of change (e.g. modification, deletion) as well as the number of added and deleted lines. The resulting data model is shown in Fig. 2 in terms of a UML class diagram.

We note that the access cookies need to be manually updated. In particular, in the first data retrieval, it might not be possible to extract all the relevant data from the repository with one single engine execution. Thus, the data is stored incrementally, updating the extraction of the unprocessed *changesets* and *workitems*, every 25 repository objects. The execution of this engine resulted in an 18.5 Mb JSON file containing data from 2678 *workitems* and 10133 *change-*

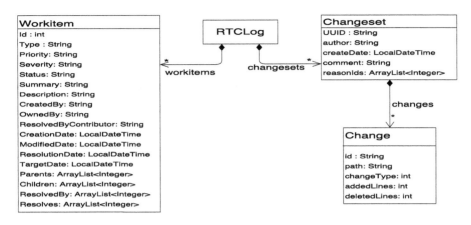

Fig. 2. Extraction engine data model (UML class diagram)

sets. Overall, such extraction required a reasonable computation (total of 8 h to extract the *changesets* and 2 h for the *workitems*), confirming that the implemented solution is lightweight and feasible with current personal computers.

A future research topic is the automatic acquisition of access cookies, as currently the authorization update procedure consists of waiting for the expiration of the cookie (that forces the termination of the engine), logging in to the web client, retrieving the access cookie and updating its value on the engine.

3.2 RTC Data Mining

We set two main goals when analyzing the extracted RTC data:

– (i) **business need** – to discover the traceability between a client requirement and changes to a source code file; and
– (ii) **source code co-change** – to identify the source code files with the most change interdependency within the repository.

Regarding the first goal, when developing new features in a software project it is crucial that the newly implemented functionalities do not invalidate the previously codified efforts. Moreover, client requirements can change during the project timeline execution. On both of these cases, the discovery of significant dependencies between requirements and source code file changes enables an improved feedback on product requirement change, as well as providing knowledge over which requirements are being significantly affected by the change on a source code file.

The construction of the dataset to analyze implies the establishment of the route between the business need and the change on a source code file. The execution of the migration from JSON data to *(Business Need, Source Code)* tuples originated 5792 analyzable pairings.

Following this data migration, we performed data distribution analysis tasks, in order to assess and pinpoint a support rate that allows the generation of relevant dependencies between business needs and source code files. The most active business need makes up to 10.75% of the complete set of available pairings. On the other hand, the most updated source code file represents 2.5% of the complete data set. As such, in the best possible case, interesting rules containing these elements will have a maximum support of 2.5% and, in general, a lower average value is expected. Thus, when applying the association rule *Apriori* algorithm [9], during the modeling phase, the minimum support rate was reduced to 0.15% to allow the extraction of a reasonable amount of traceability rules.

Turning to the second goal, one of the software development related anti-patterns with a significant contribution to the emerging of defects is shotgun surgery. This phenomenon occurs when a change to a source code implies alterations in several other files. For example, defects can surface as result of not replicating changes across the various affected files, being caused either by developer oblivion or negligence. The retrieval of relevant co-occurrences will support a developer on the conduction of maintenance tasks, providing the files that change the most simultaneously, as an attempt to mitigate the shotgun surgery hazards.

As previously explained, this case study is instantiated as a market basket analysis. Consequently, each *changeset* whose changes that contain at least one addition or deletion on a source code file is considered a transaction. Each transaction originates a record complying all the changed source code file names separated by a comma. This process allowed to obtain all the relevant source code files, leading to a total of 6655 analyzable transactions. The most frequently changed file makes up for around 2.25% of all the changed files, which is the upper bound for the support value of an association rule. Similarly to the first goal, the association rule mining was performed using the Apriori algorithm, modifying its operation to return at least two association rule elements. The extracted association rules are in the form **LHS** → **RHS**, where **LHS** and **RHS** denote the left and right hand sides of the rule, set in terms of itemsets.

We executed the association rule analysis in the R tool via the *arules* package [10]. The obtained results are analyzed in terms of rule triviality and statistical significance (in terms of the popular support, confidence and lift measures). These measures were preferred as they convey the significance of the rules within the data as well as the interdependence between the **LHS** and **RHS** elements. For confidentiality reasons, both the files names and the identifiers of business needs will be sanitized. Identifiers starting with **F** indicate source code files, whilst codes initiated with **BN** identify Business Need *workitems*. The surrogate keys are independent between the analysis scenarios.

Table 2(a) and (b) illustrate a portion of the results obtained from the association rule mining for the two main goals. The visible rules were selected using its rule support interest measure, being selected a demonstrative set of rules for each goal. Regarding the first goal, we highlight that a considerable quantity of source code files implement a single requirement, in an effect that is visible in Table 2(a) through the high confidence values on the generated rule set. Turning to the second goal, it was possible to identify the existence of trivial rules.

In the context of this project, that relies mainly on imperative programming (C language), an example of a trivial rule is *"the modification of a source code file implies a modification on its header file"*. Examples of trivial rules discovered within the rule set are shaded in Table 2(b). It is also possible to identify a strong interconnection between the changes to three distinct XML files. The generated association rules have a reduced support value. This can be an indicator that good programming practices, such as modularity and encapsulation, were adopted by the team. On the case of traceability between requirements and source code, it is visible that the very high rule confidence values convey the methodical implementation of a source code file under a single requirement, being the extracted rules useful for streamlining the development team's response to requirement change. On the analysis of simultaneous source code changes, it is visible that even though the contribution of a file from the left-hand side of the rule occurs in a low proportion, from its modification results almost always on the simultaneous modification of the files that comply the right-hand side of the association rules. Finally, we note that all extracted rules have a very high lift values, typically much higher than one.

Table 2. Snippet with example association rules results

(a) Business Need - Source Code Traceability

LHS	RHS	Support	Confidence	Lift
F1	BN1	0.005179	1	9.29695
F2	BN1	0.003108	0.9	8.36726
F3	BN2	0.002935	1	71.5062
F4	BN2	0.002762	0.9411	67.2999
F5	BN1	0.002589	0.8333	7.74745
F6	BN1	0.002417	0.8235	7.65631
F7	BN1	0.002071	1	9.29695

(b) Source Code Co-Change

LHS	RHS	Support	Confidence	Lift
F1.xml	F2.xml	0.00777	0.909	76.304
F3.xml	F2.xml	0.00777	0.869	72.986
F1.xml F3.xml	F2.xml	0.00686	0.913	76.699
F4.h	F4.cpp	0.00518	0.952	74.285
F5.h	F5.cpp	0.00466	0.972	92.756
F6.h	F6.c	0.00440	0.944	41.674

3.3   Dashboard and Overall Intelligence System

We developed a dashboard tool to present the MSR main results to the development team, since the majority of the elements that comply this project's team are not familiar with data analytics terms and concepts. Such dashboard includes statistical measures, such as the *average task resolution elapsed time*, as well as the association rules results for the two MSR goals.

The dashboard was designed using Microsoft Excel and it includes four main vertical components (Fig. 3). The leftmost component allows the selection of one or more business needs, listing the files that were most changed for each business need. The second component includes two graphs with the top changed files from the previously selected business need (top plot); and the top changed files on the global repository (bottom plot). The third component displays the list of business need traceability links, ordered by rule support measure, as well as the average and standard deviation for number of changed files by *changeset*, business need and task resolution time. Finally, the rightmost component describes the existing association rule file interdependencies (ordered by support measure, top left list in Fig. 3) and the distribution of the changed source code files (x-axis denotes the number of changed files and y-axis the *changesets*; bottom graph).

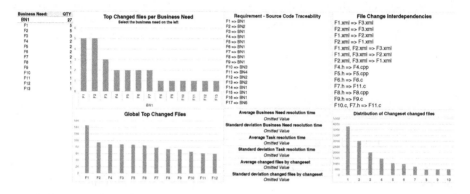

Fig. 3. Dashboard prototype (due to privacy issues, some elements are sanitized)

Overall, a very positive feedback was obtained from the project team. For instance, the results provided by the business need traceability are useful when a new change request is issued by the customer. The dashboard allows the team members to identify which files could be involved in the necessary update to fulfill such request, which helps the team to minimize the analysis and implementation time related to a change. Turning to the discovery of file co-changes, the extracted rules can inform the developer that if she/he changes a file, which other files could also require modification. This alerts the developer for possible changes that she/he could miss if she/he was not reminded by this support system. This decreases the chance for bug injection, therefore improving overall development effectiveness.

To enable an automatic update of the extracted intelligence to the development teams, we defined a data pipeline that empowers a continuous data extraction, mining and extracted knowledge presentation cycle, giving use to the several components described in the previous sections. On a time scheduled basis, a search for new *changesets* and *workitems* is performed, being the query results the input for the execution of *RTCEngine*. The successful data extraction results in an incremented JSON dataset (described in Sect. 3.1). Following this, association rules are applied to obtain intelligence in terms of several scenarios (in this paper, we approach two particular goals) and over the currently available repository data (Subsect. 3.2). Finally, the interesting rules are updated on the dashboard and presented to the development team. Figure 4 shows the adopted data pipeline. Currently, the transition between the pipeline components is operated manually, as these components are executed separately.

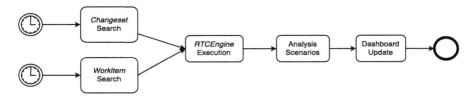

Fig. 4. Proposed data pipeline (BPMN diagram)

4   Conclusions

In this paper, we present a Mining Software Repositories (MSR) approach, where we extracted and analyzed relevant data from an ongoing two-year software project integrated lifecycle management repository, based on the IBM Rational Team Concert (RTC) tool. The MSR approach assumes three main components: RTC repository data extraction, RTC data mining and designing a dashboard with the extracted intelligence. Since the design of the first component is non-trivial and quite dependent of the analyzed repository, we implemented it from scratch, using the Java language. As such, this paper puts more focus on this component, although the other two components are also addressed.

The implemented data extraction engine allowed to obtain the relevant data from the repository on the normal working hours without causing service interruption due to computational overload. The main limitation of this engine is the necessity for manual update of the authorization cookies, which provide access to the repository data. The assurance of such conditions posed a major challenge as the standard repository access methods available are heavy, as the achieved workaround required additional time and effort to implement.

The studied analysis scenarios concentrated mainly on the assessment of source code file change patterns. In particular, two main goals were addressed: the discovery of dependencies between source code files and client requirements; and source code file co-changes. Using the popular *Apriori* algorithm [9], we extracted several association rules that were evaluated in terms of statistical measures and rule triviality. Overall, the obtained rules had high confidence and lift values but also presented a low support. We also identified some trivial rules related with usage of the C language, where a change in a source code file implies a modification on its header file. The low support values suggest that best programming practices, such as modularity or encapsulation, are quite adopted by the software project team. We also implemented a prototype of a dashboard to provide the extracted intelligence to the developers in a visual manner. Such dashboard received a positive feedback and enables the team to improve their development practices. The additional knowledge provided by the performed data mining techniques will support the improvement on the project's planning and development dynamics. For example, the results obtained by the business need traceability case study will provide input for an insightful planning and estimation of effort as response to client change requests. Results provided by the analysis of source code interdependencies also proved to be useful as it provided the developers a reminder over files that are significantly changed together. All this information aims to decrease development effort by allowing developers to spend less time in designing the solution and *implementing it right* the first time.

While interesting results were achieved, there are several improvements that could enhance the proposed MSR but that are left for future work. For example, more research is needed in order to increase automation and support the analyst during the full MSR lifecycle (e.g., automatic access to cookies in the RTC extraction component). Also, we plan to increase the set of repository mining use cases and business goals.

References

1. Hassan, A.E.: Mining software repositories to guide software development. In: International Workshop on Mining Software Repositories (MSR), Missouri, USA (2005)
2. Hassan, A.E.: The road ahead for mining software repositories. In: Frontiers of Software Maintenance, FoSM 2008, pp. 48–57 (2008)
3. de F. Farias, M.A., Novais, R., Júnior, M.C., da Silva Carvalho, L.P., Mendonça, M., Spínola, R.O.: A systematic mapping study on mining software repositories. In: Proceedings of 31st Annual ACM Symposium on Applied Computing, SAC 2016, pp. 1472–1479. ACM (2016)
4. Livshits, B., Zimmermann, T.: Dynamine: finding common error patterns by mining software revision histories. In: ACM SIGSOFT Software Engineering Notes, vol. 30, pp. 296–305. ACM (2005)
5. Hribar, L., Duka, D.: Software component quality prediction using KNN and fuzzy logic. In: 2010 Proceedings of 33rd International Convention, MIPRO, pp. 402–408. IEEE (2010)
6. Sun, X., Li, B., Duan, Y., Shi, W., Liu, X.: Mining software repositories for automatic interface recommendation. Sci. Program. **2016** (2016)
7. Kwan, I., Schröter, A., Damian, D.E.: Does socio-technical congruence have an effect on software build success? A study of coordination in a software project. IEEE Trans. Softw. Eng. **37**, 307–324 (2011)
8. Biçer, S., Bener, A.B., Çağlayan, B.: Defect prediction using social network analysis on issue repositories. In: Proceedings of 2011 International Conference on Software and Systems Process, pp. 63–71. ACM (2011)
9. Agrawal, R., Srikant, R.: Fast algorithms for mining association rules. In: Proceedings of 20th International Conference Very Large Data Bases, VLDB, vol. 1215, pp. 487–499 (1994)
10. Hahsler, M., Grün, B., Hornik, K.: Introduction to arules - mining association rules and frequent item sets. SIGKDD Explor **2**(4), 1–28 (2007)

Predictive Teaching and Learning

Cristiano Galafassi[✉], Fabiane Flores Penteado Galafassi,
and Rosa Maria Vicari

Federal University of Rio Grande do Sul, Porto Alegre, Brazil
cristianogalafassi@gmail.com,
fabiane.penteado@gmail.com, rosa@inf.ufrgs.br

Abstract. In this paper, we present a study about students' behavior based on activity logs in Moodle (an online Learning Management System LMS) analyzing three characteristics: online time (separated by its location), tasks delivered and support material views. We relate these three characteristics with the students' performance (*i.e.* success, fail and dropout) and providing a generalization of four students' groups (based on their behavior on the LMS). After analyzing these characteristics, we evaluate the correlation between each characteristic and the individual student performance, identifying a promising feature to enrich predictive algorithms. Finally, we generated a Naïve Bayes model to predict if the student will succeed, fail or dropout. To evaluate the prediction, we compared the models generated with only the performance data and the models with the enriched data, according with the previously analyzed features. The results shows that the enriched data model are more accurate and may help the teacher to identify "at risk" students.

Keywords: Learning analytics · Predictive learning · Learning management system

1 Introduction

Artificial Intelligence (AI) plays an important role in education in order to produce educationally useful computer tools. Among these tools, Intelligent Tutoring Systems (ITSs) are computer programs that are designed to incorporate techniques from AI community in order to provide tutors, which know what they teach, who they teach and how to teach (Nwana 1990). In order words, ITS attempt to help the teaching and learning process by trying to understand how students learn (Self 1990; Gluz et al. 2013). Our group in Artificial Intelligence has been researching and publishing our finds about this theme for long time. In this sense, the present work will be shown in the terms of the evolution of our previous work. In particular we are interested on the ITS component "who they teach" – the student model.

Much work has been done to evaluate students' performance, like Ranjan and Chakraborty (2015); Alturki (2016); Purarjomandlangrudi et al. (2016), and level of knowledge throughout the course. As an effort to help teachers to understand the knowledge of their students, Learning Analytics (LA) plays an important role providing tools to visualize and analyze students' profile. Through LA it is possible to measure, collect, analyze and report the data about students. It is possible too to

© Springer International Publishing AG 2017
E. Oliveira et al. (Eds.): EPIA 2017, LNAI 10423, pp. 549–560, 2017.
DOI: 10.1007/978-3-319-65340-2_45

understand and improve learning, and the environment in which it occurs. LA in this context can be defined as the analysis and reporting of educational data for optimizing the environment and learning process in which it occurs (Siemens and Gasevic 2012). On the other way, predicting algorithms act in this context aiming to predict students' future score, allowing, therefore, the teacher to intervene in the learning process. As LA and Predictive Algorithms (PA) focus on the same goal, some researchers have tried successfully to enrich predictions data with LA information, searching for more accurate response.

Predicting algorithms are usually provided with demographic, social and performance data. Some information may be difficult to obtain due to some restricted access or because it depends on specific software. On the other hand, relevant data may be extracted from the LMS. LMSs usually generate a large amount of data, which needs to be carefully analyzed to avoid noise and misinformation. Most LMSs and ITSs may integrate students' model component, which is able to analyze the given data and trace a behavioral student model. They can also getting important information for a prediction algorithm so providing teacher with the expect students' scores.

In this context, this paper aims at presenting an analysis of the online academic behavior using activity Moodle logs to describe the selected features between in class and extra class time. We presented three main features: online time on the course, tasks submitted and support resources visualized. After this analysis, we choose the main feature to enrich a predicting algorithm, trying to predict if a student will succeed, fail or dropout the class, looking to generate an initial version of a student model, capable of predict the future student performance. It is important to mention that LMSs, like Moodle, may be used to support distance and face-to-face learning and bringing a student model that is able to predict possible failures and dropouts may provide important information to the teachers.

The paper is organized as follows: Sect. 2 presents a literature review about students' performance predictors and learning analytics as a base line to our model; Sect. 3 describes the research context, the methodology and the proposed students' model; in Sect. 4 our results and discussion are presented; finally, in Sect. 5 conclusions are drawn as well as future work.

2 Related Work

Currently, numerous studies have been conducted using LA, whether in the context of institutional LMSs, MOOCs or other environments. Among them, we can mention the use of LA as a tool for identification of students' profiles, performance analysis and identification of content review needs. In the context of institutional LMSs, Casey and Gibson (2010) present a study using Moodle activity logs, which seek to validate two main points: (i) can the document/page views in Moodle be correlated with student evaluations? (ii) Does the use of Moodle in the institution or outside it makes difference in student evaluations? Based on experiments, the authors concluded that the higher the level of activity in Moodle, the better the students' grades. The authors define level of activity as the amount of online activity (online time, tasks, videos and forums) the student performed. Still, activities outside the institution and in the evening showed some correlation with better ratings. Moreover, Casey and Gibson (2010) analyzed Moodle activity logs of Computer Science courses in order to understand the behavior of students, focusing on the relationship between the number of resource views (files/pages) and the final students' grades. In this latest study, they have concluded that there is some correlation between the level of activity in Moodle and students' performance.

Still regarding work related to the Moodle activity logs, Calvo-Flores et al. (2006), sought to predict students' grades by the application of artificial neural networks in 250 students data. The characteristics used for analysis included the number of test sessions, total accesses, percentage of views of resources, the total number of each type of displayed resources, and the percentage of access per month. Corrigan (2014) applied models based on Machine Learning using a support vector machine to identify students "at risk" and alert teachers through a web application. Baker et al. (2015) have suggested a priori risk factor detection by measuring how well a final grade could be, based on assessing whether the student has opened a resource (document/page) within a certain period of time or not. Bovo et al. (2015) have created an application to monitor students' progress during the course. To this end, a number of different classifiers were tested, including logistic regression and Naïve Bayes. The characteristics used in the classifiers included login frequency, last login date, amount of time spent online, number of classes and displaying the number of completed tasks carried out. The authors used the average grade obtained in the exams as a target variable. Based on the results, the authors sought to identify best techniques to predict final students' grades.

In addition to the LMSs and ITSs, the Massive Online Open Courses (MOOCs) play an important role in the learning process. Moreover, MOOCs are one of the applications to PAs. In this way, we show some related work with PAs and MOOCs.

Still in the context of LA, Smith et al. (2012) presented a case study of the use of LA and the development of a predictive model to identify students at risk of failure in a community college. After identifying characteristics related to the use of the virtual environment such as access to the system, view resources, activity posting, access to virtual classes, among others, the authors proposed a classifier based in Naïve Bayes model. Furthermore, the input variables to the predictive model went through a correlation analysis in order to identify the relevant prediction information. Since Naïve Bayes-based methods require a great connection between the variables, the model did not get high quality results. Still, the authors raised important questions such as "What factors are effective to predict the evaluations of students in online courses in advance or on the fly?", "How does community colleges may use these factors in predictive models to predict students' ratings?" and "How does community colleges can use predictive models to perform proactive, effective and sustainable students' interventions in order to improve students' rates?". Despite the results, other studies, such as Macfadyen and Dawson (2010) identified that some variables obtained with LA worked as forecasters for excellent retention and academic performance.

Ruipérez-Valiente et al. (2015) use LA as a support for the teaching-learning process. They present the ALAS-KA module (Add-on of the LA support of the Khan Academy) to contribute to the visual analysis of the data of students registered at Khan Academy platform. This architecture allows teachers to process the huge amount of raw educational data to obtain refined information about the students. Besides the usual information, such as number of hits, number of posted jobs, correct exercises, among others, it is possible to have a broader perspective on the profile of students' point of view in terms of pedagogical aspects. For example, it is possible to analyze users who abuse the hints and even affectivity related information. The work presented by Ruipérez-Valiente et al. (2015), shows a series of indicators that can be used to support decision-making regarding the learning process. Still, the views of the ALAS-KA module may support teachers with an overview of different indicators of their classes, so that they can make the appropriate corrections, enable self-reflection of the students, or use the automatic setting of a user model based on learning styles and emotions. As this information is important for teachers, the same refined information may be used in predictive models.

3 Methodology

Analyzing the Moodle activity logs, three features may be easily extracted and may be used to trace the students' online behavior. They are Online time, Tasks delivered and Support material views.

Considering the papers presented by Młynarska et al. (2016); Casey and Gibson (2010), which indicate that the moment when students use the LMS is relevant to students' performance, the online time has been evaluated in different ways. First, we analyzed the total online time. Second, we separated this time between in class time and extra class time, verifying when students use the LMS therefore creating four profiles: (i) students that used the LMS during the class, to follow the teacher; (ii) students that used the LMS almost after the class, to review the subjects; (iii) students that used the LMS in both cases; and (iv) students who did not use the LMS at all. The second feature analyzed was when the tasks were returned: within deadline, late or not delivered. It was allowed to submit tasks after the deadline, so that students could make up for some missed tasks. Finally, in the third feature we analyzed the amount of support materials and where they were visualized: in class or extra class. Thus, as in the mentioned works, we assessed whether the students' participation in the academic environment Moodle is a good performance predictor.

After the analysis of the behavioral features, we verified which of these features may be used to enrich the prediction models, being capable of promoting improvement in its quality. Therefore, we initially checked the predictor's quality using just performance features, as a baseline. After that, we enriched the prediction models with the selected features and generated new ones. In order to evaluate these models, we have simulated an environment based in three different moments: after the first assessment (moment when most students dropout), after the second and after the third assessment. As the models use performance information (grades in each assessment), we have simulated a passage of time along the semester and, since the models were based on performance, the prediction models created were after each assessment.

Still, we had used the concept that there was a history of previous classes on the same subject. Therefore, the models were trained with complete information (simulating a class history) and used a test set with partial information. To evaluate the models, we used the cross-validation technique (10 folds), which separates the total data in ten parts, trains the model with nine of them and the last part is used as a training set.

Predictive methods are generally evaluated based on the ability to process the data and correctly predict a rating. The ratings are generally separated into four categories (Mitchell 1997). The classifications will be interpreted based on the objective prediction: True Positives (risk students provided properly as at risk), False Negatives (risk students provided erroneously as without risk), False Positives (students without risk were incorrectly predicted to be at risk) and True Negatives (students with no risk of neglect that were predicted correctly as no dropout risk).

Among the metrics for model evaluation, we emphasized the Sensitivity, the Positive Predictive Value and Accuracy (Mitchell 1997). Sensitivity indicates the ability of the model to correctly predict the final students' situation, Positive Predictive Value (PPV) indicates the probability of a prediction that matches the final students' situation and Accuracy Indicates what is the percentage of correct answers that the model obtained from the ratio between the total correct answers and the total data.

This study uses data from two introductory computing courses, taught in the first semester of 2016 in a Brazilian Federal University: Cartographic and Surveying Engineering and Bachelor in Interdisciplinary Science and Technology (BICT), with a total of 104 students. Despite the different courses, topical subjects were exposed in the same way, the three exams contained the same subjects, and the professor was the same for both groups. Students who did not achieve the expected performance during the semester were allowed to take a final exam, which would replace the lowest score of the three assessments. In this work, it is considered that successful students obtained an average grade above 6.0[1] in the three evaluations (considering the final exam). Students who had an average grade lower than 6.0 in the three evaluations (even if they have not taken the exam) are considered as failed and dropouts as they have not carried out the assessments and the exam, regardless of their frequency.

The courses consist of 15 face-to-face lessons and assessments. Each lesson is followed by supporting materials in PDF format, as well as a task to be delivered until the next class. All students were enrolled in the course in the academic environment Moodle, so that everyone knew, a priori, the schedule, the delivery dates and when the supporting materials would be available. As result, among the 104 students, 30 were successful (29%), 49 failed (47%) and 25 dropped out before the end of the semester (24%). Among the dropouts, 19 (76%) left the course after the first assessment, indicating that after verifying their partial grade, they have chosen to devote efforts to other disciplines, a common practice in the institution.

Considering this scenario, the present study aims at analyzing which features extracted from the LMS Moodle activity logs may provide good indicators about students' behavior, hence enriching students' model. Still, which of these features may be successfully associated with the students' performance to provide better prediction results. In order to validate whether these features really support the predictive methods, we used the Weka (Hall et al. 2009) to test different classifiers.

---

[1] In Brazil, the student performance is usually measured with a grade between 0 and 10.

4 Discussions

Initially we presented the data about the time spent online for the discipline in the LMS Moodle, separating the time between "in class" (*i.e.*, time spent during the class) and "extra class" (*i.e.*, time spent at home or in study rooms). It was observed that 91% of the total online time was used extra class and just 9% in class. This suggests that students took time to study and carried out the tasks after the face-to-face class. However, it is necessary to analyze the behavior of students based on their final situation in order to identify a usage pattern. Thus, Fig. 1 shows the final average time using LMS based on the situation and location of the learner.

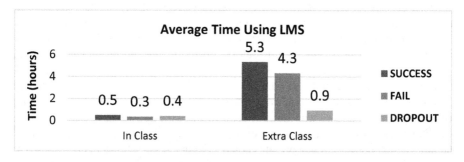

Fig. 1. Average time using LMS.

Analyzing Fig. 1, it is possible to see that the average time spent in LMS, during classes, is lower than the time of extracurricular use. This event is expected since the maximum time in class would be 4 h per week. In addition, we did not notice significant differences between the time spent during class and students' final situation. However, analyzing time extra class, we can notice a difference in the average time use among students who had succeeded and failed compared to students who dropped out. Such behavior was also pointed out by Halawa et al. (2015) where students, who dropped out the course, showed an average usage time much lower than the other students. In addition, as expected, successful students showed greater average time usage than the ones who failed.

Still on LMS usage time, it is important to notice that not all students had used Moodle in class and extra class, thus, Fig. 2 shows the percentage of students who used Moodle in every situation: only in class, only extra class, in both cases and those who did not used the LMS at all.

Considering Moodle usage profile among students, it may be seen in Fig. 2 that many students who dropped out the course did not access LMS, not even to submit an activity. As expected, among the students who persisted in the course, most used LMS in both locations. Based on this, it is possible to classify students into four distinct groups: Students who are not dedicated and succeeded; Students who are not dedicated and failed; Dedicated Students who succeeded; and Dedicated Students who failed.

Still, it can be seen that the most successful students were classified as dedicated. The same applies to students who failed. This scenario appears to be promising for

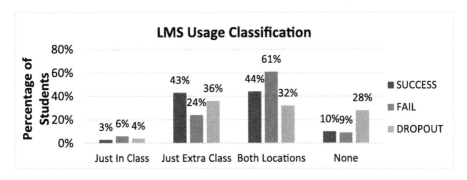

Fig. 2. LMS usage classification depending on the students' final situation.

interventions in learning process, since it is expected that students show some effort to improve their grade with the assistance of the teacher. It is noteworthy that the data presented represents the use of LMS in general, however it is crucial to analyze at what point it was used. In this sense, Fig. 3 shows the daily average time of extra class usage, where it is possible to see the assessment day.

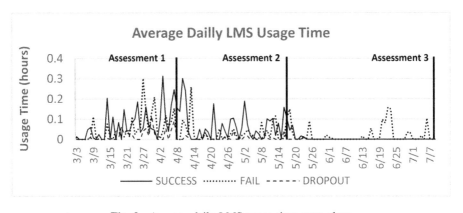

Fig. 3. Average daily LMS usage time extra class.

In Fig. 3, it can be seen that the highest average usage time occurs before the first assessment. This can be noticed for both successful and failed students, where the average usage time is similar. After the first assessment, it is possible to verify a reduction in the average usage time, which can be justified by the grades. Students who have obtained a good grade ended up reducing their dedication, managing the rest of the course. It can be verified by analyzing the time between Assessments 2 and 3 where, after de Assessment 1, there is a significant decrease in the average usage time among students who succeeded and after Assessment 2 there is almost no use. Among the students who failed it is also possible to verify a decrease in the average usage time. Much of the failed students have far below average results if compared to the first evaluation, discouraging further study. Some students continued struggling until the end of the course, in an attempt to reach a success score. Finally, dropouts have a decreasing average usage time along the course, showing an apparent lack of interest in the course. It is worth mentioning that the subject described here is taught in the first semester of the course, consisting mainly of students who have just left high school and are not yet fully aware of the differences in college education teaching process.

Another variable that describe the online academic behavior of the students is linked to the tasks that were delivered. In this context, students who succeeded delivered 58% of the total tasks, students who failed delivered 50% and students who dropped out delivered just 23% of the total tasks. According to Młynarska et al. (2016); Casey and Gibson (2010), by analyzing Moodle activity logs, students with higher level of online activity performed better. The same pattern is shown by these students where students who reached the minimum score to succeed delivered more tasks than failed ones. Moreover, to analyze in more details the characteristics of students, Fig. 4 shows the percentage of tasks delivered within the deadline, late and undelivered separated by situation of students.

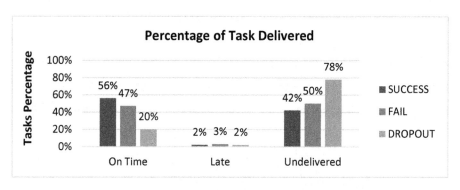

Fig. 4. Percentage of tasks delivered and not delivered on the deadline.

Observing Fig. 4, it can be seen that few activities were submitted after the deadline. What is more, among students who succeeded and failed, 98% of the late tasks were submitted after the third assessment and before the final exam, stating the purpose to be better prepared for the exam. Among the tasks submitted late by dropout students, on average, it happened a week after the deadline, which may suggest that these students were trying to make up for overdue activities. Regarding the activities undelivered by students who succeeded or failed, 92% were related to practical activities and only 8% related to theoretical ones. This feature may suggest that the practical activities involving tools such as word processors, spreadsheets and slides for presentations, were of previous knowledge of the majority or they just did not bring interest.

Finally, the third analyzed feature consisted on the support resources visualized/downloaded by students. This final analysis intended to foster the previous statement: "Students who show higher online activity on LMSs perform better". The students who succeded visualized an average of 69 files, while students who failed visualized 48 and the dropped out students visualized an average of 33 files. Once more, it is possible to verify that successful students were more active, visualizing approximately 20% more resources than students who failed. Following the analysis of the usage location, Fig. 5 shows the average visualization in class and extra-class.

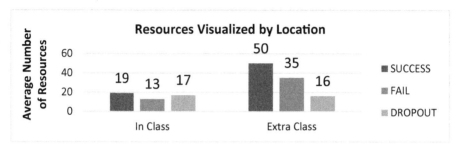

Fig. 5. Average number of resources visualized in class and extra class.

In Fig. 5, it can be observed that students who succeeded made greater use of support materials, both in class as in extra class. In summary, it is possible to verify that students who succeeded had higher level of activity in the virtual environment compared to other students. This is made clear by analyzing the data related to online time spent in LMS, both in class and extra class, the percentage of tasks delivered and the average amount of support material visualized.

Despite the general behavior of the three categories of students (success, fail and drop out) showing differences, it is important to analyze how each examined feature may be correlated to students' performance. In order to that, Table 1 shows the correlation between each studied characteristic (LMS time usage, tasks delivered and supporting resources visualized) with the final average student.

Table 1. Correlation between the studied features and the students' performance.

LMS usage time			Delivered tasks			Resources visualized		
In class	Extra class	Total	On time	Late	Undelivered	In class	Extra class	Total
0.033	**0.294**	**0.299**	**0.463**	0.041	**−0.464**	0.211	**0.425**	**0.459**

Analyzing the data in Table 1, it can be noticed that there is a moderate correlation between the resources visualized, considering extra class or total involvement. Furthermore, there is an inverse correlation with the percentage of undelivered tasks and a moderate correlation with the tasks delivered within the deadline. It is noteworthy that there is a weak correlation between LMS usage time, whether extra class or total. Based on these data, we chose to use the information about the percentage of undelivered tasks and the amount of resources visualized to enrich the predictive models.

In the second step of experiments, we analyzed three characteristics of predictive models, which are the most relevant to the proposed analysis: sensitivity, positive predictive value and accuracy. It is important to bear in mind that the predictive models are built and analyzed after each assessment, in order to compare the chosen metrics. The models are built considering a historical model, so that the model was trained with complete information about the three evaluations (simulating the knowledge about previous semesters) and we tested them with partial information using the data of the assessment mentioned.

Table 2 shows the sensitivity, PPV and accuracy of the predictive models, which were created, based on the algorithm Naive Bayes using the students' performance data and enriched data with LMS.

Table 2. Results of models based on Naive Bayes with performance data and with the enriched data.

Sensitivity						
	Assessment 1		Assessment 2		Assessment 3	
	Perform.	Enriched	Perform.	Enriched	Perform.	Enriched
Succeeded	0.85	**0.87**	**0.79**	0.77	0.89	**0.90**
Failed	0.58	**0.70**	0.70	**0.78**	0.79	**0.93**
Dropout	0.24	**0.89**	0.50	**0.57**	0.61	**0.74**
Positive predictive value						
Succeeded	0.57	**0.67**	0.57	**0.77**	0.57	**0.93**
Failed	0.80	**0.90**	**0.80**	0.73	**0.80**	**0.80**
Dropout	0.16	**0.64**	0.16	**0.64**	0.16	**0.92**
Accuracy						
	0.58	**0.77**	0.66	**0.72**	0.76	**0.87**

It is possible to notice, in Table 2, that the enriched data promoted improvements on the solutions quality, as it can be seen on the Accuracy of the models. Considering the Sensitivity results, a significant improvement is related to the Dropout students. The basic model (only performance data) can not predict dropout students because they get poor grades, as the failed ones, but, with only performance data, it is possible to verify that they really dropped out after the second assessment, when they did not show up the following assessment day. When the model is enriched with behavior information, the model is able to predict what will happen with the student. It is worth mentioning that 76% dropped out after the first assessment, which reinforces the need to correctly predict dropout students as soon as possible. Differently from dropped out students, the ones who succeeded and failed continued making an effort to improve their grades along the course and, as expected, the enriched model predicted better situations after the third assessment. The PPV also shows improvements on the solutions quality, which means that, it is more likely to a predicted situation to happen; actually it matches the real final students' situation.

5   Conclusions

This paper presented an online academic behavioral analysis using activity Moodle logs to describe the selected features. We presented three main features: online time on the course, tasks submitted and support resources visualized. These features were analyzed as a whole, however separated between final students situation and, when analyzing the online time, between in class and extra class time. After the feature analysis, we choose the main feature to enrich a predictive model, focusing at generate an initial student model that is able to predict the future student performance.

The students who showed more activity in LMS performed better than other students did. Successful students were online for average 5.8 h during the whole course, while failed students were for just 4.6 h. The activity is also higher in the other two features. Successful students submitted an average of 58% of the total tasks and visualized the support resource 69 times (in average). Students who failed did just 50% of the tasks and visualized about only 48 resources. These patterns confirm the behavior presented in Młynarska et al. (2016); Casey and Gibson (2010), where the authors found out that students who were more active in the LMS performed better than the others. Still, similar to Halawa et al. (2015) on MOOCs context, we classified students in four groups, for ease of comparison, according to the LMS usage: dedicated and successful students, dedicated students who failed, not dedicated students who succeeded and, finally not dedicated students who failed. It is important to mention that in MOOCs, the students are learning by themselves, while in our context, there were a teacher in every class and a face-to-face intervention may be applied.

An important behavior is related to the moment students mostly used LMS. It is possible to notice that the period before the first assessment is crucial to the whole course. More than 80% of the students who achieved grade higher than 6.0 in the first assessment achieved a success score. This reflects on the average time spent online in LMS, where it is higher previous to the first assessment.

After the feature analysis, the prediction models were tested. Same as Calvo-Flores et al. (2006) and Bovo et al. (2015), we presented predictive models using Moodle activity logs. Differently from the previous works, we performed a correlation analysis to evaluate a possible contribution of each feature in the predictive models solutions. We verified that there is a moderate correlation between the tasks delivered and support resources visualized. These two features were chosen to enrich a prediction model, hopping to improve its quality. The prediction tests were promoted to compare a base line model, consisting in performance information, with an enriched model, compound of the performance and behavior information. One of the most important contributions of these models is the capability to predict dropout students before they reach the second assessment. Since most students dropped out after first assessment, being able to predict this occurrence is essential to intervene in the students' learning process. This ability can not be seen in the basic models and in the previous work.

It is worth remembering that these PAs, whose main application is MOOCs, may be well applied in a student model. This student model, classical component in ITSs, is a promising technique to model the students' knowledge. We show that a LMS that does incorporate a student model may provide important information about the future student behavior.

Despite the promising results, efforts are necessary to develop a method capable of dealing with noisy data generated by LMSs. Such method could deal with the data beforehand or be aggregated with the prediction algorithm searching for better results.

References

Alturki, R.A.: Measuring and improving student performance in an introductory programming course. J.: Inf. Educ. **15**(2), 183–204 (2016)

Baker, R.S., Lindrum, D., Lindrum, M.J., Perkowski, D.: Analyzing early at-risk factors in higher education e-learning courses. In: Proceedings for the 8th International Conference on Educational Data Mining, pp. 150–155 (2015)

Bovo, A., Sanchez, S., Heguy, O., Duthen, Y.: Demonstration of a moodle student monitoring web application. In: Educational Data Mining, pp. 390–391 (2013)

Calvo-Flores, M.D., Galindo, E.G., Jimenez, M.C.P., Pineiro, O.P.: Predicting students' marks from moodle logs using neural network models. Curr. Dev. Technol.-Assist. Educ. **1**(2), 586–590 (2006)

Casey, K., Gibson, P.: (m)Oodles of data: mining moodle to understand student behaviour. In: International Conference on Engaging Pedagogy, pp. 61–71 (2010)

Corrigan, O.: Using third level educational data to help at risk students. In: Insight Student Conference (INSIGHT-SC 2014) (2014)

Gluz, J.C., Penteado, F., Mossmann, M., Vicari, R.M.: Heraclito: a dialectical tutor for logic. In: Portuguese Conference on Artificial Intelligence (EPIA), vol. 8154, pp. 1–2 (2013)

Halawa, S., Greene, D., Mitchell, J.: Dropout prediction in moocs using learner activity features. In: Proceedings of the European MOOC Summit (EMOOCs 2014) (2014)

Mitchell, T.M.: Machine Learning. McGraw-Hill, New York (1997)

Młynarska, E., Greene, D., Cunningham, P.: Indicators of good student performance in moodle activity data. Comput. Soc. (2016)

Nwana, H.S.: Intelligent tutoring systems: an overview. Artif. Intell. Rev. **4**, 215–277 (1990)

Purarjomandlangrudi, A., Chen, D., Nguyen, A.: Investigating the drivers of student interaction and engagement in online courses: a study of state-of-the-art. J.: Inf. Educ. **15**(2), 269–286 (2016)

Ranjan, R., Chakraborty, S.: Performance evaluation of Indian technical institutions using PROMETHEE-GAIA approach. J.: Inf. Educ. **14**(1), 103–125 (2015)

Ruipérez-Valiente, J.A., Muñoz-Merino, P.J., Leony, D., Kloos, C.D.: ALAS-KA: a learning analytics extension for better understanding the learning process in the Khan Academy platform. Comput. Hum. Behav. **47**(1), 139–148 (2015)

Self, J.: Theoretical foundations for intelligent tutoring systems. J. Artif. Intell. Educ. **1**(4), 3–14 (1990)

Siemens, G., Gasevic, D.: Guest editorial - learning and knowledge analytics. Educ. Technol. Soc. **15**(3), 1–2 (2012)

Smith, V.C., Lange, A., Huston, D.R.: Predictive modeling to forecast student outcomes and drive effective interventions in online community college courses. J. Asynchronous Learn. Netw. **16**(3), 51–61 (2012)

Multi-objective Learning of Neural Network Time Series Prediction Intervals

Pedro José Pereira[1], Paulo Cortez[1(✉)], and Rui Mendes[2]

[1] ALGORITMI Centre, Department of Information Systems, University of Minho,
4804-533 Guimarães, Portugal
id6927@alunos.uminho.pt, pcortez@dsi.uminho.pt
[2] Centre of Biological Engineering/ALGORITMI Centre, Department of Informatics,
University of Minho, 4710-057 Braga, Portugal
rcm@di.uminho.pt
http://www3.dsi.uminho.pt/pcortez

Abstract. In this paper, we address multi-step ahead time series Prediction Intervals (PI). We extend two Neural Network (NN) methods, Lower Upper Bound Estimation (LUBE) and Multi-objective Evolutionary Algorithm (MOEA) LUBE (MLUBE), for multi-step PI. Furthermore, we propose two new MOEA methods based on a 2-phase gradient and MOEA based learning: M2LUBET1 and M2LUBET2. Also, we present a robust evaluation procedure to compare PI methods. Using four distinct seasonal time series, we compared all four PI methods. Overall, competitive results were achieved by the 2-phase learning methods, in terms of both predictive performance and computational effort.

Keywords: Multi-objective evolutionary algorithm · Multilayer perceptron · Multi-step ahead prediction · Prediction intervals · Time series

1 Introduction

Data-driven prediction is a key tool within the context of Business Intelligence and Decision Support [12]. In particular, Time Series Forecasting (TSF) is a popular data-driven approach that models a phenomenon based on its past temporal patterns. For instance, multi-step ahead TSF is often used to assist in tactical decisions. Given the interest in TSF, there is a vast literature that approaches TSF using statistical methods, such as Holt-Winters and ARIMA [11], and computational intelligence methods, such as Neural Networks (NN) and Support Vector Machines (SVM) [16]. However, there is much less literature addressing TSF Prediction Intervals (PI), defined in terms of estimating lower and upper bounds for the future values of the output target. It should be noted that PI accounts for more sources of uncertainty (e.g., noise, error measurements, lack of input data, model misspecification) when compared with confidence intervals [10]. And PIs are invaluable in several decision making domains, since they allow to better estimate the uncertainty of key decision variables (e.g., definition of what-if scenarios for the worst and best predicted values).

© Springer International Publishing AG 2017
E. Oliveira et al. (Eds.): EPIA 2017, LNAI 10423, pp. 561–572, 2017.
DOI: 10.1007/978-3-319-65340-2_46

The quality of a PI can be measured in terms of two distinct (often conflicting) objectives [1,10]: the PI coverage and width. The former is often measured by the PI Coverage Probability (PICP), the percentage of real values that are covered by the PI, while the latter is usually measured by the Normalized Mean PI Width (NMPIW). Most PI methods proposed prior to the year of 2011 (e.g., delta, Bayesian, bootstrapping, mean-variance estimation) have two methodological drawbacks [10]. First, the PI is constructed from a data-driven model that was fit to minimize the prediction error but not the PI. Secondly, the quality of the intervals is often assessed using only PI converage (e.g., PICP). Thus, the obtained PIs may not be optimal.

A more natural approach is to directly optimize PIs when fitting the prediction model, as adopted in [1,2,10,14]. The Lower Upper Bound Estimation (LUBE) method was proposed in 2011 [10]. It uses a multilayer perceptron NN with two output nodes containing the lower and upper PI estimates. LUBE minimizes a single and nondifferentiable objective funtion that combines both PICP and NMPIW measures, called coverage width-based criterion (CWC). Thus, instead of adopting backpropagation, the NN weights are fit by using a simulated annealing metaheuristic method. LUBE achieved competitive results when compared with other PI methods (e.g., delta, Bayesian, bootstrap) for regression tasks. In 2013, the LUBEX method was proposed [14], which extends LUBE for one-step ahead TSF PI predictions by using a time-lag feature selection procedure and by considering an ensemble of NN (instead of a single NN). In the same year [1], a Multi-objective Evolutionary Algorithm (MOEA) was adopted to fit the LUBE base NN model, optimizing both the PICP and NMPIW objectives, achieving interesting results for a regression task related with oil and gas equipment. While no comparison was performed with LUBE in [1], the MOEA LUBE (MLUBE) approach is more theoretically sound, since it simultaneously optimizes the conflicting PI coverage and width objectives, while the LUBE CWC criterion tends to favor coverage, in detriment of width. More recently, in 2015 [2], the same MLUBE was adapted to fit a NN with interval-valued time series inputs, where each input example has a lower and upper limit. The NN contains just one output node and the PI is obtained by forwarding first lower input values and then the upper ones. Similarly to LUBEX, only one-step ahead PIs were considered. The proposed MLUBE was compared with an interval-valued input LUBE for wind speed data, achieving better results. However, this comparison considered only one execution and no statistical test was performed.

In this paper, we present and compare approaches that directly optimize TSF PI when fitting the data-driven models, putting more emphasis on multi-objective learning methods. In particular, we extend both LUBE and MLUBE methods to handle multi-step ahead PIs, denoted here as LUBET and MLUBET. Moreover, we propose two new MOEA variants, M2LUBET1 and M2LUBET2, both based on a 2-phase learning and that optimizes a much smaller number of NN weights when compared with MLUBET. Finally, we introduce a more robust methodology to compare PI methods based on several iterations of a realistic rolling window procedure [17] and validated by the Wilcoxon nonparametric statistical test [8]. The paper is organized as follows: Sect. 2 presents the time series data, PI methods and evaluation; Sect. 3 describes the experiments and obtained results; and Sect. 4 discusses the main conclusions.

2   Materials and Methods

2.1   Time Series Data

A time series is made of time ordered observations: $y_1, y_2, \ldots, y_L$, where y_t is the series value for the time period t and L is the length of the series. In this work, we address seasonal time series (seasonal period denoted by K), which is an important and common time series type (e.g., Sales and Production) [11]. Seasonal series are relevant in the context of multi-step ahead prediction, since previous seasonal patterns are expected to reoccur in the future. We selected four time series with different characteristics and from different domains (Table 1 and Fig. 1). Series **cradfq** and **pigs** are from the Time Series Data Library (TSDL) repository [9], **MG** is a chaotic synthetic series [6] and store is described in [4]. The first three series from Table 1 were modeled using NN and SVM in [16], while the last series was fit using SVM in [4].

Table 1. Time series data characteristics (L – series length, K – seasonal period, W – rolling window size, S – rolling window step).

Series	Description (years)	L	K	W	S
cradfq	Monthly critical radio freq. in Washington, D.C. (1934–1954)	240	12	199	1
pigs	Monthly number of pigs slaughtered in Victoria (1980–1995)	188	12	147	1
MG	Mackey-Glass chaotic series (–)	783	17	505	9
store	Daily number of human faces that entered a sports store (2013)	257	7	221	1

2.2   Prediction Interval Methods

A TSF model predicts a value for time $t+1$ based on the past: $\hat{y}_{t+1} = f(y_{t-k_I+1}, \ldots, y_{t-k_1+1})$, where f is the forecasting model function, t is the last known value of the series and the k_i denotes the sliding window with I time lags.

When performing multi-step ahead forecasting, several predictions are made at time t, ranging from $\hat{y}_{t+1}$ (1-ahead) up to $\hat{y}_{t+h}$ (h-ahead, where h denotes the horizon). Multi-step ahead forecasts can be built by iterative feedback. First an 1-ahead prediction is computed and then such 1-ahead prediction is used as the last input of the model f to generate the 2-ahead prediction, and so on [16].

LUBE [10] uses a base learner that consists in a standard NN regression model: a multilayer perceptron with bias weights, one hidden layer with H hidden

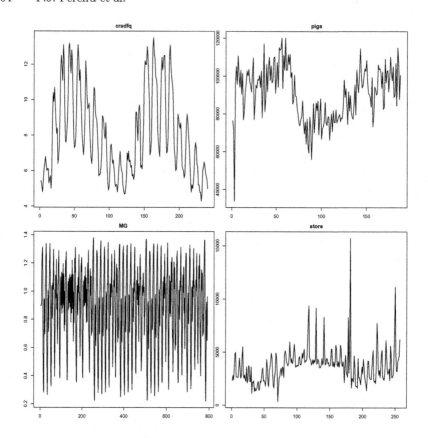

Fig. 1. Time series plots (x-axis denotes the time period t, y-axis the y_t value)

nodes and logistic activation functions, and two output linear function nodes. The total number of NN weights is $w_{\text{LUBE}} = (I + 1) \times H + (H + 1) \times 2$, where the +1 term is due to the use of bias weights. All w_{LUBE} weights are optimized by a simulated annealing which minimizes CWC:

$$
\begin{aligned}
PICP &= \tfrac{1}{n} \sum_{i=1}^{n} c_i \\
NMPIW &= \tfrac{1}{R \times n} \sum_{i=1}^{n} U_i - L_i \\
CWC &= NMPIW\big(1 + \gamma(PICP)e^{-\eta(PICP-\mu)}\big)
\end{aligned}
\tag{1}
$$

where: n is the number of PI; c_i is 1 if $y_i \in [L_i, U_i]$, otherwise $c_i = 0$; L_i and U_i denote the lower and upper bounds for input example i; η and μ are constants (set in [10] as $\eta = 50$ and $\mu = 0.90$); and γ is confidence level step function ($\gamma = 0$ if $PICP \geq \mu$; otherwise $\gamma = 1$). When PICP is higher than the confidence level (μ), CWC produces a small value that is close to NMPIW, otherwise PICP is considered unsatisfactory and CWC increases exponentially.

MLUBE uses the same base NN [1]. The difference is that all NN weights ($w_{\text{MLUBE}} = w_{\text{LUBE}}$) are optimized using the real-valued Non-dominated Sorting Genetic Algorithm-II (NSGA-II) [15], which minimizes both the PI Coverage

Error ($PICE = 1 - PICP$) and width ($NMPIW$). MLUBE uses an internal cross-validation over the training data in order to select the best number of hidden nodes (H), where "best" corresponds to the H value that produces the highest hypervolume [3]. Such hypervolume is a popular measure used to compare MOEA Pareto fronts, which contain all nondominated solutions, i.e., the best multi-objective trade-offs. As an example, the left plot of Fig. 2 shows the computed hypervolume for a two-objective minimization Pareto front with 5 solutions, corresponding to the area covered by the front when assuming a reference point (gray dot). Such reference is often set as the worst point.

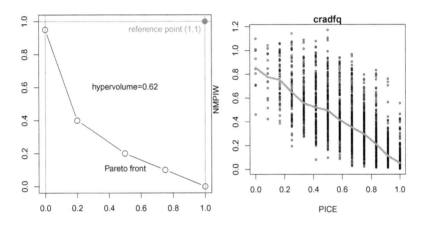

Fig. 2. Pareto front example (left) and full PI test results for MLUBET (right)

In this paper, we adapt LUBE and MLUBE to handle multi-step head TSF PI (LUBET and MLUBET). The adaptation involves computing the next ahead prediction as the middle of the PI: $\hat{y}_{t+i} = (U_{t+i} + L_{t+i})/2$, where $i \in 1, ..., h$ and L_{t+i} and U_{t+i} represent the predicted lower and upper bounds for time $t + i$. Similarly to the standard multi-step ahead TSF, the iterative feedback of the $\hat{y}_{t+i}$ values is used to generate the i-ahead PI and middle values.

We also propose two new MOEA methods based on a 2-phase learning (M2LUBET1 and M2LUBET2). In the first phase, a NN with just one output node is fit to the training data by using a backpropagation algorithm, where the goal is to directly predict 1-step ahead predictions $\hat{y}_i$, as executed in [16]. After training, the NN weights are fixed. In the second phase, two additional output nodes are added to the previous NN, aiming to output the lower and upper values. This leads to a total of $w_{\text{M2LUBET}} = (H + 1) \times 2$ new weights that are optimized by the MOEA metaheuristic algorithm. Thus, the final optimized NN contains 3 output nodes ($\hat{y}_i$, L_i and U_i). M2LUBET1 iteratively feedbacks the first output node ($\hat{y}_{t+i}$) to generate the multi-step ahead PI, while M2LUBET2 ignores such output and computes instead $\hat{y}_{t+i}$ as the PI middle point (similarly to LUBET and MLUBET). When compared to MLUBET, the 2-phase MOEA methods optimize a smaller search space, where $w_{\text{MLUBET}} \gg w_{\text{M2LUBET}}$ since MLUBET optimizes all weights while the 2-phase methods only optimize weights between the hidden layer and the output, which might translate into a better optimization. However, the M2LUBET methods are also more rigid (due to the use of frozen weights) when compared with MLUBET and thus might be more prone to local minima. Therefore, the overall performance of these PI methods needs to be accessed empirically (as executed in Sect. 3).

2.3 Evaluation

To measure the quality of the PI, we applied a fixed-size rolling window scheme [17] that allows a realistic training and testing of a large number of data-driven models. In the first iteration, the rolling window assumes a training data (also known as in-samples) of size W, from which a PI method is fit and then computes multi-step ahead PI (from $i = 1$ to $i = h$) at time $t = W$. The time period $t + 1, ..., t + h$ is considered the test set (out-of-samples) from which the forecasting PICE and NMPIW values are measured. In the second iteration, the training window is slided by discarding the oldest S elements and adding the more recent $t + S$ ones. The current time is updated ($t = W + S$), the PI model is retrained and new multi-step PI and corresponding PICE and NMPIW measures are computed, and so on. Thus, for a series of length L the rolling windows will have $U = \left(L - (W + H - 1)\right)/S$ model updates or iterations.

In this work, we assume a fixed sliding window with all time lags up to $K + 1$ ($k_i \in \{1, 2, ..., K, K + 1\}$), in order to include the seasonal period (K) plus a possible trend. Thus, all PI methods will be compared using the same $K + 1$ inputs. Also for all methods, the number of NN hidden nodes (H) is only searched in the first rolling window iteration, to reduce the computational effort. In this iteration, we use first a sequential holdout (time ordered, to preserve the temporal patterns), where the training data are split into training (70%) and validation (30%) sets. A grid search is then used to range H and select the best H value when measuring 1-step ahead PI for the whole validation set. Since the NN results are stochastic, dependent of the random initial weights, we execute a total of R runs for each H search value. For LUBET we use the average CWC measure to select what is best, while for the MOEA methods we use the average hypervolume with the reference point (1,1). Once the best H is selected, it is fixed. Then, for all rolling window iterations, including the first one, the PI method is refit by optimizing 1-step ahead PI for all training data.

For each rolling window iteration, LUBET selects just one NN, while the MOEA PI methods optimize a Pareto front with several NNs. Moreover, all PI methods are optimized using training data but the predictive evaluation is measured using test data. For the MOEA methods, this means that nondominated NN in the training data can produce dominated results in the test data, presenting several NMPIW values for the same PICE, as shown in the right of Fig. 2. In order to aggregate all rolling window results, we propose a vertical aggregation method, similar to what is used to compare ROC curves [5]. First, all test results for all U iterations, are stored. Then, to compare the PI methods, we estimate the median and 95% confidence intervals for each fixed and distinct PICE value. Such estimation is based on the Wilcoxon nonparametric statistic [8]. An example is shown in the right of Fig. 2, where the Wilcoxon median is plotted in gray color. We also compute the hypervolume of the median test curve when comparing the MOEA based methods.

3 Results

All experiments were conducted using the R tool [13] and a personal computer with an Intel i7 2.60 GHz processor and Windows 10 operating system. The NN backpropagation and simulated annealing procedures were executed using the *nnet* and *optim* R functions, while for NSGA-II the *mco* package implementation was used. We adopted the default R implementation parameters when fitting the NN, including: NSGA-II - population size of 100 and stopping criterion after 100 generations; and NN backpropagation - usage of the BFGS algorithm stopped after 100 iterations. We note that for M2LUBET methods, the first phase BFGS training is faster than the NSGA-II second stage learning. For LUBET, we set the simulated annealing temperature to 5.0 and $\eta = 50$ and $\mu = 0.90$ when computing CWC [10]. Also, to achieve a fair comparison with NSGA-II, the simulated annealing was stopped after $100 \times 100 = 10,000$ iterations.

Before fitting the NN models, the training data were first standardized to a zero mean and one standard deviation [7]. All NNs weights were randomly set within the range $[-1, 1]$. Similarly, the NSGA-II lower and upper bounds were set to optimize weights within the same range $[-1, 1]$. To speed up the optimization methods, the NN PI outputs were not initially fixed but later identified as the lowest (L_i) and highest (U_i) of the two output values during the NN evaluation. After fitting and before computing the multi-step ahead PI, the NN outputs were post-processed with the inverse of the standardized transform.

The rolling windows were set to provide a robust number of $U = 30$ iterations for all series and PI methods. The selected W and S values were adjusted to the series length and are shown in Table 1. The maximum horizon (multi-step lookahead), was set to the seasonal period $h = K$ (e.g., predict the full next week for the daily **store** series). In the first rolling window iteration, we executed ten H searches for each method, ranging the number of hidden nodes from $H = 0$ (equivalent to the simpler multiple regression model) to $H = 9$ (more complex multilayer perceptron). For each H search, we performed $R = 10$ runs. Table 2 shows the selected H values for each method and series. The results from Table 2 show that LUBET selects a smaller number of nodes when compared with the MOEA methods. We also note that when $H = 0$, MLUBET is identical to M2LUBET2, but none of the selected base NN includes the $H = 0$ case.

The obtained mult-ahead PI results are presented in Fig. 3 and Table 3. Figure 3 clearly shows that LUBET is outperformed by all MOEA methods for all time series, even when considering the region where PICE is low. When comparing the MOEA methods, the results are much closer, as indicated by the aggregated median hypervolume values of Table 3. In particular, M2LUBET2 is

Table 2. Selected number of hidden nodes (H)

Series	LUBET	MLUBET	M2LUBET1	M2LUBET2
cradfq	1	5	9	7
pigs	1	8	9	9
MG	1	8	6	4
store	1	6	9	9

clearly the best PI method for a large PICE region (from 0.0 to 0.8) and *cradfq* series. All MOEA methods have very similar performances for the *pigs* series. Both M2LUBET1 and M2LUBET2 slightly outperform MLUBET for a considerable PICE portion (from 0.1 to 0.7) for the *MG* series. And MLUBET achieves a slightly better performance for PICE=0 to PICE=0.7 and the *store* data. The median hypervolume values (Table 3) confirm M2LUBET2 as the best method for *cradfq*, both M2LUBET methods are ranked first for *pigs*, M2LUBET1 is the best method for *MG* and MLUBET outperforms other hypervolume values for *store*. Overall, the best hypervolume median (0.62) is achieved by M2LUBET2.

Table 3. Estimated median hypervolume forecasting values (best value in **bold**)

Series	MLUBET	M2LUBET1	M2LUBET2
cradfq	0.48	0.46	**0.55**
pigs	0.66	**0.68**	**0.68**
MG	0.50	**0.52**	0.51
store	**0.77**	0.76	0.75
Median	0.60	0.60	**0.62**

Table 4 shows the computational effort, measured in terms of time elapsed (in seconds) for all PI methods as measured by the proc.time() R function. LUBET requires around twice of the effort required by the MOEA methods, which might be due to implementation issues since the simulated annealing and NSGA-II R functions are coded in different packages. The MOEA computational requirements are more similar. M2LUBET1 and M2LUBET2 require the same level of computational effort, which makes sense since the optimization code is identical. While using a 2-phase learning, the M2LUBET methods require slightly less effort when compared with MLUBET. This occurs because the BGFS training is much faster than NSGA-II and the M2LUBET methods have less parameters to optimize by NSGA-II when compared with MLUBET. Table 4 also reveals that the computational effort is reasonable for current personal computers (e.g., M2LUBET2 requires round 13 min to process the *cradfq* series) and that the effort is more dependent on the series length (e.g., larger for *MG*).

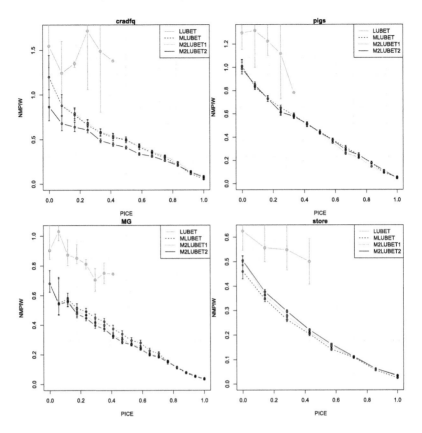

Fig. 3. Prediction Interval test results (dots denote the Wilcoxon median values and whiskers represent the respective 95% confidence intervals)

Table 4. Computational effort (in seconds)

Series	LUBET	MLUBET	M2LUBET1	M2LUBET2
cradfq	1865	984	768	804
pigs	1457	905	746	762
MG	3540	1870	1641	1636
store	1866	833	745	743
Median	1866	945	757	783

As an example of the quality of the optimization, Fig. 4 contains two plots. The left plot shows the convergence of the NSGA-II algorithm for the first rolling windows iteration, M2LUBET2 and *cradfq* data. In the plot, points denote individual NN fitnesses, while lines represent the Pareto front. Also, a gradient coloring scheme is adopted, such that first generation results are in light gray and last generation results are in black. Such plot reveals a consistent improvement of

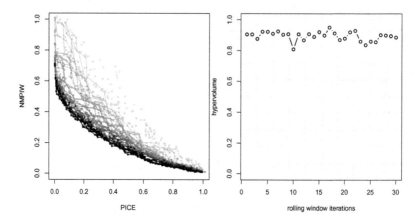

Fig. 4. Example of one M2LUBET2 Pareto front evolution (left) best training hypervolume for all rolling window iterations (right) for the *cradfq* series.

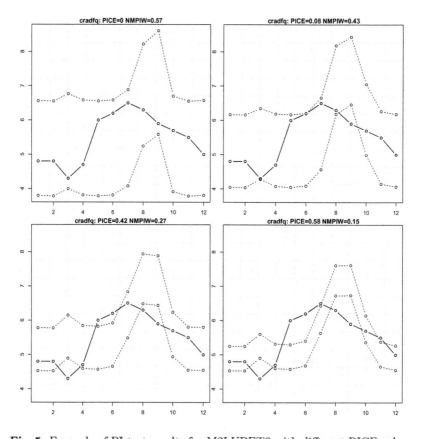

Fig. 5. Example of PI test results for M2LUBET2 with different PICE values

the Pareto front. The right graph of Fig. 4 shows the best training hypervolume obtained for all $U = 30$ rolling window iterations of M2LUBET2 and *cradfq*. In general, high quality hypervolume values were achieved, with a median value of 0.90.

For demonstration purposes, Fig. 5 shows four examples of PI and related with the last rolling window iteration twelve month ahead forecasts for the *cradfq* series. To facilitate the visual analysis, the plots are ordered in terms of the PICE values, from 0 (top left) to 0.58 (bottom right).

4 Conclusions

The Prediction of Intervals (PI) is a valuable tool to reduce uncertainty associated with important decision variables (e.g., expected sales). In this paper, we approach several PI methods based on Neural Networks (NN) for multi-step ahead Time Series Forecasting (TSF). Within our knowledge, this is the first time such an attempt is pursued. In particular, we adapt the Lower Upper Bound Estimation (LUBE) and Multi-objective Evolutionary Algorithm (MOEA) LUBE (MLUBE) for the multi-step ahead context, leading to the LUBET and MLU-BET methods. Moreover, we present two new MOEA variants (M2LUBET1 and M2LUBET2) that are based on a 2-phase learning (gradient and MOEA) and that optimize a reduced number of NN weights when compared with MLUBET. Also, we propose a robust methodology to compare PI methods based on a rolling window procedure and the Wilcoxon statistic.

Several experiments were held by considering four distinct time series. The obtained results show that LUBET achieves the worst results, even for small PI coverage error values, while the MOEA based methods exhibited similar performances. M2LUBET2 and M2LUBET1 are the best option for two of the tested series, while MLUBET is the best method in one. Overall, the best overall median value is achieved by M2LUBET2. Moreover, the M2LUBET methods require slightly less computation effort when compared with MLUBET.

In future work, we intend to explore more types of time series (including multi-variate series) and also adapt the MOEA algorithms to allow the construction of ensembles, such as executed in [14] for LUBE.

Acknowledgments. This work was supported by COMPETE: POCI-01-0145-FEDER-007043 and FCT Fundação para a Ciência e Tecnologia within the Project Scope: UID/-CEC/-00319/-2013, and project: NORTE-01-0247-FEDER-017497.

References

1. Ak, R., Li, Y., Vitelli, V., Zio, E., Droguett, E.L., Jacinto, C.M.C.: NSGA-II-trained neural network approach to the estimation of prediction intervals of scale deposition rate in oil & gas equipment. Expert Syst. Appl. **40**(4), 1205–1212 (2013)
2. Ak, R., Vitelli, V., Zio, E.: An interval-valued neural network approach for uncertainty quantification in short-term wind speed prediction. IEEE Trans. Neural Netw. Learn. Syst. **26**(11), 2787–2800 (2015)

3. Beume, N., Fonseca, C.M., López-Ibáñez, M., Paquete, L., Vahrenhold, J.: On the complexity of computing the hypervolume indicator. IEEE Trans. Evol. Comput. **13**(5), 1075–1082 (2009)

4. Cortez, P., Matos, L.M., Pereira, P.J., Santos, N., Duque, D.: Forecasting store foot traffic using facial recognition, time series and support vector machines. In: Graña, M., López-Guede, J.M., Etxaniz, O., Herrero, Á., Quintián, H., Corchado, E. (eds.) ICEUTE/SOCO/CISIS -2016. AISC, vol. 527, pp. 267–276. Springer, Cham (2017). doi:10.1007/978-3-319-47364-2_26

5. Fawcett, T.: An introduction to ROC analysis. Pattern Recogn. Lett. **27**, 861–874 (2006)

6. Glass, L., Mackey, M.: Oscillation and chaos in physiological control systems. Science **197**, 287–289 (1977)

7. Hastie, T., Tibshirani, R., Friedman, J.: The Elements of Statistical Learning: Data Mining, Inference, and Prediction, 2nd edn. Springer, New York (2008)

8. Hollander, M., Wolfe, D.A., Chicken, E.: Nonparametric Statistical Methods. Wiley, Hoboken (2013)

9. Hyndman, R.: Time Series Data Library, January 2010. http://robjhyndman.com/TSDL/

10. Khosravi, A., Nahavandi, S., Creighton, D., Atiya, A.F.: Lower upper bound estimation method for construction of neural network-based prediction intervals. IEEE Trans. Neural Netw. **22**(3), 337–346 (2011)

11. Makridakis, S., Weelwright, S., Hyndman, R.: Forecasting: Methods and Applications, 3rd edn. Wiley, New York (1998)

12. Michalewicz, Z., Schmidt, M., Michalewicz, M., Chiriac, C.: Adaptive Business Intelligence. Springer, Heidelberg (2006)

13. R Core Team. R: A Language and Environment for Statistical Computing. R Foundation for Statistical Computing, Vienna, Austria (2016)

14. Rana, M., Koprinska, I., Khosravi, A., Agelidis, V.G.: Prediction intervals for electricity load forecasting using neural networks. In: The 2013 International Joint Conference on Neural Networks (IJCNN), pp. 1–8. IEEE (2013)

15. Srinivas, N., Deb, K.: Muiltiobjective optimization using nondominated sorting in genetic algorithms. Evol. Comput. **2**(3), 221–248 (1994)

16. Stepnicka, M., Cortez, P., Donate, J.P., Stepnicková, L.: Forecasting seasonal time series with computational intelligence: on recent methods and the potential of their combinations. Expert Syst. Appl. **40**(6), 1981–1992 (2013)

17. Tashman, L.: Out-of-sample tests of forecasting accuracy: an analysis and review. Int. Forecast. J. **16**(4), 437–450 (2000)

Toward a Token-Based Approach to Concern Detection in MATLAB Sources

Miguel P. Monteiro[1]([⊠]), Nuno C. Marques[1]([⊠]), Bruno Silva[2], Bruno Palma[1], and João Cardoso[3]

[1] NOVA Laboratory for Computer Science and Informatics (NOVA-LINCS) & FCT, Universidade NOVA de Lisboa, Lisbon, Portugal
{mtpm,nmm}@fct.unl.pt
[2] IPSetubal - Escola Superior de Tecnologia de Setúbal, Setúbal, Portugal
[3] FEUP, Universidade do Porto, INESC-TEC, Porto, Portugal
jmpc@acm.org

Abstract. Matrix and data manipulation programming languages are an essential tool for data analysts. However, these languages are often unstructured and lack modularity mechanisms. This paper presents a business intelligence approach for studying the manifestations of lack of modularity support in that kind of languages. The study is focused on MATLAB as a well established representative of those languages. We present a technique for the automatic detection and quantification of concerns in MATLAB, as well as their exploration in a code base. Ubiquitous Self Organizing Map (UbiSOM) is used based on direct usage of indicators representing different sets of tokens in the code. UbiSOM is quite effective to detect patterns of co-occurrence between multiple concerns. To illustrate, a repository comprising over 35,000 MATLAB files is analyzed using the technique and relevant conclusions are drawn.

Keywords: Business intelligence · Concern metrics · Concern mining · MATLAB · Token-based technique · Self-organizing maps · Modularity

1 Introduction

This paper presents a Software Engineering Business Intelligence and Knowledge Discovery approach for advanced exploratory data analysis using Ubiquitous Self Organizing Maps (UbiSOM) [12]. The UbiSOM main algorithm was initially proposed in 1982 [7] and has become an established data mining algorithm with hundreds of applications in many scientific domains. Here, UbiSOM is used for studying the symptoms of lack of modularity in the source code under analysis. It is based on a *concern metric* [4] that is used as an indicator of the intensity of the presence of a given concern in a code file and provides the foundation for the exploratory analysis of source code bases. UbiSOM analysis is particularly effective in detecting and representing patterns of co-occurrence of multiple concerns in the same file. The technique is scalable to large code bases. The present study

© Springer International Publishing AG 2017
E. Oliveira et al. (Eds.): EPIA 2017, LNAI 10423, pp. 573–584, 2017.
DOI: 10.1007/978-3-319-65340-2_47

is focused on MATLAB since it is a classical language for matrix manipulation and of which large repositories are publicly available.

The rest of the paper is structured as follows. Section 2 provides the background for this work as well as its motivation. Section 3 describes the proposed concern mining technique and presents a repository of MATLAB code, for which an illustrating analysis is described in Sect. 4. Section 5 provides a discussion and outlines related work. Section 6 concludes the paper and mentions several opportunities for future work.

2   Background and Motivation

A *concern* is any abstraction, concept or cohesive set of functionalities that ideally is enclosed in its own module, for the sake of comprehensibility and ease of maintenance and evolution. It has long been accepted that existing programming paradigms have limitations on the ability to enclose all concerns in separate modules [6]. The root cause is that each programming paradigm provides a *single* criterion to decompose a software system. Concerns that do not align with the primary decomposition tend to cut across the system's modular structure, even when developers follow the best practices of design and programming style.

These limitations were the subject of much study in object-oriented (OO) languages, but less so in the case of Matrix and data manipulation programming languages, of which MATLAB is an important example. MATLAB's support for modularity is less sophisticated than that of OO languages. Modules are mostly MATLAB files (m-files) and MATLAB functions (m-functions). Our study is focused on m-files with at least one m-function (i.e., we presently do not consider MATLAB *scripts*). UbiSOM analysis is particularly interesting in m-files with two or more concerns, which we approach as cases of a deficient support for modularity. We consider that such files contain a *core concern* plus one or several "additional" concerns.

Past research on techniques to detect unmodularized concerns in program code were carried out mainly under the umbrella name of *aspect mining* [5], which studies tools and techniques for the automatic or semi- automatic detection of unmodularized concerns in existing systems. The approach to concern detection proposed in this paper is a pioneer approach that uses unsupervised knowledge extraction tools as part of an effort to develop a general approach for concern detection that can be used equally well to detect both modularized concerns enclosed in a single source code file and unmodularized concerns, which are therefore scattered across multiple files.

3   Concern Mining in MATLAB Systems

Concern detection builds on previous work by Monteiro et al. [2,11] which, to our knowledge, is the sole previous work on concern mining specifically tailored for MATLAB systems. The approach is based on the analysis *concern metrics* [4], which capture information about concerns present in one of more modules. This is in contrast to traditional modularity metrics [3], which capture information on individual modules. Concern metrics are particularly suitable for supporting concern mining tasks.

The main information unit are the *tokens*, i.e., the lexical elements extracted from a code file by means of some lexical analyser tool. Monteiro et al. base their work on the hypothesis that specific groups of tokens can be associated to specific concerns, in which case patterns of occurrence of such tokens can be used to detect the presence of the corresponding concerns. Individual tokens must also relate to one concern at most.

This work includes a component that performs a tokenization of all the non-comment code from each m-file from a given target repository and computes a number of metrics based on the word tokens obtained. Nonword tokens (e.g., symbols and literals, including strings) are not considered in most cases. Treatment of keywords varies according to the specific aims. A final filtering phase yields just the words that are function names, discarding the rest. Function names - particularly from standard MATLAB libraries - provide stronger guarantees of uniformity than, e.g., local variables. These metrics are then directly used by an Ubiquitous Self-Organizing Map [12] component for assisting in the multi-dimensional exploration and analysis of the extracted data.

The proposed technique uses the trial mapping between concerns and function names shown in Table 1, which was proposed by a domain expert. One of the aims of the work described here is to test and assess the technique, using this mapping. The metrics used in this work are (1) *Lines of Code* (LoC), which counts all non-comment and non-blank lines of code for each m-file; and (2) *Token Density*, which computes, for each m-file, the total count of occurrences of the tokens from a given set (e.g., 5 occurrences of 'double' count as 5), divided by LoC. This metric represents the average number of tokens per LoC, for a given concern. It parametrises the concern, i.e., the specific set of tokens considered. The mapping from Table 1 gives rise to 10 instantiations of *Token Density*. Figure 1 shows the contents of an m-file (minus blank and comment lines) whose metrics stand out for a few concerns. With just 9 LoC, it has 2 tokens indicative of *Verification of function arguments and return value* (*Token Density* 0.2(2)), 9 tokens indicative of *Data type specialisation* (*Token Density* 1.0) and 5 tokens indicative of *Memory allocation/deallocation* (*Token Density* 0.5(5)). *Token Density* is sufficient to enable the automatic detection of concerns. However, on a macro-level and just by itself, this technique is not well suited to provide a broad view of a large repository and provide a panorama of all concerns and its various co-occurrences.

The Self-Organizing Map (SOM) is an unsupervised learning artificial neural network model, based on competitive learning [7]. Standard SOM model consists of a set of topologically ordered data prototypes arranged in a rectangular lattice (the map). The SOM is widely used as a tool for projecting high-dimensional data onto the two-dimensional representation map. This projection retains the relationship between input data as faithfully as possible, thus describing a topology-preserving projection of input similarities in terms of distances in the output

Table 1. Illustrative mapping between concerns and tokens (some tokens removed due to space concerns).

Verification of function arguments and return value	nargchk, nargin, nargout, nargoutchk, varargin, varargout
Data type specialization	double, fi, fimath, int16, int32, int64, int, quantize, quantizer, sfi, single, ufi, uint16, uint32, uint64, uint
Data type verification	cast, class, intmax, intmin, isa, isboolean, iscell, ischar, $\cdots$ isquantizer, isreal, isrow, typecast, wordlength
Dynamic properties	eval, evalc, evalin, inline, feval
Console messages	annotation, assert, disp, display, error, last, lastwarn
Visualization	aaxes, axis, box, clf, close, errorbar, Figure, $\cdots$ plot, plot3, plotedit, rectangle, title, ylabel, zlabel, zoom
File I/O	diary, fgetl, fgets, fileformats, fopen, fprintf, fread, fscanf, fwrite, hgload, hgsave, load, save, saveas, uisave
System	batch, break, clear, clock, cputime, date, $\cdots$ toc, unloadlibrary, wait, weekday, who, whos, xbreak
Memory allocation/ deallocation	delete, global, ones, persistent, zeros
Parallelization	cancel, codistributed, codistributor, createParallelJob, createTask, defaultParallelConfig, demote, $\cdots$ sparse, submit, subsasgn,subsref, taskFinish, taskStartup

space. It is this special projection that, when a large enough map is used (also known as Emergent SOM), establishes as a valuable data exploratory analysis tool with special visualizations [13]. This property also makes SOM distinct from other clustering algorithms. De per si, the traditional k-means clustering is unable to compare distinct clusters and a bad setting of the k parameter could result in too generic clusters, i.e., group sets of data that may have little relation. By contrast, SOM is less "eager" in clustering together the data it processes, i.e., it significantly reduces the risk that it will group data too much. That is one reason we deem SOM more suitable for exploratory data analysis.

The proposed method uses an extension of the SOM technique called Ubiquitous SOM [12] for training maps of *Token Density* data. This technique has an easier and better defined parameterization than standard SOM and allows the detection of meaningful variations among the data, which is approached as a stream. The classical *online* SOM decreases learning parameters monotonically throughout time and requires the same observations to be presented several times, consequently considering the underlying distribution *stationary*. UbiSOM [12] also uses the classical *online* SOM update rule but with different mechanisms for estimating SOM learning parameters for non-stationary data-streams. The UbiSOM algorithm switches between an *ordering* and *learning* state. The latter is only achieved when the current distribution of the data stream is already sufficiently modeled after a previous *ordering* phase. Preference for UbiSOM [12] is justified by its dynamic visualization and data exploratory advantages over other traditional data mining tools. Moreover, UbiSOM ensures detection of distinct phenomena if new or too distinct repositories are used. This is particularly relevant if, as in this case, more code repositories are intended to be added later on.

The UbiSOM for exploring *Token Density* relations is composed of units where each position (or unit) is a vector of average values representing the *Token Density* metrics. So, each concern in a similar enough set of m-files (or micro-cluster) is associated to a particular unit/map position. This way, the method enables analyses of emergent regions of *Token Density*, enabling exploratory data analysis for concern detection and correlation in the map and dissimilar regions to detect uncommon but relevant correlation patterns.

```
function fired = nemoStep(fstim, istim_nidx, istim_current)
    if nargin < 1
        fired = nemo_mex(uint32(12), uint32(zeros(1,0)), uint32(zeros(1,0)), zeros(1, 0));
    elseif nargin < 2
        fired = nemo_mex(uint32(12), uint32(fstim), uint32(zeros(1, 0)), zeros(1, 0));
    else
        fired = nemo_mex(uint32(12), uint32(fstim), uint32(istim_nidx), istim_current);
    end
end
```
[ ] – *Verification of function arguments and return value;* [ ] – *Data type specialization;* [ ] – *Memory allocation/ deallocation;*

Fig. 1. m-file showing high values for *Token Density* in relation to 3 concerns.

The repository used for this work is one used to test the MATLAB compiler by Bispo and Cardoso [1], comprising 35,193 files organized by toolboxes and covering various application domains. 28k m-files were downloaded from Sourceforge and 2k m-files were downloaded from GitHub. Of these, 784 m-files were discarded due to the lack of useful MATLAB code inside them. For instance, we found a number of m-files with zero LoC, as they contained only comment text. After this curating, the repository comprised 34,409 m-files.

We found that in practice, m-files with too low a LoC value tend to hog results for *Token Density*. Since such small m-files are usually uninteresting, the tool was set to discard all m-files with $LoC < 5$, leaving a little over $30k$ m-files. According to the data gathered, only a small percentage of the m-files from the repository does not contain any of the concerns from Table 1. Out of the m-files with at least one concern, the biggest chunk is for m-files with *two* concerns, followed by m-files with a single concern.

4   Data Analysis and Exploration

The SOM component of our tool processes the *Token Density* data from each m-file from the repository. Our method is specifically focused on co-occurrence patterns among the various concerns from Table 1. Each pattern is formed as a vector $X = [x_{1k}, x_{2k}, \cdots, x_{Nk}]$, where each component of this vector is calculated by Eq. (1), where x_{ik} is the component for concern i for m-file k.

$$x_{ik} = \frac{log(\frac{TkDensity_{ik}}{max_c(TkDensity_{ic})} \times N + 1)}{log(N + 1)} \tag{1}$$

Each component of the vector corresponds to a row number i in Table 1, so $i = 1$ to NC, where NC=10 is the total number of concerns considered for analysis. $TkDensity_{ik}$ is the corresponding *Token Density* for concern i and m-file k and $max_c\bullet$ is the maximum of previous values of concern i for all m-files. Intuitively, the use of the logarithm of a $[0; 1]$ normalized density (i.e., the division in the numerator of equation) is needed since the *Token Density* values should be made relevant for small values of the metric and zero for zero values of the metric. The multiplication of this quantity by a factor N is used to ensure that low-frequency values of *Token Density* are distinct enough from zero. We have set $N = 6000$ after empirically testing several alternatives. The histogram with frequency analysis of distinct *Token Densities* for $N = 6000$ is shown in Fig. 2. Division by the maximum value ensures that each SOM component value is always normalized between zero and one (as required by SOM).

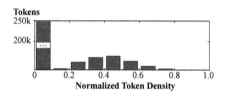

Fig. 2. Full repository normalized token density, when $N = 6000$.

Several distinct UbiSOMs were trained by filtering patterns with three or more concerns. Note that filtering improves the quality of the map, but reduces the sample for detecting patterns. Therefore, in a systematic approach, m-files with less than two simultaneous concerns with above-zero *Token Density* were filtered away and several UbiSOMs were trained with the resulting datasets. Patterns filtered with three simultaneous concerns, i.e., by selecting only the m-files with three or more above-zero *Token Density* values, were used to train a SOM that is used next, to illustrate the technique and the insights it provides. Final iterations of UbiSOM training used random resampling over the full repository. The SOM quantization error was convergent with a good reduction of quantization error during model training (final quantization error = 0.05 per component). Since no big variations were detected on the final resampling step, the current repository seems stable enough for model convergence.

The visual outputs from SOM considered in this paper comprise two components [9,12]: the *Unified Distance Matrix* (U-Matrix) and the various *Component Planes* (CP). In each CP and the U-Matrix (see for example Fig. 3), the same areas in the planes represent the same units, i.e., regions in the data that tend to have high or low values together. Throughout the rest of the paper, the regions from Fig. 4 denoted A1 to E2 also refer to the equivalent regions of the various planes from Fig. 4. However, it is important to note that the cells and colours of U-Matrix and CPs are interpreted in different ways and that regional commonalities between CPs must be interpreted in light of the specific colour pattern found in the corresponding region of the U-Matrix. It is the combination of both views that yields a proper understanding of the full dataset and their underlying patterns. The U-Matrix provides a general view of the units or patterns found in the data, while the various CPs provide the details of the various units. Here, each CP relates to one specific concern.

The average values in both the U-Matrix and the CPs are represented as a JET colour map [9], meaning that red represents high values, blue represents low values (down to zero) and green represents intermediate values. In addition (and consistently), green areas with a blue hue represent values lower than pure green, while "dirty" green areas with a red hue represent values higher than pure green. In the U-Matrix, each unit measures the average Euclidean distance of the correspondent SOM unit vector to the vectors of the eight SOM unit vectors that are its immediate neighbours. In the CPs, each position represents the density parameters for its respective concern.

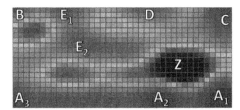

Fig. 3. U-Matrix representing the selected m-files in the MATLAB repository. The various letter annotations highlight relevant regions. (Color figure online)

Figure 3 shows an U-Matrix for the metrics data fed to the SOM, from the example used in the rest of this paper to illustrate and summarize our analyses. In general, well-separated regions (i.e. the blue "lakes" [9]) in the U-Matrix represent clearly separated patterns in the data fed to the SOM. The regions labelled A1, A2, A3 and C from Fig. 3 are good examples. In the U-Matrix, blue regions represent homogeneous regions in the SOM while red regions (e.g., region Z from Fig. 4) denote high variability among units. Green regions represent intermediate values for distance among SOM units. Blue regions in a slight

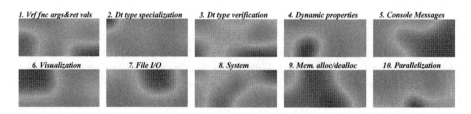

Fig. 4. Component planes showing the colour maps of the *Token Density* metric for concerns from Table 1. (Color figure online)

green hue such as B, E1, E2 and D from Fig. 3 also represent relatively homogeneous regions. Several well-defined blue and light green "lakes" can be discerned by their colour uniformity regarding neighbourhood units. These various data regions betray several well-defined concern patterns.

To analyse the data obtained for the various concerns, we look at their respective CPs (Fig. 4). For instance, we see that concerns *Data type verification* and *Verification of function arguments* share two common red regions in their respective CPs (at the bottom, to the left and right). This means that there is a significant co-occurrence between those two particular concerns. This sharing is particularly significant, because those regions are blue in the U-Matrix, meaning that the sharing is particularly uniform across the analysed data. The two concerns co-occur with high densities, though we can also see a significant overlap with concerns *Console messages* and *Memory allocation/deallocation* in regions A1 and A2.

A sharing of red regions taking place in a red rather than blue region of the U-Matrix (no such case in the present example) would depict more variable distances between units and would mean that patterns in such regions would be much more diverse (with high, low and intermediate densities). The overlap would probably not be representative of the data as a whole. It is also significant that no "blue lake" from Fig. 4 is devoid of at least one CP with high values in the same region, i.e., all red zone in the CPs correspond to blue lakes in the U-Matrix. If such region existed, it would represent some diffuse concept, possibly meaningless.

The red region in the CP for concern *Data type specialization* completely overlaps with that for concern *Visualization* (region B) though the latter's region is wider. This could suggest that in the majority of m-files where *Data type specialization* has a significant presence, *Visualization*'s presence is significant as well. There is also a relevant presence of this concern in area A2, jointly with concerns *Data type verification* and *Verification of function arguments and return value*. However, *Data type specialization* does not have enough above zero values to enable a reliable characterization in the CP. For this reason, it was discarded from subsequent analyses. A similar overlap of red regions also occurs with *Console messages* and *System* (region), though the overlap is less complete in this case.

```
function options = merge_options(default_options, varargin)
  if ~isempty(varargin) && mod(length(varargin),2) == 0
    options = merge_structs(struct(varargin{:}),default_options);
  elseif length(varargin)==1 && isstruct(varargin{1})
    options = merge_structs(varargin{1},default_options);
  elseif ~isempty(varargin)
    error('matlag_bgl:optionsParsing',...
      'There were an odd number of key-value pairs specified');
  else
    options = default_options;
  end
end
```

[ ] – *Vrf. of func. Args. and return value;*

■ – *Data type verification;*

■ – *Console messages;*

Fig. 5. m-file with high *Token Density* values relative to three of the analysed concerns.

We performed several manual checks on several m-files to confirm that red regions from the various CPs do indeed relate consistently to high values of *Token Density* with respect to their respective concerns. One example is m-file merge_options.m (shown in Fig. 5 without comment lines) - one the m-files indicated by the common blue region A1 of the U-Matrix (Fig. 3) and selected as a small representative from a shortlist of m-files with high density values for more than one concern. As expected, those m-files show several tokens associated with the concerns found in region A1, particularly *Verification of function arguments and return value* and *Data type verification* but also *Console messages*.

M-file merge_options.m is an interesting illustration of the attempt to separate concern *Verification of function arguments and return value* from other concerns. Its sole purpose seems to test the way the function is called and configure a call to another function that provides the functionality proper. However, that does not prevent merge_options.m being a clear case of code tangling in MATLAB. Throughout our work, we found several examples of this symptom, in functions that do not separate argument-checking from other concerns.

5   Discussion and Related Work

Token Density is sufficient to directly allow the selection of the top densities on any individual concern from Table 1. However, it cannot be scaled to provide an overview of a large repository spanning multiple concerns.

The SOM model presents large distances between many units, which jointly with the presence of some quantization error, suggests a good enough convergence of the model but does not yet represent some patterns in the data, i.e., the boundaries separating clusters in Fig. 4 could be "crisper". Nevertheless, the observation that most CPs have clear continuous regions in several trained SOMs, points us to a clear and concise division of the studied concern patterns under analysis. Overlapping areas in planes from the CPs (Fig. 4) are related primarily with co-occurring concerns. This is a clear indicator that the groups of tokens from Table 1 are effective in identifying the concerns to which they are associated and that those groups of tokens cover distinct programming considerations (i.e., concerns).

SOM use is marred by a high number of zeros in the *Token Density* data. The traditional technique for handling sparse data would be Principle Component

Analysis (PCA). However, PCA is not discriminating enough for our purposes, since it aggregates the several concerns in different variables. Namely, the tests performed using PCA for our problem did not improve the outcome, be in terms of the SOM, be in not reducing the quantization error. The high number of zeros of *Token Density* seems to be an instance of an exponential law on the token occurrence. A better alternative would be to use a method such Word2Vec [10], a natural language method that can build high-quality distributed vector representations that capture precise syntactic and semantic relationships. However, for a more rigorous evaluation we chose to use information provided by an expert (cf. Table 1).

The $N = 6000$ parameter used in Eq. 1 is an efficient way to give proper relevance to low *Token Density* values. M-files with one concern occurrence per 60 LoC have a normalized value of 0.5, while one concern occurrence per 200 LoC (normalized value of 0.3). Even in more than 1000 LoC (normalized value lower than 0.2) are still detectable. Preliminary experiments done without the exponential normalization (cf. Eq. 1) showed a large uniform region and few co-occurring concerns. Indeed, SOM training is known to be sensible to too many zeros. This problem is seen for concerns with a high number of zeros such as, e.g., *Data type specialization*, which tends to adjust with high error and therefore tends to appear opportunistically in several areas of the space. Manual analysis nevertheless shows that the red and green areas in this concern's CP (Fig. 4) are related with m-files relevant for this concern. Restricting the selection to m-files with more co-occurring concerns reduced this problem.

In our illustrative example, a particularly relevant result from the SOM analysis is the high correlation of the densities for concerns *Verification of function arguments* and *Data type verification* (see Fig. 4). An illustrating example of an m-file with these concerns is shown in Fig. 5. The high correlation between both these parameters is common in many analysed m-files. This result suggests that MATLAB is somewhat problematic as regards validating and verifying function arguments or data types. The problem with arguments is caused by the practice of "schizophrenic functions" that need to test multiple variations of its parameters to learn in what "mode" they were actually called. In object-oriented languages, method overloading enables the tackling of the same problem with better separation of concerns. As regards data types, Cardoso et al. propose aspect-oriented extensions to MATLAB to enable a precise control of data types without incurring the symptom of code tangling [2].

Considering the large percentage of m-files from the analysed repository that betray the presence of multiple concerns, we can conclude that the code tangling symptom is quite common.

The present work is based on concern metrics and therefore is related to past research work on that category of metrics [4]. A work with several similarities to ours is that by Maisikely and Mitropoulos [8], whose purpose is to develop an aspect mining technique that uses a SOM component to process metrics data to find similarities. It differs from ours in that the target language is Java and the mining is specifically tailored to the kind of CCCs that AspectJ is good at modularizing. As it would be expected, the metrics used are also quite different. All of those metrics reside at method level and the group seems to be centered in two dynamic (i.e., captured at runtime) versions of *method Fan-In* and *method Fan-Out*. To complement, other method-level metrics are used, namely: *Information flow* (Fan-In*Fan-Out), *Method Signature* (method name, parameter types and their order, visibility modifiers and return type), *Method Internal Coupling* and *Method External Coupling*. Maisikely and Mitropoulos report positive results from an experiment with their technique, using as target systems JHotDraw 5.41b and a small system comprising 6 classes. The present work uses token-based metrics because they seem more appropriate for a first experiment for aspect mining of MATLAB system, as argued in previous work [11].

6   Conclusions and Future Work

This paper makes the following contributions:

1. Proposes the *Token Density* metric as a direct development of some ideas proposed by Monteiro et al. [11].
2. Proposes a technique for exploratory analysis of MATLAB code, scalable to large repositories. The technique provides a precise way to identify patterns of occurrence and co-occurrence of concerns in (possibly large) repositories of MATLAB files.
3. The analysis described in this paper serves as a first validation of the *Token Density* metric.

We identify some of the opportunities for future work. Next, we highlight a few of them.

Automatize the Development of the Concern-Token Mapping. We can use a distributional representation of tokens [10] as a direct input to the UbiSOM. Finding out the best way to automatically learn this representation from MATLAB code bases is an avenue left open by this work. In future, we will further mature this technique in at least two directions: (1) automatize or semi-automatize the discovery of new, distinct patterns of occurrence that lead to new concerns and new entries for Table 1; and (2) automatically or semi-automatically refine existing entries of the Table, by applying a more fine-grained, token-level analysis that indicates the tokens that should be kept in the mapping - because patterns of occurrence confirm their usefulness - and those that should be discarded - because patterns of occurrence are too sparse and/or do not add meaningful information.

The results achieved with the proposed method are promising. The interactive and exploratory nature of SOM allows a focused search for specific concerns in code repositories. In future, this will be part of a tool for finding relevant code snippets in MATLAB repositories. There is an increasing trend in big data analytics using matrix based analysis (or N-dimensional matrices, i.e., tensors). This can be seen by the increasing number of packages and tools for matrix and data handling, e.g., Google TensorFlow, the numPy package in Python and the very relevant statistical analysis tools and languages such as SPSS and R. We plan to make a social collaborative web site with such a tool as a useful way for reusing and improving previously available code. This site will also be a forum for exchanging good practices on development of data analysis software. Empirical data collected from this site promises be a powerful means to develop this line of research.

References

1. Bispo, J., Cardoso, J.M.P.: A MATLAB subset to c compiler targeting embedded systems. Softw.: Pract. Exp. **47**(2), 249–272 (2017). http://dx.doi.org/10.1002/spe.2408, sPE-15-0162.R2
2. Cardoso, J.M., Fernandes, J.M., Monteiro, M.P.: Adding aspect-oriented features to matlab. In: Fifth International Conference on Aspect-Oriented Software Development (AOSD 2016) (2006)
3. Chidamber, S.R., Kemerer, C.F.: A metrics suite for object oriented design. IEEE Trans. Softw. Eng. **20**(6), 476–493 (1994)
4. Figueiredo, E., Sant'Anna, C., Garcia, A., Bartolomei, T.T., Cazzola, W., Marchetto, A.: On the maintainability of aspect-oriented software: a concern-oriented measurement framework. In: 12th European Conference on Software Maintenance and Reengineering, CSMR 2008, pp. 183–192. IEEE (2008)
5. Kellens, A., Mens, K., Tonella, P.: A survey of automated code-level aspect mining techniques. In: Rashid, A., Aksit, M. (eds.) Transactions on Aspect-Oriented Software Development IV. LNCS, vol. 4640, pp. 143–162. Springer, Heidelberg (2007). doi:10.1007/978-3-540-77042-8_6
6. Kiczales, G., Lamping, J., Mendhekar, A., Maeda, C., Lopes, C., Loingtier, J.-M., Irwin, J.: Aspect-oriented programming. In: Akşit, M., Matsuoka, S. (eds.) ECOOP 1997. LNCS, vol. 1241, pp. 220–242. Springer, Heidelberg (1997). doi:10. 1007/BFb0053381
7. Kohonen, T.: Self-Organizing Maps. Springer, Berlin (2001)
8. Maisikeli, S.G., Mitropoulos, F.J.: Aspect mining using self-organizing maps with method level dynamic software metrics as input vectors. In: 2010 2nd International Conference on Software Technology and Engineering (ICSTE), vol. 1, pp. V1–212. IEEE (2010)
9. Marques, N.C., Silva, B., Santos, H.: An interactive interface for multi-dimensional data stream analysis. In: 2016 20th International Conference on Information Visualisation (IV), pp. 223–229. IEEE (2016)
10. Mikolov, T., Sutskever, I., Chen, K., Corrado, G.S., Dean, J.: Distributed representations of words and phrases and their compositionality. In: Advances in Neural Information Processing Systems, pp. 3111–3119 (2013)
11. Monteiro, M., Cardoso, J., Posea, S.: Identification and characterization of cross-cutting concerns in MATLAB systems. In: Conference on Compilers, Programming Languages, Related Technologies and Applications (CoRTA 2010), Braga, Portugal, pp. 9–10. Citeseer (2010)
12. Silva, B., Marques, N.C.: The ubiquitous self-organizing map for non-stationary data streams. J. Big Data **2**(1), 1–22 (2015)
13. Ultsch, A., Herrmann: The architecture of emergent self-organizing maps to reduce projection errors. In: Verleysen, M. (ed.) Proceedings of the European Symposium on Artificial Neural Networks (ESANN 2005), pp. 1–6 (2005)

Food Truck Recommendation Using Multi-label Classification

Adriano Rivolli[1,2(✉)], Larissa C. Parker[3], and Andre C.P.L.F. de Carvalho[2]

[1] Tecnological University of Paraná, Cornélio Procópio, PR, Brazil
rivolli@usp.br
[2] Institute of Mathematics and Computer Sciences,
University of São Paulo, São Carlos, SP, Brazil
andre@icmc.usp.br
[3] Federal University of Rio Grande do Norte, Natal, RN, Brazil

Abstract. Food trucks are vehicles with which fast food, from various cuisines, is cooked and sold. They have been popular in several countries and usually offer food in different locations of a city. Frequently, several food trucks offer their dishes in music concerts, festivals and other events. When several food trucks are present in a place, the variety of possible cuisines and food dishes makes their choice by the public a challenging task. This paper describes the task of recommending food trucks using a multi-label classification approach, where more than one option can be suggested. The recommendation is made using customers' personal information and preferences. Six multi-label transformation strategies were used to induce learning models from real data obtained via a market research, where hundreds of participants provided their food preferences. The experimental results show that the strategies overcame the adopted baseline in almost all cases, with RAndom k-labELsets (RAkEL) and Binary Relevance (BR) in specific, were the ones who had the best overall result, respectively. On the other hand, it is required to investigate the matter furthermore to improve the predictive outcome of the task. From a machine learning perspective, a new way to analyze multi-label results, called confusion matrix plot, is discussed and the food truck dataset is released as a new multi-label benchmark.

Keywords: Food truck recommendation · Recommendation system · Multi-label classification · Multi-label dataset

1 Introduction

From the beginning of the 21st century, food trucks started to spread throughout the world [21]. Generally, they sell food that belongs to a wide range of cuisines, moving from one location to another, in any given region of a city, without having to settle in a specific place. In festivals, music concerts and large-scale events, it is common to have more than one of them. The large number of possibilities can make the food choice by the public a challenging task. Recommender systems,

© Springer International Publishing AG 2017
E. Oliveira et al. (Eds.): EPIA 2017, LNAI 10423, pp. 585–596, 2017.
DOI: 10.1007/978-3-319-65340-2_48

like personalized event app and iterative totems, can be used to suggest options to the public and help them select one or more options among the available alternatives.

Motivated by this emerging business, a food truck recommendation task, using data related to socioeconomic profiles and the personal information of customers like their habits and preferences, is investigated in this paper. While related works [9,15,23] recommend specific places (restaurants), in this work, the food truck recommendation is performed considering the different types of menus offered by a set of food trucks, allowing the suggestion of more than one option. The hypothesis assumed in this study is that it is possible to use machine learning (ML) techniques to recommend, with a good predictive accuracy, one or more different food truck options.

The problem is addressed using a multi-label classification (MLC) approach, a supervised ML task where each instance is related to one or more class labels [5]. In this approach, each different type of food truck is mapped to a class label and more than one class labels can be recommended to any given user. Thus, each recommendation can suggest one or more options. The data used in the learning process was obtained from a market research regarding food truck preferences conducted by one of the authors. The research was carried out in Natal, a Brazilian city, using a social media app. Overall, 407 users, who have bought from food trucks, participated in this survey. They anonymously filled-out a questionnaire describing their food truck preferences along with personal information, such as their age, address, gender, etc.

The aim of this work is to explore the task of food truck recommendation as a MLC task. Experiments were performed comparing six different MLC transformation strategies when applied to the collected food truck data. Some business opportunities that can benefit from this study are: food truck market research, discovery of trends in food truck preferences, food truck advertising and food truck recommendation apps.

Regarding ML contributions, this paper investigates, for the first time, ML for food truck/restaurant recommendation, use of MLC strategies to deal with the possibility of more than one recommendation and proposes a new alternative to analyze MLC results: the *confusion matrix plot*. This plot provides support to compare results among different MLC strategies, considering all of the labels' confusion matrices at the same time.

The rest of this paper is organized as follows: In Sect. 2, the main aspects and previous works on restaurant and food recommendation are briefly presented. Next, Sect. 3, multi-label classification is defined. Section 4 describes the food truck multi-label dataset. Then, Sect. 5 presents and analyzes the experimental results. The paper ends with a highlight of the relevant points (Sect. 6).

2   Related Works

To the best of the authors' knowledge, the use of ML for food truck recommendation has not been explored in the literature. However, restaurant recommendation has been the subject of several studies, some of them recent [9,18,23,24].

This problem has been studied in the recommender system scientific community as a specialization of the location prediction problem [15].

Restaurant recommender systems usually base their recommendation on a broad range of attributes, including user's feedback (restaurant visit via check-ins, reviews and ratings), geolocation information, demographic data (age, gender, etc.), friends' preferences and restaurant features. In some cases, the prediction is a ranking of restaurants [9] or the top-k most relevant restaurants [24]. However, neither authors modeled their tasks as a MLC problem, which supports both scenarios intrinsically.

The main approaches used for restaurant recommender systems are designed to predict specific places and their solutions are developed in a dynamic and ubiquitous environment. This work follows a different, more generic approach, addressing food truck recommendation through the recommendation of cuisine categories.

3   Multi-label Classification

In MLC tasks, an instance can be simultaneously classified in more than one of the existing class labels. Binary and multi-class classification tasks can be seen as special cases of MLC tasks [5] where a single class is predicted. To formally define MLC, let $\mathcal{L} = \{\lambda_1, \lambda_2, ..., \lambda_q\}$ be the set of q labels λ_j related to a particular problem $\mathcal{X}$, where $\mathcal{X}$ is the instance space with d attributes. The learning process results in a hypothesis $h : \mathcal{X} \rightarrow 2^{\mathcal{L}}$ that associates new instances with a subset of labels contained in $\mathcal{L}$. It is done using an inductive process that learns from available data [1].

MLC tasks are often treated by transformation strategies, which transforms the original multi-label data set into a set of single-label data sets, where conventional ML algorithms can be used [19]. Several transformation-based strategies have been proposed in the literature. This study evaluates the predictive performance obtained by six of them when applied to the food truck recommendation tasks: Binary Relevance (BR) [3]; Calibrated Label Ranking (CLR) [10]; Dependent Binary Relevance (DBR) [14]; Ensemble of Classifier Chains (ECC) [16]; multi-label learning with Label specIfic FeaTures (LIFT) [25]; and, RAndom k-LabELsets (RAkEL) [20]. These strategies were selected due to their popularity and different approaches used.

BR is the simplest and most common multi-label strategy [12]. It uses the one-versus-all approach [5] to generate q binary datasets and induce a binary model for each dataset. The final MLC prediction is the combination of all binary predictions. Similarly, LIFT creates a binary model for each label, but uses an unsupervised approach to transform the input space for each subtask. The DBR strategy is based on stacking generalization [22], thus the label values are used to increase the feature space, to model the label dependencies in the learning process. The ECC strategy is an ensemble of distinct Classifier Chains (CC) models. It organizes the binary classifiers in a chain and increment the input space with the results obtained by the previous classifiers in the chain. The CLR strategy uses a pairwise transformation where each pair of labels generates a binary dataset. The prediction is defined using a voting scheme. RAkEL is an ensemble of multi-class models. Each model is induced using a subset of labels, named labelset, and each labelset is mapped to a class.

The evaluation of the predictive performance of MLC strategies and ML techniques for MLC tasks requires the use of specific measures that are able to explore their particularities [19]. In this work, measures that evaluate different perspectives of the learning process were considered. *Accuracy* and *subset accuracy* measure the predictive quality. The first is lenient when considering the partial successes, while the second is rigid and considers only complete arrangements. *Macro-F1* and *micro-F1* are label-based measures and they are computed considering each individual labels. In practice, a macro measure gives equal weight to all labels whereas a micro measure focuses on the most common labels [11]. Finally, *hamming-loss* and *one-error* are error measures. The former computes the proportion of misclassified instance-label pairs while the later is a ranking measure that indicates whether or not the most relevant label predicted should be really predicted. A complete list of measures, definitions and formulation can be found in [26].

4   Data Description

The food truck dataset was created from the answers provided by the 407 survey participants. They either were approached in fast food festivals and popular events or anonymously received a request to fill out a questionnaire, in Portuguese, describing their personal information and preferences when it comes to their selection from food trucks[1]. This section describes the questionnaire used and analyzes the multi-label dataset.

4.1   The Survey

The form used for the survey had 15 objective questions about the habits and preferences related to food trucks and 6 objective questions about users' profile. These 21 questions were considered predictive attributes, as summarized in Table 1. Some attributes were inherently organized in categories, like gender and marital.status, however those that have some intrinsic order were converted to numeric, like scholarity and age.group. In the table, the questions and options are reduced due to space limitation. The types *num*, *categ* and *bin* are respectively abbreviations for numeric, categorical and binary.

The target attribute, the labels, was associated with food preferences and multiple alternatives could be simultaneously assigned, making the target prediction a MLC task. The form provided 12 alternatives:

arabic_food	brazilian_food	chinese_food	street_food
fitness_food	gourmet	healthy_food	italian_food
japanese_food	mexican_food	snacks	sweets_desserts

---

[1] The survey was conducted between November 15th and 20th, 2015. The Google Form tool was used to collect the responses.

Table 1. Summary of dataset attributes. The questions and options used in the survey and their respective values mapped in the dataset.

Attribute	Type	Question - Options
Habits and preferences questions		
frequency	num	Often eating out
		0 - rarely, 1 - monthly, 2 - weekly,
		3 - twice a week, 4 - almost daily or daily
time	categ	Day period of preference
		afternoon, dawn, dinner, happy hour, lunch
expenses	num	How much to spend
		15 - until R$15,00, 20 - until R$20,00, 30 - until R$30,00,
		40 - until R$40,00, 50 - without limit
motivation	categ	What is the motivation
		ads, by chance, friend, social network, web
taste	num	Importance of food taste
		1 - very low, 2 - low, 3 - medium, 4 - high, 5- very high
hygiene	num	Importance of hygiene
		1 - very low, 2 - low, 3 - medium, 4 - high, 5- very high
menu	num	Importance of menu diversity
		1 - very low, 2 - low, 3 - medium, 4 - high, 5- very high
presentation	num	Importance of food presentation
		1 - very low, 2 - low, 3 - medium, 4 - high, 5- very high
attendance	num	Importance of service quality
		1 - very low, 2 - low, 3 - medium, 4 - high, 5- very high
ingredients	num	Importance of ingredients quality
		1 - very low, 2 - low, 3 - medium, 4 - high, 5- very high
place.to.sit	num	Importance of a place to sit
		1 - very low, 2 - low, 3 - medium, 4 - high, 5- very high
takeout	num	Importance of takeout option
		1 - very low, 2 - low, 3 - medium, 4 - high, 5- very high
variation	num	Importance of varying the choices
		1 - very low, 2 - low, 3 - medium, 4 - high, 5- very high
stop.strucks	num	Importance of food truck meetings
		1 - very low, 2 - low, 3 - medium, 4 - high, 5- very high
schedule	num	Importance of food truck schedule
		1 - very low, 2 - low, 3 - medium, 4 - high, 5- very high
Profile questions		
gender	categ	Gender
		F - Female, M - Male
age.group	num	Age group
		1 - <19, 2 - 20–25, 3 - 26–30, 4 - 31–35,
		5 - 36–40, 6 - 41–45, 7 - 46–50, 8 - >50
scholarity	num	Scholarity
		0 - no study, 1 - high school, 1.5 - in graduation,
		2 - graduation, 3 - specialization, 4 - master degree,
		5 - phd
average.income	num	Average income
		1 - <2 salaries, 2 - 2–3 salaries, 3 - 3–5 salaries,
		4 - 5–10 salaries, 5 - 10–20 salaries, 6 - >20 salaries
has.work	bin	Has a work
		0 - No, 1 - Yes
marital.status	categ	Marital status
		divorced, married, single

4.2   Dataset Analysis

Table 2 shows the main aspects of the food truck dataset. The 21 attributes are composed of 16 numeric attributes, 4 categorical attributes and 1 binary attribute. The 12 labels are combined in 117 distinct ways (labelsets), where 74 of these combinations occur only once (single labelsets). Labels dependency [12] measures the averaged correlation among the labels, where the value 0.13 indicates a low correlation. The cardinality 2.28 means that each instance is tagged with two labels, on average, and a 0.19 density, averaged labels' frequency, is a value larger than is often found on the literature [12][2].

Table 2. Multi-label statistics of the food truck dataset

Characteristic	Value	Characteristic	Value
Attributes	21	Labelsets	117
Instances	407	Single labelsets	74
Labels	12	Labels dependency	0.13
Cardinality	2.28	Density	0.19

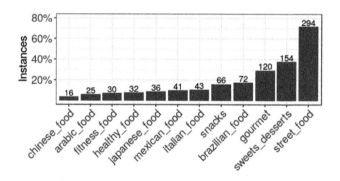

Fig. 1. Frequency of the labels present in the food truck dataset.

Figure 1 illustrates the frequency of each label in the dataset, which measures the number of instances that receives each label. Most labels appear in more than 10% of the instances and the 3 most frequent labels appear in, at least, 30% of the instances. Particularly, the street_food appears in more than 70% of the instances, which is not very common in multi-label datasets[3]. Regarding the co-occurrences of the labels, shown in Fig. 2, it is possible to notice that, given their high frequency, the 4 most popular labels are highly related to the others. Other frequent pairs of labels were observed, such as:

---

[2] 0.03 is the average density of the ML datasets available in the MULAN repository.
[3] Usually, a label is associated with less than 50% of the instances.

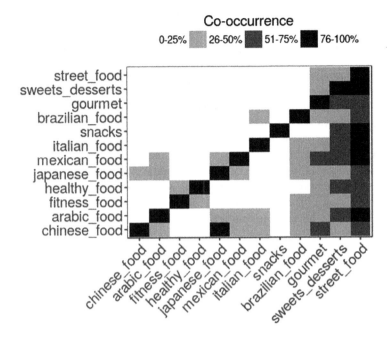

Fig. 2. Co-occurrence of the labels in the food truck dataset. The rows indicate the presence of each label and the columns reflect the co-occurrence.

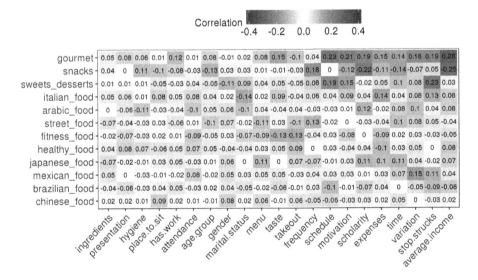

Fig. 3. Correlation coefficient among the attributes (x-axis) and the labels (y-axis). The attributes are ordered from left to right by the absolute average of the correlations. Similarly, the labels are ordered from the bottom to the top.

chinese_food ⇔ japanese_food   arabic_food ⇔ japanese_food
arabic_food ⇔ mexican_food   fitness_food ⇔ healthy_food
japanese_food ⇔ mexican_food   italian_food ⇔ brazilian_food

The food items in each pair are somewhat related, like spicy food (Arabic and Mexican), oriental cuisine (Chinese and Japanese), with many pasta dishes (Italian and Brazilian), and health-related (fitness and healthy).

Figure 3 shows the Pearson correlation coefficient between each predictive attribute and each label. The most relevant attributes, with regards to correlation, is the average.income, followed by scholarity, both of which are considered part of an individual's personal information. Gourmet is the label mostly related to the attributes and snacks is the second, although it is inversely correlated with most of the attributes. All other pairs of labels and attributes have some occurrences, however it was not possible to see a clear pattern.

5   Food Truck Recommendation

This section describes the MLC experiments carried out using the food truck dataset. It starts with the methodology and the tools used and next reports the experimental results and their analysis.

5.1   Methodology

The experiments were carried out using the R environment. The implementations of the MLC strategies used in the experiments are available in the utiml package[4] and the MLC dataset support was provided by mldr package [6]. The Random Forest [4] implementation is available in the randomForest package[5] and it was used as base algorithm for the MLC strategies.

As mentioned in Sect. 3, six distinct strategies were selected to induce MLC models for food truck recommendation. These strategies were chosen because they cover different MLC approaches. Table 3 shows the parameters used for each strategy. These are the default values specified in their original papers. The Random Forest was used as base algorithm due to its high predictive performance in several classification tasks, even without hyper-parameter tuning [8]. Thus, the Random Forest hyper-parameters used the default values defined in the randomForest package.

All of the reported results were obtained using 10-fold cross validation. The same training and testing partitions were used to obtain the average of the measures for all strategies. To ensure the same proportion of each label in each fold, the split between train and test followed the label stratification algorithm [17].

Additionally, the multi-label baseline General$_B$ [13] was considered. The idea behind this baseline consists of predicting the top most frequent labels based on the cardinality of the train data. In this case, just the 2 most frequent labels (street_food and sweets_desserts) were predicted as relevant.

---

[4] https://cran.r-project.org/package=utiml.

[5] https://cran.r-project.org/package=randomForest.

Table 3. Parameters of the MLC strategies used in the experiments

Strategy	Parameters	Strategy	Parameters
BR	-	CLR	-
DBR	-	ECC	m = 10
			subsample = 1
			attr.space = 1
			vote.schema = "maj"
LIFT	ratio = 0.1	RAkEL	k = 3
			m = 24

5.2 Analysis of the Experimental Results

Table 4 shows the MLC results obtained for each strategy, including the baseline. The bold markup indicates the best value obtained for each measure. The strategies BR and RAkEL obtained the best result for 2 measures, while the strategies CLR and ECC for one measure. The strategies BR, DBR, ECC and RAkEL outperformed the baseline for all considered measures. On average, RAkEL followed by BR obtained the best results for the measures considered in this work, as reported in the column *Averaged Ranking*.

Table 4. Results obtained from the evaluation of distinct MLC strategies.

Strategy	Accuracy↑	Macro-F1↑	Micro-F1↑	Subset accuracy↑	Hamming loss↓	One error↓	Averaged ranking
BR	0.479	0.194	**0.540**	0.255	**0.144**	0.265	2.7
CLR	0.293	**0.290**	0.455	0.002	0.375	0.260	4.8
DBR	0.467	0.173	0.516	**0.280**	0.146	0.260	3.7
ECC	0.473	0.174	0.516	0.277	0.147	**0.255**	3.3
LIFT	0.444	0.198	0.516	0.213	0.157	0.287	4.5
RAkEL	**0.483**	0.188	0.530	**0.280**	0.145	0.257	**2.1**
Baseline	0.386	0.116	0.516	0.040	0.173	0.272	-

All of the strategies, with the exception of one (the CLR strategy), presented similar results. For the measures hamming loss, micro-F1 and one-error the differences against the baseline were also small. The biggest differences between the baseline and the evaluated strategies were observed in the macro-F1 and the subset accuracy measures. The best predictive performance for the macro-F1 was obtained by the CLR strategy. Regarding the subset accuracy, the high range observed was due to the poor result obtained by the baseline.

Figure 4 shows the confusion matrix plot, where the performance of each label (x-axis) and strategy can be comparatively analyzed. The colors in each column indicate the amount of false negative (FN), false positive (FP), true negative

(TN) and true positive (TP). An optimal prediction should have only two colors (TP and TN) and the black line shows where this division should be. The labels are sorted by their frequency and the strategies arranged in alphabetical order. Based on the plot, the strategies BR, DBR, ECC, LIFT and RAkEL presented similar confusion matrices.

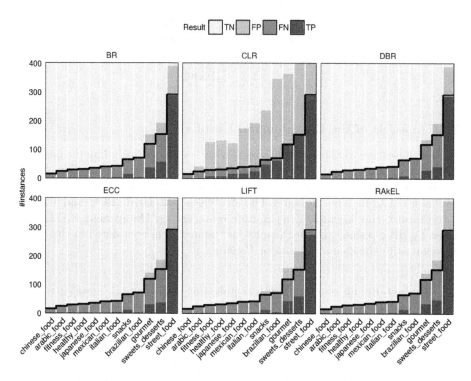

Fig. 4. Confusion matrix of each label obtained for the evaluated strategy. The colors indicate the values False Negative (FV); False Positive (FP); True Negative (TN); and, True Positive (TP). The line indicates the expected values to divide the TP from TN values considering an optimal prediction. (Color figure online)

Surprisingly, most of the strategies did not predict the presence of the labels arabic_food, brazilian_food, chinese_food, fitness_food, healthy_food, italian_food, japanese_food and mexican_food, even as false positive. Just the CLR strategy was able to overcome this limitation, at the cost of a higher number of false positive rate. Consequently, CLR obtained the best result for the macro-F1 measure and the worst results for the other measures.

It was assumed that the predictive performance was harmed by the class imbalance in the dataset. To deal with this problem, two techniques were applied: *(i)* the SMOTE [7] oversampling technique to mitigate the imbalance caused by the transformations; *(ii)* different threshold values for each label. The threshold value was selected using the SCUT algorithm [2]. Both alternatives resulted in a decrease of the MLC performance for some strategies, so these results are not reported here. Their thorough investigation are suggested as future work, especially the first option and the use of other MLC imbalance techniques.

The correlation between attributes and labels was not sufficient for the induction of models with high predictive performance. Even for the strategies capable of incorporating the label's dependencies in the learning process (DBR, ECC, LIFT and RAkEL), the results were not improved, suggesting that this MLC task is not easy to model with the currently used predictive attributes.

6   Conclusions

This paper investigated food truck recommendation using a MLC approach. The food truck options were used as class labels and the predictive attributes were personal information and user preferences. Popular multi-label strategies were applied to the food truck data set and they obtained a similar predictive performance. Although the obtained results were superior to a baseline, most of them were not able to estimate correctly the least common labels. Additionally, a confusion matrix plot was used to analyze the multi-label result, providing an overview of the performance of the investigated strategies for the different class labels.

Alternatives like increasing the number of instances and exploring new predictive attributes can improve the performance obtained. Nevertheless, the authors did not find other works investigating the use of MLC for food truck recommendation based on users' preferences.

Acknowledgments. This work is supported by the National Council for the Improvement of Higher Education (CAPES). Research developed with the computational resources of CeMEAI-FAPESP, Proc. 13/07375-0.

References

1. Abu-Mostafa, Y.S., Magdon-Ismail, M., Lin, H.T.: Learning From Data. AMLBook (2012)
2. Al-Otaibi, R., Flach, P., Kull, M.: Multi-label classification: a comparative study on threshold selection methods. In: First International Workshop on Learning over Multiple Contexts (LMCE) at ECML-PKDD 2014, Nancy, France (2014)
3. Boutell, M.R., Luo, J., Shen, X., Brown, C.M.: Learning multi-label scene classification. Pattern Recogn. **37**(9), 1757–1771 (2004)
4. Breiman, L.: Random forests. Mach. Learn. **1**(45), 5–32 (2001)
5. de Carvalho, A.C.P.L.F., Freitas, A.A.: A tutorial on multi-label classification techniques. In: Abraham, A., Hassanien, A.E., Snášel, V. (eds.) Foundations of Computational Intelligence Volume 5. Studies in Computational Intelligence, vol. 205, pp. 177–195. Springer, Heidelberg (2009). doi:10.1007/978-3-642-01536-6_8
6. Charte, F., Charte, D.: Working with multilabel datasets in R: the mldr package. R J. **7**(2), 149–162 (2015). https://journal.r-project.org/archive/2015/RJ-2015-027/index.html
7. Chawla, N.V., Bowyer, K.W., Hall, L.O., Kegelmeyer, W.P.: SMOTE: synthetic minority over-sampling technique. J. Artif. Intell. Res. **16**, 321–357 (2002)

8. Fernández-Delgado, M., Cernadas, E., Barro, S., Amorim, D.: Do we need hundreds of classifiers to solve real world classification problems? J. Mach. Learn. Res. **15**, 3133–3181 (2014)
9. Fu, Y., Liu, B., Ge, Y., Yao, Z., Xiong, H.: User preference learning with multiple information fusion for restaurant recommendation. In: Proceedings of the 2014 SIAM International Conference on Data Mining, pp. 470–478 (2014)
10. Fürnkranz, J., Hüllermeier, E., Loza Mencía, E., Brinker, K.: Multilabel classification via calibrated label ranking. Mach. Learn. **73**(2), 133–153 (2008)
11. Jackson, P., Moulinier, I.: Natural Language Processing for Online Aplications: Text Retrieval, Extraction and Categorization. John Benjamins Publishing Company, Amsterdam (2002)
12. Luaces, O., Díez, J., Barranquero, J., del Coz, J.J., Bahamonde, A.: Binary relevance efficacy for multilabel classification. Prog. Artif. Intell. **1**(4), 303–313 (2012)
13. Metz, J., de Abreu, L.F., Cherman, E.A., Monard, M.C.: On the estimation of predictive evaluation measure baselines for multi-label learning. In: Pavón, J., Duque-Méndez, N.D., Fuentes-Fernández, R. (eds.) IBERAMIA 2012. LNCS, vol. 7637, pp. 189–198. Springer, Heidelberg (2012). doi:10.1007/978-3-642-34654-5_20
14. Montañes, E., Senge, R., Barranquero, J., Ramón Quevedo, J., José Del Coz, J., Hüllermeier, E.: Dependent binary relevance models for multi-label classification. Pattern Recogn. **47**(3), 1494–1508 (2014)
15. Pazzani, M.J., Billsus, D.: Content-based recommendation systems. In: Brusilovsky, P., Kobsa, A., Nejdl, W. (eds.) The Adaptive Web. LNCS, vol. 4321, pp. 325–341. Springer, Heidelberg (2007). doi:10.1007/978-3-540-72079-9_10
16. Read, J., Pfahringer, B., Holmes, G., Frank, E.: Classifier chains for multi-label classification. Mach. Learn. **85**(3), 333–359 (2011)
17. Sechidis, K., Tsoumakas, G., Vlahavas, I.: On the stratification of multi-label data. In: Gunopulos, D., Hofmann, T., Malerba, D., Vazirgiannis, M. (eds.) ECML PKDD 2011. LNCS, vol. 6913, pp. 145–158. Springer, Heidelberg (2011). doi:10.1007/978-3-642-23808-6_10
18. Sun, J., Xiong, Y., Zhu, Y., Liu, J., Guan, C., Xiong, H.: Multi-source information fusion for personalized restaurant recommendation. In: Proceedings of the 38th International ACM SIGIR Conference on Research and Development in Information Retrieval, SIGIR 2015, pp. 983–986. ACM, New York (2015)
19. Tsoumakas, G., Katakis, I., Vlahavas, I.: Mining multi-label data. In: Maimon, O., Rokach, L. (eds.) Data Mining and Knowledge Discovery Handbook, 2nd edn, pp. 667–685. Springer, Boston (2010). doi:10.1007/978-0-387-09823-4_34. Chap. 34
20. Tsoumakas, G., Katakis, I., Vlahavas, I.: Random k-labelsets for multilabel classification. IEEE Trans. Knowl. Data Eng. **23**(7), 1079–1089 (2011)
21. Weber, D.: The Food Truck Handbook: Start, Grow, and Succeed in the Mobile Food Business. Wiley, Hoboken (2012)
22. Wolpert, D.H.: Stacked generalization. Neural Netw. **5**(2), 241–259 (1992)
23. Zhang, F., Yuan, N.J., Zheng, K., Lian, D., Xie, X., Rui, Y.: Exploiting dining preference for restaurant recommendation. In: Proceedings of the 25th International Conference on World Wide Web, WWW 2016, pp. 725–735 (2016)
24. Zhang, F., Zheng, K., Yuan, N.J., Xie, X., Chen, E., Zhou, X.: A novelty-seeking based dining recommender system. In: Proceedings of the 24th International Conference on World Wide Web, WWW 2015, pp. 1362–1372. ACM, New York (2015)
25. Zhang, M.L., Wu, L.: Lift: multi-label learning with label-specific features. IEEE Trans. Pattern Anal. Mach. Intell. **37**(1), 107–120 (2015)
26. Zhang, M.L., Zhou, Z.H.: A review on multi-label learning algorithms. IEEE Trans. Knowl. Data Eng. **26**(8), 1819–1837 (2014)

Improving Incremental Recommenders
with Online Bagging

João Vinagre[1(✉)], Alípio Mário Jorge[1,2], and João Gama[1,3]

[1] LIAAD - INESC TEC, Porto, Portugal
jnsilva@inesctec.pt, amjorge@fc.up.pt, jgama@fep.up.pt
[2] Faculty of Sciences, University of Porto, Porto, Portugal
[3] Faculty of Economics, University of Porto, Porto, Portugal

Abstract. Online recommender systems often deal with continuous, potentially fast and unbounded flows of data. Ensemble methods for recommender systems have been used in the past in batch algorithms, however they have never been studied with incremental algorithms that learn from data streams. We evaluate online bagging with an incremental matrix factorization algorithm for top-N recommendation with positive-only user feedback, often known as binary ratings. Our results show that online bagging is able to improve accuracy up to 35% over the baseline, with small computational overhead.

Keywords: Recommender systems · Bagging · Matrix factorization · Data streams

1 Introduction

In many real world recommender systems, user feedback is continuously generated at unpredictable rates and order, and is potentially unbounded. In large scale systems, the rate at which user feedback is generated can be very fast. Building predictive models from these continuous flows of data is a problem actively studied in the field of data stream mining. Ideally, algorithms that learn from data streams should be able to process data at least as fast as it arrives, in a single pass, while maintaining an always-available model [3]. Most incremental algorithms naturally have these properties, and are thus a viable solution.

Incremental algorithms for recommendation also treat user feedback data as a data stream, immediately incorporating new data in the recommendation model. In many – if not most – recommendation applications this is a desirable feature, since it gives the model the ability to evolve over time. This is important, because the task of a recommender system is to find the most relevant items to each user, individually. Naturally, users are human beings, whose preferences change over time. Moreover, in large scale systems, new users and items are permanently entering the system. A model that is immediately updated with fresh data has the capability of adjusting faster to such changes.

© Springer International Publishing AG 2017
E. Oliveira et al. (Eds.): EPIA 2017, LNAI 10423, pp. 597–607, 2017.
DOI: 10.1007/978-3-319-65340-2_49

1.1 Related Work

Ensemble methods in machine learning are convenient techniques to improve the accuracy of algorithms. Typically, this is achieved by combining results from a number of weaker sub-models. Bagging [1], Boosting [4] and Stacking [13] are three well-known ensemble methods used with recommendation algorithms. Boosting is experimented in [2,7,9,10], bagging is studied also in [7,10], and stacking in [11]. In all of these contributions, ensemble methods work with batch learning algorithms only.

In this paper we propose online bagging for incremental recommendation algorithms designed to deal with streams of positive user feedback. To our best knowledge this is the first ensemble method proposed for incremental recommender systems in the literature.

This paper is organized as follows. After this introductory section, we describe online bagging for common data mining tasks in Sect. 2. Section 3 describes our online bagging approach in recommendation problems. In Sect. 4 we present our experiments and results, along with a short discussion. Finally, we conclude in Sect. 5.

2   Online Bagging

Bagging [1] is an ensemble technique that takes a number of bootstrap samples of a dataset and trains a model on each one of the samples. Predictions from the various sub-models are then aggregated in a final prediction. This is known to improve the performance of algorithms by reducing variance, which is especially useful with unstable algorithms that are very sensitive to small changes in the data. The diversity offered by training several models with slightly different bootstrap samples of the data helps in giving more importance to the main concepts being learned – since they must be present in most bootstrap samples of the data, and less importance to noise or irrelevant phenomena that may mislead the learning algorithm.

To obtain a bootstrap sample of a dataset with size N, we perform N trials, sampling a random example with replacement from the dataset. Each example has probability of $1/N$ to be sampled at each trial. The resulting dataset will have the same size as the original dataset, however some examples will not be present whereas some others will occur multiple times. To obtain M samples, we simply repeat the process M times.

In its original proposal [1], bagging is a batch procedure requiring $N \times M$ passes through the dataset. However, it has been shown in [8] that this can be done incrementally in a single pass, if the number of examples is very large – a natural assumption when learning from data streams. Looking at the batch method above, we observe that each bootstrap sample contains K occurrences of each example, with $K \in \{0, 1, 2, \ldots\}$, and:

$$P(K = k) = \binom{N}{k} \left(\frac{1}{N}\right)^k \left(1 - \frac{1}{N}\right)^{N-k} \tag{1}$$

In an incremental setting, one could just initialize M sub-models – or bootstrap nodes – and then use (1) to train new examples K times, redrawing K for each node. The problem is that this would still require knowing N beforehand. However, if we assume that $N \to \infty$, then the distribution of K tends to a $Poisson(1)$ distribution, and therefore

$$P(K = k) = \frac{e^{-1}}{k!} \tag{2}$$

eliminating the need of any prior knowledge about the data, allowing the usage of bagging in a single pass over data.

3   Online Recommendation with Bagging

To assess the potential of online bagging, we use ISGD [12], a simple online matrix factorization algorithm for positive-only data. ISGD (Algorithm 1) uses Stochastic Gradient Descent in one pass through the data, which is convenient for data stream processing. It is designed for positive-only streams of user-item pairs (u, i) that indicate a positive interaction between user u and item i. Examples of positive interactions are users buying items in an online store, streaming music tracks from an online music streaming service, or simply visiting web pages. This is a much more widely available form of user feedback, than for example, ratings data, which is only available from systems with user rating features.

Algorithm 1. ISGD - Incremental SGD for positive-only user feedback [12]

Data: a finite set or a data stream $D = \{(u, i)_1, (u, i)_2, \ldots\}$
input : no. of latent features $feat$, no. of iterations $iter$, regularization factor λ, learn rate η
output: user and item factor matrices A and B

for $(u, i) \in D$ **do**
  if $u \notin \text{Rows}(A)$ **then**
    $A_u \leftarrow \text{Vector}(\text{size} : feat)$
    $A_u \sim \mathcal{N}(0, 0.1)$
  if $i \notin \text{Rows}(B)$ **then**
    $B_i \leftarrow \text{Vector}(\text{size} : feat)$
    $B_i \sim \mathcal{N}(0, 0.1)$
  for $n \leftarrow 1$ **to** $iter$ **do**
    $err_{ui} \leftarrow 1 - A_u \cdot B_i$
    $A_u \leftarrow A_u + \eta(err_{ui}B_i - \lambda A_u)$
    $B_i \leftarrow B_i + \eta(err_{ui}A_u - \lambda B_i)$

ISGD continuously updates factor matrices A – the user factors matrix – and B – the item factors matrix –, correcting the model to adapt to the incoming user-item pairs. If (u, i) occurs in the stream, then the model prediction $\hat{R}_{ui} = A_u \cdot B_i$

should be close to 1. Top-N recommendations to any user u is obtained by a ranking function $f = |1 - \hat{R}_{ui}|$ for all items i in ascending order, and taking the top N items.

The online bagging approach described in Sect. 2, can be easily applied to ISGD, resulting in Algorithm 2 – BaggedISGD.

Algorithm 2. BaggedISGD - Bagging version of ISGD (training algorithm)

Data: a finite set or a data stream of user-item pairs $D = \{(u,i)_1, (u,i)_2, \ldots\}$
input : no. of latent features $feat$, no. of iterations $iter$, regularization factor
$\quad\quad\quad\quad$ λ, learn rate η, no. of bootstrap nodes M
output: M user and item factor matrices A^m and B^m

for $(u,i) \in D$ **do**
$\quad$ **for** $m \leftarrow 1$ **to** M **do**
$\quad\quad$ $k \sim \text{Poisson}(1)$ $\qquad\qquad\qquad\qquad\qquad\qquad$ // eq. (2)
$\quad\quad$ **if** $k > 0$ **then**
$\quad\quad\quad$ **for** $l \leftarrow 1$ **to** k **do**
$\quad\quad\quad\quad$ **if** $u \notin \text{Rows}(A^m)$ **then**
$\quad\quad\quad\quad\quad$ $A_u^m \leftarrow \text{Vector}(\text{size} : feat)$
$\quad\quad\quad\quad\quad$ $A_u^m \sim \mathcal{N}(0, 0.1)$
$\quad\quad\quad\quad$ **if** $i \notin \text{Rows}(B^m)$ **then**
$\quad\quad\quad\quad\quad$ $B_i^m \leftarrow \text{Vector}(\text{size} : feat)$
$\quad\quad\quad\quad\quad$ $B_i^m \sim \mathcal{N}(0, 0.1)$
$\quad\quad\quad\quad$ **for** $n \leftarrow 1$ **to** $iter$ **do**
$\quad\quad\quad\quad\quad$ $err_{ui} \leftarrow 1 - A_u^m \cdot B_i^m$
$\quad\quad\quad\quad\quad$ $A_u^m \leftarrow A_u^m + \eta(err_{ui}B_i^m - \lambda A_u^m)$
$\quad\quad\quad\quad\quad$ $B_i^m \leftarrow B_i^m + \eta(err_{ui}A_u^m - \lambda B_i^m)$

BaggedISGD learns M models on M bootstrap nodes, each of them based on the online bootstrap sampling method described in Sect. 2. Similarly to ISGD, to perform the actual list of recommendations for a user u, items i are sorted by a function $f = |1 - \hat{R}_{ui}|$. However, the scores $\hat{R}_{ui}$ are actually the average score of all nodes:

$$\hat{R}_{ui} = \frac{\sum_{m=1}^{M} A_u^m \cdot B_i^m}{M} \tag{3}$$

At training time, this algorithm requires at least M times the computational resources needed for ISGD, with M bootstrap nodes. Recommendation also has the overhead of aggregating M predictions from the submodels. In our experiments, we also measure update and recommendation times, for several values of M.

4   Evaluation

To simulate a streaming environment we need datasets that maintain the natural order of the data points, as they were generated. Additionally, we need

Table 1. Dataset description

Dataset	Events	Users	Items	Sparsity
PLC-STR	588 851	7 580	30 092	99.74%
LFM-50U	1 121 520	50	159 208	85.91%
YHM-6KU	476 886	6 000	127 448	99.94%
ML1M	226 310	6 014	3 232	98.84%

positive-only data, since the tested algorithm is not designed to deal with ratings. We use 4 datasets that conciliate these two requirements – positive-only and naturally ordered, described in Table 1. ML1M is based on the Movielens-1M movie rating dataset[1]. To obtain the YHM-6KU, we sample 6000 users randomly from the Yahoo! Music dataset[2]. LFM-50U is a subset consisting of a random sample of 50 users taken from the Last.fm[3] dataset[4]. PLC-STR[5] consists of the music streaming history taken from Palco Principal[6], a Portuguese social network for non-mainstream artists and fans.

All of the 4 datasets consist of a chronologically ordered sequence of positive user-item interactions. However, ML1M and YHM-50U are obtained from ratings datasets. To use them as positive-only data, we retain the user-item pairs for which the rating is in the top 20% of the rating scale. This means retaining only the rating 5 in ML1M and rating of 80 or more in the YHM-6KU dataset. Naturally, only single occurrences of user-item pairs are available in these datasets, since users do not rate the same item more than once. PLC-STR and LFM-50 have multiple occurrences of the same user-item pairs.

We run a set of experiments using the prequential approach [5] as described in [12]. Each observation in the dataset consists of a simple user-item pair (u, i) that indicates a positive interaction between user u and item i. The following steps are performed in the prequential evaluation process:

1. If u is a known user, use the current model to recommend a list of items to u, otherwise go to step 3;
2. Score the recommended list given the observed item i;
3. Update the model with (u, i) (optionally);
4. Proceed to – or wait for – the next observation

This process is entirely applicable to algorithms that learn either incrementally or in batch mode. This is the reason why step 3 is annotated as optional. For example, instead of performing this step, the system can store the data to perform batch retraining periodically.

---

[1] http://www.grouplens.org/data [Jan 2013].
[2] https://webscope.sandbox.yahoo.com/catalog.php?datatype=r [Jan 2013].
[3] http://last.fm/.
[4] http://ocelma.net/MusicRecommendationDataset [Jan 2013].
[5] https://rdm.inesctec.pt/dataset/cs-2017-003, file: `playlisted_tracks.tsv`.
[6] http://www.palcoprincipal.com/.

Table 2. Average performance of ISGD with and without bagging. M is the number of bootstrap nodes. The last two columns contain the average update times and the average recommendation times.

Dataset	M	Rec@1	Rec@5	Rec@10	Rec@20	Upd. (ms)	Rec. (ms)
PLC-STR	ISGD	**0.127**	**0.241**	0.277	0.302	0.237	21.736
	8	0.076	0.194	0.257	0.316	2.563	64.793
	16	0.081	0.215	0.284	0.349	4.732	132.812
	32	0.088	0.229	0.302	0.370	9.508	264.846
	64	0.092	0.237	**0.313**	**0.384**	18.012	517.479
LFM-50U	ISGD	**0.034**	0.049	0.052	0.055	2.625	94.177
	8	0.023	0.044	0.052	0.058	21.449	241.452
	16	0.026	0.050	0.059	0.066	43.094	491.689
	32	0.028	0.055	0.064	0.071	84.536	984.060
	64	0.030	**0.057**	**0.067**	**0.075**	168.781	1.958s
YHM-6KU	ISGD	**0.030**	**0.063**	0.082	0.103	4.462	89.321
	8	0.011	0.033	0.051	0.076	28.529	347.422
	16	0.012	0.037	0.058	0.086	54.723	667.898
	32	0.019	0.055	0.082	0.117	158.744	990.551
	64	0.021	0.059	**0.087**	**0.123**	328.924	1.934s
ML1M	ISGD	0.005	0.021	0.034	0.055	0.069	2.557
	8	0.005	0.019	0.033	0.056	0.517	7.208
	16	0.006	0.022	0.038	0.063	1.390	21.816
	32	0.006	0.025	0.042	0.071	1.866	33.496
	64	**0.007**	**0.026**	**0.045**	**0.074**	3.999	41.090

To kickstart the evaluation process we use 10% the available data to train a base model in batch, and use the remaining 90% to perform incremental training and evaluation. We do this initial batch training to avoid *cold-start* problems, which are not the subject of our research.

In our setting, the items that users have already co-occurred with – i.e. items that users know – are not recommended. This has one important implication in the prequential evaluation process, specifically on datasets that have multiple occurrences of the same user-item pair. Evaluation at these points is necessarily penalized, since the observed item will not be within the recommendations. In such cases, we bypass the scoring step, but still use the observation to update the model.

We measure two dimensions on the evaluation process: accuracy and time. In the prequential process described above, we need to make a prediction and evaluate it at every new user-item pair (u, i) that arrives in the data stream. To do this, we use the current model to recommend a list of items to user u. We then score this recommendation list, by matching it to the actually observed item i. We use a recommendation list with at most 20 items, and then score this list as 1 if i is within the recommended items, and 0 otherwise, using Recall@C with cutoffs $C \in \{1, 5, 10, 20\}$. Using these cutoffs, we only consider the top C items in the list. For example, Recall@1 only checks whether the first item in the list matches the actual observed item i. Regardless of C, we only have one item to test against the list, which means that Recall@C can only take the values $\{0, 1\}$. We can calculate the overall Recall@C by averaging the scores at every step, which in practice gives us the hit ratio. Additionally, we can also depict it using a moving average. We also measure the update time, in milliseconds, at every step which can depicted using a moving average as well.

All experiments were run in Intel Haswell 4-core machines, with CentOS Linux 7 64 bit. The algorithms and prequential evaluation code is implemented on top of MyMediaLite [6]. The recommendation step is implemented with multi-core code – predictions from nodes are computed in parallel.

4.1 Results

To evaluate bagging, we experiment with four levels of bootstrapping $M \in \{8, 16, 32, 64\}$. Table 2 summarizes the results of our experiments. Values in Table 2 are obtained by averaging Recall and time obtained at all prequential evaluation steps. With all datasets except YHM-6KU, bagging improves the Recall, especially with $M \geq 32$. One interesting observation is that bagging has a bigger influence on higher Recall cutoffs, which suggests that improvements of the predictive ability are typically not obtained in the top 5 recommended items.

The model update times increase approximately in proportion to the number of bootstrap nodes M, which is not surprising, since the algorithm performs the update operations one time (in average) in each one of the M bootstrap nodes. However, since the baseline update time is very small, this overhead is also small. The last column of Table 2 contains the recommendation time, specifically the average time required to produce a recommendation list. The bagging algorithm needs to aggregate predictions coming from all M nodes, which is an important overhead. Results show that both the update times and recommendation times increase proportionally to M. However, the recommendation step is a far more expensive operation, even when computed in parallel. For example, using $M = 64$ with LFM-50U and YHM-6KU, recommendations are computed in nearly two seconds in average, in 4-core machines, which can reasonably be considered too much in many applications.

A useful feature of prequential evaluation is that it allows us also to depict the evolution of the outcome of Recall. In Figs. 1, 2, 3 and 4, we depict the evolution of Recall@C with $C \in \{1, 5, 10, 20\}$. This visualization reveals how the predictive ability of the algorithm performs over time, as the incremental learning process occurs.

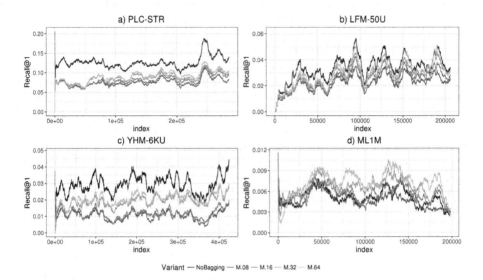

Fig. 1. Prequential evaluation of Recall@1 with ISGD with and without bagging. Lines are drawn using a moving average of Recall@1 with $n = 10000$. The first 10 000 points are drawn using the accumulated average.

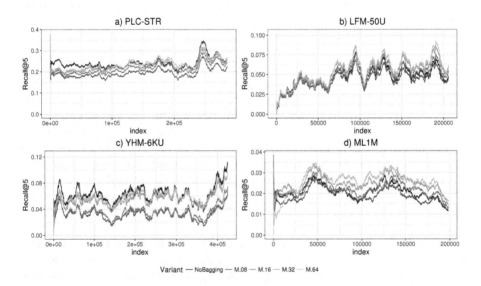

Fig. 2. Prequential evaluation of Recall@5 with ISGD with and without bagging. Lines are drawn using a moving average of Recall@5 with $n = 10000$. The first 10 000 points are drawn using the accumulated average.

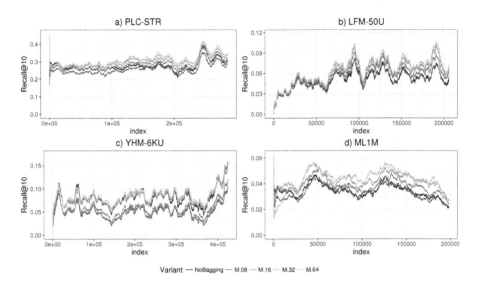

Fig. 3. Prequential evaluation of Recall@10 with ISGD with and without bagging. Lines are drawn using a moving average of Recall@10 with $n = 10000$. The first 10 000 points are drawn using the accumulated average.

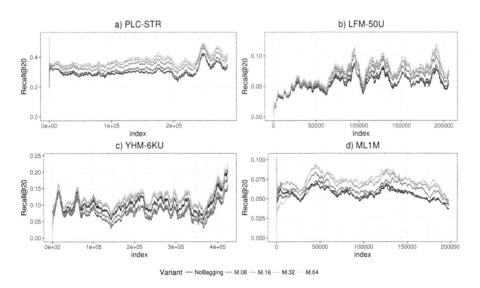

Fig. 4. Prequential evaluation of Recall@20 with ISGD with and without bagging. Lines are drawn using a moving average of Recall@20 with $n = 10000$. The first 10 000 points are drawn using the accumulated average.

4.2 Discussion

Results in Table 2 and Figs. 1, 2, 3 and 4 show that bagging is able to improve the accuracy of ISGD, with improvements of 35% over the baseline (see Table 2 LFM-50U and ML1M). This improvement is mainly observable with cutoffs $C \geq 5$ of Recall. Given that bagging reduces variance [1], this suggests that ISGD is more stable in the top few recommendations. Another observation is that improvements are not consistent with all datasets. With LFM-50U, for example, bagging only slightly outperforms the baseline ISGD – and only with $M \geq 32$, while with PLC-STR, the improvement is much higher in proportion, even with lower M.

One other observation that is particularly visible in the plotted lines in Figs. 1, 2, 3 and 4 is that as we increase the number of nodes M, the improvement potential becomes lower. In almost all experiments, regardless of the Recall cutoff and the dataset, the improvement achieved when doubling M from 16 to 32 is higher than the improvement we get when doubling M from 32 to 64, although the computational overhead in the latter case is twice as high. The optimal number of nodes is dependent on the desired trade-off between accuracy improvement and computational cost. Note that with some datasets – e.g. YHM-6KU, improvements may only be obtained with a relatively large M.

It is also clear that the time overheads grow linearly with the number of bootstrap models. However, the overhead in model update times is not very relevant in practice, given that the baseline update times are very low in ISGD – with $M = 64$ the highest update time falls below 400 ms. The overhead at recommendation time is more evident, when aggregating results from the M bootstrap nodes. Fortunately, as with most ensemble techniques, parallel processing can be trivially used to alleviate this overhead. Additionally, there may be room for code optimization or approximate methods that require less and/or more efficient computations.

5 Conclusions

Bagging is an ensemble technique successfully used with many machine learning algorithms, however it has not been thoroughly studied in recommendation problems, and particularly with incremental algorithms. In this paper, we experiment online bagging with an incremental matrix factorization algorithm that learns from unbounded streams of positive-only data. Our results suggest that with manageable overheads, accuracy clearly improves – more than 35% in some cases, especially as the number of recommended items increases. In the near future, we intend to experiment this and other online ensemble methods in a larger number of stream-based recommendation algorithms.

Acknowledgments. Project "TEC4Growth – Pervasive Intelligence, Enhancers and Proofs of Concept with Industrial Impact/NORTE-01-0145-FEDER-000020" is financed by the North Portugal Regional Operational Programme (NORTE 2020), under the PORTUGAL 2020 Partnership Agreement, and through the European

Regional Development Fund (ERDF). This work is also partially funded by the European Commission through project MAESTRA (Grant no. ICT-2013-612944). We thank Ubbin Labs, Lda. for kindly providing data from Palco Principal.

References

1. Breiman, L.: Bagging predictors. Mach. Learn. **24**(2), 123–140 (1996). doi:10.1007/BF00058655
2. Chowdhury, N., Cai, X., Luo, C.: BoostMF: boosted matrix factorisation for collaborative ranking. In: Appice, A., Rodrigues, P.P., Santos Costa, V., Gama, J., Jorge, A., Soares, C. (eds.) ECML PKDD 2015. LNCS, vol. 9285, pp. 3–18. Springer, Cham (2015). doi:10.1007/978-3-319-23525-7_1
3. Domingos, P., Hulten, G.: Catching up with the data: research issues in mining data streams. In: DMKD (2001). http://www.cs.cornell.edu/johannes/papers/dmkd2001-papers/p8_domingos.pdf
4. Freund, Y., Schapire, R.E.: Experiments with a new boosting algorithm. In: Proceedings of the 13th International Conference on Machine Learning ICML 1996, pp. 148–156. Morgan Kaufmann (1996)
5. Gama, J., Sebastião, R., Rodrigues, P.P.: On evaluating stream learning algorithms. Mach. Learn. **90**(3), 317–346 (2013). doi:10.1007/s10994-012-5320-9
6. Gantner, Z., Rendle, S., Freudenthaler, C., Schmidt-Thieme, L.: MyMediaLite: a free recommender system library. In: Proceedings of the 2011 ACM Conference on Recommender Systems, RecSys 2011, pp. 305–308. ACM (2011)
7. Jahrer, M., Töscher, A., Legenstein, R.A.: Combining predictions for accurate recommender systems. In: Proceedings of the 16th ACM SIGKDD International Conference on Knowledge Discovery and Data Mining, KDD 2010, pp. 693–702. ACM (2010). http://doi.acm.org/10.1145/1835804.1835893
8. Oza, N.C., Russell, S.J.: Experimental comparisons of online and batch versions of bagging and boosting. In: Proceedings of the 7th ACM SIGKDD International Conference on Knowledge Discovery and Data Mining, KDD 2001, pp. 359–364. ACM (2001). http://portal.acm.org/citation.cfm?id=502512.502565
9. Schclar, A., Tsikinovsky, A., Rokach, L., Meisels, A., Antwarg, L.: Ensemble methods for improving the performance of neighborhood-based collaborative filtering. In: Proceedings of the 2009 ACM Conference on Recommender Systems, RecSys 2009, pp. 261–264. ACM (2009). http://doi.acm.org/10.1145/1639714.1639763
10. Segrera, S., Moreno, M.N.: An experimental comparative study of web mining methods for recommender systems. In: Proceedings of the 6th WSEAS International Conference on Distance Learning and Web Engineering, pp. 56–61. WSEAS (2006)
11. Sill, J., Takács, G., Mackey, L.W., Lin, D.: Feature-weighted linear stacking. CoRR abs/0911.0460 (2009). http://arxiv.org/abs/0911.0460
12. Vinagre, J., Jorge, A.M., Gama, J.: Fast incremental matrix factorization for recommendation with positive-only feedback. In: Dimitrova, V., Kuflik, T., Chin, D., Ricci, F., Dolog, P., Houben, G.-J. (eds.) UMAP 2014. LNCS, vol. 8538, pp. 459–470. Springer, Cham (2014). doi:10.1007/978-3-319-08786-3_41
13. Wolpert, D.H.: Stacked generalization. Neural Netw. **5**(2), 241–259 (1992). doi:10.1016/S0893-6080(05)80023-1

Knowledge Representation and Reasoning

Tableaux for Hybrid XPath with Data

Carlos Areces[1,2], Raul Fervari[1,2(✉)], and Nahuel Seiler[1]

[1] FaMAF, Universidad Nacional de Córdoba, Córdoba, Argentina
{areces,fervari,ngs0108}@famaf.unc.edu.ar
[2] CONICET, Córdoba, Argentina

Abstract. We provide a sound, complete and terminating tableau procedure to check satisfiability of downward XPath$_=$ formulas enriched with nominals and satisfaction operators. The calculus is inspired by ideas introduced to ensure termination of tableau calculi for certain Hybrid Logics. We prove that even though we increased the expressive power of XPath by introducing hybrid operators, the satisfiability problem for the obtained logic is still PSPACE-complete.

Keywords: XPath · Hybrid logic · Tableaux · Termination · Complexity

1 Introduction

In many applications, dealing with actual data is an important challenge. For instance, applications which manage large volumes of web or medical data require, in many cases, more complex models than those that can be encoded in classical relational databases. These models are often defined and studied in the context of *semi-structured data* [9]. A semi-structured data model is based on an organization of data in labeled trees or graphs, and on query languages for accessing and updating these structures. These representations can contain labels coming from a finite alphabet (capturing the *structural* information), or from an infinite alphabet (capturing also the actual *data* in the database). Most query languages focus only on how to access the structural information, in this article we focus on languages that also handle data.

XML (eXtensible Markup Language) is the most successful data model that captures both structural information and data. An XML document is a hierarchical structure represented by an unranked finite ordered tree, where nodes have labels (either letters from a finite alphabet, or data values from an infinite alphabet). XPath is, arguably, the most widely used XML query language, with application in specification and update languages. XPath is, fundamentally, a general purpose language for addressing, searching, and matching pieces of an XML document. It is an open standard and constitutes a World Wide Web Consortium (W3C) Recommendation [11]. Core-XPath [16] is the fragment of XPath 1.0 containing the navigational behavior of XPath. It can express properties of the underlying tree structure of the XML document, such as the label (tag name)

© Springer International Publishing AG 2017
E. Oliveira et al. (Eds.): EPIA 2017, LNAI 10423, pp. 611–623, 2017.
DOI: 10.1007/978-3-319-65340-2_50

of a node, but it cannot express conditions on the actual data contained in the attributes. In other words, it is essentially a *classical modal logic* [5,6].

However, without the ability to relate nodes based on the actual data values of the attributes, the expressive power of Core-XPath is inappropriate for many applications. In fact, it is not possible to define the most important construct in a database query language: the *join*. The extension of Core-XPath with (in)equality tests between attributes of elements in an XML document is named Core-Data-XPath in [7]. Here, we will call this logic XPath$_=$. Models of XPath$_=$ are data trees which can be seen as abstractions of XML documents. A data tree is a tree whose nodes contain a label from a finite alphabet and a data value from an infinite domain (see Fig. 1 for an example). In this article we will consider the case where models can be arbitrary *graphs* and not just finite trees. XPath$_=$ allows formulas of the form $\langle \alpha = \beta \rangle$ and $\langle \alpha \neq \beta \rangle$, where α, β are path expressions that navigate the model using axes: descendant, child, ancestor, next-sibling, etc. and can make tests in intermediate nodes. The formula $\langle \alpha = \beta \rangle$ (respectively $\langle \alpha \neq \beta \rangle$) is true at a node x of a data tree if there are nodes y, z that can be reached by paths denoted by α, β, and such that the data value of y is equal (respectively different) to the data value of z. For instance, in Fig. 1 the expression *"there is a one-step descendant and a two-steps descendant with the same data value"* is satisfied at x, given the presence of u and z. The expression *"there are two children with distinct data value"* is also true at x, because y and z have different data.

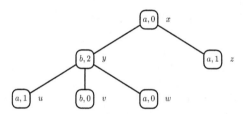

Fig. 1. An example of a data tree. Letters are labels, numbers are data.

Notice that XPath$_=$ allows to compare data values at the end of a path, by equality or inequality. However, it does not grant access to the concrete data value of nodes (in the example, 0, 1 or 2). As a result, it is possible to work with an abstraction of data trees: instead of having concrete data values in each node, we have an equivalence relation between nodes. In the data tree from Fig. 1, the relation consists of three equivalence classes: $\{x, v, w\}$, $\{u, z\}$ and $\{y\}$.

Recent articles investigate XPath$_=$ from a modal perspective. For example, satisfiability and evaluation are discussed in [13,14], while model theory and expressivity are studied in [2,15]. A Gentzen-style sequent calculus is given in [4] for a very restricted fragment of XPath$_=$. An extension of the equational axiomatic system from [10] is introduced in [1], allowing downward navigation and equality/inequality tests. [3] provides an axiomatization for the previous logic, extended with upward navigation, nominals and satisfaction operators.

Contributions. In this article we introduce a sound, complete and terminating tableau calculus for XPath$_=$ with downward navigation, where node expressions are extended with nominals (special labels that are true in only one node), and path expressions are extended with the satisfaction operator (allowing the navigation to some particular named node). We call this logic HXPath$_=(\downarrow)$.

We will follow ideas introduced in [8] to design terminating tableau calculi for hybrid logics. The main intuition is that nominals and satisfaction operators can be used in tableaux to keep track of the evaluation of a formula during an attempt to build a model. This way, tableaux rules and the completeness proof are more intuitive, obtaining a simple proof theory for XPath with data.

Organization. In Sect. 2 we define the syntax and semantics of HXPath$_=(\downarrow)$, and give examples to show its expressive power. Section 3 introduces a tableau calculus for HXPath$_=(\downarrow)$, its completeness is proved in Sect. 4, and termination in Sect. 5. We also show that the satisfiability problem for HXPath$_=(\downarrow)$ is PSPACE-complete. We include some final remarks and future work in Sect. 6.

2   Basic Definitions

We start by defining the structures that will be used to evaluate formulas in the language. We assume basic knowledge of classical modal logic [5].

Definition 1. *Let* PROP *(the set of propositional symbols) be an infinite countable set, let* NOM *(the set of nominals) be an infinite countable well-ordered[1] set such that* NOM $\cap$ PROP $= \emptyset$, *and let* ATOM $=$ PROP $\cup$ NOM *be the set of atomic formulas (or atoms for short).*

An abstract hybrid data model *is a tuple* $\mathcal{M} = \langle M, \sim, \rightarrow, label, nom \rangle$, *where* M *is a non-empty set of elements,* $\sim \subseteq M^2$ *is an equivalence relation between elements of* M, $\rightarrow \subseteq M^2$ *is an accessibility relation,* label: $M \rightarrow 2^{\mathsf{PROP}}$ *is a labeling function and nom:* NOM $\rightarrow M$ *is a function that assigns nominals to certain elements.*

Concrete data models[2] are most commonly used in application, where we encounter data from an infinite alphabet (e.g., alphabetic strings) associated to the nodes in a semi-structured database. It is easy to see that each concrete data model has an associated abstract data model where data is replaced by an equivalence relation that links all nodes with the same data. Vice-versa, each abstract data model can be "concretized" by assigning to each node its equivalence data class as data.

---

[1] The well-ordered condition will be used to prove termination.
[2] For a detailed introduction, see [3].

Definition 2. *The sets* PExp *of path expressions and* NExp *of node expressions of the language HXPath$_=(\downarrow)$ are defined by mutual recursion as follows:*

$$\text{PExp} ::= \; \downarrow \; | \; i \; | \; [\varphi] \; | \; \alpha\beta \; | \; \alpha \cup \beta$$
$$\text{NExp} ::= \; p \; | \; i \; | \; \neg\varphi \; | \; \varphi \wedge \psi \; | \; \langle \alpha = \beta \rangle \; | \; \langle \alpha \neq \beta \rangle,$$

where $p \in \text{PROP}$, $i \in \text{NOM}$, $\alpha, \beta \in \text{PExp}$ *and* $\varphi, \psi \in \text{NExp}$. *The set* Exp *of expressions of HXPath$_=(\downarrow)$ is defined as* NExp $\cup$ PExp.

NOM(ε) *denotes the set of nominals appearing in an expression* $\varepsilon \in \text{Exp}$. *If E is a set of expressions then* $\text{NOM}(E) = \bigcup_{\varepsilon \in E} \text{NOM}(\varepsilon)$.

In the rest of the article we will use the symbols i, j, k, n, m for nominals; p, q, r, for propositional symbols; α, β, γ, δ for path expressions; φ, ψ for node expressions; and ε for an arbitrary expression.

In what follows we will always use $*$ for $=$ and $\neq$. Missing Boolean operators are defined as usual. We define the following operators as abbreviations. Let α be a path expression, φ a node expression, $i \in \text{NOM}$, and $p \in \text{PROP}$:

$$\top \equiv p \vee \neg p \quad \bot \equiv \neg\top \quad \langle\alpha\rangle\varphi \equiv \langle\alpha[\varphi] = \alpha[\varphi]\rangle \quad [\alpha]\varphi \equiv \neg\langle\alpha\rangle\neg\varphi \quad i\varphi \equiv \langle i\rangle\varphi.$$

Formulas of the form $i\varphi$ for $i \in \text{NOM}$ and φ a node expression are called *at-formulas* or *prefixed-formulas* (intuitively, they express that φ holds *at* the state named by i); i is called the prefix of $i\varphi$. At-formulas will play a crucial role in the tableau calculus introduced in the next section.

Notice that we use nominals in satisfaction operators appearing in path expressions (e.g., $\downarrow i\downarrow$) and as atoms (e.g., $i \wedge p$) and prefixes (in $i\varphi$) in node expressions; the intended meaning will always be clear by context.

Also, following the standard notation in XPath logics and in modal logics, the $[\,]$ operation is overloaded: for φ a node expression and α a path expression, both $[\alpha]\varphi$ and $[\varphi]\alpha$ are well-formed expressions; the former is a node expression where $[\alpha]$ is a box modality, the latter is a path expression where $[\varphi]$ is a test.

Definition 3. *Let* $\mathcal{M} = \langle M, \sim, \rightarrow, label, nom \rangle$ *be an abstract data model, and $x, y \in M$. We define the semantics of HXPath$_=(\downarrow)$ as follows:*

$$\mathcal{M}, x, y \models \; \downarrow \; iff \; x \rightarrow y$$
$$\mathcal{M}, x, y \models i \; iff \; nom(i) = y$$
$$\mathcal{M}, x, y \models [\varphi] \; iff \; x = y \; and \; \mathcal{M}, x \models \varphi$$
$$\mathcal{M}, x, y \models \alpha\beta \; iff \; there \; is \; some \; z \in M \; s.t. \; \mathcal{M}, x, z \models \alpha \; and \; \mathcal{M}, z, y \models \beta$$
$$\mathcal{M}, x, y \models \alpha \cup \beta \; iff \; \mathcal{M}, x, y \models \alpha \; or \; \mathcal{M}, x, y \models \beta$$
$$\mathcal{M}, x \models p \; iff \; p \in label(x)$$
$$\mathcal{M}, x \models i \; iff \; nom(i) = x$$
$$\mathcal{M}, x \models \neg\varphi \; iff \; \mathcal{M}, x \not\models \varphi$$
$$\mathcal{M}, x \models \varphi \wedge \psi \; iff \; \mathcal{M}, x \models \varphi \; and \; \mathcal{M}, x \models \psi$$
$$\mathcal{M}, x \models \langle \alpha = \beta \rangle \; iff \; there \; are \; y, z \in M \; s.t. \; \mathcal{M}, x, y \models \alpha, \; \mathcal{M}, x, z \models \beta \; and \; y \sim z$$
$$\mathcal{M}, x \models \langle \alpha \neq \beta \rangle \; iff \; there \; are \; y, z \in M \; s.t. \; \mathcal{M}, x, y \models \alpha, \; \mathcal{M}, x, z \models \beta \; and \; y \not\sim z.$$

As a corollary of the definition above, the abbreviations $\langle\alpha\rangle\varphi$, $[\alpha]\varphi$ and $i\varphi$ have their classical meaning.

$$\mathcal{M}, x \models \langle\alpha\rangle\varphi \text{ iff there is } y \in M \text{ s.t. } \mathcal{M}, x, y \models \alpha \text{ and } \mathcal{M}, y \models \varphi$$
$$\mathcal{M}, x \models [\alpha]\varphi \text{ iff for all } y \in M \ \mathcal{M}, x, y \models \alpha \text{ implies } \mathcal{M}, y \models \varphi$$
$$\mathcal{M}, x \models i\varphi \text{ iff } \mathcal{M}, nom(i) \models \varphi$$

The addition of the hybrid operators to XPath increases its expressive power. The following examples should serve as illustration.

Example 1. We list below some HXPath$_=(\downarrow)$ expressions together with their intuitive meaning:

$[i]\alpha$	The current node is named i and there exists an α path to some node.
$\alpha[i]$	There exists an α path between the current node and the node named i.
$i\alpha$	There exists an α path between the node named i and some other node.
αi	There exists an α path between the current node and some other node, evaluation continues at point named i.
$\langle i = i \rangle$	It is always valid.
$\langle [i] = [i] \rangle$	The current node is named i.
$\langle i = j \rangle$	The node named i has the same data as the node named j.
$\langle \alpha = i\beta \rangle$	A node accessible from the current node by an α path has the same data than a node accessible from the point named i by a β path.

It is worth highlighting the difference between $\langle\alpha \neq \beta\rangle$ and $\neg\langle\alpha = \beta\rangle$. The first expression establishes that there is an α path from the evaluation point to some point y, and there is a β path from the evaluation point to some point z, and $y \not\sim z$ (i.e., they have different data value). The second expression says that either at least one of the α or β paths fail to exist, or they exist but they fail to have the same data value. So while in the first expression paths are necessarily realizable to make the formula true, this is not the case in the second expression. However, these formulas are equivalent if $\alpha = i$ and $\beta = j$, with $i, j \in \mathsf{NOM}$.

The next proposition collects some semantic properties that will be useful in the completeness proof of Sect. 4. The proof uses only the definition of $\models$.

Proposition 1. *Let $\mathcal{M} = \langle M, \sim, \rightarrow, label, nom \rangle$ be an abstract data model, $x, y \in M$, α, β arbitrary path expressions, and $i, j \in \mathsf{NOM}$. Then*

1. $\mathcal{M}, x \models \langle i\alpha * j\beta \rangle$ iff $\mathcal{M}, y \models \langle i\alpha * j\beta \rangle$,
2. $\mathcal{M}, x \models i$ and $\mathcal{M}, x \models \langle \alpha * \beta \rangle$ [resp. $\neg\langle \alpha * \beta \rangle$] then $\mathcal{M}, x \models \langle i\alpha * \beta \rangle$ [resp. $\neg\langle i\alpha * \beta \rangle$],
3. $nom(i) \sim nom(j)$ iff $\mathcal{M}, x \models \langle i = j \rangle$,
4. $\mathcal{M}, x \models \langle ij\alpha * \beta \rangle$ iff $\mathcal{M}, x \models \langle j\alpha * \beta \rangle$.

3   Tableau Calculus

We present a tableau calculus for HXPath$_=(\downarrow)$. We assume basic knowledge of tableau calculi for modal logics [12].

In addition to HXPath$_=$($\downarrow$)-formulas, the tableau rules contain *accessibility formulas* of the form $n \to m$, where $n, m \in$ NOM. The intended interpretation of $n \to m$ is that the node denoted by m is accessible from the node denoted by n by the accessibility relation $\to$. In the following we will use the term *formula* to denote either a formula of HXPath$_=$($\downarrow$), or an accessibility formula.

A tableau in this calculus is a well-founded, finitely branching tree in which each node is labeled by a formula, and the edges represent applications of tableau rules, in the usual way. To check satisfiability of a node expression φ, we initialize the tableau with $i\varphi$, for $i \notin$ NOM(φ). To check satisfiability of a path expression α, we initialize the tableaux with $i\langle\alpha\rangle\top$, for $i \notin$ NOM(α). Figure 2 introduces the rules of the calculus.

A branch Θ of a tableau contains a *clash* if one of the following conditions holds:

1. $\{na, n\neg a\} \subseteq \Theta$, with $a \in$ ATOM,
2. $\langle n \neq n \rangle \in \Theta$,
3. $\neg\langle n = n \rangle \in \Theta$,
4. $\{\langle n = m \rangle, \langle n \neq m \rangle\} \subseteq \Theta$,
5. $\{\langle n = m \rangle, \neg\langle n = m \rangle\} \subseteq \Theta$,

for some n, $m \in$ NOM. Conditions 1–5 are called *clash conditions*. The rules $(\neg)$, $(\downarrow)$, $(\downarrow_r)$ $(@)$, $(@_r)$, $(\neg@)$ and $(\neg@_r)$ are called *nominal generating rules*. We impose two general constraints on the construction of tableaux:

- C1: A nominal generating rule is never applied twice to the same premise on the same branch.
- C2: A formula is never added to a tableau branch where it already occurs.

A *saturated tableau* is a tableau in which no more rules can be applied that satisfy the constraints. A *saturated branch* is a branch of a saturated tableau. For ε an expression, let *Tableau(ε)* be a saturated tableau for ε. We say that a tableau branch is *closed* if it contains a clash, otherwise it is called *open*. A *closed tableau* is one in which all branches are closed, and an *open tableau* is one in which at least one branch is open. It is easy to show the calculus is sound:[3]

Theorem 1. *If ε is satisfiable then any Tableau(ε) has an open branch.*

4   Completeness

In this section we will prove that the tableau calculus we introduced is *complete*, i.e., if a formula φ appears in an open and saturated branch, then φ is satisfiable.

Definition 4. *Let Θ be a tableau branch. Define the relation $\equiv_\Theta \subseteq$ NOM(Θ)^2 as $n \equiv_\Theta m$ iff $nm \in \Theta$.*

---

[3] Some readers may call this notion "completeness", and the one introduced in the next section "soundness". However, we use the classical tableaux denomination.

Boolean

$$\frac{n\neg i}{mi}\ (\neg^1) \qquad \frac{n\neg\neg\varphi}{n\varphi}\ (\neg\neg) \qquad \frac{n(\varphi\wedge\psi)}{\begin{array}{c}n\varphi\\n\psi\end{array}}\ (\wedge) \qquad \frac{n\neg(\varphi\wedge\psi)}{n\neg\varphi \mid n\neg\psi}\ (\neg\wedge)$$

Prefix

$$\frac{n\langle\alpha*\beta\rangle}{\langle n\alpha*n\beta\rangle}\ (Int) \qquad \frac{n\neg\langle\alpha*\beta\rangle}{\neg\langle n\alpha*n\beta\rangle}\ (\neg Int)$$

Data

$$\frac{\neg\langle n\neq m\rangle}{\langle n=m\rangle}\ (DEq) \qquad \frac{\langle n=m\rangle}{\langle m=n\rangle}\ (DSym) \qquad \frac{\langle n=m\rangle\ \langle m=k\rangle}{\langle n=k\rangle}\ (DTrans)$$

Nominal

$$\frac{}{ii}\ (Ref^2) \qquad \frac{ni}{in}\ (Sym) \qquad \frac{nj\ ni\ mi}{mj}\ (Nom) \qquad \frac{n\varphi\ ni\ mi}{m\varphi}\ (Copy^3) \qquad \frac{nm}{\langle n=m\rangle}\ (Data)$$

XPath

$$\frac{\langle n[\varphi]\alpha*\beta\rangle}{\begin{array}{c}n\varphi\\\langle n\alpha*\beta\rangle\end{array}}\ (?) \qquad \frac{\neg\langle n[\varphi]\alpha*\beta\rangle}{n\neg\varphi \mid \neg\langle n\alpha*\beta\rangle}\ (\neg?) \qquad \frac{\langle n*m[\varphi]\alpha\rangle}{\begin{array}{c}m\varphi\\\langle n*m\alpha\rangle\end{array}}\ (?_r) \qquad \frac{\neg\langle n*m[\varphi]\alpha\rangle}{m\neg\varphi \mid \neg\langle n*m\alpha\rangle}\ (\neg?_r)$$

$$\frac{\langle n\downarrow\alpha*\beta\rangle}{\begin{array}{c}n\to m\\\langle m\alpha*\beta\rangle\end{array}}\ (\downarrow^1) \qquad \frac{\neg\langle n\downarrow\alpha*\beta\rangle\ \ n\to m}{\neg\langle m\alpha*\beta\rangle}\ (\neg\downarrow) \qquad \frac{\langle n*m\downarrow\alpha\rangle}{\begin{array}{c}m\to k\\\langle n*k\alpha\rangle\end{array}}\ (\downarrow_r^4) \qquad \frac{\neg\langle n*m\downarrow\alpha\rangle\ \ m\to k}{\neg\langle n*k\alpha\rangle}\ (\neg\downarrow_r)$$

$$\frac{\langle n(\alpha\cup\beta)\gamma*\delta\rangle}{\langle n\alpha\gamma*\delta\rangle \mid \langle n\beta\gamma*\delta\rangle}\ (\cup) \qquad \frac{\neg\langle n(\alpha\cup\beta)\gamma*\delta\rangle}{\begin{array}{c}\neg\langle n\alpha\gamma*\delta\rangle\\\neg\langle n\beta\gamma*\delta\rangle\end{array}}\ (\neg\cup) \qquad \frac{\langle n*m(\alpha\cup\beta)\gamma\rangle}{\langle n*m\alpha\gamma\rangle \mid \langle n*m\beta\gamma\rangle}\ (\cup_r) \qquad \frac{\neg\langle n*m(\alpha\cup\beta)\gamma\rangle}{\begin{array}{c}\neg\langle n*m\alpha\gamma\rangle\\\neg\langle n*m\beta\gamma\rangle\end{array}}\ (\neg\cup_r)$$

$$\frac{\langle ni\alpha*\beta\rangle}{\begin{array}{c}mi\\\langle m\alpha*\beta\rangle\end{array}}\ (@^1) \qquad \frac{\neg\langle ni\alpha*\beta\rangle}{\begin{array}{c}mi\\\neg\langle m\alpha*\beta\rangle\end{array}}\ (\neg@^1) \qquad \frac{\langle n*mi\alpha\rangle}{\begin{array}{c}ki\\\langle n*k\alpha\rangle\end{array}}\ (@_r^4) \qquad \frac{\neg\langle n*mi\alpha\rangle}{\begin{array}{c}ki\\\neg\langle n*k\alpha\rangle\end{array}}\ (\neg@_r^4)$$

[1] m is the smallest nominal that has not appeared in the tableau.

[2] i appears in the tableau.

[3] m is the smallest nominal making i true in the tableau.

[4] k is the smallest nominal that has not appeared in the tableau.

Fig. 2. Tableaux rules

Lemma 1. $\equiv_\Theta$ *is an equivalence relation.*

Definition 5. *Let Θ be a tableau branch, and let $n \in \mathsf{NOM}(\Theta)$. The* nominal urfather *of n on Θ (denoted $u_\Theta(n)$) is the smallest m such that $m \equiv_\Theta n$. m is called a* nominal urfather *on Θ if $m = u_\Theta(n)$ for some n.*

Lemma 2. *Let Θ be a saturated branch. If $n\varphi$ occurs on Θ then $u_\Theta(n)\varphi$ also occurs on Θ.*

Proof. Assume $n\varphi \in \Theta$. By definition of urfather, $u_\Theta(n) = m$ and $nm \in \Theta$. Since Θ is saturated we have closure under *(Copy)* and *(Ref)*. Hence, $n\varphi$, nm, $mm \in \Theta$ and $m\varphi \in \Theta$.

Lemma 3. *Let Θ be a saturated branch, and let n and m be nominals occurring on Θ. $n \equiv_\Theta m$ if and only if n and m make the same nominals true on Θ.*

Lemma 4. *Let Θ be a saturated branch. If $n \equiv_\Theta m$ then $u_\Theta(n) = u_\Theta(m)$.*

Lemma 5. *Let Θ be a saturated branch. Then n is a nominal urfather on Θ if and only if $u_\Theta(n) = n$.*

Proof. The right to left direction is direct from the definition of a nominal urfather. For the other direction, if n is a nominal urfather then $u_\Theta(m) = n$ for some m, and $n \equiv_\Theta m$. By Lemma 4, we have $u_\Theta(n) = u_\Theta(m) = n$.

Definition 6. *Let Θ be an open saturated branch, we define the extracted model $\mathcal{M}^\Theta = \langle M^\Theta, \sim^\Theta, \to^\Theta, label^\Theta, nom^\Theta \rangle$, as*

$$
\begin{aligned}
M^\Theta &= \{n \mid n\varphi \in \Theta\} \cup \{n, n' \mid n \to n' \in \Theta\} \cup \{n, n' \mid \langle n * n' \rangle \in \Theta\} \\
\sim^\Theta &= \{(n, u_\Theta(n')) \mid \langle n = n' \rangle \in \Theta\} \\
\to^\Theta &= \{(u_\Theta(n), u_\Theta(n')) \mid n \to n' \in \Theta\} \\
label^\Theta(n) &= \{p \mid np \in \Theta\} \\
nom^\Theta(i) &= \begin{cases} n_0, & \text{if } i \notin \mathsf{NOM}(\Theta) \\ u_\Theta(i), & \text{if } i \in \mathsf{NOM}(\Theta), \end{cases}
\end{aligned}
$$

where n_0 is the first prefix introduced in Θ.

Proposition 2. $\sim^\Theta$ *is an equivalence relation.*

Lemma 6. *Let $i \in \mathsf{NOM}(\Theta)$ then $u_\Theta(i) \in M^\Theta$ and $\mathcal{M}^\Theta, u_\Theta(i) \models i$.*

Proof. By definition $u_\Theta(i) = m$ and $mi \in \Theta$. Hence, by definition of M^Θ, $m \in M^\Theta$. That it satisfies i follows from the definition of nom^Θ.

We need a notion of size both for path and node expressions, and a notion of size for any tableau formula:

$$
\begin{aligned}
psize(i) &= 1 \ \text{ for } i \in \mathsf{NOM} & psize(\alpha\beta) &= psize(\alpha) + psize(\beta) \\
psize(\downarrow) &= 2 & psize(\alpha \cup \beta) &= psize(\alpha) + psize(\beta) + 1 \\
psize([\varphi]) &= nsize(\varphi) + 1 & & \\[4pt]
nsize(a) &= 1 \ \text{ for } a \in \mathsf{ATOM} & nsize(\varphi \wedge \psi) &= nsize(\varphi) + nsize(\psi) + 1 \\
nsize(\neg\varphi) &= nsize(\varphi) + 1 & nsize(\langle \alpha * \beta \rangle) &= psize(\alpha) + psize(\beta) + 2 \\[4pt]
size(n \to m) &= 0 & size(\langle \alpha * \beta \rangle) &= nsize(\langle \alpha * \beta \rangle) \\
size(i\varphi) &= nsize(\varphi) + 3. & &
\end{aligned}
$$

Notice that $size(\varphi)$ induces a well-founded order on the set of HXPath$_=$($\downarrow$)-formulas by taking $\varphi < \psi$ if and only if $size(\varphi) < size(\psi)$. The particular notion of $size$ introduced will let us prove Theorem 3.

Theorem 2. *Let Θ be an open and saturated branch and $n, m \in$ NOM. Then*

1. $n\varphi \in \Theta$ *implies* $\mathcal{M}^\Theta, u_\Theta(n) \models \varphi$.
2. (a) $\langle n\alpha * m\beta \rangle \in \Theta$ *implies* $\mathcal{M}^\Theta, k \models \langle n\alpha * m\beta \rangle$, *for any* $k \in M^\Theta$, *and*
   (b) $\neg\langle n\alpha * m\beta \rangle \in \Theta$ *implies* $\mathcal{M}^\Theta, k \models \neg\langle n\alpha * m\beta \rangle$, *for any* $k \in M^\Theta$.

Proof. We reason by structural induction (as we mentioned, $size$ induces a well-founded order on the set of formulas). Let us consider the base cases. We show some of them, the rest can be proved in a similar way:

- Cases np and $n\neg p$, with $p \in$ PROP are direct from definition of $label^\Theta$.
- $ni \in \Theta$, with $i \in$ NOM. Then $n \equiv_\Theta i$ and by Lemma 4, $u_\Theta(n) = u_\Theta(i)$. By definition of nom^Θ, $nom^\Theta(i) = u_\Theta(i)$, and $\mathcal{M}^\Theta, u_\Theta(n) \models i$.
- $n\neg i \in \Theta$. By $(\neg)$, we have $mi \in \Theta$, for some m, and by definition of $\mathcal{M}^\Theta$ we have $n, m \in M^\Theta$ (and their respective urfathers by Lemma 6). Reasoning as above, $nom^\Theta(i) = u_\Theta(i) = u_\Theta(m)$. By Lemma 2, $u_\Theta(m)i \in \Theta$, but because Θ is an open saturated branch such that $n\neg i$, $mi \in \Theta$, then $n \neq u_\Theta(m)$. Then $nom^\Theta(i) \neq n$, hence $\mathcal{M}^\Theta, n \models \neg i$.
- $\langle n = m \rangle \in \Theta$. By definition of $\mathcal{M}^\Theta$, we have $n, m \in M^\Theta$ and $n \sim^\Theta u_\Theta(m)$. By definition of urfather $nu_\Theta(n) \in \Theta$ and by $(Data)$, $\langle n = u_\Theta(n) \rangle \in \Theta$. By definition of $\sim^\Theta$, $n \sim^\Theta u_\Theta(u_\Theta(n))$, i.e., $n \sim^\Theta u_\Theta(n)$ by Lemma 5. Because, $\sim^\Theta$ is an equivalence relation, $u_\Theta(n) \sim^\Theta u_\Theta(m)$. By definition of nom^Θ, $nom^\Theta(n) \sim^\Theta nom^\Theta(m)$ and, hence, by Proposition 1 (item 3), $\mathcal{M}^\Theta, k \models \langle n = m \rangle$ for any $k \in M^\Theta$.

Now we proceed with the inductive cases:

- $n\langle \alpha * \beta \rangle \in \Theta$: by (Int), we have $\langle n\alpha * n\beta \rangle \in \Theta$. $size(n\langle \alpha * \beta \rangle) = nsize(\langle \alpha * \beta \rangle) + 3 = psize(\alpha) + psize(\beta) + 5$, and $size(\langle n\alpha * n\beta \rangle) = psize(n\alpha) + psize(n\beta) = psize(\alpha) + psize(\beta) + 4$, i.e., (Int) decrements the size of the formula. Then we can apply inductive hypothesis and get $\mathcal{M}^\Theta, x \models \langle n\alpha * n\beta \rangle$, for all $x \in M^\Theta$. In particular $\mathcal{M}^\Theta, u_\Theta(n) \models \langle n\alpha * n\beta \rangle$. Therefore (by Lemma 6 and $\models$), $\mathcal{M}^\Theta, u_\Theta(n) \models n\langle \alpha * \beta \rangle$.
- $\langle n\alpha * k\beta \rangle \in \Theta$: induction on α.
  - $\alpha = {\downarrow}\alpha'$: $\langle n{\downarrow}\alpha' * k\beta \rangle \in \Theta$, then by $(\downarrow)$ we have $n \to m$, $\langle m\alpha' * \beta \rangle \in \Theta$ (with m the smallest nominal that has not appeared in the tableau). By definition of $\mathcal{M}^\Theta$, we have $u_\Theta(n) \to^\Theta u_\Theta(m)$ $(\otimes_1)$ and by IH, $\mathcal{M}^\Theta, x \models \langle m\alpha' * k\beta \rangle$ $(\otimes_2)$, for all $x \in M^\Theta$. From $\otimes_2$, we have that in particular $\mathcal{M}^\Theta, u_\Theta(m) \models \langle m\alpha' * k\beta \rangle$, and because $u_\Theta(m)$ is the urfather of m, by Lemma 6, $\mathcal{M}^\Theta, u_\Theta(m) \models m$. Then by $\models$, $\mathcal{M}^\Theta, u_\Theta(m) \models \langle \alpha' * k\beta \rangle$ $(\otimes_3)$. From $\otimes_1$ and $\otimes_3$ we get $\mathcal{M}^\Theta, u_\Theta(n) \models \langle {\downarrow}\alpha' * k\beta \rangle$, iff $\mathcal{M}^\Theta, u_\Theta(n) \models \langle n{\downarrow}\alpha' * k\beta \rangle$, iff (by Proposition 1, item1) $\mathcal{M}^\Theta, x \models \langle n{\downarrow}\alpha' * k\beta \rangle$, for all $x \in M^\Theta$.

– $\neg\langle n\alpha * k\beta\rangle \in \Theta$: induction on α.

- $\alpha = \downarrow\alpha'$: $\neg\langle n\downarrow\alpha' * k\beta\rangle \in \Theta$, and suppose $n \rightarrow m \in \Theta$, then by $(\neg\downarrow)$ $\neg\langle m\alpha' * k\beta\rangle \in \Theta$. By definition of $\mathcal{M}^{\Theta}$, we have $u_{\Theta}(n) \rightarrow^{\Theta} u_{\Theta}(m)$ $(\otimes_1)$ and by IH, $\mathcal{M}^{\Theta}, x \models \neg\langle m\alpha' * k\beta\rangle$ $(\otimes_2)$, for all $x \in M^{\Theta}$. From $\otimes_2$, we have that in particular $\mathcal{M}^{\Theta}, u_{\Theta}(m) \models \neg\langle m\alpha' * k\beta\rangle$, and because $u_{\Theta}(m)$ is the urfather of m, by Lemma 6, $\mathcal{M}^{\Theta}, u_{\Theta}(m) \models m$. Then by $\models$, $\mathcal{M}^{\Theta}, u_{\Theta}(m) \models \neg\langle\alpha' * k\beta\rangle$ $(\otimes_3)$. From $\otimes_1$ and $\otimes_3$ we get $\mathcal{M}^{\Theta}, u_{\Theta}(n) \models \neg\langle\downarrow\alpha' * k\beta\rangle$, iff $\mathcal{M}^{\Theta}, u_{\Theta}(n) \models \neg\langle n\downarrow\alpha' * k\beta\rangle$, iff (by Proposition 1, item 1) $\mathcal{M}^{\Theta}, x \models \neg\langle n\downarrow\alpha' * k\beta\rangle$, for all $x \in M^{\Theta}$.

5 Termination

In this section we prove that any tableaux obtained by the application of the rules in Sect. 3 is finite. This proves that satisfiability for HXPath$_=$($\downarrow$) is decidable.

Definition 7. *Let* φ, φ' *be node expressions. Define* $\varphi \prec \varphi'$ *if and only if,*

1. *there are* ψ, n, m *such that* $\varphi = n\psi$, $\varphi' = m\psi$, *and* $n < m$, *or*
2. *there are no* ψ, n, m *such that* $\varphi = n\psi$ *and* $\varphi' = m\psi$, *and* $size(\varphi) < size(\varphi')$.

Proposition 3. *The relation* $\prec$ *from Definition 7 is a well-founded order.*

Proof. As we already mentioned $size$ induces a well-founded order over the set of node expressions. The relation $\prec$ orders also at-formulas which are identical except for their prefix, and hence have the same value for $size$. The order used in this case is the order given by NOM. As a result, $\prec$ cannot have infinite descending chains.

Proposition 4. *In every tableaux rule in Sect. 3 except (Ref), (Sym), (Nom), (DSym), (DTrans) and (Data) the formulas in the consequent are strictly smaller, in terms of* $\prec$, *than some of the formulas in the antecedent.*

Theorem 3. *Any tableau in the calculus from Sect. 3 is finite.*

Proof. Suppose, for contradiction, that a tableaux T is infinite. As all rules in Sect. 3 are finitely branching, T should have an infinite branch Θ. Moreover, by Propositions 3 and 4, together with the general constraints C1 and C2 imposed on the construction of tableaux, there is a point in Θ in which the only rules applied further down the branch are (DSym), (DTrans), (Ref), (Sym), (Nom) and (Data). But these rules only introduce atomic formulas built over symbols that have already appeared in Θ, and hence, at one point, by constraint C2 no further application is possible.

Theorem 4. *The satisfiability problem for formulas of HXPath$_=$($\downarrow$) is* PSPACE-*complete.*

Proof. Hardness follows from the PSPACE satisfiability problem for the basic modal logic K [5]. PSPACE completeness can be proved by designing a backtracking algorithm which uses polynomial space, based on the rules from Sect. 3. A sketch of a non-deterministic algorithm that uses only polynomial space is shown in Algorithm 1. The algorithm explores a model "depth-first" and allows the expansion of only one $\langle \alpha * \beta \rangle$ formula at a time. The following constraints are, furthermore, assumed by the procedure. Let φ be the input formula:

- Formulas of the form $i\varphi$, $\langle i * j \rangle$ and $\neg\langle i * j \rangle$ for $i, j \in \mathsf{NOM}(\varphi)$ are never removed from the tableau once generated, and they are assumed to be preserved by the Pop operation (e.g., they are copied to the previous instance of T in the stack).
- To allow the exploration of *two* branches in the model needed to check $\langle \alpha * \beta \rangle$ formulas, we assume that $(\downarrow)$ marks the data comparison formula in the consequent using a $*$ (e.g., $\langle m\alpha * \beta \rangle^*$). All other rules except $(\downarrow_r)$ pass the mark to the data comparison formula in its consequent when applied to a marked formula. $(\downarrow_r)$ never marks a data comparison formula in its consequent. Notation $\varphi^{(*)}$ indicates that $*$ may appear or not.

Algorithm 1. PSPACE Tableaux

In: The algorithm is non-deterministic, branching rules are handled in parallel runs. All variables are global. Tableau rules are applied following the constraints described in Sect. 3.

Out: φ is satisfiable if at least one run returns SAT.

```
1: T ← {0φ}, 0 not in φ
2: ST ← [ ]
3: loop
4:     SATURATE( )
5:     if CHOOSELEFT( ) then
6:         EXPLORELEFT( )
7:     else if CHOOSERIGHT( ) then
8:         EXPLORERIGHT( )
9:     else
10:        Pop ST
```

```
1: procedure SATURATE( )
2:     Apply all rules except (↓) and (↓_r)
3:         till saturation
4:     if T has a clash then
5:         exit(FAIL)
```

```
6:     if No formula waits for (↓) or (↓_r) then
7:         exit(SAT)
```

```
1: function CHOOSELEFT( )
2:     Choose from T
3:         Unexpanded φ = ⟨n↓α * β⟩^(*)
4:         s.t. n → m ∉ T
5: return φ was found in T?
```

```
1: function CHOOSERIGHT( )
2:     Let h be the highest s.t., ⟨n * h↓α⟩* ∈ T
3:     Choose from T
4:         Unexpanded φ = ⟨n * h↓α⟩*
5:     otherwise
6:         Unexpanded φ = ⟨n * m↓α⟩
7:         s.t. m → k ∉ T
8: return φ was found in T?
```

```
1: procedure EXPLORELEFT( )
2:     Push T in ST
3:     Expand T using (↓)
```

```
1: procedure EXPLORERIGHT( )
2:     Push T in ST
3:     Expand T using (↓_r)
```

---

6 Final Remarks

We have introduced a tableau calculus for the logic HXPath$_=(\downarrow)$, i.e., XPath with downward navigation and data comparison (by $=$ and $\neq$), extended with nominals and satisfaction operators. We proved that the calculus is sound, complete, and that it terminates on all inputs. As the tableaux only needs polynominal space, and the satisfiability for $HXPath_=(\downarrow)$ problem is PSPACE-hard (because it embeds the satisfiability problem for the basic modal logic K, [5]) a PSPACE-complete bound follows.

Several lines of further research are worth exploring:

- Given that XPath is commonly used as a query language for XML documents, we will consider extending the calculus with rules and clash conditions to restrict the class of models to finite data trees.
- We plan to take advantage of existing techniques and implementations of tableau procedures for hybrid logics to develop a prover for $HXPath_=(\downarrow)$.
- We will investigate extensions of $HXPath_=(\downarrow)$ and consider the inclusion of additional navigation axis like descendant $(\downarrow^*)$, ancestor $(\uparrow^*)$, father $(\uparrow)$, next-sibling $(\rightarrow)$, etc.

Acknowledgements. This work was partially supported by grant ANPCyT-PICT-2013-2011, STIC-AmSud "Foundations of Graph Structured Data (FoG)", SeCyT-UNC, the Laboratoire International Associé "INFINIS", and the European Union's Horizon 2020 research and innovation programme under the Marie Skodowska-Curie grant agreement No. 690974 for the project MIREL: MIning and REasoning with Legal texts.

References

1. Abriola, S., Descotte, M., Fervari, R., Figueira, S.: Axiomatizations for downward XPath on data trees. J. Comput. Syst. Sci. (2017, in press)
2. Abriola, S., Descotte, M., Figueira, S.: Model theory of XPath on data trees. Part II: binary bisimulation and definability. Inf. Comput. (to appear). http://www.glyc.dc.uba.ar/santiago/papers/xpath-part2.pdf
3. Areces, C., Fervari, R.: Hilbert-style axiomatization for hybrid XPath with data. In: Michael, L., Kakas, A. (eds.) JELIA 2016. LNCS, vol. 10021, pp. 34–48. Springer, Cham (2016). doi:10.1007/978-3-319-48758-8_3
4. Baelde, D., Lunel, S., Schmitz, S.: A sequent calculus for a modal logic on finite data trees. In: 25th EACSL Annual Conference on Computer Science Logic (CSL 2016), pp. 32:1–32:16 (2016)
5. Blackburn, P., de Rijke, M., Venema, Y.: Modal Logic. Cambridge Tracts in Theoretical Computer Science, vol. 53. Cambridge University Press, Cambridge (2001)
6. Blackburn, P., van Benthem, J.: Modal logic: a semantic perspective. In: Handbook of Modal Logic, pp. 1–84. Elsevier (2006)
7. Bojańczyk, M., Muscholl, A., Schwentick, T., Segoufin, L.: Two-variable logic on data trees and XML reasoning. J. ACM **56**(3), 13 (2009)
8. Bolander, T., Blackburn, P.: Termination for hybrid tableaus. J. Log. Comput. **17**(3), 517–554 (2007)
9. Buneman, P.: Semistructured data. In: ACM Symposium on Principles of Database Systems (PODS 1997), pp. 117–121 (1997)
10. ten Cate, B., Litak, T., Marx, M.: Complete axiomatizations for XPath fragments. J. Appl. Log. **8**(2), 153–172 (2010)

11. Clark, J., DeRose, S.: XML path language (XPath). W3C Recommendation (1999). http://www.w3.org/TR/xpath
12. D'Agostino, M., Gabbay, D.M., Hähnle, R., Posegga, J. (eds.): Handbook of Tableau Methods. Springer, Heidelberg (1999)
13. Figueira, D.: Decidability of downward XPath. ACM Trans. Comput. Log. **13**(4), 34 (2012)
14. Figueira, D.: On XPath with transitive axes and data tests. In: Fan, W. (ed.) ACM Symposium on Principles of Database Systems (PODS 2013), pp. 249–260. ACM Press, New York (2013)
15. Figueira, D., Figueira, S., Areces, C.: Model theory of XPath on data trees. Part I: bisimulation and characterization. J. Artif. Intell. Res. **53**, 271–314 (2015)
16. Gottlob, G., Koch, C., Pichler, R.: Efficient algorithms for processing XPath queries. ACM Trans. Database Syst. **30**(2), 444–491 (2005)

On the Properties of Atom Definability and Well-Supportedness in Logic Programming

Pedro Cabalar[1]([✉]), Jorge Fandinno[1,2], Luis Fariñas[2], David Pearce[3], and Agustín Valverde[4]

[1] Universidade da Coruña, A Coruña, Spain
{cabalar,jorge.fandino}@udc.es, jorge.fandinno@irit.fr
[2] University of Toulouse IRIT, CNRS, Toulouse, France
farinas@irit.fr
[3] Universidad Politécnica de Madrid, Madrid, Spain
david.pearce@upm.es
[4] Universidad de Málaga, Málaga, Spain
a_valverde@ctima.uma.es

Abstract. We analyse alternative extensions of stable models for non-disjunctive logic programs with arbitrary Boolean formulas in the body, and examine two semantic properties. The first property, we call *atom definability*, allows one to replace any expression in rule bodies by an auxiliary atom defined by a single rule. The second property, *well-supportedness*, was introduced by Fages and dictates that it must be possible to establish a derivation ordering for all true atoms in a stable model so that self-supportedness is not allowed. We start from a generic fixpoint definition for well-supportedness that deals with: (1) a monotonic basis, for which we consider the whole range of intermediate logics; and (2), an assumption function, that determines which type of negated formulas can be added as defaults. Assuming that we take the strongest underlying logic in such a case, we show that only Equilibrium Logic satisfies both atom definability and strict well-suportedness.

1 Introduction

Almost 30 years ago, the introduction of the *stable models* [1] semantics for normal logic programs constituted the first general semantics for default negation that was defined on any normal logic program, without limitations on the syntactic dependences among atoms and rules. Since then, many extensions of stable models have been proposed in the literature to cope with more and more general syntactic fragments that went beyond normal logic programs. If we exclusively

Partially supported by Xunta de Galicia (projects GPC ED431B 2016/035 and 2016-2019 ED431G/01 for CITIC center) and ERDF; by the Centre International de Mathématiques et d'Informatique de Toulouse (CIMI), contract ANR-11-LABEX-0040-CIMI within program ANR-11-IDEX-0002-02; by UPM RP151046021 and by Spanish MINECO project TIN2015-70266-C2-1-P.

E. Oliveira et al. (Eds.): EPIA 2017, LNAI 10423, pp. 624–636, 2017.
DOI: 10.1007/978-3-319-65340-2_51

focus on propositional connectives, rule heads were soon extended to include disjunction [2] and negative literals [3]. Going a step forward, [4] introduced a type of rule $B \to H$ where both the body B and the head H could be a so-called *nested expression*, that is, a Boolean formula allowing conjunction, disjunction and negation, but not the implication symbol, which could not be nested. The first extension of stable models to arbitrary propositional formulas, including nested implications, was actually provided with the previous definition of *Equilibrium Logic* [5] which, as proved in [6], is a conservative extension of nested expressions and, as shown in [7], can be alternatively described in terms of a formula reduct. Although Equilibrium Logic constitutes nowadays one of the most successful and better studied logical characterisations for *Answer Set Programming* (ASP), other approaches have been proposed trying to overcome some features on which no agreement seems to have been reached so far. For instance, one of those properties pursued by some authors is that stable models of a program should be *minimal* with respect to the set of their true atoms. Although this holds for disjunctive logic programs in all ASP semantics, the first proposals for negation in the head (or double negation in the body) [3] already violated minimality, this being also the case of Equilibrium Logic, which is a conservative extension. For instance, a common way to represent a choice rule in Equilibrium logic is using the expression:

$$\neg\neg p \to p \tag{1}$$

with double negation or, alternatively, its strongly equivalent disjunctive form $p \vee \neg p$ that uses negation in the head. The equilibrium models of (1) are $\emptyset$ and $\{p\}$, which is not minimal. In an attempt to guarantee minimality for programs with aggregates, Faber et al. [8] (FLP) came out with a new semantics that was generalised to arbitrary propositional formulas in [9] while keeping the minimality criterion. For instance, the unique FLP-stable model of (1) is $\emptyset$.

Apart from minimality, another property that has been recently considered by Shen et al. in [10] is the extension of Fages' *well-supportedness* [11], originally defined for normal logic programs, to rules with a more general syntax like, for instance, allowing Boolean formulas in the head or the body. Intuitively, a model M is said to be *well-supported* if its true atoms can be assigned a derivation ordering (via modus ponens) from the positive part of the program, while the interpretation of negated atoms is fixed with respect to M, acting like an assumption *a priori*. Fages proved that well-supported models coincide with stable models for normal logic programs, but did not specify how to extrapolate well-supportedness to other syntactic classes. For instance, consider rule (1) again and model $M = \{p\}$. If we consider that $\neg\neg p$ belongs to the "positive" part of the program, then it should be included in the derivation ordering, as any regular atom. However, doing so, there is no way to obtain p in a well-supported manner, since we would have to assign $\neg\neg p$ some level strictly smaller than p and find a different rule to justify $\neg\neg p$, something that does not exist. On the other hand, if $\neg\neg p$ is seen as a "negated" formula (as happens with negated atoms), then it should behave as an assumption and its truth should be fixed with respect to M *a priori* as well. For $M = \{p\}$, $\neg\neg p$ would directly hold, and so, rule (1) would just behave as a fact for p, making it true.

In this paper, we provide a general definition of *well-supportedness* for programs with a head atom and a Boolean formula in the body. This definition is parametrized in two ways: (1) the type of formulas that can be used as "assumptions," that is, whose truth is fixed with respect to some model M; and (2), the monotonic logic that defines satisfaction of a rule body before applying the rule to derive a new conclusion. For (1), we study three cases: negated atoms, negated literals, and negated arbitrary formulas. For (2), we analyse the whole range of intermediate logics, from intuitionistic to classical logic, both included. In the paper, we prove that a group of variants collapse either into Equilibrium Logic or Clark's completion. To compare the different alternatives, we analyse one more property we call *atom definability*. This property asserts that if we replace occurrences of a formula φ in one or more rule bodies by a new auxiliary atom a, and we define this atom with an additional rule $\varphi \to a$, then we should get a strongly equivalent program (modulo the original alphabet). As we will see, this is important since semantics satisfying atom definability immediately provide a way to unfold programs with double negation into regular, normal logic programs. We show that, among the analysed variants, only those collapsing to Equilibrium Logic or to Clark's completion satisfy atom definability.

2   Auxiliary Atoms and Atom Definability

In this section we introduce the property of *atom definability* and motivate its importance for one of most powerful representational features of ASP: the definition of *auxiliary atoms* or *predicates*. Auxiliary atoms constitute a fundamental part of the widespread, commonly accepted, specification methodology for problem solving in ASP called *Generate, Define and Test* (GDT) that we will illustrate with a well-known example.

Example 1 (Hamiltonian cycles). Given a graph with nodes N and edges $E \subseteq N \times N$ find cyclic paths that visit each node exactly once.

> INPUT: Facts $\{node(X) \mid X \in N\}$ and $\{edge(X, Y) \mid \langle X, Y \rangle \in E\}$.
> OUTPUT: Facts $in(X, Y)$, edges forming a cyclic path that traverses all nodes.

In what follows, we represent logic program rules as implications $B \to H$, B being the rule *body* and H the rule *head*. We also use $\wedge$ and $\neg$ instead of commas and *not*, respectively. When using a expression with variables we assume it is an abbreviation of the conjunction of its possible ground instantiations. We also assume finite domains, leaving the infinite case for the future extension to first-order. A possible ASP representation of this problem would be:

$$edge(X,Y) \rightarrow 0 \ \{in(X,Y)\} \ 1 \qquad (2)$$
$$in(X,Y) \wedge in(X,Z) \wedge Y \neq Z \rightarrow \bot \qquad (3)$$
$$in(X,Y) \wedge in(Z,Y) \wedge X \neq Z \rightarrow \bot \qquad (4)$$
$$node(X) \wedge node(Y) \wedge \neg reach(X,Y) \rightarrow \bot \qquad (5)$$
$$in(X,Y) \rightarrow reach(X,Y) \qquad (6)$$
$$in(X,Z) \wedge reach(Z,Y) \rightarrow reach(X,Y) \qquad (7)$$

The GDT methodology identifies three main groups of rules:

G = non-deterministic choices that *generate* potential solutions. In our case, we have the *choice rule* (2) so that, for each edge $edge(X,Y)$ in the graph, we may freely decide to include 0 or 1 instances of fact $in(X,Y)$ in our solution.

T = constraints that rule out undesired solutions (the *test* part). In the example, rules (3), (4), (5) check that we generate linear paths and that any pair of nodes are mutually reachable.

D = *definition* of auxiliary predicates when features for **G** and **T** cannot be directly represented in the ASP language. In the example, rules (6) and (7) define the *auxiliary predicate* $reach(X,Y)$, the transitive closure of $in(X,Y)$.

Although choice rules like (2) are already included in the standard input language *ASP Core 2.0* [12] (used for the ASP solvers competition), their semantics is actually defined in terms of auxiliary predicates. In the past, before the introduction of choices, a common way to represent (2) was:

$$edge(X,Y) \wedge \neg out(X,Y) \rightarrow in(X,Y) \qquad (8)$$
$$edge(X,Y) \wedge \neg in(X,Y) \rightarrow out(X,Y) \qquad (9)$$

using another auxiliary predicate $out(X,Y)$. An important observation, sometimes underestimated, is that these auxiliary predicates *are not a relevant part* of the problem definition. In Example 1, this problem definition involves input predicates *node* and *edge* plus the output predicate *in* describing the result. Predicates *out* and *reach* are representational resources used internally and are not to be included in the final result, as their extent is *irrelevant* for the problem solution. Think, for instance, that $out(X,Y)$ eventually collects the edges that are not $in(X,Y)$, so it does not provide new information and its use is merely technical. Moreover, if we had to compare two different ASP encodings of the Hamiltonian cycle problem, it seems obvious that predicates *out* and *reach* should not be part of the language. In fact, all ASP solvers provide some option to hide irrelevant predicates.

In the previous example, we saw a pair of features (the transitive closure and the choice rule) whose semantics could be directly defined in terms of auxiliary atoms. Of course, when doing so, *correctness* is not an issue, since the application of auxiliary atoms is done by definition. However, one may wonder what happens when we want to use auxiliary predicates to capture the meaning of some expression or formula that is not an ASP extension, but is part of the basic language from normal logic programs. Can we trust that the replacement is correct? To illustrate this idea, consider the following common situation. We introduced a large graph instance for which we expect to find some Hamiltonian cycle, but the execution of the ASP solver yields no solution. In order to identify which constraint might have been applied, we decide to replace (5) by:

$$unreach(X, Y) \rightarrow \bot \tag{10}$$

$$node(X) \wedge node(Y) \wedge \neg reach(X, Y) \rightarrow unreach(X, Y) \tag{11}$$

i.e., the constraint body is now captured by an auxiliary predicate $unreach(X, Y)$ that keeps track of pairs of disconnected nodes. We momentarily remove (10) and find a pair of nodes in the graph for which some edge was missing by mistake. Then, we decide to keep (10), (11) for repeating this debugging technique. Now, can we safely replace (5) by (10)–(11) in any context?

This question is directly related to the formal property of *strong equivalence* [6]. Let V be some *vocabulary* or set of atoms, and $\mathcal{L}_V$ a syntactic language, with signature V, for which stable models are defined. Moreover, let $\mathrm{SM}(\Gamma)$ denote the set of stable models for some $\Gamma \subseteq \mathcal{L}_V$. We say that two theories Γ, Γ' are *strongly equivalent*, written $\Gamma \cong \Gamma'$, iff $\mathrm{SM}(\Gamma \cup \Delta) = \mathrm{SM}(\Gamma' \cup \Delta)$ for any arbitrary theory $\Delta \subseteq \mathcal{L}_V$. That is, Γ and Γ' provide the same results even when joined with any arbitrary common context Δ. This definition assumes that Γ, Γ' and Δ deal with the same common signature V. However, as we discussed before, auxiliary atoms should be kept hidden inside Γ and Γ' and not used for comparison. To cope with different vocabularies, we further specialise to one of the variants considered in [13] recently named *projective strong equivalence* in [14]. Suppose that the vocabularies of Γ and Γ' are, respectively, $V \cup U$ and $V \cup U'$, where U and U' represent hidden local atoms. We write now $\mathrm{SM}_V(\Gamma)$ to stand for the set of stable models of Γ restricted to vocabulary V, that is $\mathrm{SM}_V(\Gamma) \stackrel{\mathrm{df}}{=} \{I \cap V \mid I \in \mathrm{SM}(\Gamma)\}$. Then, two theories Γ, Γ' satisfy *projective strong equivalence with respect to vocabulary V* (are *V-strongly equivalent*, for short), written $\Gamma \cong_V \Gamma'$ iff $\mathrm{SM}_V(\Gamma \cup \Delta) = \mathrm{SM}_V(\Gamma' \cup \Delta)$ for any theory $\Delta \subseteq \mathcal{L}_V$.

Using this formal concept, our example amounts to asking whether the programs $\Gamma = \{(5)\}$ and $\Gamma' = \{(10), (11)\}$ are V-strongly equivalent for any vocabulary V not containing $unreach(X, Y)$. Since (11) defines predicate $unreach$, and the latter cannot be defined anywhere else in the program, we obviously expect an affirmative answer to this question. We can even generalise this property in the following way. We say that a syntactic language $\mathcal{L}_V$ for vocabulary V is *implicational* if it contains, at least, the implication symbol $\rightarrow$. A *program* $\Gamma \subseteq \mathcal{L}_V$ from an implicational language $\mathcal{L}_V$ is a set of implications (*rules*) so that, for each rule $(\alpha \rightarrow \beta) \in \Gamma$ the formulas α (the *body*) and β (the *head*) do not contain implications[1] in their turn. Given a program Γ, let $\Gamma[\varphi/a]$ denote any theory resulting from arbitrarily replacing some occurrences of formula φ in the rule bodies of Γ by an atom a.

---

[1] We allow the exception $\varphi \rightarrow \bot$ since, as we will see later, this corresponds to $\neg\varphi$ in intermediate logics.

Definition 1 (Atom definability). *We say that a semantics for an implicational language $\mathcal{L}_V$ satisfies* atom definability *iff for any program $\Gamma \subseteq \mathcal{L}_V$, any subformula φ occurring in one or more bodies of Γ and any fresh atom $a \notin V$:*

$$\Gamma \cong_V \Gamma[\varphi/a] \cup \{\varphi \to a\}$$ □

In our example, we have replaced each ground instance of body formula $\varphi = node(c) \wedge node(d) \wedge \neg reach(c, d)$ in (5) by a new ground atom $a = unreach(c, d)$, (10) being the result $\Gamma[\varphi/a]$ of these replacements. On the other hand, it is easy to see that (11) corresponds to the new rule $\varphi \to a$. Thus, these replacements would be V-strongly equivalent to the original formula if we chose a semantics satisfying atom definability. In the general case, it seems clear that this is an interesting property that one would wish to guarantee, as it is behind the intuitive use of auxiliary predicates. However, the consequences of such a property may also affect the admissible semantics for other extensions going beyond normal or disjunctive logic programs. For instance, suppose that bodies with double negation were introduced in ASP for the first time and that no previous semantics for this extension were available. We could still see each doubly negated atom $\neg\neg p$ as an expression $\neg\varphi$ where $\varphi = (\neg p)$. Then, atom definability should allow us simply to replace $\neg\neg p$ by $\neg a$ providing that a is a fresh atom and we include a rule $\varphi \to a$ in the program. This means that atom definability immediately provides a method to remove double negation. For instance, take (1) again under this new reading: $\neg \underbrace{\neg p}_{\varphi} \to p$. Atom definability guarantees that:

$$\neg \; a \to p \tag{12}$$
$$\underbrace{\neg p}_{\varphi} \to a \tag{13}$$

is strongly equivalent to (1) relative to any original signature not containing a. In particular, as the stable models of (12)–(13) are $\{p\}$ and $\{a\}$, atom definability implies that the stable models of (1) *must be* the result of filtering out atom a, i.e., $\{p\}$ and $\emptyset$. In other words, any argument against obtaining $\{p\}$ and $\emptyset$ as stable models of (1) becomes an argument against obtaining $\{p\}$ and $\{a\}$ as regular stable models for the normal logic program (12)–(13), under the reasonable assumption that definition of auxiliary atoms works "as expected".

3   Formal Preliminaries

We recall some basic preliminaries and definitions that will be used in the rest of the paper. Here, we will restrict attention to propositional formulas, leaving first-order extensions for future work. Propositional formulas are built in the usual way over a *vocabulary* or set V of atoms plus connectives $\wedge$, $\vee$, $\to$ and $\bot$. We regard $\neg\varphi$ is an abbreviation of $\varphi \to \bot$, that $\top$ stands for $\neg\bot$ and that $\varphi \leftrightarrow \psi$ stands for $(\varphi \to \psi) \wedge (\psi \to \varphi)$. A *literal* is an atom p (*positive* literal) or its negation $\neg p$ (*negative* literal). Given a conjunction of literals B, we write B^+ and B^- to respectively stand for the conjunctions of positive and negative literals in B (empty conjunctions correspond to $\top$). As expected, a *negated literal* can be either $\neg p$ or $\neg\neg p$. Note that, in intermediate logics, $\neg\neg p$ does not need to be equivalent to p whereas operator $\rightarrow$ is independent from $\wedge$ and $\vee$ and cannot be defined in terms of the latter. We say that an occurrence of formula φ in Γ is *positive* iff φ is in the scope of an even number of implication antecedents in Γ. We also say that occurrence φ is *negated* in Γ iff φ is in the scope of negation in Γ, that is, it is in the antecedent of some implication with $\bot$ as consequent. Note that φ can be both positive and negated in Γ: for instance, p is positive and negated in $(p \rightarrow q) \rightarrow \bot$, but q is just negated. A *Boolean formula* (also known as *nested expression* [4]), is a propositional formula exclusively formed with operators $\wedge, \vee, \neg$ and $\bot$. In other words, Boolean formulas do not contain $\rightarrow$ except in negations $\varphi \rightarrow \bot$, that is, $\neg\varphi$.

Let $\mathbf{L}$ be a propositional logic and let $M \models_\mathbf{L} \varphi$ represent its satisfaction relation for an interpretation M and formula φ. M is said to be a *model* of a theory Γ, written $M \models_\mathbf{L} \Gamma$, iff it satisfies all formulas in Γ. As usual, we say that Γ *entails* a formula ψ, written $\Gamma \models_\mathbf{L} \psi$, iff all models of Γ satisfy ψ. Similarly, φ is a *tautology*, written $\models_\mathbf{L} \varphi$, if any interpretation is a model of φ. We write $\mathbf{CL}$ to stand for Classical Logic. As usual, a *classical interpretation* M is just a set of atoms $M \subseteq V$. We write $\mathbf{IL}$ for Intuitionistic Logic and briefly recall its semantics. A *frame* is a pair $\langle W, \leq \rangle$ where W is a set of points or 'worlds' and $\leq$ is a partial order on W. An interpretation has the form $\langle W, \leq, v \rangle$ where $v : W \rightarrow 2^V$ assigns a set of true atoms to each world, satisfying $v(w) \subseteq v(w')$ for all pairs of worlds $w \leq w'$. We define when $M = \langle W, \leq, v \rangle$ satisfies a formula φ at some world w, written $M, w \models_\mathbf{IL} \varphi$, in the following recursive way:

- $M, w \models p$ iff $p \in v(w)$ for any atom $p \in V$
- $M, w \not\models \bot$
- $M, w \models \alpha \wedge \beta$ iff $M, w \models \alpha$ and $M, w \models \beta$
- $M, w \models \alpha \vee \beta$ iff $M, w \models \alpha$ or $M, w \models \beta$
- $M, w \models \alpha \rightarrow \beta$ iff for all $w' \geq w$, $M, w' \not\models \alpha$ or $M, w' \models \beta$

Intuitionistic logic $\mathbf{IL}$ is strictly weaker than classical logic $\mathbf{CL}$, $\mathbf{IL} \subset \mathbf{CL}$, since many classical tautologies (such as $p \vee \neg p$) are not tautologies in $\mathbf{IL}$. By an *intermediate* logic we mean any logic $\mathbf{L}$ lying between $\mathbf{IL}$ and $\mathbf{CL}$, $\mathbf{IL} \subseteq \mathbf{L} \subseteq \mathbf{CL}$. The strongest (non-classical) intermediate logic is known as the logic of *Here-and-There*, $\mathbf{HT}$ and is defined by frames with two worlds $W = \{h, t\}$ (respectively called *here* and *there*) fixing $h \leq t$. An $\mathbf{HT}$ model can be represented as a pair $\langle H, T \rangle$ with $H \subseteq T$ corresponding to frame $\langle \{h, t\}, \leq, v \rangle$ where $v(h) = H$ and $v(t) = T$. An $\mathbf{HT}$ interpretation $M = \langle H, T \rangle$ is said to be an *equilibrium model* of a theory Γ iff $H = T$, $M \models_\mathbf{HT} \Gamma$ and there is no $H' \subset H$ such that $\langle H', T \rangle \models_\mathbf{HT} \Gamma$. *Equilibrium logic* is the logic induced by equilibrium models.

Theorem 1. *Equilibrium Logic satisfies the atom definability property (Definition 1). Moreover, this property holds even when allowing nested implications in Γ, given that the replaced occurrences of φ do not occur positively non-negated in Γ.*

The extension in Theorem 1 for nested implications does not hold if φ occurs positively non-negated in Γ. As an example, take the program Γ consisting of $((p \rightarrow q) \rightarrow p)$ and $(p \rightarrow q)$ whose only stable model is $\{p, q\}$. Assume that φ is the leftmost occurrence of p in the first formula, which occurs positively non-negated. Then, $\Gamma[\varphi/a] \cup \{\varphi \rightarrow a\}$ contains the rules $((a \rightarrow q) \rightarrow p)$, $(p \rightarrow q)$ and $(p \rightarrow a)$ yielding no stable model. The intuition for this limitation is that a positive, non-negated occurrence of a formula acts as a rule head in **HT**. In fact, $(p \rightarrow q) \rightarrow p$ is **HT**-equivalent to the pair of rules $\neg\neg q \rightarrow p$ and $\neg p \rightarrow \bot$.

Although equilibrium models are defined for arbitrary propositional theories, the syntactic fragment we will identify as *logic programs* in this paper will be more limited, since we are interested in extensions of normal programs for which we can still find a natural definition of well-supportedness. We define a *Boolean (logic) program* P to be a set of rules $B \rightarrow p$ where the body B is a Boolean formula and the head p is an atom. As usual, P is further said to be a *normal (logic) program* iff all rule bodies in P are conjunctions of literals. We assume the reader is familiar with normal programs and their stable model semantics [1]. As is well-known, equilibrium models coincide with stable models in the sense that an interpretation M is a *stable model* of a normal program P iff $\langle M, M \rangle$ is an equilibrium model of P, [5].

Clark's *completion* [15] of a normal program P, denoted as $\mathrm{COMP}(P)$, corresponds to the union of P and the implications $p \rightarrow B_1 \vee \cdots \vee B_n$ for each atom $p \in V$ where $B_1, \ldots, B_n$ are the bodies of all rules $B_i \rightarrow p$ in P for that head atom. As usual, if no rules exist for p, then the empty disjunction corresponds to $\bot$. The intuitive reading of $\mathrm{COMP}(P)$ is that each true atom in M must have some supporting rule $B_i \rightarrow p$ in P whose body is true in M, $M \models B_i$. We say that a classical interpretation M is a *supported* model of P iff $M \models_{\mathbf{CL}} \mathrm{COMP}(P)$ and, by abuse of notation, we also write $\mathrm{COMP}(P)$ to represent the supported models of P. For normal programs, it is well-known that $\mathrm{SM}(P) \subseteq \mathrm{COMP}(P)$ but the converse does not necessarily hold. The main difference relies on the behaviour of positive loops. For instance, take the program P_1:

$$q \wedge \neg r \rightarrow p \tag{14}$$

$$p \rightarrow q \tag{15}$$

Its completion is the conjunction of P_1 plus the implications $(r \rightarrow \bot)$, $(p \rightarrow q \wedge \neg r)$ and $(q \rightarrow p)$. The resulting theory is classically equivalent to $\neg r \wedge (p \leftrightarrow q)$ having two supported models $\emptyset$ and $\{p, q\}$ while only the former is stable. To overcome this difference, Fages [11] strengthened supported models as follows. A classical interpretation M is a *well-supported model* of a normal program P iff there exists a strict partial order $\prec$ on M such that, for every atom $p \in M$, there is a rule $(B_i \rightarrow p) \in P$ that satisfies: (i) $M \models B_i$ and (ii) $q \prec p$ for every positive literal q in B_i. In the example above, the supported model $M = \{p, q\}$ is not well-supported. To see why, note that the only support for p is (14) whose body holds in M. To be well-supported, we would need a strict order $\prec$ satisfying $q \prec p$ for the positive literal q in the body. However, the only support for q, in its turn, is (15) whose body also holds in M and we would also need its positive literal to satisfy $p \prec q$. If we add fact p to program P_1, then the new program P_2 has a unique well-supported model $\{p, q\}$ where p is supported by the fact and q is supported by (15) with the order $p \prec q$. Fages proved that the stable models of a normal logic program coincide with its well-supported models.

4   Well-Supported Models of Boolean Programs

Extending the definition of supported models from normal to Boolean programs is straightforward: for each true atom p in M, we must still find some rule $B_i \rightarrow p$ in the program with true body $M \models B_i$ to support it. So, we add the formulas $p \rightarrow B_1 \vee \cdots \vee B_n$ collecting all bodies B_i for head p in the program – the fact that these bodies are Boolean formulas does not affect the definition in a substantial way. For instance, the completion of (1) would become $p \leftrightarrow \neg\neg p$ which is a classical tautology, its supported models being $\emptyset$ and $\{p\}$.

Theorem 2. *Supported models of Boolean programs satisfy atom definability.*

The extension of well-supportedness to Boolean bodies, however, is not so immediate, as it depends on the syntactic form of the rule body, treating negative and positive literals in a different way. Given a candidate model M, an interesting observation is that all negative literals are directly interpreted with respect to M, regardless of the derivation order $\prec$ we choose. Thus, we can simply add them to the program as a set of axioms $\Delta_M := \{\neg p \mid p \in V \setminus M\}$ we call *assumptions*. On the other hand, for finding a supporting rule $B \rightarrow p$ for p, all atoms in B^+ must be strictly smaller than p with respect to relation $\prec$. Let us define $M_{\prec p} := \{q \in M \mid q \prec p\}$, that is, all atoms in M strictly smaller than p. Using these ideas, we can rephrase the definition of well-supported model in a way that does not depend on the rule body syntax:

Proposition 1. *M is a well-supported model of a normal program P iff there exists a well-founded strict partial order $\prec$ on M such that, for each $p \in M$, there is a rule $(B \rightarrow p) \in P$ satisfying: $M_{\prec p} \cup \Delta_M \models_{\mathbf{CL}} B$.*   □

The use of negated assumptions Δ_M shares some resemblance with McDermott and Doyle's [16] fixpoint definition of *expansion* E for non-monotonic modal logics: in that case, the epistemic negation $\neg L\varphi$ of any formula $\varphi \notin E$ can be added as assumption. As an example of Proposition 1, consider program P_3 consisting of $(b \wedge \neg c \rightarrow d)$ and fact b. Its unique well-supported model is $\{b, d\}$, associated to order $b \prec d$. It is easy to see that d is justified because the body of its rule $b \wedge \neg c$ is classically entailed by $M_{\prec d} = \{b\}$ and $\Delta_M = \{\neg c\}$. Now, Proposition 1 can be directly used to provide a definition of well-supported model for Boolean programs by simply generalising the form of rule bodies B from conjunctions of literals to Boolean formulas. Unfortunately, this direct extrapolation does not satisfy atom definability. Take (1) again and consider the interpretation $M = \{p\}$. As we only have one atom and this atom is true, $M_{\prec p} \cup \Delta_M = \emptyset$ while the only possible rule is not supported $\emptyset \not\models_{\mathbf{CL}} \neg\neg p$. However, as we explained in

Sect. 2, to respect atom definability, (1) should behave as the program (12)–(13) after removing atom a, so $\{p\}$ must be a stable model of both programs. This example apparently creates a false dilemma: either we choose well-supportedness or atom definability, but not both. We claim, however, that the apparent dilemma can be resolved by allowing the concept of well-supportedness to be parametrised in at least two different ways. A first, obvious way is to permit different logics to characterise the monotonic entailment relation in Proposition 1; so one would expect, for instance, that Equilibrium Logic corresponds to **HT** instead of **CL**. Different semantics may arise from considering other logics but, as we will show, if we focus on the whole family of intermediate logics, most variants collapse into a pair of non-monotonic alternatives, one of them being Equilibrium Logic. A second observation is that there is no reason *a priori* why the set of assumptions Δ_M should be restricted to negated atoms. As mentioned, in non-monotonic modal logics, assumptions may involve negations of more general formulas. Given a class of formulas $\mathcal{C} \subseteq \mathcal{L}_V$, we define the corresponding set of assumptions with respect to a classical interpretation M as $\Delta_M^{\mathcal{C}} := \{ \neg\varphi \mid \varphi \in \mathcal{C}, \ M \not\models_{\mathbf{CL}} \varphi \}$ that is, we collect the negation of all formulas of class $\mathcal{C}$ not satisfied by M. We are particularly interested in three classes: the set of atoms, the set of literals and the set of propositional formulas, respectively denoted with the superscripts at, lit and for. Thus, Δ_M used before corresponds now to Δ_M^{at}. This leads us to the following general definition of well-supported model.

Definition 2 (Well-supported model). *Given a logic* **L** *and a class of assumption formulas* $\mathcal{C}$, *a set of atoms* M *is a* $\mathbf{L}^{\mathcal{C}}$*-well-supported model (for short,* $\mathbf{L}^{\mathcal{C}}$*-model) of a Boolean program* P *iff there exists a strict partial order* $\prec$ *on* M *such that, for each* $p \in M$, *there is a rule* $(B \to p) \in P$ *satisfying* $M_{\prec p} \cup \Delta_M^{\mathcal{C}} \models_{\mathbf{L}} B$. □

Under this new notation, [10] corresponds now to $\mathbf{CL}^{at}$-models, that is, we use classical entailment of rule bodies and take negated atoms as assumptions. If we consider the class of literals $\mathcal{C} = lit$ as assumptions, then we obtain the following characterisations of supported and equilibrium models.

Theorem 3. *If* P *is a Boolean program and* M *a classical interpretation:*

(i) M *is a supported model of* P *iff* M *is a* $\mathbf{CL}^{lit}$*-model of* P.
(ii) $\langle M, M \rangle$ *is an equilibrium model of* P *iff it is a* $\mathbf{HT}^{lit}$*-model of* P. □

Property (i) means that we can see Clark's completion (supportedness) as a degenerate case of well-supportedness. This is because Δ_M^{lit} has M as its unique classical model, so the other part of the well-supportedness condition $M_{\prec p}$ has no effect at all. Property (ii), however, has a different reading. It means that equilibrium models are well-supported if we take negated literals as assumptions and use **HT** entailment to interpret them. Remember that $\neg\neg p$ is not **HT**-equivalent to p. Definition 2 gives us a new reading of their meanings: $\neg\neg p$ corresponds to assuming that p will not eventually become false, while p must be derived from rules under some derivation order $\prec$. Therefore, Equilibrium Logic simultaneously satisfies well-supportedness (in a non-degenerate way) besides atom definability. What happens with the rest of variants that can be obtained from Definition 2? These variants are not completely unrelated. For instance, well-supported models for $\mathbf{L}^{\mathcal{C}}$ are preserved for stronger logics or for more general assumption classes, as stated below.

Proposition 2. *Let M be a $\mathbf{L}^{\mathcal{C}}$-model of a Boolean program P. Then, for any logic $\mathbf{M} \supseteq \mathbf{L}$ and any $\mathcal{D} \supseteq \mathcal{C}$, M is also an $\mathbf{M}^{\mathcal{D}}$-model of P.*   □

As we showed that $\mathbf{CL}^{at}$-models do not satisfy atom definability because $\{p\}$ is not a $\mathbf{CL}^{at}$-model of (1), by the proposition above, $\{p\}$ will not be a well-supported model of (1) in any weaker logic either, and so:

Corollary 1. *For any $\mathbf{L} \subseteq \mathbf{CL}$, $\mathbf{L}^{at}$-models do not satisfy atom definability.*   □

The next result shows that, at least for intermediate logics, the remaining combinations for monotonic logics and where $\mathcal{C}$ includes at least the set of literals *lit*, eventually collapse into supported or equilibrium models.

Theorem 4. *Let P be a Boolean program and $\mathcal{C} \supseteq$ lit. Then:*

(i) M is a $\mathbf{CL}^{\mathcal{C}}$-model of P iff M is a supported model of P.
(ii) For any intermediate logic $\mathbf{L} \subset \mathbf{CL}$:
   M is a $\mathbf{L}^{\mathcal{C}}$-model of P iff $\langle M, M \rangle$ is an equilibrium model of P.   □

That is, we obtain the same result as in Theorem 3, even if we use any non-classical intermediate logic $\mathbf{L}$ from $\mathbf{IL}$ to $\mathbf{HT}$. Again, (i) is not surprising since, for classical logic, the set Δ_M^{lit} fixes a unique model M and the same will happen for any $\mathcal{C} \supseteq$ *lit*. So, strictly speaking, supported models are not well-supported, since they admit any arbitrary partial order relation $\prec$. This means that the only non-monotonic candidate from Definition 2 among intermediate logics that satisfies strict well-supportedness and atom definability is Equilibrium Logic.

5   Related Work and Conclusions

We have examined two properties, well-supportedness and atom definability, that we suggest might be taken as *desiderata* for a sound methodology for generalised logic programming based on the concept of stable model. Given certain assumptions and a range of possible underlying logics, it turns out that essentially only Equilibrium Logic satisfies both conditions. This may be seen as a new and strong argument in its favour.[2]

A related approach to generalising well-supportedness for Boolean programs is pursued in [10], proposing a modification of the so-called FLP-semantics of [8]. Though the approach we have taken here is related, it is less restrictive than that of [10], since assumptions there are restricted to negated atoms, Δ_M^{at} in our

---

[2] Many other properties of Equilibrium Logic, studied elsewhere, also speak in its favour, e.g. not least the characterisation of strong equivalence, [6].

notation, and logical inference is classical, based on $\models_{\mathbf{CL}}$. A fuller analysis and discussion of [10] is left for future work. However, we can already remark that the semantics proposed in [10] does not satisfy atom definability.

We plan to extend this analysis to other semantics for Boolean programs such as [17] and the ones studied in [18]. An important topic for future study is to provide a full, first-order logical account of these desiderata.

Acknowledgements. We are very thankful to the anonymous reviewers for their helpful comments and suggestions to improve the paper, especially for pointing out example after Theorem 1 which led to a more accurate reformulation.

References

1. Gelfond, M., Lifschitz, V.: The stable models semantics for logic programming. In: Proceedings of the 5th International Conference on Logic Programming, pp. 1070–1080 (1988)
2. Gelfond, M., Lifschitz, V.: Classical negation in logic programs and disjunctive databases. New Gener. Comput. **9**, 365–385 (1991)
3. Inoue, K., Sakama, C.: Negation as failure in the head. J. Log. Program. **35**(1), 39–78 (1998)
4. Lifschitz, V., Tang, L.R., Turner, H.: Nested expressions in logic programs. Ann. Math. Artif. Intell. **25**, 369–389 (1999)
5. Pearce, D.: A new logical characterisation of stable models and answer sets. In: Dix, J., Pereira, L.M., Przymusinski, T.C. (eds.) NMELP 1996. LNCS, vol. 1216, pp. 57–70. Springer, Heidelberg (1997). doi:10.1007/BFb0023801
6. Lifschitz, V., Pearce, D., Valverde, A.: Strongly equivalent logic programs. ACM Trans. Comput. Log. **2**(4), 526–541 (2001)
7. Ferraris, P.: Answer sets for propositional theories. In: Baral, C., Greco, G., Leone, N., Terracina, G. (eds.) LPNMR 2005. LNCS, vol. 3662, pp. 119–131. Springer, Heidelberg (2005). doi:10.1007/11546207_10
8. Faber, W., Leone, N., Pfeifer, G.: Recursive aggregates in disjunctive logic programs: semantics and complexity. In: Alferes, J.J., Leite, J. (eds.) JELIA 2004. LNCS, vol. 3229, pp. 200–212. Springer, Heidelberg (2004). doi:10.1007/978-3-540-30227-8_19
9. Truszczyński, M.: Reducts of propositional theories, satisfiability relations, and generalizations of semantics of logic programs. Artif. Intell. **174**(16), 1285–1306 (2010)
10. Shen, Y.D., Wang, K., Eiter, T., Fink, M., Redl, C., Krennwallner, T., Deng, J.: FLP answer set semantics without circular justifications for general logic programs. Artif. Intell. **213**, 1–41 (2014)
11. Fages, F.: Consistency of Clark's completion and existence of stable models. J. Methods Log. Comput. Sci. **1**(1), 51–60 (1994)
12. Calimeri, F., Faber, W., Gebser, M., Ianni, G., Kaminski, R., Krennwallner, T., Leone, N., Ricca, F., Schaub, T.: ASP-Core-2 input language format (2013). https://www.mat.unical.it/aspcomp2013/ASPStandardization
13. Eiter, T., Tompits, H., Woltran, S.: On solution correspondences in answer-set programming. In: Kaelbling, L.P., Saffiotti, A. (eds.) Proceedings of the Nineteenth International Joint Conference on Artificial Intelligence (IJCAI 2005), Edinburgh, Scotland, UK, pp. 97–102. Professional Book Center (2005)

14. Aguado, F., Cabalar, P., Fandinno, J., Pearce, D., Pérez, G., Vidal, C.: Forgetting auxiliary atoms in forks. In: Proceedings of the 10th Workshop on Answer Set Programming and Other Computing Paradigms (ASPOCP 2017) (2017)
15. Clark, K.L.: Negation as failure. In: Gallaire, H., Minker, J. (eds.) Logic and Databases, pp. 293–322. Plenum Press, New York (1978)
16. McDermott, D.V., Doyle, J.: Non-monotonic logic I. Artif. Intell. **13**(1–2), 41–72 (1980)
17. Tasharrofi, S.: A rational extension of stable model semantics to the full propositional language. In: Proceedings of the Twenty-Third International Joint Conference on Artificial Intelligence, IJCAI 2013, pp. 1118–1124. AAAI Press (2013)
18. Alviano, M., Faber, W.: Stable model semantics of abstract dialectical frameworks revisited: a logic programming perspective. In: Proceedings of the 24th International Joint Conference on Artificial Intelligence (IJCAI 2015), pp. 2684–2690 (2015)

haspie - A Musical Harmonisation Tool Based on ASP

Pedro Cabalar[(✉)] and Rodrigo Martín

Department of Computer Science, Universidade da Coruña, A Coruña, Spain
{cabalar,r.martin1}@udc.es

Abstract. In this paper we describe a musical harmonisation and composition assistant based on Answer Set Programming (ASP). The tool takes scores in MusicXML format and annotates them with a preferred harmonisation. If specified, it is also able to complete intentionally blank sections and create new parts of the score that fit with the proposed harmonisation. Both the harmonisation and the completion of blank parts can be seen as constraint satisfaction problems that are encoded in ASP. Although the tool is a preliminary prototype still being improved, its basic functionality already helps to illustrate the appropriateness of ASP for musical knowledge representation, which provides a high degree of flexibility thanks to its relational, declarative orientation and an efficient computation of preferred solutions.

1 Introduction

Music Theory learning is a field with a long tradition, relying on well-established methods but suffering, in many cases, from an obsolete technology. A central discipline in music learning is *Harmony*, a cornerstone for score analysis, vital for its comprehension, later interpretation and further development. Harmony studies the superposition of sounds, that is, the combination of simultaneous notes to create *chords*. In their turn, chord progressions help either to reaffirm or to blur (depending on the author's intentions) the concept of *tonality*. It is usually said that harmony constitutes the "vertical" reading of a score (that is, what is sounding at a same time) as opposed to the "horizontal" reading provided by the *melody* (that is, how a given voice progresses along time).

Apart from acquiring theoretical foundations, Harmony students must usually face a series of exercises in the form of a four-voices score partially incomplete. The goals of these exercises may comprise tasks such as annotating the chords, filling missing voice parts or both. This has to be done according to some style *rules* that may be strict or, occasionally, act as preferences or recommendations. In other words, harmony exercises constitute a natural application domain for constraint based reasoning. Moreover, musical notation (at least for harmony

This work has been partially supported by MINECO, Spain (project TIN2013-42149-P), Xunta de Galicia, Spain (projects GPC ED431B 2016/035 and 2016-2019 ED431G/01 for CITIC center) and European Regional Development Fund (ERDF).

© Springer International Publishing AG 2017
E. Oliveira et al. (Eds.): EPIA 2017, LNAI 10423, pp. 637–642, 2017.
DOI: 10.1007/978-3-319-65340-2_52

purposes) is mostly discrete and symbolic, and its knowledge involves many kinds of relations (among notes, chords, measures, etc.), becoming in this way an ideal test-bed for logical Knowledge Representation and Reasoning (KRR).

In this paper, we present `haspie`, a musical harmonisation tool based on *Answer Set Programming* (ASP) [1–3], one of the most successful KRR paradigms for practical problem solving. `haspie` aims to help Harmony students achieve a better understanding of the matter and lets them experiment earlier with composition from a harmonic point of view. The tool can be combined with a score graphic editor (`MuseScore`[1]) to create/manipulate harmony exercises that can be solved via a call to the ASP backend. The solutions can then be displayed again in the graphic editor or directly translated into MIDI files for their reproduction.

2   Tool Description

The architecture of `haspie` (Fig. 1) is a simple pipeline written in Python with a single execution path. The input format for `haspie` is *Music Extensible Markup Language* (MusicXML, or MXML), an extension of the XML format used to represent Western music. It contains not only score information but also display data such as margins, font sizes, musical notes position coordinates in the sheet, etc. The tool takes a single MusicXML file (usually generated with the graphic editor `MuseScore`) as input that is passed to the first stage of the pipeline: a parser written in C along with the Flex and Bison libraries. This module transforms the MusicXML tag information to ASP facts. The parser also performs other tasks such as fixing the measure level at which the harmonisation will take place, interpreting the instrument or voice names to determine their most common pitch ranges, reading the expected tonality via the key signature, etc.

The core of `haspie` is an ASP encoding that declares the style norms and preferences as logic program rules. Without entering into detail (see [3] for a extended explanation), ASP usually describes constraint problems with a methodology called *generate-define-test*. Some rules allow generating potential solutions, constraints (test) are used to prune undesired choices and an additional group of rules allow defining auxiliary predicates to represent some features used in generation and test. An example of a generation rule is:

```
1 { chord(HT,C) : pos_chord(C) } 1 :- htime(HT).
```

It essentially asserts that, for each time beat `HT`, exactly 1 chord `C` is (nondeterministically) assigned among all those possible chords `pos_chord(C)` defined elsewhere according to the chord harmony rules. With this rule alone, each possible assignment becomes one of the answer sets of the program, which are in one-to-one correspondence to solutions to our harmonisation exercises.

As we can see, ASP rules allow variables (in capital letters) that are replaced by their possible instances in a first stage called *grounding*. After all rules are

---

[1] https://musescore.org/.

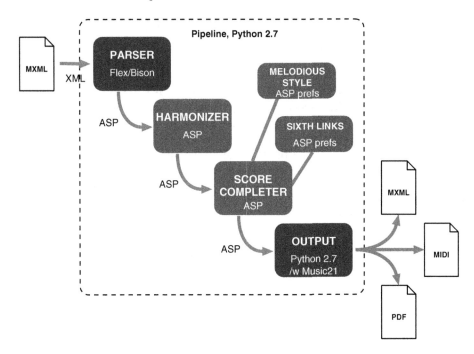

Fig. 1. haspie architecture

grounded, a second stage does the (propositional) solving. The ASP solver that haspie uses as a backend is clingo[2] which incorporates both the grounding and solving phases in a singe package. To reduce the combinatorial explosion, the ASP core for haspie has been actually divided into two modules: the harmonisation module and the score completer (see Fig. 1). The former assigns a (coherent) harmonic structure for the partial score provided as an input, whereas the latter fills the gaps once the harmony has been established.

The harmonisation module takes a file with ASP facts and uses this information to expand the general harmony rules, using some auxiliary predicates and finally assigning a chord to each specified section of the piece with the rule shown before. The possible chords poss_chord(C) are defined in separate files major_chords and minor_chords – the tool determines which one to use by inferring the mode from the extracted key signature. These chords are defined by the relative role of the notes in the (inferred) tone scale (1st grade, 2nd grade, etc.) rather than their absolute pitch (C, D, etc.). By doing so, the tool generalises the chord concept, reducing it to a tonal grade detection and then fits the best possible chord for that grade by taking all the notes in the analysed beat interval. Knowing the tonal grades of each note of the rhythmic interval, the tool then marks as mistakes those notes in strong beats not belonging to the assigned chord so that, using optimisation rules, answer sets with a minimum number of

---

[2] http://potassco.sourceforge.net/.

mistakes are chosen. The tool displays a summary of these best answers and lets the user choose one for the score completion step A temporal chord facts file is then created, that is used, along with the original logical facts to complete the blank parts or the new voices of the score.

The second half of the tool, the score completer, is called if there are blank sections (denoted using predicate `freebeat`) in the score or the creation of new parts were specified in the input options. This second half works in a similar fashion as the first half, by assigning new notes to the completable sections of the score among those in the pitch range of the specified instrument or voice type of the part. For instance, the rule:

```
1 { freebeatfigure(V,N,1,FB) : N=VL..VH } 1 :- freebeat(V,FB),
             voice_limit_low(V,VL), voice_limit_high(V,VH).
```

is a non-deterministic assignment of a note N between the lowest VL and highest VH pitches for voice V, for each time point FB marked as `freebeat` (that is, blank section to be filled). These new notes N are again generalised to their tonal grade and octave (as it is done in the very first steps of the previous half) to then being checked against the selected harmonisation. This is done by marking the incorrect ones in strong beats as mistakes, as well as checking for other melodic rules such as note distance or trying to avoid certain undesirable sounds produced among the different voices that play at the same time. By minimizing these mistakes, again, the optimal solutions are found.

The following is an example showing a hard constraint:

```
octave_jump(V,B1,B2) :- ex_note(V,N1,B1), ex_note(V,N2,B2),
                (B1+1) == B2, N2 > (N1+12), beat(B1+1).
octave_jump(V,B1,B2) :- ex_note(V,N1,B1), ex_note(V,N2,B2),
                (B1+1) == B2, N2 < (N1-12), beat(B1+1).
:- octave_jump(_,_,_).
```

The first two rules define the auxiliary predicate `octave_jump(V,B1,B2)` that detects when a given voice V moves from one note at beat B1 to another note at B1+1 with the same name but one octave higher (or lower). Rules like the one in the last line, without a head expression before ':-', correspond to constraints in ASP. In this case, the constraints rule out all octave jumps.

`haspie` has an optional module including some preferences to improve the result of the score completer. These preferences include some melodic rules trying, for instance, to minimise the size of melodic jumps:

```
melodic_jump(V,J,B1,B2) :- out_note(V,N1,B1), out_note(V,N2,B2),
                (B1+1) == B2, beat(B1+1), J = #abs(N1-N2).
#minimize[melodic_jump(_,J,_,_) = (J * weight) @ priority].
```

The `minimize` clause above assigns a penalty J * `weight` per each melodic jump of J semitones. The constant `weight` and the `priority` level for this preference can be assigned by the user, so we can tune how much influence this preference will have on the final result. The preferences module includes other optimisations. For instance, if a section melody has a rising or falling tendency, it tries to imitate that tendency in the completable sections as much as possible. Another group of preferences detects a popular type of chord progression (cadential 6/4 chords), trying to extend a sequence of this type of chords as much as possible by filling completable blank sections. The last module called by the pipeline uses the internal score representation in Python objects to export the result in the format specified by the user. This module works using the `music21` library[3] developed by the MIT.

3 Evaluation

For the tool evaluation, four pieces were chosen. For each one, the tool was asked to harmonise and complete one of its measures as well as a whole new part, measuring not only runtime but also quality of the result. The left table in Fig. 2 shows the obtained results: each measure was taken 100 times and then averaged. Harmony selection times are very good and the completion times are very promising. Nevertheless, the required time to complete new parts grows very quickly as adding more and more sections to complete makes the possibilities grow exponentially. In quality terms, the selected chords are correct, and the section completion or the new parts creation offer interesting harmonically correct solutions like the one in Fig. 3, adding an harmonically correct bass line to the well-known melody from "Greensleeves." The load tests for "Twinkle Twinkle" were performed by leaving blank measures in one of the parts. Measures were emptied in blocks of four. We also tried adding 1 and 2 voices to the piece, achieving the times in the right table of Fig. 2.

Piece	Harmonisation	Measure	New Part
Greensleeves	1.016s	1.926s	4m 49.032s
Menuet	0.631s	0.726s	3m 50.376s
Joy to the World	2.381s	3.813s	7m 17.115s
Twinkle Twinkle	0.685s	0.716s	2m 31.299s

Test	Time
4 measures	1.481s
8 measures	2.394s
12 measures	3.978s
16 measures	3.982s
20 measures	5.966s
1 voice	2m 31.299s
2 voices	25m 17.298s

Fig. 2. Some execution results.

---

[3] http://web.mit.edu/music21/.

Fig. 3. Obtained harmonisation and bass part for Greensleeves melody.

4 Conclusions and Related Work

Clearly, the closest works to haspie are ANTON [4] and CHASP [5], since both rely on ASP too. ANTON is a complex rythmic, melodic and harmonic composer for small musical pieces. Although it is more complete than haspie, it is limited to the Renaissance style of Palestrina and only two voices, so it is less suitable for harmony training. CHASP is a tiny tool created by the Potassco Group to calculate chord progressions through ASP starting from scratch (no input file), allowing the user to specify key and length of the piece.

The current prototype is only at a preliminary stage. Many open topics remain for future work. Apart from improving the input and output interfaces (like the connection to MuseScore as a plugin) a fundamental extension which is a current, important limitation, is the possibility of automated *modulation*, that is, allowing haspie to decide changes in the piece tonality in a dynamic way.

References

1. Niemelä, I.: Logic programs with stable model semantics as a constraint programming paradigm. Ann. Math. Artif. Intell. **25**(3–4), 241–273 (1999)
2. Marek, V.W., Truszczyński, M.: Stable models and an alternative logic programming paradigm. In: Apt, K.R., Marek, V.W., Truszczyński, M., Warren, D.S. (eds.) The Logic Programming Paradigm. Artificial Intelligence, pp. 375–398. Springer, Heidelberg (1999). doi:10.1007/978-3-642-60085-2_17
3. Brewka, G., Eiter, T., Truszczyński, M.: Answer set programming at a glance. Commun. ACM **54**(12), 92–103 (2011)
4. Boenn, G., Brain, M., De Vos, M., Ffitch, J.: Automatic music composition using answer set programming. Theory Pract. Log. Program. **11**(2–3), 397–427 (2011)
5. Opolka, S., Obermeier, P., Schaub, T.: Automatic genre-dependent composition using answer set programming. In: Proceedings of the 21st International Symposium on Electronic Art (ISEA 2015) (2015)

Iterative Variable Elimination in ASP

Ricardo Gonçalves, Matthias Knorr$^{(\boxtimes)}$, and João Leite

NOVA LINCS, Departamento de Informática, Faculdade de Ciências e Tecnologia,
Universidade Nova de Lisboa, 2829-516 Caparica, Portugal
mkn@fct.unl.pt

Abstract. In recent years, a large variety of approaches for forgetting in Answer Set Programming (ASP) have been proposed, in the form of specific operators, or classes of operators, following different principles and obeying different properties. A recent comprehensive overview of existing operators and properties provides a uniform picture of the landscape, including many novel results on relations between properties and operators. In this paper, we introduce four new properties not considered previously and show that these are indeed succinct and relevant additions providing novel results and insights, further strengthening established relations between existing operators. Most notably among these, the invariance to permutations of the order of forgetting a set of atoms iteratively raises interesting questions with surprising results.

1 Introduction

Forgetting – or variable elimination – is an operation that allows for the removal, from a knowledge base, of so-called *middle* variables no longer deemed relevant, whose importance is witnessed by its application to cognitive robotics [1–3], resolving conflicts [4–7], and ontology abstraction and comparison [8–11]. With its early roots in Boolean Algebra [12], it has been extensively studied within classical logic [4,13–18].

Only more recently, the operation of forgetting began to receive attention in the context of logic programming and non-monotonic reasoning, notably of Answer Set Programming (ASP) [19]. It turns out that the rule-based nature and non-monotonic semantics of ASP create very unique challenges to the development of forgetting operators, – just as to the development of other belief change operators such as those for revision and update, c.f. [20–26] – making it a special endeavour with unique characteristics distinct from those for classical logic.

Over the years, many have proposed different approaches to forgetting in ASP, through the characterization of the result of forgetting a set of atoms from a given program up to some equivalence class, and/or through the definition of concrete operators that produce a program given an input program and atoms to be forgotten [5,6,27–32]. All these approaches were typically proposed to obey some specific set of properties deemed adequate by their authors, some adapted from the literature on *classical* forgetting [28,31,33], others specifically introduced for the case of ASP [6,27–30,32].

© Springer International Publishing AG 2017
E. Oliveira et al. (Eds.): EPIA 2017, LNAI 10423, pp. 643–656, 2017.
DOI: 10.1007/978-3-319-65340-2_53

The result is a *complex* landscape filled with operators and properties, that is difficult to navigate. This problem was tackled in [34] by presenting a systematic study of *forgetting* in ASP, thoroughly investigating the different approaches found in the literature, their properties and relationships, giving rise to a comprehensive guide aimed at helping users navigate this topic's complex landscape and ultimately assist them in choosing suitable operators for each application.

However, [34] ignores to a large extent a set of postulates on forgetting in ASP introduced by Wong in [27]. This can be justified by the fact that these are limited to forgetting a single atom from a program and often their generalization has been considered independently, and also because, otherwise, they had not played a significant role in the literature on forgetting.

Whereas completing the picture presented in [34] would be sufficient reason to thoroughly investigate these postulates, recent findings in [35] made it even more relevant. It was shown in [35] that it is not always possible to forget while preserving so-called *strong persistence* – an essential property for forgetting in ASP that encodes the required preservation, under forgetting, of all relations between non-forgotten atoms – shifting the attention to the question of when (and how) it is possible to forget. This also relates to Wong's postulates, notably the one which deals with order in which atoms (or more generally sets of atoms) can be forgotten from a logic program. The possibility to change the order of atoms to be forgotten as well as the step-wise iteration of forgetting a set of atoms comes with a number of benefits. First, designing algorithms for forgetting one atom can often be easier, and forgetting a set of atoms would then simply amount to iteratively apply the resulting simpler algorithm. Second, forgetting one atom can be done without having to worry that this may impose restrictions on the possibility to forget other atom in the future. However, maybe surprisingly, investigating Wong's postulates allowed us to prove that if we want to preserve the property *strong persistence*, then a) the order of forgetting (sets of) atoms matters, and b) it may be impossible to step-wise iteratively forget a set of atoms that can be forgotten as a whole.

In this paper, we introduce new properties, which generalize four of Wong's postulates that are not trivially covered by existing properties in [34]. We show that these new properties turn out to be distinct and provide additional novel results further strengthening the relations between properties and classes of operators of forgetting as previously established. Notably, we clarify the limits of iteratively forgetting a set of atoms and permuting the order of atoms to be forgotten.

After the recalling the necessary notions, we introduce the four new properties and present our results on relations w.r.t. previously established properties and on which classes of operators satisfy which properties. We then investigate one of them with more detail, and establish the novel impossibility result concerning step-wise iterative forgetting, before concluding.

2   Preliminaries

We assume a propositional language $\mathcal{L}_{\mathcal{A}}$ over a *signature* $\mathcal{A}$, a finite set of propositional atoms. The *formulas* of $\mathcal{L}_{\mathcal{A}}$ are inductively defined using connectives $\bot$, $\wedge$, $\vee$, and $\supset$:

$$\varphi ::= \bot \mid p \mid \varphi \vee \varphi \mid \varphi \wedge \varphi \mid \varphi \supset \varphi \tag{1}$$

where $p \in \mathcal{A}$. In addition, $\neg\varphi$ and $\top$ are shortcuts for $\varphi \supset \bot$ and $\bot \supset \bot$, resp. Given a finite set S of formulas, $\bigvee S$ and $\bigwedge S$ denote resp. the disjunction and conjunction of all formulas in S. In particular, $\bigvee \emptyset$ and $\bigwedge \emptyset$ stand for resp. $\bot$ and $\top$, and $\neg S$ and $\neg\neg S$ represent resp. $\{\neg\varphi \mid \varphi \in S\}$ and $\{\neg\neg\varphi \mid \varphi \in S\}$. We assume that the underlying signature for a particular formula φ is $\mathcal{A}(\varphi)$, the set of atoms appearing in φ.

Regarding the semantics of propositional formulas, we consider the monotonic logic here-and-there (HT) and equilibrium models [36]. An *HT-interpretation* is a pair $\langle H, T \rangle$ s.t. $H \subseteq T \subseteq \mathcal{A}$. The satisfiability relation in HT, denoted $\models_{\mathsf{HT}}$, is recursively defined as follows for $p \in \mathcal{A}$ and formulas φ and ψ:

- $\langle H, T \rangle \models_{\mathsf{HT}} p$ if $p \in H$; $\qquad$ $\langle H, T \rangle \not\models_{\mathsf{HT}} \bot$;
- $\langle H, T \rangle \models_{\mathsf{HT}} \varphi \wedge \psi$ if $\langle H, T \rangle \models_{\mathsf{HT}} \varphi$ and $\langle H, T \rangle \models_{\mathsf{HT}} \psi$;
- $\langle H, T \rangle \models_{\mathsf{HT}} \varphi \vee \psi$ if $\langle H, T \rangle \models_{\mathsf{HT}} \varphi$ or $\langle H, T \rangle \models_{\mathsf{HT}} \psi$;
- $\langle H, T \rangle \models_{\mathsf{HT}} \varphi \supset \psi$ if (i) $T \models \varphi \supset \psi$,[1] and (ii) $\langle H, T \rangle \models_{\mathsf{HT}} \varphi \Rightarrow \langle H, T \rangle \models_{\mathsf{HT}} \psi$.

An *HT-interpretation* is an *HT-model* of a formula φ if $\langle H, T \rangle \models_{\mathsf{HT}} \varphi$. We denote by $\mathcal{HT}(\varphi)$ the set of *all HT-models* of φ. In particular, $\langle T, T \rangle \in \mathcal{HT}(\varphi)$ is an *equilibrium model* of φ if there is no $T' \subset T$ s.t. $\langle T', T \rangle \in \mathcal{HT}(\varphi)$. Given two formulas φ and ψ, if $\mathcal{HT}(\varphi) \subseteq \mathcal{HT}(\psi)$, then φ *entails* ψ in HT, written $\varphi \models_{\mathsf{HT}} \psi$. Also, φ and ψ are *HT-equivalent*, written $\varphi \equiv_{\mathsf{HT}} \psi$, if $\mathcal{HT}(\varphi) = \mathcal{HT}(\psi)$. For sets of atoms X, Y and $V \subseteq \mathcal{A}$, $Y \sim_V X$ denotes that $Y \setminus V = X \setminus V$. For *HT-interpretations* $\langle H, T \rangle$ and $\langle X, Y \rangle$, $\langle H, T \rangle \sim_V \langle X, Y \rangle$ denotes that $H \sim_V X$ and $T \sim_V Y$. For a set $\mathcal{M}$ of *HT-interpretations*, $\mathcal{M}_{\dagger V}$ denotes the set $\{\langle X, Y \rangle \mid \langle H, T \rangle \in \mathcal{M}$ and $\langle X, Y \rangle \sim_V \langle H, T \rangle\}$. An *(extended) logic program* P is a finite set of *rules*, i.e., formulas of the form

$$\bigwedge \neg\neg D \wedge \bigwedge \neg C \wedge \bigwedge B \supset \bigvee A, \tag{2}$$

where all elements in $A = \{a_1, \ldots, a_k\}$, $B = \{b_1, \ldots, b_l\}$, $C = \{c_1, \ldots, c_m\}$, $D = \{d_1, \ldots, d_n\}$ are atoms.[2] Such rules r are also commonly written as

$$a_1 \vee \ldots \vee a_k \leftarrow b_1, \ldots, b_l, \mathit{not}\, c_1, \ldots, \mathit{not}\, c_m, \mathit{not\ not}\, d_1, \ldots, \mathit{not\ not}\, d_n, \tag{3}$$

and we use both forms interchangeably. We denote the *head* of r by $head(r) = A$ and its *body* by $body(r) = B \cup \neg C \cup \neg\neg D$, a disjunction and a conjunction, respectively.

---

[1] $\models$ is the standard consequence relation from classical logic.
[2] Extended logic programs [37] are actually more expressive, but this form is sufficient here.

As shown by Cabalar and Ferraris [38], any set of (propositional) formulas is HT-equivalent to an (extended) logic program which is why we can focus solely on these.

This class of logic programs, $\mathcal{C}_e$, includes a number of special kinds of rules r: if $n = 0$, then we call r *disjunctive*; if, in addition, $k \leq 1$, then r is *normal*; if on top of that $m = 0$, then we call r *Horn*, and *fact* if also $l = 0$. The classes of *disjunctive*, *normal* and *Horn programs*, $\mathcal{C}_d$, $\mathcal{C}_n$, and $\mathcal{C}_H$, are defined resp. as a finite set of disjunctive, normal, and Horn rules. We have $\mathcal{C}_H \subset \mathcal{C}_n \subset \mathcal{C}_d \subset \mathcal{C}_e$.

We now recall the *answer set semantics* [39] for logic programs. Given a program P and a set I of atoms, the *reduct* P^I is $P^I = \{A \leftarrow B : r$ of the form (3) in P, $C \cap I = \emptyset, D \subseteq I\}$. A set I' of atoms is a model of P^I if, for each $r \in P^I$, $I' \models B$ implies $I' \models A$. I is minimal in a set S, denoted by $I \in \mathcal{MIN}(S)$, if there is no $I' \in S$ s.t. $I' \subset I$. I is an *answer set* of P iff I is a minimal model of P^I. Note that, for $\mathcal{C}_n$ and its subclasses, this minimal model is in fact unique. The set of all answer sets of P is denoted by $\mathcal{AS}(P)$. Note that, for $\mathcal{C}_d$ and its subclasses, all $I \in \mathcal{AS}(P)$ are pairwise incomparable. If P has an answer set, then P is *consistent*. The V-*exclusion* of a set of answer sets $\mathcal{M}$, denoted $\mathcal{M}_{\|V}$, is $\{X \setminus V \mid X \in \mathcal{M}\}$. Two programs P_1, P_2 are *equivalent* if $\mathcal{AS}(P_1) = \mathcal{AS}(P_2)$ and *strongly equivalent* if $P_1 \equiv_{\mathsf{HT}} P_2$. It is well-known that answer sets and equilibrium models coincide [36].

We also recall notions on forgetting from [34]. Given a class of logic programs $\mathcal{C}$ over $\mathcal{A}$, a *forgetting operator* is a partial function $\mathsf{f} : \mathcal{C} \times 2^{\mathcal{A}} \to \mathcal{C}$ s.t. $\mathsf{f}(P, V)$ is a program over $\mathcal{A}(P) \setminus V$, for each $P \in \mathcal{C}$ and $V \in 2^{\mathcal{A}}$. We call $\mathsf{f}(P, V)$ the *result of forgetting about V from P*. Furthermore, f is called *closed* for $\mathcal{C}' \subseteq \mathcal{C}$ if, for every $P \in \mathcal{C}'$ and $V \in 2^{\mathcal{A}}$, we have $\mathsf{f}(P, V) \in \mathcal{C}'$. Often, a set of forgetting operators is conjoined by some characteristic condition/definition. We also call such sets *classes* F *of forgetting operators*.

3   Properties of Forgetting

Previous work on forgetting in ASP has introduced a variety of desirable properties which we recall next [34]. Unless stated otherwise, F is a class of forgetting operators, and $\mathcal{C}$ the class of programs over $\mathcal{A}$ of a given $\mathsf{f} \in \mathsf{F}$.

(sC) F satisfies *strengthened Consequence* if, for each $\mathsf{f} \in \mathsf{F}$, $P \in \mathcal{C}$ and $V \subseteq \mathcal{A}$, we have $\mathcal{AS}(\mathsf{f}(P, V)) \subseteq \mathcal{AS}(P)_{\|V}$.

(wE) F satisfies *weak Equivalence* if, for each $\mathsf{f} \in \mathsf{F}$, $P, P' \in \mathcal{C}$ and $V \subseteq \mathcal{A}$, we have $\mathcal{AS}(\mathsf{f}(P, V)) = \mathcal{AS}(\mathsf{f}(P', V))$ whenever $\mathcal{AS}(P) = \mathcal{AS}(P')$.

(SE) F satisfies *Strong Equivalence* if, for each $\mathsf{f} \in \mathsf{F}$, $P, P' \in \mathcal{C}$ and $V \subseteq \mathcal{A}$: if $P \equiv_{\mathsf{HT}} P'$, then $\mathsf{f}(P, V) \equiv_{\mathsf{HT}} \mathsf{f}(P', V)$.

(W) F satisfies *Weakening* if, for each $\mathsf{f} \in \mathsf{F}$, $P \in \mathcal{C}$ and $V \subseteq \mathcal{A}$, we have $P \models_{\mathsf{HT}} \mathsf{f}(P, V)$.

(PP) F satisfies *Positive Persistence* if, for each $\mathsf{f} \in \mathsf{F}$, $P \in \mathcal{C}$ and $V \subseteq \mathcal{A}$: if $P \models_{\mathsf{HT}} P'$, with $P' \in \mathcal{C}$ and $\mathcal{A}(P') \subseteq \mathcal{A} \setminus V$, then $\mathsf{f}(P, V) \models_{\mathsf{HT}} P'$.

(NP) F satisfies *Negative Persistence* if, for each $\mathsf{f} \in \mathsf{F}$, $P \in \mathcal{C}$ and $V \subseteq \mathcal{A}$: if $P \not\models_{\mathsf{HT}} P'$, with $P' \in \mathcal{C}$ and $\mathcal{A}(P') \subseteq \mathcal{A} \setminus V$, then $\mathsf{f}(P, V) \not\models_{\mathsf{HT}} P'$.

(SI) F satisfies *Strong (addition) Invariance* if, for each f $\in$ F, $P \in \mathcal{C}$ and $V \subseteq \mathcal{A}$, we have $f(P, V) \cup R \equiv_{HT} f(P \cup R, V)$ for all programs $R \in \mathcal{C}$ with $\mathcal{A}(R) \subseteq \mathcal{A} \setminus V$.

(E$_{\mathcal{C}}$) F satisfies *Existence for $\mathcal{C}$*, i.e., F is *closed for a class of programs $\mathcal{C}$* if there exists f $\in$ F s.t. f is closed for $\mathcal{C}$.

(CP) F satisfies *Consequence Persistence* if, for each f $\in$ F, $P \in \mathcal{C}$ and $V \subseteq \mathcal{A}$, we have $\mathcal{AS}(f(P, V)) = \mathcal{AS}(P)_{\|V}$.

(SP) F satisfies *Strong Persistence* if, for each f $\in$ F, $P \in \mathcal{C}$ and $V \subseteq \mathcal{A}$, we have $\mathcal{AS}(f(P, V) \cup R) = \mathcal{AS}(P \cup R)_{\|V}$, for all programs $R \in \mathcal{C}$ with $\mathcal{A}(R) \subseteq \mathcal{A} \setminus V$.

(wC) F satisfies *weakened Consequence* if, for each f $\in$ F, $P \in \mathcal{C}$ and $V \subseteq \mathcal{A}$, we have $\mathcal{AS}(P)_{\|V} \subseteq \mathcal{AS}(f(P, V))$.

Throughout the paper, whenever we write that a single operator f obeys some property, we mean that the singleton class composed of that operator, {f}, obeys such property.

Some notions of forgetting do only require that atoms to be forgotten be *irrelevant*:

(IR) $f(P, V) \equiv_{HT} P'$ for some P' not containing any $v \in V$.

However, this is not a restriction, as argued in [34], and, implicitly, any F satisfies **(IR)**.

4   Operators of Forgetting

We now review existing approaches to operators of forgetting in ASP following [34].

Strong and Weak Forgetting [5] are based on syntactic operators for normal programs. Both start by computing a reduction corresponding to weak partial evaluation (WGPPE) [40]: for a normal program P and $a \in \mathcal{A}$, $R(P, a)$ is the set of all rules in P and all rules of the form $head(r_1) \leftarrow body(r_1) \setminus \{a\} \cup body(r_2)$ for each $r_1, r_2 \in P$ s.t. $a \in body(r_1)$ and $head(r_2) = a$. Then, they differ on how to remove rules containing a, the atom to be forgotten. In Strong Forgetting, all rules containing a are simply removed:

$$f_{strong}(P, a) = \{r \in R(P, a) \mid a \notin \mathcal{A}(r)\}$$

In Weak Forgetting, rules containing *not a* in their bodies are kept, without the *not a*.

$$f_{weak}(P, a) = \{head(r) \leftarrow body(r) \setminus \{not\ a\} \mid r \in R(P, a), a \notin head(r) \cup body(r)\}$$

The motivation for this difference is whether such *not a* is seen as support for the rule head (Strong) or not (Weak). In both cases, the actual operator for a set of atoms V is defined by the sequential application of the respective operator to each $a \in V$. Both operators are closed for $\mathcal{C}_n$. The corresponding singleton classes are defined as follows.

$$F_{strong} = \{f_{strong}\} \qquad F_{weak} = \{f_{weak}\}$$

Semantic Forgetting [6] aimed at addressing shortcomings of the previous two syntactic operators, introducing the class F_{sem} for consistent disjunctive programs:[3]

$$\mathsf{F}_{sem} = \{\mathsf{f} \mid \mathcal{AS}(\mathsf{f}(P, V)) = \mathcal{MIN}(\mathcal{AS}(P)_{\|V})\}$$

The basic idea is to characterize a result of forgetting just by its answer sets, obtained by considering only the minimal sets among the answer sets of P ignoring V. Three concrete algorithms are presented, two semantic ones and one syntactic. Unlike the former, the latter is not closed for classes[4] $\mathcal{C}_d^+$ and $\mathcal{C}_n^+$, since double negation is required.

Semantic Strong and Weak Forgetting [27][5] were introduced for disjunctive programs to focus on HT-models,[6] instead of answer sets. For program P and atom a, the set of consequences of P is $Cn(P, a) = \{r \mid r \text{ disjunctive}, P \models_{\mathsf{HT}} r, \mathcal{A}(r) \subseteq \mathcal{A}(P)\}$. $P_S(P, a)$ and $P_W(P, a)$, the results of strongly/weakly forgetting atom a from P, are:

1. Obtain P_1 by removing from $Cn(P, a)$: (i) r with $a \in body(r)$, (ii) a from the head of each r with $not\, a \in body(r)$.
2. Obtain $P_S(P, a)$ and $P_W(P, a)$ from P_1 by replacing/removing rules r as follows:

	r with $not\, a$ in body	r with a in head
S	(remove)	(remove)
W	remove only $not\, a$	remove only a

The generalization to sets of atoms V, i.e., $P_S(P, V)$ and $P_W(P, V)$, can be obtained by simply sequentially forgetting each $a \in V$, yielding the following classes of operators.

$$\mathsf{F}_S = \{\mathsf{f} \mid \mathsf{f}(P, V) \equiv_{\mathsf{HT}} P_S(P, V)\} \qquad \mathsf{F}_W = \{\mathsf{f} \mid \mathsf{f}(P, V) \equiv_{\mathsf{HT}} P_W(P, V)\}$$

While both steps are syntactic, different strongly equivalent representations of $Cn(P, a)$ exist, including one based on inference rules for HT-consequence, closed for $\mathcal{C}_d$.

HT-Forgetting [28,31] builds on properties [33] introduced in the context of modal logics, with the aim of overcoming problems with Wongs notions of forgetting [27]. It is defined for extended programs and uses representations of sets of HT-models directly.

$$\mathsf{F}_{\mathsf{HT}} = \{\mathsf{f} \mid \mathcal{HT}(\mathsf{f}(P, V)) = \mathcal{HT}(P)_{\dagger V}\}$$

---

[3] Actually, classical negation can occur in scope of not, but due to the restriction to consistent programs, this difference is of no effect [39], so we ignore it here.

[4] Here, $^+$ denotes the restriction to consistent programs.

[5] It has been shown in [34] that SE-Forgetting [32] coincides with Semantic Strong Forgetting.

[6] Without loss of generality, we consider HT-models instead of SE-models [41] as in [27].

A concrete operator is presented [31] that is shown to be closed for $\mathcal{C}_e$ and $\mathcal{C}_H$, and it is also shown that no operator exists that is closed for either $\mathcal{C}_d$ or $\mathcal{C}_n$. **SM-Forgetting** [29] was introduced for extended programs, aiming at preserving the answer sets of the original program (modulo forgotten atoms).

$$\mathsf{F_{SM}} = \{\mathsf{f} \mid \mathcal{HT}(\mathsf{f}(P,V)) \text{ is a maximal subset of}$$
$$\mathcal{HT}(P)_{\dagger V} \text{ s.t. } \mathcal{AS}(\mathsf{f}(P,V)) = \mathcal{AS}(P)_{\|V}\}$$

A concrete operator is provided that, like for $\mathsf{F_{HT}}$, is shown to be closed for $\mathcal{C}_e$ and $\mathcal{C}_H$. It is also shown that no operator exists that is closed for either $\mathcal{C}_d$ or $\mathcal{C}_n$. **Strong AS-Forgetting** [30] was introduced with the aim of preserving not only the answer sets of P itself but also those of $P \cup R$ for any R over the signature without the atoms to be forgotten. The notion is defined abstractly for classes of programs $\mathcal{C}$.

$$\mathsf{F}_{Sas} = \{\mathsf{f} \mid \mathcal{AS}(\mathsf{f}(P,V) \cup R) = \mathcal{AS}(P \cup R)_{\|V} \text{ for all}$$
$$\text{programs } R \in \mathcal{C} \text{ with } \mathcal{A}(R) \subseteq \mathcal{A}(P) \setminus V\}$$

An operator is defined for programs without disjunction, but not closed for $\mathcal{C}_n$ or $\mathcal{C}_e$.

5   Beyond Wong's Properties

The postulates introduced by Wong [27] were defined in a somewhat different way when compared to the properties presented in Sect. 3. Namely, they only consider forgetting a single atom, were defined for disjunctive programs (the maximal class of programs considered in [27]), and used a generic formulation which allowed different notions of equivalence. Here, we only consider HT-equivalence, i.e., strong equivalence, as, in the literature, this is clearly the more relevant of the two notions considered in [27] (the other one being the non-standard T-equivalence) and in line with previously presented material here and in [34]. We recall these postulates[7] adjusting them to our notation and extending them to the most general class of extended logic programs considered here.

(F0) F satisfies **(F0)** if, for each $\mathsf{f} \in \mathsf{F}$, $P, P' \in \mathcal{C}$ and $a \in \mathcal{A}$: if $P \equiv_{\mathsf{HT}} P'$, then $\mathsf{f}(P, \{a\}) \equiv_{\mathsf{HT}} \mathsf{f}(P', \{a\})$.
(F1) F satisfies **(F1)** if, for each $\mathsf{f} \in \mathsf{F}$, $P, P' \in \mathcal{C}$ and $a \in \mathcal{A}$: if $P \models_{\mathsf{HT}} P'$, then $\mathsf{f}(P, \{a\}) \models_{\mathsf{HT}} \mathsf{f}(P', \{a\})$.
(F2) F satisfies **(F2)** if, for each $\mathsf{f} \in \mathsf{F}$, $P, P' \in \mathcal{C}$ and $a \in \mathcal{A}$: if a does not appear in R, then $\mathsf{f}(P \cup R, \{a\}) \equiv_{\mathsf{HT}} \mathsf{f}(P', \{a\}) \cup R$ for all $R \in \mathcal{C}$.
(F2-) F satisfies **(F2-)** if, for each $\mathsf{f} \in \mathsf{F}$, $P \in \mathcal{C}$, and $a \in \mathcal{A}$: if $P \models_{\mathsf{HT}} r$ and a does not occur in r, then $\mathsf{f}(P, \{a\}) \models_{\mathsf{HT}} r$ for all rules r expressible in $\mathcal{C}$.

---

[7] We use the term *postulate* to follow [27] and ease readability. Technically, they are treated as every other *property*.

(F3) F satisfies **(F3)** if, for each $f \in F$, $P \in C$ and $a \in \mathcal{A}$: $f(P, \{a\})$ does not contain any atoms that are not in P.

(F4) F satisfies **(F4)** if, for each $f \in F$, $P \in C$ and $a \in \mathcal{A}$: if $f(P, \{a\}) \models_{\mathsf{HT}} r$, then $f(\{r'\}, \{a\}) \models_{\mathsf{HT}} r$ for some $r' \in Cn_\mathcal{A}(P)$.

(F5) F satisfies **(F5)** if, for each $f \in F$, $P \in C$ and $a \in \mathcal{A}$: if $f(P, \{a\}) \models_{\mathsf{HT}} A \leftarrow B \cup \neg C \cup \neg\neg D$, then $P \models_{\mathsf{HT}} A \leftarrow B \cup \neg C \cup \{\neg a\} \cup \neg\neg D$.

(F6) F satisfies **(F6)** if, for each $f \in F$, $P \in C$ and $a, b \in \mathcal{A}$: $f(f(P, \{b\}), \{a\}) \equiv_{\mathsf{HT}} f(f(P, \{a\}), \{b\})$.

These postulates represent the following: Forgetting about atom a from HT-equivalent programs preserves HT-equivalence **(F0)**; if a program is an HT-consequence of another program, then forgetting about atom a from both programs preserves this HT-consequence **(F1)**; when forgetting about an atom a, it does not matter whether we add a set of rules over the remaining language before or after forgetting **(F2)**; any consequence of the original program not mentioning atom a is also a consequence of the result of forgetting about a **(F2-)**; the result of forgetting about an atom from a program only contains atoms occurring in the original program **(F3)**; any rule which is a consequence of the result of forgetting about an atom from program P is a consequence of the result of forgetting about that atom from a single rule among the HT-consequences of P **(F4)**; a rule obtained by extending with *not a* the body of a rule which is an HT-consequence of the result of forgetting about an atom a from program P is an HT-consequence of P **(F5)**; and the order is not relevant when sequentially forgetting two atoms **(F6)**. Note that $Cn_\mathcal{A}(P)$ for **(F4)** is defined over the class of programs considered in each operator, and, likewise, that the kind of rules considered in **(F5)** is restricted according to the class of programs considered in a given operator.

Lifting of some of the postulates to the case of forgetting sets of atoms precisely coincides with existing properties, namely **(F0)**, **(F2)**, and **(F2-)** with **(SE)**, **(SI)**, and **(PP)**, resp., hence we will not further consider them. In addition, **(F3)** can also be safely ignored, since the postulate is satisfied already by definition for any class of operators and an extension to forgetting sets of atoms would not affect this.

The remaining are distinct, and thus worth further investigation. We therefore generalize them next, associating each of them with a distinctive name.

(SC) F satisfies *Strong Consequence* if, for each $f \in F$, $P, P' \in C$ and $V \subseteq \mathcal{A}$: if $P \models_{\mathsf{HT}} P'$, then $f(P, V) \models_{\mathsf{HT}} f(P', V)$.

(RC) F satisfies *Rule Consequence* if, for each $f \in F$, $P \in C$ and $V \subseteq \mathcal{A}$: if $f(P, V) \models_{\mathsf{HT}} r$, then $f(\{r'\}, V) \models_{\mathsf{HT}} r$ for some $r' \in Cn_\mathcal{A}(P)$.

(NC) F satisfies *Non-contradictory Consequence* if, for each $f \in F$, $P \in C$ and $V \subseteq \mathcal{A}$: if $f(P, V) \models_{\mathsf{HT}} A \leftarrow B \cup \neg C \cup \neg\neg D$, then $P \models_{\mathsf{HT}} A \leftarrow B \cup \neg C \cup \neg V \cup \neg\neg D$.

(PI) F satisfies *Permutation Invariance* if, for each $f \in F$, $P \in C$, and $V \subseteq \mathcal{A}$: $f(P, V) \equiv_{\mathsf{HT}} f(\ldots f(P, V_1), \ldots, V_n)$ for every partition $\{V_1, \ldots, V_n\}$ of V.

These new properties indeed generalize their corresponding postulates. Furthermore, some are related to properties previously considered.

Proposition 1. *The following relations hold for all* F*:*

1. **(SC)** *implies* **(F1)**;
2. **(RC)** *implies* **(F4)**;
3. **(NC)** *implies* **(F5)**;
4. **(PI)** *implies* **(F6)**;

5. **(W)** *and* **(PP)** *together imply* **(SC)**;
6. **(SC)** *implies* **(SE)**;
7. **(W)** *implies* **(NC)**.

Notably, 5. and 6. of Proposition 1 generalize 5. of Proposition 1 in [34], and **(NC)** is intuitively weaker than **(SC)** by 5. and 7. of Proposition 1.

One might wonder whether the original postulates also imply these novel generalizations, which turns out not to be the case.

Proposition 2. *The converse of each of 1.–4. in Proposition 1 does not hold.*

Thus, these new properties are indeed more general than the original postulates, which, together with the new results established in Proposition 1 on relations between these and the properties studied in [34], already allows us to conclude that they are indeed interesting additions to the overall landscape of properties of forgetting in ASP.

To complete the picture, we show which operators satisfy which of the new properties, which also allows us to clarify that these properties are indeed distinct.

F	sC	wE	SE	W	PP	NP	SI	CP	SP	wC	SC	RC	NC	PI
F_{strong}	×	×	×	✓	×	✓	✓	×	×	×	×	✓	✓	✓
F_{weak}	×	×	×	×	✓	×	✓	×	×	×	×	✓	✓	✓
F_{sem}	✓	✓	×	×	×	×	×	×	×	×	×	×	×	✓
F_S	×	×	✓	✓	✓	✓	×	×	×	×	✓	✓	✓	✓
F_W	✓	✓	✓	×	✓	×	✓	×	×	×	✓	✓	✓	✓
F_{HT}	×	×	✓	✓	✓	✓	✓	×	×	×	✓	✓	✓	✓
F_{SM}	✓	✓	✓	×	✓	×	×	✓	×	✓	×	×	×	✓
F_{Sas}	✓	✓	✓	×	✓	×	✓	✓	✓	✓	×	×	×	×

Fig. 1. Satisfaction of properties for known classes of forgetting operators. For class F and property **P**, '✓' represents that F satisfies **P**, and '×' that F does not satisfy **P**.

Proposition 3. *All results for properties* **(SC)***,* **(RC)***,* **(NC)** *and* **(PI)** *in Fig. 1 hold.*

Thus, **(SC)** is distinct per se, as it provides a unique set of classes of operators of forgetting for which it is satisfied. In particular, unlike the weaker property **(SE)**, F_{SM} and F_{Sas} do not satisfy **(SC)**, most likely because the premise in the condition for satisfying **(SC)** is weaker than that of **(SE)**. Also, **(RC)** turns out to be of interest as no previously studied property is satisfied by precisely the same set of classes of forgetting operators. Moreover, maybe surprisingly, even though

(NC) is implied by the existing property (W), the set of classes of forgetting operators that satisfy it does not coincide with that of the stronger property, which makes (NC) also a property of interest in the context of distinguishing existing classes of forgetting operators. Also, notably, while the properties (RC) and (NC) are different, they turn out to be satisfied by the same set of known operators. We conjecture that this is so because both are closely tied to the concrete definitions of F_S and F_W along which they were introduced. Finally, (PI) is distinct and there is no property considered in [34] which is satisfied by all classes but F_{Sas}.

On closer inspection of which classes of operators satisfy (PI), there seems to exist an inherent incompatibility between this property and F_{Sas}, a class of operators that satisfies (SP). The property (SP) has been argued to be essential for forgetting in ASP inasmuch as it is the one that adequately encodes the required preservation, under forgetting, of all relations between non-forgotten atoms. However, it was shown in [35] that it is not always possible to forget while preserving (SP), shifting the attention to the question of when it is possible to forget.

One consequence of the negative result for F_{Sas} w.r.t. (SP) is that even if it is possible to forget $V \cup V'$, it may not be possible to iteratively forget V and V' in any arbitrary order, which is also why classes such as F_{Sas} cannot satisfy (PI).

Example 1. Take $P = \{p \leftarrow not\, not\, p; a \leftarrow p; b \leftarrow not\, p\}$. Forgetting about b from P first is strongly equivalent to removing the third rule, and subsequently forgetting about p is strongly equivalent to $\{a \leftarrow not\, not\, a\}$. However, forgetting about p from P first while satisfying (SP) is simply not allowed (as shown in [35]). Hence, the order of forgetting matters for F_{Sas}.

However, this raises another important question, which hasn't been addressed before: *If a set of atoms can be forgotten as a whole, is there at least one partition that permits iterative forgetting?* Previous arguments, such as in Example 1, might suggest that there is, but it turns out not to be the case. Before we state it formally, we recall a piece of notation from [35] denoting the restriction of (SP) to a concrete instance: a forgetting operator f over $\mathcal{C}$ satisfies $(SP)_{\langle P,V \rangle}$ if $\mathcal{AS}(f(P,V) \cup R) = \mathcal{AS}(P \cup R)_{\|V}$, for all programs $R \in \mathcal{C}$ with $\mathcal{A}(R) \subseteq \mathcal{A} \setminus V$.

Theorem 1. *Let P be a logic program, $V \subseteq \mathcal{A}$, and f a forgetting operator that satisfies $(SP)_{\langle P,V \rangle}$. There may not exist any V' with $\emptyset \subset V' \subset V$ such that f satisfies $(SP)_{\langle P,V' \rangle}$.*

Hence, even if it is possible to forget a set of atoms, it may be impossible to forget arbitrary proper subsets of it, in particular, there may not exist a partition of V for which it is possible to step-wise iteratively forget the elements of V.

Corollary 1. *Let P be a logic program, $V \subseteq \mathcal{A}$, and f a forgetting operator that satisfies $(SP)_{\langle P,V \rangle}$. There may not exist any partition of V, $\{V_1, \ldots, V_n\}$, $n > 1$, such that f satisfies $(SP)_{\langle f(\ldots f(P,V_1),\ldots,V_{i-1}),V_i \rangle}$, for every $1 < i \leq n$.*

One final note to mention two variants of **(PI)** previously considered in the literature.

The first variant, here named **(PIa)**, was first discussed in [6].

(PIa) F satisfies *Permutation Invariance* if, for each $f \in F$, $P \in \mathcal{C}$, and $\{p_1, \ldots, p_n\} = V \subseteq \mathcal{A}$: $f(P, V) \equiv_{\mathsf{HT}} f(\ldots f(P, \{p_1\}), \ldots, \{p_n\})$.

Maybe not surprisingly, this variant is implied by **(PI)** though not vice-versa, although, together with **(SE)**, even the converse direction holds.

Proposition 4. **(PI)** *implies* **(PIa)**, *and* **(PIa)** *and* **(SE)** *together imply* **(PI)**.

The second variant, here named **(PIb)**, was first discussed in [29].

(PIb) F satisfies *Permutation Invariance* if, for each $f \in F$, $P \in \mathcal{C}$, and $V, V' \subseteq \mathcal{A}$: $f(P, V \cup V') \equiv_{\mathsf{HT}} f(f(P, V), V')$.

Despite appearing less general, it turns out that this variant is equivalent to **(PI)**.

Proposition 5. **(PI)** *is equivalent to* **(PIb)**.

This also shows that our formalization of permutation invariance is indeed well done, as it covers the alternative notions/formalizations existing in the literature.

6   Conclusions

We have studied four new properties of forgetting in ASP (as generalizations of postulates introduced in [27]), to fill a gap in a recent comprehensive guide on properties and classes of operators for forgetting in ASP, and relations between these [34].

Each of the four properties is in fact distinct (even though **(NC)** is implied by an existing property), and no other already existing property is satisfied by precisely the same set of classes of forgetting operators in each of these cases. They are worth being considered for inclusion in the set of relevant properties since not only they would provide further distinguishing criteria for existing classes of operators, as they would help further clarify the relation between properties **(SE)**, **(W)**, and **(PP)** considered before, and even provide additional means to *axiomatically* characterize many classes of forgetting operators.

Finally, **(PI)** is not always satisfied, but it seems that this is solely tied to the incompatibility with the crucial property, **(SP)**. Though not fundamental to distinguish known classes of operators, it helped establishing one of the fundamental results of this paper: that even if it is possible to forget a set of atoms, it may be impossible to step-wise iteratively forget its subsets.

Left open is the investigation of these properties for semantics other than ASP, such as [31] based on the FLP-semantics [42], or [30,43] based on the well-founded semantics, as well as forgetting in the context of hybrid theories

[44–46] and dynamic multi-context systems [47,48], as well as the development of concrete syntactical forgetting operators that can be integrated in reasoning tools such as [49–52].

Acknowledgments. This work was partially supported by Fundação para a Ciência e a Tecnologia (FCT) under UID/CEC/04516/2013, and grants SFRH/BPD/100906/ 2014 (R. Gonçalves) and SFRH/BPD/86970/2012 (M. Knorr).

References

1. Lin, F., Reiter, R.: How to progress a database. Artif. Intell. **92**(1–2), 131–167 (1997)
2. Liu, Y., Wen, X.: On the progression of knowledge in the situation calculus. In: Walsh, T. (ed.) Proceedings of IJCAI, pp. 976–982. IJCAI/AAAI (2011)
3. Rajaratnam, D., Levesque, H.J., Pagnucco, M., Thielscher, M.: Forgetting in action. In: Baral, C., Giacomo, G.D., Eiter, T. (eds.) Proceedings of KR. AAAI Press (2014)
4. Lang, J., Liberatore, P., Marquis, P.: Propositional independence: formula-variable independence and forgetting. J. Artif. Intell. Res. (JAIR) **18**, 391–443 (2003)
5. Zhang, Y., Foo, N.Y.: Solving logic program conflict through strong and weak forgettings. Artif. Intell. **170**(8–9), 739–778 (2006)
6. Eiter, T., Wang, K.: Semantic forgetting in answer set programming. Artif. Intell. **172**(14), 1644–1672 (2008)
7. Lang, J., Marquis, P.: Reasoning under inconsistency: a forgetting-based approach. Artif. Intell. **174**(12–13), 799–823 (2010)
8. Wang, Z., Wang, K., Topor, R.W., Pan, J.Z.: Forgetting for knowledge bases in DL-lite. Ann. Math. Artif. Intell. **58**(1–2), 117–151 (2010)
9. Kontchakov, R., Wolter, F., Zakharyaschev, M.: Logic-based ontology comparison and module extraction, with an application to DL-lite. Artif. Intell. **174**(15), 1093–1141 (2010)
10. Konev, B., Ludwig, M., Walther, D., Wolter, F.: The logical difference for the lightweight description logic EL. J. Artif. Intell. Res. (JAIR) **44**, 633–708 (2012)
11. Konev, B., Lutz, C., Walther, D., Wolter, F.: Model-theoretic inseparability and modularity of description logic ontologies. Artif. Intell. **203**, 66–103 (2013)
12. Lewis, C.I.: A survey of symbolic logic. University of California Press (1918). Republished by Dover (1960)
13. Bledsoe, W.W., Hines, L.M.: Variable elimination and chaining in a resolution-based prover for inequalities. In: Bibel, W., Kowalski, R. (eds.) CADE 1980. LNCS, vol. 87, pp. 70–87. Springer, Heidelberg (1980). doi:10.1007/3-540-10009-1_7
14. Larrosa, J.: Boosting search with variable elimination. In: Dechter, R. (ed.) CP 2000. LNCS, vol. 1894, pp. 291–305. Springer, Heidelberg (2000). doi:10.1007/ 3-540-45349-0_22
15. Larrosa, J., Morancho, E., Niso, D.: On the practical use of variable elimination in constraint optimization problems: 'still-life' as a case study. J. Artif. Intell. Res. (JAIR) **23**, 421–440 (2005)
16. Middeldorp, A., Okui, S., Ida, T.: Lazy narrowing: strong completeness and eager variable elimination. Theor. Comput. Sci. **167**(1&2), 95–130 (1996)
17. Moinard, Y.: Forgetting literals with varying propositional symbols. J. Log. Comput. **17**(5), 955–982 (2007)

18. Weber, A.: Updating propositional formulas. In: Expert Database Conference, pp. 487–500 (1986)
19. Leite, J.: A bird's-eye view of forgetting in answer-set programming. In: Balduccini, M., Janhunen, T. (eds.) LPNMR 2017. LNCS, vol. 10377, pp. 10–22. Springer, Cham (2017). doi:10.1007/978-3-319-61660-5_2
20. Alferes, J.J., Leite, J.A., Pereira, L.M., Przymusinska, H., Przymusinski, T.C.: Dynamic updates of non-monotonic knowledge bases. J. Logic Program. **45**(1–3), 43–70 (2000)
21. Eiter, T., Fink, M., Sabbatini, G., Tompits, H.: On properties of update sequences based on causal rejection. Theory Pract. Logic Program. (TPLP) **2**(6), 721–777 (2002)
22. Sakama, C., Inoue, K.: An abductive framework for computing knowledge base updates. Theory Pract. Logic Program. (TPLP) **3**(6), 671–713 (2003)
23. Slota, M., Leite, J.: Robust equivalence models for semantic updates of answer-set programs. In: Brewka, G., Eiter, T., McIlraith, S.A. (eds.) Proceedings of KR, pp. 158–168. AAAI Press (2012)
24. Slota, M., Leite, J.: A unifying perspective on knowledge updates. In: Cerro, L.F., Herzig, A., Mengin, J. (eds.) JELIA 2012. LNCS, vol. 7519, pp. 372–384. Springer, Heidelberg (2012). doi:10.1007/978-3-642-33353-8_29
25. Delgrande, J.P., Schaub, T., Tompits, H., Woltran, S.: A model-theoretic approach to belief change in answer set programming. ACM Trans. Comput. Log. **14**(2), 14 (2013)
26. Slota, M., Leite, J.: The rise and fall of semantic rule updates based on se-models. TPLP **14**(6), 869–907 (2014)
27. Wong, K.S.: Forgetting in logic programs. Ph.D. thesis, The University of New South Wales (2009)
28. Wang, Y., Zhang, Y., Zhou, Y., Zhang, M.: Forgetting in logic programs under strong equivalence. In: Brewka, G., Eiter, T., McIlraith, S.A. (eds.) Proceedings of KR, pp. 643–647. AAAI Press (2012)
29. Wang, Y., Wang, K., Zhang, M.: Forgetting for answer set programs revisited. In: Rossi, F. (ed.) Proceedings of IJCAI. IJCAI/AAAI (2013)
30. Knorr, M., Alferes, J.J.: Preserving strong equivalence while forgetting. In: Fermé, E., Leite, J. (eds.) JELIA 2014. LNCS, vol. 8761, pp. 412–425. Springer, Cham (2014). doi:10.1007/978-3-319-11558-0_29
31. Wang, Y., Zhang, Y., Zhou, Y., Zhang, M.: Knowledge forgetting in answer set programming. J. Artif. Intell. Res. (JAIR) **50**, 31–70 (2014)
32. Delgrande, J.P., Wang, K.: A syntax-independent approach to forgetting in disjunctive logic programs. In: Bonet, B., Koenig, S. (eds.) Proceedings of AAAI, pp. 1482–1488. AAAI Press (2015)
33. Zhang, Y., Zhou, Y.: Knowledge forgetting: properties and applications. Artif. Intell. **173**(16–17), 1525–1537 (2009)
34. Gonçalves, R., Knorr, M., Leite, J.: The ultimate guide to forgetting in answer set programming. In: Baral, C., Delgrande, J., Wolter, F. (eds.) Proceedings of KR, pp. 135–144. AAAI Press (2016)
35. Gonçalves, R., Knorr, M., Leite, J.: You can't always forget what you want: on the limits of forgetting in answer set programming. In: Fox, M.S., Kaminka, G.A. (eds.) Proceedings of ECAI. IOS Press (2016)
36. Lifschitz, V., Pearce, D., Valverde, A.: Strongly equivalent logic programs. ACM Trans. Comput. Log. **2**(4), 526–541 (2001)
37. Lifschitz, V., Tang, L.R., Turner, H.: Nested expressions in logic programs. Ann. Math. Artif. Intell. **25**(3–4), 369–389 (1999)

38. Cabalar, P., Ferraris, P.: Propositional theories are strongly equivalent to logic programs. TPLP **7**(6), 745–759 (2007)
39. Gelfond, M., Lifschitz, V.: Classical negation in logic programs and disjunctive databases. New Gener. Comput. **9**(3–4), 365–385 (1991)
40. Brass, S., Dix, J.: Semantics of (disjunctive) logic programs based on partial evaluation. J. Log. Program. **40**(1), 1–46 (1999)
41. Turner, H.: Strong equivalence made easy: nested expressions and weight constraints. TPLP **3**(4–5), 609–622 (2003)
42. Truszczynski, M.: Reducts of propositional theories, satisfiability relations, and generalizations of semantics of logic programs. Artif. Intell. **174**(16–17), 1285–1306 (2010)
43. Alferes, J.J., Knorr, M., Wang, K.: Forgetting under the well-founded semantics. In: Cabalar, P., Son, T.C. (eds.) LPNMR 2013. LNCS, vol. 8148, pp. 36–41. Springer, Heidelberg (2013). doi:10.1007/978-3-642-40564-8_4
44. Knorr, M., Alferes, J.J., Hitzler, P.: Local closed world reasoning with description logics under the well-founded semantics. Artif. Intell. **175**(9–10), 1528–1554 (2011)
45. Gonçalves, R., Alferes, J.J.: Parametrized logic programming. In: Janhunen, T., Niemelä, I. (eds.) JELIA 2010. LNCS, vol. 6341, pp. 182–194. Springer, Heidelberg (2010). doi:10.1007/978-3-642-15675-5_17
46. Slota, M., Leite, J., Swift, T.: On updates of hybrid knowledge bases composed of ontologies and rules. Artif. Intell. **229**, 33–104 (2015)
47. Gonçalves, R., Knorr, M., Leite, J.: Evolving multi-context systems. In: Schaub, T., Friedrich, G., O'Sullivan, B. (eds.) Proceedings of ECAI, pp. 375–380. IOS Press (2014)
48. Brewka, G., Ellmauthaler, S., Pührer, J.: Multi-context systems for reactive reasoning in dynamic environments. In: Schaub, T., Friedrich, G., O'Sullivan, B. (eds.) Proceedings of ECAI, pp. 159–164. IOS Press (2014)
49. Gebser, M., Kaufmann, B., Kaminski, R., Ostrowski, M., Schaub, T., Schneider, M.T.: Potassco: the Potsdam answer set solving collection. AI Commun. **24**(2), 107–124 (2011)
50. Ivanov, V., Knorr, M., Leite, J.: A query tool for $\mathcal{EL}$ with non-monotonic rules. In: Alani, H., et al. (eds.) ISWC 2013. LNCS, vol. 8218, pp. 216–231. Springer, Heidelberg (2013). doi:10.1007/978-3-642-41335-3_14
51. Costa, N., Knorr, M., Leite, J.: Next step for NoHR: OWL 2 QL. In: Arenas, M., et al. (eds.) ISWC 2015. LNCS, vol. 9366, pp. 569–586. Springer, Cham (2015). doi:10.1007/978-3-319-25007-6_33
52. Lopes, C., Knorr, M., Leite, J.: NoHR: integrating XSB Prolog with the OWL 2 profiles and beyond. In: Balduccini, M., Janhunen, T. (eds.) LPNMR 2017. LNCS, vol. 10377, pp. 236–249. Springer, Cham (2017). doi:10.1007/978-3-319-61660-5_22

Logic-Based Encodings for Ricochet Robots

Filipe Gouveia, Pedro T. Monteiro, Vasco Manquinho, and Inês Lynce[(⊠)]

INESC-ID/Instituto Superior Técnico, Universidade de Lisboa, Lisbon, Portugal
{filipe.gouveia,pedro.tiago.monteiro,vasco.manquinho,
ines.lynce}@tecnico.ulisboa.pt

Abstract. Studying the performance of logic tools on solving a specific problem can bring new insights on the use of different paradigms. This paper provides an empirical evaluation of logic-based encodings for a well known board game: Ricochet Robots. Ricochet Robots is a board game where the goal is to find the smallest number of moves needed for one robot to move from the initial position to a target position, while taking into account the existing barriers and other robots. Finding a solution to the Ricochet Robots problem is NP-hard. In this work we develop logic-based encodings for the Ricochet Robots problem to feed into Boolean Satisfiability (SAT) solvers. When appropriate, advanced techniques are applied to further boost the performance of a solver. A comparison between the performance of SAT solvers and an existing ASP solution clearly shows that SAT is by far the more adequate technology to solve the Ricochet Robots problem.

Keywords: Ricochet Robots · Encodings · Boolean Satisfiability · Answer Set Programming

1 Introduction

Puzzles play a key role in artificial intelligence. N-queens problem, towers of Hanoi, Sudoku and Traveling Salesman Person (TSP) are only a few examples of puzzles which are commonly used to motivate and illustrate the use of artificial intelligence in problem solving [21]. Despite not being real problems, solving such puzzles has represented a landmark in the history of artificial intelligence. A recent example is the successful case of solving the GO game. Amazingly, some years ago GO was mentioned in textbooks (e.g. [21]) as an example of a game that was simple for humans and difficult for machines to solve.

Ricochet Robots is another example of such puzzles. Ricochet Robots is a simple board game where the goal is to find the smallest number of moves for a robot to move from its initial position to some target position on the board. Allowed movements are peculiar in the sense that the robot has to be stopped to stay at a given position. A robot movement is stopped either due to a barrier

This work was partially supported by national funds through Fundação para a Ciência e a Tecnologia (FCT) with reference UID/CEC/50021/2013.

E. Oliveira et al. (Eds.): EPIA 2017, LNAI 10423, pp. 657–669, 2017.
DOI: 10.1007/978-3-319-65340-2_54

or due to another robot. What makes the Ricochet Robots game particularly interesting is the fact that it is easy for a human expert to find a solution, although it is very hard to find the best solution, i.e., the solution with as few moves as possible [6]. Finding a solution is an NP-hard problem [10].

The main contribution of this work is a set of logic-based encodings for solving Ricochet Robots. The encodings were carefully designed to achieve a good performance using logic tools, namely Boolean Satisfiability (SAT) tools. Specialized techniques have been used to further boost the efficiency of the solvers. The developed encodings are compared against recent successful solutions [12,13] encoding the problem into Answer Set Programming (ASP) [4]. Experimental results are clear: SAT is more competitive than ASP in this context.

This paper is organized as follows. Section 2 introduces Ricochet Robots. Logic-based encodings are described in Sect. 3. Experimental results are then presented in Sect. 4. Section 5 discusses other logic-based encodings and Sect. 6 concludes the paper and mentions future work.

2   Ricochet Robots

The *Ricochet Robots* board game, also known as *Rasende Roboter* or *Randolph's Robots*, was designed by Alex Randolph in Germany in 1999 [6]. The success of this game is testified by the possibility of playing Ricochet Robots online or even on your mobile.

The original board game is played by two or more players on a 16 × 16 grid. Each position of the board can have a barrier at the upper, bottom, left or right border. The board is limited by barriers all around it, *i.e.*, each position of the top row has a barrier on the top border, and analogous for the bottom row, and the leftmost and rightmost columns. In the original board game, the four positions in the middle of the board are inaccessible and surrounded by barriers. Figure 1 illustrates a Ricochet Robots board with some barriers placed and the four positions in the middle surrounded by barriers, and therefore inaccessible.

In addition to the 16 × 16 grid board, the Ricochet Robots game is composed by four robots of different colors. At the start of the game, the four robots are placed randomly on the board, such that:

- each position cannot have more than one robot;
- there are no robots in the four middle (inaccessible) positions.

A target is also placed randomly on the board, except in any of the four center positions. The color of the target corresponds to the color of one of the robots.

The goal of the game is to move any number of robots, one at a time, so that at the end the robot with the target color is on the target position. A player must place the robot in the target position with as few moves as possible. The player wins as many points as the number of moves used. Another target is randomly selected and another round with other player begins. At the end of the game, the player with fewest points wins.

The robots can move on the board with the following rules:

– A robot can move in any of the four directions (up, down, left, right);
– Once a robot moves, it **only** stops when it reaches: (i) a barrier or (ii) another robot.

Take for example the board in Fig. 1. If the blue robot moves up, then it stops in the position (12, 0) - row 12, column 0 - counting as a single move.

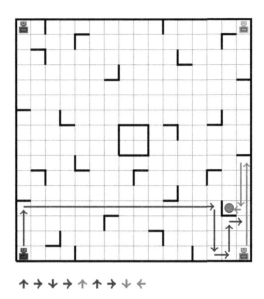

Fig. 1. 16 × 16 Ricochet Robots board. A solution is presented at the bottom. (Color figure online)

Figure 1 illustrates the minimum number of moves so that the green robot reaches the green target. In this case, 9 moves are required. Notice that in the fourth movement (blue robot going right), the blue robot stops in the position (15, 14) because the green robot in the position (15, 15) is blocking further movements.

3   Encodings of the Ricochet Robots

We start with a base model for the Ricochet Robots problem, followed by the description of a Boolean encoding for the problem.

3.1   Base Model

The Ricochet Robots board, described in Sect. 2, can be represented by a graph where each board position is a vertex. Each two adjacent positions are connected

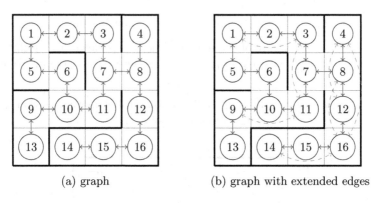

(a) graph   (b) graph with extended edges

Fig. 2. 4 × 4 board (Color figure online)

by an edge as long as there is no barrier between them. Figure 2a illustrates the graph representation of a 4 × 4 board.

Remember that a robot moves in a given direction until it reaches a barrier or another robot. The concept of extended edges is introduced taking this information into account. For each position and for each direction (vertical and horizontal), an edge to other positions in the same row or column is added if and only if there is no barrier between the two positions.

Figure 2b presents the board graph from Fig. 2a where extended edges, marked in dashed red, are added. For example, there is an extended edge connecting vertexes 1 and 3 (same row) since there are no barriers in the path between them. However, there is no extended edge between vertexes 2 and 10 (same column) due to the existence of the barrier between vertexes 2 and 6.

3.2   Boolean Encoding

We assume that a problem is encoded using the conjunctive normal form (CNF). A CNF formula is a conjunction (∧) of clauses, where a clause is a disjunction (∨) of literals and a literal is a Boolean variable (positive literal) or its negation (negative literal). A formula is said to be satisfied if all of its clauses are satisfied. A clause is satisfied if at least one of its literals is assigned value `true`. A positive (negative) literal is assigned value `true` if the corresponding variable is assigned value `true` (`false`); otherwise it is assigned value `false` (`true`). The SAT problem is to decide whether there exists an assignment to the variables of a CNF formula that satisfies the formula.

The proposed Boolean encoding for the Ricochet Robots problem follows the SAT encoding for the Cooperative Path-Finding (CPF) problem [24]. The CPF problem is very similar to the Ricochet Robots problem, differing only on the rules of movement. In the Ricochet Robots problem each robot movement corresponds to a displacement over one or more positions, only stopped either by a barrier or another robot, whereas in the CPF problem each movement corresponds to a move to an adjacent empty position.

Consider a $d \times d$ board and $G = (V, E)$ the graph representing the board where $V = \{v_1, v_2, \ldots, v_n\}$ is the set of $n = d \times d$ vertexes and E is the set of extended edges defined in Subsect. 3.1. In addition, consider $R = \{r_1, r_2, \ldots, r_\mu\}$ the set of μ robots and η the number of time steps required to achieve the goal, with $\mu, \eta \in \mathbb{N}$.

A Boolean encoding for the Ricochet Robots consists of the following propositional variables:

- $X_{j,k}^t$ with $0 \leq t \leq \eta$, $1 \leq j \leq n$ and $1 \leq k \leq \mu$. $X_{j,k}^t$ is **true** if and only if robot r_k is in position v_j at time step t.
- $Poss_{j,l}^t$ for every $0 \leq t \leq \eta - 1$ and $(v_j, v_l) \in E$. $Poss_{j,l}^t$ is **true** if it is possible to move from vertex v_j to vertex v_l at time step t. A move is possible if the path from vertex v_j to vertex v_l is clear, i.e. there are neither barriers nor robots in the path between the two vertexes and the vertex v_l is a limit when coming from vertex v_j, i.e., v_l is proceeded by a barrier or another robot considering the direction from v_j to v_l.
- M_k^t with $0 \leq t \leq \eta - 1$ and $1 \leq k \leq \mu$. M_k^t is **true** if and only if robot r_k moved at time step t.

For the sake of clarity, in what follows the concepts of position in the board and vertex in the graph are used indistinctly.

The encoding starts by encoding the facts representing the initial state of the board. For each robot r_k, a clause with one literal $X_{j,k}^0$ is added if the robot is placed in vertex v_j at the initial state. The goal state is also encoded with a clause with one literal. The clause $X_{j,k}^\eta$ is added if the goal is to have robot r_k in vertex v_j.

The following clauses are also added to the CNF formula[1]:

- A robot is placed in exactly one vertex at each time step. This is encoded with at least one and at most one constraints, respectively:
  (a) A robot must be in one vertex at each time step

$$\bigvee_{j=1}^{n} X_{j,k}^t \tag{1}$$

for every time step $0 \leq t \leq \eta$ and for each robot $r_k, 1 \leq k \leq \mu$.
  (b) A robot cannot be in two vertexes at the same time step

$$\bigwedge_{j=1}^{n} \bigwedge_{l=j+1}^{n} \neg X_{j,k}^t \vee \neg X_{l,k}^t \tag{2}$$

for every time step $0 \leq t \leq \eta$ and for each robot $r_k, 1 \leq k \leq \mu$.

---

[1] For the sake of clarity, some of the clauses are not written in CNF. In any case, the translation to CNF is trivial.

- A robot either stays in the same vertex v_l or comes from a vertex v_j, such that $(v_j, v_l) \in E$, from which a movement is possible

$$X_{l,k}^{t+1} \implies X_{l,k}^t \vee \bigvee (X_{j,k}^t \wedge Poss_{j,l}^t \wedge M_k^t) \tag{3}$$

for every time step $0 \le t \le \eta - 1$, for each robot $r_k, 1 \le k \le \mu$, for every edge $(v_j, v_l) \in E$.
- Given an edge $(v_j, v_l) \in E$, a path between vertexes v_j and v_l is clear if and only if there are no robots in any of the vertexes comprised between the source vertex v_j and the destination vertex v_l.

$$Poss_{j,l}^t \implies \bigwedge_{h \in p(j,l)} \bigwedge_{k=1}^{\mu} \neg X_{h,k}^t \tag{4}$$

for every time step $0 \le t \le \eta - 1$ and for every edge $(v_j, v_l) \in E$. Remember that $p(j,l)$ denotes the set of vertexes in the path from v_j and v_l.
- A vertex is a *stop* vertex for a given direction if there is a robot in the following vertex

$$Poss_{j,l}^t \implies \bigvee_{k=1}^{\mu} X_{m,k}^t \tag{5}$$

for every time step $0 \le t \le \eta - 1$ and for each $(v_j, v_l) \in E$, where v_m represents the next vertex adjacent to v_l considering the direction from v_j to v_l.
- Only one robot can move at each time step

$$\bigwedge_{k=1}^{\mu} \bigwedge_{h=k+1}^{\mu} \neg M_k^t \vee \neg M_h^t \tag{6}$$

for every time step $0 \le t \le \eta - 1$;

Constraint (5) is only applied if the target position of the movement is not a natural stop vertex, *i.e.*, if it is not a vertex followed by either a barrier or the end of the board.

Observe that (2) and (6) specify at most one constraints on robot locations or movements. In this paper, the pairwise encoding is used for encoding at most one cardinality constraints, since the board dimensions are small. Nevertheless, other encodings [1,7,11,16,17,20] could also be used.

The goal of the Ricochet Robots problem is to move a given robot from its initial position to the target position with the minimum number of moves.

The encoding proposed allows to check if a solution exists for a given time step limit. However, it is possible to obtain an optimal solution for this problem using this encoding following an iterative approach.

Iterative Approach. This approach consists in iteratively using a SAT solver to solve successive instances limited to a given time step η. One possible strategy is to start by considering $\eta = 0$, and whenever the resulting instance is unsatisfiable, increase η by 1. This process is repeated until a satisfiable instance is found. The solution to the satisfiable instance is clearly an optimal solution of the problem. Observe that this strategy follows an UNSAT-SAT linear search on the value of the optimal solution.

It is known that most of the optimum solutions for the Ricochet Robots problem, from the benchmark used by Gebser *et al.* [12], have at most 20 time steps. Hence, a different strategy to solve the problem is to first encode an instance considering $\eta = 20$ (or another large value where a solution is conceivably to be found). In this case, whenever the generated encoding is satisfiable, η is decreased by 1. The process is repeated until an unsatisfiable instance is found, thus proving that the last satisfiable solution is also an optimal solution to the problem. This strategy follows a SAT-UNSAT linear search on the value of the optimal solution.

If an initial upper bound can be defined, another iterative strategy would be to use a binary search, considering 0 time steps as a lower bound and 20 (or another conceivable value) as an upper bound. In this case, we can first consider $\eta = 10$. If the instance is satisfiable, then 10 is the new upper bound and update η to 5. Otherwise, if the instance is unsatisfiable, then 11 is the new lower bound and update η to 15. The binary search continues by updating η to the average value between the lower and upper bound. The optimal solution has been found when the lower bound is equal to the upper bound.

It might occur that the initial value for the upper bound in the binary search or the linear SAT-UNSAT might not result in a satisfiable instance. In this case, one can define a new upper bound (*e.g.* considering 20 more steps) and apply the same strategy.

4   Experimental Evaluation

In this section, we compare the proposed SAT encoding with the Advanced ASP encoding described in [12][2].

The experimental evaluation was performed using the 256 benchmark instances used by Gebser *et al.* [12]. These benchmarks are based on an authentic 16×16 Ricochet Robots board. In the initial state of the board, each of the four robots is placed on one of the four corners. The instances of the problem were generated by placing the target on each of the 256 possible positions. The target is to be reached always by the same robot. The experiments were run on a Linux machine with Intel Xeon CPU E5-2630 v2 2.60 GHz processors, considering a time limit of 600 s.

We consider the optimization problem of finding the optimum solution for a Ricochet Robots problem instance. For the ASP encoding, *gringo 3.0.5* [15] was used as the grounder and *clasp 3.1.4* [14] was used as the ASP solver[3]. For the

---

[2] This encoding is available from https://potassco.org/doc/apps/2016/09/20/ricochet-robots.html. Note that the more recent encoding described in [13] is not publicly available.

[3] http://potassco.sourceforge.net/.

incremental approach of the ASP encoding we used *iclingo 3.0.5*. For the SAT encoding, *glucose 4.0*[4] [3] was used.

For the optimization problem, the iterative algorithms described in Sect. 3.2 were implemented on top of the *glucose 4.0* SAT solver. Moreover, for each of the three iterative approaches (linear SAT-UNSAT, linear UNSAT-SAT and binary search), we considered both non-incremental and incremental implementations.

In the non-incremental implementations, the SAT solver is rebuilt at each iteration of the algorithm. On the other hand, in the incremental implementations the SAT solver is never rebuilt from scratch at each SAT call, thus allowing to reuse the learned clauses and other information from previous iterations. This can be achieved by using an assumption-based approach [2,9] that has proved to be effective in several domains [18,22,23].

In incremental implementations, a SAT formula ϕ is built considering an initial limit of ν time steps. In our case, we considered $\nu = 20$. Next, depending on the iterative algorithm being used, for each SAT call on ϕ, a set of assumption literals is defined such that it limits the allowed number of time steps for that specific call. If the number of allowed time steps is η for a board with μ robots, then literals $\neg M_k^t$ (with $\eta \leq t \leq \nu - 1$ and $1 \leq k \leq \mu$) are added as assumptions to the SAT solver call on ϕ. Observe that assumption literals are not unit clauses. Hence, at each SAT call we are only testing if ϕ can be satisfied by assuming that no robot can move beyond η time steps. As a result, the working formula of the optimization algorithm does not have to be rebuilt between iterations.

Table 1 shows the average run time for the solved optimization problem instances, as well as the number of timeouts considering a time limit of 600 s. First, results clearly show that SAT-based approaches outperform the ASP encodings for the tested instances of the Ricochet Robot problem, since all SAT encodings are able to optimally solve a larger set of instances. Moreover, the incremental algorithms also outperform the non-incremental, on both the number of solved instances and the average time spent on solving each instance.

Table 1. Average time (in seconds) of solved optimization instances.

	Time (s)	#Timeouts
ASP advanced optimization	59,34	81
ASP advanced incremental	41,84	79
SAT using binary search	108,37	51
SAT using incremental binary search	56,79	50
SAT using incremental linear search (UNSAT-SAT)	57,43	54
SAT using incremental linear search (SAT-UNSAT)	66,27	45

Figure 3 sheds more light on the data given in Table 1. For each one of the different approaches, represented by a different line, the CPU times used for

---

[4] http://www.labri.fr/perso/lsimon/glucose/.

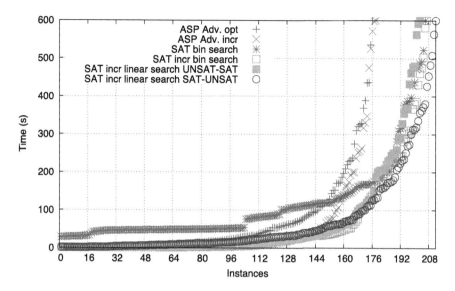

Fig. 3. Time comparison (in seconds) between ASP Advanced encodings and SAT encoding for optimization instances.

solving each of the problem instances are sorted and plotted in the graph. At the end, one has a clear picture of how many instances are solved by each approach for a given CPU time limit. Not only the SAT-based encoding is more effective, but also the incremental approaches are able to solve a larger number of problem instances. Observe that the non-incremental SAT-based binary search algorithm has a more significant overhead, but it is still a more robust approach than using ASP encodings.

Finally, it was observed that the binary search algorithm performs fewer SAT calls than the linear SAT-UNSAT algorithm. However, the time spent in each SAT call was larger. This might result from the fact that, in two consecutive iterations of the binary search algorithm, the set of assumptions has more changes since the time step limit can vary (increase or decrease) more than 1. Hence, the reuse of the previous SAT call context does not seem to be as useful in a binary search approach as when performing a linear SAT-UNSAT algorithm.

5   Other Logic-Based Encodings

The success of using SAT and ASP for solving the Ricochet Robots problem suggests the use of other logic-based tools as the next natural step. We have explored the use of Satisfiability Modulo Theories (SMT) and Constraint Programming (CP) for solving this problem. However, experimental results show that all of these encodings perform worse than ASP and SAT encodings in terms of CPU time. One can argue that these encodings can still be improved, but enough time has been invested for one to say that there should not be a straightforward SMT or CP encoding performing better than SAT or ASP encodings.

The SMT encoding developed for solving the Ricochet Robots problem corresponds to the implementation of the SAT encoding. Other SMT encodings have been tried, but at the end the SAT-like encoding was the best performing encoding. The experiments were run using $z3$ 4.5[5] [8] as the SMT solver. Incremental implementations of the Boolean encoding presented were also developed on top of the $z3$ SMT solver, similarly to the SAT approaches. Experimental results have shown that the SMT approaches solve fewer instances than the corresponding ASP (and SAT) approaches, and also have greater average times for solved instances.

The proposed CP encoding for solving the Ricochet Robots problem considers the CP language used by MiniZinc [19]. Experiments were run using *MiniZinc* $2.1.0$[6] [19] with the Gecode solver provided. Experimental results have shown that the CP approaches solve 4 to 5 times fewer instances than the SAT and ASP approaches. These results are consistent with the results obtained by Barták *et al.* [5] on a problem with similarities to the Ricochet Robots problem. The results show that CP solves far less instances than SAT, despite the instances solved by CP requiring less CPU time. In what follows, the CP encoding is described with more detail.

The CP encoding builds upon a set of integer variables. The input consists of the dimension of the board, the list of robots, the robots initial positions and goals, the list of barriers of the board and the number of time steps. The positions of the board are represented by 2 integers, one representing the line and another representing the column of the board. For each position, four variables are defined, with either value 1 or 0, representing the barriers. The four variables represent the north, south, east, and west directions and have value 1 if the position has a barrier in the corresponding direction and 0 otherwise.

Besides the variables that define the problem instance and, are therefore given as input, two sets of variables are also defined in order to have a solution for the problem. These variables are called *decision variables*. For each robot and for each time step, two variables with integer values are defined, representing the position of each robot at each time step. Similarly to the previous encoding presented, for each robot, and for each time step, a variable with value 0 or 1 is defined representing if either the robot is moving (1) or not (0) in that time step. The constraints of the problem encoding in CSP are:

- The position of a robot at time step 0 must be the initial position of the robot;
- The position of a robot at the limit time step must be the goal position, if that robot has a goal;
- At most one robot moves at each time step;
- If a robot does not move then it stays in the same position;
- If a robot moves, it moves to a valid position;
- If no robot moves in a given time step, then no robot moves in the next time step.

---

[5] https://github.com/Z3Prover/z3.

[6] http://www.minizinc.org/index.html.

Similarly to CP encoding of a similar problem [5] we found convenient to use an auxiliary predicate, valid_movement, to define if a robot moves to a valid position. The predicate valid_movement is defined according to the rules of the game, *i.e.*, it is a valid movement if the following rules are satisfied:

- The robot moves to a position on the same row or column;
- There are no robots nor barriers in the path between the initial position and the target position of the movement;
- There is a barrier on the target position considering the direction of the movement or there is a robot in the next position of the target position considering the direction of the movement.

Finally, iterative implementations were developed for the linear searches and binary search on top of the CP encoding. Moreover, the minimization native approach was considered in the experiments.

6 Conclusions and Future Work

Puzzles are common challenges in AI. Apart from their recreational interest, puzzles provide a testbed for the use and comparison of different techniques in problem solving. In this paper, new logic-based encodings for the Ricochet Robots problem are proposed. These encodings are given to SAT solvers using different algorithmic implementations such as binary search, linear search and incrementality. The new proposed encodings allowed to solve a larger set of problem instances than the previously proposed ASP encodings.

Despite clear improvements on previously proposed encodings, the use of a MaxSAT approach is yet to be fully explored, as well as the use of planning tools. Another direction will consider extending the current encodings (and the lessons learned from its development) to similar problems.

References

1. Ansótegui, C., Manyà, F.: Mapping problems with finite-domain variables into problems with Boolean variables. In: International Conference on Theory and Applications of Satisfiability Testing, pp. 1–15 (2004)
2. Audemard, G., Lagniez, J.-M., Simon, L.: Improving glucose for incremental SAT solving with assumptions: application to MUS extraction. In: Järvisalo, M., Van Gelder, A. (eds.) SAT 2013. LNCS, vol. 7962, pp. 309–317. Springer, Heidelberg (2013). doi:10.1007/978-3-642-39071-5_23
3. Audemard, G., Simon, L.: Lazy clause exchange policy for parallel SAT solvers. In: Sinz, C., Egly, U. (eds.) SAT 2014. LNCS, vol. 8561, pp. 197–205. Springer, Cham (2014). doi:10.1007/978-3-319-09284-3_15
4. Baral, C.: Knowledge Representation, Reasoning and Declarative Problem Solving. Cambridge University Press, Cambridge (2003)
5. Barták, R., Dovier, A., Zhou, N.F.: Multiple-origin-multiple-destination path finding with minimal arc usage: complexity and models. In: International Conference on Tools with Artificial Intelligence (ICTAI), pp. 91–97. IEEE (2016)

6. Butko, N., Lehmann, K.A., Ramenzoni, V.: Ricochet robots-a case study for human complex problem solving. Project thesis from the Complex System Summer School, Santa Fe Institute (2006)
7. Chen, J.: A new SAT encoding of the at-most-one constraint. In: International Workshop on Modelling and Reformulating Constraint Satisfaction Problems (2010)
8. Moura, L., Bjørner, N.: Z3: an efficient SMT solver. In: Ramakrishnan, C.R., Rehof, J. (eds.) TACAS 2008. LNCS, vol. 4963, pp. 337–340. Springer, Heidelberg (2008). doi:10.1007/978-3-540-78800-3_24
9. Eén, N., Sörensson, N.: An extensible SAT-solver. In: Giunchiglia, E., Tacchella, A. (eds.) SAT 2003. LNCS, vol. 2919, pp. 502–518. Springer, Heidelberg (2004). doi:10.1007/978-3-540-24605-3_37
10. Engels, B., Kamphans, T.: Randolphs robot game is NP-hard!. Electron. Notes Discret. Math. **25**, 49–53 (2006)
11. Frisch, A.M., Peugniez, T.J., Doggett, A.J., Nightingale, P.: Solving non-Boolean satisfiability problems with stochastic local search: a comparison of encodings. J. Autom. Reason. **35**(1–3), 143–179 (2005)
12. Gebser, M., Jost, H., Kaminski, R., Obermeier, P., Sabuncu, O., Schaub, T., Schneider, M.: Ricochet robots: a transverse ASP benchmark. In: Cabalar, P., Son, T.C. (eds.) LPNMR 2013. LNCS, vol. 8148, pp. 348–360. Springer, Heidelberg (2013). doi:10.1007/978-3-642-40564-8_35
13. Gebser, M., Kaminski, R., Obermeier, P., Schaub, T.: Ricochet Robots reloaded: a case-study in multi-shot ASP solving. In: Eiter, T., Strass, H., Truszczyński, M., Woltran, S. (eds.) Advances in Knowledge Representation, Logic Programming, and Abstract Argumentation. LNCS, vol. 9060, pp. 17–32. Springer, Cham (2015). doi:10.1007/978-3-319-14726-0_2
14. Gebser, M., Kaufmann, B., Neumann, A., Schaub, T.: clasp: a conflict-driven answer set solver. In: Baral, C., Brewka, G., Schlipf, J. (eds.) LPNMR 2007. LNCS, vol. 4483, pp. 260–265. Springer, Heidelberg (2007). doi:10.1007/978-3-540-72200-7_23
15. Gebser, M., Schaub, T., Thiele, S.: GrinGo: a new grounder for answer set programming. In: Baral, C., Brewka, G., Schlipf, J. (eds.) LPNMR 2007. LNCS, vol. 4483, pp. 266–271. Springer, Heidelberg (2007). doi:10.1007/978-3-540-72200-7_24
16. Gent, I.P., Nightingale, P.: A new encoding of All different into SAT. In: International Workshop on Modelling and Reformulating Constraint Satisfaction Problems (2004)
17. Klieber, W., Kwon, G.: Efficient CNF encoding for selecting 1 from N objects. In: International Workshop on Constraints in Formal Verification (2007)
18. Martins, R., Joshi, S., Manquinho, V., Lynce, I.: Incremental cardinality constraints for MaxSAT. In: O'Sullivan, B. (ed.) CP 2014. LNCS, vol. 8656, pp. 531–548. Springer, Cham (2014). doi:10.1007/978-3-319-10428-7_39
19. Nethercote, N., Stuckey, P.J., Becket, R., Brand, S., Duck, G.J., Tack, G.: MiniZinc: towards a standard CP modelling language. In: Bessière, C. (ed.) CP 2007. LNCS, vol. 4741, pp. 529–543. Springer, Heidelberg (2007). doi:10.1007/978-3-540-74970-7_38
20. Prestwich, S.: Variable dependency in local search: prevention is better than cure. In: Marques-Silva, J., Sakallah, K.A. (eds.) SAT 2007. LNCS, vol. 4501, pp. 107–120. Springer, Heidelberg (2007). doi:10.1007/978-3-540-72788-0_14
21. Russell, S.J., Norvig, P.: Artificial Intelligence - A Modern Approach, 3rd edn. Pearson Education, London (2010)

22. Sharma, A., Sharma, D.: An incremental approach to solving dynamic constraint satisfaction problems. In: Huang, T., Zeng, Z., Li, C., Leung, C.S. (eds.) ICONIP 2012. LNCS, vol. 7665, pp. 445–455. Springer, Heidelberg (2012). doi:10.1007/978-3-642-34487-9_54

23. Shtrichman, O.: Pruning techniques for the SAT-based bounded model checking problem. In: Margaria, T., Melham, T. (eds.) CHARME 2001. LNCS, vol. 2144, pp. 58–70. Springer, Heidelberg (2001). doi:10.1007/3-540-44798-9_4

24. Surynek, P.: Simple direct propositional encoding of cooperative path finding simplified yet more. In: Gelbukh, A., Espinoza, F.C., Galicia-Haro, S.N. (eds.) MICAI 2014. LNCS, vol. 8857, pp. 410–425. Springer, Cham (2014). doi:10.1007/978-3-319-13650-9_36

An Achilles' Heel of Term-Resolution

Mikoláš Janota[1][(✉)] and Joao Marques-Silva[2]

[1] IST/INESC-ID, Lisbon, Portugal
mikolas.janota@gmail.com
[2] LaSIGE, Faculty of Science, University of Lisbon, Lisbon, Portugal

Abstract. Term-resolution provides an elegant mechanism to prove that a quantified Boolean formula (QBF) is true. It is a dual to Q-resolution and is practically highly important as it enables certifying answers of DPLL-based QBF solvers. While term-resolution and Q-resolution are very similar, they are not completely symmetrical. In particular, Q-resolution operates on clauses and term-resolution operates on models of the matrix. This paper investigates the impact of this asymmetry. We will see that there is a large class of formulas (formulas with "big models") whose term-resolution proofs are exponential. As a possible remedy, the paper suggests to prove true QBFs by refuting their negation (*negate-refute*), rather than proving them by term-resolution. The paper shows that from the theoretical perspective this is indeed a favorable approach. In particular, negation-refutation p-simulates term-resolution and there is an exponential separation between the two calculi. These observations further our understanding of proof systems for QBFs and provide a strong theoretical underpinning for the effort towards non-CNF QBF solvers.

1 Introduction

Arguably, the interest of computer scientists in proof complexity begins with the seminal work of Cook and Reckhow who showed a relation between proof complexity and the question NP vs. co-NP [8]. This interest was further fueled by the practical success of programs for automated reasoning, such as *SMT solvers* or *SAT solvers*. Machine-verifiable proofs serve as *certificates* for such solvers. It is important that a solver can produce a certificate of its answer as the solver itself can contain bugs [6,24]. Moreover, proofs have turned out to be important artifacts for further computations, like invariant inference for example [18]. This paper follows this line of research, i.e. proof complexity and solver complication certification, with the focus on *quantified Boolean formula* (QBF). In particular, it focuses on QBFs whose propositional part is in *conjunctive normal form* (QCNF). QCNF is complete and widely popular input for QBF solvers due to its susceptibility to simple representation inside the solver.

A number of QCNF solvers take inspiration in the approach that turned out to be so successful for SAT; and that is *conflict driven clause learning* (CDCL) [17,20,21]. Since *propositional resolution* is the underlying proof principle used in SAT, an analogous proof system was developed for QCNF. In

© Springer International Publishing AG 2017
E. Oliveira et al. (Eds.): EPIA 2017, LNAI 10423, pp. 670–680, 2017.
DOI: 10.1007/978-3-319-65340-2_55

particular, *Q-resolution* [14] for false formulas, and *term-resolution* [10] for true formulas. It has been shown that CDCL-based QBF solvers [27] can be certified by these two proof systems [10]. Recently, several proof complexity analyses of Q-resolution were published. A separation result for Q-resolution and a sequent calculus by Krajíček and Pudlák [16] is shown by Egly [9]; Van Gelder shows that enabling resolution on universal-variables in Q-resolution proofs gives an exponential advantage to Q-resolution [25]. The relation between Q-resolution and expansion-based systems was investigated by Beyersdorff et al. [5]. A number of variants of Q-resolution have been considered [3]. Proof systems for QBF were also investigated in the context of preprocessing [12].

This paper brings the focus to term-resolution. While term-resolution is an elegant system because it provides a dual to Q-resolution, the two types of resolution are not perfectly symmetric. This is because Q-resolution can operate on the given clauses but term-resolution operates on the satisfying assignments of those clauses. This paper shows that this difference exposes an Achilles' heel of term-resolution.

The first result of this paper is that it shows that term-resolution proofs are large for QCNFs whose propositional part have models with a large number of universal literals. More precisely, if each model has at least k universal literals, any term-resolution proof has at least 2^k nodes. Subsequently, the paper investigates an alternative route to term-resolution and that is *refuting the negation* of the formula. The paper shows that any term-resolution proof can be translated to a negation-refutation in polynomial time. On a particular formula Ψ we show an exponential separation between negation-refutation and term-resolution, i.e. all term-resolution proofs of Ψ are exponential but there is a Q-resolution proof of $\neg\Psi$ that is polynomial.

These results have direct practical implications for QBF solving because term-resolution enables certifying DPLL-based QBF solvers. Consequently, a formula whose term-resolution proofs are exponential, will require exponential time to *solve*. These theoretical results further substantiate an observation already made in the QBF community and that is that QBF with propositional part in CNF are particularly harmful for solving [2,26].

2   Preliminaries

A *literal* is a Boolean variable or its negation. For a literal l, we write $\bar{l}$ to denote the literal *complementary* to l, i.e. $\bar{x} = \neg x$, $\overline{\neg x} = x$. A *clause* is a disjunction of finitely many literals. A formula in *conjunctive normal form* (CNF) is a conjunction of finitely many clauses. As common, whenever convenient, a clause is treated as a set of literals and a CNF formula as a set of sets of literals.

For a literal $l = x$ or $l = \bar{x}$, we write $\mathsf{var}(l)$ for x; for a clause C, $\mathsf{var}(C)$ denotes $\{\mathsf{var}(l) \mid l \in C\}$, and for a CNF ψ, $\mathsf{var}(\psi)$ denotes $\{l \mid l \in \mathsf{var}(C), C \in \psi\}$. For a set of variables X an *assignment* is a function from X to the constants 0 and 1. We say that the assignment is *complete* for X if the function is total.

A *term* is a conjunction of finitely many non-complementary literals. Whenever convenient, a term is treated as a set of literals. We say that a term T is a *model* of a CNF ϕ if for each $C \in \phi$ there is a literal l both in T and C, i.e. $C \cap T \neq \emptyset$.

There is an obvious relation between terms and assignments. A term uniquely determines a set of assignments that satisfy the term. If an assignment satisfies a model of ϕ, then it is a satisfying assignment of ϕ. Note that some definitions require a model to be a complete assignment to the variables of ϕ. The aforementioned correspondence shows that there's no substantial difference between the definitions.

Quantified Boolean Formulas (QBFs) [13] extend propositional logic with quantifiers with the standard semantics that $\forall x. \Psi$ is satisfied by the same truth assignments as $\Psi[x/0] \wedge \Psi[x/1]$ and $\exists x. \Psi$ as $\Psi[x/0] \vee \Psi[x/1]$. Unless specified otherwise, QBFs are in *closed prenex* form with a CNF *matrix*, i.e. $\mathcal{Q}_1 X_1 \ldots \mathcal{Q}_k X_k. \phi$, where X_i are pairwise disjoint sets of variables; $\mathcal{Q}_i \in \{\exists, \forall\}$ and $\mathcal{Q}_i \neq \mathcal{Q}_{i+1}$. The formula ϕ is in CNF and is defined only on variables $X_1 \cup \ldots \cup X_k$. The propositional part ϕ is called the *matrix* and the rest the *prefix*. We write QCNF to talk about formulas in this form. If a variable x is in the set X_i, we say that x is at *level i* and write $\mathsf{lv}(x) = i$; we write $\mathsf{lv}(l)$ for $\mathsf{lv}(\mathsf{var}(l))$. A closed QBF is *false* (resp. *true*), iff it is semantically equivalent to the constant 0 (resp. 1).

If a variable is universally quantified, we say that the variable is universal. For a literal l and a universal variable x such that $\mathsf{var}(l) = x$, we say that l is universal. The notions of existential variable and literal are defined analogously.

2.1   Q-Resolution

Q-resolution [14] is an extension of propositional resolution for showing that a QCNF is false. For a clause C, a universal literal $l \in C$ is *blocked* by an existential literal $k \in C$ iff $\mathsf{lv}(l) < \mathsf{lv}(k)$. $\forall$-*reduction* is the operation of removing from a clause C all universal literals that are *not* blocked by some literal. For two $\forall$-reduced clauses $x \vee C_1$ and $\bar{x} \vee C_2$, where x is an existential variable, a *Q-resolvent* [14] is obtained in two steps. (1) Compute $C_u = C_1 \cup C_2 \smallsetminus \{x, \bar{x}\}$. If C_u contains complementary literals, the Q-resolvent is undefined. (2) $\forall$-reduce C_u. For a QCNF $\mathcal{P}.\phi$, a A *Q-resolution proof* of a clause C is a finite sequence of clauses $C_1, \ldots, C_n$ where $C_n = C$ and any C_i in the sequence is part of the given matrix ϕ or it is a Q-resolvent for some pair of the preceding clauses. A Q-resolution proof is called a *refutation* iff C is the empty clause, denoted $\bot$.

In this paper Q-resolution proofs are treated as connected directed acyclic graphs so that the each clause in the proof corresponds to some node labeled with that clause. We assume that the input clauses are already $\forall$-reduced. Q-resolution steps are depicted as on the right. Note that the $\forall$-reduction step is depicted separately.

$$
\begin{array}{cc}
C_1 \vee x & C_2 \vee \bar{x} \\
\diagdown & \diagup \\
& C_u \\
& | \\
& C
\end{array}
$$

2.2   Term-Resolution

Term-resolution is analogous to Q-resolution with the difference that it operates on terms and its purpose is to prove that a QCNF is true [10]. Since the calculus operates on QBFs with CNF matrices, it needs a mechanism to generate terms to operate on. This is done by a rule that enables using models of the given matrix in the proof.

Term-resolution, resolves on universal literals and reduces existential ones. For a term T an existential literal l is *blocked*, iff there is a universal $k \in T$ such that $\mathsf{lv}(l) < \mathsf{lv}(k)$. $\exists$-reduction removes from a term T all existential literals that are *not* blocked by some universal literal. For two $\exists$-reduced terms $x \wedge T_1$ and $\bar{x} \wedge T_2$, a *term-resolvent* is defined as the $\exists$-reduction of the term $T_1 \wedge T_2$, if T_1 and T_2 do not contain complementary literals; it is undefined otherwise.

For a QCNF $P.\,\phi$ a *term-resolution proof* of the term T_m a is a finite sequence $T_1, \ldots, T_m$ of terms such that each term T_i is a model of ϕ or it was obtained from the previous terms by $\exists$-reduction or term-resolution. Such a proof *proves* $\mathcal{P}$. ϕ iff T_m is the empty term, denoted as $\top$. Those terms of the proof that are models of ϕ are said to be generated by a *model generation rule*. In the literature, terms are sometimes referred to as "cubes", especially in the context of DPLL QBF solvers that apply cube learning [27].

2.3   Proof Complexity

A *proof system* P is relation $P(\Phi, \pi)$ that is computable in polynomial time such that a formula Φ is true iff there exists a proof π for which $P(\Phi, \pi)$. A proof system P_1 *p-simulates* a proof system P_2 iff any proof in P_2 of a formula Φ can be translated into a proof in P_1 of Φ in polynomial time (cf. [8,23]).

As is common, we will count the sizes of Q-resolution and term-resolution as the number of resolution steps and number of $\forall$ / $\exists$-reductions where each reduced literal is counted separately.

3   The Achilles' Heel

This section describes a large class of formulas that have exponential term-resolution proofs. Recall that a leaf of a term-resolution proof must be generated by the model-generation rule. We will show that due to this, a refutation proof can be "forced" to generate exponentially many leafs.

First we make a simple observation that for any assignment to universal variables, there must be a leaf-term in a term-resolution proof that "agrees" with that assignment. We say that a term T *agrees* with an assignment τ iff there is no literal l such that $\bar{l} \in T$ and $\tau(l) = 1$.

Lemma 1. *For any assignment τ to universal variables and a term-resolution proof π of some QCNF $P.\,\phi$ there is a leaf-term T of π that agrees with τ.*

Proof. We construct a path from the root to some leaf such that each node on that path agrees with τ. The root of π agrees with τ because it does not contain any literals. If a term T agrees with τ and T is obtained from T' by existential-reduction, then T' also agrees with τ since τ assigns only to universal variables. If T agrees with τ and is obtained from T_1 and T_2 by term-resolution on some variable y, it has to be that y is in one of the T_1, T_2 and $\bar{y}$ in the other. Hence, at least one of the terms agrees with τ.   □

Theorem 1. *Consider a QCNF $\Phi = P.\phi$. If all models of ϕ contain at least k universal literals, then any term-resolution proof of Φ has at least 2^k leafs.*

Proof. Let V_u be the set of universal variables of Φ. Since each leaf-term of any term-resolution proof has at least k universal literals, it can agree with at most $2^{|V_u|-k}$ different complete assignments to the universal variables. Lemma 1 gives that for any of the $2^{|V_u|}$ total assignments to V_u there must be a corresponding leaf-term. Averaging gives that π has at least $\frac{2^{|V|}}{2^{|V|-k}} = 2^k$ leafs.   □

Theorem 1 gives us a powerful method of constructing formulas with large term-resolution proofs. It is sufficient to construct a true QCNF whose models have many universal literals. Let us construct one such formula. For a given parameter $N \in \mathbb{N}^+$ construct the following formula with $2N$ variables and $2N$ clauses.

$$\forall x_1, \exists y_1, \ldots, \forall x_N, \exists y_N. \bigwedge_{i \in 1..N} (\bar{x}_i \vee y_i) \wedge (x_i \vee \bar{y}_i) \tag{1}$$

Proposition 1. *Any term-resolution proof of (1) is exponential in N.*

Proof. Formula (1) is true as each of the existential variables y_i can be set to the same value as the variable x_i and thus satisfying the matrix.

Let ψ denote the matrix of (1). Each pair of clauses $\bar{x}_i \vee y_i$ and $\bar{y}_i \vee x_i$ must be satisfied by any model τ of ψ, which can be only done in two ways: the model contains the literals $\{y_i, x_i\}$ or it contains the literals $\{\bar{y}_i, \bar{x}_i\}$. Hence τ contains a literal for each x_i and for each y_i. Theorem 1 gives that at least 2^N models are needed in the leafs of any term-resolution proof.   □

4   A Possible Remedy—Negation

This section suggests a possible remedy to the weakness exposed in the previous section. Instead of proving a formula true by term-resolution, we propose to refute its negation by Q-resolution.

To construct the negation of a formula, we follow the standard equalities $\neg \forall x. \Psi = \exists x. \neg \Psi$ and $\neg \exists x. \Psi = \forall x. \neg \Psi$. In order to bring the matrix back to conjunctive normal form, we add additional (*Tseitin*) variables [22]. We use the optimization by Plaisted-Greenbaum, which enables encoding variables' seman-tics only in one direction [19]. In particular, for each clause we introduce a fresh variable that is forced to true when that clause becomes true. Using these variables, we construct a clause that requires that at least one of the clauses is false.

It would be correct to insert these fresh variables at the end of the prefix (existentially quantified) but we will see that it is useful to insert them further towards the outer levels, if possible. It has been shown elsewhere that in fact can give an exponential speedup [4].

Definition 1. *The negation of a formula $P.\phi$ is denoted as $Neg(P.\phi)$ and constructed as follows. For each clause C introduce a fresh variable n_C. Construct the prefix of $Neg(P.\phi)$ from P inverting all the quantifiers in P and inserting each of the variables the variable n_C as existential after the variable with maximal level in C. Construct a matrix of $Neg(P.\phi)$ as the following set of clauses.*

$$\{\bar{l} \vee n_C \mid l \in C, C \in \phi\} \cup \left\{\bigvee_{C \in \phi} \bar{n}_C\right\}$$

Example 1. The $Neg\left(\forall x \exists y \exists z. (\bar{x} \vee y) \wedge (x \vee z)\right)$ is equal to $\exists x \forall y \exists c_1 \forall z \exists c_2. (x \vee c_1) \wedge (\bar{y} \vee c_1) \wedge (\bar{x} \vee c_2) \wedge (\bar{z} \vee c_2) \wedge (\bar{c}_1 \vee \bar{c}_2)$.

Clearly, $Neg(\Psi)$ is false if and only if Ψ is true. We say that a QCNF Ψ is *negation-refuted* by a Q-resolution proof π iff π is a refutation of $Neg(\Psi)$.

4.1   Negation-Refutation P-Simulates Term-Resolution

The first question we should ask is whether for any term-resolution proof there is a polynomial-size negation-refutation proof. We show this is indeed the case.

Theorem 2. *Negation-refutation p-simulates term-resolution.*

Proof (sketch). Let π be a term-resolution proof of a QCNF $P.\phi$. Construct a Q-resolution of $Neg(P.\phi)$ as follows. Let M be a leaf of π. From the rules of term-resolution for each $C \in \phi$ there is a literal l s.t. $l \in C$ and $l \in M$. From the definition of Neg, the QCNF $Neg(P.\phi)$ contains the clause $\bar{n}_C \vee \bar{l}$ for such literal.

Starting with the clause $\bigvee_{C \in \phi} \bar{n}_C$, resolve each literal $\bar{n}_C$ with the clause $n_C \vee \bar{l}$, for each l s.t. $l \in C$ and $l \in M$. This results in the clause $\bigvee_{l \in M} \bar{l}$. Note that this clause does not contain contradictory literals because M must not contain contradictory literals.

Repeating this process for each leaf of π produces clauses that are negations of those leafs. Perform Q-resolutions steps and $\forall$-reductions as are done term-resolutions steps and $\exists$-reductions in π. This produces a Q-resolution proof where each derived clause is a negation of the corresponding term in π. Since π has the empty term in the root, the produced tree has the empty clause in the root. Resolutions needed to produce each of the leaf clauses requires at most $\min(|\pi|, |var(\phi)|)$ steps thus the resulting Q-resolution is at most of size $(|\Phi| + |\pi|)^2$. $\qquad\square$

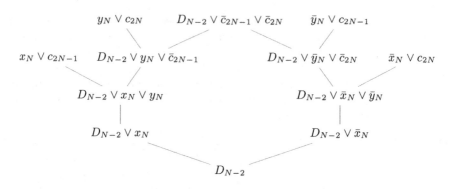

Fig. 1. Resolving away negation of (1) (where $D_{N-2} = \bar{c}_1 \vee \cdots \vee \bar{c}_{2N-3} \vee \bar{c}_{2N-2}$).

4.2 Separation Between Term-Resolution and Negation-Refutation

The previous section shows that negation-refutation is at least as powerful as term-resolution. To show that the negation-refutation proof system is in fact stronger, we recall formula (1), whose term-resolution proofs are exponential, and show it has a negation-refutation proof of linear size.

Proposition 2. *Formula (1) has a linear negation-refutation proof.*

Proof (sketch). Negation of (1) introduces variables $c_1, \ldots, c_{2N}$ representing the respective clauses. In particular, the following clauses are constructed $x_i \vee c_{2i-1}$, $\bar{y}_i \vee c_{2i-1}$, $\bar{x}_i \vee c_{2i}$, $y_i \vee c_{2i}$ for $i \in 1..N$ and the clause $\bar{c}_1 \vee \cdots \vee \bar{c}_{2N}$. With the prefix $\exists x_1 \forall y_1 \exists c_1 c_2 \ldots \exists x_1 \forall y_1 \exists c_{2N-1} c_{2N}$.

We show how to resolve away the literals $\bar{c}_{2N-1}$ and $\bar{c}_{2N}$; the rest of the c_i literals is resolved in the same fashion. For conciseness we define D_{N-2} as $\bar{c}_1 \vee \cdots \vee \bar{c}_{2N-3} \vee \bar{c}_{2N-2}$. Figure 1 shows how $\bar{c}_{2N-1}$ and $\bar{c}_{2N}$ are replaced by y_N and x_N at which point y_N is universally reduced. Analogously, the literals are replaced with $\bar{x}_N$ and $\bar{y}_N$, which enables resolving x_N away.

Using this construction, each of the literals $\bar{c}_{2i-1}, \bar{c}_{2i}$ are resolved away in 7 resolution/reduction steps thus resulting in a resolution proof with $7N$ resolution/reduction steps in total.   □

4.3 Variable Definitions

We observe that formula (1) is an example of a formula where an existential variable y is *defined*, i.e. the value of the variable is determined by values of some variables with a lower level (in the case of formula (1) the value of y_i is determined by the value of x_i). So the natural question to ask is whether any definition can be proven true by negation-refutation. We show that this is indeed the case but we will need *QU-resolution*—an extension of Q-resolution that enables resolving on *universal variables* [25].

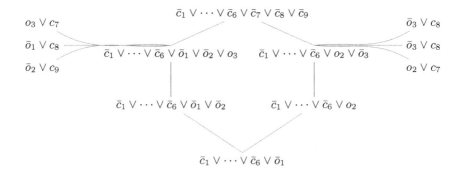

Fig. 2. Resolving definitions

We will demonstrate how negations of definitions can be refuted on the following representative example. Consider the prefix $\exists x_1 \forall x_2 \exists x_3 o_1 o_2 o_3$ and a matrix capturing the equalities $o_1 = \mathsf{NAND}(x_1, x_2)$, $o_2 = \mathsf{NAND}(x_2, x_3)$, and $o_3 = \mathsf{NAND}(o_1, o_2)$. These correspond to the following clauses (Tseitin variables that will be used for negating the clauses are indicated in parentheses).

$$(c_1)\ \bar{x}_1 \vee \bar{x}_2 \vee \bar{o}_1 \quad (c_4)\ \bar{x}_2 \vee \bar{x}_3 \vee \bar{o}_2 \quad (c_7)\ \bar{o}_1 \vee \bar{o}_2 \vee \bar{o}_3$$
$$(c_2)\ x_2 \vee o_1 \qquad\quad (c_5)\ x_2 \vee o_2 \qquad\quad (c_8)\ o_1 \vee o_3$$
$$(c_3)\ x_2 \vee o_1 \qquad\quad (c_6)\ x_2 \vee o_2 \qquad\quad (c_9)\ o_1 \vee o_3$$

After negating this formula, we obtain the following prefix.

$$\forall x_1 \exists x_2 \forall x_3 \forall o_1 \exists c_1 c_2 c_3 \forall o_2 \exists c_4 c_5 c_6 \forall o_3 \exists c_7 c_8 c_9$$

We omit the negated formula's matrix for succinctness. The Q-resolution proof proceeds in a similar fashion as the one for (1). Starting with the clause $\bar{c}_1 \vee \cdots \vee \bar{c}_9$, the $\bar{c}_i$ literals are resolved away, starting with the innermost ones.

Figure 2 shows a fragment of the proof, which resolves away the literals $\bar{c}_7, \ldots, \bar{c}_9$ (certain resolution steps are collapsed). Using the clauses determining the value of o_3, the proof generates the clauses $\bar{c}_1 \vee \cdots \vee \bar{o}_1 \vee \bar{o}_2$ and $\bar{c}_1 \vee \cdots \vee o_2$. Resolving these two clauses removes the variable o_2. Note that o_2 is universal, which is why we need QU-resolution. In order to resolve away o_1, the clause $\bar{c}_1 \vee \cdots \vee o_1$ is generated analogously. Leaving us with the clause $\bar{c}_1 \vee \cdots \vee \bar{c}_6$. Note that it was possible to $\forall$-reduce o_3 throughout the process because it is blocked only by the variables $c_7, \ldots, c_9$. In contrast, the variables o_1 and o_2 could *not* be $\forall$-reduced because they are blocked by the literals $\bar{c}_5, \ldots, \bar{c}_6$. The literals $\bar{c}_4, \ldots, \bar{c}_6$ and subsequently $\bar{c}_1, \ldots, \bar{c}_3$ are resolved in the same fashion.

An analogous proof can be carried out for any acyclic circuit of NAND gates. One picks a topological order of the gates and resolves them away as in the example above.

5 Summary, Conclusions, and Future Work

This paper investigates the strength of term-resolution: a well-established calculus for true quantified Boolean formulas. This paper exposes a significant vulnerability in the term-resolution calculus, which stems from the fact that the number of leafs of a term-resolution proof is not bound by the size of the formula in question. Instead, the model-generation rule enables generating new leafs of the proof from models of the matrix. The paper demonstrates that this lets us force the proof to generate exponentially many leafs by constructing QBF matrices with "many" universal literals.

This theoretical observation provides a further underpinning of the well-known observation that solving quantified Boolean formula with a CNF matrix can be sometimes particularly harmful [2,26]. Indeed, we demonstrate that even a very simple formula where each clause has only two literals leads to exponential term-resolution proofs.

At the practical level, in response to this issue, Zhang proposes to reason on a formula and on its negation at the same time [26]. This idea was realized with different flavors in various solvers [1,11,15]. The second part of this paper takes a similar avenue at the theoretical level. We compare the term-resolution calculus with the negation-refutation calculus, a calculus which refutes the formula's negation in order to show the formula true. The paper demonstrates that this proof system indeed has favorable theoretical properties, in particular it p-simulates term-resolution and there is an exponential separation between the two calculi.

This result is related to the well-known fact that enabling adding new variables in propositional resolution yields a more powerful proof system (extended resolution) [7]. Negation-refutation introduces new variables too. However, in extended resolution, the prover must come up with the variables' definitions. In negation-refutation, the definitions are determined by the clauses of the formula.

The last part of the paper touches upon some limitations of the negation-refutation calculus. If a variable's value is defined as a function of some other variables, through a Boolean circuit, we ask if it's possible to prove that it is always possible to come up with the right value for the variable being defined, i.e. complete the circuit. This is something that we would hope to be proven easily. We show that it is indeed possible to prove such definitions true linearly using negation-refutation but we show so with the use of QU-resolution—extension of Q-resolution that enables resolving on universal variables. This result is important from a theoretical perspective but raises further questions because existing QBF solvers use Q-resolution. It is the subject of future work to look for linear proofs for such formulas using only Q-resolution.

Acknowledgments. This work was supported by national funds through Fundação para a Ciência e a Tecnologia (FCT) with reference UID/CEC/50021/2013 and by FCT funding of LASIGE Research Unit, reference UID/CEC/00408/2013.

References

1. Goultiaeva, A., Seidl, M., Biere, A.: Bridging the gap between dual propagation and CNF-based QBF solving. In. Proceedings of International Conference on Design, Automation and Test in Europe (DATE) (2013)
2. Ansótegui, C., Gomes, C.P., Selman, B.: The Achilles' heel of QBF. In: Veloso, M.M., Kambhampati, S. (eds.) AAAI, pp. 275–281. AAAI Press/The MIT Press (2005)
3. Balabanov, V., Widl, M., Jiang, J.-H.R.: QBF resolution systems and their proof complexities. In: Sinz, C., Egly, U. (eds.) SAT 2014. LNCS, vol. 8561, pp. 154–169. Springer, Cham (2014). doi:10.1007/978-3-319-09284-3_12
4. Beyersdorf, O., Chew, L., Janota, M.: Extension variables in QBF resolution. In: Workshops at the Thirtieth AAAI Conference on Artificial Intelligence (2016)
5. Beyersdorff, O., Chew, L., Janota, M.: Proof complexity of resolution-based QBF calculi. In: Proceedings of Symposium on Theoretical Aspects of Computer Science (STACS), pp. 76–89. LIPIcs Series (2015)
6. Brummayer, R., Lonsing, F., Biere, A.: Automated testing and debugging of SAT and QBF solvers. In: Strichman, O., Szeider, S. (eds.) SAT 2010. LNCS, vol. 6175, pp. 44–57. Springer, Heidelberg (2010). doi:10.1007/978-3-642-14186-7_6
7. Cook, S.A.: A short proof of the pigeon hole principle using extended resolution. SIGACT News **8**(4), 28–32 (1976)
8. Cook, S.A., Reckhow, R.A.: The relative efficiency of propositional proof systems. J. Symb. Log. **44**(1), 36–50 (1979)
9. Egly, U.: On sequent systems and resolution for QBFs. In: Cimatti, A., Sebastiani, R. (eds.) SAT 2012. LNCS, vol. 7317, pp. 100–113. Springer, Heidelberg (2012). doi:10.1007/978-3-642-31612-8_9
10. Giunchiglia, E., Narizzano, M., Tacchella, A.: Clause/term resolution and learning in the evaluation of quantified Boolean formulas. J. Artif. Intell. Res. **26**(1), 371–416 (2006)
11. Goultiaeva, A., Bacchus, F.: Exploiting QBF duality on a circuit representation. In: AAAI (2010)
12. Heule, M.J.H., Seidl, M., Biere, A.: A unified proof system for QBF preprocessing. In: Demri, S., Kapur, D., Weidenbach, C. (eds.) IJCAR 2014. LNCS, vol. 8562, pp. 91–106. Springer, Cham (2014). doi:10.1007/978-3-319-08587-6_7
13. Kleine Büning, H., Bubeck, U.: Theory of quantified Boolean formulas. In: Handbook of Satisfiability. IOS Press (2009)
14. Kleine Büning, H., Karpinski, M., Flögel, A.: Resolution for quantified Boolean formulas. Inf. Comput. **117**(1), 12–18 (1995)
15. Klieber, W., Sapra, S., Gao, S., Clarke, E.: A non-prenex, non-clausal QBF solver with game-state learning. In: Strichman, O., Szeider, S. (eds.) SAT 2010. LNCS, vol. 6175, pp. 128–142. Springer, Heidelberg (2010). doi:10.1007/978-3-642-14186-7_12
16. Krajíček, J., Pudlák, P.: Quantified propositional calculi and fragments of bounded arithmetic. Math. Logic Q. **36**(1), 29–46 (1990)
17. Lonsing, F.: Dependency Schemes and Search-Based QBF Solving: Theory and Practice. Ph.D. thesis, Johannes Kepler Universität (2012). http://www.kr.tuwien.ac.at/staff/lonsing/diss/
18. McMillan, K.L.: Interpolation and SAT-based model checking. In: Hunt, W.A., Somenzi, F. (eds.) CAV 2003. LNCS, vol. 2725, pp. 1–13. Springer, Heidelberg (2003). doi:10.1007/978-3-540-45069-6_1

19. Plaisted, D.A., Greenbaum, S.: A structure-preserving clause form translation. J. Symb. Comput. **2**(3), 293–304 (1986)
20. Silva, J.P.M., Lynce, I., Malik, S.: Conflict-driven clause learning sat solvers. In: Biere, A., Heule, M., van Maaren, H., Walsh, T. (eds.) Handbook of Satisfiability, pp. 131–153. IOS Press (2009)
21. Silva, J.P.M., Sakallah, K.A.: Conflict analysis in search algorithms for satisfiability. In: ICTAI, pp. 467–469 (1996)
22. Tseitin, G.S.: On the complexity of derivations in the propositional calculus. In: Studies in Constructive Mathematics and Mathematical Logic (1968)
23. Urquhart, A.: The complexity of propositional proofs. Bull. EATCS **64**, 128–138 (1998)
24. Van Gelder, A.: Decision procedures should be able to produce (easily) checkable proofs. In: Workshop on Constraints in Formal Verification (in Conjunction with CP02) (2002)
25. Van Gelder, A.: Contributions to the theory of practical quantified Boolean formula solving. In: Milano, M. (ed.) CP 2012. LNCS, pp. 647–663. Springer, Heidelberg (2012). doi:10.1007/978-3-642-33558-7_47
26. Zhang, L.: Solving QBF by combining conjunctive and disjunctive normal forms. In: AAAI (2006)
27. Zhang, L., Malik, S.: Conflict driven learning in a quantified Boolean satisfiability solver. In: ICCAD (2002)

Horn Maximum Satisfiability: Reductions, Algorithms and Applications

Joao Marques-Silva[1]([⊠]), Alexey Ignatiev[1,2], and Antonio Morgado[1]

[1] LASIGE, Faculty of Science, University of Lisbon, Lisbon, Portugal
{jpms,aignatiev,ajmorgado}@ciencias.ulisboa.pt
[2] ISDCT SB RAS, Irkutsk, Russia

Abstract. Recent years have witnessed remarkable performance improvements in maximum satisfiability (MaxSAT) solvers. In practice, MaxSAT algorithms often target the most generic MaxSAT formulation, whereas dedicated solvers, which address specific subclasses of MaxSAT, have not been investigated. This paper shows that a wide range of optimization and decision problems are either naturally formulated as MaxSAT over Horn formulas, or permit simple encodings using Horn-MaxSAT. Furthermore, the paper also shows how linear time decision procedures for Horn formulas can be used for developing novel algorithms for the HornMaxSAT problem.

1 Introduction

Recent years have seen very significant improvements in MaxSAT solving technology [2,13,28,33]. Currently, the most effective MaxSAT algorithms propose different ways for iteratively finding and blocking unsatisfiable cores (or subformulas). However, and despite the promising results of MaxSAT in practical settings, past work has not investigated dedicated approaches for solving subclasses of the MaxSAT problem, with one concrete example being the MaxSAT problem over Horn formulas, i.e. HornMaxSAT[1]. The HornMaxSAT optimization problem is well-known to be NP-hard [23]. In contrast to HornMaxSAT, the decision problem for Horn formulas is well-known to be in P, with linear time algorithms proposed in the 80s [15,27]. This paper investigates practical uses of MaxSAT subject to Horn formulas, and shows that a vast number of decision and optimization problems are naturally formulated as HornMaxSAT. More importantly, as this paper also shows, a vast number of other decision and optimization problems admit simple HornMaxSAT encodings. One should observe that HornMaxSAT is NP-hard and so, by definition, any decision problem in NP admits a polynomial time reduction to HornMaxSAT. However, for

---

This work was supported by FCT funding of post-doctoral grants SFRH/BPD/103609/2014, SFRH/BPD/120315/2016, and LASIGE Research Unit, ref. UID/CEC/00408/2013.

[1] In contrast, for predicate logic and many of its specializations, Horn clauses are used ubiquitously. This includes logic programming, among many others applications.

© Springer International Publishing AG 2017
E. Oliveira et al. (Eds.): EPIA 2017, LNAI 10423, pp. 681–694, 2017.
DOI: 10.1007/978-3-319-65340-2_56

many problems in NP, such reductions are not known, and may result in large (although polynomial) encodings.

With the purpose of exploiting the observation that many optimization and decision problems have natural (and simple) reductions to HornMaxSAT, this paper also proposes a novel algorithm for HornMaxSAT. The new algorithm mimics recent Implicit Hitting Set algorithms[2] proposed for MaxSAT [13,33], which exploiting the fact that Horn formulas can be decided in polynomial (linear) time [27], and for which minimal unsatisfiable cores (or MUSes) can be computed in polynomial time [26].

The paper is organized as follows. Section 2 introduces the definitions and notation used in the remainder of the paper. Section 3 shows that a large number of well-known optimization, but also decision problems already have simple HornMaxSAT formulations which, to the best of our knowledge, have not been exploited before. Section 4 proposes a variant of recent general-purpose MaxSAT algorithms, that is dedicated to the HornMaxSAT problem. This section also shows that the new algorithm can elicit automatic abstraction mechanisms. Section 5 overviews additional applications and generic reductions to Horn-MaxSAT. The potential of the work proposed in this paper is assessed in Sects. 6, and 7 concludes the paper.

2   Preliminaries

The paper assumes definitions and notation standard in propositional satisfiability (SAT) and MaxSAT [8]. Propositional variables are taken from a set $X = \{x_1, x_2, \ldots\}$. A Conjunctive Normal Form (CNF) formula is defined as a conjunction of disjunctions of literals, where a literal is a variable or its complement. CNF formulas can also be viewed as sets of sets of literals, and are represented with letters in calligraphic font, $\mathcal{A}$, $\mathcal{F}$, $\mathcal{H}$, etc. Given a formula $\mathcal{F}$, the set of variables is $\mathsf{vars}(\mathcal{F}) \subseteq X$. A clause is a *goal clause* if all of its literals are negative. A clause is a *definite clause* if it has exactly one positive literal and all the other literals are negative; the number of negative literals may be 0. A clause is Horn if it is either a goal or a definite clause. A truth assignment ν is a map from variables to $\{0, 1\}$. Given a truth assignment, a clause is satisfied if at least one of its literals is assigned value 1; otherwise it is falsified. A formula is satisfied if all of its clauses are satisfied; otherwise it is falsified. If there exists no assignment that satisfies a CNF formula $\mathcal{F}$, then $\mathcal{F}$ is referred to as *unsatisfiable*. (Boolean) Satisfiability (SAT) is the decision problem for propositional formulas, i.e. to decide whether a given propositional formula is satisfiable. Since the paper only considers propositional formulas in CNF, throughout the paper SAT refers to the decision problem for propositional formulas in CNF. Modern SAT solvers instantiate the Conflict-Driven Clause Learning paradigm [8]. For unsatisfiable (or inconsistent) formulas, MUSes (minimal unsatisfiable subsets) represent subset-minimal subformulas that are unsatisfiable (or inconsistent),

---

[2] Throughout the paper, these are referred to as MaxHS-family of MaxSAT algorithms.

and MCSes (minimal correction subsets) represent subset-minimal subformulas such that the complement is satisfiable [8].

To simplify modeling with propositional logic, one often represents more expressive constraints. Concrete examples are cardinality constraints and pseudo-Boolean constraints [8]. A cardinality constraint of the form $\sum x_i \leq k$ is referred to as an AtMost$k$ constraint, whereas a cardinality constraint of the form $\sum x_i \geq k$ is referred to as an AtLeast$k$ constraint. Propositional encodings of cardinality and pseudo-Boolean constraints is an area of active research [1, 4–8, 10, 16, 29, 35, 37]. The (plain) MaxSAT problem is to find a truth assignment that maximizes the number of satisfied clauses. For the plain MaxSAT problem, all clauses are *soft*, meaning that these may not be satisfied. Variants of the MaxSAT can consider the existence of *hard* clauses, meaning that these must be satisfied, and also assign weights to the soft clauses, denoting the *cost* of falsifying the clause; this is referred as the weighted MaxSAT problem, WMaxSAT. When addressing MaxSAT problems with weights, hard clauses are assigned a large weight $\top$. The HornMaxSAT problem corresponds to the MaxSAT problem when all clauses are Horn. If clauses have weights, then HornWMaxSAT denotes the Horn MaxSAT problem when the soft clauses have weights.

Throughout the paper, standard graph and set notations will be used. An undirected graph $G = (V, E)$ is defined by a set V of vertices and a set $E \subseteq \{\{u, v\} \mid u, v \in V, u \neq v\}$. Given $G = (V, E)$, the *complement graph* $G = (V, E^C)$ is the graph with edges $\{\{u, v\} \mid u, v \in V, u \neq v, \{u, v\} \notin E\}$. Moreover, it is assumed some familiarity with optimization problems defined on graphs, including minimum vertex cover, maximum independent set, maximum clique, among others. Finally, $\leq_P$ is used to represent polynomial time reducibility between problems [12, Sect. 34.3].

3   Basic Reductions

This section shows that a number of well-known problems can be reduced in polynomial time to the HornMaxSAT problem. Some of the reductions are well-known; we simply highlight that the resulting propositional formulas are Horn.

3.1   Optimization Problems on Graphs

Definition 1 (Minimum Vertex Cover, MinVC). *Given an undirected graph* $G = (V, E)$, *a vertex cover* $T \subseteq V$ *is such that for each* $\{u, v\} \in E$, $\{u, v\} \cap T \neq \emptyset$. *A minimum (or cardinality minimal) vertex cover* $T \subseteq V$ *is a vertex cover of minimum size*[3].

Reduction 1 (MinVC $\leq_P$ HornMaxSAT). *For* $u \in V$, *let* $x_u = 1$ *iff* u *is not included in a vertex cover. For any* $\{u, v\} \in E$, *add a hard clause* $(\neg x_u \vee \neg x_v)$.

---

[3] This corresponds to requiring $T \subseteq V$ to be such that $\forall_{U \subseteq V} |U| < |T| \rightarrow \exists_{\{u,v\} \in E}, \{u, v\} \cap U = \emptyset$. Throughout the paper, we will skip the mathematical representation of minimum (but also maximum) size sets.

For each $u \in V$, add a soft clause (x_u). (Any non-excluded vertex $u \in V$ (i.e. $x_u = 0$) is in the vertex cover.)

Remark 1. The proposed reduction differs substantially from the one originally used for proving HornMaxSAT to be NP-hard [23], but our working assumptions are also distinct, in that we consider hard and soft clauses.

Definition 2 (Maximum Independent Set, MaxIS). *Given an undirected graph $G = (V, E)$, an independent set $I \subseteq V$ is such that for each $\{u, v\} \in E$ either $u \notin I$ or $v \notin I$. A maximum independent set is an independent set of maximum size.*

Reduction 2 (MaxIS $\leq_P$ HornMaxSAT). *One can simply use the previous encoding, by noting the relationship between vertex covers and independent sets. For any $\{u, v\} \in E$, add a hard clause $(\neg x_u \vee \neg x_v)$. For each $u \in V$, add a soft clause (x_u).*

Definition 3 (Maximum Clique, MaxClique). *Given an undirected graph $G = (V, E)$, a clique (or complete subgraph) $C \subseteq V$ is such that for two vertices $\{u, v\} \subseteq C$, $\{u, v\} \in E$. A maximum clique is a clique of maximum size.*

Reduction 3 (MaxClique $\leq_P$ HornMaxSAT). *A MaxSAT encoding for Max-Clique is the following. For any $\{u, v\} \in E^C$, add a hard clause $(\neg x_u \vee \neg x_v)$. For each $u \in V$, add a soft clause (x_u).*

Definition 4 (Minimum Dominating Set, MinDS). *Let $G = (V, E)$ be an undirected graph. $D \subseteq V$ is a dominating set if any $v \in V \setminus D$ is adjacent to at least one vertex in D. A minimum dominating set is a dominating set of minimum size.*

Reduction 4 (MinDS $\leq_P$ HornMaxSAT). *Let $x_u = 1$ iff $u \in V$ is excluded from a dominating set D. For each vertex $u \in V$ add a hard Horn clause $(\neg x_u \vee_{\{u,v\} \in E} \neg x_v)$. The soft clauses are (x_u), for $u \in V$.*

3.2 Optimization Problems on Sets

Definition 5 (Minimum Hitting Set, MinHS). *Let $\mathcal{C}$ be a collection of sets of some set S. A hitting set $H \subseteq S$ is such that for any $D \in \mathcal{C}$, $H \cap D \neq \emptyset$. A minimum hitting set is a hitting set of minimum size.*

Reduction 5 (MinHS $\leq_P$ HornMaxSAT). *For each $a \in S$ let $x_a = 1$ iff a is excluded from H. For each $D \in \mathcal{C}$, create a hard Horn clause $(\vee_{a \in D} \neg x_a)$. The soft clauses are (x_a), for $a \in S$.*

Remark 2. The minimum set cover (MinSC) is well-known to be equivalent to the minimum hitting set problem. Thus, the same reduction to HornMaxSAT can be applied.

Definition 6 (Maximum Set Packing, MaxSP). *Let $\mathcal{T} = \{T_1, \ldots, T_k\}$ be a family of sets. $\mathcal{R} \subseteq \mathcal{T}$ is a set packing if $\forall_{T_i, T_j \in \mathcal{R}} T_i \cap T_j = \emptyset$. A maximum set packing is a set packing of maxim size.*

Reduction 6 (MaxSP $\leq_P$ HornMaxSAT). *Let $x_i = 1$ iff T_i is included in the set packing. For each pair T_i, T_j, such that $T_i \cap T_j \neq \emptyset$, create a hard Horn clause $(\neg x_i \vee \neg x_j)$. The soft clauses are (x_i), for $T_i \in \mathcal{T}$.*

Remark 3. It is well-known that the maximum set packing problem can be reduced to the maximum clique problem. The reduction above exploits this result.

It also immediate to conclude that the weighted version of any of the optimization problems described in this and the previous sections can be reduced to HornWMaxSAT.

3.3 Handling Linear Constraints

This section argues that the propositional encodings of a number of linear constraints are Horn. In turn, this enables solving a number of optimization problems with HornMaxSAT.

The first observation is that *any* of the most widely used CNF encodings of AtMost$k$ constraints are composed *exclusively* of Horn clauses[4]:

Proposition 1 (CNF Encodings of AtMost$k$ constraints). *The following CNF encodings of AtMost$k$ constraints are composed solely of Horn clauses: pairwise and bitwise encodings [8, Chap. 2], totalizers [6], sequential counters [35], sorting networks [16], cardinality networks [4,5], pairwise cardinality networks [10], and modulo totalizers [29].*

Proof. Immediate by inspection of each encoding [4–6, 8, 10, 16, 29, 35]. □

For the case of the more general pseudo-Boolean constraints, $\sum a_i x_i \leq b$, with a_i, b non-negative, there also exist Horn encodings:

Proposition 2 (CNF Encodings of Pseudo-Boolean Constraints). *The Local Polynomial Watchdog [7] encoding for PB constraints is composed solely of Horn clauses.*

Proof. Immediate by inspection of the encoding in [7]. □

These observations have immediate impact on the range of problems that can be solved with HornMaxSAT and HornWMaxSAT. One concrete example is the Knapsack problem [12].

---

[4] To our best knowledge, this property of propositional encodings has not been investigated before.

Algorithm 1. HMaxHS, a MaxHS-like [13] HornMaxSAT algorithm

Input: $\mathcal{F} = \langle \mathcal{A}, \mathcal{H} \rangle$, HornMaxSAT formula
Output: $(\mu, \mathrm{Cost}(\mu))$, MaxSAT assignment and cost

1 **begin**
2 $\quad \mathcal{K} \leftarrow \emptyset$
3 $\quad$ **while** true **do**
4 $\quad \quad \mathcal{S} \leftarrow \mathrm{MinimumHS}(\mathcal{K})$
5 $\quad \quad (st, \mu, \mathcal{U}) \leftarrow \mathrm{LTUR}(\mathcal{H} \cup (\mathcal{A} \setminus \mathcal{S}))$
   $\quad \quad$ `// If st, then` μ `is a satisfying assignment`
   $\quad \quad$ `// Otherwise,` $\mathcal{U}$ `is a core/MUS`
6 $\quad \quad$ **if** st **then return** $(\mu, \mathrm{Cost}(\mu))$
7 $\quad \quad \mathcal{K} \leftarrow \mathcal{K} \cup \{\mathcal{U}\}$

8 **end**

Definition 7 (Knapsack problem). *Let* $\{1, \ldots, n\}$ *denote a set of* n *objects, each with value* v_i *and weight* w_i, $1 \le i \le n$, *and a maximum weight value* W. *The knapsack problem is to pick a subset of objects of maximum value that is consistent with the weight constraint. By letting* $x_i = 1$ *iff object* i *is picked, we get the well-known 0–1 ILP formulation* $\max \sum_i v_i x_i$; $s.t. \sum_i w_i x_i \le W$.

Reduction 7 (Knapsack $\le_P$ HornMaxSAT). *From Proposition 2, there exist Horn encodings for Pseudo-Boolean constraints. Thus, the hard constraint* $\sum_i w_i x_i \le W$ *can be encoded with Horn clauses. The soft clauses are* (x_i) *for each object* i, *each with cost* v_i. *Both the soft and the hard clauses in the reduction are Horn.*

4 HornMaxSAT Algorithm with Hitting Sets

This section develops a MaxHS-like [13,33] algorithm for HornMaxSAT. In addition, the section shows that this MaxHS-like algorithm elicits the possibility of solving large scale problems with abstraction.

4.1 A MaxHS-Like HornMaxSAT Algorithm

With the goal of exploiting the special structure of HornMaxSAT, a MaxHS-like algorithm is envisioned [13,33]. Algorithm 1 summarizes the proposed approach. The key observation is that each call to LTUR [27] runs in linear time. (Unit propagation as implemented in modern SAT solvers, will also run in polynomial time, but it will be less efficient in practice.) The original motivation for MaxHS is that finding a minimum hitting set of $\mathcal{S}$ is expected to be much easier than solving the MaxSAT problem. This is also the motivation for HMaxHS. As observed in recent work [3,26], MUSes (minimal unsatisfiable subsets) can be computed in polynomial time in the case of Horn formulas. MUS extraction, but also MCS (minimal correction subset) extraction [26], are based on the original LTUR algorithm [27]. It should be noted that some implementations of MaxHS use an ILP (Integer Linear Programming) package (e.g. CPLEX or SCIP) [13,33][5], whereas others exploit SAT solvers for computing minimum hitting sets [19,21].

4.2 Automatic Abstraction-Based Problem Solving

For some of the problems described in Sect. 3 a possible criticism of Algorithm 1 is that it will iteratively find sets $\mathcal{U}$ consisting of a single clause, and it will essentially add to $\mathcal{K}$ all the clauses in $\mathcal{H}$. Although this is in fact a possibility for some problems (but not all, as investigated in Sect. 5), this section shows that even for these problems, Algorithm 1 can provide an effective problem solving approach.

Consider the example graph in Fig. 1, where the goal is to compute a maximum independent set (or alternatively a minimum vertex cover). From the figure, we can conclude that the number of vertices is $(1 + m)k$, the number of edges is $(k(k - 1)/2 + km)$, the size of the maximum independent set is km and the size of the minimum vertex cover is k. From the inspection of the reduction from MaxIS (or MinVC) to HornMaxSAT, and the operation of Algorithm 1, one might anticipate that Algorithm 1 would iteratively declare each hard clause as an unsatisfiable core, and replicate the clause in the list $\mathcal{K}$ of sets to hit, thus requiring a number of iterations no smaller than the number of edges. (More importantly, for a MaxHS-like algorithm, the number of iterations is worst-case exponential [13].) However, and as shown below, the operation of the HMaxHS actually *ensures* this is *not* the case.

Without loss of generality, consider any of the vertices in the clique, i.e. $v_1, \ldots, v_k$, say v_i. For this vertex, no more than $k(k - 1)/2 + 2k$ edges will be replicated, i.e. added to $\mathcal{K}$. Observe that, as soon as two edges $\{v_i, u_{ij_1}\}$ and $\{v_i, u_{ij_2}\}$ are replicated, a minimum hitting set will necessarily pick v_i. As a result, after at most $k(k-1)/2+2k$ iterations, the algorithm will terminate with the answer mk. Essentially, the algorithm is capable of *abstracting* away $(m-2)k$ clauses when computing the maximum independent set. Observe that m can be made arbitrarily large. Abstraction is a well-known topic in AI, with important applications [17]. The example in this section suggests that HornMaxSAT and the HMaxHS algorithm can effectively enable automatic abstraction for solving large scale (graph) optimization problems. This remark is further investigated in Sect. 6.

It should be noted that the result above highlights what seems to be a fundamental property of the original MaxHS algorithm [13]. Although in the worst case, the algorithm can require an exponential number of steps to find the required set of clauses to remove to achieve consistency, the result above illustrates how the MaxHS can be effective at discarding irrelevant clauses, and focusing on the key parts of the formula, thus being able to compute solutions

---

[5] SCIP and CPLEX are available, respectively, from http://scip.zib.de/ and https://www-01.ibm.com/software/commerce/optimization/cplex-optimizer/.

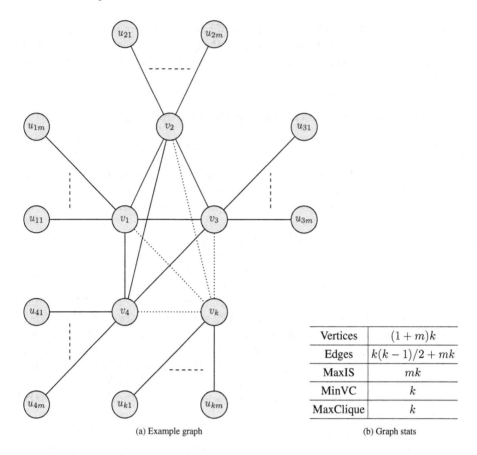

Vertices	$(1+m)k$
Edges	$k(k-1)/2 + mk$
MaxIS	mk
MinVC	k
MaxClique	k

(a) Example graph   (b) Graph stats

Fig. 1. Example graph for computing MaxIS and MinVC

in a number of iterations not much larger than the minimum number of falsified clauses in the MaxHS solution. Results from recent MaxSAT Evaluations[6] confirm the practical effectiveness of MaxHS-like algorithms.

5   HornMaxSAT in Practice

Besides the reference optimization problems analyzed in Sect. 3, a number of practical applications can also be shown to correspond to solving HornMaxSAT or can be reduced to HornMaxSAT. This section investigates some of these problems, but also proposes generic HornMaxSAT encodings for SAT and CSP.

5.1   Sample Problems

Different optimization problems in practical settings are encoded as HornMaxSAT. The winner determination problem (WDP) finds important appli-

---
[6] http://www.maxsat.udl.cat/.

cations in combinatorial auctions. An immediate observation is that the encoding proposed in [18] corresponds to HornMaxSAT. The problem of coalition structure generation (CSG) also finds important applications in multi-agent systems. An immediate observation is that some of the encodings proposed in [24] correspond to HornMaxSAT. HornMaxSAT also finds application in the area of axiom pinpointing for $\mathcal{EL}^+$ description logic, but also for other lightweight description logics. For the concrete case of $\mathcal{EL}^+$, the problem encoding is well-known to be Horn [34], with the soft clauses being unit positive. The use of LTUR-like algorithms has been investigated in [3].

As shown in the sections below, it is actually simple to reduce different decision (and optimization[7]) problems into HornMaxSAT.

5.2   Reducing SAT to HornMaxSAT

Let $\mathcal{F}$ be a CNF formula, with N variables $\{x_1 \ldots, x_N\}$ and M clauses $\{c_1, \ldots, c_M\}$. Given $\mathcal{F}$, the reduction creates a Horn MaxSAT problem with hard clauses $\mathcal{H}$ and soft clauses $\mathcal{S}$, $\langle \mathcal{H}, \mathcal{S} \rangle = \mathsf{HEnc}(\mathcal{F})$. For each variable $x_i \in X$, create new variables p_i and n_i, where $p_i = 1$ iff $x_i = 1$, and $n_i = 1$ iff $x_i = 0$. Thus, we need a hard clause $(\neg p_i \vee \neg n_i)$, to ensure that we do not simultaneously assign $x_i = 1$ and $x_i = 0$. (Observe that the added clause is Horn.) For each clause c_j we require c_j to be satisfied, by requiring that one of its literals *not* to be falsified. For each literal x_i use $\neg n_i$ and for each literal $\neg x_i$ use $\neg p_i$. Thus, c_j is encoded with a new (hard) clause c_j' with the same number of literals as c_i, but with only negative literals on the p_i and n_i variables, and so the resulting clause is also Horn. The set of soft clauses $\mathcal{S}$ is given by (p_i) and (n_i) for each of the original variables x_i. If the resulting Horn formula has a HornMaxSAT solution with at least N variables assigned value 1, then the original formula is satisfiable; otherwise the original formula is unsatisfiable. (Observe that, by construction, the HornMaxSAT solution cannot assign value 1 to more than N variables.) Clearly, the encoding outlined in this section can be subject to different improvements, e.g. not all clauses need to be goal clauses.

The transformation proposed can be related with the well-known dual-rail encoding, used in different settings [9,22,25,30,31]. To our best knowledge, the use of a dual-rail encoding for deriving a pure Horn formula has not been proposed in earlier work.

5.3   Reducing CSP to HornMaxSAT

This section investigates reductions of Constraint Satisfaction Problems (CSP) into HornMaxSAT. Standard definitions are assumed [32]. A CSP is a triple $\langle X, D, C \rangle$, where $X = \langle x_1, \ldots, x_N \rangle$ is an n-tuple of variables, D is a corresponding N-tuple of domains $D = \langle D_1, \ldots, D_N \rangle$, such that $x_i \in D_i$, and C is a t tuple of constraints $C = \langle C_1, \ldots, C_t \rangle$. C_j is a pair $\langle R_{S_j}, S_j \rangle$, where R_{S_j} is a relation

---

[7] Due to lack of space, details are omitted.

on the variables in S_j, and represents a subset of the Cartesian product of the domains of the variables in S_j.

One approach to encode CSPs as HornMaxSAT is to translate the CSP to SAT (e.g. [36]), and then apply the Horn encoder outlined in Sect. 5.2. There are however, alternative approaches, one of which we now detail. We show how to adapt the well-known direct encoding of CSP into SAT [36]. The set of variables is x_{iv}, such that $x_{iv} = 1$ iff x_i is assigned value $v \in D_i$. Moreover, we consider the *disallowed* combinations of values of each constraint C_j. For example, if the combination of values $x_{i_1} = v_{i_1} \wedge x_{i_2} = v_{i_2} \wedge \cdots \wedge x_{i_q} = v_{i_q}$ is disallowed, i.e. no tuple of the relation S_j associated with C_j contains these values, then add a (Horn) clause $(\neg x_{i_1 v_{i_1}} \vee \cdots \vee \neg x_{i_q v_{i_q}})$. For each x_i, require that no more than one value can be used: $\sum_{v \in D_i} x_{iv} \leq 1$; this AtMost1 constraint can be encoded with Horn clauses as shown in Proposition 1. Finally, the goal is to assign as many variables as possible, and so add a soft clause $(x_{i,v})$ for each x_i and each $v \in D_i$. It is immediate that the CSP is satisfiable iff the HornMaxSAT formulation has a solution with at least N satisfied soft clauses (and by construction it cannot assign value 1 to more than N variables).

5.4 Reducing PHP to HornMaxSAT

The previous sections show that the optimization and decision problems with simple reductions to HornMaxSAT are essentially endless, as any decision problem that can be reduced to SAT or CSP can also be reduced to HornMaxSAT. However, it is also possible to develop specific reductions, that exploit the original problem formulation. This section investigates how to encode the representation of the pigeonhole principle (PHP) as HornMaxSAT, for which propositional encodings are well-known and extensively investigated [11].

Definition 8 (Pigeonhole Principle, PHP [11]). *The pigeonhole principle states that if $m + 1$ pigeons are distributed by m holes, then at least one hole contains more than one pigeon. A more formal formulation is that there exists no injective function mapping $\{1, 2, \ldots, m + 1\}$ to $\{1, 2, \ldots, m\}$, for $m \geq 1$.*

Propositional formulations of PHP encode the negation of the principle, and ask for an assignment such that the $m+1$ pigeons are placed into m holes [11]. Given a propositional encoding and the reduction proposed in Sect. 5.2, we can encode PHP formulas into HornMaxSAT. We describe below an alternative reduction.

Reduction 8 (PHP $\leq_P$ HornMaxSAT). *Let $x_{ij} = 1$ iff pigeon i, with $1 \leq i \leq m + 1$, is placed in hole j, with $1 \leq j \leq m$. For each hole j, $1 \leq j \leq m$, at most 1 pigeon can be placed in hole j:*

$$\sum_{i=1}^{m+1} x_{ij} \leq 1 \qquad 1 \leq j \leq m \tag{1}$$

which can be encoded with Horn clauses, by Proposition 1.
For each pigeon i, $1 \leq i \leq m + 1$, the pigeon is placed in at most 1 hole:

$$\sum_{j=1}^{m} x_{ij} \leq 1 \qquad 1 \leq i \leq m + 1 \tag{2}$$

which can also be encoded with Horn clauses, by Proposition 1.
The soft clauses are (x_{ij}), *with* $1 \leq i \leq m+1, 1 \leq j \leq m$. *The PHP problem is satisfiable iff the HornMaxSAT problem has a solution satisfying at least* $m+1$ *soft clauses, i.e.* $m+1$ *are placed.*

6 Experimental Results

This section provides a preliminary investigation into exploiting reductions to HornMaxSAT in practice. All the experiments were run in Ubuntu Linux on an Intel Xeon E5-2630 2.60 GHz processor with 64 GByte of memory. The time limit was set to 1800 s and the memory limit to 10GByte for each process to run. Two classes of problem instances were considered. The first being a set of 46 PHP instances that were generated ranging the number of holes from 10 up to 100. The second set of benchmarks corresponds to 100 instances generated according to the example in Fig. 1, with k ranging from 10 to 100 and m ranging from k to $20k$. In the experiments six different MaxSAT solvers were considered. Some solvers are core-guide [28] (namely, OpenWBO16, WPM3, MSCG and Eva), whereas others are based on implicit hitting sets (namely, MaxHS and LMHS) [28]. Additionally, a variant of LMHS was considered for which the option "–no-equiv-seed" was set (LMHS-nes). The results are summarized in the cactus plot shown in Fig. 2. As can be observed, solvers based on implicit hitting sets (i.e. the MaxHS family of MaxSAT algorithms), but also OpenWBO16, perform very well on the instances considered[8]. The differences to the other solvers are

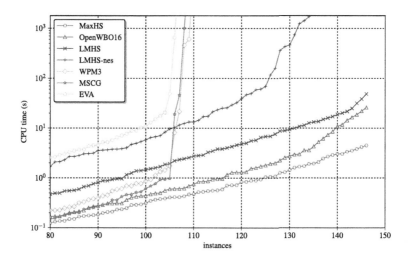

Fig. 2. Cactus plot for selected solvers on PHP and MaxIS benchmarks.

---

[8] Any implementation of the MaxHS-family of MaxSAT algorithms, by using a CDCL SAT solver, implements a basic version of the algorithm proposed in Sect. 4.

solely due to the PHP instances. While propositional encodings of PHP are well-known to be extremely hard for SAT solvers, the proposed MaxSAT encoding scales well for MaxHS-like algorithms, but also for the core-guided MaxSAT solver OpenWBO16.

Analysis of the Number of Iterations. In order to validate the abstraction mechanism described in Sect. 4.2, we considered the LMHS-nes variant, and the benchmarks generated according to the example in Fig. 1. The reason to consider LMHS-nes is that soft clauses are all unit and the set of soft clauses includes the complete set of variables of the formula. If the option is not set, then the complete CNF formula is replicated inside the MIP solver (CPLEX), *as a preprocessing step*, which results in exactly one call to CPLEX [14].

Table 1. Statistics on benchmarks generated according to the example in Fig. 1.

k	10		20		30		40		50		60		70		80		90	
m	100	200	200	400	300	600	400	800	500	1000	600	1200	700	1400	800	1600	900	1800
UB	65	65	230	230	495	495	860	860	1325	1325	1890	1890	2555	2555	3320	3320	4185	4185
#DC	9	7	13	13	27	26	25	25	50	50	49	36	70	70	48	49	63	63
#I	19	35	71	132	53	72	211	356	50	50	225	693	70	70	2140	768	747	812

Table 1 presents the results obtained, where first and second row show the k and the m parameters of the instance. The third row (UB) shows the upper bound on the number of iterations presented in Sect. 4.2. The fourth and fifth rows show the number of disjoint cores (#DC) and the number of iterations (#I) reported by LMHS-nes. As can be concluded from the table, the number of iterations is always smaller than the upper bound, suggesting that the algorithm is able to abstract clauses more effectively than in the worst case scenario. The ability of HMaxHS algorithms to find good abstractions is expected to represent a significant step into deploying HornMaxSAT problem solvers.

7   Conclusions and Research Directions

The practical success of recent MaxSAT solvers not only motivates investigating novel applications, but it also justifies considering subclasses of the general MaxSAT problem. This paper investigates the subclass of MaxSAT restricted to Horn clauses, i.e. HornMaxSAT. The paper shows that a comprehensive set of optimization and decision problems are either formulated as HornMaxSAT or admit simple reductions to HornMaxSAT. The paper also shows that fundamental decision problems, including SAT and CSP, can be reduced to HornMaxSAT. The role of HornMaxSAT in tackling the limits of resolution is investigated in recent work [20]. Although NP-hardness of HornMaxSAT guarantees that such reductions must exist, the paper develops simple reductions, some of which were unknown to our best knowledge. The paper also proposes a HornMaxSAT algorithm, based on a well-known family of MaxSAT algorithms [13,33], but which exploits the fact that the formulas to be analyzed are Horn. The experimental results show the promise of reductions of HornMaxSAT and motivate investigating further the use of HornMaxSAT as a generic problem solving approach.

This also motivates the development of more efficient implementations of HMaxHS and of alternative approaches to HMaxHS.

References

1. Abío, I., Nieuwenhuis, R., Oliveras, A., Rodríguez-Carbonell, E.: BDDs for pseudo-Boolean constraints – revisited. In: Sakallah, K.A., Simon, L. (eds.) SAT 2011. LNCS, vol. 6695, pp. 61–75. Springer, Heidelberg (2011). doi:10.1007/978-3-642-21581-0_7

2. Ansótegui, C., Bonet, M.L., Levy, J.: SAT-based MaxSAT algorithms. Artif. Intell. **196**, 77–105 (2013)

3. Arif, M.F., Mencía, C., Marques-Silva, J.: Efficient MUS enumeration of Horn formulae with applications to axiom pinpointing. In: SAT, pp. 324–342 (2015)

4. Asín, R., Nieuwenhuis, R., Oliveras, A., Rodríguez-Carbonell, E.: Cardinality networks and their applications. In: Kullmann, O. (ed.) SAT 2009. LNCS, vol. 5584, pp. 167–180. Springer, Heidelberg (2009). doi:10.1007/978-3-642-02777-2_18

5. Asín, R., Nieuwenhuis, R., Oliveras, A., Rodríguez-Carbonell, E.: Cardinality networks: a theoretical and empirical study. Constraints **16**(2), 195–221 (2011)

6. Bailleux, O., Boufkhad, Y.: Efficient CNF encoding of Boolean cardinality constraints. In: Rossi, F. (ed.) CP 2003. LNCS, vol. 2833, pp. 108–122. Springer, Heidelberg (2003). doi:10.1007/978-3-540-45193-8_8

7. Bailleux, O., Boufkhad, Y., Roussel, O.: New encodings of pseudo-Boolean constraints into CNF. In: Kullmann, O. (ed.) SAT 2009. LNCS, vol. 5584, pp. 181–194. Springer, Heidelberg (2009). doi:10.1007/978-3-642-02777-2_19

8. Biere, A., Heule, M., van Maaren, H., Walsh, T. (eds.): Handbook of Satisfiability. Frontiers in Artificial Intelligence and Applications, vol. 185. IOS Press, Amsterdam (2009)

9. Bryant, R.E., Beatty, D.L., Brace, K.S., Cho, K., Sheffler, T.J.: COSMOS: a compiled simulator for MOS circuits. In: DAC, pp. 9–16 (1987)

10. Codish, M., Zazon-Ivry, M.: Pairwise cardinality networks. In: Clarke, E.M., Voronkov, A. (eds.) LPAR 2010. LNCS, vol. 6355, pp. 154–172. Springer, Heidelberg (2010). doi:10.1007/978-3-642-17511-4_10

11. Cook, S.A., Reckhow, R.A.: The relative efficiency of propositional proof systems. J. Symb. Log. **44**(1), 36–50 (1979)

12. Cormen, T.H., Leiserson, C.E., Rivest, R.L., Stein, C.: Introduction to Algorithms, 3rd edn. MIT Press, Cambridge (2009)

13. Davies, J., Bacchus, F.: Solving MAXSAT by solving a sequence of simpler SAT instances. In: Lee, J. (ed.) CP 2011. LNCS, vol. 6876, pp. 225–239. Springer, Heidelberg (2011). doi:10.1007/978-3-642-23786-7_19

14. Davies, J., Bacchus, F.: Exploiting the power of MIP solvers in MAXSAT. In: Järvisalo, M., Van Gelder, A. (eds.) SAT 2013. LNCS, vol. 7962, pp. 166–181. Springer, Heidelberg (2013). doi:10.1007/978-3-642-39071-5_13

15. Dowling, W.F., Gallier, J.H.: Linear-time algorithms for testing the satisfiability of propositional Horn formulae. J. Log. Program. **1**(3), 267–284 (1984)

16. Eén, N., Sörensson, N.: Translating pseudo-Boolean constraints into SAT. JSAT **2**(1–4), 1–26 (2006)

17. Giunchiglia, F., Walsh, T.: A theory of abstraction. Artif. Intell. **57**(2–3), 323–389 (1992)

18. Heras, F., Larrosa, J., de Givry, S., Schiex, T.: 2006 and 2007 max-sat evaluations: contributed instances. JSAT **4**(2–4), 239–250 (2008)
19. Ignatiev, A., Morgado, A., Marques-Silva, J.: Propositional abduction with implicit hitting sets. In: ECAI, pp. 1327–1335 (2016)
20. Ignatiev, A., Morgado, A., Marques-Silva, J.: On tackling the limits of resolution in SAT solving. In: SAT (2017)
21. Ignatiev, A., Previti, A., Liffiton, M., Marques-Silva, J.: Smallest MUS extraction with minimal hitting set dualization. In: Pesant, G. (ed.) CP 2015. LNCS, vol. 9255, pp. 173–182. Springer, Cham (2015). doi:10.1007/978-3-319-23219-5_13
22. Jabbour, S., Marques-Silva, J., Sais, L., Salhi, Y.: Enumerating prime implicants of propositional formulae in conjunctive normal form. In: Fermé, E., Leite, J. (eds.) JELIA 2014. LNCS, vol. 8761, pp. 152–165. Springer, Cham (2014). doi:10.1007/978-3-319-11558-0_11
23. Jaumard, B., Simeone, B.: On the complexity of the maximum satisfiability problem for Horn formulas. Inf. Process. Lett. **26**(1), 1–4 (1987)
24. Liao, X., Koshimura, M., Fujita, H., Hasegawa, R.: Solving the coalition structure generation problem with MaxSAT. In: ICTAI, pp. 910–915 (2012)
25. Manquinho, V.M., Flores, P.F., Marques-Silva, J., Oliveira, A.L.: Prime implicant computation using satisfiability algorithms. In: ICTAI, pp. 232–239 (1997)
26. Marques-Silva, J., Ignatiev, A., Mencía, C., Peñaloza, R.: Efficient reasoning for inconsistent Horn formulae. In: Michael, L., Kakas, A. (eds.) JELIA 2016. LNCS, vol. 10021, pp. 336–352. Springer, Cham (2016). doi:10.1007/978-3-319-48758-8_22
27. Minoux, M.: LTUR: a simplified linear-time unit resolution algorithm for Horn formulae and computer implementation. Inf. Process. Lett. **29**(1), 1–12 (1988)
28. Morgado, A., Heras, F., Liffiton, M.H., Planes, J., Marques-Silva, J.: Iterative and core-guided MaxSAT solving: a survey and assessment. Constraints **18**(4), 478–534 (2013)
29. Ogawa, T., Liu, Y., Hasegawa, R., Koshimura, M., Fujita, H.: Modulo based CNF encoding of cardinality constraints and its application to MaxSAT solvers. In: ICTAI, pp. 9–17 (2013)
30. Previti, A., Ignatiev, A., Morgado, A., Marques-Silva, J.: Prime compilation of non-clausal formulae. In: IJCAI, pp. 1980–1988 (2015)
31. Roorda, J.-W., Claessen, K.: A new SAT-based algorithm for symbolic trajectory evaluation. In: Borrione, D., Paul, W. (eds.) CHARME 2005. LNCS, vol. 3725, pp. 238–253. Springer, Heidelberg (2005). doi:10.1007/11560548_19
32. Rossi, F., van Beek, P., Walsh, T. (eds.): Handbook of Constraint Programming. Foundations of Artificial Intelligence, vol. 2. Elsevier, Amsterdam (2006)
33. Saikko, P., Berg, J., Järvisalo, M.: LMHS: a SAT-IP hybrid MaxSAT solver. In: Creignou, N., Le Berre, D. (eds.) SAT 2016. LNCS, vol. 9710, pp. 539–546. Springer, Cham (2016). doi:10.1007/978-3-319-40970-2_34
34. Sebastiani, R., Vescovi, M.: Axiom pinpointing in lightweight description logics via Horn-SAT encoding and conflict analysis. In: Schmidt, R.A. (ed.) CADE 2009. LNCS, vol. 5663, pp. 84–99. Springer, Heidelberg (2009). doi:10.1007/978-3-642-02959-2_6
35. Sinz, C.: Towards an optimal CNF encoding of Boolean cardinality constraints. In: van Beek, P. (ed.) CP 2005. LNCS, vol. 3709, pp. 827–831. Springer, Heidelberg (2005). doi:10.1007/11564751_73
36. Walsh, T.: SAT v CSP. In: Dechter, R. (ed.) CP 2000. LNCS, vol. 1894, pp. 441–456. Springer, Heidelberg (2000). doi:10.1007/3-540-45349-0_32
37. Warners, J.P.: A linear-time transformation of linear inequalities into conjunctive normal form. Inf. Process. Lett. **68**(2), 63–69 (1998)

Not Too Big, Not Too Small...
Complexities of Fixed-Domain Reasoning
in First-Order and Description Logics

Sebastian Rudolph and Lukas Schweizer[⊠]

Computational Logic Group, Technische Universität Dresden, Dresden, Germany
{Sebastian.Rudolph,Lukas.Schweizer}@tu-dresden.de

Abstract. We consider reasoning problems in description logics and variants of first-order logic under the fixed-domain semantics, where the model size is finite and explicitly given. It follows from previous results that standard reasoning is NP-complete for a very wide range of logics, if the domain size is given in unary encoding. In this paper, we complete the complexity overview for unary encoding and investigate the effects of binary encoding with partially surprising results. Most notably, fixed-domain standard reasoning becomes NExpTime for the rather low-level description logics $\mathcal{ELI}$ and $\mathcal{ELF}$ (as opposed to Exp-Time when no domain size is given). On the other hand, fixed-domain reasoning remains NExpTime even for first-order logic, which is undecidable under the unconstrained semantics. For less expressive logics, we establish a generic criterion ensuring NP-completeness of fixed-domain reasoning. Amongst other logics, this criterion captures all the tractable profiles of OWL 2.

1 Introduction

Description logics [2,14] and other fragments of first-order logic are popular knowledge representation (KR) formalisms. Traditionally, the semantics underlying these formalisms do not constrain the number of elements of the described domain of interest; classical KR even admits models of infinite size. In many realistic knowledge representation scenarios, however, it is known that the domain must be finite, or even a bound on its size is given. In such scenarios, the classical semantics allowing for models of arbitrary (even infinite) size does not adequately reflect the reasoning requirements. Consequently, KR research has recently started to consider alternative semantics, leading to numerous novel (un)decidability and complexity results. The *finite model semantics*, inspired by database theory, requires models to be finite (but of arbitrary size). Finite satisfiability checking and finite query entailment have been considered for a variety of description logics [5,11,13,15]. Still, in some situations just requiring finiteness of the domain is not restrictive enough; sometimes the complete set of domain elements (or at least their precise number) are known, leading to the notion of the *fixed-domain semantics* [8]. First complexity investigations have shown that

© Springer International Publishing AG 2017
E. Oliveira et al. (Eds.): EPIA 2017, LNAI 10423, pp. 695–708, 2017.
DOI: 10.1007/978-3-319-65340-2_57

standard reasoning tasks are NP-complete for a wide range of DLs, when the elements of the fixed domain are explicitly enumerated. These results directly carry over to the case where only the number of domain elements is provided but this number is given in unary encoding.

Previous work has left open (or has been too unspecific on) important questions regarding fixed-domain reasoning. First, it was not explicitly investigated, if and how the complexity results would be affected if the domain size would be considered as a fixed parameter rather than a variable part of the input. Second, reasoning complexities of (fragments of) first-order logic (which are undecidable under classical and finite-model semantics but become decidable when fixing the domain) have not been investigated thoroughly. Third, the effect of representing the size of the domain in binary encoding has not been considered at all. In this paper, we clarify the complexity landscape for fixed-domain standard reasoning in first-order logic and description logics by making the following contributions.

- We show that for unrestricted first-order logic, standard reasoning is NExpTime, no matter if the domain size is a fixed parameter or given in unary or binary as part of the input. For fixed size or unary encoding, the complexity drops to PSpace when bounding the predicate arity, and to NP when the number of variables is bounded.
- We show that for the binary encoding, the complexity remains NExpTime, even when the logic is drastically restricted. In particular, we show corresponding hardness results for $\mathcal{ELI}$ and $\mathcal{ELF}$ terminologies.
- Finally, we establish NP-completeness for the binary encoding case for a wide range of lightweight logics by introducing a model-theoretic property shared by these logics and showing that it warrants NP-membership.

2 Preliminaries

2.1 KR Formalisms

We briefly recap syntax and semantics of the description logic $\mathcal{SROIQ}$ and some of its fragments [9].

Let N_I, N_C, and N_R be finite, disjoint sets called *individual names, concept names* and *role names* respectively. These atomic entities can be used to form complex ones as displayed in Table 1. A $\mathcal{SROIQ}$ *knowledge base* $\mathcal{K}$ is a tuple $(\mathcal{A}, \mathcal{T}, \mathcal{R})$ where $\mathcal{A}$ is an ABox, $\mathcal{T}$ is a TBox and $\mathcal{R}$ is a RBox. Table 1 presents the axiom types available in the three parts.[1]

The semantics of $\mathcal{SROIQ}$ is defined via interpretations $\mathcal{I} = (\Delta^{\mathcal{I}}, \cdot^{\mathcal{I}})$ composed of a non-empty set $\Delta^{\mathcal{I}}$ called the *domain of* $\mathcal{I}$ and a function $\cdot^{\mathcal{I}}$ mapping individual names to elements of $\Delta^{\mathcal{I}}$, concept names to subsets of $\Delta^{\mathcal{I}}$, and role names to subsets of $\Delta^{\mathcal{I}} \times \Delta^{\mathcal{I}}$. This mapping is extended to complex role and concept expressions and finally used to define satisfaction of axioms (see Table 1).

---

[1] For brevity, we omit the global restrictions of $\mathcal{SROIQ}$ as they are irrelevant in our setting.

We say that $\mathcal{I}$ *satisfies* a knowledge base $\mathcal{K} = (\mathcal{A}, \mathcal{T}, \mathcal{R})$ (or $\mathcal{I}$ is a *model* of $\mathcal{K}$, written: $\mathcal{I} \models \mathcal{K}$) if it satisfies all axioms of $\mathcal{A}$, $\mathcal{T}$, and $\mathcal{R}$. We say that a knowledge base $\mathcal{K}$ *entails* an axiom α (written $\mathcal{K} \models \alpha$) if all models of $\mathcal{K}$ are models of α. If α is a GCI, i.e., an axiom of the form $C \sqsubseteq D$ the entailment problem is also referred to as *subsumption*.

Table 1. Syntax and semantics of $\mathcal{SROIQ}$ role and concept constructors, where $a_1, \ldots a_n$ are individual names, s a role name, r a role expression and C and D concept expressions.

Name	Syntax	Semantics	
inverse role	s^-	$\{(x, y) \in \Delta^{\mathcal{I}} \times \Delta^{\mathcal{I}} \mid (y, x) \in s^{\mathcal{I}}\}$	
universal role	u	$\Delta^{\mathcal{I}} \times \Delta^{\mathcal{I}}$	
top	$\top$	$\Delta^{\mathcal{I}}$	
bottom	$\bot$	$\emptyset$	
negation	$\neg C$	$\Delta^{\mathcal{I}} \setminus C^{\mathcal{I}}$	
conjunction	$C \sqcap D$	$C^{\mathcal{I}} \cap D^{\mathcal{I}}$	
disjunction	$C \sqcup D$	$C^{\mathcal{I}} \cup D^{\mathcal{I}}$	
nominals	$\{a_1, \ldots, a_n\}$	$\{a_1^{\mathcal{I}}, \ldots, a_n^{\mathcal{I}}\}$	
univ. restriction	$\forall r.C$	$\{x \mid \forall y.(x, y) \in r^{\mathcal{I}} \rightarrow y \in C^{\mathcal{I}}\}$	
exist. restriction	$\exists r.C$	$\{x \mid \exists y.(x, y) \in r^{\mathcal{I}} \wedge y \in C^{\mathcal{I}}\}$	
Self concept	$\exists r.Self$	$\{x \mid (x, x) \in r^{\mathcal{I}}\}$	
qualified number	$\leqslant n\, r.C$	$\{x \mid \#\{y \in C^{\mathcal{I}} \mid (x, y) \in r^{\mathcal{I}}\} \leq n\}$	
restriction	$\geqslant n\, r.C$	$\{x \mid \#\{y \in C^{\mathcal{I}} \mid (x, y) \in r^{\mathcal{I}}\} \geq n\}$	
	Axiom α	$\mathcal{I} \models \alpha$, if	
role chains	$r_1 \circ \cdots \circ r_n \sqsubseteq r$	$r_1^{\mathcal{I}} \circ \cdots \circ r_n^{\mathcal{I}} \subseteq r^{\mathcal{I}}$	RBox $\mathcal{R}$
role disjointness	$\mathsf{Dis}(s, r)$	$s^{\mathcal{I}} \cap r^{\mathcal{I}} = \emptyset$	
subsumption	$C \sqsubseteq D$	$C^{\mathcal{I}} \subseteq D^{\mathcal{I}}$	TBox $\mathcal{T}$
concept assertion	$C(a)$	$a^{\mathcal{I}} \in C^{\mathcal{I}}$	ABox $\mathcal{A}$
role assertion	$r(a, b)$	$(a^{\mathcal{I}}, b^{\mathcal{I}}) \in r^{\mathcal{I}}$	
same individual	$a \doteq b$	$a^{\mathcal{I}} = b^{\mathcal{I}}$	
different individual	$a \not\doteq b$	$a^{\mathcal{I}} \neq b^{\mathcal{I}}$	

$\mathcal{EL}/\mathcal{ELI}/\mathcal{ELF}$ *Terminologies.* $\mathcal{EL}$ terminologies are knowledge bases with only axioms of the form $C \sqsubseteq D$, where C, D are concept expressions built from concept and role names using only top, conjunction, and existential quantification. We consider two extensions: $\mathcal{ELI}$ terminologies additionally allow the usage of role inverses, while $\mathcal{ELF}$ terminologies admit role functionality axioms of the shape $\top \sqsubseteq \leqslant 1\, r.C$.

$\mathsf{DL_{min}}$ *Knowledge Bases.* With $\mathsf{DL_{min}}$, we refer to a minimalistic description logic that merely allows TBox axioms of the form $A \sqsubseteq \neg B$, with $A, B \in \mathsf{N_C}$. Moreover, only atomic assertions of the form $A(a)$ are admitted. It is immediate that (finite) satisfiability checking in DL_{min} is in AC^0.

First-Order Logic. We assume the reader to be familiar with syntax and semantics of first-order predicate logic (FOL). By default, we assume that the only functions occurring are of arity zero (i.e., constants). We use $\mathsf{FOL}^=$ to denote FOL with equality. By *bounded-arity $FOL^{(=)}$* we denote $\mathsf{FOL}^{(=)}$ using only predicates of arity smaller or equal to a given bound. By *bounded-variable $FOL^{(=)}$* we denote $\mathsf{FOL}^{(=)}$ using only a bounded number of variables. For uniformity, we use the typical DL notation also for first-order interpretations and we refer to $\mathsf{FOL}^{(=)}$ sentences as $(\mathsf{FOL}^{(=)})$ axioms and to $\mathsf{FOL}^{(=)}$ as $(\mathsf{FOL}^{(=)})$ knowledge bases. We recall that virtually all mainstream DLs (including $\mathcal{SROIQ}$) can be expressed in bounded-arity $\mathsf{FOL}^=$. We also recall that Datalog denotes the function-free first-order Horn clauses.

3   Fixed-Domain Semantics

In this paper, we investigate the effects of fixing the domain size of models. Given some $s \in \mathbb{N}$, we say a knowledge base $\mathcal{K}$ is *s-satisfiable*, if it has a model $\mathcal{I} = (\Delta^{\mathcal{I}}, \cdot^{\mathcal{I}})$ with $|\Delta^{\mathcal{I}}| = s$ (referred to as an *s-model*) and an axiom φ is *s-entailed* by $\mathcal{K}$ (written: $\mathcal{K} \models_s \varphi$) if every s-model of $\mathcal{K}$ is a model of φ. We define *s-subsumption* accordingly.

Depending on how we treat the size parameter s, we distinguish three versions of the fixed-domain entailment decision problem (where, the function $|| \cdot ||$ determines the size of a knowledge base or axiom according to some usual encoding):

- assuming s fixed, the input is $(\mathcal{K}, \varphi)$; the problem size is $||\mathcal{K}|| + ||\varphi||$
- the input is $(\mathcal{K}, \varphi, s)$ with s in unary; the problem size is $||\mathcal{K}|| + ||\varphi|| + s$
- the input is $(\mathcal{K}, \varphi, s)$ with s in binary; the problem size is $||\mathcal{K}|| + ||\varphi|| + \lceil \log_2 s \rceil$

In all cases, the output is "yes" if $\mathcal{K} \models_s \varphi$ and "no" otherwise. We define the three versions of the fixed-domain satisfiability problem accordingly.

4   Fixed and Unary Encoding

4.1   Variants of First-Order Logic

We first consider the case of unrestricted first-order logic, rectifying an incorrect result from the literature. Without giving a proof, Gaggl et al. [8] claim that this problem is PSPACE-complete, sketching an argument based on the assumption that any FOL model with polynomially many domain elements can be represented in polynomial space, which, however, only holds when the maximum predicate arity is bounded (see our results below). In fact, we can show that even for domain size 2, the problem is NEXPTIME-hard (even when no constants are used). We use a reduction from the TILING-problem, as it can be found in [12], which is known to be NEXPTIME-hard.

Definition 1 ($n \times n$ **Tiling Problem**). *Given a set of square tile types $T = \{t_0, \ldots, t_k\}$, together with two relations $H, V \subseteq T \times T$ (horizontal and vertical compatibility, respectively), as well as an integer n in binary. An $n \times n$ tiling is a function $f : \{1, \ldots, n\} \times \{1, \ldots, n\} \mapsto T$ such that (a) $f(1,1) = t_0$, and (b) for all i, j $(f(i,j), f(i+1,j)) \in H$, and $(f(i,j), f(i,j+1)) \in V$. TILING is the problem of deciding, given T, H, V, and n, whether an $n \times n$ tiling exists. We refer to given T, H, V, and n as tiling system $\mathfrak{T} = (T, H, V, n)$.*

Theorem 1. *The 2-satisfiability problem for constant-free FOL is* NEXPTIME-*hard.*

Proof. We provide a reduction from TILING. Let n be the size of the grid. W.l.o.g. we assume $n = 2^m$. We now provide a FOL knowledge base (of size polynomial in m) which is satisfiable iff a tiling exists. In the following, $\vec{x}$ stands for the sequence $x_0, \ldots, x_{m-1}$ of variables (likewise $\vec{y}$ and $\vec{z}$).

$$\exists x, y.1(x) \wedge 0(y) \qquad \forall x.1(x) \leftrightarrow \neg 0(x) \tag{1}$$

$$\forall x, y.same(x, y) \leftrightarrow (1(x) \leftrightarrow 1(y)) \tag{2}$$

$$\forall \vec{x}, \vec{y}.flip_i(\vec{x}, \vec{y}) \leftrightarrow \bigwedge_{j \in \{0 \ldots i-1\}} (1(x_j) \wedge 0(y_j)) \wedge 0(x_i) \wedge 1(y_i) \wedge \bigwedge_{j \in \{i+1 \ldots m-1\}} same(x_j, y_j) \tag{3}$$

$$\forall \vec{x}, \vec{y}.next(\vec{x}, \vec{y}) \leftrightarrow \bigvee_{i \in \{0 \ldots m-1\}} flip_i(\vec{x}, \vec{y}) \tag{4}$$

$$\forall \vec{x}, \vec{y}.\neg(t_i(\vec{x}, \vec{y}) \wedge t_j(\vec{x}, \vec{y})) \tag{5}$$

$$\forall \vec{x}, \vec{y}. \bigwedge_{i \in \{0 \ldots m-1\}} (0(x_i) \wedge 0(y_i)) \rightarrow t_0(\vec{x}, \vec{y}) \tag{6}$$

$$\forall \vec{x}, \vec{y}, \vec{z}.next(\vec{x}, \vec{y}) \rightarrow \bigvee_{(t_i, t_j) \in H} t_i(\vec{x}, \vec{z}) \wedge t_j(\vec{y}, \vec{z}) \wedge \bigvee_{(t_i, t_j) \in V} t_i(\vec{z}, \vec{x}) \wedge t_j(\vec{z}, \vec{y}) \tag{7}$$

With this knowledge base and a domain of size two, we use the two elements as 0 and 1 to encode the coordinates in the grid $(0 \ldots 2^m - 1)$ in binary, using m positions in the predicate for each coordinate. With this encoding, the *next* predicate is axiomatized to contain any pair of consecutive m-bit numbers. Then the t_i predicates indicate the coordinate pairs of grid positions where the tile t_i is positioned. $\qquad \square$

A matching upper bound will be provided through Theorem 4. The proof of the preceding theorem suggests that an unbounded predicate arity is essential for the result. Indeed, when bounding the maximal arity, the complexity can be shown to be PSPACE-complete.

Theorem 2. *The fixed-domain satisfiability problem for bounded-arity FOL$^{(=)}$ is* PSPACE-*complete when the domain size is fixed or given unary.*

Proof. We show PSPACE-hardness of FOL satisfiability for domain size 2 by providing a reduction from the validity problem of quantified Boolean formulae

(QBFs). We recap that for any QBF, it is possible to construct in polynomial time an equivalent QBF that has the specific shape $\psi = Q_1 x_1 Q_2 x_2 \ldots Q_n x_n \varphi$ with $Q_1, \ldots Q_n \in \{\exists, \forall\}$ and φ being a propositional formula over the propositional variables $x_1, \ldots, x_n$. Let the first-order sentence ψ' be obtained from ψ by replacing every occurrence of a propositional variable x_i by $true(x_i)$ (thus reinterpreting the propositional variables as first-order variables and introducing $true$ as the only unary predicate). It is now easy to see that ψ is true iff $\psi' \land \exists x. true(x) \land \exists x. \neg true(x)$ has a model with two elements.

We show PSPACE membership of FOL$^{(=)}$ satisfiability checking for domain size given in unary encoding by providing a PSPACE decision procedure for a given $\mathcal{K}$ and domain size s. Let $k = ||\mathcal{K}||$ and $\ell = k + s$. Let a be the upper bound on the arity. There can be at most k predicates, hence the size needed to represent a model is upper-bounded by $k \cdot s^a \leq \ell \cdot \ell^a$, i.e., polynomial. Then we guess a polynomial size model representation and verify it in PSPACE [17]. This gives an NPSPACE algorithm which by Savitch's theorem [16] can be turned into a PSPACE one.   □

Again, inspecting the previous proof, it seems to be essential that the number of used variables is unbounded. The subsequent theorem confirms that bounding the number of variables will lead to NP-membership.

Theorem 3. *The fixed-domain satisfiability problem for bounded-variable FOL$^=$ is in NP when the domain size is given in unary encoding.*

Proof. Let v be the upper bound on the number of variables. Let $\mathcal{K}$ be a FOL knowledge base with at most v variables, let s be the prescribed domain size and let $\ell = ||\mathcal{K}|| + s$. We now describe a nondeterministic polytime procedure for checking s-satisfiability of $\mathcal{K}$. Let $\varphi = \bigwedge_{\alpha \in \mathcal{K}} \alpha$ and let $\mathcal{I}$ be a model of φ (and, hence, of $\mathcal{K}$) with $|\Delta^{\mathcal{I}}| = s$. We guess $c^{\mathcal{I}}$ for every free constant c occurring in $\mathcal{K}$. We also guess for every subformula ψ of φ the set $\mathcal{Z}_\psi$ of variable assignments $\nu : \text{freevars}(\varphi) \to \Delta^{\mathcal{I}}$ for which $\mathcal{I}, \nu \models \psi$. We determine an upper bound for the size of the guessed information: φ has not more than 2ℓ subformulae each of which has maximally v free variables, hence the size to store all $\mathcal{Z}_\psi$ is bounded by $2\ell \cdot s^v$ and hence by $2\ell \cdot \ell^v$, i.e., polynomial in the input.

Verifying that the guessed information indeed satisfies the above mentioned property requires four checks: first, $\mathcal{Z}_\varphi$ must contain the empty function. Second, every $\mathcal{Z}_\psi$ must be compatible with the variable assignments of ψ's subformulae in the following way (where δ ranges over $\Delta^{\mathcal{I}}$):

$$
\begin{aligned}
\mathcal{Z}_{\neg\psi} &= (\Delta^{\mathcal{I}})^{\text{freevars}(\psi)} \setminus \mathcal{Z}_\psi \\
\mathcal{Z}_{\psi_1 \land \psi_2} &= \{\nu \in (\Delta^{\mathcal{I}})^{\text{freevars}(\psi_1 \land \psi_2)} \mid \mathcal{Z}_{\psi_1} \subseteq \nu \text{ and } \mathcal{Z}_{\psi_2} \subseteq \nu\} \\
\mathcal{Z}_{\psi_1 \lor \psi_2} &= \{\nu \in (\Delta^{\mathcal{I}})^{\text{freevars}(\psi_1 \lor \psi_2)} \mid \mathcal{Z}_{\psi_1} \subseteq \nu \text{ or } \mathcal{Z}_{\psi_2} \subseteq \nu\} \\
\mathcal{Z}_{\exists x.\psi} &= \{\nu \in (\Delta^{\mathcal{I}})^{\text{freevars}(\exists x.\psi)} \mid \exists \delta : \nu \cup \{(x, \delta)\} \in \mathcal{Z}_\psi\} \\
\mathcal{Z}_{\forall x.\psi} &= \{\nu \in (\Delta^{\mathcal{I}})^{\text{freevars}(\forall x.\psi)} \mid \forall \delta : \nu \cup \{(x, \delta)\} \in \mathcal{Z}_\psi\}
\end{aligned}
$$

Third, for any atomic subformula ψ which is an equality atom $t_1 \doteq t_2$, we need to check that $\nu \in \mathcal{Z}_\psi$ exactly if $\nu^*(t_1) = \nu^*(t_2)$ where, given a ν, we let ν^*

denote the extension of ν to arbitrary terms, mapping constants c to $c^{\mathcal{I}}$ (as guessed before). Fourth, for any two atomic subformulae $\psi_1 = p(t_1, \ldots, t_k)$ and $\psi_2 = p(t'_1, \ldots, t'_k)$, referring to the same predicate p, we need to check that they do not contradict each other w.r.t. any k-tuple being or not being in $p^{\mathcal{I}}$. This is checked by verifying if $\{(\nu^*(t_1), \ldots, \nu^*(t_k)) \mid \nu \in \mathcal{Z}_{\psi_1})\} \cap \{(\nu^*(t'_1), \ldots, \nu^*(t'_k)) \mid \nu \in (\Delta^{\mathcal{I}})^{\mathsf{freevars}(\psi)} \setminus \mathcal{Z}_{\psi_2})\} = \emptyset$, with ν^* defined as before. Note that the sets in this condition do only have polynomially many elements. All these checks can be done in polynomial time. Hence we obtain an NP upper bound for checking satisfiability. □

4.2   Upper and Lower Bounds for DLs

We recall from Gaggl et al. [8] that fixed-domain standard reasoning in $\mathcal{SROIQ}$ with unary encoding is in NP. Note that this result is not subsumed by Theorem 3 since encoding number restrictions may require an unbounded number of variables. For one lower bound, we recall that 3-satisfiability is already NP-hard for $\mathsf{DL}_{\mathsf{min}}$ [8], a very minimalistic DL that is subsumed by all tractable profiles of OWL. To also provide a lower bound for logics without ABox, we add a hardness result for terminologies.

Proposition 1. *Deciding 3-subsumption in $\mathcal{EL}$ terminologies is* CONP*-hard.*

Proof. We provide a reduction from the 3-colorability problem to non-3-subsumption. For a graph (V, E) with $V = \{v_1, \ldots, v_n\}$, we introduce a concept name A_{v_i} for every vertex and one distinguished concept name *Clash*. Then we let the terminology $\mathcal{K}$ consist of the axioms $A_{v_i} \sqcap A_{v_j} \sqsubseteq$ *Clash* for every $\{v_i, v_j\} \in E$. Then the graph is not 3-colorable iff $\mathcal{K} \models_3 \exists r. A_{v_1} \sqcap \ldots \sqcap \exists r. A_{v_n} \sqsubseteq \exists r.$ *Clash*. □

5   Binary Encoding

5.1   NExpTime Upper Bound for FOL

Theorem 4. *The fixed-domain satisfiability problem for* FOL$^=$ *with the domain size given in binary is in* NExpTime.

Proof. Let $\mathcal{K}$ be a FOL knowledge base, s the prescribed domain size and let $\ell = ||\mathcal{K}|| + \lceil \log_2 s \rceil$. We now describe a nondeterministic exponential time procedure to check s-satisfiability of $\mathcal{K}$. Let $\varphi = \bigwedge_{\alpha \in \mathcal{K}} \alpha$. We guess a model $\mathcal{I}$ of φ (and, hence, of $\mathcal{K}$) with $|\Delta^{\mathcal{I}}| = s$ and for every subformula ψ of φ we guess the set $\mathcal{Z}_\psi$ of variable assignments $\nu : \mathsf{freevars}(\varphi) \to \Delta^{\mathcal{I}}$ for which $\mathcal{I}, \nu \models \psi$.

We determine an upper bound for the size of the guessed information: φ can contain at most ℓ different predicates and ℓ is also an upper bound for the arity of the predicates used in φ. Therefore, the size to store $\mathcal{I}$ is bounded by $\ell \cdot s^\ell$ and hence by $\ell \cdot (2^\ell)^\ell = \ell \cdot 2^{\ell^2}$. φ has not more than 2ℓ subformulae each of which has maximally ℓ free variables, hence the size to store all $\mathcal{Z}_\psi$ is bounded by $2\ell \cdot s^\ell$

and hence by $2\ell \cdot (2^\ell)^\ell = 2\ell \cdot 2^{\ell^2}$. Verifying the claimed properties of $\mathcal{I}$ and all $\mathcal{Z}_\psi$ then can be done in polynomial time w.r.t. the exponential size input. Hence we obtain a NExpTime upper bound for checking satisfiability.   □

This result subsumes NExpTime membership of fixed-domain satisfiability in all mainstream description logics. Also, by reducibility to FOL satisfiability checking, it follows that axiom entailment, conjunctive query entailment and even entailment of arbitrary Datalog queries (subsuming all kinds of navigational queries) is in co-NExpTime.

5.2   NExpTime Lower Bound for $\mathcal{ELI}$ and $\mathcal{ELF}$

We show co-NExpTime hardness for subsumption in $\mathcal{ELI}$ and $\mathcal{ELF}$ terminologies under the fixed-domain semantics in binary encoding. Note that for both logics, the problem is ExpTime-complete under the classical or finite-model semantics [10]. We show that constraining the domain size allows for encoding tiling problems. Similar constructions for much more expressive DLs have been described before [4,18].

Reducing Tiling Problems to $\mathcal{ELI}$ Subsumption. Given $\mathfrak{T} = (T, H, V, n)$ (cf. Sect. 4.1), we construct an $\mathcal{ELI}$ terminology $\mathcal{K}_\mathfrak{T}$ such that every model of $\mathcal{K}_\mathfrak{T}$ not satisfying a certain subsumption (called countermodel) represents a tiling. For simplicity, we assume $n = 2^m$. The countermodels we axiomatize shall consist of two types of domain elements: elements corresponding to grid positions and elements representing tile types. The former will be endowed with their x- and y-coordinates in binary representation, using concept names X_i^z, Y_i^z, with ($0 \leq i < m$) and $z \in \{0, 1\}$ to encode the each of the m bits of each coordinate. By means of the following axioms, we axiomatize the $n \times n$ grid:

$$\exists h^-.(X_j^0 \sqcap X_i^0) \sqsubseteq X_i^0 \quad \exists h^-.(X_j^0 \sqcap X_i^1) \sqsubseteq X_i^1 (0 \leq j < i) \tag{8}$$

$$\exists h^-.((X_0^1 \sqcap \ldots \sqcap X_{i-1}^1) \sqcap X_i^0) \sqsubseteq X_i^1 \tag{9}$$

$$\exists h^-.((X_0^1 \sqcap \ldots \sqcap X_{i-1}^1) \sqcap X_i^1) \sqsubseteq X_i^0 \tag{10}$$

$$\exists v^-.X_i^z \sqsubseteq X_i^z \quad X_i^z \sqsubseteq Grid \quad X_i^0 \sqsubseteq \exists h.Grid \tag{11}$$

$$X_i^0 \sqcap X_i^1 \sqsubseteq C_\perp \quad \exists h.C_\perp \sqsubseteq C_\perp \tag{12}$$

$$Origin \sqsubseteq X_0^0 \sqcap \ldots \sqcap X_{m-1}^0 \sqcap Y_0^0 \sqcap \ldots \sqcap Y_{m-1}^0 \tag{13}$$

with $0 \leq i < m$ and $z \in \{0, 1\}$. Likewise, we let $\mathcal{K}_\mathfrak{T}$ contain axioms obtained from axioms (8–12) where the X_i^z are replaced by Y_i^z and the roles v and h are swapped. Axioms in (8) ensure that, the value of the ith bit of the x-coordinate does not change when going in horizontal direction, if some preceding bits are set to low. Correspondingly, Axioms (9–10) ensure, that the ith bit changes its value, if all preceding bits are set to high. The axioms in (11) enforce that there is an h-successor, as long as one of the X_i^z bits is still set to low, thus stopping after 2^m consecutive h-successors. Naturally, a bit can only be set to one value which is reflected in the axioms in (12).[2] Then, instances of the first axiom in (11) merely ensure that X_i^z bit values remain unchanged when moving vertically. Finally, in (13) we use *Origin* to refer to the grid origin.

We now turn to the domain elements representing the tile types. We will make sure that every countermodel contains one element per tile type and that every grid element is associated with one tile type via the *tiledBy* role. Regarding the tiling conditions in T, H, V, the following axioms are used:

$$Tile_i \sqsubseteq Tile \quad (0 \le i \le k) \quad Tile_i \sqcap Tile_j \sqsubseteq C_\perp \quad (0 \le i < j \le k) \quad (14)$$

$$Origin \sqsubseteq \exists tiledBy. Tile_0 \tag{15}$$

$$Grid \sqsubseteq \exists tiledBy. Tile \quad Grid \sqcap Tile \sqsubseteq C_\perp \tag{16}$$

$$Origin \sqsubseteq \exists req. Tile_1 \sqcap \ldots \sqcap \exists req. Tile_k \tag{17}$$

$$\exists tiledBy. Tile_i \sqcap \exists h. \exists tiledBy. Tile_j \sqsubseteq C_\perp \tag{18}$$

$$\exists tiledBy. Tile_i \sqcap \exists v. \exists tiledBy. Tile_j \sqsubseteq C_\perp \tag{19}$$

where for each $(t_i, t_j) \notin H$ and $(t_i, t_j) \notin V$ we find an instance of (18) or (19), respectively. Axiom (15) encodes the initial tiling condition, whereas (17) enforces the existence of $Tile_i$ instances whenever *Origin* is nonempty.

Lemma 1. *For given $\mathfrak{T} = (T, H, V, n)$, let $\mathcal{K}_{\mathfrak{T}}$ be the $\mathcal{ELI}$ terminology described above, and let $s = n^2 + k + 1$. Then $\mathcal{K}_{\mathfrak{T}} \not\models_s Origin \sqsubseteq C_\perp$ iff $\mathfrak{T}$ has a tiling.*

Proof. ($\Rightarrow$) Recall that $n = 2^m$. Let $\mathcal{I} = (\Delta^{\mathcal{I}}, \cdot^{\mathcal{I}})$, with $|\Delta^{\mathcal{I}}| = 2^{2m} + k + 1 = s$, be the countermodel for the subsumption $Origin \sqsubseteq C_\perp$, i.e., there is a $\delta \in \Delta^{\mathcal{I}}$, such that $\delta \in Origin^{\mathcal{I}}$, but $\delta \notin C_\perp^{\mathcal{I}}$. Moreover, since $\mathcal{I} \models_s \mathcal{K}_{\mathfrak{T}}$, we know that there are elements $\tau_0, \ldots, \tau_k \in \Delta^{\mathcal{I}}$, with $\tau_i \in Tile_i^{\mathcal{I}}$, and in particular $(\delta, \tau_0) \in tiledBy^{\mathcal{I}}$ satisfying the initial tiling condition. Now given $x, y \in \{1, \ldots, 2^m\}$, let $x_0 x_2 \ldots x_{m-1}$ and $y_0 y_2 \ldots y_{m-1}$ be the binary representations of $x - 1$ and $y - 1$, respectively. Then we let $C_{x,y}$ denote the shorthand notation for the concept: $C_{x,y} \equiv X_0^{x_i} \sqcap \ldots \sqcap X_{m-1}^{x_{m-1}} \sqcap Y_0^{y_i} \sqcap \ldots \sqcap Y_{m-1}^{y_{m-1}}$. Axiom (13) then ensures $\delta \in C_{1,1}^{\mathcal{I}}$. It follows from Axiom (11) that, $(\delta, \delta') \in v^{\mathcal{I}}$, $(\delta, \delta'') \in h^{\mathcal{I}}$ for some $\delta', \delta'' \in \Delta^{\mathcal{I}}$, where $\delta' \in C_{1,2}^{\mathcal{I}}$ and $\delta'' \in C_{2,1}^{\mathcal{I}}$ due to axioms (8–10). Further, there must be $(\delta', \gamma') \in h^{\mathcal{I}}$ and $(\delta'', \gamma'') \in v^{\mathcal{I}}$, with $\gamma', \gamma'' \in C_{2,2}^{\mathcal{I}}$. In the same vein, by induction on x and y it follows that, for each possible (x, y), $|C_{x,y}^{\mathcal{I}}| \ge 1$, and for every $x > 1$, at least one $\beta \in C_{x,y}^{\mathcal{I}}$ has an incoming h-role from some $\beta' \in C_{x-1,y}^{\mathcal{I}}$, just as for every $y > 1$, one $\beta \in C_{x,y}^{\mathcal{I}}$ has an incoming v-role from some $\beta' \in C_{x,y-1}^{\mathcal{I}}$. Note that no element on the binary tree thus created can be in $C_{x,y}^{\mathcal{I}}$ and $C_{x',y'}^{\mathcal{I}}$ at the same time for $(x, y) \neq (x', y')$ since any $\gamma \in (C_{x,y} \sqcap C_{x',y'})^{\mathcal{I}}$ would also satisfy $\gamma \in C_\perp^{\mathcal{I}}$ leading to $\delta \in C_\perp^{\mathcal{I}}$, contradicting our assumption.

Let now $s' = \sum_{x,y} |C_{x,y}^{\mathcal{I}}|$, and assume $|C_{x,y}^{\mathcal{I}}| > 1$, i.e., there are several elements carrying the same coordinate. Recall that $k + 1$ distinct domain elements

---

[2] Disjointness ($A \sqsubseteq \neg B$) of concepts A, B are modeled in $\mathcal{ELI}$ as $A \sqcap B \sqsubseteq C_\perp$, where $C_\perp$ is a freshly introduced concept name that acts as the bottom concept in countermodels [1].

are required for the tiles, but then $s - (k + 1) = 2^{2m} < s'$. This contradicts the assumption, therefore $|C_{x,y}^{\mathcal{I}}| = 1$ for all x and y, effectively leading to all elements of $Grid$ forming an $n \times n$ grid with h and v encoding horizontal and vertical neighbourhood, respectively. Axioms (16) and (18–19) then ensure that the assignment of tiles to grid positions satisfies the horizontal and vertical compatibility constraints of H and V, respectively.

($\Leftarrow$) By the arguments above it is immediate that from every correct tiling, a countermodel for the subsumption $Origin \sqsubseteq C_\perp$ can be extracted. $\square$

We want to emphasize that the imposed domain size is crucial for (a) enforcing a grid of exponential size, and (b) for exploiting the non-deterministic choice in tile assignments.

Theorem 5. *Subsumption in $\mathcal{ELI}$ under the fixed-domain semantics with binary encoding is* CO-NEXPTIME-*hard.*

Proof. Note that for a given $\mathfrak{T} = (T, H, V, 2^m)$, the corresponding $\mathcal{ELI}$ terminology $\mathcal{K}_{\mathfrak{T}}$ is of polynomial size in m. From Lemma 1 it then follows that, subsumption in $\mathcal{ELI}$ is CO-NEXPTIME-hard. $\square$

We finish the section by showing the same complexity for $\mathcal{ELF}$ by virtue of a small adaptation of the above argument.

Theorem 6. *Subsumption in $\mathcal{ELF}$ under the fixed-domain semantics with binary encoding is* CO-NEXPTIME-*hard.*

Proof. We reuse the construction made for $\mathcal{ELI}$ with the following modification: for $r \in \{h, v\}$ we add the axioms $\top \sqsubseteq \leqslant 1\,r.\top$ and we turn every axiom of the shape $\exists r^-.C_1 \sqsubseteq C_2$ into the axiom $C_1 \sqsubseteq \exists r.C_2$. It can be readily checked that the resulting knowledge base is an $\mathcal{ELF}$ terminology. Moreover, the countermodels obtained for $\mathcal{ELI}$ satisfy the functionality restriction imposed. Finally, in the presence of functionality of r, $C_1 \sqsubseteq \exists r.C_2$ entails $\exists r^-.C_1 \sqsubseteq C_2$, hence all the arguments in Lemma 1 carry over to this case. $\square$

5.3   Logics Below NEXPTIME

We recall that even for a domain of fixed size and not part of the input, standard reasoning is already NP-hard for $\mathsf{DL}_{\min}$ knowledge bases and $\mathcal{EL}$ terminologies (cf. Sect. 4.1, Theorem 1). Obviously these hardness results carry over to the unary and binary encoding case and to any logic subsuming any of the two. We now show that a generic property that is shared by many tractable DLs ensures NP-membership of standard reasoning tasks with domain size given in binary. We start with some model-theoretic considerations.

Definition 2. *We call a model* nontrivial *if its domain size is larger than 1. A knowledge base is called* nontrivially satisfiable, *if it has a nontrivial model. A logic $\mathcal{L}$ has the* polynomial nontrivial model property *if there is a polynomial function $p : \mathbb{N} \to \mathbb{N}$ such that every nontrivially satisfiable $\mathcal{L}$ knowledge base of size k has a nontrivial model with at most $p(k)$ elements.*

This property has been shown to hold for a variety of prominent tractable logics. Among those, the recently introduced role-safety-acyclic Horn-$\mathcal{SHOIQ}$ [6] is rather general and subsumes the tractable profiles OWL QL and OWL RL of the Web Ontology Language. Another logic satisfying this property is $\mathcal{EL}^{++}$, even the version extended by reflexive roles and range restrictions [1,3] subsuming the third tractable OWL profile OWL EL. Finally, the property holds trivially for Datalog, since there is always a model containing only as many individuals as there are constants.

In the following, we will introduce two kinds of model transformations and state some logics for which modelhood is preserved under these operations.

Definition 3. *Let* $\mathcal{I} = (\Delta^{\mathcal{I}}, \cdot^{\mathcal{I}})$ *and* $\mathcal{J} = (\Delta^{\mathcal{J}}, \cdot^{\mathcal{J}})$ *be interpretations. The product interpretation of* $\mathcal{I}$ *and* $\mathcal{J}$, *denoted* $\mathcal{I} \times \mathcal{J}$ *is the interpretation* $\mathcal{K}$ *with* $\Delta^{\mathcal{K}} = \Delta^{\mathcal{I}} \times \Delta^{\mathcal{I}}$, $a^{\mathcal{K}} = (a^{\mathcal{I}}, a^{\mathcal{J}})$ *for all* $a \in N_I$, $A^{\mathcal{K}} = A^{\mathcal{I}} \times A^{\mathcal{K}}$ *for all* $A \in N_C$, *and* $r^{\mathcal{K}} = \{((\delta, \delta'), (\epsilon, \epsilon')) \mid (\delta, \epsilon) \in r^{\mathcal{I}}, (\delta', \epsilon') \in r^{\mathcal{J}}\}$ *for all* $r \in N_R$.

A very helpful observation is that the classes of models of Horn (description) logics are closed under taking products [7]: given a Horn KB $\mathcal{K}$ and two interpretations $\mathcal{I}$ and $\mathcal{J}$ with $\mathcal{I} \models \mathcal{K}$ and $\mathcal{J} \models \mathcal{K}$, it follows that $\mathcal{I} \times \mathcal{J} \models \mathcal{K}$. The next model transformation that we describe consists in picking one element and "copying" it (as well as all its atomic class memberships and relation to other elements) n times.

Definition 4. *Let* n *be a natural number, let* $\mathcal{I} = (\Delta^{\mathcal{I}}, \cdot^{\mathcal{I}})$ *be an interpretation and let* $\delta \in \Delta^{\mathcal{I}}$. *The* n-fold duplication *of* δ *in* $\mathcal{I}$ *creates an interpretation* $\mathsf{dup}^n(\mathcal{I}, \delta) = \mathcal{J}$ *with* $\Delta^{\mathcal{J}} = (\{0\} \times \Delta^{\mathcal{I}}) \cup (\{1 \ldots n\} \times \{\delta\})$ *as well as* $a^{\mathcal{J}} = (0, a^{\mathcal{I}})$ *for all* $a \in N_I$ *and for every predicate* p *of arity* k *holds* $((n_1, \delta_1), \ldots (n_k, \delta_k)) \in p^{\mathcal{J}}$ *if* $(\delta_1, \ldots, \delta_k) \in p^{\mathcal{I}}$.

Definition 5. *We call a logic* $\mathcal{L}$ non-counting, *if modelhood is preserved under arbitrary duplication of anonymous elements (i.e., elements* $\delta \in \Delta^{\mathcal{I}}$ *with* $\delta \neq a^{\mathcal{I}}$ *for all* $a \in N_I$).

Note that FOL (without equality) is non-counting, and consequently all mainstream description logics without functionality and cardinality restrictions (that is, all DLs subsumed by $\mathcal{SROI}$) are non-counting as well. Subsequent finding allows us to conclude NP-membership of satisfiability checking for a wide variety of (description) logics.

Theorem 7. *Let* $\mathcal{L}$ *be a non-counting Horn logic with bounded maximal predicate arity satisfying the polynomial nontrivial model property. Then fixed-domain satisfiability checking of* $\mathcal{L}$ *knowledge bases is in* NP *when using binary encoding.*

Proof. We describe a guess-and-check procedure. Let s be the prescribed domain cardinality and $k = ||\mathcal{K}||$ be the size of the knowledge base. Let p be the polynomial as in the definition above. If $s \leq (p(k))^2$, we guess and polytime-verify a model of size s (the guessed model takes polynomial space as $\mathcal{L}$ has bounded arity by assumption). Otherwise, we guess and polytime-verify a nontrivial model $\mathcal{I}$ of some cardinality $\tilde{s} \leq p(k)$.

It remains to show that the existence of $\mathcal{I}$ ensures the existence of a model $\mathcal{J}$ of cardinality s. Let $\mathcal{I}' = \mathcal{I} \times \mathcal{I}$. Obviously, $\mathcal{I}'$ has $\tilde{s}^2 \leq (p(k))^2$ elements and is again a model (since $\mathcal{L}$ is a Horn logic by assumption). Also by construction, $\mathcal{I}'$ contains anonymous individuals (namely all elements of the form (δ, ϵ) with $\delta \neq \epsilon$, existence guaranteed due to $\mathcal{I}$ being nontrivial). Let (δ, ϵ) be one such anonymous individual. We obtain $\mathcal{J}$ by $(s - \tilde{s}^2)$-fold duplication of (δ, ϵ). Since $\mathcal{L}$ is non-counting, $\mathcal{J}$ is a model of the knowledge base. □

Corollary 1. *Fixed-domain satisfiability checking with binary encoding is in* NP *for the logics: bounded-arity Datalog, role-safety-acyclic (RSA) Horn-$\mathcal{SHOI}$, $\mathcal{EL}{++}$ with reflexivity and ranges, and all tractable profiles of OWL: OWL EL, OWL QL, and OWL RL.*

Table 2. Overview of fixed-domain standard reasoning complexities. Complexities marked with a star have been established in this paper for which pointers to the relevant theorems are given.

	s fixed	Ref.	Unary	Ref.	Binary	Ref.	Finite
DL$_{\min}$	NP	[8]	NP	[8]	NP *	Corollary 1	AC^0
OWL QL	NP	[8]	NP	[8]	NP *	Corollary 1	NL
OWL RL	NP	[8]	NP	[8]	NP *	Corollary 1	P
$\mathcal{EL}$ terminologies	NP *	Proposition 1	NP *	Proposition 1	NP *	Corollary 1	P
OWL EL	NP	[8]	NP	[8]	NP *	Corollary 1	P
$\mathcal{EL}{++}$	NP	[8]	NP	[8]	NP *	Corollary 1	P
RSA Horn-$\mathcal{SHOI}$	NP	[8]	NP	[8]	NP *	Corollary 1	P
$\mathcal{ELI}/\mathcal{ELF}$ terminologies	NP *	Proposition 1	NP *	Proposition 1	NExpTime *	Theorems 4, 5 and 6	ExpTime
$\mathcal{ALC}$	NP	[8]	NP	[8]	NExpTime *	Theorems 4 and 5	ExpTime
$\mathcal{SHOIQ}$	NP	[8]	NP	[8]	NExpTime *	Theorems 4 and 5	NExpTime
$\mathcal{SROIQ}$	NP	[8]	NP	[8]	NExpTime *	Theorems 4 and 5	N2ExpTime
bounded-variable FOL$^{(=)}$	NP *	Theorem 3	NP *	Theorem 3	NExpTime *	Theorems 4 and 5	undec.
bounded-arity FOL$^{(=)}$	PSpace *	Theorem 2	PSpace *	Theorem 2	NExpTime *	Theorems 4 and 5	undec.
FOL$^{(=)}$	NExpTime *	Theorems 1 and 4	NExpTime *	Theorems 1 and 4	NExpTime *	Theorems 4 and 5	undec.

6 Conclusion

We investigated the complexities of standard reasoning under the fixed-domain semantics for first-order and a large range of description logics. We thereby specifically account for the encoding of the imposed domain size, and distinguish between fixed, unary, and binary. Table 2 summarizes our findings. We obtain quite uniform results of NP-completeness on the full range of description logics for the case of a fixed or unary encoded domain size. Contrariwise, in case of a binary encoding, little expressivity is needed to have standard reasoning jump to NEXPTIME where it remains for all formalisms subsumed by full first-order logic. Thus, regarding fixed-domain standard reasoning (i.e. satisfiability and non-entailment), we were able to complete the complexity landscape, and leave non-standard reasoning tasks, such as query answering as future work.

Acknowledgements. This work is supported by DFG in the Research Training Group QuantLA (GRK 1763). We thank Franz Baader for asking the right questions, and are grateful for the valuable feedback from the anonymous reviewers, which helped greatly to improve this work.

References

1. Baader, F., Brandt, S., Lutz, C.: Pushing the EL envelope. In: IJCAI, pp. 364–369. Professional Book Center (2005)
2. Baader, F., Calvanese, D., McGuinness, D., Nardi, D., Patel-Schneider, P.: The Description Logic Handbook: Theory, Implementation, and Applications, 2nd edn. Cambridge University Press, Cambridge (2007)
3. Baader, F., Lutz, C., Brandt, S.: Pushing the EL envelope further. In: OWLED, CEUR Workshop Proceedings, vol. 496. CEUR-WS.org (2008)
4. Baader, F., Sattler, U.: Expressive number restrictions in description logics. JLC **9**(3), 319–350 (1999)
5. Calvanese, D.: Finite model reasoning in description logics. In: DL, pp. 25–36. AAAI Press (1996)
6. Carral, D., Feier, C., Grau, B.C., Hitzler, P., Horrocks, I.: Pushing the boundaries of tractable ontology reasoning. In: Mika, P., et al. (eds.) ISWC 2014. LNCS, vol. 8797, pp. 148–163. Springer, Cham (2014). doi:10.1007/978-3-319-11915-1_10
7. Chang, C., Keisler, H.J.: Model Theory, Studies in Logic and the Foundations of Mathematics, vol. 73, 3rd edn. North Holland, Amsterdam (1990)
8. Gaggl, S.A., Rudolph, S., Schweizer, L.: Fixed-domain reasoning for description logics. In: ECAI, pp. 819–827. IOS Press (2016)
9. Horrocks, I., Kutz, O., Sattler, U.: The even more irresistible $\mathcal{SROIQ}$. In: KR, pp. 57–67. AAAI Press (2006)
10. Krötzsch, M., Rudolph, S., Hitzler, P.: Complexities of horn description logics. TOCL **14**(1), 2:1–2:36 (2013)
11. Lutz, C., Sattler, U., Tendera, L.: The complexity of finite model reasoning in description logics. Inf. Comput. **199**(1–2), 132–171 (2005)
12. Papadimitriou, C.H.: Computational Complexity. Addison-Wesley, Boston (1994)
13. Rosati, R.: Finite model reasoning in DL-Lite. In: Bechhofer, S., Hauswirth, M., Hoffmann, J., Koubarakis, M. (eds.) ESWC 2008. LNCS, vol. 5021, pp. 215–229. Springer, Heidelberg (2008). doi:10.1007/978-3-540-68234-9_18

14. Rudolph, S.: Foundations of description logics. In: Polleres, A., d'Amato, C., Arenas, M., Handschuh, S., Kroner, P., Ossowski, S., Patel-Schneider, P. (eds.) Reasoning Web 2011. LNCS, vol. 6848, pp. 76–136. Springer, Heidelberg (2011). doi:10.1007/978-3-642-23032-5_2
15. Rudolph, S.: Undecidability results for database-inspired reasoning problems in very expressive description logics. In: KR, pp. 247–257. AAAI Press (2016)
16. Savitch, W.J.: Relationships between nondeterministic and deterministic tape complexities. JCSS 4(2), 177–192 (1970)
17. Stockmeyer, L.J.: The complexity of decision problems in automata theory and logic. Ph.D. thesis, MIT (1974)
18. Tobies, S.: The complexity of reasoning with cardinality restrictions and nominals in expressive description logics. JAIR 12, 199–217 (2000)

Reactive Maintenance Policies over Equalized States in Dynamic Environments

Zeynep G. Saribatur[1(✉)], Chitta Baral[2], and Thomas Eiter[1]

[1] Technische Universität Wien, Vienna, Austria
{zeynep,eiter}@kr.tuwien.ac.at
[2] Arizona State University, Tempe, USA
chitta@asu.edu

Abstract. We address the problem of representing and verifying the behavior of an agent following a policy in dynamic environments. Our focus is on policies that yield sequences of actions, according to the present knowledge in the state, with the aim of reaching some main goal. We distinguish certain cases where the dynamic nature of the environment may require the agent to stop and revise its next actions. We employ the notion of maintenance to check whether a given policy can maintain the conditions of the main goal, given a respite from environment actions. Furthermore, we apply state clustering to mitigate the large state spaces caused by having irrelevant information in the states, and under some conditions this clustering might change the worst-case complexity. By preserving the behavior of the policy, it helps in checking for maintenance with a guarantee that the result also holds in the original system.

1 Introduction

Dynamic environments may change the state of the world and interfere with the behavior of a reactive agent that follows a given policy. During the execution of a plan given by the policy, a state change may require the agent to stop and examine the current situation, to determine the next steps. In such cases, rather than "achieving" certain conditions of a main goal, the focus is more on "maintaining" the conditions. Baral et al. [3] introduced maintenance given a *window of opportunity*, a respite from the environment actions. This notion enables us to distinguish the agent following a policy and doing its best to maintain the goal, if the environment does not interfere during a time period.

For an example, consider an agent that is looking for a person in a supermarket with a layout shown in Fig. 1(a). Although the agent knows the layout, it does not know where the person might be, and is given a policy (Fig. 1(b)) to follow. If the agent observes the person at any time step, then it stops and moves

This work has been supported by Austrian Science Fund (FWF) project W1255-N23, and Zeynep G. Saribatur's visit to ASU was supported by the Austrian Marshall Plan Foundation.

E. Oliveira et al. (Eds.): EPIA 2017, LNAI 10423, pp. 709–723, 2017.
DOI: 10.1007/978-3-319-65340-2_58

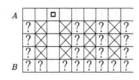

If at row A: walk towards right to the next aisle.
If reached the end of row A: walk towards row B.
If at row B: walk towards left to the next aisle.
If reached the end of row B: walk towards row A.
If observed the person: move towards the person.

(a) agent's observation in a state   (b) a policy

Fig. 1. Supermarket example

towards him. If the environment is static, i.e., the person does not move, then the agent's behavior following the policy can be represented as in [13]. However, our focus is on the dynamic nature of the environment; the person may also be moving, while the agent executes its actions. Thus, the environment actions play a role in the agent's behavior and need to be distinguished.

Different from [3], we are interested in policies that yield sequences of actions, which requires awareness of environment actions that may concurrently be made. Furthermore, while [3] considers explicit states, our focus is on implicit state representations, which allows for the use of logical formalisms to represent transitions. Moreover, the policies that we consider are defined using the representation power of logic programs, action theories or QBFs. Online planning and decision making are governed by these policies.

One concern of representing an agent's behavior for a given policy is the issue of keeping irrelevant information in the state which the policy does not use; having to represent such information adds to the state explosion problem. State clustering considered by [13] is a form of abstraction that omits such information, while preserving the behavior of the policy in static environments. We employ this notion by extending it to distinguish environment actions, which helps in defining the maintenance of a policy. Although such a clustering might not change the worst-case complexity in general, it makes a difference in practice, as one deals with information only related to the behavior. However, in certain situations the clustering may significantly decrease the complexity.

Our contributions are briefly summarized as follows:

(1) We extend the notion of maintainability to consider concurrent actions and focus on policies that yield sequences of actions (Sect. 3). We consider the possible outcomes of executing the latter in a dynamic environment. In our representation, we distinguish cases such as (a) the agent executes the actions with no interference, (b) the environment acts in a way that prevents the agent from executing the remainder of its actions, and (c) the agent realizes a way to reach the main goal, and stops executing its remaining actions. Case (c) can also occur in a static environment, but was not considered in [13].

(2) We introduce a state clustering that can distinguish environment movements and define a system that represents the policy's behavior in the dynamic

environment (Sect. 4). We show that such a system preserves the relevant information, and helps in checking the maintenance with a guarantee that the result also holds in the original system (Sect. 5).

(3) We discuss complexity issues regarding the representation, such as checking for maintainability of a system for a given policy, and the effect of the clustering (Sect. 6). We also discuss the synthesis problem, i.e., constructing some maintenance policy.

2 Preliminaries

We define a system that represents dynamic environments as follows.

Definition 2.1 (System). *A (dynamic) system is a quadruple $A = \langle \mathcal{S}, \mathcal{S}_0, \mathcal{A}, \Phi_c \rangle$, where*

- $\mathcal{S}$ *is the finite set of states;*
- $\mathcal{S}_0 \subseteq \mathcal{S}$ *is the set of initial states;*
- $\mathcal{A} = \mathcal{A}_a \cup \mathcal{A}_e$ *is the finite set of agent $(\mathcal{A}_a)$ and environment $(\mathcal{A}_e)$ actions;*
- $\Phi_c : \mathcal{S} \times \mathcal{A}_a \times \mathcal{A}_e \to 2^{\mathcal{S}}$ *is a non-deterministic transition function.*

The idle action a_{nop} (resp. e_{nop}) is included in $\mathcal{A}_a$ (resp. $\mathcal{A}_e$) and Φ_c considers concurrent actions, where for all $s \in \mathcal{S}$, $\Phi_c(s, a_{nop}, e_{nop}) = \{s\}$. A sequence $\bar{a} = a_1, a_2, \ldots, a_n$ of agent actions is executable if

$$\exists s_0, \ldots, s_n : \forall i < n, s_{i+1} \in \Phi_c(s_i, a_{i+1}, e_{nop}) \ \wedge \ a_{i+1} \neq a_{nop}.$$

We denote such *(potential) plans* by Σ_a, and by $\Sigma_a(s)$ those that are executable from s. We use the notation $\Sigma'_a = \Sigma_a \cup \{a_{nop}\}$ to also consider the idle agent action.

We consider policies that have a main goal μ in mind, and guide the agent with action sequences that are computed according to the knowledge base KB, which is the formal representation of the world's model with a transition system view (as in [13]).

Definition 2.2 (Policy). *Given a system $A = \langle \mathcal{S}, \mathcal{S}_0, \mathcal{A}, \Phi_c \rangle$ and a set Σ_a of plans with actions of $\mathcal{A}_a \subseteq \mathcal{A}$, a policy is a function $P_{\mu, KB} : \mathcal{S} \to 2^{\Sigma'_a}$ s.t. $P_{\mu, KB}(s) \subseteq \Sigma_a(s) \cup \{a_{nop}\}$.*

For any state s, $\{a_{nop}\} \subseteq P_{\mu, KB}(s)$ should hold, for the cases of a moving environment while the agent is idle. We say that $P_{\mu, KB}$ is undefined for a state s if $P_{\mu, KB}(s) = \{a_{nop}\}$. For readability, we omit subscripts of P, as they are considered to be fixed.

Notice that a plan given by the policy might become inexecutable if the environment acts. In order to consider environments that may interfere with the agent's plan execution, we will express possible outcomes of the desire towards executing the *policy plans*.

3 Behavior of a Policy in Dynamic Environments

We describe a system that represents possible outcomes of executing a policy plan in a dynamic environment, and define the maintenance by the policy.

Transitions as Action Sequences. To consider execution of action sequences, we first extend the system $A = \langle \mathcal{S}, \mathcal{S}_0, \mathcal{A}, \Phi_c \rangle$ to $A_\Sigma = \langle \mathcal{S}, \mathcal{S}_0, \Sigma, \Phi_\Sigma \rangle$, where $\Sigma = \Sigma'_a \cup \Sigma_e$ with $\Sigma_e = \mathcal{A}^*_e$ as the set of sequences of environment actions. The transition function $\Phi_\Sigma : \mathcal{S} \times \Sigma'_a \times \Sigma_e \to 2^\mathcal{S}$ yields the states resulting from executing concurrent action sequences: For $\bar{a} = \langle a_1, \ldots, a_n \rangle$ and $\bar{e} = \langle e_1, \ldots, e_n \rangle$,

$$\Phi_\Sigma(s, \bar{a}, \bar{e}) = \{s' \mid \exists s_0, \ldots, s_n : \forall i < n, s_{i+1} \in \Phi_c(s_i, a_{i+1}, e_i) \land s_0 = s \land s_n = s'\};$$

it is undefined if $|\bar{a}| \neq |\bar{e}|$. We use $\Phi_\Sigma(s, P(s), \bar{e})$ as a shorthand for $\bigcup_{\bar{a} \in P(s)} \Phi_\Sigma(s, \bar{a}, \bar{e})$.

The evolution of the world described by the system is characterized by trajectories and the closure of a system is defined using these trajectories as follows.

Definition 3.1 (Trajectory and Closure). *In a system $A_\Sigma = \langle \mathcal{S}, \mathcal{S}_0, \Sigma, \Phi_\Sigma \rangle$, an alternating sequence of states and action sequences $s_0, \sigma_1, s_1, \ldots, \sigma_n, s_n$ is a trajectory if $s_i \in \Phi_\Sigma(s_{i-1}, \bar{a}_i, \bar{e}_i), i \geq 0$, for $\sigma_i = (\bar{a}_i, \bar{e}_i) \in \Sigma$. The closure w.r.t. a set $S \subseteq \mathcal{S}$ is $Cl_\Sigma(S, A_\Sigma) = \bigcup_{s \in S}\{s_n \mid \exists trajectory\ s_0, \sigma_1, s_1, \ldots, \sigma_n, s_n\ in\ A_\Sigma, n \geq 0 : s_0 = s\}$.*

Following the Policy in a Dynamic Environment. We consider three outcomes of executing a policy plan in the dynamic environment:

(1) The environment's actions may not interfere with the execution of the plan, and the agent can execute the whole plan and reach the state that the policy was aiming for.

(2) The environment may act in a way that a state is reached, from which the remainder of the plan becomes non executable (even if the environment does no longer move).

(3) The agent may reach a state that has a possibility to reach the main goal, so that, instead of executing the remaining plan, a new plan can be determined towards the goal.

Formally, a transition function $\Psi_{P, \Sigma_e} : \mathcal{S} \times \Sigma'_a \to 2^\mathcal{S}$ yields the states by executing some plan returned by P:

$$\Psi_{P, \Sigma_e}(s, \bar{a}) = \{s' \mid \bar{a} \in P(s), \exists \bar{e} \in \Sigma_e : s' \in \Phi_\Sigma(s, \bar{a}, \bar{e})\} \cup \tag{1}$$

$$\bigcup_{\bar{a} = \bar{a}'\bar{a}'' \in P(s)} \{s' \mid \exists \bar{e} \in \Sigma_e, s' \in \Phi_\Sigma(s, \bar{a}', \bar{e}) \land \Phi_\Sigma(s', \bar{a}'', \bar{e}_{nop}) \models \bot\} \cup \tag{2}$$

$$\bigcup_{\bar{a} = \bar{a}'\bar{a}'' \in P(s)} \{s' \mid \exists \bar{e} \in \Sigma_e, s' \in \Phi_\Sigma(s, \bar{a}', \bar{e}) \land \exists s'' \in \Phi_\Sigma(s', P(s'), \bar{e}_{nop}) : s'' \models \mu\} \tag{3}$$

where for a set S of states, $S \models \alpha \Leftrightarrow \forall s \in S, s \models \alpha$ and $\bar{e}_{nop} \in \{e_{nop}\}^*$. In (2) and (3), we focus on prefixes $\bar{a}'$ of $\bar{a}$ to compute the (middle) states reached while executing $\bar{a}$.

The states reachable from s if all of the plan $\bar{a}$ can be executed are computed in (1). The states in (2) are those reached due to some environment actions $\bar{e}$ during the execution of $\bar{a}$, where the remaining plan $\bar{a}''$ is no longer executable, even if the environment is idle after this point. From the middle states in (3), the main goal μ can be reached with a new policy plan (if the environment remains idle).

We represent the case when the environment remains idle with $\Psi_{P,\bar{e}_{nop}}$, where

$$\Psi_{P,\bar{e}_{nop}}(s,\bar{a}) = \{s' \mid \bar{a} \in P(s), s' \in \Phi_{\Sigma}(s,\bar{a},\bar{e}_{nop})\} \cup$$
$$\bigcup_{\bar{a}=\bar{a}'\bar{a}'' \in P(s)} \{s' \in \Phi_{\Sigma}(s,\bar{a}',\bar{e}_{nop}) \mid \exists s'' \in \Phi_{\Sigma}(s',P(s'),\bar{e}_{nop}) : s'' \models \mu\}.$$

Notice that $\Psi_{P,\bar{e}_{nop}}(s,\bar{a}) \subseteq \Psi_{P,\Sigma_e}(s,\bar{a})$.

From a state s, a state s' reached after trying to execute a plan $\bar{a}$, i.e., $s' \in \Psi_{P,\Sigma_e}(s,\bar{a})$, is referred as a *checkpoint state* from s, where the agent determines its next policy actions. The set of all such states from a set S of states is similar to Definition 3.1 when the closure Cl_{P,Σ_e} is defined over the trajectories of Ψ_{P,Σ_e}.

Maintenance. The idea is to keep track of the checkpoint states when the policy is followed, and define the maintenance over them. First, the notion of unfolding a policy is defined as a sequence of states the system may go through if it follows the policy, while the environment remains idle, for at most some k steps.

Definition 3.2 (Unfold). *For a system* $A_{\Sigma} = \langle S, S_0, \Sigma, \Phi_{\Sigma} \rangle$ *and* $s \in S$, $Unfold_k(s, A_{\Sigma}, P)$ *is the set of all sequences* $\bar{s} = s_0, \ldots, s_l$ *where* $l \leq k$ *and* $s_0 = s$ *s.t.* $P(s_j)$ *is defined for all* $j < l$, $s_{j+1} \in \Psi_{P,\bar{e}_{nop}}(s_j, P(s_j) \backslash \{a_{nop}\})$, *and if* $l < k$, *then* $P(s_j)$ *is undefined.*

Based on this, we define the k-maintainability.

Definition 3.3 (k-Maintainability). *For a system* $A_{\Sigma} = \langle S, S_0, \Sigma, \Phi_{\Sigma} \rangle$, *the policy* P k-maintains $S \subseteq S$ *w.r.t. a goal condition* μ, *if for each state* $s \in Cl_{P,\Sigma_e}(S, A_{\Sigma})$ *and sequence* $s_0, s_1 \ldots, s_l$ *in* $Unfold_k(s, A_{\Sigma}, P)$ *some* $j \leq l$ *exists s.t.* $s_j \models \mu$.

We say that the original system A_{Σ} is k-maintained by policy P w.r.t. μ, if P k-maintains the initial states S_0 w.r.t. μ.

We illustrate over a simple example for better understanding of the concepts. We consider a basic scenario, since even a simplified (yet still interesting) supermarket example has quite a number of states and is difficult to visualize within the space limits.

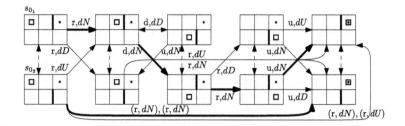

Fig. 2. Closure w.r.t. the initial states in the sliding door example

Example 3.1. Consider a sliding door scenario, where an agent, initially located at (0,0), can move right (r), down (d) or up (u), and a sliding door, located between columns 1–2, can move up (dU), down (dD) or remain still (dN). The agent can look horizontally and detect if the door is located in its row. The main goal is to reach (0,2). Consider a policy P that tells to move right whenever possible and if not possible then to move up/down (depending on which one is executable). In case (0,2) is observable, the policy returns the plan to reach that cell. Once the agent reaches (0,2), no more action is taken.

Figure 2 shows possible trajectories from the initial states s_{0_1}, s_{0_2}, including those where the agent does not move (dashed arrows). All shown states constitute the closure w.r.t. the initial states according to the policy and the possible environment actions. The trajectories in which the environment remains still gives the unfolding trajectories from the initial states (thick arrows). One can see that the system is 4-maintained by the policy.

The door scenario is simplistic, and as one adds new properties of the agent, the environment, or a more involved policy, the state space immediately gets larger. Furthermore, as in the supermarket example, the state may contain information irrelevant to the agent's behavior, which leads to a large number of states with unnecessary information.

Note that if we restrict the concurrent action transition function Φ_c to only allow for execution of (a, e_{nop}) and (a_{nop}, e), this can model an alternating execution of agent and environment actions described in [3]. The transition (a_{nop}, e_{nop}) then corresponds to having no possible actions for the agent or the environment at a state. Thus, we have the following proposition when only policies with 1-step plans are considered.

Proposition 3.1 (Connection to Baral et al. [3]). *A system $A_\Sigma = \langle \mathcal{S}, \mathcal{S}_0, \Sigma, \Phi_\Sigma \rangle$, where Φ_Σ is built over a restricted Φ_c, is k-maintained by a 1-step policy P iff the corresponding system defined as in [3] is k-maintainable, due to existence of P.*

4   Omitting Unnecessary Information

State clustering by getting rid of irrelevant information w.r.t. the policy or the observability of the environment was considered in [13] with a focus on static environments, which guarantees any information gain in a state to hold in the successor state. This allows the state clusters to become more explicit as the agent traverses the environment.

However, in case of dynamic environments, such a clustering idea is unable to distinguish the environment's movement in a state's irrelevant/unobserved part. Figure 3(a) shows some part of the system when the notion in [13] is applied to the supermarket example; the states where the agent observes the person are omitted for simplicity. The agent only knows that the environment did some actions $\overline{e}$. Therefore, whenever the person is not observed, the unobserved part is considered to be unknown, because the dynamic nature can not guarantee that some gained information holds in the next state.

To define maintenance, we must be able to distinguish the transitions where the environment does not move (especially, in the unobserved parts) and represent how this affects the knowledge about the state clusters. To this end, we use equalized d-states.

Definition 4.1. *An* equalized dynamic (d-) state *is a pair* $\langle \hat{s}, \theta \rangle$, *where*

(1) the equalized state, $\hat{s}$, contains the indistinguishable states w.r.t the policy, and
(2) the inferred state, $\hat{\theta}$, contains the states which are inferred to possibly hold by using the knowledge of the environment's movements.

The state $\hat{s}$ contains the information relevant to the policy or the observability of the environment, while the state $\hat{\theta}$ makes further inferences to represent the effect of the environment's movements; in particular, whether the environment moved or not. Thus, there can be multiple pairs with identical equalized states, but different inferred states.

Building the Clusters. We consider two *classification functions* described by surjections:

- $h : S \rightarrow \Omega$, where Ω is the set of possible equalized states, and
- $h_r : S \rightarrow 2^{\Theta}$, where Θ is the set of possible inferred states.

Necessarily, h and h_r should satisfy that for every $\langle \hat{s}, \hat{\theta} \rangle$, we have $h_r^{-1}(\hat{\theta}) \subseteq h^{-1}(\hat{s})$. A state may be mapped to more than one inferred state cluster, as these clusters depend on the previous states and the movement of the environment.

The classification function h is based on the notion of indistinguishability, as in [13]. The state clustering is done only to omit the irrelevant information w.r.t the policy, so that P returns the same output for the cluster. Formally, the clustering satisfies the condition

$$\forall s \in \mathcal{S}, P(s) = P(h(s)) \tag{4}$$

which makes sure that for states that are mapped to the same cluster, the policy returns the same plans, i.e., $\forall d, e \in \mathcal{S}, h(d) = h(e) \Rightarrow P(d) = P(e)$.

As said, inferred states depend on the previous states and the taken environment actions. In detail, the initial set of inferred states is $\Theta_0 = \{h(s) \mid s \in S_0\}$, and the clustering satisfies the constraint: for all $d, e \in \mathcal{S}$ such that $h_r(d) = h_r(e)$ it holds that $h(d) = h(e)$ and $\exists d', e': d \in \Psi_{P,\Sigma_e \backslash \bar{e}_{nop}}(d', P(d')), e \in \Psi_{P,\Sigma_e \backslash \bar{e}_{nop}}(e', P(e'))$ with $h_r(d') = h_r(e')$. In other words, only the states that can be reached from a previous state, due to some sequence of environment actions, are mapped into the inferred states. This is similarly done for the case of $\bar{e}_{nop}$, to distinguish the states reached only by $\bar{e}_{nop}$.

How to do state clustering h for action languages was shown in [13]. Inferred state clustering h_r is possible along the same lines, but not elaborated here due to space limits.

Abstract Environment Actions. Clustering the states by omitting the information about the irrelevant part of the state leads to abstracting the irrelevant environment actions. Since the main aim is to represent whether or not the environment concurrently moved, we distinguish between the actions e_{nop} and $\hat{e}$ which is an abstraction of all other environment actions; we let $\widehat{\mathcal{A}}_e = \{e_{nop}, \hat{e}\}$ and consider the mapping $\phi_h : \mathcal{A}_e \rightarrow \widehat{\mathcal{A}}_e$.

Such an abstraction can be seen as the coarsest one possible, as it only distinguishes whether the environment moved or not. It is sufficient for defining maintenance, since the focus is on cases in which the environment does not move.

Example 4.1. Figure 3(b) shows an example of equalized d-states. As expected, the inferred states have less possible locations for the person than the equalized states, since the possible locations are inferred more precisely depending on whether he/she moved or not. Furthermore, whether or not the person concurrently moves results in different inferred states. From state $\langle s_1, \theta_1 \rangle$, $\bar{e}_{nop}$ causes the cells observed at θ_1 to remain the same in θ_{2_1}, although to the agent's view, s_{2_1}, they become unknown. If the person executes some actions $\bar{\hat{e}}$, his possible locations in θ_{2_2} are inferred from θ_1. Notice that θ_{2_2} is not the same as s_{2_2}, as it shows the locations the person can move to in the same time steps as the agent. A transition may also result in the agent observing the person; then $s_{2_3} = \theta_{2_3}$ holds, since the person is obviously not in the unobserved parts.

5   Equalized Dynamic Systems

A system that represents the policy execution in a dynamic environment is defined over the original system by taking the classification functions and the policy into account.

Definition 5.1. *An* equalized dynamic system A_P^{h,h_r}, *w.r.t. the classification functions* h, h_r *and the policy* P, *is defined as* $A_P^{h,h_r} = \langle \widehat{\mathcal{S}}, \widehat{\mathcal{S}}_0, \Sigma_a', \widehat{\Sigma}_e, \widehat{\Psi}_{P,\Sigma_e} \rangle$, *where*

- $\widehat{\mathcal{S}}$ *is the finite set of equalized d-states;*

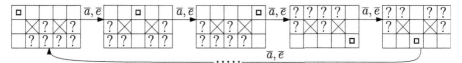

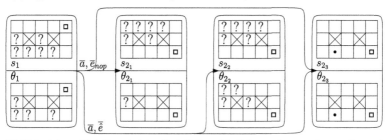

(a) Equalization is unable to distinguish the unobserved environment movements

(b) Pair states with inferred states that distinguish if the environment moved or not

Fig. 3. State clusters that distinguish environment actions

- $\widehat{S}_0 \subseteq \widehat{S}$ is the set of initial equalized d-states, if $h^{-1}(\widehat{\theta}) \cap S_0 \neq \emptyset$;
- Σ'_a is the union of the set Σ_a, possible plans with agent actions $\mathcal{A}_a$, and $\{a_{nop}\}$;
- $\widehat{\Sigma}_e = \widehat{A}^*_e$ is the set of sequences of abstract environment actions (for $\widehat{A}_e = \{e_{nop}, \hat{e}\}$);
- $\widehat{\Psi}_{P,\widehat{\Sigma}_e} : \widehat{S} \times \Sigma'_a \to 2^{\widehat{S}}$ is the policy transition function in the dynamic environment, i.e.,

$$\widehat{\Psi}_{P,\widehat{\Sigma}_e}(\langle \hat{s}, \hat{\theta} \rangle, \bar{a}) = \{\langle h(s'), h_r(s') \rangle \mid \bar{a} \in P(\hat{s}), \exists s \in h_r^{-1}(\hat{\theta}), s' \in \Psi_{P,\Sigma_e}(s, \bar{a})\}.$$

The transitions $\widehat{\Psi}_{P,\bar{e}_{nop}}$ show an idle environment. For simplicity, $\langle \hat{s}, \hat{\theta} \rangle$ is denoted as $\hat{s}\hat{\theta}$.

The equalized dynamic system is defined over the state clusters of the checkpoint states in the original system. Reduced number of states and transitions help to focus on the details important for the policy, without losing any property of the behavior.

The closure $\widehat{Cl}(\widehat{S}, A_P^{h,h_r})$ is defined akin to Definition 3.1, using the trajectories of $\widehat{\Psi}_{P,\widehat{\Sigma}_e}$.

Lemma 5.1. *For a given set S of states, any state s in $Cl_{P,\Sigma_e}(S, A_\Sigma)$, has a corresponding state $\hat{s}\hat{\theta}$ in $\widehat{Cl}(\widehat{S}, A_P^{h,h_r})$, where $\hat{s} = h(s)$ and $\hat{\theta} = h_r(s)$.*

The result holds since for every pair of successor states in A_Σ, there is a corresponding pair of equalized d-states in A_P^{h,h_r}. So any sequence of states considered in the closure of A_Σ w.r.t. a set S, has a corresponding sequence in the closure of A_P^{h,h_r} w.r.t. $\widehat{S}$.

Maintenance over the Equalized Dynamic System. We define the unfolding of the policy over the equalized d-states, similar to Definition 3.2, by considering $\widehat{\Psi}_{P,\overline{e}_{nop}}$. The clustering condition (4) ensures that no transitions will be introduced different from how the policy behaves in the original system. Furthermore, it ensures the following result.

Lemma 5.2. *For some k, for each sequence $s_0, \ldots, s_l$ in $Unfold_k(s, A_\Sigma, P)$, some sequence $\hat{s}\hat{\theta}_0, \ldots, \hat{s}\hat{\theta}_l$ in $\widehat{Unfold}_k(\hat{s}\hat{\theta}, A_P^{h,h_r})$ exists with $\hat{s}_i = h(s_i)$ and $\hat{\theta}_i = h_r(s_i), 0 \le i \le l$.*

We define the k-maintainability of the equalized dynamic system as follows, where $\hat{s}\hat{\theta} \models \mu \Leftrightarrow \forall s \in h^{-1}(\hat{s}) : s \models \mu$.

Definition 5.2 (Equalized k-Maintainability). *$A_P^{h,h_r} = \langle \widehat{S}, \widehat{S}_0, \Sigma'_a, \widehat{\Sigma}_e, \widehat{\Psi}_{P,\Sigma_e} \rangle$ is k-maintainable, if P k-maintains $\widehat{S}_0$ w.r.t. μ: For each state $\hat{s}\hat{\theta}$ in $\widehat{Cl}(\widehat{S}_0, A_P^{h,h_r})$ and sequence $\hat{s}\hat{\theta}_0, \hat{s}\hat{\theta}_1, \ldots, \hat{s}\hat{\theta}_l$ in $\widehat{Unfold}_k(\hat{s}\hat{\theta}, A_P^{h,h_r})$ some $j \le l$ exists s.t. $\hat{s}\hat{\theta}_l \models \mu$.*

Example 5.1. In the supermarket example for environment size 5×9 (Fig. 1(a)), the given policy 9-maintains the set of initial states. At any state in the closure, the person may be located at the farthest possible point, and if he does not move for at least 9 steps, then the agent will eventually observe the person and catch him.

The following theorem shows that the clustering does not introduce false positives.

Theorem 5.1 (Soundness). *If A_P^{h,h_r} is k-maintainable, then A_Σ is k-maintained by P.*

Proof. Assume that A_Σ is not k-maintained by P. Let $s \in Cl_{P,\Sigma_e}(S_0, A_\Sigma)$ be a state and $\tau = s_0, s_1 \ldots, s_l$ in $Unfold_k(s, A_\Sigma, P)$ such that $s_l \not\models \mu$. By Lemmas 5.1 and 5.2, we know that $\exists \hat{s}\hat{\theta} \in \widehat{Cl}(\widehat{S}_0, A_P^{h,h_r})$ with $\hat{s} = h(s)$ and $\exists \hat{\tau} = \hat{s}\hat{\theta}_0, \hat{s}\hat{\theta}_1 \ldots, \hat{s}\hat{\theta}_l$ in $\widehat{Unfold}_k(\hat{s}\hat{\theta}, A_P^{h,h_r})$ with $\hat{s}_i = h(s_i), 0 \le i \le l$. By assumption on s_l, $\hat{s}\hat{\theta}_l \not\models \mu$. Hence, A_P^{h,h_r} is not k-maintainable. $\square$

In order to have completeness, we need further restrictions on the state clustering h, to avoid introducing spurious trajectories. We consider the properness condition [13]

$$\hat{s}\hat{\theta}' \in \widehat{\Psi}_{P,\widehat{\Sigma}_e}(\hat{s}\hat{\theta}, \overline{a}) \iff \forall s' \in h^{-1}(\hat{s}'), \exists s \in h^{-1}(\hat{s}) : \Psi_{P,\Sigma_e}(s, \overline{a}) \quad (5)$$

which ensures that if A_P^{h,h_r} has a transition from $\hat{s}\hat{\theta}_1$ to $\hat{s}\hat{\theta}_2$, then any state mapped to $\hat{s}\hat{\theta}_2$ has a transition from some state mapped to $\hat{s}\hat{\theta}_1$. This allows for the possibility of backtracking any trajectory found in A_P^{h,h_r} and map it back to A_Σ (see details in [13]).

Theorem 5.2 (Completeness). *If A_Σ is k-maintained by P and h is proper, then A_P^{h,h_r} is k-maintainable.*

The equalized dynamic system can represent static environments by only allowing e_{nop} and can be related to the equalized static system [13]. Assuming that the actions are reversible (as in the supermarket example), if the agent's observations during a plan execution contribute to the decision making in the next state, then we get the following.

Corollary 5.1. *If the equalized dynamic system A_P^{h,h_r} is k-maintainable, then the policy P works in at most k steps in the equalized static system $A_{h,P}$.*

The result follows, since the assumptions help in emulating (3) (for $\bar{e}_{nop}$ case) in the static setting. If the agent reaches a state while also observing the main goal on the way, then the policy will have the agent reach the main goal in the next state. However, the reverse of the corollary may not hold, as the dynamic nature of the environment may have the agent end up in a state that was not considered in the static environment.

6   Computational Complexity

In this section, we consider the computational complexity of k-maintainability.

Assumptions. We assume that given states $s, s' \in \mathcal{S}$, which are given in a binary encoding, and $(a, e) \in \Sigma_a' \times \Sigma_e$, deciding $\Phi_c(s, (a, e), s')$ is in Σ_i^p, for some $i \geq 0$; this reflects theory-based specification by action theories, logic programs, or QBFs possibly with projective auxiliary variables. Checking executability of any sequences $\bar{a}$, $\bar{e}$ on $\mathcal{A}_a^*$, resp. $\mathcal{A}_e^*$, at a state s is thus in Σ_j^p, where $j = \max(1, i)$ (and complete for Σ_j^p, under mild assumptions). Consequently, deciding whether a sequence $\bar{a} \in \mathcal{A}_a^*$ may occur in $P(s)$ at all (thanks to a suitable $\bar{e}$) has the same complexity; we (reasonably) assume that $P(s)$ selects among those $\bar{a}$ only polynomially many and of polynomial length (in the state size), called *p-jump* plans, and that recognizing plans $\bar{a}$ in $P(s)$ and deciding $P(s) \neq \{a_{nop}\}$ is feasible in polynomial time (this holds e.g. if $P(s)$ is computable in logspace). Assuming that the goal test $s \models \mu$ is also in polynomial time, we obtain:

Lemma 6.1. *Deciding (i) given $s, \bar{a}$ and s' whether $\Psi_{P,\Sigma_e}(s, \bar{a}, s')$ holds is in Σ_{j+1}^p and (ii) given an action sequence $\bar{s}$ whether $\bar{s} \in Unfold_k(s, A_\Sigma, P)$ is in Σ_j^p.*

The increase to Σ_{j+1}^p in (i) is due to part (2) of $\Psi_{P,\Sigma_e}(s, \bar{a})$. The lemma also holds for goal tests in Π_i^p. If the initial state check $s \in \mathcal{S}_0$ is in Π_j^p, we obtain the following result.

Theorem 6.1 (k-Maintaining Check). *Deciding whether a system $A_\Sigma = \langle \mathcal{S}, \mathcal{S}_0, \Sigma, \Phi_\Sigma \rangle$ is k-maintained, $k \geq 0$, by a given policy P w.r.t. a goal μ is* PSpace-*complete.*

To see this, deciding $s \in Cl_{P,\Sigma_e}(S_0, A_\Sigma)$ is by Lemma 6.1.(i) in NPSpace. We can thus check the existence of a counterexample to k-maintenance (i.e., a state s violating Definition 3.3) in NPSpace, where we guess the sequence $\bar{s} = s_0, s_1, \ldots, s_l$ in $\bar{s} \in Unfold_k(s, A_\Sigma, P)$ stepwise. As NPSpace = PSpace, this yields the upper bound. On the other hand, the problem is PSpace-hard already in plain settings, with deterministic actions and simple policies, due to the PSpace-completeness of succinct graph reachability [1]. The complexity is lowered, if we assume that for $s \in Cl_{P,\Sigma_e}(S_0, A_\Sigma)$? an oracle in some class of the Polynomial Hierarchy is available and that k is polynomially bounded; in particular, for a Σ_i^p oracle, we obtain then membership in Π_j^p.

In contrast, the complexity of *synthesizing* a k-maintaining policy P is much harder, even if we require that P returns only p-jump plans.

Theorem 6.2 (k-Maintaining Synthesis). *Deciding if a system $A_\Sigma = \langle S, S_0, \Sigma, \Phi_\Sigma \rangle$ is k-maintained, $k \geq 0$, by any (p-jump) policy P w.r.t. a goal μ is* NExpTime-*complete.*

The membership part follows as we can guess in exponential time a (polynomial-jump) policy P and check in polynomial space whether P is indeed k-maintaining. The NExpTime-hardness is shown by encoding a polynomial-space branching Turing Machine (BTM) [8] into 1-maintainability of a system A_Σ; a BTM is like an alternating TM, but in a special state it moves according to a *branching instruction* that depends on the whole configuration, not only on the current scanned symbol. The acceptance problem of such BTMs is NExpTime-complete. Informally, the policy (resp. environment) mimics the existential and branching (resp. universal moves).

Equalization. We assume that given s and $\hat{s}$ (resp. $\hat{\theta}$), deciding $s \in h^{-1}(\hat{s})$ ($s \in h_r^{-1}(\hat{\theta})$) is in Σ_ℓ^p, for some $\ell \geq 0$, where $|\Theta|$ is polynomial in the number $|S|$ of states. In this setting, the transition function $\widehat{\Psi}_{P,\widehat{\Sigma}_e}(\hat{s}\hat{\theta}, \bar{a}, \hat{s}'\hat{\theta}')$ is decidable in $\Sigma_{j'}^p$, where $j' = \max(j, \ell) + 1$; thus, k-maintaining policy checking and policy synthesis have the same complexity as in the unequalized case in general, i.e., in Theorems 6.1 and 6.2.

The worst-case complexity drops if the equalization does an exponential compression, i.e., $|\Omega| = \mathcal{O}(\log |S|)$ and $|\Theta| = \mathcal{O}(\log |S|)$. Such a compression can, for instance, result by projecting away auxiliary fluents from the models of a logic program or SAT formula that serve to encode state constraints, if the number of admissible states is polynomially bounded. Each such state induces two clusters with all auxiliary fluent interpretations that admit resp. do not admit this state; all other interpretations form a further cluster.

Under exponential compression, A_P^{h,h_r} has a polynomial-size state set $\widehat{S}$, and along the discussion above the complexity of policy checking drops to $\Pi_{j'}^p$; thus policy synthesis is in $\Sigma_{j'+1}^p$. However, the problems share a smaller upper bound that is tight.

Theorem 6.3 (Compression). *For* $A_P^{h,h_r} = \langle \widehat{\mathcal{S}}, \widehat{\mathcal{S}}_0, \Sigma'_a, \widehat{\Sigma}_e, \widehat{\Psi}_{P,\Sigma_e} \rangle$ *with expo-*
nential compression, both deciding if (i) A_P^{h,h_r} *is k-maintainable w.r.t.* μ *and*
(ii) some (p-jump) policy P' *exists s.t.* $A_{P'}^{h,h_r}$ *is k-maintainable w.r.t.* μ *is* $\Theta_{j'}^p$-
complete where $k \geq 0$.

Here $\Theta_{j'}^p = \Delta_{j'}^p[\log n] = \mathsf{P}_{\|[c]}^{\Sigma_{j'-1}^p}$ are the problems decidable in polynomial time
with logarithmically many $\Sigma_{j'-1}^p$ oracle calls, or equivalently, a fixed number c
of rounds of *parallel* $\Sigma_{j'-1}^p$ oracle calls [7,14]. Not that for $i = \ell = 0$, we obtain
Θ_2^p, as $j = \max(1, i)$.

Informally, by one such round we can construct the 1-step transition graph
with nodes $\widehat{\mathcal{S}}$ and edges $\hat{s}\hat{\theta} \to \hat{s}'\hat{\theta}'$ with label (a, e) if some $s \in h_r^{-1}(\hat{\theta})$ and
$s' \in \Phi_c(s, (a, e))$ exist with $h(s') = \hat{s}'$ and $h_r(s') = \hat{\theta}'$. The k-maintainability of
policy P in (i) can then be checked, using a labeling technique on the graph and
reachability tests, in polynomial time modulo goal tests $\hat{s}\hat{\theta} \models \mu$; the latter can
be computed separately before with parallel $\Sigma_{j'-1}^p$ oracle queries, and likewise
the plans in $P(s)$.

The existence of some P' in (ii) is decided similarly, where the graph and
the goal test results are passed to an NP oracle that guesses and checks P'; this
establishes $\Theta_{j'}^p$-membership. Matching hardness is shown by a reduction from a
suitable problem on QBFs: given $\text{QBF}_{\exists,j'-1}$ instances $\Phi_1, \ldots, \Phi_m$, is the number
of satisfiable ones even?

Remark. No bound on k is imposed in this result; this is because polynomially
many steps in the size of $\widehat{\mathcal{S}}$ will be sufficient to construct a counterexample for
k-maintainability.

7   Discussion and Conclusion

In this paper, we have extended and combined the notions of equalization [13]
and maintenance [3] to represent and verify the behavior of an agent following
a policy in a dynamic environment. Equalization was extended to also consider
inferred states according to projected movements of the environment, which
helps in establishing maintenance. A more sophisticated behavior of the environment than executing any sequence of actions can easily be embedded in the
current representation of the system. Maintenance in [3] was generalized to have
concurrent actions and policies with sequences of actions that are executed under
richer behavior patterns.

The policies described in [13] determine targets with some target function
and call a planner for a conformant plan that guarantees reaching the target.
In this paper, plans need not be conformant, as no targets are considered and
all states reached by trying to execute the plan occur in the closure, and thus
matter for defining the maintenance.

Our emphasis is mainly on the verification aspect, i.e., verifying if a given
policy achieves desired properties. Such a policy testing and, in case it fails,
refining with typically small changes would be preferred over a radical change.

It also fits in the policy engineering life cycle. Eventually, we aim to bring in parameterization and verify policies in all possible sizes (up to some limit) of the environment, e.g., varying number of aisles in the supermarket. Our representation can easily be adjusted to such extensions.

Related Work. Constructing agent control functions with various tasks such as "achievement" and "maintenance" is analyzed by [15], and [10] present a method to synthesize reactive plans based on linear temporal logic. In our work, we explicitly distinguish agent and environment actions to define maintenance, and the window of opportunity for the agent. We also focus on the verification aspect, and consider policies in the style of [13]. For further discussion on related work concerning maintenance, we refer to [3].

Plan verification [4] is on checking executability and goal achievement of a given plan. We focus on a more reactive case where, depending on the current situation, rather short sequences of actions are provided by the policy, and the aim is to eventually reach the goal while the agent traverses the environment with such guidance. Such an approach comes in handy especially if there is partial observability and a dynamic environment.

Abstraction can be useful to reason over the agent's behavior [2] or to do planning [9]. Over-approximation could achieve a significant reduction of the state space. However, trajectories found in the abstract system may be spurious, which would require further abstraction refinement. In this paper, we have focused on state clustering that is a faithful form of abstraction and gets rid of irrelevant information. This allows to focus on how the policy behaves in the system, and especially if the policy is not working properly, to detect this without having to consider all possible irrelevant states. Dealing with proper (non-faithful) abstractions remains as our future work.

The notion of irrelevant information and its effects were analyzed for planning in [12], in which different heuristics were introduced to omit such information. In our case, the irrelevancy is inferred from the given policy (e.g., target determination formulas in [13]) and which information it is making use of in determining the plans.

Verification of agent behavior represented using situation calculus action theory and of multi-agent systems has been studied e.g. in [6,16] and [11], respectively. We focus on a single agent that follows the guidance of a given policy, and also consider the decision making of the policy or distinguish possible environment actions. Goal-driven agents acting in dynamic environments has been modeled with considering activities (i.e., sequences of actions meant to achieve a goal) [5], while the issue of having irrelevant information in the states was not the focus.

References

1. Balcázar, J.L.: The complexity of searching implicit graphs. AIJ **86**(1), 171–188 (1996)
2. Banihashemi, B., De Giacomo, G., Lespérance, Y.: Abstraction in situation calculus action theories. In: Proceedings of AAAI, pp. 1048–1055 (2017)
3. Baral, C., Eiter, T., Bjäreland, M., Nakamura, M.: Maintenance goals of agents in a dynamic environment: formulation and policy construction. AIJ **172**(12), 1429–1469 (2008)
4. Behnke, G., Höller, D., Biundo, S.: On the complexity of HTN plan verification and its implications for plan recognition. In: Proceedings of ICAPS, pp. 25–33 (2015)
5. Blount, J., Gelfond, M., Balduccini, M.: A theory of intentions for intelligent agents. In: Calimeri, F., Ianni, G., Truszczynski, M. (eds.) LPNMR 2015. LNCS, vol. 9345, pp. 134–142. Springer, Cham (2015). doi:10.1007/978-3-319-23264-5_12
6. De Giacomo, G., Lespérance, Y., Patrizi, F., Vassos, S.: LTL verification of online executions with sensing in bounded situation calculus. In: Proceedings of ECAI, pp. 369–374. IOS Press (2014)
7. Eiter, T., Gottlob, G.: The complexity class Θ_p^2: recent results and applications in AI and modal logic. In: Chlebus, B.S., Czaja, L. (eds.) FCT 1997. LNCS, vol. 1279, pp. 1–18. Springer, Heidelberg (1997). doi:10.1007/BFb0036168
8. Eiter, T., Lukasiewicz, T., Predoiu, L.: Generalized consistent query answering under existential rules. In: Baral, C., Delgrande, J., Wolter, F. (eds.) Proceedings of KR, pp. 359–368 (2016)
9. Hoffmann, J., Sabharwal, A., Domshlak, C.: Friends or foes? An AI planning perspective on abstraction and search. In: ICAPS, pp. 294–303 (2006)
10. Kabanza, F., Barbeau, M., St-Denis, R.: Planning control rules for reactive agents. AIJ **95**(1), 67–113 (1997)
11. Lomuscio, A., Michliszyn, J.: Verification of multi-agent systems via predicate abstraction against ATLK specifications. In: Proceedings of AAMAS, pp. 662–670 (2016)
12. Nebel, B., Dimopoulos, Y., Koehler, J.: Ignoring irrelevant facts and operators in plan generation. In: Steel, S., Alami, R. (eds.) ECP 1997. LNCS, vol. 1348, pp. 338–350. Springer, Heidelberg (1997). doi:10.1007/3-540-63912-8_97
13. Saribatur, Z.G., Eiter, T.: Reactive policies with planning for action languages. In: Michael, L., Kakas, A. (eds.) JELIA 2016. LNCS, vol. 10021, pp. 463–480. Springer, Cham (2016). doi:10.1007/978-3-319-48758-8_30
14. Wagner, K.: Bounded query classes. SIAM J. Comput. **19**(5), 833–846 (1990)
15. Wooldridge, M., Dunne, P.E.: Optimistic and disjunctive agent design problems. In: Castelfranchi, C., Lespérance, Y. (eds.) ATAL 2000. LNCS, vol. 1986, pp. 1–14. Springer, Heidelberg (2001). doi:10.1007/3-540-44631-1_1
16. Zarrieß, B., Claßen, J.: Decidable verification of Golog programs over non-local effect actions. In: Proceedings of AAAI, pp. 1109–1115 (2016)

Multi-agent Systems: Theory and Applications

Multi-agent Based File Replication and Consistency Management

Serkan Akdemir[1(✉)] and Nadia Erdoğan[2]

[1] Siemens AS, Corporate Technology Development Center Kartal,
34870 Istanbul, Turkey
srkn_akdemir@hotmail.com
[2] Faculty of Computer and Informatics, Computer Engineering Department,
Istanbul Technical University, 34469 Maslak Istanbul, Turkey
nerdogan@itu.edu.tr

Abstract. Replication is a well-known technique in distributed systems. Replication can reduce data access latency, enhance and optimize the availability and reliability of the entire system. The existence of multiple instances of data however causes additional issues. The main issue is consistency of data. In this paper we present a multi-agent based approach for file replication and consistency management. We describe the design of a multi-agent system using the JADE platform. The system presents a multi-agent based communication framework that enables the replication and maintenance of files.

Keywords: Multi-agent system · Replication · Consistency

1 Introduction

Replication [12], applied on databases, files or objects, is creating multiple copies of some data stored at multiple locations. The main advantages of replication are increased availability and performance, enhanced reliability, and fault tolerance.

An agent is a piece of software that acts like a separate application and functions to achieve a specific goal. A multi-agent system may be defined as a collection of autonomous agents that are dedicated to accomplish a task assigned by clients. JADE (Java Agent Development Framework) [10] is a software framework that allows development of multi agent applications in compliance with the FIPA [11] specifications. JADE conceptualizes an agent as an independent and autonomous process that has an identity, and that requires communication with other agents in order to fulfill its tasks. This communication is implemented through asynchronous message passing.

The goal of our work is to develop to a multi-agent based file replication management system. The system architecture consists of two applications, named Front-End and Back-End. The Front-End is developed for clients who carry out file operations, as creating, modifying and displaying files. The Front-End application provides a GUI to the clients to communicate with the Back-End. The Back-End refers to the JADE agent containers, with each agent container representing a storage service in our study.

© Springer International Publishing AG 2017
E. Oliveira et al. (Eds.): EPIA 2017, LNAI 10423, pp. 727–738, 2017.
DOI: 10.1007/978-3-319-65340-2_59

The system supports two separate modes of operation for file replication management. These modes are synchronous and asynchronous replication. On synchronous mode, all modifications are propagated simultaneously to all agent containers. On the other hand, on asynchronous mode, only current agent container storage is affected by modifications, other agent containers will only be notified by mobile agents, file update does not occur till a request is made by some client.

Replicas need to be kept consistent when one or more copies are modified. This requires us to propose a versioning mechanism [7–9]. For this purpose, both agent containers and clients holds version of files. File versions are produced by a centralized version manager agent which provides a new version number when a file is created or modified.

Asynchronous replication causes an additional issue, data conflicts. Concurrent writes to different replicas of same file lead to conflicts. As a solution, we propose token based modifications on agent containers. A token represents access right of a client and only one client can possess the token on a specific file at the same time.

JADE platform supports mobility, allowing agents (mobile agents) to move from one agent container to another. Token clearing and consistency of containers (for asynchronous replication) are provided by mobile agents.

The rest of the paper is organized as follows. Section 2 surveys related work. Section 3 presents details of the proposed architecture of the replication management system. Section 4 studies both synchronous and asynchronous replication with all scenarios. Section 5 presents the experimental results. Section 6 concludes the paper and suggests future directions in this research area.

2 Related Work

Replication techniques have been studied deeply on many researches. Geoffrey and David [1] discusses various replication strategies, classifying replication into two categories, namely, static and dynamic. Dynamic replication is further classified as synchronous where data is updated on all sites simultaneously, and asynchronous in which updates take some time. Both advantages and disadvantages of this classification are examined in detail.

Different distributed replica management strategies have been proposed in the literature [2–4]. Replication is mostly used to reduce access latency and bandwidth consumption. Number of replicas, network bandwidth and frequency of operations are crucial parameter of replica management and impacts the performance of the system.

Reptor [5], an implementation of a Replica Management System, proposes consistency of replicas with versions stored under metadata catalogue. In our study, manifest catalogues store version and system related information of files similar to Reptor implementation.

Lee and Yang [6] proposed agent-based consistency service. The agent manages grid consistency service module (GCSM) and grid transaction module (GTM). GCSM keeps track of storage space of the node, whereas GTM takes care of consistency and integrity of the replicas. GCSM and GTM coordinate with each other to make consistency. Similarly, in our proposed system, static agents reply client requests providing consistency of agent container where they exist, while mobile agents maintain storage consistency and integrity between containers.

3   System Architecture

First, we define terms and concepts that are used throughout this paper.

Versioning: All files are assigned a version representing the state of that file and modification of files result in a new version. Versioning is required to determine the latest version of files to provide consistency. Version information is stored in the manifest catalogue.

Token: File modification requests are restricted by token-based access system, a client must get the token of that file first, as only the possessor of the token is authorized to modify a file. Every file stored in the system is assigned with a single token between all agent containers. The period of validity of tokens are determined by the Back-End admin as the starting input parameter of main container. Every agent container contains a single token catalogue holding all tokens of that container along with owner client's name.

Manifest: Despite of differences in file structures, both the Front-End and the Back-End utilize manifest catalogues to track the history of files. Information such as file directory, token holder, version information etc. are kept in this file. The manifest tracks files in the same directory.

Outdated-Producer: In Asynchronous Replication Mode, all modification related information is kept in this catalogue. It is read by the mobile agent to inform other agent containers of the changes. Every agent container maintains a single Outdated-Producer catalogue.

Outdated-Consumer: In Asynchronous Replication Mode, information is kept in this catalogue when the mobile agent informs that a file has been changed by another container. Every agent container contains a single Outdated-Consumer catalogue.

Figure 1 depicts the overall design of proposed file management system and with relation between the Front-End and the Back-End. Each client interacts with fixed single agent container and all agent containers are bound to one single main container. JADE IMTP (Internal Message Transport Protocol) is used for both exchanging messages and files between agents. JADE IMTP is based upon Java RMI [13].

3.1   Front-End

The Front-End presents a simple Java Swing [14] based GUI that runs on client's computer. This GUI proposes fundamental features to the client, as displaying a file (download), creating/modifying a file (upload), token requesting/releasing. In order to create or modify a file, a client must choose a file from local computer, define an upload path of the container and send a request. Similarly, client must define a download path

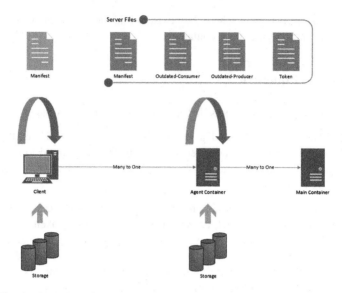

Fig. 1. Overview of interaction between the Front-End and the Back-End.

on local computer and source path of the file on agent container to download for display requests. Token request is necessary to modify a file.

All GUI requests are attached with current version of the file from manifest catalogue and unique client name on local computer for modifications. Client name is basically used to obtain the token of file.

A single JADE agent runs on the Front-End, simply forwarding client request to Back-End and similarly receiving responses of the Back-End. This agent is also responsible for maintaining manifest catalogue and all files on client's computer.

3.2 Back-End

The Back-End system can be described from two different points of view. On the one hand, the Back-End agents fulfill the demands of clients and maintain the agent container where they exist, simultaneously. This part is managed by static agents that run on the same agent container during its lifecycle. On the other hand, the Back-End mobile agents are responsible for managing consistency between agent containers.

Main Container is started up with mode selection, through a JADE provided GUI, Remote Monitoring Agent (RMA). Management of all agent containers and agents are also provided by this GUI.

Mobile agents are intelligent and decide on their own to migrate from one agent container to another agent container, when required. As shown in Fig. 2, token clearing and file consistency between agent containers are managed by two different mobile agents.

Tokens can be invalidated in three ways. First one is that client modifies a file successfully and token is revoked automatically. Second, client returns token manually

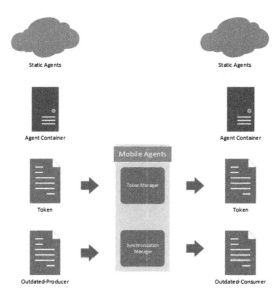

Fig. 2. Interaction between agent containers with mobile agents.

using the Front-End GUI. Finally, token is out-of-dated. In this case, expired tokens must be discovered and cleared by the system. The mobile Token Manager agent is implemented for this purpose clears all expired tokens where it stands. When all tokens are cleared, it moves itself to the next agent container.

In Asynchronous mode, data changes are not propagated immediately, instead, change logs are written to Outdated-Producer catalogue first. The Mobile Synchronization Manager agent that travels between agent containers reads the Outdated-Producer catalogue and advertises change logs to all other agent containers. Main container provides an agent that is responsible for all agent containers. Mobile agents get the lists of agent containers over this agent. Agents of notified agent containers are responsible for the rest of the process. If the copy of the mentioned file exists on that agent container, Outdated-Consumer catalogue must be updated, otherwise, notification is skipped.

4   Modes of Replication

The Back-End application presents two replication options, synchronous and asynchronous respectively. Numerous problems arise when replication is applied. In this section, all possible scenarios are studied regarding create, modify and display requests.

On Tables 1 and 2, symbol of Ø refers to the absence of field, * is used for insignificant field, α represents file version and finally X means that mentioned field is not applied for that case. In the rest of the paper, agent container of the client is called the Local Agent Container, shortly the LAC.

Table 1. Possible flow cases for synchronous replication.

FUNCTION	CASE	Client	LAC		Any Other Container(s)
		Storage	Storage	Outdated-Consumer	Storage
Display	Case 1	∅	∅	X	X
	Case 2	∅	α1	X	X
	Case 3	α1	α2	X	X
	Case 4	α1	α1	X	X
Create	Case 1	α1	*	X	X
	Case 2	∅	α1	X	X
	Case 3	∅	∅	X	X
Modify	Case 1	α1	α1	X	X
	Case 2	α1	α2	X	X
	Case 3	α1	∅	X	X
	Case 4	α2	α1	X	X

Table 2. Possible flow cases for asynchronous replication.

FUNCTION	CASE	Client	LAC		Any Other Container(s)
		Storage	Storage	Outdated-Consumer	Storage
Display	Case 1	*	∅	*	-
	Case 2	*	∅	*	α1
	Case 3	*	α1	α2	α2
	Case 4	∅	α1	∅	α1
	Case 5	α1	α2	∅	α2
	Case 6	α1	α1	∅	α1
Create	Case 1	α1	*	X	*
	Case 2	∅	α1	X	*
	Case 3	∅	∅	X	α1
	Case 4	∅	∅	X	-
Modify	Case 1	α1	α1	∅	*
	Case 2	α1	α2	∅	*
	Case 3	α1	α2	α3	α3
	Case 4	α1	∅	*	*
	Case 5	α2	α1	*	*

4.1 Synchronous Replication

Synchronous replication requires the propagation of all modification on data to all agent containers simultaneously and guarantees files to be consistent at all times. However, it brings a heavy overhead. This replication technique increases transaction response time and clients have to wait for all the other replicas to be modified. Table 1 reveals all probabilities with related conditions. Since all nodes are consistent, Outdated-Consumer catalogue is not applied and there is no need of checking storage of other agent containers.

File display scenarios:

- **Case 1:** The LAC checks the storage first and no such file is found, the LAC returns failure response to the client.
- **Case 2:** The LAC has the file in the storage, returns success response with the file, the Front-End agent saves the file then updates the manifest catalogue on client's computer.
- **Case 3:** Exactly the same scenario with Case 3, with the only difference that client has an out-of-dated file at first, actions of the Back-End is identical.
- **Case 4:** Both client and the LAC files are up-to-date; the LAC returns success response without a file.

File create scenarios:

- **Case 1:** Manifest catalogue already has versioned file on the Front-End, already existed file request is blocked on the Front-End without accessing the Back-End.
- **Case 2:** File is not versioned on client's manifest catalogue, request is sent to the Back-End. However, the Back-End has such a file in the storage (probably created by another client), the LAC returns failure response.
- **Case 3:** Both client and the LAC's manifest catalogue don't contain such a file, the LAC saves file to the storage, updates manifest catalogue relatively. The next step is to call all other containers so that the file is saved and manifest catalogue is updated on all storages. Finally, the LAC returns success response with file version, the Front-End updates manifest catalogue.

File modify scenarios:

- **Case 1:** Both the Front-End and the LAC are up-to-date. The LAC saves the file to the storage and updates the manifest catalogue. The LAC then calls all other containers to save the file to the storage and updates the manifest catalogue. Finally, the LAC returns success response with file version, the Front-End updates manifest catalogue.
- **Case 2:** Client is not up-to-date, client must update the file first with display request.
- **Case 3**: Under normal circumstances, it is impossible for clients to have a file but the LAC does not. This can only happen when a file is deleted from the container side manually. In this case, the LAC returns failure response and the manifest catalogue of client is adjusted to the LAC.
- **Case 4:** Same flow occurs as Case 3. It is impossible for clients to have greater file version than the LAC.

4.2   Asynchronous Replication

In Asynchronous replication mode, file is written to the LAC first, then copied to other agent containers on demand. Increased performance does not come without its price. For the majority of tasks, short-term occurrence of stale data on distant servers is acceptable. Modified files are not propagated to other agents, yet they are notified of changes. In this way, agent containers know that some files have been modified, and if they are interested, they can send pull request to the final copy of the file. Table 2 presents probabilities in detail.

The main problem associated with this service is the question of how to govern the trade-off between consistency and resource usage.

File display scenarios:

- **Case 1:** The LAC checks the storage first and does not find the file. All other agent containers are called to ask if any of them has the requested file. Next, the LAC waits until all containers respond. Neither the LAC nor the other containers have such a file, so the LAC returns failure response to client.
- **Case 2:** The LAC checks the storage first and does not find the file. All other agent containers are called to ask if any of them has the requested file. The LAC waits until all containers respond. The LAC requests the file from the owner agent container, saves file to the storage, updates the manifest catalogue and sends the file to the client. Similarly, client saves the file and updates manifest catalogue on his computer.
- **Case 3:** As requested file name exists in Outdated-Consumer catalogue, the LAC directly requests the file from the owner agent container. The rest is similar as in Case 2.
- **Case 4:** The LAC has the file in the storage and there is no record about the file in Outdated-Consumer catalogue, which means that the LAC is already up-to-date. The LAC sends the file to the client, client saves the file and updates the manifest catalogue on his computer.
- **Case 5:** Exactly the same scenario as in Case 4, with the only difference is that client has an out-of-date copy of file first.
- **Case 6:** This scenario is almost the same as in Case 4, except now client is also up-to-date. The LAC only sends an up-to-date flag to client.

File create scenarios:

- **Case 1:** This can only happen when a file is deleted from container side manually, the LAC returns failure response to the client and the manifest catalogue of client is adjusted to the LAC.
- **Case 2:** The LAC already has such a file, the LAC returns failure response to the client.
- **Case 3:** The LAC does not have such a file, all other agent containers are called to ask if such a file exists, if any of the containers has such a file, the LAC returns failure response to the client.
- **Case 4:** Similar as Case 3, except no container owns such a file. The LAC saves the file to the storage, updates the manifest catalogue, finally the LAC returns success response with file version, the Front-End updates the manifest catalogue.

File modify scenarios:

- **Case 1:** Both client and the LAC are up-to-date. Both client and the LAC save the file and update manifest catalogue. Additionally, the LAC updates the Outdated-Producer catalogue for asynchronous notification.
- **Case 2:** Client is not up-to-date, client must update the file first with display request.

- **Case 3:** The LAC is not up-to-date which means that client is also out-of-dated. Client must update the file first with display request.
- **Case 4:** This can only happen when a file is deleted from container side manually, the LAC returns failure response to the client and the manifest catalogue of client is adjusted to the LAC.
- **Case 5:** Same flow occurs as Case 4. It is impossible for clients to have greater file version than the LAC.

5 Experimental Results and Assessment

In this section, our goal is to evaluate the performance and compare the behavior of synchronous and asynchronous modes of replication in the same environment, under the same conditions. Results cover requests for file create, modify and display.

Throughout the experiments, we assume that all agent containers are in the same network, the distances between the clients and all containers are equal and the round-trip time of redirection is identical. All tests were run on three identical computers with 2.5 GHz Intel Core i7 processor, 16.0 GB memory, 200 GB SSD on a 64-bit Windows 7. Four agent containers were initialized on each computer, thus totally 12 agent containers were created for testing.

In order to obverse the total disk usage of the system, we have carried out experiments with different numbers of replicas and different file sizes. Figure 3 shows two graphics that demonstrate the utilization of disk space. The graphic on the left relates to the experiment where file size was fixed to 1 MB, but the number of replicas was increased. The graphic on the right gives the results of the experiment where the replica number was kept constant, specified as 12, but different file sizes were applied.

Figure 3 indicates that, under the conditions of both experiments, storage consumption is a drawback of synchronous replication for file creations. Propagations of files to all containers dramatically increase the amount of storage used. Total disk usage

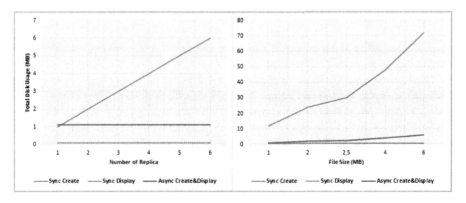

Fig. 3. Effect of the number of replicas (on the left) and the file size (on the right) on disk space consumption of create and display file requests.

is directly proportional to number of replicas and size of files. However, for the case of asynchronous replication, disk consumption was reduced considerably. However, storage space required for display request is almost zero if a local replica already exists. At this point, we can argue that, systems with frequent display operations can adopt synchronous replication at no extra memory cost, as they will always be hosting an up to date copy of the file. Both create and display requests require space as much as the size of the file regardless of number of replicas, for both types of replication.

To assess the performance of the system, we have carried out experiments to measure the response time of the system to requests, the elapsed time between the call and completion of a request. We tested our system approximately with 600 runs to observe the effect of increasing number of replicas, file sizes for both types of replication with create, modify and display requests. Graphics present average time consumptions of test results.

For asynchronous replication, the response time for a display request varies depending on the state of the file on agent container, with three cases being possible Therefore, Figs. 4 and 5 demonstrate these cases separately: display-1 refers to the case where the LAC is already up-to-date for the requested file, display-2 indicates that the LAC has the requested file but not latest version, and finally display-3 represents the case where the LAC does not have the requested file at all.

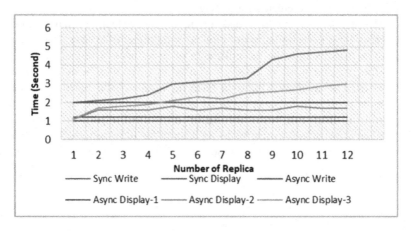

Fig. 4. Effect of the number of replicas on response time for write and display.

Due to similar performance of create and modify demands, they both are entitled as write operations in the figures. Figure 4 reflects the effect of the number of replicas on system performance. During the experiment, file size was set to 1 MB, and replicas were created on the same computer first, and then switched to the next computer. Thus, for example, transitions from node 4 to 5 and 8 to 9 are crucial.

Results depicted in Fig. 4 indicate that, number of replicas and the performance of the system are quite related to each other for synchronous write requests, as the response time grows with increasing numbers of replicas. This is due to increasing amount of processing required for larger numbers of replicas. However, synchronous display requests don't give rise to such a delay on the system because a local copy is

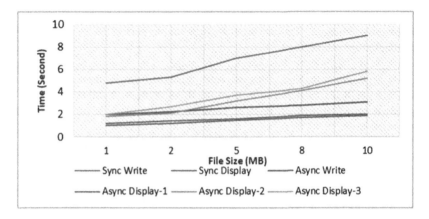

Fig. 5. Effect of file size on response time for write and display.

accessed on each request. In case of asynchronous replication, write requests have a much better performance and the total number of replicas has no effect on the response time since only the local copy is modified. On the other hand, due to pull based approach of asynchronous replication, the total performance declines when write operations are frequent on different agent containers and current container requires to get final copy of that file as shown on display 2. When write operations are not often or only occur on the LAC, time consumption decreases as shown on display 1. If the file is requested for the first time, longer response time occurs as shown on display 3.

Figure 5 introduces the results of the experiment which evaluates the performance of the system with different sized files but with a fixed number of replicas, set to 12 in this case. The results indicate that, the response time of synchronous write increases excessively with greater sized files while asynchronous writes perform much better as the file propagation to all replicas take times for synchronous replication.

On the other hand, response times of display operations are promising when compared to write requests. Synchronous display operations perform the best as file size varies. Results indicate that asynchronous replication is suitable for execution environments when write and display demands occur on the same container as shown on display 1. As reading changes from different agent container consumes time as shown on display 2, asynchronous replication is not the best approach for display requests when modification occurs often on different agent containers. If the file is requested for the first time, response time increases as shown on display 3.

6   Conclusion and Future Work

In this paper, we present a replication and consistency management system using the JADE framework. The system presents a multi-agent based communication framework that enables the replication and maintenance of files. In particular, we introduce two replication techniques. With synchronous replication, we propagate all write operations to all replicas simultaneously, and guarantee data set consistency at all times. However, performance becomes an issue and latencies occur. With the alternative technique, asynchronous replication, we can provide a preferable performance, especially when write requests are frequent.

The system we present has several advantages. One main advantage is that it simplifies access to distributed files as issues related to distribution, access and consistency are handled transparently by the underlying system. Another advantage is its being based on JADE, which ensures portability across a variety of hardware and software platforms.

As future work, we plan to assess system performance under realistic user access patterns. Replication decisions can also be made dynamically for future tasks. Security is another fundamental concern for an agent system. Security must be concerned including agent-agent and agent-client communications. In the future, we plan to implement an application with secured communication infrastructure and allow for file access with support for security.

References

1. Concurrency and Computation: Practice and Experience, vol. 24, no. 7, pp. 661–750, Wiley. New York, May 2012. Online ISSN 1532-0634
2. Coulouris, G., Dollimore, J., Kindberg, T.: Distributed Systems, Concepts and Design, 3rd edn. Addison Wesley, Boston (2001)
3. Narasimhan, N.: Transparent fault tolerance for Java remote method invocation. Ph.D dissertation, Department of Electrical and Computer Engineering, University of California, Santa Barbara, June 2001
4. Tanenbaum, A.S., van Steen, M.: Distributed Systems, Principles and Paradigms, 1st edn. Prentice Hall, Upper Saddle River (2002)
5. Guy, L., et al.: Replica management in data grids. In: Global Grid Forum, vol. 5 (2002)
6. Lee, H.-M., Yang, C.-H.: A distributed backup agent based on grid computing architecture. In: Khosla, R., Howlett, R.J., Jain, L.C. (eds.) KES 2005. LNCS, vol. 3682, pp. 1252–1257. Springer, Heidelberg (2005). doi:10.1007/11552451_173
7. Patterson, H., et al.: SnapMirror®: file system based asynchronous mirroring for disaster recovery. In: Proceedings of 1st USENIX Conference on File and Storage Technologies. USENIX Association (2002)
8. Santry, D.S., et al.: Deciding when to forget in the Elephant file system. In: ACM SIGOPS Operating Systems Review, vol. 33, no. 5. ACM (1999)
9. Craig, A.N., et al.: Metadata efficiency in versioning file systems. In: 2nd USENIX Conference on File and Storage Technologies, San Francisco, CA, March 2003
10. Bellifemine, F., Caire, G., Greenwood, D.: Developing Multi-agent Systems with JADE. Wiley Series in Agent Technology. Wiley, New York (2007). ISBN 978–0-470-05747-6
11. FIPA Specifications Web Site. http://www.fipa.org
12. Lamehamedi, H., et al.: Data replication strategies in grid environments. In: Proceedings of 5th International Conference on Algorithms and Architectures for Parallel Processing. IEEE (2002)
13. Maassen, J., et al.: Efficient Java RMI for parallel programming. ACM Trans. Program. Lang. Syst. 23(6), 747–775 (2001)
14. Loy, M., et al.: Java Swing. O'Reilly Media, Inc., Sebastopol (2002)

Online Learning for Conversational Agents

Vânia Mendonça$^{(\boxtimes)}$, Francisco S. Melo, Luísa Coheur, and Alberto Sardinha

Instituto Superior Técnico and INESC-ID, Av. Prof. Doutor Aníbal Cavaco Silva,
Porto Salvo, Portugal
{vania.mendonca,luisa.coheur,jose.alberto.sardinha}@tecnico.ulisboa.pt,
fmelo@inesc-id.pt

Abstract. Agents relying on large collections of interactions face the challenge of choosing an appropriate answer from such collections. Several works address this challenge by using offline learning approaches, which do not take advantage of how user-agent conversations unfold.

In this work, we propose an alternative approach: incorporating user feedback at each interaction with the agent, in order to enhance its ability to choose an answer. We focus on the case of adjusting the weights of the features used by the agent to choose an answer, using an online learning algorithm (the Exponentially Weighted Average Forecaster) for that purpose. We validate our hypothesis with an experiment featuring a specific agent and simulating user feedback using a reference corpus. The results of our experiment suggest that the adjustment of the agent's feature weights can improve its answers, provided that an appropriate reward function is designed, as this aspect is critical in the agent's performance.

Keywords: Online learning · Exponentially Weighted Average Forecaster · Conversational agents

1 Introduction

Several agents rely on large collections of data from where to get their answers (e.g., TV drama scripts [11], Twitter interactions [5], movie scripts [4] and subtitles [1,15]). Using such large collections makes these systems more likely to be able provide an answer to a variety of potential requests.

Given a considerably large collection of interactions (each interaction being composed of a trigger and an answer), the challenge lies in *how* to select an appropriate answer from this collection. Several works address this challenge by modelling human-agent conversations using offline learning approaches [13,18,21,22]. Approaches of this sort have the downside of not taking advantage of how user-agent conversations unfold. An alternative approach would be to incorporate user feedback in an attempt to enhance the system's ability to choose an answer at each interaction, as discussed by [7]. This approach has been followed by several works in the task of choosing a dialogue strategy, achieving promising results [9,12,17,19,20,23]. These works formulate their problems as a Markov

© Springer International Publishing AG 2017
E. Oliveira et al. (Eds.): EPIA 2017, LNAI 10423, pp. 739–750, 2017.
DOI: 10.1007/978-3-319-65340-2_60

Decision Problem and apply reinforcement learning techniques to learn policies from user feedback (either simulated or from real users).

In this work, we focus on the following scenario: given a user request, an agent retrieves a set of candidate interactions from its source of data, and then applies a set of weighted features to those candidates in order to choose the most appropriate answer to the request. Our hypothesis is that, if these weights were iteratively adjusted considering user feedback at each interaction, the agent would be more capable of retrieving an appropriate response. In this scenario, and unlike the works mentioned above, we do not explicitly model states, as there is only one state. Moreover, there is feedback for each of the agent's possible actions. Therefore, we propose the use of an online learning algorithm suitable for this kind of scenario: the Exponentially Weighted Average Forecaster [14].

To validate this hypothesis, we devised an experiment using an existing dialogue engine, Say Something Smart (SSS) [1,15]. Given a user request, SSS retrieves a set of candidate interactions from a corpus of interactions based on movie subtitles, and chooses the answer from the most voted interaction according to a set of weighted criteria. We compare the performance of weights iteratively adjusted based on feedback against the performance achieved by different sets of fixed weights, using a reference corpus of actual movie dialogues to simulate user feedback.

2   Related Work

In order to be more robust to a variety of user requests, several works on conversational agents and dialogue systems rely on large collections of data from where to get their answers. The system by Lasguido et al. [11] uses a corpus of TV drama series and retrieves the candidate answers from the dialogues that are most similar to the input in terms of syntactic and semantic features. In Bessho et al. [5], a corpus of Twitter interactions is used as the main source of candidate answers (when it cannot find a candidate within that corpus, the system delegates the request to a crowd to get a response in real time). The IRIS chatbot [4] provides answers based on a corpus of interactions extracted from movie scripts (Movie-DiC [3]). The Filipe chatbot, based on the dialogue system Say Something Smart (SSS) [2,15], follows a similar approach, but using a corpus of movie subtitles instead (Subtle [1,15]). Finally, the TickTock chatbot [24] incorporates crowdsourcing of the appropriateness of responses present in the corpus.

While the strategy of relying on large amounts of data allows these systems to provide diverse responses to most requests, these might not always be the most adequate. Some works deal with this challenge by modelling human-agent conversations, employing to this end diverse deep learning representations. This is the case of the works presented by Serban et al. [18], in which the system learns offline to emulate the training dialogues, Xu et al. [21], whose system incorporates loose-structured domain knowledge in order to capture semantic relevance between sentences in a conversation, Yao et al. [22], who propose a neural conversation model that models the intention across turns and produces specific responses from scratch, and Li et al. [13], who address the issue of the consistency of the agent's responses within a dialogue.

The aforementioned works depend on previous offline training and, in some cases, they rely on domain-specific knowledge; moreover, the machine learning representations they use might be too costly to be efficiently deployed and scalable to realistic settings. As such, several works focus on the use of learning strategies that incorporate feedback, which allows to improve the systems at each user-agent interaction, as discussed by Cuayáhuitl and Dethlefs [7]. Below we present a brief description of such works.

Levin et al. [12] follow an hybrid approach by combining supervised learning (to estimate the model of the user) with reinforcement learning, simulating a user interaction with the system, to learn the weights in the system's objective function (an application similar to our scenario).

Singh et al. [19] take a two-step approach: first, they train the system by having it interacting with users, in order to use the resulting dialogues to build a Markov Decision Problem (MDP); then they use reinforcement learning to obtain the optimal dialogue policy for the built MDP. This policy outperformed several standard policies in the experiment reported.

Gašić et al. [9] use reinforcement learning to learn a dialogue policy directly from human interaction, using a reward signal provided by users at the end of each dialogue. The authors compared this approach with the use of a random policy and an offline one in an experiment with humans. They collected the first 680 dialogues and observed that the online approach significantly outperformed the random policy and was not significantly inferior to a offline trained policy.

Pietquin et al. [17] use reinforcement learning (both online and batch approaches) to learn an optimal policy as the system interacts with (simulated) users, with the online approach obtaining the best results.

Su et al. [20] seek to simultaneously optimize both the dialogue policy and the reward model of their system by extracting the features of the previous dialogue turn. The reward model estimates the success of that turn based on the extracted features and, depending on the degree of uncertainty regarding that estimate, the user is queried for feedback. This system achieved approximately 91% of subjective success and an F-Score of 95% on the reward model evaluation.

In contrast to these works, Yu et al. [23] address a scenario of non-task oriented conversation. They use reinforcement learning to learn a policy from user feedback, simulated using the chatbot A.L.I.C.E. in one experimental setting, and coming from actual humans in another setting. The authors compared the policy learned using reinforcement learning with both a random and a greedy policy, and observed that it outperforms those policies in all metrics of interest (turn-level appropriateness, conversational depth and information gain).

3   Learning from Feedback in a Conversational Agent Scenario

Let us recall the scenario in hands: an agent receives a user request and looks for an answer in a large collection of interactions (pairs trigger-answer). For each request, the agent obtains a set of candidate interactions from that collection and then applies a set of weighted features to those candidates in order to choose the most appropriate answer to the request.

Our goal is to accommodate feedback in the process of selecting the weights assigned to each of the features used to assess the quality of different candidate answers. Ultimately, we are interested in the feedback provided by users, which imposes two important requirements:

– The algorithm should learn *incrementally* from successive feedback, allowing the performance of the system to immediately incorporate each piece of feedback provided by users;
– The learning algorithm used should be *fast* at incorporating user feedback, since user interactions are potentially expensive.

In light of the requirements above, we adopt an online approach, choosing a standard sequential learning algorithm known as Exponentially Weighted Average Forecaster (EWAF), a generalization of the Weighted Majority algorithm of Littlestone and Warmuth [14]. EWAF precisely addresses the two requirements above: it has well-established performance guarantees, which include a bound on how fast it converges [6]. We describe this algorithm in Sect. 3.1 how we applied it to our scenario in Sect. 3.2.

3.1   The Exponentially Weighted Average Forecaster

EWAF addresses sequential prediction problems with expert advice. An *expert* is defined as a function $E : H_t \to \Delta(A)$ that, at each step t, maps the history H_t of past events (we denote by $\mathcal{H}_t$ the set of all histories of events up to time t) to a distribution $E(H_t)$ over the set of alternatives $\mathcal{A}$ (we denote by $\Delta(\mathcal{A})$ the set of all distributions over $\mathcal{A}$). A sequential prediction problem with expert advice is then an iterated game between a predictor P and "nature". At each step t, the predictor has access to a set of experts $\mathcal{E} = \{E^1, \ldots, E^K\}$ and observes the distribution over $\mathcal{A}$ proposed by each expert $E^k \in \mathcal{E}$. It then proposes a distribution $P(H_t)$ over the set $\mathcal{A}$. At the same time, "nature" selects an element $a_t \in A$. Each expert $E^k \in \mathcal{E}$ incurs a loss

$$\ell_t^k = \left| E^k(H_t) - a_t \right| \tag{1}$$

and the predictor incurs a loss

$$\ell_t^P = |P(H_t) - a_t| . \tag{2}$$

The EWAF algorithm associates a weight ω^k to each expert $E^k \in \mathcal{E}$. Then, at each step t, computes

$$P_{EWAF}(a \mid H_t) = \frac{\sum_{k=1}^{K} \omega^k E^k(a \mid H_t)}{\sum_{k=1}^{K} \omega^k}. \tag{3}$$

The weights $\omega^k, k = 1, \dots, K$, are updated according to the loss incurred by each expert as

$$\omega_{t+1}^k = \omega_t^k e^{-\eta \ell_t^k}, \tag{4}$$

where η is a parameter of the algorithm. By setting $\eta = \sqrt{8 \log |\mathcal{E}| / T}$ it can be shown that

$$\sum_{t=1}^{T} \ell_t^P - \min_{k=1,\dots,K} \sum_{t=1}^{T} \ell_t^k \leq \sqrt{\frac{T}{2} \log |\mathcal{E}|}, \tag{5}$$

ensuring that the predictor P quickly reaches a performance similar to that of the best expert [6].

3.2 Learning the Agent's Feature Weights

The learning process can be formalized as follows. At each step t, the user formulates a request $u(t)$ to the agent. The user request is used to retrieve a set of candidate interactions $C(t) = \{c_1(t), \dots, c_N(t)\}$. In order to choose an answer, the agent will use K features. Each feature $f_k, k = 1, \dots, K$ gives a score to each candidate interaction $c_n(t) \in C(t)$. The "user" is provided with the highest scored candidate according to each feature, $c(t)^k = (T^k, A^k)$, and evaluates the quality of the respective answer with a reward $r_t(c(t)^k) \in [0, 1]$. Finally, the feature weights $w_1, \dots, w_K$ are updated as a function of the reward $r_t(c(t)^k)$.

In order to apply the EWAF algorithm to the learning of the feature weights, $w_1, \dots, w_K$, we associate with each feature f_k an expert $E_k, k = 1, \dots, K$ as:

$$E^k(c \mid H_t) = \begin{cases} 1 & \text{if } c = \operatorname{argmax}_{c \in C(t)} f_k(C(t), c, u(t)). \\ 0 & \text{otherwise.} \end{cases} \tag{6}$$

In other words, each expert E_k selects the interaction $c(t)^k \in C(t)$ that maximizes the feature f_k. By setting

$$w_k = \frac{\omega^k}{\sum_{k=1}^{K} \omega^k} \tag{7}$$

the agent's selection criterion becomes that of P_{EWAF}. Finally, by setting

$$\ell_t^k = -r_t(c(t)^k) \tag{8}$$

we can use the EWAF weight update to adjust the weights w_k associated with each feature $f_1, \dots, f_K$. In particular, we update the weights considering the sum of the rewards r_t^k received so far, $R^k(1, \dots, t)$, as shown in Eq. 9:

$$w^k(t+1) = e^{\eta R^k(1,...,t)} \qquad (9)$$

We compute η according to Eq. 10 (in which K is the number of experts, U is the expected number of iterations – in this case, the number of input pairs u –, and β is a configurable parameter).

$$\eta = \sqrt{\frac{\beta \log K}{U}} \qquad (10)$$

4   Evaluation

To evaluate our contribution, we start by defining the following research question: *Can iteratively adjusted weights outperform fixed weights?*. As explained in Sect. 1, our problem differs from those addressed in existing works in that we do not explicitly model states and we have feedback for each of the agent's possible action. Therefore, we cannot directly compare our contribution with those from such works.

To address our research question, we set up an experiment in a concrete scenario, using a reference corpus to simulate user input and feedback. We describe our approach to account for user feedback in Sect. 4.1; we present our choice for the scenario and reward function in Sect. 4.2; we describe the procedure followed in our experiment in Sect. 4.3, and then we present and discuss the results obtained in Sect. 4.4.

4.1   Simulating User Feedback

In a first approach to validate the proposed learning approach, we use a reference corpus to simulate the user feedback. As such, at each step t, a "user interaction" $u(t) = (T_{u(t)}, A_{u(t)})$ is selected from the reference corpus. The trigger $T_{u(t)}$ is presented to the agent as being a user request. The agent proceeds as usual, retrieving a set $C(t)$ of candidate interactions from its collection of interactions, and each expert E^k scores the different candidate interactions in $C(t)$ as described in the previous section. Then, for each expert, a user reward r_t^k is computed, using as reference the answer $A_{u(t)}$ from the user interaction $u(t)$, so that it measures how well the candidate answer A^k that received the highest score by E^k matches the reference answer, $A_{u(t)}$. The weights w^k of each expert E^k are then updated considering the sum of the rewards received so far, $R^k(1,...,t)$. In other words, we use the reference corpus to automatically compute the user feedback.

Our choice for the reference corpus was the Cornell Movie-Dialogs (CMD) corpus[1], which contains over $80,000$ conversations from different sources [8], all

---

[1] This corpus is available in http://www.cs.cornell.edu/~cristian/Cornell_Movie-Dialogs_Corpus.html (last accessed in 07/21/2016).

of them corresponding to actual movie conversations. Each entry in the conversations file of the CMD corpus lists all the lines that compose that conversation. For our purposes, we select only the first two lines of each interaction, acting as a pair $(trigger, answer)$.

4.2 Experimental Scenario: Say Something Smart

As our evaluation scenario, we decided to use Say Something Smart (SSS), the dialogue engine behind the open domain agent Filipe [2,15]. Given a user request, SSS looks up for a set of answer candidates in Subtle, a corpus of interactions built from movie subtitles [1,15], and returns the best answer according to a combination of K configurable features [15]. The interactions in Subtle were extracted from OpenSubtitles[2] and are organized as pairs of consecutive subtitles – the first element of the pair is the trigger (T), and the second is the answer (A), as illustrated in Fig. 1. The interactions are indexed using the Lucene engine [16].

```
SubId  - 100679
DialogId - 10
Diff  - 20927
T - Did you see that?
A - What is it?
```

Fig. 1. Example of an interaction in the Subtle format.

For each request u, Lucene retrieves a set of up to N candidate interactions $C = \{c_1, \ldots, c_N\}$, where each interaction c_n is a trigger-answer pair, (T_n, A_n), and N is a configurable value. SSS then has each feature f_k comparing every interaction $c_n \in C$ to the user input u and scoring them. SSS outputs the answer associated with the most voted interaction c^* as the reply to the user input u.

For the purpose of our experiment, we adapted SSS in order to include a learning module that selects a pair trigger-answer $u(t) = (T_{u(t)}, A_{u(t)})$ from the reference corpus and sends the trigger $T_{u(t)}$ to Lucene, which retrieves N candidates from the collection of interactions. Each candidate is scored by each feature f_k, and then each feature is evaluated by a reward function (simulating user feedback). We define our reward function as the similarity between the answer selected by the criterion k and the reference answer $A_{u(t)}$:

$$r_t^k = \mathrm{Jac}(A_n, A_{u(t)}). \tag{11}$$

Where Jac is the Jaccard similarity measure[3]. The value obtained is rounded by α decimal places. Finally, the weights w_k associated with each feature f_k are updated as a function of the accumulated reward $R^k(1, \ldots, t)$, as explained in the previous section. An overview of this process is shown in Fig. 2.

---

[2] http://www.opensubtitles.org/ (last accessed on 07/23/2016).

[3] The Jaccard similarity coefficient measures the similarity between two sets A and B as $Jac(A, B) = \frac{|A \cap B|}{|A \cup B|}$ [10].

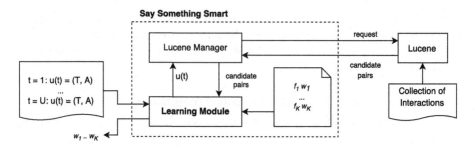

Fig. 2. SSS incorporating a learning module.

Concerning the values used in the experiment, we considered the same ones from the work of Magarreiro et al. [15]: the maximum number N of candidate interactions retrieved by Lucene was set to 20, and the criteria considered were the following:

f_1: Frequency of the answer A_n in the subtitle corpus;

f_2: Similarity between the answer A_n and the user input u using the Jaccard similarity measure;

f_3: Similarity between the trigger T_n and the user input u, also using the Jaccard similarity measure;

However, we did not consider the fourth criterion reported in Magarreiro et al. [15] (f_4 – Time difference between the trigger T_n and the answer A_n), as CMD corpus does not contain such information. In Magarreiro et al. [15], the weight for this criterion was set to zero in the configuration that achieved the best results, therefore its removal should not impact the evaluation procedure.

4.3   Experimental Procedure

In our experiment, we aim at comparing the performance of the weights learned using the online approach described in Sect. 3 against sets of fixed weights: the ones reported as best by Magarreiro et al. [15], and six sets of random weights.

Our simulation was designed in a cross-validation fashion with 10 folds. For each fold, the algorithm learns sets of weights w_k using different configurations of the algorithm's meta-parameters β (parameter of the weight update) and α (decimal places of the rounding made to the reward $r_t(c(t)^k)$). When learning, we used 60000 interactions from the CMD corpus (i.e., 80% of the corpus) as the collection of interactions used by SSS (having had converted them to the Subtle format), and 18000 (9×2000) other interactions as the reference corpus.

In order to assess the performance of the weights as they were iteratively adjusted, at each 300 iterations, we "froze" the weights obtained and ran SSS with them. We computed the accuracy of the system, i.e., the percentage of iterations in which SSS was able to choose the candidate answer that matched the input reference answer. To make this possible, the remaining 2000 interactions in the corpus were used both as the reference corpus and as the collection of interactions.

4.4   Results and Discussion

We compared the performance, in terms of accuracy (%), of the following sets of weights:

- The weights iteratively adjusted using different combinations of meta-parameters: $\alpha \in \{0, 4\}$ and $\beta \in \{4, 16\}$;
- The weights reported as best by Magarreiro et al. [15]: all the three features with the same weight: 33.3(3);
- Six sets of randomly generated weights:
  - $w_1 = 64$, $w_2 = 22$, $w_3 = 14$
  - $w_1 = 48$, $w_2 = 45$, $w_3 = 7$
  - $w_1 = 43$, $w_2 = 0$, $w_3 - 57$
  - $w_1 = 12$, $w_2 = 81$, $w_3 = 7$
  - $w_1 = 40$, $w_2 = 41$, $w_3 = 19$
  - $w_1 = 19$, $w_2 = 56$, $w_3 = 25$.

The results of this comparison are shown in Fig. 3, where each marker point over the solid lines represents the accuracy obtained by the set of weights computed at a given iteration, while the dashed line represents the accuracy of the fixed weights by Magarreiro et al. [15] and the dotted line represents the accuracy of the sets of random weights. The accuracy curves represent the average accuracy across the 10 cross-validation folds. In the case of the sets of random weights, we also averaged across different sets of weights.

The weights obtained when α was set to 0 outperformed both those of Magarreiro et al. [15] and random weights, converging within about 8000 iterations (and 4000 iterations in the case of $\beta = 16$), and achieving an accuracy of nearly 80%. In contrast, the weights obtained when α was set to 4 underperformed when compared to those of Magarreiro et al. [15] and to random weights. These results suggest that iteratively adjusting weights might or might not improve performance, showing high sensitivity to a particular meta-parameter: α. Let us recall that α regulates the rounding of the reward value. In practical terms, $\alpha = 0$ (rounding to the unit) benefits features that receive the maximum reward (1.0) often, which is the case of f_3, and penalizes those that receive a reward between 0.0 and 0.5 more often than a reward between 0.5 and 1.0, which is the case of f_1 and f_2. On the other hand, as expected, the parameter β does not impact how good the results are, but rather how fast these are obtained, since this parameter regulates how fast the weights change. From these results, we observe that the choice of reward function (and, particularly, the numerical precision of the values that can be returned by such function) is critical to its performance.

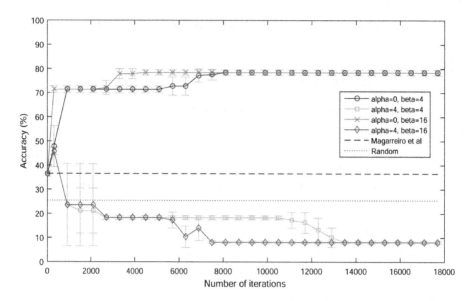

Fig. 3. Comparison in terms of accuracy between the weights iteratively adjusted using different combinations of meta-parameters α and β, the weights reported as best by Magarreiro et al. [15] and random sets of weights.

5   Conclusions and Future Work

In this work, we proposed the use of an online approach to improve an agent's performance at each interaction with a user. In particular, we applied an online algorithm, the Exponentially Weighted Average Forecaster, to the problem of adjusting the weights of the features used by a given agent to choose an answer to a given request from a large collection of interactions. We devised an experiment to validate this hypothesis, in which we adapted an existing dialogue engine, Say Something Smart, in order to incorporate the Exponentially Weighted Average Forecaster, and used a reference corpus to simulate user feedback. The results achieved indicate that adjusting the feature weights based on feedback might improve the performance of the agent, but it strongly depends on the design of the feedback (reward) function. Further exploration of the current work includes experimenting different online approaches and reward functions in the process of learning weights.

Acknowledgements. This work was supported by national funds through Fundação para a Ciência e a Tecnologia (FCT) with reference UID/CEC/50021/2013, and under project CMUP-ERI/HCI/0051/2013. Vânia Mendonça is funded by an FCT grant with reference SFRH/BD/121443/2016.

References

1. Ameixa, D., Coheur, L.: From subtitles to human interactions: introducing the SubTle Corpus from subtitles to interactions - response pairs. Technical report (2013)
2. Ameixa, D., Coheur, L., Fialho, P., Quaresma, P.: Luke, I am your father: dealing with out-of-domain requests by using movies subtitles. In: Bickmore, T., Marsella, S., Sidner, C. (eds.) IVA 2014. LNCS, vol. 8637, pp. 13–21. Springer, Cham (2014). doi:10.1007/978-3-319-09767-1_2
3. Banchs, R.E.: Movie-DiC: a movie dialogue corpus for research and development. In: Proceedings of 50th Annual Meeting of the Association for Computational Linguistics: Short Papers, ACL 2012, vol. 2, pp. 203–207. Association for Computational Linguistics, Stroudsburg (2012). http://dl.acm.org/citation.cfm?id=2390665.2390716
4. Banchs, R.E., Li, H.: Iris: a chat-oriented dialogue system based on the vector space model. In: Proceedings of ACL 2012 System Demonstrations, ACL 2012, pp. 37–42. Association for Computational Linguistics, Stroudsburg (2012). http://dl.acm.org/citation.cfm?id=2390470.2390477
5. Bessho, F., Harada, T., Kuniyoshi, Y.: Dialog system using real-time crowdsourcing and twitter large-scale corpus. In: Proceedings of 13th Annual Meeting of the Special Interest Group on Discourse and Dialogue, SIGDIAL 2012, pp. 227–231. Association for Computational Linguistics, Stroudsburg (2012). http://dl.acm.org/citation.cfm?id=2392800.2392841
6. Cesa-Bianchi, N., Lugosi, G.: Prediction, Learning and Games. Cambridge University Press, Cambridge (2006)
7. Cuayáhuitl, H., Dethlefs, N.: Dialogue systems using online learning: beyond empirical methods. In: NAACL-HLT Workshop on Future Directions and Needs in the Spoken Dialog Community: Tools and Data, SDCTD 2012, pp. 7–8. Association for Computational Linguistics, Stroudsburg (2012). http://dl.acm.org/citation.cfm?id=2390444.2390451
8. Danescu-Niculescu-Mizil, C., Lee, L.: Chameleons in imagined conversations: a new approach to understanding coordination of linguistic style in dialogs. In: Proceedings of Workshop on Cognitive Modeling and Computational Linguistics, ACL 2011 (2011)
9. Gašić, M., Jurčiček, F., Thomson, B., Yu, K., Young, S.: On-line policy optimisation of spoken dialogue systems via live interaction with human subjects. In: 2011 Proceedings of IEEE Workshop on Automatic Speech Recognition and Understanding, ASRU 2011, pp. 312–317 (2011)
10. Jaccard, P.: The distribution of the flora in the alpine zone. New Phytol. **11**(2), 37–50 (1912)
11. Nio, L., Sakti, S., Neubig, G., Toda, T., Adriani, M., Nakamura, S.: Developing non-goal dialog system based on examples of drama television. In: The International Workshop on Spoken Dialog Systems (IWSDS), Paris, France, December 2012
12. Levin, E., Pieraccini, R., Eckert, W.: A stochastic model of human-machine interaction for learning dialog strategies. IEEE Trans. Speech Audio Process. **8**, 11–23 (2000)
13. Li, J., Galley, M., Brockett, C., Gao, J., Dolan, B.: A persona-based neural conversation model. CoRR abs/1603.06155 (2016). http://arxiv.org/abs/1603.06155
14. Littlestone, N., Warmuth, M.K.: The weighted majority algorithm. Inf. Comput. **108**(2), 212–261 (1994). http://dx.doi.org/10.1006/inco.1994.1009

15. Magarreiro, D., Coheur, L., Melo, F.S.: Using subtitles to deal with out-of-domain interactions. In: SemDial 2014 - DialWatt (2014)
16. McCandless, M., Hatcher, E., Gospodnetic, O.: Lucene in Action, 2nd edn.: Covers Apache Lucene 3.0., Manning Publications Co., Greenwich (2010)
17. Pietquin, O., Geist, M., Chandramohan, S.: Sample efficient on-line learning of optimal dialogue policies with Kalman temporal differences. In: International Joint Conference on Artificial Intelligence (IJCAI 2011), Barcelona, Spain, pp. 1878–1883, July 2011
18. Serban, I.V., Sordoni, A., Bengio, Y., Courville, A., Pineau, J.: Building end-to-end dialogue systems using generative hierarchical neural network models. In: AAAI 2016 (Special Track on Cognitive Systems) (2015). https://arxiv.org/abs/1507.04808
19. Singh, S., Litman, D., Kearns, M., Walker, M.: Optimizing dialogue management with reinforcement learning: experiments with the NJFun system. J. Artif. Intell. Res. **16**, 105–133 (2002)
20. Su, P.H., Gasic, M., Mrkšić, N., Rojas Barahona, M.L., Ultes, S., Vandyke, D., Wen, T.H., Young, S.: On-line active reward learning for policy optimisation in spoken dialogue systems. In: Proceedings of 54th Annual Meeting of the Association for Computational Linguistics, Long Papers, vol. 1, pp. 2431–2441. Association for Computational Linguistics (2016). http://aclweb.org/anthology/P16-1230
21. Xu, Z., Liu, B., Wang, B., Sun, C., Wang, X.: Incorporating loose-structured knowledge into LSTM with recall gate for conversation modeling. CoRR abs/1605.05110 (2016). http://arxiv.org/abs/1605.05110
22. Yao, K., Peng, B., Zweig, G., Wong, K.: An attentional neural conversation model with improved specificity. CoRR abs/1606.01292 (2016). http://arxiv.org/abs/1606.01292
23. Yu, Z., Xu, Z., Black, A.W., Rudnicky, A.I.: Strategy and policy learning for non-task-oriented conversational systems. In: Proceedings of SIGDIAL 2016 Conference, pp. 404–412 (2016)
24. Yu, Z., Xu, Z., Black, A.W., Rudnicky, A.I.: Chatbot evaluation and database expansion via crowdsourcing. In: Proceedings of RE-WOCHAT Workshop of LREC (2016)

Social Simulation and Modelling

Simulation and Embedding

Simulating Behaviors of Children with Autism Spectrum Disorders Through Reversal of the Autism Diagnosis Process

Kim Baraka[1,2]($\boxtimes$), Francisco S. Melo[2], and Manuela Veloso[3]

[1] Robotics Institute, Carnegie Mellon University, Pittsburgh, PA 15213, USA
kbaraka@andrew.cmu.edu
[2] Instituto Superior Técnico/INESC-ID, 2744-016 Porto Salvo, Portugal
fmelo@inesc-id.pt
[3] Machine Learning Department, Carnegie Mellon University,
Pittsburgh, PA 15213, USA
mmv@cs.cmu.edu

Abstract. Children affected by Autism Spectrum Disorders (ASD) exhibit behaviors that may vary drastically from child to child. The goal of achieving accurate computer simulations of behavioral responses to given stimuli for different ASD severities is a difficult one, but it could unlock interesting applications such as informing the algorithms of agents designed to interact with those individuals. This paper demonstrates a novel research direction for high-level simulation of behaviors of children with ASD by exploiting the structure of available ASD diagnosis tools. Building on the observation that the simulation process is in fact the reverse of the diagnosis process, we take advantage of the structure of the Autism Diagnostic Observation Schedule (ADOS), a state-of-the-art standardized tool used by therapists to diagnose ASD, in order to build our ADOS-Based Autism Simulator (ABASim). We first define the ADOS-Based Autism Space (ABAS), a feature space that captures individual behavioral differences. Using this space as a high-level behavioral model, the simulator is able to stochastically generate behavioral responses to given stimuli, consistent with provided child descriptors, namely ASD severity, age and language ability. Our method is informed by and generalizes from real ADOS data collected on 67 children with different ASD severities, whose correlational profile is used as our basis for the generation of the feature vectors used to select behaviors.

Keywords: Behavioral simulation · Computational modeling · Autism · Autism Diagnostic Observation Schedule

1 Introduction

Autism Spectrum Disorders (ASD) is a set of developmental conditions that affect 1 in 68 children in the US[1] and can have varying degrees of impact on

---

[1] According to a 2014 report by the Centers for Disease Control and Prevention.

© Springer International Publishing AG 2017
E. Oliveira et al. (Eds.): EPIA 2017, LNAI 10423, pp. 753–765, 2017.
DOI: 10.1007/978-3-319-65340-2_61

social abilities, verbal and non-verbal communication, and motor and cognitive skills. These disorders have been widely studied from a developmental, neuropsychological [17] and genetic [13] point of view, whereby researchers try to explain the underlying mechanisms that cause or characterize ASD. However, apart from diagnostic procedures, efforts for understanding, classifying, formalizing and predicting the wide range of *behaviors* of individuals with ASD remain as of now limited. In particular in children, which are the focus of this work, the exhibited behaviors may be even more diverse and hard to predict compared to adults. The lack of such accurate behavioral models poses a problem in the design of autonomous agents that are expected to interact socially with children with ASD, such as avatars [12] or robots [6,14]. Several studies have shown that introducing such agents in ASD therapy session has notable benefits [3], which has encouraged researchers to design such agents in a variety of ways. However, most of the existing agents either lack autonomy or are rigid when it comes to personalizing the interaction to account for different ASD severities or types. We believe one major bottleneck comes from the lack of useful behavioral models and simulation tools to enable the agents to intelligently adapt their social interaction with the child. Without such tools, the effectiveness of the agent's reasoning, including both planning and learning, is limited.

On the other hand, several tools have been developed to diagnose ASD through observations or questionnaires. This paper specifically builds upon the Autism Diagnostic Observation Schedule (ADOS)[2], "a semi-structured, standardized assessment of communication, social interaction, play, and imagination designed for use in diagnostic evaluations of individuals referred for a possible Autism Spectrum Disorder (ASD)" [10]. Compared to other diagnostic and evaluation tools (e.g., ADI-R, CARS, SRS, etc.), the ADOS possesses enough structure to be interesting from a computational point of view. It provides us with a detailed, precise and quasi-comprehensive assessment of the characteristics of a child suspected of having an ASD, thanks to its detailed coding scheme and the inherent structure of its activities. For instance, some of these activities are 'algorithmic' in nature and use a hierarchy of 'presses' (social structures) to help the coding. We take advantage of these points and use the ADOS as a starting point for the design of a high-level behavioral simulator of children with different severities of ASD.

The basis for this paper stems from the observation that the simulation process can be seen as the reverse of the diagnosis process. While the latter maps observed behaviors to a set of coded features, the former maps features to simulated behaviors consistent with those features. Unlike existing simulation procedures for ASD, our simulator, the *ADOS-Based Autism Simulator (ABASim)*, captures the individual differences in behaviors of children with varying ASD severities. We summarize the contributions of this paper as follows:

---

[2] Our work uses version 2 of the tool, namely ADOS-2, but for simplicity we refer to it by ADOS throughout the paper.

1. We define the ADOS-based Autism Space (ABAS), which captures behavioral differences among children with ASD, through the use of ADOS-based features,
2. We provide a method for stochastically mapping high-level descriptors of a child with ASD (namely: age, ASD severity, and language ability) to a point in ABAS. To inform the mapping process, our method uses real data collected on children with different ASD severities,
3. We provide a method for mapping a point in ABAS to behaviors occurring in response to a fixed set of stimuli, corresponding to ADOS activities.

2   Background

We start by discussing some related work on simulating/modeling human behaviors. Then, we provide some details on the structure of the ADOS diagnostic tool.

2.1   Simulating/Modeling Human Behaviors

Simulating and modeling human behaviors have been a widespread practice to inform any type of decision-making involving humans. Examples include consumer modeling in market research [1,5,16], online recommendation systems [9], and driver modeling [4], to name a few. These models focus on behavior, which is predicted either using an underlying cognitive process (e.g., driver modeling) or through the use of data (e.g., recommendation systems). Moreover, a general purpose "computer based mental simulator" (NL_MAMS) has been developed and used to simulate the underlying mental processes of individuals with ASD [7].

Computational models of ASD include techniques such as neural networks or game theory to model low-level mechanisms of the brain affecting behavior [7]. These methods are good at explaining different observed autistic behaviors, but not as successful in computationally predicting high-level behavior, especially for different types or severities of ASD. Reinforcement Learning methods have been proven to be useful in modeling some high-level behaviors seen in individuals with ASD [2], but they are only able to distinguish between ASD and non-ASD populations. Individual differences, well established in available diagnostic tools, are starting to be studied from a modeling/simulation perspective [15] but the parts of the model accounting for these differences is usually simplistic. To the best of our knowledge, the simulation of high-level autistic behaviors in an *individualized* way and in response to *different types of stimuli* remains unexplored.

2.2   Autism Diagnostic Observation Schedule (ADOS) Structure

The ADOS diagnostic tool comprises 5 modules suitable for different language abilities and/or ages. Module 1 (Pre-verbal/Single Words) remains the main module used by therapists as an initial assessment of children 31 months or older, and up to 14 years of age. For this reason, we focus on this particular module in this work. However, our methods can be applied to any of the ADOS modules as they possess a very similar structure.

The ADOS Module 1 is composed of 10 standardized activities, with varying degrees of structuredness, including rather unstructured activities such as 'Free Play' (where the child is left to freely play in the room) to very structured activities such as 'Response to name' (where the therapists calls the child's name at different degrees of intensity and observes the child's response). In a typical session where the ADOS is administered, the therapist performs the activities and records behaviors of interest throughout the session. At the end of the session (i.e., after all 10 activities are over), the therapist codes the behaviors exhibited by the child throughout the whole session.

There are a total of 29 ADOS codes for different, usually exclusive, behavior types. However, of these 29 codes only 14 are used in the algorithm that returns the *total score* used for diagnosis, and those slightly vary depending on the language ability of the child. Table 1 shows the codes used for computing the total score and of interest in this work. Codes are all converted to a 0–2 integer scale before they are summed to produce a total score between 0 and 28. The total score can be further broken down into three subtotals for Communication (A2 to A8), Reciprocal Social Interaction (B1 to B12) and Restricted and Repetitive Behavior (A3 to D4). From the total score, one can compute a *comparison score* (between 1 and 10) which serves as our measure for autism severity. In this paper, we focus only on the codes of Table 1, although using more codes to get more detailed simulated behaviors is possible.

3   ADOS-Based Autism Space (ABAS)

In this section, we formally introduce our domain, based on the structure of the ADOS.

3.1   ABAS Definition

Through its use of codes to map observed behaviors to numbers, the ADOS effectively defines a *feature space* for ASD, which we will call the *ADOS-based Autism space (ABAS)*. In this space, the **features** under consideration correspond to the different ADOS codes, and ABAS points represent different individuals with different ASD characteristics. We refer to our features (codes) as $c_{i,L}$ for $i = 1, ..., 14$ and $L =$ 'No words', 'Some words', where $c_{i,L} \in \{0, 1, 2\}$. Even though some items may be originally coded by the therapist using values outside the 0–2 range, the codes are remapped to it for the algorithm's purposes. We refer to a point in ABAS using the feature vector $[c_1, ..., c_{14}]$ (ignoring the dependence on language ability for simplicity).

Table 1. Summary of the ADOS module 1 codes (features) used for computing the total score for the two different language abilities

Code name	Label	Few/no words	Some words
Frequency of vocalization directed to others	A2	✓	✓
Pointing	A7	✗	✓
Gestures	A8	✓	✓
Unusual eye contact	B1	✓	✓
Facial expressions directed to others	B3	✓	✓
Integration of gaze [etc.] during social overtures	B4	✓	✓
Shared enjoyment in interaction	B5	✓	✓
Showing	B9	✓	✓
Spontaneous initiation of joint attention	B10	✓	✓
Response to joint attention	B11	✓	✗
Quality of social overtures	B12	✓	✓
Intonation of vocalizations or verbalizations	A3	✓	✗
Stereotyped/idiosyncratic use of words or phrases	A5	✗	✓
Unusual sensory interest in play material/person	D1	✓	✓
Hand and finger and other complex mannerisms	D2	✓	✓
Unusually repetitive interests or stereotyped behaviors	D4	✓	✓

3.2 Total Score Constraint on ABAS

The total score C is defined as $\sum_{i=1}^{14} c_i$ ($C \in \{0, ..., 28\}$). Except for edge cases, there are many feature vectors (combinations of ADOS codes) that sum up to the same total score. To evaluate the impact on constraining the L1 norm of the feature vector, we solve the following equation for each of the possible values of C:

$$\sum_{i=1}^{14} c_i = C, \quad c_i \in \{0, 1, 2\} \tag{1}$$

The number of elements in the solution set of Eq. 1 as a function of C is shown in Fig. 1. For some values of the total score, the number of possible feature vectors can be very large (e.g., more than 600,000 for a total score of 14). Although mathematically feasible, we suspect that some of these feature vectors will be unlikely to occur in nature due to inevitable dependencies between the different features. This observation will be tackled in Sect. 4.2.

3.3 Descriptors

As for any simulator, it is useful to define a set of high-level variables which could be inputted by a user to create a range of simulations with different characteristics. In particular, the individual features might be too many to input by hand, or as mentioned in the previous subsection, some of the combinations of features may be unlikely to even occur in nature. Also, we may want to be able to

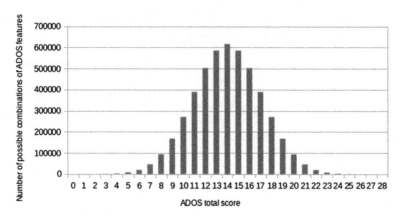

Fig. 1. Number of different possible combinations of ADOS codes (feature vectors) for a fixed total score.

stochastically generate different simulation runs for a smaller set of higher-level input variables. For these reasons, we introduce **descriptors**, defined as:

- The child's chronological *age* A,
- The child's *language ability* L ('no words' or 'some words'),
- The child's *ASD severity* S (on a scale from 1 to 10).

These descriptors are used in the ADOS, which defines a relationship between A, L, S and C in the form of a conversion table. The (A,L,S) triplet will be used as a convenient yet expressive input to our simulator.

4   Behavioral Simulation of Children with Different ASD Severities

In this section, we describe the different components along the pipeline of our ADOS-Based Autism Simulator (ABASim), which generates behavioral responses to input stimuli for specified descriptors.

4.1   ABASim Components Overview

ABASim enables the generation of a set of behaviors which, according to ADOS, are likely to occur as a response to a given stimulus, for a child with given descriptors. The stimuli we consider in this work correspond to the standardized activities performed during an ADOS session; therefore the set of behaviors ABASim is able to generate are those typically observed during or as a response to these activities.

The pipeline of our simulator is shown in Fig. 2. We use the descriptors (A, L, S) to specify the characteristics of the fictional child to be simulated. The input descriptors first get translated into a total score range, from which a single total score is randomly selected. From this total score, we stochastically generate 14 feature values whose sum matches the specified total score. The sampling process used is informed by data collected on real children suspected of having an ASD. Finally, for each of the 10 activities, we have identified a set of relevant features which dictate what kinds of behaviors are likely to be observed for the given activity. These behaviors are selected from a database of behaviors that we compiled based on the explanation of the coding scheme of the ADOS manual [10]. We now give some more detail on the different simulator components.

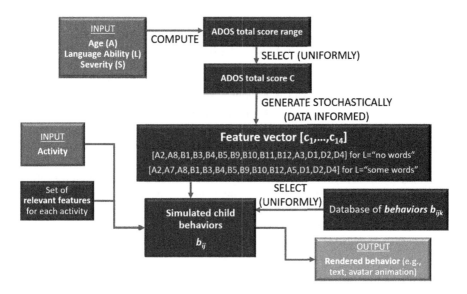

Fig. 2. ABASim pipeline: generating simulated behaviors for input descriptors and activity.

4.2 Stochastic Generation of Feature Vectors from Descriptors

As mentioned in the simulator overview, the user will be specifying the descriptors as an input to the simulator. We hence need a mapping from descriptors to a feature vector consistent with these descriptor values.

The first step is to map given descriptors to a total score C. This step is trivial since it is directly given by a conversion table present at the end of the ADOS. This table converts a given set of age, language ability, and total score range to a severity value. Reversing this conversion gives us a range for C for a given (A,L,S) triplet (the width of this range is typically between 0 and 7). We then uniformly select one integer value in that range as our total score C.

The second step is to map the obtained total score C to a feature vector $[c_1, ..., c_{14}]$ in ABAS. In other words, we are looking for a method to sample a feature vector with the property $\sum_{i=1}^{14} c_i = C$. As emphasized in Sect. 3.2 some vectors will be unlikely to occur because we do not expect to have complete independence between the features c_i. We use real data to verify and make use of this hypothesis, as explained in the following subsections.

Dataset Description and Analysis. In order to inform our method for sampling feature vectors, we gathered the Module 1 ADOS scores (feature values) of 67 children with different severities of ASD[3]. Ages ranged between 3 and 7 years and the female-to-male ratio was 11:56. The total scores in the dataset ranged between 0 and 25, with a more or less uniform distribution over total scores (no blatant skewness). We analyzed the correlation between pairs of features, as shown in Fig. 3(a). Since we are dealing with ordinal data, we used Spearman correlation coefficients; we also ignored higher-order correlations. P-values were computed for each correlation coefficient using a t-statistic. Note that, of the 14 features, only the 12 in common between the two L categories were included. Because of our small sample size, breaking down our dataset into two parts (one for each value of L) would have been problematic statistically speaking. As a workaround, we could set the value of the two remaining features randomly.

Most features turn out to be correlated (hence dependent), except for three pairs of features whose p-value is above 0.05, namely (D2,B1) ($p = 0.060$), (D2,B4) ($p = 0.068$), and (D2, B12) ($p = 0.105$). Note that all three pairs contain D2 which corresponds to 'Hand and Finger and Other Complex Mannerisms'. Furthermore, the computed correlation matrix does not contain any negative correlations, which makes sense given that all features are partial measures of ASD severity, along different dimensions, where higher means more severe.

Generating Consistent (Unconstrained) Feature Vectors. The ABAS is a very large space which inevitably makes most reasonably sized datasets sparse. In particular, with our limited dataset (67 data points), it is important to enable the simulator to generalize from data to generate synthetic feature vectors that are consistent with our limited data points. In this work, we aim to generate feature vectors according to the correlational structure between features, as obtained from our dataset. In other words, we would like to generate correlated discrete (ordinal) data according to the dataset's correlational profile. Several methods exist to achieve this, including the Gaussian copula [11], binary conversion, and mean mapping [8] methods. We use the mean mapping method, which gave best results for our application. The method takes as input the target marginal distributions and target correlation matrix of the features, and generates a set of feature vectors with (asymptotically) identical marginals and correlation matrix. The ordinal data is first mapped to the continuous space by computing a corresponding multivariate normal correlation matrix (achieved through

---

[3] The ADOS data used in this research are part of a database for autistic children that the ASD group, at the Child Development Center of the Hospital Garcia de Orta (Lisbon, Portugal), keeps for statistical purposes. All data was anonymous; only age and gender were collected from the sample for biographical characterization.

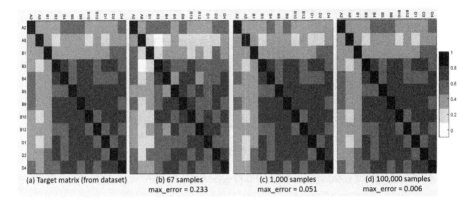

Fig. 3. Spearman correlation matrices of features for: (a) the real dataset (67 feature vectors), (b–d) synthetic datasets of size 67, 1,000, and 100,000 respectively, along with maximum absolute errors as compared to (a). Target feature marginals were set to uniform distributions.

function fitting). Multivariate normal data is then drawn according to this correlation matrix and reconverted to ordinal data. We used an R implementation of this method through the `orddata`[4] package to generate the synthetic feature vectors analyzed in Fig. 3. The figure shows the obtained correlation matrices, which are consistent with the target correlation matrix (from the real dataset) and converge to it as the number of samples increases. We report the maximum absolute errors, defined as the maximum absolute difference between the sample matrices and the target matrix over all matrix entries. In order not to bias the generated total scores, target marginals were set to the uniform distribution.

Incorporating the Constraint to Achieve the Mapping. In our feature vector generation scheme, we have so far ensured that the sampling was consistent with real data, but we have ignored the constraint on the L1 norm of the feature vector (Eq. 1). To incorporate the constraint, we iteratively generate unconstrained feature vectors until the total score constraint is satisfied. Unlike the bell-shaped distribution of Fig. 1, the statistical distribution of our generated (unconstrained) feature vectors is almost uniform, as shown in Fig. 4, which we attribute primarily to the target uniform marginals we enforced. This result suggests that the amount of computation needed to generate a feature vector for a given total score does not significantly rely on the value of that score as one might expect from the different subspace sparsities emphasized in Fig. 1.

4.3   Mapping Feature Vectors to Behaviors

The problem of mapping a feature vector in ABAS to a set of behaviors in response to stimuli is a tricky one because there are usually more than a single

---

[4] https://r-forge.r-project.org/R/?group_id=708.

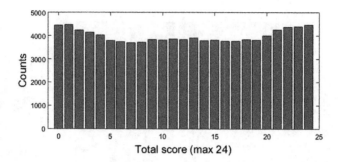

Fig. 4. Histogram of total scores for 100,000 generated feature vectors (only 12 features used).

behavior that fall under the same feature value and the degree of specificity in describing the different behaviors in the ADOS manual varies greatly. Also, there is always some level of subjectivity in the ADOS coding process which makes the generation and rendering of the different behaviors a sensitive task which would need to be backed up by extensive empirical studies if deployed in an actual system (beyond the scope of this paper).

As a first step in the mapping process, we defined a set of relevant features for each of the ADOS activities, which we summarize in Table 2. Relevant features capture the types of behaviors that are expected to be exhibited in - or are of special importance for - a particular activity. For example, in the activity 'Response to join attention', the feature 'Spontaneous Initiation of Joint Attention' (B10) is relevant but the feature 'Unusual Sensory Interest in Play Material/Person' (D1) is not. These relevant features were chosen based on the nature of the activity as well as the observational guidelines included in the ADOS manual.

Table 2. Relevant features for each activity considered (for both L = 'no words' and L = 'some words' combined).

Activity	Relevant features
Free play	A2,A7,A8,B5,B9,B10,B3,D1,D2,D4
Response to name	B1,B4,A2
Response to joint attention	B11,B1,A2,B5,B10,B12
Bubble play	B3,B10,B5,D1,D2,D4
Anticipation of a routine with objects	B10,B5,D2,D4
Responsive social smile	B3
Anticipation of a social routine	B4,B1,B3,A2,A8,B5
Functional and symbolic imitation	B4,B5
Birthday party	D4,B5,B12,B1,B3,B4
Snack	B1,A8,B3,A3,B12

On the other hand, for each feature, we extracted from the ADOS manual one or more corresponding behavior(s) b_{ijk}, where $i \in \{1, ..., 14\}$ is the feature index, $j \in \{0, 1, 2\}$ is the feature value, and $k \in \{1, ..., K_{ij}\}$ is the behavior index. The ADOS manual describes the coding process by listing more or less specific behaviors that would fall under a given value for each feature. The database of behaviors b_{ijk} was manually compiled to include all those described behaviors. The number of behaviors that fall under the same value for a given feature ranges from a single behavior to up to 8 behaviors with varying degrees of similarity.

Sample behavior database entry for feature A7 (c_2):

- $c_2 = 0$: $\{b_{201}$: "Child points with index finger to show visually directed referencing"$\}$,
- $c_2 = 1$: $\{b_{211}$: "Child produces an approximation of pointing", $b_{212} - b_{217}$: "Child (gazes)/(vocalizes) while (touching object)/(pointing to a person)/(pointing to himself/herself)" (all combinations)$\}$,
- $c_2 = 2$: $\{b_{221}$ b_{222}: "Child points when (close to)/(touching) object only, and with no gaze or vocalization", b_{223}: "Child doesn't point"$\}$.

The behavior generation for a particular activity is done by sampling a behavior for each of the features relevant to the activity according to the given value of the feature. Because of the small number of behaviors that fall under the same (feature,value) pair, we opt for a simple uniform selection rule. Note that when selecting behaviors, the algorithm has to use the L value since the corresponding features slightly differ. We render generated behaviors as text, but one could imagine other ways of rendering them, such as for instance using an animated virtual avatar.

We implemented the pipeline of Fig. 2 in Python with a GUI to control the different simulator inputs. Figure 5 shows an illustrative example of the different steps computed by ABASim for three different sets of input descriptors and activities.

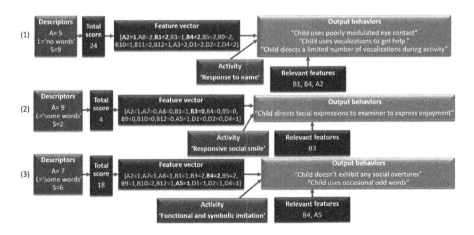

Fig. 5. Illustrative examples showing ABASim steps for three different inputs.

5   Conclusion and Future Work

We presented ABASim, a method for simulating the behaviors of children with Autism Spectrum Disorders (ASD) of different severities, as a response to a range of stimuli. While the Autism Diagnostic Observation Schedule (ADOS), a standardized tool for diagnosing ASD, maps child behaviors to a score, our method aims at mapping a score (along with the age and language ability of the child) to a set of behaviors consistent with these descriptors. We first defined the Autism-Based Autism Space (ABAS) where features correspond to ADOS codes. We then contributed a pipeline enabling us to generate behaviors from descriptors. In particular, our stochastic mapping from descriptors to a point in ABAS ensures a correlational structure between features that is consistent with actual ADOS data from 67 children suspected of having an ASD.

Our method could enable agents designed to enhance ASD therapy to reason better about interactions with children with ASD, accounting for individual behavioral differences. Another possible application that we foresee is for therapist training. Simulating the behavioral responses of virtual kids could provide new tools for therapists by enabling them to virtually interact with hypothetical children, which they cannot do only by observing videos. The simulator could also expose the therapists in training to a wide range of hypothetical cases of ASD that goes beyond the sample they physically interact with in their real professional life.

In the future, we would like to use a larger dataset to better inform our sampling process. Also, it would be useful to have some way of evaluating our generated feature vectors as well as behaviors to ensure they accurately reflect actual behavioral patterns. Finally, we are interested in integrating these simulation methods as part of the reasoning of an agent interacting with children with ASD, such as a mobile robot for therapy.

Acknowledgments. This research was supported by the FCT CMUP-ERI/HCI/ 0051/2013 grant and national funds through Fundação para a Ciência e a Tecnologia (FCT) with reference UID/CEC/50021/2013. We would like to thank the Child Development Center at Hospital Garcia de Orta (Almada, Portugal), Dr. Marta Couto, and the INSIDE project for giving us access to and assistance with the data used in this research. We also thank Patrick Lin, Jocelyn Huang, and Minji Kim for their contributions on the code. The views and conclusions contained in this document are those of the authors only.

References

1. Bagozzi, R.P.: On the concept of intentional social action in consumer behavior. J. Consum. Res. **27**(3), 388–396 (2000)
2. Behrens, T.E., Hunt, L.T., Rushworth, M.F.: The computation of social behavior. Science **324**(5931), 1160–1164 (2009)
3. Cabibihan, J.-J., Javed, H., Ang, M., Aljunied, S.M.: Why robots? A survey on the roles and benefits of social robots in the therapy of children with autism. Int. J. Soc. Robot. **5**(4), 593–618 (2013)

4. Cacciabue, P.C., Re, C., Macchi, L.: Simple simulation of driver performance for prediction and design analysis. In: Cacciabue, P.C. (ed.) Modelling Driver Behaviour in Automotive Environments, pp. 344–375. Springer, Heidelberg (2007). doi:10.1007/978-1-84628-618-6_19

5. Chen, G., Warren, J., Riddle, P.: Semantic space models for classification of consumer webpages on metadata attributes. J. Biomed. Inform. **43**(5), 725–735 (2010)

6. Feil-Seifer, D.J.: Data-driven interaction methods for socially assistive robotics: validation with children with autism spectrum disorders (Unpublished doctoral dissertation). University of Southern California

7. Galitsky, B.: Computational Models of Autism. Springer Internatinal Publishing, Cham (2016)

8. Kaiser, S., Träger, D., Leisch, F.: Generating correlated ordinal random values (2011)

9. Li, L., Chu, W., Langford, J., Schapire, R.E.: A contextual-bandit approach to personalized news article recommendation. In: Proceedings of the 19th International Conference on World Wide Web, pp. 661–670 (2010)

10. Lord, C., Rutter, M., Dilavore, P., Risi, S., Gotham, K., Bishop, S.: Autism Diagnostic Observation Schedule, 2nd edn. Western Psychological Services, Torrance (2012)

11. Madsen, L., Birkes, D.: Simulating dependent discrete data. J. Stat. Comput. Simul. **83**(4), 677–691 (2013)

12. Milne, M., Luerssen, M.H., Lewis, T.W., Leibbrandt, R.E., Powers, D.M.: Development of a virtual agent based social tutor for children with autism spectrum disorders. In: The 2010 International Joint Conference on Neural networks (IJCNN) (2010)

13. Muhle, R., Trentacoste, S.V., Rapin, I.: The genetics of autism. Pediatrics **113**(5), e472–e486 (2004)

14. Ricks, D.J., Colton, M.B.: Trends and considerations in robot-assisted autism therapy. In: 2010 IEEE International Conference on Robotics and Automation (ICRA), pp. 4354–4359 (2010)

15. Sevgi, M., Diaconescu, A.O., Tittgemeyer, M., Schilbach, L.: Social bayes: using bayesian modeling to study autistic trait-related differences in social cognition. Biol. Psychiatry **80**(2), 112–119 (2016)

16. Shen, Z.-J.M., Su, X.: Customer behavior modeling in revenue management and auctions: a review and new research opportunities. Prod. Oper. Manag. **16**(6), 713–728 (2007)

17. Sigman, M., Spence, S.J., Wang, A.T.: Autism from developmental and neuropsychological perspectives. Annu. Rev. Clin. Psychol. **2**, 327–355 (2006)

An Adaptive Simulation Tool for Evacuation Scenarios

Daniel Formolo$^{(\boxtimes)}$ ⓘ and C. Natalie van der Wal ⓘ

Department of Computer Science,
Vrije Universiteit Amsterdam, Amsterdam, Netherlands
{d.formolo,c.n.vander.wal}@vu.nl

Abstract. Building useful and efficient models and tools for a varied audience, such as evacuation simulators for scientists, engineers and crisis managers, can be tricky. Even good models can fail in providing information when the user's tools for the model are scarce of resources. The aim of this work is to propose a new tool that covers the most required features in evacuation scenarios. This paper starts with a review of current software, prototypes and models simulating evacuation scenarios, by discussing their required and desired features. Based on this overview, we propose our simulator comparing it with other models and commercial tools. Moreover, we discuss the importance of building simulators that cover the minimum requirements to avoid the risk of building inefficient models or tools that do not provide enough insights for users to take right decisions in terms of security policies in crowded events. The implications of this work are to present a new simulation tool and to start a discussion in this research field on mandatory features of evacuation simulation tools that will provide valuable information to users and to find out what the criteria are to define these features.

Keywords: Evacuation · Simulation · Crowd model · Multi-agent · Tools

1 Introduction

Incident management involving crowds is always a hard task, and the best way to deal with it is to be prepared for many possible scenarios that emerge. In that way, specialists are able to make cause-effect lists and predict countermeasures to reduce damage, injuries, and dead. People-people and people-environment interaction and other aspects that influence the start of an incident are very complex. Therefore, many unpredicted situations can happen and decisions have to be taken immediately. To help specialists make good security plans, computer evacuation models are becoming integrated into emergency prevention and management more and more. Crowd evacuation simulations have been used to analyse different phenomena, such as exit selection, queuing, herding behaviour, panic propagation, fluid behaviour, decision behaviour, escape behaviour, pushing behaviour, competitive and collaborative behaviour, jamming, clogging and following behaviour [21]. Computer models also help to design new safe environments which diminish risks in case of incidents.

© Springer International Publishing AG 2017
E. Oliveira et al. (Eds.): EPIA 2017, LNAI 10423, pp. 766–777, 2017.
DOI: 10.1007/978-3-319-65340-2_62

Usually, these models are more environment oriented, simulating people like robots taking rational decisions to reach a safe place, avoiding obstacles and suffering the influence of the environment in their speed to escape, for example, fixed barriers and the physical influence of others around that slow down the evacuation. Most of these models do not incorporate psychological and social factors. Observations of current emergencies show that people tend to be slow to respond to evacuation alarms (taking up to 10 min) and take the familiar route out instead of the nearest exit [1–3, 7, 10, 12]. These risky behaviour stem from being unfamiliar with the environment, not seeing immediate signs of danger, following others' (unsafe) behaviour. Evacuation simulation models could become more realistic by incorporating these realistic human behaviours, as currently, they do not.

This work presents a tool that can simulate evacuation scenarios with the aims: (1) Being useful for a wide variety of audiences: simple enough for end users to operate it and adaptable by social scientist and engineers to explore new theories on evacuation models; (2) Incorporating psychological and social parameters in the evacuation model, based on the lack in current evacuation models; (3) Starts a discussion of Required and Desired features to Evacuation Simulation Tools.

Before developing the current tool, a review of significant features of current crowd evacuation models and simulation tools was performed. Moreover, a survey about which features are important according to experts and current users of evacuation simulation tools was conducted. Then based on the findings, the simulator was developed. It goes beyond other products or models, by integrating behavioural and physical models, enabling users to adapt it to any kind of scenario. Different than the majority of tools, it is completely free to simulate any kind of environment. Besides, it empowers users to add or change elements of the behaviour model extending it to even more refined simulations.

2 Review of Evacuation Model Tools

A careful review of evacuation models and commercial tools was performed. The characteristics were selected based on other literature reviews, commercial softwares and a questionnaire that was applied to specialists and users of crowd simulations. The characteristics are separated into three categories: Usability, Reports and Model. Usability covers the user interactions with the tool; Reports cover the output visualisation and helping the user in making decisions; Model covers how precise the real world is translated into the model itself. These characteristics were chosen because they contain all technical needs from a wide variety of users. Haron et al. also evaluated 6 tools for a specific scenario [5], the features listed in their work are similar to those proposed in this work, which reinforces the concept of a minimum common set of characteristics.

Usability features are: 2D/3D visualisation; Scenarios; Controls (which refers to how the user can change parameters); Performance. Reports features are: Graphs; Exporting results. Model features are: Speed; Planned Routes; Fixed or dynamic routes; Floor plans; Access Areas (such as stairs, bridges and lifts).

In combination with the above features extracted from models and commercial tools, the following concepts were defined to guide the selection of features in the categories: Required and Desired.

Required Characteristic: Characteristics that impact, at least 75 s, that is 50% of the recommended average evacuation time of 150 s defined in [22]. It can have a direct impact, in case of variables of the model or indirect in case of Report and Usability helps to identify bottlenecks in evacuation situations.

Desired Characteristic: All the other characteristics not classified as Required and which helps to make security protocols and improve security in evacuation situations.

There are many approaches for computer models of crowd evacuation simulations. Zheng et al. describe seven approaches for computer evacuation models: (1) cellular automata, (2) lattice gas, (3) social force, (4) fluid dynamics, (5) agent-based, (6) game theory, (7) animal experiments [21]. The current available tools use one of these types of models inside their engines. A more recent review on crowd models by Templeton et al. concludes that current crowd simulations do not include psychological factors and therefore cannot accurately simulate large collective behaviour that has been found in extensive empirical research on crowd events [15]. The perspective that only a few works consider social and psychological aspects into models is reinforced by Santos and Aguirre's review [13]. They argue that models such as EVACNET4, EESCAPE, EGRESSPRO (flow based models), EGRESS (cellular automata) and SIMULEX, EXIT89, GridFlow (agent-based models) do not model the social dimensions, such as group decision making but focus more on the physical constraints and factors such as walking speed, walkways and stairways to find the optimal flow of the evacuation process. Agents are rational in these simulations: they can find the optimal escape route and can avoid physical obstructions and in some models even overtake another person that would obstruct their way.

Ha and Lykotrafitis [4] proposed an agent-based model in 2012 governed by social-forces described in terms of Newtonian equations. That model makes an indirect link between social aspects and equations based on particles movements, what hampers the comprehension of social aspects. Also, the interface is poor and limited to simple rooms. A user-friendlier prototype with detailed environment aspects was proposed in 2014 by Wagner and Agrawal [17] to simulate evacuation in diverse auditoriums and stadiums shapes. Again, the model focused on people-environment interaction, ignoring people-people social aspects plus, as a prototype it is not adaptable for a variety of scenarios and most of their features are hardcoded. The MASCM model [9] includes social interaction in the way of evacuation leaders. For example, evacuation leaders can communicate 'please follow me' and start to walk along the evacuation route or find an evacuee at the distance or wait for the evacuee to approach.

All these models are reflected in simulation tools. In his work, van Toll et al. [16] proposes a framework tool with which it is possible to build 3D environments and simulate crowds flowing among buildings or inside them. Other commercial tools [6, 8, 11, 14] have good 3D interfaces and editors to build the environments in details but again are target-oriented and do not include social aspects. Besides, their models are black boxes, therefore adaptations in the models are limited. For example, only for [6] and [11] it is possible to set up specific evacuation time curves for groups of agents, for the others it is hard coded, dependent of customised solution, case by case.

Incontrol [6], MassMotion [11] and SimWalk [14] are the 3 commercial tools that were analysed. These three commercial tools were chosen because they are part of the industry leaders in this domain, with many applicable projects in real situations and they cover most of the characteristics present in other tools. Concerning Usability, all of them provide 2/3D visualisations as well as import scenarios from CAD like files and other pictures formats. They also allow users to edit them or build an entire scenario from scratch. Some basic controls are available, such as: start to evacuate time for each agent; pre-defined evacuation routes; number of agents and their initial position. For Reports, they provide many types of graphs are generated like Flow Output; Density Graphs; Multiple Evacuation graphs. All of them also export results of simulations to common file formats like CSV.

The internal Models, handle individual Speed of each agent, and all of them work with multiple floors and access areas. MassMotion differs from others by offering pre-defined evacuation actions. Each individual can be programmed to do tasks, i.c. take his belongings, before starting to evacuate. Incontrol provides footstep logs to follow each agent in the scenario and playback simulations to not miss any detail. It also offers adding elements to the scenario during the simulation and scripts to customise events in the simulation. In SimWalk it is possible to distinguish agents by age, size and gender, and add goals like Oasys tool.

After reviewing the state-of-the-art, a questionnaire was applied to professionals of crisis management and risk assessment, familiar with evacuation simulations. In total, 13 specialists from areas of railways (23.1%), maritime (7.7%), aviation (38.5%), medicine (7.7%) and other (23.1%) were asked to classify many aspects (below each bar in Fig. 1) of evacuation simulation scenarios from 1 = Not Necessary to 5 = Highly Required. Before they started classifying, the definitions of Required and Desired Characteristics were informed to them. The questions were divided into 3 categories: Usability, Reports and Model. Figure 1 shows a compiled overview of their answers. The aspects rated with a 4 or above (solid bars) have been classified as Required while others as Desired.

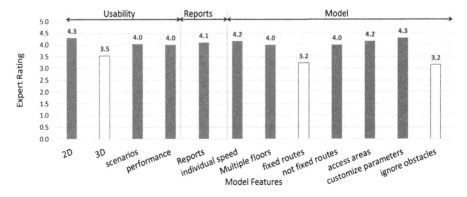

Fig. 1. Results overview of questionnaire applied to specialists in risk management.

Next, we wanted to determine the effect of social impact on evacuation time, to determine the necessity of including social and psychological factors in evacuation models. There are no available statistics about the impact of social impact on evacuation time. In order to get an estimation of the influence of this factor we used the model proposed in [18] on our developed tool to measure the influence of social impact on evacuation time. A neutral scenario was chosen, composed of a square room (20 × 20 meters) layout of a building, with no barriers and four exits (top, down, left, right, main exit = down), see Fig. 3. All environmental and personal factors such as width of the doors, gender, age and level of compliance were kept constant among simulations. When social impact is on, agents influence each other sharing their fears and believes, familiarity with the environment, helping behavior, differentiation in agents among adults, elderly and children (impacting on compliance and speed of agents) and groups of two people (children are always accompanied for an adult or elderly). The results of evacuation time with and without social behavior were compared in a low, medium and high crowded environment (2, 4 or 8 people/m2, respectively). On average, social impact reduces the evacuation time with 20%, (78.85 s), mostly because agents are influenced by the fear conveyed by others. Other social and cultural elements also have substantial influence on evacuation time, between decreasing it by 30% to increasing it by 3%, as described in [19]. Here, we consider the social impact as a global measurement.

Based on these results and the qualitative analyses of prototypes, academic models and commercial tools, the minimum set of needed characteristics of evacuation simulator tools are classified in next subsection which discuss Required and Desirable features for Usability, Reports and Model.

2.1   Discussion of Usability, Reports and Model Features

All commercial tools have very good 2D/3D visualisations, while most of the non-commercial prototypes and academic models are limited to 2D or only mathematical equations with no visualisation. 2D interfaces provide the most necessary aspects of analysing the simulation and taking decisions about security protocols, furniture, fixed barriers and escape areas. These physical aspects are the most important in influencing the evacuation time of a population from an environment. 3D interfaces add more realism to simulations, providing more intuitive orientations about possible problems in a real evacuation scenario, especially when referring to details in rooms and corridors. The capability if import scenario's floor plans is a feature present in all commercial tools and useful to not miss environment details that can reverberate in bottlenecks of evacuation flow.

In a simulation, it is important to test as many variations as possible in the population, environment and their relations. Tools have to provide easy-to-use Controls to facilitate these variations in the simulations. The Controls could also provide interaction with the simulation in real time to test specific situations, like an incident in a specific point of the scenario, or to provide an interface that can easily setup pre-programed characteristics like: routes of agents, actions that they take, the number of agents, gender, initial position, belonging to a group, size of the group, response time, number of incidents, start of the incidents, etc. Evacuation Simulations can become very detailed in terms of relations among population and relation with detailed environments, 2D and especially 3D interfaces cost long processing time. The number of repetitions and variations in the same scenario can make the simulation time rise exponentially. Due to these reasons, it is important to design a scalable and multithread tool. Based on the above analysis and the review of current tools and models, required and desirable features of Usability are shown in Table 1.

Table 1. Required and desirable features.

Feature	Required	Desirable
Usability		
2D/3D	2D visualization	3D visualization
Controls	All controls related to characteristics of the model that cause high impact in evacuation time. These are: Add incidents, e.g. block exits; Quantity of people; Speed; Start and end locations of agents; Social Features	Controls with low impact on safe evacuation but that can help to design a more safe environment
Performance	There is not a restriction requirement for performance. The only consequence is delaying of results	If performance is not required it can be classified as desirable
Reports		
Graphs	The minimum set of variables is: Evacuation time; response time; Number of agents that take each exit Flow density for each area	Any other variable related to the model that can be tracked
Export of results	There is not a restriction requirement for export of results	All data used to generate graphs
Model		
People	Occupied area of each agent; Physical effects of barriers and other agents over the agents; Evacuation speed; At least a statistical distribution of routes taken by the agents; Social Aspects	Non-pre-fixed evacuation routes
Environment	The Possibility of adding floors to buildings; Access areas with a configurable delay for each area; Fixed Barriers	Non-flat terrains and different type of terrains; Non-fixed barriers, i.e. furniture
Incident	Fix one or more incident points in the scenario; Define the size of the incident; Property of block paths; intelligent elements blocking areas for some time, i.e. terrorists	Property of gradually increasing the size of the incident along the simulation
Understandability	Provides a manner of understanding the results of simulations and the consequences of each event in the scenarios simulated	The parts not important to the final result can be kept hidden from users

The Reports are divided in Graphs and Export Results. Commercial tools provide very good graphs to analyse many aspects of the simulation, they are helpful to understand the simulation and in support decisions. The final evacuation time is not the only important measurement to be observed. Some other important variables are: response times, to observe when people start to evacuate. Escape rate along simulation and flow density on each area are especially good to identify bottlenecks. All cited measurements can lead to security measurements that have a direct impact one final evacuation time. The capability to export details of the simulation is also desirable. Required and desirable features of Reports are shown in Table 1.

The Model was divided into People, Environment, Incident and Understandability. All models consider the area occupied by each person and guarantee that one does not walk through others or walls, this is the main aspect behind models based on a fluid or particles. Some of the models have prefixed routes for the agents considering the best route, pre-programming the agents to follow the signs of the environment or even making a statistic distribution of people on the routes. Both are much used and provide a reasonable approximation of reality. Other important aspects are related to the characteristics of the people, like speed and the decision to evacuate or not. More detailed models consider age, gender and groups of people moving together. In general, most models use the basic aspects. The environment has a clear division, the simplest models consider a flat scenario with fixed barriers. Commercial tools add slopes on the surface and distinguish terrains in the scenario. These two characteristics have an impact mainly on the speed of the agents. Other essential aspects are Access Areas that connect floors. They have their own characteristics, influencing the speed of people and consequently their evacuation time. Few environments provide non-fixed barriers like furniture that do not impede agents to move forward but can delay their evacuation a lot. Some tools, prototypes and models ignore an incident in a specific location of the environment, assuming that the simulation is like an evacuation exercise. That could be enough for many situations but is far from covering the entire range of possibilities. Some incidents can affect the mobility in part of the environment. One example is a partial collapse of a floor, explosions or an incident that starts at one or more points and grows along the time like fire. Incontrol [6] partially covers these situations because users are able to add elements in the simulation while it is running. None of the tools or models cover terrorist attacks, simulating intelligent elements moving in the scenario or intentionally blocking corridors or exits.

All these aspects can influence the dynamics of the evacuation. Depending on the size of the environment, not all people starting to evacuate at the same time, even if the incident was announced and everybody is aware of it. For groups of people distanced from the incident, the jeopardy sensation can be low. As a consequence, they take more time to decide to evacuate. The situations described above are a taste of the immense number of possibilities that can happen. Some of these variants can provoke a deep impact on the evacuation time. A not much mentioned characteristic is the understandability of the model. It is especially desirable to understand the limitations of the model and what is expected from it. The backends of commercial tools are black boxes while other models are described in terms of equations or rules. In general, the more refined the model the more complex its understandability. It is a challenge to keep it easy to analyse and at the same time providing refined and detailed simulations. It is also mandatory that the tools being open to simulate diverse scenarios and not only standard ones. The commercial tools do this job very well, importing floor plans or providing the possibility of building a whole new scenario from scratch. The required and desirable model features are shown in Table 1.

3   Evacuation Simulator

Based on the features found in the literature cited in Sect. 2 and together with the results of the questionnaire, a Simulator tool was developed and the model described in [18] was integrated into it. The Netlogo language was chosen to be the core of the Simulator. This language is multi-agent modelling oriented [20], providing facilities for incorporating models, extending them and making user interfaces. Concerning Usability features, it also incorporates a tool to run many parallel simulations with different parameter setups, facilitating the generation of results and making the simulation scalable. More specifically, concerning the Controls features, the simulator was developed in modules, making a clear distinction between its parts, see the Component Diagram of Fig. 2. The predefined Model that simulates the behaviour of agents and their social aspects as well as the physical aspects of the scenario is easily identified in the code and can be updated or changed by another one. The behaviour of the agents, their social aspects and the influence of physical aspects are defined inside the Model.

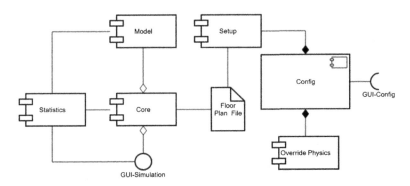

Fig. 2. Simulator's UML component diagram.

The internal model was developed using simple rules that make relations between internal states and external stimuli. The code below shows an example rule. In this rule, an agent takes the action of evacuating only if the internal desire of evacuation is bigger than the desire to walk around. If the agent falls on the floor, then the action of moving to the exit is suppressed. The simple rules that form the model are isolated from the rest of the code. The users still have access to all inputs of the agents and their possible actions. That allows users to change the model in a very deep way and experience variances in all levels of the simulation.

```
if st_desire_evacuate >= st_desire_walkrand[ set
st_intention_evacuate ETA_BODY * st_desire_evacuate]
if st_fall = 1 [ set st_action_movetoexit  0]
```

The physical aspects can be changed in the Override Physics, inside Config Module, with the possibility to change the effect of non-fixed furniture on evacuation speed and control events along the simulation like incidents, public announcements, fire alarm, etc. Still, inside Config, another submodule is responsible to set up the initial conditions or change pre-defined configurations of the agents such as: start to evacuate time, distribution of agents on the environment or the final location of the agents. One can set up the system directly in Config Module. It is also possible to setup the system through an interface that generates it, unfortunately, the graphical part is not implemented at moment, but it is feasible and is indicated in Fig. 2 by GUI-Config. The rule below is an example of changing the defined speed of the agents. If the function is left blank, the simulator uses its default speed. A set of functions similar to the below example is available, each one of the specific parts of the environment. With this approach, the simulator guarantees free access to change the physical behaviour into the environment.

```
to-report calculate-evacuation-speed-alternative
    jump 1.2; changes the speed of all agents to 1.2
report TRUE
end
```

The model interacts with the system Core, which is responsible for connecting configurations, model, statistics and graphical interface. Concerning Usability, other tools presented in this work have advantages, such as importing CAD floor plans and 3D. Both have pre-fixed Controls but in the proposed tool they are flexible and extensible. Users can easily add new controls related to internal variables. The statistics are fed by the model while the Core shows them and the simulation through a graphical interface GUI-Simulation. The Floor Plan File is imported from PNG picture. Based on the configurations of Config Module it is possible to define simple environments like that shown in Fig. 3, or complex ones with many floors, exits, alternative routes, fixed barriers and non-fixed barriers. The colours in the Floor Plan File have to match with the configurations in the Config Module, which means that a specific colour is interpreted by the Simulator as Exit areas (Blue in case of Fig. 3), fixed barriers are considered Black and Gray, while free areas are White and Access Areas Yellow. All these parameters are changeable for each kind of scenario. In Fig. 3, the red square represents an incident. The size and place where it happens are configurable. Users can setup multiple incidents occurring along the simulation. The pink agents are aware of the hazard and decide to start to evacuate, while black agents are still acting as of no incident has occurred. The orange agents have fallen because of the action of other agents and their own speed. After some time, they stand up and continue to evacuate.

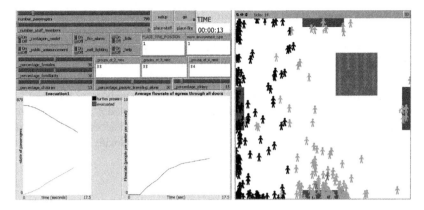

Fig. 3. Simple environment simulation of an empty room with 4 exits. (Color figure online)

Figure 4 shows the activity diagram of the simulator focusing on the internal model. The system updates internal states and actions of each agent. After that, it finalises the cycle updating statistics. The simulation stops when all agents either evacuated or died. At any moment, the user can change the parameters available on the interface and influence environment or agents. Concerning Reports features, the statistics are fed by the model while the Core shows them and the simulation through a graphical interface named GUI-Simulation. The simulator is prefixed with the most common controls and graphs. If necessary users easily add more of them to the interface. That is possible due to the large set of statistics and tuning parameters available. With this approach, the Simulators guarantee flexibleness to be used by many end-users that import their own environments and take advantages of pre-fixed controls and reports. Despite the huge number of reports available in commercial tools, the proposed one has the main statistics, all of them exportable to CSV files.

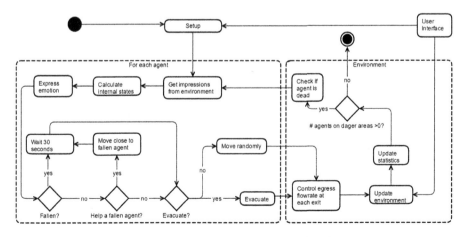

Fig. 4. General activity diagram of the simulator.

The biggest advantages of the simulator are in the Model. In relation to the Model features, they are equivalent in environment features, but the proposed one provides more features to customise each agent with their own personality, influencing others via social interaction. Incidents can be programmed and placed on the environment, provoking injuries in agents or blocking their paths, while not all the other tools have this feature available. Moreover, commercial tools are a blackbox for the most part of the models. Users are dependent on companies to adapt the model to specific scenarios. With the proposed tool, users can change or adapt the model according to their needs, they are free to go deep on customizations or use what is already available.

4   Conclusions

In this work, we proposed an evacuation simulator tool that covers the main Required aspects of this type of application. The development of this tool was based on expert impressions and a review of software, prototypes and models that can simulate evacuation scenarios. It is clear from the literature review and the survey applied to crisis management experts, that some basic features are present in all commercial applications, while prototypes and models are much more diverse in their embedded features, most of them are limited and contain a basic set of features. Models can be very detailed but do not present good interfaces. Prototypes combine models and interfaces but in general, they do it with a hardcoded interface and model. Otherwise, commercial softwares are not clear in all aspects of real scenarios they can simulate. In most cases, they are able to run simple evacuation scenarios simplifying many aspects covered by specialised evacuation models.

Moreover, there is no research known by the authors that define which are the required and desired features for an Evacuation Scenario Simulator. In this research, we have taken the first steps in this direction by proposing a minimum and not strictly defined set of mandatory requirements for this type of application. It also suggests desirable features that can provide more insights for users to take decisions based on the results of simulations. The absence of the basic required features in a tool can lead to errors in guaranteeing the safety of events or even design of buildings, stadiums and event centres.

The proposed Evacuation Scenarios Simulator was designed to cover required aspects already cited. This Simulator is very flexible and attends basic and specialised users providing the possibility of easily extending its already detailed model, it still is behind of commercial tools in terms of Visualization and Reports, but covers the required aspects of Visualization, provides a minimum set of reports and is more generic in covers Model's aspects. For future work, the visualisation aspects will be improved and the system will be evaluated by final users, comparing their results with evaluations of other tools.

Acknowledgments. This research was undertaken as part of the EU HORIZON 2020 Project IMPACT (GA 653383) and Science without Borders – CNPq (scholarship reference: 233883/2014-2). We would like to thank our Consortium Partners and stakeholders for their input and the Brazilian Government.

References

1. Challenger, R., Clegg, C.W., Robinson, M.A., Leigh, L.: Understanding crowd behaviours, vol. 1: Practical guidance and lessons identified. London: The Stationery Office (TSO) (2010). https://www.gov.uk/government/publications/understanding-crowd-behaviours-documents
2. Donald, I., Canter, D.: Intentionality and fatality during the King's Cross underground fire. Eur. J. Soc. Psychol. **22**, 203–218 (1992)
3. Grosshandler, W.L., Bryner, P., Madrzykowski, D.M., Kuntz, K.: Report of the Technical Investigation of The Station Nightclub Fire (NIST NCSTAR 2), vol. 1. National Construction Safety Team Act Reports (NIST NCSTAR) – 2 (2005)
4. Ha, V., Lykotrafitis, G.: Agent-based modeling of a multi-room multi-floor building emergency evacuation. Phys. A: Stat. Mech. Appl. **391**(8), 2740–2751 (2012)
5. Haron, F., Alginahi, Y.M., Kabir, M.N., Mohamed, A.I.: Software evaluation for crowd evacuation software evaluation for crowd evacuation–case study: Al case study: Al case study: Al-masjid an masjid an-nabawi. Int. J. Comput. Sci. Issues – IJCSI **9**, 128–134 (2012)
6. Incontrol Simulation Solutions: Pedestrian Dynamics (2017). http://www.pedestrian-dynamics.com/
7. Kobes, M., Helsloot, I., de Vriesc, B., Posta, J.G.: Building safety and human behaviour in fire: a literature review. Fire Saf. J. **45**(1), 1–11 (2010)
8. Legion (2017). http://www.legion.com/
9. Murakami, Y., Minami, K., Kawasoe, T., Ishida, T.: Multi-agent simulation for crisis management. In: 2002 Proceedings. IEEE Workshop Knowledge Media Networking, pp. 135–139. IEEE (2002)
10. McConnell, N.C., Boyce, K.E., Shields, J., Galea, E.R., Day, R.C., Hulse, L.M.: The UK 9/11 evacuation study: analysis of survivors' recognition and response phase in WTC1. Fire Saf. J. **45**(1), 21–34 (2010)
11. Oasys Software: MassMotion (2017). http://www.oasys-software.com/
12. Proulx, G., Fahy, R.F.: The time delay to start evacuation: review of five case studies. Fire Saf. Sci. **5**, 783–794 (1997)
13. Santos, G., Aguirre, B.E.: A critical review of emergency evacuation simulation models (2004)
14. SimWalk (2015). http://www.simwalk.com/
15. Templeton, A., Drury, J., Philippides, A.: From mindless masses to small groups: conceptualizing collective behavior in crowd modeling (2015)
16. van Toll, W., Jaklin, N., Geraerts, R.: Towards believable crowds: a generic multi-level framework for agent navigation (2015)
17. Wagner, N., Agrawal, V.: An agent-based simulation system for concert venue crowd evacuation modeling in the presence of a fire disaster. Expert Syst. Appl. **41**(6), 2807–2815 (2014)
18. van der Wal, C.N., Formolo, D., Robinson, M., Minkov, M., Bosse, T.: An agent-based evacuation model with social contagion mechanisms and cultural factors. In: Proceedings of IEA/AIE 2017 (2017). In Press
19. van der Wal, C.N., Formolo, D., Robinson, M., Minkov, M., Bosse, T.: Developing a crowd evacuation model with socio-cultural, cognitive, and emotional elements. Trans. Comput. Collect. Intell. (2017). In Press
20. Wilensky, U.: NetLogo. http://ccl.northwestern.edu/netlogo/. Center for Connected Learning and Computer-Based Modeling, Northwestern University, Evanston, IL (1999)
21. Zheng, X., Zhong, T., Liu, M.: Modeling crowd evacuation of a building based on seven methodological approaches. Build. Environ. **44**(3), 437–445 (2009)
22. Massachusetts State: Emergency Evacuation Safety Plan Guidelines Handbook Department of Developmental Services (2009)

A Stochastic Approach of SIRC Model Using Individual-Based Epidemiological Models

Arlindo Rodrigues Galvão Filho[1]([✉]), Telma Woerle de Lima[1],
Anderson da Silva Soares[1], and Clarimar Jose Coelho[2]

[1] Universidade Federal de Goiás, Goiânia, Goiás, Brazil
argfilho@gmail.com, telma.woerle@gmail.com, engsoares@gmail.com
[2] Pontiícia Universidade Católica de Goiás, Goiânia, Goiás, Brazil
clarimarc@gmail.com

Abstract. Mathematical models are important instruments in epidemiology to assist in analyzing epidemiological dynamics as well as possible dissemination controls. Classical model uses differential equations to describe dynamics of population over time. A widely used example is susceptible-infected-recovered (SIR) compartmental model. Such model has been used to obtain optimum control policies in different scenarios. This model has been enhanced to include dynamics of reinfection of disease including a new compartment, known as susceptible-infected-recovered-cross-immune (SIRC). An alternative model is to consider each individual as a string or vector of characteristic data and simulate the contagion and recovery processes by computational means. This type of model, referred in literature as individual based model (IBM) has advantage of being flexible as characteristics of each individual can be quite complex, involving, for instance, age, sex, pre-existing health conditions, environmental factors, social, and habits. However, it was not found in literature equivalence in an IBM model for SIRC model. Some works have shown the possibility of equivalence between IBM and SIR models, in order to simulate similar scenarios with models of different natures, in deterministic and stochastic case respectively. In this context, this work proposes implementation of an IBM stochastic model equivalent to SIRC model. Results show that equivalence is also possible only with the proper configuration of parameters of IBM model. Accuracy of equivalent model showed better with reduction of time step end increase the size of population.

Keywords: Mathematical epidemiology · SIRC · IBM

1 Introduction

Epidemiology is an area of science that involves the quantitative and qualitative study of phenomena associated with the health of populations, and also potential risk factors that can cause disease [1]. Within this area, an important research

© Springer International Publishing AG 2017
E. Oliveira et al. (Eds.): EPIA 2017, LNAI 10423, pp. 778–788, 2017.
DOI: 10.1007/978-3-319-65340-2_63

field is called in mathematical epidemiology, which is characterized by the use of mathematical models for the development of control strategies and prevention of epidemics [8].

There are several types of epidemiological models, including different aspects of the population and the infectious disease considered, such as the availability of vaccination, acquisition of immunity after a first infection, possibility of the presence of healthy infected, among others. One of the most used models considers that the population can be divided into three compartments, or classes: Susceptible, infected and recovered (SIR). The dynamics of the epidemic are then represented by a set of deterministic differential equations that describe the temporal evolution of the number of individuals in each of the classes [4,19,22]. This model has provided good results for investigation of general aspects related to the spread of various infectious diseases [21,24,25].

One limitation of classic SIR is that only way to add susceptible individuals to the model is by birth, which limits their use in relation to some dynamics of relapsing diseases. There are several enhancements and adaptations of the SIR model for different dynamics [3,7,10,20]. One improvement that has come to stand out is the susceptible, infected, recovered and cross-immune (SIRC), proposed by Casagrandi [14] to represent the dynamics of Influenza A [2,6,9, 13]. It is a similar to SIR model, but with a new intermediate stage between a susceptible and a recovered individual, called cross-immune. This new class enables susceptible individuals to be exposed more than once to the disease, that individuals naturally lose immunity, among other characteristics that make it closer to an actual application compared to SIR model.

An alternative model proposed by Cisternas [5] is the individual-based model (IBM) [18]. It's a stochastic model that represents each individual of the population as a unique and discrete entity, possessing at least one characteristic that changes throughout its life cycle. In this way, it is possible to include attributes such as sex, age, social habits, housing conditions, profession, hygiene conditions, among others. Cisternas and Galvão Filho [5,18] shown that is possible to obtain equivalence of the SIR model with IBM model by properly configuring IBM model parameters. This result was valid both in homogeneous and heterogeneous scenarios.

Thus, it would be interesting if the SIRC model were implemented as an IBM model. Such an approach would enable both an analysis of the dynamics on a stochastic approach and the inclusion of heterogeneities at individual levels. In this context, this work proposes the use of SIRC to simulate the dynamics of a case study for Influenza A, together with an equivalent IBM model.

2   Epidemiological Models

2.1   SIRC Model

Similar to SIR model, SIRC model is also constituted by a system of continuous nonlinear differential equations. It divides a population into four classes: susceptible (S), infected (I), recovered (R) and cross-immune (C). The main advantage compared to SIR is additional class of cross-immune individuals (C) in the model. Susceptible are people who have never been infected or who once recovered have lost immunity of disease, and are subject to contagion through contact with infected people. Those infected are people who have disease in question and can pass it on to susceptible or cross-immune people. Those recovered are people who have already been infected and acquired immunity, but not definitive cure of disease. Finally, cross-immune individuals are recovered and may now lose immunity making them susceptible or due to new contact with an infected individual become recovered if disease does not settle or become infected if they have contracted the disease. Cross-immune class can be interpreted as an intermediate stage between a susceptible and a recovered individual [2,14].

Figure 1 presents the main elements of SIRC model [2,14]. Newborns are considered susceptible, with no vertical transmission of disease or immunity by the parents. μ is birth rate of new individuals per unit of time. Mortality rate, denoted by v, is the same for all three classes. Coefficients β and α represent disease rates of transmission and recovery, respectively. Coefficient σ can be interpreted as rate of re-infection of the disease. Δ represents rate of loss of immunity and γ is rate at which subjects become susceptible again. Total number of individuals is denoted by N.

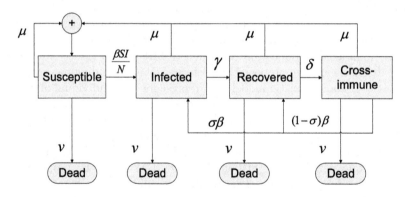

Fig. 1. Schematic representation of SIRC model.

In SIRC model it will also be considered that population size remains constant over time, i.e., it is assumed that birth rates (μ) and mortality (v) are equal. The SIRC model is given by

$$
\begin{aligned}
dS/dt &= \mu N - \mu S - \beta IS/N + \gamma C \\
dI/dt &= \beta IS/N + \sigma \beta CI/N - \mu I - \alpha I \\
dR/dt &= \beta CI/N - \sigma \beta CI/N + \alpha I - \mu R - \delta R \\
dC/dt &= \delta R - \beta CI/N - \mu C - \gamma C
\end{aligned}
\tag{1}
$$

where $S(t) + I(t) + R(t) + C(t) = N$.

2.2 IBM Model

In IBM model, proposed by [5], each individual of the population is described by a set of characteristics of epidemiological relevance. The main characteristic is current epidemiological condition, which can follow, for example, categorization adopted in SIR model (susceptible, infected, or recovered). In addition, it is possible to contemplate characteristics such as age, time in which individual is infected and spatial location within a certain region. Such characteristics can be taken into account in the birth, contagion and death processes throughout the simulation of model.

Formally, d-th individual is associated with a vector of n characteristics, defined by

$$I_d(t) = [C_{d1}(t) \, C_{d2}(t) \, \cdots \, C_{dn}(t)]^T \tag{2}$$

where t is a instant of time considered. At this point, population of N individuals is then represented by the following matrix of dimensions $N \times n$:

$$P(t) = [I_1 I_2 \cdots I_N]^T. \tag{3}$$

2.3 IBM-SIRC Model

Figure 2 shows flowchart for simulation of respective IBM to SIRC (IBM-SIRC model).

Initially, population size (N), as well as initial (t_0) and final (t_f) time instants of simulation are defined, and time increment between iterations (Δ). Also defined are values of parameters Q_p, P_{infec}, $P_{reinfec}$, P_{cross}, P_{sucep}, P_{rec} and P_{mor}, which are employed in steps described below.

IBM simulation has a stochastic character because it involves random events related to infection, reinfection, cross-immunity, loss of immunity, recovery and death processes [12,17,18].

At the beginning of each iteration, pairs of individuals to be considered in infection and re-infection processes are drawn. For each pair of form (S,I) or (I,S) a random number is then generated from a distribution $U[0,1]$ (uniform distribution in the range [0,1]). If such a number is less than a given infection probability P_{infec}, susceptible individual (S) of the pair becomes infected (I) condition.

Subsequently, for each pair of form (C,I) or (I,C), a random number is generated from a distribution $U[0,1]$. If such a number is less than a given probability of P reinfection, cross-immune individual (C) of the pair becomes infected (I) condition. However, if the random number is higher, cross-immune individual (C) of the pair becomes recovered condition (R). Other types of pairs do not give rise to occurrence of infection or re-infection.

The algorithm proceeds to cross-immunity step. This process is done by generating a random number from a distribution $U[0,1]$ for each recovered individual. If such a number is less than a given probability of cross-immunity P_{cross},

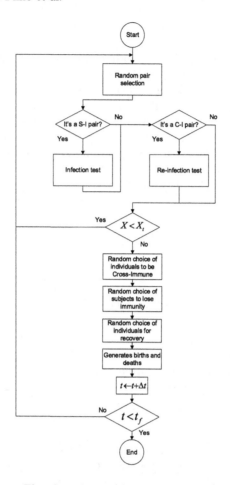

Fig. 2. Flowchart for simulation of the IBM-SIRC.

individual in question becomes cross-immune (C). Then process of natural loss of immunity occurs.

A random number is generated from a $U[0,1]$ distribution for each cross-immune individual. If such number is less than a given probability of loss of immunity P_{sucep}, individual in question becomes susceptible (S) condition.

Next step is recovery. A random number is generated from a $U[0,1]$ distribution for each infected individual. If such a number is less than a given recovery probability P_{rec}, individual in question becomes recovered (R) condition.

Finally, a similar procedure is employed in death stage, in which each of N individuals of population may die with probability P_{mor}. Deceased individuals are replaced by new susceptible individuals, considering that mortality and birth rates are such that size of population remains constant.

2.4   Equivalence Parameters

As discussed in [5,17,18], it is possible to similarly choose the parameters Q_p, P_{infec}, $P_{reinfec}$, P_{cross}, P_{sucep}, P_{rec} and P_{mor} of the IBM model in order to obtain results equivalent, on average, to those of SIRC model presented in Eq. 1. Given a time step Δt to be used in the IBM simulation, such equivalence is obtained by imposing:

- $Q_p = \frac{N\Delta t}{2}$
- $P_{infec} = \beta$
- $P_{reinfec} = \beta\sigma$
- $P_{cross} = \delta\Delta t$
- $P_{sucep} = \gamma\Delta t$
- $P_{rec} = \alpha\Delta t$
- $P_{mor} = \mu\Delta t$

Additionally, the population size N should be same in both models.

2.5   Case Study

A very recurrent disease in the human population is Influenza. In Brazil, according to the Ministry of Health, 750 million hospitalizations for influenza were recorded in the year of 2011 [11]. According to the World Health Organization, influenza results in about 250 to 500 thousand deaths worldwide [23].

Several works show the SIR and SIRC are good models to simulate dynamics of influenza [2,5,16]. The SIR model is limited to represent only influenza virus infection by a specific virus, without taking into account possible mutations over considered period of time. This limitation causes the individual once recovered not to become contaminated again. SIRC covers precisely this limitation, including reinfection of individual, loss of immunity, and so on.

For the purpose of case study, the parameters used in SIRC model specifically for Influenza A. They were chosen based on works of authors [2,6,9,13,14]. To exemplify such scenario, IBM-SIRC simulation algorithm was coded to match equivalent SIRC. For this purpose, SIRC model was simulated using the Dormand-Prince numerical method [15]. Models were configured to obtain equivalence with a SIRC model with the following parameters [5,17,18]:

$$\mu = 1/75$$
$$\beta = 150$$
$$\gamma = 1/2$$
$$\sigma = 0.078$$
$$\delta = 1$$
$$\alpha = 365/6$$

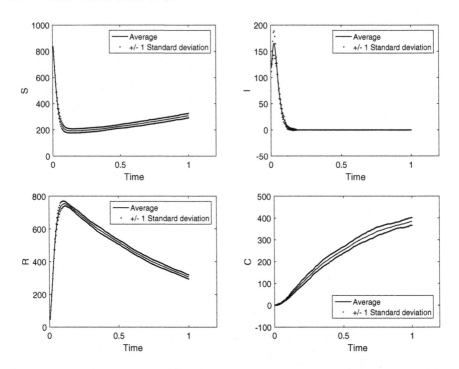

Fig. 3. Results of IBM-SIRC simulations for $N = 1000$ and $\Delta t = 0,005$, for each state.

3   Results

Figures 3 and 4 show the mean of the MBI-SIRC realizations with $+/-$ 1 standard deviation. These results are presented for each S, I, R and C state separately. Figure 3 shows the simulation results for $N = 1000$ and $\Delta t = 0,005$, while Fig. 4 shows the results for $N = 8000$ and $\Delta t = 0,0001$. If both figures are compared, it is possible to observe a greater approximation of the avearage and standard deviations as N is increased and Δt is reduced.

Figure 5(a), (b) and (c) shows the comparison between the SIRC models and proposed IBM-SIRC model. The results presented were obtained in three different simulations performed with different population size values (N) and time step in the IBM model (Δt). Trajectories of IBM-SIRC consist of average of ten simulation realizations. As expected, results obtained with IBM tend to approximate those generated by SIRC model as N increases and Δt decreases.

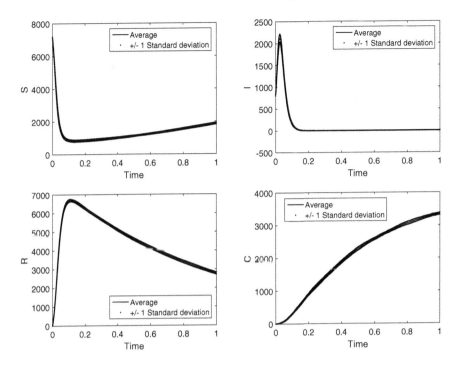

Fig. 4. Results of IBM-SIRC simulations for $N = 8000$ and $\Delta t = 0,0001$, for each state.

4 Conclusion

The proposed IBM model was on average equivalent to the SIRC model for case study presented here. Such equivalence is directly dependent on parameters N and Δt. As the values of N increases and Δt decreases the trajectories tend to approach. Each state was individually analyzed, showing standard deviations that accompany the mean thresholds. It was also possible to observe that as the parameters were duly changed, as previously mentioned, standard deviation tends to approach the mean. For this case of study, values of $N = 8000$ and $\Delta t = 0.0001$ were considered sufficient for equivalence between models.

5 Future Work

With equivalence between two models it is possible to obtain epidemiological control policies in SIRC deterministic model and test it in an IBM-SIRC stochastic equation model. In future works, it is intend to explore possible controls considering insertion of uncertainty coming from IBM approach. It is hoped that in this case the results of control policy to be applied will be closer to reality. In addition, we will investigate IBMs who consider aspects of population heterogeneity, further enriching the model, and consequently approaching even more of a more realistic scenario.

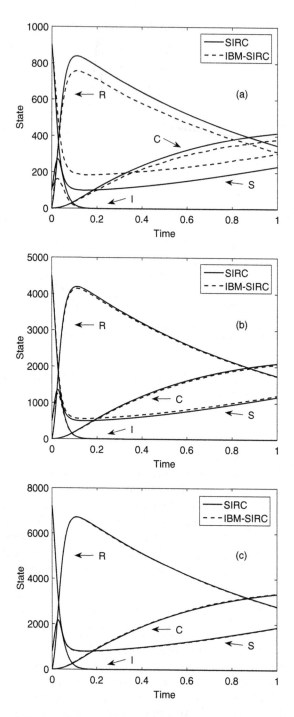

Fig. 5. Results of the simulation confronting SIRC and IBM-SIRC for (a) $N = 1000$ and $\Delta t = 0,005$, (b) $N = 5000$ and $\Delta t = 0,001$ and (c) $N = 8000$ and $\Delta t = 0,0001$.

Acknowledgments. Authors would like to thank the brazilian research agencies CAPES, FAPEG and CNPq for the financial support provided to this work.

References

1. Filho, N.A., Rouquayrol, M.Z.: Introduo epidemiologia. Guanabara Koogan, Rio de Janeiro (2006)
2. Iacoviello, D., Stasio, N.: Optimal control for SIRC epidemic outbreak. Comput. Methods Programs Biomed. **110**, 333–342 (2013)
3. Capone, F., De Cataldis, V., De Luca, R.: On the nonlinear stability of an epidemic SEIR reaction-diffusion model. Ricerche di Matematica **62**(1), 161–181 (2013)
4. Behncke, H.: Optimal control of deterministic epidemics. Optim. Control Appl. Methods **21**(6), 269–285 (2000)
5. Cisternas, J., William, G.C., Levin, S., Kevrekidis, I.G.: Equation-free modelling of evolving diseases: coarse-grained computations with individual-based models. In: Proceedings of the Royal Society of London A: Mathematical, Physical and Engineering Sciences, vol. 460, pp. 2761–2779. The Royal Society (2004)
6. Jódar, L., et al.: Nonstandard numerical methods for a mathematical model for influenza disease. Math. Comput. Simul. **79**(3), 622–633 (2008)
7. Nie, L.-F., Teng, Z.-D., Guo, B.-Z.: A state dependent pulse control strategy for a SIRS epidemic system. Bull. Math. Biol. **75**(10), 1697–1715 (2013)
8. Anderson, R.M., May, R.M.: Infectious Diseases of Humans: Dinamics and Control. Oxford University Press, Oxford (1992)
9. El-Shahed, M., Alsaedi, A.: The fractional SIRC model and influenza A **2011**, 9 (2011)
10. Wu, M., Wang, L., Li, M., Long, H.: An approach based on the SIR epidemic model and a genetic algorithm for optimizing product feature combinations in feature fatigue analysis (2013)
11. Ministério da Saúde Brasil. Boletim informativo de influenza (2012). http://portalsaude.saude.gov.br/portalsaude/noticia/6651/785/boletim-informativo-de-influenza:-semana-epidemiologica-32.html. acessado 1-maio-2013
12. Giancotti, K.H.O., de Assis Dias, F., Teixeira, W.W.M., Nepomuceno, E.G., Kurcbart, S.M.: Anlise da estrutura do MBI: sensibilidade da taxa de infeco e da populao. In: Anais do XVIII Congresso Brasileiro de Automtica, Bonito, MS, In Em (2010)
13. Samanta, G.P.: Global dynamics of a nonautonomous SIRC model for influenza A with distributed time delay. Differ. Equ. Dyn. Syst. **18**(4), 341–362 (2010)
14. Casagrandi, R., et al.: The SIRC model and influenza A. Math. Biosci. **200**(2), 156–169 (2006)
15. Dormand, J.R., Prince, P.J.: A family of embedded Runge-Kutta formulae. J. Comput. Appl. Math. **6**(1), 19–26 (1980)
16. Galvão Filho, A.R., Galvão, R.K.H., Yoneyama, T.: Otimização da alocação temporal de recursos para combate a epidemias com transmissão sazonal atraves de metodos de barreira. In: Proceeding Series of the Brazilian Society of Computational and Applied Mathematics, pp. 1–6 (2013)
17. Galvão Filho, A.R., Galvão, R.K.H., Yoneyama, T., Arruda, F.: Programação paralela cuda para simulação de modelos epidemiológicos baseados em indivíduos. In: Anais do X Simpósio Brasileiro de Automação Inteligente, pp. 241–246 (2011)

18. Galvão Filho, A.R., et al.: CUDA parallel programming for simulation of epidemiological models based on individuals. Math. Methods Appl. Sci. **39**(3), 405–411 (2016)
19. Morton, R., Wickwire, K.H.: On the optimal control of a deterministic epidemic. Adv. Appl. Probab. **6**(4), 622–635 (1974)
20. Arif, S., Olariu, S.: Efficient solution of a stochastic SI epidemic system. J. Supercomput. **62**, 1385–1403 (2012)
21. Grenfell, B.T., Bjørnstad, O.N., Finkenstädt, B.F.: Dynamics of measles epidemics: scaling noise, determinism, and predictability with the TSIR model. Ecol. Monogr. **72**(2), 185–202 (2002)
22. Kermack, W.O., Mckendrick, A.G.: A contribution to the mathematical theory of epidemics. In: Proceedings of the Royal Society of London A: Mathematical, Physical and Engineering Sciences, vol. 115, no. 772, pp. 700–721 (1927). The Royal Society
23. World Health Organization. Influenza (seasonal): Fact sheet n211 (2009). http://www.who.int/mediacentre/factsheets/fs211/en/. acessado 13-maio-2013
24. Yoshida, N., Hara, T.: Global stability of a delayed SIR epidemic model with density dependent birth and death rates. J. Comput. Appl. Math. **201**(2), 339–347 (2007)
25. Lu, Z., Chi, X., Chen, L.: The effect of constant and pulse vaccination on SIR epidemic model with horizontal and vertical transmission **36**, 1039–1057 (2002)

Incorporating Learning into Decision Making in Agent Based Models

Pia Ramchandani$^{(\boxtimes)}$ ⓘ , Mark Paich ⓘ , and Anand Rao ⓘ

PricewaterhouseCoopers, New York, USA
ramchandani.pia@gmail.com

Abstract. Most of the current work in social simulation is focused on building multi-agent systems that cooperate and collaborate together to exhibit some kind of a collective or social behavior. These agents are coded as rule-based or state-transition based systems. Often, the choice function of the agents is either hard-wired or dependent on environmental changes, but there is no explicit learning based on historical performance. There has been some recent work exploring methods for incorporating machine learning into multi-agent systems to capture adaptive behaviors. The goal of this paper is to expand upon the discussion around designing adaptive behaviors in agent based models by comparing multiple techniques for modeling learning, including: (1) applying machine learning and symbolic regression to use historical patterns to design learning mechanisms, (2) modeling behavioral economic principles to capture "irrational" or non-optimal learning, and (3) simulating reinforcement learning techniques such as q-learning to model a direct reward structure to improve learning outcomes at both the individual and group level. An example model has been built that applies these three learning techniques to simulate how people invest for retirement. Then, the outcomes of each learning technique simulated are used to identify lessons learned on when each technique should be applied.

Keywords: Adaptive decision making · behavioral economics · agent based models

1 Introduction

Agent based models (Rao-Georgeff) are useful tools for modeling social systems at the individual level to understand emergent trends at the aggregate level. However, to effectively capture the dynamics of a social system, it is important to simulate how agents perceive their environment and adjust their behavior over time to learn from personal experiences or experiences of other agents in the system (Gilbert). Designing the structure of these types of adaptive agents in social systems is a challenge that modelers face (Junges), frequently resulting in the construction of simple rules to modulate agent behavior that include elements of the environment in the rule to adjust the agent behavior based on changes in the environment during the simulation (Macal). Designing simple rules to simulate adaptive behavior in social systems is challenging because:

© Springer International Publishing AG 2017
E. Oliveira et al. (Eds.): EPIA 2017, LNAI 10423, pp. 789–800, 2017.
DOI: 10.1007/978-3-319-65340-2_64

1. Humans can be "economically irrational": Humans can seem "irrational" from a social perspective but "rational" from an individual perspective.
2. Behavioral Economics: Humans can also be actually irrational, not optimizing their decisions in regards to any goals (Thaler 1981).
3. Resource-bounded reasoning: Humans may not have the ability to compute the optimal outcome for every decision due to restrictions on time, mental capacity and access to information.

There has been some recent research done exploring more complex approaches for designing adaptive agents within ABMs to more realistically represent how humans learn and act (Rand). For example, some work has focused on incorporating neural nets and other machine learning algorithms into agents that learn over time during the simulation to capture more fundamental learning where the internal decision making process for an agent adapts to altering circumstances (Gilbert). More research is needed to:

1. Understand the best ways for incorporating the growing amount of data on social system behaviors into designing adaptive behaviors for ABMs (Janssen),
2. Better capture human irrationality into adaptive decision making structures in ABMs, and
3. Compare methodologies to determine which are the most useful for different types of social systems.

The goal of this paper is to discuss and compare three methods for designing adaptive decision making behavior in ABMs in social systems by applying them to an example model on retirement planning. The techniques for modeling learning in ABMs that are explored include: (1) applying machine learning and symbolic regression to use historical patterns to design learning mechanisms, (2) modeling behavioral economic principles to capture "irrational" or non-optimal learning, and (3) simulating reinforcement learning techniques such as q-learning to model a direct reward structure to improve learning outcomes at both the individual and group level.

2 Structure of Example Model

Retirement planning is an important social behavior to understand in order to find ways for improving retirement outcomes for individuals. There is currently a retirement crisis in the United States, where 80% of Americans between ages 30–54 believe they will not have enough saved for retirement and 36% of Americans over 65 years old are completely dependent on social security, a government funded program that is running out of money (Frankel 2016). Retirement planning ABMs (Lombardi et al. 2012 and Rao et al. 2014) can be used to better understand the robustness of the state of retirement readiness in the United States and design intervention strategies to improve conditions. However, the challenge with modeling retirement decision making is that individuals' behavior is both irrational and evolves over time as they learn from societal trends/interactions, past experiences and market changes. Therefore, it is a useful example to compare methods for embedding learning into decision making for agents in ABMs. We consider two primary decisions of retirement planning:

Decision #1: How much to invest in retirement accounts as a percentage of an individual's income stream, and

Decision #2: How to allocate retirement savings into cash, equities and bonds.

In the example model, individuals are represented by agents that have attributes such as income, wealth, age, gender, savings and employment that change over time. Each individual has an employment state chart that includes states for being employed, unemployed, and retired with transitions based on the environmental unemployment rate and the agent's age. An individual's income grows based off of their employment status and a wage growth rate that depends on the state of the economy in the simulated environment. During each time-step, individuals make decisions around how much of their income to allocate to their retirement accounts, how much to spend and how much to add to their savings to accumulate wealth. Periodically, the agents will make decisions around how to allocate their retirement investments across cash, bonds and equity. The allocation of retirement assets will impact the returns that retirement accounts experience under varying economic conditions. These two decisions on investment amount and allocation are structured using different learning techniques (see Sect. 2.1–2.3 for details on design structure) and the outcomes are compared in section 3. The model time step is 1 month with a simulated time period of 45 years.

The population is placed in a regimen switching economy environment that was developed using economic data from the Federal Reserve Economic Data (FRED) portal (see Fig. 1), a reliable government source for economic data in the United States. FRED was used to categorize the economy into 3 states: Good, Normal and Recession. The last 60 years of economic data was used to compute the transition probabilities between these states and the distributions of the durations of these states. Then, distributions for key economic factors such as unemployment, equity returns, treasury rates, bond rates and wage inflation were computed for each economic state and applied to simulate a dynamic economic environment. The economic factors impact the attributes of the population, causing changes to income, growth of wealth and employment.

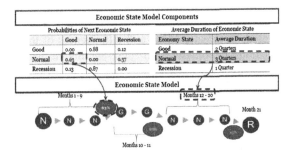

Fig. 1. Regimen switching economy environment

2.1   Using Machine Learning to Design Learning Structures

Machine learning (ML) is a growing subfield of artificial intelligence that can be used
to identify patterns in data and develop algorithms to represent those patterns. Machine
learning can be useful for designing components of ABMs by applying these techniques to large sets of historical data and uncovering patterns of interest to modelers.
ML can also be used to develop a set of hypotheses on the model structure driving
behaviors and test out multiple hypotheses in an ABM to understand the impact on
model outcomes (Pruyt 2014). When there is significant historical data on human
decision making over time, ML can be used to understand how decision making was
evolving and develop representative decision-making model structures from the data
that can then be embedded in ABMs. This is particularly useful because historical time
series data at the individual level can be very noisy and difficult to extract useful
information from for designing models. To illustrate this, ML was used to design the
structure for modeling Decision #1 on how much of an individual's income is invested
into their retirement accounts in a particular month. Two ML techniques were compared for designing agents that can adapt their behavior or decisions based on their past
behavior/outcomes: 1. Symbolic regression and 2. Random forest. These two techniques were selected because of the transparency that these algorithms provide,
allowing modellers to understand the mechanisms leading to particular outcomes.

2.1.1   Symbolic Regression

Symbolic regression is a type of regression analysis that doesn't require a model
structure to be specified, but rather tests out a series of model structures based on a set
of mathematical operator inputs (e.g. +, −, *, exp, cos). The initial expressions are
formed randomly using the input operators, then new equations are formed by combining the best performing prior equations. This genetic programming technique provides a series of equations that best represent the patterns and intrinsic relationships in
the data rather than forcing a pre-specified model structure as many traditional statistical techniques do (e.g. other regressions such as linear or logistic have a defined
model structure that is then fit to the data). This is a significant benefit for using
symbolic regression to model adaptive decision making because frequently,
pre-specified model structures don't fit the human decision making process well
(Zhang). Symbolic regression can be used to look at tradeoffs between complexity of
the equations generated, fit to actual data, and intuitiveness of the functional form to
select a set of equations hypothesized to represent the decision making behavior
(Smits). These hypothesized structures representing decision making can be embedded
into an agent's decision making process to compare the impact each form has on model
outputs.

    For the example model of simulating retirement investment and allocation deci-
sions, symbolic regression was used to identify potential structural forms that represent
how much of an individual's income is invested into retirement accounts. Data was
taken from the Strategic Business Insights (SBI) MacroMonitor survey, a detailed cross
sectional household level dataset that includes 4300+ variables on household financials
such as demographics, household income statement fields, household balance sheet
fields (all products owned and size), and financial attitudinal variables. The SBI data

from 2010 was used in the symbolic regression process, then the resulting equations were tested on prior years of data to validate the fit. While longitudinal data would be preferred for analyzing adaptive behavior over time, datasets with the level of granularity and breadth as SBI frequently come in cross sectional studies but can still be useful for designing decision structures due to the extensive fields covered in the data.

The symbolic regression was run using a tool called Eureqa (Edwards 2009) but could also be done in other tools such as R, Matlab, or Python. The resulting equations were reviewed by subject matter experts to select one that had an equation structure that intuitively aligned with behavioral research on retirement investing and had a good fit to the data. The ultimate equation chosen to test in the example model was:

$$Contributio(\$) = .0307 * Income(\$) + 0.01 * RetirementAssets(\$)$$
$$+ 1e - 13 * RetirementAssets * Income * Home\ Value(\$).0001296$$
$$* age^2 + 1e - 12 * RetirementAssets^2$$

$$(1)$$

This functional form developed by applying the ML symbolic regression algorithm to historical retirement contribution data matched a heuristic that subject matter specialists follow when determining expected contributions. The heuristic is that individuals apply a base rate of their income and then an adjustment factor based on their current assets and how far they are from retirement.

These functional forms that are developed from applying symbolic regression to historical data can then be embedded in an ABM as a decision rule to define the behavior of an agent. This is a useful approach for designing decision rules in ABMs by combining heuristics with data. Multiple functional forms can also be built into the decision making process for agents, either to compare the outcomes across different forms or to have distinct decision rules for different types of agents.

2.1.2 Random Forest

Human decision making can become quite complex with a large set of factors influencing behaviors. In addition, there are situations where there might not be heuristics or intuitive model structures that fit known information such as prior behavioral studies or historical data. For these situations, more advanced forms of ML that don't have equational forms can be used to fit an ML model to data and embed that ML model directly into the dynamic simulation. For example, ML techniques such as neural nets or deep learning, random forest, and support vector machines don't have a defined equational form that can be coded into an agent but may fit historical data very well. An ABM can be setup to include the relevant structure for the agents being modeled, then an ML algorithm can be trained on historical data and embedded into one specific decision for the agent to determine the decision outcomes or next state of the agent. A pre-trained ML model can also be a useful starting point for embedding an ML algorithm into an ABM, but then the training can be updated during runtime for each agent to capture how the agent is learning overtime in different simulated environments.

For the example model, a random forest algorithm was used for simulating Decision #1 of determining contribution rates into retirement accounts. The same example model on retirement planning discussed in the rest of the paper was used, but the computation for the particular variable around contribution rates was setup to call a random forest model to compute the value.

A random forest model is an ML classifier algorithm that constructs multiple decision trees for a set of options and outputs the mode of the classification or mean prediction amongst all the trees in the forest. Decision trees are commonly used in behavioral research to understand the process of making decisions, thus can be informative when designing decision making structures in dynamic models. Random forest models can be used purely to explore historical data before designing ABMs because the resulting decision trees can provide insight into decision making process patterns seen in the data. However, random forest models can also be embedded directly into a dynamic model.

The same SBI dataset used in Technique 1a was used to train a random forest classifier in Python on retirement contributions to classify which category of contribution rates an individual followed: 0%, .1–2%, 2–4%, 6–8%, 10%+. Then, the example agent based model of retirement planning was setup to call the python random forest classifier to calculate the contribution rate for each individual. A great strength of random forests is the transparency of the algorithm because the decision trees within the forest can be visualized to determine if they make sense. Other ML algorithms, particularly deep learning and neural nets, don't currently have many methods for making the algorithm transparent and thus are less helpful in purely exploring patterns of decision making or validating the behaviors of agents in the simulation over time to ensure that they make sense.

2.2 Incorporating Behavioral Economics into Dynamic Models

Behavioral economics focuses on understanding how in the real world, peoples' decisions are subject to "bounded rationality" (Simon 1955). Certain decisions can be too complex and overwhelm people during their decision making process. Additionally, individuals can have "bounded self-control" (Mullainathan and Thaler 2000), with limited willpower to execute optimal behaviors. Researchers in the field have used social experiments to develop heuristics on how people make decisions and these resulting heuristics can be applied to decisions across topic areas. There has been increasing literature on how behavioral economics applies to retirement planning to help understand behavioral drivers and identify strategies for improving outcomes for retirees. While there are many examples of how behavioral economics is seen in retirement planning, the following three were chosen because of their relevance to Decision #2 in the example model of retirement account investment allocation to equities, bonds and cash:

1. **Loss Aversion:** Kahneman and Tversky (1979) modeled individuals with an s-shaped value function (see Fig. 2) where incremental gains and losses influence the perceived value of a choice for an individual. Additionally, the steeper slope of

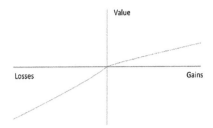

Fig. 2. Prospect theory value function from Kahneman and Tversky (1979)

the loss function means individuals will experience losses more acutely than gains of an equal size. From experiments, they suggest that the loss-aversion index is 2.5, meaning a loss is 2.5 times as painful as an equivalent dollar gain.

2. **Overconfidence:** Once individuals are experiencing positive outcomes, excessive optimism can occur, leading the individual to construct forecasts of the future that are typically rosier than reality (Mitchell and Utkus 2003).

3. **Framing:** The structure of how a decision or question is shown to an individual changes their final decision. For example, an investor could use market performance to frame fund performance, "The fund saw only a −2% return while the market average was a −5% return" (Mitchell and Utkus 2003).

These three behavioral economic principles were used to design a decision making structure for Decision #2 in which individuals make a periodic decision on how much of their retirement account to allocate to bonds, equities and cash. In the example model, individuals are setup to have different frequencies of reviewing their account and determining allocations. Individuals will check recent gains or losses that alter their confidence in the market. Loss aversion is applied by creating larger declines in an individual's market confidence when a loss on their portfolio occurs than a gain of the same size. Loss accumulates into a loss pain for an individual, so large or frequent losses will compound to decay market confidence. However, with time, loss pain will decay as individuals experience better outcomes. With consistent recent gains, market confidence will grow and can result in overconfident, more bullish market strategies by increasing investments in equities. When market confidence is low, individuals shift more of their investments into conservative accounts such as bonds and treasuries. Finally, individuals each have a different frequency of reviewing their accounts, which impacts the framing of their decision because they will see returns either over a longer term of 1 year or a shorter term of 4 months (see Fig. 3).

A full calibration process to minimize the error between model produced behaviors and historical data was not executed because the focus of this example model is to demonstrate and compare multiple techniques for structuring models around individual learning behavior but not to run robust scenario analysis around retirement planning for policy making. However, research was used to identify a set of points to roughly calibrate the model to achieve realistic ranges of simulated model results under different conditions. For example, one experiment found that individuals that viewed returns on a shorter term basis of 1 year versus long-term returns allocated just 41% to

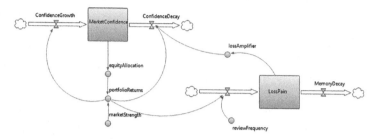

Fig. 3. Representative stock-flow diagram of decision making dynamics implemented at the individual level for Decision #2 on retirement account allocation to equities, cash and bonds. Stock-flow diagrams were developed in the system dynamics field. These diagrams use stocks to model accumulations (e.g MaketConfidence), flows to capture growth/decay rates, and dynamic variables (e.g. equityAllocation) to incorporate driving factors.

stocks, whereas those that saw the long-term returns allocated 82% to stocks (Benartzi and Thaler 1999). This experiment illustrates how the framing effect can be compounded with loss aversion because those viewing equity returns at a shorter time period see more volatility and down turns than those seeing long-term returns. This experiment along with data from SBI and Kahneman and Tversky's 2.5 loss aversion index were used to develop a model with simulation results with a reasonable range of outcomes under different scenarios.

2.3   Reinforcement Learning at the Individual and Group Level

Reinforcement learning is a field in machine learning where agents take an action in their environment in order to maximize a reward function. Overtime, agents accumulate a set of experiences in different states that are mapped to rewards and store this in a knowledge base. This knowledge base is then used to select the best decision given a specific state based on prior rewards.

One frequently used reinforcement learning technique is called q-learning. Q- learning problems contain an agent, a set of states and a set of allowed actions per state. When an agent takes an action, it will move from state to state and receive a reward depending on the action chosen. The action that is optimal for each state is the one that has the highest long-term reward. Before the learning process is started, the agent has a specific "exploration" time in which random actions are chosen at a decreasing probability in order to develop an initial knowledge base of state, action, reward pairs.

Q-learning was applied to the example model Decision #2 for allocation of retirement assets into equities, cash and bonds. The state was modeled as the prior 3 quarters of the economy (good, normal or recession), actions allowed were "Buy", "Sell" or "Hold" equity amounts and the reward function was computed as the returns during the time period since the last action taken. Each agent in the model started with a probability of 1 for random exploration that causes them to pick a random action. State, action, value pairs are then are stored experiences in their knowledge base to represent historical rewards achieved for actions taken in different states. For example, a state, action, value pair that could be stored is:

State: "Recession, Recession, Normal"
Action: "Buy"
Value: -.12%

As random actions are chosen, the individual's knowledge base begins to grow and they learn which actions have higher rewards under different conditions. Then, the probability of selecting a random action decreases over time and the agent begins to pick the strategy with the highest score based on their state, action, value pairs within their knowledge base. When the equivalent state has not been experienced and thus, does not have an associated "reward" for each action, the most similar state is chosen. The example q-learning model for retirement asset allocation was then expanded to include "group learning", in which individuals learn from the collective social experiences of people in their networks. Networks for the agents simulated were selected at random, but could be enhanced to include clustering algorithms that combine individuals with similar attributes or attitudes.

3 Model Outcomes

In order to compare the performance of the behavioral economics (BE) approach explored in technique 2 and the reinforcement learning (RL) approach implemented in technique 3, the example retirement investment allocation simulation model was run for the same population of 1,000 individuals under each technique for 3,000 economic scenarios using the regimen switching economy, as the base case scenario. In addition, the population was run with a completely randomized version of reinforcement learning where individuals continue to pick actions at random with a probability of 1 rather than implement their learnings to compare the outcomes against those attempting to learn.

Simulation scenario results across the 3,000 economic scenarios are shown in Fig. 4. Overall performance of the individual level reinforcement learning does show an improvement to randomized equity allocation when comparing final outcomes for retirement assets, outperforming random actions 70% overall, 90% during the 1,000 worse economies and 86% during the 1,000 best economies. The difference between the overall performance across 3,000 scenarios versus the subsets of good and recessionary economies could be explained with the ability for random actions to have reasonable results with a normal economy because return ranges are smaller, with lower gains and losses. Group learning outperforms individual RL 86% across scenarios, 91% during good economies and only 15% during recessionary economies. The BE decision structure outperforms individual and group RL during 68% overall, but only 25% during poor economies and 72% during good economies.

Drilling in further to the scenarios, Fig. 5 shows the final retirement account balances and equity allocations across all scenarios and the 1,000 worst economic scenarios. In the individual RL and group RL simulations, individuals are learning that a higher allocation to equities results in better returns. The increase in equity allocations

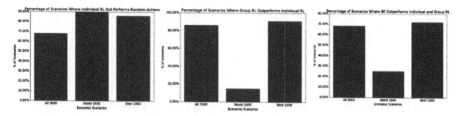

Fig. 4. Performance comparison across 4 learning techniques under different economic conditions.

from the group reinforcement learning technique illustrate how learning from other successes in each network has taught individuals that higher equity allocation yields a higher reward even if they haven't had that experience themselves. An interesting outcome during the 1,000 worst economic scenarios is that the group reinforcement learning approach performance is lower than across all scenarios, only outperforming the individual RL 15% of the time. This could be because recessionary economic scenarios have more volatility in returns than normal and good economic conditions. Therefore, individuals learning from other's recent experiences investing more in equities may not provide a useful strategy when returns are quite volatile.

The behavioral economics technique out performs the random allocation, individual RL and group RL approaches when looking across all 3,000 scenarios. This could be due to the overconfidence effect where individuals have a rosier view of the economy when they've had recent returns during good economies, ultimately investing more in equities. However, when examining the final retirement asset values and equity allocations in Fig. 5, it shows that the behavioral economics approach results in the widest ranges of allocations and outcomes due to the different experiences people are having under different economies. During bad economies, the loss aversion included in the BE model causes people to significantly cut back on equity allocations because of the accumulated pain felt from recent losses, resulting in lower final values for retirement assets. The overconfidence and loss aversion dynamics explains why the BE approach outperformed individual and group RL in 72% of good economic scenarios but only in 25% of recessionary economic scenarios.

When comparing these techniques to US historical data, the BE approach comes closest to matching actual investment dynamics. It has been found that the best strategy for retirement investments is to maintain a consistently high allocation to stocks (Kitces and Pfau 2015), which is also demonstrated in the scenario results of this example model. However, historical data has shown that equity allocation does grow in strong economic times and decrease during recessions (Benartzi and Thaler 2007). Investment behavior for the overall population seems to be driven by numerous behavioral factors, including other concepts such as how many funds are shown to individuals, how questions are phrased and what advice individuals are given from advisors (Benartzi and Thaler 2007). There may be a subset of individuals focused on investment that look more rationally at prior returns in different conditions and match closer to the reinforcement learning decision structure, however the multi-faceted and complex decisions around retirement frequently end up driven by emotions and framing.

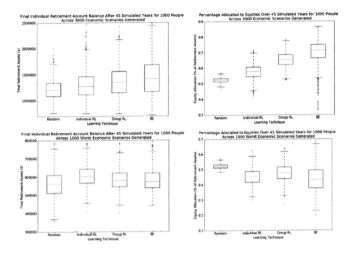

Fig. 5. Simulation results for the 4 learning techniques implemented in the example model of retirement allocation behaviors.

4   Conclusion

This paper explored 3 techniques for modeling the evolution of human decision making through different learning or adaptation mechanisms. Most systems of focus in dynamic models are impacted on some level by how humans make decisions and how that behavior changes over time. When determining which type of learning structure design is appropriate for a particular problem, it is important to ask the following questions:

- How much data is available?
- Is there relevant behavioral research on similar decision structures available?
- Is the decision complex or simple?
- Is there an outcome or reward associated with the decision?

From the outcomes of the example model on retirement planning, it seems that technique 1 of training a machine learning model on historical data is beneficial when sufficient data is available but limited behavioral research has been done. It can also be useful to combine the machine learning approach in technique 1 with the BE approach in technique 2 to understand if any heuristics seen in related behavioral research are validated through ML. The BE approach in technique 2 is useful when decisions are complex, forcing individuals to simplify their decision making processes to heuristics. BE research has also been conducted across industries leading to a wealth of studies available that can be used to inform model structures. Reinforcement learning would be a structure to consider for human decisions that are made frequently, are simple and have a clear reward function that people understand because this makes it easier for people to pick optimal options. In addition, the reinforcement learning approach can be expanded for any situation in which an individual is expected to optimize their decision making. In more complex state spaces, RL can be combined with deep learning to run deep neural nets that map states to the values achieved for each action.

References

Benartzi, S., Thaler, R.H.: Heuristics and Biases in Retirement Savings Behavior. J. Econ. Perspect. **21**, 81–104 (2007)

Benartzi, S., Thaler, R.H.: Risk aversion or myopia? Choices in repeated gambles and retirement investments. Manag. Sci. **45**(3), 364–381 (1999)

Edwards, L.: Eureqa, the Robot Scientist (2009). http://www.physorg.com/news179394947.html

Matthew, F.: 20 retirement stats that will blow you away. The Motley Fool (2016)

Nigel, G.: How to build and use agent-based models in social systems. Center for Research and Simulation for Social Sciences, University of Surrey

Janssen, M.: Empirically, agent based models. Ecol. Soc. **11**(2), 37 (2006)

Robert, J.: How to design agent based models using agent learning. In: Proceedings of the 2012 Winter Simulation Conference (2012)

Kahneman, D., Tversky, A.: Prospect theory: an analysis of decision under risk. Econometrica **47** (2), 263–291 (1979)

Kirman, A.: Learning in agent based models. Eastern Econ. J. **1**, 20–27 (2010)

Kitces, M., Pfau, W.D.: Retirement risk, rising equity glide paths, and valuation-based asset allocation. J. Financ. Plan. **28**(3), 38–48 (2015)

Lombardi, L., Paich, M., Rao, A.S.: Behavioral Simulations: Using Agent-based modeling to understand policyholder behavior. Society of Actuaries (2012)

Macal, C.M.: Tutorial on agent based modeling and simulation. J. Simul. **4**, 151–162 (2010)

Mitchell, O., Utkus, S.: Lessons from behavioral finance for retirement plan design. The Wharton Financial Institutions Center (2003)

Mullainathan, S., Thaler, R.H.: Behavioral economics. NBER Working Paper 7948 (2000)

Pruyt, E.: From data-poor to data-rich: system dynamics in the era of big data. In: Proceedings of the 32nd International Conference of the System Dynamics Society, pp. 2458–2469 (2014)

Rao, A.S., Georgeff, M.P.: BDI agents: from theory to practice. In: International Conference on Multi-Agent Systems (ICMAS), pp. 312–319 (1995)

Rao, A.S., Gates, D., Ray, P.: Retirement readiness: rule of thumb vs behavioral simulation. Retirement Management Journal, Spring Issue 2014, Retirement Income Industry Association (2014)

Rand, W.: Machine learning meets agent based modeling: when not to go to a bar. Northwestern University

Simon, H.A.: A behavioral model of rational choice. Q. J. Econ. **69**, 99–118 (1955)

Sanchez, S.M., Lucas, T.W.: Exploring the world of agent-based simulations: simple models, complex analyses. In: Proceedings of the Winter Simulation Conference, San Diego, CA, USA, vol. 1, pp. 116–126 (2002)

Smits, G., Mark, K.: Pareto-front exploitation in symbolic regression. In: O'Reilly, U.-M., Yu, T., Riolo, R., Worzel, B. (eds.) Genetic programming theory and practice II, vol. 8, pp. 283–299. Springer, Heidelberg (2005)

Thaler, R.H.: Some empirical evidence on dynamic inconsistency. Econ. Lett. **8**(3), 201–207 (1981). doi:10.1016/0165-1765(81)90067-7

Chi, Z.: Genetic Programming for Symbolic Regression. University of Tennessee Knoxville, TN 37996

Text Mining and Applications

The Complementary Nature of Different NLP Toolkits for Named Entity Recognition in Social Media

Filipe Batista$^{(\boxtimes)}$ and Álvaro Figueira

CRACS/INESC TEC and University of Porto, Rua do Campo Alegre, 1021/1055, 4169-007 Porto, Portugal
filipe.batista@fe.up.pt, arf@dcc.fc.up.pt

Abstract. In this paper we study the combined use of four different NLP toolkits—Stanford CoreNLP, GATE, OpenNLP and Twitter NLP tools—in the context of social media posts. Previous studies have shown performance comparisons between these tools, both on news and social media corporas. In this paper, we go further by trying to understand how differently these toolkits predict Named Entities, in terms of their precision and recall for three different entity types, and how they can complement each other in this task in order to achieve a combined performance superior to each individual one. Experiments on two publicly available datasets from the workshops WNUT-2015 and #MSM2013 show that using an ensemble of toolkits can improve the recognition of specific entity types - up to 10.62% for the entity type PERSON, 1.97% for the type LOCATION and 1.31% for the type ORGANIZATION, depending on the dataset and the criteria used for the voting. Our results also showed improvements of 3.76% and 1.69%, in each dataset respectively, on the average performance of the three entity types.

Keywords: Named Entity Recognition · Social medria · Ensemble of NLP toolkits · Text-mining · Machine learning

1 Introduction

Following the rapid growth of social networks, Named Entity Recognition (NER) on texts from social media sources such as Twitter, has received increasing attention over the last decade.

While Named Entity Recognition has been studied for a long time, and some tools achieved what could be considered very good results, most of these tools were essentially tested on formal texts, as news articles, scientific articles, or books. Two state-of-the-art tools for this task are Stanford CoreNLP [10], a complete NLP pipeline widely used as a NER reference and the OpenNLP library, a "machine learning based toolkit for the processing of natural language text" [12].

However, when applied to texts from social media, "out-of-the-box" tools tend to show significant decrease in performance [15], mainly due to the informal

© Springer International Publishing AG 2017
E. Oliveira et al. (Eds.): EPIA 2017, LNAI 10423, pp. 803–814, 2017.
DOI: 10.1007/978-3-319-65340-2_65

nature of those texts, which is expressed by the absence of context, the lack of proper punctuation, wrong capitalization, the use of characters to represent *emoticons*, spelling errors and even the use of different languages in the same text.

To overcome these problems different studies have been conducted at different levels in the NLP pipeline to deal with specific problems such as tokenization on tweets [9] or capitalization restoration [11].

Entire pipelines with the specific purpose of Named Entity Recognition on tweets have also been proposed. Twitter NLP tools, proposed by Ritter et al. [15], is an example of a rebuilt NLP pipeline, with part-of-speech tagging, chunking and named-entity recognition. Another example of an entire social media NLP pipeline is TwitIE [3], a sequence of modules including language identification, tokenization, spelling and orthographic corrector, Stanford POS tagger adapted to Twitter, and a Named Entity Recognizer.

Most of these tools implement different algorithms to perform NER, and their performances on different entity types varies significantly [1,13,16]. Moreover, it is common to find disagreements between these tools regarding specific tokens and their corresponding named entity. Therefore, it is our intuition that the simultaneous use of different toolkits might help achieve better results than using them separately. Apart from the obvious benefit that some of these toolkits predict different sets of entity types, complementing each other that way, we will analyze, for a standard set of core entities (PERSON, LOCATION, ORGANIZATION), if a ponderation between toolkits reveals to be beneficial.

In this regard, along this paper we will try to answer the following research questions (regarding the English language only):

- Can an ensemble of different toolkits achieve overall higher NER performance than any of the involved toolkits, independently, for the same task?
- What is the best way to resolve conflicts/disagreements between different toolkits regarding their entity predictions?

The remainder of this paper is presented as follows: in Sect. 2, we review previous toolkit comparisons and the conclusions regarding their individual performances per each entity type; in Sect. 3 we describe our experimental setup, including details on the datasets used, brief descriptions of the toolkits used and the necessary steps taken to obtain their results for our analysis, the ensemble itself and the different voting protocols tested, as well as the performance measures used; in Sect. 4 we present the results and discuss them in detail; finally, in Sect. 5 we present our conclusions and ideas for future work.

2   Related Work

While ensemble methods have been proposed in literature for the task of NER, usually these methods were applied at the level of the machine learning algorithms, rather than at the level of ready-to-use toolkits. An example of previous use of ensemble methods for NER, proposed by Wu, Chia-Wei, et al. [18], consisted in applying a memory-based ensemble method on Chinese datasets to achieve better results than using individual classifiers. Another example of the same use was proposed by S. Saha and A. Ekbal [17], once again showing that combining different learning algorithms can improve the performance of Named Entity Recognition.

Differently from these works, in this study we will not be implementing algorithms from scratch, but instead using widely recognized toolkits which provide already solid out-of-the-box performances, presumably optimized by many contributors over the years. As a first approach, we chose Stanford CoreNLP [10], a reference toolkit in NER, OpenNLP and the Twitter specific NLP pipelines: "Twitter NLP tools" by Ritter et al. [15] and TwitIE [3].

To the best of our knowledge, there have been few attempts to simultaneously use different out-of-the-box toolkits to perform Named Entity Recognition on social media texts. The idea of combining toolkits was applied in one of the submissions to the Making Sense of Microposts challenge in 2013 [4]. In this study the authors combined different toolkits using machine learning techniques, and their results showed that several classification models could achieve better results than the best individual tools [4]. In our work, besides machine learning techniques we also tried manually defining protocols for the ensembles' voting system, and our experiments were conducted on a different set of toolkits, combining social media-oriented NLP toolkits with general text toolkits.

A more recent example of combining toolkits used two different toolkits (SpaCy and CoreNLP) together to create an hybrid NER tool [8]. This hybrid tool was tested on formal texts rather than social media texts, as in our study.

3 Experimental Setup

3.1 Datasets

For comparison purposes, every toolkit used equally pre-tokenized datasets, following Ritter's [15] tokenization method. We also chose to focus only on the entities PERSON, LOCATION and ORGANIZATION. The reason for this choice was that these entities are the only three entities detected by all the toolkits tested.

For the first experiment, an original dataset of tweets from our project [6] was partially used. This dataset consists of 840 entries: 420 tweets, 107 Facebook posts and 313 Facebook comments, retrieved by a crawler about 6 topics highly discussed in 2016: "Refugees Syria", "Elections US", "Olympic Games", "Terrorism", "Daesh" and "Referendum UK EU".

This original dataset was then tokenized. Therefore, instead of 840 entries, the tokenized dataset had 28172 entries (one per token). From the tokenized dataset, a subset of 3474 tokens was extracted. The final dataset contains one token per row, and one entity for each token. The ground truth for this dataset was manually annotated by the authors of this paper.

For the second experiment, a dataset from WNUT NER - Workshop on Noisy User-generated Text [2]- was used. This dataset used the same format seen in

Twitter NLP tools by Ritter et al., including less common entity types that were dropped for the purpose of this study, which focuses only on the 3 core entities PERSON, LOCATION and ORGANIZATION.

In the third experiment, we tested the dataset from the 3rd workshop on 'Making Sense of Microposts' (#MSM13) [4], which took place in 2013. It is important to note that for this dataset we used the PTBTokenizer available as part of the CoreNLP libraries. The reason for this choice was that in the conversion process we had to tokenize both the entities and the text of the tweets, and for the tokenizations to match we needed a deterministic tokenizer.

Finally, in the last experiment, we used machine learning algorithms instead of manually defined voting rules. Dataset 1 was rather small for the purpose, and Dataset 2 had to suffer multiple conversions as will be explained in the next section. Therefore, we decided to partially use Dataset 3.

Therefore, our testing datasets were:

- **Dataset 1**: Our dataset - 3474 entries (tokens)
- **Dataset 2**: WNUT NER - 48 862 entries (tokens)
- **Dataset 3**: #MSM2013 - 62 494 entries (tokens)
- **Dataset 4**: Subset of #MSM2013 - 10 000 entries (tokens)

3.2 Toolkits and Data Preparation

Stanford CoreNLP[1] was run using the default toolkit via command line [10]. This toolkit accepts as input format the tokenized text and the output format in a tab formatted file, convenient for this study.

Since there was not enough labeled data for training our own model, as the data was manually annotated by the authors and that is a very costly task time-wise, we used the "3 class model" provided by CoreNLP, which was trained on both MUC 6 and MUC 7 training data sets with some additional data (including ACE 2002 and other generated data).

GATE Using TwitIE Plugin[2] provides a graphical interface which was used in this study to run the TwitIE [3] pipeline, available as part of the Twitter plugin.

The output format consists in surrounding any detected entity with XML tags. In order to convert this type of output to the tab separated format, a small script using regular expressions was written in Python.

While GATE is able to detect many other entity types, we used only the three core entities (PERSON, LOCATION and ORGANIZATION). We used the default configurations of the TwitIE pipeline.

Twitter NLP Tools[3] were run via command line, following the usage presented in the Twitter NLP tools Github repository.

---

[1] https://stanfordnlp.github.io/CoreNLP/.

[2] https://gate.ac.uk/download/.

[3] https://github.com/aritter/twitter_nlp.

Twitter NLP tools [15] output is by default in the IOB format [14] (B for beginning of a Named Entity (NE), I for inside an NE, O for outside of NE), and the "token/ENTITY" format. The IOB format was dropped, so instead of B-ENTITY and I-ENTITY we opted to use ENTITY only. Besides, 2 entity types were converted: COMPANY to ORGANIZATION, and GEO-LOCATION to LOCATION, while all the remaining entity types (except PERSON) were simply dropped.

We used this tool as is, without any re-training or tuning.

OpenNLP[4] is a Java library which supports several common NLP tasks, including Named Entity Recognition.

OpenNLP can be used directly as a tool, or via its API. We decided to use the API in a small Java project in order to easily output the entities to the tab-separated format.

We used the pre-trained models for the OpenNLP 1.5 series, for each entity type used.

3.3 Ensemble Voting Methods

In order to study the viability of a NER toolkit ensemble, all the outputs from the previous toolkits previously mentioned were merged to a single *comma-separated values* file, one column for the tokens, another column for the ground truth entities, and one column for each of the entities predicted from each toolkit.

The first step was to compute the precision, recall and F1 measure for each toolkit individually, using the ground truth obtained by manual labeling.

The second step was to define different voting protocols to resolve the conflicts between the different toolkits predictions.

Finally, we used different machine learning algorithms taking as input features the predictions of each tool.

Protocol Use 1: A token is tagged with entity type A if and only if at least one of the following conditions are met:

- 50% of the toolkits predicted entity type A and the other 50% did not predict any entity type
- At least 75% of the toolkits predicted entity type A

Protocol Use 2: A token is tagged with entity type A if and only if at least one of the following conditions are met:

- 50% of the toolkits predicted entity type A and the other 50% did not agree on any other entity between them.
- At least 75% of the toolkits predicted entity type A

---

[4] https://opennlp.apache.org/.

Machine Learning Approach: The models for predicting the combined output were obtained by running each of the following ML algorithms on a training set, with 10-fold cross validation, and then tested on an independent test set.

Both the train and test sets were subsets, each of 10 000 entries, of the previously mentioned MSM2013 dataset. Every ML experiment was performed in RapidMiner Studio. The algorithms used were Naïve Bayes, Random Forest, k-nearest neighbors (k-NN) and Neural Network. The features used consisted of the 4 individual outputs of each tool.

3.4   Performance Evaluation

Performance in classification systems is measured by comparing the output of a classifier on unseen data with a golden standard - made by human annotators, and assumed as correct. A certain prediction can be either Positive or Negative, and according to the golden standard, that prediction can be True or False.

There are different ways of counting true positives. In the strict way, only exact matches are considered, while in the lenient way partially correct (shorter, longer, overlapping at either end) are also considered as correct [7]. In this study we chose to use the lenient way.

The metrics we used to measure performance of classification tasks include Precision, Recall and F1-score.

Although it is important to understand how the system is behaving, recall and precision measures are not sufficient when used independently, meaning that knowing recall without knowing precision, or vice-versa, does not provide enough information about the performance of the system. The most common way to combine Recall and Precision in one single measure is the F-measure.

F-Measure: Calculates the harmonic mean of precision and recall. The relative importance (weight) of each component (precision and recall) is controlled by the β parameter (higher values of β mean more weight on recall) [5].

$$F_\beta = \frac{(\beta^2 + 1) \times P \times R}{\beta * P + R} \equiv F_1 = \frac{2 \times P \times R}{P + R}, \beta = 1 \tag{1}$$

F1-Score: Used when both measures have the same importance ($\beta = 1$)

4   Experimental Results

In this Section we explore the performances of each toolkit and compare them to the ensembles' performances using different protocols and datasets. $Ensemble_n$ (E_n) will be the notation used to refer to the ensemble using protocol number n, previously defined. Bold will be used to highlight the highest results.

For the first dataset we provide a more extensive analysis, providing not only the F1-score results but also the Precision and Recall. For the other datasets we present only the F1-scores and discuss them briefly, given that the results of precision and recall led to the same conclusions in every experiment.

For dataset 4 more experiments were added using ML algorithms.

4.1   Dataset 1 - Our Dataset

F1-Score Analysis

Ensemble 1:
Looking at Table 1 we can see that $Ensemble_1$ achieved the highest F1-score for detecting the entity PERSON. In terms of LOCATION and ORGANIZATION entities, while $Ensemble_1$ was better than CoreNLP, Twitter NLP tools and OpenNLP, it did not perform better than TwitIE.

Table 1. Precision, recall and F_1 scores on dataset 1

	Person			Location			Organization			Average		
	Precision	Recall	F1	Precision	Recall	F1	Precision	Recall	F1	Precision	Recall	F1
CoreNLP	58.18	**80**	67.37	96.92	65.63	78.26	100	16.67	28.57	85.03	54.1	58.07
TwitIE	67.5	67.5	67.5	89.77	**82.29**	85.87	84.62	**30.56**	**44.90**	80.63	**60.12**	**66.09**
TwitterNLP	37.93	55	44.90	88.33	61.46	72.84	80	5.56	10.39	69.11	40.67	42.71
OpenNLP	80.77	52.5	63.63	88.33	55.21	67.95	37.5	16.67	23.08	63.13	41.46	51.55
Ensemble1	**85.71**	75	**80.00**	**98.61**	73.96	84.52	100	18.06	30.59	**94.79**	55.67	65.04
Ensemble2	73.17	75	74.07	96.30	81.25	**88.14**	100	18.06	30.59	89.82	58.10	64.27

On average, TwitIE still achieved the best F1 measure, with 66%, followed immediately by the ensemble, which achieved an average F_1 of 65%. This is not surprising, given that TwitIE was, among all the 4 toolkits, the one to achieve better results for every entity type.

Nevertheless, it was possible to achieve an improvement of 12.5% on the detection of the entity Person by using $Ensemble_1$.

Ensemble 2:
$Ensemble_2$ also achieved the best F_1 score for the entity type PERSON when compared to any other toolkit individually, however its F_1 score was lower than $Ensemble_1$.

On the other hand, $Ensemble_2$ scored higher than $Ensemble_1$ and any other toolkit and in terms of detecting the entity LOCATION.

On average, $Ensemble_2$ was worse than $Ensemble_1$, which in turn was worse than TwitIE.

While for this dataset our ensembles did not outperform the best individual toolkit, TwitIE, there were still visible improvements in specific entity types, namely PERSON and LOCATION.

Recall Analysis

Ensemble 1:
In terms of recall, it is possible to see in Table 1 that the $Ensemble_1$ ranked second for every entity type. The toolkit able to detect more PERSON entities was Stanford CoreNLP, while TwitIE was the toolkit to achieve higher recall for the entities LOCATION and ORGANIZATION.

Ensemble 2:
$Ensemble_2$ ranked better than $Ensemble_1$ for the entity type LOCATION, but scored the same for PERSON and ORGANIZATION.

The fact that protocol 2 was less strict than protocol 1 is the likely reason for the improve in recall from $Ensemble_1$ to $Ensemble_2$.

Precision Analysis

Ensemble 1:
In terms of precision, $Ensemble_1$ ranked first for every entity type, as we can see in Table 1. This result makes sense and indicates that using this protocol helped significantly in detecting entities efficiently, by eliminating predictions with less than a certain level of confidence (see protocol 1).

Ensemble 2:
$Ensemble_2$ overall precision dropped when compared to $Ensemble_1$, 12.54% on PERSON and 2.31% on ORGANIZATION. Once again it makes sense that reducing the strictness of the protocol would likely reduce the precision.

4.2   Dataset 2 - WNUT NER

In Table 2 we can see that for this dataset the results were generally low for all the toolkits, when compared to the performances obtained from the other datasets tested. Since this dataset used Twitter NLP tools format, it had to suffer the same conversion explained in Sect. 3.2.3, which probably led to the worse results.

Table 2. F1-scores on dataset 2

	PERSON	LOCATION	ORGANIZATION	Avg
CoreNLP	56.62	32.5	20	36.37
TwitIE	59.95	**48.14**	38.23	48.77
TwitterNLP	52.78	34.9	**45.12**	44.27
OpenNLP	43	34.79	6.59	28.13
$Ensemble_1$	**70.57**	41.45	42.37	51.46
$Ensemble_2$	70.44	44.53	41.73	**52.53**

Nevertheless, we can see that both Ensembles achieved better F-scores on average than any other toolkit alone, which is the question we sought to answer in this work.

4.3   Dataset 3 - #MSM2013

Looking at Table 3 it is possible to see that once again ensemble 2 performed better on average than any other toolkit individually. $Ensemble_1$, while not

Table 3. F1-scores on dataset 3

	PERSON	LOCATION	ORGANIZATION	Avg
CoreNLP	69.20	54.18	27.09	50.16
TwitIE	77.06	**67.96**	43.95	62.99
Ritter	55.04	41.91	16.18	37.71
OpenNLP	55.40	47.68	25.47	42.85
$Ensemble_1$	79.93	62.20	41.37	61.17
$Ensemble_2$	**82.36**	66.42	**45.26**	**64.68**

better than TwitIE on average still performed reasonably well with only 1.82% less F1-score.

Also, once again, both Ensembles outperformed every toolkit on the entity type PERSON, and $Ensemble_2$ on the entity type ORGANIZATION.

4.4   Dataset 4 - Subset of #MSM2013

We extracted a subset of 20000 entries (i.e. tokens) from #MSM2013 and split it into two equally sized datasets for training and testing purposes.

Looking at Table 4, we can see that Naïve Bayes was the best method on average (74.02% F1), followed by the Neural Network (74.00% F1), and our manually defined $Ensemble_2$ (73.48% F1). Every ML algorithm that we experimented, except kNN with k = 3, performed better than TwitIE (the best among the tools).

Table 4. F1-scores on dataset 4

	PERSON	LOCATION	ORGANIZATION	Avg
CoreNLP	54.21	65.64	40.20	53.35
TwitIE	71.13	82.20	**61.02**	71.45
TwitterNLP	51.73	55.59	15.85	41.06
OpenNLP	52.80	63.05	41.20	52.35
$Ensemble_1$	80.08	77.07	53.57	70.24
$Ensemble_2$	**81.26**	81.45	57.74	73.48
Random Forest	80.68	82.58	51.4	71.55
Naïve Bayes	80.88	83.82	57.37	**74.02**
kNN, k = 3	75.09	**84.17**	47.76	69.00
kNN, k = 10	80.68	82.53	53.16	72.12
Neural net	79.62	83.71	58.68	74.00

In terms of individual entity types, our $Ensemble_2$ was the best for PERSON, achieving 81.26% of F1, an improvement of 10.13% against TwitIE. For

LOCATION, the best achieved was 84.17%, using kNN with $k = 3$, an increase of 1.97% (again against TwitIE). For the entity type ORGANIZATION none of our ensembles was able to perform better than TwitIE.

An interesting fact to note is that the best ensemble on average (Naïve Bayes) was not the best ensemble for any specific entity type alone.

4.5   Results Summary

Differently from results previously shown in literature [13, 15], in our experiments Twitter NLP tools achieved overall worse performances than other toolkits across all the 3 tested datasets. We believe this performance difference was related to the way we converted the output of this toolkit for our study. We expose our rationale for this.

Firstly, Twitter NLP recognizes multiple entity types, but those entities do not include ORGANIZATION nor LOCATION. Instead, they include COMPANY and GEO-LOCATION, which were converted directly to ORGANIZATION and LOCATION. We are aware that the former is probably not optimal, since a company does not need to be an organization and vice-versa.

Secondly, there is also the fact that Twitter NLP tools recognizes other entity types that we decided to ignore in this study (such as SPORTSTEAM, BAND, and MOVIE) which could be, in some cases, sub-categories of more general entity types (for example a SPORTSTEAM could be seen as an ORGANIZATION/COMPANY). Therefore, ignoring such entity types could be another reason for the comparatively worse results obtained by Twitter NLP tools in our experiments.

Finally, we did not include optional features based on POS and chunk tags, which leads to faster but lower quality results [15].

For the first dataset, while TwitIE has remained better than both ensembles on average, we witnessed a positive boost of PERSON detection using Protocol 1, achieving more 12.5% F1-score than the best individual toolkit (TwitIE with 67.5%), and a boost in LOCATION detection using Protocol 2, achieving more 2.27% F1-score than the best individual toolkit (TwitIE with 85.871%).

On the second dataset, both ensembles have beaten the best individual toolkit. The performance boost was very noticeable on the entity type PERSON (up to 10.62%), and the ensembles managed to keep a reasonable performance on the detection of ORGANIZATIONS (42.37% and 41.73% respectively), given that two of the toolkits (CoreNLP and OpenNLP) achieved very low results for this entity type (20% and 6.59% respectively).

In our third experiment, the boost on the entity type person remained noticeable for both ensembles (2.87% and 5.3% higher than the best toolkit). $Ensemble_2$ performed better on average than any other toolkit, achieving 1.69% higher F1-score than TwitIE, the best individual toolkit with 62.99% F1-score.

In terms of precision and recall, the conclusions were the same as for every dataset: the stricter protocol ($Ensemble_1$) had less recall but more precision than the less strict protocol ($Ensemble_2$).

Finally, our last experiment showed that there were some ML algorithms able to outperform TwitIE and even our *Ensemble₂*, namely Naive Bayes and the Neural Network.

5 Conclusions and Future Work

The first conclusion of this study is that using an ensemble of toolkits with a voting system can improve the performance of NER on tweets, answering the first question of our research.

As for the second question, we can say that both manually defined protocols were, to some extent, naïve yet they achieved promising results. This indicates that a more refined protocol will probably improve these results even further. It proves to be false, this approach could still be used with a combination of both protocols for the entities PERSON and LOCATION, and keeping ORGANIZATION predicted by TwitIE. We also showed that using machine learning algorithms for predicting entities based on the outputs of each toolkit is viable.

As future work we intend to train most of the toolkits using a training dataset, instead of using already trained models, since in some of these toolkits the models were not trained on social media texts. We also want to set up an "out-of-the-box" multi-threading ensemble NER toolkit, available and easy to use for anyone intending to extract entities from social media posts.

In terms of the results, a deeper analysis could be conducted in the future in order to better understand the behaviours observed in each toolkit, as well as the differences across corpora. Statistical tests would also be interesting to check if improvements between tools are statistically significant or not.

For the machine learning algorithms, more complex features and hyperparameters could be tried and analyzed. It would also be interesting to apply the ML approach to different datasets and compare the results.

Acknowledgments. This work is supported by the ERDF European Regional Development Fund through the COMPETE Programme (operational programme for competitiveness) and by National Funds through the FCT (Portuguese Foundation for Science and Technology) within project "Reminds/UTAP-ICDT/EEI-CTP/0022/2014".

References

1. Atdağ, S., Labatut, V.: A comparison of named entity recognition tools applied to biographical texts. In: 2013 2nd International Conference on Systems and Computer Science (ICSCS), pp. 228–233. IEEE (2013)
2. Baldwin, T., De Marneffe, M.C., Han, B., Kim, Y.-B., Ritter, A., Xu, W.: Shared tasks of the: Twitter lexical normalization and named entity recognition. In: Proceedings of the Workshop on Noisy User-generated Text (WNUT 2015), Beijing, China (2015)
3. Bontcheva, K., Derczynski, L., Funk, A., Greenwood, M.A., Maynard, D., Aswani, N.: Twitie: an open-source information extraction pipeline for microblog text. In: RANLP, pp. 83–90 (2013)

4. Cano Basave, A.E., Varga, A., Rowe, M., Stankovic, M., Dadzie, A.-S.: Making sense of microposts (# msm2013) concept extraction challenge (2013)
5. Clark, A., Fox, C., Lappin, S.: The Handbook of Computational Linguistics and Natural Language Processing. Wiley, Hoboken (2013)
6. Figueira, A., Sandim, M., Fortuna, P.: An approach to relevancy detection: contributions to the automatic detection of relevance in social networks. In: Rocha, A., Correia, A.M., Adeli, H., Reis, L.P., Teixeira, M.M. (eds.) ITEM 2014. AISC, vol. 444, pp. 89–99. Springer, Cham (2016). doi:10.1007/978-3-319-31232-3_9
7. Gate.ac.uk - wiki/twitie.html. https://gate.ac.uk/wiki/twitie.html. Accessed 06 Oct 2017
8. Jiang, R., Banchs, R.E., Li, H.: Evaluating and combining named entity recognition systems. In: ACL 2016, p. 21 (2016)
9. Laboreiro, G., Sarmento, L., Teixeira, J., Oliveira, E.: Tokenizing micro-blogging messages using a text classification approach. In: Proceedings of the Fourth Workshop on Analytics for Noisy Unstructured Text Data, pp. 81–88. ACM (2010)
10. C. D. Manning, M. Surdeanu, J. Bauer, J. R. Finkel, S. Bethard, and D. McClosky. The stanford corenlp natural language processing toolkit. In ACL (System Demonstrations), pp. 55–60 (2014)
11. Nebhi, K., Bontcheva, K., Gorrell, G.: Restoring capitalization in# tweets. In: Proceedings of the 24th International Conference on World Wide Web, pp. 1111–1115. ACM (2015)
12. Apache opennlp. https://opennlp.apache.org/. Accessed 06 Oct 2017
13. Pinto, A., Gonçalo Oliveira, H., Oliveira Alves, A.: Comparing the performance of different nlp toolkits in formal and social media text. In: OASIcs-OpenAccess Series in Informatics, vol. 51. Schloss Dagstuhl-Leibniz-Zentrum fuer Informatik (2016)
14. Ramshaw, L.A., Marcus, M.P.: Text chunking using transformation-based learning. In: Armstrong, S., Church, K., Isabelle, P., Manzi, S., Tzoukermann, E., Yarowsky, D. (eds.) Natural Language Processing Using Very Large Corpora, vol. 11, pp. 157–176. Springer, Heidelberg (1999). doi:10.1007/978-94-017-2390-9_10
15. Ritter, A., Clark, S., Etzioni, O., et al.: Named entity recognition in tweets: an experimental study. In: Proceedings of the Conference on Empirical Methods in Natural Language Processing, pp. 1524–1534. Association for Computational Linguistics (2011)
16. Rodriquez, K.J., Bryant, M., Blanke, T., Luszczynska, M.: Comparison of named entity recognition tools for raw OCR text. In: KONVENS, pp. 410–414 (2012)
17. Saha, S., Ekbal, A.: Combining multiple classifiers using vote based classifier ensemble technique for named entity recognition. Data Knowl. Eng. 85, 15–39 (2013)
18. Wu, C.-W., Jan, S.-Y., Tsai, R.T.-H., Hsu, W.-L.: On using ensemble methods for Chinese named entity recognition. In: Proceedings of the 5th SIGHAN Workshop on Chinese Language Processing, pp. 142–145 (2006)

Aspect-Based Opinion Mining in Drug Reviews

Diana Cavalcanti[(⊠)] and Ricardo Prudêncio

Centro de Informática, Universidade Federal de Pernambuco, Recife, PE, Brazil
{dcc2,rbcp}@cin.ufpe.br

Abstract. Aspect-based opinion mining can be applied to extract relevant information expressed by patients in drug reviews (e.g., adverse reactions, efficacy of a drug, symptoms and conditions of patients). This new domain of application presents challenges as well as opportunities for research in opinion mining. Nevertheless, the literature is still scarce of methods to extract multiple relevant aspects present in drug reviews. In this paper we propose a method to extract and classify aspects in drug reviews. The proposed solution has two main steps. In the aspect extraction, a method based on syntactic dependency paths is proposed to extract opinion pairs in drug reviews, composed by an aspect term associated to a sentiment modifier. In the aspect classification, a supervised classification is proposed based on domain and linguistics resources to classify the opinion pairs by aspect type (e.g., condition, adverse reaction, dosage and effectiveness). In order to evaluate the proposed method we conducted experiments with datasets related to three different diseases: ADHD, AIDS and Anxiety. Promising results were obtained in the experiments and various issues were identified and discussed.

Keywords: Opinion mining · Aspect extraction · Aspect classification · Natural language processing · Machine learning · Drugs reviews

1 Introduction

Opinion mining is the process of detecting and analyzing subjective information, sentiments and opinionated aspects in large volumes of texts using computational methods [4]. Opinion mining has been applied in different domains, specially to evaluate the acceptance of products and services, as well as the general sentiment about people and brands. In our work, we are focused on opinion mining in drug reviews, in which patients express their experiences and opinions about treatments or medicines. This domain of application has received a great interest in recent years [1]. Specifically in pharmacovigilance, drug manufacturers can benefit from opinion mining since particular adverse reactions to a drug can be traced more quickly from public repositories or posts in social networks.

Previous works on opinion mining in drug reviews have focused on classifying the sentiment about a drug (e.g., positive or negative) expressed in the users' reviews [5,6]. A more refined (and possibly useful) task is to identify the Adverse Drug Reactions (ADRs) mentioned in a drug review, which have been commonly

© Springer International Publishing AG 2017
E. Oliveira et al. (Eds.): EPIA 2017, LNAI 10423, pp. 815–827, 2017.
DOI: 10.1007/978-3-319-65340-2_66

reported by patients. ADRs are harmful reactions caused by medication intake resulting in an intervention related to the use of the product. Due to various limitations in clinical trials, it is not possible to fully evaluate the consequences of using a particular drug before being released [1–3]. An ADR may not be detected before the product go to the market and can take some time after its sale to track new ADRs and relate them to the drug's label [9].

In this work, we focused on *aspect-based opinion mining* [4] in drug reviews. The aim is to identify in a drug review fragments of text that can be associated to specific aspects of interest like, adverse reactions, effectiveness, patient conditions, among others. The identification of ADRs can be seen as an example of task related to aspect-based opinion mining. Although ADR is in fact an important information to be identified, it is not the only aspect of interest mentioned in drug reviews. Patient conditions, for instance, once extracted, can be useful to reveal wrong uses of a medicine among patients. Other aspects can provide a better assessment of the reported patients' experience as well as a better summarization of the reviews associated to a drug. The extraction of multiple relevant aspects in drug reviews is a lack in the literature that we aim to focus on.

In the current work, a method for extracting and classifying aspects is proposed. In the aspect extraction, a linguistic method based on dependency paths in the syntactic tree of the reviews is adopted to extract *opinion pairs* (i.e., an aspect term and its opinion term). In the aspect classification, a supervised learning algorithm is adopted to classify opinion pairs in one of four aspects types: Condition, ADR, Dosage or Effectiveness. Previous work only focused on classifying ADRs. Experiments were performed in three datasets related to different diseases and drugs. The results revealed a gain in performance to extract relevant aspects (in terms of F-Measure) compared to previous work.

The current work filled in a gap in the literature by investigating and proposing effective methods for mining multiple aspects in drug reviews. We can mention the following contributions:

- Proposal of a method for extracting aspects in drug reviews based on syntactic dependency paths, with a good performance;
- Production of a corpus of drug reviews labeled by aspects, which can be adopted for new experiments;
- A supervised method based on domain resources and linguistic features for aspect type classification.

The remainder of this paper is organized as follows. Section 2 provides a brief introduction on opinion mining in drug reviews. In Sect. 3 we present the proposed approach. Section 4 presents the results of our experiments. Finally, Sect. 5 concludes the paper, along with recommendations for future work.

2   Opinion Mining in Drugs Reviews

Recent studies have focused on mining reviews of drugs (available in social networks, forums, web,...) in order to provide useful information for pharmacovigilance. Two common tasks can be identified in the literature of opinion mining in drug reviews: (1) classification of reviews; and (2) extraction of opinion aspects.

Concerning the first task, a review can be automatically classified according to its sentiment about the drug (usually positive, negative or neutral) [5,6]. Sentiment classification can be useful for filtering relevant reviews to be inspected (e.g., reviews classified as negative have a high chance of mentioning a negative side effect). A related task is to directly classify whether a review mentions an ADR or not [7,10]. This is more specific and focused than simply classifying the sentiment of a review. The sentiment classification task can be dealt with both machine learning (e.g., [7,10]) and knowledge-based approaches (e.g., [5,6]).

The second task is to extract specific aspects in drug reviews. Hence, the aim is not only to classify whether a review mentions an ADRs, for instance, but also to extract the reaction itself or any other aspect considered as relevant [9]. In literature, this task is called *aspect-based opinion mining*, which aims to extract the main aspects mentioned about an item or entity and to provide the classification of the opinion given on every aspect [4]. According to [5,6], six aspects (see examples in Table 1) are common in drug reviews:

- **Overall:** The general opinion of a medicinal product or when the clause is not mentioned any of the other five categories of aspects;
- **Effectiveness:** Changes noted after the use of the medicine, linked to the patient's condition or disease;
- **Side effects:** The reactions that are not related to the medicine. ADR is a negative side effect;
- **Dosage:** Reports the amount, frequency or the treatment period in which the medicine was used.
- **Condition:** Corresponds to a description of the patient's condition, e.g., a disease or health problems in general.
- **Cost:** Corresponds the cost/price of a medicine.

Table 1. Opinion sentence by aspects in drugs reviews

Aspect	Opinion sentence
Overall	Adderall is overall a **good** ADD **medicine**.
Effectiveness	It **helped** me stay **focused** on any tasks.
Side effects	I have only one side effect which is **dry mouth**.
Condition	I **had** clinical **depression/anxiety** for years.
Cost	I hate that the **price** is so **high**.
Dosage	I take **30 mg twice a day**

As in the classification task, previous work on aspect-based opinion mining can be split in the two categories: (1) machine learning; and (2) knowledge-based approaches. In the machine learning approach, sequential learning algorithms like Conditional Random Fields (CRFs) and Hidden Markov Models (HMMs) have been adopted specially to extract ADRs, but also other aspects [1,2]. The idea is to treat aspect extraction as a sequence labeling task: each word in a review is labeled with a tag associated to an aspect and sequences of words with the same tag are extracted. Sequential learning also requires labeled corpora for training the models. The need for a large training set can be even more critical for sequential learning, since whole sequences of inputs have to be classified.

Few attempts have been identified in the literature to build knowledge-based techniques for aspect extraction in drug reviews, although such techniques are very common in the general application of aspect-based opinion mining (e.g., for product reviews). Additionally, the existing works are not completely adequate for the task. For instance, in [8], a knowledge-based approach is proposed for extracting text fragments in a review that express an opinion about an entity. Although this approach can be used for filtering relevant opinions in the reviews, it does not directly extract specific aspects (like ADRs). In [5,6], text fragments are extracted from reviews with the focus on classifying sentiments. Although some of the extracted information can coincide with aspects of interest, this approach is also not focused on aspect-based extraction.

3   Proposed Solution

In this paper, a method for extracting and classifying aspects in drug reviews is proposed. Our proposed method for mining aspects in drugs reviews is comprised of three main steps: Pre-processing, Aspect Extraction and Aspect Type Classification (see Fig. 1). Initially, given an input review, the Pre-processing step normalizes the review's text. In the Aspect Extraction step, we extended an algorithm, in which dependency paths in the syntactic trees of the reviews are adopted to extract opinion pairs in the review's sentences (i.e., an aspect plus a sentiment modifier). This approach does not require to train an extraction model (e.g., by using a sequential learning algorithm), which is usually very expensive. Additionally, it will be useful to find low frequent aspects terms. Finally, in the Aspect Type Classification step, each opinion pair is classified into one of the

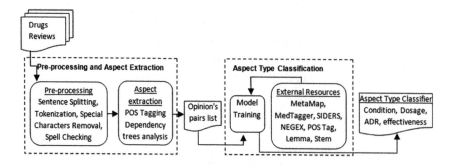

Fig. 1. An overview of the proposed approach

four aspect types: Condition, Side Effects, Dosage or Effectiveness. For this a conventional supervised learning algorithm is adopted. To the best of our knowledge, there is no previous work which identifies multiple aspect classes in drugs reviews. Previous work only focused on classifying ADRs, which is limited compared to our work. In the following sections we describe the implementation details for each step of the proposed approach.

3.1 Pre-processing

Each review in collected data were splited in sentences and tokenized by Stanford CoreNLP tool[1]. We performed spelling correction to correcting words that were misspelled frequently by users using the Google spell checking API[2] and special symbols were removed. Finally, the term *meds* and *med* frequently cited on corpus were replaced to *medicine*. Stopwords were not removed as it may infer wrong syntactic tree parse process.

3.2 Aspect Extraction Task

Knowledge-based approaches which adopted linguistic rules are an interesting alternative for aspect mining. Previous techniques successfully adopted in other domains (like product reviews) can be investigated in the domain of drug reviews, thus filling in a gap in the literature. Obviously, adaptation of previous methods has to be addressed to fit the specific characteristics of the drug review domain.

In the current work, we proposed an aspect extraction method for drug reviews, which is an extension of the *Aspectator* method [11]. This work was originally developed to automatically detect aspects of products on user feedback. It analyzes dependency paths in the syntactic tree of a review to find opinions expressed on candidates aspects. The selection and extraction is based on pairs of words or phrases called *opinion pairs* as illustrated in Fig. 2. The first term called *sentiment modifier* is the word around the aspect that expresses an opinion and the second term called *aspect mention* is the mention of an aspect.

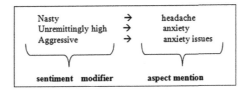

Fig. 2. Examples of opinion pairs in drug reviews.

---

[1] https://stanfordnlp.github.io/CoreNLP/.

[2] https://code.google.com/archive/p/google-api-spelling-java/.

Dependency path	Dependency paths examples	Opinion pair
amod VB	*amod* Some people note increased aggression DT NNS VBP VBN NN	\<increased ; agression\>
amod_conj	*conj:and* *amod* *cc* Night sweats with intense anxiety and nausea NNP VBZ IN JJ NN CC NN	\<intense; anxiety\> \<intense; nausea\>
amod_nsubj	*nsubj* *amod* *advmod* The therapeutic effects are still evident DT JJ NNS VBP RB JJ	\<still evident; therapeutic effects\>
dobj NN_VB	*dobj* he has developed seizures PRP VBZ VBN NNS	\<developed; seizures\>
nsubj_xcomp VB	*nsubj* *xcomp* My metabolism slowed down immensely PRPS NN VBD IN RB	\<immensely slowed; metabolism\>
nsubj_xcomp VB_JJ	*nsubj xcomp* I felt very groggy PRP VBD RB JJ	\<very groggy; felt\>.
nsubj_xcomp VB_VB	*nsubj* *xcomp* I mainly feel relaxed PRP RB VBP VBN	\<mainly relaxed; feel\>
nsubj VB	*nsubj* *neg* This medicine is n't helping DT NN VBZ RB VBG	\<n't helping; medicine\>
nsubj_conj	*conj:and* *nsubj* *cc* behavior is uncontrollable and very irritable NN VBZ JJ CC RB JJ	\<very irritable; behaviors\> \<uncontrollable; behaviors\>

Fig. 3. New dependency paths: aspectator algorithm adaptation to medical domain

The original approach focuses on extracting opinion pairs based on nouns and adjectives, except to "nsubjpass-advmod" path. In our domain of interest, Sarker [2] comments that verbs have an important role when patients express their experiences in a review. Thus, important aspects cannot be extracted by the original *Aspectator*. For instance, in the expression *reduced my pain*, the term *reduced* is a verb (a verb not related by an adverb as suggested in "nsubjpass-advmod" path) and thus the effectiveness aspect of the drug would not be identified. This paper proposes to extend the algorithm and adapt it to the medical domain in order to overcome this limitation as well as other gaps identified.

Figure 3 presents the new dependency paths proposed in our work. All paths considered relations between nouns and adjectives or verbs. For instance, in the dependency paths "nsubj-xcomp VB-JJ" and "nsubj-xcomp VB-VB", a verb is considered as aspect mention and an adjective or verb respectively are sentiment modifiers. In our work, dependency trees were computed using the Universal Dependency Relations embedded in the Stanford CoreNLP tool.

3.3   Aspect Type Classification

In this step, each opinion pair is labeled as Condition, Side Effects, Dosage or Effectiveness. A model built by supervised learning is adopted in our solution. An important issue in this classification is the set of features used to describe the opinion pairs and thus adopted as predictor attributes by the classifier. We adopted in our work seven sets of features that were combined in the classification. Initially, the aspect and modifier in a pair are associated to their grammatical class indicated by the **POS tagging** tool. Additionally, named entity recognition tools were used to tag both the aspect and modifier with semantical types. Three knowledge based databases were adopted, containing lists of terms associated to different semantical types:

- **MetaMap:** The Unified Medical Language System (UMLS)[3] is a metathesaurus which contains over a million medical and general English concepts grouped in more than 130 semantic types. Each one belongs to one of the 15 semantic groups, e.g., the term *muscle tension* belongs to the semantic type *Sign* or *Symptom* from the *Disorders* semantic group. We used the MetaMap Java API[4] to tag the aspects and modifiers with UMLS semantic types.
- **SIDER**[5]**:** The SIDER side effect resource contains a list of terms tagged as precondition or indication of adverse reaction. The resource contains associations between drugs and adverse reactions terms extracted from pharmaceutical literature. For example, the term *Bipolar Disorder* is tagged as precondition and *Fever* is tagged as indication.
- **MedTagger**[6]**:** The MedTagger is a suite of programs including indexing based on dictionaries, syntactic parsing to detect concept mentions in clinical text, and named entity recognizers. Dictionary-based concept in MedTagger was used to tag aspects and modifiers matching a list of terms labeled with semantic groups like disorder (DISO), anatomy (ANAT), among others.

We also use **NegEX**[7], an open source Java tool for negation detection of events in medical documents. In our work, this tool was applied to indicate whether an opinion pair event is negated. NegEX contains a list of negation phrases tagged with default labels. We considered only terms tagged with the label *definiteNegatedExistence*. Finally it was included as attributes, the **Lemma** and **Stem** of the aspect and modifier in the opinion pair.

The Random Forest algorithm classifier implemented in Weka tool[8] was adopted to built the classifier. As it will be seen, the classifier was learned by using a manually labeled corpus of opinion pairs.

4   Experiments and Results

In this section we describe the experiments to evaluate the proposed approach. Three drug review datasets [14] (see Table 2) were manually collected from the website *drugs.com* regarding to the clinical conditions: ADHD, AIDS and Anxiety.

---

[3] https://www.nlm.nih.gov/research/umls/knowledge_sources/metathesaurus/.
[4] https://metamap.nlm.nih.gov.
[5] sideeffects.embl.de/.
[6] https://sourceforge.net/projects/ohnlp/files/MedTagger/.
[7] https://code.google.com/archive/p/negex/.
[8] http://www.cs.waikato.ac.nz/ml/weka/.

In order to create a gold standard for evaluation, initially the opinion pairs present in each drug review were manually extracted. After extraction, each opinion pair was manually labeled (by one annotator) as Condition (C), Side Effects (ADR), Dosage (D) or Effectiveness (E), Overall aspect was considered as Effectiveness and Cost was not considered to the experiment due to the low frequency in the database. The aspect extraction step will be evaluated according to its capability of retrieving the gold standard opinion pairs. The labeled pairs will be used to evaluate the predictive performance of the classification step. Following we present the experiments and obtained results respectively for the aspect extraction and the classification tasks.

Table 2. Corpus of experiments related to three different clinical conditions

	ADHD	AIDS	Anxiety
Drug's name	8	4	4
Total reviews	802	201	500
Labeled aspect	6,528	1,841	3,955

4.1 Aspect Extraction

In order to evaluate the aspect extraction step, we computed classical metrics: precision, recall and F-measure. Precision (P) is defined by the number of automatically extracted opinion pairs that occur in the labeled corpus (i.e., relevant pairs extracted - Opa) divided by number of automatically opinion pairs extracted (Opi). Recall (R) is measured as the number of relevant opinion pairs extracted divided by the number opinion pairs present in the labeled dataset (Opn). The F-Measure (F) is the harmonic mean between precision and recall. A comparative analysis was performed with previous approaches:

- Zheng et al. [12]: developed an unsupervised dependency analysis-based approach to extract Appraisal Expression Patterns (AEPs). The AEP is applied to represent the syntactic relationship between aspect and sentiment words by using Shortest Dependency Path (SDP) that connects two words in the dependency graph. The AEP information is incorporated into the AEP-LDA model for mining aspect and sentiment words simultaneously. We compare our dependencies patterns with relations generated in the AEP.
- Samha [13]: proposed an approach undertakes Dependency Parsing, Lemma, and POS tagging in order to obtain the syntactic structure of sentences by means of a dependency relation rule. Dependency Relations is applied to map the dependencies between all words within the sentence in the form of relation (a grammatical relation holds between a head and a dependent).
- Original Aspectator.

Table 3. Precision, Recall and F-Measure

	ADHD			AIDS			Anxiety		
Method	P	R	F	P	R	F	P	R	F
Zheng et al. [12]	0,459	0,561	0,505	0,502	0,578	0,537	0,515	0,543	0,529
Samha [13]	0,580	0,540	0,560	0,643	0,604	0,623	0,624	0,550	0,585
Aspectator	0,816	0,514	0,631	0,772	0,554	0,645	0,828	0,582	0,683
Proposed Method	0,780	0,665	0,718	0,752	0,678	0,713	0,787	0,658	0,717

Table 3 presents the obtained results to baselines, original Aspectator and new dependency paths. Original *Aspectator* achieved the highest precision for all datasets, but lower recall levels. The other baselines were not competitive due to the low values of precision in turn. The proposed method obtained the best trade-off between precision and recall, i.e., the best results in terms of F-Measure.

Table 4. Recall to each aspect type

Dataset	Overall	Effectiveness	ADR	Dosage	Condition	Cost
ADHD	0,796	0,696	0,629	0,708	0,713	0,615
AIDS	0,879	0,796	0,651	0,511	0,582	0,60
Anxiety	0,780	0,764	0,725	0,601	0,777	0,778

Table 4 presents the recall relative to each aspect type. Cost aspect retrieved the lowest frequency, only 27 pairs in all bases, users usually do not discuss about price in drug reviews. Dosage and Anxiety to ADHD had a higher occurrence than to AIDS, we noted, drugs belonging to ADHD and Anxiety are available in different dosages (capsule, tablet or liquid), then users have more options to discuss about different dosages. Therefore, aspect type is quite dependent of disease type. For certain aspects like condition, the recall is lower, which could be explained by the difficulty in handling some domain dependent terms.

We also note Efficacy or Side Effects aspects are frequently expressed using quantitative values, mainly in the AIDS database, e.g., *"My **CD4** count was at **89** and **Viral Load** up to **182,000/mL**. After 6 weeks of treatment my **CD4** count had jumped to **394**, and **VL** dropped to **2,185**."*, implies positive review about the medicine. The *Aspectator* is not prepared to handle with quantitative terms.

Table 5 presents the precision to original and new *Aspectator* paths. As it can be seen, most rules have good precision values. We consider "nsubj-dobj" path not relevant to our domain due to its lower frequency and low precision. The path "nsubj NN-VB" resulted high frequency and low precision, we observed that is necessary filtering the occurrence of some verbs types. For example, verbs "is", "do", "went", "does", "been" are frequent extracted as *sentiment modifier*.

The path "dobj NN-VB" reached high precision and solves the expression *reduced my pain* previously mentioned. The path "nsubj-xcomp VB-VB - VB-JJ" is able to extract verbs as *aspect mention*. Drugs reviews have high frequency of sentences in first person, as *I feel extremely anxious*, resulting opinion pair <extremely anxious; feel>. In addition, we considered the new dependency paths proposed relevant to drugs reviews domain.

Table 5. Precision by Dependency Path

Path	ADHD			AIDS			Anxiety		
Original Paths	Opa	Opi	P	Opa	Opi	P	Opa	Opi	P
amod NN-JJ	1302	1627	**0,8**	591	787	**0,75**	1220	1493	**0,82**
nsubj-dobj NN-JJ	1	3	0,33	1	1	1	1	2	0,5
nsubj-xcomp NN-JJ	50	55	**0,91**	17	19	**0,89**	42	47	**0,89**
nsubj-cop NN-JJ	158	164	**0,96**	92	101	**0,91**	125	132	**0,95**
nsubjpass-advmod NN-VB	14	20	**0,7**	5	6	**0,83**	15	21	**0,71**
New Paths									
amod NN-VB	46	49	**0,94**	14	15	**0,93**	43	45	**0,96**
amod-conj NN-VB/JJ	46	73	0,63	24	50	0,48	48	74	0,65
amod-nsubj NN-VB/JJ	113	161	**0,7**	82	110	**0,75**	106	149	**0,71**
dobj NN-VB	813	1127	**0,72**	285	394	**0,72**	750	1040	**0,72**
nsubj-xcomp NN-VB	50	108	0,46	15	29	0,52	42	84	0,5
nsubj-xcomp VB-JJ	237	247	**0,96**	51	53	**0,96**	209	215	**0,97**
nsubj-xcomp VB-VB	19	25	**0,76**	2	3	0,67	5	8	0,63
nsubj NN-VB	364	907	0,4	137	319	0,43	342	767	0,45
nsubj-conj NN-VB	13	18	**0,72**	8	11	**0,73**	15	21	**0,71**

4.2   Aspect Type Classification

In this section, we initially evaluated the predictive performance of the RF algorithm and measured the impact of the feature sets adopted. For this, the RF algorithm was evaluated with 10-fold cross-validation using different sets of features, as presented in Table 6 (first column). In each experiment, a new set is included to augment the description of the opinion pairs. The simplest set is the *Postag* set, which is considered as a baseline for comparison.

As it can be seen in Table 6, for all datasets, a gain in performance was observed when MetaMap was included in comparison to only using the Postag set. Although better results can be achieved by including other feature sets, the significance over the combination Postag+MetaMap was not verified. For instance, the best accuracy values were obtained when all domain feature sets were considered. However only a very small gain in performance was obtained over Postag+MetaMap. In some cases, including more features can even harm accuracy, which was specially observed when Stemming was adopted. One reason for high accuracy using MetaMap that this feature in addition to identifying medical terms also covers quantitative, qualitative, and temporal terms like 30 mg, better, great, daily in which are quite frequent in the experiment dataset.

Table 6. Correctly Classified Instances (in %).

Features Used	ADHD	AIDS	Anxiety
Postag	72.87	74.75	72.89
Postag + Metamap	76.08	77.34	75.9
Postag + Metamap + Medtagger	75.85	76.75	76
Postag + Metamap + Medtagger + Siders	76.31	77.4	76.25
Postag + Metamap + Medtagger + Siders + Negex	**76.86**	**78.16**	**76.78**
Postag + Metamap + Medtagger + Siders + Negex + Lemma	75.79	76.58	75.77
Postag+Metamap+Medtagger+Siders+Negex+Lemma+Stem	72.69	73.38	72.97

Table 7 presents the confusion matrix resulted from the best feature set presented in Table 6. The classifier has mainly failed in the ADR and Conditions classes, which were commonly classified as Effectiveness. In the same way. Effectiveness was commonly assigned as Condition or ADR. We observed that the occurrence of modifiers terms like *low, lower, higher, declined, stopped, lost, less, etc.*, are leading the classifier to errors. For example, observe the opinion pairs: <lost;focus> labeled as Condition, <lost;appetite> as ADR and <lost;pounds> as Effectiveness, the word *lost* was referenced in different ways as modifier, but their aspects are not sufficient for the classifier to distinguish different classes.

Table 7. Confusion matrix from using the optimal set of features

ADHD					AIDS					Anxiety				
	ADR	C	D	E		ADR	C	D	E		ADR	C	D	E
ADR	1391	121	3	290	ADR	313	10	0	111	ADR	602	106	2	202
C	185	571	4	455	C	22	375	10	121	C	85	672	13	225
D	4	3	586	72	D	0	4	66	12	D	0	6	397	48
E	211	142	20	2470	E	41	66	6	684	E	101	109	21	1366

We also observed that the same opinion pair may occur as Condition or ADR, as in the sentences: (1) "I **had** constant **headache** and horrible migraines which I am treated for by a neurologist" and (2) "The generic did nothing for me except to make me agitated/jittery for few hours, then crashed and **had** a **headache**".

The opinion pair <had;headache> in sentence (1) is described as Condition and in sentence (2) is described as ADR.

Another error to mention is false negative opinion pair. For example, consider the sentence *I was more satisfied with this one than any of the medicines. I **never had headaches** (with some I had terrible headaches!) the time release worked very well.* The opinion pair <had;never;headaches> indicates Effectiveness, but the classifier predicted as Condition. We highlight that the use of the resource Negex is not enough to address problem.

All these examples are inducing the classifier to wrong predictions. Some of these errors can be dealt with by including other features to describe the opinion pairs. Additionally, it can be relevant to analyze frequent terms before and after each opinion pair in order to identify specific patterns. Sampathkumar et al. [9] defines a list of keywords and phrases that denote the causal relationship of a drug causing a side-effect. For example, expressions like *Caused by, Have been getting, Made me feel* could be adopted to distinguish ADR aspects.

We also observed that patients often use different verbs to describe different aspects. For example, terms like *diagnosed, suffering* and *have* are usually used to describe Condition (e.g., *I have been diagnosed, I was suffering, I have ADHD, I have psychotic symptoms*). For ADRs, terms like *felt* and *have been* are commonly used (e.g., *I have been losing my appetite, I felt very confused, I felt suicidal*). The verbs *work* and *help* are usually used to describe Effectiveness (e.g., *it helps me concentrate, Adderall really helps me focus, didn't work well, Concerta worked wonders.* For Dosage, common verbs are *prescribed, take, taken* and *took up*.

5   Conclusion and Further Work

In this work, we developed a method for extracting and classifying aspects in drug reviews. Initially, we extend the algorithm *Aspectator* suggesting new dependency paths to extract relevant opinion pairs to medical domain. We tested each path in three datasets of drugs reviews. The proposed solution achieved very competitive results compared to baseline methods (the highest values of F-Measure were observed for all datasets). We highlight that the solution can be easily adapted to other languages since it does not require labeled data. We also report an aspect term classification model based on Random Forest classifier. Evaluation on the dataset shows encouraging results that need further investigation and analysis of many ways to improve the performance of the system.

Other datasets can be considered in the future covering other medicines and diseases. We also aim to explore other supervised machine learning methods, hybrid approaches and new lexical resources in order to achieve improvements in results. Finally review analysis of comparative sentences can be performed in order to consider citations between drugs.

References

1. Denecke, K., Deng, Y.: Sentiment analysis in medical settings: new opportunities and challenges. Artif. Intell. Med. **64**(1), 17–27 (2015)

2. Sarker, A., et al.: Utilizing social media data for pharmacovigilance: a review. J. Biomed. Inform. **54**, 202–212 (2015)
3. Gosal, G.P.S.: Opinion mining and sentiment analysis of online drug reviews as a pharmacovigilance technique. Int. J. Recent Innov. Trends Comput. Commun. **3**, 4920–4925 (2015)
4. Liu, B.: Sentiment Analysis and Opinion Mining. Synthesis Lectures on Human Language Technologies. Morgan & Claypool Publishers, San Rafael (2012)
5. Na, J.-C., Kyaing, W.Y.M., Khoo, C.S.G., Foo, S., Chang, Y.-K., Theng, Y.-L.: Sentiment classification of drug reviews using a rule-based linguistic approach. In: Chen, H.-H., Chowdhury, G. (eds.) ICADL 2012. LNCS, vol. 7634, pp. 189–198. Springer, Heidelberg (2012). doi:10.1007/978-3-642-34752-8_25
6. Na, J.C., Kyaing, W.Y.M.: Sentiment analysis of user-generated content on drug review websites. J. Inf. Sci. Theory Pract. **1**(1), 6–23 (2015)
7. Egger, D., et al.: Adverse drug reaction detection using an adapted sentiment classifier. In: Social Media Mining Shared Task Workshop at PSB (2015)
8. Noferesti, S., Shamsfard, M.: Resource construction and evaluation for indirect opinion mining of drug reviews. PLoS ONE **10**, e0124993 (2015)
9. Sampathkumar, H., et al.: Mining adverse drug reactions from online healthcare forums using hidden Markov model. BMC Med. Inf. Decis. Making **14**, e0124993 (2014)
10. Jonnagaddala, J., et al.: Binary classification of Twitter posts for adverse drug reactions. In: Social Media Mining Shared Task Workshop at PSB (2016)
11. Bancken, W., Alfarone, D., Davis, J.: Automatically detecting and rating product aspects from textual customer reviews. In: 1st international workshop, DMNLP (2014)
12. Zheng, X., et al.: Incorporating appraisal expression patterns into topic modeling for aspect and sentiment word identification. Knowl.-Based Syst. **61**, 29–47 (2014)
13. Samha, A.K.: Aspect-based opinion mining using dependency relations. Int. J. Comput. Sci.Trends Technol. (IJCST) 4 (2016)
14. Drugs Reviews Dataset. https://github.com/spdiana/DrugsReviewsCorpus

Unsupervised Approaches for Computing Word Similarity in Portuguese

Hugo Gonçalo Oliveira[✉]

CISUC, Department of Informatics Engineering,
University of Coimbra, Coimbra, Portugal
hroliv@dei.uc.pt

Abstract. This paper presents several approaches for computing word similarity in Portuguese and is motivated by the recent availability of state-of-the-art distributional models of Portuguese words, which add to several lexical knowledge bases (LKBs) for this language, available for a longer time. The previous resources were exploited to answer word similarity tests, also recently available for Portuguese. We conclude that there are several valid approaches for this task, but not one that outperforms all the others in every single test. For instance, distributional models seem to capture relatedness better, but LKBs are better suited for computing genuine similarity.

Keywords: Semantic similarity · Word similarity · Lexical knowledge bases · Lexical semantics · Word embeddings · Distributional semantics

1 Introduction

Semantic similarity is a key problem in natural language processing (NLP) and understanding (NLU). Specifically, word similarity aims at determining the likeness of meaning transmitted by two words, and is generally a necessary step towards computing the semantic similarity of larger units, such as phrases or sentences. This is why there are many automatic approaches for computing word similarity, as well as several benchmarks that enable the assessment and comparison of distinct approaches for this purpose.

As for other NLP tasks, most related work targets English, because it is widely spoken, which also results in more benchmarks in this language. Yet, especially since word embeddings – vector representations of words learned with a deep neural network [17] – became a trend in NLP, researchers have developed both benchmarks and approaches for computing semantic similarity in other languages, including Portuguese.

This work uses recently released word similarity tests in Portuguese and answers them with unsupervised approaches that either exploit the structure of existing lexical knowledge bases (LKBs) or distributional models of words, including word embeddings. The goal of the automatic procedures is to score

© Springer International Publishing AG 2017
E. Oliveira et al. (Eds.): EPIA 2017, LNAI 10423, pp. 828–840, 2017.
DOI: 10.1007/978-3-319-65340-2_67

the similarity of two words, which may then be assessed by comparison with the scores in the benchmark test, in this case, based on human judgements.

The main contribution of this work is a comparison of several procedures employed for word similarity in Portuguese, which might support the choice of approaches to adopt in more complex tasks, such as semantic textual similarity (for Portuguese, see ASSIN [7]) or other tasks involved in a NLU pipeline (useful for e.g. conversational agents), or in a semantically-enriched search engine. Indirectly, the resources underlying each approach end up also being compared. For instance, results provide cues on the most suitable LKBs for computing word similarity, also a strong hint on the quality and coverage of these resources. Overall, this work involved different procedures for computing word similarity and several resources, namely: two different procedures applied to eight open Portuguese LKBs, plus two LKBs that combine the previous; three procedures applied to a fuzzy wordnet; one procedure based on the co-occurrence of words in articles of the Portuguese Wikipedia; and one procedure that computes similarity from three different models of word embeddings available for Portuguese.

The remainder of this paper starts with a brief overview on semantic similarity, variants, common approaches, and a focus on this topic for Portuguese. After this, the benchmarks used are presented and the tested approaches are described. Before concluding, the results obtained for each approach are reported and discussed. In general, the best results obtained are highly correlated with human judgements. Yet, depending on the nature of the dataset, both the best approach and underlying resource is different. For instance, when it comes to genuine similarity, exploiting LKBs outperformed similarity computed with trendy word embeddings.

2 Related Work

Semantic similarity measures the likeness of the meaning transmitted by two units, which can either be instances in an ontology or linguistic units, such as words or sentences. This involves comparing the features shared by each meaning, which sets their position in a taxonomy, and considers semantic relations such as synonymy, for identical meanings, or hypernymy, hyponymy and co-hyponymy, for meanings that share several features. Semantic relatedness goes beyond similarity and considers any other semantic relations that may connect meanings. For instance, the concepts of *dog* and *cat* are semantically similar, but they are not similar to *bone*. On the other hand, *dog* is more related to *bone* than *cat* is, because *dogs* like and are often seen with *bones*.

Word similarity tests are collections of word pairs with a similarity score based on human judgements. To answer such tests, humans would either look for the words in a dictionary or search for their occurrence in large corpora, possibly with the help of a search engine. This has a parallelism with the common approaches for determining word similarity automatically and unsupervisedly: (i) corpus-based approaches, also known as distributional, resort to a large corpus and analyse the distribution of words; (ii) knowledge-based approaches exploit the contents of a dictionary or lexical knowledge base (i.e. a machine-friendly representation of dictionary knowledge). It should be noted that the distinction of similarity and relatedness is not very clear for everyone. Therefore, whether the test scores reflect similarity or relatedness is also not always completely clear. Nevertheless, approaches for one are often applied to the other.

Corpus-based approaches rely on the distributional hypothesis – words that occur in similar contexts tend to have similar meanings [12] – and often represent words in a vector space model [28]. Recent work uses deep learning techniques to learn vectors from very large corpora, which are more accurate and computationally efficient at the same time. Sucessfull models of this kind include word2vec [17] and fastText [4].

The similarity of two words may also be computed from their probability of occurrence in a corpus. Pointwise Mutual Information (PMI) [27] quantifies the discrepancy between the probability of two words, a and b, co-occurring ($P(a, b)$), given their joint distribution and their individual distributions ($P(a)$ and $P(b)$), and assuming their independence. PMI can be computed according to Eq. 1, where probabilities can be obtained from the number of hits of the analysed words in a search engine.

$$PMI(a, b) = log \frac{P(a, b)}{P(a) * P(b)} = log \frac{Hits(a \cap b)}{Hits(a) * Hits(b)} \tag{1}$$

Knowledge-based approaches for computing word similarity exploit the contents of a dictionary [14] or lexical knowledge-base (LKB), often WordNet [5], a resource where synonyms are grouped together in synsets and semantic relations (e.g. hypernymy, part-of) are held between synsets.

Distributional word representations consider how language is used, while LKBs are more theoretical and often based on the work of lexicographers. In the former, several types of relation are present, but not explicit, while in LKBs semantic relations are explicit, but limited to a small set of types. For instance, despite the presence of a few other relations, WordNet is mainly focused on synonymy and hypernymy. This is why it is better-suited to measure similarity, but is outperformed by corpus-based approaches when it comes to measuring relatedness. Some authors have thus adopted hybrid approaches, where distributional and knowledge-based approaches are combined [1, 26].

State of the art results for well-known English similarity tests can be found in the ACL Wiki[1]. For Portuguese, however, research in the area is quite recent, because resources (e.g. LKBs and word vectors) and benchmarks, are only becoming available in recent years.

Related work for Portuguese has tackled mostly paraphrasing [2] or semantic textual similarity [21], which consists of computing the similarity of larger units of text. A shared task was recently organised on the latter [7]. In this case, supervised approaches typically perform better, by exploiting several features, including semantic features that might involve word similarity measures.

---

[1] https://www.aclweb.org/aclwiki/index.php?title=Similarity_(State_of_the_art).

When it comes to word similarity, Granada et al. [11] created a Portuguese test for this purpose, compared the judge agreement with other languages, and applied a distributional approach, based on Wikipedia, to answer it. Wilkens et al. [29] compiled the B²SG test and used it to assess distributional similarity measures. But B²SG is slightly different from the tests used in this work because, instead of a similarity score, a related word is to be selected from a group where it is shuffled with distractors.

3 Benchmarks

Four Portuguese word similarity tests were used as bechmarks. One is based on the RG-65 similarity test [23], which contains 65 pairs of nouns and their similarity of meaning, between 0 and 4, computed from 51 human judgements. RG-65 was translated to Portuguese by Granada et al. [11] and similarity was re-scored from the opinions of 50 native speakers of Portuguese. It was renamed to PT-65 and is freely available[2].

The other three tests – SimLex-999, WordSim-353 and RareWords – were also created originally for English, but recently translated to Portuguese, to be used in the assessment of the LX-DSemVectors [22] word embeddings. They are also available online[3].

SimLex-999 [13] contains 999 word pairs (666 noun-noun, 222 verb-verb, 111 adjective-adjective) and their similarity score, based on the opinion of approximately 50 judges. This is the only dataset where judges were specifically instructed to differentiate between similarity and relatedness and rate regarding the former only. Its authors thus claim that it targets genuine similarity[4].

WordSim-353 [6] contains 353 word pairs, their relatedness score from 0 to 10, based on the judgement of 13 to 16 human judges, and the name of the relation between them, though the later information was not used in this work. RareWords [15] contains 2,034 word pairs. The first words of each pair are rare, in the sense that they occur only 5,000 to 10,000 times in Wikipedia, while the second words are related to the first, according to WordNet.

Tables 1 and 2 illustrate the contents of the Portuguese SimLex-999 and WordSim-353, respectively. The other two tests have a similar format, but each line contains no additional columns besides the words and the score.

4 Approaches

Different unsupervised procedures were employed to answer the similarity tests, including some based on models of distributional similarity and others that exploit the structure of open Portuguese lexical knowledge bases (LKBs).

---

[2] http://www.inf.pucrs.br/linatural/wikimodels/similarity.html.

[3] http://metashare.metanet4u.eu/.

[4] RG-65 also targets similarity but, as far as we know, the process of differentiating similarity and relatedness was much more thorough in SimLex-999.

Table 1. First two adjectives, nouns and verbs of the Portuguese SimLex-999, with original English translation.

Word#1	Word#2	POS	Similarity
velho (old)	*novo* (new)	A	0.00
esperto (smart)	*inteligente* (intelligent)	A	8.33
esposa (wife)	*marido* (husband)	N	5.00
livro (book)	*texto* (text)	N	5.00
ir (go)	*vir* (come)	V	3.33
levar (take)	*roubar* (steal)	V	6.67

Table 2. First five lines of the Portuguese WordSim-353 test with original English translation. Identified relations are: topically related (t), first is hyponym of the second (h), identical tokens (i), second is part of the first (M).

Relation	Word#1	Word#2	Relatedness
t	*amor* (love)	*sexo* (sex)	6.77
h	*tigre* (tiger)	*gato* (cat)	7.35
i	*tigre* (tiger)	*tigre* (tiger)	10.00
t	*livro* (book)	*papel* (paper)	7.46
M	*computador* (computer)	*teclado* (keyboard)	7.62

4.1 Distributional Approaches

Two distinct models of distributional similarity were used, namely PMI, computed on the Portuguese Wikipedia, and distinct word embeddings learned from Portuguese corpora.

It was only recently that word embeddings trained in Portuguese corpora became available. Several models of this kind are available[5] as LX-DSemVectors [22]. Besides a vanilla model, trained with the default parameters, more than 30 additional models were trained with different parameters. In this work, two models trained in Wikipedia were used: the vanilla model (LX-vanilla) and model 17 (LX-p17), which has shown to be the most accurate [22].

We also used the fastText models [4] for Portuguese, available[6] and also trained in the Portuguese Wikipedia. The main difference of these models is that they are based on character n-grams, which can still be used to obtain word representations, from the sum of the vectors of their characters. This is especially relevant for morphologically rich languages.

As in other word-based vector space models, in a word embedding, computing the similarity of two words, a and b, is just a matter of computing the cosine of their vectors: $sim(a, b) = cos(\vec{a}, \vec{b})$.

---

[5] https://github.com/nlx-group/lx-dsemvectors/.

[6] https://github.com/facebookresearch/fastText/blob/master/pretrained-vectors.md.

4.2 Knowledge-Based Approaches

For comparison with the distributional similarity models, open Portuguese LKBs were also used to answer the word similarity tests. Those included:

- Two wordnets: OpenWordNet-PT (OWN.PT) [18] and PULO [25];
- Two synset-based thesauri: TeP [16] and OpenThesaurus.PT[7] (OT.PT);
- Three lexical-semantic networks extracted from Portuguese dictionaries: PAPEL [10] and relations from Dicionário Aberto [24] and Wiktionary.PT[8];
- The semantic relations available in Port4Nooj [3], a set of linguistic resources.

Although all the previous are theoretical models of Portuguese words and their meanings, they do not share exactly the same structure. Therefore, to enable comparison, they were all reduced to a network of relation instances of the kind "x related-to y", where x and y are lexical items (nodes) and related-to is a relation name (link). For synset-based LKBs, synsets had to be deconstructed. For example, the synset-based instance {cão, cachorro} memberOf {matilha} resulted in: (cão synonymOf cachorro), (cão memberOf matilha), (cachorro memberOf matilha). Adopted relation names were those defined in the project PAPEL [10], which covered the types in all the LKBs, though a few names were normalized.

Moreover, in order to analyse the benefits of combining the previous LKBs, they were combined in two additional LKBs: (i) one with the relation instances in all the LKBs (All-LKB); (ii) another with only the relation instances in at least two of them (Redun2).

Despite other advantages, such as explicitly-named semantic relations, the computation of a similarity score for two words, a and b, from a LKB, is not as straightforward as in a vector space, and requires an algorithm that exploits the network structure. In this work, two different algorithms were applied to compute $sim(a, b)$:

- Similarity of the adjacencies of each word in the target LKB, i.e. directly-connected words, computed with the Jaccard coefficient (Adj-Jac) and the cosine similarity (Adj-Cos);
- PageRank vectors, inspired by Pilehvar et al. [19]. For each word of a pair, Personalized PageRank is first run in the target LKB, for 30 iterations, using the word as context, and a vector is created with the resulting rank of each other word in the LKB. The similarity between the vectors of the two words is computed with the Jaccard coefficient between the sets of words in these vectors (PR-Jac) and with the cosine of the vectors (PR-CosV). Due to their large sizes, vectors were trimmed to the top$-N$ ranked words. Different sizes N were tested, from 50, to 3200.

In addition, the previous methods were tested using all the relations of each LKB, or only synonymy and hypernymy relations. Table 3 presents the LKBs used and their sizes, in terms of distinct words and relation instances. It is clear

---

[7] http://paginas.fe.up.pt/~arocha/AED1/0607/trabalhos/thesaurus.txt.
[8] http://pt.wiktionary.org (2015 dump).

Table 3. Size of the LKBs used in terms of words and relation instances.

LKB	#Words	#Instances
OWN-PT	40,940	151,731
PULO	7,943	44,198
TeP	40,499	480,932
OT	12,782	51,410
PAPEL	94,165	191,497
DA	95,188	139,404
Wikt.PT	45,345	80,071
Port4Nooj	12,641	20,340
Redun2	56,565	145,429
All-LKB	178,903	791,182

that there are LKBs with significantly different sizes. A deeper analysis into the content and redundancy of these LKBs, and on the creation redundancy-based LKBs, is found elsewhere [9].

An alternative model of LKB was also used. CONTO.PT [8] is a fuzzy wordnet, freely available[9], and which also happens to combine all of the previous LKBs. The main difference between CONTO.PT and a common wordnet is that there are confidence values assigned to the decisions taken during its automatic creation: words have fuzzy memberships to synsets (μ) and relations between synsets also have a confidence value (ν). The version of CONTO.PT used here contains 107,482 words (less than the All-LKB) and 140,195 fuzzy word senses, organised in 32,684 fuzzy synsets, connected in a network of 24,229 fuzzy relations.

To compute $sim(a,b)$ from CONTO.PT, three approaches were tested:

- Memberships (μ): if there is a synset S with both a and b, $sim(a,b) = \mu_S(a) + \mu_S(b)$; if there are two synsets S_a and S_b, such that $a \in S_a \wedge b \in S_b$, and a relation instance R, such that $R = (S_a$ related-to $S_b)$, $sim(a,b) = \mu_{S_a}(a) * \mu_{S_b}(b) * \nu(R)$; otherwise, $sim(a,b) = 0$;
- Weighted adjacencies intersection: each word is represented by a vector, $\vec{a}$ and $\vec{b}$, where its adjacencies are weighted based on the memberships to the same synsets and confidence of direct connections. After this, $sim(a,b) = cos(\vec{a},\vec{b})$.
- Adjacencies intersection: similar to the previous, but $\vec{a}$ and $\vec{b}$ are binary vectors, with 1, if the words are adjacent (no matter their weight) or 0, if they are not.

5   Results

The described approaches were adopted to answer the four similarity tests automatically. As usual in this kind of tests, the performance of each approach was

[9] http://ontopt.dei.uc.pt/.

Table 4. Results overview for the PT-65 test.

Resource	Relations	Algorithm	ρ
All-LKB	All	Adj-Cos	0.84
All-LKB	All	PR-CosV$_{1600}$	0.83
All-LKB	All	PR-CosV$_{800}$	0.83
All-LKB	Syn+Hyp	Adj-Cos	0.82
All-LKB	All	PR-CosV$_{3200}$	0.82
Redun2	All	Adj-Cos	0.77
CONTO.PT	All	μ	0.76
fastText	–	–	0.75
OWN-PT	Syn+Hyp	Adj-Cos	0.69
PAPEL	All	Adj-Cos	0.67
LX-p17	–	–	0.66
PMI	–	–	0.66
DA	All	Adj-Cos	0.64
TeP	All	Adj-Cos	0.63
LX-vanilla	–	–	0.57
Wikc.PT	Syn+Hyp	Adj-Jac	0.57
PULO	Syn+Hyp	Adj-Cos	0.52
OT	All	Adj-Int	0.42
Port4Nooj	Syn+Hyp	Adj-Cos	0.39

Table 5. Results overview for the SimLex-999 test.

Resource	Relations	Algorithm	ρ
All-LKB	Syn+Hyp	PR-CosV$_{400}$	0.60
All-LKB	Syn+Hyp	PR-CosV$_{50}$	0.56
All-LKB	Syn+Hyp	PR-CosV$_{100}$	0.58
All-LKB	Syn+Hyp	PR-CosV$_{200}$	0.59
All-LKB	Syn+Hyp	PR-CosV$_{800}$	0.59
All-LKB	Syn+Hyp	Adj-Cos	0.57
PAPEL	All	PR-Jac$_{800}$	0.49
Redun2	Syn+Hyp	PR-Jac$_{50}$	0.48
CONTO.PT	Syn+Hyp	μ	0.45
OWN-PT	Syn+Hyp	Adj-Cos	0.44
Wikt.PT	All	PR-Jac$_{1600}$	0.42
DA	All	PR-Jac$_{400}$	0.38
TeP	Syn+Hyp	Adj-Jac	0.36
OT.PT	Syn+Hyp	Adj-Cos	0.34
fastText	–	–	0.34
LX-p17	–	–	0.33
PULO	Syn+Hyp	Adj-Cos	0.29
LX-vanilla	–	–	0.23
PMI	–	–	0.22
Port4Nooj	All	Adj-Jac	0.19

assessed with the Spearman correlation (ρ) between the automatically-computed similarities and the gold ones in the test.

Tables 4, 5, 6 and 7 show the results obtained, respectively for PT-65, Simlex-999, WordSim-353 and RareWords. For each test, we present the top 5 results and the best results for each other resource not in the top 5. Besides the identification of each LKB and the resulting ρ, the relation set and the algorithm are also revealed for each result.

5.1 Best Results

We note that the best results are always obtained by different approaches. The only resource with the best results for two tests is the All-LKB, in PT-65 and SimLex-999, though with different algorithms and relation sets. This confirms the benefits of combining different LKBs, which end up complementing each other. In fact, LKBs had to be combined to outperform the fastText embeddings in the PT-65 test. None of the individual LKBs were enough for it, and only two, OWN-PT and PAPEL, outperformed the LX-p17 embeddings and PMI. Another conclusion taken from the PT-65 results is that better results are obtained with larger LKBs, which suggest that their size matters.

For SimLex-999, the best results used only synonymy and hypernymy relations, while for PT-65 all relations were used. In these tests, the distributional

Table 6. Results overview for the WordSim-353 test.

Resource	Relations	Algorithm	ρ
PMI	–	–	0.49
LX-p17	–	–	0.48
fastText	–	–	0.43
All-LKB	All	Adj-Cos	0.38
All-LKB	All	PR-CosV$_{200}$	0.38
OWN-PT	All	Adj-Cos	0.37
LX-vanilla	–	–	0.36
PAPEL	Syn+Hyp	Adj-Cos	0.29
Redun2	All	Adj-Cos	0.29
Port4Nooj	Syn+Hyp	Adj-Cos	0.28
DA	All	Adj-Jac	0.27
Wikt.PT	All	Adj-Jac	0.27
CONTO.PT	All	μ	0.23
PULO	All	Adj-Cos	0.22
TeP	All	Adj-Jac	0.16
OT.PT	All	Adj-Cos	0.15

Table 7. Results overview for the RareWords test.

Resource	Relations	Algorithm	ρ
CONTO.PT	All	μ	0.38
TeP	All	Adj-Cos	0.38
TeP	All	Adj-Jac	0.38
All-LKB	All	Adj-Jac	0.38
CONTO.PT	Syn+Hyp	μ	0.38
LX-p17	–	–	0.35
fastText	–	–	0.34
PAPEL	All	Adj-Jac	0.33
Redun2	All	Adj-Cos	0.32
Wikt.PT	All	Adj-Jac	0.29
PMI	–	–	0.29
OT.PT	All	Adj-Cos	0.27
OT.PT	All	Adj-Jac	0.27
DA	Syn-Hyp	Adj-Jac	0.28
LX-vanilla	–	–	0.27
OWN-PT	All	Adj-Jac	0.26
PULO	All	Adj-Jac	0.13
Port4Nooj	Syn+Hyp	Adj-Cos	0.07

approaches were behind the majority of the knowledge-based approaches. We recall that SimLex-999 is the only test that targets genuine similarity because judges were explicitly instructed to score this feature and not relatedness, while in PT-65 and RareWords there could still be some confusion on these concepts. We recall that similarity is mainly represented through synonymy and hypernymy relations, while relatedness involves virtually any kind of semantic relation. Therefore, distributional models are better-suited to capture relatedness rather than similarity (e.g. see Sect. 5.3).

This is confirmed by the best performances in WordSim-353, focused on relatedness, where the three best results are obtained by three distributional approaches, in the following order: PMI, LX-p17 and fastText. The best LKB was, once again, the All-LKB, with a significantly lower ρ, but comparable to LX-vanilla, which we recall to have been trained with the default parameters, and has a lower accuracy than the other distributional models.

Finally, the best results for the RareWords test were obtained with CONTO.PT, the fuzzy wordnet, using all relations, though with no significant differences to TeP and to the All-LKB. LX-p17 and fastText were only a few points below. This makes some sense for a dataset of not so frequent words, which were probably left out from smaller resources, but are covered by the larger ones, namely CONTO.PT, All-LKB and TeP.

5.2 Comparing LKBs

As mentioned earlier, combining all the LKBs in a single one leads to the best results. Looking at individual LKBs, PAPEL and OWN-PT performed generally well, except for the RareWords test, where the latter got one of the lowest performances. This can be due to a lower coverage of words by OWN-PT. On the other hand, TeP matched the best performance in RareWords. Again, although TeP only covers synonymy and antonymy, its huge number of relation instances has played an important role.

A remark should be given on the presented results, which are not only influenced by the contents and structure of the LKBs, but also by the applied algorithms. Therefore, although they provide useful hints, our results are only valid for the tested algorithms, and better results could possibly be obtained by alternative ways of exploiting the LKBs.

5.3 Comparison with State-of-the-art

To the best of our knowledge, there are not published results for the Portuguese versions of SimLex-999, WordSim-353 nor RareWords, because they were only translated recently. On the other hand, our results for PT-65 clearly outperform experimental results by Granada et al. [11], who used a LSA distributional model based on the Portuguese Wikipedia and achieved $\rho = 0.53$.

State-of-the-art results for the English versions of RG-65, SimLex-999 and WordSim-353 can be found in the ACL Wiki. Although with different distances, all our results are below the best results for English, all quite recent. For RG-65 ($\rho = 0.920$), the best results were obtained with a knowledge-based approach [19] that exploits Wiktionary [20]. The best results for WordSim-353 ($\rho = 0.828$) were obtained with hybrid approaches, including one that exploited the ConceptNet knowledge graph and two distributional models (word2vec and GloVe) [26]. The best results for SimLex-999 ($\rho = 0.642$, not far from our 0.60) were obtained by combining distributional knowledge with WordNet [1]. Although not in the ACL Wiki, a $\rho = 0.46$ was recently reported for the English RareWords test, using the fastText embeddings [4]. As in our experiments, this is also the test with lower state-of-the-art results.

6 Discussion

Several approaches for computing word similarity in Portuguese, using different available resources, were presented. Results, assessed through word similarity tests that recently became available for Portuguese, confirm that there are several valid approaches for this purpose, but the best depends on the nature of the test. An important conclusion is that, in their current state, Portuguese word embeddings are not the best for every similarity test. In fact, when it comes to genuine similarity, not relatedness, they are clearly outperformed by LKBs.

We believe that the presented results can be seen as a reference for future work on the development of new word models, LKBs, or algorithms for computing semantic similarity in Portuguese. In our case, some experiments were left undone, such as exploiting the wordnet structure of OWN-PT and PULO and applying a similar procedure as those applied to CONTO.PT, though always considering a membership of 1. Furthermore, although the combination of different LKBs was tested, the combination of one or more LKBs with the word embeddings was not. In the future, we will consider adapting state-of-the-art approaches of this kind to the Portuguese resources.

Finally, there are other tasks, not explored here but with available tests, where word embeddings have shown to be accurate, such as finding analogies through simple algebraic operations. To the best of our knowledge, this task has not been explored with the Portuguese LKBs, and we are unsure on the possible results. But it would possibly require to identify analogous nodes in the network of relations, which can easily become a complex task.

References

1. Banjade, R., Maharjan, N., Niraula, N.B., Rus, V., Gautam, D.: Lemon and tea are not similar: measuring word-to-word similarity by combining different methods. In: Gelbukh, A. (ed.) CICLing 2015. LNCS, vol. 9041, pp. 335–346. Springer, Cham (2015). doi:10.1007/978-3-319-18111-0_25
2. Barreiro, A.: ParaMT: a paraphraser for machine translation. In: Teixeira, A., Lima, V.L.S., Oliveira, L.C., Quaresma, P. (eds.) PROPOR 2008. LNCS, vol. 5190, pp. 202–211. Springer, Heidelberg (2008). doi:10.1007/978-3-540-85980-2_21
3. Barreiro, A.: Port4NooJ: an open source, ontology-driven Portuguese linguistic system with applications in machine translation. In: Proceedings of the 2008 International NooJ Conference (NooJ 2008). Newcastle-upon-Tyne: Cambridge Scholars Publishing, Budapest, Hungary (2010)
4. Bojanowski, P., Grave, E., Joulin, A., Mikolov, T.: Enriching word vectors with subword information. arXiv preprint arXiv:1607.04606 (2016)
5. Budanitsky, A., Hirst, G.: Evaluating wordnet-based measures of lexical semantic relatedness. Comput. Linguist. **32**(1), 13–47 (2006)
6. Finkelstein, L., Gabrilovich, E., Matias, Y., Rivlin, E., Solan, Z., Wolfman, G., Ruppin, E.: Placing search in context: the concept revisited. ACM Trans. Inf. Syst. **20**(1), 116–131 (2002)
7. Fonseca, E.R., dos Santos, L.B., Criscuolo, M., Aluísio, S.M.: Visão geral da avaliação de similaridade semântica e inferência textual. Linguamática **8**(2), 3–13 (2016)
8. Gonçalo Oliveira, H.: CONTO.PT: groundwork for the automatic creation of a fuzzy Portuguese wordnet. In: Silva, J., Ribeiro, R., Quaresma, P., Adami, A., Branco, A. (eds.) PROPOR 2016. LNCS, vol. 9727, pp. 283–295. Springer, Cham (2016). doi:10.1007/978-3-319-41552-9_29
9. Gonçalo Oliveira, H.: Comparing and combining Portuguese lexical-semantic knowledge bases. In: Proceedings of the 6th Symposium on Languages, Applications and Technologies (SLATE 2017), pp. 16:1–16:14. OASICS, Schloss Dagstuhl - Leibniz-Zentrum fuer Informatik (2017)

10. Gonçalo Oliveira, H., Santos, D., Gomes, P., Seco, N.: PAPEL: a dictionary-based lexical ontology for Portuguese. In: Teixeira, A., Lima, V.L.S., Oliveira, L.C., Quaresma, P. (eds.) PROPOR 2008. LNCS, vol. 5190, pp. 31–40. Springer, Heidelberg (2008). doi:10.1007/978-3-540-85980-2_4
11. Granada, R., Trojahn, C., Vieira, R.: Comparing semantic relatedness between word pairs in Portuguese using wikipedia. In: Baptista, J., Mamede, N., Candeias, S., Paraboni, I., Pardo, T.A.S., Volpe Nunes, M.G. (eds.) PROPOR 2014. LNCS, vol. 8775, pp. 170–175. Springer, Cham (2014). doi:10.1007/978-3-319-09761-9_17
12. Harris, Z.: Distributional structure. Word **10**(2–3), 146–162 (1954)
13. Hill, F., Reichart, R., Korhonen, A.: Simlex-999: evaluating semantic models with genuine similarity estimation. Comput. Linguist. **41**(4), 665–695 (2015)
14. Lesk, M.: Automatic sense disambiguation using machine readable dictionaries: how to tell a pine cone from an ice cream cone. In: Proceedings of the 5th Annual International Conference on Systems Documentation (SIGDOC 1986), NY, USA, pp. 24–26 (1986)
15. Luong, T., Socher, R., Manning, C.: Better word representations with recursive neural networks for morphology. In: Proceedings of the Seventeenth Conference on Computational Natural Language Learning, pp. 104–113. ACL Press, Sofia, Bulgaria, August 2013
16. Maziero, E.G., Pardo, T.A.S., Felippo, A.D., Dias-da-Silva, B.C.: A Base de Dados Lexical e a Interface Web do TeP 2.0 - Thesaurus Eletrônico para o Português do Brasil. In: VI Workshop em Tecnologia da Informação e Linguagem Humana, pp. 390–392. TIL (2008)
17. Mikolov, T., Chen, K., Corrado, G., Dean, J.: Efficient estimation of word representations in vector space. In: Proceedings of the Workshop Track of the International Conference on Learning Representations (ICLR), Scottsdale, Arizona (2013)
18. de Paiva, V., Rademaker, A., de Melo, G.: OpenWordNet-PT: an open brazilian wordnet for reasoning. In: Proceedings of 24th International Conference on Computational Linguistics. COLING (Demo Paper) (2012)
19. Pilehvar, M.T., Jurgens, D., Navigli, R.: Align, disambiguate and walk: a unified approach for measuring semantic similarity. In: Proceedings of the 51st Annual Meeting of the Association for Computational Linguistics, ACL 2013, Sofia, Bulgaria, vol. 1: Long Papers, pp. 1341–1351. ACL Press (2013)
20. Pilehvar, M.T., Navigli, R.: From senses to texts: an all-in-one graph-based approach for measuring semantic similarity. Artif. Intell. **228**, 95–128 (2015)
21. Pinheiro, V., Furtado, V., Albuquerque, A.: Semantic textual similarity of Portuguese-language texts: an approach based on the semantic inferentialism model. In: Baptista, J., Mamede, N., Candeias, S., Paraboni, I., Pardo, T.A.S., Volpe Nunes, M.G. (eds.) PROPOR 2014. LNCS, vol. 8775, pp. 183–188. Springer, Cham (2014). doi:10.1007/978-3-319-09761-9_19
22. Rodrigues, J., Branco, A., Neale, S., Silva, J.: LX-DSemVectors: distributional semantics models for Portuguese. In: Silva, J., Ribeiro, R., Quaresma, P., Adami, A., Branco, A. (eds.) PROPOR 2016. LNCS, vol. 9727, pp. 259–270. Springer, Cham (2016). doi:10.1007/978-3-319-41552-9_27
23. Rubenstein, H., Goodenough, J.B.: Contextual correlates of synonymy. Commun. ACM **8**(10), 627–633 (1965)
24. Simões, A., Sanromán, Á.I., Almeida, J.J.: Dicionário-Aberto: a source of resources for the Portuguese language processing. In: Caseli, H., Villavicencio, A., Teixeira, A., Perdigão, F. (eds.) PROPOR 2012. LNCS, vol. 7243, pp. 121–127. Springer, Heidelberg (2012). doi:10.1007/978-3-642-28885-2_14

25. Simões, A., Guinovart, X.G.: Bootstrapping a Portuguese wordnet from galician, spanish and english wordnets. In: Navarro Mesa, J.L., Ortega, A., Teixeira, A., Hernández Pérez, E., Quintana Morales, P., Ravelo García, A., Guerra Moreno, I., Toledano, D.T. (eds.) IberSPEECH 2014. LNCS, vol. 8854, pp. 239–248. Springer, Cham (2014). doi:10.1007/978-3-319-13623-3_25
26. Speer, R., Chin, J., Havasi, C.: Conceptnet 5.5: an open multilingual graph of general knowledge. In: Proceedings of 31st AAAI Conference on Artificial Intelligence, San Francisco, California, USA, pp. 4444–4451 (2017)
27. Turney, P.D.: Mining the web for synonyms: PMI-IR versus LSA on TOEFL. In: Raedt, L., Flach, P. (eds.) ECML 2001. LNCS, vol. 2167, pp. 491–502. Springer, Heidelberg (2001). doi:10.1007/3-540-44795-4_42
28. Turney, P.D., Pantel, P.: From frequency to meaning: vector space models of semantics. J. Artif. Intell. Res. **37**(1), 141–188 (2010)
29. Wilkens, R., Zilio, L., Ferreira, E., Villavicencio, A.: B^{2}SG: a TOEFL-like task for Portuguese. In: Proceedings of 10th International Conference on Language Resources and Evaluation. LREC, ELRA (2016)

Gradually Improving the Computation of Semantic Textual Similarity in Portuguese

Hugo Gonçalo Oliveira[1]([⊠]), Ana Oliveira Alves[1,2]([⊠]), and Ricardo Rodrigues[1,3]

[1] CISUC, DEI, University of Coimbra, Coimbra, Portugal
{hroliv,ana,rmanuel}@dei.uc.pt
[2] ISEC, Polytechnic Institute of Coimbra, Coimbra, Portugal
[3] ESEC, Polytechnic Institute of Coimbra, Coimbra, Portugal

Abstract. There is much research on Semantic Textual Similarity (STS) in English, specially since its inclusion in the SemEval evaluations. For other languages, it is not as common, mostly due to the unavailability of benchmarks. Recently, the ASSIN shared task targeted STS in Portuguese and released training and test collections. This paper describes an incremental approach to ASSIN, where the computed similarity is gradually improved by exploiting different features (e.g., token overlap, semantic relations, chunks, and negation) and approaches. The best reported results, obtained with a supervised approach, would get second place overall in ASSIN.

Keywords: Natural language processing · Semantic Textual Similarity · Semantic relations · Supervised machine learning

1 Introduction

Computing the similarity of words or sentences in terms of their meaning is an active area of research in natural language processing (NLP) and understanding. This is confirmed by the shared tasks organised on STS, such as SemEval STS [1,2], which required the manual compilation of annotated data for benchmarking this specific task. Briefly, STS aims at computing a score for the semantic similarity between two sentences. Most successful approaches for English learn a similarity function that combines different metrics, such as word or chunk overlap, semantic relations, or distributional similarity.

Since their beginning, STS tasks have targeted English and had an increasing number of participants. For instance, the 2016 edition had more than 100 runs submitted by a total of 43 teams. We can therefore say that, for English, STS is becoming a mature task. On the other hand, excluding Spanish, included in recent editions of SemEval, this task is in its earliest days for other languages, including Portuguese. In fact, until recently, there was not a public dataset for computing semantic similarity between Portuguese sentences. Last year, this started to change, after the ASSIN shared evaluation [3] and the release of a dataset of STS in Portuguese.

© Springer International Publishing AG 2017
E. Oliveira et al. (Eds.): EPIA 2017, LNAI 10423, pp. 841–854, 2017.
DOI: 10.1007/978-3-319-65340-2_68

This paper presents a post-evaluation approach to ASSIN and the gradual improvement of the results as features and techniques are added. Most features are inspired by related work for English, but adapted for Portuguese. More than describing a winning approach, which it is not, we detail every single step towards improving the baselines that rely exclusively on the surface text.

The remainder of this paper starts with a brief overview of related work, with the best results of English STS together with commonly used features. We address this task for Portuguese, focusing on ASSIN, its collections and best approaches. The pre-processing tools used here are then described, and results based on set similarity measures presented. After this, information in Portuguese LKBs is considered to compute similarity without supervision. Before concluding, the best supervised measures are combined with lexical and syntactic features to learn a similarity function, this time with supervision, with different regression algorithms and training datasets. Though some features were left unexplored, the final results are very close to the best position overall in ASSIN.

2   Related Work

The SemEval shared evaluations include STS tasks since 2012 [1,2]. Results are typically assessed by the correlation (e.g., Pearson, hereafter ρ, between -1 and 1—the higher, the better) and the Mean Squared Error (MSE—the lower, the better) between the values computed by the system and those given by several human judges, for the same collection of pairs.

Most successful approaches are supervised. To learn a similarity function, they combine different features, some of which as basic as token or n-gram overlap, but also similarity measures computed in WordNet [4] or other semantic networks, topic models, or distributional similarity models. In recent editions, deep semantic models have been successfully used, including by the best systems in SemEval 2016 [5,6]. Best ρ has ranged from 0.618, in SemEval 2013, to 0.824, in SemEval 2012. For the adopted baseline—the cosine of the vectors that represent the words in each sentence of the pair—this number has ranged from 0.311, in 2012, to 0.587, in 2015. For Spanish STS, the best system [7] in SemEval 2015 achieved $\rho = 0.69$, also with an approach that combined string similarity, semantic similarity and alignment features.

Another related task, in SemEval 2014, was the *Evaluation of Compositional Distributional Semantic Models on Full Sentences through Semantic Relatedness* [8]. The main difference is that it evaluates compositionality. It is thus more focused on issues like lexical variation, syntactic alternations, negation, and does not require dealing with multiword expressions or accessing world knowledge, including named entities. Yet, the system with the best results [9] tackled it as STS and achieved $\rho = 0.827$ and $MSE = 0.325$. Another system that participated in both the previous tasks, though with less success, was ASAP [10,11].

An earlier approach to STS in Portuguese [12] exploited a knowledge base to identify related words in different sentences. The proposed measure was tested in natural language descriptions of bugs in software engineering projects, which had their similarity annotated by two human judges. But it was not until 2015 that Portuguese NLP researchers could tackle STS and compare it with other approaches, using common benchmarks. The ASSIN shared task [3] targeted precisely Semantic Similarity and Textual Entailment in Portuguese. Announced in late 2015, the evaluation took 6 days, starting on 27 February 2016. Training data comprised 3,000 sentence pairs for Brazilian Portuguese (PT-BR) and another 3,000 for European Portuguese (PT-PT). Test data comprised 2,000 PT-BR pairs and 2,000 PT-PT pairs. Both collections are available in XML, together with the evaluation tools[1]. While recent editions of English STS have used text from varied sources, including news, glosses, forum posts, forum answers or image descriptions, sentences in the ASSIN collections were obtained exclusively from Google News. Table 1 shows three pairs in the ASSIN training collections, including their ids, their two sentences (t, for text, and h, for hypothesis), and the average similarity given by four human judges that followed the same guidelines. Similarity values range from 1 (completely different sentences, on different subjects) to 5 (sentences mean essentially the same).

Table 1. Examples from the training collections.

Collection	Id	Pair	Sim
PT-PT	2675	**t:** *O Chelsea só conseguiu reagir no final da primeira parte.*	1.25
		h: *Não podemos aceitar outra primeira parte como essa.*	
PT-PT	315	**t:** *Todos que ficaram feridos e os mortos foram levados ao hospital.*	3.0
		h: *Além disso, mais de 180 pessoas ficaram feridas.*	
PT-BR	1282	**t:** *As multas previstas nos contratos podem atingir, juntas, 23 milhões de reais.*	5.0
		h: *Somadas, as multas previstas nos contratos podem chegar a R$ 23 milhões.*	

ASSIN had 6 participating teams, which submitted 14 runs for the similarity task in PT-BR and 17 in PT-PT. The best official runs were obtained by different systems for PT-PT and PT-BR. For PT-BR, the best run [13] achieved $\rho = 0.70$ with $MSE = 0.38$, obtained by computing the cosine similarity of a vector representation of each sentence, based on the sum of the TF-IDF scores and word2vec [14] vectors of each word. For PT-PT, the best run [15] achieved $\rho = 0.73$ with $MSE = 0.61$, obtained after learning a similarity function with a Kernel Ridge Regression that used several similarity metrics as input, computed between the two sentences of each pair, including overlap and set similarity measures on multiple text representations (lowercase, character trigrams,...). An adaptation to Portuguese of ASAP, dubbed ASAPP [16], also participated

---

[1] http://nilc.icmc.usp.br/assin/.

in ASSIN, with best runs achieving $\rho = 0.65$ and $MSE = 0.44$, for PT-BRE, and $\rho = 0.68$ and $MSE = 0.70$ for PT-PT. This work revisits ASAPP.

3 Sentences Pre-processing

Our approach for computing the similarity of the pairs in the ASSIN collections starts with a pre-processing step, where sentences are split by tokens, part-of-speech (POS) tagged and lemmatized. Tokenization and POS tagging were performed by a set of tools based on the Apache OpenNLP Toolkit[2], targeting Portuguese. Besides basic tokenization operations, the tokenizer separates contractions, handles clitics and normalizes some abbreviations. Identified tokens are used by the basic OpenNLP Portuguese POS tagger, trained with a Maximum Entropy model. The lemmatizer converts words to their dictionary form, considering the output of the POS tagger, a morphology lexicon and a set of handcrafted rules [17]. Chunks and named entities were also identified with OpenNLP-based tools. These tools are freely available[3].

Alternatively to lemmatization, tokens can be stemmed with the PTStemmer tool, also freely available[4]. The main difference is that a lemma is still a word, though in the masculine singular form, if a noun or an adjective (e.g., *jogo* for *jogos*), or in the infinitive, if a verb (e.g., *jogar* for *joga* or *jogaram*), while stems are just the roots of the words (e.g., *jog* for *jogos*, *joga* and *jogaram*).

4 Sentence Similarity as Set Similarity

After pre-processing, simple computations were performed for each pair. Each sentence was considered as a set of words—T and H—and their overlap was computed with measures typically used for set similarity, including Jaccard, Overlap and Dice, respectively in Eqs. 1, 2, and 3. The cosine of the word vectors built from the words in the sentences was also computed as a set similarity measure (see Eq. 4).

$$Jacc(T,H) = \frac{|T \cap H|}{|T \cup H|} \qquad (1) \qquad Dice(T,H) = \frac{|T \cap H|}{|T| + |H|} \qquad (3)$$

$$Ovl(T,H) = \frac{|T \cap H|}{|min(T,H)|} \qquad (2) \qquad Cos(T,H) = \frac{|T \cap H|}{\sqrt{|T|}\sqrt{|H|}} \qquad (4)$$

In order to select basic parameters and set our baselines, the previous measures were computed for each pair of sentences and combinations of the following:

- Normalization: tokens could be matched exactly as they occur, after lemmatization, or after stemming;

---

[2] http://opennlp.apache.org/.
[3] NLP tools available from https://github.com/rikarudo/.
[4] PTStemmer is available from https://code.google.com/archive/p/ptstemmer/.

Table 2. Set similarity results for PT-PT.

Closed	Lem	POS	Sim	ρ	MSE
×	×	×	Cos	0.622	0.850
✓	×	×	Ovl	0.640	0.529
✓	×	×	Cos	0.664	0.552
×	✓	×	Ovl	0.618	0.550
×	✓	×	Dice	0.653	0.621
✓	✓	×	Cos	**0.698**	**0.446**
×	×	✓	Ovl	0.577	0.775
×	×	✓	Cos	0.605	0.918
✓	×	✓	Ovl	0.624	0.564
✓	×	✓	Cos	0.649	0.618
×	✓	✓	Ovl	0.599	0.601
×	✓	✓	Cos	0.632	0.675
✓	✓	✓	Ovl	0.642	0.484
✓	✓	✓	Cos	0.675	0.544
✓	stems		Jacc	0.700	1.140
✓	stems		Dice	0.703	0.458
✓	stems		Cos	**0.706**	**0.443**

Table 3. Set similarity results for PT-BR.

Closed	Lem	POS	Sim	ρ	MSE
×	×	×	Cos	0.539	0.718
✓	×	×	Ovl	0.574	0.583
✓	×	×	Cos	0.587	0.591
×	✓	×	Cos	0.560	0.598
✓	✓	×	Jacc	**0.610**	0.921
✓	✓	×	Cos	**0.610**	**0.484**
×	×	✓	Jacc	0.521	1.357
×	×	✓	Cos	0.519	0.784
✓	×	✓	Jacc	0.571	1.049
✓	×	✓	Ovl	0.557	0.545
×	✓	✓	Dice	0.538	0.648
✓	✓	✓	Cos	0.585	0.523
✓	stems		Jacc	0.625	0.853
✓	stems		Dice	0.609	0.489
✓	stems		Cos	**0.626**	**0.467**

- All tokens (except punctuation signs) could be considered, or only open-class words (nouns, verbs, adjectives and adverbs);
- A match could require just the same token/lemma or also the same POS.

As all the measures used output values between 0 (sets have no common elements) to 1 (sets have exactly the same elements), they were normalized to the 1–5 interval, as in the ASSIN collection. Tables 2 and 3 show a selection of results of set similarity and different configurations in the training collections. For each combination of parameters, we show the best correlation ρ and MSE.

These experiments lead to relevant conclusions. First, they are higher than all the baselines considered in editions of the SemEval English STS, which suggests that this exercise might be easier. Better results are obtained when using all tokens and not only open-class words, even better when tokens are normalized. However, matching also the POS leads to worse results. This can be caused by noise in the POS tagger or because lemmatization differentiates the base form of words depending on their category (e.g., noun, verb, and adjective). Best results were obtained with stems instead of lemmas, *grouping* words of the same family, regardless of their POS. The best configuration for both training collections used the Cosine of the stem vectors of all words and reached $\rho = 0.706$ and $MSE = 0.443$ for PT-PT, and 0.626 and 0.467 for PT-BR. With lemmas,

Cosine was also the best measure, but with lower ρ and MSE, respectively 0.698 and 0.446 for PT-PT and 0.610 and 0.484 for PT-BR.

5 Exploiting Known Semantic Relations

Language is flexible in such a way that the same idea can be transmitted through different words, generally related by well-known semantic relations. For instance, synonyms may be used to denote the same meaning (e.g., *big* and *large*) and hypernyms are generalisations of their hyponyms (e.g., *animal* and *dog*). Those relations are implicitly mentioned in dictionaries, and explicitly encoded in LKBs, such as WordNet [4].

5.1 Portuguese Lexical Knowledge Bases

As it seemed natural to explore semantic relations when computing semantic similarity, we decided to use a LKB for Portuguese. After analysing the land-scape of alternatives, we extracted semantic relation instances of different types, represented as "*a* related-to *b*" from 9 LKBs, namely: WordNet.Br [18] (just verbs), OpenWordNet-PT (OWN.PT) [19] and PULO [20]—three wordnets; TeP [21] and OpenThesaurus.PT[5]—two synonymy-based thesauri; PAPEL [22] and relations from Dicionário Aberto [23] and Wiktionary.PT[6]—three lexical networks extracted from Portuguese dictionaries; and the semantic relations of Port4Nooj [24]—a set of linguistic resources.

The aforementioned LKBs have substantially different sizes and the creation of most involved some degree of automation, which means that they contain noise, including rarely used words and meanings, not so useful relations, and also actual errors. Therefore, we decided to rely on redundancy to build more reliable and useful semantic networks, namely *Redun2* and *Redun3*, which include all the the relation instances respectively in at least two or three of the exploited LKBs. Table 4 shows the number of distinct relation instances in all the LKBs (≥ 1) and the types with more instances, side-by-side with the same number for *Redun2* (≥ 2) and *Redun3* (≥ 3), and two examples for each relation type. A comparison of the LKBs and the creation of the redundancy-based LKBs is described in detail elsewhere [25].

5.2 Combining Semantic Relations and Sentence Overlap

In order to consider semantic relations, set similarity was first computed and then adjusted, considering the semantic network distances of the lemmas of the non-overlapping tokens (T' and H'). The later was computed according to Eq. 5—for each lemma in $T'_i \in T'$ we used the maximum similarity with a lemma $H'_j \in H'$— and summed in a factor γ (Eq. 6). The set similarity measure was adjusted by

---

[5] http://paginas.fe.up.pt/~arocha/AED1/0607/trabalhos/thesaurus.txt.
[6] http://pt.wiktionary.org.

Table 4. Relations of the semantic networks and their redundancy.

Relation	≥1	≥2	≥3	Examples
Synonymy	327,316	94,525	29,750	(realçar, sublinhar), (afronta, ofensa)
Hypernymy	277,764	29,879	4,639	(mover, tremer), (campo, prado)
Causation	15,373	4,705	1,590	(frio, crestar), (distinção, preferência)
Property-of	52,365	6,934	877	(oral, boca), (defeituoso, ter_defeito)
Antonymy	50,171	1,727	470	(tristeza, alegria), (próximo, distante)
Part-of	24,656	2,036	153	(núcleo, átomo), (mês, ano)
Purpose-of	17,348	1,410	134	(polir, lixa), (traçar, compasso)
Other	29,590	3,130	298	–
Total	794,583	144,346	37,983	

adding γ to the numerator, which, for all measures used, was the intersection of the tokens/lemmas/stems. Equation 7 shows how Jaccard becomes Jaccard$^+$. The other measures were analogously adapted. Considering that the maximum similarity (1, before normalization) is achieved when the tokens/lemmas/stems are the same, for each lemma in T', similarity had to be lower than 1, therefore $0 \leq \gamma \leq |T'|$. After several experiments in the training collections, we empirically set the values of the similarity equation to $\alpha = 0.75$ and $\beta = 0.05$.

$$Sim(T'_i, H'_j) = \begin{cases} \alpha, & \text{if } distance(T'_i, H'_j) = 1 \\ \beta, & \text{if } distance(T'_i, H'_j) = 2 \\ 0, & \text{otherwise} \end{cases} \tag{5}$$

$$\gamma = \sum_{i=1}^{|T'|} \sum_{j=1}^{|H'|} Max(Sim(T'_i, H'_j)) \quad (6) \quad Jacc^+(T, H) = \frac{|T \cap H| + \gamma}{|T \cup H|} \tag{7}$$

The adapted measures were computed with each semantic network, individually, and with *Redun2* and *Redun3*. Although some differences were insignificant, *Redun3* lead more consistently to the best results. Tables 5 and 6 present, respectively for the PT-PT and for the PT-BR training collections, a selection of the best results obtained with different similarity measures and a different kind of normalization using all the relations of *Redun3*. The lower part of the tables shows a selection of the best results when using only synonymy and hypernymy relations, *Redun2*, and when using each LKB individually.

Cosine was again the best measure. Jaccard was very close in terms of correlation, but with considerably higher MSE. Moreover, although we would think that synonymy and hypernymy relations would fit this task better, using all relation types shown to be a better choice. Although lower than expected, the baseline results were improved. For PT-PT, correlation went from 0.706 to 0.721 and for PT-BR it went from 0.626 to 0.632.

Table 5. Results for PT-PT training pairs when semantic networks are exploited.

Norm	LKB	Rels	Sim	ρ	MSE
Lem	Redun3	All	Jacc$^+$	0.709	1.116
Lem	Redun3	All	Dice$^+$	0.708	0.448
Lem	Redun3	All	Cos$^+$	0.712	0.431
Stem	Redun3	All	Jacc$^+$	0.717	1.049
Stem	Redun3	All	Dice$^+$	0.717	0.419
Stem	Redun3	All	Cos$^+$	**0.721**	0.388
Stem	Redun3	Syn+Hyp	Jacc$^+$	0.713	1.007
Stem	Redun3	Syn+Hyp	Cosine$^+$	0.717	0.394
Stem	Redun2	All	Jacc$^+$	0.715	1.034
Stem	Redun2	All	Cos$^+$	0.712	0.404
Stem	Wikt.PT	All	Cos$^+$	0.720	0.388
Stem	PAPEL	All	Cos$^+$	0.719	**0.383**

Table 6. Results for PT-BR training pairs when semantic networks are exploited.

Norm	LKB	Rels	Sim	ρ	MSE
Lem	Redun3	All	Jacc$^+$	0.621	0.843
Lem	Redun3	All	Dice$^+$	0.617	0.466
Lem	Redun3	All	Cos$^+$	0.62	0.464
Stem	Redun3	All	Jacc$^+$	**0.632**	0.778
Stem	Redun3	All	Dice$^+$	0.628	0.456
Stem	Redun3	All	Cos$^+$	0.631	**0.453**
Stem	Redun3	Syn+Hyp	Jacc$^+$	0.631	0.787
Stem	Redun3	Syn	Cos$^+$	0.631	**0.453**
Stem	Redun2	All	Jacc$^+$	**0.632**	0.727
Stem	Redun2	All	Cos$^+$	0.624	0.466
Stem	TeP	Syn	Jacc$^+$	0.629	0.771
Stem	OT	Syn	Cos$^+$	0.628	0.458

5.3   Unsupervised Test Results

From the previous experiments on the training collections, we selected three configurations, based on the best combined results and used them to compute the similarity of the pairs in the ASSIN test collections. Table 7 shows the obtained results for PT-PT and PT-BR and the results of the best training baseline in the test collection.

Table 7. Test results when semantic networks are exploited, plus the Cosine baseline.

Normalization	Network	Relations	Measure	PT-PT		PT-PBR	
				ρ	MSE	ρ	MSE
Stem	Redun2	All	Jacc$^+$	0.669	0.746	0.669	0.764
Stem	Redun3	All	Jacc$^+$	0.669	0.723	0.666	0.825
Stem	Redun3	All	Cos$^+$	**0.677**	**0.686**	**0.667**	0.454
(baseline) Stem	–	–	Cos	0.656	0.658	0.653	**0.445**

In PT-PT, performance was lower than for the training, but in PT-BR it was higher. For both of them, the highest ρ and lowest MSE are obtained with the Cos$^+$ and Redun3. In the ASSIN evaluation, this would be the fifth best run and fourth best system for PT-PT, in terms of ρ, and the third best run and system in terms of MSE. For PT-BR, it would get the third best ρ, second best system, and seventh best MSE, fourth best system. For an unsupervised approach, we see these results as very interesting, and would be ranked first considering only unsupervised approaches to ASSIN. Towards better results, some of these measures were combined with additional features in different learning methods.

6   Learning a Similarity Model

To improve the previous results, some of the unsupervised measures were used together with a set of additional features to learn a similarity function from each training collection and, later, from both. Here, we enumerate the features used, describe the learning algorithms explored, and report on the training and test results achieved.

6.1   Features

From the previous experiments, we selected the best baselines—Jaccard and Cosine—both with lemmas and stems, as well as two of the best configurations of the unsupervised approach—Jaccard$^+$ and Cosine$^+$—again with lemmas and stems. The previous were considered together with the following additional features, some of which also exploited in related work:

- **Lexical features:** number of negation words (*não, nada, nenhum, de modo algum,...*) in each sentence of the pair and their absolute difference; number of common tokens; number of common lemmas; and number of common stems.
- **Syntactic features:** number of noun, verb and prepositional chunks in each sentence of the pair and their absolute difference.
- **Semantic features:** number of named entities of each type (abstraction, product, event, number, organization, person, place, thing and time) in each sentence of the pair and their absolute difference; number of semantic relations of four types (synonymy, hypernymy, antonymy and other) between lemmas in one sentence of the pair and lemmas in the other, for each LKB.

6.2   Learning Algorithms

Three different regression algorithms, provided by the Weka [26] machine learning toolkit, were used to learn the similarity function. Table 8 presents the setup of the three best-peforming algorithms, after an exhaustive set of runs, namely:

- *M5Rules* [27] generates a decision list for regression problems using a separate-and-conquer strategy. In each iteration, it builds a model tree using the M5 algorithm and turns the "best" leaf into a rule.
- *Random Subspace* [28] is an ensemble learning algorithm that builds a decision tree classifier. It consists of random subspacing regression ensembles composed of multiple trees constructed systematically by pseudo-randomly selected subsets of components of the feature vector.
- Regression algorithm to infer the similarity function based on *Gaussian Processes* [29], in this case with a Radial Basis Function (RBF) Kernel as the Gaussian function. This implementation is simplified in Weka: it does not apply hyper-parameter-tuning and uses normalization to the target class (similarity value), so the features simplify the choice of a noise level.

Table 8. Weka setup for the three learning algorithms used.

Algorithm	Weka setup
M5Rules	`weka.classifiers.rules.M5Rules -M 4.0`
RandomSubspace w/M5	`weka.classifiers.meta.RandomSubSpace -P 0.5 -S 1 -num-slots 1 -I 10 -W` `weka.classifiers.trees.M5P -- -M 4.0`
Gaussian Process w/RBF Kernel	`weka.classifiers.functions.GaussianProcesses -L 1.0 -N 0` `-K"weka.classifiers.functions.supportVector.RBFKernel -G 0.01 -C 250007"`

6.3 Training and Testing

Table 9 shows the average training performance for the three learning models in a 10-fold cross validation, for PT-PT and PT-BR individually. They are clearly higher than the unsupervised results in the training collections.

Table 10 shows the results of the learned models in the ASSIN test collections. Though using the same algorithm, different models were used for PT-PT and PT-BR, respectively trained in the PT-PT and on the PT-BR training collection. When compared to our unsupervised approach, there is a clear improvement—ρ is 0.032 points higher for PT-PT and 0.019 for PT-BR—but results are still below the best official ASSIN results. They would get second position in both collections, considering both ρ and MSE.

Table 9. Performance when training in the PT-PT and PT-BR collections.

Method	PT-PT		PT-BR	
	ρ	MSE	ρ	MSE
M5Rules	0.742	0.472	0.657	0.518
RandomSubspace	**0.756**	**0.457**	**0.662**	**0.515**
GaussianProcess	0.739	0.479	0.658	0.520

Table 10. Test results for models trained in the respective training collection.

Method	PT-PT		PT-BR	
	ρ	MSE	ρ	MSE
M5Rules	0.703	0.714	0.678	0.411
RandomSubspace	**0.709**	**0.698**	**0.686**	**0.403**
GaussianProcess	0.694	0.725	0.683	0.406

6.4 Training on both Collections

As a complementary experiment, we adopted a different training strategy. Since they are just variants of the same language, instead of training independent models for PT-PT and PT-BR, we concatenated the training collections and learned new (variant-ignoring) models from the resulting larger collection, which comprised 6,000 pairs. Tables 11 and 12 show, respectively, the training performance of the same learning algorithms on a 10-fold cross-validation in the larger collection, and the results of the new models in each test collection.

Despite the lower training performance, when using the Random Subspace ensemble, there are minor improvements in ρ, both for PT-PT and PT-BR, which is enough to match the correlation of the best official run for PT-BR — although the official results reported 0.70 correlation, they were rounded to two

Table 11. Training performance in a collection with both PT-PT and PT-BR training pairs.

Method	ρ	MSE
M5Rules	0.705	0.493
RandomSubspace	0.713	0.486
GaussianProcess	0.701	0.493

Table 12. Test results for models trained with both PT-PT and PT-BR training pairs.

Method	PT-PT		PT-BR	
	ρ	MSE	ρ	MSE
M5Rules	0.702	0.648	0.690	0.505
RandomSubspace	**0.711**	**0.657**	**0.697**	**0.499**
GaussianProcess	0.691	0.678	0.684	0.509

decimal places. Regarding MSE, it is slightly better for PT-PT, but worst for PT-BR. Also, the lower differences between training and test suggest that the variant specific features were more clear in the training than in the test, but a deeper analysis would be needed for this claim.

7 Concluding Remarks

An incremental approach to the ASSIN shared task on Portuguese STS was described. Simple similarity measures based on the surface text were first used and gradually improved after exploiting Portuguese LKBs and combining different features in a supervised approach. The reported experiments should be seen as the development of ASAPP [16], an approach to ASSIN.

The best results achieved would get second place overall in ASSIN. To beat the best official results, more experiments would be needed and additional features explored. Our approach would probably benefit from distributional features based on a vector representation for words, such as word embeddings [14] for Portuguese (e.g., [30]), as well as topic distributions (e.g., using LDA [31]) and n-gram overlap. Adding those features will be the next steps of this work, which will also explore feature reduction methods.

Acknowledgements. This work was financed by the ERDF European Regional Development Fund through the COMPETE Programme (operational programme for competitiveness) and by National Funds through the FCT Fundação para a Ciência e a Tecnologia (Portuguese Foundation for Science and Technology) within project REMINDS – UTAP-ICDT/EEI-CTP/0022/2014.

References

1. Agirre, E., Banea, C., Cer, D., Diab, M., Gonzalez-Agirre, A., Mihalcea, R., Rigau, G., Wiebe, J.: Semeval-2016 task 1: semantic textual similarity, monolingual and cross-lingual evaluation. In: Proceedings of the 10th International Workshop on Semantic Evaluation (SemEval-2016), San Diego, California, pp. 497–511. ACL Press, June 2016

2. Agirre, E., Diab, M., Cer, D., Gonzalez-Agirre, A.: Semeval-2012 task 6: a pilot on semantic textual similarity. In: Proceedings of the 1st Joint Conference on Lexical and Computational Semantics, vol. 1: Proceedings of the Main Conference and the Shared Task, and Proceedings of the Sixth International Workshop on Semantic Evaluation, vol. 2, pp. 385–393. ACL Press (2012)

3. Fonseca, E., Santos, L., Criscuolo, M., Aluísio, S.: Visão geral da avaliação de similaridade semântica e inferência textual. Linguamática **8**(2), 3–13 (2016)

4. Fellbaum, C. (ed.): WordNet: An Electronic Lexical Database (Language, Speech, and Communication). The MIT Press, Cambridge (1998)

5. Rychalska, B., Pakulska, K., Chodorowska, K., Walczak, W., Andruszkiewicz, P.: Samsung Poland NLP team at SemEval-2016 task 1: necessity for diversity; combining recursive autoencoders, wordnet and ensemble methods to measure semantic similarity. In: Proceedings of 10th International Workshop on Semantic Evaluation (SemEval-2016), San Diego, California, pp. 602–608. ACL Press, June 2016

6. Brychcín, T., Svoboda, L.: UWB at semeval-2016 task 1: semantic textual similarity using lexical, syntactic, and semantic information. In: Proceedings of the 10th International Workshop on Semantic Evaluation (SemEval-2016), San Diego, California, pp. 588–594. ACL Press, June 2016

7. Hänig, C., Remus, R., de la Puente, X.: ExB themis: extensive feature extraction from word alignments for semantic textual similarity. In: Proceedings of the 9th International Workshop on Semantic Evaluation (SemEval 2015), Denver, Colorado, pp. 264–268. ACL Press, June 2015

8. Marelli, M., Bentivogli, L., Baroni, M., Bernardi, R., Menini, S., Zamparelli, R.: Semeval-2014 task 1: evaluation of compositional distributional semantic models on full sentences through semantic relatedness and textual entailment. In: Proceedings of the 8th International Workshop on Semantic Evaluation (SemEval 2014), Dublin, Ireland, pp. 1–8. ACL Press, August 2014

9. Zhao, J., Zhu, T., Lan, M.: ECNU: one stone two birds: ensemble of heterogenous measures for semantic relatedness and textual entailment. In: Proceedings of the 8th International Workshop on Semantic Evaluation (SemEval 2014), Dublin, Ireland, pp. 271–277. ACL Press, August 2014

10. Alves, A., Ferrugento, A., Lourenço, M., Rodrigues, F.: ASAP: automatic semantic alignment for phrases. In: Proceedings of the 8th International Workshop on Semantic Evaluation (SemEval 2014), Dublin, Ireland, pp. 104–108. ACL Press, August 2014

11. Alves, A., Simões, D., Gonçalo Oliveira, H., Ferrugento, A.: ASAP-II: from the alignment of phrases to textual similarity. In: Proceedings of 9th International Workshop on Semantic Evaluation (SemEval 2015), Denver, Colorado, pp. 184–189. ACL Press, June 2015

12. Pinheiro, V., Furtado, V., Albuquerque, A.: Semantic textual similarity of portuguese-language texts: an approach based on the semantic inferentialism model. In: Proceedings of the 11th Conference on the Computational Processing of the Portuguese Language, PROPOR 2014, São Carlos/SP, Brazil, pp. 183–188, 6–8 October 2014 (2014)

13. Hartmann, N.: Solo queue at ASSIN: combinando abordagens tradicionais e emergentes. Linguamática **8**(2), 59–64 (2016)

14. Mikolov, T., Chen, K., Corrado, G., Dean, J.: Efficient estimation of word representations in vector space. In: Proceedings of the Workshop track of the International Conference on Learning Representations (ICLR), Scottsdale, Arizona (2013)

15. Fialho, P., Marques, R., Martins, B., Coheur, L., Quaresma, P.: INESC-ID@ASSIN: medição de similaridade semântica e reconhecimento de inferência textual. Linguamática **8**(2), 33–42 (2016)
16. Alves, A., Gonçalo Oliveira, H., Rodrigues, R.: ASAPP: alinhamento semântico automático de palavras aplicado ao português. Linguamçtica **8**(2), 43–58 (2016)
17. Rodrigues, R., Gonçalo-Oliveira, H., Gomes, P.: LemPORT: a high-accuracy cross-platform lemmatizer for portuguese. In: Proceedings of the 3rd Symposium on Languages, Applications and Technologies (SLATE 2014), OASICS, Germany, Schloss Dagstuhl–Leibniz-Zentrum für Informatik, pp. 267–274. Dagstuhl Publishing, June 2014
18. Dias-da-Silva, B.C.: Wordnet.Br: an exercise of human language technology research. In: Proceedings of 3rd International WordNet Conference (GWC), GWC 2006, South Jeju Island, Korea, pp. 301–303, January 2006
19. Paiva, V., Rademaker, A., Melo, G.: OpenWordNet-PT: an open Brazilian wordnet for reasoning. In: Proceedings of 24th International Conference on Computational Linguistics, COLING (Demo Paper) (2012)
20. Simões, A., Guinovart, X.G.: Bootstrapping a Portuguese wordnet from Galician, Spanish and English wordnets. In: Navarro Mesa, J.L., Ortega, A., Teixeira, A., Hernández Pérez, E., Quintana Morales, P., Ravelo García, A., Guerra Moreno, I., Toledano, D.T. (eds.) IberSPEECH 2014. LNCS, vol. 8854, pp. 239–248. Springer, Cham (2014). doi:10.1007/978-3-319-13623-3_25
21. Maziero, E., Pardo, T., Felippo, A., Dias-da-Silva, B.: A Base de Dados Lexical e a Interface Web do TeP 2.0 - Thesaurus Eletrônico para o Português do Brasil. In: VI Workshop em Tecnologia da Informação e da Linguagem Humana (TIL), pp. 390–392 (2008)
22. Gonçalo Oliveira, H., Santos, D., Gomes, P., Seco, N.: PAPEL: a dictionary-based lexical ontology for Portuguese. In: Teixeira, A., Lima, V.L.S., Oliveira, L.C., Quaresma, P. (eds.) PROPOR 2008. LNCS, vol. 5190, pp. 31–40. Springer, Heidelberg (2008). doi:10.1007/978-3-540-85980-2_4
23. Simões, A., Sanromán, Á.I., Almeida, J.J.: Dicionário-Aberto: a source of resources for the Portuguese language processing. In: Caseli, H., Villavicencio, A., Teixeira, A., Perdigão, F. (eds.) PROPOR 2012. LNCS, vol. 7243, pp. 121–127. Springer, Heidelberg (2012). doi:10.1007/978-3-642-28885-2_14
24. Barreiro, A.: Port4NooJ: an open source, ontology-driven portuguese linguistic system with applications in machine translation. In: Proceedings of the 2008 International NooJ Conference (NooJ 2008), Budapest, Hungary, Newcastle-upon-Tyne: Cambridge Scholars Publishing (2010)
25. Gonçalo Oliveira, H.: Comparing and combining Portuguese lexical-semantic knowledge bases. In: Proceedings of 6th Symposium on Languages, Applications and Technologies (SLATE 2017), OASICS, Schloss Dagstuhl - Leibniz-Zentrum fuer Informatik. pp. 16: 1–16: 14 (2017)
26. Hall, M., Frank, E., Holmes, G., Pfahringer, B., Reutemann, P., Witten, I.: The WEKA data mining software: an update. SIGKDD Explor. **11**(1), 10–18 (2009)
27. Holmes, G., Hall, M., Prank, E.: Generating rule sets from model trees. In: Foo, N. (ed.) AI 1999. LNCS, vol. 1747, pp. 1–12. Springer, Heidelberg (1999). doi:10.1007/3-540-46695-9_1
28. Ho, T.K.: The random subspace method for constructing decision forests. IEEE Trans. Pattern Anal. Mach. Intell. **20**(8), 832–844 (1998)
29. Mackay, D.: Introduction to Gaussian processes. In: Bishop, C.M. (ed.) Neural Networks and Machine Learning. Springer, Berlin (1998)

30. Rodrigues, J., Branco, A., Neale, S., Silva, J.: LX-DSemVectors: distributional semantics models for Portuguese. In: Silva, J., Ribeiro, R., Quaresma, P., Adami, A., Branco, A. (eds.) PROPOR 2016. LNCS, vol. 9727, pp. 259–270. Springer, Cham (2016). doi:10.1007/978-3-319-41552-9_27
31. Blei, D., Ng, A., Jordan, M.: Latent dirichlet allocation. J. Mach. Learn. Res. **3**, 993–1022 (2003)

Towards a Mention-Pair Model for Coreference Resolution in Portuguese

Gil Rocha[(✉)] and Henrique Lopes Cardoso

LIACC/DEI, Faculdade de Engenharia, Universidade do Porto,
Rua Dr. Roberto Frias, 4200-465 Porto, Portugal
{gil.rocha,hlc}@fe.up.pt

Abstract. The aim of coreference resolution is to automatically determine all linguistic expressions included in a piece of text that refer to the same entity. Following the mention-pair model, we employ machine learning techniques to address coreference resolution from text written in Portuguese. Based on a modest annotated corpus, we highlight the impact that different training-set creation strategies have on the quality of the predictions made by the system. We conclude that enriching the system with semantic-based features significantly improves the overall performance of the system.

1 Introduction

Coreference resolution is a natural language processing (NLP) task that aims to automatically determine all linguistic expressions included in a piece of text that refer to the same entity. A natural language expression used to perform a reference is called a *referring expression* (also known as *mention*), while the entity that is being referred is called the *referent* (e.g. person, company, event) [15].

Automatic recognition of coreferring expressions for entities and events is recognized by the NLP community as a challenging and important step in order to conceptualize computational systems capable of processing and understanding natural language, with high impact in several sub-tasks that are currently being addressed by the community. Coreference resolution corresponds to a very important pre-processing step for several NLP subtasks, such as document summarization, question answering, information extraction, and argumentation mining. The use of coreferences is prevalent in natural language texts, and occurs in varied ways – oftentimes different coreferences to a same entity are found in a single text. This practice is typically associated with natural language ambiguity found in text documents, and is commonly reported as one of the major sources of errors in several NLP sub-tasks. As an example of the task that we aim to address in this work, consider the following passage (extracted from [15]):

> "Victoria Chen, Chief Financial Officer of Megabucks Banking Corp since 2004, saw her pay jump 20%, to $1.3 million, as the 37-year-old also became the Denver-based financial-services company's president. It has been ten years since she came to Megabucks from rival Lotsabucks."

© Springer International Publishing AG 2017
E. Oliveira et al. (Eds.): EPIA 2017, LNAI 10423, pp. 855–867, 2017.
DOI: 10.1007/978-3-319-65340-2_69

In this excerpt, each underlined piece of text corresponds to a *referring expression* that is being used by the writer to denote one entity in particular, the *referent* (*i.e.* entity or person whose name is *Victoria Chen*).

The set of referential expressions that can be found in natural language is quite rich indeed, where referential phenomena can be used to express new or given information. Different types of coreferences were identified and are extensively studied in linguistics [15].

A *coreference chain* (also denoted as *entity*) is a group (or cluster) of referring expressions that refer to the same referent (*i.e.* linguistic expressions that corefer). Thus, a coreference chain is associated to an entity and is composed of all mentions in a discourse that refer to this entity.

Given a text document as input, the goal of a coreference resolution system is to determine all the coreference chains included in the text. By automatically detecting coreferences and being able to aggregate different mentions in the same coreference chain, we are able to disambiguate some of the meaning of the text and, therefore, contribute to a better understanding of the text. In this paper, we aim to study: (a) how semantic-based features may improve the performance of a baseline coreference resolution system containing features at the lexical, syntactic, morphological and structural level and, (b) how different heuristic-based strategies to generate balanced datasets following the mention-pair model may influence the quality of the predictions made by the system.

This paper is structured as follows: Sect. 2 presents related work on coreference resolution, focusing on text written in the Portuguese language. Section 3 introduces the resources that were used in our experiments, namely the corpus (Sect. 3.1) and external semantic resources (Sect. 3.2). Then, in Sect. 4 we describe the methods that were used to address the task of coreference resolution. Section 5 presents the results obtained by the system described in this work. Finally, Sect. 6 concludes and points to directions of future work.

2 Related Work

General and complete coreference resolution systems receive as input text written in natural language and return as output the set of coreference chains present in the text. In [22], the authors divided this process in three main components: *mention detection, characterization of mentions*, and *resolution*.

The first component of the coreference resolution process is the *detection of mentions* from text written in natural language. The aim of this component is to find the exact boundaries of each mention present in the text document. These mentions can be proper nouns, pronouns, definite noun phrase and indefinite noun phrases and, may refer different types of entities, namely: person, place, organization, event, thing, time, amongst others. In the *characterization of mentions* step, identified referring expressions are characterized with all the available knowledge about them and their possible relations with other mentions. Depending on the approach, it may involve the extraction of lexical, syntactic, structural and semantic knowledge for each referring expression. Finally, in the *resolution* step we aim to determine the coreference chains for all mentions that were identified and characterized by the previous components of the system.

Several paradigms to address the task of coreference resolution have been explored: rule-based [16], heuristic-based (e.g. based on the centering theory of the discourse [14,25]), based on constraint satisfaction (e.g. [21]) and machine learning (including mention-pair models, mention-ranking models and entity-mention models [22]). Since in this paper we aim to address the task of coreference resolution using machine learning (ML) techniques, the remainder of this section will focus on related work following this paradigm; moreover, a special focus will be given to work based on Portuguese text.

In [11], Garcia and Gamallo propose a coreference resolution approach focusing on entities of the type person, entitled *Link-People*. They have built their own corpus for this purpose [12]. Their model combines an entity-centric approach containing a set of constraints and rules specially designed to deal with pronouns, anaphoras and cataphoras for person entities, and a multi-pass architecture that dynamically enriches an entity with new features in every iteration. They report results for three different languages, achieving 87.4% of F1-measure in the MUC metric [24] for Portuguese. Coreixas [3] proposes a coreference resolution system for Brazilian-Portuguese based on a ML approach and focusing on semantic categories of named entities, such as *Person, Location, Organization, Event* and *Other*. Coreixas claims that the approach that included semantic categories of entities provided improvements (in about 17% of the cases) in terms of performance to determine coreference relations between pairs of mentions. Resources used in this work include: the *HAREM* corpus [9] for semantic categories, *PALAVRAS* parser [2] and, the *Summ-it* corpus [5] for coreference resolution. Finally, Coreixas emphasizes the importance of world knowledge for this line of work, since some semantic categories such as *Event* and *Organization* did not show satisfactory results. Using Decision Trees they reported 64% and 75% F1-score, for coreferent mention-pairs and non-coreferent mention-pairs, respectively.

Fonseca *et al.* [6] propose a supervised ML system to address coreference resolution for text written in Portuguese-Brazilian, following the mention-pair model. The authors used the *Summ-it* corpus [5] to train the proposed system. They focus only on pairs whose noun-phrases are proper nouns. Then, in [7], Fonseca *et al.* consider all noun phrases pairs and they present some improvements to the feature set. In addition, they study the problem of dealing with imbalanced datasets. Using Decision Trees, they reported an average F-measure of 65.6% and 74.4% for coreferent/non-coreferent mention-pairs in a "1 to 1" balancing level (1 coreferent for each non-coreferent mention-pair) and an average F-measure of 55.6% and 85.9% in a "1 to 2" balancing level. Finally, in [8], the authors show that exploring semantic resources the performance of the system can be improved. They explored external resources to add new semantic features, including the *PALAVRAS* parser (for entity semantic-category based features) and Onto-PT (for synonyms, hyperonyms and meronyms). They reported an average F-measure of 66.45% for coreferent mention-pairs and 74.88% for non-coreferent mention-pairs in a "1 to 1" balancing level.

3   Resources

We here introduce the corpora used in our experiments and the external semantic resources used by the mention-pair classifier to employ semantic-based features.

3.1   Corpora

The availability of a collection of annotated documents (corpus) with coreference chains occurring in natural language textual resources is an important requirement in order to address the task of coreference resolution using supervised machine learning techniques. English corpora for this task date back to the Message Understanding Conferences (MUC) and ACE corpora. MUC corpora cover all noun phrases in text, but represent small training and test sets. The ACE corpora, on the other hand, have much more annotation, but are restricted to a small subset of entities. They are also less consistent, in terms of inter-annotator agreement. More recently, the *CoNLL-2011* shared task on coreference resolution was based on the English portion of the *OntoNotes* 4.0 corpus [20], a large-scale and accurate corpus (in terms of inter-annotator agreement). The complete corpus contains annotations in English, Arabic and Chinese. For the English language, it contains a total of 1300000 tokens and 34290 coreference chains, extracted from 2999 text documents [20]. There is no limit on the semantic types of noun phrase entities that can be considered for coreference, which corresponds to a significant improvement in relation to previous available corpora (for instance, it is not limited to the *ACE* types).

To the best of our knowledge, current available corpora annotated with referring expressions and coreference chains from text written in Portuguese are the following. The Garcia and Gamallo corpus [10] contains 91 journalistic documents with approximately 34000 tokens and 6 encyclopedia documents with approximately 17000 tokens. The coreferential annotations were manually made by two linguists following the *SemEval* 2010 guidelines. These annotations are restricted to persons and pronouns. This corpus contains texts from Portugal, Brazil, Mozambique and Angola. The *HAREM* corpus [9] contains manually annotated named entities distributed in ten semantic categories. Relations between these entities have also been manually annotated in four types: identity, inclusion, placement and other. Contains approximately 887 coreference chains annotated from 129 documents. However, a detailed analysis of the annotations regarding referring entities showed that some of these relations were annotated considering semantic relations between named entities instead of coreference relations including different types of entities as described in previous sections of this paper. Finally, the Summ-it++ corpus [5] consists of fifty journalistic articles from the Science section of the Brazilian newspaper entitled "Folha de São Paulo". The corpus contains a total of 560 coreference chains (manually annotated) with an average of 3 referring expressions in each coreference chain. The largest chain contains 16 referring expressions. There are 20000 tokens in total. The annotation of coreferences follows the *SemEval* style.

In the experiments presented in this paper we used the *Summ-it++* corpus to validate the approach described in Sect. 4. Even though this corpus corresponds to the linguistic resource containing the lowest number of text documents annotated for this task, we concluded, after a manual analysis (we randomly selected a small portion of documents to analyze the annotations that were made in each corpora), that *Summ-it++* corpus contains the most reliable annotations of coreference chains from text written in Portuguese.

Summ-it++ corpus follows the typical annotation format used in corpora provided in previous editions of the *SemEval* and *CoNLL* NLP challenges related to the task of coreference resolution, in which each data instance is a complete text document (e.g. a complete news article) that was annotated and is included in the corpus in a tabular format, where (a) each line contains one of the tokens extracted from the original text, and (b) each column contains information related to each token, namely: the word lemma, part-of-speech tagging, gender, number, head word indicator, semantic category (comprising the semantic classes of *Abstraction*, *Event*, *Organization*, *Other*, *Person*, *Place*, *Thing*, *Time*, *Value*, and *Work*), relation descriptor between a pair of named entities, and coreference indicator. Furthermore, this corpus provides the necessary resources to focus on the resolution component and assume that the expected output of the mention detection component is given as input.

3.2 External Semantic Resources

We explore large external semantic resources in order to improve the performance of our coreference resolution approach, augmenting the feature set created in the mention-pair classification sub-step (Sect. 4.2) with semantic knowledge. This aims at better dealing with the diversity and ambiguity of natural language text.

Knowledge about the words of a language and their semantic relations with other words can be exploited with large-scale lexical databases. Similarly to WordNet [4] for the English language, CONTO.PT [13] is a fuzzy wordnet for Portuguese, which groups words into sets of cognitive synonyms (called synsets), each expressing a distinct concept. In addition, synsets are interlinked by means of conceptual-semantic and lexical relations (e.g. "hyperonym" and "part-of"). The synsets included in CONTO.PT were automatically extracted from several linguistic resources and include degrees of membership where higher values mean that the word belongs to the corresponding synset with more certainty.

Finally, we exploit a distributed representation of words (word embeddings). These distributions map a word from a dictionary to a feature vector in high-dimensional space, without human intervention, from observing the usage of words on large (non-annotated) corpora. This real-valued vector representation tries to arrange words with similar meanings close to each other based on the occurrences of these words in a corpora. Then, from these representations, interesting features can be explored, such as semantic and syntactic similarities. In our experiments, we used a model provided by the *Polyglot*[1] tool [1], in which a neural network architecture was trained on Portuguese *Wikipedia* articles.

4   Method

To address the task of coreference resolution in Portuguese text we employ supervised machine learning. In previous related work (see Sect. 2), these techniques have shown promising results. Given a set of mentions extracted from a text document, $M = \{m_1, m_2, \ldots, m_n\}$, where n corresponds to the number of mentions present in the text document, we aim to address the task of detecting all the coreference chains contained in the text, where each coreference chain aggregates all the mentions $m_i \in M$ that refer to the same entity.

In this paper, we follow the *mention-pair model*. Even taking into account the well known limitations of this model (e.g. lack of global information and contradictions in classification) [22], given the current lack of a large scale annotated corpora for the task of coreference resolution in Portuguese we argue that a mention-pair approach is the most adequate for this task, since we can generate more training instances to train the supervised machine learning classifiers. On the other hand, mention-ranking models and entity-mention models optimize the learning problem globally and, therefore, require a considerable amount of learning instances that we do not have at our disposal using the *Summ-it++* corpus (which has 50 documents). Consequently, we formulate the problem as a binary classification problem: classifiers are trained to classify pairs of mentions as coreferent (CO) or non-coreferent (NC). This approach can be divided in three main steps, namely: training set creation, mention-pair classification and coreference chains generation. In the remainder of this section, a detailed description of each of these steps is presented.

4.1   Training Set Creation

To transform the annotations available in the *Summ-it++* corpus into a set of training instances suitable for the learning process, we need to develop methods that take in consideration the approach that will be used: the mention-pair model. Consequently, we need to transform annotations of coreference chains into a pairwise combination of referring expressions indicating whether the pair of referring expressions is coreferent (*CO* label) or not (*NC* label) in the original text document, according to the *Summ-it++* corpus. To generate training instances, we explored the following methods:

Closest Antecedent: Given a mention m_j, a positive example $\langle m_i, m_j, CO \rangle$ is generated with m_j and its closest preceding coreference m_i; a set of negative examples $\langle m_k, m_j, NC \rangle$ is generated with m_j and any other mention m_k occurring between m_i and m_j. This method of negative instance selection is explained in detail in Soon *et al.* [23].

---

[1] http://polyglot.readthedocs.io/en/latest/index.html.

Most Confident Antecedent: Given a mention m_j, a positive example $\langle m_i, m_j, CO \rangle$ is generated with m_j and (a) its closest non-pronomial preceding coreference m_i, if m_j is non-pronomial, or (b) its closest preceding coreference m_i, otherwise; a set of negative examples $\langle m_k, m_j, NC \rangle$ is generated similarly to the *closest antecedent* method. This method is described in Ng and Cardie [18].

All Antecedents: A set of positive examples $\langle m_i, m_j, CO \rangle$ is generated with any pair m_i and m_j annotated in the same coreference chain; a set of negative examples $\langle m_i, m_j, NC \rangle$ is generated from the rest of mention pairs.

Most Confident Antecedent Neighbors (MCAN): This method is similar to the *closest antecedent* method, but instead of generating a negative example $\langle m_k, m_j, NC \rangle$ for each antecedent m_k occurring between m_i and m_j, it generates only up to k negative examples with the antecedents of m_j occurring closer to the mention m_i (*i.e.* if $k = 2$, $\{\langle m_{i+1}, m_j, NC \rangle, \langle m_{i+2}, mj, NC \rangle\}$). In addition, to generate the positive examples (CO pairs), this method follows the restrictions described in the *Most Confident antecedent* method. This method was conceived to generate a training set containing a balanced number of coreferent (CO) and non-coreferent (NC) training instances which takes into account the characteristics of the formulation previously presented. By only considering as negative examples the mention pairs occurring more closely to the positive example, we provide to the classifier the most relevant training examples for the task being tackled: we aim that the classifier learns to distinguish CO pairs from NC pairs and, therefore, this distinction is critical for neighboring pairs.

4.2 Mention-Pair Classification

In this paper, we formulate the problem of coreference resolution as a binary classification problem: classifiers are trained to classify each mention-pair as coreferent (CO) or non-coreferent (NC).

In order to apply machine learning algorithms it is necessary to represent the training instances by a set of numerical features. Following the mention-pair model, the feature set should be designed taking into account that the training instances correspond to mention-pairs and, therefore, should not only represent each mention individually but also capture the coreference relation between the pair of mentions. The feature set used to represent each mention-pair is depicted in Table 1. This feature set contains features at the lexical, syntactic, morphological, structural and semantic level. For the first four, we obtained the necessary information from the labels and annotations extracted from the *Summ-it++* corpus (described in Sect. 3.1). For semantic level features we extracted the necessary information from external semantic resources (see Sect. 3.2). Two mentions are considered synonyms if they occur in the same synset. One mention m_i is considered hyperonym of m_j if at least one word contained in m_i can be found in an hyperonym relation ("hyperonym_of") with at least one word contained in m_j. One mention m_i is considered meronym of m_j if at least one word contained in m_i can be found in an meronymy relation ("part_of" or "member_of") with at least one word contained in m_j. In order to obtain a score indicating the similarity between two mentions, we compute the cosine similarity between the vectors that represent each of the mentions in the high-dimensional space. Each mention is projected into the embedding space as $\vec{m_i} = \sum_{k=1}^{n} \vec{e}(w_k)n^{-1}$, where $\vec{e}(w_k)$ represents the embedding vector of the word w_k and n corresponds to the number of words contained in mention m_i.

Table 1. Feature set for mention-pair classification. A star (*) indicates that an additional pre-processing step was performed in which all prepositions, adverbs, punctuation marks and numbers were removed

Feature	Description
Lexical	
Exact_Str_Match*	If the words of m_i match the words of m_j, return 1; else return 0
Substr_Match*	If intersection of words in m_i and m_j is empty, return 0; else 1
Syntactical	
Pronoun_1	If m_i is a pronoun return 1; else return 0
Pronoun_2	If m_j is a pronoun return 1; else return 0
Definite_2	If m_j starts with the word-lemma "o" or "de"
Demonstrative_2	If m_j starts with the demonstrative word-lemma, return 1; else 0
ProperNouns	If m_i and m_j are both proper nouns, return 2; If exactly one of the mentions is proper noun, return 1; else return 0
Morphological	
Number	If m_i and m_j agree in number, return 2; If they disagree, return 1; If undefined, return 0
Gender	If m_i and m_j agree in gender, return 2; If they disagree, return 1; If undefined, return 0
Structural	
Appositive	If m_i and m_j are in an appositive relationship, return 1; else 0
Sentence_dist	Absolute distance between m_i and m_j in number of sentences
Mentions_dist	Number of mentions between m_i and m_j
Semantical	
Synonym*	If m_i and m_j are synonyms return 1; else return 0
Hyperonym*	If m_i is hyperonym of m_j or if m_j is hyperonym of m_i return 1; else return 0
Meronym*	If m_i is meronym of m_j or if m_j is meronym of m_i return 1; else return 0
Cosine_Similarity*	Cosine similarity between the embedding vector $\vec{e}(m_i)$ and the embedding vector $\vec{e}(m_j)$

Regarding ML algorithms used in our experiments, we made several experiments with the following algorithms: *Decision Tree*, *SVM* (with *Sequential Minimal Optimization* training), *SVM* (with *Stochastic Gradient Descendent* training), *Naïve bayes*, *AdaBoost* (using *Decision Trees* as weak classifiers). These algorithms were implemented using the library *scikit-learn* [19] for the *Python* programming language. Given the set of features, each classifier learns, from a training set generated by one the methods described in Sect. 4.1, to classify each pair of mentions as Coreferent (CO) or Non-Coreferent (NC). In Sect. 4.3, methods to generate the final output of the coreference resolution system are presented.

4.3   Coreference Chains Generation

In this step, we aim to automatically partition the set of mentions M clustered in the corresponding coreference chains, where each coreference chain represents one entity that is referred in the text by all the mentions contained in the cluster.

Given that to generate the training instances we processed the text from left to right and, for each active mention, mention-pairs are generated from right to left, we must consider that a classifier trained following this approach is biased to learn how to classify each pair of mentions in this setting. Therefore, the set of instances that we aim to make predictions should be presented following a similar procedure. Based on the approach described by Soon *et al.* [23], we employ the *closest-first strategy* to generate coreference chains: for each mention m_j a mention-pair test instance is created, in turn, with each preceding mention m_i and is presented to the coreference classifier. For each pair, the classifier returns the predicted label indicating whether the pair of mentions are Coreferent (CO) or Non-Coreferent (NC). This procedure terminates as soon as an antecedent is found for m_j or the beginning of the text is reached. This process is repeated for each mention occurring in the text. In the end, some of the mentions are connected pairwise and, possibly, some of them are not connected to any other mention. Then, a cluster is created for each set of connected mentions (representing one coreference chain) and the mentions that are not connected to any other mention constitute singletons (clusters whose coreference chain contains only one mention). In the end of this process, we obtain the set of coreference chains predicted by the mention-pair model.

5   Results

The results presented in this section were obtained using the mention-pair model (described in Sect. 4) and using the annotations available in the *Summ-it++* corpus (described in Sect. 3.1).

The best overall results obtained in each scenario presented in this section were obtained using the *AdaBoost* algorithm with *Decision Trees* as weak classifiers. For this reason, the results reported in this section were all obtained using this supervised machine learning algorithm. In order to assess the role of semantic features in the coreference resolution task, we report here on two sets of experiments, with and without such features (while the remaining features listed in Table 1 are used in all cases). The results shown in Table 2 were obtained using ten-fold cross-validation. The evaluation metrics computed for each label are *precision, recall* and *F1-score*.

We obtained better overall results when creating the training set using the *All Antecedents* method (0.92 of overall F1-score), which we associate with the higher number of training instances that were created with this method. However, as shown in Table 2, the dataset is very unbalanced and the performance scores for label CO are very low. To overcome this problem, we made several experiments aiming to increase the performance of the algorithm for CO mention-pairs. From Table 2, we conclude that the methods used to generate a training set with a balanced number of CO and NC mention-pairs improve the performance of the system in the classification of CO pairs, while decreasing the overall performance of the system. Therefore, different methods to create training sets for the mention-pair model can have a significant impact in the quality of the predictions made by the system (in particular for CO mention-pairs).

Furthermore, we used two different approaches towards obtaining more balanced datasets: methods for training set generation that use heuristics taking into account the characteristics of the approach (see Sect. 4.1); and simple methods (*Random Undersampling*) to generate balanced training sets [17], by randomly removing some of the learning instances from the learning instances generated with the "All Antecedents" method. The latter are used as a baseline approach to analyze the impact that the methods described in Sect. 4.1 have on the overall performance of the system. Comparing results of "Most Confident" and "Closest Antecedent" (which have a similar number of instances) with "Random Undersampling 1", and "MCAN" with "Random Undersampling 2", we conclude that using more sophisticated (heuristic) methods to generate balanced training sets brings better results.

Table 2. Mention-pair classifier scores.

Methods/metrics	CO label				NC label			
	# Instances	Prec.	Rec.	f1	# Instances	Prec.	Rec.	f1
Without semantic-based features								
All Antecedents	3320	0.72	0.20	0.31	38759	**0.94**	**0.99**	**0.96**
Most Confident	1267	0.84	0.27	0.40	8812	0.90	**0.99**	0.95
Closest Antecedent	1273	**0.86**	0.25	0.39	8701	0.90	**0.99**	0.95
MCAN	2871	0.64	0.41	0.50	4351	0.69	0.85	0.76
With semantic-based features								
All Antecedents	3320	0.76	0.23	0.35	38759	**0.94**	**0.99**	**0.96**
Most Confident	1267	0.78	0.41	0.54	8812	0.92	0.98	0.95
Closest Antecedent	1273	0.75	0.40	0.52	8701	0.92	0.98	0.95
MCAN	2871	0.79	0.51	**0.62**	4351	0.74	0.91	0.82
Rand Undersample 1	1267	0.74	0.31	0.44	8812	0.91	0.98	0.94
Rand Undersample 2	2871	0.74	**0.53**	**0.62**	4351	0.74	0.88	0.80

Finally, we conclude that exploring semantic-based features significantly improves the performance of the system (Table 2). These features allowed the system to solve some coreferences between noun phrases (*i.e.* semantic similar words, synonyms, hyperonyms, meronyms) that were not captured in the previous experimental setup. Furthermore, semantic-based features are relevant to make the system able to generalize better for unseen data. Conversely, we also noticed that these features are responsible for some errors made by the system, due to (a) the importance that the classifier gives to this set of features and (b) lack of semantic knowledge about some of the words presented in the corpus (coverage of the external semantic resources).

We observed that the overall performance of the system presented in this paper is slightly better than the systems presented in related work (as described in Sect. 2). More precisely, our system performs better in the classification of NC pairs and performs worst in the classification of CO pairs, when compared with [8] (based on a similar experimental setup).

6   Conclusions

In this paper, we described an approach to address the problem of coreference resolution from text written in the Portuguese language. We addressed this problem using the mention-pair model and exploring features at the lexical, morphological, syntactic, structural and semantic level. In addition, we explored different methods to generate the training set from an annotated corpus. We conclude that semantic-based features and heuristic-based methods to generate balanced datasets according to the mention-pair model can improve the quality of the predictions made by the system.

In future work, we expect to improve our results using more sophisticated ways to compute semantic-based features (e.g. metrics to calculate semantic similarity between words based on the information provided by external resources), addressing the problem of pronominalization and exploring different approaches to address the task of coreference resolution in Portuguese (*i.e.* mention-ranking models and entity-based models).

Acknowledgments. The first author is partially supported by a doctoral grant from Doctoral Program in Informatics Engineering (ProDEI) from the Faculty of Engineering of the University of Porto (FEUP).

References

1. Al-Rfou, R., Perozzi, B., Skiena, S.: Polyglot: distributed word representations for multilingual NLP. In: Proceedings of 17th Conference on Computational Natural Language Learning, pp. 183–192. ACL, Sofia, August 2013
2. Bick, E.: Multi-level NER for Portuguese in a CG framework. In: Mamede, N.J., Trancoso, I., Baptista, J., das Graças Volpe Nunes, M. (eds.) PROPOR 2003. LNCS, vol. 2721, pp. 118–125. Springer, Heidelberg (2003). doi:10.1007/3-540-45011-4_18
3. Coreixas, T.: Resolução de correferência e categorias de entidades nomeadas. Master's thesis, Pontifícia Universidade Católica do Rio Grande do Sul (2010)

4. Fellbaum, C. (ed.): WordNet: An Electronic Lexical Database. Language, Speech, and Communication. MIT Press, Cambridge (1998)
5. Fonseca, E.B., Antonitsch, A., Collovini, S., do Amaral, D.O.F., Vieira, R., Figueira, A.: Summ-it++: an enriched version of the summ-it corpus. In: Proceedings of 10th International Conference on Language Resources and Evaluation, Portorož, Slovenia (2016)
6. Fonseca, E.B., Vieira, R., Vanin, A.A.: Coreference resolution in Portuguese: detecting person, location and organization. J. Braz. Comput. Intell. Soc. **12**, 86–97 (2014)
7. Fonseca, E.B., Vieira, R., Vanin, A.A.: Dealing with imbalanced datasets for coreference resolution. In: Proceedings of 28th International Florida Artificial Intelligence Research Society Conference, FLAIRS, Hollywood, Florida, 18–20 May, pp. 169–174 (2015)
8. Fonseca, E., Vieira, R., Vanin, A.: Improving coreference resolution with semantic knowledge. In: Silva, J., Ribeiro, R., Quaresma, P., Adami, A., Branco, A. (eds.) PROPOR 2016. LNCS, vol. 9727, pp. 213–224. Springer, Cham (2016). doi:10.1007/978-3-319-41552-9_21
9. Freitas, C., Mota, C., Santos, D., Oliveira, H.G., Carvalho, P.: Second harem: advancing the state of the art of named entity recognition in portuguese. In: Calzolari, N., Choukri, K., Maegaard, B., et al. (eds.) Proceedings of Seventh International Conference on Language Resources and Evaluation (LREC). ELRA, Valletta, Malta, May 2010
10. Gamallo, P., García, M.: Multilingual open information extraction. In: Proceedings of Progress in Artificial Intelligence - 17th Portuguese Conference on Artificial Intelligence, EPIA 2015, Coimbra, Portugal, 8–11 September 2015, pp. 711–722 (2015)
11. García, M., Gamallo, P.: An entity-centric coreference resolution system for person entities with rich linguistic information. In: 25th International Conference on Computational Linguistics: Technical Papers, 23–29 August, Dublin, Ireland, pp. 741–752 (2014)
12. Garcia, M., Gamallo, P.: Multilingual corpora with coreferential annotation of person entities. In: The 9th edn. of the Language Resources and Evaluation Conference, pp. 3229–3233. European Language Resources Association (2014)
13. Gonçalo Oliveira, H.: CONTO.PT: groundwork for the automatic creation of a fuzzy portuguese wordnet. In: Silva, J., Ribeiro, R., Quaresma, P., Adami, A., Branco, A. (eds.) PROPOR 2016. LNCS, vol. 9727, pp. 283–295. Springer, Cham (2016). doi:10.1007/978-3-319-41552-9_29
14. Grosz, B.J., Joshi, A.K., Weinstein, S.: Providing a unified account of definite noun phrases in discourse. In: Proceedings of the 21st Annual Meeting on ACL, pp. 44–50. ACL 1983. ACL, Stroudsburg (1983)
15. Jurafsky, D., Martin, J.H.: Speech and Language Processing, 2nd edn. Prentice-Hall Inc., Upper Saddle River (2009)
16. Lee, H., Peirsman, Y., Chang, A., Chambers, N., Surdeanu, M., Jurafsky, D.: Stanford's multi-pass sieve coreference resolution system at the CoNLL-2011 shared task. In: Proceedings of the Fifteenth Conference on CoNLL: Shared Task, pp. 28–34. ACL, Stroudsburg (2011)
17. More, A.: Survey of resampling techniques for improving classification performance in unbalanced datasets. Computing Research Repository (CoRR) (2016)
18. Ng, V., Cardie, C.: Improving machine learning approaches to coreference resolution. In: Proceedings of the 40th Annual Meeting on Association for Computational Linguistics, pp. 104–111. ACL 2002. ACL, Stroudsburg (2002)

19. Pedregosa, F., Varoquaux, G., Gramfort, A., et al.: Scikit-learn: machine learning in Python. J. Mach. Learn. Res. **12**, 2825–2830 (2011)
20. Pradhan, S., Ramshaw, L., Marcus, M., Palmer, M., Weischedel, R., Xue, N.: CoNLL-2011 shared task: modeling unrestricted coreference in ontonotes. In: Proceedings of the Fifteenth Conference on Computational Natural Language Learning: Shared Task, pp. 1–27. CONLL Shared Task 2011. ACL, Stroudsburg (2011)
21. Rich, E., LuperFoy, S.: An architecture for anaphora resolution. In: Proceedings of the Second Conference on ANLC, pp. 18–24. ACL, Stroudsburg (1988)
22. Sapena, E., Padró, L., Turmo, J.: A constraint-based hypergraph partitioning approach to coreference resolution. Comput. Linguist. **39**(4), 847–884 (2013)
23. Soon, W.M., Ng, H.T., Lim, D.C.Y.: A machine learning approach to coreference resolution of noun phrases. Comput. Linguist. **27**(4), 521–544 (2001)
24. Vilain, M., Burger, J., Aberdeen, J., Connolly, D., Hirschman, L.: A model-theoretic coreference scoring scheme. In: Proceedings of the 6th Conference on Message Understanding. pp. 45–52. MUC6 1995. ACL (1995)
25. Walker, M., Joshi, A., Prince, E.: Centering Theory in Discourse. Clarendon Press, Wotton-under-Edge (1998)

Recognizing Textual Entailment
and Paraphrases in Portuguese

Gil Rocha[✉] and Henrique Lopes Cardoso

LIACC/DEI, Faculdade de Engenharia,
Universidade do Porto, rua Dr. Roberto Frias, 4200-465 Porto, Portugal
{gil.rocha,hlc}@fe.up.pt

Abstract. The aim of textual entailment and paraphrase recognition is to determine whether the meaning of a text fragment can be inferred (is entailed) from the meaning of another text fragment. In this paper, we address the task of automatically recognizing textual entailment (RTE) and paraphrases from text written in the Portuguese language employing supervised machine learning techniques. Firstly, we formulate the task as a multi-class classification problem. We conclude that semantic-based approaches are very promising to recognize textual entailment and that combining data from European and Brazilian Portuguese brings several challenges typical with cross-language learning. Then, we formulate the task as a binary classification problem and demonstrate the capability of the proposed classifier for RTE and paraphrases. The results reported in this work are promising, achieving 0.83 of accuracy on the test data.

1   Introduction

Recognizing Textual Entailment (RTE) [8] in natural language text is a task seeking to find entailment relations between text fragments. Given two text fragments, typically denoted as 'Text' (T) and 'Hypothesis' (H), RTE is the task of determining whether the meaning of the Hypothesis (H, *e.g.* "Joe Smith contributes to academia") is entailed (can be inferred) from the Text (T, *e.g.* "Joe Smith offers a generous gift to the university") [28]. In other words, a sentence T entails another sentence H if after reading and knowing that T is true, a human would infer that H must also be true.

We may think of textual entailment and paraphrasing in terms of logical entailment ($\models$) [4]. If the logical meaning representations of T and H are Φ_T and Φ_H respectively, then $\langle T, H \rangle$ corresponds to a textual entailment pair if and only if $(\Phi_T \wedge B) \models \Phi_H$, where B is a knowledge base containing postulates that correspond to knowledge that is typically assumed to be shared by humans (*i.e.* common sense reasoning and world knowledge). Similarly, if the logical meaning representations of text fragments T_1 and T_2 are Φ_1 and Φ_2 respectively, then T_1 is a paraphrase of T_2 if and only if $(\Phi_1 \wedge B) \models \Phi_2$ and $(\Phi_2 \wedge B) \models \Phi_1$.

It is well known that writers tend to avoid repetition of words (*e.g.* making use of different referring expressions) and omit implicit knowledge in order

© Springer International Publishing AG 2017
E. Oliveira et al. (Eds.): EPIA 2017, LNAI 10423, pp. 868–879, 2017.
DOI: 10.1007/978-3-319-65340-2_70

to obtain a more fluent reading experience and capture a reader's attention. Writers often appeal to commonsense knowledge and inferring capabilities they assume the target reading audience to have, to convey information about the world. These assumptions turn out to pose very difficult challenges to computational systems aiming to automatically process and reason about information expressed in natural language texts. Furthermore, this phenomena is often associated with ambiguity presented in text written in natural language. Taking into account the characteristics of natural language text previously presented, the *NLP* community typically adopts a relaxed definition of textual entailment [4], so that T entails H if a human knowing that T is true would be expected to infer that H must also be true in a given context. A similar relaxed definition can be formulated for paraphrases.

RTE has been recently proposed as a general task that captures major semantic inference needs in several NLP applications [4,7], including question answering [22], information extraction [21], document summarization [19], machine translation [23] and argumentation mining [18,26].

Between 2004 and 2013, eight *RTE Challenges* [6] were organized aiming to provide concrete datasets that could be used by the research community to evaluate and compare different approaches. However, RTE from Portuguese text remains little explored. Recently, at the *PROPOR 2016* international conference, the ASSIN ("Avaliação de Similaridade Semântica e Inferência Textual") challenge was proposed [12]. This challenge introduced a corpus annotated for the semantic similarity and textual inference tasks from text written in Portuguese, providing the necessary resources for the development of NLP systems using machine learning (ML) techniques to address this challenging task.

In this paper, we aim to explore different approaches to address the task of recognizing textual entailment and paraphrases from text written in the Portuguese language, using supervised ML algorithms.

This paper is structured as follows: Sect. 2 presents related work on recognizing textual entailment and paraphrases, focusing approaches based on text written in the Portuguese language. Section 3 introduces the corpus that was used in our experiments to validate the approach presented in this work. Section 4 describes the methods that were used to address the task of recognizing textual entailment and paraphrases using supervised machine learning algorithms. Section 5 presents the results obtained by the system described in this paper. Finally, Sect. 6 concludes and points to directions of future work.

2   Related Work

State-of-the-art systems for RTE and paraphrase in natural language text typically follow a supervised machine learning approach. These systems rely on heavily engineered NLP pipelines, extensive manual creation of features, several external resources (e.g. WordNet [10]) and specialized sub-components to address specific auxiliary sub-tasks [4,7,27], such as negation detection, semantic similarity and paraphrase detection [5,9,16]. Existing approaches differ mainly on the initial assumptions and specific goals. In [4], the authors divided these systems in two main dimensions: (a) whether they focus on *paraphrasing* or *textual entailment* between text fragment pairs, and (b) whether they perform *recognition, generation* or *extraction* of paraphrases or textual entailment pairs. Since, in this paper, we focus on the recognition of paraphrase and textual entailment between each pair of sentences, the remainder of this section will focus on related work for this specific task. The main input given to a paraphrase or textual entailment recognizer is a pair of sentences, possibly in a particular context. The desired output is a (probabilistic) judgment, indicating whether or not the text fragments are paraphrases or a textual entailment pair.

For English text several challenges have been proposed, namely the RTE Challenges [6], SICK [20] and STS at SemEval [1].

The ASSIN challenge [12] follows similar guidelines and introduces the first corpus containing entailment and semantic similarity annotations between pairs of sentences in two Portuguese variants, European and Brazilian, suitable for the exploration of supervised machine learning techniques to address these tasks. To the best of our knowledge, the best ML approaches for RTE and paraphrases in Portuguese texts are presented in the ASSIN challenge. In [15], Hartmann followed the supervised machine learning paradigm with an approach based on the cosine similarity of the vectorial representation of each sentence. These sentence representations were obtained from the sum of the vectors representing each word in a sentence using two language models: *TF-IDF* and *word2vec*. Then, Hartmann computes cosine similarity metrics for each pair of sentences from the two representations (*TF-IDF* and *word2vec*) and uses them as features that are given to a linear classifier.

Fialho *et al.* [11] extracted several metrics for each pair of sentences, namely edit distance, words overlap, *BLEU* [24] and *ROUGE* [17], amongst others. They reported several experiments considering different preprocessing steps in the NLP pipeline, namely: original sentences, removing stop-words, lower-case words and clusters of words. A feature set containing more than 90 features to represent each pair of sentences was used as input for a *SVM* classifier. Fialho *et al.* also reported experiments merging the original ASSIN corpus with annotated data from the SICK corpus translated from English to Portuguese. They added 9191 examples from the *SICK* corpus to the 6000 examples from the ASSIN training set in one of their experiments. The results reported on the augmented version of the training data were worst than the results reported on the original training data. The authors associate these results to translation errors that were probably made during the process. In addition, they trained their model in one of the Portuguese variants of the ASSIN corpus and evaluated the performance of the model in the other Portuguese variant. Reported results following this experimental setup were worst when compared with the model trained and tested in the same variant, but were better than the results obtained in the augmented version of the original dataset (with the *SICK* data). They obtained the best results for recognizing textual entailment in the ASSIN challenge: 0.843 of accuracy and 0.66 of macro F1-score.

In [3], Alves *et al.* explored two different approaches for RTE and paraphrases: a supervised ML approach ("Reciclagem" system) and a heuristic-based approach ("ASAPP" system). The "Reciclagem" system is based on lexical and semantic knowledge that calculates the similarity and relations of two sentences without any kind of supervised machine learning methods. This system was used as a baseline for the "ASAPP" system and to evaluate the quality of different lexical and semantic resources for Portuguese. The "ASAPP" system follows the supervised ML approach and adds to "Reciclagem" features based on the syntactic and structural information extracted from the pair of sentences, such as: number of tokens, overlapping words, synonyms, hyperonyms, meronyms, antonyms and number of words with negative connotation, type of named entities, amongst others. In their experiments, the authors explored different strategies to divide the training data, to combine results from different classifiers and several feature selection techniques. They reported 0.731 of accuracy and 0.43 of macro F1-score on the European-Portuguese test data.

3   Data

A corpus with sentence pairs labeled with the type of relation (*Entailment, Paraphrase* or *None*) is an important requirement in order to address the task of recognizing textual entailment and paraphrases using supervised ML techniques. The ASSIN corpus [12] is, to the best of our knowledge, the first corpus annotated with pairs of sentences written in Portuguese that is suitable for this task. The corpus contains pairs of sentences extracted from news articles written in European-Portuguese (EP) and Brazilian-Portuguese (BP), obtained from *Google News* Portugal and Brazil, respectively.

The ASSIN challenge [12] included two tasks, both using the ASSIN corpus: (a) semantic similarity and (b) textual entailment and paraphrase recognition. We will focus on the latter: the "entailment" label is the attribute that will be used as target label for the proposed task.

In total, the ASSIN corpus contains 10.000 pairs, half in each of the Portuguese variants. The distribution of $\langle T, H \rangle$ pairs between each "entailment" label and between texts written in BP and EP is shown in Table 1. It is important to notice that the corpus is unbalanced in relation to the "entailment" and "paraphrase" labels. This can bring some issues that should be taken into account.

Table 1. Distribution of labels in ASSIN corpus.

Label/partition	BP		EP	
	Train	*Test*	*Train*	*Test*
None	2331	1553	2046	1386
Entailment	529	341	729	481
Paraphrase	140	106	225	133

The inter-annotator agreement metrics related to this corpus are the following: *Fleiss's* $\mathcal{K}$ of 0.61 and Concordance of 0.8. The *Fleiss's* $\mathcal{K}$ value is relatively low, demonstrating the subjectivity associated with the annotation process [12]. However, these values are not very different from the values reported in other corpora used for the same task: for instance, in the RTE Challenges the values ranged from 0.6 in the first RTE Challenge to 0.75 or more in the following challenges [6,12].

Table 2 shows one example of the content and annotations available in the ASSIN corpus for each of the labels.

Table 2. Annotated examples from the ASSIN corpus (extracted from [12]).

Label	Pair of Sentences
None	As apostas podem ser feitas até as 19h (de Brasília). (T)
	As apostas podem ser feitas em qualquer lotérica do país. (H)
Entailment	Como não houve acordo, a reunião será retomada nesta terça, a partir das 10h. (T)
	As partes voltam a se reunir nesta terça, às 10h. (H)
Paraphrase	Vou convocar um congresso extraordinário para me substituir enquanto presidente. (T)
	Vou organizar um congresso extraordinário para se realizar a minha substituição como presidente. (H)

4   Methods

We here describe the approach we followed to address the task of entailment and paraphrase recognition from natural language Portuguese text. We formulate the problem following two different settings. First, as a multi-class classification problem, in which we aim to classify each $\langle T, H \rangle$ with one of the labels *Entailment* (if $T \models H$), *Paraphrase* (if $T \models H$ and $H \models T$, *i.e.*, if T is paraphrase of H), or *None* (if T and H are not related with one of the previous labels). Second, as a binary classification problem, aiming to distinct each $\langle T, H \rangle$ with one of the labels *Entailment* or *None*. We employed supervised ML techniques given a set of annotated data, the ASSIN corpus.

To transform each sentence into the corresponding set of tokens and to obtain for each token the corresponding lemma and part-of-speech information (including syntactic function, person, number, tense, amongst others) we used the *CitiusTagger* [13] NLP tool. This tool includes a named entity recognizer trained in natural language text written in Portuguese.

Several experiments were made using different NLP techniques to process the sentences received as input: removing stop-words, removing auxiliary words (*i.e.* words relevant for the discourse structure but not domain specific, such as:

prepositions, determiners, conjunctions, interjections, numbers and some adverbial groups) and lemmatization. Transforming each token in the corresponding lemma is a promising approach because it will make explicit that some of the words are repeated in both sentences even if small variations of these words are used in each sentence (*e.g.* different verb tenses). After this step, each sentence contained in T and H from the pair $\langle T, H \rangle$ under analysis were represented in a structured format (set of tokens) and annotated with some additional information regarding the content of the text (*e.g.* part-of-speech tags).

In order to apply ML algorithms we need to represent the training instances by a set of numerical features. Since in this problem we receive a pair of sentences as input and we aim to automatically classify the relation between them as output, the feature set should be designed taking special attention to the properties that characterize such relation. To represent each pair $\langle T, H \rangle$ we employed a set of features (listed in Table 3) at the lexical, syntactic and semantic level. The first four lexical features listed in Table 3 aim to capture the overlap of information expressed in T in relation to H and vice-versa. Feature *T_Bigger_H* tries to capture the intuition that in a relation of *Entailment*, sentence H is usually smaller than sentence T. Regarding syntactic features, changes in verb tense are typically not expected to occur in *Paraphrase* relations, but rewriting the same sentence using alternation between passive and active voice is the most common case of paraphrase relations. Semantic features were employed for tokens in one of the sentences that do not occur in the other, after removing named entities (to avoid overlap with lexical features). The first three features capture semantic relations between each pair of tokens using knowledge extracted from a Portuguese wordnet. The last two features explore the word embeddings model and aim to capture different ways of measuring semantic relations between H and T, after projecting each sentence in the embedding space.

Table 3. Feature set

Type	Feature	Description
Lexical	Overlap_T	% of (unique) tokens in T that exist in H
	Overlap_H	% of (unique) tokens in H that exist in T
	NE_T	% of (unique) named entities in T that exist in H
	NE_H	% of (unique) named entities in H that exist in T
	T_Bigger_H	If $|T| > |H|$ returns 1. Returns 0, otherwise
Syntactic	Tense	If T and H are written in the same grammatical tense
	Voice	If T and H are written in the same grammatical voice
Semantic	Synonym	% of tokens in T synonyms of tokens in H. And vice-versa
	Hyperonym	% of tokens in T hyperonyms of tokens in H. And vice-versa
	Meronym	% of tokens in T meronyms of tokens in H. And vice-versa
	Cos_Sim	cosine similarity between $\vec{e}(T)$ and $\vec{e}(H)$
	Entail_Versor	entailment versor ($\hat{d}$) in the word embeddings space

Knowledge about the words of a language and their semantic relations with other words can be exploited with large-scale lexical databases. To enrich the feature set shown in Table 3 with semantic knowledge, we explored external semantic resources. By exploiting these resources we aim to enable the system to deal better with the diversity and ambiguity of natural language text. Similarly to WordNet [10] for the English language, CONTO.PT [14] is a fuzzy wordnet for Portuguese, which groups words into sets of cognitive synonyms (called *synsets*), each expressing a distinct concept. In addition, synsets are interlinked by means of conceptual and semantic relations (*e.g.* "hyperonym" and "part-of"). Synsets included in CONTO.PT were automatically extracted from several linguistic resources. All the relations represented in CONTO.PT (i.e. relations between words and synsets, as well as relations between synsets) include degrees of membership. Two tokens (obtained after tokenization and lemmatization) are considered synonyms if they occur in the same synset. One token T_i is considered hyperonym of T_j if there exists a hyperonym relation ("hyperonym_of") between the synset of T_i and the synset of T_j. Similarly, T_i is considered meronym of T_j if there exists a meronym relation ("part_of" or "member_of") between the synset of T_i and the synset of T_j.

Finally, we exploit a distributed representation of words (word embeddings) to compute the last two features described in Table 3. These distributions map a word from a dictionary to a feature vector in high-dimensional space, without human intervention, from observing the usage of words on large (non-annotated) corpora. This real-valued vector representation tries to arrange words with similar meanings close to each other based on the occurrences of these words in large-scale corpora. Then, from these representations, interesting features can be explored, such as semantic and syntactic similarities. In our experiments, we used a pre-trained model provided by the *Polyglot*[1] tool [2], in which a neural network architecture was trained with Portuguese *Wikipedia* articles.

In order to obtain a score indicating the similarity between two text fragments, T_i and T_j, we compute the cosine similarity between the vectors that represent each of the text fragments in the high-dimensional space. Each text fragment is projected into the embedding space as $\vec{T_i} = \sum_{k=1}^{n} \vec{e}(w_k)n^{-1}$, where $\vec{e}(w_k)$ represents the embedding vector of the word w_k and n corresponds to the number of words contained in the text fragment T_i. Then, we compute the final value of the cosine similarity $\delta_{\vec{T_i},\vec{T_j}} = \cos(\vec{T_i}, \vec{T_j})$, $\delta_{\vec{T_i},\vec{T_j}} \in [-1,1]$ followed by the following rescaling and normalization: $(1.0 - \delta_{\vec{T_i},\vec{T_j}})/2.0$. The entailment versor $(\hat{d})$ corresponds to the normalized direction vector obtained by subtracting the projection of T in the embedding space, $\vec{e}(T)$, by the projection of H, $\vec{e}(H)$.

For each classification task, we have run several experiments exploring some well known state-of-the-art algorithms, namely: *Support Vector Machine* (SVM) using linear and polynomial kernels, *Maximum Entropy model* (MaxEnt), *Adaptive Boosting* algorithm (AdaBoost) using *Decision Trees* as weak classifiers, *Random Forrest Classifier* using *Decision Trees* as weak classifiers, and

---

[1] http://polyglot.readthedocs.io/en/latest/index.html.

Multilayer Perceptron Classifier (Neural Net) with one hidden layer. All the ML algorithms previously mentioned were employed using the *scikit-learn* library [25] for the *Python* programming language. Since the best overall results reported in all the evaluation scenarios were obtained using a *SVM* with a *linear* kernel, all the results reported in Sect. 5 were obtained using this classifier.

5   Experiments and Results

We investigate four evaluation scenarios. First, we report 10-fold cross validation results over all the training examples of the European-Portuguese partition of the ASSIN corpus, using a simple set of features, namely the lexical and syntactic-based features presented in Sect. 4. We also report on the results obtained by the learned model on a separate test set from the ASSIN corpus containing examples annotated in European-Portuguese. The system obtained in this scenario corresponds to our baseline. The second evaluation scenario follows a similar setting but using a more sophisticated set of features, in which semantic-based features were included (complete set of features described in Sect. 4). In this evaluation scenario we aim to determine the impact semantic-based features have in correctly identifying entailment relations. In the third evaluation scenario, we report 10-fold cross validation results over all the training examples available in the ASSIN corpus, including both the European-Portuguese and the Brazilian-Portuguese partitions, using the complete set of features described in Sect. 4. In this evaluation scenario we aim to validate our intuition that increasing the training set with more training data, regardless of the differences between European-Portuguese and Brazilian-Portuguese, should increase the performance of the system for the task of recognizing textual entailment and paraphrases from text written in Portuguese.

Table 4. Evaluation results for each evaluation scenario of the multi-class setting.

	Train						Test	
	N	E	P	Total			Total	
	F1	F1	F1	F1	Macro-F1	Acc.	Macro-F1	Acc.
EP	0.89	0.69	**0.60**	0.82	**0.73**	0.823	0.69	0.817
EP and Semantic	**0.9**	**0.7**	0.59	**0.83**	**0.73**	0.824	**0.71**	0.821
EP+BP and Semantic	**0.9**	0.65	0.52	0.82	0.69	0.819	**0.71**	**0.827**

Table 4 summarizes the results obtained in our experiments regarding the multi-class formulation. Each line corresponds to the results obtained in each of the evaluation scenarios previously described. The first three columns correspond to the averaged F1-score evaluation metric obtained after performing 10-fold cross validation on the training data for each label considered in the classification problem, namely *None* (N), *Entailment* (E) and *Paraphrase* (P). The last three columns, also regarding the results obtained in the training set, correspond to the overall results obtained for each evaluation metric, namely *micro F1-score* (F1), *macro F1-score* (Macro-F1) and *accuracy* (Acc.). Finally, the last two columns correspond to the overall *macro F1-score* and *accuracy* obtained in the test set.

In general, we obtained better overall results in the recognition of the *None* relation (0.9), followed by *Entailment* relations (0.7) and by *Paraphrase* relations (0.6). We associate these results to the higher number of learning instances available in the corpus for each of the labels *None* and *Entailment*, respectively.

From the analysis of the results we conclude that enhancing the feature set with semantic-based features improved the overall results, but such improvements are not statistically significant. We expected these improvements to be more significant, since it seems intuitive that semantic-based features are relevant for the task of recognizing textual entailment and paraphrases. After performing feature and error analysis, we associate these results with the following: (a) the system gave too much importance to the "percentage of overlapping tokens" feature (*i.e.* when the value of the feature "Overlap_T" is very high the system tends to predict *Paraphrase*, when the feature "Overlap_H" is very high the system tends to predict *Entailment*, and when these values are both very low the system tends to predict *None*); (b) the coverage of semantic-based features is relatively low, causing this feature to have null values in some situations.

Comparing the results obtained by the system using the European-Portuguese and the Brazilian-Portuguese training set of the ASSIN corpus, we observed that increasing the training set with the Brazilian-Portuguese partition reduced the overall performance of the system. These results suggest that some characteristics of entailment and paraphrase relations between two text fragments of the Brazilian-Portuguese partition are different from the European-Portuguese partition. Furthermore, syntactic and semantic differences between the two variants are responsible for the majority of the errors made by the system. The best overall results in the test data were obtained in the last evaluation scenario, which we associate to the highest number of training examples that were provided to the system during the training phase. These resulted in a system that is able to generalize better for unseen data, explaining the results shown in Table 4. Comparing the results reported in this paper with the systems participating in the *ASSIN Challenge*, our approach would be ranked in a second place, obtaining an overall score that is very close to the results presented by the best system: 0.8385 of accuracy and 0.7 of macro F1-score ("L2F/INESC-ID" team).

Finally, in a fourth evaluation scenario, we address the problem in a different perspective, motivated by the characteristics of the ASSIN corpus. As shown in Table 1, the distribution of classes in the ASSIN corpus is very unbalanced, with a much lower number of examples for the *Paraphrase* class. As introduced in Sect. 1, a *Paraphrase* can be formulated as a bidirectional entailment. In this experimental setup we formulate the problem of recognizing textual entailment as a binary classification problem between the classes *Entailment/Paraphrase* and *None*. The training set was built as follows: (a) each *Paraphrase* example from the ASSIN corpus was transformed into two new *Entailment* examples (*i.e.* T entails H and H entails T); (b) the remaining *None* and *Entailment* examples from the ASSIN corpus were added. The test set comprises the same examples of the ASSIN corpus, where the *Entailment* and *Paraphrase* classes were aggregated in the same class (E+P). We aim to demonstrate the ability of the approach proposed in this paper to distinguish situations where the text sentence (T) entails the hypothesis sentence (H) from when this is not the case. The results obtained in this experimental setup are shown in Table 5. The first two lines correspond to the results obtained for each of the target classes: *None* (N) and *Entailment/Paraphrase* (E+P). For each of the partitions (training and test set) of the ASSIN corpus containing annotations for European-Portuguese, the first column presents the total number of samples used in the experiments and the last two columns correspond to the accuracy and averaged micro F1-score evaluation metrics obtained after performing 10-fold cross validation. The results obtained in the binary formulation show that this binary classification task makes the decision boundaries easier to distinguish.

Table 5. Evaluation results for the binary classification setting

	Train			Test		
	# samples	Acc.	F1	# samples	Acc.	F1
N	2046	0.87	0.88	1386	0.86	0.88
E + P	1179	0.81	0.79	614	0.78	0.74
Total/avg	3225	0.85	0.85	2000	0.83	0.84

6 Conclusions

In this paper, we presented a preliminary approach to address the NLP task of recognizing textual entailment and paraphrases from text written in the Portuguese language. Firstly, we formulated this task as a multi-class classification problem. The overall results reported in this paper are promising (accuracy of 0.827 in the test set). A close assessment of obtained results shown that the number of annotated sentence pairs may not be sufficient to build a system that generalizes well for unseen data since the implemented classifiers tend to prefer labels that contain more training instances simply because they are more representative of the training data in statistical terms. Looking at the obtained results, we conclude that the overall system performance improved with semantic-based features, but not significantly. Notwithstanding, a detailed analysis points that this is one of the most promising directions for future work. Increasing the training set with the Brazilian-Portuguese partition of the ASSIN corpus had an unexpected impact in the overall performance of the system. We associate this result to syntactic and semantic differences between European and Brazilian Portuguese and because some of the external resources that were employed (*i.e.* fuzzy wordnet, part-of-speech tagger, word embeddings model) are based on the European-Portuguese language. Consequently, some lexical, syntactic and semantic Brazilian-Portuguese linguistic phenomena may be missing or misleading in this approach. Then, we formulate the problem as a binary classification task and demonstrate the ability of the system to recognize textual entailment.

In future work, we would like to enhance the semantic-based features employed in our system, including: metrics to evaluate semantic similarity between fragments of text using the fuzzy wordnet described in this paper, sentence-level representations (e.g. using a dependency parser) and, more sophisticated computations using distributed representation models. These are promising directions for future work that we intend to pursue.

Acknowledgments. The first author is partially supported by a doctoral grant from Doctoral Program in Informatics Engineering (ProDEI) from the Faculty of Engineering of the University of Porto (FEUP).

References

1. Agirre, E., Banea, C., Cardie, C., Cer, D.M., Diab, M.T., Gonzalez-Agirre, A., Guo, W., Lopez-Gazpio, I., Maritxalar, M., Mihalcea, R., Rigau, G., Uria, L., Wiebe, J.: Semeval-2015 task 2: semantic textual similarity, english, spanish and pilot on interpretability. In: Cer, D.M., Jurgens, D., Nakov, P., Zesch, T. (eds.) Proceedings of the 9th International Workshop on Semantic Evaluation, Denver, USA, pp. 252–263. ACL (2015)
2. Al-Rfou, R., Perozzi, B., Skiena, S.: Polyglot: distributed word representations for multilingual NLP. In: Proceedings of Seventeenth Conference on Computational Natural Language Learning, pp. 183–192. ACL, Sofia, Bulgaria, August 2013
3. Alves, A.O., Oliveira, H., Rodrigues, R.: ASAPP: Alinhamento Semântico Automático de Palavras aplicado ao Português. Linguamática **8**(2), 43–58 (2016)
4. Androutsopoulos, I., Malakasiotis, P.: A survey of paraphrasing and textual entailment methods. J. Artif. Int. Res. **38**(1), 135–187 (2010)
5. Beltagy, I., Roller, S., Cheng, P., Erk, K., Mooney, R.J.: Representing meaning with a combination of logical and distributional models. Comput. Linguist. **42**(4), 763–808 (2016)
6. Bentivogli, L., Dagan, I., Dang, H.T., Giampiccolo, D., Magnini, B.: Fifth PASCAL recognizing textual entailment challenge. In: Proceedings of Text Analysis Conference (2009)
7. Dagan, I., Glickman, O., Magnini, B.: The PASCAL recognising Textual entailment challenge. In: Quiñonero-Candela, J., Dagan, I., Magnini, B., d'Alché-Buc, F. (eds.) MLCW 2005. LNCS, vol. 3944, pp. 177–190. Springer, Heidelberg (2006). doi:10.1007/11736790_9
8. Dagan, I., Roth, D., Sammons, M., Zanzotto, F.M.: Recognizing Textual Entailment: Models and Applications. Synthesis Lectures on Human Language Technologies. Morgan & Claypool Publishers, San Rafael (2013)
9. De Marneffe, M., Rafferty, A.N., Manning, C.D.: Finding contradictions in text. In: Association for Computational Linguistics (2008)
10. Fellbaum, C. (ed.): WordNet: an electronic lexical database Language, speech, and communication. MIT Press, Cambridge (1998)
11. Fialho, P., Marques, R., Martins, B., Coheur, L., Quaresma, P.: INESC-ID@ASSIN: Medição de Similaridade Semântica e Reconhecimento de Inferência Textual. Linguamática **8**(2), 33–42 (2016)
12. Fonseca, E., Santos, L., Criscuolo, M., Aluisio, S.: ASSIN: avaliacao de similaridade semantica e inferencia textual. In: Computational Processing of the Portuguese Language - 12th International Conference, Tomar, Portugal, 13–15 July (2016)

13. Garcia, M., Gamallo, P.: Yet another suite of multilingual NLP tools. In: Sierra-Rodríguez, J.-L., Leal, J.P., Simões, A. (eds.) SLATE 2015. CCIS, vol. 563, pp. 65–75. Springer, Cham (2015). doi:10.1007/978-3-319-27653-3_7

14. Gonçalo Oliveira, H.: CONTO.PT: groundwork for the automatic creation of a fuzzy portuguese wordnet. In: Silva, J., Ribeiro, R., Quaresma, P., Adami, A., Branco, A. (eds.) PROPOR 2016. LNCS, vol. 9727, pp. 283–295. Springer, Cham (2016). doi:10.1007/978-3-319-41552-9_29

15. Hartmann, N.S.: Solo Queue at ASSIN: Combinando Abordagens Tradicionais e Emergentes. Linguamática **8**(2), 59–64 (2016)

16. Lai, A., Hockenmaier, J.: Illinois-LH: a denotational and distributional approach to semantics. In: Proceedings of 8th International Workshop on Semantic Evaluation (SemEval 2014), pp. 329–334. ACL, Dublin, Ireland, August 2014

17. Lin, C.Y., Och, F.J.: Automatic evaluation of machine translation quality using longest common subsequence and skip-bigram statistics. In: Proceedings of 42nd Annual Meeting Association for Computational Linguistics, Stroudsburg, PA, USA (2004)

18. Lippi, M., Torroni, P.: Argumentation mining: state of the art and emerging trends. ACM Trans. Internet Technol. **16**(2), 10:1–10:25 (2016)

19. Madnani, N., Dorr, B.J.: Generating phrasal and sentential paraphrases: a survey of data-driven methods. Comput. Linguist. **36**(3), 341–387 (2010)

20. Marelli, M., Bentivogli, L., Baroni, M., Bernardi, R., Menini, S., Zamparelli, R.: Semeval-2014 task 1: evaluation of compositional distributional semantic models on full sentences through semantic relatedness and textual entailment. In: Nakov, P., Zesch, T. (eds.) Proceedings of 8th International Workshop on Semantic Evaluation, COLING, Dublin, Ireland, pp. 1–8. ACL (2014)

21. Moens, M.F.: Information Extraction: Algorithms and Prospects in a Retrieval Context. Springer, Heidelberg (2009)

22. Mollá, D., Vicedo, J.L.: Question answering in restricted domains: an overview. Comput. Linguist. **33**(1), 41–61 (2007)

23. Padó, S., Galley, M., Jurafsky, D., Manning, C.: Robust machine translation evaluation with entailment features. In: Proceedings of Joint Conference of the 47th Annual Meeting of the ACL and the 4th International Joint Conference on Natural Language Processing of the AFNLP, vol. 1, pp. 297–305. ACL, Stroudsburg, PA, USA (2009)

24. Papineni, K., Roukos, S., Ward, T., Zhu, W.J.: Bleu: A method for automatic evaluation of machine translation. In: Proceedings of 40th Annual Meeting Association Computational Linguistics, pp. 311–318. ACL, Stroudsburg, PA, USA (2002)

25. Pedregosa, F., Varoquaux, G., Gramfort, A., Michel, V., Thirion, B., Grisel, O., Blondel, M., Prettenhofer, P., Weiss, R., Dubourg, V., Vanderplas, J., Passos, A., Cournapeau, D., Brucher, M., Perrot, M., Duchesnay, E.: Scikit-learn: machine learning in python. J. Mach. Learn. Res. **12**, 2825–2830 (2011)

26. Rocha, G., Lopes Cardoso, H., Teixeira, J.: ArgMine: a framework for argumentation mining. In: 12th International Conference on Computational Processing of the Portuguese Language - PROPOR 2016, Student Research Workshop, Tomar, Portugal, 13–15 July (2016)

27. Rocktäschel, T., Grefenstette, E., Hermann, K.M., Kociský, T., Blunsom, P.: Reasoning about entailment with neural attention. CoRR abs/1509.06664 (2015)

28. Sammons, M., Vydiswaran, V., Roth, D.: Recognizing textual entailment. In: Bikel, D.M., Zitouni, I. (eds.) Multilingual Natural Language Applications: From Theory to Practice, pp. 209–258. Prentice Hall, Upper Saddle River (2012)

Learning Word Embeddings from the Portuguese Twitter Stream: A Study of Some Practical Aspects

Pedro Saleiro[1,2]([✉]), Luís Sarmento[1,2,3], Eduarda Mendes Rodrigues[1],
Carlos Soares[1,3], and Eugénio Oliveira[1,2]

[1] FEUP, Universidade do Porto, Porto, Portugal
pssc@fe.up.pt
[2] LIACC, Universidade do Porto, Porto, Portugal
[3] INESC TEC, Universidade do Porto, Porto, Portugal

Abstract. This paper describes a preliminary study for producing and distributing a large-scale database of embeddings from the Portuguese Twitter stream. We start by experimenting with a relatively small sample and focusing on three challenges: volume of training data, vocabulary size and intrinsic evaluation metrics. Using a single GPU, we were able to scale up vocabulary size from 2048 words embedded and 500K training examples to 32768 words over 10M training examples while keeping a stable validation loss and approximately linear trend on training time per epoch. We also observed that using less than 50% of the available training examples for each vocabulary size might result in overfitting. Results on intrinsic evaluation show promising performance for a vocabulary size of 32768 words. Nevertheless, intrinsic evaluation metrics suffer from over-sensitivity to their corresponding cosine similarity thresholds, indicating that a wider range of metrics need to be developed to track progress.

1 Introduction

Word embeddings have great practical importance since they can be used as pre-computed high-density *features* to ML models, significantly reducing the amount of training data required in a variety of NLP tasks. However, there are several inter-related challenges with computing and consistently distributing word embeddings concerning the:

- **intrinsic properties of the embeddings**. How many dimensions do we actually need to store all the "useful" semantic information? How big should the embedded vocabulary be to have practical value? How do these two factors interplay?
- **type of model** used for generating the embeddings. There are multiple possible models and it is not obvious which one is the "best", both in general or in the context of a specific type of applications.

© Springer International Publishing AG 2017
E. Oliveira et al. (Eds.): EPIA 2017, LNAI 10423, pp. 880–891, 2017.
DOI: 10.1007/978-3-319-65340-2_71

- the size and properties of **training data**: What is the minimum amount of training data needed? Should we include out of vocabulary words in the training?
- optimization techniques to be used, **model hyperparameter** and *training parameters.*

Not only the space of possibilities for each of these aspects is large, there are also challenges in performing a consistent large-scale evaluation of the resulting embeddings [1]. This makes systematic experimentation of alternative word-embedding configurations extremely difficult.

In this work, we make progress in trying to find good combinations of some of the previous parameters. We focus specifically in the task of computing word embeddings for processing the Portuguese Twitter stream. User-generated content (such as twitter messages) tends to be populated by words that are specific to the medium, and that are constantly being added by users. These dynamics pose challenges to NLP systems, which have difficulties in dealing with out of vocabulary words. Therefore, learning a semantic representation for those words directly from the user-generated stream - and as the words arise - would allow us to keep up with the dynamics of the medium and reduce the cases for which we have no information about the words.

Starting from our own implementation of a neural word embedding model, which should be seen as a flexible baseline model for further experimentation, our research tries to answer the following practical questions:

- how large is the vocabulary the one can realistically embed given the level of resources that most organizations can afford to buy and to manage (as opposed to large clusters of GPU's only available to a few organizations)?
- how much data, as a function of the size of the vocabulary we wish to embed, is enough for training meaningful embeddings?
- how can we evaluate embeddings in automatic and consistent way so that a reasonably detailed systematic exploration of the previously describe space of possibilities can be performed?

By answering these questions based on a reasonably small sample of Twitter data (5M), we hope to find the best way to proceed and train embeddings for Twitter vocabulary using the much larger amount of Twitter data available (300M), but for which parameter experimentation would be unfeasible. This work can thus be seen as a *preparatory study* for a subsequent attempt to produce and distribute a large-scale database of embeddings for processing Portuguese Twitter data.

2   Related Work

There are several approaches to generating word embeddings. One can build models that *explicitly* aim at generating word embeddings, such as Word2Vec or GloVe [2,3], or one can extract such embeddings as by-products of more general models, which implicitly compute such word embeddings in the process of solving other language tasks.

Word embeddings methods aim to represent words as real valued continuous vectors in a much lower dimensional space when compared to traditional bag-of-words models. Moreover, this low dimensional space is able to capture lexical and semantic properties of words. Co-occurrence statistics are the fundamental information that allows creating such representations. Two approaches exist for building word embeddings. One creates a low rank approximation of the word co-occurrence matrix, such as in the case of Latent Semantic Analysis [4] and GloVe [3]. The other approach consists in extracting internal representations from neural network models of text [2,5,6]. Levy and Goldberg [7] showed that the two approaches are closely related.

Although, word embeddings research go back several decades, it was the recent developments of Deep Learning and the word2vec framework [2] that captured the attention of the NLP community. Moreover, Mikolov et al. [8] showed that embeddings trained using word2vec models (CBOW and Skip-gram) exhibit linear structure, allowing analogy questions of the form "man:woman::king:??." and can boost performance of several text classification tasks.

One of the issues of recent work in training word embeddings is the variability of experimental setups reported. For instance, in the paper describing GloVe [3] authors trained their model on five corpora of different sizes and built a vocabulary of 400K most frequent words. Mikolov et al. [8] trained with 82K vocabulary while Mikolov et al. [2] was trained with 3M vocabulary. Recently, Arora et al. [9] proposed a generative model for learning embeddings that tries to explain some theoretical justification for nonlinear models (e.g. word2vec and GloVe) and some hyper parameter choices. Authors evaluated their model using 68K vocabulary.

SemEval 2016-Task 4: Sentiment Analysis in Twitter organizers report that participants either used general purpose pre-trained word embeddings, or trained from Tweet 2016 dataset or "from some sort of dataset" [10]. However, participants neither report the size of vocabulary used neither the possible effect it might have on the task specific results.

Recently, Rodrigues et al. [11] created and distributed the first general purpose embeddings for Portuguese. Word2vec gensim implementation was used and authors report results with different values for the parameters of the framework. Furthermore, authors used experts to translate well established word embeddings test sets for Portuguese language, which they also made publicly available and we use some of those in this work.

3   Our Neural Word Embedding Model

The neural word embedding model we use in our experiments is heavily inspired in the one described in [5], but ours is one layer deeper and is set to solve a slightly different word prediction task. Given a sequence of 5 words - w_{i-2} w_{i-1} w_i w_{i+1} w_{i+2}, the task the model tries to perform is that of predicting the middle word, w_i, based on the two words on the left - w_{i-2} w_{i-1} - and the two words on the right - w_{i+1} w_{i+2}: $P(w_i|w_{i-2}, w_{i-1}, w_{i+1}, w_{i+2})$. This should produce embeddings that closely capture distributional similarity, so that words that belong to the same semantic class, or which are synonyms and antonyms of each other, will be embedded in "close" regions of the embedding hyper-space.

Our neural model is composed of the following layers:

- a **Input Word Embedding Layer**, that maps each of the 4 input words represented by a 1-hot vectors with $|V|$ dimensions (e.g. 32k) into a low dimension space (64 bits). The projections matrix - W_{input} - is shared across the 4 inputs. This is *not* be the embedding matrix that we wish to produce.
- a **Merge Layer** that *concatenates* the 4 previous embeddings into a single vector holding all the context information. The concatenation operation ensures that the rest of the model has explicit information about the **relative position** of the input words. Using an *additive* merge operation instead would preserve information onlu about the presence of the words, not their sequence.
- a **Intermediate Context Embedding Dense Layer** that maps the preceding representation of 4 words into a lower dimension space, still representing the entire context. We have fixed this context representation to 64 dimensions. This ultimately determines the dimension of the resulting embeddings. This intermediate layer is important from the point of view of performance because it isolates the still relatively high-dimensional input space (4×64 bits input word embeddings) from the very high-dimensional output space.
- a final **Output Dense Layer** that maps the takes the previous 64-bit representation of the entire input context and produces a vector with the dimensionality of the word output space ($|V|$ dimensions). This matrix - W_{output} - is the one that stores the word embeddings we are interested in.
- A **Softmax Activation Layer** to produces the final prediction over the word space, that is the $P(w_i|w_{i-2}, w_{i-1}, w_{i+1}, w_{i+2})$ distribution

All neural activations in the model are sigmoid functions. The model was implemented using the Syntagma[1] library which relies on Keras [12] for model development, and we train the model using the built-in ADAM [13] optimizer with the default parameters.

4   Experimental Setup

We are interested in assessing two aspects of the word embedding process. On one hand, we wish to evaluate the semantic quality of the produced embeddings. On the other, we want to quantify how much computational power and training data are required to train the embedding model as a function of the size of the vocabulary $|V|$ we try to embed. These aspects have fundamental practical

---

[1] https://github.com/sarmento/syntagma.

importance for deciding how we should attempt to produce the large-scale database of embeddings we will provide in the future. All resources developed in this work are publicly available[2].

Apart from the size of the vocabulary to be processed ($|V|$), the hyperparameters of the model that we could potentially explore are (i) the dimensionality of the input word embeddings and (ii) the dimensionality of the output word embeddings. As mentioned before, we set both to 64 bits after performing some quick manual experimentation. Full hyperparameter exploration is left for future work.

Our experimental testbed comprises a desktop with a nvidia TITAN X (Pascal), Intel Core Quad i7 3770K 3.5 GHz, 32 GB DDR3 RAM and a 180 GB SSD drive.

4.1   Training Data

We randomly sampled 5M tweets from a corpus of 300M tweets collected from the Portuguese Twitter community [14]. The 5M comprise a total of 61.4M words (approx. 12 words per tweets in average). From those 5M tweets we generated a database containing 18.9M distinct 5-g, along with their frequency counts. In this process, all text was down-cased. To help anonymizing the n-gram information, we substituted all the twitter handles by an artificial token "T_HANDLE". We also substituted all HTTP links by the token "LINK". We prepended two special tokens to complete the 5-g generated from the first two words of the tweet, and we correspondingly appended two other special tokens to complete 5-g centered around the two last tokens of the tweet.

Tokenization was perform by *trivially* separating tokens by blank space. No linguistic pre-processing, such as for example separating punctuation from words, was made. We opted for not doing any pre-processing for not introducing any linguistic bias from another tool (tokenization of user generated content is not a trivial problem). The most direct consequence of not performing any linguistic pre-processing is that of increasing the vocabulary size and diluting token counts. However, in principle, and given enough data, the embedding model should be able to learn the correct embeddings for both actual words (e.g. "ronaldo") and the words that have punctuation attached (e.g. "ronaldo!"). In practice, we believe that this can actually be an advantage for the downstream consumers of the embeddings, since they can also relax the requirements of their own tokenization stage. Overall, the dictionary thus produced contains approximately 1.3M distinct entries. Our dictionary was sorted by frequency, so the words with lowest index correspond to the most common words in the corpus.

We used the information from the 5-gram database to generate all training data used in the experiments. For a fixed size $|V|$ of the target vocabulary to be embedded (e.g. $|V| = 2048$), we scanned the database to obtain *all* possible 5-g for which all tokens were among the top $|V|$ words of the dictionary (i.e. the top $|V|$ most frequent words in the corpus). Depending on $|V|$, different numbers of

---

[2] https://github.com/saleiro/embedpt.

valid training 5-g were found in the database: the larger $|V|$ the more valid 5-g would pass the filter. The number of examples collected for each of the values of $|V|$ is shown in Table 1.

Table 1. Number of 5-g available for training for different sizes of target vocabulary $|V|$

$|V|$	# 5-g
2048	2,496,830
8192	6,114,640
32768	10,899,570

Since one of the goals of our experiments is to understand the impact of using different amounts of training data, for each size of vocabulary to be embedded $|V|$ we will run experiments training the models using 25%, 50%, 75% and 100% of the data available.

4.2 Metrics Related with the Learning Process

We tracked metrics related to the learning process itself, as a function of the vocabulary size to be embedded $|V|$ and of the fraction of training data used (25%, 50%, 75% and 100%). For all possible configurations, we recorded the values of the training and validation loss (cross entropy) after each epoch. Tracking these metrics serves as a minimalistic sanity check: if the model is not able to solve the word prediction task with some degree of success (e.g. if we observe no substantial decay in the losses) then one should not expect the embeddings to capture any of the distributional information they are supposed to capture.

4.3 Tests and Gold-Standard Data for Intrinsic Evaluation

Using the gold standard data (described below), we performed three types of tests:

- **Class Membership Tests**: embeddings corresponding two member of the same semantic class (e.g. "Months of the Year", "Portuguese Cities", "Smileys") should be close, since they are supposed to be found in mostly the same contexts.
- **Class Distinction Test**: this is the reciprocal of the previous Class Membership test. Embeddings of elements of different classes should be different, since words of different classes ere expected to be found in significantly different contexts.

- **Word Equivalence Test**: embeddings corresponding to *synonyms, antonyms, abbreviations* (e.g. "porque" abbreviated by "pq") and *partial references* (e.g. "slb and benfica") should be almost equal, since both alternatives are supposed to be used be interchangeable in all contexts (either maintaining or inverting the meaning).

Therefore, in our tests, two words are considered:

- *distinct* if the cosine of the corresponding embeddings is lower than **0.70** (or **0.80**).
- to *belong to the same class* if the cosine of their embeddings is higher than **0.70** (or **0.80**).
- equivalent if the cosine of the embeddings is higher that **0.85** (or **0.95**).

We report results using different thresholds of cosine similarity as we noticed that cosine similarity is skewed to higher values in the embedding space, as observed in related work [15,16]. We used the following sources of data for testing Class Membership:

- AP+Battig data. This data was collected from the evaluation data provided by [11]. These correspond to 29 semantic classes.
- Twitter-Class - collected manually by the authors by checking top most frequent words in the dictionary and then expanding the classes. These include the following 6 sets (number of elements in brackets): smileys (13), months (12), countries (6), names (19), surnames (14) Portuguese cities (9).

For the Class Distinction test, we pair each element of each of the gold standard classes, with all the other elements from other classes (removing duplicate pairs since ordering does not matter), and we generate pairs of words which are supposed belong to different classes. For Word Equivalence test, we manually collected equivalente pairs, focusing on abbreviations that are popular in Twitters (e.g. "qt" $\simeq$ "quanto" or "lx" $\simeq$ "lisboa" and on frequent acronyms (e.g. "slb" $\simeq$ "benfica"). In total, we compiled 48 equivalence pairs.

For all these tests we computed a *coverage* metric. Our embeddings do not necessarily contain information for all the words contained in each of these tests. So, for all tests, we compute a *coverage* metric that measures the fraction of the gold-standard pairs that could actually be tested using the different embeddings produced. Then, for all the test pairs actually covered, we obtain the success metrics for each of the 3 tests by computing the ratio of pairs we were able to correctly classified as (i) being distinct (cosine < 0.7 or 0.8), (ii) belonging to the same class (cosine > 0.7 or 0.8), and (iii) being equivalent (cosine > 0.85 or 0.95).

It is worth making a final comment about the gold standard data. Although we do not expect this gold standard data to be sufficient for a wide-spectrum evaluation of the resulting embeddings, it should be enough for providing us clues regarding areas where the embedding process is capturing enough semantics, and where it is not. These should still provide valuable indications for planning how to produce the much larger database of word embeddings.

5   Results and Analysis

We run the training process and performed the corresponding evaluation for 12 combinations of size of vocabulary to be embedded, and the volume of training data available that has been used. Table 2 presents some overall statistics after training for 40 epochs.

Table 2. Overall statistics for 12 combinations of models learned varying $|V|$ and volume of training data. Results observed after 40 training epochs.

Embeddings	# Training data tuples	Avg secs/epoch	Training loss	Validation loss
$|V| = 2048$	561,786 (25% data)	4	3.2564	3.5932
$|V| = 2048$	1,123,573 (50% data)	9	3.2234	3.4474
$|V| = 2048$	1,685,359 (75% data)	13	3.2138	3.3657
$|V| = 2048$	2,496,830 (100% data)	18	3.2075	3.3074
$|V| = 8192$	1,375,794 (25% data)	63	3.6329	4.286
$|V| = 8192$	2,751,588 (50% data)	151	3.6917	4.0664
$|V| = 8192$	4,127,382 (75% data)	187	3.7019	3.9323
$|V| = 8192$	6,114,640 (100% data)	276	3.7072	3.8565
$|V| = 32768$	2,452,402 (25% data)	388	3.7417	5.2768
$|V| = 32768$	4,904,806 (50% data)	956	3.9885	4.8409
$|V| = 32768$	7,357,209 (75% data)	1418	4.0649	4.6
$|V| = 32768$	10,899,570 (100% data)	2028	4.107	4.4491

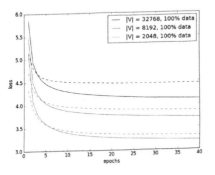
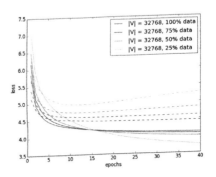

Fig. 1. Continuous line represents loss in the training data while dashed line represents loss in the validation data. Left side: effect of increasing $|V|$ using 100% of training data. Right side: effect of varying the amount of training data used with $|V| = 32768$.

The average time per epoch increases first with the size of the vocabulary to embed $|V|$ (because the model will have more parameters), and then, for each $|V|$, with the volume of training data. Using our testbed (Sect. 4), the total time of learning in our experiments varied from a minimum of 160 s, with $|V| = 2048$ and 25% of data, to a maximum of 22.5 h, with $|V| = 32768$ and using 100% of the training data available (extracted from 5M tweets). These numbers give us an approximate figure of how time consuming it would be to train embeddings from the complete Twitter corpus we have, consisting of 300M tweets.

We now analyze the learning process itself. We plot the training set loss and validation set loss for the different values of $|V|$ (Fig. 1 left) with 40 epochs and using all the available data. As expected, the loss is reducing after each epoch, with validation loss, although being slightly higher, following the same trend. When using 100% we see no model overfitting. We can also observe that the higher is $|V|$ the higher are the absolute values of the loss sets. This is not surprising because as the number of words to predict becomes higher the problem will tend to become harder. Also, because we keep the dimensionality of the embedding space constant (64 dimensions), it becomes increasingly hard to represent and differentiate larger vocabularies in the same hyper-volume. We believe this is a specially valuable indication for future experiments and for deciding the dimensionality of the final embeddings to distribute.

On the right side of Fig. 1 we show how the number of training (and validation) examples affects the loss. For a fixed $|V| = 32768$ we varied the amount of data used for training from 25% to 100%. Three trends are apparent. As we train with more data, we obtain better validation losses. This was expected. The second trend is that by using less than 50% of the data available the model tends to overfit the data, as indicated by the consistent increase in the validation loss after about 15 epochs (check dashed lines in right side of Fig. 1). This suggests that for the future we should not try any drastic reduction of the training data to save training time. Finally, when not overfitting, the validation loss seems to stabilize after around 20 epochs. We observed no phase-transition effects (the model seems simple enough for not showing that type of behavior). This indicates we have a practical way of safely deciding when to stop training the model.

5.1 Intrinsic Evaluation

Table 3 presents results for the three different tests described in Sect. 4. The first (expected) result is that the coverage metrics increase with the size of the vocabulary being embedded, i.e., $|V|$. Because the Word Equivalence test set was specifically created for evaluating Twitter-based embedding, when embedding $|V| = 32768$ words we achieve almost 90% test coverage. On the other hand, for the Class Distinction test set - which was created by doing the cross product of the test cases of each class in Class Membership test set - we obtain very low coverage figures. This indicates that it is not always possible to re-use previously compiled gold-standard data, and that it will be important to compile gold-standard data directly from Twitter content if we want to perform a more precise evaluation.

The effect of varying the cosine similarity decision threshold from 0.70 to 0.80 for Class Membership test shows that the percentage of classified as correct test cases drops significantly. However, the drop is more accentuated when training with only a portion of the available data. The differences of using two alternative thresholds values is even higher in the Word Equivalence test.

Table 3. Evaluation of resulting embeddings using Class Membership, Class Distinction and Word Equivalence tests for different thresholds of cosine similarity.

Embeddings |V|, %data	Class Membership Coverage	Acc. @0.70	Acc. @0.80	Class Distinction Coverage	TN @0.70	TN @0.80	Word Equivalence Coverage	Acc. @0.85	Acc. @0.95
2048, 25%	12.32%	30.71%	4.94%	1.20%	100%	100%	31.25%	26.67%	2.94%
2048, 50%		29.13%	12.69%		100%	100%		26.67%	2.94%
2048, 75%		29.13%	18.12%		100%	100%		33.33%	2.94%
2048, 100%		32.28%	26.77%		100%	100%		33.33%	6.67%
8192, 25%	29.60%	14.17%	4.94%	6.54%	100%	100%	70.83%	14.71%	2.94%
8192, 50%		22.41%	12.69%		99%	100%		20.59%	2.94%
8192, 75%		27.51%	18.12%		99%	100%		20.59%	2.94%
8192, 100%		33.77%	21.91%		97%	100%		29.41%	5.88%
32768, 25%	47.79%	17.73%	5.13%	18.31%	98%	100%	89.58%	16.28%	2.33%
32768, 50%		52.30%	21.06%		83%	98%		34.88%	9.30%
32768, 75%		85.15%	49.41%		44%	88%		58.14%	23.26%
32768, 100%		95.59%	74.80%		13%	57%		72.09%	34.88%

The Word Equivalence test, in which we consider two words equivalent word if the cosine of the embedding vectors is higher than 0.95, revealed to be an extremely demanding test. Nevertheless, for $|V| = 32768$ the results are far superior, and for a much larger coverage, than for lower $|V|$. The same happens with the Class Membership test.

On the other hand, the Class Distinction test shows a different trend for larger values of $|V| = 32768$ but the coverage for other values of $|V|$ is so low that becomes difficult to hypothesize about the reduced values of True Negatives (TN) percentage obtained for the largest $|V|$. It would be necessary to confirm this behavior with even larger values of $|V|$. One might hypothesize that the ability to distinguish between classes requires larger thresholds when $|V|$ is large. Also, we can speculate about the need of increasing the number of dimensions to be able to encapsulate different semantic information for so many words.

5.2   Further Analysis Regarding Evaluation Metrics

Despite already providing interesting practical clues for our goal of trying to embed a larger vocabulary using more of the training data we have available, these results also revealed that the intrinsic evaluation metrics we are using are overly sensitive to their corresponding cosine similarity thresholds. This sensitivity poses serious challenges for further systematic exploration of word embedding architectures and their corresponding hyper-parameters, which was also observed in other recent works [16].

By using these absolute thresholds as criteria for deciding similarity of words, we create a dependency between the evaluation metrics and the *geometry* of the embedded data. If we see the embedding data as a graph, this means that metrics will change if we apply scaling operations to certain parts of the graph, even if its structure (i.e. relative position of the embedded words) does not change.

For most practical purposes (including training downstream ML models) absolute distances have little meaning. What is fundamental is that the resulting embeddings are able to capture topological information: similar words should be *closer to each other* than they are to words that are dissimilar to them (under the various criteria of similarity we care about), independently of the absolute distances involved.

It is now clear that a key aspect for future work will be developing additional performance metrics based on topological properties. We are in line with recent work [17], proposing to shift evaluation from absolute values to more exploratory evaluations focusing on weaknesses and strengths of the embeddings and not so much in generic scores. For example, one metric could consist in checking whether for any given word, all words that are known to belong to the same class are closer than any words belonging to different classes, independently of the actual cosine. Future work will necessarily include developing this type of metrics.

6   Conclusions

Producing word embeddings from tweets is challenging due to the specificities of the vocabulary in the medium. We implemented a neural word embedding model that embeds words based on n-gram information extracted from a sample of the Portuguese Twitter stream, and which can be seen as a flexible baseline for further experiments in the field. Work reported in this paper is a preliminary study of trying to find parameters for training word embeddings from Twitter and adequate evaluation tests and gold-standard data.

Results show that using less than 50% of the available training examples for each vocabulary size might result in overfitting. The resulting embeddings obtain an interesting performance on intrinsic evaluation tests when trained a vocabulary containing the 32768 most frequent words in a Twitter sample of relatively small size. Nevertheless, results exhibit a skewness in the cosine similarity scores that should be further explored in future work. More specifically, the Class Distinction test set revealed to be challenging and opens the door to evaluation of not only similarity between words but also dissimilarities between words of different semantic classes without using absolute score values.

Therefore, a key area of future exploration has to do with better evaluation resources and metrics. We made some initial effort in this front. However, we believe that developing new intrinsic tests, agnostic to absolute values of metrics and concerned with topological aspects of the embedding space, and expanding gold-standard data with cases tailored for user-generated content, is of fundamental importance for the progress of this line of work.

Furthermore, we plan to make public available word embeddings trained from a large sample of 300M tweets collected from the Portuguese Twitter stream. This will require experimenting producing embeddings with higher dimensionality (to avoid the cosine skewness effect) and training with even larger vocabularies. Also, there is room for experimenting with some of the hyper-parameters of the model itself (e.g. activation functions, dimensions of the layers), which we know have impact on final results.

Acknowledgements. We gratefully acknowledge the support of NVIDIA Corporation with the donation of the Titan X Pascal GPU used for this research.

References

1. Levy, O., Goldberg, Y., Dagan, I.: Improving distributional similarity with lessons learned from word embeddings. Trans. Assoc. Comput. Linguist. **3**, 211–225 (2015)
2. Mikolov, T., Sutskever, I., Chen, K., Corrado, G.S., Dean, J.: Distributed representations of words and phrases and their compositionality. In: NIPS (2013)
3. Pennington, J., Socher, R., Manning, C.D.: Glove: global vectors for word representation. In: EMNLP, vol. 14, pp. 1532–1543 (2014)
4. Deerwester, S., Dumais, S.T., Furnas, G.W., Landauer, T.K., Harshman, R.: Indexing by latent semantic analysis. J. Am. Soc. Inf. Sci. **41**(6), 391 (1990)
5. Bengio, Y., Ducharme, R., Vincent, P., Jauvin, C.: A neural probabilistic language model. J. Mach. Learn. Res. **3**(Feb), 1137–1155 (2003)
6. Collobert, R., Weston, J.: A unified architecture for natural language processing: deep neural networks with multitask learning. In: Proceedings of the 25th International Conference on Machine Learning, pp. 160–167. ACM (2008)
7. Levy, O., Goldberg, Y.: Neural word embedding as implicit matrix factorization. In: Advances in Neural Information Processing Systems, pp. 2177–2185 (2014)
8. Mikolov, T., Yih, W.-T., Zweig, G.: Linguistic regularities in continuous space word representations. In: HLT-NAACL, vol. 13 (2013)
9. Arora, S., Li, Y., Liang, Y., Ma, T., Risteski, A.: Rand-walk: a latent variable model approach to word embeddings. arXiv preprint arXiv:1502.03520 (2015)
10. Nakov, P., Ritter, A., Rosenthal, S., Sebastiani, F., Stoyanov, V.: Semeval-2016 task 4: sentiment analysis in Twitter. In: Proceedings of SemEval, pp. 1–18 (2016)
11. Rodrigues, J., Branco, A., Neale, S., Silva, J.: LX-DSemVectors: distributional semantics models for portuguese. In: Silva, J., Ribeiro, R., Quaresma, P., Adami, A., Branco, A. (eds.) PROPOR 2016. LNCS, vol. 9727, pp. 259–270. Springer, Cham (2016). doi:10.1007/978-3-319-41552-9_27
12. Chollet, F.: Keras (2015). https://github.com/fchollet/keras
13. Kingma, D., Ba, J.: Adam: a method for stochastic optimization. arXiv preprint arXiv:1412.6980 (2014)
14. Bošnjak, M., Oliveira, E., Martins, J., Mendes Rodrigues, E., Sarmento, L.: Twitterecho: a distributed focused crawler to support open research with Twitter data. In: Proceedings of the 21st International Conference on World Wide Web, pp. 1233–1240. ACM (2012)
15. Dinu, G., Lazaridou, A., Baroni. M.: Improving zero-shot learning by mitigating the hubness problem. arXiv preprint arXiv:1412.6568 (2014)
16. Faruqui, M., Tsvetkov, Y., Rastogi, P., Dyer, C.: Problems with evaluation of word embeddings using word similarity tasks. In: ACL 2016, p. 30 (2016)
17. Gladkova, A., Drozd, A., Center, C.: Intrinsic evaluations of word embeddings: what can we do better? In: ACL 2016, p. 36 (2016)

Correction to: Flower Pollination Algorithm Applied to the Economic Dispatch Problem with Multiple Fuels and Valve Point Effect

Rafael Ochsendorf G. Souza, Ezequiel Silva Oliveira,
Ivo Chaves Silva Junior, André Luís Marques Marcato,
and Marcos T.B. de Oliveira

Correction to:
Chapter "Flower Pollination Algorithm Applied
to the Economic Dispatch Problem with Multiple Fuels
and Valve Point Effect" in: E. Oliveira et al. (Eds.):
Progress in Artificial Intelligence, **LNAI 10423,**
https://doi.org/10.1007/978-3-319-65340-2_22

In the originally published version of this paper the name of the fifth author was inadvertently published with a spelling error. The name "Marcos T.B. de Olveira" was corrected to "Marcos T.B. de Oliveira".

The updated version of this chapter can be found at
https://doi.org/10.1007/978-3-319-65340-2_22

© Springer International Publishing AG 2019
E. Oliveira et al. (Eds.): EPIA 2017, LNAI 10423, p. C1, 2019.
https://doi.org/10.1007/978-3-319-65340-2_72

Author Index

Printed in the United States
By Bookmasters